1999

M I L L E R

GAAP

G U I D E

PROFESSIONAL EDUCATION SERVICES, LP
The Professional's Choice for Quality CPE

8303 Sierra College Blvd., Suite 146
Roseville, CA 95661

Order: 1-800-998-5024
Customer Service: 1-800-990-2731
Fax: (916) 791-4099

1999

MILLER

GAAP

G U I D E

Restatement and Analysis of Current FASB Standards

JAN R. WILLIAMS, Ph.D., CPA

HARCOURT BRACE PROFESSIONAL PUBLISHING

A Division of

Harcourt Brace & Company

SAN DIEGO   NEW YORK   LONDON

The publisher has not sought nor obtained approval of this publication from any other organization, profit or not-for-profit, and is solely responsible for its contents.

Printed in Canada.

ISBN: 0-15-606312-3 (hardcover)
ISBN: 0-15-606311-5 (softcover)
ISBN: 0-03-021118-2 (college edition)

99 00 01 02 WBC 4 3 2 1

1999 *Miller GAAP Guide*

Contents

Table of Contents

Specialized Industry Accounting Principles

1999 *Miller GAAP Implementation Manual*
Contents

Generally Accepted Accounting Principles

Accounting Policies and Standards
Advertising
Balance Sheet Classification
Bankruptcy and Reorganization
Business Combinations
Changing Prices
Contingencies, Risks, and Uncertainties
Equity Method
Extinguishment of Debt
Financial Instruments
Foreign Operations and Exchange
Income Taxes
Intangible Assets
Interest on Receivables and Payables
Interim Financial Reporting
Inventory Pricing and Methods
Investment Tax Credit
Investments in Debt and Equity Securities
Leases
Long-Term Construction Contracts
Nonmonetary Transactions
Pension Plans—Employers
Pension Plans—Settlements and Curtailments
Personal Financial Statements
Postemployment and Postretirement Benefits Other
   Than Pensions
Research and Development Costs
Results of Operations
Revenue Recognition
Segment Reporting
Stockholders' Equity
Stock Issued to Employees
Troubled Debt Restructuring

Self-Study CPE Program
Index

1999 *Miller GAAP Implementation Manual:* EITF
Contents

Generally Accepted Accounting Principles

Specialized Industry Accounting Principles

Our Commitment to You

Thank you for ordering the 1999 *Miller GAAP Guide*. Each year we bring you the best accounting and auditing reference guides on the market. To confirm the technical accuracy and quality control of our materials, Harcourt Brace voluntarily submitted to a peer review of our publishing system and products.

We were not surprised when the SEC of the AICPA Division for CPA Firms accepted the unqualified peer review report reproduced on the following page of this Guide. (You should provide a copy of this report to your peer review team captain the next time you undergo a peer review.)

In addition to peer review, our products undergo strict technical and content reviews by qualified practitioners. This ensures that our products meet "real-world" standards and applicability. We also rely on our twenty years' experience of working to bring you the products you need.

In other words, our products are reviewed every step of the way—from conception through production—to ensure you of the finest products on the market.

In response to favorable feedback, we continue to publish the most portable product on the market, putting critical answers at your fingertips when and where you need them. Our products also contain low-cost, self-study CPE, another way you can make use of the knowledge you'll gain from using our Guides.

Peer-reviewed, technically accurate, convenient, and practical—the 1999 *Miller GAAP Guide* shows our appreciation for the value of your time and our commitment to creating products you can trust.

Peer Review Statement

Caldwell, Becker, Dervin, Petrick & Co., L.L.P.
CERTIFIED PUBLIC ACCOUNTANTS

January 14, 1997

The Board of Directors
Harcourt Brace & Company

We have reviewed the system of quality control for the development and maintenance of <u>GAAP Guide</u>, 1996 edition ("materials") of Harcourt Brace & Company (the company) in effect for the year ended December 31, 1996 and the resultant materials in effect at December 31, 1996 in order to determine whether the materials are reliable aids to assist users in conforming with those professional standards the materials purport to encompass. Our review was conducted in accordance with the standards for reviews of quality control materials and guidelines for review of continuing professional education programs promulgated by the peer review committee of the SEC practice section of the AICPA Division for CPA Firms.

In performing our review, we have given consideration to the following general characteristics of a system of quality control. A company's system for the development and maintenance of quality control materials and continuing professional education programs encompasses its organizational structure and the policies and procedures established to provide the users of its materials with reasonable assurance that the materials are reliable aids to assist them in conforming with professional standards in conducting their accounting and auditing practices. The extent of a company's quality control policies and procedures for the development and maintenance of the materials and the manner in which they are implemented will depend upon a variety of factors, such as the size and organizational structure of the company and the nature of the materials provided to users. Variance in individual performance and professional interpretation affects the degree of compliance with prescribed quality control policies and procedures. Therefore, adherence to all policies and procedures in every case may not be possible. As is customary in a review of quality control materials and continuing professional education programs, we are issuing a letter under this date that sets forth comments related to certain policies and procedures or compliance with them or to the resultant materials. None of these matters were considered to be of sufficient significance to affect the opinion expressed in this report.

Our review and tests were limited to the system of quality control for the development and maintenance of the aforementioned materials of Harcourt Brace & Company and to the materials themselves and did not extend to the application of these materials by users of the materials nor to the policies and procedures of individual users.

In our opinion, the system of quality control for the development and maintenance of the quality control materials and continuing professional education programs of Harcourt Brace & Company was suitably designed and was being complied with during the year ended December 31, 1996 to provide users of the materials with reasonable assurance that the materials are reliable aids to assist them in conforming with those professional standards the materials purport to encompass. Also, in our opinion, the materials referred to above are reliable aids at December 31, 1996.

Caldwell, Becker, Dervin, Petrick & Co., L.L.P.
CALDWELL, BECKER, DERVIN, PETRICK & CO., L.L.P.

20750 Ventura Boulevard, Suite 140 · Woodland Hills, CA 91364
(818)704-1040 · (213)873-1040 · FAX (818)704-5536

Preface

As part of **The Complete** *Miller GAAP Library for Business,* the 1999 *Miller GAAP Guide* explains and analyzes promulgated accounting principles in the highest level of the GAAP hierarchy in use today. This edition is current through the issuance of FASB Statement 133.

New Pronouncements and Outstanding Exposure Drafts

- FASB Statement 132   Employers' Disclosures about Pensions and Other Postretirement Benefits

- FASB Statement 133   Accounting for Derivative Instruments and Hedging Activities

- Consolidated Financial Statements: Policy and Procedures

- Accounting for Certain Liabilities Related to Closure or Removal of Long-Lived Assets

- Accounting for Mortgage-Backed Securities and Other Interests Retained After the Securitization of Mortgage Loans Held for Sale by a Mortgage Banking Enterprise

IMPRESS™ Cross-References

IMPRESS stands for the Integrated Miller Professional Reference and Engagement Series System. It is the system by which all Miller publications are thoroughly cross-referenced to one another on a chapter-by-chapter basis. The system is designed to facilitate comprehensive research and to assure that you will always find the complete answers you need. The IMPRESS™ Comprehensive Table of Contents shows the system in its entirety across all Miller publications. The IMPRESS™ Cross-References at the beginning of each chapter refer you to corresponding chapters in other publications as well as to related chapters in the 1999 *Miller GAAP Guide.*

The foundation of the IMPRESS™ system is the GAAP hierarchy of authoritative accounting pronouncements, established by Statement on Auditing Standards (SAS) 69. The 1999 *Miller GAAP Guide* is based on Category A pronouncements—the highest level in the hierarchy. The 1999 *Miller GAAP Implementation Manual* covers Categories B through D, and the 1999 *Miller GAAP Implementation Manual: EITF* focuses on specific guidance in Category C. See "About the GAAP Hierarchy" for more about this structure.

How to Use the 1999 *Miller GAAP Guide*

The 1999 *Miller GAAP Guide* organizes accounting pronouncements alphabetically by topic under two general areas: generally accepted accounting principles and specialized industry accounting principles. Pronouncements covering the same subject are compiled and incorporated in a single chapter so that the authoritative information is immediately accessible.

The *Miller GAAP Guide* is written in clear, understandable language. Each pronouncement is discussed in a comprehensive format that makes it easy to understand and apply. Illustrations and figures demonstrate and clarify specific accounting principles. Many of these are new to this edition.

The *Practice Pointers* throughout this edition do just that: they point out in plain English how to apply the standards just discussed.

Paragraphs called *Observations* enrich the discussion by presenting interesting aspects of GAAP, such as conflicts within the authoritative literature. Although no attempt is made to resolve apparent errors and conflicts in the promulgated pronouncements, these items are brought to your attention.

To facilitate research, the *Miller GAAP Guide* includes extensive codification references to pertinent paragraphs of the original pronouncements. Also, the Tables of Contents of all three books in **The Complete *Miller GAAP Library for Business*** are provided in the beginning of each volume so you can find pertinent topics in the Library easily.

The end-of-book material comprises, first, a *Disclosure Index*, which contains both required and recommended disclosures currently in use. It was designed to assist the preparer or reviewer of financial statements in determining whether the necessary and most current disclosures have been made. The *Self-Study CPE Program* divides the material in the 1999 *Miller GAAP Guide* into four separate modules for efficient and thorough study. The *Topical Index* provides quick, accurate reference to needed information.

The 1999 *Miller GAAP Guide* meets accounting industry standards overseen by the peer review system. A document covering the peer review of this book is reprinted for your reference.

Acknowledgments

The author thanks Joseph V. Carcello, Ph.D., CPA, University of Tennessee, for suggesting many improvements to the 1999 *Miller GAAP Guide*. He would also like to thank Shelly Bowen for her tireless efforts, as well as her patience, in bringing this edition to press.

Abbreviations

The following abbreviations are used throughout the text to represent accounting and auditing principles:

APB	Accounting Principles Board Opinions
ARB	Accounting Research Bulletins
ASR	Accounting Series Release
FAS	FASB Statements of Financial Accounting Standards
FIN	FASB Interpretations
SAS	Statement on Auditing Standards
SOP	AICPA Statements of Position

About the Author

Jan R. Williams, Ph.D., CPA, is the Ernst & Young Professor of Accounting and Associate Dean in the College of Business Administration at the University of Tennessee, Knoxville, where he has been on the faculty since 1977. Formerly, he was on the faculties of the University of Georgia and Texas Tech University. He received a Ph.D. in business administration, major in accounting, from the University of Arkansas and is a CPA licensed in Arkansas and Tennessee.

Dr. Williams has, for many years, been actively involved in the American Institute of Certified Public Accountants, the Tennessee Society of Certified Public Accountants, and several other professional organizations. Throughout his career, he has taught continuing professional education for CPAs. In 1994, Dr. Williams received both the Tennessee Society of CPAs and the AICPA Outstanding Accounting Educator Award. At the time this book is being printed, he has been nominated for the position of president of the American Accounting Association.

About the GAAP Hierarchy

The meaning of the term *generally accepted accounting principles* (GAAP) has varied over time. Originally, GAAP referred to accounting policies and procedures that were widely used in practice. As standards-setting bodies and professional organizations increasingly became involved in recording practices and recommending preferred practices, the term came to refer more and more to the pronouncements issued by particular accounting bodies, such as the Committee on Accounting Procedure and the Accounting Principles Board, both committees of the AICPA, and more recently the FASB. Today, many different series of authoritative literature exist, some of which are still in effect but are no longer being issued, like APB Opinions and AICPA Accounting Research Bulletins. Others—such as FASB Statements and Interpretations—continue to be issued by accounting organizations.

To better organize and make clear what is meant by GAAP, Statement on Auditing Standards (SAS) No. 69 (The Meaning of "Present Fairly in Conformity with Generally Accepted Accounting Principles" in the Independent Auditor's Report) established what is commonly referred to as the GAAP hierarchy. The purpose of the hierarchy is to instruct financial statement preparers, auditors, and users of financial statements concerning the relative priority of the different sources of GAAP used by auditors to judge the fairness of presentation in financial statements. While the GAAP hierarchy appears in the professional auditing literature, its importance goes beyond auditors: preparers, users, and others interested in financial statements must understand the sources of GAAP that underlie those statements.

SAS-69 defines the GAAP hierarchy by outlining four categories of established accounting principles. Because these sources of accounting principles arose over five decades and were promulgated by different groups, some conflicts exist among them. The four categories of GAAP as set forth by SAS-69 correspond to these principles' relative authoritativeness. Sources of accounting principles in higher categories carry more weight and must be followed when conflicts arise. When two or more sources of GAAP within a given level of the hierarchy disagree on the accounting for a particular type of transaction, the approach that better portrays the substance of the transaction should be followed.

In addition to the four levels of established accounting principles, the GAAP hierarchy recognizes other types of accounting literature that may be useful in resolving financial reporting problems when issues have not been covered in established sources of GAAP.

The following figure displays the GAAP hierarchy's four levels of established principles that are supported by authoritative accounting literature, as well as the additional sources of GAAP. The *Miller GAAP Guide* is based on Category A, which is the highest level of the established accounting principles.

Hierarchy of Generally Accepted Accounting Principles

Level A • FASB Statements of Financial Accounting Standards (FAS)
  • FASB Interpretations (FIN)
  • APB Opinions (APB)
  • Accounting Research Bulletins (ARB)

Level B • FASB Technical Bulletins (FTB)
  • AICPA Industry Audit and Accounting Guides
  • AICPA Statements of Position (SOP)

Level C • Consensus Positions of the Emerging Issues Task Force (EITF)
  • AICPA AcSEC Practice Bulletins (PB)

Level D • AICPA Accounting Interpretations (AIN)
  • FASB Implementation Guides (FIG)
  • Industry practices widely recognized and prevalent

Other Accounting Literature

  • FASB Concepts Statements (CON)
  • APB Statements
  • AICPA Issues Papers
  • International Accounting Standards Committee Statements
  • GASB Statements, Interpretations, and Technical Bulletins
  • Pronouncements of other professional associations and regulatory bodies
  • AICPA Technical Practice Aids
  • Accounting textbooks, handbooks, and articles

Accounting Resources on the Web

The following World Wide Web addresses are just a few of the resources on the Internet that are available to practitioners. Because of the evolving nature of the Internet, some addresses may change. In such a case, refer to one of the many Internet search engines, such as Yahoo! (http://www.yahoo.com).

AICPA http://www.aicpa.org/

American Accounting Association http://www.rutgers.edu/accounting/raw/aaa/

FASB http://www.rutgers.edu:80//Accounting/raw/fasb/

Federal Tax Code Search http://www.tns.lcs.mit.edu:80/uscode/

Fedworld http://www.fedworld.gov

GASB http://www.rutgers.edu/Accounting/raw/gasb/gasbhome.html

General Accounting Office http://www.gao.gov/

Harcourt Brace Professional Publishing http://www.hbpp.com

House of Representatives http://www.house.gov/

IRS Digital Daily http://www.irs.ustreas.gov/prod/cover.html

Library of Congress http://lcweb.loc.gov/homepage/

Office of Management and Budget http://www.gpo.gov/omb/omb001.html

Securities and Exchange Commission http://www.sec.gov/

Thomas Legislative Research http://thomas.loc.gov/

Integrated Miller Professional Reference and Engagement Series System

IMPRESS stands for the Integrated Miller Professional Reference and Engagement Series System. It is the system by which all Miller publications are thoroughly cross-referenced to one another on a chapter-by-chapter basis. The system is designed to facilitate comprehensive research and to assure that you will always find the complete answers you need.

Comprehensive Table of Contents

Generally Accepted Accounting Principles

MILLER GUIDE CHAPTER

IMPRESS™ Topic	1999 Miller GAAP Guide	1999 Miller GAAP Implementation Manual	1999 Miller GAAP Implementation Manual: EITF	1999 Miller Not-for-Profit Reporting	1999 Miller GAAS Guide	1999 Miller Governmental GAAP Guide
Accounting Changes	1	—	1	1	3, 8, 11	—
Accounting Policies	2	1	—	9	3	—
Advertising	—	2	—	2	—	—

IMPRESS™ Topic	1999 Miller GAAP Guide	1999 Miller GAAP Implementation Manual	1999 Miller GAAP Implementation Manual: EITF	1999 Miller Not-for-Profit Reporting	1999 Miller GAAS Guide	1999 Miller Governmental GAAP Guide
Balance Sheet Classification	—	3	2	2	—	—
Bankruptcy and Reorganization	—	4	—	—	—	—
Business Combinations	3	4, 13	3	2, 7	11	6
Capitalization and Expense Recognition Concepts	—	—	4	5, 6, 16	—	—
Cash Flow Statement	4	—	5	10	—	5, 6
Changing Prices	5	6	—	—	—	—
Consolidated Financial Statements	6	—	6	2, 7	8	—

IMPRESS™ Topic	1999 Miller GAAP Guide	1999 Miller GAAP Implementation Manual	1999 Miller GAAP Implementation Manual: EITF	1999 Miller Not-for-Profit Reporting	1999 Miller GAAS Guide	1999 Miller Governmental GAAP Guide
Contingencies, Risks, and Uncertainties	7	7	7	2	11	20
Convertible Debt and Debt with Warrants	8	—	8	—	—	—
Current Assets and Current Liabilities	9	3	2	2	—	13, 16
Deferred Compensation Contracts	10	—	—	—	—	27
Depreciable Assets and Depreciation	11	—	—	5	—	13, 24, 30

IMPRESS™ Topic	1999 Miller GAAP Guide	1999 Miller GAAP Implementation Manual	1999 Miller GAAP Implementation Manual: EITF	1999 Miller Not-for-Profit Reporting	1999 Miller GAAS Guide	1999 Miller Governmental GAAP Guide
Development Stage Enterprises	12	27	—	—	—	—
Earnings per Share	13	—	9	—	—	—
Equity Method	14	8	6	7	8	13
Extinguishment of Debt	15	9	10	2, 6, 11	—	16
Financial Instruments	16	10	11, 29	2	11	13
Foreign Operations and Exchange	17	11	12	2, 11	—	—

IMPRESS™ Topic	1999 Miller GAAP Guide	1999 Miller GAAP Implementation Manual	1999 Miller GAAP Implementation Manual: EITF	1999 Miller Not-for-Profit Reporting	1999 Miller GAAS Guide	1999 Miller Governmental GAAP Guide
Futures Contracts	18	—	—	—	—	—
Government Contracts	19	—	—	15	—	—
Impairment of Loans and Long-Lived Assets	20	—	13	—	—	—
Income Taxes	21	12	14	2, 13	—	—
Installment Sales Method of Accounting	22	—	—	—	—	—
Intangible Assets	23	13	15	2	—	—
Interest Costs Capitalized	24	—	—	6	—	—

IMPRESS™ Topic	1999 Miller GAAP Guide	1999 Miller GAAP Implementation Manual	1999 Miller GAAP Implementation Manual: EITF	1999 Miller Not-for-Profit Reporting	1999 Miller GAAS Guide	1999 Miller Governmental GAAP Guide
Interest on Receivables and Payables	25	14	16	2	—	—
Interim Financial Reporting	26	15	17	—	13	—
Inventory Pricing and Methods	27	16	18	—	8	13
Investment Tax Credit	28	17	—	—	—	—
Investments in Debt and Equity Securities	29	18	19	2, 5, 9	8	13, 14, 15
Leases	30	19	20	—	—	19, 29, 30

IMPRESS™ Topic	1999 Miller GAAP Guide	1999 Miller GAAP Implementation Manual	1999 Miller GAAP Implementation Manual: EITF	1999 Miller Not-for-Profit Reporting	1999 Miller GAAS Guide	1999 Miller Governmental GAAP Guide
Long-Term Construction Contracts	31	20	—	—	8, 18	24
Long-Term Obligations	32	—	—	2, 6, 11	—	29
Nonmonetary Transactions	33	21	21	2, 10, 14	—	—
Pension Plans—Employers	34	22	23	16	8, 20	21, 28
Pension Plans—Settlements and Curtailments	35	23	—	—	—	17
Personal Financial Statements	—	24	—	—	—	—

IMPRESS™ Topic	1999 Miller GAAP Guide	1999 Miller GAAP Implementation Manual	1999 Miller GAAP Implementation Manual: EITF	1999 Miller Not-for-Profit Reporting	1999 Miller GAAS Guide	1999 Miller Governmental GAAP Guide
Postemployment and Post-retirement Benefits Other Than Pensions	36	25	24	—	8, 20	22
Product Financing Arrangements	37	—	—	—	—	—
Property Taxes	38	—	—	—	9	—
Quasi-Reorganizations	39	—	—	—	—	—
Related Party Disclosures	40	—	—	2	8	—
Research and Development Costs	41	26	—	—	—	—

IMPRESS™ Topic	1999 Miller GAAP Guide	1999 Miller GAAP Implementation Manual	1999 Miller GAAP Implementation Manual: EITF	1999 Miller Not-for-Profit Reporting	1999 Miller GAAS Guide	1999 Miller Governmental GAAP Guide
Results of Operations	42	27	25	2, 11	—	5
Revenue Recognition	43	28	26	2, 3, 9, 11	—	9
Segment Reporting	44	29	—	7, 11	—	26
Stockholders' Equity	45	30	27	—	—	—
Stock Issued to Employees	46	31	28	—	—	—
Transfer and Servicing of Financial Assets	47	—	29	—	—	—
Troubled Debt Restructuring	48	32	30	2, 6	—	—

IMPRESS™ Topic	1999 Miller GAAP Guide	1999 Miller GAAP Implementation Manual	1999 Miller GAAP Implementation Manual: EITF	1999 Miller Not-for-Profit Reporting	1999 Miller GAAS Guide	1999 Miller Governmental GAAP Guide
SPECIALIZED INDUSTRY ACCOUNTING PRINCIPLES						
Computer Software	41	—	32	—	—	—
Entertainment Broadcasters	50	—	—	—	—	—
Cable Television	51	—	—	—	—	—
Motion Picture Films	52	—	—	—	—	—
Records and Music	53	—	—	—	—	—
Financial Institutions Banking and Thrift Institutions	49	—	22, 31	—	19	—

IMPRESS™ Topic	1999 Miller GAAP Guide	1999 Miller GAAP Implementation Manual	1999 Miller GAAP Implementation Manual: EITF	1999 Miller Not-for-Profit Reporting	1999 Miller GAAS Guide	1999 Miller Governmental GAAP Guide
Mortgage Banking Industry	57	—	34	—	—	—
Franchising	54	—	—	—	—	—
Health Care	—	40	—	—	21	—
Insurance Insurance Enterprises	55	—	33	—	—	—
Title Plant	56	—	—	—	—	11
Not-for-Profit Organizations	58	—	—	2, 8	22	31, 32, 33

IMPRESS™ Topic	1999 Miller GAAP Guide	1999 Miller GAAP Implementation Manual	1999 Miller GAAP Implementation Manual: EITF	1999 Miller Not-for-Profit Reporting	1999 Miller GAAS Guide	1999 Miller Governmental GAAP Guide
Oil and Gas Producing Companies	59	—	—	—	—	—
Pension Plan Financial Statements	60	—	—	—	—	27
Real Estate Costs and Initial Rental Operations	61	—	36	—	—	—
Recognition of Sales	62	—	36	—	—	—
Regulated Industries	63	—	35	—	—	—

Cross-Reference

This locator provides instant cross-reference between an original pronouncement and the chapter(s) in this publication in which a pronouncement is covered. Original pronouncements are listed chronologically on the left and the chapter(s) in which they appear in the 1999 *Miller GAAP Guide* on the right. When an original pronouncement has been superseded, cross-reference is made to the succeeding pronouncement.

ACCOUNTING RESEARCH BULLETINS (ARBs)

(Accounting Research Bulletins 1–42 were revised, restated, or withdrawn at the time ARB No. 43 was issued.)

ORIGINAL PRONOUNCEMENT	1999 *MILLER GAAP GUIDE* REFERENCE
ARB No. 43 (Restatement and Revision of Accounting Research Bulletins)	
Chapter 1—Prior Opinions	
1-A: Rules Adopted by Membership	Portions amended by FAS-111. Consolidated Financial Statements, ch. **6** Current Assets and Current Liabilities, ch. **9** Installment Sales Method of Accounting, ch. **22** Stockholders' Equity, ch. **45**
1-B: Opinion Issued by Predecessor Committee	Portions amended by APB-6. Stockholders' Equity, ch. **45**
Chapter 2—Form of Statements	
2-A: Comparative Financial Statements	Portions amended by APB-20. Consolidated Financial Statements, ch. **6**
2-B: Combined Statement of Income and Earned Surplus	Superseded by APB-9
Chapter 3—Working Capital	
3-A: Current Assets and Current Liabilities	Portions amended by APB-6, 21, FAS-6, 78, 111, and 115. Current Assets and Current Liabilities, ch. 9
3-B: Application of United States Government Securities Against Liabilities for Federal Taxes on Income	Superseded by APB-10
Chapter 4 Inventory Pricing	Inventory Pricing and Methods, ch. **27**
Chapter 5 Intangible Assets	Superseded by APB-16 and APB-17

Chapter 6

Contingency Reserves   Superseded by FAS-5

Chapter 7—Capital Accounts
7-A: Quasi-Reorganization or Corporate
Readjustment   Portions amended by FAS-111.
                                              Quasi-Reorganizations, ch. **39**

7-B: Stock Dividends and Stock Split-Ups   Portions amended by APB-6.
                                              Stockholders' Equity, ch. **45**

7-C: Business Combinations   Superseded by ARB-48

Chapter 8:
Income and Earned Surplus   Superseded by APB-9

Chapter 9—Depreciation
9-A: Depreciation and High Costs   Depreciable Assets and Depreciation,
                                              ch. **11**

9-B: Depreciation on Appreciation   Superseded by APB-6

9-C: Emergency Facilities—Depreciation,
Amortization, and Income Taxes   Portions amended or superseded by APB-6
                                              and 11, FAS-96 and 109.
                                              Depreciable Assets and Depreciation, ch. **11**

Chapter 10—Taxes
10-A: Real and Personal Property Taxes   Portions amended by APB-9 and FAS-111.
                                              Property Taxes, ch. **38**

10-B: Income Taxes   Superseded by APB-11, FAS-96 and 109.

Chapter 11—Government Contracts
11-A: Cost-Plus-Fixed-Fee Contracts   Government Contracts, ch. **19**

11-B: Renegotiation   Portions amended or superseded by APB-9,
                                              11, FAS-96, 109 and 111.
                                              Government Contracts, ch. **19**

11-C: Terminated War and Defense
Contracts   Government Contracts, ch. **19**

Chapter 12
Foreign Operations and Foreign Exchange   Superseded by FAS-52 and 94

Chapter 13—Compensation
13-A: Pension Plans—Annuity Costs
Based on Past Service   Superseded by APB-8

13-B: Compensation Involved in Stock
Optionand Stock Purchase Plans   Portions amended by APB-25 and FAS-123.
                                              Stock Issued to Employees, ch. **46**

Chapter 14
Disclosures of Long-Term Leases in
Financial Statements of Lessees   Superseded by APB-5

Chapter 15
Unamortized Discount, Issue Cost, and
Redemption Premium on Bonds Refunded   Superseded by APB-26

ARB No. 44
Declining-Balance Depreciation — Superseded by ARB-44 (Revised)

ARB No. 44 (Revised)
Declining-Balance Depreciation — Superseded by FAS-96 and FAS-109

ARB No. 45
Long-Term Construction-Type Contracts — Long-Term Construction Contracts, ch. **31**

ARB No. 46
Discontinuance of Dating Earned Surplus — Quasi-Reorganizations, ch. **39**

ARB No. 47
Accounting for Costs of Pension Plans — Superseded by APB-8

ARB No. 48
Business Combinations — Superseded by APB-16

ARB No. 49
Earnings per Share — Superseded by APB-9

ARB No. 50
Contingencies — Superseded by FAS-5

ARB No. 51
Consolidated Financial Statements — Portions amended or superseded by APB-10, 11, 16, 18, 23, FAS-58, 71, 94, 96, 109, and 111. Consolidated Financial Statements, ch. **6**

ACCOUNTING PRINCIPLES BOARD OPINIONS (APBs)

ORIGINAL PRONOUNCEMENT — 1999 *MILLER GAAP GUIDE* REFERENCE

APB Opinion No. 1
New Depreciation Guidelines and Rules — Superseded by FAS-96 and 109

APB Opinion No. 2
Accounting for the "Investment Credit" — Portions amended or superseded by APB-4, FAS-71 and 109. Investment Tax Credit, ch. **28**

APB Opinion No. 2—Addendum
Accounting Principles for Regulated Industries — Superseded by FAS-71

APB Opinion No. 3
The Statement of Source and Application of Funds — Superseded by APB-19

APB Opinion No. 4
Accounting for the "Investment Credit" — Investment Tax Credit, ch. **28**

APB Opinion No. 5
Reporting of Leases in Financial Statements
of Lessee   Superseded by FAS-13

APB Opinion No. 6
Status of Accounting Research Bulletins   Portions amended or superseded by APB-11,
                                              16, 17, 26, 28, FAS-8, 52, 71, 96, 109, and 111.
                                              Depreciable Assets and Depreciation, ch. **11**
                                              Stockholders' Equity, ch. **45**

APB Opinion No. 7
Accounting for Leases in Financial Statements
of Lessors   Superseded by FAS-13

APB Opinion No. 8
Accounting for the Cost of Pension Plans   Superseded by FAS-87

APB Opinion No. 9
Reporting the Results of Operations   Portions amended or superseded by APB-13,
                                              15, 20, 30, FAS-16 and 111
                                              Results of Operations, ch. **42**

APB Opinion No. 10
Omnibus Opinion—1966   Portions amended or superseded by APB-12,
                                              14, 16, 18, FAS-111 and 129.
                                              Current Assets and Current Liabilities, ch. **9**
                                              Income Taxes, ch. **21**
                                              Installment Sales Method of Accounting,
                                              ch. **22**

APB Opinion No. 11
Accounting for Income Taxes   Superseded by FAS-96 and FAS-109

APB Opinion No. 12
Omnibus Opinion—1967   Portions amended or superseded by APB-14,
                                              FAS-87, 106, and 111.
                                              Deferred Compensation Contracts, ch. **10**
                                              Depreciable Assets and Depreciation, ch. **11**
                                              Postemployment and Postretirement Benefits
                                              Other Than Pensions, ch. **36**
                                              Stockholders' Equity, ch. **45**

APB Opinion No. 13
Amending Paragraph 6 of APB Opinion No. 9,
Application to Commercial Banks   Results of Operations, ch. **42**

APB Opinion No. 14
Accounting for Convertible Debt and Debt
Issued with Stock Purchase Warrants   Convertible Debt and Debt with
                                              Warrants, ch. **8**
                                              Stockholders' Equity, ch. **45**

APB Opinion No. 15
Earnings per Share   Superseded by FAS-128 for periods ending
                                              after December 15, 1997

APB Opinion No. 27
Accounting for Lease Transactions by
Manufacturer or Dealer Lessors   Superseded by FAS-13

APB Opinion No. 28
  Interim Financial Reporting   Portions amended or superseded by FAS-3,
                                         95, 96, 109, and 128.
                                         Interim Financial Reporting, ch. **26**
                                         Inventory Pricing and Methods, ch. **27**

APB Opinion No. 29
  Accounting for Nonmonetary Transactions   Portions amended or superseded by FAS-71,
                                         96, 109, and 123.
                                         Nonmonetary Transactions, ch. **33**

APB Opinion No. 30
Reporting the Results of Operations—
Reporting the Effects of Disposal of a
Segment of a Business, and Extraordinary,
Unusual, and Infrequently Occurring
Events and Transactions   Portions amended or superseded by FAS-4,
                                         16, 60, 83, 96, 97, 101, 109, and 128.
                                         Results of Operations, ch. **42**

APB Opinion No. 31
Disclosure of Lease Commitments by Lessees   Superseded by FAS-13

ACCOUNTING PRINCIPLES BOARD STATEMENTS

ORIGINAL PRONOUNCEMENT   *1998 MILLER GAAP GUIDE* REFERENCE

APB Statement No. 3
Financial Statements Restated
for General Price-Level Changes   Changing Prices, ch. **5**

FINANCIAL ACCOUNTING STANDARDS BOARD STATEMENTS (FASs)

ORIGINAL PRONOUNCEMENT   *1998 MILLER GAAP GUIDE* REFERENCE

FASB Statement No. 1
Disclosure of Foreign Currency Translation
Information   Superseded by FAS-8 and 52

FASB Statement No. 2
Accounting for Research and Development
Costs   Portions amended or superseded by FAS-71
                                         and 86.
                                         Inventory Pricing and Methods, ch. **27**
                                         Research and Development Costs, ch. **41**

FASB Statement No. 3
Reporting Accounting Changes in Interim
Financial Statements   Accounting Changes, ch. **1**

FASB Statement No. 4

Reporting Gains and Losses from Extinguishment of Debt

Portions amended or superseded by FAS-71 and 64.

Extinguishment of Debt, ch. **15**

FASB Statement No. 5

Accounting for Contingencies

Portions amended or superseded by FAS-11, 16, 60, 71, 87, 111, 112, 113, 114, and 123.

Contingencies, Risks, and Uncertainties, ch. **7**

FASB Statement No. 6

Classification of Short-Term Obligations Expected to Be Refinanced

Current Assets and Current Liabilities, ch. **9**

FASB Statement No. 7

Accounting and Reporting by Development Stage Enterprises

Portions amended or superseded by FAS-71 and 95.

Development Stage Enterprises, ch. **12**

FASB Statement No. 8

Accounting for the Translation of Foreign Currency Transactions and Foreign Currency Financial Statements

Superseded by FAS-52

FASB Statement No. 9

Accounting for Income Taxes—Oil and Gas Producing Companies

Superseded by FAS-19

FASB Statement No. 10

Extension of "Grandfather" Provisions for Business Combinations

Business Combinations, ch. **3**

FASB Statement No. 11

Accounting for Contingencies—Transition Method

No longer relevant

FASB Statement No. 12

Accounting for Certain Marketable Securities

Superseded by FAS-115

FASB Statement No. 13

Accounting for Leases

Portions amended or superseded by FAS-17, 22, 23, 26, 27, 28, 29, 34, 71, 77, 91, 96, 98, 109, and 125.

Leases, ch. **30**

FASB Statement No. 14

Financial Reporting for Segments of a Business Enterprise

Segment Reporting, ch. **44**

(Superseded by FAS-131 for periods beginning after December 15, 1997)

FASB Statement No. 15

Accounting by Debtors and Creditors for Troubled Debt Restructurings

Portions amended or superseded by FAS-71, 111, 114, and 121.

Troubled Debt Restructuring, ch. **48**

FASB Statement No. 16
Prior Period Adjustments

Portions amended or superseded by FAS-71, 96, and 109.
Results of Operations, ch. **42**

FASB Statement No. 17
Accounting for Leases—Initial Direct Costs

Superseded by FAS-91

FASB Statement No. 18
Financial Reporting for Segments of a Business Enterprise—Interim Financial Statements

Segment Reporting, ch. **44**
(Superseded by FAS-131 for periods beginning after December 15, 1997)

FASB Statement No. 19
Financial Accounting and Reporting by Oil and Gas Producing Companies

Portions amended or superseded by FAS-25, 69, 71, 96, 109, and 121.
Oil and Gas Producing Companies, ch. **59**

FASB Statement No. 20
Accounting for Forward Exchange Contracts

Superseded by FAS-52

FASB Statement No. 21
Suspension of the Reporting of Earnings per Share and Segment Information by Nonpublic Enterprises

Segment Reporting, ch. **44**
(Superseded by FAS-131 for periods beginning after December 15, 1997)

FASB Statement No. 22
Changes in the Provisions of Lease Agreements Resulting from Refundings of Tax-Exempt Debt

Portions amended or superseded by FAS-71, 76, 95, 123, 125, and 128.
Extinguishment of Debt, ch. **15**
Leases, ch. **30**

FASB Statement No. 23
Inception of the Lease

Leases, ch. **30**

FASB Statement No. 24
Reporting Segment Information in Financial Statements That Are Presented in Another Enterprise's Financial Report

Segment Reporting, ch. **44**
(Superseded by FAS-131 for periods beginning after December 15, 1997)

FASB Statement No. 25
Suspension of Certain Accounting Requirements for Oil and Gas Producing Companies

Superseded by FAS-111.

FASB Statement No. 26
Profit Recognition on Sales-Type Leases of Real Estate

Superseded by FAS-98

FASB Statement No. 27
Classification of Renewals or Extensions of Existing Sales-Type or Direct Financing Leases

Leases, ch. **30**

FASB Statement No. 28
Accounting for Sales with Leasebacks

Portions amended by FAS-66.
Leases, ch. **30**

FASB Statement No. 29
Determining Contingent Rentals

Portions amended by FAS-98.
Leases, ch. **30**

FASB Statement No. 30
Disclosure of Information About Major
Customers

Government Contracts, ch. **19**
Segment Reporting, ch. **44**
(Superseded by FAS-131 for periods
beginning after December 15, 1997)

FASB Statement No. 31
Accounting for Tax Benefits Related to U.K.
Tax Legislation Concerning Stock Relief

Superseded by FAS-96 and FAS-109

FASB Statement No. 32
Specialized Accounting and Reporting Prin-
ciples and Practices in AICPA Statements of
Position and Guides on Accounting and
Auditing Matters

Superseded by FAS-111

FASB Statement No. 33
Financial Reporting and Changing Prices

Superseded by FAS-89

FASB Statement No. 34
Capitalization of Interest Cost

Portions amended or superseded by FAS-42,
58, 62, 71, 75, and 121.
Interest Costs Capitalized, ch. **24**

FASB Statement No. 35
Accounting and Reporting by Defined Benefit
Pension Plans

Portions amended or superseded by FAS-59,
75, and 110.
Pension Plan Financial Statements, ch. **60**

FASB Statement No. 36
Disclosure of Pension Information

Superseded by FAS-87

FASB Statement No. 37
Balance Sheet Classification of Deferred
Income Taxes

Superseded by FAS-109

FASB Statement No. 38
Accounting for Preacquisition Contingencies
of Purchased Enterprises

Portions amended or superseded by FAS-96
and 109.
Business Combinations, ch. **3**
Contingencies, Risks, and Uncertainties, ch. **7**

FASB Statement No. 39
Financial Reporting and Changing Prices:
Specialized Assets—Mining and Oil and Gas

Superseded by FAS-89

FASB Statement No. 40
Financial Reporting and Changing Prices:
Specialized Assets—Timberlands and
Growing Timber

Superseded by FAS-89

FASB Statement No. 41
Financial Reporting and Changing Prices:
Specialized Assets—Income-Producing Real
Estate

Superseded by FAS-89

FASB Statement No. 42
Determining Materiality for Capitalization
of Interest Cost

Interest Costs Capitalized, ch. **24**

FASB Statement No. 43
Accounting for Compensated Absences

Portions amended or superseded by FAS-71,
112, and 123.
Current Assets and Current Liabilities, ch. **9**

FASB Statement No. 44
Accounting for Intangible Assets of Motor
Carriers

Portions amended by FAS-96 and 109.
Intangible Assets, ch. **23**

FASB Statement No. 45
Accounting for Franchise Fee Revenue

Franchise Fee Revenue, ch. **54**

FASB Statement No. 46
Financial Reporting and Changing Prices:
Motion Picture Films

Superseded by FAS-89

FASB Statement No. 47
Disclosure of Long-Term Obligations

Portions superseded by FAS-129.
Long-Term Obligations, ch. **32**

FASB Statement No. 48
Revenue Recognition When Right of Return
Exists

Revenue Recognition, ch. **44**

FASB Statement No. 49
Accounting for Product Financing
Arrangements

Portions superseded by FAS-71.
Product Financing Arrangements, ch. **37**

FASB Statement No. 50
Financial Reporting in the Record and Music
Industry

Records and Music, ch. **53**

FASB Statement No. 51
Financial Reporting by Cable Television
Companies

Portions superseded by FAS-71.
Cable Television, ch. **51**

FASB Statement No. 52
Foreign Currency Translation

Portions amended by FAS-96 and 109.
Foreign Operations and Exchange, ch. **17**

FASB Statement No. 53
Financial Reporting by Producers and
Distributors of Motion Picture Films

Motion Picture Films, ch. **52**

FASB Statement No. 54
Financial Reporting and Changing Prices:
Investment Companies

Superseded by FAS-89

FASB Statement No. 55
Determining Whether a Convertible
Security Is a Common Stock Equivalent

Superseded by FAS-111

FASB Statement No. 56
Designation of AICPA Guide and Statement of
Position (SOP) 81-1 on Contractor Accounting
and SOP 81-2 Concerning Hospital-Related
Organizations as Preferable for Purposes of
Applying APB Opinion 20　　　　　　　　　Superseded by FAS-111

FASB Statement No. 57
Related Party Disclosures　　　　　　　　　Portions amended by FAS-95, 96, and 109.
　　　　　　　　　　　　　　　　　　　　　Related Party Disclosures, ch. **40**

FASB Statement No. 58
Capitalization of Interest Cost in Financial
Statements That Include Investments
Accounted For by the Equity Method　　　　Interest Costs Capitalized, ch. **24**

FASB Statement No. 59
Deferral of the Effective Date of Certain
Accounting Requirements for Pension
Plans of State and Local Governmental Units　Superseded by FAS-75

FASB Statement No. 60
Accounting and Reporting by Insurance
Enterprises　　　　　　　　　　　　　　　Portions amended or superseded by FAS-91,
　　　　　　　　　　　　　　　　　　　　　96, 97, 109, 113, 114, 115, 120, 121, and 124.
　　　　　　　　　　　　　　　　　　　　　Insurance Enterprises, ch. **55**

FASB Statement No. 61
Accounting for Title Plant　　　　　　　　　Portions amended by FAS-121.
　　　　　　　　　　　　　　　　　　　　　Insurance Enterprises, ch. **55**
　　　　　　　　　　　　　　　　　　　　　Title Plant, ch. **56**

FASB Statement No. 62
Capitalization of Interest Cost in Situations
Involving Certain Tax-Exempt Borrowings
and Certain Gifts and Grants　　　　　　　Interest Costs Capitalized, ch. **24**

FASB Statement No. 63
Financial Reporting by Broadcasters　　　　Broadcasters, ch. **50**

FASB Statement No. 64
Extinguishments of Debt Made to Satisfy
Sinking-Fund Requirements　　　　　　　　Extinguishment of Debt, ch. **15**

FASB Statement No. 65
Accounting for Certain Mortgage Banking
Activities　　　　　　　　　　　　　　　　Portions amended or superseded by FAS-91,
　　　　　　　　　　　　　　　　　　　　　115, 122, 124, and 125.
　　　　　　　　　　　　　　　　　　　　　Mortgage Banking Industry, ch. **57**

FASB Statement No. 66
Accounting for Sales of Real Estate　　　　Portions amended or superseded by FAS-98
　　　　　　　　　　　　　　　　　　　　　and 121.
　　　　　　　　　　　　　　　　　　　　　Real Estate-Recognition of Sales, ch. **62**

FASB Statement No. 67
Accounting for Costs and Initial Rental
Operations of Real Estate Projects　　　　　Real Estate Costs and Rental Operations,
　　　　　　　　　　　　　　　　　　　　　ch. **61**

FASB Statement No. 68
Research and Development Arrangements

Research and Development Costs, ch. **41**

FASB Statement No. 69
Disclosures about Oil and Gas Producing
Activities

Portions amended or superseded by FAS-89,
95, 96, 109, 111, and 121.
Oil and Gas Producing Companies, ch. **59**

FASB Statement No. 70
Financial Reporting and Changing Prices:
Foreign Currency Translation

Superseded by FAS-89

FASB Statement No. 71
Accounting for the Effects of Certain Types
of Regulation

Portions amended or superseded by FAS-90,
92, 86, 96, 109, and 121.
Regulated Industries, ch. **63**

FASB Statement No. 72
Accounting for Certain Acquisitions of
Banking or Thrift Institutions

Business Combinations, ch. **3**
Intangible Assets, ch. **23**
Banking and Thrift Institutions, ch. **49**

FASB Statement No. 73
Reporting a Change in Accounting for
Railroad Track Structures

Accounting Changes, ch. **1**

FASB Statement No. 74
Accounting for Special Termination Benefits
Paid to Employees

Superseded by FAS-88

FASB Statement No. 75
Deferral of the Effective Date of Certain
Accounting Requirements for Pension
Plans of State and Local Governmental
Units

Pension Plan Financial Statements, ch. **60**

FASB Statement No. 76
Extinguishment of Debt

Superseded by FAS-125

FASB Statement No. 77
Reporting by Transferors for Transfers of
Receivables with Recourse

Superseded by FAS-125

FASB Statement No. 78
Classification of Obligations That Are
Callable by the Creditor

Current Assets and Current Liabilities, ch. **9**

FASB Statement No. 79
Elimination of Certain Disclosures for Business
Combinations by Nonpublic Enterprises

Business Combinations, ch. **3**

FASB Statement No. 80
Accounting for Futures Contracts

Portions amended by FAS-115.
Futures Contracts, ch. **18**

FASB Statement No. 81
Disclosure of Postretirement Health Care and
Life Insurance Benefits

Superseded by FAS-106

FASB Statement No. 82
Financial Reporting and Changing Prices:
Elimination of Certain Disclosures — Superseded by FAS-89

FASB Statement No. 83
Designation of AICPA Guides and Statement
of Position on Accounting by Brokers and
Dealers in Securities, by Employee Benefit
Plans, and by Banks as Preferable for Purposes
of Applying APB Opinion 20 — Rescinded by FAS-111

FASB Statement No. 84
Induced Conversions of Convertible Debt — Convertible Debt and Debt with Warrants, ch. **8**

FASB Statement No. 85
Yield Test for Determining whether a
Convertible Security Is a Common Stock
Equivalent — Superseded by FAS-128 for periods ending after December 15, 1997

FASB Statement No. 86
Accounting for the Costs of Computer
Software to Be Sold, Leased, or Otherwise
Marketed — Research and Development Costs, ch. **41**

FASB Statement No. 87
Employers' Accounting for Pensions — Portions amended or superseded by FAS-96, 106, and 109.
Pension Plans—Employers, ch. **34**

FASB Statement No. 88
Employers' Accounting for Settlements and
Curtailments of Defined Benefit Pension
Plans and for Termination Benefits — Pension Plans—Settlements and Curtailments, ch. **35**

FASB Statement No. 89
Financial Reporting and Changing Prices — Portions amended by FAS-96 and 109.
Changing Prices, ch. **5**
Oil and Gas Producing Companies, ch. **59**

FASB Statement No. 90
Regulated Enterprises—Accounting for
Abandonments and Disallowances of Plant
Costs — Portions amended or superseded by FAS-92, 96, and 109.
Regulated Industries, ch. **63**

FASB Statement No. 91
Accounting for Nonrefundable Fees and Costs
Associated with Originating or Acquiring
Loans and Initial Direct Costs of Leases — Portions amended or superseded by FAS-98, 114, 115, and 124.
Leases, ch. **30**
Banking and Thrift Institutions, ch. **49**
Insurance Enterprises, ch. **55**
Mortgage Banking Industry, ch. **57**

FASB Statement No. 92
Regulated Enterprises—Accounting for
Phase-in Plans — Regulated Industries, ch. **63**

FASB Statement No. 93
Recognition of Depreciation by Not-for-
Profit Organizations
      Portions amended by FAS-99.
      Not-for-Profit Organizations, ch. **58**

FASB Statement No. 94
Consolidation of all Majority-Owned
Subsidiaries
      Consolidated Financial Statements, ch. **6**
      Equity Method, ch. **14**

FASB Statement No. 95
Statement of Cash Flows
      Portions amended by FAS-102, 104, and 117.
      Cash Flow Statement, ch. **4**

FASB Statement No. 96
Accounting for Income Taxes
      Superseded by FAS-109

FASB Statement No. 97
Accounting and Reporting by Insurance
Enterprises for Certain Long-Duration
Contracts and for Realized Gains and
Losses from the Sale of Investments
      Portions amended or superseded by FAS-113,
      115, and 120.
      Insurance Enterprises, ch. **55**

FASB Statement No. 98
Accounting for Leases:
• Sale-Leaseback Transactions
  Involving Real Estate
• Sales-Type Leases of Real Estate
• Definition of the Lease Term
• Initial Direct Costs of Direct
  Financing Leases
      Leases, ch. **30**
      Real Estate—Recognition of Sales, ch. **62**

FASB Statement No. 99
Deferral of the Effective Date of
Recognition of Depreciation by
Not-for-Profit Organizations
      Not-for-Profit Organizations, ch. **58**

FASB Statement No. 100
Accounting for Income Taxes—Deferral of
the Effective Date of FASB Statement No. 96
      Superseded by FAS-103, 108, and 109.

FASB Statement No. 101
Regulated Enterprises—Accounting for
the Discontinuation of Application
of FASB Statement No. 71
      Portions amended by FAS-121.
      Regulated Industries, ch. **63**

FASB Statement No. 102
Statement of Cash Flows—Exemption of
Certain Enterprises and Classification
of Cash Flows from Certain Securities
Acquired for Resale
      Portions amended by FAS-115.
      Cash Flow Statement, ch. **4**

FASB Statement No. 103
Accounting for Income Taxes—Deferral of
the Effective Date of FASB Statement No. 96
      Superseded by FAS-108 and 109.

FINANCIAL ACCOUNTING STANDARDS BOARD
INTERPRETATIONS (FINs)

FASB Interpretation No. 5
Applicability of FASB Statement No. 2 to
Development Stage Enterprises   Superseded by FAS-7

FASB Interpretation No. 6
Applicability of FASB Statement No. 2 to
Computer Software   Portions amended or superseded by FAS-86.
                                              Research and Development Costs, ch. **41**

FASB Interpretation No. 7
Applying FASB Statement No. 7 in
Financial Statements of Established
Operating Enterprises   Development Stage Enterprises, ch. **12**

FASB Interpretation No. 8
Classification of a Short-Term Obligation
Repaid Prior to Being Replaced by a
Long-Term Security   Current Assets and Current Liabilities, ch. **9**

FASB Interpretation No. 9
Applying APB Opinions No. 16 and 17
When a Savings and Loan Association or a
Similar Institution Is Acquired in a Business
Combination Accounted for by the
Purchase Method   Portions amended by FAS-72.
                                              Business Combinations, ch. **3**
                                              Intangible Assets, ch. **23**
                                              Banking and Thrift Institutions, ch. **49**

FASB Interpretation No. 10
Application of FASB Statement No. 12 to
Personal Financial Statements   Rescinded by FAS-83

FASB Interpretation No. 11
Changes in Market Value after the Balance
Sheet Date   Superseded by FAS-115

FASB Interpretation No. 12
Accounting for Previously Established
Allowance Accounts   Superseded by FAS-115

FASB Interpretation No. 13
Consolidation of a Parent and Its Subsidiaries
Having Different Balance Sheet Dates   Superseded by FAS-115

FASB Interpretation No. 14
Reasonable Estimation of the Amount of a Loss   Contingencies, Risks, and Uncertainties, ch. **7**

FASB Interpretation No. 15
Translation of Unamortized Policy Acquisition
Costs by a Stock Life Insurance Company   Superseded by FAS-52

FASB Interpretation No. 16
Clarification of Definitions and Accounting for
Marketable Equity Securities That Become
Nonmarketable   Superseded by FAS-115

FASB Interpretation No. 17
Applying the Lower of Cost or Market Rule in
Translated Financial Statements   Superseded by FAS-52

FASB Interpretation No. 18
Accounting for Income Taxes in Interim
Periods   Portions amended or superseded by FAS-71,
                                              96, 109, and 111
                                              Income Taxes, ch. **21**

CHAPTER 1
ACCOUNTING CHANGES

CONTENTS

CHAPTER 1
ACCOUNTING CHANGES

OVERVIEW

Accounting changes are broadly classified as (*a*) changes in an accounting principle, (*b*) changes in an accounting estimate, and (*c*) changes in the reporting entity. *Corrections of errors in previously issued financial statements are not accounting changes but are covered in the same accounting literature because of their similarity.*

Three accounting methods are identified in promulgated GAAP to account for accounting changes and corrections of errors: (1) current and prospective method, (2) cumulative effect method, and (3) retroactive restatement method. These methods are not alternatives—the authoritative literature is specific concerning which method is to be used for each type of accounting change or correction of error.

GAAP for accounting changes apply to financial statements prepared in conformity with GAAP and are found in the following authoritative literature:

APB-20	Accounting Changes
FAS-3	Reporting Accounting Changes in Interim Financial Statements
FAS-73	Reporting a Change in Accounting for Railroad Track Structures
FAS-111	Rescission of FASB Statement No. 32 and Technical Corrections
FIN-1	Accounting Changes Related to the Cost of Inventory
FIN-20	Reporting Accounting Changes under AICPA Statements of Position

CROSS-REFERENCES

1999 Miller GAAP Guide: Chapter 2, "Accounting Policies"; Chapter 13, "Earnings per Share"; Chapter 26, "Interim Financial Reporting"; Chapter 42, "Results of Operations"

1999 MILLER GAAP IMPLEMENTATION MANUAL: EITF: Chapter 1, "Accounting Changes"

1999 MILLER NOT-FOR-PROFIT REPORTING : Chapter 1, "Introduction"

1999 MILLER GAAS GUIDE: Chapter 3, "Generally Accepted Accounting Principles"; Chapter 8, "Evidence"; Chapter 11, "Auditor's Reports"

BACKGROUND

Changes in accounting principle, estimate, and entity are described in the authoritative literature as follows:

- *Change in accounting principle*—Results from the adoption of a generally accepted accounting principle different from the one used previously for financial reporting purposes. The term *principle* includes not only principles and practices, but also methods of applying them (APB-20, par. 7).

- *Change in accounting estimate*—Necessary consequence of periodic presentations of financial statements and the many estimates and assumptions that underlie those statements. Future events and their effects cannot be known with certainty; estimating and the exercise of judgment are required in the preparation of financial statements (APB-20, par. 10).

- *Change in accounting entity*—A special type of change in accounting principle that results when the reporting entity is different from that of previous periods. This type of change is limited mainly to (*a*) presenting consolidated or combined financial statements in place of individual company statements, (*b*) changing specific subsidiaries that make up the group of companies for which consolidated financial statements are presented, and (*c*) changing the companies included in combined financial statements (APB-20, par. 12).

Corrections of errors are not accounting changes. They are sufficiently similar, however, that the authoritative literature discusses them with accounting changes. Errors in financial statements result from mathematical mistakes, mistakes in the application of accounting principles, and the oversight or misuse of facts that existed at the time financial statements were prepared. A change from an unacceptable accounting principle or method to an acceptable one is also considered a correction of an error (APB-20, par. 13).

Three approaches for dealing with accounting changes and corrections of errors are included in APB-20: (1) the current and prospective method, (2) the cumulative effect method, and (3) the retroactive restatement method. In the current and prospective method, the impact of the change is reflected in current and future financial statements without adjustment for prior years. In the cumulative effect method, the effect of the change on prior years is recognized in the determination of income in the year of change. In the retroactive restatement method, prior years' financial statements are revised to include the effect of the change.

The authoritative literature specifies which method is appropriate in each individual circumstance, as summarized below:

Type of Change/ Correction	*Method of Accounting*		
	Current and Prospective	*Cumulative Effect*	*Retroactive Restatement*
Change in principle			
General Rule		X	
Limited special cases			X
Change in estimate	X		
Change in entity			X
Correction of errors			X

The following areas are not considered changes in an accounting principle (APB-20, par. 8):

1. A principle, practice, or method adopted for the first time on new or previously immaterial events or transactions

2. A principle, practice, or method adopted or modified because of events or transactions that are clearly different in substance

☞ **PRACTICE POINTER:** A situation that is not mentioned in APB-20, but generally is not considered a change in accounting principle, is changing from an accelerated depreciation method to the straight-line method at a point in the life of the asset, provided the change is planned at the time the accelerated method is adopted and the policy is applied consistently.

A change in the composition of the elements of cost (material, labor, and overhead) included in inventory is an accounting change that must be justified based on the rule of preferability (FIN–1, par. 5).

FAS-111 amends APB-20 to recognize the hierarchy of accounting principles set forth in Statement on Auditing Standards (SAS) No. 69 (The Meaning of "Present Fairly in Conformity with Generally Accepted Accounting Principles" in the Independent Auditor's Report). SAS-69 defines four categories of established accounting principles. Sources of accounting principles in higher categories carry more weight and should be followed when conflicts arise. When two sources within the same category provide conflicting guidance, the approach that better portrays the substance of the transaction should be selected. (See the section of the 1999 *Miller GAAP Guide* titled "About the GAAP Hierarchy," for further information.)

REPORTING A CHANGE IN ACCOUNTING PRINCIPLE

The following are some common changes in accounting principles (APB-20, par. 9):

1. A change in the method of pricing inventory, such as LIFO to FIFO or FIFO to LIFO

2. A change in the method of depreciating previously recorded assets, such as from straight-line to accelerated method or from accelerated to straight-line method

3. A change in the method of accounting for long-term construction-type contracts

Although the presumption is that once an accounting principle has been adopted it should not be changed, when a change is necessary it generally is recognized by including the cumulative effect of the change in the net income of the period of change (APB-20, par. 18). The cumulative effect of a change in an accounting principle is the total direct effects (less related taxes) that the change has on prior periods (i.e., on retained earnings at the beginning of the period). For example, if the total direct effects of a change in a depreciation method has the effect of increasing prior years' income by $100,000 and if the appropriate income tax rate is 40%, the cumulative effect of the change in the depreciation method is $60,000 [$100,000 x (1 – .40)].

☞ **PRACTICE POINTER:** When computing the cumulative effect of a change in accounting principle, do *not* include the difference between the previous principle and the newly adopted principle for the current period. Compute the cumulative effect as the difference in retained earnings at the beginning of the period of change. Thus, the timing of the change within an annual period is not important because the amount of the cumulative effect is the same regardless of when the change is made. Timing may be important, however, in reporting at interim dates within an annual period.

The cumulative effect is not an extraordinary item, but it is shown in the income statement net of related tax effects between extraordinary items and net income, as follows (numbers assumed for illustrative purposes) (APB-20, par. 20):

Income before extraordinary items (including the effect of a change in an accounting principle for the current year)	$700,000
Extraordinary loss (Note:_____)— net of $28,000 of related tax effect	(42,000)
Cumulative effect of a change in an accounting principle—net of $40,000 of related tax effect	60,000
Net income	$718,000

Earnings per share shown on the face of the income statement should include the per share amount attributable to the cumulative effects of the accounting change (net of related taxes).

The authoritative literature specifies that certain changes in accounting principle be accounted for by restating prior years' financial statements. The following changes in accounting principle are exceptions to the general rule of presenting the cumulative effect in income, and prior-period financial statements that are presented for comparative purposes must be retroactively restated in reporting a change in an accounting principle (FAS-73, par. 2):

1. Change from LIFO method of inventory pricing to another method

2. Change in accounting for long-term construction-type contracts

3. Change to or from the "full cost" method of accounting in the extractive industries

4. Change from the retirement-replacement-betterment method of accounting for railroad track structures to the depreciation method of accounting (FAS-73, par. 2)

In addition, a one-time change in accounting principles for closely held corporations in conjunction with a public offering of equity securities, or when such a company first issues financial statements to (1) obtain additional equity capital, (2) effect a business combination, or (3) register securities, is accounted for by retroactively restating financial statements of previous periods (APB-20, par. 29).

> ☞ **PRACTICE POINTER:** The cumulative effect method and retroactive restatement method both require the same information. The effect of the accounting change on all prior periods must be determined. In a retroactive restatement, this effect is charged or credited to beginning retained earnings in the year of change. In the cumulative effect method, the total effect appears in the income statement of the year of change as a separate item immediately above net income. Under both methods, the newly adopted accounting principle or practice is used in determining net income of the year of change.

Calculating the Cumulative Effect

In computing the cumulative effect of a change in an accounting principle, the *direct effects* of the change are always included, but the *nondiscretionary effects* (indirect effects) are included only if they are being recorded on the books as a result of the change. Direct effects of a change in accounting principle are those adjustments that are necessary to apply the change to all affected prior periods. Nondiscretionary effects (indirect) are *secondary effects* that sometimes arise from applying the newly adopted accounting principle to the prior years involved in the change. For example, a change from an accelerated depreciation method to the straight-line method will directly affect the net income of the prior periods in which the accelerated method was used. Profit-sharing expense, incentive compensation costs, and royalties based on net income, however, are affected only if the base on which they were computed (net income, income before extraordinary items, etc.) is changed. For example, if in prior years a manager had been receiving a bonus of 10% of net income, and a change in an accounting principle affects the prior years' bonuses, a nondiscretionary effect results. If an adjustment is to be made to the manager's bonus in the current year (recorded on the books), the nondiscretionary effects, less related taxes, are included in the calculation of the cumulative effect of the change in an accounting principle. If the company is owed money by the manager as a result of the bonus adjustment and the company does not intend to collect, however, the nondiscretionary effect is not included in the cumulative effect, because it is not recorded on the books (APB-20, footnote 6).

When a change in an accounting principle involves depreciation, an adjustment is made to the accumulated depreciation account (APB-20, par. 22). Assume that a change in an accounting principle involves a change from an accelerated method to the straight-line method for a particular asset. The direct effect of such a change is the difference in depreciation expense for all prior years in which the particular asset was depreciated. Assume that the difference in the depreciation methods resulted in an increase to prior years' income of $100,000. Thus, the cumulative effect of the change in depreciation methods, before related taxes, is $100,000. If the income tax rate is 40%, deferred taxes would have to be adjusted for the tax on the $100,000 cumulative effect. The journal entry to record the cumulative effect of a change in an accounting principle and its related tax effect is as follows:

Accumulated depreciation	$100,000	
Deferred income taxes		$40,000
Cumulative effect of a change in accounting principle		$60,000

A new depreciation method may be adopted for newly acquired long-lived assets and future assets of the same class and at the same time, older long-lived assets of the same class may be depreciated under a different method. This type of change in an accounting principle does not require an adjustment, but APB-20 does require disclosure of the change and its effect on income before extraordinary items and on net income of the period of change, along with related per share data (APB-20, par. 24).

If an accounting change is considered immaterial in the year of change but is reasonably expected to become material in subsequent periods, it should be disclosed fully in the year of change (APB-20, par. 38).

Pro Forma Disclosures

In reporting a change in an accounting principle in the income statement, pro forma disclosure of certain information is required. The pro forma portion of the income statement presentation includes (*a*) income before extraordinary items, (*b*) net income, and (*c*) related per share data for both primary and fully diluted earnings. For comparative purposes pro forma information must be disclosed for the current period and all prior periods presented. The pro forma portion is presented as if the newly adopted accounting principle had been used in prior years. Thus, the direct effects (less related taxes) of the newly adopted accounting principle and the indirect effects (less related taxes) are used in determining the pro forma amounts. However, the indirect effects are used only if they are to be recorded on the books. The cumulative effect of a change in an accounting principle does not appear in the pro forma presentation (APB-20, par. 21).

Illustration of Regular and Pro Forma Income Statement Presentations Required by APB-20

	in thousands	
Regular portion:	*19X2*	*19X1*
Income before extraordinary item(s) and cumulative effect of a change in an accounting principle	$1,243	$1,540
Extraordinary item(s) [describe]	—	787
Cumulative effect on prior years (to December 31, 19X1) of a change in an accounting principle	(133)	—
Net income	$1,110	$2,327
Per share amounts (100,000 shares of common stock outstanding):		
Income before extraordinary item(s) and cumulative effect of a change in an accounting principle	$12.43	$15.40
Extraordinary item(s)		7.87
Cumulative effect on prior years (to December 31, 19X1) of a change in an accounting principle	(1.33)	—
Net income	$11.10	$23.27
Pro forma portion:		
Income before extraordinary item(s), assuming accounting change is applied retroactively	$1,243	$1,450
Earnings per share	$12.43	$14.50
Net income	$1,243	$2,237
Earnings per share	$12.43	$22.37

Note: As required by GAAP, extraordinary items and the cumulative effect on prior years are both shown on financial statements net of any related tax.

Cumulative Effect Not Determinable

Determining the cumulative effect on retained earnings at the beginning of the period in which a change in accounting principle is made may not be practical or even possible in some situations. The principal example is a change in inventory pricing to LIFO. In this situation, no cumulative effect is presented in income. Disclosure consists of showing the effect of the change on the results of operations for the current period, including earnings per share, and explaining the reason for omitting the cumulative effect and other disclosures, including the pro forma amounts (APB-20, par. 26).

The following points summarize GAAP for changes in accounting principle (other than those for which restatement of prior years is required) (APB-20, par. 19):

1. Prior-period comparative financial statements are presented as previously reported.

2. The cumulative effect of changing to a new accounting principle is included in net income of the period of the change and is shown in the income statement between extraordinary items and net income.

3. The earnings per share information on the face of the income statement includes the per share amount of the cumulative effect of the change.

4. The earnings per share for income before extraordinary items and net income should be shown on the face of the income statement for all periods presented.

Justifying a Change in Accounting Principle

The nature, justification, and preferability (if applicable) of a change in an accounting principle and its effects on income must be clearly disclosed in the financial statements of the period in which the change is made. This usually is accomplished in a note to the financial statements (APB-20, par. 28).

FAS-111 states that a pronouncement issued by the FASB or by other bodies constitutes sufficient support for making a change in accounting principle, provided the hierarchy established by SAS-69 is followed.

When an AICPA Industry Audit and Accounting Guide or Statement of Position requires a change in accounting, the manner of reporting that change (the retroactive restatement method or the cumulative effect method) specified in the Guide or SOP should be followed (APB-20, par. 4, and FIN-20, par. 5).

Reporting Changes in Principles in Interim Periods

The cumulative effect of a change in accounting principle is included in net income of the first interim period of the year in which a change is made, regardless of the period during the year in which the change occurs. If the accounting change occurs in other than the first interim period, the current and prior interim statements are restated to include the newly adopted accounting principle. The cumulative effect of the change in an accounting principle is included only in the net income of the first interim period (FAS-3, pars. 9 and 10).

When the cumulative effects of a change in an accounting principle cannot be determined, the pro forma amounts cannot be computed. In this event, the cumulative effect and pro forma amounts are omitted. The amount of the effect of adopting the new accounting principle and its per share data for each interim period and year-to-date amounts are disclosed in a footnote to the financial statements, however, along with the reasons for omitting the cumulative effect and pro forma information (FAS-3, par. 12).

Publicly traded companies that do not issue separate fourth-quarter reports must disclose in a note to their annual reports any effect of an accounting change made during the fourth quarter. This is similar to other disclosure requirements of publicly traded companies that do not issue fourth-quarter interim reports (FAS-3, par. 14).

The following disclosures concerning a cumulative effect-type accounting change should be made in interim financial reports (FAS-3, par. 11):

1. The nature and justification of the change made in the interim period in which the new accounting principle is adopted

2. The effects of the accounting change on income from continuing operations, net income, and related per share data for:
    a. The interim period in which the change is made
    b. Each, if any, prior interim period of the same year
    c. Each, if any, restated prior interim period of the same year
    d. Year-to-date and last twelve-months-to-date financial reports that include the adoption of the new accounting principle
    e. Interim financial reports of the fiscal year, subsequent to the interim period in which the accounting change was adopted

3. The pro forma effects of the accounting change on income from continuing operations, net income, and related per share data for:

   a. The interim period in which the change is made

   b. Any interim period of prior fiscal years for which financial information is presented

   c. Year-to-date and last twelve-months-to-date financial reports that include the adoption of the new accounting principle

If no interim periods of prior fiscal years are presented, note disclosure for the corresponding interim period of the immediate fiscal year in which the accounting change occurred is made for actual and pro forma income from continuing operations, net income, and related per share data.

REPORTING A CHANGE IN ACCOUNTING ESTIMATE

A change in an accounting estimate usually is the result of new events, changing conditions, more experience, or additional information, any of which requires the revision of previous estimates. Estimates are necessary in determining depreciation and amortization of long-lived assets, uncollectible receivables, provisions for warranty, and a multitude of other items involved in preparing financial statements (APB-20, par. 10).

A change in an accounting estimate caused in part or entirely by a change in an accounting principle is reported as a change in an accounting estimate (APB-20, par. 11).

A change in an accounting estimate is not accounted for by restating prior years' financial statements or by including the cumulative effect of the change in income. The effect of a change in accounting estimate is accounted for (*a*) in the period of change, if the change affects only that period or (*b*) in the period of change and future periods, if the change affects both (APB-20, par. 31).

If a change in an accounting estimate affects future periods, the effect on income before extraordinary items, net income, and the related per share information of the current period should be disclosed in the income statement (APB-20, par. 33).

☛ **PRACTICE POINTER:** Distinguishing between a *change in accounting estimate* and the *correction of an error* may be difficult and may require significant professional judgment. In the final analysis, the difference comes down to the timing of the availability of the information upon which the change or correction is made. If the information is newly available, the adjustment is a change in accounting estimate. If the information was previously available but was not used or was misused, the adjustment is a correction of an error. This classification is important because the change in estimate is accounted for prospectively, while the correction of an error requires restatement of previously issued financial statements.

REPORTING A CHANGE IN ENTITY

A change in entity results when financial statements are those of a different entity from previous accounting periods. This type of accounting change is illustrated by the following (APB-20, par. 12):

1. Presenting consolidated or combined financial statements in place of statements of individual companies

2. Changing specific subsidiaries comprising the group of companies for which consolidated financial statements are presented

3. Changing the companies included in combined financial statements

Restatement of prior years' financial statements is necessary when an accounting change results in financial statements that are actually statements of a different reporting entity (APB-20, par. 34). All prior and current periods presented are restated to reflect financial information for the new reporting entity.

The nature of the change and the reason for it must be disclosed. Changes in income before extraordinary items, net income, and related earnings per share data must be adequately disclosed (APB-20, par. 35).

REPORTING CORRECTIONS OF ERRORS

Errors in financial statements discovered subsequently to their issuance are reported as prior-period adjustments. Errors result from mistakes in mathematics and application of an accounting principle or from misjudgment in the use of facts. While corrections of errors and changes in estimate are similar and are sometimes confused, they are different in that a change in estimate is based on new (revised) information that was not previously available. A change from an unacceptable accounting principle to a generally accepted one is considered a correction of an error for financial reporting purposes (APB-20, par. 13).

Corrections of errors are incorporated into financial statements by retroactively restating prior periods' financial statements. The nature of the error and the effect of its correction on income before extraordinary items, net income, and the related per share data shall be disclosed fully in the period the error is discovered and corrected (APB-20, par. 37).

FINANCIAL SUMMARIES

The presentation of accounting changes, including pro forma amounts, in financial summaries, including five-year summaries, should be presented in the same way as primary financial statements (APB-20, par. 39).

Illustration of Current and Prospective Method

In 19X5, Martin Co. paid $150,000 for a building that was expected to have a 10-year life with an estimated value at the end of that period of $25,000. Straight-line depreciation was used through 19X8. In 19X9, management's reassessment of the useful lives of all assets resulted in a decision that the useful life would be 15 years from the time of purchase, at which time the estimated value would be $10,000.

The book value of the asset at the time of the change is computed as follows:

Cost	$150,000
Accumulated depreciation [($150,000 − $25,000)/10] x 4	(50,000)
	$100,000

Depreciation for 19X9 and each of the next 11 years (15 years total − 4 years depreciated to date) is computed and recorded as follows:

Depreciable base ($100,000 − $10,000)	$90,000
Estimated residual value	(10,000)
Depreciable cost	$80,000
Depreciation per year (80,000/11)	$7,273

Entry: Depreciation Expense	7,273	
Accumulated Depreciation		7,273

No cumulative effect is recorded. Disclosure is required of the nature of the change and the impact on income ($12,500 − $7,273 = $5,227) as follows:

During 19X9, management determined that the useful life of the building was longer than originally expected. A change in accounting estimate was recognized to reflect this decision, resulting in an increase in net income of $5,227.

Illustration of Cumulative Effect Method

At the end of 19X9, a company decides to change from an accelerated method of recording depreciation on plant equipment to the straight-line method. The direct effect of this change is $600,000 (19X9—$100,000; 19X8—$60,000; 19X7—$100,000; 19X6—$140,000; 19X5 and prior—$200,000). The indirect items (nondiscretionary) affected by the change in an accounting principle are an incentive bonus plan and royalties, which are 10% of the annual net income. Any adjustment for indirect effects is to be recorded on the books. The income tax rate is 40%. The company has 1,000,000 shares of common stock outstanding and no potential dilution. The comparative income statements for 19X9 and 19X8 reflect the following without any adjustments for the accounting change:

	19X9	19X8
Income before extraordinary item(s)	$2,400,000	$2,200,000
Less: Extraordinary loss(es) (Note:___)	(70,000)	—
Net income	$2,330,000	$2,200,000
Earnings per share:		
Income before extraordinary item(s)	$ 2.40	$ 2.20
Extraordinary item(s)	(0.07)	—
Net income	$ 2.33	$ 2.20

The following adjustments are needed in the previous information to account for the change in the accounting principle:

Regular Portion

1. For the current year (19X9), income before extraordinary items and cumulative effect of a change in an accounting principle is calculated as follows:

Before adjustment	$2,400,000
Adjustment for direct effects ($100,000 less 40% taxes)	60,000
Adjustment for indirect effects (10% of $100,000 less 40% taxes)	(6,000)
As adjusted	$2,454,000

Note: Incentive bonuses and royalties of $240,000 had already been recorded on the books (10% of $2,400,000). However, the adjustment for the direct effects results in a net increase of $60,000 to income. Thus, the net indirect effects of $6,000 must be included in the calculation. The net indirect effects of $6,000 reduces income because it is an expense (incentive bonus and royalties).

2. Extraordinary items are presented in the usual manner and require no adjustment.

3. The cumulative effect on prior years of the change in an accounting principle is computed as follows:

Direct effect of the change in accounting principle on all years except the current year	$ 500,000
Less: 40% taxes	(200,000)
Indirect effect of the change in accounting principle on all years except the current year	(50,000)
Less: 40% taxes	20,000
Net cumulative effect on prior years	$ 270,000

Note: Both direct and indirect effects are included because indirect effects are to be recorded on the books for the current year.

4. Any prior years presented are disclosed at their previously reported amounts.

Pro Forma Portion

1. The pro forma portion is presented as if the newly adopted accounting principle had always been used. In addition, indirect effects of the change are considered if they are to be recorded on the books.

2. For the prior year presented (19X8), income before extraordinary items is calculated as follows:

Before adjustment	$2,200,000
Adjustment for direct effects ($60,000 less 40% taxes)	36,000
Adjustment for indirect effects (10% of $60,000 less 40% taxes)	(3,600)
As adjusted	$2,232,400

Note: Incentive bonuses and royalties of $220,000 had already been recorded on the books (10% of $2,200,000). However, the adjustment for the direct effects results in a net increase of $36,000 to income. Thus, the net indirect effects of $3,600 must be included in the calculation. The net indirect effects of $3,600 reduces income because it is an expense (incentive bonus and royalties).

The statement presentation for our illustration, taking into consideration the effects of the change in using a different depreciation method is:

	19X9	19X8
Income before extraordinary item(s) and cumulative effect of a change in accounting principle	$2,454,000	$2,200,000
Extraordinary loss (Note: ___)	(70,000)	—
Cumulative effect on prior years (to December 31, 19X8) of changing to a different depreciation method (Note: ___)	270,000	—
Net income	$2,654,000	$2,200,000
EPS before extraordinary item(s)	$ 2.45	$ 2.20
Extraordinary item	(0.07)	—
Cumulative effect on prior years (to December 31, 19X8) of changing to a different depreciation method	.27	—
Net income	$ 2.65	$ 2.20
Pro forma amounts assuming the new depreciation method is applied retroactively:		
Income before extraordinary item(s)	$2,454,000	$2,232,400
Earnings per share	$ 2.45	$ 2.23
Net income	$2,384,000	$2,232,400
Earnings per share	$ 2.38	$ 2.23

Illustration of Retroactive Restatement Method

The following is an illustration of presenting a correction of an error by the retroactive restatement method.

In 19X5, Warren, Inc., purchased equipment for $20,000 that was erroneously expensed rather than being capitalized. Depreciation policy calls for the straight-line method over five years with a salvage value of 10% of cost and a full year's depreciation recognized in the year of purchase.

The analysis and correcting entry for the discovery of this error in 19X7 are as follows:

Cost	$20,000	
Accumulated depreciation		
[($20,000 – $2,000)/5] x 2	(7,200)	
	$12,800	

Entry: Equipment	20,000	
Accumulated Depreciation		7,200
Retained Earnings		12,800

Depreciation for 19X7 and the next two years is recorded in the usual manner at $3,600 per year: ($20,000 – $2,000)/5 = $3,600.

If the error was also made for income tax purposes and additional taxes are owed, the following correction is required, assuming a 35% income tax rate and no temporary difference:

Retained Earnings	4,480	
Income Taxes Payable		4,480
($12,800 x .35)		

In the statement of retained earnings or statement of (changes in) stockholders' equity, beginning retained earnings for each year presented is adjusted for the portion of the correction of the error that is included in that figure. Disclosure is required of the nature of the error and the impact on income, as follows:

During 19X7, a 19X5 error was discovered in which equipment with an estimated five-year life was erroneously charged to expense. This error was corrected by restating the amount of retained earnings. The effects of the error were to understate 19X5 net income by $10,660 and overstate 19X6 net income by $2,340, a net overstatement of $8,320.

Note: The above income effects assume the tax effects and are computed as follows:

19X5: Cost of equipment	$20,000	
19X5 depreciation	(3,600)	
Understatement before tax	$16,400	
Income tax rate	35%	
Net-of-tax effect		
[$16,400 x (1 – .35)]	$10,660	

19X6: Overstatement before tax		
(19X6 depreciation)	$ (3,600)	
Income tax rate	35%	
Net-of-tax effect		
[$3,600 x (1 – .35)]	$ (2,340)	

CHAPTER 2
ACCOUNTING POLICIES

CONTENTS

CHAPTER 2
ACCOUNTING POLICIES

OVERVIEW

Accounting policies are important considerations in understanding the content of financial statements. FASB standards require the disclosure of accounting policies as an integral part of financial statements when those statements are intended to present financial position, cash flows, and results of operations in conformity with GAAP.

The following pronouncement is the primary source of promulgated GAAP concerning disclosure of accounting policies:

APB-22   Disclosure of Accounting Policies

CROSS-REFERENCES

1999 MILLER GAAP GUIDE: Chapter 1, "Accounting Changes"

1999 MILLER GAAP IMPLEMENTATION MANUAL: Chapter 1, "Accounting Policies and Standards"

1999 MILLER NOT-FOR-PROFIT REPORTING: Chapter 9, "Note Disclosures"

1999 MILLER GAAS GUIDE: CHAPTER 3, "Generally Accepted Accounting Principles"

BACKGROUND

All financial statements that present financial position, cash flows, and results of operations in accordance with GAAP must include disclosure of significant accounting policies. This includes financial statements of not-for-profit entities. Unaudited interim financial statements that do not include changes in accounting policies since the end of the preceding year are not required to disclose accounting policies in those interim statements (APB-22, pars. 8–10).

SIGNIFICANT ACCOUNTING POLICIES

GAAP require a description of all significant accounting policies of a reporting entity as an integral part of the financial statements. The preferable presentation of disclosing accounting policies is in the first footnote of the financial statements, under the caption "Summary of Significant Accounting Policies." APB-22 specifically states this preference, but recognizes the need for flexibility in the matter of formats (APB-22, par. 15).

Examples of areas of accounting for which policies are required to be disclosed are (APB-22, par. 13):

- Basis of consolidation
- Depreciation methods
- Inventory methods
- Amortization of intangibles
- Recognition of profit on long-term construction contracts
- Recognition of revenue from franchising and leasing operations

DISCLOSURE STANDARDS

Accounting principles and methods of applying them should be disclosed. Informed professional judgment is necessary to select for disclosure those principles that materially affect financial position, cash flows, and results of operations. Accounting principles and their method of application in the following areas are considered particularly important (APB-22, par. 12):

1. A selection from existing acceptable alternatives
2. The areas peculiar to a specific industry in which the entity functions
3. Unusual and innovative applications of GAAP

Disclosure of accounting policies should not duplicate information presented elsewhere in the financial statements. In disclosing accounting policies, it may become necessary to refer to items presented elsewhere in the report, such as in the case of a change in an accounting principle that requires specific treatment (APB-22, par. 14).

☛ **PRACTICE POINTER:** Many pronouncements require disclosure of information about accounting policies. For example,

FAS-95 (Statement of Cash Flows) requires disclosure of the accounting policy for defining the term *cash equivalents*. Because there are so many requirements of this type embedded in the authoritative accounting literature, a financial statement disclosure checklist is a very useful tool to guard against the inadvertent omission of required information.

Illustration of Disclosure of Significant Accounting Policies

Principles of consolidation The consolidated financial statements include the assets, liabilities, revenues, and expenses of all significant subsidiaries. All significant intercompany transactions have been eliminated in consolidation. Investments in significant companies that are 20% to 50% owned are accounted for by the equity method, which requires the corporation's share of earnings to be included in income. All other investments are carried at market value or amortized cost in conformity with FAS-115 (Accounting for Certain Investments in Debt and Equity Securities).

Cash equivalents Securities with maturities of three months or less when purchased are treated as cash equivalents in presenting the statement of cash flows.

Plant assets and depreciation Plant assets are carried at cost, less accumulated depreciation. Expenditures for replacements are capitalized, and the replaced items are retired. Maintenance and repairs are charged to operations. Gains and losses from the sale of plant assets are included in income. Depreciation is calculated on a straight-line basis utilizing the assets' estimated useful lives. The corporation and its subsidiaries use other depreciation methods (generally accelerated) for tax purposes where appropriate.

Inventories Inventories are stated at the lower of cost or market using the last-in, first-out (LIFO) method for substantially all qualifying domestic inventories and the average cost method for other inventories.

Patents, trademarks, and goodwill Amounts paid for purchased patents and trademarks and for securities of newly acquired subsidiaries in excess of the fair value of the net assets of such subsidiaries are charged to patents, trademarks, and goodwill. The portion of these amounts determined to be attributable to patents and trademarks is amortized over their remaining lives and the remainder is amortized over the estimated period of benefit but not more than 40 years.

Earnings per share Earnings per share is based on the weighted-average number of shares of common stock outstanding in each year. There would have been no material dilutive effect on net income per share for 19X1 or 19X2 if convertible securities had been converted and if outstanding stock options had been exercised.

Pension plans The company has pension plans that cover substantially all employees. Benefits are based primarily on each employee's years of service and average compensation during the last five years of employment. Company policy is to fund annual periodic pension cost to the maximum allowable for federal income tax purposes.

Income taxes Income taxes are accounted for by the asset/liability approach in accordance with FAS-109 (Accounting for Income Taxes). Deferred taxes represent the expected future tax consequences when the reported amounts of assets and liabilities are recovered or paid. They arise from differences between the financial reporting and tax bases of assets and liabilities and are adjusted for changes in tax laws and tax rates when those changes are enacted. The provision for income taxes represents the total of income taxes paid or payable for the current year, plus the change in deferred taxes during the year.

Interest costs Interest related to construction of qualifying assets is capitalized as part of construction costs in accordance with FAS-34 (Capitalization of Interest Cost).

Revenue recognition on long-term contracts The company recognizes revenue on long-term contracts by the percentage-of-completion method of accounting. In accordance with that method, revenue is estimated during each financial reporting period encompassed by the contract based on the degree of completion.

☛ **PRACTICE POINTER:** APB-22 states a preference for all accounting policies to be presented together, and for that presentation to be between the financial statements and their notes or to be the first note. In meeting this requirement, some companies present detailed information in the policy statement that is not directly related to accounting policy. For example, in addition to stating the inventory cost method used, a company also may indicate the dollar breakdown of raw materials, work-in-process, and finished goods. This tends to obscure the accounting policy information. A preferable approach is to limit information presented in the policy statement to content about accounting policy and to present other information in other notes, possibly with cross-references. For example, in the section of the policy statement that states inventory policy, a cross-reference to another note covering in detail information about the amount of various types of inventory may be appropriate.

CHAPTER 3
BUSINESS COMBINATIONS

CONTENTS

CHAPTER 3
BUSINESS COMBINATIONS

OVERVIEW

A business combination occurs when two or more entities combine to form a single entity. An *asset combination* results when one company acquires the assets of one or more other companies, or when a new company is formed to acquire the assets of two or more existing companies. In an asset combination, the target companies cease to exist as operating entities and may be liquidated or become investment companies. An *acquisition of stock combination* occurs when one company acquires more than 50% of the outstanding voting common stock of one or more target companies, or when a new company is formed to acquire controlling interest in the outstanding voting common stock of two or more target companies.

There are two basic methods of accounting for the above types of business combinations: (1) the purchase method and (2) the pooling of interests method. The pooling method is required when certain criteria regarding the nature of the consideration given and the circumstances of the exchange are met. If the pooling criteria are not met, the purchase method of accounting must be used to record the combination.

In a purchase method combination, the combined entity reports the assets and liabilities of the target company at fair market value on the date of acquisition. Any excess of the fair market value of the consideration given over the fair market value of the net assets acquired is reported as goodwill. If the fair market value of the consideration given is less than the fair market value of the net assets acquired, the resulting negative goodwill is immediately written off against identifiable long-term assets before a deferred credit for negative goodwill is recorded. The operating statements for purchase method combinations report combined results only for the period subsequent to the combination.

In a pooling of interests combination, the combined entity reports the assets and liabilities of the target company at the book values previously reported by the combining entities. In a pooling transaction, only voting common stock may be given as consideration, and it is recorded in an amount equal to the net book value of the combined assets and liabilities; thus, no goodwill is recorded in a pooling transaction. The operating statements for pooling of interests combinations are combined for the full year in the year of the combination regardless of the specific date the pooling occurs. Comparative prior years' financial statements are restated retroactively to reflect the pooled status.

GAAP for business combinations are found in the following authoritative pronouncements:

APB-16   Business Combinations

APB-17   Intangible Assets

FAS-38   Accounting for Preacquisition Contingencies of Purchased Enterprises

FAS-72   Accounting for Certain Acquisitions of Banking or Thrift Institutions

FAS-79   Elimination of Certain Disclosures for Business Combinations by Nonpublic Enterprises

FIN-9   Applying APB Opinions No. 16 and 17 When a Savings and Loan Association or a Similar Institution Is Acquired in a Business Combination Accounted for by the Purchase Method

CROSS-REFERENCES

1999 MILLER GAAP GUIDE: Chapter 6, "Consolidated Financial Statements"; Chapter 14, "Equity Method"; Chapter 21, "Income Taxes"; Chapter 23, "Intangible Assets"; Chapter 35, "Pension Plans—Employers"; Chapter 36, "Postemployment and Postretirement Benefits Other Than Pensions"

1999 MILLER GAAP IMPLEMENTATION MANUAL: Chapter 4, "Business Combinations"; Chapter 13, "Intangible Assets"

1999 MILLER GAAP IMPLEMENTATION MANUAL: EITF: Chapter 3, "Business Combinations"

1999 MILLER NOT-FOR-PROFIT REPORTING: Chapter 2, "Overview of Current Pronouncements"; Chapter 7, "Organizational Issues"

1999 MILLER GAAS GUIDE: Chapter 11, "Auditor's Reports"

BACKGROUND

The authoritative GAAP for business combinations are centered around APB-16. APB-16 applies to both incorporated and unincorporated entities. Certain types of transactions, however, are not covered by APB-16. These are:

1. Acquisition of any minority interests in a subsidiary (APB-16 does require the use of the purchase method for this type of transaction.)

2. Creation by a corporation of a newly formed corporation for the purpose of transferring the corporation's net assets to the newly formed corporation

3. Transfer of net assets or exchange of shares of stock between companies under common control

Other pronouncements, issued subsequent to APB-16, also address issues related to business combinations. For example:

- FAS-109 (Accounting for Income Taxes) requires that a liability or asset be recognized for the deferred tax consequences of differences between the assigned values and the tax bases of the assets and liabilities (other than nondeductible goodwill and leveraged leases) recognized in a purchase business combination.

- FAS-87 (Employers' Accounting for Pensions) requires that assets and liabilities recorded under the purchase method include a liability for the projected benefit obligation in excess of plan assets or an asset for plan assets in excess of the projected benefit obligation, thereby eliminating any previously existing unrecognized net gain or loss, unrecognized prior service cost, or unrecognized net obligation or net asset existing prior to the business combination.

Each of the above issues relating to business combinations is addressed in this chapter.

PURCHASE METHOD

Business combinations accounted for by the purchase method are recorded at cost. Cost is determined as the fair value of the net assets acquired or as the fair value of the consideration given, whichever is more objectively determinable. In exchanges involving cash, the net assets are recorded in the amount of cash disbursed. In exchanges involving the issuance of securities, normally the market value of the securities can be referred to as a basis for recording the acquisition. If the securities given are debt securities, their fair market value can be determined by computing the present value of the debt, discounted at the market rate of interest for the class of debt involved (APB-16, par. 72). Any resulting difference between par value and present value of the debt is reflected in the financial statements of the combined entity as discount or premium on the debt, in accordance with APB-21 (Interest on Receivables and Payables).

> ☞ **PRACTICE POINTER:** The market price of traded securities usually is evidence of fair value. However, the market price of a traded security issued in a business combination may have to be adjusted for the quantity issued, price fluctuations, and issue costs. One way of incorporating these factors into the transaction is to use the average market value before and after the business combination (APB-16, par. 74). Independent appraisals of the identifiable assets acquired may also be necessary to determine whether goodwill should be recorded (APB-16, par. 87).

The recorded cost of an acquisition is equal to the determinable amount of cash and other net assets that are unconditionally surrendered at the date of acquisition. Any contingent additional consideration is disclosed fully in the financial statements but is not recorded as a liability. Contingently issuable debt or equity securities are not recognized as outstanding until the contingency is resolved. The fact that contingently issuable debt or equity securities are held by an independent escrow agent does not alter this latter treatment (APB-16, par. 78).

Contingent considerations may be on the basis of maintaining or achieving specific earning levels over future periods, or on a security maintaining or achieving a specific market price. When a contingent consideration based on earnings is achieved, the acquiring company records the current fair value of the additional consideration. At this juncture, it is more than likely that the increase in the cost of the acquisition will be in the form of goodwill (APB-16, par. 80). As detailed in APB-17 (Intangible Assets), goodwill is amortized over the remaining life of the acquired asset, but not for more than 40 years.

When contingent consideration arises on the basis of maintaining or exceeding a specific market price for the securities issued to consummate the acquisition, the acquiring company will have to issue additional securities or transfer other assets in accordance with the contingency arrangements. The issuance of the additional contingency securities is based on their then-current fair value, but does not increase the overall cost of the acquisition because the recorded cost of the original securities issued is reduced by the same amount. The only item that changes is the total number of shares issued for the acquisition (APB-16, pars. 81 and 82).

Illustration of Contingent Consideration

MRK Company issues 1,000 shares of its common stock to a seller for an acquisition. The market price of the stock, at the date of the sale, is $12 per share, and MRK guarantees that if, at the end of two years, the market price is less than $12 per share, it will issue additional shares to make up any difference. Under the agreed-upon conditions MRK deposits 500 shares of stock with an independent escrow agent. At the end of the two years the market price of the stock is $10 per share, and the escrow agent delivers 200 shares to the seller in accordance with the seller's instructions. The remainder of the shares is returned to MRK.

In accordance with APB-16, MRK records the acquisition at $12,000 ($12 per share x 1,000). MRK records the issuance of the 200 additional shares at the current market price of $10 per share for a total of $2,000, and correspondingly reduces the original stock issued to $10 per share, for a total of $10,000. The total acquisition price remains $12,000, and only the number of shares issued changes from 1,000 to 1,200.

When debt securities are issued in an acquisition and additional debt securities are issued subsequently as contingent consideration, the reduction in value results in the recording of a discount on the debt securities. Discounts arising in this manner are amortized over the life of the securities, commencing from the date the additional securities are issued (APB-16, par. 82).

Contingent consideration that provides compensation for services or use of property are accounted for as expenses of the appropriate period upon resolution of the contingency (APB-16, par. 86).

Interest or dividends paid or accrued on contingent securities during the contingency period are accounted for in the same manner as the underlying security. Therefore, interest expense or dividend distributions on contingent securities are not recorded until the contingency is resolved. In the event a contingency is resolved that results in the payment of an amount for interest or dividends, that amount is added to the cost of the acquisition at the date of distribution (APB-16, par. 84).

Allocating Cost

Acquired assets are recorded at their fair market value. Any excess of the purchase price over the fair market value of identifiable assets acquired less liabilities assumed is recorded as goodwill, which is amortized by the straight-line method in accordance with APB-16 (APB-16, par. 90). Goodwill cannot be written off as a lump sum to paid-in capital or retained earnings, or be reduced to a nominal amount, at or immediately after acquisition.

> **OBSERVATION:** Some people believe that the requirement to carry goodwill as an intangible asset rather than writing it off as a lump sum upon purchase places companies that are subject to U.S. GAAP at a disadvantage compared with companies subject to the reporting requirements of countries that permit or require goodwill be be written off immediately. The primary basis for this concern is that under U.S. GAAP, earnings are reduced when goodwill is amortized in periods subsequent to the purchase.

In cases in which the values assigned to the net assets exceed the cost (defined as a *bargain purchase element* or *negative goodwill*), the noncurrent assets acquired (excluding long-term investments in marketable securities) are reduced proportionately. Excess of net assets over cost (negative goodwill) is not recorded in the financial statements unless all the identifiable noncurrent assets (excluding long-term investments in marketable securities) have been reduced to zero. If this circumstance arises, the bargain purchase element is recorded as a deferred credit, "excess of [fair market value] over cost of assets acquired in business combinations" and amortized to income over the period of expected benefit but not more than 40 years (APB-16, par. 91).

This approach requires that interest-bearing assets be recorded at present value, using appropriate current interest rates, less allowances for uncollectibility and collection. Likewise, liabilities are recorded at the present value of amounts to be paid, using appropriate current interest rates. Inventories should be recorded at net realizable value less a reasonable profit, except raw materials, which should be valued at current replacement cost. Marketable securities should be recorded at net realizable value. Plant and equipment and identifiable intangible assets should be appraised in accordance with intended use (APB-16, par. 88).

Registration and issue costs of equity securities given in a business combination accounted for by the purchase method are deducted from the fair value of the securities. Any direct costs incurred are treated as consideration and are included as part of the total cost of the acquisition (APB-16, par. 76). Liabilities and commitments for expenses of closing a plant that is being acquired are direct costs of the acquisition and are recorded at the present values of amounts to be paid (APB-16, par. 88). However, the costs incurred in closing facilities already owned by the acquiring company that duplicate other facilities which are being acquired are not recognized as part of the cost of acquisition. Direct costs include only out-of-pocket costs incurred in effecting the business combination. These include finders' fees and fees paid to outside consultants for accounting and legal services, engineering evaluations, and appraisals. Internal costs incurred in a purchase business combination must be expensed as incurred.

Acquisition of Pension Plan Assets and Liabilities

When a single-employer defined benefit pension plan is acquired as part of a business combination accounted for by the purchase method, an excess of the projected benefit obligation over the plan assets is recognized as a liability and an excess of plan assets over the projected benefit obligation is recognized as an asset. The recognition of a new liability or new asset by the purchaser, at the date of a business combination accounted for by the purchase method, results in the elimination of any (*a*) previously existing unrecognized net gain or loss, (*b*) unrecognized prior service cost, and (*c*) unrecognized net obligation or net asset that existed at the date of initial application of FAS-87 (FAS-87, par. 74).

In subsequent periods, the differences between the purchaser's net pension cost and contributions will reduce the new liability or new asset recognized at the date of combination to the extent that the previously unrecognized net gain or loss, unrecognized prior service cost, or unrecognized net obligation are considered in determining the amounts of contributions to the plan. In addition, the effects of an expected plan termination or curtailment are considered by the purchaser in calculating the amount of the projected benefit obligation at the date of a business combination accounted for by the purchase method (FAS-87, par. 74).

FAS-106 (Employers' Accounting for Postretirement Benefits Other Than Pensions) makes a similar amendment to APB-16 relating to the purchase of assets and liabilities of a postretirement benefit plan other than pensions, discussed in the *GAAP Guide* chapter titled "Postemployment and Postretirement Benefits Other Than Pensions."

Contingent Assets and Liabilities

A portion of the total cost of acquiring an enterprise under the purchase method is allocated to contingent assets, contingent liabilities, and contingent impairments of assets, if any, provided that the following conditions are met (FAS-38, par. 5):

1. It is probable that the contingent item existed at the consummation date of the business combination accounted for by the purchase method.

2. After the consummation date, but prior to the end of the *allocation period*, the facts in (1) above are confirmed.

3. The amount of the asset, liability, or impairment can be estimated reasonably.

The *allocation period* is the period that is required by the purchaser to identify and quantify the acquired assets and assumed liabilities for the purposes of allocating the total cost of the acquisition in accordance with APB-16. The allocation period usually will not exceed one year from the closing date of the purchase transaction (FAS-38, par. 4).

After the allocation period is over, any subsequent adjustments for contingent items are included in net income of the period in which the adjustment is recognized. In other words, adjustments for contingent items arising from a purchased acquisition are charged to net income if they occur after the end of the allocation period (FAS-38, par. 6).

Type of Purchase Business Combinations

A purchase method business combination may be approached in one of two ways. The acquiring company may purchase the assets (asset acquisition) of the target company. In this instance, normally the target company is liquidated and only one entity continues. Alternatively, the acquiring company may purchase more than 50% (up to 100%) of the outstanding voting common stock of the target company. In this instance, the financial statements of the two entities are consolidated in accordance with ARB-51 (Consolidated Financial Statements), as amended by FAS-94 (Consolidation of All Majority-Owned Subsidiaries).

In an asset purchase, entries are made to record the assets and assume the liabilities of the target company on the books of the acquiring company. If the purchase price exceeds the fair market value of the net assets, goodwill is recorded in the acquisition entry. If the fair market value of identifiable assets exceeds the purchase price, the resulting bargain purchase element is allocated to reduce the recorded value of the identifiable long-term assets other than investments in marketable securities. If the bargain purchase element is so large that it allows the value of identifiable long-term assets (other than investments in marketable securities) to be reduced to zero, the resulting deferred credit is amortized over the period benefited, but not more than 40 years (APB-16, pars. 87 and 91).

Illustration of Asset Purchase

On July 1, 19X7, S Company sold all its net assets and business to P Company for $415,000. The following is S Company's balance sheet as of July 1, 19X7:

Balance Sheet

Cash	$ 20,000
Accounts receivable	72,000
Allowance for doubtful accounts	(8,000)
Inventory	120,000
Plant and equipment (net)	260,000
Total assets	$464,000
Accounts payable	$ 60,000
Accrued expenses	5,000
Mortgage payable—plant	120,000
Common stock	200,000
Retained earnings	79,000
Total liabilities and equity	$464,000

Additional Information:

Confirmation of the accounts receivable revealed that $10,000 was uncollectible.

The physical inventory count was $138,000 (fair value).

The fair value of the plant and equipment was $340,000.

The journal entry to record the investment on the books of P Company is:

Cash	$ 20,000	
Accounts receivable	72,000	
Inventory	138,000	
Plant & equipment	340,000	
Goodwill	40,000	
Allowance for doubtful accounts		$ 10,000
Accounts payable		60,000
Accrued expenses		5,000
Mortgage payable		120,000
Investment in S Company		415,000

The computation of goodwill involved in the transaction is:

Computation of Goodwill

Assets	$464,000
Liabilities ($60,000 + $5,000 + $120,000)	(185,000)
Total	$279,000

Additional uncollectibles	(2,000)
Increase in inventory	18,000
Increase in plant and equipment	80,000
Adjusted net assets	$375,000
Cost of purchase	(415,000)
Goodwill	$ 40,000

Now assume that the purchase price was $350,000.

Adjusted net assets	$375,000
Cost of purchase	(350,000)
Negative goodwill	$ 25,000

Negative goodwill is not recorded, because noncurrent assets (plant and equipment) are reduced to $315,000.

In an acquisition of stock, entries are made to record the investment in the stock of the investee. An analysis of the difference between the cost of the investment and the underlying book value is required to prepare consolidated financial statements for the parent and subsidiary that will reflect the fair market value of the identifiable assets and goodwill as of the date of acquisition. Using data from the previous example, the only entry required to record the combination is:

Investment in S Company	$415,000	
Cash		$415,000

At the financial statement date, consolidated financial statements will be prepared that combine the assets and liabilities of the parent and subsidiary companies. At that time, the account "Investment in S Company" is eliminated from the statements along with the stockholders' equity in S Company. In addition, the identifiable assets of S Company are adjusted to fair market value and the goodwill of $40,000 is recorded in the consolidated balance sheet. Operating expenses, depreciation, and amortization of the combined entities are adjusted to reflect the revised asset values. In cases in which more than one class of stock is outstanding, the analysis is more complex.

Illustration of Stock Acquisition

For $1,500,000, P Company purchased 90% of the common stock and 50% of the preferred stock of S Company. At the date of acquisition, S Company's stockholders' equity was:

Stockholders' Equity

Common stock, 100,000 shares, $5 par, all authorized, issued, and outstanding	$ 500,000
5% preferred stock, 10,000 shares, all authorized, issued, and outstanding	1,000,000
Paid-in capital	200,000
Retained earnings	300,000
Total stockholders' equity	$2,000,000

The computation of the goodwill involved in the transaction is:

Computation of Goodwill

Cost of 90% common and 50% preferred	$1,500,000
Less: Company S equity:	
Common stock ($500,000 x 90%)	$ 450,000
Preferred stock ($1,000,000 x 50%)	500,000
Paid-in capital ($200,000 x 90%)	180,000
Retained earnings ($300,000 x 90%)	270,000
Total	$1,400,000
Excess of cost over book value (goodwill)	$ 100,000

The journal entry to record the investment is:

Investment in S Company	$1,500,000	
Cash		$1,500,000

Goodwill is not necessarily the difference between cost and book value of an investment, unless the book value is equal to the fair value of the underlying assets. The underlying assets represented by an investment individually are assigned a fair value at the date of acquisition, and if the assigned fair values are less than the amount of the investment, the difference is goodwill (APB-16, par. 68). For consolidation purposes, the acquisition of a stock investment may be considered the purchase price paid for an interest in the underlying net assets of a business.

If any excess of cost over acquired book value is allocated to depreciable or amortizable assets, the depreciation or amortization expense of subsequent periods must be increased to spread the amount of such excess over the remaining life of the assets.

If after assigning values to the underlying assets of an investment there is resulting goodwill, it must be amortized over a period of 40 years or less, starting from the acquisition date of the investment. *Since consolidating adjustments and eliminations are never posted on the books, however, it is necessary to reduce the beginning consolidated retained earnings, in the years subsequent to the first year, by the amount of depreciation or amortization of prior years.* Alternatively, the full equity method may be employed in accounting for the investment in the subsidiary in accordance with APB-18 (The Equity Method of Accounting for Investments in Common Stock).

Illustration of Goodwill Amortization

If P Company amortizes $10,000 of the excess of cost over book value (goodwill) over a 10-year period, the consolidated adjustment for the second full year would be:

Consolidated retained earnings	$1,000	
Amortization, current year	1,000	
Goodwill		$2,000

Goodwill is not recorded when it is obvious that the underlying assets in a stock interest purchase or the net assets in a straight asset purchase are undervalued. Any excess cost over book value at the date of acquisition is assigned specifically to these undervalued assets. When the excess cost over book value is assigned to specific assets, it is depreciated or amortized on the consolidated working papers (APB-16, par. 69).

Illustration of Cost-Book Differential Assigned to Plant Assets

Excess cost over book value of $25,000 is assigned (a) $5,000 to a parcel of land and (b) $20,000 to the building located on the land. The building has a 20-year life, and the following adjusting journal entry is made on the consolidated working papers (assume one full year):

Land	$ 5,000	
Building	20,000	
Investment		$25,000
Depreciation	$ 1,000	
Accumulated depreciation		$ 1,000

Since consolidated adjusting journal entries are never posted on the books, these entries must be repeated each year on the worksheet for consolidated statements. In addition, assuming the partner company accounts for the investments using the cost method, a correcting entry must be made for the depreciation for prior years. For example, for the second year, the above entries are made as well as the following entry:

Consolidated retained earnings	$1,000	
Accumulated depreciation		$1,000

For the third year, the correction would be for $2,000; for the fourth year, $3,000; etc. If the full equity method were used in accounting for the investments in the subsidiary, this correction would not be needed.

Financial Institutions

When a savings and loan association is acquired in a business combination accounted for by the purchase method, the assets and liabilities acquired are recorded at their fair values on the date of acquisition. This approach is called the *separate-valuation method,* as opposed to the *net-spread method,* which values the purchase as a whole, based on the spread between interest rates received on the mortgage portfolio and interest rates paid on savings accounts. The net-spread method is *not* an acceptable accounting practice (FIN-9, par. 4).

Goodwill arising from the purchase of savings and loan associations or similar institutions may be amortized using accelerated methods under the following conditions (FIN-9, pars. 8 and 9):

1. Part or all of the recorded goodwill includes one or more of the following factors, which could not be determined separately:

   a. Capacity of existing savings accounts and loan accounts to generate future income and/or additional business or new business

   b. Nature of territory served

2. The anticipated benefits to be received from the factors in (1) above are expected to decline over their estimated lives.

In addition, FAS-72 requires that goodwill arising in the acquisition of a troubled banking or thrift institution be amortized over a relatively short period because of the uncertainty about the nature and extent of the estimated future benefit related to the goodwill (FAS-72, par. 5).

Different Classes of Capital Stock

In computing a parent's investment in a subsidiary, an important consideration is to isolate those elements of the subsidiary's stockholders' equity to which the parent company is actually entitled. For instance, if the subsidiary had a minority interest, it must be excluded in computing the parent's interest. Other items that must be considered are different classes of stock, dividends in arrears, and liquidating dividends. If another class of stock is participating, it must share in the retained earnings of the subsidiary to the extent of its participation. If another class of stock is cumulative as to dividends, and dividends are in arrears, the amount of dividends in arrears must be deducted from retained earnings before determining the parent's interest in the subsidiary's stockholders' equity.

The following are guidelines for preferred stock issues:

1. Nonparticipating and noncumulative preferred stocks require no apportionment of retained earnings.

2. Nonparticipating and cumulative preferred stocks require an apportionment only to the extent of any dividends in arrears.

3. Participating preferred stock requires an apportionment of retained earnings, under all circumstances. The apportionment is made based on the total dollar amount of the par or stated values of the securities involved.

Illustration of Different Classes of Capital Stock

On January 1, 19X7, for $5,200,000, P Company acquires 80% of the common stock and 60% of the 5% preferred stock of S Company. On the date of acquisition, the stockholders' equity in S Company consisted of:

	Shares	Dollars
Common stock ($1 par)	1,000,000	$1,000,000
5% preferred stock ($100 par) nonparticipating and cumulative	50,000	5,000,000
3% preferred stock ($10 par) fully participating and noncumulative	200,000	2,000,000
Retained earnings		2,000,000

The 5% preferred stock has a liquidating preference value of $105 per share, and dividends of $350,000 are in arrears. The parent's share of the subsidiary's stockholders' equity as of the date of acquisition is determined as follows:

Apportionment of Retained Earnings

Total retained earnings	$2,000,000
Less: Dividends in arrears—Preferred	350,000
Balance	$1,650,000

Less: Liquidating preference dividend $5	250,000
Balance	$1,400,000
Less: 20% minority interest	280,000
Balance to apportion	$1,120,000
3% preferred, 2/3	(746,667)
Balance to P Company	$ 373,333

The 3% preferred stock ($10 par) participates fully with the common stock ($1 par) in the earnings of the company. The apportionment is made based on the total par or stated value dollar amounts of the common and 3% preferred, which are $1,000,000 and $2,000,000, respectively. Therefore, the apportionment of retained earnings after all adjustments is 1/3 to common shareholders and 2/3 to the 3% participating preferred shareholders.

Computation of P's Investment

	Minority Interests 20%	5% Preferred	Participating Preferred	P Company 80%
Common stock	$200,000			$ 800,000
5% preferred		$5,000,000		
3% preferred— participating			$2,000,000	
Retained earnings	280,000		746,667	373,333
Dividend—arrears		350,000		
Liquidating dividend		250,000		
Totals	$480,000	$5,600,000	$2,746,667	$1,173,333
60% of preferred to P		(3,360,000)		3,360,000
Totals	$480,000	$2,240,000	$2,746,667	$4,533,333
Cost of 80% of common and 60% of preferred				5,200,000
Goodwill				$ 666,667

Acquisition of Stock Directly from Target Company

A stock interest may be acquired directly from the investee. That is, a target company will sell some of its own capital stock to another company. In this event, the amount paid for capital stock is added to the stockholders' equity before determining the acquirer's stock interest.

Illustration of Acquisition of Stock Directly from Target Company

S Company had 100,000 shares of $1 par capital stock outstanding ($100,000) and $60,000 of retained earnings. On January 1, 19X7, S Company authorized an additional 200,000 shares of capital stock ($1 par) and sold them to P Company for $250,000. Determine P Company's stock interest in S Company.

Computation of S Company's Stockholders' Equity

Common stock ($1 par) (300,000 shares)	$300,000
Paid-in capital—common	50,000
Retained earnings	60,000
Total	$410,000

Computation of P's Investment in S

	Minority Interest 33 1/3%	P Company 66 2/3%
Common stock	$100,000	$200,000
Paid-in capital	16,667	33,333
Retained earnings	20,000	40,000
Totals	$136,667	$273,333
Cost of P's 66 2/3%		(250,000)
Negative goodwill		$ 23,333

Step-by-Step Acquisition

A corporation may acquire a target company in more than one transaction. In this case, any goodwill or negative goodwill involved is computed at the time of each step-by-step transaction. When control is achieved, it is necessary to adjust to the equity method any earlier step acquisition accounted for by the cost method. The result of this treatment is that the parent's portion of the undistributed earnings of the subsidiary for the period prior to achieving control is added to the investment account of the parent.

Illustration of Step-by-Step Acquisition

P Company acquired an interest in S Company in two steps: (1) acquiring 20% of the outstanding common stock for $200,000 and (2) the following year acquiring an additional 60% for $500,000. At the first and second dates of acquisition, the equity book value for S Company was $900,000 and $1,100,000, respectively.

Computation of Excess of Cost over Book Value

First Acquisition:

Cost of 20% acquired	$ 200,000
20% of equity book value of $900,000	(180,000)
Excess of cost over book value (goodwill)	$ 20,000

Second Acquisition:

Cost of 60% acquired	$ 500,000
60% of equity book value of $1,100,000	(660,000)
Excess of book value over cost (negative goodwill)	$(160,000)

As of the date of the second acquisition, P Company adjusts its investment account balance to the amount that would exist if the equity method had been used for the 20% holding, with the following entry:

Investments in S Company	$40,000	
Retained earnings		$40,000
($200,000 increase in S Company equity x 20%)		

The above entry may be made on the consolidated worksheet only, but subsequent consolidations would require that it be repeated each year. The simplest arrangement is to record this entry on the parent company's books.

Stock Exchanges—Companies under Common Control

In an exchange of stock between two of its subsidiaries, one or both of which is partially owned, a parent company accounts for its minority interest at historical cost, if the minority shareholders are not a party to the exchange transaction. Under this circumstance, the minority interest remains outstanding and is not affected by the transaction. The acquisition of all or part of a minority interest between companies under common control, regardless of how acquired, is never considered a transfer or exchange by the companies under common control.

The term *business combination* does not apply to the transfer of net assets or the exchange of shares between companies under common control (APB-16, par. 5). Therefore, the acquisition of some or all of the stock held by minority shareholders of a subsidiary is not a business combination. The acquisition of some or all of the stock held by minority stockholders of a subsidiary, whether acquired by the parent, the subsidiary itself, or another affiliate, should be accounted for by the purchase method (fair value) (APB-16, par. 43). Under this circumstance, the minority interest is affected by the transaction and the result is that a new minority interest is created in a different subsidiary. AICPA Accounting Interpretation No. 26 of APB-16 describes the following transactions in which purchase accounting applies: (*a*) a parent company exchanges its common stock or assets or debt for common stock held by minority shareholders of its subsidiary, (*b*) the subsidiary buys as treasury stock the common stock held by minority shareholders, or (*c*) another subsidiary of the parent exchanges its common stock or assets or debt for common stock held by the minority shareholders of an affiliated subsidiary.

Disclosure for the Purchase Method

The following disclosures are required in the period in which a business combination occurs and is accounted for by the purchase method (APB-16, par. 95):

1. Name, brief description, and total cost of the acquisition

2. Method of accounting (i.e., the purchase method)

3. Period for which results of operations of the acquisition are included in the income statement (usually starts at the date of acquisition)

4. If applicable, the number of shares of stock issued or issuable, including the amount assigned to the issued and issuable shares

5. Description of the plan for amortization of acquired goodwill, including the amortization method and period

6. Other pertinent information such as contingent payments, options, or other commitments

7. Combining several minor acquisitions for disclosure purposes is acceptable.

The following supplemental information should be disclosed in the notes to the financial statements of an acquiring company in the year of acquisition (APB-16, par. 96):

1. Results of operations for the current period, combining the acquisition as though it were acquired at the beginning of the period.

2. If comparative statements are presented, results of operations should include the acquisition as though it were acquired at the beginning of the comparative statement period (APB-16, par. 96).

> **OBSERVATION:** FAS-79 provides that nonpublic enterprises do not have to disclose the above supplemental information. For the purposes of FAS-79, a nonpublic enterprise is an enterprise other than one (a) whose debt or equity securities are traded in a public market, on a stock exchange, or in the over-the-counter market or (b) whose financial statements are filed with a regulatory agency in preparation for the sale of any class of securities (FAS-79, pars. 4 and 5).

POOLING OF INTERESTS METHOD

The pooling of interests method is intended for a combination in which the shareholders of the combining entities become shareholders in a combined company. The essence of a pooling is that the shareholders of the combining companies neither withdraw nor invest assets, but exchange shares in accordance with a ratio that preserves their interests in the combined corporation. Twelve specific conditions must be met in order for a combination to be accounted for as a pooling. If any of these conditions is not met, the combination must be accounted for by the purchase method. The conditions can be divided into three categories: (1) attributes of combining companies, (2) manner of combining interests, and (3) absence of planned transactions (APB-16, par. 45).

Attributes of Combining Companies

Two criteria describe this aspect of a pooling of interests:

1. Each of the combining companies must be autonomous and not have been a subsidiary or division of another corporation within two years before the plan of combination is initiated (APB-16, par. 46a).

   The initiation date is the *earlier* of:

   a. The date of public announcement, or notification to the shareholders of any one of the combining companies, of the major terms of the plan, including the ratio of exchange or a formula that provides for the ratio of exchange.

    b. The date that shareholders of a combining company are notified in writing of an exchange offer.

A new company, incorporated within the last two years, qualifies unless it was in any way a successor to a company that would not have been considered autonomous.

It is irrelevant whether a parent company or any of its wholly owned subsidiaries distribute voting common stock of the parent company to effect a combination, as long as the condition of autonomy is met.

2. At the date of initiation and at the date of consummation of the combination plan, each combining company is independent of the other. An intercorporate investment of 10% or less of the total outstanding voting common stock of any combining company is acceptable and will not impair the independence test (APB-16, par. 46b).

In addition, the term *business combination* does not apply to the transfer of net assets or the exchange of shares between companies under common control (APB-16, par. 5). Therefore, the exchange by a partially owned subsidiary of its common stock for the outstanding voting common stock of its parent (a downstream merger) cannot be accounted for by the pooling of interests method (FTB 85-5, pars. 13 and 14). The acquisition of some or all of the stock held by minority stockholders of a subsidiary, whether acquired by the parent, the subsidiary itself, or another affiliate, should be accounted for by the purchase method (fair value) (APB-16, par. 43).

AICPA Accounting Interpretation No. 26 of APB-16 specifically requires that purchase accounting be applied to downstream mergers. Under this Interpretation, the exchange by a partially owned subsidiary of its common stock for the outstanding voting stock of its parent should be accounted for as if the parent had exchanged its common stock for common stock held by minority shareholders of its subsidiary. Purchase accounting is applied whether a subsidiary acquires its parent or a parent acquires the minority interest of the subsidiary, because the end result is a single shareholder group. Furthermore, if a new corporation exchanges its common stock for the common stock of the parent and the common stock of the subsidiary held by the minority shareholders, the accounting treatment would be the same.

Manner of Combining Interests

Criteria (#3 to #9) describe this aspect of a pooling of interests.

3. After a plan is initiated, it must be completed within one year in accordance with a specific plan, or completed in a single transaction (APB-16, par. 47a).

> **OBSERVATION:** A pooling of interests is, in essence, a combining of existing shareholders' voting common stock in which the separate shareholder interests lose their identity, resulting in the mutual combination of risks and rights.
> Any change in the exchange ratio or terms thereof creates a new initiation date for the plan of combination. Any change in the relative voting rights that result in preferential treatment for some common stockholder groups is incompatible to a pooling of interests.

Litigation or proceedings of a governmental authority that delay the completion of a plan of combination are excepted from the one-year rule, providing they are beyond the control of any of the combining companies.

4. At the consummation date of the plan, the acquiring company offers and issues its majority class of stock (voting rights) for no less than 90% of the *voting common stock interests* of the combining company being acquired. The 90% or more of the voting common stock interests being acquired is determined at the date the plan is consummated (APB-16, par. 47b).

> **OBSERVATION:** The consummation date generally is considered the date the assets are transferred to the issuing company.

> ☞ **PRACTICE POINTER:** Although the authoritative literature specifically states "wholly owned subsidiary," AICPA Accounting Interpretation No. 18 of APB-16 suggests that the parent should own substantially all of the subsidiary's outstanding voting stock and that under no circumstances would less than 90% be considered substantially all.

This 90% requirement can be related to the requirement that intercorporate investments of 10% or less, in any company being acquired, are acceptable for the independence rule [see condition (2) above].

The determination of whether the acquiring company acquires 90% or more of the outstanding voting common stock interests at the date of consummation excludes the following shares of the company being acquired:

a. Any shares acquired for any form of consideration and held at the date of initiation of the combination plan by the acquiring parent or its subsidiaries

b. Any shares acquired and held after the date of initiation by the acquiring parent or its subsidiaries, except those shares acquired by the issuance of the acquiring company's own voting stock

☛ **PRACTICE POINTER:** In other words, intercorporate investments in the company being acquired, except those acquired by the issuance of voting common stock after the date of initiation, are excluded in calculating the number of voting common stock interests that are exchanged at the consummation date.

The larger the intercorporate investment an acquirer has in an acquisition that was acquired prior to the initiation date, the more difficult the 90% requirement will be to achieve.

An investment in the voting common stock of the acquiring company held by a company being acquired must be restated in an equivalent number of shares of the company being acquired. The equivalent number of shares is determined by the exchange ratio of the combination plan and then deducted from the number of voting common shares actually exchanged on the consummation date. The resulting number of shares of the company being acquired must equal 90% or more of its total outstanding voting common shares at the date of consummation.

Illustration of Equivalent Shares Analysis

S has 100,000 shares of voting common stock outstanding and owns an investment in P of 1,000 shares of voting common stock. P initiated a plan of combination to acquire S by offering four shares of its voting common stock (majority class) for each share of S's voting common stock. At the date of consummation, 91,000 shares of S's stock are tendered to P. However, the 1,000 shares of voting common stock of P held by S must be restated into an equivalent amount of S's stock in accordance with the exchange ratio of four to one, which equals 250 shares. In other words, at the consummation date, S is theoretically the owner of 250 shares of its own stock when restated in terms of the exchange ratio. The 250 shares are deducted from the 91,000 shares tendered, which equals 90,750 shares, and then compared to 90% of the outstanding voting common stock of S at the date of consummation, which in this case is 90,000 shares (90% of 100,000).

As a result, P's acquisition of 91,000 shares is restated to 90,750 shares, which meets the 90% requirement, and the transaction can be accounted for as a pooling of interests.

When two or more companies are acquired in a plan of combination, each condition necessary for a pooling of interests must be met by each company. However, 90% of each combining company must be exchanged for voting common stock of the acquiring company. Intercompany investments between any of the combining companies are excluded in calculating whether 90% or more of the voting common stock interests are exchanged, but are included in computing the total amount of voting common stock interests outstanding.

A plan of combination may not include a pro rata cash distribution but may, within limits, include a cash distribution for fractional shares and for shares purchased from dissenting shareholders. Cash also may be used in a plan of combination to retire, or redeem, callable debt and equity securities.

A transfer of all the net assets at the date the plan is consummated in exchange for voting common stock (majority class) of the acquiring company qualifies as an exchange of substantially all (90% or more) of the *voting common stock interests*. Although the requirement is for *all the net assets* of the company being acquired, temporary cash, receivables, and marketable securities may be retained to settle liabilities, disputed items, or contingencies. In a net asset transaction, both voting common stock and other stock may be issued by the acquiring company, if the company whose net assets are being acquired has both voting common stock and other stock outstanding. However, the voting common stock and other stock must be issued in proportion to the voting common stock and other stock outstanding of the company being acquired, at the date of consummation of the combination plan.

In determining the independence rule [see condition (2) above] in an exchange of voting common stock for net assets, intercorporate investments of 10% or less are evaluated in terms of the issuing company's voting common stock, as follows:

a. The number of voting common shares being issued at the date of consummation for all the net assets is allocated between outstanding voting common stock and the other outstanding stock, if any. The net assets being acquired should include any intercorporate investment in the acquiring company.

b. A ratio is computed between the number of shares of voting common stock outstanding, at the date of consummation, for the company whose net assets are being acquired, and the number of voting common shares of the acquirer allocated [in (*a*) above] to the acquisition of voting common stock interests.

c. An intercorporate investment of the issuer in the voting common stock of the company whose assets are being acquired is restated in equivalent shares of the ratio computed in (*b*) above.

d. An intercorporate investment in the issuing company by the company whose net assets are being acquired is not restated, because the number of shares is already stated in terms of the issuing company's stock.

e. To meet the 90% test, all intercorporate investments (when restated in terms of the stock of the issuing company) cannot exceed 10% of the number of issued shares of voting common stock allocated and issued for the acquisition of the voting common stock interests being acquired.

Illustration of Independence Rule Test

P owns 12,000 shares of S's voting common stock that was acquired prior to initiation date. P issues 100,000 shares of its voting common stock to acquire all the net assets of S, which include 1,000 shares of P's voting common stock. The 100,000 shares of P's stock is allocated 70% to outstanding voting common stock and 30% to other outstanding stock. S has 210,000 shares of voting common stock outstanding.

P has allocated 70,000 (70% of 100,000) shares of its stock to acquire the 210,000 shares of S's voting common stock at the consummation date. This results in a ratio of one share of P for three shares of S.

The 12,000 shares of S that are owned by P are converted to 4,000 shares of P. The 1,000 shares of P that are owned by S are already stated in P's stock. The 4,000 equivalent shares plus the 1,000 shares of P equal 5,000 shares, which are compared to 10% of the 70,000 shares of P's voting common stock that have been allocated for the acquisition of the voting common stock interests in S. The 5,000 equivalent shares of P are less than the 10% of the 70,000 shares allocated by P for the acquisition; thus, the combination qualifies for a pooling of interests.

---

5. No changes in the equity interests of the voting common stock of any combining company may be made in contemplation of a pooling of interests. This restriction is for a period beginning two years prior to the initiation date of the plan of combination and for the period between the initiation date and the consummation date (APB-16, par. 47c).

   Normal distributions based on earnings and/or prior policy are permitted.

   The organizational form of a mutual or cooperative enterprise does not have equity interests of voting common stock. The conversion of a mutual or cooperative enterprise to equity interests of voting common stock represents a change in the form of organization, not a change in the equity interests of voting common stock. Therefore, the conversion of a mutual or cooperative enterprise to stock ownership within two years before a plan of combination is initiated or between the dates a combination is initiated and consummated does not preclude accounting for such a combination as a pooling of interests (FTB 85-5, pars. 21 and 22).

6. The reacquisition of voting common stock by any combining company is allowed except for purposes of business combinations. In addition, any reacquisition of voting common stock between the initiation and the consummation dates must be no more than a normal amount (APB-16, par. 47d).

A *normal amount* of reacquired shares is determined by reference to a company's pattern of reacquisition prior to the initiation of a plan of combination.

A systematic pattern of reacquisition of voting common stock established for stock option or compensation plans is permitted.

After a plan is initiated, the acquisition of voting common stock of the issuing company by any combining company is considered the same as if the issuing company reacquired its own shares.

The important point in this provision of APB-16 is that shares are not reacquired in substance or form to effect a business combination.

7. Each common stockholder to a plan of combination must receive a voting common stock interest exactly in proportion to his or her voting common stock interest prior to the combination (APB-16, par. 47e).

A business combination cannot be accounted for as a pooling of interests if the issuer retains a right of first refusal to repurchase the shares issued in certain circumstances, even if the shares issued are identical to other outstanding common shares (FTB 85-5, pars. 16 and 17).

Generally, restrictions imposed on the sale of stock to the public in compliance with governmental regulations do not violate the provisions of APB-16, providing that subsequent to the combination the issuer has started the process of registering the stock or had agreed to register the stock (AIN-APB-16, #11).

8. The common stockholders to a plan of combination must receive the voting rights they are entitled to and must not be deprived or restricted in any way from exercising those rights (APB-16, par. 47f).

9. The entire plan of combination must be effected on the date of consummation (APB-16, par. 47g).

This provision prohibits contingent shares that are to be issued at a later date, except for contingently issuable shares that will be used to adjust differences in amounts represented at the consummation date by management. These differences are recorded as an adjustment to combined stockholders' equity and reflected in net income of the period of resolution or as a prior-period adjustment of the correction of an error of a prior period.

Illustration of Stock Issuance in a Pooling of Interests

Assume that A Company issues 10,000 shares of $1 par common stock for all of the outstanding common stock of B Company in an acquisition accounted for as a pooling of interests. Also assume that the stockholders' equity accounts of B Company immediately before the pooling were as follows:

Common stock, $1 par	$ 25,000
Paid-in capital	10,000
Retained earnings	25,000
Total	$ 60,000

The journal entry to record the pooling on the books of A Company would appear as follows:

Investment in B Company	$ 60,000	
Common stock		$ 10,000
Paid-in capital		25,000
Retained earnings		25,000

The investment in B Company is recorded at B Company book value. The common stock issued by A Company is recorded at par value. The credit to A Company's paid-in capital is determined by subtracting the par value of the shares issued from the total *contributed capital* of B. Finally, A Company records retained earnings equal to the retained earnings on the books of B Company.

Next assume that A issues 40,000 shares of $1 par value common stock for all the outstanding common shares of B and that before the acquisition, A Company has a balance of $50,000 in paid-in capital. The entry to record the acquisition would be as follows:

Investment in B Company	$ 60,000	
Paid-in capital	5,000	
Common stock, $1 par		$ 40,000
Retained earnings		25,000

In this entry, the paid-in capital is debited for the excess of the par value issued over the total contributed capital of B Company. Paid-in capital may be debited only if Company A has a balance in paid-in capital equal to or greater than the required debit.

Finally, assume that A Company issues 40,000 shares of $1 par value common stock for all of the outstanding common shares of B Company and that before the acquisition of B Company, A Company *has no paid-in capital balance*. In this case, A Company must credit retained earnings for an amount equal to the excess of the book value of the combined equity acquired over the par value of the shares issued in the business combination:

Investment in B Company	$ 60,000	
Common stock, $1 par		$ 40,000
Retained earnings		20,000

Absence of Planned Transactions

No subsequent transactions may counteract the effect of the combining of stockholder interests, or the pooling method will not be allowed.

10. The combined corporation may not agree to reacquire or retire any of the stock issued to effect the combination (APB-16, par. 48a).

11. The combined corporation may not enter into any agreements to the benefit of the former shareholders of the combiners, such as loan guarantees secured by issuer company stock (APB-16, par. 48b).

12. The combined corporation may not plan to dispose of substantial amounts of the assets of the combiners within two years of the date of the combination other than routine transactions in the ordinary course of business or to eliminate excess capacity (APB-16, par. 48c).

Application of the Pooling of Interests Method

All the conditions for a pooling of interests must be met before a business combination can be accounted for as such. The mechanics of applying the pooling of interests method are:

1. At the date the combination is consummated, the assets and liabilities of the issuer and combiners are recorded at historical cost (APB-16, par. 52). Issuer common stock is recorded at combiner book value, and the combiner retained earnings is recorded on the issuer's books. If the combination is an acquisition of stock, an investment is recorded in the amount of the combiner book value.

2. If an acquiring company issued treasury stock to effect part or all of a plan of combination, the treasury stock first must be treated as though it were retired (gain or loss is recorded), and then it is considered the same as any other previously unissued shares (APB-16, par. 54).

3. Intercorporate investments in the acquiring company are treated as treasury stock in combined financial statements. Intercorporate investments, other than in the acquiring company stock, are treated as retired stock of the combination (APB-16, par. 55).

4. All financial statements for the period in which the combination occurred should be reported as though the combination occurred at the beginning of the period (APB-16, par. 56).

5. Prior-year financial statements should be restated on a combined basis (APB-16, par. 57).

6. Expenses relating to the combination are expenses of the combined group and should be deducted from combined net income. Examples of such expenses are registration fees, finders' and consultants' fees, and costs and losses resulting from combining the separate companies (APB-16, par. 58).

7. If within two years after a combination, a material profit or loss results from the disposal of a significant portion of the assets of the previously separate companies, full disclosure, as an extraordinary item (net of tax effects), should be made in the combined financial statements (APB-16, par. 60).

8. Prior to the consummation date of a plan of combination, the investment on the books of the acquiring company (investor) should be accounted for by the equity method, if acquired for voting common stock, and at cost if the investment was acquired for cash (APB-16, par. 62).

In a pooling of interests, the stockholders' equities of the separate companies are combined. The combined corporation records as capital the capital stock and capital in excess of par or stated value of the outstanding stock of the separate companies. Retained earnings or deficits of the separate companies are combined and recognized as the retained earnings of the combined corporation. The amount of the par or stated value of the outstanding stock of the combined corporation may exceed the total amount of capital stock of the separate combining corporations. The excess should be deducted first from the combined contributed capital in excess of par or stated value and then from the combined retained earnings (APB-16, par. 53).

Disclosure for Pooling of Interests Combinations

The following disclosures should be made to the financial statements in the period in which the pooling occurs (APB-16, par. 64):

1. Brief description of the companies combined
2. Method of accounting for the combination (i.e., the pooling of interests method)
3. Description and amount of shares of stock issued to effect the combination
4. Details of the results of operations for each separate company, prior to the date of combination, that are included in the current combined net income
5. Description of the nature of adjustments in net assets of the combining companies to adopt the same accounting policies
6. If any of the combining companies changed their fiscal year as a result of the combination, full disclosure of any changes in stockholders' equity that were excluded from the reported results of operations
7. Revenue and earnings previously reported by the acquiring company reconciled with the amounts shown in the combined financial statements

Any plan of combination that has been initiated but not consummated at a balance sheet date must be disclosed fully, including the effects of the plan on combined operations and any changes in accounting methods (APB-16, par. 65).

In the period that a pooling of interests is consummated, recurring intercompany transactions should be eliminated to the greatest extent possible from the beginning of the period. However, nonrecurring intercompany transactions involving long-term assets and liabilities need not be eliminated, but in that event they should be disclosed fully (APB-16, par. 56).

CHAPTER 4
CASH FLOW STATEMENT

CONTENTS

CHAPTER 4
CASH FLOW STATEMENT

OVERVIEW

A statement of cash flows is required as part of a complete set of financial statements prepared in conformity with GAAP for all business enterprises. Within that statement, cash receipts and payments are classified as operating, investing, and financing activities, which are presented in a manner to reconcile the change in cash from the beginning to the end of the period.

Promulgated GAAP for the presentation of the cash flow statement are included in the following pronouncements:

FAS-95   Statement of Cash Flows

FAS-102   Statement of Cash Flows—Exemption of Certain Enterprises and Classification of Cash Flows from Certain Securities Acquired for Resale

FAS-104   Statement of Cash Flows—Net Reporting of Certain Cash Receipts and Cash Payments and Classification of Cash Flows from Hedging Transactions

> **OBSERVATION:** FAS-95 is amended by FAS-133 (Accounting for Derivative Instruments and Hedging Activities). This is effective for fiscal years beginning after June 15, 1999. FAS-133 applies in interim financial statements for periods that begin after the same date (e.g., the quarter beginning July 1, 1999). FAS-133 is covered in Chapter 16 of the 1999 *Miller GAAP Guide.*
>
> Because the effective date of FAS-133 is delayed as indicated above, and the first calendar year for which FAS-133 will be in effect is the year 2000, the impact of FAS-133 on FAS-95 is not reflected in the 1999 *Miller GAAP Guide.*

CROSS-REFERENCES

1999 MILLER GAAP GUIDE: Chapter 9, "Current Assets and Current Liabilities"

1999 MILLER GAAP IMPLEMENTATION MANUAL: EITF: Chapter 5, "Cash Flow Reporting"

1999 MILLER NOT-FOR-PROFIT REPORTING: Chapter 10, "Cash Flows"

1999 MILLER GOVERNMENTAL GAAP GUIDE: Chapter 5, "Governmental Financial Reporting"; Chapter 6, "Reporting Cash Flows of Proprietary and Similar Funds"

BACKGROUND

Information in a statement of cash flows, when used in conjunction with information available in other financial statements and related disclosures, is expected to be helpful to investors, creditors, and others users to:

1. Assess the enterprise's ability to generate positive future net cash flows

2. Assess the enterprise's ability to meet its obligations, pay dividends, and satisfy its needs for external financing

3. Assess the reasons for differences between net income and associated cash receipts and payments

4. Assess the effects on an enterprise's financial position of both its cash and noncash investing and financing transactions

FAS-95 requires that a *statement of cash flows* be included as part of a full set of general purpose financial statements that are externally issued by any business enterprise. All business enterprises are required to comply with the provisions of FAS-95 except not-for-profit organizations. FAS-95 was subsequently amended by FAS-102 and FAS-104.

FAS-102 was issued to provide exemptions from the provisions of FAS-95 to (*a*) certain employee benefit plans that report their financial information in accordance with FAS-35 (Accounting and Reporting by Defined Benefit Pension Plans) and (*b*) highly liquid investment companies that meet certain conditions.

FAS-102 also provides that cash receipts and cash payments resulting from transactions in certain securities, other assets, and loans acquired specifically for resale must be classified as *operating cash flows* in a statement of cash flows.

FAS-104 amends FAS-95 to permit banks, savings institutions, and credit unions to report net cash flows from certain transactions instead of gross cash flows required by the provisions of FAS-95. FAS-104 also amends FAS-95 by allowing an enterprise that meets certain conditions to classify the cash flow of a hedging transaction and the cash flow of its related hedged item in the same category of cash flow (operating activity, investing activity, or financing activity).

STATEMENT OF CASH FLOWS—GENERAL

A statement of cash flows specifies the amount of net cash provided or used by an enterprise during a period from (*a*) operating activities, (*b*) investing activities, and (*c*) financing activities. The statement of cash flows indicates the net effect of these cash flows on the enterprise's cash and cash equivalents. A reconciliation of beginning and ending cash and cash equivalents is included in the statement of cash flows. FAS-95 also requires that the statement of cash flows contain separate related disclosures about all investing and financing activities of an enterprise that affect its financial position but do not directly affect its cash flows during the period (FAS-95, par. 6). Descriptive terms such as *cash* or *cash and cash equivalents* are required in the statement of cash flows, whereas ambiguous terms such as *funds* are inappropriate (FAS-95, par. 7).

Cash Equivalents

Under FAS-95, cash equivalents are short-term, highly liquid investments that are (*a*) readily convertible to known amounts of cash and (*b*) so near their maturities that they present insignificant risk of changes in value because of changes in interest rates. As a general rule, only investments with original maturities of three months or less qualify as cash equivalents (FAS-95, par. 8). Examples of items commonly considered to be cash equivalents include Treasury bills, commercial paper, money market funds, and federal funds sold (FAS-95, par. 9).

> ☛ **PRACTICE POINTER:** An enterprise must disclose its policy for determining which items are treated as cash equivalents. Any change in that policy is accounted for as a change in accounting principle and is effected by restating financial statements of earlier years that are presented for comparative purposes (FAS-95, par. 10). FAS-95 does not specify the accounting treatment of amounts in bank accounts that are unavailable for immediate withdrawal, such as compensating balances in the bank account of a borrower. Logically, these amounts should be treated as cash, with disclosure of any material restrictions on withdrawal.

Gross and Net Cash Flows

As a general rule, FAS-95 requires an enterprise to report the gross amounts of its cash receipts and cash payments in the statement of cash flows. For example, outlays for acquisitions of property, plant, and equipment should be reported separately from proceeds from the sale of these assets. Similarly, proceeds from borrowing are reported separately from repayments. The gross amounts of cash receipts and cash payments usually are presumed to be more relevant than net amounts. It may be sufficient in some circumstances, however, to report the net amounts of certain assets and liabilities instead of their gross amounts (FAS-95, par. 11).

The net changes during a period may be reported for those assets and liabilities in which turnover is quick, amounts are large, and maturities are short (FAS-95, par. 12). These include cash receipts and cash payments pertaining to (*a*) investments (other than cash equivalents), (*b*) loans receivable, and (*c*) debt, provided the original maturity of the asset or liability is three months or less (FAS-95, par. 13).

FAS-104 permits banks, savings institutions, and credit unions to report net amounts for (*a*) deposits placed with other financial institutions and withdrawals of deposits, (*b*) time deposits accepted and repayments of deposits, and (*c*) loans made to customers and principal collections of loans.

Classification of Cash Receipts and Cash Payments

Under FAS-95, an enterprise is required to classify its cash receipts and cash payments into operating activities, investing activities, or financing activities (FAS-95, par. 14).

> *Operating Activities*—Include all transactions and other events that are not defined as investing or financing activities. Operating activities generally involve producing and delivering goods and providing services (i.e., transactions that enter into the determination of net income) (FAS-95, par. 21).

Cash inflows:

1. Cash receipts from sales of goods or services, including receipts from collection or sale of accounts and short-term and long-term notes arising from such sales
2. Cash receipts from returns on loans, other debt instruments of other entities, and equity securities
3. All other cash receipts not classified as investing or financing activities

Cash outflows:

1. Cash payments for materials for manufacture or goods for resale, including principal payments on accounts and short-term and long-term notes to suppliers
2. Cash payments to other suppliers and employers for other goods and services
3. Cash payments to governments for taxes, duties, fines, and other fees or penalties
4. Cash payments to lenders and others for interest
5. All other cash payments not classified as investing or financing activities

Investing Activities—Include making and collecting loans and acquiring and disposing of debt or equity instruments and property, plant, and equipment and other productive assets; that is, assets held for or used in the production of goods or services by the enterprise (other than materials that are part of the enterprise's inventory) (FAS-95, par. 15). Acquiring and disposing of certain loans or other debt or equity instruments that are acquired specifically for resale are excluded from investing activities (FAS-102, par. 10).

Cash inflows:

1. Receipts from collections or sales of loans and of others' debt instruments
2. Receipts from sales of equity instruments of other enterprises and from returns of investments in those instruments
3. Receipts from sales of property, plant, and equipment and other productive assets

Cash outflows:

1. Payments for loans made by the enterprise and to acquire debt instruments of other entities
2. Payments to acquire equity instruments in other enterprises
3. Payments at the time of purchase or soon thereafter to acquire property, plant, and equipment and other productive assets

Financing Activities—Include obtaining resources from owners and providing them with a return on, and return of, their investment; borrowing money and repaying amounts borrowed, or otherwise settling the obligation; and obtaining and paying for other resources obtained from creditors on long-term credit (FAS-95, par. 18).

Cash inflows:

1. Proceeds from issuing equity instruments
2. Proceeds from issuing bonds, mortgages, notes, and other short-term or long-term borrowing

Cash outflows:

1. Payments of dividends or other distributions to owners, including outlays to reacquire the enterprise's equity instruments
2. Repayments of amounts borrowed
3. Other principal payments to creditors that have extended long-term credit

☛ **PRACTICE POINTER:** Classify cash received from sales of inventory to customers as cash from operating activities, whether received at the time of sale or collected at some other time, on open account or on a note (short-term, long-term, or installment). Similarly, classify cash paid to suppliers for inventory as cash used for operating activities, whether paid at time of purchase or paid at some other time, on open account or on a note (short-term, long-term, or installment).

A cash receipt or a cash payment that can qualify for more than one cash flow activity is appropriately classified as the activity that is likely to be the predominant source of cash flows for that item. For example, the acquisition and sale of equipment used by an enterprise or rented to others generally are investing activities. If the intention of an enterprise is to use or rent the equipment for a short period of time and then sell it, however, the cash receipts and cash payments associated with the acquisition or production of the equipment and the subsequent sale are considered cash flows from operating activities (FAS-95, par. 24).

☛ **PRACTICE POINTER:** Take care in classifying certain cash flows. The FASB has indicated how to classify certain items that might fit logically in more than one of the major categories of the statement of cash flows. Following are examples of these items:

Interest paid Presented as an operating activity, despite the fact that dividends paid are presented as a financing activity.

Interest and dividends received Presented as an operating activity, despite their close association with other activities presented as investing activities.

Gains and losses on asset and liability transactions (e.g., sale of plant assets, extinguishment of debt) Presented as investing and financing activities, although the gain/loss was included in net income.

Income taxes Presented entirely as an operating activity, despite the fact that gains and losses that may affect income taxes are presented as investing and financing activities.

As a general rule, each cash receipt or cash payment is required to be classified according to its source (operating, investing, or financing) without regard to whether it arose as a hedge of another item. FAS-104, however, specifies that the cash flow of a hedging transaction may be classified in the same category as the cash flow of its related hedged item, provided that the enterprise (*a*) discloses this accounting policy and (*b*) reports the gain or loss on the hedging instrument in the same accounting period as the offsetting gain or loss on the hedged item (FAS-104, par. 7).

FAS-102 provides that cash receipts and cash payments must be classified as operating cash flows in a statement of cash flows when such cash receipts and cash payments result from the acquisition or sale of (*a*) securities and other assets that are acquired specifically for resale and carried at market value in a trading account and (*b*) loans that are acquired specifically for resale and carried at market value or the lower of cost or market value (FAS-102, par. 8). The cash receipts and cash payments from the sale of loans originally acquired as investments, however, are classified as investing cash flows in a statement of cash flows, regardless of any subsequent change in the purpose of holding those loans (FAS-102, par. 9).

Foreign Currency Cash Flows

An enterprise with foreign currency translations or foreign operations shall report, in its statement of cash flows, the reporting currency equivalent of foreign currency cash flows using the exchange rates in effect at the time of the cash flows. An appropriately weighted average exchange rate for the period may be used in lieu of the actual currency rates at the dates of the cash flows, provided that the results are substantially the same. The effect of exchange rate changes on cash balances held in foreign currencies is reported in the statement of cash flows as a separate part of the reconciliation of the change in cash and cash equivalents during the period (FAS-95, par. 25).

Exemption for Certain Employee Benefit Plans

FAS-102 provides an exemption from the provisions of FAS-95 for (*a*) defined benefit pension plans that present their financial information in accordance with FAS-35 and (*b*) other employee benefit plans that present their financial information similar to that required by FAS-35, including those employee benefit plans that present their plan investments at fair value. Thus, these employee benefit pension plans are not required to include a statement of cash flows in their financial presentations. However, FAS-102 encourages all employee benefit pension plans to include a statement of cash flows as part of their financial presentation in those circumstances in which such a statement would provide relevant information concerning a plan's ability to meet its future obligations (FAS-102, par. 5).

Exemption for Certain Investment Companies

FAS-102 was issued to provide for certain exemptions from the provisions of FAS-95. One of these exemptions provides that certain investment-type entities that meet all of the conditions specified in FAS-102 are not required to include a statement of cash flows as part of their complete financial presentation in accordance with GAAP. The entities entitled to this exemption are as follows (FAS-102, par. 6):

a.   Investment companies that are subject to the registration and regulatory requirements of the Investment Company Act of 1940 (1940 Act)

b.   Investment enterprises that have essentially the same characteristics as investment companies subject to the 1940 Act

c.   Common trust funds, variable annuity accounts, or similar funds maintained by a bank, insurance company, or other enterprise in its capacity as a trustee, administrator, or guardian for the collective investment and reinvestment of moneys

Under FAS-102, the investment-type entities specified above are not required to include a statement of cash flows in their financial presentations, provided that they meet all of the following conditions (FAS-102, par. 7):

a.   Substantially all investments owned by the enterprise were highly liquid during the period covered by the financial statements (highly liquid investments include, but are not limited to, marketable securities and other assets that can be sold through existing markets).

b. Substantially all of the investments owned by the enterprise are carried at market value including securities for which market value is calculated by the use of matrix pricing techniques (described in the AICPA Industry Audit and Accounting Guide titled *Audits of Investment Companies*). Securities that do not meet this condition are those for which (*a*) market value is not readily ascertainable and (*b*) fair value must be determined in good faith by the board of directors of the enterprise.

c. Based on average debt outstanding during the period, the enterprise had little or no debt in relation to average total assets. For purposes of FAS-102, average debt outstanding generally may exclude obligations from (*a*) redemption of shares by the enterprise, (*b*) unsettled purchases of securities or similar assets, or (*c*) written covered options.

d. The enterprise provides a statement of changes in net assets.

CONTENT AND FORM OF STATEMENT OF CASH FLOWS

A statement of cash flows shall disclose separately the amount of net cash provided or used during a period from an enterprise's (*a*) operating activities, (*b*) investing activities, and (*c*) financing activities. The effect of the total amount of net cash provided or used during a period from all sources (operating, investing, and financing) on an enterprise's cash and cash equivalents shall be clearly disclosed in a manner that reconciles beginning and ending cash and cash equivalents (FAS-95, par. 26).

In reporting cash flows from *operating activities* in the statement of cash flows, FAS-95 encourages but does not require an enterprise to use the *direct method* (FAS-95, par. 27). Enterprises that do not use the direct method to report their cash flows from operating activities may use the *indirect method* (also referred to as the reconciliation method). There is no difference in reporting the cash flows from investing and financing activities, regardless of whether the direct or indirect method is used to report cash flows from operations.

Direct Method

A presentation of a statement of cash flows by the direct method reflects the gross amounts of the principal components of cash receipts and cash payments from operating activities, such as cash received from customers and cash paid to suppliers and employees. Using the direct method, the amount of net cash provided by or used in operating activities during the period is equal to the difference between the total amount of gross cash receipts and the total amount of gross cash payments arising from operating activities.

FAS-95 requires enterprises using the direct method of reporting the amount of net cash flow provided from or used by operating activities to present separately, at a minimum, in their statement of cash flows, the following principal components of operating cash receipts and operating cash payments (FAS-95, par. 27):

- Cash collected from customers, including lessees, licensees, and other similar receipts

- Interest and dividends received

- Any other operating cash receipts

- Cash paid to employees and other suppliers of goods or services including suppliers of insurance, advertising, and other similar cash payments

- Any other operating cash payments, including interest paid, income taxes paid, and other similar cash payments

☛ **PRACTICE POINTER:** An enterprise may use an alternate method of computation to arrive at the amounts shown in a statement of cash flows. For example, when preparing a direct method statement of cash flows, an enterprise may make an alternate computation to determine the amount of cash received from customers; i.e., it may start with total sales for the period and adjust that figure for the difference between beginning and ending accounts receivable.

The provisions of FAS-95 encourage, but do not require, an enterprise to include in its statement of cash flows other meaningful details pertaining to its cash receipts and cash payments from operating activities. For example, a retailer or manufacturer might decide to subdivide cash paid to employees and suppliers into cash payments for costs of inventory and cash payments for selling, general, and administrative expenses (FAS-95, par. 27).

OBSERVATION: The use of the direct method is encouraged by FAS-95 because it reflects the gross amounts of the principal components of cash receipts and cash payments from operating activities, while the indirect method does not. This presentation is more compatible with the manner of presenting cash flows from financing and investing activities than is the indirect method.

Indirect Method

Enterprises that choose not to provide information about major classes of operating cash receipts and cash payments by the direct method, as encouraged by FAS-95, can indirectly determine and report the same amount of net cash flow from operating activities by reconciling net income to net cash flow from operating activities (the indirect or reconciliation method). The adjustments necessary to reconcile net income to net cash flow are made to net income to remove (*a*) the effects of all deferrals of past operating cash receipts and cash payments, such as changes during the period in inventory, deferred income and the like, (*b*) the effects of all accruals of expected future operating cash receipts and cash payments, such as changes during the period in receivables and payables, and (*c*) the effects of all items classified as investing or financing cash flows, such as gains or losses on sales of property, plant, and equipment and discontinued operations (investing activities), and gains or losses on extinguishment of debt (financing activities) (FAS-95, par. 28).

Reconciliation of Net Income to Net Cash Flow

Regardless of whether an enterprise uses the direct or indirect method of reporting net cash flow from *operating* activities, FAS-95 requires that a reconciliation of net income to net cash flow be provided in conjunction with the statement of cash flows. The reconciliation of net income to net cash flow from operating activities provides information about the net effects of operating transactions and other events that affect net income and operating cash flows in different periods. This reconciliation separately reflects all major classes of reconciling items. For example, major classes of deferrals of past operating cash receipts and payments and accruals of expected future operating cash receipts and payments, including at a minimum changes during the period in receivables and payables pertaining to *operating* activities, are reported separately. Enterprises are encouraged to further break down those categories they consider meaningful. For example, changes in trade receivables for an enterprise's sale of goods or services might be reported separately from changes in other operating receivables (FAS-95, par. 29).

If an enterprise uses the direct method, the reconciliation of net income to net cash flow from operating activities is provided in a separate schedule accompanying the statement of cash flows (FAS-95, par. 30).

If an enterprise uses the indirect method, the reconciliation may be *either* included within and as part of the statement of cash flows *or* provided in a separate schedule, with the statement of cash flows reporting only the net cash flow from operating activities. If the reconciliation is included within and as part of the statement of cash flows, all adjustments to net income to determine net cash flow from operating activities shall be clearly identified as reconciling items (FAS-95, par. 30).

Regardless of whether the direct or the indirect method is used to report net cash flow from operating activities, FAS-95 requires the separate disclosure of the amounts of interest paid (net of amounts capitalized) and income taxes paid during the period (FAS-95, par. 29).

Noncash Investing and Financing Activities

Disclosures in conjunction with the statement of cash flows must contain information about all investing and financing activities of an enterprise during a period that affect recognized assets or liabilities but that do not result in cash receipts or cash payments. These disclosures may be either narrative or summarized in a schedule, and they shall clearly relate the cash and noncash aspects of transactions involving similar items. Examples of noncash investing and financing transactions include:

- Converting debt to equity
- Acquiring assets by assuming directly related liabilities (e.g., capital leases, purchasing a building by incurring a mortgage to the seller)
- Exchanging noncash assets or liabilities for other noncash assets or liabilities

Only the cash portion of a part-cash, part-noncash transaction is reported in the statement of cash flows (FAS-95, par. 32).

Cash Flow per Share

An enterprise is prohibited from reporting any amount representing cash flow per share in its financial statements (FAS-95, par. 33).

FINANCIAL INSTITUTIONS

FAS-102 primarily affects the statements of cash flows of financial institutions. Cash receipts and payments associated with securities that are carried in *trading accounts* by banks, brokers, and dealers in securities are classified as cash flows from operating activities. On the other hand, if securities are acquired for investment purposes, the related cash receipts and cash payments are classified as cash flows from investing activities. Loans are given similar treatment. The cash receipts and cash payments associated with mortgage loans that are held for resale by a bank or mortgage broker are classified as cash flows from operating activities. If the mortgage loans are held for investment purposes, however, the related cash receipts and cash payments are classified as cash flows from investing activities (FAS-102, pars. 8 and 9).

Instead of reporting gross amounts of cash flows in their statements of cash flows, as would be required by FAS-95, banks, savings institutions, and credit unions are permitted by FAS-104 to report *net* amounts of cash flows that result from (*a*) deposits and deposit withdrawals with other financial institutions, (*b*) time deposits accepted and repayments of deposits, and (*c*) loans to customers and principal collections of loans (FAS-104, par. 7). Thus, an enterprise has the following choices in reporting cash flows in its statement of cash flows:

1. To report the gross amount of all cash receipts and disbursements

2. To report the net cash flows in the limited situations allowed by FAS-95, such as loans with maturities of three months or less, and to report gross amounts for all other transactions

3. If the enterprise is a bank, savings institution, or credit union, to report net cash flows in the limited situations allowed by FAS-104, such as time deposits, and to report gross amounts for all other transactions

4. If the enterprise is a bank, savings institution, or credit union, to report net cash flows in the situations allowed by FAS-95 and also those allowed by FAS-104, and to report gross amounts for all other transactions

> **OBSERVATION:** The choices outlined above may produce a lack of comparability among the statements of cash flows of various enterprises.

If a consolidated enterprise includes a bank, savings institution, or credit union that uses net cash reporting as allowed by FAS-104, the statement of cash flows of the consolidated enterprise must report separately (*a*) the net cash flows of the financial institution and (*b*) the gross cash receipts and cash payments of other members of the consolidated enterprise, including subsidiaries of a financial institution that are not themselves financial institutions (FAS-104, par. 7).

> **OBSERVATION:** The above provision requires separate reporting of net cash flows and gross cash flows in a consolidated statement, if the net cash flows are allowed by FAS-104. It would seem desirable, along similar lines, to require separate

reporting of net cash flows and gross cash flows, if the net cash flows are allowed by the exceptions contained in FAS-95, such as loans with maturities of three months or less. However, neither FAS-95 nor FAS-104 expressly requires separate reporting in these situations.

Illustration of Basic Procedure in Preparing a Statement of Cash Flows*

The purpose of the comprehensive illustration that follows is to demonstrate the basic procedure in preparing a statement of cash flows. Ordinarily, a statement of cash flows would contain the current year and the immediate prior year for comparison purposes. To keep the illustration as simple as possible, however, only the current year is shown, and, in addition, the provisions of FAS-102 have been excluded. Thus, the statement of cash flows in the following illustration is for enterprises other than financial institutions.

The starting point for the preparation of a statement of cash flows, in accordance with the provisions of FAS-95, is the computation of the increases and decreases in balance sheet accounts from the previous period to the current period. After all of the increases and decreases have been calculated, each one must be analyzed to determine its effect, if any, on the net cash provided or used in either the operating, investing, or financing activities of the enterprise. If an increase or decrease consists of more than one transaction, each one must be analyzed separately. In addition to the cash flow worksheet, which depicts the increases and decreases in the balance sheet accounts from one period to another, a condensed income statement is necessary.

Reference numbers have been provided throughout this illustration to allow the reader to follow each transaction from its original source to the place it appears on the statement of cash flows. Statements of cash flows prepared by both direct and indirect methods are illustrated.

This illustration consists of the following documents, in order of their appearance:

Cash Flow Worksheet—This worksheet reflects the increases and decreases in the balance sheet accounts of the AAA Accounting Corporation from 19X1 to 19X2. A condensed statement of income of the AAA Accounting Corporation also appears on this worksheet. Reference numbers are parenthesized.

Schedule of Transactions—This schedule contains a separate analysis of each increase and decrease that appears on the cash flow worksheet. Reference numbers are parenthesized.

Schedule of Cash Flows from Operating Activities by the Direct Method— This schedule illustrates how cash flow information for the direct method is obtained.

Consolidated Statement of Cash Flows (Indirect Method)—Prepared in accordance with the provisions of FAS-95.

Cash Flow Worksheet:

AAA Accounting Corporation
Cash Flow Worksheet
December 31, 19X2

	Increase or (Decrease)	Purchase of XYZ Co.	Increase or (Decrease) Without XYZ
ASSETS			
Cash & cash equivalents	$ 1,500	$ 300 (1)	$ 1,200 (4)
Accounts receivable—net	9,000	2,000	7,000 (5)
Notes receivable	(7,000)		(7,000)
Inventories	6,000	3,000	3,000 (10)
Prepaid expenses	1,000		1,000 (11)
Property, plant, & equipment	17,000	10,000	7,000
Accumulated depreciation & amortization	(5,000)		(5,000)
Investment in affiliated companies	2,100		2,100
Intangible assets	1,400	2,000	(600) (19)
	$26,000	$17,300 (2)	$ 8,700

LIABILITIES & EQUITIES			
Short-term notes payable— banks	$ (4,000)		$ (4,000)
Accounts payable & accrued expenses	5,350	$ 1,500	3,850
Long-term debt	14,000	7,800	6,200
Capital lease obligations	1,600		1,600
Deferred income taxes	1,000		1,000 (30)
Common stock	3,000		3,000
Retained earnings	5,050		5,050
	$26,000	$ 9,300 (3)	$16,700

Adapted with permission from the Journal of Accountancy, copyright © 1988 by the American Institute of Certified Public Accountants, Inc.

Income Statement

Sales	$150,000 (33)
Other income	10,000 (34)
Costs of sales	(122,000) (35)
Selling & administrative	(15,400) (36)
Depreciation & amortization	(8,600) (37)
Equity in net income of investees	3,000 (38)
Gain on sale of equipment	2,500 (39)
Interest expense	(5,500) (40)
Income tax expense	(6,000) (41)
Net income	$ 8,000 (42)
Dividends paid to shareholders	(2,950) (43)
	$ 5,050

Schedule of Transactions:

AAA Accounting Corporation
Schedule of Transactions
For the Year Ended December 31, 19X2

1. *Acquisition of XYZ Company*   During 19X2, AAA purchased the common stock of XYZ Company for $8,000 cash. The purchase price was allocated based on these fair values of XYZ's assets and liabilities at the date of acquisition:

Cash	$ 300
Accounts receivable	2,000
Inventory	3,000
Property, plant, & equipment	10,000
Goodwill & other intangible assets	2,000
Accounts payable & accrued expenses	(1,500)
Long-term debt	(7,800)
	$ 8,000
Assets acquired	$17,300 (2)
Less: Liabilities assumed	(9,300) (3)
Cash paid	$ 8,000
Less: Cash acquired in transaction	(300) (1)
Net assets acquired, excluding cash	$ 7,700

2. *Accounts receivable*   Accounts receivable net of allowances of $900 in 19X2 and $500 in 19X1 were $29,000 and $20,000 at December 31, 19X2 and 19X1, respectively. AAA wrote off $350 in bad debts and recognized a

provision for losses on receivables (in selling & administrative expense) of $750.

Accounts receivable 12/31/X2	$29,000	
Accounts receivable 12/31/X1	(20,000)	
Increase in accounts receivable	$ 9,000	
Less: Accounts receivable acquired from XYZ	(2,000)	
Increase in accounts receivable without XYZ	$ 7,000	(5)
Add back provision for bad debts	750	(6)
Increase in accounts receivable before bad debts	$ 7,750	(7)

3. *Accounts payable & accrued expenses* Accounts payable and accrued expenses were $33,000 and $27,650 on December 31, 19X2 and 19X1, respectively. Included are accruals for income taxes payable of $3,500 and $3,000 and for interest payable of $2,300 and $2,000.

Accounts payable & accrued expenses 12/31/X2	$33,000	
Accounts payable & accrued expenses 12/31/X1	(27,650)	
Increase in accounts payable & accrued expenses	$ 5,350	
Less: Accounts payable & accrued expenses from XYZ Co.	(1,500)	
Increase in accounts payable & accrued expenses	$ 3,850	
Increase consists of:		
Increase in accrual for income taxes	$ 500	(22)
Increase in accrual for interest payable	300	(23)
Increase in accounts payable from 19X1 to 19X2	3,050	(24)
Total increase	$ 3,850	

4. *Notes receivable* AAA collected principal of $2,500 on an installment note receivable related to a product sale and $4,500 on a note receivable from a prior year's sale of a plant.

Payment received on installment note receivable	$ 2,500	(8)
Payment received on prior year's sale of plant	4,500	(9)
Decrease in notes receivable	$ 7,000	

5. *Capital lease obligation* AAA entered into a capital lease for equipment with a fair value of $2,000. Principal payments on this and other lease obligations amounted to $400 during the year.

New capital lease	$ 2,000	(28)
Principal payments on new capital lease	(400)	(29)
Increase in capital lease obligations	$ 1,600	

6. *Long-term debt*   AAA borrowed $9,000 on a long-term basis during the
year and made payments of $1,800 on long-term debt.

Increase in long-term debt	$14,000
Less: Assumed in the XYZ acquisition	7,800
Increase in long-term debt without XYZ	$ 6,200
Increase consists of:	
New long-term borrowing	$ 9,000 (25)
Repayment of long-term borrowing	(1,800) (26)
Conversion of common stock (see #12)	(1,000) (27)
Increase in long-term debt without XYZ	$ 6,200

7. *Short-term revolving credit agreement*   AAA borrowed $5,500 and re-
paid $9,500 under a revolving credit agreement with an original maturity of
one year. At the time of the agreement, AAA signed a single note with a one-
year term for the maximum amount available.

Proceeds—borrowings via revolving line of credit	$ 5,500 (20)
Repayments—borrowings via revolving line of credit	(9,500) (21)
Decrease in short-term notes payable to banks	$ (4,000)

8. *Dividend from affiliated company*   An affiliate paid AAA a $900 divi-
dend. It was accounted for using the equity method of accounting.

Increase in equity in net income of investees	$ 3,000 (17)
Dividend received from equity investee	(900) (18)
Increase in investment in affiliated companies	$ 2,100

9. *Sale of equipment & construction of warehouse*   AAA received $6,500
from the sale of equipment, which had a book value of $4,000 and an original
cost of $7,000. In addition, AAA built a warehouse for $12,000 (including
$300 of capitalized interest).

Purchase of property, plant, & equipment	$12,000 (12)
Original cost of equipment sold	(7,000) (13)
Acquisition of equipment under capital lease	2,000 (14)
Increase in property, plant, & equipment	$ 7,000

10. *Depreciation & amortization expense*   AAA's 19X2 depreciation expense and amortization of intangibles were $8,000 and $600, respectively.

Depreciation expense for 19X2	$ (8,000) (15)
Accumulated depreciation on equipment sold	3,000 (16)
Decrease in accumulated depreciation account	$ (5,000)
Amortization of intangible assets	$ (600) (19)
Decrease in intangible assets	$ 600
Total depreciation & amortization expense	$ 8,600 (37)

11. *Deferred income taxes* AAA's 19X2 provision for deferred taxes was $1,000.

Provision for deferred income taxes	$ 1,000
Increase in deferred income taxes	$ 1,000 (30)

12. *Common stock issued* In 19X2, AAA issued $3,000 of additional common stock ($2,000 for cash and $1,000 upon the conversion of debt).

Sale of common stock for cash	$ 2,000 (31)
Issuance of common stock—conversion of debt	1,000 (32)
Increase in common stock	$ 3,000

13. *Dividends paid to shareholders* AAA paid dividends of $2,950 to shareholders in 19X2.

Dividends paid to shareholders	$ 2,950 (43)

14. *Cash & cash equivalents* Cash & cash equivalents were $7,500 and $6,000 on December 31, 19X2 and 19X1, respectively.

Cash & cash equivalents December 31, 19X2	$ 7,500
Cash & cash equivalents December 31, 19X1	(6,000)
Increase in cash & cash equivalents	$ 1,500 (1) + (4)

Direct Method:

AAA Accounting Corporation
Consolidated Statement of Cash Flows
(Direct Method)

Increase (Decrease) in Cash & Cash Equivalents
for the Year Ended December 31, 19X2

Cash flows from operating activities:

Cash received from customers (see separate computation)		$144,750
Cash paid to suppliers and employees (see separate computation)		(137,600)
Cash dividend received from affiliate	(18)	900
Other operating cash receipts	(34)	10,000
Interest paid in cash (net of amounts capitalized)	(40) – (23)	(5,200)
Income taxes paid in cash	(41) – (30) – (22)	(4,500)
Net cash provided (used) by operating activities		$ 8,350

Computation of cash received from customers during the year:

Sales	(33)	$150,000
Collection of installment payment for sale of product	(8)	2,500
		$152,500
Gross accounts receivable—beginning of year	$ 20,500	
Accounts receivable acquired in XYZ deal	2,000	
Accounts receivable written off	(350)	
Gross accounts receivable—end of year	(29,900)	
Excess of new accounts receivable over collections from customers	(7)	(7,750)
Cash received from customers during the year		$144,750

Computation of cash paid to suppliers and employees during the year:

Cost of sales	(35)	$122,000
Selling & administrative expenses	(36) $ 15,400	
Noncash expenses (provision for bad debts)	(6) (750)	
Net expenses requiring cash payments		$ 14,650
Consolidated increase in inventory	$ 6,000	
Inventory acquired in purchase of XYZ Co.	(3,000)	
Net increase in inventory from AAA's operations	(10)	3,000
Increase in prepaid expenses	(11)	1,000
Adjustments—changes in accounts payable & accrued expenses:		
Balance—beginning of year	$ 27,650	
Amounts related to income taxes and interest at beginning of year	(5,000)	
Accounts payable & accrued expenses assumed in purchase of XYZ Co.	1,500	

Balance—end of year	(33,000)	
Amounts related to income taxes and interest at end of year	5,800	
Amounts charged to expense but not paid during the year	(3,050)	
Cash paid to suppliers & employees during the year		$137,600

Indirect Method:

AAA Accounting Corporation
Consolidated Statement of Cash Flows
(Indirect Method)

Increase (Decrease) in Cash & Cash Equivalents
for the Year Ended December 31, 19X2

Cash flows from operating activities:

Net income	(42)	$	8,000
Adjustments to reconcile net income to net cash provided by operating activities:			
Depreciation and amortization	(15) + (19)	$ 8,600	
Provisions for doubtful accounts receivable	(6)	750	
Provision for deferred income taxes	(30)	1,000	
Undistributed earnings of affiliate	(17) + (18)	(2,100)	
Gain on sale of equipment	(39)	(2,500)	
Payment received on installment sale of product	(8)	2,500	
Changes in operating assets and liabilities net of effects from purchase of XYZ Company:			
Increase in accounts receivable	(7)	(7,750)	
Increase in inventory (Note 1)	(10) + (11)	(4,000)	
Increase in accounts payable and accrued expenses (Note 1)	(22) + (23) + (24)	3,850	
Total adjustments to net income			350
Net cash provided (used) by operating activities			$ 8,350

Cash flows from investing activities:

Purchase of property, plant, & equipment	(12)	$(12,000)
Purchase of XYZ Company (net of cash acquired)	(2) – (3) – (1)	(7,700)
Proceeds from sale of equipment (Note 2)	(13) – (16) + (39)	6,500
Payment received on note for sale of plant (Note 2)	(9)	4,500
Net cash provided (used) by investing activities		$ (8,700)

Cash flows from financing activities:

Proceeds from revolving line of credit	(20)	$5,500
Principal payments on revolving line of credit	(21)	(9,500)
Principal from long-term borrowings	(25)	9,000
Principal payments on long-term borrowings	(26)	(1,800)
Principal payment on capital lease obligation	(29)	(400)
Proceeds from sale of common stock	(31)	2,000
Dividends paid	(43)	(2,950)
Net cash provided (used) by financing activities		1,850
Net increase (decrease) in cash & cash equivalents		$1,500
Cash & cash equivalents—beginning of year		6,000
Cash & cash equivalents—end of year		$7,500

Supplemental disclosures of cash flow information:

- *Accounting policy note:* The company considers all highly liquid investments with a maturity of three months or less at the date of acquisition to be cash equivalents.

- *Debt or property, plant, & equipment note:* (Note 3) During 19X2, the company incurred interest cost of $5,800 [(40) + $300 capitalized]. Interest paid was $5,500 [$5,800 − (23)] during 19X2. (See Note 4).

- *Income tax note:* (Note 3) The company made income tax payments of $4,500 [(41) − (30) − (22)] during 19X2.

- *Acquisitions note:* (Note 3) In connection with the acquisition of all of the common stock of XYZ Co. for $8,000 [(2) − (3)], the company acquired assets with a fair value of $17,300 (2) and assumed liabilities of $9,300 (3).

- *Leases note:* (Note 3) During 19X2, the company incurred a capital lease obligation of $2,000 (28) in connection with lease agreements to acquire equipment.

- *Shareholders' equity note:* (Note 3) On June 11, 19X2, the company called for redemption of all 5.75% convertible debentures outstanding. Debenture holders of securities with a carrying amount of $1,000 [(27), (32)] elected to convert the debentures into 20,000 shares of common stock.

Note 1—FAS-95 requires separate presentation of changes in inventory, in receivables, and in payables relating to operating activities. The idea is to allow users to estimate amounts that would be reported when using the direct method of reporting. It is probably acceptable to present line items that include other reconciling items (in this case the changes in prepaid expenses and accrued expenses) as long as all the items combined would affect a single line item under a direct-method presentation.

Note 2—It is probably acceptable to combine these cash receipts into a single line item, such as "proceeds from sales of property, plant, and equipment."

Note 3—The location of this disclosure is not specified by FAS-95. Many enterprises present the disclosures required by FAS-95 in existing notes discussing related matters.

Note 4—Alternatively, interest paid (net of interest capitalized) of $5,200 ($5,500 – $300).

CHAPTER 5
CHANGING PRICES

CONTENTS

CHAPTER 5
CHANGING PRICES

OVERVIEW

Financial statements prepared in conformity with GAAP are based on the assumption of a stable monetary unit. That is, the assumption is made that the monetary unit used to convert all financial statement items into a common denominator (i.e., dollars) does not vary sufficiently over time that distortions in the financial statements are material. Also, financial statements prepared in conformity with GAAP are primarily historical-cost based (i.e., the characteristic of most financial statement items that is measured and presented is the historical cost of the item).

Over the years, two approaches have been proposed and procedures developed to compensate for changes in the monetary unit and changes in the value of assets and liabilities after their acquisition—current value accounting and general price-level accounting. Current value accounting substitutes a measure of current value for historical cost as the primary measurement upon which the elements of financial statements are based. General price-level accounting adheres to historical cost, but substitutes a current value of the dollar for historical dollars through the use of price indexes. Neither current value accounting nor general price-level accounting is required at the present time. Procedures are established in the accounting literature for use by those enterprises that choose to develop either general price-level or current value financial statements. In FAS-89, the FASB has developed disclosure standards that are optional for dealing with the problem of the impact of changing prices on financial statements.

Promulgated GAAP in the area of changing prices are found in the following pronouncement:

FAS-89 Financial Reporting and Changing Prices

CROSS-REFERENCES

1999 Miller GAAP Guide: Chapter 17, "Foreign Operations and Exchanges"

1999 MILLER GAAP IMPLEMENTATION MANUAL: Chapter 6, "Changing Prices"

BACKGROUND

FAS-33 (Financial Reporting and Changing Prices), issued in 1979, required certain large enterprises to disclose the effects of changing prices via a series of supplemental disclosures. Several later FASB Statements and Technical Bulletins provided additional guidance on this matter.

FAS-89 subsequently specified that such disclosures are encouraged, but not required (FAS-89, par. 3). An appendix to FAS-89 provides guidelines on the disclosure of the effects of changing prices. These guidelines are substantially the same as prior FASB pronouncements, except that the guidelines are not mandatory.

REPORTING UNDER FAS-89

Net Monetary Position

Assets and liabilities are identified as monetary items if their amounts are fixed or determinable without reference to future prices of specific goods and services. Cash, accounts and notes receivable in cash, and accounts and notes payable in cash are examples of monetary items (FAS-89, par. 44).

Monetary items lose or gain general purchasing power during inflation or deflation as a result of changes in the general price-level index (FAS-89, par. 41). For example, a holder of a $10,000 promissory note executed 10 years ago and due today will receive exactly $10,000 today, in spite of the fact that $10,000 in cash today is worth less than $10,000 was worth 10 years ago.

Assets and liabilities that are not fixed in terms of the monetary unit are called nonmonetary items. Inventories, investment in common stocks, property, plant, and equipment, and deferred charges are examples of nonmonetary items (FAS-89, par. 41). A nonmonetary asset or liability is affected (a) by the rise or fall of the general price-level index and (b) by the increase or decrease of the fair value of the nonmonetary item. Holders of nonmonetary items lose or gain with the rise or fall of the general price-level index if the nonmonetary item does not rise or fall in proportion to the change in the price-level index. For example, the purchaser of 10,000 shares of common stock 10 years ago was subject (a) to the decrease in purchasing power of the dollar and (b) to the change in the fair value of the stock. Only if the decrease in purchasing power exactly offsets an increase in the price of the stock is the purchaser in the same economic position today as 10 years ago.

The difference between monetary assets and monetary liabilities at any specific date is the net monetary position. The net monetary position may be either positive (monetary assets exceed monetary liabilities) or negative (monetary liabilities exceed monetary assets).

In periods in which the general price-level is rising (inflation), it is advantageous for a business to maintain a net negative monetary position. The opposite is true during periods in which the general price-level is falling (deflation). In periods of inflation, a business that has a net negative monetary position will experience general price-level gains, because it can pay its liabilities in a fixed number of dollars that are declining in value over time. In contrast, in periods of inflation a business that has a net positive monetary position will experience general price-level losses, because it holds more monetary assets than liabilities and the value of the dollar is declining.

> ☛ **PRACTICE POINTER:** Some assets and liabilities have characteristics of both monetary and nonmonetary items. Convertible debt, for example, is monetary in terms of its fixed obligation, but nonmonetary in terms of its conversion feature. Whether an item is monetary or nonmonetary is determined as of the balance sheet date. Therefore, if convertible debt has not been converted as of that date, classify it as a monetary item. Additionally, classify a bond receivable held for speculation as nonmonetary, because the amount that will be received when the bond is sold is no longer fixed in amount, as it would be if the same bond were held to maturity. FAS-89 (pars. 96–108) contains a table that reflects the monetary/nonmonetary classification of most assets and liabilities.

Current Cost Accounting

Current cost accounting is a method of measuring and reporting assets and expenses associated with the use or sale of assets at their current cost or lower recoverable amount at the balance sheet date or at the date of use or sale. Current cost/constant purchasing power accounting is a method of accounting based on measures of current cost of lower recoverable amounts in units of currency that each have the same general purchasing power. For operations for which the U.S. dollar is the functional currency, the general purchasing power of the dollar is used. For operations for which the functional currency is other than the U.S. dollar, the general purchasing power of either *(a)* the dollar or *(b)* the functional currency is used (FAS-89, par. 44).

Determining Current Costs

Current cost is the current cost to purchase or reproduce a specific asset. Current reproduction cost must contain an allocation for current overhead costs (direct costing is not permitted).

The current cost of inventory owned by an enterprise is the current cost to purchase or reproduce that specific inventory. The current cost of property, plant, and equipment owned by an enterprise is the current cost of acquiring an asset that will perform or produce in a manner similar to the owned asset (FAS-89, pars. 17 and 18).

An enterprise may obtain its current cost information internally or externally, including independent appraisals, and may apply the information to a single item or to groups of items. An enterprise is expected to select the types of current cost information that are most appropriate for its particular circumstances. The following types and sources of current cost information may be utilized by an enterprise (FAS-89, par. 19):

1. Current invoice prices

2. Vendor firms' price lists, quotations, or estimates

3. Standard manufacturing costs that reflect current costs

4. Unit pricing, which is a method of determining current cost for assets, such as buildings, by applying a unit price per square foot of space to the total square footage in the building

5. Revision of historical cost by the use of indexation, based on:

   a. Externally generated price indexes for the goods or services being restated, or

   b. Internally generated indexes for the goods or services being restated

Depreciation Methods

Depreciation methods, useful lives, and salvage values used for current cost purposes are generally the same as those used for historical cost purposes. If historical cost computations already include an allowance for changing prices, then a different method may be used for current cost purposes. However, any material differences shall be disclosed in the explanatory notes to the supplementary information (FAS-89, par. 22).

Recoverable Amounts

Recoverable amounts may be determined by reference to net realizable values or values in use. They reflect write-downs during a current period, from the current cost amount to a lower recoverable amount. These reductions reflect a permanent decline in the value of inventory, or property, plant, and equipment.

Net Realizable Value

Net realizable value is the expected amount of net cash or other net equivalent to be received from the sale of an asset in the regular course of business. Net realizable value is used only if the specific asset is about to be sold (FAS-89, par. 29).

Value in Use

Value in use is the total present value of all future cash inflows that are expected to be received from the use of an asset. Value in use is used only if there is no immediate intention to sell or otherwise dispose of the asset. Value in use is estimated by taking into consideration an appropriate discount rate that includes an allowance for the risk involved in the circumstances (FAS-89, par. 44).

Income Tax Expense

Income tax expense and the provision for deferred taxes, if any, are not restated in terms of current cost and are presented in the supplementary information at their historical cost. Disclosure is required in the supplementary information to the effect that income tax expense for the current period is presented at its historical cost.

Minimum Supplementary Information under FAS-89

Under FAS-89, an enterprise is encouraged to disclose certain minimum supplementary information for each of its five most recent years. In addition, if income from continuing operations as shown in the primary financial statements differs significantly from income from continuing operations determined on a current cost/constant purchasing power basis, certain additional disclosures relating to the components of income from continuing operations for the current year also should be disclosed (FAS-89, par. 11).

The minimum supplementary information encouraged by FAS-89 is disclosed in average-for-the-year units of constant purchasing power. The Consumer Price Index for All Urban Consumers (CPI-U) is used to restate the current cost of an item in average-for-the-year units of constant purchasing power. Alternatively, an enterprise may disclose the minimum supplementary information in dollars having a purchasing power equal to that of dollars of the base period used in calculating the CPI-U. The level of the CPI-U used for each of the five most recent years should be disclosed (FAS-89, par. 8).

An enterprise is encouraged to disclose the following minimum supplementary information for the five most recent years (FAS-89, par. 7):

- Net sales and other operating revenue
- Income from continuing operations on a current cost basis
- Purchasing power gain or loss on net monetary items
- Increase or decrease in the current cost or lower recoverable amount of inventory and property, plant, and equipment, net of inflation
- Aggregate foreign currency translation adjustment on a current cost basis, if applicable
- Net assets at the end of each fiscal year on a current cost basis
- Income per common share from continuing operations on a current cost basis
- Cash dividends declared per common share
- Market price per common share at year-end
- Average level of the CPI-U for each year

Each of the above disclosures included in the five-year summary of selected financial data is discussed below.

Net Sales and Other Operating Revenue

Net sales and other operating revenue for each of the five most recent years is restated in average-for-the-year units of constant purchasing power using the CPI-U.

Income from Continuing Operations on a Current Cost Basis

Income from continuing operations on a current cost basis for each of the five most recent years is computed in accordance with FAS-89 and then restated in average-for-the-year units of constant purchasing power using the CPI-U. For purposes of the minimum supplementary information, only certain items that are included in income from continuing operations in the primary financial statements have to be adjusted to compute income from continuing operations on a current cost basis. Under FAS-89, these items are adjusted to compare income from continuing operations on a current basis (FAS-89, par. 32):

a. *Cost of goods sold* Determined on a current cost basis or lower recoverable amount at the date of a sale or at the date on which resources are used on or committed to a specific contract

b. *Depreciation, depletion, and amortization* Determined based on the average current cost of the assets' service potentials or lower recoverable amounts during the period of use

c. *Gain or loss on the sale, retirement, or write-down of inventory, property, plant, and equipment* Equal to the difference between the value of the consideration received or the written-down amount and the current cost or lower recoverable amount of the item prior to its sale, retirement, or write-down

All other revenue, expenses, gains, and losses that are included in the primary financial statements are not adjusted in computing income from continuing operations on a current cost basis.

Income tax expense that is included in the primary financial statements is not adjusted in computing income from continuing operations on a current cost basis (FAS-89, par. 33). Disclosure must be made in the minimum supplementary information to the effect that income tax expense for the current period is presented at its historical cost.

Purchasing Power Gain or Loss on Net Monetary Items

The purchasing power gain or loss on net monetary items for each of the five most recent years is computed and then restated in average-for-the-year units of constant purchasing power using the CPI-U. The purchasing power gain or loss on net monetary items is determined by restating in units of constant purchasing power the opening and closing balances of, and transactions in, monetary assets and monetary liabilities (FAS-89, par. 40).

Increase or Decrease in Inventory, Property, Plant, and Equipment at Current Costs

The increase or decrease in current costs for inventory and property, plant, and equipment for each of the five most recent years must be restated in average-for-the-year units of constant purchasing power using the CPI-U. The increase or decrease in the current cost amounts represents the difference between the measures of the assets at their entry dates for the year and at their exit dates for the year. The entry date is the beginning of the year or the date of acquisition, whichever is applicable. The exit date is the end of the year or the date of use, sale, or commitment to a specific contract, whichever is applicable (FAS-89, par. 34).

The increase or decrease in the current cost amounts of inventory, property, plant, and equipment for the five-year summary is reported after the effects of each year's general inflation. The increase or decrease in the current cost amounts for the current year is reported both before and after the effects of general inflation (FAS-89, par. 35).

Aggregate Foreign Currency Translation Adjustment (if Applicable)

The aggregate foreign currency translation adjustment (if applicable) for each of the five most recent years is computed on a current cost basis and then restated in average-for-the-year units of constant purchasing power using the CPI-U.

Current cost information for operations measured in a foreign functional currency is measured either *(a)* after translation and based on the CPI-U (the translate-restate method) or *(b)* before translation and based on a broad measure of the change in the general purchasing power of the functional currency (the restate-translate method). In this event, the same method must be used for all operations measured in foreign functional currencies and for all periods presented. Appendix A of FAS-89 contains illustrative calculations of current cost/constant purchasing power information (FAS-89, par. 37).

Net Assets at End of Each Fiscal Year

For purposes of the minimum supplementary information required by FAS-89, net assets at the end of each fiscal year are equal to all of the net assets appearing in the basic historical cost financial statements except that inventories, property, plant, and equipment are included at their current costs or at a lower recoverable amount. (Total net assets at historical cost less inventories, property, plant, and equipment at historical cost, plus inventories, property, plant, and equipment at current costs or lower recoverable amounts, equals net assets as encouraged by FAS-89.) The amount computed for net assets at end of each fiscal year is then restated in average-for-the-year units of constant purchasing power using the CPI-U (FAS-89, par. 27).

When comprehensive restatement of financial statements is made in lieu of the minimum supplementary information, net assets for the five-year summary of selected financial data may be reported at the same amount shown in the comprehensive restated financial statements (FAS-89, par. 28).

Income per Common Share from Continuing Operations on a Current Cost Basis

Income per common share from continuing operations for each of the five most recent years is computed and then restated in average-for-the-year units of constant purchasing power using the CPI-U. Income per common share from continuing operations on a current cost basis is found by dividing the outstanding number of shares of common stock into the total restated income from continuing operations on a current cost basis.

Cash Dividends Declared per Common Share

Cash dividends declared per common share for each of the five most recent years are restated in average-for-the-year units of constant purchasing power using the CPI-U.

Market Price per Common Share at Year-End

Market price per common share at year-end for each of the five most recent years is restated in average-for-the-year units of constant purchasing power using the CPI-U.

Average Level of CPI-U

The average level of CPI-U for each of the five most recent years is disclosed in a note to the minimum supplementary information. If an enterprise presents comprehensive current cost/constant purchasing power financial statements measured in year-end units of purchasing power, the year-end level of the CPI-U for each of the five most recent years is disclosed (FAS-89, par. 8).

Explanatory Disclosures

An enterprise shall provide an explanation of the disclosures encouraged by FAS-89 and a discussion of their significance in the circumstances of the enterprise. These explanatory statements should be detailed sufficiently so that a user who possesses reasonable business acumen will be able to understand the information presented (FAS-89, par. 10).

Additional Disclosures for the Current Year

If income from continuing operations as shown in the primary financial statements differs significantly from income from continuing operations determined on a current cost/constant purchasing power basis, certain other disclosures for the current year are encouraged by FAS-89 in addition to the minimum supplementary information.

Income from continuing operations for the current year on a current cost basis is computed in accordance with FAS-89 and then restated in average-for-the-year units of constant purchasing power using the CPI-U. The information for income from continuing operations for the current year on a current cost basis is presented in either a *statement format*, or a *reconciliation format*, which discloses all adjustments between the supplementary information and the basic historical cost financial statements (see illustrations in Appendix A of FAS-89). The same categories of revenue and expense that appear in the basic historical cost financial statements are used for the presentation of income from continuing operations for the current year on a current cost basis. Account classifications may be combined if they are not individually significant for restating purposes, or if the restated amounts are approximately the same as the historical cost amounts (FAS-89, par. 12).

Income from continuing operations for the current year on a current cost basis does not include (*a*) the purchasing power gain or loss on net monetary items; (*b*) the increase or decrease in the current cost or lower recoverable amount of inventory and property, plant, and equipment, net of inflation; and (*c*) the translation adjustment (if applicable). However, an enterprise may include this information after the presentation of income from continuing operations for the current year on a current cost basis (see illustrations in Appendix A of FAS-89) (FAS-89, par. 12).

Only certain items that are included in income from continuing operations in the primary financial statements have to be adjusted to compute income from continuing operations for the current year on a current cost basis. Under FAS-89, these items are (FAS-89, par. 32):

a. *Cost of goods sold* Determined on a current cost basis or lower recoverable amount at the date of sale or at the date on which resources are used on or committed to a specific contract

b. *Depreciation, depletion, and amortization* Determined based on the average current cost of the assets' service potentials or lower recoverable amounts during the period of use

c. *Gain or loss on the sale, retirement, or write-down of inventory, property, plant, and equipment* Equal to the difference between the value of the consideration received or the written-down amount and the current cost or lower recoverable amount of the item prior to its sale, retirement, or write-down

Other revenues, expenses, gains, and losses that are included in the primary financial statements are not adjusted and may be measured at amounts included in those statements.

Income tax expense that is included in the primary financial statements is not adjusted in computing income from continuing operations for the current year on a current cost basis (FAS-89, par. 33). Disclosure must be made in the minimum supplementary information to the effect that income tax expense for the current period is presented at its historical cost.

Disclosure must also include (FAS-89, par. 13):

- Separate amounts for the current cost or lower recoverable amount at the end of the current year of (*a*) inventory and (*b*) property, plant, and equipment (see illustrations in Appendix A of FAS-89).

- The increase or decrease in current cost or lower recoverable amount before and after adjusting for the effects of inflation of (*a*) inventory and (*b*) property, plant, and equipment.

- The principal types and sources of information used to calculate current costs for the current year.

- The differences, if any, in depreciation methods, useful lives, and salvage values used in (*a*) the primary financial statements and (*b*) the disclosure of current cost information for the current year.

Specialized Assets

Timberlands, growing timber, mineral ore bodies, proved oil and gas reserves, income-producing real estate, and motion picture films are classified as specialized assets. Specialized assets are considered unique, and the determination of their current costs frequently is difficult, if not impossible. For example, the current cost of an existing oil field may be difficult to determine because the oil field is one of a kind and cannot be duplicated. Yet, the definition of current cost is the current cost to purchase or reproduce the specific asset, and the current cost of property that is owned is the current cost of acquiring an asset that will perform or produce in a manner similar to that of the owned property.

FAS-89 provides special rules for determining the current costs of specialized assets. As a substitute for the current cost amounts and related expenses, the historical cost amounts of specialized assets may be adjusted for changes in specific prices by the use of a broad index of general purchasing power (FAS-89, par. 25).

> **OBSERVATION:** FAS-89 provides additional guidance on reporting the effects of changing prices on timber assets and mineral resource assets. Other types of specialized assets mentioned above do not receive detailed discussion in the Statement.

Timber Assets

In the event an enterprise estimates the current cost of growing timber and timber harvested by adjusting historical costs for changes in specific prices, the historical costs may include either *(a)* only costs that are capitalized in the primary financial statements or *(b)* all direct costs of reforestation and forest management, even if such costs are not capitalized in the primary financial statements. Reforestation and forest management costs include planting, fertilization, fire protection, property taxes, and nursery stock (FAS-89, par. 26).

Mineral Resource Assets

The requirements for determining the current cost amounts for mineral resource assets are flexible because there is no generally accepted approach for measuring the current cost of finding mineral reserves. In determining the current cost amounts of mineral resource assets, FAS-89 permits the use of specific price indexes applied to historical costs, market buying prices, and other statistical data to determine current replacement costs. FAS-89 encourages the disclosure of the types of data or information that are used to determine current cost amounts (FAS-89, par. 23).

FAS-89 contains the following definitions relating to mineral resource assets (FAS-89, par. 44):

> **Mineral resource assets** Assets that are directly associated with and derive value from all minerals extracted from the earth. Such minerals include oil and gas, ores containing ferrous and nonferrous metals, coal, shale, geothermal steam, sulphur, salt, stone, phosphate, sand, and gravel. Mineral resource assets include mineral interests in properties, completed and uncompleted wells, and related equipment and facilities, and other facilities required for purposes of extraction (FAS-19, Financial Accounting and Reporting by Oil and Gas Producing Companies, par. 11). The definition does not cover support equipment, because that equipment is included in the property, plant, and equipment for which current cost measurements are required by this appendix.

> **Proved mineral reserves** In extractive industries other than oil and gas, the estimated quantities of commercially recoverable reserves that, based on geological, geophysical, and engineering data, can be

demonstrated with a reasonably high degree of certainty to be recoverable in the future from known mineral deposits by either primary or improved recovery methods.

Probable mineral reserves In extractive industries other than oil and gas, the estimated quantities of commercially recoverable reserves that are less well defined than proved.

For enterprises that own significant mineral reserves, the following information on owned mineral reserves, excluding oil and gas, is encouraged to be disclosed for each of the five most recent years (FAS-89, par. 14):

1. The estimated amount of proved or of proved and probable mineral reserves on hand at the end of the year. A date during the year may be used, but the date must be disclosed.
2. The estimated quantity of each significant mineral product that is commercially recoverable from the mineral reserves in (1) above. The estimated quantity may be expressed in percentages or in physical units.
3. The quantities of each significant mineral produced during the year. The quantity of each significant mineral produced by milling or similar processes also must be disclosed.
4. The quantity of mineral reserves (proved or proved and probable) purchased or sold in place during the year.
5. The average market price of each significant mineral product. If transferred within the enterprise, the equivalent market price prior to further use should be disclosed.

In classifying and detailing the above information, current industry practices should prevail.

The following procedures shall be used in determining the quantities of mineral reserves that should be reported (FAS-89, par. 15):

1. In consolidated financial statements, 100% of the quantities of mineral reserves attributable to both the parent company and all consolidated subsidiaries shall be reported regardless of whether a subsidiary is partially or wholly owned.
2. In a proportionately consolidated investment, an investor shall include only its proportionate share of the investor's mineral reserves.
3. Mineral reserve quantities attributable to an investment accounted for by the equity method shall not be included at all. If significant, however, the mineral reserve quantities should be reported separately by the investor.

APPENDIX A: CURRENT VALUE ACCOUNTING

Background

Current value accounting deals with the measurement of profits and the valuation of a business entity during periods of changing prices. In current value accounting, historical costs are replaced by current values that attempt to measure the current worth of financial statement elements.

There are no promulgated GAAP on current value accounting, and its general use for basic financial statements is prohibited under existing GAAP. However, current value data may be utilized to supplement the historical cost financial statements required by GAAP or to present information that is not intended to conform to GAAP.

Current Value Methods

A major problem encountered in implementing current value accounting is the measurement of current value. The broad approaches to measuring current value are the entry value system and the exit value system.

The entry value system is based on cost of replacement or reproduction. Replacement cost is the estimated cost of acquiring new and equivalent property at current prices after adjusting for depreciation, and may be approximated through the use of a specific price index. Reproduction cost is the estimated cost of producing new and equivalent property at current prices after adjusting for depreciation.

The exit value system usually is based on net realizable value in the ordinary course of business, or sometimes on discounted future cash flow. Net realizable value is the estimated selling price of the asset less any costs to complete or dispose. Discounted future cash flow is the present value of estimated cash inflows, or cost savings, discounted at an appropriate rate of interest.

☛ **PRACTICE POINTER:** In an entry value system, financial statement items are measured in terms of acquiring the item (i.e., bringing the item into the enterprise) under current circumstances reather than historical circumstances. For assets, this means measurement at current replacement cost or the equivilent. For liabilities, this means measurement at the current cost of borrowing. In an exit value system, financial statement items are measured in terms of eliminating or disposing the item. For assets, this means measurement at an amount that would be received by selling or otherwise disposing of the item. For liabilities, this means measurement at an amount required to extinguish the item.

Monetary and Nonmonetary Items

To apply current value accounting methods, assets and liabilities must be separated into monetary and nonmonetary. Monetary assets or liabilities are fixed in terms of currency and usually are contractual claims. Because these amounts are fixed, there is no need to restate monetary assets and liabilities. Examples of monetary assets and liabilities are cash, accounts and notes receivable, and accounts and notes payable.

Nonmonetary assets or liabilities are those other than monetary assets or liabilities. Nonmonetary assets generally are restated for changes in current value. Examples of nonmonetary assets and liabilities are inventory, investments in common stock, property, plant and equipment, liability for advance rent collected, and common stock.

Because monetary assets are stated in fixed amounts of currency, they represent the amount of cash that is expected to be realized by them in the near future. Therefore, monetary assets are effectively stated at their net realizable value and usually do not have to be restated for current value financial statements.

Nonmonetary assets are not stated in fixed amounts of currency and thus do not reflect their net realizable value. Therefore, nonmonetary assets must be restated to their present current worth for current value financial statements.

Holding Gains and Losses

Holding gains and losses result from changes in the current value of an asset while it is held. Realized holding gains and losses result from the disposal of an asset, either by sale or use, during an accounting period. Unrealized holding gains and losses result from increases or decreases in current values of assets during an accounting period in which such assets are retained by the entity.

Controversy exists as to whether holding gains and losses should be reported in the current value income statement or in a separate statement intended to report holding gains and losses.

Current Value Income

Under the current value concept, current operating income is the result of deducting from actual revenues the cost of goods sold and other expenses based on current values. Realized income is determined by adding (deducting) realized holding gains (losses) to net operating income (current operating income less income taxes). Current value income is obtained by adding (deducting) unrealized holding gains (losses) to realized income. The following illustration shows the steps required to determine current value income, assuming the typical situation of a holding gain.

Revenues (actual)

Less: Current value of cost of goods sold and other expenses

Current operating income

Less: Income taxes

Net operating income

Plus: Realized holding gains

Realized income

Plus: Unrealized holding gains

Current value income

Illustration of Computation of Current Value Income, Both Realized and Unrealized Holding Gains

Fair Value, Inc., paid $1,200,000 in December 19X6 for certain of its inventory. In December 19X7, one half of the inventory was sold for $1,000,000, when the replacement cost of the original inventory was $1,400,000. Ignoring income taxes, the current value income resulting from the above facts in a current fair value accounting income statement for 19X7 is as follows:

Proceeds of sale	$1,000,000
Less: Current value of inventory sold (1/2 of $1,400,000)	700,000
Current operating income	300,000
Plus: Realized holding gain—Inventory ($700,000 current value – $600,000 historical cost)	100,000
Realized income	400,000
Plus: Unrealized holding gains—Inventory	100,000
Current value income	$500,000

Illustration Comparing Historical Cost Accounting to Current Value Method of Accounting

Balance Sheet

Assets	Historical Cost	Current Value
Current assets:		
Cash	$1,700	$1,700
Accounts receivable	5,500	5,500
Investments	200	200
Inventory	2,500	3,000
Fixed assets:		
Plant	4,000	5,000
Accumulated depreciation	(400)	(500)
Total assets	$13,500	$14,900

Liabilities		
Current liabilities	$ 5,000	$ 5,000
Stockholders' equity:		
Common stock	4,000	4,000
Retained earnings	4,500	2,900
Revaluation reserve		3,000
Total liabilities and stockholders' equity	$13,500	$14,900

Comments:
Under the current value accounting method, monetary assets and liabilities are not restated, because they represent amounts fixed in terms of currency. However, nonmonetary assets and liabilities (inventory, plant, and stockholders' equity) are restated to their net realizable values.

Statement of Income

	Historical Cost		Current Value	
Sales		$13,000		$13,000
Less: Cost of goods sold		4,000		5,500
Gross margin		$9,000		$7,500
Less: Expenses:				
Depreciation	$200		$250	
Others	600	800	600	850

Income before taxes	$8,200	
Current operating income		$6,650
Less: Provision for taxes	4,100	4,100
Net income	$4,100	
Net operating income		$2,550
Plus: Realized holding gains applicable to:		
Sale of inventory	$1,500	
Depreciation of plant	50	1,550
Realized income		$4,100
Plus: Unrealized holding gains applicable to:		
Replacement at cost of inventory at year-end	$500	
Undepreciated value of plant	950	1,450
Current value income		$5,550

Comments:

Under the traditional historical cost method, net income is $4,100, whereas current value income is $5,550. Both methods use actual sales, but the current value method uses current values (replacement cost) in computing cost of goods sold and other expenses. In periods of inflation, gross margins under current value accounting usually will be less than under historical cost accounting, because current values are used. Realized income under current value accounting equals net income under the historical cost method.

Holding gains and losses are identified separately in current value income statements but are not identified separately in historical cost statements. The only difference in total dollar amounts between the two methods is unrealized holding gains and losses. A current value income statement includes unrealized holding gains and losses, but they are not included in an historical cost income statement.

The provision for income taxes is the same for both historical cost and current value income statements. Depreciation expense is computed on the current value of an asset for current value accounting; historical cost is used for historical cost purposes.

A statement showing the cumulative amount of holding gains (losses) may be prepared. The following example uses information from the previous example, which included a holding gain.

Statement of Changes in Revaluation Reserve (Holding Gains)

Revaluation reserve (holding gains), beginning of the year	—

Realized holding gains applicable to:

Inventory sold	$1,500	
Depreciation on plant (5% of $1,000)	50	$1,550

Unrealized holding gains applicable to:

Inventory at year-end	500	
Undepreciated value of plant	950	1,450

Total revaluation reserve (holding gains)		$3,000

Comments:

The revaluation reserve ($3,000) is a stockholders' equity account, which reflects the difference between historical cost and current value.

Statement of Retained Earnings

	Historical Cost	Current Value
Beginning balance	$400	$400
Add: Net income	4,100	
Current value income		5,550
Total	4,500	5,950
Less: Backlog depreciation		50
Revaluation reserve		3,000
Ending retained earnings	$4,500	$2,900

Comments:

Backlog depreciation (sometimes referred to as the amortization gap) is the difference between accumulated depreciation under historical cost and accumulated depreciation based on current value.

APPENDIX B: GENERAL PRICE-LEVEL ACCOUNTING

Background

The degree of inflation or deflation in an economy may become so great that conventional statements lose much of their significance, and general price-level statements may become more meaningful.

The unit of measure used is the basic difference between historical and general price-level financial statements. General price-level financial statements do not represent replacement cost or an appraisal value, but merely represent what historical cost statements reflect in general purchasing power, at a specific date. GAAP used in historical cost financial statements also are used in general price-level financial statements. Changes in the general price level are measured in terms of price index numbers; the base year is given the index number of 100, and changes are expressed as percentages of the base year.

Procedures for restating financial statements for general price-level changes are contained in APB Statement No. 3 (Financial Statements Restated for General Price-Level Changes), which was issued in June 1969. APB Statement No. 3 was rescinded by SOP 93-3 (Rescission of APB Statements) to clarify that it does not, and never did, have standing as rules or standards under the AICPA Code of Professional Conduct. APB Statement No. 3 provides a comprehensive model for general price-level restatement, however, and is useful to the extent that it is not inconsistent with FAS-89.

Price Indexes

Price-level changes are measured by price indexes. Price indexes are stated in percentages to a base year, which is assigned a value of 100.

By using a price index, dollars of general purchasing power in one period can be restated to dollars of general purchasing power of another period. The formula for restating dollars of one period to those of another is:

$$\frac{\text{New index (converting to)}}{\text{Old index (converting from)}}$$

For example, assume that the current ending price index is 120, and a parcel of land was purchased for $10,000 in a year in which the price index was 80. The conversion would be:

$$(120/80) \times \$10,000 = \$15,000$$

Alternatively, the two index numbers may be combined into a single conversion index:

$$(120/80) = 1.5$$

That index is then applied to the historical cost of all items to which the index applies. For the $10,000 item of land, the conversion is:

$$\$10,000 \times 1.5 = \$15,000$$

This conversion does not mean that the land is worth $15,000. Rather, it means that land which cost $10,000 at an earlier date would cost $15,000 in terms of today's dollars. Restatement can be made in either direction—to current purchasing power or to purchasing power of a prior year.

The conversion index approach is efficient because many financial statement items will be subject to conversion by the same price index number (i.e., 80 in the above example).

General Price-Level Gain or Loss

Monetary items automatically gain or lose general purchasing power as a result of changes in price indexes. Assume that a comparative balance sheet showed cash of $10,000 and notes payable of $25,000 at both balance sheet dates in a year in which the price index went from 110 to 117. The current year's $10,000 in cash cannot purchase what the prior year's $10,000 in cash could. Using the formula, the conversion of the current year to general price levels would be:

$$(117/110) \times \$10,000 = \$10,636$$

To purchase the same value today, $10,636 is required. The $636 is a loss in the general purchasing power of the cash as measured by the change in the price indexes.

On the other hand, the current year's $25,000 of notes payable will be paid with cheaper dollars than the prior year's $25,000 in notes payable:

$$(117/110) \times \$25,000 = \$26,591$$

The $1,591 ($26,591 − $25,000) is a gain in general purchasing power, because the liability will be paid with dollars of less general purchasing power.

If the company has no other monetary assets and liabilities besides the $10,000 cash and $25,000 notes payable, it would have a net general price-level gain of $955 ($1,591 − $636) for the year.

A change in the price index from one period to another can be expressed as a percentage. When the index moves from 110 to 117, it has increased seven points, or 6.36% (7/110 = .0636). Applying this percentage increase to the $10,000 cash and $25,000 notes payable in the preceding example:

Price-level loss on cash: $10,000 x 6.36% = $ (636)

Price-level gain on notes payable: $25,000 x 6.36% = 1,590

Net price-level gain
for the period $ 954*

---

*The $1 difference between the two results ($955 and $954) is due to rounding.

Instead of computing a gain or loss on each individual monetary item, it is easier to calculate the net monetary position. In our last example, the net monetary position (negative) was $15,000 ($10,000 cash less $25,000 notes payable). We can now restate the beginning net monetary position for the change in the price index and then subtract the actual net monetary position at the end of the period, as follows:

Net monetary position (negative)

$15,000 x (117 / 110) = $15,955

Less: Ending net monetary position	$15,000*
Net general price-level gain	$ 955

---

*$10,000 cash less the $25,000 notes payable on the current year's balance sheet

Advantages of Restatement

Advantages of general price-level financial statements are:

1. The dollar is not stable, and changes in its monetary value should be reflected in financial statements to produce more realistic information.
2. General price-level financial statements provide more meaningful information in terms of current economic conditions.
3. Management's effectiveness in periods of inflation or deflation can be more readily determined.
4. General price-level balance sheets more clearly approximate current values.

Disadvantages of Restatement

Disadvantages of general price-level financial statements are:

1. Historical-dollar financial statements are based on verifiable information.
2. There is no general agreement as to which price-level index to use and how it should be applied.
3. Many assets and liabilities may have been recently acquired and are already valued close to current price levels.
4. Historical costs have been employed traditionally over many years with satisfactory results.

Schedule of General Price-Level Gain or Loss

The previous discussion has been simplified to demonstrate the nature of general price-level gains or losses.

In reality, a business will have many transactions that cause a change in net monetary assets or liabilities. Cash and credit sales increase the net monetary position; purchases, operating expenses, and cash dividends decrease the net monetary position. Depreciation and amortization have no effect on the net monetary position. The procedure for preparing a schedule of general price-level gain or loss is:

1. Determine the net monetary position (positive or negative) at the beginning of the period (usually the monetary assets less the monetary liabilities at the end of the prior period) adjusted to the general price-level index at the end of the period.

2. Add all increases in net monetary items from all sources (sales, miscellaneous revenue, proceeds from the sale of fixed assets, proceeds from the issuance of debt or stock, etc.), adjusted to the general price-level at the end of the period.

3. Deduct all decreases in net monetary items from all sources (expenditures for purchases, operating expenses, acquisition of assets, miscellaneous expenses, and the retirement of debt or stock), adjusted to the general price-level index at the end of the period.

4. Arrive at the *estimated* net monetary position at the end of the period, which is the difference between steps 1, 2, and 3 above.

    (1 + 2 − 3) = Estimated net monetary position at the end of the period

5. Compute the *actual* net monetary position at the end of the period (monetary assets less monetary liabilities), and subtract this from the estimated net monetary position calculated in step 4.

Note: The difference between the estimated net monetary items at the end of the period and the actual net monetary items at the end of the period is the general price-level gain or loss for the period. If the estimated net monetary items exceed the actual, a loss results. If the estimated net monetary items are less than the actual, a gain results.

This general price-level gain or loss is shown in the income statement as the item immediately preceding net income.

General Price-Level Financial Statements

The following are general rules for preparing price-level adjusted financial statements:

1. All financial statements presented, including those of prior years, are restated to the purchasing power of the dollar at the most recent balance sheet date. This is called rolling over the previously restated statements. The prior restated statements are simply restated again to the current price level. This serves two purposes. It converts last year's statements into current-year dollars (comparability), and it translates last year's ending retained earnings into current-year dollars for use in the current-year statement of retained earnings.
2. Sales and expenses incurred evenly throughout the year are converted using the average general price index for the year.
3. The inventory method (FIFO, LIFO, etc.) will dictate the price index to use for restating inventory.
4. Depreciation is restated by using the price index of the related asset.
5. Buildings, equipment, and other fixed assets are restated by using the price index existing at the time of their purchase.
6. Common stock is restated by using the price index existing at the time the stock was issued.

Illustration of Restating Financial Statements for General Price-Level Changes

ABC Corporation's financial statements for the year ended December 31, 19X5, are shown below:

Balance Sheet
As of December 31, 19X5

Cash	$100,000
Accounts receivable	200,000
Inventory (FIFO)	50,000
Fixed assets	250,000
Total assets	$600,000
Accounts payable	$70,000
Common stock	200,000
Retained earnings	330,000
Total liabilities and equity	$600,000

Income Statement
For the year ended December 31, 19X5

Sales		$900,000

Cost of goods sold:

Beginning inventory	$50,000	
Add: Purchases	700,000	
Total	750,000	
Less: Ending inventory	50,000	
Cost of goods sold		700,000
Gross profit		200,000

Operating expenses:

Depreciation	20,000
Other	80,000
Total operating expenses	100,000
Income before taxes	100,000
Income tax expense	20,000
Net income	$80,000

Relevant price indexes:

Beginning of year	104
End of year	108
Average	106
Fixed assets acquired	92
Formation of company	90

Additional data:

The company's net monetary position at December 31, 19X4, was $130,000. Inventories are priced on a FIFO basis.

The first step in this problem is to compute the amount of the general price-level gain or loss.

The essence of creating the schedule of general price-level gain or loss is to compare the monetary items at year-end with the amount at which the items would have been stated if they were nonmonetary items.

The steps in preparing this schedule are explained below.

1. The net monetary position at the beginning of the year (December 31, 19X4) is given as $130,000. Restate this to current dollars as follows:

$$\$130,000 \times (108/104) = \$135,000$$

The beginning index of 104 is used because this is the net monetary position at the beginning of the period.

2. Assemble all increases in monetary items and convert them, using the appropriate index.

Increases:

Sales	$900,000
Total increases	$900,000
Conversion factor	108/106
Adjusted sales	$916,981

The average index of 106 is used because sales are assumed to occur evenly throughout the year unless otherwise indicated.

3. Assemble all decreases in monetary items and convert them, using the appropriate index.

Decreases:

Purchases	$700,000
Other expenses	80,000
Income tax expense	20,000
Total decreases	$800,000
Conversion factor	108/106
Adjusted expenses	$815,094

The average index of 106 is used because purchases and expenses, including income tax expense, are assumed to be incurred evenly throughout the year unless otherwise indicated.

4. The net estimated monetary position at year-end is calculated as follows:

Net monetary position—beginning	$135,000
Plus: Increases	916,981
Less: Decreases	815,094
Net estimated monetary position—ending	$236,887

5. The actual net monetary position at the end of the period is calculated from actual amounts appearing on the balance sheet for the end of the period, as follows:

Monetary assets:	
Cash	$100,000
Accounts receivable	200,000
Total actual monetary assets	300,000
Monetary liabilities:	
Accounts payable	(70,000)
Total actual monetary liability	(70,000)
Net monetary position (positive)	$230,000

The general price-level gain or loss can now be calculated as follows:

Actual net monetary items	$230,000
Estimated net monetary items	(236,887)
General price-level gain (loss)	$(6,887)

Since the estimated net monetary position exceeds the actual net monetary position, there is a loss.

The workpapers for the restatement of the financial statements of ABC Corporation follow:

Income Statement
For the year ended December 31, 19X5

	Historical	Conversion Factor	Adjusted
Sales	$900,000	108/106	$916,981
Cost of goods sold:			
Beginning inventory	50,000	108/104	51,923
Add: Purchases	700,000	108/106	713,208
Total	750,000		765,131
Less: Ending inventory	50,000	108/108	50,000
Cost of goods sold	700,000		715,131
Gross profit	200,000		201,850
Operating expenses:			
Depreciation	$20,000	108/92	$23,478
Other	80,000	108/106	81,509
Total	100,000		104,987
Net income before taxes	100,000		96,863
Income tax expense	20,000	108/106	20,377
Net income	$80,000		76,486
General price-level gain (loss)			(6,887)
Net income—adjusted for changes in general price levels			$69,599

Schedule of General Price-Level Gain (Loss)

Historical		Converted for Price-Level Changes
$130,000	Beginning net monetary position [index at beginning of year (104) index at end of year (108) = conversion factor 108/104]	$135,000
900,000	Increases in monetary items during the year: sales $900,000 [average index during the year (106), index at end of year (108) = conversion factor 108/106]	916,981
(800,000)	Decreases in monetary items during the year: purchases $700,000, other expenses $80,000, income tax expense $20,000 [average index during the year (106), index at end of year (108) = conversion factor 108/106]	(815,094)
230,000	Ending estimated net monetary position	236,887
$230,000	Ending actual net monetary position*	$230,000
—	General price-level gain or (loss)	$ (6,887)

*Monetary assets—end of period	$300,000
Less: Monetary liabilities—end of period	70,000
Actual net monetary position—end of period	$230,000

Balance Sheet
As of December 31, 19X5

	Historical	Conversion Factor	Adjusted
Cash			$100,000
108/108	$100,000		
Accounts receivable	200,000	108/108	200,000
Inventory		50,000	108/108
50,000			
Fixed assets	250,000	108/92	293,478
Total assets	$600,000		$643,478

Accounts payable	$ 70,000	108/108	$ 70,000
Common stock	200,000	108/90	240,000
Retained earnings	330,000		333,478
Total liabilities and equity	$600,000		$643,478

Note: Only the nonmonetary assets and liabilities are restated on the general price-level balance sheet. The changes in the net monetary assets and liabilities have already been taken into account in the general price-level income statement as a general price-level gain or loss. The retained earnings figure in the adjusted balance sheet is the amount required to balance the statement.

CHAPTER 6
CONSOLIDATED FINANCIAL STATEMENTS

CONTENTS

CHAPTER 6
CONSOLIDATED FINANCIAL STATEMENTS

OVERVIEW

Consolidated financial statements represent the results of operations, statement of cash flows, and financial position of a single entity, even though multiple, separate legal entities are involved. Consolidated financial statements are presumed to present more meaningful information than separate financial statements and must be used in substantially all cases in which a parent directly or indirectly controls the majority voting interest (over 50%) of a subsidiary. Consolidated financial statements should not be used in those circumstances in which (*a*) the parent's control of the subsidiary is temporary, or (*b*) there is significant doubt concerning the parent's ability to control the subsidiary.

The promulgated accounting standards and reporting principles for consolidated financial statements, combined financial statements, and comparative financial statements are:

ARB-43	Chapter 1A, Rules Adopted by Membership Chapter 2A, Comparative Financial Statements
ARB-51	Consolidated Financial Statements (as amended)
FAS-94	Consolidation of All Majority-Owned Subsidiaries

CROSS-REFERENCES

1999 MILLER GAAP GUIDE: Chapter 3, "Business Combinations"; Chapter 14, "Equity Method"; Chapter 17, "Foreign Operations and Exchange"; Chapter 45, "Stockholders' Equity"

1999 MILLER GAAP IMPLEMENTATION MANUAL: EITF: Chapter 6, "Consolidation and the Equity Method"

1999 MILLER NOT-FOR-PROFIT REPORTING: Chapter 2, "Overview of Current Pronouncements"; Chapter 7, "Organizational Issues"

1999 MILLER GAAS GUIDE: Chapter 8, "Evidence"

BACKGROUND

ARB-43, Chapter 1A, contains six rules that were adopted by the Professional Organization of Certified Public Accountants in 1934. The third rule deals with consolidated financial statements and requires that a subsidiary company's retained earnings created prior to the date of its acquisition cannot be considered part of the consolidated retained earnings of the parent company and its subsidiaries, although APB-16 (Business Combinations) requires the combining of retained earnings for business combinations qualifying as a pooling of interests. Furthermore, any dividends declared out of such retained earnings cannot be included in the net income of the parent company.

ARB-43, Chapter 2A, discusses the desirability of presenting comparative financial statements in annual reports, because such a presentation is likely to provide much more information than noncomparative statements.

ARB-51, as amended by FAS-94, is the main source of GAAP relating to consolidated financial statements. Under ARB-51, a consolidated financial statement represents the results of operations, statement of cash flows, and financial position of a single entity. FAS-94 amended ARB-51 to require, with few exceptions, a parent company to consolidate all of its majority-owned subsidiaries.

Retained earnings of a subsidiary accounted for as a purchase at the date of acquisition are not treated as part of consolidated retained earnings (ARB-51, par. 9). The retained earnings, other capital accounts, and contributed capital of a purchased subsidiary at the date of acquisition represent the book value that is eliminated in preparing consolidated statements.

A parent company should not exclude a majority-owned subsidiary from consolidation because it has a different fiscal year. For consolidation purposes, a subsidiary usually can prepare financial statements that correspond with its parent's fiscal period. If a subsidiary's fiscal year is within three months or less of its parent's fiscal year, it is acceptable to use those fiscal-year financial statements for consolidation purposes, provided that adequate disclosure is made of any material events occurring within the intervening period (ARB-51, par. 4).

MAJORITY-OWNED SUBSIDIARIES

ARB-51, as amended by FAS-94, requires that all investments in which a parent company has a controlling financial interest represented by the direct or indirect ownership of a majority voting interest (more than 50%) be consolidated, except those in which (*a*) control of the subsidiary is temporary, or (*b*) significant doubt exists regarding the parent's ability to control the subsidiary. For example, a subsidiary in legal reorganization or bankruptcy is controlled by the receiver or trustee and not by the parent company (FAS-94, par. 13).

> ☛ **PRACTICE POINTER:** In determining whether consolidated financial statements are required in a particular situation, a reasonable starting point is to assume that if majority ownership exists, consolidation is appropriate. For that point, consider those rare circumstances in which majority interest does exist but consolidation would not be appropriate. However, such circumstances are clearly intended to be exceptions to a policy of consolidation in most situations of majority ownership.

FAS-94 also added a new paragraph 19 to ARB-51, which requires a parent company to disclose summarized information concerning the assets, liabilities, and results of operations (or separate financial statements) for all majority-owned subsidiaries that were previously unconsolidated for fiscal years 1986 and 1987 that are consolidated for fiscal years ending after December 15, 1988, in accordance with FAS-94 (FAS-94, par. 14).

FAS-94 amends Chapter 12 of ARB-43 by superseding paragraphs 8 and 9 (Consolidation of Foreign Subsidiaries), which had permitted the exclusion from consolidation of majority-owned foreign subsidiaries because of foreign currency and/or exchange restrictions. FAS-94 requires that the exchange restrictions or other governmental controls in a foreign subsidiary be so severe that they "cast significant doubt on the parent's ability to control the subsidiary." This amendment narrows the exception for a majority-owned foreign subsidiary from one that permits exclusion from consolidation of any or all foreign subsidiaries to one that effectively eliminates distinctions between foreign and domestic subsidiaries (FAS-94, par. 9). Thus, a majority-owned subsidiary must be consolidated unless significant doubt exists regarding the parent's control of the subsidiary or the parent's control is temporary. FAS-52 (Foreign Currency Translation) contains special rules for translating foreign currency financial statements of foreign subsidiaries that operate in countries with highly inflationary economies.

FAS-94 amends APB-18 (The Equity Method of Accounting for Investments in Common Stock) by removing the requirement of APB-18 to report unconsolidated majority-owned subsidiaries by the equity method. In addition, FAS-94 eliminates the provisions of APB-18 applying to "parent-company financial statements prepared for issuance to stockholders as the financial statements of the primary reporting entity" (FAS-94, par. 15).

☞ **PRACTICE POINTER:** FAS-94 comes close to requiring that all majority-owned subsidiaries be consolidated. Exceptions are situations where (1) control is temporary or (2) control does not rest with the majority owner, as when a subsidiary is in legal reorganization or bankruptcy. APB-18, on the other hand, is amended by FAS-94 to eliminate the requirement that unconsolidated subsidiaries be accounted for by the equity method. In the rare instances indicated above, where (majority-owned) subsidiaries are not consolidated, the authoritative literature apparently does not specify a particular method of accounting, although the equity method may be judged the appropriate method to use in the circumstances.

ACCOUNTING AND REPORTING ON SUBSIDIARIES

The common stock or net assets of a subsidiary may be purchased (*a*) for book value, (*b*) in excess of book value, and (*c*) for less than book value. If purchased for more than book value, there may be resulting goodwill; if purchased for less than book value, there may be a deferred credit, sometimes referred to as *negative goodwill.*

When a subsidiary's common stock is acquired by the purchase method in more than one transaction, each purchase should be determined on a step-by-step basis and consolidation usually is not made until control (more than 50%) is achieved. In the year that control is achieved, the percentage amount of net income from the purchased subsidiary will probably vary (ARB-51, par. 10). ARB-51 suggests two methods for the inclusion of income from a subsidiary in periods in which there are several purchases. The preferable method usually is to include the subsidiary in the consolidation as if it had been acquired at the beginning of the period, and to deduct at the bottom of the consolidated income statement the net income of the subsidiary that does not accrue to the parent (ARB-51, par. 11).

OBSERVATION: Apparently, when this method is being used, all the revenue and expense accounts of the subsidiary remain in the consolidated income statement, since only the net income that the parent is not entitled to is deducted from the consolidated net income at the bottom of the statement.

The other method that ARB-51 suggests is to include in the parent's consolidated income statement only the subsidiary's revenue and expenses subsequent to the date that control was obtained (ARB-51, par. 11).

In the disposal of a subsidiary during the year, ARB-51 suggests that it may be preferable to omit from the consolidated income statement all details of the operation of the subsidiary and to show only the equity of the parent in the earnings of the subsidiary, prior to disposal, as a separate item in the consolidated income statement (the equity method) (ARB-51, par. 12).

Consolidated financial statements are prepared in the same manner for a pooling of interests as they are for a purchase. In the purchase method, fair values are assigned to identifiable assets and any excess cost is recorded as goodwill. In a pooling of interests, the cost of an acquisition is the book value of the net assets of the target company, and goodwill is not recorded.

CONSOLIDATION ISSUES

Combined Financial Statements

Consolidated financial statements usually are justified on the basis that one of the consolidating entities exercises control over the affiliated group. When there is no such control, combined financial statements may be used to accomplish the same results. For example, a group of companies controlled by an individual shareholder, or a group of unconsolidated subsidiaries that could otherwise not be consolidated, should utilize combined financial statements. Combined financial statements are prepared on the same basis as consolidated financial statements, except that no company in the group has a controlling interest in the other (ARB-51, pars. 22 and 23).

Comparative Financial Statements

Comparative financial statements reveal much more information than noncomparative statements and furnish useful data about differences in the results of operations for the periods involved or in the financial position at the comparison dates (ARB-43, Ch. 2A, par. 1).

Consistency is a major factor in creating comparability. Prior-year amounts and classifications must be, in fact, comparable with the current period presented, and exceptions must be disclosed clearly (ARB-43, Ch. 2A, par. 2).

Consolidation versus Equity Method

The income and balance sheet effects of intercompany transactions are eliminated in equity method adjustments as well as in the financial statements of consolidated entities (ARB-51, par. 6). In consolidated financial statements, the details of all entities to the consolidation are reported in full. In the equity method, the investment is shown as a single amount in the investor balance sheet, and earnings or losses generally are shown as a single amount in the income statement. This is the reason the equity method is frequently referred to as *one-line consolidation.*

> ☛ **PRACTICE POINTER:** While their impact on reporting income is the same, the equity method and consolidation differ in the extent of detail each reflects in the financial statements. The authoritative literature clearly states that the equity method is not necessarily an appropriate alternative to consolidation, or vice versa. Generally, consolidation is appropriate where majority interest exists, and the equity method is appropriate where the investor has the ability to exert significant influence over the investee but lacks majority ownership.

Consolidated Work Papers and Intercompany Transactions

The preparation of consolidated financial statements is facilitated by the preparation of a consolidated statements worksheet. Traditionally, this worksheet was prepared by hand and the adjustments and eliminations required for consolidation were not posted to the books of the individual companies. Computerization of accounting processes, including the preparation of worksheets to assist in the preparation of consolidated financial statements, has modernized this process and all eliminations and adjustments are posted.

Following is a brief discussion of some of the most frequently encountered intercompany transactions.

Sales and Purchases

The gross amount of all intercompany sales and/or purchases is eliminated on the consolidated work papers. When the adjustment has already been made in the trial balance for ending inventory, the eliminating entry is made by debiting sales and crediting cost of sales. When no adjustment has been made for ending inventory, the eliminating entry is made by crediting the purchases account. In this latter case, a more straightforward approach is to make an adjusting entry establishing the cost of sales and then eliminating intercompany sales by crediting cost of sales.

Receivables and Payables

Intercompany receivables and payables include:

1. Accounts receivable and accounts payable.
2. Advances to and from affiliates.
3. Notes receivable and notes payable.
4. Interest receivable and interest payable.

The gross amounts of all intercompany receivables and payables are eliminated on the consolidated work papers. Care must be exercised when a receivable is discounted with one of the consolidated companies (no contingent liability). If the balance sheet reflects a discounted receivable with another affiliate, the amount must be eliminated by a debit to discounted receivables and a credit to receivables. If one affiliate discounts a receivable to another affiliate, who in turn discounts it to an outsider, a real contingent liability still exists, and must be shown on the consolidated balance sheet.

Unrealized Profits in Inventory

Regardless of any minority interests, all (100%) of any intercompany profits in ending inventory is eliminated on the consolidated work papers. In addition, the cost of sales account must be adjusted for intercompany profit in beginning inventory arising from intercompany transactions in the previous year. If the adjustment for intercompany profits in inventories is not made, consolidated net income will be incorrect and consolidated ending inventory will be overstated.

Illustration of Profit in Inventory

P Company purchased $200,000 and $250,000 of merchandise in 19X1 and 19X2, respectively, from its subsidiary S at 25% above cost. As of December 31, 19X1 and 19X2, P had on hand $25,000 and $30,000 of merchandise purchased from S. The following is the computation of intercompany profits:

Computation of Intercompany Profits

Beginning inventory	$25,000	=	125%
Cost to S	(20,000)	=	(100%)
Intercompany profit	$ 5,000		25%
Ending inventory	$30,000	=	125%
Cost to S	(24,000)	=	(100%)
Intercompany profit	$ 6,000		25%

The adjustment is different for a consolidated balance sheet than for a consolidated income statement and balance sheet. If intercompany profit adjustments have not been recorded in equity method entries on P Company's books, for a consolidated balance sheet only the elimination entry is:

Retained earnings	$6,000	
Inventory		$6,000

Assuming no equity method adjustments are made, and a perpetual inventory system is used, for a consolidated income statement and balance sheet the following adjustments are necessary:

Sales	$250,000	
Costs of sales		$250,000
To eliminate intercompany sales.		
Consolidated retained earnings	$ 5,000	
Cost of sales		$ 5,000
To reverse consolidated adjustment of 12/31/X1.		
Cost of sales	$ 6,000	
Inventory		$ 6,000
To eliminate intercompany profit in ending inventory.		

The adjustment to consolidated retained earnings is necessary because the intercompany profit was eliminated on the prior year's consolidated work papers. (Consolidated adjustments and eliminations are not posted to the books of the individual companies. Therefore, the beginning inventory for P still reflected the prior year's intercompany inventory profits from S.)

If merchandise containing an intercompany inventory profit is reduced from the purchase price to market value and the reduction is equal to, or more than, the actual intercompany inventory profit, no deferral of profit entry is required in consolidation. For example, if merchandise costing one affiliate $10,000 is sold to another affiliate for $12,000, who reduces it to market value of $11,000, the consolidated work paper adjustment for unrealized intercompany inventory profits should be only $1,000.

Minority interests do not affect the adjustment for unrealized intercompany profits in inventories. Consolidated net income and minority interests in the net income of a subsidiary are affected by the adjustment, however, because the reduction or increase in beginning or ending inventory of a partially owned subsidiary does affect the determination of net income.

Unrealized intercompany losses in inventory are accounted for in the same manner as unrealized profits, except that they have the opposite effect. Profits or losses on sales and/or purchases prior to an affiliation are not recognized as a consolidated adjustment.

Unrealized Profits in Long-Lived Assets

Regardless of any minority interests, all (100%) of any intercompany profits on the sale and/or purchase of long-lived assets between affiliates is eliminated on the consolidated work papers.

When one affiliate constructs or sells a long-lived asset to another affiliate at a profit, the profit is eliminated on the consolidated work papers. As with unrealized intercompany profits or losses in inventory, minority interests do not affect any consolidated adjustment for profits in intercompany sales of long-lived assets between affiliates. Net income of the subsidiary involved in the intercompany profit on a long-lived asset is affected by the adjustment, however, which in turn affects consolidated net income and minority interests.

If a nondepreciable asset is involved in an intercompany profit on a long-lived asset, the profit is eliminated by a debit to either retained earnings, in the case of an adjusted consolidated balance sheet, or to gain on sale, in the case of a consolidated income statement.

Depreciable assets require the same adjustment for intercompany profit as nondepreciable long-lived assets, and an adjustment must also be made for any depreciation recorded on the intercompany profit.

Illustration of Profit in Long-Lived Assets

S Company, an 80%-owned subsidiary, sells to P Company for $100,000 a piece of machinery that cost $80,000. The sale was made on July 1, 19X1, and consolidated statements are being prepared for December 31, 19X1. P Company depreciates machinery over 10 years on a straight-line basis and records one-half year's depreciation on the purchased machinery.

The first entry eliminates the $20,000 of intercompany profit, as follows:

Gain on sale of machinery	$20,000	
Machinery		$20,000

Since P Company has recorded one-half year's depreciation on the machinery, the following additional entry is made:

Accumulated depreciation	$1,000	
Depreciation expense		$ 1,000

Because consolidated eliminations and adjustments are never posted to any books, additional entries are required in the following year. Assuming that intercompany profit adjustments were not made under the equity method on P Company's books, the following eliminations are needed:

Retained earnings—P Company	$16,000	
Retained earnings—S Company	4,000	
Machinery		$20,000

To eliminate intercompany profit
on prior year's sale of machinery.

Accumulated depreciation	$ 3,000	
Retained earnings—P Company		$ 800
Retained earnings—S Company		200
Depreciation expense		2,000

To eliminate the $2,000
depreciation expense on
intercompany profit on the sale
of machinery and to eliminate
the $1,000 depreciation expense
for prior year's depreciation.

If the intercompany sale had been made from P Company to S Company, the retained earnings adjustments would have been made only to P Company's accounts.

The process of eliminating the depreciation expense on the intercompany profit on the sale of long-lived assets continues until the asset is fully depreciated. Thereafter, until the asset is disposed of or retired, adjustments are needed to the machinery and accumulated depreciation accounts. In the example, the following entry would be made every year on the consolidated work papers after the asset is fully depreciated and before it is disposed of or retired.

Accumulated depreciation	$20,000	
Machinery		$20,000

An affiliate that makes an intercompany profit on the sale of long-lived assets to another affiliate may pay income taxes on the gain. This occurs usually when the affiliated group does not file consolidated tax returns and the gain cannot be avoided for tax purposes. In such cases, the intercompany profit on the sale should be reduced by the related tax effects in computing the consolidated adjusting entry.

Intercompany Bondholdings

Intercompany bonds purchased by an affiliate are treated in the year of acquisition as though they have been retired. Any gain or loss is recognized in the consolidated income statement for the year of acquisition.

The amount of gain or loss on an intercompany bond purchase is the difference between the unamortized bond premium or discount on the books of the issuer and the amount of any purchase discount or premium.

An intercompany gain or loss on bonds does not occur when an affiliate makes the purchase directly from the affiliated issuer, because the selling price will be exactly equal to the cost.

Illustration of Intercompany Bonds

An affiliate purchases $20,000 face value 6% bonds from an affiliated issuer for $19,500.
On the affiliated investor's books the following entry is made:

Investment in bonds	$19,500	
Cash		$19,500

On the affiliated issuer's books the entry is:

Cash	$19,500	
Discount on bonds payable	500	
Bonds payable		$20,000

The consolidated elimination is:

Bonds payable	$20,000	
Discount on bonds payable		$ 500
Investment in bonds		19,500

An intercompany gain or loss on bonds does not occur when the purchase price is exactly the same as the carrying value on the books of the affiliated issuer.

The following conditions must exist for an affiliated investor to realize a gain or loss on intercompany bondholdings:

1. The bonds are already outstanding.
2. The bonds are purchased from outside the affiliated group.
3. The price paid is different from the carrying value of the affiliated issuer.

Illustration of Intercompany Bonds with Gain/Loss

Company S acquires $50,000 of face amount 6% bonds from an outsider. These bonds were part of an original issue of $300,000 made by the parent of Company S. The purchase price was $45,000, and the bonds mature in four years and nine months (57 months). Interest is payable on June 30 and December 31, and the purchase was made on March 31.

The journal entry on the books of Company S to record the purchase is:

Investment in bonds	$45,000	
Accrued interest receivable	750	
Cash		$45,750

On the consolidated work papers at the end of the year, the following entries are made:

Investment in bonds	$ 5,000	
Gain on intercompany bondholdings		$ 5,000

To adjust the investment in bonds to face amount and record the gain.

Bonds payable—Co. P	$50,000	
Investment in bonds—Co. S		$50,000

To eliminate intercompany bondholdings.

Interest income—Co. S	$ 2,250	
Interest expense—Co. P		$ 2,250

To eliminate intercompany interest on bonds that was actually paid.

Interest income—Co. S	$ 788	
Investment in bonds		$ 788

To eliminate amortization of $5,000 discount on bonds recorded on Co. S's books. (9/57 of $5,000 = $788)

Accrued interest payable	$ 1,500	
Accrued interest receivable		$ 1,500

To eliminate accrued interest payable on Dec. 31 by Co. P, and the accrued interest receivable on Dec. 31 by Co. S.

This example contains all the possible adjustments except for an issuer's premium or discount. Assume the following additional information on the original issue:

Face amount	$300,000
Issued at 96	288,000
Date of issue	1/1/X1
Maturity date	1/1/Y0

Company S had purchased its $50,000 face amount when the issue had four years and nine months left to maturity.

On the parent company's books, this discount is being amortized over the life of the bond issue at the rate of $1,200 per year ($12,000 discount divided by 10 years). An adjustment is made on the consolidated work papers to eliminate the portion of the unamortized bond discount existing at the date of purchase that is applicable to the $50,000 face amount purchased by Company S.

Total discount on issue	$12,000
1/6 applicable to Co. S's purchase	$ 2,000
Amount of discount per month ($2,000 divided by 120 months)	$ 16.67
Four years and nine months equal 57 months x $16.67	$ 950

The amount of unamortized bond discount on Co. P's books applicable to the $50,000 purchase made by Company S was $950 at the date of purchase. This $950 would have entered into the computation of the gain or loss on intercompany bondholdings. In the example, the gain or loss on intercompany bondholdings of $5,000 would have been reduced by $950 ($4,050) and the following additional consolidated elimination would have been made:

Gain or loss on intercompany bondholdings	$950	
Unamortized bond discount		$950

In addition, the amortization on the intercompany portion of the bond discount would be reversed in the consolidated worksheet (9 months x $16.67):

Unamortized bond discount	$150	
Interest expense		$150

Intercompany Dividends

Intercompany dividends are eliminated on the consolidated work papers. Consolidated retained earnings should reflect the accumulated earnings of the consolidated group arising since acquisition that have not been distributed to the shareholders of, or capitalized by, the parent company. In the event that a subsidiary capitalizes earnings arising since acquisition by means of a stock dividend, or otherwise, a transfer to paid-in capital is not required in consolidating (ARB-51, par. 18).

Intercompany Stockholdings

Shares of the parent held by a subsidiary should not be treated as outstanding stock in the consolidated balance sheet. Such shares are treated as "treasury stock" on the consolidated balance sheet and subtracted from consolidated stockholders' equity.

Income Tax Considerations

Income taxes are deferred on any intercompany profits where the asset still exists within the consolidated group (ARB-51, par. 17). If consolidated tax returns are filed, however, no adjustment need be made for deferred income taxes, because intercompany profits are eliminated in computing the consolidated tax liability.

Minority Interests

Consolidated financial statements are prepared primarily for the benefit of creditors and shareholders.

Minority interests in net income are deducted to arrive at consolidated net income. Minority interests are theoretically limited to the extent of their equity capital, however, and losses in excess of minority interest equity capital are charged against the majority interest. Subsequently, when the losses reverse, the majority interests should be credited with the amount of minority interest losses previously absorbed before credit is made to the minority interests (ARB-51, par. 15).

Disclosure

The consolidation policy should be disclosed fully on the financial statements or in footnotes thereto (ARB-51, par. 5).

Disclosure of Minority Interests

The *parent company theory* is used in practice almost exclusively for disclosing minority interests in a consolidated balance sheet. Under the parent company theory, minority interests are *not* considered part of stockholders' equity and are disclosed in the consolidated balance sheet between the liability section and the stockholders' equity section. Whereas minority interests are insignificant and do not warrant a separate classification in the consolidated balance sheet, some enterprises have seen fit to disclose minority interests among other liabilities. Minority interests in consolidated net income are shown as a deduction in arriving at consolidated net income.

Under the *entity theory*, minority interests are disclosed within and as part of the consolidated stockholders' equity section of the consolidated balance sheet. Although the entity theory has much more theoretical support, it is seldom used in practice.

6.18 Consolidated Financial Statements

Illustration of Computing Minority Interest and Consolidated Net Income

Computing minority interests in a complex father-son-grandson affiliation may be demonstrated by using the following diagram (dollar amounts are income figures for the separate entities):

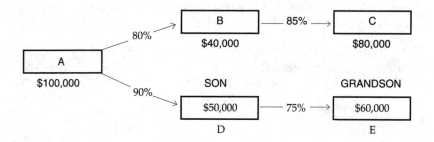

The computations of minority interests and consolidated net income follow:

	E	D	C	B	A
Net income	$60,000	$50,000	$80,000	$ 40,000	$100,000
75% to D	(45,000)	45,000			
		$95,000			
90% to A		(85,500)			85,500
85% to B			(68,000)	68,000	
				$108,000	
80% to A				(86,400)	86,400
Minority interests	$15,000	$ 9,500	$12,000	$ 21,600	

Consolidated net income $271,900

In a situation in which a subsidiary owns shares of the parent company, consolidated net income may be found algebraically, as the following depicts:

Company	Unconsolidated Income (excluding income from investees)	
A	$40,000	A, the parent, owns 80% of B
B	20,000	B owns 70% of C
C	10,000	C owns 20% of A

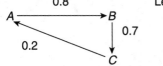

Let A = A's *consolidated basis* net income
B = B's *consolidated basis* net income
C = C's *consolidated basis* net income

The figures and relationships can be put into algebraic form so as to compute *consolidated net income.*

$$A = 40,000 + 0.8B$$
$$B = 20,000 + 0.7C$$
$$C = 10,000 + 0.2A$$

Solving for A, we have:

$$A = 40,000 + 0.8 (20,000 + 0.7C)$$
$$A = 40,000 + 16,000 + 0.56C$$
$$A = 56,000 + 0.56C$$
$$A = 56,000 + 0.56 (10,000 + 0.2A)$$
$$A = 56,000 + 5,600 + 0.112A$$
$$0.888A = 61,600$$
$$A = 69,369$$

Company A's income on an equity basis, which equals consolidated income, is determined by multiplying by the 80% interest outstanding (i.e., the remaining 20% is held within the consolidated entity):

$69,369 x 0.8 = $55,495 consolidated net income

The minority interests in the two subsidiaries are determined as follows:

$$C = \$10,000 + 0.2(\$69,369)$$
$$= \$23,874$$

Minority interest share of C $= 0.3(\$23,874)$
$$= \$7,162$$

$$B = \$20,000 + 0.7(\$23,874)$$
$$= \$36,712$$
$$\text{Minority interest share of } B = 0.2(\$36,712)$$
$$= \$7,342$$

CONSOLIDATED FINANCIAL STATEMENTS
IMPORTANT NOTICE FOR 1999

As the 1999 *Miller GAAP Guide* goes to press, the FASB continues to deliberate issues concerning consolidation policies and procedures.

An Exposure Draft of a proposed FASB statement was issued in 1995. Among the more important requirements incorporated in the Exposure Draft are the following:

1. A controlling (parent) entity would be required to consolidate all entities that it controls (subsidiaries) unless control is temporary. *Control* of an entity is defined as the power to use or direct the use of the individual assets of another entity in essentially the same ways as the controlling entity can use its own assets.

2. The aggregate amount of the uncontrolling interest in subsidiaries that are not wholly owned by the parent would be reported in the consolidated balance sheet as a separate component of equity. In the income statement, the amount of net income or loss that is attributable to the noncontrolling interest would be deducted from consolidated net income to compute net income attributable to the controlling interest.

3. Intercompany balances and transactions would be eliminated in the preparation of consolidated financial statements. The effect of eliminating intercompany profits and losses on assets that remain within the group would be allocated between the controlling and noncontrolling interests based on their ownership interests in the selling affiliate.

4. At the date the parent-subsidiary relationship is established, the purchase price of the subsidiary would be assigned to the identifiable assets acquired and liabilities assumed at their fair values. The excess of the cost over the parent's share of the net amount assigned to the assets acquired and the liabilities assumed is goodwill.

5. Changes in a parent's ownership interest that occur after a subsidiary is acquired that do not result in a loss of control would be accounted for as transactions in the equity of the consolidated entity. No gain or loss would be recognized.

The FASB has held extensive deliberations concerning this project. It has tentatively decided to modify and clarify the Exposure Draft's definition of control and discussion of the characteristics of control. Tentatively, the FASB is defining *control* as the power to direct the policies and management that guide the activities of another entity so as to benefit from its activities. The FASB has decided to focus first on consolidation policy and to defer further discussion of consolidation procedures until completion of the policy phase of the project.

A revised Exposure Draft is currently scheduled for the third quarter of 1998.

CHAPTER 7
CONTINGENCIES, RISKS, AND UNCERTAINTIES

CONTENTS

CHAPTER 7
CONTINGENCIES, RISKS, AND UNCERTAINTIES

OVERVIEW

Accounting for contingencies is an important feature of the preparation of financial statements in accordance with GAAP, because of the many uncertainties that may exist at the end of each accounting period. Standards governing accounting for loss contingencies require accrual and/or note disclosure when specified recognition and disclosure criteria are met. Gain contingencies generally are not recognized in financial statements but may be disclosed.

GAAP concerning accounting for contingencies are provided in the following pronouncements:

FAS-5   Accounting for Contingencies

FAS-38   Accounting for Preacquisition Contingencies of Purchased Enterprises

FIN-14   Reasonable Estimation of the Amount of a Loss

FIN-34   Disclosure of Indirect Guarantees of Indebtedness of Others

Closely related to the authoritative literature on accounting for contingencies are the requirements in SOP 94-6 to disclose information about significant risks and uncertainties. Under SOP 94-6 (Disclosure of Certain Significant Risks and Uncertainties), information is required about the nature of an entity's operations, use of estimates in the preparation of financial statements, certain significant estimates, and current vulnerability due to certain concentrations.

CROSS-REFERENCES

1999 MILLER GAAP GUIDE: Chapter 3, "Business Combinations"; Chapter 9, "Current Assets and Current Liabilities"; Chapter 43, "Revenue Recognition"

BACKGROUND

A *contingency* is an existing condition, situation, or set of circumstances involving varying degrees of uncertainty that may, through one or more related future events, result in the acquisition or loss of an asset or the incurrence or avoidance of a liability, usually with the concurrence of a gain or loss. The resulting gain or loss is referred to as a *gain contingency* or a *loss contingency*.

The existence of a loss contingency may be established on or before the date of the financial statements, or after the date of the financial statements but prior to the issuance date of the financial statements. After a loss contingency is established, the probability of its developing into an actual loss must be evaluated. Accounting for a loss contingency is based upon the degree of probability that one or more future events will occur that will confirm that a loss occurred. Gain contingencies are ordinarily not recorded until they are actually realized, although footnote disclosure in the financial statements may be necessary.

Loss contingencies may arise from the risk of exposure resulting from items such as the following (FAS-5, par. 4):

- Collectibility of receivables
- Property loss by fire, explosion, or other hazards
- Expropriation of assets
- Pending or threatened litigation, claims, or assessments
- Product warranties or defects
- Catastrophic losses of property

☞ **PRACTICE POINTER:** Not all uncertainties in the accounting process are *contingencies*, as that term is used in FAS-5. Many estimates that are inherent in the financial reporting process are *not* contingencies, and the authoritative literature covered in this section does *not* apply. For example, depreciable assets have a reasonably estimated life, and depreciation expense is used to allocate the cost of the asset systematically over its estimated useful life. Estimates, such as depreciation and similar accrued amounts, are not contingencies as described in FAS-5.

OBSERVATION: Many risks and uncertainties are important in evaluating an enterprise's financial position, results of operations, and cash flow prospects. The many risks and uncertainties confronted by an enterprise underscore the tentative nature of financial statements that are based on relatively short periods of time. While Statements of Position of the AICPA are generally not covered in the 1999 *Miller GAAP Guide,* SOP 94-6 is a particularly important document in the authoritative accounting literature in terms of required disclosure of risks and uncertainties and, as a result, is covered in this chapter.

LOSS CONTINGENCIES

Classification

A loss contingency will develop into an actual loss only upon the occurrence of one or more future events, whose likelihood of occurring may vary significantly. The likelihood that future events will confirm a loss must be classified as (a) probable (likely to occur), (b) reasonably possible (between *probable* and *remote*), or (c) remote (slight chance of occurring) (FAS-5, par. 3).

The accounting treatment for loss contingencies flows logically from the three ranges of probability described in the previous paragraph. Figure 7-1 provides the general structure of accounting that is required.

Accounting and Reporting

Depending upon whether a loss contingency is classified as probable, reasonably possible, or remote, it may be (a) accrued as a charge to income as of the date of the financial statements, (b) disclosed by note to the financial statements, or (c) neither accrued nor disclosed.

The following two conditions must be met for a *loss contingency* to be accrued as a charge to income as of the date of the financial statements (FAS-5, par. 8):

- It is *probable* that as of the date of the financial statements an asset has been impaired or a liability incurred, based on information available before the actual issuance date of the financial statements.

    It is implicit in this condition that it must be *probable* that one or more future events will occur to confirm the loss.

- The amount of loss can be estimated reasonably.

> ☞ **PRACTICE POINTER:** If a loss contingency is classified as *probable* and only a range of possible loss (similar to a minimum–maximum) can be established, then the **minimum** amount in the range is accrued, unless some other amount within the range appears to be a better estimate (FIN-14, par. 3). The range of possible loss must also be disclosed.

Loss contingencies that are accrued ordinarily require note disclosure so that the financial statements are not misleading. This disclosure ordinarily consists of the nature of the contingency and, in some circumstances, the amount accrued (FAS-5, par. 9).

Illustration of Accrued Contingent Liability

Following is a pro forma illustration of disclosure of a loss contingency for which the probability of future events confirming a loss is high and for which an amount can be reasonably estimated:

> During 19XX, the Company became aware of past circumstances (describe nature of contingency) that management believes are likely to require recognition of a loss(es) in future year(s). While the exact amount of this (these) loss(es) is not known, a reasonable estimate, based on information currently available, is $XXX. This amount has been recognized as a loss in the current year and appears as a contingent liability (provide title) in the 19XD statement of financial position. Recognition of this loss had the impact of reducing net income and earnings per share by $XX and $XX, respectively, in 19XX.

If one or both conditions for the accrual of a loss contingency are not met and the loss contingency is classified as *probable* or *reasonably possible*, financial statement disclosure of the loss contingency is required. The disclosure shall contain a description of the nature of the loss contingency and the range of possible loss, or include a statement that no estimate of the loss can be made (FAS-5, par. 10).

Litigation, Claims, or Assessments

If both conditions for the accrual of a loss contingency are met, an accrual for the estimated amount of pending or threatened litigation and actual or possible claims or assessments is required. Some of the factors that should be considered in determining whether the conditions for accrual have been met are the (*a*) nature of the litigation, claim, or assessment, (*b*) progress of the case, including progress after the date of the financial statements but before the issuance date of the financial statements, (*c*) opinions of legal counsel, and (*d*) management's intended response to the litigation, claim, or assessment (FAS-5, par. 36).

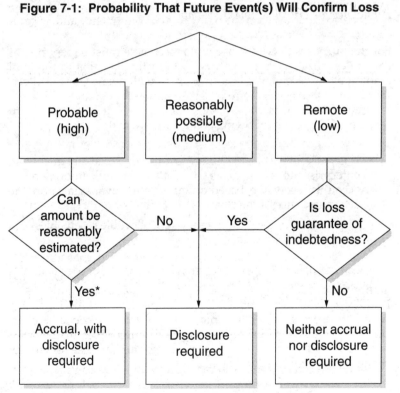

Figure 7-1: Probability That Future Event(s) Will Confirm Loss

* Includes estimation of a range of loss, in which case the minimum amount is accrued and the amount of the range is disclosed.

Illustration of Disclosed Loss Contingency

Following is a pro forma illustration of disclosure of a loss contingency for which the probability of future events confirming the loss is reasonably possible and for which the outcome is sufficiently uncertain that accrual is not appropriate:

> During 19XX, a suit was filed against the company by a former employee alleging that the company engaged in discriminatory employment practices. The suit requests damages of $1,000,000. Management has indicated its plans to vigorously contest this suit and believes that the loss, if any, resulting from the suit will not have a material impact on the company's financial position, results of operations, or cash flows in future years.

Allowance for Uncollectible Receivables

For the purposes of GAAP, accounts receivable must be reported at their net realizable value. Net realizable value is equal to the total amount of the receivables less an estimated allowance for uncollectible accounts.

Under FAS-5, an accrual for a loss contingency must be charged to income if both of the following conditions are met:

- It is *probable* that as of the date of the financial statements an enterprise does not expect to collect the full amount of its accounts receivable, based on information available before the actual issuance of the financial statements.

- The amount of loss contingency (uncollectible receivables) can be *reasonably estimated*.

If both of these conditions are met, an accrual for the estimated amount of uncollectible receivables must be made even if the uncollectible receivables cannot be identified specifically (FAS-5, par. 22). An enterprise may base its estimate of uncollectible receivables on its prior experience, the experience of other enterprises in the same industry, the debtor's ability to pay, and/or an appraisal of current economic conditions (FAS-5, par. 23).

☞ **PRACTICE POINTER:** A significant uncertainty exists in the ultimate collection of accounts receivable if an enterprise is unable to estimate reasonably the amount of its uncollectible receivables. If a significant uncertainty does exist in the collection of the receivables, use the installment sales method, cost-recovery method, or some other method of revenue recognition (APB-10, par. 12).

Product or Service Warranty Obligation

A product or service warranty obligation is a contingency under the provisions of FAS-5, because of the potential claims that may result from the warranty. If both of the conditions for the accrual of a loss contingency are met, an accrual for the estimated amount of a warranty obligation must be made even if the warranty obligation cannot be identified specifically. An enterprise may base its estimate of a warranty obligation on its prior experience, the experience of other enterprises in the same industry, and/or an appraisal of current economic conditions. If an enterprise is unable to estimate reasonably the amount of its warranty obligation and the range of possible loss is wide, significant uncertainty exists as to whether a sale should be recorded (FAS-5, par. 25). If a significant uncertainty does exist in estimating a warranty obligation, a sale shall not be recorded and the installment sales method, cost-recovery method, or some other method of revenue recognition shall be used (APB-10, par. 12).

Loss Contingencies Arising after the Date of the Financial Statements

A loss contingency that is classified as *probable* or *reasonably possible,* that occurs after the balance sheet date but before the issuance date of the financial statements, may have to be disclosed to avoid misleading financial statements. If professional judgment deems this type of disclosure necessary, the disclosure shall contain a description of the nature of the loss contingency and the range of possible loss, or include a statement that no estimate of the loss can be made. It may be desirable to disclose this type of loss contingency by supplementing the historical financial statements with pro forma statements reflecting the loss as if it occurred at the date of the financial statements (FAS-5, par. 11).

> ☛ **PRACTICE POINTER:** Disclosing loss contingencies that arise after the date of the financial statements may require either adjustment to the financial statements or note disclosure, depending on the nature of the loss contingency. If the subsequent event confirms or provides additional information on a condition that existed at the financial statement date, make an adjustment to the financial statements. Otherwise, disclose the loss contingency, which, in some cases, may be made best by

presenting pro forma restated financial information as a part of the note disclosure.

Unasserted Claims or Assessments

An *unasserted claim* is one that has not been asserted by the claimant because the claimant has no knowledge of the existing claim or has not elected to assert the existing claim. If it is *probable* that an unasserted claim will be asserted by the claimant and it is *probable* or *reasonably possible* that an unfavorable outcome will result, the unasserted claim must be disclosed in the financial statements. If these conditions are not met, however, disclosure is not required for unasserted claims or assessments in which the potential claimant apparently has no knowledge of the claim's existence (FAS-5, par. 38).

Disclosure of Remote Loss Contingencies

As a general rule, financial statement disclosure of loss contingencies that have a *remote* possibility of materializing is not required by FAS-5. Loss contingencies that may occur as the result of a *guarantee*, however, must be disclosed in the financial statements, even if they have a *remote* possibility of materializing.

Guarantees to repurchase receivables or related property, obligations of banks under letters of credit or *standby agreements*, guarantees of the indebtedness of others, and unconditional obligations to make payments are examples of the types of guarantee contingencies that must be disclosed even if they have a *remote* possibility of materializing. The nature and amount of the guarantee must be disclosed in the financial statements. In addition, consideration should be given to disclosing the amount, if estimable, that can be recovered in the event the guarantor is called upon to satisfy the guarantee (FAS-5, par. 12).

FIN-34 was issued to clarify that the term *guarantee of indebtedness of others* (FAS-5, par. 12) includes both direct and indirect guarantees. FIN-34 describes the following agreements as indirect guarantees of indebtedness of others:

- A guarantor is obligated to transfer funds to a debtor if a specific event occurs. The funds transferred must be legally available to the debtor's creditors, who also expressly have the right to enforce the terms of the agreement in the event of default.
- A guarantor is obligated to transfer funds to a debtor if the debtor's income, working capital, and/or coverage of fixed charges are not maintained at specified amounts.

In both a direct and indirect guarantee of indebtedness of others, three parties are involved: (1) the debtor, (2) the creditor, and (3) the guarantor. In a direct guarantee, the guarantor agrees to make payment directly to the creditor if the debtor fails to do so. The guarantee runs directly from the guarantor to the creditor. Thus, the creditor has a direct claim against the guarantor if the debtor defaults. In an indirect guarantee, the guarantor agrees to transfer funds to the debtor if a specified event occurs. The guarantee runs directly from the guarantor to the debtor, but the creditor is an indirect beneficiary of the guarantee. Thus, the creditor has an indirect claim against the guarantor because he or she may exercise the debtor's claim against the guarantor in the event of default. After the guarantor transfers the funds to the debtor, they may become available to the creditor (FIN-34, pars. 2 and 9).

> **OBSERVATION:** FIN-34 states that the funds transferred to the debtor will become legally available to creditors. This does not necessarily mean, however, that any creditor will actually receive the transferred funds. The agreement may specifically require the debtor to use the funds for purposes other than the payment of creditors. For example, the agreement may require that the debtor retain the transferred funds to maintain its working capital at or above a specified minimum.
>
> Another possibility is that competing creditor claims may be made against the transferred funds, in which event litigation may be the only solution.

Disclosure of Noninsured Property

An enterprise may be underinsured or not insured at all against the risk of future loss or damage to its property by fire, explosion, or other hazard. The fact that an enterprise's property is underinsured or not insured at all constitutes an existing uncertainty as defined by FAS-5. The absence of insurance does not mean, however, that an asset has been impaired or a liability incurred as of the date of the financial statements (FAS-5, par. 28). Therefore, FAS-5 does not require financial statement disclosure of noninsurance or underinsurance of possible losses, but specifically states that it does not discourage this practice (FAS-5, par. 103).

> ☛ **PRACTICE POINTER:** The removal of insurance does not, in and of itself, mean that a loss has already been incurred and that a contingent liability should be recorded. While the uninsured enterprise assumes greater risk than an insured one, a contingent loss results from a past event and the removal of insurance does not qualify for such an event.

Appropriations of Retained Earnings

FAS-5 does not prohibit an enterprise from appropriating specific amounts of retained earnings for potential loss contingencies. The amount of appropriated retained earnings, however, must be reported within the stockholders' equity section of the balance sheet and clearly identified as an appropriation of retained earnings. In addition, the following rules must be observed (FAS-5, par. 15):

1. No costs or losses shall be charged against the appropriated retained earnings and no part of the appropriated retained earnings may be transferred to income or in any way used to affect the determination of net income for any period.

2. The appropriated retained earnings shall be restored intact to retained earnings when the appropriation is no longer considered necessary.

Preacquisition Contingencies

A portion of the total cost of acquiring an enterprise under the purchase method (APB-16, Business Combinations) must be allocated to contingent assets, contingent liabilities, and contingent impairments of assets, provided that the following conditions are met (FAS-38, par. 4):

- It is probable that the contingent item existed at the consummation date of the business combination.

- After the consummation date, but prior to the end of the "allocation period," it is confirmed that the contingent item did exist at the consummation date of the business combination.

- The amount of the asset, liability, or impairment can be estimated reasonably.

If the above conditions are met, a portion of the total cost of acquiring an enterprise under the purchase method must be allocated to any contingent items (FAS-38, par. 5).

The *allocation period* is the period that is required by the purchaser to identify and quantify the acquired assets and assumed liabilities for the purposes of allocating the total cost of the acquisition in accordance with APB-16.

Any adjustment for contingent items arising from a purchase transaction that occurs after the end of the allocation period is included in net income of the period in which the adjustment is recognized (FAS-38, par. 6).

GAIN CONTINGENCIES

Gain contingencies may be disclosed in the financial statements by note, but should not be reflected in income, because doing so may result in recognizing revenue prior to its realization. Care should be exercised in disclosing gain contingencies to avoid misleading implications as to the recognition of revenue prior to its realization (FAS-5, par. 17).

DISCLOSURE OF SIGNIFICANT RISKS AND UNCERTAINTIES

Volatility and uncertainty in the business and economic environment result in the need for disclosure of information about the risks and uncertainties confronted by reporting entities. SOP 94-6 requires disclosure of significant risks and uncertainties that confront entities in the following areas: nature of operations, use of estimates in the preparation of financial statements, certain significant estimates, and current vulnerability due to certain concentrations.

> ☞ **PRACTICE POINTER:** Take care to not overlook the broad-based disclosure requirements of SOP 94-6. Many Statements of Position are industry specific and not applicable in all or many situations. SOP 94-6, however, is an exception and requires disclosures that are applicable to many reporting entities. For example, disclosing the nature of operations, the use of estimates, and significant estimates used in the preparation of financial statements affects virtually all entities. While vulnerability from concentrations may not be as prevalent as the previously mentioned areas, it applies in many situations.

Nature of Operations

Financial statements should include a description of the major products or services an entity sells or provides and its principal markets and locations of those markets. Entities that operate in more than one market must indicate the relative importance of their operations in each market. Disclosures concerning the nature of operations are not required to be quantified, and relative importance may be described by terms such as *predominantly, about equally, major and other* (SOP 94-6, par. 10).

Use of Estimates

Financial statements should include an explanation that their preparation in conformity with GAAP requires the application of management's estimates (SOP 94-6, par. 11).

Significant Estimates

Disclosure regarding an estimate is required when *both* of the following conditions are met:

1. It is at least reasonably possible that the estimate of the effect on the financial statements of a condition, situation, or set of circumstances that existed at the date of the financial statements will change in the near term due to one or more future confirming events.
2. The effect of the change would have a material effect on the financial statements (SOP 94-6, par. 13).

The disclosure requirements of FAS-5 for contingencies are supplemented by SOP 94-6 as follows:

- If an estimate requires disclosure under FAS-5 or another pronouncement, an indication also shall be made that it is at least reasonably possible that a change in the estimate will occur in the near term.

- An estimate that does not require disclosure under FAS-5 (such as estimates associated with long-term operating assets and amounts reported under profitable long-term contracts) may meet the standards described above and, if so, requires disclosure of (a) its nature, and (b) an indication that it is reasonably possible that a change in the estimate will occur in the near term (SOP 94-6, par. 16).

Following are examples of the types of situations that may require disclosure in accordance with SOP 94-6, assuming the conditions stated above are present:

- Inventory subject to rapid technological obsolescence
- Specialized equipment subject to technological obsolescence
- Valuation allowances for deferred tax assets based on future taxable income
- Capitalized motion picture film production costs
- Capitalized computer software costs
- Deferred policy acquisition costs of insurance enterprises
- Valuation allowances for commercial and real estate loans
- Environmental remediation-related obligations
- Litigation-related obligations

- Contingent liabilities for obligations of other entities
- Amounts reported for long-term obligations (e.g., pensions and other post-retirement benefits)
- Estimated net proceeds recoverable, the provisions for expected loss to be incurred, etc., on disposition of a business or assets
- Amounts reported for long-term contracts (SOP 94-6, par. 18)

Vulnerability from Concentrations

Vulnerability from concentrations exists because of an enterprise's greater exposure to risk than would be the case had the enterprise mitigated its risk through diversification. Financial statements should disclose concentrations if *all* of the following conditions are met:

1. The concentration existed at the date of the financial statements.
2. The concentration makes the enterprise vulnerable to the risk of a near-term severe impact.
3. It is reasonably possible that the events that could cause the severe impact will occur in the near term (SOP 94-6, par. 21).

Information sufficient to inform financial statement users of the general nature of the risk associated with the concentration is required for the following specific concentrations:

1. Concentrations in the volume of business transacted with a particular customer, supplier, lender, grantor, or contributor
2. Concentrations in revenue from particular products, services, or fund-raising events
3. Concentrations in the available sources of supply of materials, labor, or services, or of licenses or other rights used in the entity's operations
4. Concentrations in the market or geographic area in which an entity conducts its operations (SOP 94-6, par. 22)

In addition, for concentrations of labor subject to collective bargaining agreements, disclosure shall include both the percentage of the labor force covered by a collective bargaining agreement and the percentage of the labor force covered by a collective bargaining agreement that will expire within one year. For concentrations of operations located outside the entity's home country, disclosure shall include the carrying amounts of net assets and the geographic areas in which they are located (SOP 94-6, par. 24).

CHAPTER 8
CONVERTIBLE DEBT AND DEBT
WITH WARRANTS

CONTENTS

CHAPTER 8
CONVERTIBLE DEBT AND DEBT
WITH WARRANTS

OVERVIEW

Debt may be issued with a conversion feature or a feature that permits the separate purchase of other securities, usually common stock of the issuing company. These "hybrid" debt/equity securities generally derive some portion of their value from the equity component (i.e., the conversion feature or the separate purchase option) that is included in the issue price. The significant accounting question that arises is the recognition, if any, of the equity feature when a hybrid security is issued. That treatment, in turn, affects the subsequent accounting when the conversion feature or separate purchase option is exercised.

GAAP in the area of convertible debt and debt issued with purchase options are included in the following pronouncements:

APB-14	Accounting for Convertible Debt and Debt Issued with Stock Purchase Warrants
FAS-84	Induced Conversions of Convertible Debt

CROSS-REFERENCES

1999 MILLER GAAP GUIDE: Chapter 13, "Earnings per Share"; Chapter 15, "Extinguishment of Debt"; Chapter 45, "Stockholders' Equity"

1999 MILLER GAAP IMPLEMENTATION MANUAL: EITF: Chapter 8, "Convertible Debt and Debt with Warrants"

BACKGROUND

Convertible debt is convertible into the common stock of the issuer or an affiliated enterprise. Common characteristics of convertible debt are (APB-14, par. 3):

- The interest rate is lower than the interest rate on an equivalent, but not convertible, security.

- The initial conversion price is greater than the market value of the underlying security.

- The conversion price does not change (except pursuant to certain antidilutive considerations).

- The security usually is callable by the issuer.

- The debt usually is subordinate to the nonconvertible debt of the issuer.

Conversion of the convertible debt requires the holders to relinquish their status as debtholders to become stockholders.

Debt also may be issued with detachable purchase warrants that usually permit the holders to purchase shares of common stock at a set price for a specified period. The holders of the detachable warrants are not required to relinquish their status as debtholders to become stockholders.

CONVERTIBLE DEBT

Issuance

Under current GAAP, when convertible debt is issued, no portion of the proceeds is accounted for as attributable to the conversion feature. At that time, the debt issue is treated entirely as debt and no formal accounting recognition is assigned to the value inherent in the conversion feature. In reaching this conclusion, APB-14 placed greater weight on the inseparability of the debt and the conversion feature, and less weight on practical problems of valuing the conversion feature (APB-14, par. 12).

> **OBSERVATION:** In considering alternative methods of accounting for convertible debt, some felt that the value of the equity component (conversion feature) should be recognized at the time the convertible debt is issued; others felt that it should be given formal recognition not at that time, but later when conversion occurs. APB-14 concluded that the most important reason for accounting for convertible debt solely as debt at the time of issuance is the inseparability of the debt and conversion option. The holder must give up rights as a debtholder to become a stockholder. The alternatives are mutually exclusive.

Illustration of Convertible Bond Issuance

Alpha Company issues $1,000,000 of convertible bonds at 98% of par value. Each $1,000 bond is convertible into 10 shares of the company's common stock. The bond issue is recorded as if there were no conversion feature, as follows:

Cash ($1,000,000 x 98%)	$980,000	
Discount on bonds payable	20,000	
Bonds payable		$1,000,000

Disclosure of the features of the bond, including the conversion option, is required. The entry above, however, is the same as it would be had the bonds not been convertible.

Conversion

When a convertible debt security with an inseparable conversion feature is converted into equity securities of the debtor in accordance with the original conversion terms, the convertible debt security is surrendered by the holder and the debt is retired by the debtor. The issuer substitutes equity for debt in its balance sheet. The following is an illustration of such a transaction.

Illustration of Convertible Debt Security
Converted into Equity Security

Blue Corporation has outstanding $20,000,000 of 8% convertible bonds, with an unamortized bond premium balance of $800,000. Each $1,000 bond is convertible into 10 shares of Blue Corporation's $5 par value common stock. On April 1, 19X1, all of the convertible bonds were converted by the bondholders.

8% convertible bonds payable	$20,000,000	
Unamortized bond premium	800,000	
Common stock ($5 par x 200,000)		$ 1,000,000
Capital in excess of par		
(common stock)		19,800,000

Under current accounting practice, no gain or loss is recognized on the conversion of convertible bonds to common stock if the conversion is made in accordance with the original conversion terms.

Generally, convertible debt is issued in anticipation that it will be converted into equity securities, and that the issuer will not have to pay the face amount of the debt at its maturity date. Although most convertible debt issues provide for the issuance of common equity shares upon conversion, the terms of a convertible debt security may provide for the issuance of preferred or other type of equity security upon conversion. When an enterprise converts debt to common equity shares, the liability for the debt is eliminated and the number of common equity shares outstanding is increased, which may affect the computation of earnings per share (EPS). When debt is converted to common equity shares, the pretax net income of the enterprise also increases by the amount of interest expense that was previously paid on the convertible debt.

> ☛ **PRACTICE POINTER:** Convertible debt generally is converted
> by a holder when the market value of its underlying equity
> securities into which the debt can be converted exceeds the
> face amount of the debt. If a convertible bondholder does not
> convert, the issuer may exercise the call provision in the debt
> to force conversion.

Convertible debt usually is not converted when the market value of its underlying equity securities is less than the face amount of the debt. Under this circumstance, the issuer may (*a*) exercise the call provision in the debt and pay the bondholders the face amount of the convertible debt, (*b*) offer the bondholders an inducement to convert that exceeds the original conversion terms, or (*c*) not pay off the debt until the scheduled maturity date (APB-14, par. 4).

Induced Conversion

FAS-84 applies to conversions of convertible debt in which the original conversion terms are changed by the debtor to encourage the holder of the convertible debt to convert to equity securities of the debtor. Changes in the original conversion terms may include (*a*) the reduction of the original conversion price to increase the number of shares of equity securities received by the bondholder, (*b*) the issuance of warrants or other securities, or (*c*) the payment of cash or some other type of consideration (FAS-84, par. 2).

FAS-84 applies only to induced conversions that (*a*) are exercisable for a limited period of time and (*b*) include the issuance of no less than the number of shares of equity securities required by the original conversion terms for each convertible bond converted. Thus, for each convertible bond that is converted, the debtor must issue, at a minimum, the amount of equity securities required by the original conversion terms (FAS-84, par. 2).

☞ **PRACTICE POINTER:** FAS-84 applies to only those induced conversions that are offered for a "limited period of time." This phrase is not explicitly defined by the standard, however.

Example 1 of Appendix A of FAS-84 appears to indicate that 60 days is a "limited period of time." Example 2 indicates that 30 days is considered a limited period of time. However, paragraph 32 of FAS-84 seems to indicate that a "limited period of time" may even be longer than 60 days.

In an induced conversion of convertible debt under FAS-84, a debtor does not recognize any gain or loss on the amount of equity securities that are required to be issued under the original conversion terms for each convertible bond converted. However, the fair value of any equity securities or other consideration paid or issued by the debtor that exceeds the amount of equity securities required to be issued for each convertible bond converted under the original conversion terms is recognized as current expense on the date the inducement offer is accepted by the bondholder (FAS-84, par. 3).

If the additional inducement consists of equity securities, the market value of such securities is credited to capital stock, and if necessary to capital in excess of par, with an offsetting debit to debt conversion expense. If the additional inducement consists of assets other than the debtor's equity securities, the market value of such assets is credited with an offsetting debit to debt conversion expense.

The fair value of the securities or other consideration is measured as of the date the inducement offer is accepted by the debtholder. This usually is the date the debtholder converts the debt into equity securities or enters into a binding agreement to do so (FAS-84, par. 4).

☞ **PRACTICE POINTER:** If individual bondholders accepted an inducement offer on many different days during the "limited period of time" allowed by FAS-84, a separate computation of the fair value of the incremental consideration would be required if the fair value of the debtor's common stock changes from day to day.

Illustration of Induced Conversion

Black Corporation has outstanding 100 10% convertible bonds, issued at par value and due on December 31, 19X1. Each $1,000 bond is convertible into 20 shares of Black Corporation $1 par value common stock. To induce bondholders to convert to its common stock, Black Corporation increases the conversion rate from 20 shares per $1,000 bond to 25 shares per $1,000 bond. This offer was made by Black Corporation for a limited period of 60 days commencing March 1, 19X2.

On April 1, when the market price of Black's common stock was $60, one bondholder tendered a $1,000 convertible bond for conversion. Under FAS-84, the amount of incremental consideration is equal to the fair value of the additional five shares of Black Corporation's common stock on April 1. Thus, the amount of incremental consideration is $300 (5 shares x $60 per share). The journal entry to record the transaction is:

Convertible bonds payable	$1,000	
Debt conversion expense	300	
Common stock ($1 par value)		
($1 x 25 shares)		$ 25
Capital in excess of par		
(common stock)		1,275

The incremental consideration paid or issued by a debtor may also be calculated as the difference between (*a*) the fair value of the equity securities and/or other consideration required to be issued under the original terms of the conversion privilege and (*b*) the fair value of the equity securities and/or other consideration that is actually issued.

Market value of securities based on inducement (25 x $60)	$1,500
Market value of securities based on original terms (20 x $60)	(1,200)
Fair value of incremental consideration	$ 300

OBSERVATION: There is a significant difference between extinguishment accounting and conversion accounting. As a rule, gain or loss is recognized in extinguishment accounting, while no gain or loss is recognized in conversion accounting. Extinguishment accounting results in the **extinguishment** of a debt, while conversion accounting results in the issuance of equity securities and the **retirement** of a debt. Although FAS-84 refers to both extinguishment and conversion accounting, it does not distinguish between the two.

OBSERVATION: When an enterprise gives up **assets** or increases its **liabilities** to induce the conversion of its convertible debt to its equity securities, there is little question that a cost is incurred. Serious doubt exists, however, about whether an enterprise incurs a cost when it gives up its own **equity securities** as an inducement for the conversion of convertible debt. CON-3 states that expenses represent outflows or other using up of assets or incurrences of liabilities (or a combination of both) during a period. There is no outflow or other using up of assets or incurrence of liabilities when, as a conversion inducement, an enterprise issues its equity securities and records their fair market value as debt conversion expense. FAS-84 appears to contradict the fact that the issuance of capital stock is a capital transaction, and under current accounting practice described in APB-9 (Reporting the Results of Operations), capital transactions do not enter into the income determination of an enterprise.

DEBT WITH DETACHABLE PURCHASE WARRANTS

Issuance

In contrast to accounting for convertible debt, when detachable purchase warrants are issued in conjunction with debt, APB-14 requires that separate amounts attributable to the debt and the purchase warrants be computed and accounting recognition be given to each component. The allocation to the two components of the hybrid debt/equity security is based on the relative market values of the two securities at the time of issuance (APB-14, par. 16). This conclusion is based primarily on the fact that the options available to the debtholder are *not* mutually exclusive—bondholders can become stockholders and retain their status as bondholders.

Illustration of Issuance of Debt with Detachable Warrants

Xeta Corporation issues 100 $100-par-value, 5% bonds with a detachable common stock warrant to purchase one share of Xeta's common stock at a specified price. At the time of issuance, the quoted market price of the bonds was $97, and the stock warrants were quoted at $2 each. The proceeds of the sale to Xeta Corporation were $9,900. The transaction is accounted for as follows:

Cash	$9,900	
Discount on 5% bonds payable (100 x $3)	300	
5% bonds payable		$10,000
Paid-in capital (stock warrants) (100 x $2)		200

The bonds and warrants are recorded separately at their market values:

Bonds: $10,000 x 97% = $9,700, recorded at $10,000 par value, less $300 discount

Warrants: 100 x $2 = $200

Exercise of Warrants

Once a separate purchase feature, such as a detachable stock purchase warrant, is issued, it usually is traded separately from its related convertible debt security. The separate purchase feature has its own market price, and conversion requires (*a*) the surrender of the purchase option and (*b*) the payment of any other consideration required by the terms of the warrant.

Under current accounting practice (APB-14), when a separate purchase feature is exercised in accordance with the original purchase terms, no gain or loss is recognized on the transaction. The amount previously credited to paid-in capital for the purchase feature at issuance is eliminated, the amount of cash received, if any, is recorded, and the par value of the capital stock issued and the appropriate amount of capital stock in excess of par is recorded. The following is an illustration of such a transaction.

Illustration of Exercise of Separate Purchase Feature

Ace Corporation previously issued debt securities with detachable stock purchase warrants. A credit of $10 for each warrant was recorded in paid-in capital at the date of issuance, representing the relative market value of each warrant. There was no discount or premium on the issuance of the related debt with detachable stock purchase warrants. Each stock purchase warrant permitted the purchase of 50 shares of Ace's $1 par value common stock, upon the payment of $200 and the surrender of the warrant. Assuming that one warrant was exercised, the journal entry would be:

Cash	$200	
Paid-in capital (stock warrants)	10	
Capital stock ($1 par value)		$ 50
Capital in excess of par (common stock)		160

The conversion of a separate conversion feature, such as a detachable stock purchase warrant, is accounted for solely as an equity transaction, and no gain or loss is recorded.

☛ **PRACTICE POINTER:** The accounting described in this section applies to "detachable" stock purchase warrants and other similar instruments, meaning that the stock purchase warrant can be exercised without affecting the other security from which it is detachable. Occasionally, a stock purchase warrant is encountered that is inseparable from another security (i.e., a nondetachable stock purchase warrant), and the related security must be surrendered to effect the stock purchase. In this case, although the name may imply otherwise, the stock purchase warrant effectively is part of a convertible security and should be accounted for as such.

OBSERVATION: APB-14 recognized that it is not practical to discuss all possible types of debt with conversion features and debt issued with purchase warrants, or debt issued with a combination of the two. It states that securities not explicitly dealt with in APB-14 should be accounted for in accordance with the substance of the transaction in a manner consistent with APB-14 (APB-14, par. 18).

CHAPTER 9
CURRENT ASSETS AND CURRENT LIABILITIES

CONTENTS

CHAPTER 9
CURRENT ASSETS AND
CURRENT LIABILITIES

OVERVIEW

The distinction between current and noncurrent assets and liabilities in a classified balance sheet is an important feature of financial reporting. There is considerable interest in the liquidity of the reporting enterprise, and the separate classification of current assets and liabilities is an important part of liquidity analysis.

GAAP concerning current assets and current liabilities are found in the following pronouncements:

ARB-43	Chapter 1A, Receivables from Officers, Employees, or Affiliated Companies
	Chapter 3A, Current Assets and Current Liabilities
APB-10	Omnibus Opinion—1966
FAS-6	Classification of Short-Term Obligations Expected to Be Refinanced
FAS-43	Accounting for Compensated Absences
FAS-78	Classification of Obligations That Are Callable by the Creditor
FIN-8	Classification of a Short-Term Obligation Repaid Prior to Being Replaced by a Long-Term Security
FIN-39	Offsetting of Amounts Related to Certain Contracts

CROSS-REFERENCES

1999 MILLER GAAP GUIDE: Chapter 4, "Cash Flow Statement"; Chapter 7, "Contingencies, Risks, and Uncertainties"; Chapter 16, "Financial Instruments"; Chapter 27, "Inventory Pricing and Methods"; Chapter 29, "Investments in Debt and Equity Securities"; Chapter 47, "Transfer and Servicing of Financial Assets"

1999 MILLER GAAP IMPLEMENTATION MANUAL: Chapter 3, "Balance Sheet Classification"

1999 MILLER GAAP IMPLEMENTATION MANUAL: EITF: Chapter 2, "Balance Sheet Classification"

1999 MILLER NOT-FOR-PROFIT REPORTING: Chapter 2, "Overview of Current Pronouncements"

1999 MILLER GOVERNMENTAL GAAP GUIDE: Chapter 13, "Assets"; Chapter 16, "Liabilities"

BACKGROUND

In the ordinary course of business there is a continuing circulation of capital within the current assets. For example, with a manufacturer, cash is expended for materials, labor, and factory overhead that are converted into finished inventory. After being sold, inventory usually is converted into trade receivables and, on collection of receivables, is converted back to cash. The average time elapsing between expending the cash and receiving the cash back from the trade receivable is called an *operating cycle*. One year is used as a basis for segregating current assets when more than one operating cycle occurs within a year. When the operating cycle is longer than one year, as with the lumber, tobacco, and distillery businesses, the operating cycle is used for segregating current assets. *In the event that a business clearly has no operating cycle, the one-year rule is used* (ARB-43, Ch. 3A, par. 5).

Frequently, businesses have a *natural business year*, at the end of which the company's activity, inventory, and trade receivables are at their lowest point. This is often the point in time selected as the end of the entity's accounting period for financial reporting purposes.

BASIC DEFINITIONS

Current Assets

Resources that are expected to be realized in cash, sold, or consumed during the next year (or longer operating cycle) are classified as current assets. Current assets are sometimes called circulating or working assets; cash that is restricted as to withdrawal or use for other than current operations is not classified as a current asset (ARB-43, Ch. 3A, par. 6).

There are several basic types of current assets (ARB-43, Ch. 3A, par. 4):

Cash

Includes money in any form, for example, cash on deposit, cash awaiting deposit, and cash funds available for use.

Secondary Cash Resources

The most common type of secondary cash resources is marketable securities.

Receivables

Include accounts receivable, notes receivable, and receivables from officers and employees.

Inventories

Include merchandise, raw materials, work in process, finished goods, operating supplies, and ordinary maintenance material and parts.

Prepaid Expenses

Include prepaid insurance, interest, rents, taxes, advertising, and operating supplies. Prepaid expenses, unlike other current assets, are not expected to be converted into cash; but, if they had not been paid in advance, they would require the use of current assets during the operating cycle.

Current Liabilities

Current liabilities are obligations for which liquidation is reasonably expected to require the use of current assets or the creation of other current liabilities.

> ☞ **PRACTICE POINTER:** The definition of current liabilities is based on the asset category from which the liability is expected to be retired rather than on a specific period of time. As a practical matter, most current liabilities are those that are expected to be retired during the period of time encompassed by the definition of current asset. Be careful, however, to identify instances where liabilities that are due in the near future should be classified as noncurrent because they will not

require the use of current assets. Examples are short-term obligations expected to be refinanced, and noncurrent liabilities that are near their maturity but that will be paid from noncurrent assets (e.g., bond sinking funds).

There are several basic types of current liabilities (ARB-43, Ch. 3A, par. 7):

Payables from Operations

Include items that have entered the operating cycle, which include trade payables and accrued liabilities such as wages and taxes.

Debt Maturities

Include amounts expected to be liquidated during the current operating cycle, such as short-term notes and the currently maturing portion of long-term debt.

Revenue Received in Advance

Includes collections received in advance of services, for example, prepaid subscriptions and other deferred revenues.

Other Accruals

Include estimates of accrued amounts that are expected to be required to cover expenditures within the year for known obligations (*a*) when the amount can be determined only approximately (provision for accrued bonuses payable) or (*b*) when the specific person(s) to whom payment will be made is (are) unascertainable (provision for warranty of a product) (ARB-43, Ch. 3A, par. 8).

Working Capital and Related Ratios

Working capital is the excess of current assets over current liabilities, and it is sometimes used as a measure of the liquidity of an enterprise (ARB-43, Ch. 3A, par. 3).

Changes in Each Element of Working Capital

The changes in each element of working capital are the increases or decreases in each current asset and current liability over the amounts in the preceding year.

Illustration of Determining Working Capital

	19X1	19X2	Working Capital Increase or (Decrease)
Current Assets:			
Cash	$10,000	$ 15,000	$ 5,000
Accounts receivable	25,000	35,000	10,000
Inventory	50,000	60,000	10,000
Prepaid expenses	1,000	500	(500)
Total current assets	$86,000	$110,500	$24,500
Current Liabilities:			
Accounts payable	$10,000	$ 15,000	$ (5,000)
Notes payable-current	20,000	15,000	5,000
Accrued expenses	1,000	1,500	(500)
Total current liabilities	$31,000	$ 31,500	$ (500)
Net working capital	$55,000	$ 79,000	
Increase in working capital			$24,000

The *current ratio*, or *working capital ratio*, is a measure of current position and is useful in analyzing short-term credit. The current ratio is computed by dividing the total current assets by the total current liabilities.

Illustration of Current Ratio

	19X1	19X2
Current assets	$86,000	$110,500
Current liabilities	(31,000)	(31,500)
Working capital	$55,000	$ 79,000
Current ratio	2.8 : 1	3.5 : 1

The *acid-test ratio* (also called the *quick ratio*) is determined by dividing those assets typically closest to cash by total current liabilities. The assets used to calculate this ratio consist of only the most liquid assets, typically cash, receivables, and marketable securities.

☞ **PRACTICE POINTER:** Only receivables and securities *convertible into cash* are included; restricted cash and securities are excluded.

Illustration of Acid-Test Ratio

	19X1	19X2
Cash	$10,000	$15,000
Receivables, net	25,000	35,000
Total *quick* assets	$35,000	$50,000
Total current liabilities	$31,000	$31,500
Acid-test ratio	1.1 : 1	1.6 : 1

RECEIVABLES

Accounts receivable are reported in the financial statements at net realizable value. Net realizable value is equal to the gross amount of receivables less an estimated allowance for uncollectible accounts.

Two common procedures of accounting for uncollectible accounts are (*a*) the direct write-off method and (*b*) the allowance method.

Direct Write-Off Method

This method recognizes a bad debt expense only when a specific account is determined to be uncollectible. The conceptual weaknesses of the direct write-off method are:

1. Bad debt expense is not *matched* with the related sales.

2. Accounts receivable are overstated, because no attempt is made to account for the unknown bad debts included therein.

Ordinarily, the direct write-off method is not considered GAAP, because it results in a mismatching of revenues and expenses (i.e., expenses are recognized in a later period than the revenue to which they relate). The method may be acceptable in situations where uncollectible accounts are immaterial in amount.

Allowance Method

The allowance method recognizes an estimate of uncollectible accounts each period, even though the specific individual accounts that will not be collected are not known at that time. Estimates of uncollectible accounts usually are made as a percentage of credit sales or ending receivables. This method is consistent with FAS-5 (Accounting for Contingencies), as explained below.

Under FAS-5, a contingency exists if, at the date of the financial statements, an enterprise does not expect to collect the full amount of its accounts receivable. Under this circumstance, an accrual for a loss contingency must be charged to income, if both of the following conditions exist:

- It is *probable* that as of the date of the financial statements an asset has been impaired or a liability incurred, based on information available before the issuance of the financial statements.

- The amount of the loss can be *estimated reasonably*.

If both of the above conditions are met, an accrual for the estimated amount of uncollectible receivables is made even if the specific uncollectible receivables cannot be identified. An enterprise may base its estimate of uncollectible receivables on its prior experience, the experience of other enterprises in the same industry, the debtor's ability to pay, or an appraisal of current economic conditions. Significant uncertainty may exist in the ultimate collection of receivables if an enterprise is unable to estimate reasonably the amount that is uncollectible. If a significant uncertainty exists in the ultimate collection of the receivables, the installment sales method, cost-recovery method, or some other method of revenue recognition should be used. In the event that both of the above conditions for accrual are not met and a loss contingency is at least *reasonably possible*, certain financial statement disclosures are required by FAS-5.

Illustration of Accounting for Uncollectible Accounts by the Allowance Method

AMB Co. estimates uncollectible accounts at 1% of credit sales. For the current year, credit sales totaled $1,000,000. The year-end balances in accounts receivable and the unadjusted allowance for uncollectible accounts are $250,000 and $15,000, respectively.

The entry to record uncollectible accounts ($1,000,000 x 1% = $10,000) is as follows:

Bad debt expense	$10,000	
Allowance for uncollectible accounts		$10,000

The balance sheet will include accounts receivable of $250,000, allowance for uncollectible accounts of $25,000 ($15,000 + $10,000), and net accounts receivable of $225,000 (250,000 – $25,000).

When a specific uncollectible account is written off (e.g., $2,100), the following entry is required:

Allowance for uncollectible accounts	$2,100	
Accounts receivable (specific account)		$2,100

This entry has no effect on the amount of net accounts receivable, because both the receivables balance and the allowance balance are reduced by the same amount.

If the estimate of uncollectibles had been based on the ending balance of accounts receivable, the same procedure would have been followed, except that the existing balance in the allowance would require consideration. For example, if uncollectible accounts were estimated at 9% of the ending balance in accounts receivable, the bad debt expense for the year would be $7,500, computed as follows:

Required allowance ($250,000 x 9%)	$22,500
Balance before adjustment	(15,000)
Required adjustment	$ 7,500

The balance sheet would include accounts receivable of $250,000, an allowance of $22,500, and a net receivables amount of $227,500.

A variation on the previous method is to "age" accounts receivable, a procedure that provides for recognizing an increasing percentage as uncollectible as accounts become increasingly delinquent. For example, applying this procedure to the $250,000 receivables balance above might result in the following:

	Not Yet Due	30 Days Overdue	60 Days Overdue	Past 60 Days Overdue
Accounts receivable balance	$120,000	$50,000	$50,000	$30,000
Uncollectible %	2%	7%	12%	25%
Uncollectible balance	$ 2,400	$ 3,500	$ 6,000	$ 7,500

The total uncollectible balance is $19,400, resulting in the recognition of bad debt expense of $4,400, assuming a previous allowance balance of $15,000 ($19,400 – $15,000 = $4,400).

Discounted Notes Receivable

Discounted notes receivable arise when the holder endorses the note (with or without recourse) to a third party and receives a sum of cash. The difference between the amount of cash received by the holder and the maturity value of the note is called the discount. If the note is discounted with recourse, the assignor remains contingently liable for the ultimate payment of the note when it becomes due. If the note is discounted without recourse, the assignor assumes no further liability.

The account discounted notes receivable is a contra account, which is deducted from the related receivables for financial statement purposes. The following is the procedure for computing the proceeds of a discounted note:

1. Compute the total maturity value of the note, including interest due at maturity.

2. Compute the discount amount (the maturity value of the note multiplied by the discount rate for the time involved).

3. The difference between the two amounts (1, less 2) equals the proceeds of the note.

Illustration of Discounted Notes Receivable

A $1,000 90-day 10% note is discounted at a bank at 8% when 60 days are remaining to maturity.

Maturity—$1,000 x 102.5% (1/4 of 10% plus face)	$1,025.00
Discount—$1,025 x 1.333% (1/6 of 8%)	(13.66)
Proceeds of note	$1,011.34

Factoring

Factoring is a process by which a company converts its receivables into cash by assigning them to a factor either with or without recourse. *With recourse* means that the assignee can return the receivable to the company and get back the funds paid if the receivable is uncollectible. *Without recourse* means that the assignee assumes the risk of losses on collections. Under factoring arrangements, the customer may or may not be notified.

Pledging

Pledging is the process whereby the company uses existing accounts receivable as collateral for a loan. The company retains title to the receivables but pledges that it will use the proceeds to pay the loan.

CASH SURRENDER VALUE OF LIFE INSURANCE

The proceeds of a life insurance policy usually provide some degree of financial security to one or more beneficiaries named in the policy. Upon death of the insured, the insurance company pays the beneficiary the face amount of the policy, less any outstanding indebtedness.

Insurable Interest

An owner of an insurance contract must have an insurable interest in the insured individual in order for the contract to be valid. An insurable interest in life insurance need only exist at the time the policy is issued, while an insurable interest in property insurance must exist at the time of a loss. An insurable interest is a test of financial relationship. A husband may insure the life of his wife, an employer the life of an employee, a creditor the life of a debtor, and a partner the life of a copartner.

An investment in a life insurance policy is accounted for at the amount that can be realized by the owner of the policy as of the date of its statement of financial position. Generally, the amount that can be realized from a life insurance policy is the amount of its *cash surrender value*. The increase in the cash surrender value of an insurance policy for a particular period is recorded by the owner of the policy as an asset in its statement of financial position. The insurance expense for the same period is the difference between the total amount of premium paid and the amount of increase in the cash surrender value of the policy.

Illustration of Insurable Interest

An enterprise is the owner and sole beneficiary of a $200,000 life insurance policy on its president. The annual premium is $16,000. The policy is starting its fourth year, and the schedule of cash values indicates that at the end of the fourth year the cash value increases $25 per thousand. The enterprise pays the $16,000 premium, and the journal entry to record the transaction is as follows:

Life insurance expense—officers	$11,000	
Cash surrender value—life insurance policy (200 x $25)	5,000	
Cash		$16,000

The cash surrender value of a life insurance policy is classified either as a current or noncurrent asset in the policy owner's statement of financial position, depending upon the intentions of the policy owner. If the policy owner intends to surrender the policy to the insurer for its cash value within its normal operating cycle, the cash surrender value is classified as a current asset in the statement of financial position. If there is no intention of collecting the policy's cash value within the normal operating cycle of the policy owner, the cash surrender value is classified as a noncurrent asset in the statement of financial position.

LIABILITY CLASSIFICATION ISSUES

Current Obligations Expected to Be Refinanced

FAS-6 and FIN-8 establish GAAP for classifying a short-term obligation that expected to be refinanced into a long-term liability or stockholders' equity. FAS-6 applies only to those companies that issue classified balance sheets (FAS-6, par. 7).

A short-term obligation can be excluded from current liabilities only if the company intends to refinance it on a long-term basis and the intent is supported by the ability to refinance that is demonstrated in one of the following ways (FAS-6, pars. 9–11):

1. A long-term obligation or equity security whose proceeds are used to retire the short-term obligation is issued after the date of the balance sheet but before the issuance of the financial statements.

2. Before the issuance of the financial statements, the company has entered into an agreement that enables it to refinance a short-term obligation on a long-term basis. The terms of the agreement must be clear and unambiguous and must contain the following provisions:

   a. The agreement may not be canceled by the lender or investor, and it must extend beyond the normal operating cycle of the company. (If the company has no operating cycle or the operating cycle occurs more than once a year, then the one-year rule is used.)

b. At the balance sheet date and at its issuance, the company was not in violation, nor was there any information that indicated a violation, of the agreement.

c. The lender or investor is expected to be financially capable of honoring the agreement.

The amount of short-term obligation that can be reclassified cannot exceed the actual proceeds received from the issuance of the new long-term obligation or the amount of available refinancing covered by the established agreement. The amount must be adjusted for any limitations in the agreement that indicate the full amount obtainable will not be available to retire the short-term obligations. In addition, if the agreement indicates that the amount available for refinancing will fluctuate, then the most conservative estimate must be used. If no reasonable estimate can be made, then the agreement does not fulfill the necessary requirements and the full amount of current liabilities must be presented (FAS-6, par. 12).

An enterprise may intend to seek alternative financing sources besides those in the established agreement when the short-term obligation becomes due. If alternative sources do not materialize, however, the company must intend to borrow from the source in the agreement (FAS-6, par. 13).

☛ **PRACTICE POINTER:** If the terms of the agreement allow the prospective lender or investor to set interest rates, collateral requirements, or similar conditions that are unreasonable to the company, the intent to refinance may not exist.

FIN-8 addresses the issue of a short-term obligation that is repaid and is subsequently replaced with a long-term debt obligation or equity securities. Because cash is temporarily required to retire the short-term obligation, the obligation should be classified as a current liability in the balance sheet (FIN-8, par. 3).

Any *rollover agreements* or *revolving credit agreements* must meet the above provisions to enable a company to classify the related short-term obligations as noncurrent (FAS-6, par. 14). The financial statements must contain a footnote disclosing the amount excluded from current liabilities and a full description of the financial agreement and new obligations incurred or expected to be incurred or the equity securities issued or expected to be issued (FAS-6, par. 15).

Callable Obligations

FAS-78 establishes GAAP for the current/noncurrent classification in the debtor's balance sheet of obligations that are payable on demand or callable by the creditor.

FAS-78 is applied to a classified balance sheet to determine whether the obligation should be classified as current or noncurrent for balance sheet purposes. FAS-78 is applied to both classified and unclassified balance sheets to determine the maturity dates of obligations disclosed by footnotes. For example, an unclassified balance sheet may contain footnote disclosures of the maturity dates of obligations, despite the fact that the obligations are not classified in the unclassified balance sheet, or may not be identified separately from other obligations in the unclassified balance sheet (FAS-78, par. 4).

At the debtor's balance sheet date, an obligation may, by its terms, be payable on demand. This includes long-term obligations that are callable because a violation of an objective acceleration clause in a long-term debt agreement may exist at the date of the debtor's balance sheet. Such callable obligations must be classified as a current liability at the debtor's balance sheet date unless (FAS-78, par. 5):

1. The creditor has waived the right to demand payment for a period that extends beyond the debtor's normal operating cycle, or

2. The debtor has cured the violation after the balance sheet date, but prior to the issuance date of the financial statements, and the obligation is not callable for a period that extends beyond the debtor's normal operating cycle.

A long-term debt agreement may provide for a grace period that commences after the occurrence of a violation of an objective acceleration clause. FAS-78 requires that such an obligation be classified as a current liability at the debtor's balance sheet date, unless the two criteria above are met and, in addition, the unexpired grace period extends beyond the debtor's normal operating cycle (FAS-78, par. 5).

> **OBSERVATION:** FAS-78, which amends ARB-43, Chapter 3A, requires that an obligation be classified as current or noncurrent, based solely on whether the legal terms of the loan agreement require payment within the debtor's normal operating cycle.

A creditor may have waived the right to demand payment on a specific obligation for a period that extends beyond the debtor's normal operating cycle. In this event, the debtor shall classify the obligation as a noncurrent liability.

Acceleration Clauses

An *objective acceleration clause* in a long-term debt agreement is one that contains objective criteria that the creditor must use as the basis for calling part or all of the loan, such as a specified minimum amount of working capital or net worth requirement.

In the event of a violation of an objective acceleration clause, most long-term obligations become immediately callable by the creditor, or become callable after a grace period that is specified in the loan agreement. When this occurs, the creditor can demand payment of part or all of the loan balance, in accordance with the terms of the debt agreement.

A subjective acceleration clause is one that permits the lender to unilaterally accelerate part or all of a long-term obligation. For example, the debt agreement might state that "if, in the opinion of the lender, the borrower experiences recurring losses or liquidity problems, the lender may at its sole discretion accelerate part or all of the loan balance...."

Acceleration clauses are accounted for in the same manner as other loss contingencies. If it is *probable* that the subjective acceleration clause will be exercised by the creditor, the amount of the long-term obligation that is likely to be accelerated shall be classified as a current liability by the debtor. On the other hand, if it is only *reasonably possible* that the subjective acceleration clause will be exercised by the creditor, footnote disclosure may be all that is required. Finally, if the possibility of subjective acceleration is *remote*, no disclosure may be required.

COMPENSATED ABSENCES

FAS-43 establishes GAAP for employees' compensated absences and is concerned only with the proper accrual of the liability for compensated absences rather than the allocation of such costs to interim accounting periods. FAS-43 does not apply to the following (FAS-43, par. 2):

1. Severance or termination pay
2. Stock or stock options issued to employees
3. Deferred compensation
4. Postretirement benefits
5. Group insurance, disability pay, and other long-term fringe benefits
6. Certain sick pay benefits that accumulate

Compensated absences arise from employees' absences from employment because of illness, holiday, vacation, or other reasons. When an employer expects to pay an employee for such compensated absences, a liability for the estimated probable future payments must be accrued if all the following conditions are met (FAS-43, par. 6):

1. The employee's right to receive compensation for the future absences is attributable to services already performed by the employee.
2. The employee's right to receive the compensation for the future absences is vested, or accumulates.
3. It is probable that the compensation will be paid.
4. The amount of compensation is reasonably estimable.

The fact that an employer meets the first three conditions and not the fourth condition must be disclosed in the financial statements.

Vested rights are those that have been earned by the employee for services already performed. They are not contingent on any future services by the employee and are an obligation of the employer even if the employee leaves the employer. Rights that accumulate are nonvesting rights to compensated absences that are earned and can be carried forward to succeeding years. Rights that accumulate increase an employee's benefits in one or more years subsequent to the year in which they are earned. An employer does not have to accrue a liability for nonvesting rights to compensated absences that expire at the end of the year in which they are earned, because they do not accumulate (FAS-43, par. 13).

Nonvesting sick pay benefits that accumulate and can be carried forward to succeeding years are given special treatment by FAS-43. An employer generally does not have to accrue a liability for such sick pay benefits, as is required for other nonvesting rights that accumulate. This is an exception to the general rule in FAS-43. If payment of nonvesting accumulating sick pay benefits depends on the future illness of the employee, an employer does not have to accrue a liability for such payments. The reasons cited in FAS-43 for this exception are (*a*) the cost/benefit rule, (*b*) the materiality rule, and (*c*) the reliability of estimating the days an employee will be sick in succeeding years. This exception does not apply in circumstances in which the employer pays the sick pay benefits even though the employee is not actually sick. An employer's general policy for the payment of nonvesting accumulating sick pay benefits should govern the accounting for such payments (FAS-43, par. 7).

☛ **PRACTICE POINTER:** One issue that must be resolved in recognizing the expense and liability for compensated absences is the rate of compensation to use—the current rate or the rate expected to apply when the compensated absence is taken by the employee. In situations in which the rate of compensation increases rapidly and/or a long period of time lapses between the time the compensated absence is earned and taken by the employee, the rate of compensation used may be significant. FAS-43 does not provide guidance on this issue. Other authoritative standards may provide some help in making this decision. For example, net periodic pension cost is determined in FAS-87 (Employers' Accounting for Pensions) based on the projected benefit obligation, which includes expected future increases in compensation. If the difference in the measurement of compensated absences, when measured by the current and expected future rates of compensation is material, the latter more faithfully measures the obligation and expense of the employer.

OFFSETTING ASSETS AND LIABILITIES

Offsetting is the display of a recognized asset and a recognized liability as one net amount in a financial statement. If the amount of the recognized asset is the same as the amount of the recognized liability, then the net or combined amount of both is zero, and, as a result, no amount would appear in the financial statement. If the two amounts are not exactly the same, the net amount of the two items that have been offset is presented in the financial statement and classified in the manner of the larger item.

APB-10 (Omnibus Opinion—1966) discusses the general principle of offsetting in the balance sheet in the context of income tax amounts. APB-10 includes the following statements:

- Offsetting assets and liabilities in the balance sheet is improper except where a right of setoff exists.

- This includes offsetting cash or other assets against a tax liability or other amounts owed to governments that are not, by their terms, designated specifically for the payment of taxes.

- The only exception to this general principle occurs when it is clear that a purchase of securities that are acceptable for the payment of taxes is in substance an advance payment of taxes that are payable in the relatively near future.

The general principle of financial reporting, which holds that offsetting assets and liabilities is improper except where a right of setoff exists, usually is considered in the context of unconditional receivables from and payables to another party. FIN-39 extends this general principle to *conditional* amounts recognized for contracts under which the amounts to be received or paid or items to be exchanged depend on future interest rates, future exchange rates, future commodity prices, or other factors.

FIN-39 specifies four criteria that must be met for the right of setoff to exist (FIN-39, par. 5):

- Each party owes the other party specific amounts.

- The reporting party has the right to set off the amount payable, by contract or other agreement, with the amount receivable from the other party.
- The reporting party intends to set off.
- The right of setoff is enforceable at law.

> **OBSERVATION**: The importance of managerial intent is apparent in the third criterion, which states that the reporting party **intends** to set off its payable and receivable. When all of these conditions are met, the reporting entity has a valid right of setoff and may present the net amount of the payable or receivable in the balance sheet.

Generally, debts may be set off if they exist between mutual debtors, each acting in its capacity as both debtor and creditor. State laws and the U.S. Bankruptcy Code may impose restrictions on or prohibitions against the right of set off in bankruptcy under certain circumstances.

Application of these general principles to repurchase/reverse repurchase agreements is covered in FIN-41, which is discussed in the *GAAP Guide* chapter titled "Financial Instruments."

Illustration of Offsetting Assets and Liabilities

The offsetting of assets and liabilities is an important issue to consider when determining financial statement presentation of current assets and current liabilities. Any time items are set off, information that would otherwise be available is lost. In addition, important financial statement relationships may be altered when assets and liabilities are set off. Consider the following example:

	Assets	
Receivable from M Co.	$100	
Other assets	400	
	$500	

	Liabilities	
Payable to M Co.	$ 75	
Other liabilities	175	
	$250	
Current ratio (500/250)	2:1	

Again, consider the same situation, except the $75 payable to M Co. is offset against the $100 receivable from M Co.:

Assets

Net receivable from M Co.	
($100 – $75)	$ 25
Other assets	400
	$425

Liabilities

Other liabilities	$175
Current ratio (425/175)	2.4:1

When offsetting is applied, the individual amounts of the receivable and payable are not presented, and only the net amount of $25 is present in the balance sheet. Further, the current ratio is significantly altered by the offsetting activity. This is a simple example, but it illustrates the impact of offsetting, and thus its importance as a financial statement reporting issue.

Many sources of authoritative accounting standards specify accounting treatments that result in offsetting or in a balance sheet presentation that has an effect similar to offsetting. FIN-39 is not intended to modify the accounting treatment in any of those particular circumstances.

The specific sources of GAAP that are covered by this exemption are (FIN-39, par. 7):

- FASB Statements and Interpretations
- APB Opinions
- Accounting Research Bulletins
- FASB Technical Bulletins
- AICPA Accounting Interpretations
- AICPA Audit and Accounting Guides
- AICPA Industry Audit Guides
- AICPA Statements of Position

DISCLOSURE STANDARDS

Current assets and current liabilities must be identified clearly in the financial statements, and the basis for determining the stated amounts must be disclosed fully (ARB-43, Ch. 3A, par. 3). The following are the more common disclosures that are required for current assets and current liabilities in the financial statements or in footnotes thereto:

1. Classification of inventories and the method used (FIFO, LIFO, average cost, etc.)
2. Restrictions on current assets
3. Current portions of long-term obligations
4. Description of accounting policies relating to current assets and current liabilities

Accounts receivable and notes receivable from officers, employees, or affiliated companies, if material, must be reported separately in the financial statements (ARB-43, Chapter 1A, par. 5).

CHAPTER 10
DEFERRED COMPENSATION
CONTRACTS

CONTENTS

CHAPTER 10
DEFERRED COMPENSATION
CONTRACTS

OVERVIEW

Deferred compensation contracts are accounted for individually on an accrual basis. Such contracts ordinarily include certain requirements such as continued employment for a specified period of time, availability for consulting services, and agreements not to compete after retirement. The estimated amounts to be paid under each contract are accrued in a systematic and rational manner over the period of active employment from the initiation of the contract, unless it is evident that future services expected to be received by the employer are commensurate with the payments or a portion of the payments to be made. If elements of both current and future services are present, only the portion applicable to the current services is accrued.

GAAP for deferred compensation contracts are found in the following pronouncements:

APB-12   Omnibus Opinion—1967 (Deferred Compensation Contracts)

FAS-106   Employers' Accounting for Postretirement Benefits Other Than Pensions

CROSS-REFERENCES

BACKGROUND

The main source of promulgated GAAP for deferred compensation contracts is APB-12, paragraphs 6–8, as amended by FAS-106. If individual deferred compensation contracts, as a group, are tantamount to a pension plan, they are accounted for in accordance with the GAAP for pension plans, discussed in the 1999 *Miller GAAP Guide* chapter titled "Pension Plans—Employers."

If individual deferred compensation contracts are, as a group, tantamount to a plan for postretirement benefits other than pensions, they are accounted for in accordance with the GAAP on postretirement benefits, discussed in the 1999 *Miller GAAP Guide* chapter titled "Postemployment and Postretirement Benefits Other Than Pensions."

> **OBSERVATION:** Professional judgment is required to determine whether individual contracts are tantamount to a pension or postretirement plan.

ACCOUNTING STANDARDS

According to APB-12, deferred compensation contracts shall be accounted for on an individual basis for each employee. If a deferred compensation contract is based on current and future employment, only the amounts attributable to the current portion of employment are accrued (APB-12, par. 6).

If a deferred compensation contract contains benefits payable for the life of a beneficiary, the total liability is based on the beneficiary's life expectancy or on the estimated cost of an annuity contract that would provide sufficient funds to pay the required benefits (APB-12, par. 7).

The total liability for deferred compensation contracts is determined by the terms of each individual contract. The amount of the periodic accrual, computed from the first day of the employment contract, must total no less than the then present value of the benefits provided for in the contract. The periodic accruals are made systematically over the active term of employment (FAS-106, par. 13).

Illustration of Calculating Deferred Compensation

A deferred compensation contract provides for the payment of $50,000 per year for five years, beginning one year after the end of the employee's 10-year contract. A 10% interest rate is appropriate.

The present value for the five $50,000 payments at the end of 10 years is determined as follows:

Present value of $50,000 in five years	$ 31,045
Present value of $50,000 in four years	34,150
Present value of $50,000 in three years	37,565
Present value of $50,000 in two years	41,320
Present value of $50,000 in one year	45,455
Total present value of benefits at end of employment	$189,535

In order to have available the funds required to pay the benefits in accordance with the contract, $189,535 must be accumulated over 10 years. To find the amount of the annual accrual that earning 10% interest will total $189,535 at the end of 10 years, the following formula for the value of an annuity due may be used:

$$\$189,535 \ = \ R\,[\ (1\ +\ .10)\ ^{10}\,]$$
$$R\ =\ \$10,811$$

The annual accrual, $10,811, is made at the beginning of each year.

FAS-106 amends APB-12 with regard to the method of accruing an employer's obligation under deferred compensation contracts that are not tantamount to a plan for pension or other postretirement benefits. FAS-106 requires the employer to make periodic accruals, so that the cost of the deferred compensation is attributed to the appropriate years of an employee's service, in accordance with the terms of the contract between the employer and that employee (FAS-106, par. 13).

> ☞ **PRACTICE POINTER:** The employer must make the attribution in a systematic and rational manner. By the time an employee becomes fully eligible for the deferred compensation specified in the contract, the accrued amount should equal the then present value of the expected future payments of deferred compensation.

Illustrations of Accruals Required by FAS-106

Example 1: *Employee must remain in service for a number of years to be eligible for the deferred compensation.*

A deferred compensation contract with a newly hired employee provides for a payment of $100,000 upon termination of employment, provided the employee remains in service for at least four years.

The employer makes annual accruals during each of the first four years of this employee's service, to recognize the portion of deferred compensation cost attributable to each of these years. To make these annual accruals, the employer starts by making reasonable assumptions about (*a*) the employee's anticipated retirement date and (*b*) the discount rate for making computations of present value.

If the employer assumes that the employee will remain in service for a total of nine years (including five years after becoming fully eligible for the deferred compensation), and the discount rate is 8%, the present value of the $100,000 deferred compensation at the end of the fourth year will be $68,058 (present value of $100,000 payable at the end of five years at 8% discount).

Accruals are made for each of the first four years, so that the balance in the accrued liability account at the end of the fourth year will be $68,058. The simplest way to accomplish this is on a straight-line basis, as follows:

Accrued amount anticipated at end of fourth year	$68,058
Annual accrual during each of first four years (1/4 of $68,058)	$17,015

This computation results in the recognition of $17,015 deferred compensation cost during each of the first four years of the employee's service. The balance in the accrued liability account at the end of the fourth year, when the employee is eligible to terminate and collect the deferred compensation, is $68,058, the present value of the $100,000 deferred compensation payable five years later. (The five years represent the anticipated total service of nine years, less the four years already served.)

Next, assume the employee remains in service throughout the fifth year and is still expected to complete the nine-year term originally anticipated. The accrued liability is adjusted as of the end of the fifth year to reflect the present value of the deferred compensation, which is $73,503 (present value of $100,000 payable at the end of four years at 8% discount).

The cost recognized for the fifth year will therefore be $5,445, determined as follows:

Accrued amount at end of fifth year	$ 73,503
Accrued amount at end of fourth year	(68,058)
Cost recognized in fifth year	$ 5,445

Example 2: *Employee is eligible in the same year the contract is signed.*

An employee is hired on January 1, 19X2. The contract provides for a payment of $20,000 upon termination of employment, provided the employee remains in service for at least six months. The employer anticipates that the employee will remain in service for three years. The assumed discount rate is 8%.

The employee is still in service at the end of calendar year 19X2. Having completed at least six months of service, the employee is eligible to terminate and collect the deferred compensation. The accrual as of December 31, 19X2, is $17,147, the present value of $20,000 payable at the end of two years at 8% discount. (The two years represent the originally anticipated service of three years, less the one year of 19X2 already served.) The entire amount of the accrual is recognized as a deferred compensation cost in 19X2, since the employee achieved full eligibility by the end of the year.

If the employee remains in service throughout 19X3 and all assumptions remain unchanged, the amount of the accrued liability as of December 31, 19X3, is adjusted to $18,519, the present value of $20,000 at the end of one year at 8% discount.

The cost recognized in 19X3 is therefore $1,372, determined as follows:

Accrued amount at end of 19X3	$18,519
Accrued amount at end of 19X2	(17,147)
Cost recognized in 19X3	$ 1,372

If the contracts provide postretirement health or welfare benefits, employers apply the general transition provisions and effective dates of FAS-106, discussed in the 1999 *Miller GAAP Guide* chapter titled "Postemployment and Postretirement Benefits Other Than Pensions."

If the contracts do not provide postretirement health or welfare benefits, employers should recognize the transition as the effect of a change in accounting principle (APB-20, pars. 17–21).

CHAPTER 11
DEPRECIABLE ASSETS AND DEPRECIATION

CONTENTS

CHAPTER 11
DEPRECIABLE ASSETS AND
DEPRECIATION

OVERVIEW

Recognition of depreciation is required in general-purpose financial statements that present financial position, cash flows, and results of operations. Depreciation is an area where a variety of methods are available in practice.

GAAP in the area of depreciable assets and depreciation are established in the following pronouncements:

APB-6	Paragraph 17, Depreciation on Appreciation
	Paragraph 20, Declining Balance Depreciation
APB-12	Paragraphs 4 and 5, Disclosure of Depreciable Assets and Depreciation
ARB-43	Chapter 9A, Depreciation and High Costs
	Chapter 9C, Emergency Facilities
FAS-109	Accounting for Income Taxes

CROSS-REFERENCES

1999 MILLER GAAP GUIDE: Chapter 1, "Accounting Changes"; Chapter 5, "Changing Prices"; Chapter 20, "Impairment of Loans and Long-Lived Assets"; Chapter 21, "Income Taxes"; Chapter 23, "Intangible Assets"; Chapter 24, "Interest Costs Capitalized"; Chapter 30, "Leases"; Chapter 33, "Nonmonetary Transactions"; Chapter 58, "Not-for-Profit Organizations"

1999 MILLER NOT-FOR-PROFIT REPORTING: Chapter 5, "Assets"

1999 MILLER GOVERNMENTAL GAAP GUIDE: Chapter 13, "Assets"; Chapter 24, "Capital Projects Funds"; Chapter 30, "General Fixed Assets Account Group"

1998/1999 MILLER AUDIT PROCEDURES: Chapter 12, "Property, Plant, and Equipment"

1999 MILLER HUD AUDIT PROCEDURES: Appendix E: "Property and Equipment"

1998/1999 MILLER LOCAL GOVERNMENT AUDITS: Chapter 23, "Fixed Assets and Capital Expenditures"

BACKGROUND

Fixed assets, also referred to as *property, plant, and equipment,* or *plant assets,* are used in production, distribution, and services by all enterprises. Examples include land, buildings, furniture, fixtures, machinery, equipment, and vehicles. The nature of the assets employed by a particular enterprise is determined by the nature of its activities.

Fixed assets have two primary characteristics:

1. They are acquired for use in operations and enter into the revenue-generating stream indirectly. They are held primarily for use, not for sale.

2. They have relatively long lives.

GAAP generally require fixed assets to be recorded at their cost, which is written off periodically, or depreciated, in a systematic and rational manner. Commonly used depreciation methods include straight-line, units of production, sum-of-the-years'-digits, and declining balance, although other methods may meet the criteria of *systematic* and *rational.*

PRINCIPLES OF ACCOUNTING FOR
DEPRECIABLE ASSETS

Asset Cost

The basis of accounting for depreciable fixed assets is cost, and all normal expenditures of readying an asset for use are capitalized. However, unnecessary expenditures that do not add to the utility of the asset are charged to expense. For example, an expenditure for repairing a piece of equipment that was damaged during shipment should be charged to expense.

Razing and removal costs (less salvage value) of structures located on land purchased as a building site are added to the cost of the land. Land itself is never depreciated.

> **OBSERVATION:** Promulgated GAAP (ARB-43, Ch. 9A, par. 7) require that assets be recorded at cost, except in the case of quasi-reorganizations (corporate readjustments) in which it is permissible to write up or write down assets to market values (APB-6, par. 17).
> When price-level accounting methods are used as supplemental statements, the distortion of assets and related depreciation resulting from inflation is somewhat ameliorated.

Salvage Value

Salvage or *residual value* is an estimate of the amount that will be realized at the end of the useful life of a depreciable asset. Frequently, depreciable assets have little or no salvage value at the end of their estimated useful life and, if immaterial, the amount(s) may be ignored.

Estimated Useful Life

The *estimated useful life* of a depreciable asset is the period over which services are expected to be rendered by the asset (ARB-43, Ch. 9C, par. 5). An asset's estimated useful life may differ from company to company or industry to industry. A company's maintenance policy may affect the longevity of a depreciable asset.

> **OBSERVATION:** Total utility of an asset, expressed in time, is called the *physical life*. The utility of an asset to a specific owner, expressed in time, is called the *service life*.

Valuation of Assets

Under specific circumstances, assets may be valued in the following ways:

Historical Cost

The actual amount paid at the date of acquisition, including all normal expenditures of readying an asset for use.

Replacement Cost

The amount that it would cost to replace an asset. Frequently, replacement cost is the same as fair value.

Fair Market Value

The price at which a willing seller would sell to a willing buyer, neither of them being under any compulsion to buy or to sell.

Present Value

The value today of something due in the future.

General Price-Level Restatement

The value of an asset restated in terms of current purchasing power.

Leasehold Improvements

Leased assets may provide the lessee (i.e., party acquiring use of the assets) with many of the benefits of ownership. The lessee may invest in improvements on leased assets to enhance their usefulness. These investments are referred to as *leasehold improvements*.

Leasehold improvements frequently are made to property for which the lease extends over a relatively long period. For example, improvements to a leased building might range from relatively inexpensive improvements to extensive remodeling to prepare the leased asset for the intended use of the lessee.

Leasehold improvements are established in a separate account at cost and amortized over the shorter of the life of the improvement or the length of the lease. Amortization or depreciation policy is usually the same as similar expenditures for owned assets. If no similar assets are owned, amortization or depreciation must employ a method that is systematic and rational (as discussed above) and based on reasonable assumptions.

> ☛ **PRACTICE POINTER:** The authoritative literature does not specify requirements for amortizing or depreciating leasehold improvements; use professional judgment to apply the general rule stated above. For example, if the lessee constructs a street, curbs, and lighting on land leased for 15 years, depreciate those improvements over their estimated useful lives or 15 years, whichever is less. The method of depreciation (most

likely straight-line) should generally be that of similar assets (i.e., streets, curbs, lighting) that the company has installed on owned land. Because improvements will revert to the lessor at the end of the lease term, the period of depreciation should not exceed the term of the lease. Again, use judgment in assessing the probability of renewal when an option to renew the lease is available. If the above lease is likely to be renewed for an additional 10 years at the end of the initial 15-year term, the maximum period for depreciation of the improvements becomes 25 years (the total of the initial 15-year term and the 10-year expected renewal term).

The depreciation method used for depreciating leasehold improvements will vary with the nature of the asset. If improvements are made to leased equipment that is depreciated by an accelerated depreciation method, logically those improvements may be depreciated by the same accelerated method, with the period of depreciation limited to the lesser of the lease term or the estimated useful life of the improvements.

Self-Constructed Fixed Assets

When a business constructs a depreciable asset for its own use, the following procedure is appropriate:

1. All *direct costs* are included in the total cost of the asset.

2. *Fixed overhead costs* are not included unless they are increased by the construction of the asset.

3. *Interest costs* may or may not be capitalized as part of construction cost of the fixed assets.

> **OBSERVATION:** Interest costs that are material must be capitalized on certain qualifying assets under the provisions of FAS-34 (Capitalization of Interest Cost). (See the 1999 *Miller GAAP Guide* chapter titled "Interest Costs Capitalized.")

Illustration of Self-Constructed Depreciable Assets

A company takes advantage of excess capacity to construct its own machinery. Costs associated with the construction are as follows:

Direct material	$100,000
Direct labor	50,000
Overhead —Variable	25,000
—Fixed	35,000
	$210,000

The machinery has an estimated useful life of 5 years, with an expected salvage value of 10% of its cost.

The cost of the machine is $175,000, which includes all of the scheduled costs above except fixed overhead. Because fixed overhead is unaffected by the construction of the machinery, to capitalize fixed overhead as part of the cost would relieve operations of expenses that should be charged to them.

The amount subject to depreciation is computed as follows:

$$\$175,000 - .10 \ (\$175,000) = \$157,500$$

Write-Up of Assets to Appraisal Values

GAAP generally prohibit the write-up of fixed assets to market or appraisal values. At the same time, however, GAAP state that if fixed assets are written up to market or appraisal values, depreciation should be based on the written-up amounts (APB-6, par. 17).

Improvement of Depreciable Assets

Expenditures that increase the capacity or operating efficiency or extend the useful life of an asset, if they are substantial, are capitalized. Minor expenditures usually are treated as period costs even though they may have the characteristics of capital expenditures. When the cost of improvements is substantial or when there is a change in the estimated useful life of an asset, depreciation charges for future periods are revised based on the new book value and the new estimated remaining useful life.

The revision of an asset's estimated useful life is measured prospectively and accounted for in the current and future periods. No adjustment is made to prior depreciation.

Illustration of Improvement of Depreciable Assets

A machine that originally cost $100,000 was being depreciated (no salvage value) over 10 years, using the straight-line method. At the beginning of the fifth year, $20,000 was expended, which considerably improved the operating efficiency of the machine and extended its useful life four years.

Original cost	$100,000
Less: Four years' depreciation	(40,000)

Book value	$ 60,000
New expenditures	20,000
New depreciable base	$ 80,000
Divided by: Useful life (6 + 4) in years	10
Amount of annual depreciation	$ 8,000

Impairment of Assets

In certain specified circumstances, depreciable assets are subject to a write-down of their recorded amount to reflect an impairment of value. This procedure generally is followed only when unusual circumstances indicate that the value of the asset is below its recorded amount or carrying value.

Specific procedures for identifying assets subject to write-down for impairment, as well as standards for measuring the amount of the write-down, are included in FAS-121 (Accounting for the Impairment of Long-Lived Assets and for Long-Lived Assets to Be Disposed Of) and covered in the chapter of the 1999 *Miller GAAP Guide* titled "Impairment of Loans and Long-Lived Assets."

DEPRECIATION

Types of Depreciation

Physical depreciation is related to a depreciable asset's wear and deterioration over a period.

Functional depreciation arises from obsolescence or inadequacy of the asset to perform efficiently. Obsolescence may arise when there is no further demand for the product that the depreciable asset produces or from the availability of a new depreciable asset that can perform the same function for substantially less cost.

Depreciation Methods

The goal of depreciation methods is to provide for a reasonable, consistent matching of revenue and expense by allocating the cost of the depreciable asset systematically over its estimated useful life.

The accumulation of depreciation in the books is accomplished by using a contra account, called accumulated depreciation or allowance for depreciation.

The amount subject to depreciation—*depreciable base*—is the difference between cost and estimate of residual or salvage value.

Straight-Line Method

Straight-line depreciation is determined by the formula:

$$\frac{\text{Cost less salvage value}}{\substack{\text{Estimated useful life} \\ \text{in years}}}$$

The straight-line method of depreciation is appropriate when the asset use is expected to be relatively even over its estimated useful life or there is no discernible pattern of decline in service potential.

Illustration of Straight-Line Method of Depreciation

A machine with an invoice price of $500,000 has an expected useful life of 8 years. Costs to transport, install, and test the machine were $25,000. The salvage value of the machine at the end of its 8-year life is estimated to be $50,000.

Straight-line depreciation is the same each year. It is computed by adding the $25,000 costs to prepare the asset for its intended use to the $500,000 invoice price, reducing that amount by the estimated salvage value, and dividing by the estimated years of useful life:

$$\frac{(\$500,000 + \$25,000) - \$50,000}{8 \text{ years}} = \$59,375$$

Units-of-Production Method

The *units-of-production method* relates depreciation to the estimated production capability of an asset and is expressed in a rate per unit or hour. The formula is:

$$\frac{\text{Cost less salvage value}}{\text{Estimated units or hours}}$$

Illustration of Units-of-Production Method of Depreciation

A machine is purchased at a cost of $850,000 and has a salvage value of $100,000. It is estimated that the machine has a useful life of 75,000 hours.

$$\frac{\$850{,}000 - \$100{,}000}{75{,}000} = \$10 \text{ per hour depreciation}$$

In an accounting period during which the machine was used 12,500 hours, depreciation would be $125,000 (12,500 x $10).

The units-of-production method is used in situations in which the usage of the depreciable asset varies considerably from period to period, and in those circumstances in which the service life is more a function of use than passage of time.

Sum-of-the-Years'-Digits Method

The *sum-of-the-years'-digits method* is an accelerated method of depreciation that provides higher depreciation expense in the early years and lower charges in later years.

To find the sum of the years' digits, the digit of each year is progressively numbered and then added up. For example, the sum of the years' digits for a five-year life would be:

$$5 + 4 + 3 + 2 + 1 = 15$$

For four years:

$$4 + 3 + 2 + 1 = 10$$

For three years:

$$3 + 2 + 1 = 6$$

When dealing with an asset with a long life, it is helpful to use the following formula for finding the sum of the years' digits, S, where N is the number of years in the asset's life.

$$S = N \left(\frac{N + 1}{2} \right)$$

To find the sum of the years' digits for an asset with a 50-year life:

$$S = 50 \left(\frac{50 + 1}{2} \right)$$

$$S = 50 \,(25\,1/2)$$
$$S = 1{,}275$$

The sum of the years' digits becomes the denominator, and the digit of the highest year becomes the first numerator. In the first example, the first year's depreciation for a five-year life would be 5/15 of the depreciable base of the asset, the second year's depreciation would be 4/15, and so on.

Illustration of Sum-of-the-Years'-Digits Method of Depreciation

Assume that an asset costing $11,000 has a salvage value of $1,000 and an estimated useful life of four years.
    The first step is to determine the depreciable base:

Cost of asset	$11,000
Less: Salvage value	1,000
Depreciable base	$10,000

The sum of the years' digits for four years is: 4 + 3 + 2 + 1 = 10

    The first year's depreciation is 4/10, the second year's 3/10, the third year's 2/10, and the fourth year's 1/10, as follows:

4/10 of $10,000	=	$ 4,000
3/10 of $10,000	=	3,000
2/10 of $10,000	=	2,000
1/10 of $10,000	=	1,000
Total depreciation		$10,000

Declining-Balance Methods

The most common accelerated method is the *double-declining-balance method*, although other alternative (lower than double) methods are acceptable. Under double-declining balance, depreciation is computed at double the straight-line rate and this percentage is applied to the remaining book value. No allowance is made for salvage until the book value (cost less accumulated depreciation) reaches estimated salvage value. At that time, depreciation recognition ceases.

Illustration of Double-Declining-Balance Method of Depreciation

An asset costing $10,000 has an estimated useful life of 10 years. Using the double-declining-balance method, depreciation expense is computed as follows.

First, the regular straight-line method percentage is determined, which in this case is 10% (10-year life). This amount is doubled to 20% and applied each year to the remaining book value, as follows:

Year	Percentage	Remaining book value	Depreciation expense
1	20	$10,000	$2,000
2	20	8,000	1,600
3	20	6,400	1,280
4	20	5,120	1,024
5	20	4,096	819
6	20	3,277	655
7	20	2,622	524
8	20	2,098	420
9	20	1,678	336
10	20	1,342	268
Salvage value		1,074	

In this example, a book value (i.e., portion of cost not depreciated) of $1,074 remains after recognizing 10 years of depreciation. Should the asset remain in service, depreciation would continue to be recognized until the asset is no longer used or the book value approaches zero. Should the salvage value be a greater amount (e.g., $1,500), depreciation would cease to be recognized when a total of $8,500 is reached ($10,000 cost − $8,500 accumulated depreciation = $1,500 book value). In the above example, under this assumption, only $178 of depreciation would be recognized in the ninth year, leaving a book value of $1,500. No depreciation would be recognized in the 10th year.

Had the preceding illustration been 150% of declining balance, the rate would have been 15% of the remaining book value (i.e., 150% of 10%). The declining-balance method is one that meets the requirements of being systematic and rational. If the expected productivity or revenue-earning power of the asset is relatively greater during the early years of its life, or where maintenance charges tend to increase during later years, the declining-balance method may provide the most satisfactory allocation of cost (FAS-109, par. 288).

Partial-Year Depreciation

When an asset is placed in service during the year, the depreciation expense is taken only for the portion of the year that the asset is used. For example, if an asset (of a company on a calendar-year basis) is placed in service on July 1, only six months' depreciation is taken.

Alternatively, a company may adopt a simplifying assumption concerning partial-year depreciation which, applied consistently, usually is considered a reasonable approximation of depreciation computed to the nearest month. For example, the following policies are sometimes encountered:

- A half year of depreciation in the year of purchase and in the year of disposal
- A full year of depreciation taken in the year of purchase and none taken in the year of sale (or the opposite)

These policies are particularly appropriate when a large number of fixed assets are placed in service and removed from service on a constant basis.

Illustration of Partial-Year Depreciation

A calendar-year company purchased a machine on March 7. The machine cost $64,000, and at the end of its expected five-year life it will have a salvage value of $10,000.
　　Depreciation on a monthly basis is calculated as follows:

$$\frac{\$64,000 - \$10,000}{5 \text{ years}} = \$10,800$$

$$\frac{\$10,800}{12 \text{ months}} = \$900 \text{ per month}$$

Depreciation for the year of purchase under three different policies is as follows:

Policy	Depreciation for Year of Purchase
Computed to nearest full month	10 months x $900 = $9,000
Full year's depreciation in year of purchase; none in last year of asset's useful life	$10,800
Half year's depreciation in first and last years of asset's life	$10,800 x 1/2 = $5,400

Other Types of Depreciation

GAAP require that depreciation be determined in a manner that systematically and rationally allocates the cost of an asset over its estimated useful life. Straight-line, units-of-production, sum-of-the-years'-digits, and declining-depreciation methods are considered acceptable, provided they are based on reasonable estimates of useful life and salvage value. Other methods that are used less frequently are:

Replacement Depreciation

The original cost is carried on the books, and the replacement cost is charged to expense in the period the replacement occurs.

Retirement Depreciation

The cost of the asset is charged to expense in the period it is retired.

Present-Value Depreciation

Depreciation is computed so that the return on the investment of the asset remains constant over the period involved.

> ☛ **PRACTICE POINTER:** For financial accounting purposes, companies should not use depreciation guidelines or other tax regulations issued by the IRS, but should estimate useful lives and calculate depreciation expense according to generally accepted procedures. Only when the difference between a GAAP depreciation method and the write-off taken for tax purposes is immaterial is the letter acceptable in financial statements. When fixed asset write-offs for tax purposes differ from depreciation for financial accounting purposes, deferred income taxes are recognized.

In periods of inflation, depreciation charges based on historical cost of the original fixed asset may not reflect current price levels, and hence may not be an appropriate matching of revenues and expenses for the current period. In 1953, promulgated GAAP (ARB-43, Ch. 9A, par. 6) took the position that it was acceptable to provide an appropriation of retained earnings for replacement of fixed assets, but not acceptable to depart from the traditional cost method in the treatment of depreciation, because a radical departure from the generally accepted procedures would create too much confusion in the minds of the readers of financial statements. Although inflation has become quite serious from time to time, depreciation based on historical cost remains the official, promulgated accounting principle.

DEPLETION

Depletion is the process of allocating the cost of a natural resource over its estimated useful life in a manner similar to depreciation. An estimate is made of the amount of natural resources to be extracted, in units or tons, barrels, or any other measurement. The estimate of total recoverable units is then divided into the total cost of the depletable asset, to arrive at a depletion rate per unit. The annual depletion expense is the rate per unit times the number of units extracted during the fiscal year. If at any time there is a revision of the estimated number of units that are expected to be extracted, a new unit rate is computed. The cost of the natural resource property is reduced each year by the amount of the depletion expense for the year. This process is similar to the units-of-production depreciation explained earlier.

DISCLOSURE

Accumulated depreciation and depletion are deducted from the assets to which they relate. The following disclosures of depreciable assets and depreciation are required in the financial statements or notes thereto (APB-12, par. 5):

1. Depreciation expense for the period
2. Balances of major classes of depreciable assets by nature or function
3. Accumulated depreciation allowances by classes or in total
4. The methods used, by major classes, in computing depreciation

> **OBSERVATION:** GAAP (APB-12, par. 5) require that the above disclosures be made in the financial statements or in notes. In addition, APB-20 (Accounting Changes) requires disclosure of the effect of a change from one depreciation method to another (APB-20, par. 24).

DEPRECIABLE ASSETS AND DEPRECIATION
IMPORTANT NOTICE FOR 1999

As the 1999 *Miller GAAP Guide* goes to press, the FASB has outstanding an Exposure Draft* of a Statement of Financial Accounting Standards, "Accounting for Certain Liabilities Related to Closure and Removal of Long-Lived Assets." This project is intended to provide guidance for accounting for legal and constructive obligations associated with the retirement of long-term tangible assets. Obligations with the following characteristics would be affected:

* The obligation is incurred in the acquisition, construction, development, or early operation of a long-lived asset.

* The obligation is related to the closure or removal of a long-lived asset and cannot be satisfied until the current operation or use of that asset ceases.

* The obligation cannot realistically be avoided if the asset is operated for its intended purpose.

The Exposure Draft proposed that (*a*) obligations be recognized as a liability when incurred, (*b*) the liability be measured at its present value, and (*c*) the offsetting debit be recognized as an increase in the long-lived asset associated with the obligation.

The Exposure Draft was issued February 7, 1996. During the second quarter of 1997, the FASB deferred further deliberations on the Exposure Draft while it dealt with other priorities.

The FASB has broadened the scope of the project and changed the title to "Accounting for Obligations Associated with the Retirement of Long-Lived Assets." Criteria for the identification of constructive obligations are being developed, and the issue of whether asset retirement obligations should be capitalized is being considered.

A revised Exposure Draft is expected in the fourth quarter of 1998.

---

* Note: For in-depth discussion and analysis of this Exposure Draft, read *Miller GAAP Update Service* Commentary Number 35.

CHAPTER 12
DEVELOPMENT STAGE ENTERPRISES

CONTENTS

CHAPTER 12
DEVELOPMENT STAGE ENTERPRISES

OVERVIEW

A development stage company is one for which principal operations have not commenced or principal operations have generated an insignificant amount of revenue. GAAP require that these entities issue the same financial statements as other enterprises and include additional disclosures.

GAAP for development stage companies are established in the following pronouncements:

FAS-7   Accounting and Reporting by Development Stage Enterprises

FIN-7   Applying FASB Statement No. 7 in Financial Statements of Established Operating Enterprises

CROSS-REFERENCES

1999 MILLER GAAP GUIDE: Chapter 41, "Research and Development Costs"

1999 MILLER GAAP IMPLEMENTATION MANUAL: Chapter 27, "Results of Operation"

BACKGROUND

A development stage company devotes most of its activities to establishing a new business. Planned principal activities have not commenced, or have commenced and have not yet produced significant revenue (FAS-7, par. 8). Typical development stage activities include raising capital, building production facilities, acquiring operating assets, training personnel, developing markets, and starting production.

☞ **PRACTICE POINTER:** FAS-7 does not provide guidance on what constitutes "significant" revenue; therefore, use judgment to determine whether a company is a development stage enterprise. An enterprise involved in the following activities can be said to be in the development stage (FAS-7, par. 9):

- Financial planning
- Raising capital
- Exploring for natural resources
- Developing natural resources
- Research and development
- Establishing sources of supply
- Acquiring property, plant, equipment, and other operating assets
- Training personnel
- Developing markets

Once the company's primary attention is turned to routine, ongoing activities, it ceases to be a development stage enterprise. The point at which an enterprise ceases to be in the development stage is a matter of judgment and must be evaluated on a case-by-case basis.

ACCOUNTING AND REPORTING STANDARDS

A development stage company issues the same basic financial statements as any other enterprise, and such statements should be prepared in conformity with GAAP. Accordingly, capitalized or deferred costs are subject to the same assessment of realizability as for an operating enterprise (FAS-7, par. 10).

In the case of a subsidiary or a similar type of enterprise, the determination of expensing or capitalizing costs is made within the context of the entity presenting the financial statements. Thus, it would be possible to expense an item in the financial statements of a subsidiary and capitalize the same expense in the financial statements of the parent company. For example, if a subsidiary purchases a machine that will be used only for research and development, it would expense the cost of the item in the year of acquisition. The parent company could capitalize the same machine, however, if in its normal course of business such a machine has an alternative future use elsewhere in the company (FIN-7, par. 4).

OBSERVATION: Some observers have taken the position that development stage companies should be permitted to apply standards that are different from those of established operating enterprises. For example, because significant revenue has yet to be generated, some believe that operating costs during a start-up period would be capitalized rather than expensed and amortized over the early years of operations. This was a common practice before FAS-7 was issued. The FASB took a position contrary to this view when it required development stage enterprises to present financial statements based on the same GAAP as established operating enterprises, with additional disclosures during the development stage.

DISCLOSURE STANDARDS

FAS-7 concentrates on establishing reporting and disclosure requirements for development stage companies. The required financial statements and additional information, summarized in Table 12-1, are as follows (FAS-7, par. 11):

1. A balance sheet, presenting accumulated losses as "deficit accumulated during the development stage"
2. An income statement, including revenues and expenses for each period being presented and also a cumulative total of both amounts from the company's inception. This provision also applies to dormant companies that have been reactivated at the development stage. In such cases, the totals begin from the time that development stage activities are initiated.
3. A statement of cash flows, showing cumulative totals of cash inflows and cash outflows from the company's inception and amounts for the current period
4. A statement of stockholders' equity, containing the following information:
   a. The date and number of shares of stock (or other securities) issued for cash or other consideration and the dollar amount assigned
   b. For each issuance of capital stock involving noncash consideration, a description of the nature of the consideration and the basis for its valuation

☞ **PRACTICE POINTER:** A company can combine separate transactions of equity securities, provided that the same type of securities, consideration per equity unit, and type of consideration are involved and the transactions are made in the same fiscal period.

Modification of the statement of stockholders' equity may be required for a combined group of companies that form a development stage company or for an unincorporated development stage entity.

> **OBSERVATION:** GAAP do not indicate the types of modifications that might be necessary. Therefore, judgment must be exercised in the preparation of financial statements of development stage enterprises.

5. The financial statements are to be identified as those of a development stage company and contain a description of the proposed business activities (FAS-7, par. 12).

6. The financial statements for the first year that the company is no longer in the development stage shall indicate that in the prior year it was in the development stage. If the company includes prior years for comparative purposes, the cumulative amounts specified in 2 and 3 are not required (FAS-7, par. 13).

Table 12-1: Disclosure Requirements for Development Stage Companies

Category of Disclosure	Additional Information Required
Balance sheet	Accumulated losses during development stage, identified as "deficit accumulated during the development stage"
Income statement	Cumulative totals of revenues and expenses from the company's inception
Statement of cash flows	Cumulative totals of cash inflows and cash outflows from the company's inception
Statement of stockholde equity	Date and number of shares of stock issued for cash and other consideration and dollar amounts assigned; nature of consideration and basis for valuation for each issuance of capital stock for noncash consideration
Notes to financial statements	Identification of enterprise as development stage and proposed line of business

When a development stage company that is a subsidiary adopts a new accounting principle, the parent should also reflect this accounting change by making the necessary adjustments on its financial statements in compliance with APB-20 (Accounting Changes) (FIN-7, par. 5).

CHAPTER 13
EARNINGS PER SHARE

CONTENTS

CHAPTER 13
EARNINGS PER SHARE

OVERVIEW

Earnings per share (EPS) is an important measure of corporate performance for investors and other users of financial statements. EPS figures are required to be presented in the income statement of publicly held companies and are presented in a manner consistent with the captions included in the income statement. Certain securities, such as convertible bonds, preferred stock, and stock options, permit their holders to become common stockholders or add to the number of shares of common stock already held. When potential reduction, called *dilution*, of EPS figures is inherent in a company's capital structure, a dual presentation of EPS is required—primary and fully diluted EPS.

GAAP governing the calculation and presentation of EPS information in financial statements are found in the following pronouncements:

APB-30   Reporting the Results of Operations—Reporting the Effects of Disposal of a Segment of a Business, and Extraordinary, Unusual, and Infrequently Occurring Events and Transactions

FAS-21   Suspension of the Reporting of Earnings per Share and Segment Information by Nonpublic Enterprises

FAS-128   Earnings per Share

CROSS-REFERENCES

1999 MILLER GAAP GUIDE: Chapter 1, "Accounting Changes"; Chapter 3, "Business Combinations"; Chapter 8, "Convertible Debt and Debt with Warrants"; Chapter 16, "Financial Instruments—Disclosure"; Chapter 42, "Results of Operations"

1999 MILLER GAAP IMPLEMENTATION MANUAL: EITF: Chapter 9, "Convertible Debt and Debt with Warrants"

BACKGROUND

EPS figures are used to evaluate the past operating performance of a business in forming an opinion concerning its potential and in making investment decisions. EPS figures are commonly presented in prospectuses, proxy material, and financial reports to shareholders. They are also used in the compilation of business earnings data for the press, statistical services, and other publications. They generally are believed to be of value to investors in weighing the significance of a corporation's current net income and of changes in its net income from period to period in relation to the shares the investor holds or may acquire.

In 1969, the AICPA issued APB-15 (Earnings per Share), which required companies with complex capital structures to make a dual presentation of earnings per share (EPS)—primary and fully diluted. Companies with simple capital structures were required to make a single EPS presentation. By 1971, 102 interpretations of APB-15 had been issued. Given the importance of EPS figures, the primary objective of APB-15 and its many interpretations was to standardize the calculation and presentation of EPS so that figures would be computed on a consistent basis and presented in the most meaningful manner.

An important dimension of APB-15 was the inclusion of common stock equivalents in the determination of primary EPS. This accounts for much of the uniqueness of U.S. GAAP when compared with practices in other parts of the world. In fact, only two other countries require presentations of primary EPS. All others require the presentation of only basic EPS, or basic and diluted EPS.

In 1993, the International Accounting Standards Committee (IASC) issued a draft on EPS for public comment. In recognition of the widespread importance of EPS, this proposed international standard was intended to begin a common approach to the determination and presentation of EPS that would permit global comparisons. The FASB simultaneously pursued a project that would help achieve international harmonization by requiring EPS be computed in a manner similar to that in the proposed IASC standard. FAS-128 was issued at the same time as IASC-33 (Earnings per Share) and includes provisions that are substantially the same.

FAS-128 applies to entities with publicly held common stock or potential common stock (e.g., financial instruments or contracts that could result in the issuance of additional shares). It simplified the standards in APB-15 (Earnings per Share) for computing EPS by replacing primary earnings per share with basic EPS and by altering the calculation of diluted EPS, which replaces fully diluted EPS. Basic EPS excludes potential dilution and is calculated by dividing income available to common stockholders by the weighted average number of outstanding common shares.

FAS-128 superseded APB-15 and its 102 interpretations. It also amended several other accounting pronouncements that make reference to primary and fully diluted EPS.

FAS-128 is effective for financial statements issued for periods ending after December 15, 1997, including interim periods. All prior-period EPS figures that are presented are required to be restated.

SIMPLE AND COMPLEX CAPITAL STRUCTURES

FAS-128 applies to all entities that have issued common stock or potential common stock that trades in a public market (i.e., in a stock exchange or in an over-the-counter market, including securities that trade only locally or regionally). *Potential common stock* consists of other securities and contractual arrangements that may result in the issuance of common stock in the future, such as (FAS-128, par. 6):

- Options
- Warrants
- Convertible securities
- Contingent stock agreements

Additional guidance on the applicability of FAS-128 includes the following (FAS-128, par. 6):

1. The standard applies in situations in which an entity has made a filing, or is in the process of making a filing, with a regulatory agency in anticipation of selling securities in the future.
2. The standard does *not* require the presentation of EPS by investment companies or in financial statements of wholly owned subsidiaries.
3. The standard applies to entities that are not required to present EPS but choose to do so.

For purposes of presenting earnings per share, a distinction is made between enterprises with a simply capital structure and those with a complex capital structure.

Simple Capital Structures

A simple capital structure is one that consists of capital stock and includes no potential for dilution via conversions, exercise of options, or other arrangements that would increase the number of shares outstanding. For organizations with simple capital structures, the presentation of EPS using assumed income numbers and 50,000 shares of common stock outstanding in the income statement would appear as follows:

	19X2	19X1
Income before extraordinary item	$175,000	$160,000
Extraordinary item (describe)	15,000	—
Net income	$190,000	$160,000
Earnings per common share:		
Income before extraordinary item	$ 3.50	$ 3.20
Extraordinary item	.30	—
Net income per share	$ 3.80	$ 3.20

Complex Capital Structures

For organizations with complex capital structures, two EPS figures are presented with equal prominence on the face of the income statement. The captions for the two EPS figures are "Earnings per common share" and "Earnings per common share—assuming dilution" (or other similar descriptions).

The first of these captions is referred to as *basic EPS* and the second as *diluted EPS*. The difference between basic EPS and diluted EPS is that basic EPS considers only outstanding common stock, whereas diluted EPS incorporates the potential dilution from all potentially dilutive securities that would have reduced EPS.

Based on the information presented in the previous section and assuming 60,000 shares of stock outstanding for basic EPS and 75,000 for diluted EPS, EPS for a complex capital structure might appear as follows:

	19X2	19X1
Earnings per common share		
Income before extraordinary item	$2.92	$2.67
Extraordinary item	.25	—
Net income	$3.17	$2.67

Earnings per share assuming dilution

Income before extraordinary item	$2.33	$2.13
Extraordinary item	.20	—
Net income	$2.53	$2.13

CALCULATING EPS

Objectives and General Guidance

The objectives and general approach for measuring basic and diluted EPS are presented in Table I:

Table I—Basic EPS vs. Diluted EPS

	Basic EPS	Diluted EPS
Objective	To measure the performance of an entity over the reporting period base on its outstanding common stock	To measure the performance of an enity over the reporting period based on its outstanding common stock and to give effect to all dilutive potential common shares that were outstanding during the period
Computation	Income attributable to common stock ÷ Weighted-average number of common shares outstanding	(Income attributable to common stock + Adjustments for changes in income [loss] that are consistent with the issuance of dilutive potential common shares) ÷ (Weighted-average number of common shares outstanding + Dilutive potential common shares)

Additional guidelines for determining **basic EPS** are (FAS-128, pars. 8–10):

1. Shares issued and acquired (e.g., treasury stock) during the period are weighted for the portion of the period they were outstanding.

2. The amount of income (or loss) attributable to common stock is reduced (or increased) by dividends declared on preferred stock (whether or not paid) and by dividends on cumulative preferred stock (whether or not paid).

3. Contingently issuable shares (i.e., shares that are issuable for little or no cash consideration upon the satisfaction of certain conditions) are treated as outstanding and included in computing basic EPS as of the date that the conditions required for their issuance have been satisfied.

Additional guidelines for computing **diluted EPS** are as follows (FAS-128, pars. 11–12):

1. The denominator is similar to that for basic EPS, except that dilutive potential common shares are added.

2. Numerator adjustments are required that are consistent with the assumed issuance of dilutive potential common shares. For example, if shares issuable upon conversion of a convertible bond are added to the denominator, the after-tax interest savings is added to the numerator.

3. The denominator of diluted EPS is based on the most advantageous conversion rate or exercise price from the standpoint of the security holder (i.e., the maximum number of shares that would be issued).

4. Once EPS figures have been published, they are not retroactively restated for subsequent conversions or changes in the market price of the common stock.

Illustration of Determining Weighted Average Shares

Common stock outstanding, 1/1/X2	200,000 shares
Preferred stock (convertible into 2 shares of common stock) outstanding, 1/1/X2	50,000 shares
Convertible debentures (convertible into 100 shares of common stock for each $1,000 bond)	$100,000

On March 31, ABC reacquired 5,000 shares of its own common stock.
On May 1, 20,000 shares of ABC preferred stock were converted into common stock.
On July 1, $50,000 of ABC convertible debentures was converted into common stock.
On September 30, ABC reacquired 5,000 shares of its common stock.

Computation of Weighted Average Shares

1. Common stock outstanding, 1/1/X2	200,000
2. Common stock reacquired, 3/31/X2	(3,750)
3. Conversion of preferred stock on 5/1/X2	26,667
4. Conversion of convertible debentures on 7/1/X2	2,500
5. Common stock reacquired on 9/30/X2	(1,250)
Total weighted average shares, 19X2	224,167

1. **Common stock outstanding** Because the 200,000 shares of common stock were outstanding for the entire year, all the shares are included in the weighted average shares.

2. **Common stock reacquired** On March 31, 19X2, 5,000 shares were reacquired, which means that 9/12 of the year they were not outstanding. Since the 5,000 shares are already included in the 200,000 shares (1. above), that portion which was not outstanding during the full year must be deducted. Thus, 9/12 of the 5,000 shares, or 3,750 shares, are excluded from the computations, which means that only 196,250 of the 200,000 shares were outstanding for the full year.

3. **Conversion of preferred** On May 1, 19X2, 20,000 shares of the preferred were converted into common stock. Since the conversion rate is 2 for 1, an additional 40,000 shares were outstanding from May 1 to the end of the year. Thus, 8/12 of the 40,000 shares, or 26,667 shares, are included in the weighted average shares outstanding for the year.

4. **Conversion of convertible debentures** On July 1, 19X2, $50,000 of the convertible debentures were converted into common stock. The conversion rate is 100 shares for each $1,000 bond, which means that the $50,000 converted consisted of fifty $1,000 bonds, or 5,000 shares of common stock. Since the conversion was on July 1, only 6/12 of the 5,000 shares (2,500) are included in the weighted average shares outstanding for the year.

5. **Common stock reacquired** 5,000 additional shares out of the 200,000 shares outstanding at the beginning of the year were reacquired on September 30, which means that for 3/12 of the year they were not outstanding. Thus, 3/12 of 5,000 shares, or 1,250 shares, must be excluded from the computation of weighted average shares outstanding for the year.

Any stock splits or stock dividends (or reverse splits or dividends) are retroactively recognized in all periods presented in the financial statements. A stock split or stock dividend is recognized if it occurs after the close of the period but before issuance of the financial statements. If this situation occurs, it must be disclosed fully in the statements. Also, the dividends per share must be reported in terms of the equivalent number of shares outstanding at the time the dividend is declared.

Antidilution

The term *antidilution* refers to increases in EPS or decreases in loss per share.

Diluted EPS computed in accordance with FAS-128 is intended to be a conservative measure of performance and, accordingly, is intended to reflect the potential reduction in EPS resulting from issuance of additional common shares. Thus, potential issuances that would increase EPS or reduce loss per share generally are excluded from the calculation.

Illustration of Antidilution

A company reports net income of $100,000 and has 50,000 shares of outstanding common stock. Basic EPS is $2.00 ($100,000/50,000 shares). The same company has 15,000 shares of potential common stock.

Situation 1

Assume the numerator adjustment for the potential common shares is $15,000. Including these potential common shares, EPS is computed as follows:

$$\frac{\$100,000 + \$15,000}{50,000 + 15,000} = \frac{\$115,000}{65,000} = \$1.77 \text{ per share}$$

In this situation, the potential common shares are *dilutive* (i.e., they reduce EPS), and diluted EPS is $1.77.

Situation 2

Assume the numerator adjustment for the potential common shares is $50,000. Including these potential common shares, EPS is computed as follows:

$$\frac{\$100,000 + \$50,000}{50,000 + 15,000} = \frac{\$150,000}{65,000} = \$2.31 \text{ per share}$$

In this situation, the potential common shares are *antidilutive* (i.e., they increase EPS), and would not be included in diluted EPS.

In applying the antidilution provisions of FAS-128, the following guidelines are important (FAS-128, pars. 13–16):

1. In determining whether potential common shares are dilutive or antidilutive, each issue or series of issues of potential common shares is considered se-parately.

2. In cases in which multiple issuances of potential common shares exist, one may be dilutive on its own but antidilutive when combined with other potential common shares. To reflect maximum dilution, each issue or series of issues of potential common shares is considered in sequence, starting with the most dilutive and moving to the least dilutive.

3. An entity may report more than one income figure in its income statement (e.g., income from continuing operations, income before extraordinary item or income before accounting change, as well as net income). For purposes of determining whether potential common stock is dilutive, the diagram in Exhibit I shows which income figure should be used.

Once an issue or series of issues of potential common shares is determined to be *dilutive* using the appropriate income figure in Exhibit I, that issue or series of issues is considered to be outstanding in computing diluted EPS on all income amounts, even if it is antidilutive in one or more of those amounts. Similarly, once an issue or series of issues of potential common shares is determined to be *antidilutive* using the appropriate income figure in Exhibit I, that issue or series of issues is omitted in computing diluted EPS on all income amounts, even if it would have been dilutive in one or more of those amounts.

Options and Warrants

The dilutive effect of options and warrants generally is determined by the *treasury stock method* (FAS-128, pars. 17–19). That method involves three interrelated steps, as follows:

Step 1:   Exercise is assumed to have taken place and common shares are assumed to have been issued.

Step 2:   The proceeds from the issuance of common stock are assumed to have been used to purchase treasury stock at the average market price for the period.

Step 3:   The incremental shares issued (i.e., shares sold in Step 1 reduced by share repurchased in Step 2) are added to the denominator of the diluted EPS computation.

Exhibit I—Control Income Figure for Judging Dilution

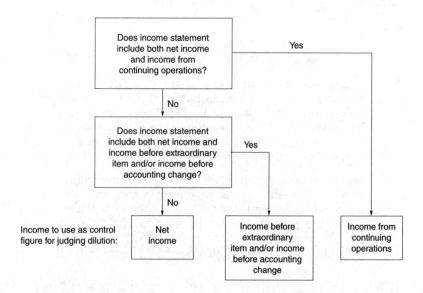

Under this method, options and warrants will have a dilutive effect on EPS when the average market price of the stock (used for assumed repurchase in Step 2) exceeds the issuance price (used for assumed sale in Step 1), because of an assumed net increase in the number of outstanding shares. In this situation, options and warrants are described as "in the money." When options and warrants are outstanding for only part of the period, the amount determined by applying the treasury stock method is weighted for the part of the period the options and warrants were outstanding.

Illustration of Application of the Treasury Stock Method

By dividing its $100,000 net income by 100,000 shares of outstanding common stock, a company determines its basic EPS to be $1. In addition, options are outstanding that permit the purchase of 10,000 shares of common stock at $25. The average market price of the stock is $40. The treasury stock method is applied as follows:

Step 1: 10,000 shares sold at $25: 10,000 x $25 = $250,000 in proceeds

Step 2: $250,000 used to purchase treasury stock at $40: $250,000 / $40 = 6,250

Step 3: Net increase in outstanding shares: 10,00 − 6,250 = 3,750

Diluted EPS is computed as follows:

$$\frac{\$100,000}{100,000 + 3,750} = \frac{\$100,000}{103,750} = \$.96$$

> **OBSERVATION:** The application of the treasury stock method in FAS-128 is simplified from that required in APB-15. In APB-15, the average market price of the common stock was used to compute primary EPS, while the ending market price was used to compute fully diluted EPS if it was higher than the average market price, resulting in a stronger dilutive impact. Under FAS-128, the average market price is used for diluted EPS. In addition, under APB-15, a 15% limit existed on the number of treasury shares that could be assumed to be purchased. Proceeds from the assumed sale of shares in excess of the quantity needed to purchase 15% of the outstanding common stock were assumed to have been used to reduce debt or to have been invested. This limitation on the application of the treasury stock method does not exist in FAS-128.

The theory behind the treasury stock method is that any number of shares of common stock that could have been purchased on the open market with the exercised price funds from the options or similar instruments are not additional outstanding stock and have no dilutive effect on EPS.

> ☞ **PRACTICE POINTER:** A shortcut method of calculating the net increase in the number of outstanding shares of common stock by the treasury stock method is as follows:
>
> $$\text{Incremental shares outstanding} = \frac{M - E}{M} \times \text{Number of shares obtainable}$$
>
> where M = the market price and E = the exercise price.
>
> For example, assume a company has 10,000 options outstanding that permit the purchase of 1 share of common stock each at $16. The average market price is $25. Applying the three-step process of the treasury stock method indicates a net increase of 3,600 shares:
>
> 1. Proceeds = 10,000 x $16 = $160,000
> 2. Repurchase of shares = $160,000/25 = 6,400 shares
> 3. Net increase = 10,000 − 6,400 = 3,600 shares
>
> The short-cut calculation is as follows:
>
> $$\frac{\$25 - \$16}{\$25} \times 10,000 = 3,600$$

When the market price of common stock rises significantly during the year, computation of the weighted average on a quarterly basis is preferred.

Illustration of Computation of Incremental Shares for Stock Options and Similar Instruments

A company has 10,000 stock options outstanding, which are exercisable at $60 each. Given the following market prices, determine the incremental shares by quarters, and the number of shares that are included in diluted EPS.

	Quarters			
	1	2	3	4
Average market price	56	64	70	68
Ending market price	60	68	72	64

Determining the incremental shares by quarters for diluted EPS follows:

1st quarter: no calculation $\qquad$ = $\qquad$ 0

2nd quarter: $10,000 - \dfrac{10,000 \times \$60}{\$64}$ = 625

3rd quarter: $10,000 - \dfrac{10,000 \times \$60}{\$70}$ = 1,429

4th quarter: $10,000 - \dfrac{10,000 \times \$60}{\$68}$ = 1,176

Total incremental shares = 3,230

Divided by 4 quarters = 808

* The exercise price of $60 is higher than the average market price.

The total is divided by four quarters because four quarters entered into the computation. The 808 shares must be included in the computation of diluted EPS.

Stock-Based Compensation Arrangements

Fixed awards and nonvested stock to be issued to an employee under a stock-based compensation plan are considered options for purposes of computing diluted EPS. Guidelines for including these arrangements in diluted EPS are (FAS-128, pars. 20–23):

1. They are considered to be outstanding as of the grant date, even though their exercise may be contingent upon vesting.
2. They are included even if the employee may not receive the stock until some future date.
3. Their impact is determined by applying the treasury stock method, and they are included only if their impact is dilutive.

In applying the treasury stock method, an important determination to make is the amount of proceeds due the issuing entity. FAS-128 identifies three components of the amount of proceeds from stock-based compensation arrangements:

1. The amount, if any, the employee must pay
2. The amount of compensation cost attributed to future services and not yet recognized
3. The amount of current and deferred tax benefits, if any, that would be credited to additional paid-in capital upon exercise of the options

These paragraphs make several other important observations. First, if stock-based compensation arrangements are payable in common stock or in cash at the discretion of either the employee or the employer, the determination of whether they are potential common shares is based on the provisions of paragraph 29 (covered below). Second, if the plan permits the employee to choose between types of equity instruments, diluted EPS is computed based on the terms used in the computation of compensation expense for the period. Finally, performance awards and targeted stock price options are subject to FAS-128's provisions on contingently issuable shares (covered below).

Written Put Options and Purchased Options

Certain contracts may require an entity to repurchase its own stock. Examples are written put options and forward purchase contracts. These contracts are reflected in the calculation of diluted EPS if their effect is dilutive when the *reverse treasury stock method* is applied. As the name implies, that method is the reverse of the treasury stock method for requirements to repurchase, rather than issue, shares of common stock in stock option plans (FAS-128, par. 24).

The steps in the reverse treasury stock method are analogous to those in the treasury stock method:

Step 1: It is assumed that enough common shares were issued at the average market price to raise enough proceeds to satisfy the contract.

Step 2: The proceeds are assumed to be used to buy back the shares required in the contract.

Step 3: The increase in number of shares (i.e., shares sold in Step 1 reduced by the shares purchased in Step 2) are added to the denominator of the diluted EPS computation.

Applying the reverse treasury stock method will result in dilution of EPS if the options are "in the money" (i.e., the exercise price is above the average market price).

Contracts held by an entity on its own stock (e.g., purchased put options and purchased call options) are not included in the determination of diluted EPS, because to do so would be antidilutive due to the reduced number of outstanding shares (FAS-128, par. 25).

Convertible Securities

Incorporating the dilutive effect of convertible securities into EPS figures requires application of the *if-converted method* (FAS-128, pars. 26–28). The method derives its name from the underlying assumption that both the numerator and the denominator of the EPS calculation are restated to what they would have been if the convertible security had already been converted into common stock for the period. This usually requires the numerator to be adjusted for the amount of the preferred dividend (convertible preferred stock) or the interest expense (convertible debt instrument).

Specific guidelines for applying the if-converted method are as follows:

1. For convertible preferred stock, the amount of the preferred dividend deducted in determining income attributable to common stockholders is added back in the numerator.

2. For convertible debt securities, the numerator is adjusted for the following:
    a. Interest charges applicable to the security are added back to the numerator.
    b. To the extent nondiscretionary adjustments based on income would have been computed differently if the inter-

est on convertible debt had never been recognized, the numerator is adjusted appropriately (e.g., for profit-sharing and royalty arrangements).

   c. The above adjustments are made net-of-tax.

3. Convertible preferred stock and convertible debt are treated as having been converted at the beginning of the period or at the time of issuance, if later.

4. Conversion is not assumed if the effect is antidilutive. (This effect occurs when the preferred dividend per common share or the interest net of tax and nondiscretionary adjustments per common share exceeds basic EPS.)

Illustration of the If-Converted Method

A company had $100,000 of net income for the year and 100,000 shares of common stock outstanding. Consider the following two independent situations:

Situation 1

25,000 shares of 6%, $10 par-value convertible preferred stock are outstanding, and are convertible into 25,000 shares of common stock.

Basic EPS:
$$\frac{\$100,000 - \$15,000^*}{100,000 \text{ shares}} = \frac{\$85,000}{100,000} = \$.85$$

*Preferred dividend = 25,000 shares x $10 par x .06

Diluted EPS:
$$\frac{\$100,000 - \$15,000 + \$15,000}{100,000 + 25,000 \text{ shares}} = \frac{\$100,000}{125,000} = \$.80$$

Explanation: The $15,000 preferred dividend is deducted to determine basic EPS. To determine diluted EPS, the preferred dividend is added back to the numerator, and the 25,000 equivalent common shares are added to the denominator. This reduces EPS from $.85 to $80.

Situation 2

100 convertible bonds, 10%, 1,000 par value, are outstanding, and each is convertible into 150 shares of common stock. The income tax rate is 35%, and interest already has been deducted in determining net income.

Basic EPS:
$$\frac{\$100,000}{100,000 \text{ shares}} = \$1.00$$

Diluted EPS:
$$\frac{\$100,000 + \$6,500^*}{100,000 + (100 \times 150) \text{ shares}} = \frac{\$106,500}{115,000} = \$.93$$

*After-tax interest: (100 bonds x $1,000 par x .10) x (1 – .35)

Explanation: Basic EPS is calculated based on $100,000 of net income and 100,000 shares of common stock outstanding. To include the dilutive effect of the convertible bonds in diluted EPS, the after-tax effect of the interest is added to the numerator (i.e., interest that would have been avoided and the accompanying increase in income taxes), and the equivalent number of common shares (150 per bond) is added to the denominator. The impact is a reduction in EPS from $1.00 to $.93.

Contracts Subject to Settlement in Stock or Cash

Entities may issue a contract that allows either the entity or the holder to elect settlement in either common stock or cash. The impact of this type of arrangement on EPS is determined on the basis of the facts available each period. Usually it will be assumed that the contract will be settled in common stock if the effect of that assumption is more dilutive than an assumption that the contract will be settled in cash. If past experience or stated policy provides a reasonable basis for assuming that the contract will be settled in cash, however, the assumption that it will be settled in common stock may be overcome.

A contract that is reported as an asset or liability in the financial statements may require an adjustment to the numerator for any change in income or loss that would have taken place if the contract had been reported as an equity instrument. This is similar to the numerator adjustment for a convertible security presented earlier (i.e., the if-converted method) (FAS-128, par. 29).

Contingently Issuable Shares

Contingently issuable shares are shares that must be issued upon the satisfaction of certain conditions. They are considered outstanding and are included in diluted EPS as follows (FAS-128, par. 30):

1. *All conditions for issuance satisfied by the end of the period*—
    Contingently issuable shares are included as of the beginning

of the period in which the conditions were satisfied, or as of the date of the contingent stock agreement, if later.

2. *All conditions for issuance not satisfied by the end of the period—* The number of contingently issuable shares included in diluted EPS is based on the number of shares, if any, that would be issuable if the end of the reporting period were the end of the contingency period.

In applying these procedures, the following guidance is provided (FAS-128, pars. 31–35):

Condition for Issuance of Stock	Treatment of Contingent Issuance in Diluted EPS, If Dilutive
Attainment or maintenance of a specified level of earnings, and that amount has been attained	Additional shares that would be issued, based on current earnings, are included in diluted EPS.
Future market price of stock	Additional shares that would be issued, based on the current market price, are included in diluted EPS.
Future earnings and market price of stock	Additional shares that would be issued, based on both current earnings and current market price of stock, are included in diluted EPS only if both conditions are met.
Condition other than earnings and/or market price of stock	Additional shares that would be issued under an assumption that the current status will remain unchanged are included in diluted EPS.
Other contingently issuable potential common shares (e.g., contingently issuable convertible securities)	Additional shares that would be issuable under current conditions based on appropriate sections of FAS-128 for options and warrants, convertible securities, and contracts that may be settled in stock or cash are included in diluted EPS.

INCOME STATEMENT PRESENTATION
AND DISCLOSURE

Entities with simple capital structures (i.e., without potential common shares) and entities with complex capital structures (i.e., with potential common shares) are required to present EPS on the face of the income statement as follows (FAS-128, par. 36):

> *Simple capital structure*—Basic EPS on income from continuing operations (or income before extraordinary item and/or change in accounting) and net income

> *Complex capital structure*—Basic and diluted EPS (with equal prominence) on income from continuing operations (or income before extraordinary item and/or change in accounting) and net income

An entity that reports discontinued operations, an extraordinary item, or a cumulative effect of an accounting change shall include basic and diluted EPS on these items either on the face of the income statement or in related notes. If an entity chooses to present EPS figures on other items, those figures must be in notes to the financial statements, along with an indication of whether the EPS figures are pretax or net-of-tax (FAS-128, par. 37).

Several other guidelines for the presentation of EPS figures are as follows (FAS-128, pars. 38–39):

1. EPS figures are required for all periods for which an income statement (or summary of earnings) is presented.

2. If diluted EPS is presented for one period, it must be presented for all periods presented, even if it is the same as basic EPS for one or more periods.

3. The terms "basic EPS" and "diluted EPS" are used in FAS-128, but are not required to be used in financial statements. Alternative titles, such as "earnings per common share" and "earnings per common share—assuming dilution" are acceptable.

In addition to specifying the EPS content on the face of the financial statement, FAS-128 also requires the following disclosures (FAS-128, par. 40):

1. A reconciliation of the numerators and denominators used to compute basic and diluted EPS for income from continuing operations (or income before extraordinary item and/or cumulative effect of accounting change or net income, as appropriate)

2. The amount of preferred dividend deducted in arriving at the amount of income attributable to common stockholders

3. Potential common stock that was not included in the calculation of diluted EPS because it is antidilutive in the current period

4. Description of any transaction that occurred after the end of the most recent period that would have materially affected the number of common shares outstanding or potential common shares if the transaction had occurred before the end of the reporting period

---

Illustration of Basic and Diluted EPS

In 1996, Stahl, Inc., a public company, had 52,500 shares of common stock outstanding at January 1, sold 10,500 shares on March 1, and repurchased 2,000 shares on November 1. Net income for the year was $375,000, and the appropriate income tax rate was 35%. Stahl's common stock sold for an average of $25 during the year and ended the year at $28.

Other financial instruments in the company's capital structure are as follows:

- Preferred stock—10,000 shares outstanding, $50 par, 6% dividend (cumulative)
- Stock options—15,000 options to purchase one share each of common stock stock at $20 each
- Convertible bonds—$200,000 par, 10%, convertible into 20 shares of common stock per $1,000 bond

Basic and diluted EPS are determined as follows:

Preliminary Calculations

Weighted-average number of common shares outstanding

Jan. 1	52,500 x 2 months	=	105,000
	10,500		
March 1	63,000 x 8 months	=	504,000
	(2,000)		
Nov. 1	61,000 x 2 months	=	122,000
			731,000
	731,000 / 12 months	=	60,917

Preferred dividend

10,000 shares x $50 par value x .06 = $30,000

Treasury stock method applied to stock options

Sale of common stock	15,000 shares x $20	=	$300,000
Repurchase of common stock	$300,000 / $25	=	12,000
Net increase in outstanding shares	15,000 – 12,000	=	3,000

If-converted method applied to convertible bonds

Numerator increase	$200,000 x .10 x (1 – .35)	=	$13,000
Denominator increase	20 shares x 200 bonds	=	4,000
Dilutive effect	$13,000 / 4,000 shares	=	3.25

Basic and diluted EPS

Numerator	Net income	$375,000
	Preferred income	(30,000)
		$345,000 Basic
	Impact of potential common shares:	
	Convertible bonds	13,000
		$358,000 Diluted
Denominator	Weighted-average outstanding shares	60,917 Basic
	Impact of potential common shares:	
	Convertible bonds	4,000
	Stock options	3,000
		67,917 Diluted

Basic EPS	$345,00 / 60,917	=	$5.66
Diluted EPS	$358,000 / 67,917	=	$5.27

☞ **PRACTICE POINTER:** Normally, antidilutive potential common stock is omitted in determining diluted EPS. In applying the specific provisions of FAS-128, however, there are some instances in which potential common stock that is antidilutive is required to be included. There are also instances in which potential common stock that appears to be dilutive must be excluded. Take care to include or exclude the potential common stock in determining diluted EPS, even though doing this may seem counter-intuitive to the assumptions and intent underlying diluted EPS.

Two situations in which this is the case are as follows:

Including antidilution

If the income statement includes more than one income figure [e.g., income (loss) from continuing operations, income (loss) before extraordinary item, net income (loss)], the one that appears first in the income statement is the benchmark number for determining whether potential common stock is included. If the potential diluter dilutes that income figure, it is included in determining diluted EPS for both or all three income figures, even though it may be antidilutive in the second or third income figure presented. For example, a company may report income as follows:

Income before extraordinary item	$100,000
Extraordinary loss	(125,000)
Net loss	($25,000)

Stock options that would dilute EPS on income before extraordinary item are outstanding, because the market price of the stock exceeds the exercise price of the options. Those same options, however, are antidilutive when included in determining the net loss per share, because the $25,000 loss would be spread over an increased number of shares.

In this case, the stock options are considered to be potential common stock in determining earnings (loss) per share on *both* income before extraordinary item and net loss, even though they are dilutive in the first figure and antidilutive in the second.

Excluding dilution

Where multiple convertible securities exist, test them for dilution in their order of dilutive effect, beginning with the most dilutive and proceeding to the least dilutive. EPS adjusted for previously considered convertible securities becomes the basis for judging the potential of each convertible security in the ordered considered.

For example, assume a company has basic EPS of $1.00 and has two convertible bond issues outstanding. These two convertibles have ratios of numerator adjustment (interest net of tax) to denominator adjustment (number of shares) as follows:

Bonds A	$.90
Bonds B	$.95

Bonds A are more dilutive than Bonds B ($.90 is less than $.95), so they are considered first. Assume that including Bonds A reduces EPS from $1.00 to $.97. The $.95 figure for Bonds B is compared with $.97, determined to be further dilutive, and included in determining diluted EPS. On the other hand, if including Bonds A had reduced EPS from $1.00 to $.85, Bonds B would have been judged antidilutive and excluded from the determination of diluted EPS, even though they would have been dilutive if considered alone.

CHAPTER 14
EQUITY METHOD

CONTENTS

CHAPTER 14
EQUITY METHOD

OVERVIEW

The equity method of accounting for investments in common stock is appropriate if an investment enables the investor to influence the operating or financial decisions of the investee. In these circumstances, the investor has a degree of responsibility for the return on its investment, and it is appropriate to include in the investor's results of operations its share of the earnings or losses of the investee. The equity method is not intended as a substitute for consolidated financial statements when the conditions for consolidation are present.

The following pronouncements are the sources of promulgated GAAP concerning the equity method:

APB-18   The Equity Method of Accounting for Investments in Common Stock

FAS-94   Consolidation of All Majority-Owned Subsidiaries

FIN-35   Criteria for Applying the Equity Method of Accounting for Investments in Common Stock

CROSS-REFERENCES

1999 MILLER GAAP GUIDE: Chapter 3, "Business Combinations"; Chapter 6, "Consolidated Financial Statements"; Chapter 21, "Income Taxes"; Chapter 29, "Investments in Debt and Equity Securities"

1999 MILLER GAAP IMPLEMENTATION MANUAL: Chapter 8, "Equity Method"

1999 MILLER GAAP IMPLEMENTATION MANUAL: EITF: Chapter 6, "Consolidation and the Equity Method"

1999 MILLER NOT-FOR-PROFIT REPORTING: Chapter 7, "Organizational Issues"

1999 MILLER GAAS GUIDE: Chapter 8, "Evidence"

1999 MILLER GOVERNMENTAL GAAP GUIDE: Chapter 13, "Assets"

1998/1999 MILLER AUDIT PROCEDURES: Chapter 9, "Investments"

1999 MILLER HUD AUDIT PROCEDURES: Appendix B, "Investments"

BACKGROUND

Domestic and foreign investments in common stock and corporate joint ventures shall be presented in financial statements on the *equity basis* by an investor whose investment in the voting stock and other factors give it the ability to *exercise significant influence over the operating and financial policies* of the investment.

The equity method of accounting is not required in accounting for unconsolidated majority-owned subsidiaries in consolidated financial statements (FAS-94, par. 15).

Under the equity method of accounting for investments in common stock, net income during a period includes the investor's proportionate share of the net income reported by the investee for the periods subsequent to acquisition. *The effect of this treatment is that net income for the period and stockholders' equity at the end of the period are the same as if the companies had been consolidated.* Any dividends received are treated as adjustments of the amount of the investment under the equity basis.

When appropriate, investors use the equity method to account for investments in common stock, corporate joint ventures, and in other common stock investments (domestic and foreign) in which ownership is less than 50%.

PRESUMPTION OF SIGNIFICANT INFLUENCE

Evidence that the investor has significant influence over the investee includes the following (APB-18, par. 17):

1. Investor has representation on the board of directors of the investee.

2. Investor participates in the policy-making process of the investee.

3. Material intercompany transactions occur between the investor and the investee.

4. There is an interchange of managerial personnel between the investor and the investee.

5. Technological dependency of the investee on the investor exists.

6. There exists significant extent of ownership of the investor in relation to the concentration of other shareholders.

Absent evidence to the contrary, an investment (directly or indirectly) of less than 20% of the voting stock of an investee is presumed to indicate lack of significant influence, and the use of the equity method or consolidated statements is not required.

Absent evidence to the contrary, *an investment (directly or indirectly) of 20% or more of the voting stock of an investee is presumed to indicate the ability to exercise significant influence, and the equity method is required for a fair presentation* (APB-18, par. 17).

> ☞ **PRACTICE POINTER:** There is also a presumption in APB-18 that significant influence does not exist in an investment of less than 20%. However, APB-18 makes clear that this presumption may be overcome by evidence to the contrary. Thus, significant influence over the operating and financial policies of an investment of less than 20% can occur. The 20% cut-off is intended to be a guideline, subject to individual judgment, rather than a rigid rule.
>
> For example, an investor might own only 15% of the voting common stock of an investee, be responsible for a substantial amount of the sales of the investee, and be represented on the investee's board of directors. In this case, the equity method may be the appropriate method of accounting by the investor, even though the investor holds only 15% of the voting stock.

Even with an investment of 20% or more, evidence may exist to demonstrate that the investor cannot exercise significant influence over the operating and financial policies of the investee. Thus, the presumption of significant influence in investments of 20% or more may be overcome by sufficient evidence.

The 20% ownership is based on current outstanding securities that have voting privilege. Potential ownership and voting privileges should be disregarded (APB-18, par. 18).

The following conditions may indicate that an investor is *unable* to exercise significant influence over the operating and financial policies of an investee (FIN-35, par. 4):

1. The investee opposes the investment and files a lawsuit or complaint, indicating that the investor does not have significant influence.

2. An agreement is executed between the investee and the investor that indicates that significant influence does not exist.

> **OBSERVATION:** These types of agreements generally are referred to as *standstill agreements* and frequently are used to settle disputes between an investor and an investee. They may

contain information as to whether the investor can or cannot exercise significant influence over the investee. The following are some typical provisions of a standstill agreement:

a. The investee agrees to use its best efforts to obtain representation for the investor on its board of directors.

b. The investor agrees not to seek representation on the investee's board of directors.

c. The investee may agree to cooperate with the investor.

d. The investor may agree to limit its ownership in the investee.

e. The investor may agree not to exercise its significant influence over the investee.

f. The investee may acknowledge or refute the investor's ability to exercise significant influence.

If a standstill agreement contains provisions indicating that the investor has given up some significant rights as a shareholder, the agreement is regarded, under FIN-35, as a factor in determining that the equity method should not be used.

3. Significant influence is exercised by a small group of shareholders other than the investor representing majority ownership of the investee.

4. The investor attempts, but cannot obtain, the financial information that is necessary to apply the equity method.

☞ **PRACTICE POINTER:** The *Codification of Statements on Auditing Standards* (AU 332.09) states, "The refusal of an investee to furnish necessary financial data to the investor is evidence (but not necessarily conclusive evidence) that the investor does not have the ability to exercise significant influence over operating and financial policies of the investee such as to justify the application of the equity method of accounting for investments in 50% or less owned companies in accordance with the provisions of APB-18."

5. The investor attempts and fails to obtain representation on the investee's board of directors.

OBSERVATION: FIN-35 implies that the investor must actually try to obtain financial information or representation on the investee's board. It seems logical that the same effect should result in the event that the investor had prior knowledge that it would fail in these attempts and, therefore, did not even attempt them.

Many other factors, not listed above, may affect an investor's ability to exercise significant influence over the operating and financial policies of an investee. An investor must evaluate all existing circumstances to determine whether factors exist that overcome the presumption of significant influence in an investment of 20% or more of an investee.

> **OBSERVATION:** On the other hand, an investor must also evaluate existing circumstances in an investment of less than 20% of an investee. The presumption that significant influence does not exist in an investment of less than 20% may be overcome by factors that indicate that significant influence does exist.
>
> If there is not enough evidence to reach a definitive conclusion at the time that the investment is made, it may be advisable to wait until more evidence becomes available.

Change in Significant Influence

Because of the purchase or sale of investment shares, and for other reasons that may affect the assessment of the ability to significantly influence the investee, an investor may be required to change to or from the equity method. The following procedures are applied in the following circumstances (APB-18, par. 19):

1. If an investment in voting stock falls below the 20% level, or other factors indicate that the investor can no longer exercise significant influence, the presumption is that the investor has lost the ability to exercise significant influence and control, in which case the equity method should be discontinued. The carrying amount at the date of discontinuance becomes the cost of the investment. Subsequent dividends are accounted for by the cost method from the date the equity method was discontinued.

2. An investor who, because of other factors, obtains significant influence or who acquires more than 20% ownership in an investee after having had less than 20% *must retroactively adjust its accounts to the equity method based on a step-by-step acquisition of an investment.* In this event, at the date of each step in the acquisition, the carrying value of the investment is compared with the underlying net assets of the investee to determine the existence of differences between investment cost and the underlying book value of the investee's net assets. Such differential is amortized as an addition to or a deduction from investment income.

☞ **PRACTICE POINTER:** In applying the equity method on a step-by-step basis, use the actual percentage of common stock owned in past periods, even if at that time the investment did *not* qualify for equity-method accounting. For example, assume that a company owned 10% of the common stock of an investee in 19X1 and 19X2, increased its ownership to 15% for 19X3, and again increased its ownership to 24% in 19X4, at which time the company adopted the equity method. The step-by-step restatement would include 10% of income for 19X1 and 19X2 and 15% of income for 19X3, even though those ownership percentages did not justify the use of the equity method during those years.

APPLYING THE EQUITY METHOD

Under the equity method, the original investment is recorded at cost and is adjusted periodically to recognize the investor's share of earnings or losses after the date of acquisition. *Dividends received reduce the basis of the investment.* Continuing operating losses from the investment may indicate the need for an adjustment in the basis of the investment in excess of those recognized by the application of the equity method.

An investor's share of earnings or losses from its investment usually is shown as a *single amount* (called a *one-line consolidation*) in the income statement. The following procedures are appropriate in applying the equity method (APB-18, par. 19):

1. Intercompany profits and losses are eliminated by reducing the investment balance and the income from investee for the investor's share of the unrealized intercompany profits and losses.

2. Any difference between the underlying equity in net assets of the investee and the cost of the investment is amortized over the period of the remaining lives of the investee assets that give rise to the difference.

3. The investment is shown in the investor's balance sheet as a single amount and earnings or losses are shown as a single amount (one-line consolidation) in the income statement, *except for the investor's share of (a) extraordinary items and (b) prior-period adjustments, which are shown separately.*

4. Capital transactions of the investee that affect the investor's share of stockholders' equity are accounted for as if the investee were consolidated.

5. Gain or loss is recognized when an investor sells the common stock investment, *equal to the difference between the selling price and the carrying amount of the investment at the time of sale.*

6. If the investee's financial reports are not timely enough for an investor to apply the equity method currently, the investor may use the most recent available financial statements, and

the lag in time created should be consistent from period to period.

7. Other than temporary declines, a loss in value of an investment should be recognized in the books of the investor.

8. When the investee has losses, applying the equity method decreases the basis of the investment. The investment account generally is not reduced below zero, at which point the use of the equity method is discontinued, unless the investor has guaranteed obligations of the investee or is committed to provide financial support. The investor resumes the equity method when the investee subsequently reports net income and the net income exceeds the investor's share of any net losses not recognized during the period of discontinuance.

9. Dividends for cumulative preferred stock of the investee are deducted before the investor's share of earnings or losses is computed, whether the dividend was declared or not.

10. The investor's shares of earnings or losses from an investment accounted for by the equity method are based on the outstanding shares of the investee without regard to common stock equivalents (APB-18, par. 18).

Joint Ventures

A *joint venture* is an entity that is owned, operated, and jointly controlled by a group of investors. A joint venture might be organized as a partnership or a corporation, or be unincorporated (each investor holding an undivided interest).

Technically, APB-18 applies only to corporate joint ventures. If the criteria for applying the equity method are met, investments in corporate joint ventures must use the equity method. In 1979, the AICPA Accounting Standards Executive Committee (AcSEC) published an Issues Paper titled *Joint Venture Accounting* that made several recommendations regarding accounting for joint ventures:

1. The equity method should be applied to investments in unincorporated joint ventures subject to joint control.

2. Majority interests in unincorporated joint ventures should be consolidated.

3. Investments in joint ventures not subject to joint control should be accounted for by proportionate consolidation.

4. Additional supplementary disclosures regarding the assets, liabilities, and results of operations are required for all material investments in unincorporated joint ventures.

Income Taxes

Applying the equity method results in the recognition of income based on the undistributed earnings of the investee. If the investee is not an S corporation, the investor has no tax liability for equity method income until those earnings are distributed. Thus, application of the equity method gives rise to temporary differences that should be considered when deferred tax assets and liabilities are measured.

Intercompany Profits and Losses

If transactions between an investor and an investee result in assets that contain unrealized profits from intercompany sales, both the investment account and the income from investee account must be adjusted to eliminate the intercompany profits. These adjustments also give rise to deferred tax adjustments.

Illustration of Elimination of Intercompany Profits

An equity-method investor sells inventory "downstream" to an investee. At the end of the year, $50,000 of profit remains in inventory from intercompany sales. The investor has a 40% interest in the voting stock of the investee, and the income tax rate is 30%. The entry for the elimination of intercompany profits is made as follows:

Income from investee ($50,000 x 40%)	$20,000	
Deferred tax asset ($20,000 x 30%)	6,000	
Investment in investee		$20,000
Income tax expense		6,000

If the intercompany sales were "upstream" (i.e., from the investee to the investor), the elimination entry would be as follows:

Income from investee [$20,000 x (1 − .30)]	$14,000	
Deferred tax asset	6,000	
Inventory		$20,000

DISCLOSURE STANDARDS

Disclosure must be made for investments accounted for by the equity method and include (APB-18, par. 20):

1. The name of the investment
2. The percentage of ownership
3. The accounting policies of the investor in accounting for the investment
4. The difference between the carrying value of the investment and the underlying equity in the net assets, and the accounting treatment of such difference
5. The quoted market price of the investment, except if it is a subsidiary
6. If material, a summary of the assets, liabilities, and results of operations presented as a footnote or as separate statements
7. The material effect on the investor of any convertible securities of the investee

If the equity method is not used for an investment of 20% or more of the voting stock, disclosure of the reason is required. Conversely, if the equity method is used for an investment of less than 20%, disclosure of the reason is required.

☞ **PRACTICE POINTER:** In evaluating the extent of disclosure, the investor must weigh the significance of the investment in relation to its financial position and results of operations.

Illustration of Equity Method

On December 31, 19X1, LKM Corporation acquired a 30% interest in Nerox Company for $260,000. Total stockholders' equity on the date of acquisition consisted of capital stock (common $1 par) of $500,000 and retained earnings of $250,000. During 19X2, Nerox Company had net income of $90,000 and paid a $40,000 dividend. LKM has an income tax rate of 35%. Any excess of cost over book value acquired is amortized over 10 years.

Entries to record the investment, the dividends and net income of the investee, and the amortization of the excess of cost over book value acquired are as follows:

Investment in Nerox	$260,000	
Cash		$260,000
Cash ($40,000 x 30%)	$12,000	
Investment in Nerox		$12,000
Investment in Nerox	$ 23,500	
Income from investee		$23,500
Income tax expense	$4,025	
Deferred income taxes		$4,025

The $23,500 amount in the third entry is determined as follows:

    30% of 19X2 income:
        30% x $90,000 $27,000
    Amortization of excess of cost over book value:

        $260,000 − 30% ($500,000 + $250,000)
                   10 Years   (3,500)
                                                      $23,500

The deferred income tax is determined as follows:

$$($23,500 - $12,000) \times 35\% = $4,025$$

On December 31, 19X2, the investment account on the balance sheet would show $271,500 ($260,000 − $12,000 + $23,500) and the income statement would show $23,500 as income from investee. Income tax expense and deferred income tax liability would increase by $3,450.

The balance in the investment account equals the investment percentage multiplied by the stockholders' equity of the investee, adjusted for any unamortized goodwill. This reconciliation for the above example is as follows:

Stockholders' equity, beginning of 19X2	$750,000
Add: 19X2 net income	90,000
Deduct: 19X2 dividends	(40,000)
Stockholders' equity, end of 19X2	$800,000
Ownership percentage	30%
Pro rata share of stockholders' equity	$240,000
Investment balance, end of 19X2	$271,500
Less: Unamortized goodwill ($35,000 − $3,500)	(31,500)
Investment balance adjusted for unamortized goodwill	$240,000

CHAPTER 15
EXTINGUISHMENT OF DEBT

CONTENTS

CHAPTER 15
EXTINGUISHMENT OF DEBT

OVERVIEW

An *extinguishment of debt* is the reacquisition of debt, or removal of debt from the balance sheet, prior to or at the maturity date of that debt. Gain or loss on the extinguishment is the difference between the total reacquisition cost of the debt to the debtor and the net carrying amount of the debt on the debtor's books at the date of extinguishment.

GAAP for the extinguishment of debt are found in the following authoritative pronouncements:

APB-26	Early Extinguishment of Debt
FAS-4	Reporting Gains and Losses from Extinguishment of Debt
FAS-22	Changes in the Provisions of Lease Agreements Resulting from Refundings of Tax-Exempt Debt
FAS-64	Extinguishments of Debt Made to Satisfy Sinking-Fund Requirements
FAS-125	Accounting for Transfers and Servicing of Financial Assets and Extinguishments of Liabilities

The authoritative literature carefully defines when debt has been extinguished and generally requires any gain or loss on extinguishment of debt to be included in the determination of net income in the period of the extinguishment transaction.

CROSS-REFERENCES

1999 MILLER GAAP GUIDE: Chapter 7, "Contingencies, Risks, and Uncertainties"; Chapter 8, "Convertible Debt and Debt with Warrants"; Chapter 16, "Financial Instruments"; Chapter 30, "Leases"; Chapter 42, "Results of Operations"

BACKGROUND

Prior to the establishment of GAAP for extinguishment of debt, differences in practice existed with regard to the recognition of gains and losses from refunding of debt issues. APB-26 was issued to narrow these differences in practice by requiring that gains and losses from early extinguishment of debt be included in net income of the period of extinguishment. FAS-4 and FAS-64, taken together, require that gains or losses on extinguishment of debt are to be presented as extraordinary items unless they result from transactions intended to satisfy sinking fund requirements that must be met within one year. In this case, the gain or loss is not classified as extraordinary.

FAS-76 defined more clearly those circumstances in which debt is considered extinguished, including (*a*) repayment of the debt, (*b*) release of the debtor judicially or by the creditor, and (*c*) in-substance defeasances. FAS-76 was superseded by FAS-125 for extinguishment transactions occurring after December 31, 1996.

When a refunding is desired because of lower interest rates or some other reason, the old debt issue may not be callable for several years. This is the usual circumstance for an advance refunding. In an advance refunding, a new debt issue is sold to replace the old debt issue that cannot be called. The proceeds from the sale of the new debt issue are used to purchase high grade investments, which are placed in an escrow account. The earnings from the investments in the escrow account are used to pay the interest and/or principal payments on the existing debt, up to the date that the existing debt can be called. On the call date of the existing debt, whatever remains in the escrow account is used to pay the call premium, if any, and all remaining principal and interest due on the existing debt.

WHEN DEBT IS EXTINGUISHED

According to FAS-125, debt is extinguished and should be derecognized in the debtor's financial statements only in the following circumstances (FAS-125, par. 16):

1. The debtor pays the creditor and is relieved of its obligations for the liability. This includes (*a*) the transfer of cash, other financial assets, goods, or services or (*b*) the debtor's reacquisition of its outstanding debt securities, whether the securities are cancelled or held as treasury bonds.

2. The debtor is legally released from being the primary obligor under the liability, either judicially or by the creditor. If a third party assumes nonrecourse debt in conjunction with the sale of an asset that serves as sole collateral for that debt, the sale and related assumption effectively accomplish a legal release of the seller-debtor for purposes of applying FAS-125.

☞ **PRACTICE POINTER:** FAS-76, which was superseded by FAS-125, permitted a third type of transaction to be accounted for as an extinguishment of debt—an in-substance defeasance. For transactions occurring after December 31, 1996, that alternative is no longer available. This is an important change, and individuals who have accounted for in-substance defeasance transactions as extinguishments of debt in the past, or who may have been planning to do so in the future, should not overlook it.

ACCOUNTING FOR EXTINGUISHMENTS OF DEBT

Under APB-26, all extinguishments of debt prior to maturity are basically alike, and accounting for such transactions is the same, regardless of the method used to achieve the extinguishment (APB-26, par. 19). Therefore, in terms of gain or loss recognition, there is no difference in accounting for an extinguishment of debt by (*a*) cash purchase, (*b*) exchange of stock for debt, (*c*) exchange of debt for debt, or (*d*) any other method.

Gain or loss on the extinguishment of debt is the difference between the reacquisition price and the net carrying amount of the debt on the date of the extinguishment (APB-26, par. 20).

Reacquisition Price

The amount paid for the extinguishment. Includes call premium and any other costs of reacquiring the portion of the debt being extinguished (APB-26, par. 3). When extinguishment is achieved through the exchange of securities, the reacquisition price is the total present value of the new securities being issued.

Net Carrying Amount

The amount due at the maturity of the debt, adjusted for any unamortized premium or discount and any other costs of issuance (legal, accounting, underwriter's fees, etc.) (APB-26, par. 3).

Gain or Loss on Extinguishment of Debt

The gain or loss on the extinguishment of debt is recognized immediately, in the year of extinguishment, and, if material, is reported as an extraordinary item, net of related tax effects (FAS-4, par. 8). Under the provisions of FAS-64, however, gains or losses from the extinguishment of debt made within one year to meet sinking fund requirements are not classified as extraordinary items, but are included in income from continuing operations. This also applies to any debt that has the same characteristics as sinking fund requirements, such as a required annual extinguishment of a specific percentage of outstanding debt prior to its maturity (FAS-64, par. 4). Gains or losses from the maturity of serialized debt are classified as extraordianry items, however, because under FAS-4 serial debt does not have the same characteristics as debt pursuant to sinking fund requirements.

> ☞ **PRACTICE POINTER:** Appropriate accounting recognition shall be given to any stated or unstated rights or privileges arising from an extinguishment of debt. In the early extinguishment of a debt, the recorded value of the new debt should not be affected in any way by the amount of the old debt.

REFUNDING OF TAX-EXEMPT DEBT

If a change in a lease occurs as a result of a refunding by the lessor of tax-exempt debt and (*a*) the lessee receives the economic advantages of the refunding and (*b*) the revised lease qualifies and is classified either as a capital lease by the lessee or as a direct financing lease by the lessor, the change in the lease shall be accounted for on the basis of whether or not an extinguishment of debt has occurred, as follows (FAS-22, par. 12):

1. Accounted for as an extinguishment of debt:
   a. The lessee adjusts the lease obligation to the present value of the future minimum lease payments under the revised agreement, using the effective interest rate of the new lease agreement. Any gain or loss shall be treated as a gain or loss on an early extinguishment of debt.
   b. The lessor adjusts the balance of the minimum lease payments receivable and the gross investment in the lease (if affected) for the difference between the present values of the old and new or revised agreement. Any gain or loss shall be recognized in the current period.
2. Not accounted for as an extinguishment of debt:
   a. The lessee accrues any costs connected with the refunding that it is obligated to reimburse to the lessor. The interest method is used to amortize the costs over the period from the date of the refunding to the call date of the debt to be refunded.
   b. The lessor recognizes as revenue any reimbursements to be received from the lessee for costs paid related to the debt to be refunded over the period from the date of the refunding to the call date of the debt to be refunded.

DISCLOSURE STANDARDS

Gains or losses from the early extinguishment of debt that are classified as extraordinary items should be disclosed in the financial statements or in properly cross-referenced notes thereto, as follows (FAS-4, par. 9):

1. A description of the transaction, including the sources, if identifiable, of any funds used to extinguish the debt
2. The income tax effect for the period of extinguishment
3. The gain or loss per share, net of any related income taxes

Illustration of Reacquisition Loss on Extinguishment

On December 31, 19X5, a corporation decides to retire $500,000 of an original issue of $1,000,000 8% debentures, which were sold on December 31, 19X0, for $98 per share and are callable at $101 per share. Legal and other expenses for issuing the debentures were $30,000. Both the original discount and the issue costs are being amortized over the 10-year life of the issue by the straight-line method.

Amount of original expenses of issue	$30,000
Amount of original discount (2% of $1,000,000)	$20,000
Amount of premium paid for redemption	
(debentures callable at 101, 1% of $500,000)	$ 5,000
Date of issue	12/31/X0
Date of maturity	12/31/Y0
Date of redemption	12/31/X5

Given that the original expenses of $30,000 are being amortized over the 10-year life of the issue and five years have elapsed since the issue date, half of these expenses have been amortized, leaving a balance of $15,000 at the date of redemption. Only half of the outstanding debentures are being retired, however, which leaves $7,500 to account for in the computation of gain or loss.

The original discount of $20,000 (debentures sold at $98) is handled the same as the legal and other expenses. Because half of the discount has already been amortized, leaving a $10,000 balance at the date of redemption, and because only half of the issue is being redeemed, $5,000 must be included into the computation of gain or loss.

Based on the above information, the loss on reacquisition is computed as follows:

Reacquisition price:		
$500,000 x 101%		$505,000
Net carrying amount:		
Face value	$500,000	
Discount	(5,000)	
Legal and other expenses	(7,500)	
		(487,500)
Loss on reacquisition		$ 17,500

CHAPTER 16
FINANCIAL INSTRUMENTS

CONTENTS

CHAPTER 16
FINANCIAL INSTRUMENTS

OVERVIEW

The FASB is involved in a long-term project intended to improve GAAP for financial instruments. Because of the complexity of the issues surrounding financial instruments, the project has been separated into several phases. The project's final output is expected to be broad standards that will assist in resolving financial reporting and other issues about various financial instruments and other related transactions.

GAAP established by the FASB for financial instruments are contained in the following pronouncements:

FAS-105	Disclosure of Information about Financial Instruments with Off-Balance-Sheet Risk and Financial Instruments with Concentrations of Credit Risk (superseded by FAS-133 effective for interim and annual periods beginning after June 15, 1999)
FAS-107	Disclosures about Fair Value of Financial Instruments (amended by FAS-133 effective for all interim and annual periods beginning after June 15, 1999)
FAS-119	Disclosure about Derivative Financial Instruments and Fair Value of Financial Instruments (superseded by FAS-133 effective for interim and annual periods beginning after June 15, 1999)
FAS-126	Exemption from Certain Required Disclosures about Financial Instruments for Certain Nonpublic Entities
FAS-133	Accounting for Derivative Instruments and Hedging Activities (effective for all interim and annual periods beginning after June 15, 1999)
FIN-39	Offsetting of Amounts Related to Certain Contracts
FIN-41	Offsetting of Amounts Related to Certain Repurchase and Reverse Repurchase Agreements

CROSS-REFERENCES

1999 MILLER GAAP GUIDE: Chapter 2, "Accounting Policies"; Chapter 7, "Contingencies, Risks, and Uncertainties"; Chapter 9, "Current Assets and Current Liabilities"; Chapter 15, "Extinguishment of Debt"; Chapter 29, "Investments in Debt and Equity Securities"; Chapter 47, "Transfer of Receivables with Recourse"; Chapter 48, "Troubled Debt Restructuring"; Chapter 57, "Mortgage Banking Industry"

1999 MILLER GAAP IMPLEMENTATION MANUAL: Chapter 10, "Financial Instruments"

1999 MILLER GAAP IMPLEMENTATION MANUAL: EITF: Chapter 11, "Financial Instruments"; Chapter 29, "Troubled Debt Restructuring"

1999 MILLER NOT-FOR-PROFIT REPORTING: Chapter 2, "Overview of Current Pronouncements"

1999 MILLER GAAS GUIDE: Chapter 11, "Auditor's Reports"

1999 MILLER GOVERNMENTAL GAAP GUIDE: Chapter 13, "Assets"

BACKGROUND

There has been an explosion of different types of financial instruments in recent years. The newly developed financial instruments include interest rate swaps, forward contracts, interest rate caps and floors, repurchase agreements, and various forms of financial guarantees. Under current accounting practice, exchanges between enterprises or individuals usually are recorded when the actual transfer of resources, services, or obligations occurs. If a significant period elapses between the execution and subsequent performance of a contract, a problem may arise as to when, if at all, the assets or liabilities created by the contract should be recognized by the contracting parties. Under existing accounting standards, assets or liabilities that are created by a contract may not be recognized to their full extent in the financial statements or they may not be recognized at all. These assets and liabilities are referred to as off-balance-sheet items.

FAS-105 was promulgated to close the information gap on off-balance-sheet financial instruments and to provide disclosure of the potential accounting loss associated with off-balance-sheet items.

FAS-105 represents the first phase of the FASB project devoted to financial statement disclosure of information relating to financial instruments. It covers *all* types of entities, including not-for-profit organizations, and addresses the disclosure of information about (*a*) the extent, nature, and terms of financial instruments with off-balance-sheet credit or market risk and (*b*) significant concentrations of credit risk for *all* financial instruments. FAS-105 also promulgated bringing the level of financial statement disclosure of information about financial instruments with off-balance-sheet risk up to that of existing disclosure requirements for on-balance-sheet instruments.

FAS-107 represents the second phase of the FASB project. It considers disclosures about fair value of all financial instruments, both for assets and liabilities recognized and for those not recognized in the statement of financial position. The FASB decided to proceed with the second phase of its financial instruments project because it concluded that fair value information is relevant and that the benefits of disclosing information about fair value, when such disclosure is practicable, justify the costs involved.

> **OBSERVATION:** The issue of disclosing information about the current value of assets and liabilities has been debated for many years. Proponents of current value information have argued that it is superior to historical-cost-based information, which underlies many generally accepted accounting principles, and that current value information should be the primary basis for recognizing and reporting items in the financial statements. Opponents have argued that it lacks relevance and, perhaps more significantly, that it lacks reliability. Between these extremes are numerous proposals from organizations and individuals calling for dual reporting of current value information and historical-cost-based information. FAS-107 requires fair value disclosure in addition to, but not in place of, historical-cost-based information, for a variety of financial instruments. While information about the value of certain elements of financial statements has been required by other authoritative standards, FAS-107 is the first standard to require the disclosure of value-based information for many financial instruments, including instruments that are not currently recognized in financial statements.

FAS-107 was later amended by FAS-126 (Exemption from Certain Required Disclosures about Financial Instruments for Certain Nonpublic Entities) to exclude the requirement of fair-value disclosure for nonpublic entities with assets totaling less than $100 million.

Neither FAS-105 nor FAS-107 deals with the issues of measurement and recognition of financial instruments, a subject that is included in the remaining phases of the FASB's financial instruments project.

FAS-119 requires disclosure about derivative financial instruments, including futures; forward, swap, and option contracts; and other financial instruments with similar characteristics. It requires disclosure of information about financial instruments that are not subject to the requirements of FAS-105. It requires that a distinction be made between financial instruments held or used for trading purposes and financial instruments held or used for purposes other than trading, and it amends FAS-105 and FAS-107 to require that distinction in certain disclosures required by those Statements.

FAS-125 amends FAS-105 and FAS-107 and establishes accounting and reporting standards for transfers and servicing of financial assets and extinguishments of liabilities. It requires the consistent application of the financial-components approach. That approach requires the recognition of financial assets and servicing assets that are controlled by the reporting entity, the derecognition of financial assets when control is surrendered, and the derecognition of liabilities when they are extinguished.

FAS-133 establishes accounting standards for derivative instruments and requires that they be classified in one of four categories and be accounted for at fair value. The treatment of the change in fair value depends on the category in which the instrument is classified. When FAS-133 becomes effective, it will replace FAS-105 and FAS-119, and amend FAS-107. FAS-133 does not become effective until mid-1999—for interim and annual periods beginning after June 15, 1999. Thus, FAS-105, FAS-107, and FAS-119 remain in effect through 1998 and even for 1999 calendar years, although it is effective for interim periods beginning after June 15, 1999.

DISCLOSURE OF INFORMATION ABOUT OFF-BALANCE-SHEET RISK AND CONCENTRATIONS OF CREDIT RISK (FAS-105)

Definitions

> **OBSERVATION:** FAS-105 is superseded by FAS-133; this is effective for interim and annual periods beginning after June 15, 1999. FAS-133 is covered in this chapter.

FAS-105, as amended by FAS-107, broadly defines the term *financial instrument* to cover the multitude of financial instruments in use today and those that may be developed in the future. Under the provisions of FAS-105, a *financial instrument* is defined as cash, evidence of an ownership interest in an entity, or a contract that meets the following criteria (FAS-105, par. 6):

1. Imposes on one entity an obligation (*a*) to deliver cash or another financial instrument to a second entity, or (*b*) to exchange other financial instruments on potentially unfavorable terms with the second entity

2. Conveys to that second entity a contractual right (*a*) to receive cash or another financial instrument from the first entity, or (*b*) to exchange other financial instruments on potentially favorable terms with the first entity

A financial instrument contract may contain unconditional rights and obligations or conditional rights and obligations. A right or obligation is unconditional when only the passage of time is necessary for it to mature. On the other hand, a right or obligation is conditional when it matures only upon the occurrence of one or more events specified in the contract.

FAS-105 defines *financial instruments with off-balance-sheet risk of accounting loss* as those in which the risk of loss, *even if remote*, exceeds the amount recognized, if any, in the financial statements (FAS-105, par. 40). FAS-105 defines an *accounting loss* as a loss that arises from exposure to credit risk and market risk that may have to be recognized as a direct result of conditional rights and obligations in the financial instrument's contract. The risk of accounting loss associated with a financial instrument includes (*a*) the failure of another party to perform in accordance with the contract terms (credit risk), (*b*) future changes in market prices that increase or decrease the value of the financial instrument (market risk), and (*c*) theft or physical loss of the financial instrument (FAS-105, par. 7). Examples of financial instruments with off-balance-sheet risk of accounting loss are loan commitments, letters of credit, financial guarantees, interest rate caps and floors, obligations to repurchase receivables sold, futures contracts, and interest rate swaps (FAS-105, par. 13).

Disclosure of Extent, Nature, and Terms of Financial Instruments with Off-Balance-Sheet Risk

Except for those financial instruments that are excluded or partially excluded from the disclosure requirements of FAS-105 (FAS-105, pars. 14 and 15), the following information about each class of all other financial instruments with off-balance-sheet risk should be disclosed by an entity in its financial statements or notes thereto (FAS-105, par. 17):

- The face or contract amount (or the notional amount if there is no face or contract amount)

- The nature and terms, including at a minimum, a discussion of credit and market risk, cash requirements of the instrument, and the related accounting policies

> **OBSERVATION:** FAS-5 (Accounting for Contingencies) requires the financial statement disclosure of the nature and amount of guarantees, even if they have only a remote possibility of materializing. Guarantees to repurchase receivables, obligations under letters of credit or standby agreements, guarantees of indebtedness of others, and unconditional obligations to make payments are examples of guarantee contingencies that must be disclosed even if it is only remotely possible that they will occur. Disclosure of both direct and indirect guarantees of the indebtedness of others is required by FIN-34 (Disclosure of Indirect Guarantees of Indebtedness of Others).

The face, contract, notional, or principal amount should be disclosed by class (category) of financial instrument with off-balance-sheet risk, in the financial statements or footnotes thereto. Classification of financial instruments with off-balance-sheet risk should be based on those classes of financial instruments with off-balance-sheet risk that have developed over the years in various financial and regulatory reports and, as a result, have become generally accepted (FAS-105, par. 17).

The discussion of credit risk should include an evaluation of the possibility that another party will fail to perform in accordance with the financial instrument contract. The discussion of market risk should include an evaluation of the possibility that the value of the financial instrument may increase or decrease as a result of future changes in market prices. The cash requirements, if any, of each class of financial instrument with off-balance-sheet risk of accounting loss should also be disclosed. FAS-105 also requires a disclosure of the accounting policies related to financial instruments with off-balance-sheet risk of accounting loss. An entity's accounting policies should be disclosed in accordance with APB-22 (Disclosure of Accounting Policies) (FAS-105, par. 17).

Disclosure of Credit Risk of Financial Instruments with Off-Balance-Sheet Credit Risk

Except for those financial instruments with off-balance-sheet risk of accounting loss that are excluded or partially excluded from the disclosure requirements of FAS-105, the following information about each class of all other financial instruments with off-balance-sheet credit risk should be disclosed by an entity in its financial statements or notes thereto (FAS-105, par. 18):

- The maximum amount of off-balance-sheet risk accounting loss that would be incurred if any party failed completely to perform according to the terms of the financial instrument contract, even if this were a remote possibility and the collateral or other security for the amount due, if any, were absolutely worthless (in other words, a "worst case" scenario)
- The entity's existing policy for determining the amount of collateral or other security required to support financial instruments subject to credit risk, information about the entity's access to that collateral or other security, and the nature and a brief description of the collateral or other security (in other words, an entity's policy for requiring security and a brief description of the security supporting the financial instruments with off-balance-sheet risk of accounting loss)

FAS-105 encourages the disclosure of additional information about the extent of the collateral because it may provide a better indication of the extent of credit risk (FAS-105, par. 19).

Disclosure of Concentrations of Credit Risk of All Financial Instruments

Except for those financial instruments that are completely excluded from the disclosure requirements of FAS-105, an entity should disclose the following information for all *significant* individual or group concentrations of credit risk associated with all owned financial instruments that both have and do not have off-balance-sheet risk of accounting loss (FAS-105, par. 20):

- Information that identifies the activity, region, or economic characteristics of each significant concentration of credit risk

  OBSERVATION: The FASB did not define the terms *significant* and *concentrations* because it found "persuasive the view that management judgment about concentrations and significance is in and of itself useful information."

- The maximum amount of accounting loss that would be incurred if the individual or group that makes up the concentration of credit risk failed completely to perform according to the terms of the financial instrument contract, even if this is a remote possibility, and the collateral or other security for the amount due, if any, was absolutely worthless (in other words, a "worst case" scenario)
- The entity's existing policy for determining the amount of collateral or the amount of other security required to support

financial instruments subject to credit risk, information about the entity's access to that collateral or other security, and the nature and a brief description of the collateral or other security (in other words, an entity's policy for requiring security and a brief description of the security supporting the financial instruments)

Individual concentrations of credit risk may exist in a specific industry or in a particular region. For example, a retailer who sells merchandise on credit in its three stores located in Mountainside is exposed to a regional concentration of credit risk confined geographically to the city of Mountainside. In another example, ABC Corporation's business activity is with customers nationwide, and as of December 31, 19XX, the bulk of ABC's accounts receivable of $22 million were from companies in the semiconductor industry. Under the provisions of FAS-105, ABC Corporation is exposed to a concentration of credit risk in the amount of $22 million from companies in a specific industry.

Group concentrations of credit risk exist if two or more parties are engaged in similar activities and have similar economic characteristics, so that a change in economic or other conditions would cause similar effects on the ability of each of these parties to meet its contractual obligations (FAS-105, par. 20). For example, an entity's trade accounts receivable from various companies in the same industry is a group concentration of credit risk.

> ☞ **PRACTICE POINTER:** A description of the principal activities of an entity could include the disclosure of its industry and/or regional concentrations of credit risk, which should be sufficient to meet the requirements of FAS-105. For example, a local retail store may adequately disclose information about concentrations of credit risk in a description of the store's business, location, and policy for granting credit to local customers.

Financial Instruments Excluded from FAS-105

The two groups of financial instruments that are excluded or partially excluded from the above disclosure requirements of FAS-105 are accounting and disclosure standards established by other authoritative pronouncements. The first group is excluded from *all* of the disclosure requirements of FAS-105, regardless of whether the instrument is written or held (FAS-105, par. 14):

* *Most insurance contracts*—Other than financial guarantees and investment contracts, all insurance contracts that are discussed

in FAS-60 (Accounting and Reporting by Insurance Enterprises), and FAS-97 (Accounting and Reporting by Insurance Enterprises for Certain Long-Duration Contracts and for Realized Gains and Losses from the Sale of Investments)

- *Long-term obligations subject to FAS-47*—All unconditional purchase obligations that are subject to the disclosure requirements of FAS-47 (Disclosure of Long-Term Obligations) (**Note:** All unconditional purchase obligations that are *not* subject to FAS-47 are subject to FAS-105.)

- *Pension, insurance, stock options, etc.*—Employers' and plans' obligations for pension benefits, postretirement health-care and life insurance benefits, employee stock option and stock purchase plans, and other forms of deferred compensation arrangements, as defined in FAS-35 (Accounting and Reporting by Defined Benefit Pension Plans), FAS-87 (Employers' Accounting for Pensions), FAS-106 (Employers' Accounting for Postretirement Benefits Other Than Pensions), FAS-43 (Accounting for Compensated Absences), APB-25 (Accounting for Stock Issued to Employees), and APB-12 (Omnibus Opinion—1967)

- *Pension plan financial instruments*—Financial instruments of a pension plan, including plan assets, when subject to the accounting and reporting requirements of FAS-87 (**Note:** Pension plan financial instruments, except obligations for pension benefits, *are included* in the scope of FAS-105, if the financial instruments are subject to the accounting and reporting provisions of FAS-35.)

- *Extinguished debt subject to FAS-76*—In-substance defeasance of debt subject to the disclosure requirements of FAS-76 (Extinguishment of Debt) and any assets held in trust in connection with an in-substance defeasance of debt

The financial instruments in the second group are *excluded* from disclosure requirements of FAS-105 concerning (*a*) the extent, nature, and terms of financial instruments with off-balance-sheet risk and (*b*) the credit risk of financial instruments with off-balance-sheet risk. They are not excluded from complying with disclosure requirement (*c*), which requires the disclosure of the concentration of credit risk in financial instruments with or without off-balance-sheet risk of accounting loss. The following financial instruments are in the second group (FAS-105, par. 15):

- *Lease contracts*—Lease contracts as defined in FAS-13 (Accounting for Leases)

- *Accruals denominated in foreign currency*—Accounts and notes payable and other financial instruments that result in accruals or other amounts denominated in a foreign currency and included in the balance sheet at translated or remeasured amounts under FAS-52 (Foreign Currency Translation), *except* obligations under (*a*) financial instruments that have off-balance-sheet risk from other risks in addition to foreign exchange risk (such as a commitment to lend foreign currency or an option written to exchange foreign currency for a bond that either is or is not denominated in a foreign currency) and (*b*) foreign currency exchange contracts (such as a forward exchange contract, a currency swap, a foreign currency futures contract, or an option to exchange currencies)

The financial statement disclosures of financial instruments that are required by FAS-105 are in addition to all other financial statement disclosures of financial instruments that are required by other existing GAAP (FAS-105, par. 16).

DISCLOSURE OF INFORMATION ABOUT FAIR VALUE (FAS-107/126)

Definitions and Scope

> **OBSERVATION:** FAS-107 is amended by FAS-133; this is effective for interim and annual periods beginning after June 15, 1999. FAS-133 is covered in this chapter.

The FAS-107 definition of the term *financial instruments,* which was stated earlier, includes minor editorial changes from the original definition of the term in FAS-105. *Fair value* is defined in FAS-107 as the amount at which an instrument could be exchanged in a transaction between willing parties, other than a forced or liquidation sale (FAS-107, par. 5).

> **OBSERVATION:** The use of the term *fair value* represents a shift from the term *market value* used in the December 1990 Exposure Draft that preceded FAS-107. Some respondents to the 1990 ED suggested that the term *market value* did not precisely apply to every financial instrument covered by the proposed Statement. The respondents associated the term *market value* only with instruments traded on active secondary markets (e.g., stock exchanges). This was not the intent of the FASB, however, because the ED described the term as being applicable whether the market for an item was active or inactive, primary or secondary. The FASB decided, nonetheless, to use the term *fair value* in FAS-107 to avoid further confusion and to be consistent with terminology used in similar disclo-

sure proposals made recently by other standard-setting organizations. While the phrase *fair value* is different from *market value* used in the December 1990 ED, the meaning is the same.

Disclosure Requirements

FAS-107 establishes specific disclosure requirements and certain procedures that must be followed in estimating the fair value of financial instruments, as follows:

- An entity shall disclose, either in the body of the financial statements or in the accompanying notes, the fair value of financial instruments for which it is practicable to estimate that value. An entity also shall disclose the method(s) and significant assumptions used to estimate the fair value of financial instruments (FAS-107, par. 10).

- Quoted market prices, if available, are the best evidence of the fair value of financial instruments. If quoted market prices are not available, management's best estimate of fair value may be based on the quoted market price of a financial instrument with similar characteristics or on valuation techniques (for example, the present value of estimated future cash flows using a discount rate commensurate with the risks involved, option pricing models, or matrix pricing models) (FAS-107, par. 11).

- In estimating the fair value of deposit liabilities, a financial entity shall not take into account the value of its long-term relationships with depositors, commonly known as core deposit intangibles, which are separate intangible assets, not financial instruments. For deposit liabilities with no defined maturities, the fair value to be disclosed is the amount payable on demand at the reporting date. FAS-107 does not prohibit an entity from disclosing separately the estimated fair value of any of its nonfinancial intangible and tangible assets and nonfinancial liabilities (FAS-107, par. 12).

- If it is not practicable for an entity to estimate the fair value of a financial instrument, or a class of financial instruments, the entity shall disclose information pertinent to estimating the fair value, such as the carrying amount, effective interest rate, and maturity, and provide an explanation of why it is not practicable to estimate fair value (FAS-107, par. 14).

OBSERVATION: FAS-107 is a "disclosure-only" standard. While some advocates of current or fair value information would prefer value-based accounting procedures to replace historical-cost-based procedures in accounting for items in the financial statements, FAS-107 made an important, but less dramatic, change by requiring disclosure of fair value information without changing existing recognition or measurement practices. FAS-107 may be an important signal for the future of financial reporting. A great deal of interest currently exists about regulators and standard-setters in value-based accounting. Preparers and auditors of financial statements can expect increasing use of fair value information and may want to consider investing time and other resources in developing procedures to estimate and audit fair value information.

Situations Not Covered by FAS-107

While FAS-107 is intended to require disclosure of fair value information about a wide spectrum of financial instruments, a number of instruments and other items are exempt. These exemptions fall into three categories (FAS-107, par. 8):

1. Items subject to reporting and disclosure requirements of other authoritative pronouncements (e.g., pensions, extinguished debt, insurance contracts other than financial guarantees and investment contracts, leases, and equity method investments). FAS-107 does not change existing disclosure requirements for these items.

2. Other items explained in terms of certain definitional problems that the FASB was unable to resolve at the time (e.g., insurance contracts other than those mentioned above, lease contracts, warranty obligations, and unconditional purchase obligations that may have both financial and nonfinancial components). The FASB believes that definitional and valuation difficulties for these contracts and obligations require further consideration before decisions can be made about the appropriateness of fair value disclosure requirements.

3. The FAS-107 disclosures are intended to apply only to financial assets and liabilities, thereby excluding items such as minority interests in consolidated subsidiaries and an entity's own equity instruments included in stockholders' equity.

FAS-126 makes the fair value disclosures of FAS-107 optional for entities meeting the following criteria:

1. The entity is a nonpublic entity.

2. The entity is small enough that it comes under the size criterion of less than $100 million of total assets on the date of the financial statements.

3. The entity has not held or issued any derivative financial instruments other than loan commitments during the reporting period.

In applying the third condition, the definition of *derivative* in FAS-119 is used. That standard defines a *derivative financial instrument* as a futures, forward, swap, or option contract, or other financial instrument with similar characteristics.

> **OBSERVATION:** Public accountants serving smaller nonpublic entities informed the FASB that the practicability provisions of FAS-107 were useful in reducing the costs of compliance, but a cost is still incurred simply to document compliance, even if the fair value information is deemed to be not practicable.
>
> The FASB observed that smaller nonpublic entities are less likely than larger entities to engage in complex financial transactions. These smaller entities' financial assets tend to consist of traded securities, investments in other closely held entities, and balances with related parties. Their financial liabilities tend to be trade payables and variable-rate and fixed-rate loans. The FASB also observed that the types of financial instruments commonly held by smaller nonpublic entities, such as trade receivables and payables and variable-rate instruments, already are carried at amounts that approximate fair value, or that information about fair values already is required by other authoritative pronouncements, such as FAS-115 (Accounting for Certain Investments in Debt and Equity Securities) and FAS-124 (Accounting for Certain Investments Held by Not-for-Profit Organizations). Taken together, these mutually reinforcing observations led the FASB to conclude that the FAS-107 disclosure requirements should be optional for smaller nonpublic companies.

Estimating Fair Value

One of the greatest challenges in applying FAS-107 is estimating the fair value of financial instruments. FAS-107 provides examples of procedures for estimating the fair value of financial instruments. The examples are illustrative and are not meant to portray all possible ways of estimating the fair value of a financial instrument to comply with FAS-107.

Fair value information frequently is based on information from market sources, of which there are four types (FAS-107, par. 19):

a. *Exchange market*—provides high visibility and order to the trading of financial instruments. Closing prices and volume levels are typically available.

b. *Dealer market*—Dealer readiness to trade—either buy or sell—provides liquidity to the market. Current bid and ask prices are more readily available than information about closing prices and volume levels. ("Over-the-counter" markets are considered dealer markets.)

c. *Brokered market*—Brokers attempt to match buyers with sellers. Brokers know the prices bid and asked by the respective parties, but each party is typically unaware of the other party's price requirements. Prices of completed transactions may be available.

d. *Principal-to-principal market*—Transactions are negotiated independently, with no intermediary. Little information typically is released publicly.

Financial Instruments with Quoted Prices

Quoted market prices are the best evidence of fair value of financial instruments. The price from the most active market is the best indicator of fair value. In some cases, management may decide to provide further information about fair value of a financial instrument. For example, an entity may want to explain why the fair value of its long-term debt is less than the carrying amount and why it may not be possible or prudent to settle the debt (FAS-107, par. 21).

Financial Instruments with No Quoted Prices

The entity should provide its best estimate of fair value. Judgments about the methods and assumptions to be used must be made by those preparing and attesting to the entity's financial statements (FAS-107, par. 22). FAS-107 offers the following guidelines for making these judgments:

• For some short-term financial instruments, the carrying amount may approximate fair value because of the relatively short period of time between origination and expected realization. Likewise, for loans that reprice frequently at market rates, the carrying amount may be close enough to fair value to satisfy disclosure requirements, provided there has been no significant change in the credit risk of the loans (FAS-107, par. 23).

• Some financial instruments may be "custom-tailored" and, thus, may not have a quoted market price. Examples include interest rate swaps and foreign currency contracts. Fair value may be estimated based on the quoted market price of a similar instrument, adjusted for the effects of the tailoring. Alternatively, the estimate might be based on the estimated current replacement cost of the financial instrument (FAS-107, par. 24).

• Other financial instruments that are commonly "custom-tailored" include options (e.g., put and call options on stock, foreign currency, or interest rate contracts). A variety of option pricing models have been developed, such as the Black–Sholes model, and may be useful in estimating fair value (FAS-107, par. 25).

- An estimate of fair value of a loan or group of loans may be based on the discounted value of the future cash flows expected to be received from the loan or group of loans. A single discount rate could be used to estimate the fair value of a homogenous category of loans. A discount rate commensurate with the credit, interest rate, and prepayment risks involved, which could be the rate at which the same loans would be made under current conditions, may be appropriate. A discount rate that reflects the effects of interest rate changes and then makes adjustments to reflect the effects of changes in credit risk may be appropriate (FAS-107, par. 27).

- Fair value for financial liabilities for which quoted market prices are not available can generally be estimated using the same technique used for estimating the value of financial assets. For example, a loan payable to a bank can be valued at the discounted amount of future cash flows, using the entity's current incremental borrowing rate for a similar liability. Alternatively, the discount rate could be the rate that an entity would pay to a creditworthy third party to assume its obligation (FAS-107, par. 28).

- For deposit liabilities with defined maturities (e.g., certificates of deposit), an estimate of fair value may be based on the discounted value of the future cash flows expected to be paid on the deposits. The discount rate could be the current rate offered for similar deposits with the same remaining maturities. For deposit liabilities with no defined maturities, the fair value should be the amount payable on demand at the reporting date (FAS-107, par. 29).

☛ **PRACTICE POINTER:** An important dimension of FAS-107 is the latitude that entities have in deciding whether applying procedures such as those described above is "practicable." *Practicable* means that an entity can estimate fair value without incurring excessive costs. It is a dynamic concept—what is practicable in one year may not be in another. Cost considerations are important in judging practicability and may affect the precision of the estimate, leading to determination of fair value for a class of financial instruments, an entire portfolio (rather than individual instruments), or a subset of a portfolio. Whatever is practicable to determine must be disclosed. The burden of this decision rests on the reporting entity and its auditor; if the decision is made that determining fair value is not practicable, reasons for not disclosing the information must be given. The explanation will normally be found in notes to the financial statement (FAS-107, par. 15).

DISCLOSURE OF INFORMATION ABOUT
DERIVATIVE FINANCIAL INSTRUMENTS
AND FAIR VALUE (FAS-119)

Definitions and Scope

> **OBSERVATION:** FAS-119 is superseded by FAS-133; this is effective for interim and annual periods beginning after June 15, 1999. FAS-133 is covered in this chapter.

A *derivative financial instrument* is a futures, forward, swap, or option contract, or other financial instrument with similar characteristics (FAS-119, par. 5). Examples of other financial instruments with characteristics similar to option contracts include interest rate caps or floors and fixed-rate loan commitments. Variable-rate loan commitments and other variable-rate financial instruments also may have characteristics similar to option contracts. Examples of other financial instruments with characteristics similar to forward contracts include various kinds of commitments to purchase stocks and bonds, forward interest rate agreements, and interest rate collars (FAS-119, par. 6).

This definition of derivative financial instruments excludes all on-balance-sheet receivables and payables, including those that derive their value or contractually require cash flows from the price of some other security or index, such as mortgage-backed securities, interest-only and principal-only obligations, and indexed debt instruments. It also excludes optional features that are embedded within an on-balance-sheet receivable or payable, such as the conversion feature and call provision embedded in convertible bonds (FAS-119, par. 7).

> ☞ **PRACTICE POINTER:** One of the most significant challenges facing the accountant in determining the appropriate disclosures for financial instruments is identifying all of the instruments that an enterprise has engaged in that require disclosure. This is particularly true with derivative financial instruments, many of which will have not been recorded in the financial statements. Be familiar with the enterprise's contracts and risk-management strategies in order to be in a position to determine the necessity and adequacy of disclosure.

Disclosure Requirements

FAS-119 requires and encourages information about derivative financial instruments in several categories:

Required Disclosure about All Derivative Financial Instruments

For many derivative financial instruments, information about their amounts, nature, and terms is already required to be disclosed because they are included in the scope of FAS-105.

For options held and other derivative financial instruments that are not included in the scope of FAS-105, because they do not have off-balance-sheet risk of accounting loss, the following is required to be disclosed, either in the body of the financial statements or accompanying notes (FAS-119, par. 8):

1. The face or nominal amount (or notional principal amount if there is no face or contract amount)
2. The nature and terms, including at a minimum a discussion of:
   a. The credit and market risk of those instruments
   b. The cash requirements of those instruments
   c. The related accounting policy pursuant to the requirements of APB-22 (Disclosure of Accounting Policies)

Required Disclosure about Purposes for Which Derivative Financial Instruments Are Held or Issued

The disclosure requirements listed above shall distinguish between derivative financial instruments held or issued for (FAS-119, par. 9):

1. Trading purposes, including dealer and other activities reported in a trading account and measured at fair value
2. Purposes other than trading

Required Disclosure about Derivative Financial Instruments Held or Issued for Trading Purposes

For derivative financial instruments that are held or issued for purposes of trading, the following information is required to be disclosed (FAS-119, par. 10):

1. The average and end-of-period amounts of fair value, distinguishing between assets and liabilities
2. The net gains or losses (often referred to as net trading revenues) arising from derivative financial instruments trading activities during the period, disaggregated by class, business activity, risk, or other category that is consistent with management of those activities, and when those net trading gains and losses are reported in the income statement

Required Disclosure about Derivative Financial Instruments Held or Issued for Purposes Other Than Trading

The following information about derivative financial instruments that are held or issued for purposes other than trading is required (FAS-119, par. 11):

1. A description of the entity's objectives for holding or issuing the derivative financial instrument, the context needed to understand those objectives, and the entity's strategies for achieving those objectives

2. A description of how the derivative financial instruments are reported in the financial statements, including:

    a. Policies for recognizing and measuring the derivative financial instruments held or issued

    b. When recognized, and where those instruments are reported in the statement of financial position and income statement

3. For derivative financial instruments that are held or issued for the purpose of hedging anticipated transactions:

    a. A description of the anticipated transactions for which risks are hedged with derivative financial instruments, including the period of time until the anticipated transactions are expected to occur

    b. A description of the classes of derivative financial instruments used to hedge the anticipated transactions

    c. The amount of hedging gains and losses explicitly deferred

    d. A description of the transactions or other events that result in the recognition of earnings of gains or losses deferred by hedge accounting

Encouraged Disclosure about All Derivative Financial Instruments Held or Issued

Entities are encouraged, but not required, to disclose quantitative information about interest rate, foreign exchange, commodity price, or other market risks of derivative financial instruments. This information must be consistent with the way the entity manages or adjusts those risks, and it must be useful for comparing the results of applying the entity's strategies with its objectives for holding or issuing the derivative financial instruments. This information is even more useful if similar information, classified by type of risk, also is disclosed about the risks of other financial instruments and nonfinancial assets and liabilities to which the derivative financial instruments are related by a risk management or other strategy (FAS-119, par. 12).

Possible means of reporting this quantitative information include (FAS-119, par. 13):

1. More details about current positions and perhaps activity during the period
2. The hypothetical effects on equity or annual income of several possible changes in market prices
3. A gap analysis of interest rate repricing or maturity dates
4. The duration of the financial instruments
5. The entity's value at risk from derivative financial instruments and from other positions at the end of the reporting period and the largest value at risk level during the year

Illustration of Selected Disclosures of Information Concerning Financial Instruments

Following are examples of disclosures of information concerning financial instruments (numbers in thousands, assumed for illustrative purposes).

Fair Value of Financial Instruments

	19X4		19X5	
	Carrying Amount	Fair Value	Carrying Amount	Fair Value
Financial asset:				
Long-term receivables	$ 300	$ 400	$500	$ 625
Financial liabilities:				
Long-term debt	75	70	200	250
Off-balance sheet derivative financial instruments held for purposes other than trading				
Interest rate swaps	40	(24)		
Foreign currency contracts	10			

Fair value amounts are estimated by management based on available market information and appropriate valuation methodologies.

Concentration of Credit Risk

Accounts receivable subject the company to concentration credit risk, because they are concentrated in the construction industry, which is subject to business cycle variations. This risk is limited because of the large number of customers included in the company's customer base and the geographic dispersion of those customers.

Derivative Financial Instrument Policy—Interest Rate Swap

The company enters into interest rate swap agreements to manage its interest rate exposure. *Interest rate swaps* are agreements to exchange interest rate payment streams based on a notional principle amount. Company policy requires settlement accounting principles for interest rate swaps in which net interest rate differentials to be paid or received are recorded currently as adjustments to interest expense.

Foreign Currency Contracts

At December 31, 19X1, the company held currency swap contracts with an aggregate notional value of $1,000,000. These contracts have maturity dates extending from 19X2 through 19X6. Under separate contracts, the company is obligated to purchase certain foreign currencies totaling $1,400,000 and to sell certain foreign currencies totaling $675,000, which mature in 19X2.

ACCOUNTING FOR DERIVATIVE INSTRUMENTS AND HEDGING ACTIVITIES

FAS-133 (Accounting for Derivative Instruments and Hedging Activities) was issued in June 1998 and is effective for fiscal periods (both years and quarters) beginning after June 15, 1999. It establishes accounting and reporting standards for derivative instruments, including derivative instruments that are embedded in other contracts, as well as for hedging activities.

Types of Derivatives and Hedging Activities

FAS-133 requires the recognition of all derivatives (both assets and liabilities) in the statement of financial position and the recognition of their measurement at fair value. In accordance with FAS-133, each derivative instrument is classified in one of the following four categories: *(1)* no hedge designation, *(2)* fair value hedge, *(3)* cash flow hedge, and *(4)* foreign currency hedge. Changes in the fair value of derivative instruments in each category are accounted for as indicated in the following table:

Type of Derivative in Fair Value	Accounting for Changes
No hedge designation	Included in current income
Fair value hedge	Included in comprehensive income (outside of net income)

Cash flow hedge	Included in current income
Foreign currency hedge	Included in comprehensive income (outside of net income) as part of the cumulative translation adjustment

No Hedge Designation

The instrument does not qualify as a fair value hedge, a cash flow hedge, or a foreign currency hedge. The change in its fair value is recognized currently in net income.

Fair Value Hedge

Certain instruments are designated as hedging the exposure to changes in the fair value of an asset or liability or an identified portion thereof that is attributed to a particular risk. A fair value hedge must meet all of the following criteria:

1. At the inception of the hedge, there is formal documentation of the hedging relationship and the entity's risk management objective and strategy for undertaking the hedge. This must include identification of (a) the hedged instrument, (b) the hedged item, (c) the nature of the risk being hedged, and (d) how the hedging instrument's effectiveness in offsetting the exposure to changes in the fair value of the hedged item will be assessed.

2. Both at the inception of the hedge and on an ongoing basis, the hedging relationship is expected to be highly effective in achieving offsetting changes in fair value attributed to the hedged risk during the period that the hedge is designated. An assessment is required whenever financial statements or earnings are reported, and at least every three months.

3. If a written option is designated as hedging a recognized asset or liability, the combination of the hedged item and the written option provides at least as much potential for gains as the exposure to losses from changes in the combined fair values.

An asset or liability is eligible for designation as a hedged item in a fair value hedge if all of the following criteria are met:

1. The hedged item is specifically identified as either all or a specified portion of a recognized asset or a recognized li-

ability or an unrecognized firm commitment. The hedged item is a single asset or liability (or specified portion thereof) or is a portfolio of similar assets or a portfolio of similar liabilities (or a specified portion thereof).

2. The hedged item presents an exposure to changes in fair value attributable to the hedged risk that could affect reported earnings. (This does not apply to an entity that does not report earnings as a separate caption in a statement of financial performance, such as a not-for-profit organization.)

3. The hedged item is not (a) an asset or liability that is remeasured with the changes in fair value attributable to the hedged risk reported currently in earnings, (b) an investment accounted for by the equity method, (c) a minority interest in one or more consolidated subsidiaries, (d) an equity investment in a consolidated subsidiary, (e) a firm commitment either to enter into a business combination or to acquire or dispose of a subsidiary, a minority interest, or an equity method investee, or (f) an equity instrument issued by the entity and classified as stockholders' equity in the statement of financial position.

4. If the hedged item is all or a portion of a debt security that is classified as held-to-maturity by FAS-115 (Accounting for Certain Investments in Debt and Equity Securities), the designated risk being hedged is the risk of changes in its fair value attributable to changes in the obligor's creditworthiness. If the hedged item is an option component of a held-to-maturity security that permits its repayment, the designated risk being hedged is the risk of changes in the entire fair value of that option component.

5. If the hedged item is a nonfinancial asset or liability other than a recognized loan servicing right or a nonfinancial firm commitment with financial components, the designated risk being hedged is the risk of changes in the fair value of the entire hedged asset or liability.

6. If the hedged item is a financial asset or liability, a recognized loan servicing right, or a nonfinancial firm commitment with financial components, the designated risk being hedged is (a) the risk of changes in the overall fair value of the entire hedged item, (b) the risk of changes in its fair value attributable to changes in market interest rates, (c) the risk of changes in its fair value attributable to changes in the related foreign currency exchange rates, or (d) the risk of changes in its fair value attributable to changes in the obligor's creditworthiness.

Changes in the fair value of derivative instruments that qualify as fair value hedges are recognized currently in earnings. The gain or loss on the hedged item attributable to the hedged risk adjusts the carrying amount of the hedged item and is recognized currently in earnings.

> **OBSERVATION:** While FAS-133 generally requires accounting for derivative instruments at fair value, those qualifying as fair value hedges are the only types of derivatives for which the change in value is included currently in determining net income. This accounting distinguishes fair value hedges from cash flow hedges and foreign currency hedges and can be expected to result in some volatility in reported income.

An entity shall discontinue prospectively accounting for a fair value hedge if *any* of the following occurs:

- Any criterion of a fair value hedge, or hedged item, is no longer met.
- The derivative expires, or is sold, terminated, or exercised.
- The entity removes the designation of the fair value hedge.

An asset or liability that is designated as a fair value hedge is subject to the applicable GAAP requirement for assessment of impairment (asset) or recognition of an increased obligation (liability).

Cash Flow Hedge

A derivative instrument may be designated as hedging the exposure to variability in expected future cash flows attributed to a particular risk. That exposure may be associated with an existing recognized asset or liability (e.g., variable rate debt) or a forecasted transaction (e.g., a forecasted purchase or sale). Designated hedging instruments and hedged items or transactions qualify for cash flow hedge accounting if all of the following criteria are met:

1. At the inception of the hedge, there is formal documentation of the hedging relationship and the entity's risk management objective and strategy for undertaking the hedge. This must include identification of *(a)* the hedging instrument, *(b)* the hedged transaction, *(c)* the nature of the risk being hedged, and *(d)* how the hedging instrument's effectiveness hedges the risk to the hedged transaction's variability in cash flows attributable to the hedged risk will be assessed.

2. Both at the inception of the hedge and on an ongoing basis, the hedging relationship is expected to be highly effective in achieving offsetting cash flows attributable to the hedged risk during the term of the hedge. An assessment is required when financial statements or earnings are reported, and at least every three months.

3. If a written option is designated as hedging the variability in cash flows for a recognized asset or liability, the combination of the hedged item and the written option provides at least as much potential for favorable cash flows as the exposure to unfavorable cash flows.

4. If a hedging instrument is used to modify the interest receipts or payments associated with a recognized financial asset or liability from one variable rate to another variable rate, the hedging instrument must be a link between an existing designated asset with variable cash flows and an existing designated liability with variable cash flows and must be highly effective in achieving offsetting cash flows.

A forecasted transaction is eligible for designation as a hedged transaction in a cash flow hedge if all of the following additional criteria are met:

1. The forecasted transaction is specifically identified as a single transaction or a group of individual transactions.

2. The occurrence of the forecasted transaction is probable.

3. The forecasted transaction is with a party external to the reporting entity.

4. The forecasted transaction is not the acquisition of an asset or incurrence of a liability that will subsequently be remeasured with changes in fair value attributed to the hedged risk reported currently in earnings.

5. If the variable cash flows of the forecasted transaction relate to a debt security that is classified as held-to-maturity under FAS-115, the risk being hedged is the risk of changes in its cash flows attributable to default or the risk of changes in the obligor's creditworthiness.

6. The forecasted transaction does not involve a business combination subject to the provisions of APB-16 (Business Combinations) and is not a transaction involving *(a)* a parent company's interest in consolidated subsidiaries, *(b)* a minority interest in a consolidated subsidiary, *(c)* an equity-method investment, or *(d)* an entity's own equity instruments.

7. If the hedged transaction is the forecasted purchase or sale of a nonfinancial asset, the designated risk being hedged is

(a) the risk of changes in the functional-currency-equivalent cash flows attributable to changes in the related foreign currency exchange rates, or (b) the risk of changes in the cash flows relating to all changes in the purchase price or shares price of the asset.

8. If the hedged transaction is the forecasted purchase or sale of a financial asset or liability or the variable cash inflow or outflow of an existing financial asset or liability, the designated risk being hedged is (a) the risk of changes in the cash flows of the entire asset or liability, (b) the risk of changes in its cash flows attributable to changes in market interest rates, (c) the risk of changes in the functional-currency-equivalent cash flows attributable to changes in the related foreign currency exchange rates, or (d) the risk of changes in cash flows attributable to default or the risk of changes in the obligor's creditworthiness.

The effective portion of the gain or loss (i.e., change in fair value) on a derivative designated as a cash flow hedge is reported in other comprehensive income (outside net income). The ineffective portion is reported in earnings. Amounts in accumulated other comprehensive income are reclassified into earnings (net income) in the same period in which the hedged forecasted transaction affects earnings.

> **OBSERVATION:** Changes in the fair value of cash flow hedges are not included currently in determining net income as they are with fair value hedges. Rather, they are included in "other comprehensive income," outside the determination of net income. Thus, they are treated like changes in the fair value of available-for-sale investments in this regard. This means that they are recognized initially in other comprehensive income and subsequently recognized in net income when they are realized.

An entity shall discontinue prospectively accounting for cash flow hedges as specified above if *any* of the following occurs:

- Any criterion for a cash flow hedge, or the hedged forecasted transaction is no longer met.
- The derivative expires, or is sold, terminated, or exercised.
- The entity removes the designation of the cash flow hedge.

If cash flow hedge accounting is discontinued, the accumulated amount in other comprehensive income remains and is reclassified into earnings when the hedged forecasted transaction affects earnings. Existing GAAP for impairment of an asset or recognition of an increased liability apply.

Foreign Currency Hedge

Consistent with the functional currency concept of FAS-52 (Foreign Currency Translation), FAS-133 indicates that an entity may designate the following types of hedges as hedges of foreign currency exposure:

1. A fair value hedge of an unrecognized firm commitment or an available-for-sale security

2. A cash flow hedge of a forecasted foreign-currency-denominated transaction or a forecasted intercompany foreign-currency-denominated transaction

3. A hedge of a net investment in a foreign operation

Foreign currency fair value hedges and cash flows hedges are generally subject to the fair value and cash flow hedge accounting requirements, respectively, covered earlier.

The change in fair value of a derivative instrument that qualifies as a hedge of net investment of a foreign operation is reported in other comprehensive income (outside net income) as part of the cumulative translation adjustment in accordance with FAS-52 (Foreign Currency Translation).

> **OBSERVATION:** Foreign currency hedges build on the standards for fair value and cash flow hedges presented earlier, and on accounting for the cumulative translation adjustment requirements of FAS-52 (Foreign Currency Translation). If a foreign currency hedge satisfies the FAS-133 criteria as a fair value or cash flow hedge, it is treated accordingly. On the other hand, if the foreign currency hedge is a hedge of net investment in a foreign operation, it is treated as a part of the cumulative translation adjustment. In this latter case, it is included in other comprehensive income (much like a cash flow hedge), but it is embedded in the cumulative translation adjustment rather than separately disclosed.

Required Disclosures

General

For instruments that qualify as hedging instruments, the following are required:

*   Objectives for holding or issuing the instruments
*   The context needed to understand these objectives

- The entity's strategies for achieving these objectives
- Distinction concerning the above between derivative instruments designated as fair value hedging instruments, cash flow hedging instruments, hedges of the foreign currency exposure of a net investment in a foreign operation, and all other derivatives
- The entity's risk management policy for each type of hedge, including a description of the items or transactions for which risks are hedged
- For instruments not designated as hedging instruments, the purpose of the derivative activity

Fair Value Hedges

Fair value hedges for derivative instruments, as well as nonderivative instruments that may give rise to foreign currency transaction gains or losses under FAS-52, that have been designated and qualify as fair value hedging instruments, include the following:

- The net gain or loss recognized in earnings during the period representing:
  - The amount of the hedges' ineffectiveness.
  - The component of the derivative instruments' gain or loss, if any, excluded from the assessment of hedge effectiveness.
  - A description of where the net gain or loss is reported in the statement of income or other statement of financial performance.
- The amount of net gain or loss recognized in earnings when a hedged firm commitment no longer qualifies as a fair value hedge.

Cash Flow Hedges

Cash flow hedges for derivatives that have been designated and qualify as cash flow hedging instruments and the related hedged transactions include the following:

- The net gain or loss recognized in earnings during the reporting period representing:
  - The amount of the hedges' ineffectiveness.
  - The component of the derivative instruments' gain or loss, if any, excluded from the assessment of hedge effectiveness.

> — A description of where the net gain or loss is reported in the statement of income or other statement of financial performance.

- A description of the transactions or other events that will result in the reclassification into earnings of gains or losses that are reported in accumulated other comprehensive income and the estimated net amount of the existing gains or losses at the reporting date that is expected to be reclassified into earnings within the next 12 months

- The maximum length of time over which the entity is hedging its exposure to the variability in future cash flows for forecasted transactions excluding those forecasted transactions related to the payment of variable interest on existing financial instruments

- The amount of gains and losses reclassified into earnings as a result of the discontinuance of cash flow hedges, because it is probable that the original forecasted transactions will not occur

Hedges of Net Investment in a Foreign Operation

Hedges of a net investment in a foreign operation for derivative instruments, as well as nonderivative instruments that may give rise to foreign currency transaction gains or losses under FAS-52, that have been designated and qualify as hedging instruments for hedges of the foreign currency exposure of a net investment in a foreign operation include:

- The net amount of gains and losses included in the cumulative translation adjustment during the reporting period.

Changes in Components of Comprehensive Income

Changes in components of comprehensive income are the following:

- Within other comprehensive income, a separate classification of the net gain or loss on derivative instruments designated and qualifying as cash flow hedging instruments

- As part of the disclosure of accumulated other comprehensive income in accordance with FAS-130 (Reporting Comprehensive Income), the beginning and ending accumulated derivative gain or loss, the related net change associated with current period hedging transactions, and the net amount of any reclassification into earnings

Effective Date and Transition

FAS-133 is effective for all fiscal periods (both annual and interim) beginning after June 15, 1999. Following is guidance on making the transition to FAS-133:

- Initial adoption shall be as of the beginning of an entity's fiscal quarter; on that date, hedging relationships shall be designated anew and documented as indicated in FAS-133.

- Earlier application of FAS-133 is encouraged, but is permitted only as of the beginning of any fiscal quarter that begins after the issuance of FAS-133.

- Earlier application of selected provisions of FAS-133 is not permitted.

- FAS-133 shall not be applied retroactively to financial statements of prior periods.

- At the date of initial application, an entity shall recognize all freestanding derivative instruments in the statement of financial position as either assets or liabilities, measured at fair value.

- The transition adjustments required to implement FAS-133 shall be presented as the cumulative effect of a change in accounting principle in accordance with APB-20 (Accounting Changes).

OFFSETTING OF FINANCIAL INSTRUMENTS

FIN-39 specifies that offsetting of assets and liabilities in the balance sheet is improper except when the right of setoff exists. The Interpretation specifically applies the general principles of offsetting to financial instruments. Unless the conditions established for the right of setoff exist (see the *GAAP Guide* chapter titled "Current Assets and Current Liabilities"), the fair value of contracts in a loss position shall not be offset against the fair value of contracts in a gain position. Similarly, amounts recognized as accrued receivables should not be offset against amounts recognized as accrued payables unless a right of setoff exists (FIN-39, par. 8).

One variation of this general policy stated in FIN-39 is that fair value amounts may be offset when they are recognized for forward, interest rate swap, currency swap, option, other conditional or exchange contracts executed with the same counterparty under a master netting arrangement. The reporting entity may choose to offset in this case, and the policy selected must be followed consistently (FAS-107, par. 10).

FIN-41 specifies the following criteria that must be met for an enterprise to offset amounts recognized as payables under repurchase agreements and amounts recognized as receivables under reverse repurchase agreements (FIN-41, par. 3):

1. The agreements are executed with the same counterparty.

2. The agreements have the same settlement date, set forth at inception.

3. The agreements are executed in accordance with a master netting arrangement.

4. The securities under the agreements exist in "book entry" form and can be transferred only by means of entries in the records of the transfer system operator or securities custodian.

5. The agreements will be settled on a securities transfer system that operates in the manner described below, and the enterprise must have associated banking arrangements in place as described below. Cash settlements for securities transferred are made under established banking arrangements that provide that the enterprise will need available cash on deposit only for any net amounts that are due at the end of the business day. It must be *probable* that the associated banking arrangements will provide sufficient *daylight overdraft or other intraday credit* at the settlement date for each of the parties.

6. The enterprise intends to use the same account at the clearing bank (or other financial institution) to settle its receivable (i.e., cash inflow from the reverse purchasing agreement) and its payable (i.e., cash outflow to settle the offsetting repurchase agreement).

If these six conditions are met, the enterprise has the option to offset. That choice must be applied consistently.

The third criterion refers to a "master netting arrangement." A master netting arrangement exists if the reporting entity has multiple contracts, whether for the same type of conditional or exchange contract or for different types of contracts, with a single counterparty that are subject to a contractual agreement that provides for the net settlement of all contracts through a single payment in a single currency in the event of default on or termination of any one contract (FIN-39).

The fourth criterion refers to "book-entry" form. FIN-41 sees this as a key element because it provides control over the securities. The controlling record for a "book entry" security is maintained by the transfer system operator. A securities custodian that has a security account with the transfer system operation may maintain "subsidiary" records of "book entry" securities and may transfer the securities within its subsidiary records; however, a security cannot be traded from the account of that custodian to a new custodian without a "book entry" transfer of the security over the securities transfer system. This form of accounting record facilitates repurchase and reverse repurchase agreement transactions on securities transfer systems.

For a transfer system for repurchase and reverse repurchase agreements to meet the fifth criterion, cash transfers must be initiated by the owner of record of the securities notifying its securities custodian to transfer those securities to the counterparty to the arrangement. Under associated banking arrangements, each party to a same-day settlement of both a repurchase agreement and a reverse repurchase agreement would be obligated to pay a gross amount of cash for the securities transferred from its counterparty, but the party would be able to reduce that gross obligation by notifying its securities custodian to transfer other securities to that counterparty the same day (FIN-41, par. 4).

In the fifth criterion, the term *probable* has the same definition as in FAS-5 (Accounting for Contingencies), meaning that a transaction or event is more likely to occur than not. The phrase "daylight overdraft or other intraday credit" refers to the feature of the banking arrangement that permits transactions to be completed during the day when insufficient cash is on deposit, provided there is sufficient cash to cover the net cash requirement at the end of the day.

CHAPTER 17
FOREIGN OPERATIONS AND EXCHANGE

CONTENTS

CHAPTER 17
FOREIGN OPERATIONS
AND EXCHANGE

OVERVIEW

There are two major areas of foreign operations:

- Translation of foreign currency financial statements for purposes of consolidation, combination, or reporting on the equity method (one-line consolidation)
- Accounting and reporting of foreign currency transactions, including forward exchange contracts

GAAP for foreign operations and exchange are found in the following pronouncements:

FAS-52	Foreign Currency Translation
FIN-37	Accounting for Translation Adjustments upon Sale of Part of an Investment in a Foreign Entity

> **OBSERVATION:** FAS-52 is amended by FAS-133 (Accounting for Derivative Instruments and Hedging Activities). This is effective for fiscal years beginning after June 15, 1999. FAS-133 applies in interim financial statements for periods that begin after the same date (e.g., the quarter beginning July 1, 1999). FAS-133 is covered in Chapter 16 of the 1999 *Miller GAAP Guide.*
> Because the effective date of FAS-133 is delayed as indicated above, and the first calendar year for which FAS-133 will be in effect is the year 2000, the impact of FAS-133 on FAS-52 is not reflected in the 1999 *Miller GAAP Guide.*

CROSS-REFERENCES

1999 MILLER GAAP GUIDE: Chapter 1, "Accounting Changes"; Chapter 5, "Changing Prices"; Chapter 6, "Consolidated Financial Statements"; Chapter 14, "Equity Method"; Chapter 21, "Income Taxes"

1999 MILLER GAAP IMPLEMENTATION MANUAL: Chapter 11, "Foreign Operations and Exchange"

1999 MILLER GAAP IMPLEMENTATION MANUAL: EITF: Chapter 12, "Foreign Currency Transactions"

1999 MILLER NOT-FOR-PROFIT REPORTING: Chapter 2, "Overview of Current Pronouncements"; Chapter 11, "Display of Certain GAAP Transactions"

BACKGROUND

Business transactions and foreign operations that are recorded in a foreign currency must be restated in U.S. dollars in accordance with generally accepted accounting principles.

Transactions occur at various dates, and exchange rates tend to fluctuate considerably. Before an attempt is made to translate the records of a foreign operation, the records should be in conformity with GAAP. In addition, if the foreign statements have any accounts stated in a currency other than their own, they must be converted into the foreign statement's currency before translation into U.S. dollars or any other reporting currency.

A brief summary of FAS-52 follows:

1. Foreign currency financial statements must be in conformity with GAAP before they are translated.

2. Assets, liabilities, and operations of an entity must be expressed in the functional currency of the entity. The functional currency of an entity is the currency of the primary economic environment in which the entity operates.

3. The current rate of exchange is used to translate the assets and liabilities of a foreign entity from its functional currency into the reporting currency.

   a. The weighted-average exchange rate for the period is used to translate revenue, expenses, and gains and losses of a foreign entity from its functional currency to the reporting currency.

   b. The current rate of exchange is used to translate changes in financial position other than those items found in the income statement, which are translated at the weighted-average exchange rate for the period.

4. Gain or loss on the translation of foreign currency financial statements is not recognized in current net income but is reported as a separate component of stockholders' equity. If remeasurement from the recording currency to the functional

currency is necessary prior to translation, however, gain or loss on remeasurement is recognized in current net income.

5. The amounts accumulated in the separate component of stockholders' equity are realized on the sale or substantially complete liquidation of the investment in the foreign entity.

6. The financial statements of a foreign entity in a country that has had cumulative inflation of approximately 100% or more over a three-year period (highly inflationary) must be remeasured into the functional currency of the reporting entity.

7. A foreign currency transaction is one that requires settlement in a currency other than the functional currency of the reporting entity.

8. Gains or losses from foreign currency transactions are recognized in current net income, except for:

   a. Gain or loss on a designated and effective economic hedge of a net investment in a foreign entity

   b. Gain or loss on certain long-term intercompany foreign currency transactions

   c. Gain or loss on a designated and effective economic hedge of a firm, identifiable, foreign currency commitment that meets certain conditions

9. Taxable foreign exchange gains or losses that do not appear in the same period in taxable income and either (*a*) financial accounting income (books) or (*b*) a separate component of stockholders' equity (books) are temporary differences for which deferred taxes must be provided in accordance with existing GAAP.

10. Certain specific disclosures are required by FAS-52.

TRANSLATION OBJECTIVES

FAS-52 establishes accounting and reporting standards for (*a*) foreign currency transactions and (*b*) translation of foreign currency financial statements that are included by consolidation, combination, or the equity method in a parent company's financial statements. Foreign financial statements must conform to U.S. generally accepted accounting principles before they can be translated into dollars (FAS-52, par. 4).

An important objective in translating foreign currency is to preserve the financial results and relationships that are expressed in the foreign currency. This is accomplished by using the *functional currency* of the foreign entity. The functional currency is then translated into the *reporting currency* of the reporting entity. FAS-52 assumes that the reporting currency for an enterprise is U.S. dollars. The reporting currency may be a currency other than U.S. dollars, however.

> **OBSERVATION:** Perhaps the ultimate objective of translating foreign transactions and financial statements is to produce the same results that each individual underlying transaction would have produced on the date it occurred, if it had then been recorded in the reporting currency.

FUNCTIONAL CURRENCY

FAS-52 requires that the assets, liabilities, and operations of an entity be measured in terms of the functional currency of that entity. The functional currency is the currency of the primary economic environment in which an entity generates and expends cash. The functional currency generally is the currency of the country in which the entity is located. The functional currency of a foreign operation may be the same as a related affiliated enterprise, however, if the foreign operation is a direct and integral component or extension of the related affiliated enterprise (FAS-52, par. 5).

> **OBSERVATION:** For example, if a foreign entity's books of record are kept in French francs and the functional currency is British pounds, the books of record are remeasured into British pounds before the financial statements are translated into the currency of the reporting entity. Any translation gain or loss from French francs to British pounds is included in the remeasured net income. If the functional currency of the foreign entity is the French franc, only translation to the reporting currency is necessary. If the functional currency of the foreign entity is that of the reporting entity, only remeasurement from French francs to the reporting currency is required.

For the purposes of determining functional currency under FAS-52, foreign operations may be separated into two models. The first model is the self-contained foreign operation, located in a particular country, whose daily operations are not dependent on the economic environment of the parent's functional currency. This type of foreign operation primarily generates and expends local currency; the net cash flows that it produces in local currency may be reinvested, or converted and distributed to its parent company. The functional currency for this type of foreign operation is its local (domestic) currency (FAS-52, par. 6).

The second model of foreign operation usually is a direct and integral component or extension of the parent company's operation. Financing usually is in U.S. dollars and frequently is supplied by the parent. The purchase and sale of assets usually are made in U.S. dollars. In other words, the daily operations of this type of foreign operation are dependent on the economic environment of the parent's currency. In addition, the changes in the foreign operation's individual assets and liabilities directly affect the cash flow of the parent company. The functional currency for this type of foreign operation is the U.S. dollar (FAS-52, par. 6).

In the event that the facts in a given situation do not clearly identify the functional currency, the determination rests on the judgment of management. The FASB has developed the following guidelines, based on certain indicators, that should be considered in determining the functional currency of a foreign operation (FAS-52, par. 42):

Cash Flow Indicators

The foreign operation's cash flows are mostly in foreign currency that does not directly affect the parent company's cash flows. Under these circumstances, the functional currency is the local currency.

The foreign operation's cash flows directly affect the parent company's cash flows on a current basis and usually are available for remittance through intercompany account settlement. Under these circumstances, the functional currency is the parent company's currency.

Sales Price Indicators

The foreign operation's sales prices for its products are primarily determined (on a short-term basis) by local competition or local government regulation, and not by exchange rate changes. Under these circumstances, the functional currency is the local currency.

The foreign operation's sales prices for its products are mostly responsive (on a short-term basis) to exchange rate changes, such as worldwide competition and prices. Under these circumstances, the functional currency is the parent company's currency.

Sales Market Indicators

The foreign operation has an active local sales market for its products, although there also may be significant amounts of exports. Under these circumstances, the functional currency is the local currency.

The foreign operation's sales market is mostly in the parent's country, or sales contracts are mostly made in the parent company's currency. Under these circumstances, the functional currency is the parent company's currency.

Expense Indicators

The foreign operation's costs of production (labor, material, etc.) or service are mostly local costs, although there also may be imports from other countries. Under these circumstances, the functional currency is the local currency.

The foreign operation's costs of production or service, on a continuing basis, are primarily costs for components obtained from the parent's country. Under these circumstances, the functional currency is the parent company's currency.

Financing Indicators

Financing for the foreign operation is in local currency, and funds generated by the foreign operation are sufficient to service debt obligations. Under these circumstances, the functional currency is the local currency.

Financing for the foreign operation is provided by the parent company or is obtained in U.S. dollars. Funds generated by the foreign operation are insufficient to service its debt. Under these circumstances, the functional currency is the parent company's currency.

Intercompany Transactions

There is little interrelationship between the operations of the foreign entity and the parent company, except for competitive advantages, such as trademarks, patents, etc. Intercompany transactions are of a low volume. Under these circumstances, the functional currency is the local currency.

There is an extensive interrelationship between the operations of the foreign entity and the parent company. Intercompany transactions are numerous. Under these circumstances, the functional currency is the parent company's currency.

The functional currency of a foreign entity must be used consistently from one fiscal year to another, unless significant changes in economic facts and circumstances dictate a change (FAS-52, par. 9).

> ☛ **PRACTICE POINTER:** Account for a change in functional currency as a change in an accounting estimate. Thus, the change is accounted for in the period of change and/or future periods (prospectively).
>
> If a change in functional currency occurs, do not remove the translation adjustments for prior periods from the separate component of stockholders' equity. Thus, the translated amounts of nonmonetary assets at the end of the period prior to the change in functional currency become the accounting basis for subsequent periods.

REMEASURING FINANCIAL STATEMENTS
TO THE FUNCTIONAL CURRENCY

The following is a brief review of the translation provisions of FAS-52 for the remeasurement process from the recording currency to the functional currency, prior to translation from the functional currency to the reporting currency.

Two categories of exchange rates are used in remeasuring financial statements. Historical exchange rates are those that existed at the time of the transaction, and the current exchange rate is the rate that is current at the date of remeasurement.

Monetary assets and liabilities are those that are fixed in amount, such as cash, accounts receivable, and most liabilities. Monetary assets and liabilities are translated at the current rate of exchange. All other assets, liabilities, and stockholders' equity are remeasured by reference to money price exchanges based on the type of market and time.

1. *Past purchase exchange*—the historical or acquisition cost, because it is based on the actual past purchase price

2. *Current purchase exchange*—the replacement cost, because it is measured by the current purchase price of a similar resource

3. *Current sale exchange*—the market price, because it is based on the current selling price of the resource

4. *Future exchange*—the present value of future net money receipts, discounted cash flow, or the discounted net realizable value, because it is based on a future resource

All other assets, liabilities, and stockholders' equity are remeasured based on the four money price exchanges, as follows:

1. Accounts based on past purchase exchanges (historical or acquisition cost) are remeasured at historical exchange rates.

2. Accounts based on current purchase, current sale, and future exchanges are remeasured at the current exchange rate.

Revenue and expense transactions are remeasured at the average exchange rate for the period, except those expenses related to assets and liabilities, which are remeasured at historical exchange rates. For example, depreciation and amortization are remeasured at historical exchange rates, the rate that existed at the time the underlying related asset was acquired.

The following is a list of assets, liabilities, and stockholders' equity items and their corresponding remeasurement rates under FAS-52:

	Remeasurement Rates	
	Current	*Historical*
Cash (in almost all forms)	X	
Marketable securities—at cost		X
Marketable securities—at market	X	
Accounts and notes receivable	X	
Allowance for receivables	X	
Inventories—at cost		X
Inventories—at market, net realizable value, selling price	X	
Inventories—under fixed contract price	X	

	Remeasurement Rates	
	Current	*Historical*
Prepaid expenses		X
Refundable deposits	X	
Advances to subsidiaries	X	
Fixed assets		X
Accumulated depreciation		X
Cash surrender value—life insurance	X	
Intangible assets (all)		X
Accounts and notes payable	X	
Accrued expenses	X	
Accrued losses on firm commitments	X	
Taxes payable	X	
All long-term liabilities	X	
Unamortized premium or discount on long-term liabilities	X	
Obligations under warranties	X	
Deferred income		X
Capital stock		X
Retained earnings		X
Minority interests		X

Revenue and expenses not related to any balance sheet items are remeasured at the average currency exchange rate for the period. The average may be based on a daily, weekly, monthly, or quarterly basis or on the weighted-average rate for the period, which will probably result in a more meaningful conversion. Revenue and expense items that are related to a balance sheet account, such as deferred income, depreciation, and beginning and ending inventories, are remeasured at the same exchange rate as the related balance sheet item.

In remeasuring the lower-of-cost-or-market rule, the remeasured historical cost is compared to the remeasured market, and whichever is lower in functional currency is used. This may require a write-down in the functional currency from cost to market, which was not required in the foreign currency financial statements. On the other hand, if market was used on the foreign statements and in remeasuring to the functional currency market exceeds historical cost, the write-down to market on the foreign statements will have to be reversed before remeasuring, which would then be done at the historical rate. Once inventory has been written down to market in remeasured functional currency statements, the resulting carrying amount is used in future translations until the inventory is sold or a further write-down is necessary. This same procedure is used for assets, other than inventory, that may have to be written down from historical cost.

> **OBSERVATION:** The reason for the above procedure in applying the lower-of-cost-or-market rule in remeasuring foreign financial statements is that exchange gains and losses are a consequence of remeasurement and not of applying the lower-of-cost-or-market rule. This means that remeasured market is equal to replacement cost (market) in the foreign currency remeasured at the current exchange rate, except that:
>
> 1. Remeasured market cannot exceed net realizable value in foreign currency translated at the current exchange rate.
> 2. Remeasured market cannot be less than (1) above, reduced by an approximate normal profit translated at the current exchange rate.

For remeasurement purposes, the current exchange rate is the one in effect as of the balance sheet date of the foreign statements. Therefore, if the parent company's financial statements are at a date different from the date(s) of its foreign operation(s), the exchange rate in effect at the date of the foreign subsidiary's balance sheet is used for remeasurement and translation purposes.

Any translation adjustment arising from the remeasurement process is included in remeasured net income. In other words, any gain or loss resulting from the remeasurement process that is required by FAS-52 is included in net income in the remeasured financial statements (FAS-52, par. 47).

After the foreign entity's financial statements are remeasured in the functional currency, they are ready for translation. If the functional currency of a foreign entity is the U.S dollar and the reporting currency of the parent is also the U.S. dollar, there will be no translation adjustment.

TRANSLATION OF FOREIGN OPERATIONS— HIGHLY INFLATIONARY ECONOMIES

FAS-52 defines a highly inflationary economy as one in which the cumulative inflation over a three-year consecutive period approximates 100%. In other words, the inflation rate in an economy must be rising at the rate of about 30–35% per year for three consecutive years to be classified as highly inflationary.

For the purposes of FAS-52, a foreign entity in a highly inflationary economy does not have a functional currency. The functional currency of the reporting entity is used as the functional currency of the foreign entity in a highly inflationary economy. Thus, the financial statements for a foreign entity in a highly inflationary economy are remeasured into the functional currency of the reporting entity. The remeasurement process required by FAS-52 is the same as that required for a foreign entity's financial statements that are not expressed in the functional currency (FAS-52, par. 11).

> **OBSERVATION:** Apparently, exchange adjustments resulting from the remeasurement process for foreign entities in highly inflationary economies are included in the determination of remeasured net income, rather than reported as a separate component of stockholders' equity. Paragraph 11 of FAS-52 is not clear on this point, but does state that the remeasurement process must be done in accordance with paragraph 10.

The International Monetary Fund (IMF) publishes monthly statistics on international inflation rates. After the financial statements of a foreign entity in a highly inflationary economy are expressed in the functional currency of the reporting entity, they are ready for translation. Since the financial statements are now expressed in the reporting currency, however, there will be no translation adjustment.

TRANSLATION OF FOREIGN CURRENCY STATEMENTS

Foreign currency financial statements must be in conformity with GAAP before they are translated into the functional currency of the reporting entity. FAS-52 covers the translation of financial statements from one functional currency to another for the purposes of consolidation, combination, or the equity method of accounting. Translation of financial statements for any other purpose is beyond the scope of FAS-52 (FAS-52, par. 2).

> **OBSERVATION:** If the functional currency of a foreign operation is the same as that of its parent, there is no need for

translation. A translation adjustment occurs only if the foreign operation's functional currency is a functional currency different from that of its parent.

The translation of foreign currency financial statements to the functional currency of the reporting entity does not produce realized exchange gains or losses. Instead, the gains or losses are considered unrealized and are recorded and reported as a separate component of stockholders' equity (FAS-52, par. 13).

> **OBSERVATION:** Paragraph 12 of FAS-52 states, "All elements of financial statements shall be translated by using a current exchange rate." This statement is potentially misleading because common stock, paid-in capital, donated capital, retained earnings, and similar items are not translated at the current exchange rate. Translation of these elements of the financial statements is made as follows:
>
> *Capital accounts* are translated at their historical exchange rates when the capital stock was issued, or at the historical exchange rate when the capital stock was acquired.
>
> *Retained earnings* are translated at the translated amount at the end of the prior period, plus the translated amount of net income for the current period, less the translated amount of any dividends declared during the current period.

Assets and liabilities are translated from the foreign entity's functional currency to the reporting entity's functional currency using the current exchange rate at the balance sheet date of the foreign entity (FAS-52, par. 12). If a current exchange rate is not available at the balance sheet date of the foreign entity being translated, the first exchange rate available after the balance sheet date is used (FAS-52, par. 26).

Revenue, expenses, and gains and losses are translated from the foreign entity's functional currency to produce the approximate results that would have occurred if each transaction had been translated using the exchange rate in effect on the date that the transaction was recognized. Since the separate translation of every transaction is impractical, an appropriate weighted-average exchange rate for the period should be used (FAS-52, par. 12).

Gains or losses on the translation of foreign currency financial statements for the purposes of consolidation, combination, or reporting on the equity method are not included in current net income. All adjustments resulting from the translation of foreign currency financial statements are recorded and reported as a separate component of stockholders' equity. Thus, these adjustments are treated as unrealized gains and losses, similar to unrealized gains and losses of available-for-sale securities (FAS-15, Accounting for Certain Investments in Debt and Equity Securities).

To summarize, the translation process embodied in FAS-52 includes the following steps:

1. Financial statements must be in conformity with U.S. GAAP prior to translation.
2. The functional currency of the foreign entity is determined.
3. The financial statements are expressed in the functional currency of the foreign entity. Remeasurement of the financial statements into the functional currency may be necessary. Gains or losses from remeasurement are included in remeasured current net income.
4. If the foreign entity operates in a country with a highly inflationary economy, its financial statements are remeasured into the functional currency of the reporting entity.
5. The functional currency financial statements of the foreign entity are translated into the functional currency of the reporting entity using the current rate of exchange method. Gains or losses from translation are not included in current net income.

REALIZATION OF SEPARATE COMPONENT OF STOCKHOLDERS' EQUITY

Upon part, complete, or substantially complete sale or upon complete liquidation of an investment in a foreign entity, a *pro rata* portion of the accumulated translation adjustments attributable to that foreign entity, which has been recorded as a separate component of stockholders' equity, is included in determining the gain or loss on the sale or other disposition of that foreign investment (FIN-37, par. 2). Thus, if an enterprise sells a 50% ownership interest in a foreign investment, 50% of the accumulated translation adjustments related to that foreign investment is included in determining the gain or loss on the sale of the interest.

> **OBSERVATION:** Any required provision for the permanent impairment of a foreign investment is determined before translation and consolidation (FAS-52, par. 118). Apparently, this means that the amounts accumulated in the separate component of stockholders' equity for a specific foreign investment are not included in determining whether the investment has become permanently impaired.

FOREIGN CURRENCY TRANSACTIONS

A foreign currency transaction is one that requires settlement in a currency other than the functional currency of the reporting entity.

Generally, gains and losses on foreign currency transactions are recognized in current net income (FAS-52, par. 15). The following transactions, however, may require different treatment:

1. Gain or loss resulting from a foreign currency transaction that is designated as an economic hedge of a net investment in a foreign entity

2. Gain or loss resulting from intercompany foreign currency transactions of a capital nature or long-term financing nature, between an investor and investee where the investee entity is consolidated, combined, or accounted for by the equity method by the investor

3. Forward exchange contracts

If the exchange rate changes between the time a purchase or sale is contracted for and the time actual payment is made, a foreign exchange gain or loss results.

Illustration of Foreign Currency Translation

Alex Co. purchased goods for 100,000 pesos when the exchange rate was 10 pesos to a dollar. The journal entry in dollars is:

| Purchases | $10,000 | |
| Accounts payable | | $10,000 |

Assuming that when the goods are paid for, the exchange rate is 12:1, the journal entry in dollars is:

Accounts payable	$10,000	
Cash		$ 8,333
Foreign exchange gain		1,667

At a 12:1 exchange rate, the $8,333 can purchase 100,000 pesos. The difference between the $8,333 and the original recorded liability of $10,000 is a foreign exchange gain. If payment is made when the exchange rate is less than 10 pesos to a dollar, a foreign exchange loss would result.

A foreign exchange gain or loss is computed at each balance sheet date on all recorded foreign transactions that have not been settled. The difference between the exchange rate that could have been used to settle the transaction at the date it occurred, and the exchange rate that can be used to settle the transaction at a subsequent balance sheet date, is the gain or loss recognized in current net income. Generally, the current exchange rate is the rate that is used to settle a transaction on the date it occurs, or on a subsequent balance sheet date (FAS-52, par. 16).

Forward Exchange Contracts

A forward exchange contract is a foreign currency transaction. A forward exchange contract is an agreement to exchange, at a future specified date and rate, currencies of different countries. Generally, a forward exchange contract is entered into either as a hedge or for speculation. Gains or losses on all foreign exchange contracts and foreign currency transactions usually are recognized in net income of the period in which the exchange rate changes (FAS-52, par. 17). Gains and losses that are exceptions to this general rule are deferred and are discussed in a later section.

FAS-52 specifies two methods of determining gain or loss on forward exchange contracts, depending upon whether the contract is (1) a hedge (whether or not deferred) or (2) speculative.

Hedge Contracts

Gain or loss is the difference between the balance sheet date spot exchange rate and the spot exchange rate at the inception of the contract, multiplied by the principal amount of foreign currency (FAS-52, par. 18).

Speculative Contracts

Gain or loss is the difference between the contracted forward exchange rate and the forward exchange rate available for the remaining maturity of the contract, multiplied by the principal amount of foreign currency (FAS-52, par. 19).

> **OBSERVATION:** The spot or forward exchange rate last used to measure gain or loss on a forward exchange contract for an earlier period may be used for either hedge or speculative contracts, if necessary.

The discount or premium involved in a hedge forward exchange contract is the difference between the forward rate and the spot rate on the date of purchase, multiplied by the principal amount of foreign currency. There is no discount or premium on a speculative forward contract. Discounts and premiums are accounted for as follows:

Hedge of a Net Asset or Liability Position

Separately accounted for and amortized to net income over the life of the contract.

Hedge of a Net Investment in a Foreign Entity

Either separately accounted for and amortized to net income over the life of the contract or included in the amount of equity adjustment from translation.

Hedge of an Identifiable Commitment

Discounts and premiums may be separately accounted for and amortized to net income over the life of the forward exchange contract or deferred and treated as adjustments of the transaction price.

Deferred Foreign Currency Transactions

Certain gains and losses on forward exchange contracts and certain types of foreign currency transactions are not included in current net income but are either (*a*) reported in the separate component of stockholders' equity, along with translation adjustments, or (*b*) included in the overall gain or loss of the related foreign currency transaction. These deferred gains and losses may be classified as follows (FAS-52, par. 20):

1. Gain or loss on a designated and effective economic hedge of a net investment in a foreign entity
2. Gain or loss on certain long-term intercompany foreign currency transactions
3. Gain or loss on a designated and effective economic hedge of a firm, identifiable, foreign currency commitment

The accounting required by FAS-52 commences with the designation date of the transaction (FAS-52, par. 21).

> **OBSERVATION:** As an example of a foreign currency transaction intended to be an economic hedge of a net investment in a foreign entity, take the case of a U.S. parent company with a net investment in a Greek subsidiary that borrows Greek currency in the amount of its net investment in the Greek subsidiary.

The U.S. company designates the loan as an economic hedge of its net investment in the Greek subsidiary. In other words, the U.S. parent computes its net investment in the foreign currency of its foreign subsidiary and then borrows the same amount of foreign currency as the amount of its net investment. In this event, if the net investment in the foreign subsidiary declines because of a change in exchange rates, the change is made up in the foreign currency loan. The U.S. company can buy a larger amount of the subsidiary's foreign currency with fewer U.S. dollars. When the net investment in the foreign subsidiary and the loan in the foreign currency of the foreign subsidiary are both translated into U.S. dollars, the change in the net investment in the foreign subsidiary (an asset) should be approximately equal to the change in the foreign currency loan, except for taxes, if any. Thus, the foreign currency loan acts as a hedge against any increase or decrease in the net foreign investment that is attributable to a change in the exchange rate.

FAS-52 requires that both translated amounts be recorded and reported in a separate component of stockholders' equity. If the translated amount of the foreign currency loan (after taxes, if any) exceeds the translated amount of the net investment in the foreign subsidiary that was hedged, however, the gain or loss that is allocable to the excess must be included in net income, and not recorded and reported as a separate component of stockholders' equity.

Gains or losses on intercompany foreign currency transactions of a capital or long-term nature are not included in current net income, but are reported in the separate component of stockholders' equity, along with translation adjustments. The entities involved in the intercompany foreign currency transactions reported in this manner must be consolidated, combined, or accounted for by the equity method. Gain or loss on intercompany foreign currency transactions that are not of a permanent nature are included in net income (FAS-52, par. 20).

Gain or loss on a forward exchange contract or foreign currency transaction that is intended and effective as a hedge of a firm, identifiable, foreign currency commitment is deferred and included in the overall gain or loss from the firm, identifiable, foreign currency commitment. However, a loss is not deferred if it is estimated that the loss would be recognized in later periods. Thus, any loss that is expected to be recognized in later periods is not deferred. The foreign currency transaction must be firm, and must be designated and effective as a hedge of a foreign currency commitment. The accounting required by FAS-52 commences with the designation date of the transaction (FAS-52, par. 21).

> **OBSERVATION:** For example, a U.S. company purchases a large piece of equipment from a Mexican company for 100,000

pesos when the exchange rate is 10:1 (10 pesos to one dollar). Delivery of the equipment will be made in one year, at which time the purchase price must be paid in Mexican pesos. To hedge against the rise or fall in the exchange rate of the peso, the U.S. company purchases, for $1,000, a forward exchange contract to purchase 100,000 Mexican pesos in one year at the exchange rate of 10:1. At the end of six months, financial statements are prepared and the exchange rate of Mexican pesos is 12:1. Thus, at the end of six months, the cost of the equipment in U.S. dollars is $8,333, or 100,000 Mexican pesos, while at the date of purchase the cost in U.S. dollars was $10,000 or 100,000 Mexican pesos. At the end of the year, the company will receive 100,000 Mexican pesos from the forward exchange contract upon payment of $10,000. At the interim six-month date, however, there is a deferred loss on the forward exchange contract of $2,667 ($1,667, plus the cost of the forward exchange contract of $1,000). This loss is not deferred if the total cost of the asset, including the deferred loss on the forward exchange contract, is expected to exceed the estimated net realizable value of the asset.

For the purposes of FAS-52, the amount of the forward exchange contract or foreign currency transaction cannot exceed the amount of the firm, identifiable, foreign currency commitment. If the amount of the transaction exceeds the amount of firm commitment, the gain or loss pertaining to the excess amount over the commitment may be deferred only to the extent that the transaction provides a hedge on an after-tax basis. When gain or loss pertaining to amounts in excess of the foreign currency commitment is deferred, it is included as an offset to the related tax effects in the period in which such tax effects are recognized. Gains or losses in excess of the amount of commitment on an after-tax basis cannot be deferred. In addition, any gains or losses on a forward exchange contract or foreign currency transaction that are attributable to a period after the transaction date of the related commitment cannot be deferred (FAS-52, par. 21).

Deferred gain or loss on a hedge of a foreign currency commitment that is sold or terminated is not recognized until the related identifiable transaction is consummated, unless the identifiable transaction is reasonably expected to result in a loss (FAS-52, par. 21).

Deferred Taxes

FAS-52 requires that deferred taxes be recognized on taxable foreign currency transactions and taxable translation adjustments of foreign currency financial statements, regardless of whether the exchange gain or loss is charged to current net income or recorded and reported as a separate component of stockholders' equity. Thus, all taxable foreign exchange gains or losses that do not appear in the same period in taxable income and either (*a*) financial accounting income or (*b*) the separate component of stockholders' equity are temporary differences, for which deferred taxes must be provided (FAS-52, par. 22). The amount of the deferred taxes should be determined in accordance with existing GAAP (FAS-52, par. 23).

> **OBSERVATION:** Historically, there has been a presumption in GAAP that all undistributed earnings of a subsidiary (domestic or foreign) would eventually be transferred to the parent company. Hence, GAAP have always considered undistributed income from foreign and domestic subsidiaries to be a temporary difference, requiring a provision for deferred income taxes. FAS-109 (Accounting for Income Taxes) does not require deferred taxes to be provided for the excess of the book basis over the tax basis of an investment in a foreign subsidiary, if the excess is considered to be relatively permanent. An important reason that such an excess might exist is undistributed income from foreign subsidiaries. Paragraph 31 of FAS-109 states:
>
>> A deferred tax liability is not recognized for the following types of temporary differences unless it is apparent that those temporary differences will reverse in the foreseeable future:
>>
>>> a. An excess of the amount for financial reporting over the tax basis of an investment in a foreign subsidiary or a foreign corporate joint venture as defined in APB-18 (The Equity Method of Accounting for Investments in Common Stock) that is essentially permanent in duration.
>
> In the basis for conclusions of FAS-109, the FASB states that the hypothetical nature of the tax allocation calculations for undistributed income from foreign subsidiaries "introduces significant implementation issues." Thus, tax allocation is not required for undistributed income of foreign subsidiaries that is essentially permanent in nature or for any other difference between the book basis and tax basis of investments of permanent nature.

Intraperiod income tax allocation is also required in the preparation of financial statements. The total income tax expense for a period should be allocated properly to (*a*) income before extraordinary items, (*b*) extraordinary items, (*c*) adjustments of prior periods, and (*d*) direct entries to other stockholders' equity accounts. Therefore, the portion of income tax expense for a period that is attributable to items in the separate component of stockholders' equity is allocated to the separate component of stockholders' equity, and does not appear as an increase or decrease of income tax expense for the period. In other words, deferred taxes related to items in the separate component of stockholders' equity account are charged or credited to the separate component of stockholders' equity account (FAS-52, par. 24). The illustration on page 17.22 demonstrates this concept.

> **OBSERVATION:** All aspects of income tax allocation are complicated, and these provisions of FAS-52 require careful application to the specific facts of each situation. In particular, intercompany transactions of a long-term nature and the discontinuation of a foreign operation may present peculiar problems.

Elimination of Intercompany Profits

The exchange rate to be used to eliminate intercompany profits is the rate that existed on the date of the intercompany transaction. The use of approximations and/or averages is permitted as long as they are reasonable (FAS-52, par. 25).

> **OBSERVATION:** Intercompany profits occur on the date of sale or transfer. Thus, the exchange rate on the date of sale or transfer is used to determine the amount of intercompany profit to be eliminated.

EXCHANGE RATES

The balance sheet date of the foreign entity that is consolidated, combined, or accounted for by the equity method is used for translation purposes, if different from the balance sheet date of the reporting entity. Thus, the current exchange rate for the translation of foreign currency financial statements is the rate in effect on the balance sheet date of the foreign entity that is being translated (FAS-52, par. 28). If a current exchange rate is not available at the foreign entity's balance sheet date, the first exchange rate available after the balance sheet date is used. The current rate used for the above translations is the rate applicable to currency conversion for the purpose of dividend remittances (FAS-52, par. 27).

Conditions may exist when it will be prudent to exclude a foreign entity from financial statements that are consolidated, combined, or accounted for by the equity method. Disruption of a foreign operation caused by internal strife or severe exchange restrictions may make it impossible to compute meaningful exchange rates. Under these circumstances, it is best to include earnings of a foreign operation only to the extent that cash has been received in unrestricted funds. Adequate disclosure should be made of any foreign subsid-

Illustration of How an Enterprise Determines the Beginning Balance of the Separate Component of Stockholders' Equity

	Beginning of the Year			Beginning of the Year		
	Functional currency	FAS-52 exchange rates	U.S. dollars	Functional currency	Current exchange rates	U.S. dollars
Current Assets						
Cash	F 1,000	C*1.25	$ 800	F 1,000	C 1.25	$ 800
Accounts receivable	4,000	C 1.25	3,200	4,000	C 1.25	3,200
Inventory	10,000	H†2.00	5,000	10,000	C 1.25	8,000
Total	F15,000		$ 9,000	F15,000		$12,000
Property, plant, & equipment	F75,000	H 1.50	$50,000	F75,000	C 1.25	$60,000
Total assets	F90,000		$59,000	F90,000		$72,000
Current Liabilities	F20,000	C 1.25	$16,000	F20,000	C 1.25	$16,000
Deferred income taxes	5,000	H 2.00	2,500	5,000	C 1.25	4,000
Long-term obligations	20,000	C 1.25	16,000	20,000	C 1.25	16,000
Total liabilities	F45,000		$34,500	F45,000		$36,000
Net assets (equals stockholders' equity)	F45,000		$24,500	F45,000		$36,000

Computation of the Beginning Balance of the Separate Component of Stockholders' Equity

Net assets at beginning of the year at current exchange rate	$36,000
Net assets at beginning of the year at FAS-52 rates	($24,500)
Beginning balance of separate component of stockholders' equity	$11,500

C* = Current exchange rate. H† = Historical exchange rate.

iary or investment that is excluded from the financial statements of the parent or investor. This may be accomplished by separate supplemental statements or a summary describing the important facts and information.

Financial Statement Disclosure

The aggregate transaction gain or loss that is included in determining net income for the period, including gain or loss on forward exchange contracts, shall be disclosed in the financial statements or footnotes thereto (FAS-52, par. 30).

> **OBSERVATION:** Transaction gains or losses of dealers in foreign exchange may be accounted for as dealer gains or losses, instead of transaction gains or losses under FAS-52.

An analysis of the changes in the separate component of stockholders' equity account for cumulative translation adjustments for the period shall be disclosed in either (*a*) a separate financial statement or (*b*) notes to the financial statements, or (*c*) be included as part of a stockholders' equity or a similar statement. The following is the minimum information that must be disclosed in the analysis (FAS-52, par. 31):

1. Beginning and ending cumulative balances
2. The aggregate increase or decrease for the period from translation adjustments and gains and losses from (*a*) hedges of a net investment in a foreign entity and (*b*) long-term intercompany transactions
3. The amount of income taxes for the period allocated to translation adjustments
4. The amount of translation adjustment transferred to net income during the period as a result of a sale or complete or substantially complete liquidation of a foreign investment

Disclosure of exchange rate changes and related effects on foreign currency transactions that occur subsequent to the balance sheet date should be disclosed, if the effects are material. No adjustment should be made to the financial statements for exchange rate changes that occur subsequent to the balance sheet date (FAS-52, par. 32).

CHAPTER 18
FUTURES CONTRACTS

CONTENTS

CHAPTER 18
FUTURES CONTRACTS

OVERVIEW

The primary issue dealt with in the authoritative literature for futures contracts is how to account for a change in the market value of a futures contract. The general principle set forth is that a change in market value of a futures contract should be accounted for as a gain or loss in the period of change unless the contract qualifies as a hedge of certain exposures to price or interest rate risk.

Standards of accounting for exchange-traded futures contracts, other than contracts for foreign currencies, are found in the following pronouncement:

FAS-80   Accounting for Futures Contracts

> **OBSERVATION:** FAS-80 is superseded by FAS-133 (Accounting for Derivative Instruments and Hedging Activities). This is effective for fiscal years beginning after June 15, 1999. FAS-133 applies in interim financial statements for periods that begin after the same date (e.g., the quarter beginning July 1, 1999). FAS-133 is covered in Chapter 16 of the 1999 *Miller GAAP Guide*.

CROSS-REFERENCES

1999 MILLER GAAP GUIDE: Chapter 16, "Financial Instruments—Disclosures"; Chapter 17, "Foreign Operations and Exchange"; Chapter 57, "Mortgage Banking Industry"

BACKGROUND

FAS-80 establishes GAAP for reporting futures contracts that are traded on commodities and other exchanges. Neither foreign currency futures contracts nor forward placement or delayed delivery contracts are covered by FAS-80. Foreign currency futures contracts are accounted for in accordance with FAS-52 (Foreign Currency Translation). Forward placement or delayed delivery contracts are accounted for in accordance with prevailing accepted accounting principles and practices. FAS-80 applies to general purpose financial statements of all enterprises. The thrust of FAS-80 is that changes in the market value of a futures contract are recognized in the period of change, unless the futures contract qualifies as a hedge.

Many types of commodities are traded on various commodity exchanges. Examples of traded commodities include grains such as wheat, barley, corn, and oats; metals such as gold, silver, platinum, copper, lead, and zinc; meats such as beef, pork bellies, and turkey; financial instruments such as commercial paper, Treasury bills, bonds and notes, and GNMA mortgages; and miscellaneous items such as cotton, plywood, eggs, and soybeans. Commodities, like securities, may be purchased long or sold short. Each commodity contract involves a specified quantity of the commodity.

A commodity may be traded in the form of a spot contract or a futures contract. A spot contract is for the current month and usually involves paying cash and taking physical delivery of the commodity. However, many commodity transactions involve futures contracts. This is because most investors do not want actual delivery of the commodity and therefore *cover* their positions before the spot month (the month in which the commodity contract expires). Some commodity contracts, such as stock index futures and Eurodollar time deposit futures, do not involve the delivery of a commodity. All outstanding contracts are settled for cash on their last day of trading. For every *buy* or *long* futures contract there must be a corresponding *sell* or *short* futures contract.

Futures contracts are traded on the basis that an investor agrees to buy or sell a certain quantity of a specific commodity in a specific future month and at a specific price. Thus, in June 19X1 an investor can agree to buy 100 ounces of gold in June 19X2 at a price that is agreed upon at the inception of the contract (June 19X1). If the price of gold rises six months later, the value of the June 19X2 gold futures contract will increase proportionately. In this event, the investor can make a profit by disposing of his or her *long* position. On the other hand, if the investor thought that the price of gold was going to decrease over the next year, a contract for 100 ounces of June 19X2 gold should be sold short. In this event, if the price of gold does decline, the investor can make a profit by disposing of his or her *short* position. The difference between the purchase price and selling price of a contract, less brokerage commission, is the investor's profit. If commodities are purchased or sold on margin, an investor's profit is decreased by the amount of interest paid on the margin account.

The commodity markets play an important role in the economy of the United States. The hedging process is an integral part of many businesses and would not be possible without the existing commodity futures markets. Over the past few years, there has been a significant increase in the volume of futures transactions involving prime financial paper and future interest rates. Most of the increase in activity can be associated with hedging transactions. For example, savings and loan associations frequently hedge their actual position in GNMA mortgages by buying or selling futures contracts of GNMA mortgages that trade on the Chicago Board of Trade. Farmers, food processors, metal manufacturers, millers, and others who must store large quantities of commodities as inventory can minimize their exposure to price fluctuation by hedging their positions. For example, if a farmer believes that the price of his or her crop of corn is going to be substantially less at the expected harvest time, the farmer can sell corn futures today and make actual delivery of the corn when the crop is ready for harvest. Alternatively, the farmer can close out a short position by purchasing spot contracts of corn in the month the farmer is ready to sell the crop. The profit made on the commodity contracts will offset the decline in the market value of the farmer's corn.

Some commodities are regulated by the Commodities Exchange Act, and some commodities are not regulated. Most regulated commodities are in the agricultural industries, such as grains, eggs, potatoes, cotton, and soybeans. The most important federal regulations (*a*) require that commodity exchange members submit daily reports of their commodity trading activity and (*b*) limit the number of futures contracts in any one commodity that any one person or enterprise can acquire for speculation purposes.

Transactions on commodity exchanges are cleared and settled by a clearing association appointed by the exchange. Thus, all buy and sell transactions in futures commodity contracts are handled by a clearing association. A settlement price for all open commodity contracts is established at the close of business each day by all commodity exchanges. This process is referred to as *marking-to-market*. Each broker must settle his or her net difference on all open contracts in cash each day with the clearing association. On the broker's books, the daily settlement is posted to a contract difference account, which is subsequently posted to each customer's account to reflect any gain or loss.

ACCOUNTING FOR FUTURES CONTRACTS

Speculative Futures Contracts

The minimum contract deposit that is paid to a commodity broker for the purchase of a futures contract usually is recorded by an enterprise as an asset (due from commodity broker). The recorded asset is then increased or decreased during the period the futures contract is outstanding to take into account the changes in the market value of the futures contract. For a futures contract that does not meet the hedge criteria established by FAS-80 (see below), the changes in the market value are reported by an enterprise as a gain or loss in the period in which the change occurs (FAS-80, par. 3). A change in the market value of a futures contract is calculated by multiplying the size of the contract by the change in the contract's quoted market price.

☛ **PRACTICE POINTER:** Capitalize brokers' commissions and related costs as part of the cost of acquiring the asset.

Hedge Criteria Established by FAS-80

A futures contract that hedges an existing or anticipated exposure to price or interest rate changes qualifies as a hedge if all of the following conditions are met (FAS-80, par. 4):

1. **Must be designated as a hedge**   A futures contract must be designated by an enterprise as a hedge of identifiable assets, liabilities, firm commitments, or anticipated transactions. A futures contract cannot be accounted for as a hedge until the date it is designated as a hedge by the enterprise. To be designated as a hedge, a futures contract must effectively reduce the enterprise's exposure to the risk of changes in price or interest rate.

☛ **PRACTICE POINTER:** FAS-80 gives management the opportunity to choose how to report changes in the market value of futures contracts that relate to hedge situations. If management designates the contract as a hedge (and all the other criteria are satisfied), do not reflect a change in the market value of the contract in income until the related transaction is completed. On the other hand, if management does not designate the contract as a hedge, recognize a change in the market value of the contract as gain or loss when it appears.

2. **Exposure to the risk of changes in price or interest rates**   The hedged item must be exposed to the risk of changes in market prices or interest rates. Thus, in order for the transaction to qualify as an economic hedge, the hedged item must contribute to the enterprise's risk associated with changes in prices or interest rates. The existence of risk associated with changes in prices or interest rates, and whether a futures contract reduces that risk, may be apparent or may require extensive

analysis and judgment. However, FAS-80 does not permit a futures contract to be accounted for as a hedge of any item that is already effectively hedged by other assets, liabilities, commitments, or other transactions of an enterprise.

The assessment of price risk may be done on a decentralized basis if an enterprise cannot otherwise assess such risk based on the enterprise as a whole and the risk management activities can be assessed on a decentralized basis.

3. **Must reduce exposure to the risk of changes in price or interest rates** The changes in the market value of a futures contract must be highly correlated, at the inception of the contract and throughout the hedge period, to the changes in the fair value of the hedged item(s). It must also be *probable* that changes in the market value of the futures contract will substantially offset the price changes or interest rate changes associated with the hedged item. Thus, the underlying commodity or financial instrument of a futures contract should be identical to the commodity or financial instrument which is hedged. The underlying commodity or financial instrument of a futures contract may differ from the underlying item being hedged, however, if (*a*) there is a clear economic relationship between the prices of the two commodities or financial instruments, and (*b*) a high degree of price correlation is *probable*.

4. **Hedged items reported at fair value** For an item to qualify as an economic hedge under FAS-80, it must generally be accounted for at historical cost or the lower of cost or market, such as investments carried at cost, liabilities carried at historical proceeds, and inventories carried at the lower of cost or market. Thus, enterprises that hedge assets reported at fair value, in accordance with generally accepted accounting principles or specialized industry practices, are required to include the changes in value of both the hedged assets and the related futures contracts in income of the same accounting period (FAS-80, par. 5).

Hedge Accounting

Changes in the market value of a futures contract associated with a hedged item are not recognized in income until the related change in the fair value of the hedged item is also recognized in income. To recognize a change in the market value of a futures contract in a different period from the related change in the fair value of the hedged item would negate the underlying economic effect of the hedging transaction. FAS-80 recognizes the underlying economic effect of a hedging transaction by providing for delayed income recognition of the changes in the market value of futures contracts that meet the hedge criteria. However, FAS-80 does not change current accounting principles or practices for assets, liabilities, or commitments.

Accounting for Hedges of Existing Items

If a futures contract qualifies under FAS-80 as a hedge of an existing asset, liability, or firm commitment, changes in the market value of the futures contract are recognized in income at the same time as the effects of the price or interest rate changes of the hedged item (FAS-80, par. 6). Adjustments of the carrying amount of a hedged item must be accounted for in the same manner as the carrying amount of the item, except for hedged interest-bearing financial instruments that are otherwise reported at amortized cost. Adjustments of the carrying amount of hedged interest-bearing financial instruments that are otherwise reported at amortized cost must begin on the date the hedge is closed out and are amortized as either interest income or interest expense over the expected remaining life of the instrument (FAS-80, par. 7). If a futures contract qualifies under FAS-80 as a hedge of a firm commitment to purchase or sell a commodity or financial instrument at a fixed price, changes in the market value must be included in the ultimate gain or loss on the transaction.

If it is *probable* that both the hedged item and the futures contract will be retained to the delivery date specified in the futures contract, an enterprise may recognize the premium or discount on a hedge contract in income over the life of the contract. The premium or discount is computed at the inception of the hedge by reference to the contracted futures price and the fair value of the hedged item (FAS-80, par. 6).

> **OBSERVATION:** A futures contract may qualify as a hedge of a fixed-rate financial instrument that an enterprise intends to hold to maturity, if the funding for the enterprise's assets has been made with instruments having earlier maturities or repricing dates.

Commodity dealers and others who use futures contracts to hedge a net exposure consisting of inventory held for sale and firm commitments to purchase and sell similar assets may find it impractical to associate specific futures contracts with related hedges, because of the volume and frequency of transactions. In this event, it is permissible to make reasonable allocations of the results of futures contracts between the assets on hand or specific commitments on hand at the end of a reporting period and the assets sold during the period (FAS-80, par. 8).

Assessment of Correlation

An ongoing assessment must be made of the correlation between the changes in the market value of a futures contract and the changes in the fair value of the related hedged item to determine the effectiveness of the hedged transaction. If a high correlation has not been achieved, the enterprise must cease to account for the futures contract as a hedge and must recognize, as a gain or loss in current income, the amount of change in the market value of the futures contract since inception that has not been offset by the change in the fair value of the hedged item (FAS-80, par. 11).

Accounting for Certain Anticipated Transactions

A futures contract may be used to hedge a purchase or sale transaction that an enterprise expects, but is not legally required, to enter into. This type of futures contract is referred to as an *anticipatory hedge*. In an anticipatory hedge, the futures contract does not relate to an enterprise's existing assets, liabilities, or firm commitments (FAS-80, par. 9).

To qualify as an anticipatory hedge, a futures contract must meet the hedge criteria established by FAS-80 (see above). If a futures contract qualifies under FAS-80 as an anticipatory hedge, changes in the market value of the futures contract are included in the ultimate gain or loss on the hedged transaction. If gain or loss in the fair value of an asset or liability will be recognized in income subsequent to its acquisition or issuance, gain or loss on the related futures contract must be recognized at the same time. If the futures contract is closed out before the date of the anticipated transaction, however, the accumulated change in the market value of the contract must be carried forward and included in the ultimate gain or loss on the transaction. When it becomes *probable* that the quantity of the anticipated transaction will be less than originally identified, a pro rata portion of the changes in the market value of the futures contract must be recognized as a gain or loss, and a pro rata portion must be included in the ultimate gain or loss on the transaction (FAS-80, par. 10).

Subject to the limitations described above, changes in the market value of a futures contract that hedges an anticipated transaction that an enterprise expects to occur must be included in the ultimate gain or loss on the anticipated transaction if both of the following conditions are met (FAS-80, par. 9):

1. An enterprise must identify the significant terms of the anticipated transaction, including (*a*) the commodity or type of

financial instrument involved, (*b*) the quantity to be purchased or sold, and (*c*) the expected date of the transaction. As long as all other conditions are met for each possible transaction, an enterprise may identify more than one similar transaction if identification of a single transaction is not possible.

2. It must be *probable* that the anticipated transaction will occur during the normal course of an enterprise's business. In other words, there must be a high level of assurance that the anticipated transaction will occur. The probability that the anticipated transaction will occur must be supported by observable facts and should not be based on management's intent. The likelihood that the anticipated transaction will occur is not sufficiently probable if the anticipated transaction can be abandoned by the enterprise with little cost or disruption of operations.

DISCLOSURE

Enterprises that apply the accounting required by FAS-80 for hedges and anticipated transactions must disclose the following information in their financial statements (FAS-80, par. 12):

- The nature of the items that are hedged or related to futures contracts

- The accounting method(s) used for the futures contracts

- A description of the events or transactions that will result in recognition in income of the changes in value of the futures contracts

Illustration of Nonhedge Contract

On September 14, 19X1 Wallace Company purchased as an investment 10 March 19X2 U.S. Treasury bill (T-bill) futures contracts at 87.50. Each contract was for a three-month $1,000,000 face amount T-bill. On that date, Wallace made an initial cash margin deposit of $40,000 with a broker. Wallace held the contracts through November 15, 19X1, when it closed out all contracts.

The quoted market price of March 19X2 T-bill contracts increased during September to 88.00 and during October to 88.30, and it declined in November to 87.90. Wallace withdrew funds from its margin account at various times in September ($11,500) and October ($4,000), deposited additional funds in November ($5,500) to meet its margin calls, and withdrew the entire balance when the futures position was closed out. Changes in the margin account are summarized as follows:

	September	October	November
Beginning balance	-0-	$41,000	$44,500
Deposit initial margin	$40,000	—	—
Change in market value of futures contracts*	12,500	7,500	(10,000)
Payments to/ withdrawals from account	(11,500)	(4,000)	5,500
Withdrawal of initial margin	—	—	(40,000)
Ending balance	$41,000	$44,500	—

* Each margin point in the price of a T-bill is equal to a $25 change in value. Changes in value are determined for each month as follows:

September: 88.00 – 87.50 = 50 basis points
50 basis points x $25 x 10 contracts = $12,500 gain
October: 88.30 – 88.00 = 30 basis points
30 basis points x $25 x 10 contracts = $7,500 gain
November: 87.90 – 88.30 = 40 basis points
40 basis points x $25 x 10 contracts = $10,000 loss

Wallace Company's financial statements at the end of September and October would show $41,000 and $44,500, respectively, due from its broker. Gains of $12,500 (September) and $7,500 (October) and a loss of $10,000 (November) would be recognized.

Illustration of Hedge of an Anticipated Purchase

Foster Company determined, on November 1, 19X1, that it will need 120,000 bushels of grain in the last week of February 19X2. (The finished product is not sold forward under fixed-price contracts, but is sold at the going market price at the date of sale.) Market conditions indicated that the selling price of the finished product was not likely to be affected significantly during the next few months by changes in the price of grain.

On November 1, Foster purchased 24 March 19X2 futures contracts, each of which was for 5,000 bushels of grain at $3 per bushel. December 31, 19X1 is the end of Foster's financial reporting year, and on that date the closing price of the March 19X2 contract was $2.80 per bushel. On February 24, 19X2, Foster purchased 100,000 bushels of grain through normal channels and closed out the future contracts at $3.15 per bushel.

Changes in the value of the contracts from November 1 to December 31, 19X1, and from January 1 to February 24, 19X2, were as follows:

Nov. 1 – Dec. 31: 24 contracts x 5,000 bushels x ($3.00 – $2.80)
= $24,000 decline

Jan. 1 – Feb. 24: 24 contracts x 5,000 bushels x ($3.15 – $2.80)
= $42,000 increase

If the transaction qualifies as a hedge under FAS-80 and evidence at December 31 indicates that the $24,000 will be recovered on the sale of the finished product, Foster would not recognize the $24,000 loss in its 19X3 financial statements. On February 24, 19X4, the cumulative change of $18,000 ($42,000 – $24,000) would be treated as a reduction in the cost of the grain acquired.

CHAPTER 19
GOVERNMENT CONTRACTS

CONTENTS

CHAPTER 19
GOVERNMENT CONTRACTS

OVERVIEW

Government contracts often include certain unique features, such as being based on the costs incurred by the contractor (i.e., cost-plus-fixed-fee) and being subject to renegotiation and termination.

GAAP for governmental contracts are found in the following pronouncements:

ARB-43   Chapter 11, Government Contracts

           A. Cost-Plus-Fixed-Fee Contracts

           B. Renegotiations

           C. Terminated War and Defense Contracts

FAS-30   Disclosure of Information about Major Customers

CROSS-REFERENCES

1999 MILLER GAAP GUIDE: Chapter 9, "Current Assets and Current Liabilities"; Chapter 31, "Long-Term Construction Contracts"; Chapter 44, "Segment Reporting"

1999 MILLER NOT-FOR-PROFIT REPORTING: Chapter 15, "Office of Management and Budget"

BACKGROUND

Usually, government contracts are performed under a cost-plus-fixed-fee arrangement, which provides for possible renegotiation if the contracting officer for the government believes that excess profits were made by the contractor. These contracts usually also provide that the government may terminate the contract at its convenience.

COST-PLUS-FIXED-FEE CONTRACTS

Cost-plus-fixed-fee (CPFF) contracts generally provide that the government must pay a fixed fee in addition to all costs involved in fulfilling the contract. The contract may include the manufacture of a product or only the performance of services, and the government may or may not withhold a specified percentage of the interim payments until completion of the entire contract. Furthermore, CPFF contracts usually are cancellable by the government. When such contracts are terminated, the contractor is entitled to reimbursement for all costs, plus an equitable portion of the fixed fee (ARB-43, Ch. 11C, par. 13).

One of the main problems in accounting for CPFF contracts is determining when profits should be recognized. As a general rule, profits are not recognized until the right to full payment becomes unconditional, which usually is when the product has been delivered and accepted or the services fully rendered (completed-contract method).

When CPFF contracts extend over several years, however, the percentage-of-completion method is acceptable, provided that costs and profits can be reasonably estimated and realization of the contract is assured reasonably (ARB-43, Ch. 11A, par. 13).

Illustration of Percentage-of-Completion on CPFF Contract

A company enters into a contract with the government that calls for a 20% profit on costs. The percentage-of-completion method is appropriate because costs and profits can be reasonably estimated.

Accumulated costs through the end of the third year of the contract totaled $1,200,000. Profits recognized in the first and second years of the contract were $100,000 and $75,000, respectively.

Profit recognized in the third year of the contract is computed as follows:

Accumulated costs to date	$1,200,000
CPFF percentage	20%
Estimated profit to date	$ 240,000
Profits recognized in previous years ($100,000 + $75,000)	(175,000)
Profit recognized in third year	$ 65,000

☛ **PRACTICE POINTER:** When CPFF contracts involve the manufacture and delivery of products, the reimbursable costs and
fees ordinarily are included in appropriate sales or other rev-

enue accounts. When CPFF contracts involve only services, only the fees ordinarily should be included in revenues.

An advance payment by the government may not be offset as a payment on account, unless it is expected to be applied as such with reasonable certainty. In the event that an advance is offset, it must be disclosed clearly (ARB-43, Ch. 11A, par. 5).

A distinction should be made in the balance sheet between unbilled costs and fees and billed amounts (ARB-43, Ch. 11A, par. 4).

RENEGOTIATION

Renegotiation involves the adjustment of the original selling price or contract. Since the government makes renegotiation adjustments an integral part of a contract, a provision for such probable adjustments is necessary. A provision for renegotiation is based on the contractor's past experience or on the general experience of the particular industry, and it is shown in the income statement as a reduction of the related sales or income. If a reasonable estimate cannot be made, that fact should be disclosed in the financial statements or accompanying notes. The provision for renegotiation is reported as a liability in the balance sheet (ARB-43, Ch. 11B, par. 4). Classification as a current liability is appropriate if the criteria established in ARB-43, Chapter 3A (Current Assets and Current Liabilities) are met.

☛ **PRACTICE POINTER:** In those unusual cases in which collection is not reasonably assured, it may be preferable to employ the installment-sale or cost-recovery method in accounting for a government contract.

When a provision for renegotiation is made in a particular year and the subsequent final adjustment differs materially, show the difference in the income statement of the year of final determination.

Disclosure

When a significant portion of a company's business is derived from government contracts, such disclosure should be made in the financial statements or notes thereto, indicating the uncertainties involved and the possibility of renegotiation in excess of the amount provided. In addition, the basis of determining the provision for renegotiation should be disclosed (prior experience, industry experience, etc.) (ARB-43, Ch. 11B, par. 5). Disclosure is required if 10% or more of an enterprise's revenue is derived from sales to the federal government, a state government, a local government, or a foreign government (FAS-30, par. 6).

TERMINATED WAR AND DEFENSE CONTRACTS

ARB-43, Chapter 11C deals with both fixed-price and CPFF contracts. It addresses the problems involved in the termination of a government contract by the government; it does not cover terminations resulting from default of the contractor (ARB-43, Ch. 11C, par. 1).

The determination of profit or loss on a terminated government contract is made as of the effective date of termination. This is the date that the contractor accrues the right to receive payment on that portion of the contract that has been terminated (ARB-43, Ch. 11C, par. 3).

Although most government contracts provide for a minimum profit percentage formula in the event agreement cannot be reached, the amount of profit to be reported in the case of termination for the convenience of the government is the difference between all allowable costs incurred and the amount of the termination claim (ARB-43, Ch. 11C, pars. 16 and 17).

If a reasonable estimate of the termination claim for reporting purposes cannot be made, full disclosure of this fact should be made by note to the financial statements, which should describe the uncertainties involved (ARB-43, Ch. 11C, par. 4).

Termination claims are classified as current assets if the criteria in ARB-43, Chapter 3A are met. Prior to termination notice, advances received are deducted from termination claims receivable for reporting purposes. Loans received on the security of the contract or termination claim are shown separately as current liabilities (ARB-43, Ch. 11C, par. 6).

The cost of items included in the termination claim that are subsequently reacquired by the contractor is recorded as a new purchase, and the amount is applied as a reduction of the termination claim. These types of reductions from the termination claim generally are referred to as *disposal credits* (ARB-43, Ch. 11C, par. 8).

Disclosure

Material amounts of termination claims are classified separately from other receivables in the financial statements (ARB-43, Ch. 11C, par. 5).

Termination claims are stated at the amount estimated as collectible, and adequate provision or disclosure should be made for items of a controversial nature (ARB-43, Ch. 11C, par. 19).

CHAPTER 20
IMPAIRMENT OF LOANS AND LONG-LIVED ASSETS

CONTENTS

CHAPTER 20
IMPAIRMENT OF LOANS AND
LONG-LIVED ASSETS

OVERVIEW

Recognition of impairment of assets generally is required when events and circumstances indicate that the carrying amount of those assets will not be recovered in the future. For loans, recognition of an impairment loss is required when it is probable that the creditor will not be able to collect all amounts due according to the contractual terms of the loan agreement, including both the contractual interest and the principal receivable. For long-lived plant and identifiable intangible assets that are to be held and used, impairment is indicated when the carrying amount of the asset exceeds the undiscounted future cash flows expected from the asset. For similar assets that are to be disposed of, an impairment loss is recognized when the carrying amount exceeds its net realizable value or its fair value less cost to sell.

GAAP for recognizing impairment of loans and long-lived assets in most situations are found in the following authoritative pronouncements:

FAS-114 Accounting by Creditors for Impairment of a Loan

FAS-118 Accounting by Creditors for Impairment of a Loan— Income Recognition and Disclosures

FAS-121 Accounting for the Impairment of Long-Lived Assets and for Long-Lived Assets to Be Disposed Of

CROSS-REFERENCES

1999 Miller GAAP Guide: Chapter 7, "Contingencies, Risks, and Uncertainties"; Chapter 15, "Extinguishment of Debt"; Chapter 25, "Interest on Receivables and Payables"; Chapter 42, "Results of Operations"; Chapter 48, "Troubled Debt Restructuring"

1999 MILLER GAAP IMPLEMENTATION MANUAL: EITF: Chapter 13, "Impairment of Long-Lived Assets"

BACKGROUND

The issue of impairment of loans was raised primarily because the guidance provided in AICPA Audit and Accounting Guides for different types of financial institutions was inconsistent. This inconsistent guidance resulted in differences in when and how different types of financial institutions recognize losses for impaired loans. FAS-114 was issued to address the accounting by creditors for the impairment of certain loans. FAS-118 subsequently amended FAS-114 with regard to income measurement and disclosure.

Long-lived assets, such as plant and equipment, intangibles, and other similar assets, are initially recorded at cost, which is usually the fair value at the date of acquisition. For most assets, cost is subsequently reduced by depreciation or amortization in a manner that allocates an asset's cost to periods in which the asset is used. This process is referred to as "matching," and it is an important part of the periodic determination of net income. The practice of systematically allocating the cost of a long-lived asset to expense over its estimated useful life was modified in some circumstances in which the value of the asset was believed to be impaired, resulting in a write-down to a new (lower) carrying amount that is less than the remaining unamortized cost. A loss was recognized for such a write-down. This practice was not consistently followed, however, because accounting standards generally did not address when an impairment loss of this type should be recognized or how it should measured.

FAS-121 was issued to standardize practice in this area by providing authoritative guidance on when an impairment loss should be recognized and how the amount of that loss should be measured.

> **OBSERVATION:** FASB Statement of Financial Accounting Concepts 5 (Recognition and Measurement in Financial Statements of Business Enterprises) describes circumstances in which expenses and losses are recognized, indicating that they generally are recognized when economic benefits are used up and the related assets are therefore expected to provide reduced or no future benefits. Concerning the loss or lack of future benefits, CON-5 indicates that a loss is recognized if it becomes evident that previously recognized future economic benefits of an asset have been reduced or eliminated.
>
> Generally, Statements of Financial Accounting Concepts are not intended to establish standards of reporting, but rather to provide a basis upon which those standards will be devel-

oped and evaluated over time. Before the issuance of FAS-121, standards for the recognition and measurement of the impairment of long-lived assets usually were not found in the authoritative literature, and therefore the description cited above from CON-5 was not applied in a consistent manner.

IMPAIRMENT OF LOANS

FAS-114 defines a *loan* as "a contractual right to receive money on demand or on fixed or determinable dates that is recognized as an asset in the creditor's statement of financial position." It addresses how allowances for credit losses related to certain loans should be determined. The Statement has wide applicability, establishing standards for all creditors for impairment of loans (FAS-114, par. 4).

FAS-114 does not specify how a creditor should identify loans that are to be evaluated for collectibility. A creditor may apply its normal loan review procedures in making that judgment. Guidance for this decision is found in the AICPA's Audit Procedure Study *Auditing the Allowance for Credit Losses of Banks* and includes the following items:

- Materiality criterion
- Regulatory reports of examination
- Internally generated listings such as "watch lists," past due reports, overdraft listings, and listings of loans to insiders
- Management reports of total loan amounts by borrower
- Historical loss experience by type of loan
- Loan files lacking current financial data related to borrowers and guarantors
- Borrowers experiencing problems such as operating losses, marginal working capital, inadequate cash flow, or business interruptions
- Loans secured by collateral that is not readily marketable or that is subject to deterioration in realizable value
- Loans to borrowers in industries or countries experiencing economic instability
- Loan documentation and compliance exception reports

Direct write-downs of an impaired loan and assessment of overall adequacy of the allowance for credit losses are not covered in FAS-114.

OBSERVATION: The FASB believes that accounting for impaired loans should be consistent among all creditors and types of loans, except those specifically identified above as loans to which FAS-114 does not apply. The Board was unable to identify any compelling reasons why the lending process for consumer, mortgage, commercial, and other loans—whether uncollateralized or collateralized—is fundamentally different. In addition, the Board could not identify any compelling reasons why different types of creditors should account for impaired loans differently, or why financial statement users for a particular industry or size of entity would be better served by accounting that differs from that of other creditors.

Recognition of Impairment

FAS-114 ties accounting for an impairment of a loan directly to the criteria established in FAS-5 (Accounting for Contingencies) for recognizing a loss contingency. Specifically, FAS-114 indicates that a loan is impaired when it is *probable* that a creditor will be unable to collect all amounts due, including principle and interest, according to the contractual terms and schedules of the loan agreement. Normal loan review procedures are to be used in making that judgment. A loan is not considered impaired if (FAS-114, par. 8):

- There is merely an insignificant delay or shortfall in amounts of payments.

- The creditor expects to collect all amounts due, including interest accrued at the contractual interest rate for the period of the delay.

> **OBSERVATION:** Use of the term *probable* in FAS-114 is consistent with its use in FAS-5. FAS-5 indicates a range of probability that must be considered in the decision to accrue a loss contingency, including *probable, reasonably possible,* and *remote.* Virtual certainty is not required before a loss can be accrued. While FAS-114 changes the wording of FAS-5 as it relates to loan impairments that require accrual, it does not change the overall intent of applying FAS-5 standards (FAS-114, par. 10).

Measurement of Impairment

The process of measuring impaired loans requires judgment and estimation, and the eventual outcomes may differ from the estimates. Following is guidance concerning the measurement of impaired loans under FAS-114. Measurement may be on a loan-by-loan or an aggregate basis (FAS-114, par. 12).

- Impairment generally is based on the present value of expected future cash flows discounted at the loan's effective interest rate. As a practical matter, a creditor may measure impairment based on a loan's observable market price or on the fair value of the collateral if the loan is collateral dependent (FAS-114, par. 13).

- A loan is considered collateral dependent when the creditor determines that foreclosure is probable and the loan is expected to be repaid solely by the underlying collateral (FAS-114, par. 13).

- Estimated costs to sell, on a discounted basis, may be a factor in measuring impairment if those costs are expected to reduce the cash flow available to repay or otherwise satisfy the loan (FAS-114, par. 13).

- If the measurement of the impaired loan is less than the recorded investment in the loan (including accrued interest, net deferred loan fees or costs, and unamortized premium or discount), the creditor shall recognize the impairment by creating or adjusting a valuation allowance with a corresponding charge to bad-debt expense (FAS-114, par. 13).

- The present value amount, based on estimated future cash flows of an impaired loan, is discounted at the loan's contractual interest rate. That rate is the rate of return implicit in the loan (FAS-114, par. 14).

  — For a loan restructured in a troubled debt restructuring, present value is based on the original contractual rate, not on the rate specified in the restructuring agreement.

  — If the loan's contractual rate varies based on changes in an independent factor, such as an index or a rate, the loan's effective interest rate may be calculated based on the factor as it changes over the life of the loan, or it may be fixed at the rate that is in effect at the date the loan meets the impairment criteria. (The alternative chosen shall be applied consistently for all loans whose contractual interest rate varies based on subsequent changes in an independent factor.)

- In estimating expected future cash flows, all available evidence should be considered—including the estimated costs to sell if those costs are expected to reduce the cash flows available to repay or otherwise satisfy the loan. The weight given to the evidence should be commensurate with the extent to which the evidence can be objectively verified (FAS-114, par. 15).

- After the initial measurement of impairment, any significant change in the amount or timing of an impaired loan's expected or actual future cash flows should be reflected by a recalculation of the impairment and an adjustment to the allowance account (FAS-114, par. 16).

> **OBSERVATION:** FAS-114 requires that impairment be measured based on the loan's effective interest rate. Alternatively, impairment can be measured based on a new direct measurement of the asset, reflecting the current market rate of interest. The Board concluded that the measurement of impairment should recognize the change in the net carrying amount of the loan based on new information about expected future cash flows, rather than on other factors that may cause a change in the fair value of an impaired loan.

Income Measurement

FAS-118 amends FAS-114 to indicate that guidance is not provided concerning how a creditor should recognize, measure, or display interest income on an impaired loan. Some accounting methods for recognizing income may result in a recorded investment in an impaired loan that is less than the present value of expected future cash flows (or other basis for valuing the loan). In this case, no additional impairment would be recognized. Those accounting methods include recognition of interest income using a cost-recovery method, a cash-basis method, or some combination of those methods. The recorded investment in an impaired loan also may be less than the present value of expected future cash flows (or other basis for valuing the loan) because the creditor has charged off part of the loan (FAS-118, par. 6g).

Disclosures

FAS-118 requires that the following information be disclosed, either in the body of the financial statements or in accompanying notes, for loans that meet the definition of an impaired loan:

1. As of the date of each statement of financial position, the total recorded investment in the impaired loan at the end of each period and (*a*) the amount of that recorded investment for which there is a related allowance for credit losses determined in accordance with FAS-118 and (*b*) the amount of the recorded investment for which there is no allowance for credit losses in accordance with FAS-118

2. The creditor's policy for recognizing interest income on impaired loans, including how cash receipts are recorded

3. For each period for which results of operations are presented, the average recorded investment in the impaired loans during each period, the related amount of interest income recognized during the time within that period that the loans were im-

paired, and, if practicable, the amount of interest income recognized using a cash-basis method of accounting during the time within that period that the loans were impaired

For each period for which results of operations are presented, a creditor shall disclose the activity in the total allowance for credit losses related to loans, including the beginning balances at the beginning and end of the period, additions charged to operations, direct write-downs charged against the allowance, and recoveries of amounts previously charged off (FAS-118, par. 6i).

IMPAIRMENT OF LONG-LIVED ASSETS

FAS-121 applies to long-lived assets (i.e., plant or fixed assets), to certain identifiable intangibles, to goodwill related to those assets to be held and used, and to long-lived assets and certain identifiable intangible assets to be disposed of. FAS-121 applies to all entities. It does *not* apply to the following types of assets (FAS-121, par. 3):

- Financial instruments
- Long-term customer relationship of a financial institution (e.g., core deposit intangibles and credit cardholder intangibles)
- Mortgage and other servicing rights
- Deferred policy acquisition costs
- Deferred tax assets

Certain FASB Statements establish separate standards of accounting for specific long-lived assets in specialized situations. FAS-121 does not change those standards. Specifically, assets whose accounting is prescribed in the following pronouncements are *not* changed by FAS-121 (FAS-121, par. 4):

- FAS-50—Financial Reporting in the Record and Music Industry
- FAS-53—Financial Reporting by Producers and Distributors of Motion Picture Films
- FAS-63—Financial Reporting by Broadcasters
- FAS-86—Accounting for the Costs of Computer Software to Be Sold, Leased, or Otherwise Marketed
- FAS-90—Regulated Enterprises—Accounting for Abandonments and Disallowances of Plant Costs

Appendix B of FAS-121 provides detailed guidance on the pronouncements that refer to impairment or disposal of assets and indicates whether the standards in those pronouncements are amended by FAS-121 or remain effective after the adoption of FAS-121.

Assets to Be Held and Used

Recognition of Impairment

The first step in applying FAS-121 is to identify assets to be held and used for which an impairment in value may have occurred. This requires a review of long-lived assets and intangible assets when certain events or changes in circumstances indicate that the carrying amount of the asset may not be recoverable.

FAS-121 provides several examples of circumstances that may indicate a problem of recoverability, including the following (FAS-121, par. 4):

1. A significant decrease in the asset's market value

2. A significant change in the way an asset is used

3. A significant physical change in the asset

4. A significant change in legal factors or in business climate that could affect the asset's value or cause an adverse action by a regulator

5. An accumulation of costs significantly in excess of the amount originally expected to acquire or construct the asset

6. A current period or history of operating or cash flow losses that implies continuing losses associated with an asset used to generate revenue

This list includes *examples* of situations that may indicate a need to assess an asset for recoverability and possible impairment. It is not intended to be comprehensive. If these or other circumstances indicate that the carrying amount of an asset that is intended to be held and used may not be recoverable, FAS-121 requires the accountant to determine the future cash flows expected to be generated by the asset, less the future cash flows expected to be required to obtain those inflows. If the sum of these flows is less than the carrying amount of the asset, an impairment loss must be recognized.

☛ **PRACTICE POINTER:** The approach identified in FAS-121 requires the investigation of potential impairments on an **exception basis**. The requirement to compare undiscounted future cash flows with the carrying amount of the asset represents a "trigger mechanism" to assist in identifying those assets that require further analysis. In explaining its conclusions, the FASB states that an asset must be tested for recoverability only if there is reason to believe that the asset is impaired. The FASB expects that the approach of comparing the asset's carrying amount with undiscounted future cash flows will be relatively easy to apply based on information that is generally available to the entity and without incurring the costs of actually projecting future cash flows.

If an impairment loss is recognized and evidence also suggests the need to review the depreciation policy related to the asset, the impairment should be recognized first. In circumstances in which an impairment loss is considered, but not recognized, a review of depreciation policy may also be appropriate. For example, the future cash flows may exceed the carrying value, but the useful life of the asset may be shorter than originally planned.

Measurement of Impairment

Once the need to recognize an impairment loss is established, the amount of that loss is measured as the excess of the carrying amount of the asset over the fair value of the asset. The carrying amount of the asset is its cost less any accumulated depreciation or amortization. The *fair value* of the asset is the amount at which the asset could be bought or sold in a current transaction between willing parties. Fair value, however, is not intended to be determined by the value in a forced or liquidation sale.

FAS-121 identifies three methods of determining fair value (FAS-121, par. 7):

1. Quoted market prices in active markets
2. Estimate based on prices of similar assets
3. Estimate based on valuation techniques

The third method includes the determination of the present value of estimated future cash flows using an appropriate discount rate and other appropriate methods available for valuing the specific asset in question (e.g., option pricing models, matrix pricing, option-adjusted spread models, and fundamentals analysis).

☞ **PRACTICE POINTER:** FAS-121 does not include a strict ranking of the three approaches for valuing impaired assets. However, they are **presented** in the above order, and the surrounding discussion implies a preference for the most direct approach possible. For assets for which an active market exists, valuation by reference to that market is more appropriate than the other two methods. For assets for which there is no active market, but an active market does exist for similar assets, reference to that market is the most appropriate valuation method. The third approach—estimating the value based on an appropriate estimation technique—is more indirect; use it only if the first two methods are not available.

When fair value is estimated on the basis of the present value of expected future cash flows, assets should be grouped at the lowest level for which there are identifiable cash flows that are largely independent of the cash flows of other groups of assets (FAS-121, par. 8). For example, assume a company has four long-lived assets identified as A, B, C, and D. Evidence suggests that the value of Asset A is impaired. If the cash flows of the four assets can be separately identified, those associated with Asset A alone are used to measure the fair value of that asset. On the other hand, if the cash flows of Assets A and B are intermingled such that separate identification of cash flows of each asset is impossible, the joint cash flows of these two assets must be considered in measuring the fair value of Assets A and B combined, even though evidence does not suggest that the value of Asset B is impaired.

☛ **PRACTICE POINTER:** As the level of aggregation of assets in applying FAS-121 goes up, the likelihood that a loss will be recognized goes down. This is because when assets are aggregated, the impairment loss that may exist within one asset is offset by the excess of fair value over carrying amount for the other assets that are part of the aggregation. For example, if impairment appears to exist for Asset A, and if Asset A can be valued independently, a loss is recognized. On the other hand, if the fair value of Asset A cannot be determined independently of Assets B and C, the excess of fair value over carrying amount of these two assets must be overcome by the impairment loss of Asset A before a loss is recognized. When assets are aggregated in applying FAS-121, it is reasonable to conclude that some—perhaps many—impairment losses are never recognized, because they are offset against the fair value in excess of carrying amount of other assets.

Other guidelines in estimating fair value via the present value of expected future cash flows are as follows (FAS-121, par. 9):

- The best estimates based on reasonable and supportable assumptions and projections should be used.
- All available evidence should be considered.

- The weight given to evidence should be commensurate with the extent to which the evidence can be verified objectively.

- If a range is determined for factors underlying the estimate of fair value, the likelihood of possible outcomes shall be considered in determining the best estimate of future cash flows.

In limited circumstances, it is possible for an asset not to have identifiable cash flows that are independent from other asset groupings. If such an asset is not expected to provide service potential to the entity, the asset should be accounted for as an abandonment or held for disposal (covered later in this chapter). If the asset is expected to provide service potential, an impairment loss should be recognized if the sum of the expected future cash flows (undiscounted and without interest charges) for the entity is less than the carrying amount of the entity's assets covered by FAS-121 (FAS-121, par. 10).

Once an impairment loss has been recognized, the new (reduced) carrying amount is considered its cost. For a depreciable asset, that cost is recognized as depreciation over the asset's remaining useful life. An impairment loss on an asset to be held and used, once recognized, cannot be restored (FAS-121, par. 11).

Illustration of Recognizing an Impairment Loss on Assets to Be Held and Used

Zeta Company has machinery for which circumstances indicate a potential impairment in value. The machinery cost $100,000 and has accumulated depreciation of $35,000, resulting in a carrying amount of $65,000. The first step is to determine how the undiscounted future cash flows compare with $65,000. Assuming that those cash flows are estimated to be $50,000, an impairment loss is evident. The next step is to determine the fair value of the asset by the appropriate method (i.e., quoted market price, estimate based on similar assets, estimate based on an appropriate valuation technique). If the fair value is determined to be $40,000, the result is an impairment loss of $25,000, computed as follows:

Asset cost	$100,000
Less: Accumulated depreciation	35,000
Carrying amount	$ 65,000
Less: Fair value	40,000
Impairment loss	$ 25,000

An impairment loss of $25,000 is recognized, and $40,000 is now considered the cost of the asset for future accounting and depreciation purposes. Notice that the undiscounted future cash flow of $50,000 is used only to identify the need to measure the amount of the impairment loss. That amount is not used directly to determine of the amount of the loss, although it may be useful if the fair value is determined by estimating the present value of future cash flows.

Goodwill

Assets that were acquired in a purchase business combination in which goodwill arose may be tested for recoverability. In determining this recoverability, the goodwill that arose should be included as part of the asset grouping. If only some of the assets acquired in that transaction are being tested, goodwill should be allocated to the assets being tested on a pro rata basis, using the relative fair values of the long-lived and other identifiable intangibles unless another method is more appropriate. When goodwill is identified in this way with assets that are subject to impairment loss, the carrying amount of the identifiable goodwill should be eliminated before the carrying amount of any other assets is reduced (FAS-121, par. 12).

Illustration of Recognizing an Impairment Loss with Related Goodwill

Alpha Company has property, plant, and equipment costing $1,000,000 that it acquired in a purchase business combination that resulted in the recognition of $400,000 of goodwill. The amount of other assets acquired is relatively small and the entire goodwill is related to the property, plant, and equipment. Several years later, depreciation has reduced the carrying amount of the property, plant, and equipment to $600,000 and the amortization has reduced the carrying amount of the goodwill to $300,000. Now, machinery with an original cost of $250,000 requires recognition of an impairment loss in accordance with FAS-121 because its undiscounted future cash flows are only $140,000. Its fair value is determined to be only $135,000. The amount of the loss is determined as follows:

Asset cost	$250,000
Less: Accumulated depreciation*	(100,000)
Carrying amount	$150,000
Plus: Related goodwill**	75,000
Asset basis for determining loss	$225,000
Fair value of impaired asset	(135,000)
Impairment loss	$ 90,000

> *40% of asset cost, determined by applying accumulated depreciation percentage to $1,000,000 cost. Depreciation percentage = ($1,000,000 − $600,000)/$1,000,000 = 40%. 40% x $250,000 = $100,000.

> **25% of carrying amount of goodwill, determined by calculating the relative cost of the impaired assets to the total cost: $250,000/$1,000,000 = 25%. 25% x $300,000 goodwill = $75,000.

The $90,000 impairment loss is recognized by first writing off $75,000 of goodwill and then writing off $15,000 of machinery.

Reporting and Disclosure

An impairment loss recognized for assets to be held and used is to be reported as a component of income from continuing operations before income taxes (1) in the income statement for a profit-seeking organization and (2) in the statement of activities for a not-for-profit organization. If the entity chooses to report a subtotal such as "income from operations," that amount must include the impairment loss (FAS-121, par. 13).

The following information must be included in the period in which an impairment loss is recognized (FAS-121, par. 14):

1. Description of the impaired assets, including the facts and circumstances leading to the impairment

2. Amount of the impairment loss and how fair value was determined

3. Location of the impairment loss in the income statement (e.g., separate caption, parenthetical disclosure, or specification of the caption in the income statement [or statement of activities] in which the impairment loss is aggregated)

4. Business segment(s) affected (if applicable)

Accounting for an impairment loss for assets held and used involves a series of steps. It begins with events and circumstances that suggest the need to consider the existence of an impairment loss, and it ends with the actual measurement and recognition of that loss as the excess of the asset's carrying amount over its fair value. That process is summarized in Figure 20-1.

Assets to Be Disposed Of

Recognition and Measurement

FAS-121 ties accounting for impairment of assets to be disposed of to APB-30 (Reporting the Results of Operations—Reporting the Effects of Disposal of a Segment of a Business, and Extraordinary, Unusual, and Infrequently Occurring Events and Transactions). APB-30 specifies accounting for the disposal of a segment of a business and requires certain assets included in that type of transaction to be measured at the lower of carrying amount or net realizable value. Long-lived and intangible assets subject to the requirements of FAS-121 that are not covered by APB-30 should be reported at the lower of carrying amount or fair value less cost to sell. Fair value is determined in the same manner as it is determined for assets to be held and used (covered earlier in this chapter) (FAS-121, par. 15).

Figure 20-1: Impairment of Assets Held and Used

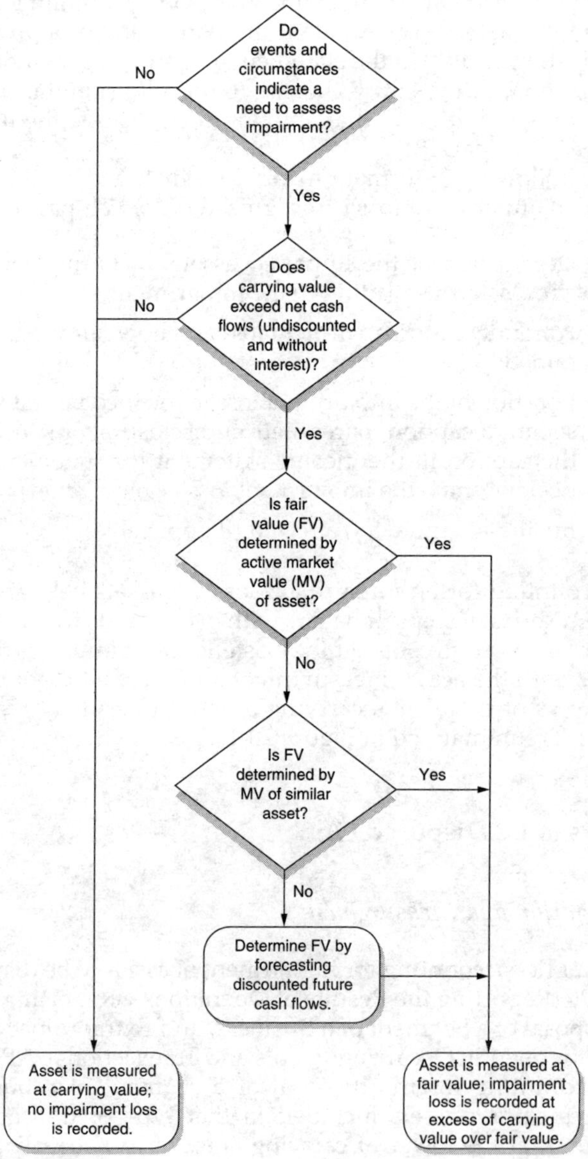

Determining the cost to sell an asset to be disposed of may require significant judgment. FAS-121 contains the following guidelines for determining fair value less cost to sell (FAS-121, par. 16):

1. Incremental direct costs to transact the sale of the asset, such as broker commissions, legal and title transfer fees, and closing costs, are generally *included* in the cost to sell.

2. Costs that are generally *excluded* from the cost to sell are insurance, security services, utility expense, and other costs of protecting or maintaining the asset.

3. If the fair value of the asset is determined by discounting expected future cash flows and if the sale is expected to occur beyond one year, the cost to sell the asset is discounted.

4. Depreciation is not recognized on assets to be disposed of while they are held for disposal.

☛ **PRACTICE POINTER:** Many estimates are required to determine the fair value of and the cost to sell such an asset. Revisions in estimates of fair value less cost to sell are appropriately reported as adjustments to the carrying amount of the asset, subject to the limitation that the asset's carrying amount cannot exceed its carrying amount before adjustment was made to reflect the decision to dispose of the asset.

Accounting for the impairment of assets held for disposal is summarized in Figure 20-2.

Reporting and Disclosure

FAS-121 indicates reporting and disclosure requirements for impairment in value of assets to be disposed of.

OBSERVATION: FAS-121, paragraph 17, may result in an increase or a decrease in the carrying amount of the impaired asset to be disposed of, subsequent to the initial recognition of an impairment loss. This appears to be a difference in accounting for assets to be held and used and assets to be disposed of. Once an impairment loss is recognized on assets to be held and used, it cannot be restored.

Adjustment to reflect the impairment of an asset to be disposed of is reported in the same manner as a similar adjustment for assets to be held and used—as a component of income from continuing operations before income taxes in the income statement (profit-seeking entities) or the statement of activities (not-for-profit entities). Any subtotal identified as "income from operations" or other similar description must include the amount recognized for the impairment of the asset to be disposed of (FAS-121, par. 18):

Additional information that must be disclosed in the financial statement or related notes includes (FAS-121, par. 19):

1. Description of assets to be disposed of, including the facts and circumstances leading to the expected disposal, the expected disposal date, and the carrying amount of the assets

2. The business segment(s) in which the assets to be disposed of are held (if applicable)

3. The loss, if any, resulting from the application of FAS-121 or APB-30

4. The gain or loss, if any, resulting from changes in the carrying amounts of assets to be disposed of that arise subsequent to the initial recognition of impairment

5. The location in the income statement (or statement of activities) in which the items included in (3) and (4) are presented if they are not presented as a separate caption or reported parenthetically

6. The results of operations for assets to be disposed of to the extent those results are included in results of operations and can be identified

Figure 20-2: Impairment of Assets for Disposal

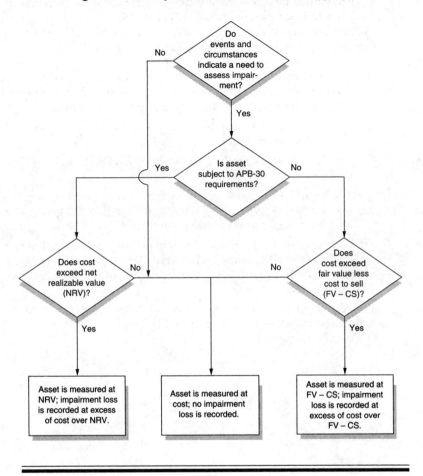

CHAPTER 21
INCOME TAXES

CONTENTS

CHAPTER 21
INCOME TAXES

OVERVIEW

The tax consequences of many transactions recognized in the financial statements are included in determining income taxes currently payable in the same accounting period. Sometimes, however, tax laws differ from the recognition and measurement requirements of financial reporting standards. Differences arise between the tax bases of assets or liabilities and their reported amounts in the financial statements. These differences are called *temporary differences* and they give rise to deferred tax assets and liabilities.

Temporary differences ordinarily reverse when the related asset is recovered or the related liability is settled. A *deferred tax liability* or *deferred tax asset* represents the increase or decrease in taxes payable or refundable in future years as a result of temporary differences and carryforwards at the end of the current year.

The objectives of accounting for income taxes are to recognize:

- The amount of taxes payable or refundable for the current year

- The deferred tax liabilities and assets that result from future tax consequences of events that have been recognized in the enterprise's financial statements or tax returns

GAAP for accounting for income taxes are in the following pronouncements:

APB-10	Paragraph 6, Tax Allocation Accounts—Discounting Paragraph 7, Offsetting Securities against Taxes Payable
APB-23	Accounting for Income Taxes—Special Areas
FAS-109	Accounting for Income Taxes
FIN-18	Accounting for Income Taxes in Interim Periods

CROSS-REFERENCES

1999 MILLER GAAP GUIDE: Chapter 26, "Interim Financial Reporting"; Chapter 28, "Investment Tax Credit "; Chapter 39, "Quasi-Reorganizations"; Chapter 42, "Results of Operations"

1999 MILLER GAAP IMPLEMENTATION MANUAL: Chapter 12, "Income Taxes"

1999 MILLER GAAP IMPLEMENTATION MANUAL: EITF: Chapter 14, "Income Taxes"

1999 MILLER NOT-FOR-PROFIT REPORTING: Chapter 2, "Overview of Current Pronouncements"; Chapter 13, "Tax Reporting Requirements"

1998/1999 MILLER AUDIT PROCEDURES: Chapter 16, "Income Taxes"

1999 MILLER HUD AUDIT PROCEDURES: Appendix I, "Income Taxes"

BACKGROUND

FAS-109 superseded FAS-96 (Accounting for Income Taxes) and addresses financial accounting and reporting for income taxes. FAS-109 changed accounting for income taxes from the deferred method, required by APB-11 (Accounting for Income Taxes), to the asset/liability method, commonly referred to as simply the *liability method*.

The *deferred method* placed primary emphasis on the matching of revenues and expenses. Income tax expense was determined by applying the current income tax rate to pretax accounting income. Any difference between the resulting expense and the amount of income taxes payable was an adjustment to deferred income taxes. The deferred method focused first on the income statement, and adjustments to balance sheet elements were determined by the measurement of income tax expense.

The *asset/liability method* places primary emphasis on the valuation of current and deferred tax assets and liabilities. The amount of income tax expense recognized for a period is the amount of income taxes currently payable or refundable, plus or minus the change in aggregate deferred tax assets and liabilities. The method focuses first on the balance sheet, and the amount of income tax expense is determined by changes in the elements of the balance sheet.

THE ASSET/LIABILITY METHOD

FAS-109 requires income taxes to be accounted for by the asset/liability method. Its main effects on financial statements include the following:

1. Primary emphasis is placed on the recognition and measurement of deferred tax assets and liabilities. Deferred income tax expense is determined residually (i.e., as the difference between the beginning and required ending balances in deferred tax assets and liabilities for the period).

2. Deferred tax asset and liability amounts are remeasured when tax rates change to approximate more closely the amounts at which those assets and liabilities will be realized or settled.

3. Deferred tax assets are recognized for operating loss and other carryforwards. Deferred tax assets are subject to reduction by a valuation allowance if evidence indicates that it is *more likely than not* that some or all of the deferred tax assets will not be realized. Determining this valuation allowance is similar to accounting for reductions in receivables to net realizable value.

4. Disclosure requirements result in the presentation of a significant amount of information in the notes to the financial statements.

GENERAL PROVISIONS OF FAS-109

Scope

FAS-109 requires what traditionally has been referred to as "comprehensive income tax allocation," as opposed to partial allocation or nonallocation. This means that the income tax effects of all revenues, expenses, gains, losses, and other events that create differences between the tax bases of assets and liabilities and their amounts for financial reporting are required to be recognized (FAS-109, par. 3).

FAS-109 is applicable to (FAS-109, par. 4):

1. Domestic federal income taxes and foreign, state, and local taxes based on income.

2. An enterprise's domestic and foreign operations that are consolidated, combined, or accounted for by the equity method.

3. Foreign enterprises in preparing financial statements in accordance with U.S. GAAP.

Three important financial statement issues are specifically set aside and not covered by FAS-109 (FAS-109, par. 5):

1. Accounting for the investment tax credit (ITC)
2. Accounting for income taxes in interim periods
3. Discounting deferred income taxes

Accounting for the ITC and accounting for income taxes in interim periods are covered by existing authoritative pronouncements, which FAS-109 does not affect. Accounting for the ITC is covered in APB-2 (Accounting for the "Investment Credit") and APB-4 (Accounting for the "Investment Credit"), and accounting for income taxes in interim periods is discussed in APB-28 (Interim Financial Reporting) and FIN–18. The issue of discounting deferred income taxes is beyond the scope of FAS-109 and is included in a separate broad project the FASB currently has underway concerning discounting in financial statements.

Basic Principles of the Asset/Liability Method

The objectives of accounting for income taxes are identified in terms of elements of the balance sheet (FAS-109, par. 6):

1. To recognize the amount of taxes currently payable or refundable
2. To recognize the deferred tax assets and liabilities for the future tax consequences of events that have been recognized in the financial statements or in tax returns

This emphasis on the balance sheet is consistent with the liability method of accounting for income taxes incorporated in FAS-109.

Four basic principles are particularly important in understanding the liability method and the procedures that are developed in FAS-109 for accounting for income taxes. Each basic principle focuses on the elements of the balance sheet relating to income taxes (FAS-109, par. 8):

1. Recognize a *tax liability or asset* for the amount of taxes currently payable or refundable.
2. Recognize a *deferred tax liability or asset* for the estimated future tax effects of temporary differences or carryforwards.
3. Measure *current* and *deferred tax assets* and *liabilities* based on provisions of enacted tax laws.
4. Reduce the amount of any deferred *tax assets* by a valuation allowance, if necessary, based on available evidence.

The following are exceptions to these basic principles (FAS-109, par. 9):

1. Certain exceptions to the requirements for recognition of deferred tax assets and liabilities for the areas addressed by APB-23 as amended by FAS-109, paragraphs 31–34, notably the investments in foreign subsidiaries and joint ventures

2. Special transitional procedures for temporary differences related to deposits in statutory reserve funds by U.S. steamship enterprises

3. Accounting for leveraged leases as required by FAS-13 (Accounting for Leases) and FIN-21 (Accounting for Leases in a Business Combination)

4. Prohibition of the recognition of a deferred tax liability or asset related to goodwill for which amortization is not deductible for tax purposes

5. Accounting for income taxes under ARB-51 (Consolidated Financial Statements)

6. Prohibition of the recognition of a deferred tax liability or asset for differences related to assets and liabilities accounted for under FAS-52 (Foreign Currency Translation)

Temporary Differences

Deferred tax assets and liabilities that result from temporary differences are based on the assumption that assets and liabilities in an entity's balance sheet eventually will be realized or settled at their recorded amounts (FAS-109, par. 11).

The following major categories of temporary differences refer to events that result in differences between the tax bases of assets and liabilities and their reported amounts in the financial statements (FAS-109, par. 11):

1. Revenues or gains that are taxable after they are recognized in accounting income (e.g., receivables from installment sales)

2. Expenses or losses that are deductible for tax purposes after they are recognized in accounting income (e.g., a product warranty liability)

3. Revenues or gains that are taxable before they are recognized in accounting income (e.g., subscriptions received in advance)

4. Expenses or losses that are deductible for tax purposes before they are recognized in accounting income (e.g., depreciation expense)

Other less common examples of temporary differences are:

1. Investment tax credits accounted for by the deferred method.
2. Business combinations accounted for by the purchase method.

Taxable and Deductible Temporary Differences

An important distinction in applying the procedures required to account for income taxes by the asset/liability method under FAS-109 is the difference between *taxable* and *deductible* temporary differences. A *taxable temporary difference* is one that will result in the payment of income taxes in the future when the temporary difference reverses. A *deductible temporary difference* is one that will result in reduced income taxes in future years when the temporary difference reverses (FAS-109, par. 13). Taxable temporary differences give rise to deferred tax liabilities; deductible temporary differences give rise to deferred tax assets. Table 21-1 further illustrates this important difference between taxable and deductible temporary differences.

The expanded definition of *temporary differences* in FAS-109 includes some items that do not appear in the company's balance sheet. For example, a company may expense organization costs when they are incurred but recognize them as a tax deduction in a later year. Between the two events, no balance-sheet item exists for this type of temporary difference (FAS-109, par. 15).

The identification of temporary differences may require significant professional judgment. Similar items may be temporary differences in one instance and not in another. For example, the excess of the cash surrender value of life insurance over premiums paid is a temporary difference and results in deferred taxes if the cash surrender value is expected to be recovered by surrendering the policy, but it is not a temporary difference and does not result in deferred taxes if the asset is expected to be recovered upon the death of the insured (FAS-109, par. 14). Management intent and professional judgment are important factors in making the appropriate determination of the nature of assets and liabilities of this type.

☞ **PRACTICE POINTER:** Developing a system for identifying and tracking the amounts of all temporary differences and carry-forwards is an important implementation issue for FAS-109. Theoretically, differences should be identified by comparing items and amounts in the entity's balance sheets for accounting purposes and for tax purposes. Many companies do not maintain tax-basis balance sheets, though this may be the most logical way to identify and track temporary differences in relatively complex situations in which FAS-109 is applied.

Table 21-1: Examples of Taxable and Deductible Temporary Differences

Nature of Temporary Difference	Explanation	Deferred Tax
Taxable Temporary Differences		
Depreciable assets	Use of modified accelerated cost recovery system (MACRS) for tax purposes and straight-line for accounting purposes makes the tax basis of the asset less than the accounting basis	Liability, to be paid as MACRS deduction becomes less than straight-line depreciation
Installment sale receivable	Sales recognized for accounting purposes at transaction date and deferred for tax purposes until collection, resulting in a difference between the tax and accounting basis of the installment receivable	Liability, to be paid when the sale is recognized for tax purposes
Deductible Temporary Differences		
Warranty liability	Expense recognized on accrual basis for accounting purposes and on cash basis for tax purposes, resulting in a liability that is recognized for financial reporting purposes but has a zero basis for tax purposes	Asset, to be recovered when deduction is recognized for tax purposes
Accounts receivable/ allowance for doubtful accounts	Expense recognized on an accrual basis for accounting purposes and deferred for tax purposes	Asset, to be recovered when uncollectible account is written off for tax purposes

FAS-109 carries forward the APB-11 concept of *permanent differences*, although that term is not used. FAS-109 points out that certain differences between the tax basis and the accounting basis of assets and liabilities will not result in taxable or deductible amounts in future years, and no deferred tax asset or liability should be recognized (FAS-109, par. 14).

Recognizing and Measuring Deferred Tax Assets and Liabilities

The emphasis placed on the balance sheet by the asset/liability method of accounting for income taxes is evident from the focus on the recognition of deferred tax liabilities and assets. The change in these liabilities and assets is combined with the income taxes currently payable or refundable to determine income tax expense (FAS-109, par. 16).

Five steps are required to complete the annual computation of deferred tax liabilities and assets (FAS-109, par. 17):

1. Identify the types and amounts of existing temporary differences and the nature and amount of each type of operating loss and tax credit carryforward and the remaining length of the carryforward period.

2. Measure the total deferred tax liability for taxable temporary differences using the applicable tax rate.

3. Measure the total deferred tax asset for deductible temporary differences and operating loss carryforwards using the applicable tax rate.

4. Measure deferred tax assets for each type of tax credit carryforward.

5. Reduce deferred tax assets by a valuation allowance if it is more likely than not that some or all of the deferred tax assets will not be realized.

Valuation Allowance and Tax-Planning Strategies

Determining the need for and calculating the amount of the valuation allowance requires the following steps at the end of each accounting period (FAS-109, par. 21):

1. Determine the amount of the deferred tax asset recognized on each deductible temporary difference, operating loss, and tax credit carryforward. (These are not offset by the deferred tax liability on taxable temporary differences.)

2. Assess the sources of future taxable income which may be available to recognize the deductible differences and carryforwards by considering the following:

   a. Taxable income in prior carryback year(s) if carryback is permitted under tax law

   b. Future reversals of existing taxable temporary differences

   c. Tax-planning strategies that would make income available at appropriate times in the future that would otherwise not be available

   d. Future taxable income exclusive of reversing differences and carryforwards

☛ **PRACTICE POINTER:** The four sources of income are organized differently here than in FAS-109 in order to emphasize the implementation of the standard. In identifying income to support the recognition of deferred tax assets (and thereby supporting a case that an allowance is not required), a logical approach is to consider sources of income in order from the most objective to the least objective. Income in prior carryback years is most objective, followed by the income from the reversal of taxable temporary differences, income resulting from tax planning strategies, and finally, future income from other sources.

3. Based on all available evidence, make a judgment concerning the realizability of the deferred tax asset.

4. Record the amount of the valuation allowance, or change in the valuation allowance (the example below assumes that the allowance is being recorded for the first time or is being increased for $100,000).

Income tax expense	$100,000	
Allowance to reduce deferred		
tax asset to lower recoverable		
value		$100,000

OBSERVATION: FAS-109 relaxes the criteria for recognizing deferred tax assets by requiring the recognition of deferred tax assets for all deductible temporary differences and all operating loss and tax credit carryforwards. An important adjunct to this provision, however, is the requirement to determine the need for, and amount of, a valuation allowance to reduce the deferred tax asset to its realizable value. The valuation allowance aspects of FAS-109 require significant judgment on the part of accountants and auditors of financial statements. A valuation allowance is required if it is more likely than not that some or all of the deferred tax assets will not be realized. *More likely than not* is defined as a likelihood of more than 50%.

Applicable Tax Rate

Reference to the applicable tax rate is made in the four steps identified above. The *applicable tax rate* is that rate expected to apply to
taxable income in the periods in which the deferred tax liability or
asset is expected to be settled or realized based on enacted tax law. If
the entity's taxable income is low enough to make the graduated tax
rates a significant factor, the entity uses the average graduated tax
rate applicable to the amount of estimated annual taxable income in
the periods in which the deferred tax liability or asset is expected to
be settled or realized (FAS-109, par. 18). For example, if a company
has taxable temporary differences of $20,000 that are expected to
reverse in a year when no other income is expected, the applicable
tax rate under current tax law is 15% and the deferred tax liability is:

$$\$20,000 \times 15\% = \$3,000$$

If the taxable temporary differences total $60,000, graduated tax
rates become a factor (the tax rate changes at $50,000); deferred taxes
are $10,000:

$$\$50,000 \times 15\% = \$\ 7,500$$
$$\$10,000 \times 25\% = \underline{\ \ 2,500}$$
$$\underline{\underline{\$10,000}}$$

The average applicable tax rate is 16.67%.

$$\$10,000 / \$60,000 = 16.67\%$$

☛ **PRACTICE POINTER:** Determining the applicable tax rate may
be a very simple task, or it may require careful analysis and
professional judgment. When an entity has been consistently
profitable at sufficiently high levels that graduated tax rates are
not a significant factor, use the single flat tax rate at which all
income is used to compute the amount of deferred taxes on
cumulative temporary differences. If a company experiences
intermittent tax loss and tax income years, or if the company is
consistently profitable at a level low enough that the graduated
tax rates are a significant factor, greater judgment is required to
determine the applicable tax rate under FAS-109.

Deferred tax assets and liabilities are remeasured at the end of
each accounting period and adjusted for changes in the amounts of
cumulative temporary differences and for changes in the applicable
income tax rate, as well as for other changes in the tax law (FAS-109,
par. 27). As a result of this procedure, the deferred tax provision is a
combination of two elements:

1. The change in deferred taxes because of the change in the amounts of temporary differences

2. The change in deferred taxes because of a change in the tax rate caused by new enacted rates or a change in the applicability of graduated tax rates (or other changes in the tax law)

Treating the change in income tax rates in this manner is consistent with accounting for a change in estimate under APB-20 (Accounting Changes).

Tax-Planning Strategies

Consideration of tax-planning strategies is also required by FAS-109. Tax-planning strategies are an important part of determining the need for, and the amount of, the valuation allowance for deferred tax assets. FAS-109 describes tax-planning strategies as actions that (FAS-109, par. 22):

1. Are prudent and feasible

2. The entity might not ordinarily take, but *would* take to prevent an operating loss or tax credit carryforward from expiring before it is used

3. Would result in the realization of deferred tax assets

Examples include actions the entity could take to accelerate taxable income to utilize expiring carryforwards, to change the character of taxable or deductible amounts from ordinary income or loss to capital gain or loss, and to switch from tax-exempt to taxable investments.

Negative Evidence

If negative evidence is present, such as cumulative losses in recent years, it is difficult to conclude that a valuation allowance is not necessary. Other examples of negative evidence are (FAS-109, par. 23):

1. A history of operating loss or tax credit carryforwards expiring before they are used

2. Losses expected in early future years

3. Unsettled circumstances that, if unfavorably resolved, would adversely affect future operations and profit levels on a continuing basis in future years

4. A carryback or carryforward period that is so brief that it significantly limits the probability of realizing deferred tax assets

Positive Evidence

Positive evidence supports a conclusion that a valuation allowance is *not required*. Examples of positive evidence are (FAS-109, par. 24):

1. Existing contracts or firm sales backlog that will produce more than enough taxable income to realize the deferred tax asset based on existing sales prices and cost structures
2. An excess of appreciated asset value over the tax basis of the entity's net assets in an amount sufficient to realize the deferred tax asset
3. A strong earnings history exclusive of the loss that created the future deductible amount, coupled with evidence indicating that the loss is an aberration rather than a continuing condition

> ☛ **PRACTICE POINTER:** Projecting the reversal of temporary differences for each future year individually is commonly referred to as "scheduling." Does FAS-109 require scheduling? On the one hand, the requirement to recognize deferred tax assets and liabilities for all taxable and deductible temporary differences, as well as for all carryforwards, seems to diminish or eliminate the need to schedule. Also, using a flat tax rate in determining the amount of deferred tax assets and liabilities, as described earlier, diminishes the need to schedule individual future years. On the other hand, scheduling may help determine the need for, and amount of, a valuation allowance, including the consideration of tax-planning strategies. To determine the availability of taxable income in the appropriate years—to take advantage of deferred tax assets and to make the judgments concerning the valuation allowance—projecting taxable income from known or estimated sources by year may still be important.

Professional judgment is required in considering the relative impact of negative and positive evidence to determine the need for, and amount of, the valuation allowance for deferred tax assets. The weight given the effect of negative and positive evidence should be commensurate with the extent to which it can be objectively verified. The more negative evidence exists, the more positive evidence is needed to conclude that a valuation allowance is not required (FAS-109, par. 25).

The effect of a change in the valuation allowance that results from a change in circumstances, which in turn causes a change in judgment about the realizability of the related deferred tax asset, is included in income from continuing operations with limited exceptions (FAS-109, par. 26).

SPECIALIZED APPLICATIONS OF FAS-109

Several specialized applications of FAS-109 are summarized briefly below:

Change in Tax Status

An enterprise's tax status may change from nontaxable or taxable or taxable to nontaxable. A deferred tax liability or asset shall be recognized for temporary differences at the date that a nontaxable enterprise becomes a taxable enterprise. A deferred tax liability or asset shall be eliminated at the date an enterprise becomes a nontaxable enterprise (FAS-109, par. 28).

Regulated Enterprises

Regulated enterprises are *not* exempt from the requirements of FAS-109. Specifically, FAS-109 (FAS-109, par. 29):

1. Prohibits net-of-tax accounting and reporting
2. Requires recognition of a deferred tax liability for tax benefits that flow through to customers when temporary differences originate and for the equity component of the allowance for funds used during construction
3. Requires adjustment of a deferred tax liability or asset for an enacted change in tax laws or rates

If as a result of an action by a regulator, it is probable that the future increase or decrease in taxes payable for items (2) and (3) above will be restored from or returned to customers through future rates, an asset or a liability is recognized for that probable future revenue or reduction in future revenue in accordance with FAS-71 (Accounting for the Effects of Certain Types of Regulation). That asset or liability is a temporary difference for which a deferred tax liability or asset is required.

Business Combinations

A deferred tax asset or liability is recognized for differences between the assigned values (i.e., allocated portion of historical cost) and the tax bases of assets and liabilities resulting from a business combination (in contrast to the recording of these items on a net-of-tax basis, as required by APB-11). If a valuation allowance is recognized for the deferred tax asset for an acquired entity's deductible temporary differences, operating loss, or tax credit carryforward at the acquisition date, the tax benefits for those items that are first recognized in financial statements after the acquisition date are applied in the following order (FAS-109, par. 30):

1. Reduce to zero any goodwill related to the acquisition.
2. Reduce to zero other noncurrent intangible assets related to the acquisition.
3. Reduce income tax expense.

APB-23 and U.S. Steamship Enterprises

A deferred tax liability is not recognized for the following temporary differences unless it becomes apparent that they will reverse in the foreseeable future (FAS-109, par. 31):

1. An excess of the amount for financial reporting over the tax basis of an investment in a foreign subsidiary or a foreign corporate joint venture as defined in APB-18 (The Equity Method of Accounting for Investments in Common Stock) that is essentially permanent in nature
2. For a domestic subsidiary or a domestic corporate joint venture that is essentially permanent in duration, undistributed earnings that arose in fiscal years beginning on or before December 15, 1992
3. "Bad debt reserves" for tax purposes of U.S. savings and loan associations and other qualified thrifts that arose in tax years beginning before December 31, 1987
4. Policyholders' surplus of stock life insurance companies that arose in fiscal years beginning on or before December 15, 1992

A deferred tax liability is recognized for the following types of taxable temporary differences (FAS-109, par. 32):

1. An excess of the amount of accounting basis over the tax basis of an investment in a domestic subsidiary that arises in fiscal years beginning after December 15, 1992
2. An excess of the amount for accounting purposes over the tax basis of an investment in a 50%-or-less-owned investee except as provided in FAS-109 for a foreign corporate joint venture that is essentially permanent in nature

3. "Bad debt reserves" for tax purposes of U.S. savings and loan associations and other qualified thrifts that arise in tax years beginning after December 31, 1987

Whether an excess of the amount for accounting purposes over the tax basis of an investment in a more-than-50%-owned domestic subsidiary is a taxable temporary difference must be assessed. It is not a taxable temporary difference if the tax law provides a means by which the reported amount of that investment can be recovered tax-free and the enterprise expects that it will ultimately use that means (FAS-109, par. 33).

A deferred tax asset is recognized for an excess of the tax basis over the amount for accounting purposes of an investment in a subsidiary or corporate joint venture that is essentially permanent in duration only if it is apparent that the temporary difference will reverse in the foreseeable future (FAS-109, par. 34).

Intraperiod Tax Allocation

Income tax expense or benefit for the year shall be allocated among continuing operations, discontinued operations, extraordinary items, and items charged or credited directly to shareholders' equity. The amount allocated to continuing operations is the tax effect of the pretax income or loss from continuing operations that occurred during the year, plus or minus income tax effects of:

- Changes in circumstances that cause a change in judgment about the realization of deferred tax assets
- Changes in tax laws or rates
- Changes in tax status
- Tax-deductible dividends paid to shareholders, except for dividends paid on unallocated shares held by an employee stock ownership plan (ESOP)

The remainder is allocated to items other than continuing operations (FAS-109, par. 35).

The tax effects of the following items are charged or credited directly to the related components of stockholders' equity (FAS-109, par. 36):

1. Adjustments of the opening balance of retained earnings for certain changes in accounting principles or to correct an error
2. Gains and losses included in comprehensive income but excluded from net income
3. An increase or decrease in contributed capital

4. An increase in the tax basis of assets acquired in a taxable business combination accounted for as a pooling of interests and for which a tax benefit is recognized at the date of the business combination

5. Expenses for employee stock options recognized differently for accounting and tax purposes

6. Dividends that are paid on unallocated shares held by an ESOP and that are charged to retained earnings

7. Deductible temporary differences and carryforwards that existed at the date of a quasi-reorganization

Generally, the tax benefit of an operating loss carryforward or carryback is reported in the same manner as the source of the income or loss in the current year, and not in the same manner as (a) the source of the operating loss carryforward or taxes paid in a prior year or (b) the source of expected future income that will result in realization of deferred tax assets for an operating loss carryforward from the current year. Exceptions to this general rule are:

1. Tax effects of deductible temporary differences and carryforwards that existed at the date of a purchase business combination and for which a tax benefit is recognized initially in subsequent years in accordance with FAS-109, par. 30

2. Tax effects of deductible temporary differences and carryforwards that are allocated to shareholders' equity in accordance with FAS-109, par. 36

If there is only one item other than continuing operations, the portion of income tax expense or benefit that remains after the allocation to continuing operations is allocated to that item. If there are two or more items, the amount that remains after the allocation to continuing operations is allocated among those other items in proportion to their individual effects on income tax expense or benefit for the year (FAS-109, par. 38).

Quasi-Reorganizations

The tax benefits of deductible temporary differences and carryforwards as of the date of a quasi-reorganization ordinarily are reported as a direct addition to contributed capital if the tax benefits are recognized in subsequent years. The only exception is for enterprises that previously adopted FAS-96 and affected a quasi-reorganization involving only the elimination of a deficit in retained earnings by a noncurrent reduction in contributed capital prior to adopting FAS-109. For those enterprises, subsequent recognition of the tax benefit of prior deductible temporary differences and carryforwards is included in income, reported as required by FAS-109, and then reclassified from retained earnings to contributed capital (FAS-109, par. 39).

Separate Financial Statements of a Subsidiary

The allocation of income taxes among the members of a group that files a consolidated tax return must be based on a method that is systematic, rational, and consistent with the broad principles established in FAS-109, although FAS-109 does not require a single allocation method. A method that allocates current and deferred taxes to members of the group by applying FAS-109 to each member as if it were a separate taxpayer meets those criteria. Examples of methods that are *not* consistent with the broad principles of FAS-109 include (FAS-109, par. 40):

1. A method that allocates only current taxes payable to a member of the group that has taxable temporary differences
2. A method that allocates deferred taxes to a member of the group using a method fundamentally different from the asset and liability method
3. A method that allocates no current or deferred tax expense to a member of the group that has taxable income because the consolidated group has no current or deferred tax expense

Miscellaneous Topics

The following pronouncements are essentially unchanged by FAS-109:

- APB-10, paragraph 6
- APB-10, paragraph 7
- APB-23
- FIN-18

APB-10 indicates that deferred taxes should not be discounted (paragraph 6), and that offsetting of assets and liabilities (including tax assets and liabilities) is prohibited unless a legal right of setoff exists (paragraph 7).

APB-23, covered earlier in this chapter, indicates several situations in which deferred taxes are not recognized for certain temporary differences unless it becomes apparent that those differences will reverse in the foreseeable future.

FIN-18 provides guidance in accounting for income taxes in interim periods in accordance with the provisions of APB-28. APB-28 generally requires an estimated annual effective tax rate to be used to determine the interim period income tax provision.

> **OBSERVATION:** The special applications of FAS-109 discussed in this section illustrate the pervasive nature of accounting for income taxes. Income tax considerations affect many parts of the financial statements and many kinds of business transactions. This dimension of accounting for income taxes makes FAS-109 a very important pronouncement and accounts at least partially for the long and difficult process of making the transition from the deferred method under APB-11 to the asset/liability method under FAS-109.

FINANCIAL STATEMENT PRESENTATION AND DISCLOSURE ISSUES

FAS-109 requires deferred tax assets and liabilities to be presented in a classified balance sheet in current and noncurrent categories. The following policies are included for applying this requirement (FAS-109, pars. 41 and 42):

1. If the temporary difference giving rise to the deferred tax asset or liability is reflected in a balance-sheet asset or liability, the classification of the deferred tax is governed by that related asset or liability. For example, the temporary difference for depreciable assets is classified as noncurrent because the related asset (i.e., property, plant and equipment) is noncurrent.

2. If the deferred tax does not relate to an underlying asset or liability on the balance sheet, classification is based on the expected timing of reversal. For example, if organization costs are expensed when incurred for accounting purposes but deferred and deducted later for tax purposes, there is no related balance sheet asset or liability.

3. For a particular taxpaying component of an enterprise and within a particular tax jurisdiction (e.g., federal and state), all current deferred tax liabilities and assets are offset and presented as a single amount; the same procedure is followed for all noncurrent deferred tax liabilities and assets. Deferred tax liabilities and assets that are attributable to different taxpaying components of the enterprise or to different tax jurisdictions are *not* offset.

> **OBSERVATION:** The classification of deferred tax assets and liabilities as current or noncurrent based on the underlying asset is conceptually inferior to classifying then based on the

current/noncurrent classification—namely, to isolate as current those assets and liabilities expected to have cash flow consequences in the near future. Classifying a deferred tax asset or liability based on the underlying asset or liability appears to have been part of an effort by the FASB to reduce complexity and eliminate, to the extent possible, procedures that would require scheduling of taxable income for individual future years in determining the amounts of deferred tax assets and liabilities and their classifications.

Disclosures

The following components of the net deferred tax liability or asset recognized in an enterprise's balance sheet must be disclosed (FAS-109, par. 43):

1. The total of all deferred tax liabilities for taxable temporary differences
2. The total of all deferred tax assets for deductible temporary differences and loss and tax credit carryforwards
3. The total valuation allowance recognized for deferred tax assets
4. The net change during the year in the total valuation allowance

Earlier, several exceptions were identified under APB-23 for which deferred taxes are not recognized. Whenever a deferred tax liability is not recognized because of those exceptions, the following information is required to be disclosed (FAS-109, par. 44):

1. A description of the types of temporary differences for which a deferred tax liability has not been recognized and the types of events that would cause those temporary differences to become taxable
2. The cumulative amount of each type of temporary difference
3. The amount of the unrecognized deferred tax liability for temporary differences related to investments in foreign subsidiaries and foreign corporate joint ventures that are essentially permanent in duration if determination of that liability is practicable, or a statement that determination is not practicable
4. The amount of the deferred tax liability for temporary differences other than those in item (3) above that is not recognized based on exceptions granted by APB-23

Disclosure of significant components of income tax expense attributable to continuing operations for each year presented is required in the financial statements or related notes (FAS-109, par. 45):

1. Current tax expense or benefit
2. Deferred tax expense or benefit
3. Investment tax credit
4. Government grants (to the extent recognized as reductions in income tax expense)
5. Tax benefits of operating loss carryforwards
6. Tax expense that results from allocating tax benefits (*a*) directly to contributed capital or (*b*) to reduce goodwill or other noncurrent intangible assets of an acquired entity
7. Adjustments to a deferred tax liability or asset for enacted changes in tax laws or rates or for a change in the tax status of the enterprise
8. Adjustments of the beginning balance of the valuation allowance because of a change in circumstances that causes a change in judgment about the realizability of the related deferred tax asset in the future

> **OBSERVATION:** The effect of two unique features of the asset/liability method can be seen in the disclosure requirements listed above. Item (7) requires disclosure of the amount of the adjustment to deferred tax assets and liabilities for enacted changes in tax laws or rates. Item (8) requires disclosure of the amount of the adjustment of the beginning balance of the valuation allowance on deferred tax assets made as a result of a change in judgment about the realizability of that item.

The amount of income tax expense or benefit allocated to continuing operations and amounts separately allocated to other items shall be disclosed for each year for which those items are presented.

Several distinctions are made in the disclosures required by public enterprises and those required by nonpublic enterprises. The two most significant ones are summarized as follows (FAS-109, pars. 43 and 47):

	Public/Nonpublic Company Disclosures	
	Public	*Nonpublic*
Temporary Differences and Carryforwards	Approximation of tax effect of each type	Description of types
Statutory Reconciliation	Reconciliation in percentages or dollars	Description of major reconciling items

Companies with operating loss and tax credit carryforwards must disclose the amount and expiration dates. Disclosure is also required for any portion of the valuation allowance for deferred tax assets for which subsequently recognized tax benefits will be allocated (*a*) to reduce goodwill or other noncurrent intangible assets of an acquired entity or (*b*) directly to contributed equity (FAS-109, par. 48).

An entity that is a member of a group that files a consolidated tax return shall disclose the following in its separately issued financial statements (FAS-109, par. 49):

1. The aggregate amount of current and deferred tax expense for each statement of earnings presented and the amount of any tax-related balances due to or from affiliates as of the date of each statement of financial position presented

2. The principal provisions of the method by which the consolidated amount of current and deferred tax expense is allocated to members of the group and the nature and effect of any changes in that method during the year

---

Illustration of Major Provisions of FAS-109*

This illustration considers Power Company for three consecutive years, with the objective of preparing the year-end income tax accrual and income tax information for the company's financial statements. Power Company's first year of operations is 19X1. During that year, the company reported $160,000 of pretax accounting income. Permanent and temporary differences are combined with pretax financial income to derive taxable income, as follows:

Pretax financial income	$160,000
Permanent difference:	
Interest on municipal securities	(5,000)
Pretax financial income subject to tax	$155,000
Temporary differences:	
Depreciation	(28,000)
Warranties	10,000
Revenue received in advance	7,000
Taxable income	$144,000

The $5,000 interest on municipal securities represents nontaxable income, and the $28,000 depreciation temporary difference represents the excess of accelerated write-off for tax purposes over straight-line depreciation for financial reporting purposes. Warranties are expensed at the time of sale on an estimated basis, but are deductible for income tax purposes only when paid. In 19X1, $10,000 more was accrued than paid. Revenue received in advance is taxable at the time received, but is deferred for financial reporting purposes until earned. In 19X1, $7,000 was received that was not earned by year-end. Depreciation is a *taxable temporary difference* that reduces current tax payable and gives rise to a deferred tax liability. The warranties and revenue received in advance are *deductible temporary differences* that increase current tax payable and give rise to deferred tax assets.

Exhibit A presents analyses that facilitate the preparation of the year-end tax accrual, as well as information for the financial statements. Similar analyses are used for each of the three years in this Illustration. The analysis in the upper portion of Exhibit A "rolls forward" the amount of the temporary differences from the beginning to the end of the year. Since 19X1 is the first year for Power Company, the beginning balances are all zero. The change column includes the amounts used in the earlier calculation to determine taxable income from pretax accounting income. The numbers without parentheses are deductible temporary differences; those in parentheses are taxable temporary differences. The company is in a net taxable temporary difference position at the end of the year because the net amount of temporary differences is $(11,000), due to the large amount of the depreciation difference.

The lower portion of Exhibit A converts these temporary differences to amounts of deferred income taxes based on those differences. Again, the beginning balances are all zero and the ending balances are computed at 34%, the assumed income tax rate for 19X1 in this Illustration. The amounts in parentheses are deferred tax liabilities, based on taxable temporary differences. The numbers without parentheses are deferred tax assets, based on deductible temporary differences.

---

* Adapted excerpts from *Intermediate Accounting*, Fourth Edition, by Jan R. Williams, Keith G. Stanga, and William W. Holder, copyright © 1992 by Harcourt Brace & Company, reprinted by permission of the publisher.

**EXHIBIT A: Analysis of Cumulative Temporary Differences
and Deferred Taxes, 19X1**

Cumulative Temporary Differences (TD)

	Beginning Balance 19X1	Change	Ending Balance 19X1
Deductible TD:			
Warranties	0	$ 10,000	$ 10,000
Revenue received in advance	0	7,000	7,000
(Taxable) TD:			
Depreciation	0	(28,000)	(28,000)
	0	$(11,000)	$(11,000)

Deferred Income Taxes

	Beginning Balance @—%	Ending Balance @34%	Change	Classification Current	Classification Non-current
Assets:					
Warranties	0	$ 3,400	$ 3,400		$ 3,400
Revenue received in advance	0	2,380	2,380	$2,380	
(Liabilities):					
Depreciation	0	(9,520)	(9,520)		(9,520)
	0	$(3,740)	$(3,740)	$2,380	$(6,120)

The classification columns on the lower right side of Exhibit A separate the ending balances into current and noncurrent for balance sheet classification purposes. This distinction is based on the asset or liability (if one exists) underlying the temporary difference. If no such asset or liability exists, classification is based on the timing of the expected cash flow. In this case, the warranty period is assumed to be five years, so the related temporary difference is noncurrent, as is depreciation, because of the noncurrent classification of the underlying plant assets. The revenue received in advance is expected to be earned in the coming period, and thus is a current liability.

The December 31, 19X1, entry to record the income tax accrual for Power Company is as follows:

Dec. 31, 19X1

Income tax expense ($48,960 + $3,740)	$52,700	
Deferred income tax—Current	2,380	
Income tax payable ($144,000 x 34%)		$48,960
Deferred income tax—Noncurrent		6,120

Notice that the amounts of deferred income taxes—current and noncurrent—are taken from the lower analysis in Exhibit A. The income tax payable is determined by multiplying the $144,000 taxable income by the 34% tax rate. An important point to understand is that income tax expense is determined last: It is the net of the other three numbers and can be computed only after the remaining elements of the entry have been determined.

An important step to complete before moving to 19X2 is a proof of the numbers obtained, commonly referred to as a *statutory rate reconciliation*. For 19X1, this calculation is as follows:

Pretax financial income @ statutory rate ($160,000 x 34%)	$54,400
Less: Permanent differences ($5,000 x 34%)	(1,700)
Income tax expense	$52,700

Effects of these calculations on the balance sheet and income statement will be considered after all three years of analysis are completed.

Power Company's second year of operations is 19X2, in which pretax financial income is $150,000. Municipal interest is $12,000 and temporary differences for depreciation and warranties are $(35,000) and $12,000, respectively. Of the revenue received in advance in 19X1, $5,000 is earned and an additional $9,000 is received in 19X2 that is expected to be earned in 19X3. A new temporary difference is the litigation loss that results from the $10,000 accrual on an estimated basis for accounting purposes. This loss will be deductible for tax purposes when the suit is settled, which is expected to occur in 19X3.

Taxable income for 19X2 is determined as follows:

Pretax financial income	$150,000
Permanent difference:	
Interest on municipal securities	(12,000)
Pretax financial income subject to tax	$138,000
Temporary differences:	
Depreciation	(35,000)
Warranties	12,000
Revenue received in advance ($9,000 – $5,000)	4,000
Litigation loss	10,000
Taxable income	$129,000

Exhibit B includes a 19X2 analysis similar to the 19X1 analysis in Exhibit A. During 19X2, new tax legislation increases the income tax rate for 19X2 and all future years to 40%. The amounts in 19X2 simply are moved forward from the end of 19X1. In the lower portion of Exhibit B, the change column is calculated by determining the change required to move the beginning balance to the desired ending balance. The litigation loss is classified as current because of its expected settlement in 19X3, when it will be deductible for income tax purposes.

The entry to record income taxes at the end of 19X2 is as follows:

Dec. 31, 19X2

Income tax expense ($51,600 + $4,260)	$55,860	
Deferred income tax—Current ($8,400 – $2,380)	6,020	
Income tax payable ($129,000 x 40%)		$51,600
Deferred income tax—Noncurrent ($16,400 – $6,120)		10,280

Notice that the debits and credits to deferred income tax—current and noncurrent, respectively—are calculated as the changes in those accounts. It is not necessary to deal with that consideration in 19X1 because it was the company's first year. The desired ending balances of current and noncurrent deferred income taxes from Exhibit B are compared with the balances from Exhibit A and the differences are debited or credited into the deferred tax accounts, as appropriate, to produce the desired ending balances. For example, deferred income tax—noncurrent must have a credit (liability) balance of $16,400 at the end of 19X2. The account began with a credit balance of $6,120, requiring a credit of $10,280 in the year-end tax accrual. Similarly, the required debit (asset) balance for deferred income taxes—current is $8,400; with a debit balance of $2,380 at the end of 19X1, the adjustment is $6,020 ($8,400 – $2,380). This illustrates the basic approach of the liability method of accounting for income taxes: The desired balance sheet figures are determined first and the expense is recognized in the amount required to meet the balance sheet objective.

The statutory rate reconciliation has an additional component in 19X2, because of the tax rate change from 34% to 40%. This change has the effect of increasing deferred taxes and, therefore, tax expense, as indicated in the following reconciliation:

Pretax financial income at statutory rate ($150,000 x 40%)	$ 60,000
Less: Permanent differences ($12,000 x 40%)	(4,800)
Plus: Tax increase on beginning cumulative temporary differences [$11,000 x (40% – 34%)]	660
Income tax expense	$ 55,860

Notice that the adjustment for the tax increase is calculated only for the beginning balance of cumulative temporary differences. The temporary differences originating in 19X2 have already been taxed at 40%. As indicated earlier, the balance sheet and income statement presentation of deferred tax information will be considered after the analysis for 19X3.

During the third year of this Illustration, Power Company's activities took a significant downturn. Because of negative economic trends and a loss of several important contracts, the company reported a pretax financial *loss* of $275,000.

An analysis of the pretax financial loss, permanent and temporary differences, and the amount of loss for tax purposes are analyzed as follows:

Pretax financial (loss)	$(275,000)
Permanent difference:	
Interest on municipal securities	(15,000)
Pretax financial (loss) subject to tax	$(290,000)
Temporary differences:	
Depreciation	(40,000)
Warranties	18,000
Revenue received in advance ($15,000 – $10,000)	5,000
Litigation loss	(10,000)
Taxable (loss)	$(317,000)

This analysis is similar to those for 19X1 and 19X2, except for the negative amount entered as pretax financial loss. Revenue of $10,000 received in advance that was previously taxed was recognized in accounting income and an additional $15,000 was received that was deferred for accounting purposes, but taxed currently. The litigation of 19X2 was completed and the $10,000 loss was deducted for tax purposes.

Notice that the loss for tax purposes is $317,000. Assume that Power Company decides to carry back the loss to the extent possible and receive a refund for income taxes paid in the carryback period. While the loss can be carried back three years, in this case the company has existed for only two years, so the loss can be carried back only to 19X1 and 19X2. For Power Company for 19X3, the amount of the refund to be received is $100,560:

19X1:	$144,000 x 34%	=	$ 48,960
19X2:	$129,000 x 40%	=	51,600
			$100,560

**EXHIBIT B: Analysis of Cumulative Temporary Differences
and Deferred Taxes, 19X2**

Cumulative Temporary Differences (TD)

	Beginning Balance 19X2	Change	Ending Balance 19X2
Deductible TD:			
Warranties	$10,000	$12,000	$22,000
Revenue received in advance	7,000	4,000	11,000
Litigation	0	10,000	10,000
(Taxable) TD:			
Depreciation	(28,000)	(35,000)	(63,000)
	$(11,000)	$(9,000)	$(20,000)

Deferred Income Taxes

	Beginning Balance @34%	Ending Balance @40%	Change	Classification Current	Classification Non-current
Assets:					
Warranties	$ 3,400	$ 8,800	$ 5,400		$ 8,800
Revenue received in advance	2,380	4,400	2,020	$4,400	
Litigation loss	0	4,000	4,000	4,000	
(Liabilities):					
Depreciation	(9,520)	(25,200)	(15,680)		(25,200)
	$(3,740)	$ (8,000)	$ (4,260)	$8,400	$(16,400)

The determination of deferred tax balances in Exhibit C is similar to those
in the two previous exhibits with modifications necessary to include the loss
carryforward of $44,000, which is determined by subtracting the amount of
loss that is carried back from the total loss for tax purposes for 19X3:

$$\$317,000 - (\$144,000 + \$129,000) \; = \; \$44,000$$

Notice that a category for the loss carryforward has been added to the
analysis at the top of Exhibit C and the $44,000 loss carryforward in 19X3
has been included. The loss carryforward gives rise to a deferred tax asset,
as indicated in the analysis at the bottom of Exhibit C. This item is classified
as noncurrent on the assumption that, given the large loss encountered by

tion) of using the 19X3 loss to receive the refund of 19X1 and 19X2 income taxes and to offset income taxes that would otherwise have to be paid after 19X3.

The 19X3 statutory rate reconciliation can now be prepared as follows:

Pretax financial (loss) at statutory rate [($275,000) x 40%] $(110,000)

EXHIBIT C: Analysis of Cumulative Temporary Differences and Deferred Taxes, 19X3

Cumulative Temporary Differences (TD)

	Beginning Balance 19X3	Change	Ending Balance 19X3
Deductible TD:			
Warranties	$ 22,000	$ 18,000	$ 40,000
Revenue received in advance	11,000	5,000	16,000
Litigation	10,000	(10,000)	0
(Taxable) TD:			
Depreciation	(63,000)	(40,000)	(103,000)
Loss Carryforward:			
19X3 Loss*	0	44,000	44,000
	$(20,000)	$ 17,000	$ (3,000)

Deferred Income Taxes

	Beginning Balance @40%	Ending Balance @40%	Change	Classification Current	Classification Non-current
Assets:					
Warranties	$ 8,800	$16,000	$ 7,200		$16,000
Revenue received in advance	4,400	6,400	2,000	$6,400	
Litigation loss	4,000	0	(4,000)		
Loss carryforward	0	17,600	17,600		17,600
(Liabilities):					
Depreciation	(25,200)	(41,200)	(16,000)		(41,200)
	$(8,000)	$(1,200)	$6,800	$6,400	$(7,600)

* [$317,000 – ($144,00 + $129,000)]

Power Company in 19X3, it will be several years before the company returns to profitable operations and is able to recognize the benefit of the loss carryforward. That item is treated in the same manner as a deductible temporary difference for purposes of determining deferred tax assets and liabilities.

> ☛ **PRACTICE POINTER:** Accumulating the information required to implement FAS-109 is facilitated by preparing a workpaper like those in Exhibits A, B, and C. Such a workpaper includes the following major components:
>
> 1. A record of the cumulative temporary differences and carryforwards, including:
>   a. Separation of temporary differences into taxable and deductible categories
>   b. Beginning balances, the increase or decrease in the cumulative temporary differences, and the ending balances
> 2. A record of cumulative amounts of carryforwards identified by year
> 3. A record of deferred income taxes, including:
>   a. Separate classifications of deferred tax liabilities and assets
>   b. Beginning balances, ending balances, and the resulting changes in deferred taxes for the year
>   c. The classification of the ending balances of deferred tax assets and liabilities into current and noncurrent balance sheet categories

The journal entry to record income taxes at the end of 19X3 is as follows:

Dec. 31, 19X3

Receivable for past income taxes		
[($144,000 x 34%) + ($129,000 x 40%)]	$100,560	
Deferred income tax—Noncurrent		
($16,400 – $7,600)	8,800	
Deferred income tax—Current		
($8,400 – $6,400)		$ 2,000
Income tax benefit ($100,560 + $6,800)		107,360

As shown in the two right-hand columns of Exhibits B and C, the balances of both deferred income taxes—current (debit) and deferred income taxes—noncurrent (credit) declined from 19X2 to 19X3. The two most significant differences are the reversal of the temporary difference from the litigation loss and the inclusion of the loss carryforward, both of which are relatively large amounts.

In the journal entry above, income tax expense has been replaced by the account income tax benefit, which indicates the positive impact (loss reduc-

Less: Permanent differences ($15,000 x 40%)	(6,000)
Plus: Loss carryback at 34% [$144,000 x (40% – 34%)]	8,640
Income tax (benefit)	$(107,360)

The last item in the reconciliation, identified as "loss carryback at 34%," is required because the 19X1 part of the carryback was determined at 34%, the 19X1 income tax rate, rather than the current (19X3) rate of 40%.

Now that the three-year analysis of the cumulative temporary differences and the loss carryforward, the related deferred tax assets and liabilities, and the year-end journal entries to record income taxes is completed, attention should be focused on the amounts that will be presented in the balance sheet and income statement. That information is presented in Exhibit D. For each year, a portion of deferred taxes appears in the current asset section of the balance sheet. This amount represents the net amount of deferred taxes on temporary differences on assets and liabilities that are classified as current in the balance sheet. In addition, in 19X3, a current asset is presented for the $100,560 receivable of 19X1 and 19X2 taxes resulting from the 19X3 carryback. For 19X1 and 19X2, a current liability is presented for income taxes payable—$48,960 and $51,600 in 19X1 and 19X2, respectively.

EXHIBIT D: Financial Statement Presentation of Income Taxes, 19X1–19X3

Balance Sheet

	19X1	19X2	19X3
Current assets:			
Receivable for past income taxes			$ 100,560
Deferred income taxes	$ 2,380	$ 8,400	6,400
Current liabilities:			
Income taxes payable	48,960	51,600	
Noncurrent liabilities:			
Deferred income taxes	6,120	16,400	7,600

Income Statement

	19X1	19X2	19X3
Income (loss):			
Before income tax	$160,000	$150,000	$(275,000)
Income tax expense (benefit):			
Current	48,960	51,600	(100,560)
Deferred	3,740	4,260	(6,800)
	52,700	55,860	(107,360)
Net income (loss)	$107,300	$ 94,140	$(167,640)

Among noncurrent liabilities, each year includes a deferred tax amount that represents deferred taxes resulting from temporary differences classified as noncurrent, and from the loss carryforward. The amount of noncurrent deferred taxes declines between 19X2 and 19X3 because of the loss carryforward, which partially offsets the large deferred tax liability related to the depreciation temporary difference for the first time in 19X3.

The income statement presentation for each year displays pretax financial income (loss), followed by income tax expense (benefit), separated into current and deferred components. In 19X1 and 19X2, income tax expense reduces the amount of net income reported, as would be expected given the profitability reported by the company in those years. In 19X3, however, the benefit of the carryback and carryforward results in a reduction in the amount of loss that would otherwise have been reported because of the refund of past taxes and the anticipation of reduced taxes in the future, when the carryforward is realized.

To examine the accounting procedures required when a valuation allowance is established for deferred tax assets, return to Exhibit C. Assume that, after careful consideration, management determines it is more likely than not that 25% of the deferred tax assets will not be realized. This requires a valuation allowance of $10,000, determined as follows, based on the information from Exhibit C:

Current deferred tax assets:
Revenue received in advance		$ 6,400

Noncurrent deferred tax assets:
Warranties	$16,000	
Loss carryforward	17,600	33,600
		$40,000

Valuation allowance: 25% x $40,000		$10,000

Allocation to current/noncurrent:
Current: ($6,400/$40,000) x $10,000	$ 1,600
Noncurrent: ($33,600/$40,000) x $10,000	8,400
	$10,000

This allocation results in a $1,600 *reduction* in the current deferred tax asset and a $8,400 *addition* to the net noncurrent deferred tax liability. In the following comparative analysis, the impact of the valuation allowance is determined as indicated in the right-hand column, and is compared with the figures presented earlier without a valuation allowance in the left-hand column.

	Without Valuation Allowance	*With Valuation Allowance*
Current deferred tax asset	$ 6,400	$ 6,400
Less: Allowance	0	(1,600)
	$ 6,400	$ 4,800

Noncurrent deferred tax liability:

Asset component	$33,600	$ 33,600
Less: Allowance	0	(8,400)
	$33,600	$ 25,200
Liability component	(41,200)	(41,200)
	$ (7,600)	$(16,000)
Total deferred tax	$ (1,200)	$(11,200)

The difference between the totals in the two columns is $10,000, exactly the amount of the valuation allowance.

The journal entry to record income taxes at the end of 19X3 under these revised assumptions, and including the valuation allowance, is as follows:

Dec. 31, 19X3

Receivable for past income taxes	
[($144,000 x 34%) + ($129,000 x 40%)]	$100,560
Deferred income tax—Noncurrent	
($16,400 – $7,600)	8,800
Allowance to reduce deferred tax assets	
to lower recoverable value	$10,000
Deferred income tax—Current	
($8,400 – $6,400)	2,000
Income tax benefit	
($100,560 + $6,800 – $10,000)	97,360

The statutory rate reconciliation for 19X3, including the recognition of the valuation allowance, is as follows:

Pretax financial income (loss) at statutory rate	
[($275,000) x 40%]	$(110,000)
Less: Permanent differences ($15,000 x 40%)	(6,000)
Plus: Loss carryback at 34% [$144,000 x (40% – 34%)]	8,640
Increase in valuation allowance	10,000
Income tax (benefit)	$ (97,360)

The valuation allowance is evaluated at the end of each year, considering positive and negative evidence about whether the asset will be realized. At that time, the allowance will either be increased or reduced; reduction could result in the complete elimination of the allowance if positive evidence indicates that the value of the deferred tax assets is no longer impaired and the allowance is no longer required.

CHAPTER 22
INSTALLMENT SALES METHOD
OF ACCOUNTING

CONTENTS

CHAPTER 22
INSTALLMENT SALES METHOD
OF ACCOUNTING

OVERVIEW

The installment sales method of accounting defers the recognition of gross profit on installment sales until cash is collected. It is commonly used for income tax purposes, but is acceptable for purposes of financial reporting in limited situations.

GAAP for the installment sales method are found in the following pronouncements:

APB-10   Paragraph 12, Omnibus Opinion—1966 (Installment Method of Accounting)

ARB-43   Chapter 1, Prior Opinions
    A. Rules Adopted by Membership

CROSS-REFERENCES

1999 MILLER GAAP GUIDE: Chapter 43, "Revenue Recognition"

BACKGROUND

GAAP prohibit accounting for sales by the installment sales method except under unusual circumstances in which collectibility cannot be reasonably estimated or assured. The doubtfulness of collectibility can be caused by the length of an extended collection period or because no basis of estimation can be established. In such cases, a company may consider using either the installment sales method or the even more conservative cost recovery method (APB-10, par. 12).

INSTALLMENT SALES METHOD

Under the installment sales method of accounting, gross profit is recognized only to the extent that cash has been collected. Each payment collected consists of *part* recovery of cost and *part* gross profit, in the same ratio that these two elements existed in the original sale.

> ☛ **PRACTICE POINTER:** Because gross profit ratios are different for many products and departments and may vary from year to year, keep a separate record of sales by year, product line, and department. Keep separate accounts and records for receivables, realized gross profit, unrealized gross profit, and repossessions for each category of product. Under the installment sales method, charge selling and administrative costs to expense in the period they are incurred.

Generally, the seller will protect its interest in an installment sale by retaining title to the goods through a conditional sales contract, lease, mortgage, or trustee. In the event of a default on an installment sales contract, the related account receivable and unrealized gross profit are written off. In many cases of default, the goods are repossessed by the seller. The loss (or gain) on a default of an installment sales contract is determined as follows:

$$\text{Loss (or Gain)} = \begin{bmatrix} \text{balance of} \\ \text{account} \\ \text{receivable} \end{bmatrix} \text{less} \begin{bmatrix} \text{unrealized} \\ \text{gross} \\ \text{profit} \end{bmatrix} \text{less} \begin{bmatrix} \text{inventory carrying} \\ \text{amount of} \\ \text{repossessed} \\ \text{merchandise} \\ \text{(if any)} \end{bmatrix}$$

When goods are repossessed, one of the major problems is determining the value of these inventory goods. Some of the methods of determining their value include:

1. Fair market value

2. Unrecovered cost (results in no gain or loss)

3. Resale value less reconditioning costs plus a normal profit (net realizable value)

4. No value—a good method when no other method is appropriate, particularly when the actual value is minor

> ☛ **PRACTICE POINTER:** Care should be taken in valuing repossessed goods at unrecovered cost because a loss that should be recorded may be overlooked.

Illustration of Installment Sales Method

A furniture dealer sells for $100 a chair that cost $70. The gross profit percentage for this sale is 30%. The dealer would recognize 70% of each payment as a recovery of cost and 30% as realized gross profit.

The entries to record the initial sale, assuming the use of a periodic inventory system and no down payment, are:

Accounts receivable—installment sales	$100	
Installment sales		$100

Cost of installment sales	70	
Inventory		70

At the end of the period, the company closes out the installment sales account and the cost of installment sales to unrealized gross profit on installment sales account, which in this example is $30. The entry is:

Installment sales	$100	
Cost of installment sales		$ 70
Unrealized gross profit on installment sales		30

In the period that the company collects $40, the entries are:

Cash	$ 40	
Accounts receivable—installment sales		$ 40

Unrealized gross profit on installment sales	12	
Realized gross profit on installment sales		12

The $40 collected includes $28 recovery of cost and $12 of realized gross profit on installment sales (a 70%/30% relationship).

If the first payment of $40 was the only payment the company received and the goods were not repossessed, the journal entry to record the default and loss would be:

Unrealized gross profit	$18	
Loss on installment sales	42	
Accounts receivable—installment sales		$60

If the goods were repossessed and had an inventory value of $25, the journal entry would be:

Unrealized gross profit	$18	
Loss on installment sales	17	
Inventory	25	
Accounts receivable—installment sales		$60

COST RECOVERY METHOD

The cost recovery method is used in very unusual situations in which recovery of cost is undeterminable or extremely questionable. The procedure is simply that all cost is recovered before any profit is recognized. Once all cost has been recovered, any other collections are recognized as profit. The only expenses remaining to be charged against such revenue are those relating to the collection process.

Illustration of Cost Recovery Method

If a company sells for $100 an item that cost $40 and receives no down payment, the first $20 collected, regardless of the year collected, is considered recovery of half the cost. The next $20 collected is recovery of the balance of the cost, regardless of the year collected. The remaining $60 (all gross profit) is recognized as income when received. The only additional expenses that are charged against the remaining $60 are those directly related to the collection process.

DEFERRED INCOME TAXES

The installment sales method is acceptable for income tax purposes, because the government attempts to collect taxes when the taxpayer has the cash available rather than basing collection on a theoretical analysis of accounting principles. The use of installment accounting for tax purposes and the accrual method for financial reporting purposes often results in a temporary difference and creates a deferred tax liability.

DISCLOSURE

Accounts receivable on installment sales are shown separately in the balance sheet. They are classified as current assets in accordance with the normal operating cycle of the entity, which may extend for more than one year. The amounts maturing each period for each class of installment receivable should also be disclosed.

Unrealized gross profit is presented in the balance sheet as a separate caption, usually as a contra account to the related installment receivable.

CHAPTER 23
INTANGIBLE ASSETS

CONTENTS

CHAPTER 23
INTANGIBLE ASSETS

OVERVIEW

Intangible assets are long-lived assets used in the production of goods and services. They are similar to property, plant, and equipment except for their lack of physical properties. Examples of intangible assets include copyrights, patents, trademarks, and goodwill. They generally are subject to amortization over their estimated useful lives, subject to certain limitations for intangibles acquired on or before October 31, 1970.

The following pronouncements contain GAAP for intangible assets:

APB-16	Business Combinations
APB-17	Intangible Assets
FAS-44	Accounting for Intangible Assets of Motor Carriers
FAS-72	Accounting for Certain Acquisitions of Banking or Thrift Institutions
FIN-9	Applying APB Opinions No. 16 and 17 When a Savings and Loan Association or a Similar Institution Is Acquired in a Business Combination Accounted for by the Purchase Method

CROSS-REFERENCES

1999 MILLER GAAP GUIDE: Chapter 3, "Business Combinations"; Chapter 12, "Development Stage Enterprises"; Chapter 14, "Equity Method"; Chapter 41, "Research and Development Costs"; Chapter 49, "Banking and Thrift Institutions"

1999 MILLER GAAP IMPLEMENTATION MANUAL: Chapter 13, "Intangible Assets"

1999 MILLER GAAP IMPLEMENTATION MANUAL: EITF: Chapter 15, "Intangible Assets"

BACKGROUND

The term *intangible asset* refers to certain long-lived legal rights and competitive advantages developed or acquired by a business enterprise.

Intangible assets differ considerably in their characteristics, useful lives, and relationship to operations of an enterprise and may be classified as follows:

Identifiability

Patents, copyrights, franchises, trademarks, and other similar intangible assets that can be specifically identified with reasonably descriptive names. Other types of intangible assets lack specific identification, the most common being goodwill.

Manner of Acquisition

Intangible assets may be purchased or developed internally and may be acquired singly, in groups, or in business combinations.

Determinate or Indeterminate Life

Patents, copyrights, and most franchises are examples of intangible assets with determinate lives, established by law or by contract. Other intangible assets such as organizational costs, secret processes, and goodwill have no established term of existence, and the expected period of benefit may be indeterminate at the time of acquisition.

Transferability

The rights to a patent, copyright, or franchise can be identified separately and bought or sold. Organization costs are an inseparable part of a business, and it is unlikely that a purchaser would purchase the organizational costs without the business. Similarly, goodwill is inseparable from a business and is transferable only as an inseparable intangible asset of an enterprise.

BASIC ACCOUNTING PROCEDURES

Cost of Intangibles

A company records as assets the costs of intangible assets acquired from other enterprises or individuals. Costs of developing, maintaining, or restoring intangible assets that are not specifically identifiable, have indeterminate lives, or are inherent in a continuing business and related to an enterprise as a whole are deducted from income when incurred (APB-17, par. 24).

The cost of an intangible asset is measured by (*a*) the amount of cash disbursed or the fair value of other assets distributed, (*b*) the present value of amounts to be paid for liabilities incurred, and (*c*) the fair value of consideration received for stock issued (cost may be determined either by the fair value of the consideration given or by the fair value of the property acquired, whichever is more clearly evident) (APB-17, par. 25).

The cost of an intangible asset, including goodwill acquired in a business combination, may *not* be written off as a lump sum to paid-in capital or to retained earnings, or be reduced to a nominal amount at or immediately after acquisition (APB-17, par. 28). Accounting for intangible-related costs is summarized in Figure 23-1.

Amortization

The cost of intangible assets is amortized by systematic charges to income over the period estimated to be benefited, but not to exceed 40 years (APB-17, par. 29).

> ☛ **PRACTICE POINTER:** In applying the requirement to amortize the cost of intangible assets, determining the period of amortization is particularly difficult because of the uncertainties surrounding intangible assets. While APB-17 states a maximum period of 40 years, and some intangibles have determinable legal or contractual lives, amortization is often over a much shorter period than either the maximum period or the legal or contractual period.
>
> Factors that may imply that a period of amortization shorter than the maximum, legal, or contractual life is appropriate include:
>
> - Effects of obsolescence
> - The service lives of employees who are critical to the realization of the asset
> - Expected actions of competitors or others

Figure 23-1: Summary of Accounting
for Intangible-Related Costs

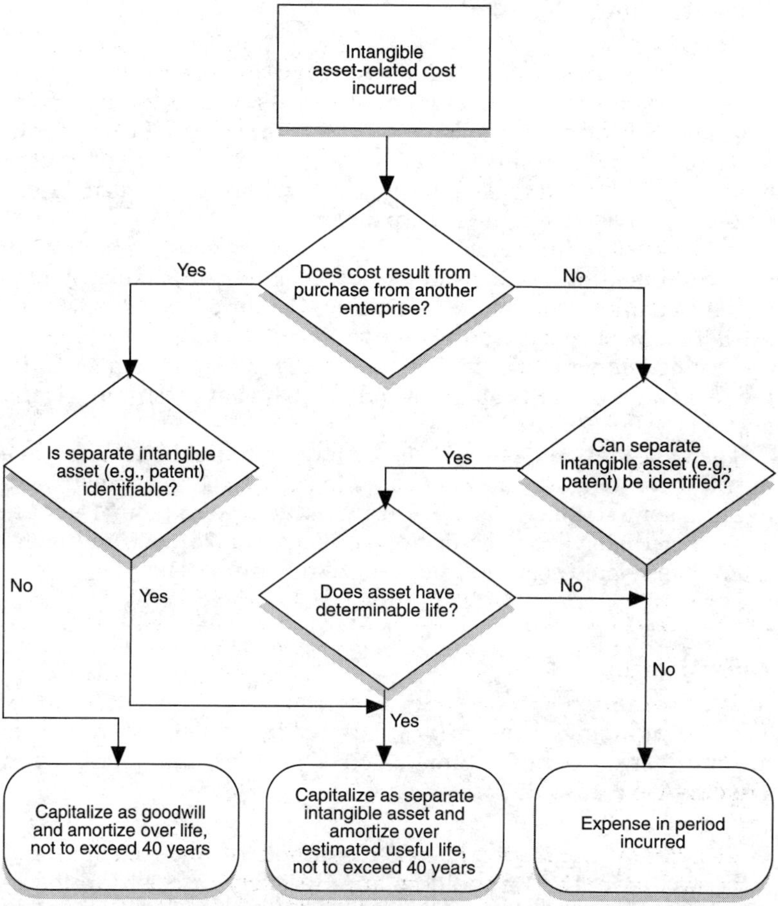

	Intangible asset-related cost incurred

Does cost result from purchase from another enterprise?

- Yes →
- No →

Is separate intangible asset (e.g., patent) identifiable?
- No
- Yes

Can separate intangible asset (e.g., patent) be identified?
- Yes
- No

Does asset have determinable life?
- No
- Yes

Capitalize as goodwill and amortize over life, not to exceed 40 years

Capitalize as separate intangible asset and amortize over estimated useful life, not to exceed 40 years

Expense in period incurred

The straight-line method of amortization is required unless a company demonstrates that another systematic method is more appropriate (APB-17, par. 30).

> **OBSERVATION**: Amortizing the cost of intangible assets on arbitrary bases in the absence of evidence of limited lives or decreased values may cause expenses and decreases of assets to be recognized prematurely. However, delaying amortization of the cost until a loss is evident may cause recognition of the decreases after the fact.

A business enterprise should evaluate the periods of amortization continually to determine if later circumstances warrant revision of estimated useful lives. If estimates are changed, the unamortized cost is allocated to the number of years in the revised useful life, but not to exceed 40 years from the date of acquisition (APB-17, par. 31).

> ☞ **PRACTICE POINTER:** APB-17 became effective for intangible assets acquired after October 31, 1970, and provided that intangible assets acquired prior to November 1, 1970, could continue to be accounted for in accordance with the preceding GAAP which permitted the permanent capitalization of the cost of certain intangible assets. Because APB-17 was not required to be applied retroactively to intangible assets acquired on or before October 31, 1970, the balance sheets of some enterprises continue to reflect the cost of certain intangible assets which have not been amortized.

Disclosure

A description of intangible assets, method of amortization, and estimated useful lives should be appropriately disclosed in the financial statements or in footnotes (APB-17, par. 30).

In the event that a large part or all of the unamortized cost of an intangible asset is included as an extraordinary charge in the determination of net income, the reasons for the extraordinary deduction should be disclosed fully (APB-17, par. 31).

GOODWILL

The cost of unidentifiable intangible assets is measured by the difference between the total price paid for the group of assets or of the enterprise acquired and the sum of the costs assigned to identifiable assets acquired, less liabilities assumed. Cost of identifiable assets do not include goodwill (APB-17, par. 26).

FAS-72 is applicable to that portion of goodwill that arises from the excess of fair value of assumed liabilities over the fair value of acquired identifiable assets that may result from the acquisition of a troubled banking or thrift institution. FAS-72 provides for a different method of amortization over a shorter period than that required by APB-17. In addition, FIN-9 provides guidance for recording the acquisition of a banking or thrift institution by the use of the net-spread method and the separate-valuation method. For a complete discussion of FAS-72 and FIN-9, refer to the 1999 *Miller GAAP Guide* chapter titled "Banking and Thrift Institutions," in the specialized industry accounting principles section of this guide.

> **OBSERVATION:** FAS-72 concludes that goodwill arising in the acquisition of a troubled banking or thrift institution should be amortized over a relatively short period because of the uncertainty about the nature and extent of the estimated future benefits related to the goodwill (see the 1999 *Miller GAAP Guide* chapter titled "Banking and Thrift Institutions").

Step-by-Step Acquisitions

If an enterprise purchases, on a step-by-step basis, a subsidiary that is consolidated or an investment that is accounted for under the equity method, the fair value of the underlying assets acquired and the goodwill for each step purchased must be identified separately.

Illustration of Excess Cost Over Book Value

Assume that Company P acquired an interest in Company S in two steps: (1) It acquired 20% of the outstanding common stock for $200,000. (2) The following year it acquired an additional 60% for $500,000. At the dates of acquisition, the equity book values for Company S were $900,000 and $1,100,000, respectively.

Computation of Excess of Cost over Book Value

First Acquisition

Cost of 20% acquired	$200,000
20% of equity book value of $900,000	(180,000)
Excess of cost over book value (goodwill)	$ 20,000

Second Acquisition

Cost of 60% acquired	$500,000
60% of equity book value of $1,100,000	(660,000)
Excess of book value over cost (negative goodwill)	($160,000)

Hence, as of the date of the second acquisition, Company P had an investment of $700,000 for 80% of Company S. Company S at the second acquisition date had an equity book value of $1,100,000, and Company P's 80% is $880,000, for which it paid $700,000. Had Company P been recording its first acquisition of 20% on the equity method, it would have recorded its 20% of the $200,000 increase in Company S's book value (assuming that no dividends or other distributions were made to Company P by Company S). Thus, the adjusted equity in Company S on the books of Company P would include the original $200,000 purchase price plus 20% of the $200,000 increase in book value (from $900,000 to $1,100,000), or a total of $220,000 ($180,000 + $40,000). The cost of the second acquisition of 60% for $500,000 and the adjusted basis for the 20% at $220,000 equals $720,000, which represents 80% of $1,100,000, or $880,000. The difference of $160,000 is the excess of book value over cost (negative goodwill), indicated by the computation for the second acquisition of 60%.

Disposal of Goodwill

Because goodwill is associated with an enterprise as a whole, it ordinarily cannot be disposed of apart from the enterprise itself. However, an acquired company, or a large segment or separate group of assets of an acquired company, may be sold or otherwise disposed of, and all or part of the unamortized goodwill recognized in the acquisition should be included in the cost of the assets sold (FAS-17, par. 32).

Negative Goodwill

The measurement or valuation of cost in financial accounting usually means the historical or acquisition cost. The sum of the market or appraised values of identifiable assets less liabilities assumed may exceed the cost of the assets or business enterprise being acquired. Under these circumstances, the values assigned to the noncurrent assets being acquired are reduced proportionately (except long-term investments in marketable securities) to absorb the excess value. A deferred credit for an excess of assigned values of identifiable assets over cost (*negative goodwill*) is not recorded unless the noncurrent assets have been reduced to zero. If, after reducing the noncurrent assets (except long-term investments in marketable securities) to zero, a deferred credit still remains, it is recorded as an excess of acquired net assets over cost, and amortized systematically to income over the period expected to benefit, but not in excess of 40 years. The method and period of amortization should be disclosed adequately in the financial statements. No part of the excess of acquired net assets over cost (negative goodwill) should be credited directly to stockholders' equity at the date of acquisition (APB-16, pars. 91 and 92).

Illustrations of Goodwill

The following examples depict the computation of goodwill using different facts.

Example 1

Company P acquires an 80% interest in the outstanding common stock of Company S for $725,000. At the date of acquisition, Company S has capital stock of $600,000 and retained earnings of $150,000.

At the Date of Acquisition

Cost of investment in Company S		$725,000
Less: Company S stockholders' equity:		
Capital stock	$600,000	
Retained earnings	150,000	
Total	750,000	
Acquired by Company P	80%	
Equity acquired by Company P		600,000
Excess of cost over book value (goodwill)		$125,000

Example 2

Company P acquires all the assets and liabilities of Company S for $500,000. An appraisal at the date of acquisition reflects the following values.

Accounts receivable (net)	$ 75,000
Inventories	125,000
Fixed assets	400,000
Long-term marketable securities	100,000
Total	700,000
Liabilities assumed (present values)	(250,000)
Value of underlying assets	450,000
Cost of assets acquired	(500,000)
Excess of cost over assets acquired (goodwill)	$ 50,000

If the cost of the assets acquired were $400,000, noncurrent assets, *except long-term marketable securities,* would be adjusted downward, but not below zero. The result would be that fixed assets are reduced to $350,000, and *no negative goodwill is recorded.* However, negative goodwill would have been recorded on the books if all the noncurrent assets (except long-term marketable securities) were reduced to zero and a balance of the excess of book value over cost still remained.

Example 3

When preferred stock is involved in an acquisition of a subsidiary, caution must be taken when (*a*) dividends are in arrears or (*b*) there is any preference in liquidation.

Company P acquires 75,000 shares of Company S common stock for $900,000. At the date of acquisition, Company S has 100,000 shares of common stock outstanding with a stated value of $1,000,000, and 5,000 shares of 5% preferred stock $100 par outstanding with dividends in arrears of $50,000; the preferred stock is entitled to $105 per share in the event of liquidation. Retained earnings and paid-in capital are $225,000 and $100,000 respectively.

Computation of Excess of Cost over Book Value

	Preferred	Common
5,000 shares of preferred stock par $100	$500,000	
Stated value of common stock		$1,000,000
Dividends in arrears	50,000	(50,000)
Liquidation preference on preferred stock	25,000	(25,000)
Retained earnings		225,000
Paid-in capital		100,000
Totals	$575,000	$1,250,000
75% of common equity acquired by P		$ 937,500
Cost of common equity acquired		900,000
Excess of book value over cost (negative goodwill)		$ 37,500

INTANGIBLE ASSETS OF MOTOR CARRIERS

Enactment of the Motor Carrier Act of 1980, which deregulated motor carriers, raised questions about intangible assets of motor carriers. Specifically, the question was raised whether motor carriers should continue to report as assets certain intangible assets that existed before the enactment. FAS-44 required motor carriers to classify intangible assets as (*a*) interstate operating rights, (*b*) other identifiable assets, or (c) goodwill (FAS-44, par. 3). If a company found it impractical or impossible to classify its intangible asset costs in this manner, all costs were assigned to interstate operating rights (FAS-44, par. 5). Intangible assets representing interstate operating rights to transport goods with limited competition were required to be charged to income and, if material, reported as an extraordinary item (FAS-44, par. 6).

> **OBSERVATION:** FAS-44 deals with accounting issues that relate to 1980 legislation. Accordingly, it has relatively little ongoing relevance, other than that it establishes standards that may have some application for similar legislation. For example, FAS-44 indicates that the cost of intrastate operating rights shall be accounted for in accordance with the standard if a state deregulates motor carriers with effects similar to the Motor Carrier Act of 1980 (FAS-44, par. 7).

CHAPTER 24
INTEREST COSTS CAPITALIZED

CONTENTS

CHAPTER 24
INTEREST COSTS CAPITALIZED

OVERVIEW

Under certain conditions, interest is capitalized as part of the acquisition cost of an asset. Interest is capitalized only during the period of time required to complete and prepare the asset for its intended use, which may be either *sale or use within the business*. Capitalization of interest is based on the principle that a better measure of acquisition cost is achieved when certain interest costs are capitalized. This results in a better matching of revenue and costs in future periods.

Promulgated GAAP for the capitalization of interest costs are found in the following pronouncements:

FAS-34   Capitalization of Interest Cost

FAS-42   Determining Materiality for Capitalization of Interest Cost

FAS-58   Capitalization of Interest Cost in Financial Statements That Include Investments Accounted for by the Equity Method

FAS-62   Capitalization of Interest Cost in Situations Involving Certain Tax-Exempt Borrowings and Certain Gifts and Grants

FIN-33   Applying FASB Statement No. 34 to Oil and Gas Producing Operations Accounted for by the Full Cost Method

CROSS-REFERENCES

1999 Miller GAAP Guide: Chapter 12, "Development Stage Enterprises"; Chapter 14, "Equity Method"; Chapter 25, "Interest on Receivables and Payables"; Chapter 30, "Leases"

1999 MILLER NOT-FOR-PROFIT REPORTING: Chapter 6, "Liabilities"

BACKGROUND

The basis of accounting for depreciable fixed assets is cost, and all normal expenditures of readying an asset for use are capitalized as part of acquisition cost. Unnecessary expenditures that do not add to the utility of the asset should be charged to expense.

FAS-34 covers the promulgated GAAP on the capitalization of interest costs on certain qualifying assets that are undergoing activities to prepare them for their intended use. FAS-42 amends FAS-34 and requires that the same materiality tests applied regular GAAP be applied to the materiality of capitalizing interest cost.

FAS-58 extends the provisions of FAS-34 to provide for capitalization of interest cost on equity funds, loans, and advances made by investors to certain investees that are accounted for by the equity method as described by APB-18 (The Equity Method of Accounting for Investments in Common Stock).

FAS-62 amends FAS-34 to provide special treatment in capitalizing interest costs on qualifying assets that are acquired with (*a*) the proceeds of tax-exempt borrowings and (*b*) gifts or grants that are restricted for the sole purpose of acquiring a specific asset.

> **OBSERVATION:** The basis of capitalizing certain interest costs is that the cost of an asset should include all costs necessary to bring the asset to the condition and location for its intended use. The requirements of FAS-34 to capitalize interest cost may result in a lack of comparability among reporting entities, depending on their method of financing major asset acquisitions. For example, Company A and Company B both acquire an identical asset for $10 million that requires three years to complete for its intended use. Company A pays cash, and at the end of three years, the total cost of the asset is $10 million. In addition, assume that Company A also had net income of $2 million a year for each of the three years and had no interest expense. Assume also that Company B had $1.5 million net income for each of the three years after deducting $500,000 of interest expense per year. If Company B qualifies for capitalized interest costs under FAS-34, it would reflect $2 million per year net income and not show any interest expense. On the balance sheet of Company B at the end of three years, the identical asset would appear at a cost of $11.5 million. Future depreciation charges will vary between the two companies by a total of $1.5 million. Although the interest cost may be necessary to Company B, it does not add to the utility of the asset.

QUALIFYING ASSETS

Acquisition Period

Interest cost must be capitalized for all assets that require an *acquisition period* to get them ready for their intended use. *Acquisition period* is defined as the period commencing with the first expenditure for a qualifying asset and ending when the asset is substantially complete and ready for its intended use. Thus, before interest costs can be capitalized, expenditures must have been made for the qualifying asset, providing an investment base on which to compute interest, and activities that are required to get the asset ready for its intended use must actually be in progress (FAS-34, par. 8).

FAS-42 was issued to reaffirm that the usual rules of materiality embodied in GAAP must be followed in determining the materiality for the capitalization of interest costs. One of the purposes of FAS-42 was to eliminate language in FAS-34 that implies capitalization of interest costs can be avoided in certain circumstances. Thus, in applying the provisions of FAS-34, all the usual materiality tests used in applying other promulgated GAAP should also be used in determining the materiality for capitalization of interest costs.

Intended Use

Capitalization of interest cost is applicable for assets that require an acquisition period to prepare them for their intended use. Assets to which capitalized interest must be allocated include both (1) assets acquired for a company's own use and (2) assets acquired for sale in the ordinary course of business (FAS-34, par. 9). Thus, inventory items that require a long time to produce, such as a real estate development, qualify for capitalization of interest costs. However, interest costs are not capitalized for inventories that are routinely produced in large quantities on a repetitive basis (FAS-34, par. 10).

> **OBSERVATION:** The FASB concluded that the benefit of capitalizing interest costs on inventories that are routinely produced in large quantities does not justify the cost. Thus, interest costs should not be capitalized for inventories that are routinely produced in large quantities.

FAS-34 does not allow the capitalization of interest cost (*a*) for assets that are ready for their intended use or that are actually being used in the earning activities of a business and (*b*) for assets that are not being used in the earning activities of a business and that are not undergoing the activities required to get them ready for use (FAS-34, par. 10).

COMPUTING INTEREST COST TO BE CAPITALIZED

The amount of interest cost that may be capitalized for any accounting period may not exceed the actual interest cost (from any source) that is incurred by an enterprise during that same accounting period (FAS-34, par. 15). In addition to interest paid and/or accrued on debt instruments, interest imputed in accordance with APB-21 (Interest on Receivables and Payables) and interest recognized on capital leases in accordance with FAS-13 (Accounting for Leases) are available for capitalization. FAS-34 specifically prohibits imputing interest costs on any equity funds. In consolidated financial statements, this limitation on the maximum amount of interest cost that may be capitalized in a period should be applied on a consolidated basis.

> **OBSERVATION:** Footnote 4 to paragraph 16 of FAS-87 (Employers' Accounting for Pensions) states that, "The interest cost component of net periodic pension cost shall not be considered to be interest for purposes of applying FASB Statement No. 34, Capitalization of Interest Cost."
>
> Similarly, footnote 8 to paragraph 22 of FAS-106 (Employers' Accounting for Postretirement Benefits Other Than Pensions) states that, "The interest cost component of postretirement benefit cost shall not be considered interest for purposes of applying FASB Statement No. 34, Capitalization of Interest Cost."

> ☛ **PRACTICE POINTER:** A logical starting point for applying FAS-34 and related pronouncements is to determine the total amount of interest that was incurred and that is available for capitalization as a cost of a qualifying asset. If a company incurs little or no qualifying interest on debt instruments, interest imputed in accordance with APB-21, or interest on capital leases, the requirement to capitalize interest may not be effective, even though the company may have invested in assets that would otherwise require interest capitalization.

Average Accumulated Expenditures

To compute the amount of interest cost to be capitalized for a particular accounting period, the average accumulated expenditures for the qualifying asset during that period must be determined. To determine the average accumulated expenditures, each expenditure must be *weighted* for the time it was outstanding during the particular accounting period.

Illustration of Computing Average Accumulated Expenditures

In the acquisition of a qualifying asset, a calendar year company expends $225,000 on January 1, 19X5; $360,000 on March 1, 19X5; and $180,000 on November 1, 19X5. The average accumulated expenditures for 19X5 are computed as follows:

Amount of Expenditure	Period from Expenditure to End of Year	Average Expenditure
$225,000	12 months (12/12)	$225,000
360,000	10 months (10/12)	300,000
180,000	2 months (2/12)	30,000
$765,000		$555,000

Identification of Interest Rates

If a specific borrowing is made to acquire the qualifying asset, the interest rate incurred on that borrowing may be used to determine the amount of interest costs to be capitalized. That interest rate is applied to the average accumulated expenditures for the period to calculate the amount of capitalized interest cost on the qualifying asset. Capitalized interest cost on average accumulated expenditures in excess of the amount of the specific borrowing is calculated by the use of the weighted-average interest rate incurred on other borrowings outstanding during the period (FAS-34, par. 13).

If no specific borrowing is made to acquire the qualifying asset, the weighted-average interest rate incurred on other borrowings outstanding during the period is used to determine the amount of interest cost to be capitalized. The weighted-average interest rate is applied to the average accumulated expenditures for the period to calculate the amount of capitalized interest cost on the qualifying asset. Judgment may be required to identify and select the appropriate specific borrowings that should be used in determining the weighted-average interest rate. The objective should be to obtain a reasonable cost of financing for the qualifying asset that could have been avoided if the asset had not been acquired (FAS-34, par. 14).

☞ **PRACTICE POINTER:** In determining the weighted average interest rate for purposes of capitalizing interest, take care not to overlook interest that is available for capitalization even though it has another specific purpose. For example, a company might have interest on mortgage debt on buildings and plant assets. Unless that interest already is being capitalized into a different asset under FAS-34, it is available for capitalization despite the fact that it was incurred specifically to finance the acquisition of a different asset.

Progress payments received from the buyer of a qualifying asset are deducted in the computation of the average amount of accumulated expenditures during a period. Nonetheless, the determination of the average amount of accumulated expenditures for a period may be reasonably estimated (FAS-34, par 16).

Illustration of Calculating Weighted-Average Interest Rate

A company has the following three debt issues outstanding during a year in which interest must be capitalized as part of the cost of a plant assets:

$1,000,000 par value, 8% interest rate
$1,500,000 par value, 9% interest rate
$1,200,000 par value, 10% interest rate

The weighted-average interest rate is computed as follows:

$1,000,000 x 8%	=	$ 80,000
1,500,000 x 9%	=	135,000
1,800,000 x 10%	=	180,000
$4,300,000	=	$395,000

$395,000/$4,300,000 = 9.19%

Interest available for capitalization is $395,000. Assuming none of the debt issues relates directly to the asset for which interest is being capitalized, interest is charged to the cost of the asset at a 9.19% interest rate applied to the average expenditure made on the asset during the year. If, instead, one of the debt issues relates directly to the asset for which interest is being capitalized, interest may be charged at the interest rate applicable to that debt issue on the investment equal to the amount of that debt. Interest on any remaining investment is calculated at the weighted-average interest rate for the remaining debt.

Capitalization Period

The interest capitalization period starts when three conditions are met (FAS-34, par. 17):

a. Expenditures have occurred.

b. Activities necessary to prepare the asset (including administrative activities before construction) have begun.

c. Interest cost has been incurred.

Interest is not capitalized during delays or interruptions, except for brief interruptions, that occur during the acquisition or development stage of the qualifying asset (FAS-34, par. 17).

When the qualifying asset is substantially complete and ready for its intended use, the capitalization of interest ceases. The qualifying asset may be completed in independent parts (i.e., the parts can be used separately from the rest of the project, like units in a condominium) or in dependent parts (i.e., parts that, although complete, cannot be used until other parts are finished, like subassemblies of a machine). Interest capitalization ceases for an independent part when it is substantially complete and ready for its intended use. For dependent parts of a qualifying asset, however, interest capitalization does not stop until all dependent parts are substantially complete and ready for their intended use (FAS-34, par. 18).

SPECIAL APPLICATIONS

Equity Method Investments

Under the provisions of FAS-58, an investor's qualifying assets, for the purposes of capitalizing interest costs under FAS-34, include equity funds, loans, and advances made to investees accounted for by the equity method (FAS-58, par. 5). Thus, an investor must capitalize interest costs on such qualifying assets if, during that period, the investee is undergoing activities necessary to start its planned principal operations and such activities include the use of funds to acquire qualifying assets for its operations. The investor does not capitalize any interest costs on or after the date that the investee actually begins its planned principal operations (FAS-58, par. 6).

> ☛ **PRACTICE POINTER:** The term *planned principal operations* has the same meaning as used in FAS-7 (Accounting and Reporting for Development Stage Enterprises). Under the provisions of FAS-7, a development stage company is one that devotes substantially all of its efforts to establishing a new business and (a) planned principal operations have not commenced or (b) planned principal operations have commenced, but there has been no significant revenue therefrom.

For the purposes of FAS-58, the term *investor* means both the parent company and all consolidated subsidiaries (FAS-58, par. 3). Thus, all qualifying assets of a parent company and its consolidated subsidiaries that appear in the consolidated balance sheet are subject to the interest capitalization provisions of FAS-34 (as amended). FAS-58 expressly states that it does not affect the accounting of reporting of capitalized interest cost in an investee's separate financial statements (FAS-58, par. 4).

Capitalized interest costs on an investment accounted for by the equity method are included in the carrying amount of the investment (FAS-58, par. 7). Up to the date on which the planned principal operations of the investee begin, the investor's carrying amount of the investment, which includes capitalized interest costs (if any), may exceed the underlying equity in the investment. If the investor cannot relate the excess carrying amount of the investment to specific identifiable assets of the investee, the difference is considered goodwill [APB-18, par. 19(n)].

Any interest cost capitalized under the provisions of FAS-58 is not changed in restating financial statements of prior periods. Thus, if an unconsolidated investee is subsequently consolidated in the investor's financial statements as a result of increased ownership or a voluntary change by the reporting entity, interest costs capitalized in accordance with FAS-58 are not changed if restatement of financial statements is necessary (FAS-58, par. 8).

Tax-Exempt Borrowings and Gifts and Grants

Under the provisions of FAS-34, capitalized interest cost for a qualifying asset is determined by applying either a specific interest rate or a weighted-average interest rate to the average accumulated expenditures during a particular period for the qualifying asset. An underlying premise in FAS-34 is that borrowings usually cannot be identified with specific qualifying assets. The financing policies of most enterprises are planned to meet general funding objectives, and the identification of specific borrowings with specific assets is considered highly subjective.

FAS-62 concludes that different circumstances are involved in the acquisition of a qualifying asset with tax-exempt borrowings, such as industrial revenue bonds and pollution control bonds. The tax-exempt borrowings, temporary interest income on unused funds, and construction expenditures for the qualifying asset are so integrated that they must be accounted for as a single transaction (FAS-62, par. 2). Thus, FAS-62 amends FAS-34 to provide for the capitalization of interest cost for any portion of a qualifying asset that is acquired with tax-exempt borrowings, as follows (FAS-62, par. 4):

Capitalization Period

Interest cost is capitalized from the date of the tax-exempt borrowings to the date that the qualifying asset is ready for its intended use (FAS-62, par. 7).

Amount of Capitalized Interest Cost

The amount of capitalized interest cost allowable under FAS-62 is equal to the total actual interest cost on the tax-exempt borrowing, less any interest income earned on temporary investments of the tax-exempt funds. The net cost of interest on the tax-exempt borrowing is capitalized and added to the acquisition cost of the related qualifying asset (FAS-62, par. 4).

External Restriction Requirement

FAS-62 applies only when the qualifying asset is financed by tax-exempt borrowing, in which the use of the borrowed funds is restricted to acquiring the assets or servicing the related debt. The restriction must be *external*, that is, imposed by law, contract, or other authority outside the enterprise that borrows the funds.

FAS-62 does not permit the capitalization of interest cost on any portion of a qualifying asset that is acquired with a gift or grant that is restricted to the acquisition of the specified qualifying asset. Restricted interest income on temporary investment of funds is considered an addition to the restricted gift or grant (FAS-62, par. 5).

> **OBSERVATION**: FAS-62 concludes that no interest cost should be capitalized on qualifying assets acquired by restricted gifts or grants, because there is no economic cost of financing involved in acquiring an asset with a gift or grant. In addition, any interest earned on temporary investment of funds from a gift or grant is, in substance, part of the gift or grant.

Full Cost Method in Extractive Industries

FIN-33 covers the application of FAS-34 to oil and gas producing activities that are being accounted for by the full cost method.

Unproved properties and major developments that represent unusually significant investments are assets which qualify for capitalization of interest costs, if the following conditions are met (FIN-33, par. 2):

a. Exploration or development activities are in progress.

b. The assets are not currently being depreciated, depleted, or amortized.

Other assets that qualify for capitalization of interest costs are significant properties or projects within a nonproducing cost center on which exploration or development activities are in progress (FAS-34, par. 11).

All assets that are currently being depreciated, depleted, or amortized are considered in use in the earning activities of the business and do not qualify for capitalization of interest costs (FAS-34, par. 10).

Disposition of Capitalized Interest

If capitalized interest costs are added to the overall cost of an asset, the total cost of the asset, including capitalized interest, may exceed the net realizable or other lower value of the asset that is required by GAAP. In this event, FAS-34 requires that the provision to reduce the asset cost to the lower value required by GAAP be increased. Thus, the total asset cost, including capitalized interest, less the provision, will equal the lower value for the asset that is required by GAAP (FAS-34, par. 19).

Capitalized interest costs become an integral part of the acquisition costs of an asset and should be accounted for as such in the event of disposal of the asset (FAS-34, par. 20).

DISCLOSURE REQUIREMENTS

The total amount of interest costs incurred and charged to expense during the period and the amount of interest costs, if any, which has been capitalized during the period, should be disclosed in the financial statements or notes thereto (FAS-34, par. 21).

Illustration of the Application of FAS-34

On January 1, 19X5, Poll Powerhouse borrowed $300,000 from its bank at an annual rate of 12%. The principal amount plus interest is due on January 1, 19X7. The funds from this loan are specifically designated for the construction of a new plant facility. On February 1, 19X5, Poll paid $15,000 for architects' fees and for fees for filing a project application with the state government.

On March 1, 19X5, Poll received state approval for the project and began construction. The following summarizes the costs incurred on this project.

19X5	
February 1 (architects' and filing fees)	$ 15,000
April 1	150,000
September 1	60,000
19X6	
January 1	1,000
March 1	360,000
November 1	180,000
Total Project Cost	$766,000

The $1,000 is a miscellaneous cost and was expensed in 19X6, since it was determined by Poll to be immaterial.

The following schedule summarizes the additional borrowings of Poll as of December 31, 19X6:

Borrowing Date	Amount	Maturity Date	Annual Interest Rate
March 1, 19X5	$1,000,000	Feb. 28, 19X7	13%
October 1, 19X6	$ 500,000	Sept. 30, 19X8	14%

From February 1, 19X6, to March 31, 19X6, a major strike of construction workers occurred, halting all construction activity during this period.

In August 19X6, Poll voluntarily halted construction for the entire month because the chief executive officer did not want construction to continue without her supervision during her scheduled vacation.

Calculation of Interest

Poll's new plant facility is a qualifying asset under the provisions of FAS-34 and is subject to interest capitalization. The interest capitalization period begins on the first date that an expenditure is made by Poll, which was for architects' fees, February 1, 19X5.

To compute the interest capitalization for 19X5, the average accumulated expenditures for 19X5 are first calculated as follows:

Amount of Expenditure	Period from Expenditure to End of Year	Average Expenditure
$ 15,000	11 months (11/12)	$ 13,750
150,000	9 months (9/12)	112,500
60,000	4 months (4/12)	20,000
$225,000		$146,250

Next, the average expenditures are multiplied by the interest rate on the borrowing (12%). This rate is used because Poll has specifically associated the borrowing with the construction of the new plant facility, and the average accumulated expenditures ($146,250) do not exceed the amount of the borrowing ($300,000). Therefore, the interest capitalized for 19X5 is computed as follows:

Average accumulated expenditures	$146,250
Interest rate	12%
Capitalizable interest cost—19X5	$ 17,550

Since Poll incurred $144,333 of interest costs [($300,000 x 12%) + ($1,000,000 x 13% x 10/12)], the full $17,550 must be capitalized.

The expenditures for 19X5 are included as part of the base to compute 19X6 capitalizable interest cost. One further adjustment is necessary to calculate the average accumulated expenditures for 19X6. The plant facility was completed on December 31, 19X6, but there were two interruptions in construction in 19X6. Interest is capitalized during delays or interruptions that are externally imposed, or during delays inherent in acquiring the qualifying asset. However, interest is not capitalized during delays or interruptions that are caused internally by an enterprise, unless they are brief. Thus, in this problem, interest capitalization continues during the externally imposed strike. However, interest capitalization ceases during August 19X6, because the CEO's vacation is a voluntary interruption.

The average accumulated expenditures for 19X6 are computed as follows:

Amount of Expenditure	Period from Expenditure to End of Year, Less One Month of Interruption	Average Expenditure
$225,000	11 months (11/12)	$206,250
360,000	9 months (9/12)	270,000
180,000	2 months (2/12)	30,000
$765,000		$506,250

Note: The $180,000 was expended on November 1, 19X6, after the interruption, so no adjustment need be made to the average expenditure of $30,000 for the interruption.

The $1,000 miscellaneous cost is not included, since Poll decided that this amount was immaterial and expensed it.

If the average accumulated expenditures for the qualifying asset exceed the amount of the specific borrowing made to construct the asset, the capitalization rate applicable to the excess is the weighted-average interest rate incurred on other borrowings. In this problem, the computation of the excess expenditures over the original loan amount is as follows:

Average expenditures through December 31, 19X6	$506,250
Less: Amount of original loan	300,000
Excess expenditures	$206,250

Thus, in 19X6, interest on $206,250 of the $506,250 average expenditures is capitalized using the weighted-average borrowing rate, whereas interest on the balance of $300,000 is capitalized using the interest rate on the original loan made specifically to acquire the qualifying asset. The weighted-average rate on the other borrowings is computed as follows:

Amount	Weighted Amount	Rate	Annual Interest
$1,000,000	$1,000,000	13%	$130,000
500,000	125,000 (3 mos.)	14%	$ 17,500
$1,500,000	$1,125,000		$147,500

$$\frac{\$147,500}{\$1,125,000} = 13.11\% \text{ weighted-average interest rate}$$

The interest cost to be capitalized for 19X6 is computed as follows:

$300,000	x	12.00%	=	$36,000
206,250	x	13.11%	=	27,039
$506,250				$63,039

Since Poll incurred $183,500 [($300,000 x 12%) + ($1,000,000 x 13%) + ($500,000 x 14% x 3/12)] of interest, the full $63,039 is capitalizable as part of the acquisition cost of the asset in 19X6.

The total interest capitalized on the asset is $80,589 ($17,550 in 19X5 plus $63,039 in 19X6). The total asset cost at the end of 19X6 is as follows:

Expenditures other than interest	$765,000
Interest cost capitalized	$ 80,589
	$845,589

CHAPTER 25
INTEREST ON RECEIVABLES AND PAYABLES

CONTENTS

CHAPTER 25
INTEREST ON RECEIVABLES
AND PAYABLES

OVERVIEW

Business transactions often involve the exchange of cash or other assets for a note or other instrument. When the interest rate on the instrument is consistent with the market rate at the time of the transaction, the face amount of the instrument is assumed to be equal to the value of the other asset(s) exchanged. An interest rate that is different from the prevailing market rate, however, implies that the face amount of the instrument may not equal the value of the other asset(s) exchanged. In this case, it may be necessary to impute interest that is not stated as part of the instrument, or to recognize interest at a rate other than that stated in the instrument.

Promulgated GAAP in the area of recognizing interest on receivables and payables are found in the following pronouncement:

APB-21   Interest on Receivables and Payables

CROSS-REFERENCES

1999 MILLER GAAP GUIDE: Chapter 11, "Depreciable Assets and Depreciation"; Chapter 24, "Interest Costs Capitalized"

1999 MILLER GAAP IMPLEMENTATION MANUAL: Chapter 14, "Interest on Receivables and Payables"

1999 MILLER GAAP IMPLEMENTATION MANUAL: EITF: Chapter 16, "Interest on Receivables and Payables"

1999 MILLER NOT-FOR-PROFIT REPORTING: Chapter 2, "Overview of Current Pronouncements"

BACKGROUND

APB-21 is the main source of GAAP on imputing interest on receivables and payables. However, APB-21 excludes receivables and payables under the following conditions (APB-21, par. 3):

1. They arise in the ordinary course of business and are due in approximately one year or less.

2. Their repayment will be applied to the purchase price of the property, goods, or services to which they relate rather than requiring a transfer of cash.

3. They represent security or retainage deposits.

4. They arise in the ordinary course of business of a lending institution.

5. They arise from transactions between a parent and its subsidiaries, or between subsidiaries of a common parent.

6. Their interest rate is determined by a governmental agency.

Receivables and payables that are not specifically excluded from the provisions of APB-21 and that are contractual rights to receive or pay money at a fixed or determinable date must be recorded at their present value if (*a*) the interest rate is not stated or (*b*) the stated interest rate is unreasonable (APB-21, par. 12).

> **OBSERVATION:** This is an application of the basic principle of substance over form in that the substance of the instrument (interest-bearing), rather than the form of the instrument (noninterest-bearing or bearing interest at an unreasonable rate), becomes the basis for recording.

CIRCUMSTANCES REQUIRING IMPUTED INTEREST

A note issued or received in a noncash transaction contains two elements to be valued: (1) the principal amount for the property, goods, or services exchanged and (2) an interest factor for the use of funds over the period of the note. These types of notes must be recorded at their present value. Any difference between the face amount of the note and its present value is a discount or premium that is amortized over the life of the note.

☛ **PRACTICE POINTER:** It is generally presumed that the interest stated on a note, resulting from a business transaction entered into at arm's length, is fair and adequate. If no interest is stated or if the interest stated appears unreasonable, however, record the substance of the transaction. Further, if rights or privileges are attached to the note, evaluate them separately.

For example, a beer distributor lends $5,000 for two years at no interest to a customer who wishes to purchase bar equipment. There is a tacit agreement that the customer will buy the distributor's products. In this event, a present value must be established for the note receivable, and the difference between the face of the note ($5,000) and its present value must be considered an additional cost of doing business for the beer distributor.

Circumstances requiring interest to be imputed as specified in APB-21 are summarized in Figure 25-1.

The present value techniques used in APB-21 should not be applied to estimates of a contractual property or other obligations that are assumed in connection with a sale of property, goods, or services such as an estimated warranty for product performance.

OBSERVATION: Interest that is imputed on certain receivables and payables in accordance with APB-21 is eligible for capitalization under the provisions of FAS-34 (see the 1999 *Miller GAAP Guide* chapter titled "Interest Costs Capitalized").

APPLYING APB-21 PRINCIPLES

Determining Present Value

There is no predetermined formula for computing an appropriate interest rate. *However, the objective is to approximate what the rate would have been, using the same terms and conditions, if it had been negotiated by an independent lender.* The following factors should be considered (APB-21, par. 13):

1. Credit rating of the borrower

2. Restrictive covenants or collateral involved

3. Prevailing market rates

4. Rate at which the debtor can borrow funds

The appropriate interest rate depends on a combination of the above factors.

Figure 25-1: Circumstances Indicating a Need to Impute Interest

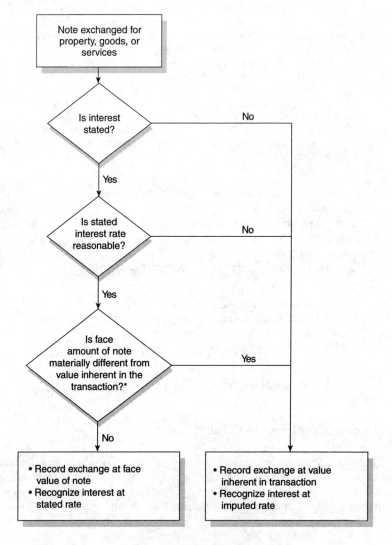

* Value inherent in transaction is the fair value of the property, goods, or services or the market value of the note, whichever is more readily determinable.

☞ **PRACTICE POINTER:** In determining an appropriate interest rate for purposes of imputing interest for the purchaser in a transaction, a starting point might be the most recent borrowing rate. The more recent the borrowing, the more appropriate that rate may be. Even if the borrowing rate is recent, however, give consideration to the impact that the additional debt from the earlier borrowing would likely have on the company's *next* borrowing. The size of the transaction for which interest is being imputed relative to other outstanding debt also may be an important factor in determining an appropriate rate.

Discount and Premium

The difference between the present value and the face amount of the receivable or the payable represents the amount of premium or discount. A discount exists if the present value of the total cash flow of the note (face amount plus stated interest), using the appropriate rate of interest, is *less* than the face amount of the note. A premium exists if the present value of the total proceeds of the note (face amount plus stated interest), using the appropriate rate of interest, is *more* than the face amount of the note.

The premium or discount is amortized over the life of the note, using a constant rate on any outstanding balance. This method is called the *interest method* and illustrated at the end of this chapter (APB-21, par. 15).

The premium or discount that arises from the use of present values on cash and noncash transactions is inseparable from the related asset or liability. Therefore, premiums and discounts are added to or deducted from their related asset or liability in the balance sheet. Discounts or premiums resulting from imputing interest are not classified as deferred charges or credits (APB-21, par. 16).

Disclosure

A description of the receivable or payable, the effective interest rate, and the face amount of the note should be disclosed in the financial statements or footnotes thereto. Issue costs are reported separately in the balance sheet as deferred charges (APB-21, par. 16).

Illustration of Interest Imputed and Accounted for on a Noninterest-Bearing Note

A manufacturer sells a machine for $10,000 and accepts a $10,000 note receivable bearing no interest for five years; 10% is an appropriate interest rate. The initial journal entry would be:

Note receivable	$10,000.00	
Sales (present value at 10%)		$6,209.00
Unamortized discount on note		3,791.00

The manufacturer records the note at its face amount but records the sale at the present value of the note because that is all the note is worth today. The difference between the face amount of the note and its present value is recorded as *unamortized discount on note*.

The *interest method* is used to produce a constant rate, which is applied to any outstanding balance. In the above example, the present value of $6,209 was recorded for the $10,000 sale using the appropriate interest rate of 10% for the five-year term of the note. The difference between the $10,000 sale and its present value of $6,209 is $3,791, which was recorded as unamortized discount on note. Since the present value was determined by using the 10% rate for five years, the same 10% rate, when applied to each annual outstanding balance for the same five years, will result in full amortization of the discount on the note, as follows:

		Amortization of Discount on the Note
Original balance	$ 6,209.00	$3,791.00
Year 1, 10%	620.90	(620.90)
Remaining balance	$ 6,829.90	$3,170.10
Year 2, 10%	682.99	(682.99)
Remaining balance	$ 7,512.89	$2,487.11
Year 3, 10%	751.29	(751.29)
Remaining balance	$ 8,264.18	$1,735.82
Year 4, 10%	826.42	(826.42)
Remaining balance	$ 9,090.60	$ 909.40
Year 5, to clear accounts	909.40	(909.40)
Remaining balance	$10,000.00	$ -0-

Following are the journal entries to record imputed interest at the end of each year and the final collection of the note.

End of 1st year:

Unamortized discount on note	$ 620.90	
Interest income		$ 620.90

End of 2nd year:

Unamortized discount on note	$ 682.99	
Interest income		$ 682.99

End of 3rd year:

Unamortized discount on note	$ 751.29	
Interest income		$ 751.29

End of 4th year:

Unamortized discount on note	$ 826.42	
Interest income		$ 826.42

End of 5th year:

Unamortized discount on note	$ 909.40	
Interest income		$ 909.40
Cash	$10,000.00	
Note receivable		$10,000.00

Illustration of Recording a Note with an Unreasonable Rate of Interest

A company purchases a $10,000 machine and issues for payment a $10,000 four-year note bearing 2% compound interest per year; 10% is considered an appropriate rate of interest. The initial journal entry is:

Machine (present value of $10,824 @ 10%)	$ 7,393	
Unamortized discount on note	3,431	
Note payable		$10,000
Deferred interest payable		824

1st year:

Interest expense	$ 739	
Unamortized discount on note		$ 739
(10% on $7,393)		

2nd year:

Interest expense	$ 813	
Unamortized discount on note		$ 813
[10% on ($7,393 + $739)]		

3rd year:

Interest expense	$ 895	
Unamortized discount on note		$ 895
[10% on ($7,393 + $739 + $813)]		

4th year:

Interest expense	$ 984	
Unamortized discount on note		$ 984
[10% on ($7,393 + $739 + $813 + $895)]		

In the fourth year, when the note and the 2% interest are paid, the following journal entry is made:

Note payable	$10,000	
Deferred interest payable	824	
Cash		$10,824

The future amount of the note is $10,824 ($10,000 x 1.0824, which compounds the 2% for four periods). The company records a note payable ($10,000) and the deferred interest ($824). The machine is recorded at the present value of this amount ($7,393), determined by discounting the $10,824 at 10% (the reasonable interest rate) for four years. This is because today the $10,824 is worth only $7,393, which is the amount at which the sale is recorded. The difference between the total amount due in four years ($10,824) and its present value ($7,393) is deferred interest ($3,431) for the use of the seller's funds and is amortized by the interest method over the term of the note.

CHAPTER 26
INTERIM FINANCIAL REPORTING

CONTENTS

CHAPTER 26
INTERIM FINANCIAL REPORTING

OVERVIEW

Interim financial reports may be issued quarterly, monthly, or at other intervals, and may include complete financial statements or summarized data. In addition, they usually include the current interim period and a cumulative year-to-date period, or last 12 months to date, with comparative reports on the corresponding periods of the immediately preceding fiscal year.

GAAP for interim financial statements are found primarily in the following pronouncement:

APB-28   Interim Financial Reporting

CROSS-REFERENCES

1999 MILLER GAAP GUIDE: Chapter 1, "Accounting Changes"; Chapter 7, "Contingencies, Risks, and Uncertainties"; Chapter 21, "Income Taxes"; Chapter 27, "Inventory Pricing and Methods"; Chapter 42, "Results of Operations"; Chapter 44, "Segment Reporting"

1999 MILLER GAAP IMPLEMENTATION MANUAL: Chapter 15, "Interim Financial Reporting"

1999 MILLER GAAP IMPLEMENTATION MANUAL: EITF: Chapter 17, "Interim Financial Reporting"

1999 MILLER GAAS GUIDE: Chapter 13, "Interim Reviews, Condensed Financials, Filings Under Federal Securities Statutes, and Letters to Underwriters"

BACKGROUND

The majority of GAAP have been developed with annual financial reporting in mind. These reporting standards generally are also applicable to interim financial reports. Some problems exist, how-ever, in attempting to apply GAAP intended primarily for annual reporting purposes to financial reporting for shorter periods of time.

Two opposing approaches explain the relationship between in-terim financial reports and annual financial reports. The *discrete* approach, sometimes called the *independent* approach, views an in-terim period in the same way as an annual period. Within this approach accounting principles for an annual period are equally appropriate for periods of differing lengths of time and are applied in the same manner. Opposite that view is the *integral* approach, sometimes called the *dependent* approach, which views an interim period as a component, or *integral* part, of the annual period rather than a separate or discrete period. Within this approach, the purpose of interim financial reporting is to provide information over the course of the annual period that helps anticipate annual results.

APB-28 endorses aspects of both the discrete and integral ap-proaches, but generally favors the *integral*, or *dependent*, approach to financial reporting for interim periods. Accordingly, certain proce-dures that are used in reporting for annual periods are modified in reporting for interim periods.

☛ **PRACTICE POINTER:** Take care in preparing and reviewing interim financial statements *not* to assume that GAAP appro-priate for *annual* financial statements are appropriate for *in-terim* statements. Examples where GAAP differ are the determi-nation of cost of goods sold where a LIFO inventory layer has been eroded in an early interim period, accounting for income taxes on a cumulative year-to-date basis, and the determina-tion of the materiality of items in interim financial statements.

ACCOUNTING AND REPORTING IN INTERIM PERIODS

Each interim period should be viewed as an integral part of the annual period. An important objective of interim reporting is for the user of the information to become progressively better informed about annual information as time passes. Accounting principles and reporting practices generally are those of the latest annual reports of the entity, with limited exceptions, such as a change in an accounting principle (APB-28, par. 10). A change in an accounting principle during an interim period is discussed in the *GAAP Guide* chapter titled "Accounting Changes."

Revenues are recognized as earned on the same basis as fiscal periods (APB-28, par. 11).

As closely as possible, product costs are determined as those for the fiscal period with some exceptions for inventory valuation, as follows (APB-28, pars. 13 and 14):

1. Companies using the gross profit method to determine interim inventory costs, or other methods different from those used for annual inventory valuation, should disclose the method used at the interim date and any significant adjustments that result from reconciliation(s) with the annual physical inventory.

2. A liquidation of a base-period LIFO inventory at an interim date that is expected to be recovered by the end of the annual period is valued at the expected cost of replacement. Cost of sales for the interim period includes the expected cost of replacement and not the cost of the base-period LIFO inventory.

3. Inventory losses from market declines are included in the interim period in which they occur, and gains in subsequent interim periods are recognized in such interim periods but cannot exceed the losses included in prior interim periods. (*Temporary* market declines that are expected to be made up by the end of the annual period need not be recognized in interim periods.)

4. Inventory and product costs computed by the use of a standard cost accounting system are determined by the same procedures used at the end of a fiscal year. Variances from standard costs that are expected to be made up by the end of the fiscal year need not be included in interim-period statements.

Other costs and expenses are charged or allocated to produce a fair presentation of the results of operation, cash flows, and financial position for all interim periods. The following apply in accounting for other costs and expenses (APB-28, par. 15):

1. A general rule in preparing interim-period financial statements is that costs and expenses that clearly benefit more than one period are allocated to the periods affected. This procedure should be applied consistently.

2. Companies that have material seasonal revenue variations must take care to avoid the possibility that interim-period financial statements become misleading. Disclosure of such variations should be made in the interim-period financial statements. In addition, it is desirable to disclose results for a full year, ending with the current interim period.

3. Unusual and infrequent transactions that are material and not designated as extraordinary items, such as the effects of a disposal of a segment of business, are reported separately in the interim periods in which they occur (APB-28, par. 21).

4. All other pertinent information, such as accounting changes, contingencies, seasonal results, and purchase or pooling transactions, is disclosed to provide the necessary information for the proper understanding of the interim financial statements.

Interim reports should not contain arbitrary amounts of costs or expenses. Estimates should be reasonable and based on all available information applied consistently from period to period (APB-28, par. 17). An effective tax rate is used for determining the income tax provision in interim periods, applied on a cumulative year-to-date basis (APB-28, par. 19). Income taxes for interim-period reports are discussed in the *GAAP Guide* chapter titled "Income Taxes."

Material contingencies and other uncertainties that exist at an interim date are disclosed in interim reports in the same manner as that required for annual reports. These interim-date contingencies and uncertainties should be evaluated in relation to the annual report. The disclosure for such items must be repeated in every interim and annual report until the contingency is resolved or becomes immaterial (APB-28, par. 22).

SUMMARIZED INTERIM FINANCIAL INFORMATION

Publicly traded companies reporting summarized financial information at interim dates should include the following (APB-28, par. 30):

1. Gross revenues, provision for income taxes, extraordinary items, effects of changes in accounting principles, and net income

2. Primary and fully diluted earnings-per-share data

3. Material seasonal variations of revenues, costs, or expenses

4. Significant changes in estimates or provisions for income taxes

5. Disposal of a segment of a business and extraordinary, unusual, or infrequently occurring items

6. Contingent items

7. Changes in accounting principles or estimates

8. Significant changes in financial position

> ☞ **PRACTICE POINTER:** To satisfy the above disclosure requirements, companies may present abbreviated financial statements, separate information items, or both. For example, a company may present an abbreviated income statement and selected information items from the balance sheet and statement of cash flows. Another company will present abbreviated versions of all three financial statements. In all approaches, companies typically omit most of the detailed note disclosures that are required in annual financial statements.

When summarized financial information is reported regularly on a quarterly basis, the above information should be furnished for the current quarter, the current year-to-date, or the last twelve months to date, with comparable information for the preceding year (APB-28, par. 30). (The illustration at the end of this chapter suggests a format for this information.)

> ☛ **PRACTICE POINTER:** Summarized interim financial statements based on these minimum disclosures *do not* constitute a fair presentation of financial position and results of operations in conformity with GAAP. Care should be taken that statements do not imply that interim information is in accordance with GAAP, unless it is (which is rarely the case).

In the event that fourth-quarter results are not issued separately, the annual report should include disclosures for the fourth quarter on the aggregate effect of material year-end adjustments and infrequently occurring items, extraordinary items, and disposal of business segments that occurred in the fourth quarter (APB-28, par. 31).

Illustration of Format for Presenting Interim Financial Information

When quarterly information is regularly reported by publicly held companies, APB-28 requires (1) minimum disclosure of specific information items for the current quarter and comparable information for the same quarter of the previous year and (2) current year-to-date or twelve-months-to-date information and comparable information for the same period of the previous year.

The following is a suggested format, using illustrative dates and numbers, for the presentation of this information:

Hypothetical Company
Interim Financial Information
For Quarter Ending June 30, 19X4, and Comparable Periods
(in thousands)

	Current Quarter		Twelve-Months-To-Date	
	3 months ending 6/30/19X4	*3 months ending 6/30/19X3*	*Year ending 6/30/19X4*	*Year ending 6/30/19X3*
[Information item]	$50	$40	$425	$575

CHAPTER 27
INVENTORY PRICING AND METHODS

CONTENTS

CHAPTER 27
INVENTORY PRICING AND METHODS

OVERVIEW

The preparation of financial statements requires careful determination of an appropriate dollar amount of inventory. Usually, that amount is presented as a current asset in the balance sheet and is a direct determinant of cost of goods sold in the income statement; as such, it has a significant impact on the amount of net income. When the matching principle is applied in determining net income, the valuation of inventories is of primary importance.

GAAP for the measurement of inventories are found in the following pronouncements:

APB-28   Interim Financial Reporting

ARB-43   Chapter 4, Inventory Pricing

FAS-2   Accounting for Research and Development Costs

FIN-1   Accounting Changes Related to the Cost of Inventory

> **OBSERVATION:** ARB 43, Chapter 4, is amended by FAS-133 (Accounting for Derivative Instruments and Hedging Activities). This is effective for fiscal years beginning after June 15, 1999. FAS-133 applies in interim financial statements for periods that begin after the same date (e.g., the quarter beginning July 1, 1999). FAS-133 is covered in Chapter 16 of the 1999 *Miller GAAP Guide*.
>
> Because the effective date of FAS-133 is delayed as indicated above, and the first calendar year for which FAS-133 will be in effect is the year 2000, the impact of FAS-133 on ARB 43 is not reflected in the 1999 *Miller GAAP Guide*.

CROSS-REFERENCES

BACKGROUND

Inventories of goods must periodically be compiled, measured, and recorded in the books of accounts of a business. Inventory usually is classified as (*a*) finished goods, (*b*) work in process, or (*c*) raw materials (ARB-43, Ch. 4, Statement 1). Inventories exclude long-term assets that are subject to depreciation.

Inventories are classified as current assets, except when there are excessive quantities that may not reasonably be expected to be used or sold within the normal operating cycle of a business. In this event, the excess inventory is classified as noncurrent.

The basis of accounting for inventories is cost, which is the price paid or consideration given to acquire the asset. In inventory accounting, cost is the sum of the expenditures and charges, direct and indirect, in bringing goods to their existing condition or location (ARB-43, Ch. 4, Statement 3).

While the principle of measuring inventory at cost can be easily stated, the application of the principle, particularly to work-in-process items and finished goods, is difficult because of the problem involved in allocating various costs and charges. For example, idle factory expense, excessive spoilage, double freight, and rehandling costs can be so abnormal that they may have to be charged to the current period, rather than be treated as elements of inventory cost. Selling expenses are not part of inventory costs. *The exclusion of all overhead from inventory costs* (direct or variable costing) *is an unacceptable accounting procedure* (ARB-43, Ch. 4, par. 5).

INVENTORY SYSTEMS

Periodic System

Inventory is determined by a physical count as of a specific date. As long as the count is made frequently enough for reporting purposes, it is not necessary to maintain extensive inventory records. The inventory shown in the balance sheet is determined by the physical count and is priced in accordance with the inventory method used. The net change between the beginning and ending inventories enters into the computation of the cost of goods sold.

Perpetual System

In a perpetual system, inventory records are maintained and updated continuously as items are purchased and sold. The system has the advantage of providing inventory information on a timely basis but requires the maintenance of a full set of inventory records. Theoretically, physical counts are not necessary, but they are normally taken to verify the inventory records. GAAP require that a physical check of perpetual inventory records be made periodically.

LOWER OF COST OR MARKET

When the utility of the goods in the ordinary course of business is no longer as great as their cost, a departure from the cost principle of measuring the inventory is required. Whether the cause is obsolescence, physical deterioration, changes in price levels, or any other, the difference should be recognized by a charge to income in the current period. This usually is accomplished by stating the goods at a lower level designated as market (lower of cost or market principle) (ARB-43, Ch. 4, Statement 5).

In the phrase *lower of cost or market*, the term *market* means current replacement cost, whether by purchase or by reproduction, *but is limited to the following maximum and minimum amounts* (ARB-43, Ch. 4, Statement 6):

1. *Maximum:* the estimated selling price less any costs of completion and disposal, referred to as net realizable value

2. *Minimum:* net realizable value, less an allowance for normal profit

The purpose of reducing inventory to the lower of cost or market is to reflect fairly the income of the period. When market is lower than cost, the purposes of the maximum and minimum limitations are:

1. The maximum prevents a loss in future periods by at least valuing the inventory at its estimated selling price less costs of completion and disposal.

2. The minimum prevents any future periods from realizing any more than a normal profit.

Illustration of How Maximum and Minimum Constraints Impact Lower of Cost or Market Determination

Item	Cost	Replacement Cost	(1) Selling Price	(2) Cost of Completion	(1 – 2) Maximum*	(3) Normal Profit	[(1 – 2) – 3] Minimum
1	$20.50	$ 19.00	$ 25.00	$ 1.00	$ 24.00	$ 6.00	$ 18.00
2	26.00	20.00	30.00	2.00	28.00	7.00	21.00
3	10.00	12.00	15.00	1.00	14.00	3.00	11.00
4	40.00	55.00	60.00	6.00	54.00	4.00	50.00
	$96.50	$106.00	$130.00	$10.00	$120.00	$20.00	$100.00

*The maximum is equal to the net realizable value.

Applying the lower of cost or market to the above four items individually results in the following amounts:

Item 1	$19.00	Item 3	$10.00
Item 2	$21.00	Item 4	$40.00

The lower of cost or market principle may be applied to a single item, a category, or the total inventory, provided that the method most clearly reflects periodic income (ARB-43, Ch. 4, Statement 7). The basic principle of consistency must be applied in the valuation of inventory, and the method should be disclosed in the financial statements (ARB-43, Ch. 4, Statement 8).

The write-down of inventory to market usually is reflected in cost of goods sold, unless the amount is unusually material, in which case the loss should be identified separately in the income statement (ARB-43, Ch. 4, Statement 14).

In the event that a significant change occurs in the measurement of inventory, disclosure of the nature of the change and, if material, the effect on income should be made in the financial statements.

Exceptional cases, such as precious metals having a fixed determinable monetary value with no substantial cost of marketing, may be stated at such monetary value. When inventory is stated at a value in excess of cost, this fact should be disclosed fully in the financial statements (ARB-43, Ch. 4, Statement 9).

To apply this exception to other types of inventory, there must be: (*a*) immediate marketability at quoted prices, (*b*) inability to determine approximate costs, and (*c*) interchangeability of units.

INVENTORY COST METHODS

For inventory purposes, cost may be determined by specific identification or by the association of the flow of cost factors—first-in, first-out (FIFO), last-in, first-out (LIFO), and average cost.

In selecting an inventory cost method, an important objective is the selection of the method that under the circumstances most clearly reflects periodic income. When similar goods are purchased at different times, it may not be possible or practical to identify and match the specific costs of the item sold. Frequently, the identity of goods and their specific related costs are lost between the time of acquisition and the time of use or sale. This has resulted in the general acceptance of several assumptions with respect to the flow of cost factors to provide practical bases for the measurement of periodic income (ARB-43, Ch. 4, Statement 4).

First-In, First-Out Method (FIFO)

The *FIFO method* of identifying inventory is based on the assumption that costs are charged against revenue in the order in which they occur. The inventory remaining on hand is presumed to consist of the most recent costs.

Theoretically, FIFO approximates the results that would be obtained by the specific identification method if items were sold in the order in which they were purchased.

Last-In, First-Out Method (LIFO)

The LIFO method matches the most recent costs incurred with current revenue, leaving the first cost incurred to be included as inventory. LIFO requires that records be maintained as to the base-year layer and additional layers that may be created or used up. An additional LIFO layer is created in any year in which the quantity of ending inventory is more than the beginning inventory and is priced at the earliest or average costs of the year in which it was created.

When the quantity of ending inventory is less than the beginning inventory, one or more LIFO layers may be used up. Once a LIFO layer is used up, any future new LIFO layer is priced at the cost of the year in which it is created, and not by reinstating a prior LIFO layer cost.

In addition to the disclosure of significant accounting policies required by APB-22 (Disclosure of Accounting Policies) and of composition of inventories (ARB-43, Ch. 4, Statement 8), a business using the LIFO method of reporting inventory must disclose the following, if it reports to the SEC:

1. Current replacement value of the LIFO inventories at each balance sheet date presented

2. The effect on the results of operations for any reduction of a LIFO layer

☛ **PRACTICE POINTER:** While using LIFO inventory method is sometimes justified on the basis of a superior matching of current revenues and current costs, the primary catalysts for using it are its acceptance for income tax purposes and the lower taxable income that it produces. Income tax law requires a company that uses LIFO for tax purposes to also use LIFO for financial reporting purposes. In changing from another inventory cost method to the LIFO method for financial reporting purposes, the company must present a justification. Changing an accounting method for financial reporting purposes because of its preferability for tax purposes generally is not acceptable. Therefore, changing to LIFO usually is justified by reasons such as higher quality earnings that result from matching current revenues with current costs, and bringing the company into conformity with normal industry practice.

Weighted-Average Method

The weighted-average method of inventory valuation assumes that costs are charged against revenue based on an average of the number of units acquired at each price level. The resulting average price is applied to the ending inventory to find the total ending inventory value. The weighted average is determined by dividing the total costs of the inventory available, including any beginning inventory, by the total number of units.

Illustration of Application of FIFO, LIFO, and the Weighted-Average Methods of Inventory Valuation

Assume the following facts:

Units Purchased During the Year

Date	Units	Cost per Unit	Total Cost
January 15	10,000	$5.10	$ 51,000
March 20	20,000	5.20	104,000
May 10	50,000	5.00	250,000
June 8	30,000	5.40	162,000
October 12	5,000	5.30	26,500
December 21	5,000	5.50	27,500
Totals	120,000		$621,000

Beginning inventory consisted of 10,000 units at $5.

Ending inventory consisted of 14,000 units.

Under *FIFO*, the first units in stock are the first units out, which means that the ending inventory is of the units purchased last. Since the ending inventory is 14,000 units and December purchases were only 5,000 units, go back to October purchases for another 5,000 units and to June purchases for another 4,000 units, as follows:

December purchases	5,000 units	@	$5.50	=	$27,500
October purchases	5,000 units	@	5.30	=	26,500
From June purchases	4,000 units	@	5.40	=	21,600
Ending inventory using FIFO	14,000 units				$75,600

Under *LIFO*, the last units in stock are the first units out, which means that the ending inventory is composed of the units purchased first. Using LIFO, go back to the earliest inventory to start the calculations. The earliest inventory available is the *beginning inventory* of 10,000 units at $5, but the ending inventory is 14,000 units. Thus, go to the next earliest purchase, which is January, and use 4,000 units at the January price to complete the ending inventory valuation, as follows:

Beginning inventory	10,000 units	@	$5.00	=	$50,000
From January purchase	4,000 units	@	5.10	=	20,400
Ending inventory using LIFO	14,000 units				$70,400

Under the *weighted-average* method, multiply the weighted-average cost per unit by the 14,000 units in the ending inventory, thus:

	Units	Cost per Unit	Total Cost
Beginning inventory	10,000	$5.00	$ 50,000
Purchases:			
January 15	10,000	5.10	51,000
March 20	20,000	5.20	104,000
May 10	50,000	5.00	250,000
June 8	30,000	5.40	162,000
October 12	5,000	5.30	26,500
December 21	5,000	5.50	27,500
Totals	130,000		$671,000

Weighted average	= Total costs divided by total units
	= $671,000 divided by 130,000
	= $5.1615 per unit
Ending inventory	= 14,000 x $5.1615 per unit = $72,261

Comparison of the Three Methods

Ending inventory, FIFO	$75,600
Ending inventory, LIFO	70,400
Ending inventory, weighted average	72,261

In periods of inflation, the FIFO method produces the highest ending inventory, resulting in the lowest cost of goods sold and the highest gross profit. LIFO produces the lowest ending inventory, resulting in the highest cost of goods sold and the lowest gross profit. The weighted-average method yields results between those of LIFO and FIFO.

Moving-Average Method

The moving-average method can be used only with a perpetual inventory. The cost per unit is recomputed after every addition to the inventory.

Illustration of Moving-Average Method

	Total Units	Total Cost	Unit Cost
Beginning inventory	1,000	$ 5,000	$5.00
Sales of 200 units	800	4,000	5.00
Purchase of 1,200 @ $6	2,000	11,200*	5.60
Sales of 1,000 units	1,000	5,600	5.60
Purchase of 1,000 @ $5	2,000	10,600**	5.30

* $4,000 + (1,200 @ $6) = $11,200; $11,200 / 2,000 units = $5.60/unit
** $5,600 + (1,000 @ $5) = $10,600; $10,600 / 2,000 units = $5.30/unit

Note: Only purchases change the unit price; sales are taken out at the prior moving-average unit cost.

Under the moving-average method, the ending inventory is costed at the last moving-average unit cost for the period.

Dollar-Value LIFO Method

A variation of the conventional LIFO method is the dollar-value LIFO method. Under the regular LIFO method, units of inventory are priced at unit prices. Under the dollar-value LIFO method, the base-year inventory is priced in dollars; for inventories of all subsequent years, price indices are used, with the base year as 100.

Illustration of Dollar-Value LIFO Method

Year	Inventory at Base-Year Prices	Price Index	LIFO Inventory Amount
1	$100,000	100	$100,000
2	20,000	105	21,000
3	10,000	110	11,000
4	20,000	120	24,000
5	20,000	125	25,000
Totals	$170,000		$181,000

Retail Inventory Method

Because of the great variety and quantity of inventory in some types of businesses, the reversed markup procedure of inventory pricing, such as the retail inventory method, may be both practical and appropriate.

The retail inventory method requires the maintenance of records of purchases at both cost and selling price. A ratio of cost to retail is calculated and applied to the ending inventory at retail to compute the approximate cost.

Illustration of Basic Retail Inventory Method

	Cost	Retail
Inventory, at beginning of period	$ 100,000	$ 150,000
Purchases during the period	1,100,000	1,850,000
Totals (ratio of cost to retail 60%)	$1,200,000	$2,000,000
Sales during the period		(1,800,000)
Estimated ending inventory at retail		$ 200,000
Estimated ending inventory at cost (60% x $200,000)		$ 120,000

Physical inventories measured by the retail method should be taken periodically as a check on the accuracy of the estimated inventories.

Original selling prices may be modified, thus necessitating an understanding of the following terminology:

Original retail—The first selling price at which goods are offered for sale

Markup—The selling price raised above the original selling price

Markdown—The selling price lowered below the original selling price

Markup cancellation—Markup selling price decreased, but not below the original selling price

Markdown cancellation—Markdown selling price increased, but not above the original selling price

Net markup—Markup less markup cancellation

Net markdown—Markdown less markdown cancellation

Markon—Difference between the cost and the original selling price, plus any net markups

---

Illustration of Markups and Markdowns

Original cost	$100
Original selling price ($50 markon)	$150
Markup	50
Original selling price plus markup	200
Markup cancellation	(25)
Original selling price plus net markup	175
Markdown (consists of $25 markup cancellation and a $25 markdown)	(50)
Original selling price less markdown	125
Markdown	(25)
Original selling price less markdown	100
Markdown cancellation	25
Original selling price less net markdown	125
Markup (consists of a $25 markdown cancellation and a $25 markup)	50
Original selling price plus net markup	$175

Theoretically, the last selling price consists of:

$50	markup
(25)	markup cancellation
(25)	markup cancellation
(25)	markdown
(25)	markdown
25	markdown cancellation
25	markdown cancellation
25	markup
$25	net plus change

Now the goods are priced at the original selling price plus a net markup of $25, or a total of $175.

The purpose of the conventional retail inventory method is to produce an inventory valuation closely approximating what would be obtained by taking a physical inventory and pricing the goods at the lower of cost or market.

The basic assumption of the retail inventory method is that there exists an equal distribution of goods (high-cost ratio and low-cost ratio) between sales, beginning inventory, and ending inventory. In instances in which this basic premise does not prevail, cost ratios should be determined by departments or small units. This requires keeping separate sales, purchases, markups, markdowns, and beginning and ending inventories by departments.

Lower of Cost or Market Application

To approximate the lower of cost or market in the computations, *markdowns and markdown cancellations are excluded in calculating the ratio of cost to retail and are added to the retail inventory after the ratio is determined.*

In calculating the cost-to-retail ratio, any adjustment to the retail value will necessarily affect the ratio and the resulting cost figure. Adjustments that decrease the denominator of the ratio increase the ratio and the value for ending inventory at cost, increasing gross profit. In the interest of conservatism, as well as for other reasons, adjustments that decrease the retail figure should be avoided. Markups, which increase the denominator, however, are included *net* of cancellations.

Net markdowns (markdowns less markdown cancellations) are an example of adjustments that decrease the denominator. Including them in the retail figure violates the lower-of-cost-or-market rule. As shown below, net markdowns are not included in the calculation of the ratio but *are* included in the determination of ending inventory after computing the ratio. The rationale for this is that the cost-to-retail ratio is presumed to be based on normal conditions, and markdown is not a normal condition. When *applying* the ratio, however, to conform to the lower-of-cost-or-market rule, the retail value must be reduced by the amount of the markdowns.

Employee discounts apply only to goods sold, not those remaining on hand. A sale at less than normal retail price to an employee does not represent a valid reduction to lower of cost or market, nor does it represent a valid adjustment of the cost-to-retail ratio or the value of the ending inventory. Therefore, employee discounts should not enter into any of the calculations, but are deducted from retail in the same way as markdowns after the computation of the cost-to-retail ratio.

Inventory spoilage and shrinkage affect the ending inventory figure but do not enter into the cost-to-retail ratio calculation. When arriving at the final figure for inventory at cost, the amount of shrinkage is deducted either at cost or at retail depending upon whether shrinkage is stated at cost or at retail.

Illustration of Retail Method/Lower-of-Cost-or-Market Application

	Cost	Retail
Inventory, at beginning of period	$200,000	$ 300,000
Purchases	550,000	800,000
Transportation-in	50,000	
Markups		100,000
Markup cancellations		20,000
Markdowns		70,000
Markdown cancellations		10,000

The calculations are as follows:

	Cost	Retail
Inventory, at beginning of period	$200,000	$ 300,000
Purchases	550,000	800,000
Transportation-in	50,000	
Markups		100,000
Markup cancellations		(20,000)
Totals (ratio of cost to retail 67.8%)	$800,000	$1,180,000
Markdowns		(70,000)
Markdown cancellations		10,000
Total goods at retail		$1,120,000
Less: Sales during the period		(860,000)
Inventory, ending (at retail)		$ 260,000
Inventory, ending (67.8% x $260,000)*		$ 176,280

*At estimated lower of cost or market

LIFO Application

The LIFO method of evaluating inventory can be estimated via the retail inventory method by using procedures somewhat different from the conventional retail method. Basically, two differences have to be taken into consideration:

1. Since the LIFO method produces a valuation approximating cost, and the conventional retail method produces a valuation approximating the lower of cost or market, to apply the LIFO concept to the conventional retail method it is necessary

to include all markdowns as well as markups in determining the ratio of cost to retail.

2. With the LIFO method, the quantity of inventory on hand is from the earliest purchases during the year or from prior years' LIFO layers. The cost-to-retail ratio considers the current relationship between cost and selling price. Therefore, the beginning inventory is omitted from the cost-to-retail ratio, because it may cause a distortion.

Illustration of Retail Method/LIFO Application

Information from the previous example is restated on a LIFO basis, as follows:

	Cost	Retail
Inventory, beginning of period	omitted	omitted
Purchases	$550,000	$ 800,000
Transportation-in	50,000	
Markups		100,000
Markup cancellations		(20,000)
Markdowns		(70,000)
Markdown cancellations		10,000
Totals (ratio of cost to retail 73.2%)	$600,000	$ 820,000
Add: Inventory, beginning of period		300,000
Total goods at retail		$1,120,000
Less: Sales during period		(860,000)
Inventory, ending of period (at retail)		$ 260,000

Since the $260,000 ending LIFO inventory (at retail) is less than the $300,000 beginning LIFO inventory (at retail), a prior LIFO layer was partially depleted:

	Retail
Beginning inventory	$300,000
Ending inventory	(260,000)
LIFO layer depleted	$ 40,000

The $40,000 difference is multiplied by the beginning inventory cost-to-retail ratio ($200,000/$300,000 = 66.7%) and then subtracted from the beginning inventory at cost, as follows:

	Cost
Beginning inventory	$200,000
$40,000 x 66.7%	(26,680)
Ending inventory (at cost)	$173,320

If the ending LIFO inventory (at retail) had been greater than the beginning LIFO inventory (at retail), a new LIFO layer would have been created which would have been costed at the new cost-to-retail ratio (73.2%).

MISCELLANEOUS INVENTORY ISSUES

Title to Goods

Legal title to merchandise usually determines whether or not it is included in the inventory of an enterprise. Title to goods passes from the seller to the buyer in any manner and on any conditions explicitly agreed on by the parties. If no conditions are explicitly agreed on, title to goods passes from the seller to the buyer at the time and place at which the seller completes its performance with reference to the physical delivery of the goods. Title passes to the buyer at the time and place of shipment if the seller is required only to send the goods. If the contract requires delivery at destination, however, title passes when the goods are tendered at the destination. The following is the most commonly used terminology in passing title from the seller to the buyer:

F.O.B.—Means *free on board* and requires the seller, at its expense, to deliver the goods to the destination indicated as F.O.B.

F.A.S.—Means *free alongside* and usually is used in conjunction with a dock or a seaport. The seller must, at its expense, deliver the goods to the vessel indicated on the F.A.S.

C.I.F.—Means that the price of the goods includes the cost of the goods and the insurance and freight to the named destination.

C & F—Means that the price of the goods includes the cost of the goods and the freight to the named destination.

C.O.D.—Means *collect on delivery* and requires the buyer to pay for the goods at the time and place of delivery.

Standard Costs

The use of standard costs is a management tool that identifies favorable or unfavorable variances from predetermined estimates established by past performance or time and motion studies. Inventory valuation by the use of standard costs is acceptable, if adjusted at reasonable intervals to reflect the approximate costs computed under one of the recognized methods, and adequate disclosure is made in the financial statements.

At the end of the reporting period, the physical inventory is costed at LIFO, FIFO, or some other generally accepted method. Any variation between this result and the carrying value of the inventory at standard cost must be closed out to cost of goods sold and ending inventory such that the reported figure represents that which the generally accepted method would yield.

Relative Sales Value Costing

Determining the relative sales cost of inventory items is used when costs cannot be determined individually. Joint products, lump-sum purchase of assets (basket purchase), and large assets that are subdivided (real estate tracts) are examples of items that would be costed by their relative sales value.

Illustration of Relative Sales Value Costing

ABC Company purchases inventory consisting of four large pieces of machinery for $100,000. At the time of purchase, an appraisal discloses the following fair values:

Machine #1	$ 12,000
Machine #2	28,000
Machine #3	40,000
Machine #4	30,000
Total	$110,000

The cost of each machine is an allocated amount, based on relative fair values, as follows:

Machine #1	12/110 x $100,000	=	$ 10,909
Machine #2	28/110 x $100,000	=	25,455
Machine #3	40/110 x $100,000	=	36,364
Machine #4	30/110 x $100,000	=	27,272
Total cost allocated			$100,000

Alternatively, a percentage of total cost to the price paid can be computed: $100,000/$110,000 = 90.91%. That percentage is then applied to the value of each item to determine its cost. For example, cost for Machine #1 is $12,000 x 90.91% = $10,909.

Firm Purchase Commitments

Losses on firm purchase commitments for inventory goods are measured in the same manner as inventory losses and, if material, recognized in the accounts and disclosed separately in the income statement (ARB-43, Ch. 4, Statement 10).

The recognition of losses, which are expected to arise from firm, noncancelable commitments and which arise from the decline in the utility of a cost expenditure, should be disclosed in the current period income statement. In addition, all significant firm purchase commitments must be disclosed in the financial statements or in footnotes, whether or not any losses are recognized.

Discontinued Segments

Inventories used in discontinued segments of a business should be written down to their net realizable value and the amount of write-down included as part of the gain or loss recognized on the disposal of the discontinued segment. Such a write-down, however, should not be attributable to any inventory adjustment that should have been recognized prior to the measurement date of the loss on disposal. In this event, the loss on the write-down is included in the operating results of the discontinued segment in accordance with APB-30 (Reporting the Results of Operations—Reporting the Effects of Disposal of a Segment of a Business and Extraordinary, Unusual, and Infrequently Occurring Events and Transactions).

Interim Financial Reporting

Generally, the same principles and methods are used to value inventories for interim financial statements as are used for annual reports. For practical purposes, however, APB-28 specifies certain exceptions (APB-28, par. 14):

1. An estimated gross profit frequently is used to determine the cost of goods sold during an interim period. This is acceptable for GAAP, as long as periodic physical inventories are taken to adjust the gross profit percentage used. Companies using the

gross profit method for interim financial statements should disclose that fact and any significant adjustments that may occur in amounts determined by a physical count.

2. When the LIFO method is used for interim financial statements and a LIFO layer is depleted, in part or in whole, that is expected to be replaced before the end of the fiscal period, it is acceptable to use the expected cost of replacement for the depleted LIFO inventory in determining cost of goods sold for the interim period.

3. Inventory losses from market declines, other than those expected to be recovered before the end of the fiscal year, are included in the results of operations of the interim period in which the loss occurs. Subsequent gains from market price recovery in later interim periods are included in the results of operation in which the gain occurs, but only to the extent of the previously recognized losses.

4. Standard costs are acceptable in determining inventory valuations for interim financial reporting. Unplanned or unanticipated purchase price, volume, or capacity variances should be included in the results of operations of the interim period in which they occur. Anticipated and planned purchase price, volume, or capacity variances that are expected to be recovered by the end of the fiscal year are deferred at interim dates. In general, the same procedures for standard costs used at the end of the fiscal year should be used for interim financial reporting.

☛ **PRACTICE POINTER:** While all four of these procedures are acceptable in interim financial statements, they are not considered GAAP for purposes of annual financial statements. Some may result in material differences in the amount of net income (e.g., using the replacement cost for erosion of a LIFO layer in an early interim period), and care should be taken that a similar procedure is not used in annual financial statements.

Business Combinations

GAAP pertaining to the valuation of inventory acquired as the result of a business combination are contained in APB-16 (Business Combinations).

Inventory acquired in a business combination accounted for by the purchase method is valued as follows (APB-16, par. 88c):

Raw materials—Current replacement cost

Finished goods—Net realizable value less costs of disposal and a reasonable profit for the selling effort

Work in process—Net realizable value for finished goods, less costs to complete and dispose, and a reasonable profit for the completion and selling effort

Inventories acquired in a business combination accounted for as a pooling of interests are valued at the same cost as that to the acquired entity (APB-16, par. 51).

Terminated Contracts

When inventory is acquired for a specific customer contract that is subsequently terminated for any purpose, the carrying value of such inventory should be adjusted to reflect any loss in value.

Research and Development

FAS-2 contains GAAP relevant to inventory expense allocation. Inventories of supplies used in research and development activities are charged to expense unless they clearly have an alternative use or can be used in future research and development projects.

When research and development activities consume goods, supplies, or materials from other sources within an organization, the carrying value of such inventory is charged to research and development expense. Goods produced by research and development activities that may be used in the regular inventory of the organization may be transferred physically to regular inventory, at which time a credit in the amount of the costs assigned to the goods should be made to the research and development department (FAS-2, par. 11).

Intercompany Profits

Regardless of any minority interest, all intercompany profits in inventory are eliminated for consolidated financial statements and investments in common stocks accounted for by the equity method.

Long-Term Construction-Type Contracts

The construction in progress account used in both the completed-contract and percentage-of-completion methods of accounting for long-term construction-type contracts is an inventory account.

Income Taxes

Inventories accounted differently for financial accounting and tax purposes may create temporary differences for which the recognition of deferred taxes may be necessary.

Accounting Change

An accounting change involving inventories in interim or annual reports necessitates accounting for the cumulative effect of the change and/or restatement of prior-period reports, including certain required PRO FORMA information in accordance with APB-20 (Accounting Changes).

Nonmonetary Exchanges

A nonmonetary exchange of inventory held for sale in the ordinary course of business for similar property to be held for the same purpose does not complete the earning process and no gain or loss is recognized. The inventory received in the nonmonetary exchange should be recorded at the book value of the inventory surrendered, unless cash is also involved in the transaction, in accordance with APB-29 (Accounting for Nonmonetary Transactions).

Inventory Profits

Profits from the sale of inventory, whose cost and selling price have increased significantly since acquisition, may include *ghost profits* or *inventory profits*. These profits are abnormal, because the cost to replace the inventory has increased significantly and the normal gross profit on the inventory is considerably less than the gross profit containing the ghost or inventory profits.

During periods of rapid inflation, a significant portion of reported net income of a business may actually be ghost or inventory profits. The use of the LIFO method for pricing inventories may offset part or all of any ghost or inventory profits, because current purchases or production costs are matched against current revenue, leaving the earliest inventory on hand.

Certain publicly held companies are required by the SEC to disclose in a supplemental statement the current replacement cost for cost of goods sold, inventories, and resulting ghost or inventory profits.

DISCLOSURE

The general disclosure requirements for inventories are:

1. A description of accounting principles used and the methods of applying those principles (APB-22, par. 12).
2. Any accounting principles or methods that are peculiar to a particular industry (APB-22, par. 12).
3. Classification of inventories (ARB-43, Ch. 4, Statement 8).
4. Basis of pricing inventories (ARB-43, Ch. 4, Statement 8).

Businesses that depend on a limited number of sources for raw material or inventory or upon precarious sources (labor problems, foreign governments, etc.) should disclose the pertinent facts in their financial statements or footnotes thereto.

CHAPTER 28
INVESTMENT TAX CREDIT

CONTENTS

CHAPTER 28
INVESTMENT TAX CREDIT

OVERVIEW

The investment tax credit (ITC) was a selective reduction in income taxes based on the reporting entity's investment in qualifying property. GAAP permit two methods of accounting for the ITC: (1) the *deferral method*, in which the benefit of the ITC is amortized over the period that the qualifying property is used, and (2) the *flow-through method*, in which the benefit is recognized entirely in the year in which the qualifying property is acquired. The Accounting Principles Board (APB) first stated a preference for the deferral method, because the philosophy at that time emphasized income reporting via matching, which led to the conclusion that the ITC was effectively a reduction of the cost of the qualifying asset. The APB later indicated that both methods are acceptable. The flow-through method has been more widely used in practice.

Promulgated GAAP for ITCs are found in the following pronouncements:

APB-2   Accounting for the "Investment Credit"

APB-4   Accounting for the "Investment Credit"

FAS-109   Accounting for Income Taxes

CROSS-REFERENCES

BACKGROUND

Current tax legislation does not permit ITCs, but ITC carryforwards remain. The ITC has been proposed by federal government policymakers and could be reinstated at some time in the future. When applicable, the ITC can be a significant factor in determining income. The primary financial reporting issue is when the ITC is reflected in the income statement. According to APB-2 and APB-4, two methods were permitted: (1) a reduction of tax expense for the period in which the credit arises and (2) amortization over the life of the property.

The case to support amortization of the ITC (deferral method) is based on the premise of matching costs with revenue, which was the primary philosophy of the APB. The ITC was viewed as an effective reduction of the cost of the asset purchased, to be reflected in income in proportion to the deprecation of the asset. The support for deducting the ITC from tax expense in the year the ITC arose (flow-through method) is based on the interpretation of the Internal Revenue Code that the ITC is a credit against taxes due. Under an asset/liability perspective, the amount of the tax expense should reflect the current and deferred tax liabilities and assets. Moreover, the deferred ITC that would be reported under the deferral method represents neither a valid liability nor a reduction of an asset. FAS-109 is consistent with the flow-through method, but under FAS-109 the deferral method is still permitted. The SEC issued ASR-96 to the effect that the only two acceptable methods are (1) amortization of the ITC over the life of the acquired property and (2) a direct reduction of taxes in the year in which the credit arose.

ACCOUNTING FOR THE ITC

Under the flow-through method, accounting for the ITC is straightforward. Under FAS-109, the amount of income tax expense is the amount of income tax currently payable or refundable, plus or less the change in net deferred tax asset or liability. (See the *GAAP Guide* chapter titled "Income Taxes" for details.) Therefore, the amount of the ITC used in a year reduces the amount of income tax currently payable for the year, and thereby reduces income tax expense. Thus the ITC flows into income.

Under the deferral method, the ITC reduces the current tax liability in the year it arises, but the ITC is recognized as a reduction in tax expense on a pro rata basis over the life of the asset that gives rise to the ITC. Unamortized deferred ITC is a deferred tax credit that will be recognized in the determination of income over time.

Any ITC carryforward is a deferred tax asset. Under FAS-109, a valuation allowance may be needed to reduce all or a portion of the deferred tax asset to an amount that is more likely than not to be realized (FAS-109, par. 17). FAS-109 defines "more likely than not" as a likelihood of more than 50%, meaning that a valuation allowance is required if the likelihood is greater than 50% that some or all of the deferred tax asset will not be realized. In making this judgment, reversals of existing deferred tax liabilities and a history of continuous profitable operations can be considered, among other things. Realization of a deferred tax asset for ITC carryforwards is seldom an issue for consistently profitable companies.

Illustration of Accounting for Investment Tax Credit

Frank Company acquired an item of equipment costing $400,000 in 19X1. This asset qualified for a 10% ITC and had an expected useful life of eight years. During 19X1, Frank earned $250,000 in income before income taxes, and the appropriate income tax rate was 35%.

The asset purchase and ITC would be recorded as follows for the deferral and flow-through methods:

Journal Entries: Deferral Method			Transaction Description	Journal Entries: Flow-Through Method		
Equipment	400,000		Acquisition of	Equipment	400,000	
Cash		400,000	equipment	Cash		400,000
Tax expense	87,500		Income tax	Tax expense	47,500	
Deferred ITC		40,000	accrual for	Tax payable		47,500
Tax payable		47,500	19X1			
Computation				**Computation**		
Tax on $250,000				Tax expense		
$250,000 x .35 =	$87,500			$87,500 − $40,000 = $47,500		
Deferred ITC						
$400,000 x .10 =	$40,000					
Tax payable						
$87,500 − $40,000 =	$47,500					
Deferred ITC	5,000		Amortization	None		
Tax expense		5,000	of ITC			
Computation						
$40,000/8 years =	5,000					
Tax payable	47,500		Payment of	Tax payable	47,500	
Cash		47,500	tax liability	Cash		47,500

Frank Company's financial statement presentation for 19X1 for both the deferral method and the flow-through method would be as follows:

	Deferral	Flow-Through
Income statement		
Income tax expense	$82,500	$47,500
Balance sheet		
Deferred ITC	$35,000	0
Statement of cash flows		
Cash paid for income taxes	$47,500	$47,500

OTHER CONSIDERATIONS

As directed by FAS-13 (Accounting for Leases), in accounting for leveraged leases, the lessor was required to use the deferral method of accounting for the ITC, or the lease must be accounted for as a direct financing lease (FAS-13, par. 42).

Under FAS-109, assets and liabilities are measured on a before-tax basis in a business combination. Any deferred tax assets and liabilities of the combining companies are remeasured at the time of combination. Therefore, any deferred tax assets from ITC carryforwards must be determined at the time of the combination. The need for a valuation allowance, if any, is determined by the likelihood of realization of the ITC carryforward for the consolidated entity, depending on whether separate or consolidated tax returns are filed (FAS-109, par. 271).

☞ **PRACTICE POINTER:** The deferral and flow-through methods of accounting for the ITC are alternative accounting policies. Once an enterprise chooses the method to use, it should follow that method consistently, as with other alternative accounting policies.

DISCLOSURE

The two most acceptable forms of balance sheet presentation for the ITC under the deferral method are (1) as a deduction from the corresponding asset and (2) as a deferred credit.

In the first case, the income statement shows a lower depreciation expense for the year because the depreciable base of the asset has been reduced by the credit; the credit would not appear on the income statement. If, however, the current year's credit amount is shown directly on the income statement, then the depreciation charge for the year should be higher by the same amount.

Regardless of which method was used to account for the ITC, disclosure of the method and amounts involved was required, as were material amounts of unused ITCs (APB-4, par. 11). Separate disclosure of the benefit of the ITC is required by FAS-109 (FAS-109, par. 45).

CHAPTER 29
INVESTMENTS IN DEBT AND EQUITY SECURITIES

CONTENTS

CHAPTER 29
INVESTMENTS IN DEBT AND
EQUITY SECURITIES

OVERVIEW

The primary issue in accounting and reporting for debt and equity investments is the appropriate use of market value. GAAP for many investments are included in the following pronouncement:

FAS-115   Accounting for Certain Investments in Debt and Equity Securities

FAS-115 addresses accounting and reporting for (*a*) investments in equity securities that have readily determinable fair values and (*b*) all investments in debt securities. It requires that these securities be classified in three categories and given specific accounting treatments, as follows:

Classification	Accounting Treatment
Held-to-maturity Debt securities with the intent and ability to hold to maturity	Amortized cost
Trading securities Debt and equity securities bought and held primarily for sale in the near term	Fair value, with unrealized holding gains and losses included in earnings
Available-for-sale Debt and equity securities not classified as held-to-maturity or trading	Fair value, with unrealized holding gains and losses excluded from earnings and reported as a separate component of shareholders' equity

CROSS-REFERENCES

1999 Miller GAAP Guide: Chapter 6, "Consolidated Financial Statements"; Chapter 9, "Current Assets and Current Liabilities"; Chapter 14, "Equity Method"; Chapter 16, "Financial Instruments"; Chapter 17, "Foreign Operations and Exchange"; Chapter 42, "Results of Operations"; Chapter 57, "Mortgage Banking Industry"

1999 Miller GAAP Guide Implementation Manual: Chapter 18, "Investments in Debt and Equity Securities"

1999 Miller GAAP Implementation Manual: EITF: Chapter 19, "Investments in Debt and Equity Securities"

1999 Miller Not-for-Profit Reporting: Chapter 2, "Overview of Current Pronouncements"; Chapter 5, "Assets"; Chapter 9, "Note Disclosures"

1999 Miller GAAS Guide: Chapter 8, "Evidence"

1999 Miller Governmental GAAP Guide: Chapter 13, "Assets"; Chapter 14, "Accounting and Financial Reporting for Certain Investments and External Investment Pools"; Chapter 15, "Deposit and Investment Portfolio Disclosures and Reverse Repurchase Agreements"

1998/1999 Miller Audit Procedures: Chapter 9, "Investments"

1999 Miller HUD Audit Procedures: Appendix B, "Investments"

1998/1999 Miller Local Government Audits: Chapter 18, "Cash and Investments"

BACKGROUND

FAS-115 defines *debt securities* and *equity securities* as follows:

Debt Security

A *debt security* is any security that represents a creditor relationship with an enterprise. It includes preferred stock that must be redeemed by the issuing enterprise or that is redeemable at the option of the investor. It also includes a collateralized mortgage obligation that is issued in equity form but is required to be accounted for as a nonequity instrument, regardless of how that instrument is classified in the issuer's statement of financial position. Other examples of debt securities are the following:

- U.S. Treasury securities
- U.S. government agency securities
- Municipal securities
- Corporate bonds
- Convertible debt
- Commercial paper
- All securitized debt instruments, such as collateralized mortgage obligations and real estate mortgage investment conduits
- Interest-only and principal-only strips

The following items are *not* debt securities:

- Option contracts
- Financial futures contracts
- Forward contracts
- Lease contracts
- Trade accounts receivable arising from sales on credit by industrial or commercial enterprises
- Loans receivable arising from consumer, commercial, and real estate lending activities of financial institutions

These last two items are examples of receivables that do not meet the definition of *security* unless they have been securitized, in which case they *do* meet the definition.

Equity Security

An *equity security* is any security representing an ownership interest in an enterprise (e.g., common, preferred, or other capital stock) or the right to acquire or dispose of an ownership interest in an enterprise at fixed or determinable prices (e.g., warrants, rights, call options, and put options).

ACCOUNTING FOR INVESTMENTS BY FAS-115

Scope

FAS-115 establishes standards of financial accounting and reporting for (*a*) investments in equity securities that have readily determinable fair values and (*b*) all investments in debt securities. Following are guidelines for the determination of fair value (FAS-115, par. 3):

• Fair value of an equity security is readily determinable if sales prices and bid-and-asked quotations are currently available on a securities exchange registered with the Securities and Exchange Commission or in the over-the-counter market, assuming the over-the-counter securities are publicly reported by the National Association of Securities Dealers Automated Quotations system or by the National Quotation Bureau. Restricted stock (i.e., equity securities whose sale is restricted by governmental or contractual requirement) does not have a readily determinable fair value.

• Fair value of an equity security traded only on a foreign market is considered readily determinable if that foreign market is of a breadth and scope comparable to one of the U.S. markets referred to above.

• Fair value of an investment in a mutual fund is readily determinable if the fair value per share is determined and published and is the basis for current transactions.

FAS-115 does not apply to the following (FAS-115, par. 4):

• Investments in equity securities accounted for by the equity method

• Investments in consolidated subsidiaries

• Enterprises whose specialized accounting practices include accounting for substantially all investments in debt and equity securities at market or fair value, with changes in value recognized in earnings or in the change in net assets

• Not-for-profit organizations

> **OBSERVATION:** The FASB limited the scope of this project because of its desire to expedite resolution of the urgent problems with current accounting and reporting practices for investment securities. In placing this limitation on the project, they addressed only certain financial assets and did not change accounting for financial liabilities at that time.

Classifications of Debt and Equity Securities

FAS-115 requires that an enterprise classify all debt securities and selected equity securities into one of three categories: (1) held-to-maturity, (2) trading, or (3) available-for-sale. The enterprise should reassess the classification at each reporting date (FAS-115, par. 6).

> ☞ **PRACTICE POINTER:** FAS-115 provides little guidance on how management should determine the appropriate classification of debt and equity investments. Classification is based primarily on management's intent for holding a particular investment:
>
> - Trading securities (both debt and equity) provide a source of ready cash when needed, with the hope of gain from holding the investment for a short period of time.
> - Held-to-maturity investments (debt only) are positively intended to be retained until maturity.
> - Available-for-sale investments (both debt and equity) rest somewhere between these extremes.
>
> Management's past patterns of practices with regard to securities are an important consideration in determining appropriate classification, as are projections of cash requirements that may imply a need to liquidate investments.

Held-to-Maturity Securities

The *held-to-maturity* category is limited to debt securities. They are measured at amortized cost in the statement of financial position only if the reporting enterprise has the intent and ability to hold them to maturity (FAS-115, par. 7). In certain circumstances, a company may change its intent concerning securities originally classified as held-to-maturity, resulting in their sale or reclassification, without calling into question the company's intent to hold other securities to maturity. FAS-115 identifies the following circumstances in which the sale or transfer of held-to-maturity investments is not considered to be inconsistent with their original classification (FAS-115, par. 8):

- Significant deterioration in the issuer's creditworthiness
- Change in tax law that eliminates or reduces the tax-exempt status of interest on the debt security
- A major business combination or major disposition that necessitates the sale or transfer of the security to maintain the enterprise's existing interest rate risk position or credit risk policy

- A change in statutory or regulatory requirements significantly modifying either what constitutes a permissible investment or the maximum level of investments in certain kinds of securities
- A significant increase by the regulator in the industry's capital requirements that causes a need to downsize by selling held-to-maturity securities
- A significant increase in the risk weights of debt securities used for regulatory risk-based capital purposes
- Other events that are isolated, nonrecurring, and unusual and that could not have been reasonably anticipated by the enterprise

A debt security is not classified as held-to-maturity if the investing enterprise intends to hold the security for only an indefinite period. A debt security is not appropriately classified as held-to-maturity, for example, if it is available for sale in response to the following circumstances (FAS-115, par. 9):

- Changes in market interest rates and related changes in the security's prepayment risk
- Need for liquidity
- Changes in the availability of and the yield on alternative investments
- Changes in funding sources and terms
- Changes in foreign currency risk

Trading Securities

The *trading securities* category includes both debt securities and equity securities with readily determinable fair values. They are measured at fair value in the statement of financial position. Trading securities (FAS-115, par. 12):

- Are bought and held primarily for purposes of selling them in the near term
- Reflect active and frequent buying and selling
- Generally are used with the objective of generating profits on short-term differences in price

Mortgage securities that are held for sale in conjunction with mortgage banking activities in accordance with FAS-65 (Accounting for Certain Mortgage Banking Activities) are classified as trading securities.

Available-for-Sale Securities

The *available-for-sale* category of debt securities includes those debt securities that are not classified in either the held-to-maturity category or the trading category (FAS-115, par. 12).

Standards of Accounting and Reporting Subsequent to Classification

After debt and equity investments are classified as held-to-maturity, trading, and available-for-sale, three important accounting issues must be addressed: (1) reporting changes in fair value, (2) transfers between categories, and (3) impairment of securities.

Reporting Changes in Fair Value

Investments in debt and equity securities classified as trading and available-for-sale are required to be carried at fair value in the statement of financial position. Unrealized holding gains and losses represent the net change in fair value of a security, *excluding*:

- Dividend or interest income recognized but not yet received
- Any write-downs for permanent impairment

Unrealized holding gains and losses are accounted for as follows (FAS-115, par. 13):

Trading—Included in earnings

Available-for-sale—Excluded from earnings and reported as a net amount in a separate component of shareholders' equity until realized

> ☛ **PRACTICE POINTER:** The accumulated amount of unrealized holding gains and losses on available-for-sale investments that is included in stockholders' equity is *not* a direct adjustment to retained earnings. It is carried in a separate component of stockholders' equity—a positive amount (credit balance) for accumulated unrealized gains and a negative amount (debit balance) for accumulated unrealized losses. Adjust this account each time the portfolio of available-for-sale investments is revalued (e.g., at the end of each accounting period) as an element of comprehensive income. Recognize the accumulated unrealized gain or loss for a particular security as an element of net income when that security is sold and recognize it in income at that time.

Dividend and interest income, including amortization of premium and discount arising at acquisition, are included in earnings for all three categories of investments. Also, realized gains and losses for securities classified as available-for-sale and held-to-maturity are reported in earnings (FAS-115, par. 14).

Transfers Between Categories

Transfers of securities between categories of investments are accounted for at fair value with an unrealized holding gain or loss treated as indicated in the following summarization (FAS-115, par. 15):

Transfer*		Accounting Treatment
From	To	
T	A or H	Unrealized holding gain or loss was already recognized in earnings during prior period(s) and is not reversed.
A or H	T	Unrealized holding gain or loss at the date of transfer is immediately recognized in earnings.
H	A	Unrealized holding gain or loss at the date of transfer is recognized in a separate component of shareholders' equity.
A	H	Unrealized holding gain or loss continues to be reported in a separate component of shareholders' equity and is amortized over the remaining life of the security as an adjustment of yield.

*T = Trading; A = Available-for-sale; H = Held-to-maturity

Given the criteria for classification of debt securities in the held-to-maturity category, transfers from that category should be rare. Also, because of the securities' nature, transfers to or from trading are rare (FAS-115, par. 15).

Impairment of Securities

For individual securities classified as either available-for-sale or held-to-maturity, when fair value declines below amortized cost an enterprise should determine whether the decline is temporary or permanent. If the decline in fair value is permanent, the following standards apply (FAS-115, par. 16):

- The cost basis of the individual security is written down to fair value as a new cost basis.
- The amount of the write-down is included in current earnings (i.e., accounted for as a realized loss).
- The new cost basis is not changed for subsequent recoveries in fair value; subsequent increases in fair value of available-for-sale securities are included in the separate component of equity; any subsequent decreases in fair value, if temporary, are also included in the separate component of equity.

☛ **PRACTICE POINTER:** Professional judgment is required to determine whether a decline in fair value of an available-for-sale investment is temporary or other than temporary. A starting point is to judge whether the decline in value results from company-specific events, industry developments, general economic conditions, or other reasons. Once the general reason for the decline is identified, further judgments are required as to whether those causal events are likely to reverse and, if so, whether that reversal is likely to result in a recovery of the fair value of the investment. To help make these judgments, consider how similar circumstances have affected other debt and equity securities.

OBSERVATION: The accounting standards outlined above represent significant changes in accounting practice away from historical cost and in the direction of fair value accounting. The requirement to account for trading and available-for-sale debt and equity investments at fair value is particularly noteworthy in that *unrealized* gains and losses are reflected in the statement of financial position. To mitigate criticisms of fair value accounting, the FASB included these requirements:

1. Because fair values are not as relevant for debt securities that are held to maturity as they are for other investments, unrealized holding gains and losses are not recognized for those investments.

2. Because valuing some assets at fair value, without valuing related liabilities similarly, might result in volatility in reported earnings, unrealized gains and losses on debt and equity investments classified as available-for-sale are reported in shareholders' equity.

Financial Statement Presentation and Disclosures

Financial statement presentation of debt and equity investment activities subject to FAS-115 are summarized as follows:

1. In the statement of financial position (FAS-115, par. 17):
   - *Trading securities*—Current assets
   - *Held-to-maturity and available-for-sale securities*—Current or noncurrent, subject to provisions of ARB-43, Chapter 3A (Current Assets and Current Liabilities)
2. In the statement of cash flows (FAS-115, par. 18):
   - *Trading securities*—Cash flows from purchases, sales, and maturities classified as operating activities
   - *Held-to-maturity and available-for-sale*—Cash flows from purchases, sales, and maturities classified as investing activities and reported gross for each classification

☛ **PRACTICE POINTER:** For available-for-sale and held-to-maturity investments, the usual classification in the statement of financial position would be noncurrent, inasmuch as those securities that are held primarily for *liquidity purposes* should be in the trading category. In certain circumstances, however, these investments may qualify for inclusion among current assets. For example, when held-to-maturity (debt) investments are within one year of maturity, they are expected to provide near-term cash and would be classified appropriately as current assets. Similarly, management intent concerning available-for-sale securities that have been held for a period of time may qualify those securities for classification as current, whereas in the past they would have been considered noncurrent.

Treating cash flows from trading securities in the operating category in the statement of cash flows is consistent with the fact that trading securities involve active and frequent buying and selling, and are used generally with the objective of generating profits. Classifying cash flows from held-to-maturity and available-for-sale securities as investing cash flows is consistent with the longer-term nature of those investments.

FAS-115 disclosure requirements are as follows:

Available-for-sale and held-to-maturity (separately) (FAS-115, par. 19):

- Aggregate fair value
- Gross unrealized holding gains
- Gross unrealized holding losses
- Amortized cost basis by major security category type [In complying with this requirement, financial institutions shall include the following major types of securities, although additional types may also be included as appropriate:

— Equity securities

— Debt securities issued by the U.S. Treasury and other U.S. government corporations and agencies

— Debt securities issued by states of the United States and political subdivisions of the states

— Debt securities issued by foreign governments

— Corporate debt securities

— Mortgage-backed securities

— Other debt securities]

- Contractual maturities as of the date of the most recent statement of financial position (FAS-115, par. 20). [In complying with this requirement, financial institutions shall disclose the fair value and amortized cost of debt securities in at least four maturity groupings:

— Within one year

— One to five years

— Five to 10 years

— After 10 years]

For each period for which the results of operations are presented, the following disclosures are required (FAS-115, par. 21):

- Proceeds from the sale of available-for-sale securities and the gross unrealized gains and losses on those sales

- The basis on which cost was determined in computing realized gain or loss (i.e., specific identification, average cost, or other)

- Gross gains and losses from transfers of securities from the available-for-sale category to the trading category that are included in earnings

- Change in net unrealized holding gains or losses on available-for-sale securities that are included in the separate component of shareholders' equity

- Change in net unrealized holding gain or loss on trading securities that are included in earnings

For each period for which results of operations are presented, the following information is required for held-to-maturity investments (FAS-115, par. 22):

- The amortized amount of any sold or transferred security

- The related realized or unrealized gain or loss

- The circumstances leading to the decision to sell or transfer the security

☞ **PRACTICE POINTER:** If a company has more than one category of debt and equity investments, an efficient way to make many of the required disclosures is to prepare a table: Use columns for investment type (e.g., trading, available-for-sale, and/or held-to-maturity) and rows for the specific information items (e.g., aggregate fair value, unrealized holding gains and losses). This approach not only saves space, but is relatively easy for users of the financial statements to read and understand. If a company has only one category of investments, presentation of information may be more efficient in paragraph form.

Illustration of General Application of FAS-115

To illustrate the general application of FAS-115, consider the case of Marble Co., which invests in two securities on January 1, 19X1, as follows:

Debt investment—$100,000 par value, 9% Paper Co. bonds priced to yield 10%, maturity date 12/31/X5

Equity investment—5,000 shares of Plastic Co. $25 par value common stock at $30 per share

FAS-115 is applied to each investment from the date of purchase. Assume that the debt investment pays interest annually and matures five years from purchase. The purchase price of the two securities is as follows:

Paper Co. bonds:

Present value of interest payments ($100,000 x 9% x 3.79079*)	$ 34,117
Present value of maturity value ($100,000 x .62092**)	62,092
	$ 96,209

Plastic Co. common stock:

5,000 shares @ $30 per share	$150,000

Total	$246,209

The discount on the Paper Co. bonds is amortized over the five-year period to maturity by the effective-interest method, as follows:

---

*Present value of annuity at 10%, compounded annually, five periods.

**Present value of one at 10%, five periods.

	(A) Interest Income	(B) Cash Rec'd	(C) Discount Amortization	(D) Remaining Discount	(E) Carrying Amount
1/1/X1	—	—	—	$3,791	$96,209
12/31/X1	$9,621	$9,000	$621	3,170	96,830
12/31/X2	9,683	9,000	683	2,487	97,513
12/31/X3	9,751	9,000	751	1,736	98,264
12/31/X4	9,826	9,000	826	910	99,090
12/31/X5	9,910	9,000	910	—	100,000

(A) Previous carrying amount (E) x 10%
(B) $100,000 x 9%
(C) [(A) – (B)]
(D) [Previous-year (D)] – [Current-year (C)]
(E) $100,000 – (D)

Market values for the investments are as follows:

	12/31/X1	12/31/X2
Paper Co. bond	$ 98,000	$ 97,500
Plastic Co. common	155,000	152,000
	$253,000	$249,500

Trading Securities

Assume that Marble Co. classifies the investments described above as trading securities. The securities are initially recorded at cost when they are purchased; discount is amortized on the bond investments to state interest income properly; interest and dividend income are recorded as they are received; and the securities are adjusted to market value at the end of the year with the unrealized gain or loss recognized in income. Assuming dividends of $4 per share are received on October 31, 19X1, on the Plastic Co. common, entries to record all events for 19X1 are as follows:

1/1/X1	Investments (trading)	$ 96,209	
	Cash		$ 96,209
	Purchase of bonds as trading investment.		
1/1/X1	Investments (trading)	150,000	
	Cash		150,000
	Purchase of common as trading investment.		
10/31/X1	Cash (5,000 shares @ $4)	20,000	
	Dividend income		20,000
	Dividends received on common stock investment.		

12/31/X1	Investments (trading)	621	
	Cash	9,000	
	Interest income		9,621
	Interest received and amortization of discount on bond investment.		

12/31/X1	Investments (trading)	6,170	
	Unrealized gain on investments		6,170
	Market value adjustment for trading investments.		

The $6,170 unrealized gain is determined as follows:

Market value of trading securities at 12/31/X1 ($98,000 + $155,000)	$253,000
Carrying amount of trading securities at 12/31/X1 ($96,830 + $150,000)	(246,830)
Unrealized gain	$ 6,170

FAS-115 requires the presentation of trading securities in the balance sheet as current assets and cash flows from trading securities to be classified as operating activities in the statement of cash flows. Those presentations are illustrated later in this example.

Continuing the example into 19X2, assume that the Plastic Co. common pays a $3 per share dividend on October 31. Entries for 19X2 are as follows:

10/31/X2	Cash (5,000 x $3)	15,000	
	Dividend income		15,000
	Dividend received on trading investment.		

12/31/X2	Investments (trading)	683	
	Cash		9,000
	Interest income		9,683
	Interest and amortization of discount on bond investment.		

12/31/X4	Unrealized loss on investments	4,183	
	Investments (trading)		4,183
	Market value adjustment for trading investments.		

The market value adjustment is determined as follows:

Market value at 12/31/X2 ($97,500 + $152,000)	$249,500
Carrying amount at 12/31/X2 ($98,683 + $155,000)	(253,683)
Unrealized loss	$ 4,183

The carrying amount of the bond investment is the 12/31/X1 market value, adjusted for the discount amortization ($98,000 + $683).

The financial statement presentation for 19X1 and 19X2 for the trading securities is illustrated as follows:

	19X1	19X2
Balance Sheet:		
Current assets: Trading investments	$253,000	$249,500
Income Statement:		
Interest income	$ 9,621	$ 9,683
Dividend income	20,000	15,000
Unrealized gain (loss) on investments	6,170	(4,183)
Statement of Cash Flows:		
Operating activities:		
Dividends	$ 20,000	$ 15,000
Interest	9,000	9,000
Purchase of investments	246,209	—

Available-for-Sale

Now assume that these same investments are classified by management as available-for-sale. All entries for 19X1 and 19X2 are the same, except as follows:

- The investments account is subtitled "available-for-sale" rather than "trading."
- The year-end market value adjustment is not recognized in income, but rather is accumulated and presented as an element of stockholders' equity.

The final entries for 19X1 and 19X2 are as follows:

12/31/X1	Investments (available-for-sale)	$6,170	
	Accumulated unrealized gains/		
	losses on investments		$6,170
	Market value adjustment for available-		
	for-sale investments.		

12/31/X2	Accumulated unrealized gains/losses		
	on investments	4,183	
	Investments (available-for-sale)		4,183
	Market value adjustment for available-		
	for-sale investments.		

In 19X2, the accumulated unrealized gains/losses on investments account is used to accumulate the net unrealized gains and losses over the two years. That account has a positive (credit) balance of $6,170 at the end of 19X1; it has a positive (credit) balance of $1,987 ($6,170 − $4,183) at the end of 19X2. FAS-115 indicates that available-for-sale securities may be classified in the balance sheet as either current or noncurrent. Assuming currently marketable investments, that decision would be made primarily on the basis of managerial intent. Cash flows from the purchase and sale of available-for-sale securities are classified in the statement of cash flows as investing activities.

The financial statement presentation for 19X1 and 19X2 for the available-for-sale securities is as follows:

	19X1	19X2
Balance Sheet:		
Assets: Available-for-sale investments	$253,000	$249,500
Stockholders' equity: Accumulated unrealized gains/losses on investments	6,170	1,987
Income Statement:		
Interest income	$ 9,621	$ 9,683
Dividend income	20,000	15,000
Statement of Cash Flows:		
Operating activities:		
Dividends	$ 20,000	$ 15,000
Interest	9,000	9,000
Investing activities:		
Purchase of investments	$246,209	—

Held-to-Maturity

Now assume that the bond investment used in the previous illustrations is classified as held-to-maturity. (The stock investment is not included in the continuation of the illustration, because the held-to-maturity classification is available for debt investments only.)

The entries relative to the purchase of the bond investment and the receipt of interest and amortization of discount are also appropriate for the held-to-maturity classification, assuming the investment account is properly identified as held-to-maturity. No entry is made, however, to recognize the change in market value of the investment at the end of each year, because the appropriate method of accounting for the portfolio is amortized cost. Held-to-maturity investments ordinarily would be classified in the balance sheet as noncurrent, except when the maturity date is within the period used to identify current assets (e.g., one year). Cash flows from transactions involving held-to-maturity investments are classified as investing activities in the statement of cash flows.

The financial statement presentation for the held-to-maturity investment for 19X1 and 19X2 is as follows:

	19X1	19X2
Balance Sheet:		
Assets: Held-to-maturity investments	$96,830	$97,513
Income Statement:		
Interest income	$ 9,621	$9,683
Statement of Cash Flows:		
Operating activities:		
Interest	$ 9,000	$9,000
Investing activities:		
Purchase of investments	$96,209	—

CHAPTER 30
LEASES

CONTENTS

CHAPTER 30
LEASES

OVERVIEW

A *lease* is an agreement that conveys the right to use property, usually for a specified period. Leases typically involve two parties: the owner of the property (lessor) and the party contracting to use the property (lessee). Because of certain tax, cash flow, and other advantages, leases have become an important alternative to the outright purchase of property by which companies (lessees) acquire the resources needed to operate.

Leases include agreements that, while not nominally referred to as leases, have the characteristic of transferring the right to use property (e.g., heat supply contracts), and agreements that transfer the right to use property even though the contractor may be required to provide substantial services in connection with the operation or maintenance of the assets.

The term *lease*, as used in promulgated GAAP, does *not* include the following:

- Agreements that are contracts for services that do not transfer the right to use property from one contracting party to another
- Agreements that concern the right to explore for or exploit natural resources such as oil, gas, minerals, and timber
- Agreements that represent licensing agreements for items such as motion picture films, plays, manuscripts, patents, and copyrights

A central accounting issue associated with leases is the identification of those leases that are treated appropriately as sales of the property by lessors and as purchases of the property by lessees (*capital leases*). Those leases that are not identified as capital leases are called *operating leases* and are not treated as sales by lessors and as purchases by lessees. Rather, they are treated on a prospective basis as a series of cash flows from the lessee to the lessor.

GAAP for leases include the largest number of authoritative accounting pronouncements of any single subject in accounting literature. Pronouncements that follow FAS-13 explain, interpret, or amend that pronouncement in a variety of ways; many of them arose as a result of attempts to implement FAS-13. Following are pronouncements that collectively establish promulgated GAAP for lease accounting:

FAS-13   Accounting for Leases

FAS-22   Changes in the Provisions of Lease Agreements Resulting from Refundings of Tax-Exempt Debt

FAS-23   Inception of the Lease

FAS-27   Classification of Renewals or Extensions of Existing Sales-Type or Direct Financing Leases

FAS-28   Accounting for Sales with Leasebacks

FAS-29   Determining Contingent Rentals

FAS-91   Accounting for Nonrefundable Fees and Costs Associated with Originating or Acquiring Loans and Initial Direct Costs of Leases

FAS-98   Accounting for Leases:
- Sale-Leaseback Transactions Involving Real Estate
- Sales-Type Leases of Real Estate
- Definition of the Lease Term
- Initial Direct Costs of Direct Financing Leases

FIN-19   Lessee Guarantee of the Residual Value of Leased Property

FIN-21   Accounting for Leases in a Business Combination

FIN-23   Leases of Certain Property Owned by a Governmental Unit or Authority

FIN-24   Leases Involving Only Part of a Building

FIN-26   Accounting for Purchase of a Leased Asset by the Lessee during the Term of the Lease

FIN-27   Accounting for a Loss on a Sublease

Following is a brief overview of the eight Statements of Financial Accounting Standards included in the promulgated GAAP for leases.

FAS-13   defines a lease as an agreement that conveys the right to use assets (tangible or intangible) for a stated period. A lease that transfers substantially all the benefits and risks inherent in the ownership of property is called a *capital lease.* Such a lease is accounted for by the lessee as the acquisition of an asset and the incurrence of a liability. The lessor accounts for such a lease as a sale (sales-type lease) or financing (direct financing lease). All other leases are referred to as *operating leases.*

FAS-22   addresses an inconsistency between FAS-13 and APB-26 (Early Extinguishment of Debt) arising from refundings of tax-exempt debt, including advance refundings that are accounted for as early extinguishments of debt. FAS-22 is covered in more detail later in this chapter.

FAS-23   amends FAS-13 to specify that, if the leased property is yet to be constructed or acquired by the lessor at the inception of the lease, the lessor's criterion pertaining to "no important uncertainties of unreimbursable costs yet to be incurred by the lessor" is applied at the date that construction of the property is completed or the property is acquired. FAS-23 amends FAS-13 to specify that any increases in the minimum lease payments that have occurred during the preacquisition or preconstruction period as a result of an escalation clause are to be considered in determining the fair value of the leased property at the inception of the lease. FAS-23 also amends FAS-13 to limit the amount that can be recorded by the lessor for the residual value of leased property to an amount not greater than the estimate as of the inception of the lease. FAS-23 is discussed more fully throughout this chapter.

FAS-27 modifies FAS-13 to require a lessor to classify a renewal or an extension of a sales-type or direct financing lease as a sales-type lease if the lease would otherwise qualify as a sales-type lease and the renewal or extension occurs at or near the end of the lease term. Otherwise, FAS-13 prohibits the classification of a renewal or extension of a sales-type or direct financing lease as a sales-type lease at any other time during the lease term.

FAS-28 amends FAS-13 to specify the appropriate accounting for sale-leaseback transactions depending on the percentage amount of the property that the seller-lessee leases back (substantially all of the property, a minor portion of the property, or more than a minor portion of the property but less than substantially all) and whether the lease is classified as a capital lease or an operating lease.

FAS-29 amends FAS-13 to provide a new definition for *contingent rentals* as those that cannot be determined at the inception of the lease because they depend on future factors or events. Rental payments based on future sales volume, future machine hours, future interest rates, and future price indexes are examples of contingent rentals. Contingent rentals can either increase or decrease lease payments.

FAS-91 establishes accounting and reporting standards for nonrefundable fees and costs associated with lending, committing to lend, or purchasing a loan or group of loans. Under FAS-91, direct loan origination fees and costs, including initial direct costs incurred by a lessor in negotiating and consummating a lease, are offset against each other and the net amount is deferred and recognized over the life of the loan as an adjustment to the yield on the loan. The provisions of FAS-91 apply to all types of loans, including debt securities, and to all types of lenders, including banks, thrift institutions, insurance companies, mortgage bankers, and other financial and nonfinancial institutions. However, FAS-91 does not apply to nonrefundable fees and costs that are associated with originating or acquiring loans which are carried at market value.

FAS-98 amends FAS-13 to establish a new definition of *penalty* and *lease term* for all leasing transactions. FAS-98 specifies the appropriate accounting for a seller-lessee in a sale-leaseback transaction involving real estate, including real estate with equipment, such as manufacturing facilities, power plants, furnished office buildings, etc. FAS-98 establishes the appropriate accounting for a sale-lease-back transaction in which property improvements or integral equipment is sold to a purchaser-lessor and leased back by the seller-lessee who retains the ownership of the underlying land. FAS-98 also provides the appropriate accounting for sale-leaseback transactions involving real estate with equipment that include separate sale and leaseback agreements for the real estate and the equipment (*a*) with the same entity or related parties and (*b*) that are consummated at or near the same time, suggesting that they were negotiated as a package.

CROSS-REFERENCES

1999 MILLER GAAP GUIDE: Chapter 3, "Business Combinations"; Chapter 6, "Consolidated Financial Statements"; Chapter 15, "Extinguishment of Debt"; Chapter 32, "Long-Term Obligations"; Chapter 62, "Real Estate—Recognition of Sales"

1999 MILLER GAAP IMPLEMENTATION MANUAL: Chapter 19, "Leases"

1999 MILLER GAAP IMPLEMENTATION MANUAL: EITF: Chapter 20, "Leases"

1999 MILLER GOVERNMENTAL GAAP GUIDE: Chapter 19, "Leases"; Chapter 29, "General Long-Term Debt Account Group"; Chapter 30, "General Fixed Assets Account Group"

BACKGROUND

Some lease agreements are such that an asset and a related liability should be reported on the balance sheet of the lessee enterprise. The distinction is one of *substance over form* when the transaction actually *transfers substantially all the benefits and risks inherent in the ownership of the property.*

Established in GAAP are criteria to determine whether a lease transaction is in substance a transfer of the incidents of ownership. If, *at its inception,* a lease meets one or more of the following four criteria, the lease is classified as a capital lease:

1. By the end of the lease term, ownership of the leased property is transferred to the lessee.

2. The lease contains a bargain purchase option.

3. The lease term is substantially (75% or more) equal to the estimated useful life of the leased property.

4. At the inception of the lease, the present value of the minimum lease payments, with certain adjustments, is 90% or more of the fair value of the leased property.

These criteria are examined in more detail later in this chapter.

TERMINOLOGY

The authoritative literature includes many terms that are important for an understanding of lease accounting. Several of these terms are explained below.

Capital Lease

A capital lease transfers the benefits and risks inherent in the ownership of the property to the lessee, who accounts for the lease as an acquisition of an asset and the incurrence of a liability (FAS-13, par. 6a).

Sales-Type Lease

A sales-type lease is a type of capital lease that results in a manufacturer's or dealer's profit or loss to the lessor and transfers substantially all the benefits and risks inherent in the ownership of the leased property to the lessee; in addition, (*a*) the minimum lease payments are reasonably predictable of collection and (*b*) no important uncertainties exist regarding costs to be incurred by the lessor under the terms of the lease (FAS-13, par. 6b).

In a sales-type lease, the *fair value* of the leased property at the inception of the lease differs from the cost or carrying amount because a manufacturer's or dealer's profit or loss exists. Fair value usually is the *normal selling price* of the property.

Direct Financing Lease

A direct financing lease is a type of capital lease that does *not* result in a manufacturer's or dealer's profit or loss to the lessor, but does transfer substantially all the benefits and risks inherent in the ownership of the leased property to the lessee; in addition, (*a*) the minimum lease payments are reasonably predictable of collection and (*b*) no important uncertainties exist regarding costs to be incurred by the lessor under the terms of the lease (FAS-13, par. 6b).

Separately identifying sales-type and direct financing leases is an accounting issue for the lessor only, who accounts for the two types of capital leases differently, as described later in this chapter. Both types of leases transfer substantially all the benefits and risks inherent in the ownership of the leased property to the lessee, who records the transaction as a *capital lease*.

Fair Value

Fair value is the price for which the leased property could be sold between unrelated parties in an arm's length transaction (FAS-13, par. 5c).

For the manufacturer or dealer, fair value usually is the normal selling price less trade or volume discounts. Fair value may be less than the normal selling price, however, and sometimes less than the cost of the property.

For others, fair value usually is cost less trade or volume discounts. Fair value may be less than cost, however, especially in circumstances in which a long period elapses between the acquisition of the property by the lessor and the inception of a lease.

Fair Rental

Fair rental is the rental rate for similar property under similar lease terms and conditions.

Related Parties

Related parties are one or more entities subject to the significant influence over the operating and financial policies of another entity (FAS-13, par. 5a).

Executory Costs

Executory costs are items such as insurance, maintenance, and taxes paid in connection with the leased property (FAS-13, par. 5j).

Bargain Purchase Option

A bargain purchase option is a lessee's option to purchase the leased property at a sufficiently low price that makes the exercise of the option relatively certain (FAS-13, par. 5d).

Bargain Renewal Option

A bargain renewal option is a lessee's option to renew the lease at a sufficiently low rental that makes the exercise of the option relatively certain (FAS-13, par. 5e).

Estimated Economic Life

Estimated economic life is the estimated remaining useful life of the property for the purpose for which it was intended, regardless of the term of the lease (FAS-13, par. 5g).

Estimated Residual Value

Estimated residual value is the estimated fair value of the leased property at the end of the lease term. The estimated residual value shall not exceed the amount estimated at the inception of the lease except for the effect of any increases that result during the construction or preacquisition period, because of escalation provisions in the lease (FAS-13, par. 5h).

Unguaranteed Residual Value

Unguaranteed residual value is the estimated fair value of the leased property at the end of the lease term that is not guaranteed by either the lessee or a third party unrelated to the lessor. A guarantee by a third party related to the lessee is considered a lessee guarantee (FAS-13, par. 5i).

Lessee's Incremental Borrowing Rate

The lessee's incremental borrowing rate is the rate of interest that the lessee would have had to pay at the inception of the lease to borrow the funds, on similar terms, to purchase the leased property (FAS-13, par. 5l).

Inception of Lease

The inception of the lease is the date of the lease agreement *or* the date of a written commitment signed by the parties involved that sets forth the principal provisions of the lease transaction. A written commitment that does not contain all of the principal provisions of the lease transaction does not establish the inception date (FAS-23, par. 6).

Interest Rate Implicit in the Lease

The interest rate implicit in the lease is the rate that, when applied to certain items (enumerated below), results in an aggregate present value equal to the fair value of the leased property at the beginning of the lease term, less any investment credit expected to be realized and retained by the lessor. The discount rate is applied to (*a*) the minimum lease payments, excluding executory costs such as insurance, maintenance, and taxes (including any profit thereon) that are paid by the lessor and (*b*) the estimated fair value of the property at the end of the lease term, exclusive of any portion guaranteed by either the lessee or a third party unrelated to the lessor (unguaranteed residual value) (FAS-13, par. 5k).

Initial Direct Costs

The definition of *initial direct costs* is as follows (FAS-91, par. 24):

> *Initial direct costs.** Only those costs incurred by the lessor that are (*a*) costs to originate a lease incurred in transactions with independent third parties that (i) result directly from and are essential to acquire that lease and (ii) would not have been incurred had that leasing transaction not occurred and (*b*) certain costs directly related to specified activities performed by the lessor for that lease. Those activities are: evaluating the prospective lessee's financial condition; evaluating and recording guarantees, collateral, and other security arrangements; negotiating lease terms; preparing and processing lease documents; and closing the transaction. The costs directly related to those activities shall include only that portion of the employees' total compensation and payroll-related fringe benefits directly related to time spent performing those activities for that lease and other costs related to those activities that would not have been incurred but for that lease. Initial direct costs shall not include costs related to activities performed by the lessor for advertising, soliciting potential lessees, servicing existing leases, and other ancillary activities related to establishing and monitoring credit policies, supervision, and administration. Initial direct costs shall not include administrative costs, rent, depreciation, any other occupancy and equipment costs, and employees' compensation and fringe benefits related to activities described in the previous sentence, unsuccessful origination efforts, and idle time.

---

*Initial direct cost shall be offset by nonrefundable fees that are yield adjustments as prescribed in FAS-91.

In determining the net amount of initial direct costs in a leasing transaction under FAS-13, a lessor shall apply the provisions of FAS-91 relating to loan origination fees, commitment fees, and direct loan origination costs of completed loans. Initial direct costs are accounted for by lessors as part of the investment in a direct financing lease.

> **OBSERVATION:** The recognition of a portion of the unearned income at the inception of a lease transaction to offset initial direct costs is not permitted (FAS-91, par. 23).

Contingent Rentals

Contingent rentals are those that cannot be determined at the inception of the lease because they depend on future factors or events. Rental payments based on future sales volume, future machine hours, future interest rates, and future price indexes are examples of contingent rentals. Contingent rentals can either increase or decrease lease payments (FAS-29, par. 11).

Increases in minimum lease payments that occur during the preacquisition or construction period as a result of an escalation clause in the lease are not considered contingent rentals.

Lease Term

The lease term includes all of the following (FAS-98, par. 22a):

1. Any fixed noncancelable term
2. Any period covered by a bargain renewal option
3. Any period in which penalties are imposed in an amount that at the inception of the lease reasonably assures the renewal of the lease by the lessee
4. Any period covered by ordinary renewal options during which a guarantee by the lessee of the lessor's debt that is directly or indirectly related to the leased property is expected to be in effect or a loan from the lessee to the lessor that is directly or indirectly related to the leased property is expected to be outstanding

   Note: The phrase *indirectly related to the leased property* is used to cover situations that in substance are guarantees of the lessor's debt or loans to the lessor by the lessee that are related to the leased property, but are structured in such a manner that they do not represent a direct guarantee or loan.

5. Any period covered by ordinary renewal options preceding the date on which a bargain purchase option is exercisable

6. Any period representing renewals or extensions of the lease at the lessor's option

A lease term does not extend beyond the date a bargain purchase option becomes exercisable.

Noncancelable Lease Term

A noncancelable lease term is a provision in a lease agreement that specifies that the lease may be canceled only (*a*) on some remote contingency, (*b*) with permission of the lessor, or (*c*) if the lessee enters into a new lease with the same lessor (FAS-98, par. 22a).

Penalty

The term *penalty* refers to any outside factor or provision of the lease agreement that does or can impose on the lessee the requirement to disburse cash, incur or assume a liability, perform services, surrender or transfer an asset or rights to an asset or otherwise forego an economic benefit, or suffer an economic detriment (FAS-98, par. 22b).

MINIMUM LEASE PAYMENTS

Normal minimum lease payments for the lessee include (FAS-13, par. 5j):

1. The minimum rent called for during the lease term

2. Any payment or guarantee that the lessee must make or is required to make concerning the leased property at the end of the lease term (residual value), including:
   a. Any amount stated to purchase the leased property
   b. Any amount stated to make up any deficiency from a specified minimum
   c. Any amount payable for failure to renew or extend the lease at the expiration of the lease term

When a lease contains a *bargain purchase option*, the minimum lease payments include only (*a*) the *minimum rental payments over the lease term* and (*b*) *the payment required to exercise the bargain purchase option*.

The following are excluded in determining minimum lease payments (FAS-13, par. 5j):

1. A guarantee by the lessee to pay the lessor's debt on the leased property

2. The lessee's obligation (separate from the rental payments) to pay executory costs (insurance, taxes, etc.) in connection with the leased property

3. Contingent rentals (FAS-29, par. 10)

> **OBSERVATION:** FIN-19 clarifies certain guarantees of the residual value of leased property made by a lessee, as follows:
>
> 1. A guarantee by a lessee to make up a residual value deficiency caused by damage, extraordinary wear and tear, or excessive usage is similar to a contingent rental, since the amount is not determinable at the inception of the lease. Therefore, this type of lessee guarantee does not constitute a lessee guarantee of residual value for purposes of computing the lessee's minimum lease payments (FIN-19, par. 3).
>
> 2. A lessee's guarantee to make up a residual value deficiency at the end of a lease term is limited to the specified maximum deficiency called for by the lease (FIN-19, par. 4).
>
> 3. Unless the lessor explicitly releases the lessee, a guarantee of residual value by an unrelated third party for the benefit of the lessor does not release the obligation of the lessee. Therefore, such a guarantee by an unrelated third party shall not be used to reduce the lessee's minimum lease payments. Costs incurred in connection with a guarantee by an unrelated third party are considered executory costs and are not included in computing the lessee's minimum lease payments (FIN-19, par. 5).

The minimum lease payments to a lessor are the sum of (FAS-13, par. 5j):

1. The minimum lease payments under the lease terms

2. Any guarantee by a third party, unrelated to the lessee and lessor, of the residual value or rental payments beyond the lease term, providing such guarantor is financially capable of discharging the potential obligation

LEASE CLASSIFICATION

Lessees

If one or more of the following four criteria is present at the inception of a lease, it is classified as a capital lease by the lessee (FAS-13, par. 7):

1. Ownership of the property is transferred to the lessee by the end of the lease term.

2. The lease contains a bargain purchase option.

3. The lease term, at inception, is substantially (75% or more) equal to the estimated economic life of the leased property, including earlier years of use. (*Exception:* This criterion cannot be used for a lease that begins within the last 25% of the original estimated economic life of the leased property. *Example:* A jet aircraft that has an estimated economic life of 25 years is leased for five successive five-year leases. If the first four five-year leases were classified as operating leases, the last five-year lease cannot be classified as a capital lease, because the lease would commence within the last 25% of the estimated economic life of the property and would fall under this exception.)

4. The present value of the minimum lease payments at the beginning of the lease term, excluding executory costs and profits thereon to be paid by the lessor, is 90% or more of the fair value of the property at the inception of the lease, less any investment tax credit retained and expected to be realized by the lessor. (*Exception:* This criterion cannot be used for a lease that begins within the last 25% of the original estimated economic life of the leased property.)

A lessee's incremental borrowing rate is used to determine the present value of the minimum lease payments, except that the lessor's implicit rate of interest is used if it is known and it is lower (FAS-13, par. 7d).

☞ **PRACTICE POINTER:** While the criteria for identifying a capital lease appear very specific, significant professional judgment must be exercised in implementing them. For example:

- Except in the simplest cases, determining the lease term may involve judgment.

- Several of the criteria include terms that require judgment when they are applied to a specific lease. These include "bargain purchase option," "estimated useful life of the property," and "fair value of the property."

- The lease term and the present value of minimum lease payments criteria are not available for leases that begin within the last 25% of the asset's estimated useful life, which is subject to judgment.

- Determining the minimum lease payments for the lessee may require use of that party's incremental borrowing rate, which may involve judgment.

Lessors

If, at inception, a lease meets any one (or more) of the four criteria indicating that substantially all the benefits and risks of ownership have been transferred to the lessee, and it *meets both the following conditions*, the lease is classified by the lessor as a sales-type or direct financing lease, whichever is appropriate:

1. *Collection of the minimum lease payments is reasonably predictable.* A receivable resulting from a lease subject to an estimate of uncollectibility based on experience is not precluded from being classified as either a sales-type or a direct financing lease (FAS-98, par. 22f).

2. *No important uncertainties exist for unreimbursable costs yet to be incurred by the lessor under the lease.* Important uncertainties include extensive warranties and material commitments beyond normal practice. *Executory costs*, such as insurance, maintenance, and taxes, are not considered important uncertainties (FAS-13, par. 8b).

   Note: In the event the leased property is not acquired or constructed before the inception of the lease, this condition is not applied until such time as the leased property is acquired or constructed by the lessor (FAS-23, par. 7).

In applying the fourth basic capitalization criterion—the present value of the lease equals or exceeds 90% of the fair value of the property—a lessor computes the present value of the minimum lease payments, using the interest rate *implicit in the lease* (FAS-13, par. 7d).

A lease involving real estate is not classified by the lessor as a sales-type lease unless the title to the leased property is transferred to the lessee at or shortly after the end of the lease term (FAS-98, par. 22c).

Classification of a lease as a capital or operating lease is summarized in Figure 30-1.

CHANGING A PROVISION OF A LEASE

If a change in a provision of a lease results in a different lease classification at the inception of the lease because it meets different criteria, a new lease agreement is created that must be reclassified according to its different criteria. Renewal, extension, or a new lease under which the lessee continues to use the same property is not considered a change in a lease provision (FAS-13, par. 9).

Any action that extends the lease term, except to void a residual guarantee, or a penalty for failure to renew the lease at the end of the

Figure 30-1: Classification of a Lease as a Capital or Operating Lease

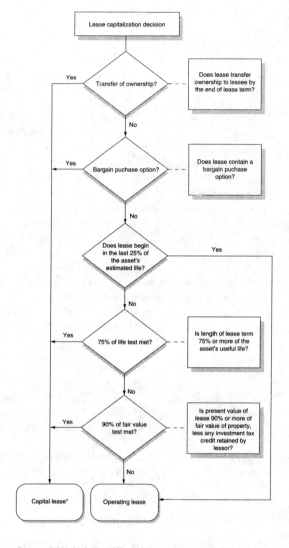

*Lessor must determine that two additional criteria are met to account for the lease as a capital lease:

1. Collection of minimum lease payments is reasonably predictable.
2. No important uncertainties exist for unreimbursable costs to be incurred by the lessor.

lease term, is considered a new lease agreement that is classified according to the different criteria.

Changes in estimates or circumstances do not cause a reclassification.

Refunding of Tax-Exempt Debt

If a change in a lease occurs as a result of a refunding by the lessor of tax-exempt debt and (*a*) the lessee receives the economic advantages of the refunding, and (*b*) the revised lease qualifies and is classified either as a capital lease by the lessee or as a direct financing lease by the lessor, the change in the lease shall be accounted for on the basis of whether or not an extinguishment of debt has occurred, as follows (FAS-22, par. 12):

1. Accounted for as an extinguishment of debt:
   a. The lessee adjusts the lease obligation to the present value of the future minimum lease payments under the revised agreement, using the effective interest rate of the new lease agreement. Any gain or loss is treated as a gain or loss on an early extinguishment of debt.
   b. The lessor adjusts the balance of the minimum lease payments receivable and the gross investment in the lease (if affected) for the difference between the present values of the old and new or revised agreement. Any gain or loss is recognized in the current period.
2. Not accounted for as an extinguishment of debt:
   a. The lessee accrues any costs connected with the refunding that are obligated to be reimbursed to the lessor. The interest method is used to amortize the costs over the period from the date of the refunding to the call date of the debt to be refunded.
   b. The lessor recognizes as revenue any reimbursements to be received from the lessee for costs paid related to the debt to be refunded over the period from the date of the refunding to the call date of the debt to be refunded.

ACCOUNTING AND REPORTING BY LESSEES

Capital Leases

Initial Recording

The lessee records a capital lease as an asset and a corresponding liability. The initial recording value of a lease is the *lesser* of the fair value of the leased property or the present value of the minimum lease payments, excluding any portion representing executory costs and profit thereon to be paid by the lessor. Fair value is determined as of the inception of the lease, and the present value of the minimum lease payments is computed at the beginning of the lease term. The inception of the lease and the beginning of the lease term are not necessarily the same dates (FAS-13, par. 10).

Since the lessee's minimum lease payments *exclude* a lessee's obligation to pay executory costs, executory costs paid by the lessee are expensed as paid or appropriately accrued. If such costs are included in the rental payments and are not identified separately (which is the most likely case), an estimate of the amount is necessary.

A lessee's incremental borrowing rate is used to determine the present value of the minimum lease payments unless the lessor's implicit rate of interest is known and is lower (FAS-13, par. 7d).

Leases with Escalation Clauses

In lease agreements or written commitments in which the leased property is to be acquired or constructed by the lessor, there may be a provision for the escalation of the minimum lease payments during the construction or preacquisition period. Usually, the escalation is based on increased costs of acquisition or construction of the leased property. A provision to escalate the minimum lease payments during the construction or preacquisition period can also be based on other measures of cost or value, including general price-level changes or changes in the consumer price index.

The relationship between the total amount of minimum lease payments and the fair value of a lease is such that when one increases so does the other. For example, assume that the total minimum lease payments of a particular lease are $100,000 payable in five equal annual installments, and the fair value of the same lease is $350,000. If the minimum lease payments are increased 20% to $120,000, it is likely that the fair value of the lease will increase correspondingly, because the lease is then worth more to an investor.

FAS-23 requires that increases in the minimum lease payments that occur during the preacquisition or construction period as a result of an escalation clause be considered in determining the fair value of the leased property at the inception of the lease for the purposes of the initial recording of the lease transaction by the lessee, or where fair value is used as a basis of allocation (FAS-23, par. 8).

The initial recording value of a lease transaction by the lessee, which is required by FAS-13, is the lesser of the fair value of the leased property or the present value of the minimum lease payments. FAS-23 changes the lessee's determination of fair value for leases that contain escalation clauses from the fair value on the inception date to a fair value amount that includes the effect of any increases which have occurred as a result of the escalation clause. The changes embodied in FAS-23 are intended to create lease classifications that more closely reflect the substance of a lease transaction.

> **OBSERVATION:** The question arises as to when leases of this type should be recorded on the books of the lessee. FAS-23 appears to indicate that the initial recording should be made only after the effects of the escalation clause on the fair value of the leased property are determined. Otherwise, FAS-23 is silent in all respects as to when the lease transaction should be recorded. In the case of significant amounts of leases, it appears illogical to wait several years to record the transaction. If this is the only viable alternative, however, full disclosure of all pertinent facts pertaining to the lease agreement or commitment should be made in a prominent footnote.
>
> The other alternative is to record these types of lease transactions immediately at the inception of the lease, utilizing whatever information is available and subsequently adjusting the recorded amounts when the effects of the escalation clauses are known. This alternative does not appear to be viable because of the difficulties mentioned in the following paragraphs.
>
> The last-enumerated criterion in FAS-13 for capitalizing a lease is when the present value of the minimum lease payments is 90% or more of the fair value of the leased property at the inception of the lease. When this criterion is considered for capitalizing a lease in conjunction with the alternative of recording lease transactions covered by FAS-23 at the inception of the lease and then subsequently adjusting the recorded amounts when the effects of the escalation clauses become known, the following problems arise, which are not addressed by either FAS-13 or FAS-23.
>
> 1. If we assume that FAS-23 requires that the fair value of leases with escalation clauses be determined at a future date, what fair value should be used to determine whether the lease is or is not a capital lease in accordance with the criterion of whether the present value of the minimum lease payments is 90% or more of the fair value of the leased property at the inception of the lease?
>
> 2. What if a lease of this type is capitalized in accordance with the criterion that the present value of the minimum lease payments is 90% or more of the fair value at inception of the lease, and subsequently, as a result of the escalation clause, the present value becomes less than 90% of the fair value, so that the lease should not have been capitalized?

3. Suppose a lease with an escalation clause is properly classified as an operating lease at inception of the lease and subsequently, as a result of the escalation clause, the lease qualifies as a capital lease.

The above are just a few of the complications that could arise in applying the provisions of FAS-23 to lease transactions.

FAS-23 also permits increases in the estimated residual value (see definition) that occur as a result of escalation provisions in leases in which the leased property is to be acquired or constructed by the lessor. For example, if the estimated residual value is 10% of the fair value at the inception of a lease and during the construction or preacquisition period of the leased property the effects of the escalation clause increase the fair value, then the estimated residual value also is allowed to increase above the amount that was estimated at the date of the inception of the lease (FAS-23, par. 9).

Amortization

The asset recorded under a capital lease is amortized in a manner consistent with the lessee's normal depreciation policy for other owned assets. The period for amortization is either (*a*) the estimated economic life or (*b*) the lease term, depending on which criterion was used to classify the lease. If the criterion used is either of the first two criteria (ownership of the property is transferred to the lessee by the end of the lease term or the lease contains a bargain purchase option), the asset is amortized over its estimated economic life. In all other cases, the asset is amortized over the lease term. Any *estimated residual value* is deducted from the asset to determine the amortizable base (FAS-13, par. 11).

☛ **PRACTICE POINTER:** Determining the appropriate amortization period for capital leases is an important issue where the lease term is significantly less than the expected useful life of the asset. A simple rule of thumb is simply to determine which party to the lease is expected to have use of the property during the period between the end of the lease period and the end of the expected life of the asset. If the lease is capitalized by the first or second capitalization criteria (transfer of title and bargain purchase option), the underlying assumption is that the lessee will become the legal owner of the asset by the end of the lease term and will have use of it for the remainder of the asset's expected life. Thus, the estimated life of the asset is the logical period of amortization. On the other hand, an assumption of the transfer of legal title does not underlie the lease if it is capitalized because of the third or fourth criteria (lease term and the present value of minimum lease payments). In either of these circumstances, the lease term is the logical period for amortization of the leased asset. Generally, if the same lease satisfies one or both of the first two criteria and one or both of the second criteria, use the expected life of the asset as the period of amortization.

Interest Expense: Interest Method

The interest method, sometimes referred to as the *effective interest method,* is used to produce a constant rate of interest on the remaining lease liability. A portion of each minimum lease payment is allocated to interest expense and/or amortization, and the balance is applied to reduce the lease liability. Any *residual guarantee(s)* by the lessee or penalty payments are automatically taken into consideration by using the interest method and will result in a balance at the end of the lease term equal to the amount of the guarantee or penalty payments at that date (FAS-13, par. 12).

Illustration of Interest Method

Jones Company leases a tractor-trailer for $8,000 per year on a noncancelable five-year lease. Jones guarantees to the lessor that the tractor-trailer will have a residual value of at least $5,000 at the end of the lease term.

Assume that all other assumptions have been eliminated and that a 12% interest rate is used.

Present value of $8,000 payments for five years at 12% =		$28,838*
Present value of $5,000 guaranteed residual value in five years at 12%	=	2,837**
Total asset and lease obligation		$31,675

---

* $8,000 x 3.60478
**$5,000 x .56743

A schedule of interest expense, amortization, and reduction of the lease obligation of $31,675 to the $5,000 residual guarantee using the interest method follows:

Book Value Lease Obligation Beginning of Year	Rental Payments	12% Interest on Beginning Book Value	Amortization	Book Value Lease Obligation End of Year
$31,675	$ 8,000	$ 3,801	$ 4,199	$27,476
27,476	8,000	3,297	4,703	22,773
22,773	8,000	2,733	5,267	17,506
17,506	8,000	2,101	5,899	11,607
11,607	8,000	1,393	6,607	5,000
	$40,000	$13,325	$26,675	

Change in Lease Terms

If a guarantee or penalty is rendered inoperative because of a renewal or other extension of the *lease term*, or if a new lease is consummated in which the lessee continues to lease the same property, an adjustment must be made to the asset and lease obligation for the difference between the present values of the old and the revised agreements. In these cases, the present value of the future minimum lease payments under the new or revised agreement is computed using the original rate of interest on the initial lease (FAS-13, par. 12).

Other lease changes are accounted for as follows (FAS-13, par. 14):

1. If a lease change results in revised minimum lease payments, but also is classified as a capital lease, an adjustment is made to the asset and lease obligation for the difference between the present values of the old and the new or revised agreement. The present value of the future minimum lease payments under the new or revised agreement is computed using the original rate of interest used on the initial lease.

2. If a new or revised agreement results from a lease change and is classified as an operating lease, gain or loss is recognized and the asset and lease obligation is eliminated from the books of account.

3. A renewal, extension, or new lease under which the lessee continues to use the same property, except when a guarantee or penalty is rendered inoperative (see above), is accounted for as follows:

   a. *Renewal or extension classified as a capital lease:* An adjustment is made for the difference between the original and revised present values, using the original discount rate.

   b. *Renewal or extension classified as an operating lease:* The existing lease continues to be accounted for as a capital lease to the end of its lease term, and the renewal or extension is accounted for as an operating lease.

When leased property under a capital lease is purchased by the lessee, it is accounted for as a renewal or extension of a capital lease. Thus, any difference between the carrying amount and the purchase price on the date of purchase is treated as an adjustment of the carrying amount of the property (FIN-26, par. 5).

Termination of a Lease

Gain or loss, if any, is recognized on the termination of a capital lease, and the asset and lease liability is removed from the books (FAS-13, par. 14).

Illustration of Capital Lease (Lessee)

Paine Corporation leases a computer under a noncancelable five-year lease for annual rental payments of $10,000. The fair value of the computer at the inception of the lease is $36,048, and the incremental borrowing rate of Paine is 10%. There are no executory costs, and no investment tax credit is available. The annual rent of $10,000 is considered a fair rental as opposed to a bargain rental. The estimated economic life of the computer is 10 years.

Classification of Lease

A review is made of the criteria involved in the provisions of the lease to determine its classification.

1. Criterion (1) is not met, because there is no transfer of the ownership of the leased property before the end of the lease term.

2. Criterion (2) is not met, because the lease does not contain a bargain purchase option.

3. Criterion (3) is not met, because the lease term (five years) is not equal to 75% or more of the estimated economic life (10 years) of the leased property. [**Note:** There are no other provisions affecting the lease term other than the five-year noncancelable term.]

4. Criterion (4) is met, because the present value ($37,908) of the minimum lease payments, excluding executory costs and profits thereon paid by the lessor, is 90% or more of the fair value ($36,048) of the leased property. [**Note:** The present value computations are given below.]

Paine Corporation should record the transaction as a capital lease.

Accounting for the Lease

The initial recording value of the leased property, at the inception of the lease, is the lesser of the fair value of the leased property or the present value of the minimum lease payments, excluding any portion that represents executory costs and profit thereon to be paid by the lessor.

The discount rate used by the lessee to find the present value of the minimum lease payments is its incremental borrowing rate of 10%, unless the lessee has knowledge of the lessor's implicit interest rate in the lease, and that rate is lower.

The lessor's interest rate implicit in the lease in this example is 12%. As a rule, the interest rate implicit in the lease is equal to the discount rate that, when applied to the minimum lease payments of $10,000 per year for five years and, if any, the unguaranteed residual value of the leased property, results in a present value equal to the fair value of the leased property at the inception of the lease. (For simplicity, this definition excludes any unusual factors that a lessor might recognize in determining its rate of return.)

This means that Paine must use its incremental borrowing rate of 10% to discount the minimum lease payments to their present value, which is $37,908.

The initial recording value of the leased property is the lesser of the fair value of the leased property at inception or the present value of the minimum lease payments using the lower interest rate. Therefore, the $36,048 fair value is less than the minimum lease payments of $37,908 (computed by using the lower incremental borrowing rate) and is used to initially record the lease, as follows:

Lease property, capital leases	$36,048	
Obligations, capital leases		$36,048

Amortization by Lessee

The asset(s) recorded under a capital lease is amortized in a manner consistent with lessee's normal depreciation policy for other owned assets. The period for amortization is either (*a*) the estimated economic life or (*b*) the lease term, depending on which criterion was used to classify the lease. If the criterion used to classify the lease as a capital lease was either criterion (1) (ownership of the property is transferred to the lessee by the end of the lease term) or criterion (2) (lease contains a bargain purchase option), the asset is amortized over its economic life. In all other cases, the asset is amortized over the lease term. Any residual value is deducted from the asset to determine the amortizable base.

Since the Paine Corporation's lease qualified under criterion (4) (present value of the minimum lease payments, excluding executory costs and profit thereon paid by the lessor, is 90% or more of the fair value of the leased property), the amortization period is over the lease term.

A schedule of amortization, interest expense, and lease obligation payments for Paine Corporation's computer lease, using the interest method, follows:

Book Value Lease Obligation Beginning of Year	Rental Payments	12% Interest on Beginning Book Value	Amortization	Book Value Lease Obligation End of Year
$36,048	$10,000	$ 4,326	$ 5,674	$30,374
30,374	10,000	3,645	6,355	24,019
24,019	10,000	2,882	7,118	16,901
16,901	10,000	2,028	7,972	8,929
8,929	10,000	1,071	8,929	—
	$50,000	$13,952	$36,048	

Note: The interest rate used is 12%, which is the interest rate implicit in the lease.

Operating Leases

Leases that do not qualify as capital leases in accordance with the provisions of FAS-13 are classified as operating leases. The cost of property covering an operating lease is included in the lessor's balance sheet as property, plant, and equipment. FAS-13 requires that rental income and expense relating to an operating lease be amortized over the periods in which the lessee derives benefit from the physical usage of the leased property. Thus, rental expense is amortized over the lease term on a straight-line basis, unless some other systematic and rational basis is more representative of the time pattern in which the benefits of the leased property are derived by the lessee (FAS-13, par. 15).

> ☞ **PRACTICE POINTER:** Use care when implementing account-ing standards for sales-type leases involving real estate. FAS-98 amended FAS-13 to require that the lessor shall not classify a lease involving real estate as a sales-type lease unless title to the leased property is transferred to the lessee at or shortly after the end of the lease term. As a result, a lessor may be required to classify a lease involving real estate as an operating lease, instead of a sales-type lease, because the lease agreement does not provide for the transfer of the leased property to the lessee by the end of the lease term. In this event, the lessor must recognize a loss at the inception of an operating lease involv-ing real estate if the fair value of the leased property is less than its cost or carrying amount, whichever is applicable. The amount of loss is equal to the difference between the fair value of the leased property and its cost or carrying amount at the inception of the lease.

Contingent Rental Expense

Some operating lease agreements provide for rental increases or decreases based on one or more future conditions, such as future sales volume, future machine hours, future interest rates, or future price indexes. These types of rental increases or decreases are classi-fied as *contingent rentals*. Contingent rentals are defined as those that cannot be determined at the inception of the lease because they depend on future conditions or events. A lessee's contingent rental payments are deducted as an expense in the period in which they arise (FAS-29, par. 11).

Scheduled Rent Increases or Decreases

To accommodate the lessee, a lessor may structure an operating lease agreement to provide for smaller rental payments in the early years of the lease and higher rental payments toward the end of the lease. *Example:* A six-year operating lease agreement may provide for rental payments of $1,000 per month for the first two years; $1,500 per month for the next two years; and $2,000 per month for the last two years; for a total rental payment of $108,000 for the six years. Under this circumstance, FAS-13 requires that the $108,000 total rental payments be amortized over the six-year lease term on a straight-line basis. The monthly amortization for the first two years of the lease term is $1,500, even though only $1,000 per month is paid by the lessee under the terms of the lease (FAS-13, par. 15).

> **OBSERVATION:** A reasonable argument can be made that in the early years of the above type of lease agreement, the lessee receives not only the use of the leased property, but also the temporary use of cash, equal to the excess of the fair rental value of the leased property over the actual rental payments. Theoretically, to recognize the economic substance of this lease transaction, both the lessee and the lessor should record imputed interest on the difference between the actual amount of rental payments and the computed amount of level rental payments. FAS-13, however, precludes the use of the time value of money as a factor in recognizing rentals under operating leases.

Right to Control Physical Use of Leased Property

In accounting for leases, there is a significant distinction between lease agreements that grant the lessee the right to control the use of the leased property at the beginning of the lease term and lease agreements that do not. A lease agreement may contain a rent escalation clause that is based on the lessee's utilization of the leased property. *Example:* A lease agreement covering a 10,000 square foot warehouse provides for a rent increase at the time the lessee utilizes more than 5,000 square feet of the warehouse. In this example, the lessee has control of the entire leased property at the beginning of the lease term. On the other hand, a lease agreement may contain a rent escalation clause for property that was originally leased, which becomes effective at the time the lessee leases additional property from the lessor. For example, a master lease provides for an increase in rent on property that was originally leased, at the time the lessee leases additional property from the lessor. In this example, the lessee does not have control of the additional leased property at the beginning of the lease term.

The right to control the use of leased property is considered to be the equivalent of the physical use of the property. In a lease agreement that gives the lessee control of the use of the leased property from the beginning of the lease term, the lessee and the lessor recognize, as part of the minimum lease payments, rental expense and rental revenue, including escalated amounts, on a straight-line basis over the lease term. On the other hand, when the lease agreement provides for the lessee to gain control over additional property, the escalated rent related to the original leased property is accounted for by the lessee as rental expense on the original leased property and recognized in proportion to the additional leased property in the years that the lessee has control over the use of the additional leased property. The lessor recognizes the escalated rents on the original leased property as additional rental revenue.

Lease Incentives in Operating Leases

To induce a prospective tenant to lease property, a lessor may offer (a) to make cash payments directly to the prospective tenant, (b) to reimburse the prospective tenant's moving expenses, or (c) to assume the obligation of the prospective tenant to a third party under a preexisting lease. These inducements are accounted for as either (a) an incentive for the lessee and an incentive for the lessor or (b) a reduction of rental expense by the lessee and a reduction of rental revenue by the lessor. Incentives or concessions that are paid to, or incurred by, the lessor on behalf of the lessee are accounted for as reductions of rental expense and/or rental revenue and recognized over the term of the new lease on a straight-line basis.

Losses incurred by the lessor as a result of assuming the lessee's obligation to a third party under a preexisting lease are accounted for as incentives by both the lessor and the lessee. In this circumstance, the lessee and the lessor shall estimate independently the amount of loss related to the assumption of the preexisting lease with a third party. The lessee may estimate the amount of loss related to the incentive by comparing the new lease to the prevailing market rate for similar leased property or by comparing the prevailing market rate for similar property reduced by the value of the lease obligation assumed by the new lessor. The lessor may estimate the amount of loss related to the incentive by subtracting from the total assumed obligation the expected benefits, if any, that the new lessor may derive from the use of the assumed leased property, including income from a sublease.

Illustration of Lease Incentives

As an incentive to execute a new operating lease for eight years, a lessor assumes the obligation on the lessee's preexisting lease which has four years remaining. The new lease payments are $8,000 per year and the lease payments on the lessee's preexisting lease are $6,000 per year. The estimated loss on the assumption of the lessee's preexisting lease is $2,400 based on the fact that the lessor can sublease the property for $450 per month for the remaining four years left on the lease. Based on a comparison with current market rates for similar leased property, the lessee calculates its amount of estimated loss as $1,600 for the remaining four years left on the lease.

The following are the lessor's and lessee's journal entries relating to this lease transaction:

Lessor Accounting

Incentive to lessee	$2,400	
Liability on sublease assumed		$2,400

To record deferred cost and liability at the inception of the lease, related to the loss on assumption of remaining lease.

Liability on sublease assumed ($2,400/4 years)	$ 600	
Sublease expense ($450 x 12 months)	5,400	
Cash		$6,000

To record cash payment on sublease assumed and amortization of the liability on the sublease assumed.

[**Note:** The above journal entry is an annualized version of entries that may be recorded monthly.]

Cash	$5,400	
Sublease revenue ($450 x 12 months)		$5,400

To record cash received from sublease of property.

[**Note:** The above journal entry is an annualized version of entries that may be recorded monthly.]

Cash	$8,000	
Rental revenue		$7,700
Incentive to lessee ($2,400/8 years)		300

[**Note:** The above journal entry is an annualized version of entries that may be recorded monthly.]

Lessee Accounting

Loss on sublease assumed by lessor	$1,600	
Incentive from lessor		$1,600

To record loss on sublease assumed by lessor in conjunction with new lease.

Lease expense	$7,800	
Incentive from lessor ($1,600/8 years)	200	
Cash		$8,000

To record cash payment on new lease and amortization of incentive over the new lease.

[**Note:** The above journal entry is an annualized version of entries that may be recorded monthly.]

Financial Statement Disclosure

General Disclosure

A general description of the lessee's leasing arrangements, including (*a*) basis of contingent rental payments; (*b*) terms of renewals, purchase options, and escalation clauses; and (*c*) restrictions imposed by lease agreements, such as additional debt, dividends, and leasing limitations, must be disclosed (FAS-13, par. 16).

Capital Leases

Assets, accumulated amortization, and liabilities from capital leases are reported separately in the balance sheet and classified as current or noncurrent in the same manner as other assets and liabilities (FAS-13, par. 13).

Current amortization charges to income must be disclosed clearly, along with additional information (FAS-13, par. 16):

1. *Gross assets:* as of each balance sheet date presented, in aggregate and by major property categories (this information may be combined with comparable owned assets)

2. *Minimum future lease payments:* in total and for each of the next five years, showing deductions for executory costs, including any profit thereon, and the amount of imputed interest to reduce the net minimum lease payments to present values

3. *Minimum sublease income:* due in future periods under noncancelable subleases

4. Total contingent rentals actually incurred for each period for which an income statement is presented

Operating Leases

The following financial statement disclosure is required for all operating leases of lessees having noncancelable lease terms in excess of one year (FAS-13, par. 16):

1. *Minimum future rental payments:* in total and for each of the next five years

2. *Minimum sublease income:* due in future periods under noncancelable subleases

3. *Schedule of total rental expense:* showing the composition by minimum rentals, contingent rentals, and sublease income (excluding leases with terms of a month or less that were not renewed)

Following is an illustration of a lessee's financial statement disclosure (using assumed numbers).

Illustration of Lessee's Financial Statement Disclosure

Lessee's Balance Sheet
(in thousands)

	December 31	
	19X8	19X7
Assets:		
Leased property:		
Capital leases, less accumulated		
amortization (Note:_____)	$ 2,200	$ 2,050
Liabilities:		
Current:		
Obligations under capital leases		
(Note:_____)	$ 365	$ 340
Noncurrent:		
Obligations under capital leases		
(Note:_____)	$ 1,368	$ 1,260

Capital Leases
Gross Assets and Accumulated Amortization
(in thousands)

	December 31	
	19X8	19X7
Type of Property		
Manufacturing plants	$ 1,500	$ 1,100
Retail stores	1,200	840
Other	300	210
Total	$ 3,000	$ 2,150
Less: Accumulated amortization	800	550
Capital leases, net	$ 2,200	$ 1,600

Capital Leases
Minimum Future Lease Payments and
Present Values of the Net Minimum Lease Payments
(in thousands)

Year Ended
December 31

19X9	$ 406
19Y0	1,232
19Y1	160
19Y2	125
19Y3	100
After 19Y3	450
Total minimum lease payments	$ 2,473
Less: Executory costs (estimated)	250
Net minimum lease payments	$ 2,223
Less: Imputed interest	490
Present value of net minimum lease payments	$ 1,733

In addition to the foregoing statements and schedules, footnotes describing minimum sublease income and contingent rentals should be included, if required.

Operating Leases
Schedule of Minimum Future Rental Payments
(in thousands)

Year Ended
December 31

19X9	$ 815
19Y0	2,400
19Y1	320
19Y2	250
19Y3	200
After 19Y3	900
Total minimum future rental payments	$ 4,885

In addition to the above information on operating leases, a note should be included describing minimum sublease income due in the future under noncancelable subleases.

Operating Leases
Composition of Total Rental Expense
(in thousands)

| | December 31 | |
	19X8	*19X7*
Minimum rentals	$1,100	$1,050
Contingent rentals	100	125
Less: Sublease rental income	(200)	(150)
Total rental expense, net	$1,000	$1,025

Note: The above schedule of total rental expense excludes leases with
terms of one month or less that were not renewed.

In addition to the foregoing information on capital and operating leases, a
footnote describing the general disclosure policy for the lessee's leases
should be included, containing (*a*) general leasing arrangements, (*b*) basis
of contingent rental payments, (*c*) terms of renewals, purchase options, and
escalation clauses, and (*d*) restrictions imposed by lease agreements, such
as additional debt, dividends, and leasing limitations.

ACCOUNTING AND REPORTING BY LESSORS

Leases are classified for the lessor as either (*a*) sales-type, (*b*) direct
financing, or (*c*) operating. Both sales-type and direct financing are
forms of capital leases.

Sales-type leases usually are used by sellers of property to increase the marketability of expensive assets. The occurrence of a
manufacturer's or dealer's profit or loss generally is present in a
sales-type lease.

Direct financing leases do not give rise to a manufacturer's or
dealer's profit or loss, and the fair value usually is the cost or the
carrying amount of the property.

Capital Leases

Recording Sales-Type Leases

The lessor's *gross investment* in the lease is the sum of (*a*) the lessor's
minimum lease payments less any executory costs and profit thereon
to be paid by the lessor and (*b*) any unguaranteed residual value
accruing to the benefit of the lessor (this is the estimated fair value of

the leased property at the end of the lease term, which is not guaranteed). (**Note:** If the residual value is guaranteed, it is included in the minimum lease payments) (FAS-13, par. 17a).

The estimated residual value used to compute the unguaranteed residual value accruing to the benefit of the lessor shall not exceed the amount estimated at the inception of the lease (FAS-13, par. 17d).

Using the interest rate implicit in the lease, the lessor's gross investment in the lease is discounted to its present value. The present value of the lessor's gross investment in the lease represents the sales price of the property that is included in income for the period. (**Note:** When using the interest rate implicit in the lease, the present value will always be equal to the fair value) (FAS-13, par. 17c).

The cost or carrying amount of the property sold plus any initial direct costs (costs incurred by the lessor to negotiate and consummate the lease, such as legal fees and commissions), less the present value of the unguaranteed residual value (if any) accruing to the benefit of the lessor is charged against income in the period in which the corresponding sale is recorded (FAS-13, par. 17c).

The difference between the lessor's gross investment in the lease and the sales price of the property is recorded as unearned income, which is amortized to income over the lease term by the interest method. The unearned income is included in the balance sheet as a deduction from the related gross investment, which results in the net investment in the lease (FAS-13, par. 17b).

A lease involving real estate is not classified by the lessor as a sales-type lease unless the title to the leased property is transferred to the lessee at or shortly after the end of the lease term (FAS-98, par. 22c).

Recording Direct Financing Leases

The lessor's *gross investment* in the lease is computed, which is equal to the sum of (*a*) the lessor's minimum lease payments less any executory costs and profit thereon to be paid by the lessor and (*b*) any unguaranteed residual value accruing to the benefit of the lessor (this is the estimated fair value of the lease property at the end of the lease term, which is not guaranteed). If the residual value is guaranteed, it is included in the minimum lease payments (FAS-98, par. 22h).

Under FAS-91, loan origination fees and direct loan origination costs, including initial direct costs incurred by the lessor in negotiating and consummating the lease, are offset against each other and the resulting net amount is deferred and recognized over the life of the loan as an adjustment to the yield on the loan (FAS-91, par. 5).

The difference between the lessor's gross investment in the lease and the cost or carrying amount of the leased property, if different, is recorded as unearned income, which is amortized to income over the lease term by the interest method. The unearned income is included in the balance sheet as a deduction from the related gross investment, which results in the net investment in the lease (FAS-98, par. 22i).

> **OBSERVATION:** The practice of recognizing a portion of the unearned income at the inception of the lease to offset initial direct costs is no longer acceptable (FAS-91, par 5).

Balance Sheet Classification

The resulting net investment in both sales-type and direct financing leases is subject to the same treatment as other assets in classifying as current or noncurrent (FAS-98, par. 22i).

Annual Review of Residual Values

The unguaranteed residual values of both sales-type and direct financing leases should be reviewed at least annually to determine whether a decline, other than temporary, has occurred in their estimated values. If a decline is not temporary, the accounting for the transaction should be revised using the new estimate, and the resulting loss should be recognized in the period that the change is made. *Upward adjustments are not allowed* (FAS-13, pars. 17d and 18d).

Accounting for Lease Changes

The definition of lease term includes any periods in which penalties are imposed in an amount that reasonably assures the renewal of the lease by the lessee. The definition of minimum lease payments includes any payments or guarantees that the lessee is required to make concerning the leased property, including any amount (*a*) to purchase the leased property, (*b*) to make up any deficiency from a specified minimum, and (*c*) for failure to renew or extend the lease at the expiration of the lease term. Guarantees and penalties such as these usually are canceled and become inoperative in the event the lease is renewed, is extended, or a new lease for the same property is consummated.

If a sales-type or direct financing lease contains a residual guarantee or a penalty for failure to renew and is rendered inoperative as a result of a lease renewal or other extension of the lease term, or if a new lease is consummated in which the lessee continues to lease the same property, an adjustment must be made to the unearned income account for the difference between the present values of the old and the revised agreements. The present value of the future minimum lease payments under the new agreement is computed by using the original rate of interest used for the initial lease (FAS-13, par. 17e).

In sales-type and direct financing leases that do not contain residual guarantees or penalties for failure to renew, an adjustment is made to account for lease changes, renewals, or other extensions, including a new lease in which the lessee continues to lease the same property. If the classification of the lease remains unchanged or is classified as a direct financing lease and the amount of the remaining minimum lease payments is changed, an adjustment is made to unearned income to account for the difference between the present values of the old and the new agreements (FAS-13, par. 17f). If a new classification results in a sales-type lease, it is classified and treated as a direct financing lease, unless the transaction occurs within the last few months of the original lease, in which case it is classified as a sales-type lease (FAS-27, par. 6).

If the classification of a lease is changed to an operating lease, the accounting treatment depends upon whether the operating lease starts immediately or at the end of the existing lease. If the operating lease starts immediately, the remaining net investment is eliminated from the accounts and the leased property is recorded as an asset using the lower of (*a*) original cost, (*b*) present fair value, or (*c*) present carrying amount. The difference between the remaining net investment and the new recorded value of the asset is charged to income in the period of change (FAS-13, par. 17f).

If the operating lease starts at the end of the existing lease, the existing lease continues to be accounted for as a sales-type or direct financing lease until the new operating lease commences, at which time the accounting treatment is the same as if the operating lease started immediately. Renewals and extensions usually commence at the end of the original sales-type or direct financing lease. Under these circumstances there should not be any remaining investment to eliminate from the books and the leased property is not recorded as an asset (FAS-13, par. 17f).

Termination of a Lease

Termination of a lease is recognized in the income of the period in which the termination occurs by the following journal entries (FAS-13, par. 17f):

1. The remaining net investment is eliminated from the accounts.

2. The leased property is recorded as an asset using the lower of the (*a*) original cost, (*b*) present fair value, or (*c*) present carrying amount.

Operating Leases

Leases that do not qualify as capital leases in accordance with the provisions of FAS-13 are classified as operating leases. The cost of the property leased to the lessee is included in the lessor's balance sheet as property, plant, and equipment. The lessor's income statement will normally include the expenses of the leased property (unless it is a net lease), such as depreciation, maintenance, taxes, insurance, and other related items. Material initial direct costs (those directly related to the negotiation and consummation of the lease) are deferred and allocated to income over the lease term (FAS-13, pars. 19a and 19c).

FAS-13 requires that rental income from an operating lease be amortized over the periods in which the lessor's benefits in the leased property are depleted. Thus, rental income is amortized over the lease term on a straight-line basis, unless some other systematic and rational basis is more representative of the time pattern in which the benefits of the leased property are depleted (FAS-13, par. 19b).

FAS-98 amended FAS-13 to require that a lease involving real estate not be classified by the lessor as a sales-type lease unless title to the leased property is transferred to the lessee at or shortly after the end of the lease term. As a result, an enterprise may be required to classify a lease involving real estate as an operating lease, instead of a sales-type lease, because the lease agreement does not provide for the transfer of the leased property to the lessee by the end of the lease term. In this event, the lessor recognizes a loss at the inception of an operating lease involving real estate if the fair value of the leased property is less than its cost or carrying amount, whichever is applicable. The amount of loss is equal to the difference between the fair value of the leased property and its cost or carrying amount at the inception of the lease (FAS-98, par. 22c).

Contingent Rental Income

Contingent rental income is defined as that which cannot be determined at the inception of the lease because it depends on future conditions or events. A lessor's contingent rental income is accrued in the period in which it arises (FAS-29, par. 13).

Money-Over-Money Operating Lease Transactions

A money-over-money lease transaction is one in which a lessor manufactures or purchases an asset, leases the asset to a lessee, and obtains nonrecourse financing in excess of the asset's cost using the leased asset and the future lease rentals as collateral. A money-over-money lease transaction may result either in (*a*) an operating lease, (*b*) a direct financing lease, or (*c*) a sales-type lease.

A lessor shall account for a money-over-money lease transaction as (*a*) the purchase or manufacture of an asset, (*b*) the leasing of that asset under an operating lease, direct financing lease, or sales-type lease in accordance with the provisions of FAS-13, and (*c*) the borrowing of funds.

If a money-over-money transaction results in an operating lease, the lessor records an asset and liability on its statement of financial position. If the transaction results in a direct financing lease or a sales-type lease, the lessor records a lease receivable and a liability on its statement of financial position.

Residual Value of a Leased Asset

Lease brokers or other enterprises may acquire an interest in the residual value of a leased asset by the payment of cash, the assumption of liabilities, and/or the payment of other consideration, including services rendered by the lease broker.

An interest in the residual value of a leased asset may be acquired by an enterprise in the form of an unconditional interest in the leased asset or the right to receive all or a portion of the proceeds from the sale of the leased asset at the end of the lease term without acquiring the related lease. For example, a lease broker may receive an interest in the residual value of a leased asset as a fee for services rendered. An interest in the residual value of a leased asset can also be acquired directly from a lessor. For example, a lessor may sell substantially all of the minimum rental payments associated with a sales-type, direct financing, or leveraged lease and retain an interest in the residual value of the leased asset.

The acquisition of an interest in the residual value of a leased asset generally includes the right to receive all or part of the future benefit that may be derived from the residual value of the leased asset. For example, an enterprise may acquire from a lessor the unconditional right to own and possess, at the end of the lease term, an asset subject to a lease; or an enterprise may acquire the right to receive all or a portion of the proceeds from the sale of a leased asset at the end of the lease term. Both of these transactions should be recorded as the acquisition of an asset, since both transactions involve the acquisition of an interest in the residual value of a leased asset.

The cost of an interest in the residual value of a leased asset is measured by (*a*) the amount of cash disbursed, (*b*) the fair value of other consideration given, and (*c*) the present value of liabilities assumed at the date the right is acquired. If it is more clearly evident, however, the fair value of the interest in the residual value of the leased asset at the date of the agreement is used instead of the fair value of the assets surrendered, services rendered, or liabilities assumed.

An enterprise accounts for the acquisition of an interest in the residual value of a leased asset at no more than the acquisition cost of the asset. Furthermore, an enterprise does not recognize any increases in the residual value of the leased asset over the remaining term of the related lease, regardless of the lessor's classification and accounting for the leased asset.

If in subsequent periods there is a decline, other than temporary, in the fair value of the interest in the residual value of a leased asset, the carrying amount of the asset is reduced to the new fair value and the amount of write-down recognized as a current loss. In this event, the new fair value becomes the new carrying amount for the asset, and the new carrying amount shall not be increased in any subsequent period prior to the sale or other disposition of the interest in the residual value of the leased asset.

After the sale of substantially all of the minimum rental payments of a sales-type, direct financing, or leveraged lease, a lessor reports any remaining interest in the residual value of the lease at its carrying amount at the date of the sale of the lease payments. In addition, the lessor does not recognize any increases in the residual value of the leased asset over the remaining term of the related lease.

If in subsequent periods there is a decline, other than temporary, in the fair value of the interest in the residual value of a leased asset, the carrying amount of the asset is reduced to the new fair value and the amount of write-down recognized as a current loss. In this event, the new fair value becomes the new carrying amount for the asset, and the new carrying amount is not increased in any subsequent period prior to the sale or other disposition of the interest in the residual value of the leased asset.

A guarantee of the residual value of a leased asset does not change the nature of an interest in the residual value of a leased asset or its historical acquisition cost.

Lease Sale or Assignment to Third Parties

Sale or assignment of a sales-type or a direct financing lease does not negate the original accounting treatment. Profit or loss is recognized at the time of sale or assignment, unless the seller assumes *substantial risks* (FAS-13, par. 20).

Frequently, a sale of property *subject to an operating lease* is complicated by some type of indemnification agreement by the seller. The seller may guarantee that the property will remain leased or may agree to reacquire the property if the tenant does not pay the specified rent. These types of transactions cannot be accounted for as a sale because of the substantial risk assumed by the seller. The principle of *substance over form* must be applied to such situations and treated accordingly. Examples of *substantial risk* on the part of the seller are (FAS-13, par. 21):

1. Agreements to reacquire the property or lease
2. Agreements to substitute another existing lease
3. Agreements to use "best efforts" to secure a replacement buyer or lessee

Examples of *nonsubstantial risk* situations on the part of the seller are (FAS-13, par. 21):

1. Execution of a remarketing agreement that includes a fee for the seller
2. Situations in which the seller does not give priority to the releasing or other disposition of the property owned by a third party

If a sale to a third party purchaser is not recorded as a sale because of the substantial risk factor assumed by the seller, it is accounted for as a *borrowing*. The proceeds from the "sale" are recorded as an obligation on the books of the seller. Rental payments made by the lessee under the operating lease are recorded as revenue to the seller, even if the rentals are paid to the third party. Each rental payment shall consist of imputed interest, and the balance of the payment shall be applied as a reduction of the obligation. Any sale or assignment of lease payments under an operating lease is accounted for as a borrowing (FAS-13, par. 22).

Financial Statement Disclosure

The following financial statement disclosure is required by lessors whose *significant business activity is leasing* (not including *leveraged* leasing):

General Disclosures

General disclosures for leases of lessors: a general description of the lessor's leasing arrangements FAS-13, par. 23c).

Capital Leases

For sales-type and direct financing leases (FAS-13, par. 23a and FAS-91, par. 25d):

1. A schedule of the components of the *net investment* in leases, as of each balance sheet date, including:
   a. Future minimum lease payments

b. Executory costs

c. Allowance for uncollectibles

d. Unguaranteed residual values accruing to the benefit of the lessor

e. Unearned income

f. Contingent rentals

2. A schedule of the minimum lease payments, in total and for the next five years

Operating Leases

For operating leases (FAS-13, par. 23b):

1. A schedule of the investment in property on operating leases, and property held for lease, by major categories, less accumulated depreciation, as of each balance sheet presented

2. A schedule of future minimum rentals on noncancelable operating leases, in total for the next five years

3. The amount of contingent rentals included in each income statement presented

Following is an illustration of a lessor's disclosure (using assumed numbers).

Illustration of Lessor's Financial Statement Disclosure

Lessor's Balance Sheet
(in thousands)

	December 31	
	19X8	19X7
Assets:		
Current assets:		
Net investment in sales-type and direct financing leases (Note:___)	$ 208	$ 200
Noncurrent assets:		
Net investment in sales-type and direct financing leases (Note:___)	$ 972	$ 830
Property on operating leases and property held for leases (net of accumulated depreciation of $450 and $400 for 19X8 and 19X7, respectively) (Note:___)	$1,800	$1,600

Schedule of Components—Net Investment in Leases
Sales-Type and Direct Financing Leases
(in thousands)

	19X8	19X7
Total minimum lease payments receivable	$1,450	$1,250
Less: Estimated executory costs, including profit thereon	150	125
Minimum lease payments	$1,300	$1,125
Less: Allowance for uncollectibles	65	60
Net minimum lease payments receivable	$1,235	$1,065
Add: Estimated unguaranteed residual values of leased properties	240	215
	$1,475	$ 1280
Less: Unearned income	295	250
Net investment in sales-type and direct financing leases	$1,180	$1,030

A footnote should be included for contingent rentals.

Schedule of Minimum Lease Payments
(in thousands)

Year Ended
December 31

19X9	$ 260
19Y0	195
19Y1	156
19Y2	132
19Y3	125
After 19Y3	432
Total minimum lease payments receivable, net of executory costs	$1,300

Schedule of Investment in Property
on Operating Leases and Property Held
for Lease (by Major Class Categories)
(in thousands)

Data-processing equipment	$ 900
Transportation equipment	700
Construction equipment	400
Other	200
Total	$2,200
Less: Accumulated depreciation	400
Net investment	$1,800

*Schedule of Future Minimum Rentals
on Noncancelable Operating Leases
(in thousands)*

Year Ended
December 31

19X9	$ 200
19Y0	175
19Y1	165
19Y2	125
19Y3	110
After 19Y3	200
Total future minimum rentals	$ 975

A footnote should be included for contingent rentals.

LEASES INVOLVING REAL ESTATE

Leases involving real estate are categorized as follows (FAS-13, par. 24):

1. Land only
2. Land and building(s)
3. Land, building(s), and equipment
4. Only part of a building(s)

Review of Classification of Leases by Lessees

A review of the classifications of leases by lessees is necessary because accounting for leases involving real estate depends primarily on the criteria for classifying leases.

If one or more of the following four criteria are present at the inception of a lease, it is classified as a capital lease by the lessee:

1. Ownership of the property is transferred to the lessee by the end of the lease term.
2. The lease contains a bargain purchase option.
3. The lease term, at inception, is substantially (75% or more) equal to the estimated economic life of the leased property, including earlier years of use. (*Exception:* This criterion cannot be used for a lease that begins within the last 25% of the original estimated economic life of the leased property.)

4. The present value of the minimum lease payments at the beginning of the lease term, excluding executory costs and profits thereon to be paid by the lessor, is 90% or more of the fair value of the property at the inception of the lease, less any investment tax credit retained and expected to be realized by the lessor. (*Exception:* This criterion cannot be used for a lease that begins within the last 25% of the original estimated economic life of the leased property.)

These criteria are referred to by number in the following discussion.

Leases Involving Land Only

A *lessee* accounts for a lease involving land only as a capital lease if either criterion (1) or criterion (2) is met. All other leases involving land only are classified as operating leases by the lessee.

A *lessor* classifies a lease involving land only as a sales-type lease and accounts for the transaction as a sale under the provisions of FAS-66, if the lease gives rise to a manufacturer's or dealer's profit (or loss) and criterion (1) is met. A lessor classifies a lease involving land only as a direct financing lease or a leveraged lease, whichever is applicable, if the lease does not give rise to a manufacturer's or dealer's profit (or loss), criterion (1) is met, and (*a*) the collection of the minimum lease payments is reasonably predictable and (*b*) no important uncertainties exist regarding costs yet to be incurred by the lessor under the lease. A lessor classifies a lease involving land only as a direct financing lease, a leveraged lease, or an operating lease, whichever is applicable, if criterion (2) is met, and (*a*) the collection of the minimum lease payments is reasonably predictable and (*b*) no important uncertainties exist regarding costs yet to be incurred by the lessor under the lease. All other leases involving land only are classified as operating leases by the lessor (FAS-98, par. 22k).

Leases Involving Land and Building(s)

Leases involving land and building(s) may be categorized as follows:

A. Leases that meet criterion (1) or criterion (2)
B. Leases in which the fair value of the land is less than 25% of the total fair value of the leased property at the inception of the lease
C. Leases in which the fair value of the land is 25% or more of the total fair value of the leased property at the inception of the lease

A. Leases That Meet Criterion (1) or Criterion (2)

Leases that meet either criterion (1) or criterion (2) are accounted for as follows:

Lessee The present value of the minimum lease payments, less executory costs and profits thereon (to be paid by the lessor), is allocated between the land and building(s) in proportion to their fair value at the inception of the lease. The present value assigned to the building(s) is amortized in accordance with the lessee's normal depreciation policy (FAS-13, par. 26a).

Lessor If a lease gives rise to a manufacturer's or dealer's profit (or loss) and criterion (1) is met, a lessor classifies a lease involving land and building(s) as a sales-type lease and accounts for the transaction as a sale under the provisions of FAS-66. If a lease does not give rise to a manufacturer's or dealer's profit (or loss) and criterion (1) is met, a lessor classifies a lease involving land and building(s) as a direct financing lease or a leveraged lease, whichever is applicable, providing that (*a*) collection of the minimum lease payments are reasonably predictable and (*b*) no important uncertainties exist regarding costs yet to be incurred by the lessor under the lease (FAS-98, par. 22l).

If a lease gives rise to a manufacturer's or dealer's profit (or loss) and criterion (2) is met, a lessor classifies a lease involving land and building(s) as an operating lease. If the lease does not give rise to a manufacturer's or dealer's profit (or loss) and criterion (2) is met, a lessor classifies a lease involving land and building(s) as a direct financing lease or a leveraged lease, whichever is applicable, providing that (*a*) collection of the minimum lease payments is reasonably predictable and (*b*) no important uncertainties exist regarding costs yet to be incurred by the lessor under the lease (FAS-98, par. 22l).

All other leases involving land and building(s) are classified as operating leases by the lessor.

B. Fair Value of the Land Is Less Than 25% of the Total Fair Value of the Leased Property at the Inception of the Lease

When applying criteria (3) and (4), both the lessee and the lessor consider the land and building(s) as a single unit, and the estimated economic life of the building(s) is the estimated economic life of the single unit. This type of lease is accounted for as follows:

Lessee The land and building(s) are accounted for as a single capitalized asset and amortized in accordance with the lessee's normal depreciation policy over the lease term if either criterion (3) or criterion (4) is met (FAS-13, par. 26b).

Lessor   If a lease gives rise to a manufacturer's or dealer's profit (or loss) and criterion (3) or criterion (4) is met, a lessor classifies a lease involving land and building(s), in which the fair value of the land is less than 25% of the total fair value of the leased property at the inception of the lease as an operating lease. If the lease does not give rise to a manufacturer's or dealer's profit (or loss) and criterion (3) or criterion (4) is met, a lessor classifies a lease involving land and building(s) in which the fair value of the land is less than 25% of the total fair value of the leased property at the inception of the lease as a direct financing lease or a leveraged lease, whichever is applicable, providing that (*a*) collection of the minimum lease payments is reasonably predictable and (*b*) no important uncertainties exist regarding costs yet to be incurred by the lessor under the lease. All other leases involving land and building(s) are classified as operating leases by the lessor (FAS-98, par. 22m).

C. Fair Value of the Land Is 25% or More of the Total Fair Value of the Leased Property at the Inception of the Lease

When applying criteria (3) and (4), both the lessee and the lessor shall consider the land and building(s) separately. To determine the separate values of the land and building(s), the lessee's incremental borrowing rate is applied to the fair value of the land to determine the annual minimum lease payments applicable to the land. The balance of the minimum lease payments remaining is attributed to the building(s). This type of lease is accounted for as follows (FAS-13, par. 26b):

Lessee   The building(s) portion is accounted for as a capital lease and amortized in accordance with the lessee's normal depreciation policy over the lease term if the building(s) portion meets either criterion (3) or criterion (4). The land portion is accounted for separately as an operating lease.

Lessor   If a lease gives rise to a manufacturer's or dealer's profit (or loss) and criterion (3) or criterion (4) is met, a lessor classifies a lease involving land and building(s) in which the fair value of the land is 25% or more of the total fair value of the leased property at the inception of the lease as an operating lease. If the lease does not give rise to a manufacturer's or dealer's profit (or loss) and criterion (3) or (4) is met, a lessor shall classify the building(s) portion of a lease in which the fair value of the land is 25% or more of the total fair value of the leased property at the inception of the lease as a direct financing lease or a leveraged lease, whichever is applicable, providing that (*a*) collection of the minimum lease payments is reasonably predictable and (*b*) no important uncertainties exist regarding costs yet to be incurred by the lessor under the lease. The land portion is accounted for separately as an operating lease.

All other leases involving land and building(s) are classified as operating leases by the lessor.

Leases Involving Land, Building(s), and Equipment

Equipment values, if material, should not be commingled with real estate values in leases. The minimum lease payments attributed to the equipment shall, if necessary, be estimated appropriately and stated separately. The criteria for the classification of leases are applied separately to the equipment to determine proper accountability (FAS-13, par. 27).

Leases Involving Only Part of a Building(s)

If the cost and fair value of a lease involving only part of a building(s) can be determined objectively, the lease classification and accountability are the same for any other land and building(s) lease. An independent appraisal of the leased property or replacement cost can be made as a basis for the objective determination of fair value (FIN-24, par. 6). In the event that cost and fair value cannot be determined objectively, leases involving only part of a building(s) are classified and accounted for as follows (FAS-13, par. 28):

Lessee

The lessee classifies the lease only in accordance with criterion (3) as follows: The lease term, at inception, is substantially (75% or more) equal to the estimated economic life of the leased property, including earlier years of use. (*Exception*: This particular criterion cannot be used for a lease that begins within the last 25% of the original estimated economic life of the leased property.)

In applying the above criterion, the estimated economic life of the building(s) in which the leased premises are located is used.

In the event the above criterion is met, the leased property is capitalized as a single unit and amortized in accordance with the lessee's normal depreciation policy over the lease term. In all other cases, the lease is classified as an operating lease.

Lessor

In all cases in which the cost and fair value are indeterminable, the lessor accounts for the lease as an operating lease.

SALE-LEASEBACK TRANSACTIONS

A sale-leaseback is a transaction in which an owner sells property and then leases back part or all of the same property. Such an owner is referred to as the seller-lessee. The purchaser-lessor is the party who purchases the property and leases back the same property to the seller-lessee. Sale-leaseback transactions involving real estate are addressed in FAS-98. All other sale-leaseback transactions are covered by FAS-28.

Non-Real Estate

Profit or loss on the sale is the amount that would have been recognized on the sale by the seller-lessee, assuming there was no leaseback (FAS-28, par. 3).

Accounting for the sale-leaseback by the seller-lessee is determined by the degree of rights in the remaining use of the property the seller-lessee retains, as follows:

1. Substantially all

2. Minor

3. More than minor but less than substantially all

Substantially All or Minor

Under the terms of the lease, the seller-lessee may have a *minor* portion or *substantially all* of the rights to the remaining use of the property. This is determined by the present value of a total *reasonable rental* for the rights to the remaining use of the property retained by the seller-lessee. The seller-lessee has transferred *substantially all* of the rights to the remaining use of the property to the purchaser-lessor if the present value of the total *reasonable rental* under the terms of the lease is 10% or less than the fair value of the property sold at the inception of the lease. The seller-lessee has transferred a *minor* portion of the remaining rights to the purchaser-lessor if the terms of the leaseback include the entire property sold and qualify as a capital lease under FAS-13 (FAS-28, par. 3a).

> **OBSERVATION:** FAS-28 does not define *reasonable rental* or *fair value*. FAS-13, however, defines *fair value* as the price the leased property could be sold for between unrelated parties in an arm's length transaction. FAS-13 defines *fair rental* as the rental rate for similar property under similar lease terms and conditions.

Whether the lease is recorded as a capital lease or an operating lease, any profit or loss (see definition) on the sale by the seller-lessee must be deferred and amortized as follows:

Capital lease   For a capital lease, the deferred profit or loss on the sale is amortized in proportion to the amortization of the leased property.

Operating lease   For an operating lease, the deferred profit or loss on the sale is amortized in proportion to the gross rental charged to expense over the lease term.

Whether a capital lease or an operating lease, if the leased asset is land only, the amortization of the deferred profit or loss on the sale must be on a straight-line basis over the lease term.

If the seller-lessee retains the rights to a *minor* portion of the remaining use in the property, the seller-lessee accounts for the sale and leaseback as two independent transactions based on their separate terms. The lease must provide for a reasonable amount of rent, however, considering prevailing market conditions at the inception of the lease. The seller-lessee must increase or decrease the profit or loss on the sale by an amount, if any, which brings the total rental for the leased property to a reasonable amount. Any amount created by this adjustment is amortized, as follows:

Capital lease   For a capital lease, the deferred or accrued amount is amortized in proportion to the amortization of the leased property.

Operating lease   For an operating lease, the deferred or accrued amount is amortized in proportion to the gross rental charged to expense over the lease term.

Whether a capital lease or an operating lease, if the leased asset is land only, the amortization of the deferred or accrued amount must be on a straight-line basis over the lease term.

☛ **PRACTICE POINTER:** If the total rental on the lease is less than a reasonable amount compared to prevailing market conditions at the inception of the lease, increase a profit on the sale and decrease a loss on the sale.

For an operating lease, the journal entry is a debit to prepaid rent and a credit to profit or loss. Amortize the prepaid rent in an amount that increases the periodic rental expense over the lease term to a reasonable amount. Conversely, if the total rental on the lease is more than a reasonable amount compared to prevailing market conditions at the inception of the lease, decrease a profit on the sale and increase a loss on the sale. The journal entry is a debit to profit or loss and a credit to deferred rent. Amortize the deferred rent in an amount that decreases the periodic rental expense over the lease term to a reasonable amount.

For a capital lease, make no debit to prepaid rent or credit to deferred rent. Instead, the debit or credit increases or decreases the amount that is recorded for the leased property. Then, amortize the leased property in the usual manner.

More Than Minor but Less Than Substantially All

If the seller-lessee retains the rights to more than minor but less than substantially all of the remaining use in the property, the seller-lessee shall recognize any excess profit (not losses) determined at the date of sale as follows (FAS-28, par. 36):

Capital lease The excess profit (if any) on a sale-leaseback transaction is equal to the amount of profit that exceeds the seller-lessee's recorded amount of the property as determined under the provisions of FAS-13 (the lesser of the fair value of the leased property or the present value of the minimum lease payments). For example, if the seller-lessee's recorded amount of the sale-leaseback property is $100,000 as determined under the provisions of FAS-13, and the amount of profit on the sale-leaseback transaction is $120,000, the excess profit that is recognized by the seller-lessee is $20,000. The balance of the profit ($100,000) is deferred and amortized in proportion to the amortization of the leased property.

Operating lease The excess profit (if any) on a sale-leaseback transaction is equal to the amount of profit that exceeds the present value of the minimum lease payments over the term of the lease. The amount of profit on the sale-leaseback transaction that is not recognized at the date of the sale is deferred and amortized over the lease term in proportion to the gross rentals charged to expense.

Whether a capital lease or an operating lease, if the leased property is land only, the amortization of the deferred profit (if any) must be on a straight-line basis over the lease term.

Real Estate

Under the provisions of FAS-98, the definition of *sale-leaseback accounting* is analogous to the definition of the *full accrual method of accounting*. Under sale-leaseback accounting, the sale portion of a sale-leaseback transaction is recorded as a sale by the seller-lessee, the property sold and all of its related liabilities are eliminated from the seller-lessee's balance sheet, gain or loss on the sale portion of the sale-leaseback transaction is recognized by the seller-lessee in accordance with the provisions of FAS-13 (as amended by FAS-28, FAS-66, and FAS-98), and the lease portion of the sale-leaseback transaction is accounted for in accordance with the provisions of FAS-13 (as amended by FAS-28).

Under FAS-98, a seller-lessee applies sale-leaseback accounting only to those sale-leaseback transactions that include payment terms and provisions that provide for (*a*) a normal leaseback (as defined by FAS-98), (*b*) an adequate initial and continuing investment by the purchaser-lessor (as defined by FAS-66), (*c*) the transfer of all of the other risks and rewards of ownership to the purchaser-lessor, and (*d*) no other continued involvement by the seller-lessee, other than the continued involvement represented by the lease portion of the sale-leaseback transaction (FAS-98, par. 7).

Normal Leaseback

Under FAS-98, a normal leaseback is one in which the seller-lessee actively uses substantially all of the leased property in its trade or business during the lease term. The seller-lessee may sublease a minor portion of the leased property, equal to 10% or less of the reasonable rental value for the entire leased property, and the lease will still qualify as a normal leaseback. Thus, to qualify as a normal leaseback, the seller-lessee must actively use substantially all of the leased property in its trade or business in consideration for rent payments, which may include contingent rentals that are based on the seller-lessee's future operations (FAS-98, par. 8).

If occupancy by the seller-lessee's customers is transient or short-term, the seller-lessee may provide ancillary services, such as house-keeping, inventory control, entertainment, bookkeeping, and food service. Thus, active use by a seller-lessee in its trade or business includes the use of the leased property as a hotel, bonded ware-house, parking lot, or some other similar business.

Adequate Initial and Continuing Investment by the
Purchaser-Lessor

To qualify for sale-leaseback accounting under FAS-98, the purchaser-lessor's initial and continuing investment in the property must be adequate as prescribed by FAS-66 (Accounting for Sales of Real Estate) (FAS-98, par. 10). Under FAS-66, the purchaser's minimum initial investment must be made at or before the time of sale in cash or cash equivalents. A purchaser's note does not qualify for the minimum initial investment unless payment of the note is unconditionally guaranteed by an irrevocable letter of credit from an established unrelated lending institution. A permanent loan commitment by an independent third party to replace a loan made by the seller shall not be included in the purchaser's initial investment. Any funds that have been loaned or will be loaned, directly or indirectly, to the purchaser by the seller must be deducted from the purchaser's initial investment to determine whether the required minimum has been met. For the purposes of this provision, the seller must be exposed to a potential loss as a result of the funds loaned to the purchaser. For example, if a purchaser made an initial cash investment of $200,000 in a real estate transaction, $25,000 of which was a loan from the seller, the purchaser's minimum initial investment would be $175,000. If an unrelated banking institution unconditionally guaranteed the timely repayment of the $25,000 to the seller, however, the entire $200,000 would be eligible as the purchaser's initial investment. (A discussion of the detailed provisions of FAS-66 and FAS-98 are found in the 1999 *Miller GAAP Guide* chapter "Real Estate—Recognition of Sales."

Accounting for Certain Losses on Sale-Leasebacks

Under any circumstances, if the fair value of the property at the time of the sale-leaseback is less than its undepreciated cost, the seller-lessee recognizes immediately a loss in an amount not to exceed the difference between the fair value and the undepreciated cost of the property sold (FAS-28, par. 3c).

> **OBSERVATION:** Paragraph 33c of FAS-13, as amended by paragraph 3 of FAS-28, states that the maximum indicated loss may not be more than the difference between the undepreciated cost of the property sold and its fair value. On the other hand, paragraph 18 of FAS-28 states that the maximum indicated loss may not be more than the difference between the carrying amount of the property sold and its fair value. Thus, it is not clear whether the undepreciated cost or the carrying amount of the property should be used in calculating the maximum loss that is recognized immediately.

OTHER LEASE ACCOUNTING ISSUES

Wrap Lease Transactions

In a wrap lease transaction, a lessor leases equipment to a lessee and obtains nonrecourse financing from a financial institution using the lease receivable and the asset as collateral. The lessor sells the asset subject to the lease and the nonrecourse financing to a third-party investor and then leases the asset back. Thus, the original lessor remains the principal lessor, who continues to service the lease. The transaction with the third-party investor may or may not occur at the same time that the original lease is executed with the original equipment user. As a matter of fact, it is not unusual in a wrap lease transaction for the subsequent nonrecourse financing or sale to a third-party to occur up to six months after the original lease agreement is executed.

In exchange for the sale of the asset to a third-party investor, the lessor may receive a combination of cash, a note, an interest in the residual value of the leased asset, and certain other rights or contingent rights, such as the right to remarket the asset at the end of the lease term. Depending on the terms of the specific transaction, (*a*) the lessor may or may not be liable for the leaseback payments if the primary lessee defaults, (*b*) the lessor may or may not receive a fee for servicing the lease, (*c*) payments under the leaseback may or may not approximate collections under the note, and (*d*) the terms of the leaseback may or may not correspond with the terms of the original equipment lease.

A wrap lease transaction consists primarily of a sale-leaseback of property and is accounted for as such under FAS-13 or FAS-98, whichever is applicable. If the property involved in a wrap lease transaction is other than real estate, the provisions of FAS-13, as amended by FAS-28, must be followed. On the other hand, if the property involved is real estate, the provisions of FAS-98 must be observed in accounting for the sale-leaseback transaction.

Under sale-leaseback accounting, the sale portion of a sale-leaseback transaction is recorded as a sale by the seller-lessee. The property sold and all of its related liabilities are eliminated from the seller-lessee's balance sheet. Gain or loss on the sale portion of the sale-leaseback transaction is recognized by the seller-lessee in accordance with paragraph 33 of FAS-13, as amended by FAS-28. The lease portion of the sale-leaseback transaction should be classified as a capital lease or an operating lease in accordance with paragraph 6 of FAS-13 and accounted for by the seller-lessee in accordance with paragraph 33 of FAS-13 (FAS-28, par. 3).

The purchaser-lessor records a sale-leaseback transaction as a purchase and a direct financing lease if the lease portion of the sale-leaseback meets the criteria of a capital lease under FAS-13. Otherwise, the purchaser-lessor records the transaction as a purchase and an operating lease (FAS-13, par. 34).

The main difference in accounting for a sale-leaseback under FAS-13 and FAS-98 is that under the provisions of FAS-98, the sale portion of the sale-leaseback must meet all of the criteria for sales recognition under the provisions of FAS-66. FAS-98 prohibits a lease involving real estate from being classified as a sales-type lease unless the lease agreement provides for the title of the leased property to be transferred to the lessee at or shortly after the end of the lease term.

In reporting a wrap lease transaction, an enterprise's statement of financial position should include (*a*) the amount of the retained residual interest in the leased property, (*b*) the amount of the gross sublease receivable, (*c*) the amount of the nonrecourse third-party debt, (*d*) the amount of the leaseback obligation, and (*e*) the amount of the note receivable from the investor.

Illustration of Wrap Lease Transactions

Assume that a lessor leases an asset with an undepreciated cost of $1,000 to a lessee for five years at $19.12 a month. The residual value of the leased asset at the end of the lease term is estimated to be $164.53 and the interest rate implicit in the lease is 10%. The lessor would classify the lease as a direct financing lease under the provisions of FAS-13 and record the following journal entry:

Lease receivable (60 x $19.12)	$1,147.20	
Residual value of leased asset	164.53	
Asset		$1,000.00
Unearned income—lease receivable		247.20
Unearned income—residual		64.53

Note: For financial reporting purposes, FAS-13 requires that the lease receivable and residual value of the leased asset be combined and reported as the gross investment in the lease. In addition, the unearned income amounts must also be combined.

Using the lease receivable and the asset as collateral, the lessor enters into a nonrecourse financing arrangement with a financial institution for $900.00 (the present value of the $19.12 monthly lease payment for 60 months discounted at 10%) at a rate of 10%. The lessor would record the following journal entry to reflect the liability for the nonrecourse debt:

Cash	$900.00	
Nonrecourse debt		$900.00

The lessor then sells the asset subject to the lease and the nonrecourse debt to a group of equity partners and leases the asset back for five years at $19.12 a month (for simplicity, assume that the lease, the nonrecourse financing, and the sale to the equity partners occur at the same time). The lessor is now the lessee-sublessor and remains the obligor with the financial institution that financed the nonrecourse debt. In return for the asset, the lessor receives the following:

1. Cash of $50, representing the sale of 50% of the residual value of the leased asset

2. An additional $103.66 in cash, representing the transfer of tax benefits [for purposes of this illustration, the $103.66 represents the discounted tax benefits associated with the transaction using 1985 tax laws, and includes the investment tax credit (ITC)]

3. A note receivable for $900.00 bearing interest at 10% with 60 monthly payments of $19.12 (60 payments at $19.12 represent a gross note of $1,147.20 and unearned income of $247.20)

4. The right to receive a fee of $82.27 for remarketing the asset at the end of the initial lease term (the present value of an $82.27 payment 60 months in the future discounted at 10% equals $50.00)

5. In addition, the lessor retains a 50% interest in the proceeds of the residual value of the leased asset at the end of the lease term

Subleases and Similar Transactions

Unless the original lease agreement is replaced by a new agreement, the original lessor continues to account for the lease as before (FAS-13, par. 36).

A termination of a lease is recognized by a lessor in the income of the period in which termination occurs, as follows (FAS-13, par. 37):

1. The remaining net investment is eliminated from the accounts.

2. The leased property is recorded as an asset using the lower of the (*a*) original cost, (*b*) present value at termination, or (*c*) present carrying amount at termination.

If an original lessee is relieved of the primary obligation under an original lease, the transaction is accounted for by the lessee as follows (FAS-13, par. 38):

Capital leases   Termination of the lease occurs and gain or loss is recognized in income of the period. A loss contingency should also be provided for if the original lessee remains secondarily liable on the lease.

Operating leases   A loss contingency is provided for if the original lessee remains secondarily liable on the lease.

When a lessee subleases leased property, the original lease continues and a simultaneous new lease is created in which the lessee becomes a sublessor. The results are that the original lessee is both a lessee in the original lease and, at the same time, a sublessor in the new lease. In situations like this, the original lease continues to be accounted for as if nothing happened, but the new lease is classified and accounted for separately.

If an original lessee is not relieved of the primary obligation under an original lease, the transaction is accounted for by the original lessee-sublessor as follows (FAS-13, par. 39):

1. If the criterion for the original lease was criterion (1) (ownership of the property is transferred before the end of the lease term) or (2) (lease contains a bargain purchase option), the new lease is classified based on its own new criteria. If the new lease qualifies for capitalization, it is accounted for as a sales-type or a direct financing lease, whichever is appropriate, and the unamortized balance of the asset under the original lease is treated as the cost of the leased property to the sublessor (original lessee).

   In the event that the new lease does not qualify for capitalization, it is treated as an operating lease.

2. If the criterion for the original lease was criterion (3) (lease term is substantially—75% or more—equal to the estimated economic life of the leased property at the inception of the lease) or (4) (present value of the minimum lease payments— excluding executory costs—is 90% or more of the fair value at inception), the new lease is capitalized only if it meets criterion (3) and (*a*) the collection of the minimum lease payments is reasonably predictable and (*b*) no important uncertainties exist regarding costs yet to be incurred by the lessor under the lease. If the new lease meets the criteria above, it is accounted for as a direct financing lease, with the amortized balance of the asset under the original lease as the cost of the leased property.

   If the new lease does not meet the specific conditions above, it is accounted for as an operating lease.

In any event, if the original lease is an operating lease, the sublease also is accounted for as an operating lease (FAS-13, par. 39c).

Even though the sublessor (original lessee) remains primarily obligated under an original lease, a loss may be recognized on a sublease. The loss is measured as the difference between the unamortized cost of the leased property (net carrying amount) and the present value of the minimum lease payments which will be received under the terms of the sublease (FIN-27, par. 2).

> **OBSERVATION:** FIN-27 is silent as to recognition of any gain on subleases in which the sublessor (original lessee) remains primarily obligated under the original lease. FAS-13, paragraph 39, however, implies that **both** gain and loss may be recognized on sales-type and direct financing leases.

FIN-27 also reaffirms that estimated costs and expenses directly associated with a decision to dispose of a business segment should include future rental payments on long-term leases less any future rentals to be received from subleases of the same properties (APB-30, par. 17). The gain or loss is measured as the difference between the unamortized cost of the leased property (net carrying amount) and the present value of the minimum lease payments that will be received under the terms of the sublease. The gain or loss is included in the overall gain or loss on the disposal of the business segment (FIN-27, par. 3).

> **OBSERVATION:** FIN-27 is not clear on its coverage of subleases that are classified as operating leases. There is a strong argument that gain or loss on an operating sublease be included as part of the overall gain or loss on disposal of a business segment. APB-30 specifically states that all costs and expenses that are directly associated with the decision to dispose of a business segment be included in the overall gain or loss on the disposal. If a business segment has a long-term operating lease that is subleased and classified as an operating lease as part of the overall disposal of the segment, then any gain or loss would be associated directly with management's decision to dispose of the segment. The gain or loss would be measured as the difference between the present value of the future rental payments that must be paid on the original lease and the present value of the future rental receipts that will be collected on the operating sublease. The journal entry to record a loss would be a debit to the gain or loss account for disposal of the business segment and a credit to a deferred account. The deferred credit account would be amortized each year in an amount that would make up the difference between the payment made on the original lease and the rental collected on the operating sublease.

Leases Involving Governmental Units

Leases with governmental units usually lack fair values, have indeterminable economic lives, and cannot provide for transfer of ownership. These special provisions usually prevent their classification as any other than operating leases (FAS-13, par. 28).

Leases involving governmental units, however, are subject to the same criteria as any other lease unless all of the following conditions exist; and in that event, these leases are classified as operating leases (FIN-23, par. 8):

1. A governmental unit or authority owns the leased property.
2. The leased property is operated by or on behalf of a governmental unit or authority and is part of a larger facility, such as an airport.

3. The leased property cannot be moved to another location because it is a permanent structure or part of a permanent structure.

4. Any governmental unit or authority can terminate the lease agreement at any time under the terms of the lease agreement, existing statutes, or regulations.

5. Ownership is not transferred to the lessee and the lessee cannot purchase the leased property.

6. Equivalent property in the same area as the leased property cannot be purchased or leased from anyone else.

Related Party Leases

Except in cases in which the substance of a lease transaction indicates clearly that the terms and conditions have been significantly influenced by the related parties, related party leases are classified and accounted for as if the parties were unrelated (FAS-13, par. 29).

It is important to note that, generally, a subsidiary whose principal business activity is leasing property to its parent must be consolidated with the parent's financial statements (FAS-13, par. 31).

> **OBSERVATION:** Specific financial statement disclosures pertaining to related parties are required by FAS-57 (Related Party Disclosures).

Leveraged Leases

A lessee classifies and accounts for *leveraged* leases in the same manner as *nonleveraged* leases. *Only a lessor* must classify and account for leveraged leases in the specific manner prescribed herein (FAS-13, par. 41).

FAS-13 defines a *leveraged lease* as a lease having all the following characteristics (FAS-13, par. 42):

1. A leveraged lease meets the definition of a *direct financing lease* as follows:

   A direct financing lease is a lease that does not result in a manufacturer's or dealer's profit or loss because the fair value of the leased property at the inception of the lease is the same as the cost or carrying amount. In a direct financing lease, substantially all the benefits and risks inherent in the ownership of the lease property are transferred to the lessee. In addition, the following requirements must be met:

    a. The minimum lease payments are reasonably predictable of collection.

    b. No important uncertainties exist regarding costs to be incurred by the lessor under the terms of the lease.

2. It involves at least three parties: (*a*) a lessee, (*b*) a lessor, and (*c*) a long-term creditor. (**Note:** The lessor is sometimes referred to as the *equity participant*.)

3. The financing is sufficient to provide the lessor with substantial leverage in the transaction and is nonrecourse as to the general credit of the lessor.

4. Once the lessor's net investment is completed, it declines in the early years and rises in later years before being liquidated. These fluctuations in the lessor's net investment can occur more than once in the lease term.

☛ **PRACTICE POINTER:** Leveraged leases are complex contracts that meet very specific criteria. Accounting for leveraged leases is unique in certain ways (e.g., offsetting assets and liabilities) and, therefore, determining whether a given lease is a leveraged lease is particularly important. A lease must meet *all* of the following specific criteria (taken from the definition of a leveraged lease) to be accounted for as a leveraged lease:

1. The lease is a direct financing lease.
2. The lease involves three parties rather than the normal two.
3. The lease provides the lessor with substantial leverage.
4. The pattern of the lessor's investment declines then rises.

Only when all four of these conditions are met is the lease subject to leveraged lease accounting.

If the investment tax credit is accounted for as provided herein and a lease meets the preceding definition, it is classified and accounted for as a leveraged lease (FAS-13, par. 42).

The initial and continuing investment of the lessor in a leveraged lease is recorded *net* of the nonrecourse debt, as follows (FAS-13, par. 43):

1. Rentals receivable, net of that portion applicable to principal and interest on the nonrecourse debt

2. A receivable for the amount of the investment tax credit to be realized on the transaction

3. The estimated residual value of the leased property

4. Unearned and deferred income consisting of (*a*) the estimated pretax lease income or loss, after deducting initial direct costs of negotiating and consummating the lease transaction, that

remains to be allocated to income over the lease term and (*b*) the investment tax credit that remains to be allocated to income over the lease term

The investment in a leveraged lease, less applicable deferred taxes, represents the lessor's net investment for purposes of computing periodic net income from the leveraged lease (FAS-13, par. 43). The following method is used to compute periodic net income (FAS-13, par. 44):

1. A projected cash flow analysis is prepared for the lease term.

2. The rate of return on net investment in the years it is positive is computed (usually by trial and error).

3. Every year the net investment is increased or decreased by the difference between the net cash flow and the amount of income recognized, if any.

The amount of net income that is recognized each year consists of (FAS-13, par. 44):

1. Pretax lease income or loss (allocated from the unearned income portion of the net investment)

2. Investment tax credit (allocated from the deferred income portion of the net investment)

3. The tax effect of the pretax lease income or loss recognized (which is reflected in tax expense for the year)

Any tax effect on the difference between pretax accounting income or loss and taxable income or loss is charged or credited to deferred taxes.

All the important assumptions affecting the estimated net income from the leveraged lease, including any estimated residual values, should be reviewed at least annually.

If, at the inception or at any time during the lease, the projected net cash receipts over the initial or remaining lease term are less than the lessor's initial or current investment, the resulting loss is immediately recognized (FAS-13, par. 45).

Upward adjustments of the estimated residual value are not permitted (FAS-13, par. 46).

The lessor's financial statement disclosure for leveraged leases shall include the amount of deferred taxes stated separately. When leveraged leasing is a significant part of the lessor's business activity, a schedule of the components of the net investment in leveraged leases shall be disclosed fully in the footnotes to the financial statements (FAS-13, par. 47).

Lessor's Existing Asset in a Leveraged Lease

Only a direct financing lease may qualify as a leveraged lease (FAS-13, par. 42a). One of the requirements of a direct financing lease is that it may not result in a manufacturer's or dealer's profit or loss. It is difficult for an existing asset of a lessor to qualify for leveraged lease accounting because the carrying amount (cost less accumulated depreciation) of an asset previously placed in service is not likely to be the same as its fair value. An existing asset of a lessor may qualify for leveraged lease accounting, however, if its carrying amount is equal to its fair value, without any write-down or other adjustment to its fair value.

Business Combinations

A business combination, in itself (FIN-21, pars. 13–14), does not affect the classification of a lease. If as a result of a business combination, however, a lease is revised or modified to the extent that under FAS-13 it is considered a new agreement, it is reclassified based on its revision or modification.

Ordinarily, under the purchase method or pooling-of-interests method of effecting a business combination, a lease retains its previous classification under FAS-13 and is accounted for in the same manner as it was prior to the combination.

The acquiring company in a business combination accounted for by the purchase method accounts for a leveraged lease by assigning a fair value (present value, net of tax) to the net investment in a leveraged lease based on the remaining future cash flows with appropriate recognition for any future estimated tax effects. After the fair value (present value, net of tax) of the net investment is determined, it is allocated to net rentals receivable, estimated residual value, and unearned income. Thereafter, a company accounts for the leveraged lease by allocating the periodic cash flow between the net investment and the lease income (FIN-21, par. 16).

In a business combination in which an acquired lease has not been conformed to FAS-13, the acquiring company classifies such a lease to conform retroactively to FAS-13 (FIN-21, par. 17).

CHAPTER 31
LONG-TERM CONSTRUCTION CONTRACTS

CONTENTS

CHAPTER 31
LONG-TERM CONSTRUCTION CONTRACTS

OVERVIEW

Long-term construction contracts present a difficult financial reporting problem primarily because of their large dollar amounts and their relatively long duration (i.e., they span more than one accounting period, sometimes beginning and ending several years apart). GAAP in the area of revenue recognition for long-term construction contracts deal with this situation by permitting two methods—the *percentage-of-completion method* and the *completed-contract method*. The percentage-of-completion method is appropriate in situations in which reliable estimates of the degree of completion are possible, in which case a pro rata portion of the income from the contract is recognized in each accounting period covered by the contract. If reliable estimates are not available, the completed-contract method is used, in which income is deferred until the end of the contract period.

GAAP for long-term construction contracts are found in the following pronouncement:

ARB-45   Long-Term Construction-Type Contracts

CROSS-REFERENCES

1999 MILLER GAAP GUIDE: Chapter 19, "Government Contracts"; Chapter 43, "Revenue Recognition"

1999 MILLER GAAP IMPLEMENTATION MANUAL: Chapter 20, "Long-Term Construction Contracts"

1999 MILLER GOVERNMENTAL GAAP GUIDE: Chapter 24, "Capital Projects Funds"

1999 MILLER GAAS GUIDE: Chapter 8, "Evidence"; Chapter 18, "Audits of Construction Contractors"

BACKGROUND

Because of the length of time involved in long-term construction contracts, a problem exists as to when income should be recognized. The completed-contract method and the percentage-of-completion method generally are followed to account for these long-term contracts.

> **OBSERVATION:** The specialized accounting and auditing practices for construction contractors appear in the AICPA Industry Audit and Accounting Guide titled "Construction Contractors." Specialized accounting practices also appear in the AICPA Statement of Position 81-1 (Accounting for Performance of Construction-Type and Certain Production-Type Contracts).
>
> The "Construction Contractors" guide and SOP 81-1 were issued concurrently in 1981 and supersede the previous Audit Guide ("Audits of Construction Contractors") issued in 1965. The "Construction Contractors" guide primarily focuses on the construction industry, whereas SOP 81-1 makes recommendations on accounting issues that apply to a broad range of contracting activities.
>
> In the case of construction-type contracts, revenue may be recognized either by the completed-contract method or by the percentage-of-completion method. The percentage-of-completion method is preferable when the estimated cost to complete the contract and the extent of progress made on the contract are reasonably determinable. When estimates are unreliable, the completed-contract method is required.

COMPLETED-CONTRACT METHOD

The completed-contract method recognizes income only on completion or substantial completion of the contract. *A contract is regarded as substantially complete if the remaining costs are insignificant* (ARB-45, par. 9).

Any excess of accumulated costs over related billings is reflected in the balance sheet as a current asset; any excess of accumulated billings over related costs is reflected as a current liability. In the case of more than one contract, the accumulated costs or liabilities should be stated separately on the balance sheet. The preferred terminology for the balance sheet presentation is *(Costs) (Billings) of uncompleted contracts in excess of related (billings) (costs)* (ARB-45, par. 12).

In some cases, it is preferable to allocate general and administrative expenses to contract costs as opposed to period income. In years in which no contracts are completed, a better matching of costs and revenues is achieved by carrying general expense as a charge to the contract. If a contractor has many jobs, however, it is more appropriate to charge these expenses to current periods (ARB-45, par. 10).

Although income is not recognized until completion of the contract, a provision for an expected loss should be recognized when it becomes evident that a loss will occur. (ARB-45, par. 11).

Illustration of the Completed-Contract Method

A construction company has a balance in its construction-in-progress account of $500,000, representing the costs incurred to date on a project. While the project was initially expected to be profitable, management now expects a loss on the project at completion of $75,000. At the time of this determination, the following entry should be made:

Estimated loss on construction project	$75,000	
Construction in progress		$75,000

This entry reduces the construction (inventory) account by $75,000 and recognizes the loss in income of the period in which the determination of the loss is estimable. Assuming the estimate of the loss is accurate, future costs will be charged to the construction account as incurred and the balance in that account will equal the revenue on the contract.

The primary advantage of the completed-contract method is that it is based on final results rather than on estimates. The primary disadvantage of this method is that it does not reflect current performances when the period of the contract extends over more than one accounting period (ARB-45, pars. 13 and 14).

Accounting for the Completed-Contract Method

The following are important points in accounting for contracts under the completed-contract method:

1. Overhead and direct costs are charged to a construction-in-progress account (an asset).

2. Billings and/or cash received are charged to advances on construction-in-progress account (a liability).

3. At completion of the contract, gross profit or loss is recognized as follows:

Contract price − total costs = gross profit or loss

4. At balance sheet dates that occur during the contract period, the excess of either the construction-in-progress account or the advances account over the other is classified as a current asset or a current liability. It is a *current* asset or a *current* liability because of the *normal operating cycle concept.*

5. Expected losses are recognized in full in the year they are identified. An expected loss on the total contract is determined by:

    a. Adding estimated costs to complete to the recorded costs to date to arrive at total contract costs

    b. Adding to advances any additional revenue expected to arrive at total contract revenue

    c. Subtracting (*b*) from (*a*) to arrive at total estimated loss on contract

PERCENTAGE-OF-COMPLETION METHOD

Revenues generally are recognized when (*a*) the earning process is complete or virtually complete and (*b*) an exchange has taken place.

Accounting for long-term construction contracts by the percentage-of-completion method is a modification of the general practice of realization at the point of sale. Realization is based on the evidence that the ultimate proceeds are available and the consensus that the result is a better measure of periodic income (matching-of-revenue-and-cost principle).

The principal advantages of the percentage-of-completion method are the reflection of the status of the uncompleted contracts and the periodic recognition of the income currently rather than irregularly as contracts are completed. The principal disadvantage of this method is the necessity of relying on estimates of the ultimate costs (ARB-45, pars. 7 and 8).

The percentage-of-completion method recognizes income as work progresses on the contract. The method is based on an estimate of the income earned to date, less income recognized in earlier periods. Estimates of the degree of completion usually are based on one of the following (ARB-45, par. 4):

-   The relationship of costs incurred to date to expected total costs for the contract
-   Other measures of progress toward completion, such as engineering estimates

During the early stages of a contract, all or a portion of items such as material and subcontract costs may be excluded if it appears that the results would produce a more meaningful allocation of periodic income (ARB-45, par. 4).

When current estimates of the total contract costs indicate a loss, a provision for the loss on the entire contract should be made. When a loss is indicated on a total contract that is part of a related group of contracts, however, the group may be treated as a unit in determining the necessity of providing for losses (ARB-45, par. 6).

> ☛ **PRACTICE POINTER:** Income to be recognized under the percentage-of-completion method at various stages ordinarily should not be measured by interim billings.

Accounting for the Percentage-of-Completion Method

The following are important points in accounting for contracts under the percentage-of-completion method:

1. Journal entries and balance sheet treatment are the same as for the completed-contract method, *except* that the amount of estimated gross profit earned in each period is recorded by charging the construction-in-progress account and crediting realized gross profit.

2. Gross profit or loss is recognized in each period by the following formula:

$$\left[\begin{array}{c} \text{percentage} \\ \text{of} \\ \text{completion} \end{array} \times \begin{array}{c} \text{total estimated} \\ \text{gross profit or} \\ \text{loss} \end{array} \right] - \begin{array}{c} \text{gross profit} \\ \text{recognized to} \\ \text{date} \end{array} = \begin{array}{c} \text{realized gross} \\ \text{profit} \end{array}$$

3. An estimated loss on the total contract is recognized immediately in the year it is discovered. Any gross profit (or loss) reported in prior years, however, must be added (or deducted) from the total estimated loss.

> ☛ **PRACTICE POINTER:** The completed-contract and percentage-of-completion methods are *not* alternative methods of accounting for the same contract. Each is appropriate in certain circumstances, but do *not* consider them *equally appropriate in the same circumstances.* Where reasonable estimates of the percentage of completion are possible, the percentage-of-completion method constitutes GAAP and should be used. On the other hand, if reasonable estimates of the percentage are *not* possible, the completed-contract method constitutes GAAP and should be used.

Illustration of Accounting for the Completed-Contract and Percentage-of-Completion Methods

The following data pertain to a $2,000,000 long-term construction contract:

	19X5	19X6	19X7
Costs incurred during the year	$ 500,000	$700,000	$ 300,000
Year-end estimated costs to complete	1,000,000	300,000	—
Billing during the year	400,000	700,000	900,000
Collections during the year	200,000	500,000	1,200,000

The journal entries for both the completed-contract method and the percentage-of-completion method for the three years are as follows, assuming the degree of completion is determined based on costs incurred:

19X5	Completed Contract		% of Completion	
Construction in progress	$ 500,000		$ 500,000	
Cash or liability		$ 500,000		$ 500,000
Accounts receivable	400,000		400,000	
Advance billings		400,000		400,000
Cash	200,000		200,000	
Accounts receivable		200,000		200,000
Construction in progress	no entry		166,667	
Realized gross profit (P&L)				166,667

19X6	Completed Contract		% of Completion	
Construction in progress	$ 700,000		$ 700,000	
Cash or liability		$ 700,000		$ 700,000
Accounts receivable	700,000		700,000	
Advance billings		700,000		700,000
Cash	500,000		500,000	
Accounts receivable		500,000		500,000
Construction in progress	no entry		233,333	
Realized gross profit (P&L)				233,333

19X7	Completed Contract		% of Completion	
Construction in progress	$ 300,000		$ 300,000	
Cash or liability		$ 300,000		$ 300,000
Accounts receivable	900,000		900,000	
Advance billings		900,000		900,000
Cash	1,200,000		1,200,000	
Accounts receivable		1,200,000		1,200,000
Construction in progress	no entry		100,000	
Realized gross profit (P&L)				100,000
Advance billings	2,000,000		2,000,000	
Construction in progress		1,500,000		2,000,000
Realized gross profit (P&L)		500,000		—

Computation of Realized Gross Profit

19X5

$$\frac{\$500,000}{\$1,500,000} \times \$500,000^* - 0 = \$166,667$$

19X6

$$\frac{\$1,200,000}{\$1,500,000} \times \$500,000 - \$166,667 = \$233,333$$

19X7

$$\frac{\$1,500,000}{\$1,500,000} \times \$500,000 - (\$166,667 + \$233,333) = \$100,000$$

Total gross profit $\quad\quad\quad \$500,000^*$

$^*\$2,000,000 - (\$500,000 + \$1,000,000) = \$500,000$

At the end of each year during which the contract is in progress, the excess of the construction-in-progress account over the advance billings account is presented as a current asset:

19X5: ($500,000 + $166,667) – $400,000 = $266,667

19X6: ($500,00 + $166,667 + $700,00 + $233,333)
$\quad\quad$ – ($400,000 + $700,00) = $500,000

In this illustration, the estimated gross profit of $500,000 was the actual gross profit on the contract. If changes in the estimated cost to complete the contract had been appropriate at the end of 19X5 and/or 19X6, or if the actual costs to complete had been determined to be different when the contract was completed in 19X7, those changes would have been incorporated into revised estimates during the contract period. For example, if at the end of 19X6 the costs to complete were estimated to be $400,000 instead of $300,000, the 19X6 gross profit of $133,333 would have been determined as follows:

$$\left(\frac{\$1,200,000}{\$1,600,000^*} \right) \times (2,000,000 - \$1,6000,000) = \$300,000$$

$$\$300,000 - \$166,667 = \$133,333$$

---

*$500,000 (19X5) + $700,000 (19X6) + $400,000 (19X7 estimated) = $1,600,000

CHAPTER 32
LONG-TERM OBLIGATIONS

CONTENTS

CHAPTER 32
LONG-TERM OBLIGATIONS

OVERVIEW

The authoritative accounting literature contains disclosure requirements for many types of long-term obligations. These include unrecorded obligations (e.g., unrecorded unconditional purchase obligations), as well as recorded obligations (e.g., recorded purchase obligations, debt maturities, required stock redemptions).

The general source of GAAP for disclosure of long-term obligations is the following pronouncement:

FAS-47   Disclosure of Long-Term Obligations

Other pronouncements cover disclosure requirements for specific
types of obligations (e.g., FAS-13 [Accounting for Leases]).

For unrecorded unconditional purchase obligations, FAS-47 requires disclosure of the nature and terms of the obligation, amounts
of the obligation at the latest balance sheet date, and for each of the
next five years, a description of any variable portion of the obligation
and amounts purchased under the obligation for each period for
which an income statement is presented. Similar disclosures are
required for recorded obligations, including purchase obligations,
debt maturities, and capital stock redemption requirements.

CROSS-REFERENCES

1999 MILLER GAAP GUIDE: Chapter 7, "Contingencies, Risks, and
Uncertainties"; Chapter 8, "Convertible Debt and Debt with War-
rants"; Chapter 30, "Leases"; Chapter 37, "Product Financing
Arrangements"

1999 MILLER NOT-FOR-PROFIT REPORTING: Chapter 2, "Overview of Current Pronouncements"; Chapter 6, "Liabilities"; Chapter 11, "Display of Certain GAAP Transactions"

1999 MILLER GOVERNMENTAL GAAP GUIDE: Chapter 29, "General Long-
Term Debt Account Group"

BACKGROUND

Enterprises and/or individuals frequently acquire assets or liabilities by written contract. A contract may contain unconditional rights and obligations or conditional rights and obligations. A right or obligation is unconditional when only the passage of time is necessary for it to mature. A conditional right or obligation is one that matures only on the occurrence of one or more events that are specified in the contract.

If a significant period elapses between the execution and subsequent performance of a contract, a problem may arise as to when, if at all, the assets and/or liabilities created by the contract should be recognized by the contracting parties. Under existing accounting practices, assets and/or liabilities that are created by a contract may not be recognized at all, or may be either recognized in the accounts or disclosed in a note to the financial statements.

Under existing accounting principles, exchanges between enterprises or individuals usually are recorded when the transfer of resources, services, and/or obligations occurs. Unfulfilled purchase commitments for the future exchange of resources, services, and/or obligations, however, are not recorded until the commitment is at least partially fulfilled by one of the contracting parties. Exceptions to the general rule for unfulfilled purchase commitments are certain leases and losses on firm noncancelable purchase commitments, which are recorded under existing accounting principles.

> ☛ **PRACTICE POINTER:** The disclosure of certain contractual rights or obligations is sometimes confused with the disclosure of a contingency. The disclosure of a contingency is necessary only when a contingent *gain* or *loss* exists in accordance with the provisions of FAS-5. If there is no contingent *gain* or *loss*, disclosure is not required. On the other hand, the disclosure of information on certain contractual rights or obligations may be required by GAAP to avoid financial statements that are misleading.
>
> A situation may arise in which the disclosure of a contractual obligation is required by GAAP and—at the same time—a *loss contingency* may exist involving the same contractual obligation. In this event, disclose the information concerning both the obligation and the contingency in accordance with GAAP.

PURCHASE OBLIGATIONS

Unconditional Purchase Obligations

For the purposes of FAS-47, an *unconditional purchase obligation* is one in which one party is required to transfer funds to another party in return for future delivery of specified quantities of goods or services at specified prices.

> **OBSERVATION:** In contrast, an unconditional purchase obligation to transfer assets other than funds to another party in return for specified quantities of goods or services at specified prices is not considered an unconditional obligation and, apparently, would not be covered by FAS-47.

For FAS-47 disclosure requirements to apply, an unconditional purchase obligation must be associated with the financing arrangements (*a*) for the facilities that will provide the contracted goods or services or (*b*) relating to the costs of the contracted goods or services (such as carrying costs). Unconditional purchase obligations that have a remaining term of one year or less are excluded from the provisions of FAS-47. An unconditional purchase obligation qualifies for disclosure even though it is cancelable because of (FAS-47, par. 6):

1. A remote contingency
2. Permission of the other party
3. A replacement agreement between the same parties
4. A provision for a penalty payment in an amount that reasonably assures the continuation of the agreement

The provisions in FAS-47 dealing with unrecorded purchase obligations are primarily directed to take-or-pay contracts and throughput contracts.

> **OBSERVATION:** In a *take-or-pay contract,* a buyer agrees to pay certain periodic amounts for certain products or services. The buyer must make the specified periodic payments, even though it does not take delivery of the products or services.
>
> In a *throughput contract,* one party agrees to pay certain periodic amounts to another party for the transportation or processing of a product. The periodic payments must be made, even though the minimum quantities specified in the agreement in each period have not been sent to the other party for transporting or processing.
>
> In take-or-pay contracts and throughput contracts, the periodic payments are unconditional and are not dependent on the occurrence of a specified event or the fulfillment of a condition.

Disclosure of Unrecorded Unconditional Purchase Obligations

FAS-47 does not change GAAP in terms of the recording of liabilities in conjunction with unconditional purchase obligations or other similar obligations. It does, however, require disclosure of information for unrecorded unconditional purchase obligations that are (*a*) substantially noncancelable, (*b*) associated with the financing arrangements for the facilities that will provide the contracted goods or services or related to the costs of the contracted goods or services (such as carrying costs), and (*c*) for a remaining term in excess of one year. The following information is to be disclosed (FAS-47, par. 7):

1. A description of the nature and term of the obligation

2. The total determinable amount of unrecorded unconditional purchase obligations as of the latest balance sheet date, and the total determinable amount of unrecorded unconditional purchase obligations for each of the five years after the latest balance sheet date

3. A description of the nature of any variable component of the unrecorded unconditional purchase obligations

4. For each income statement presented, the amounts actually purchased under the unconditional purchase obligations

> **OBSERVATION**: An unconditional obligation may consist of a determinable portion and a variable portion. The determinable portion is quantified and disclosed in accordance with item (2) above. The variable portion need not be quantified, but the nature of such amounts must be disclosed in accordance with item (3) above.

Similar or related obligations may be combined and disclosures are not required if the aggregate commitment of all unrecorded unconditional purchase obligations is immaterial.

Minimum lease payments that are required to be disclosed in accordance with FAS-13 need not be disclosed in accordance with FAS-47. Minimum lease payments that are not required to be disclosed in accordance with FAS-13, however, must be disclosed in accordance with FAS-47 if they meet the requirements for disclosure outlined in FAS-47 (FAS-47, par. 6).

> **OBSERVATION**: Apparently, FAS-47 requires the disclosure of certain leases that were specifically excluded from FAS-13, if such leases are (a) substantially noncancelable, (b) part of the financing arrangements for the facilities that will provide specified goods or services, or related to the costs of the specified goods or services, and (c) for a remaining term in excess of one year. The following types of leases and similar agreements were expressly excluded from FAS-13 and may require disclosure under the provisions of FAS-47:

1. Natural resource leases, including oil, gas, minerals, and timber

2. Leases involving services only

3. Licensing agreements, including motion picture films, plays, manuscripts, patents, and copyrights

Furthermore, despite the similarity to take-or-pay contracts, "nuclear fuel heat supply contracts" are specifically included in FAS-13 as leases and therefore are not covered by FAS-47.

FAS-47 does not require, but does encourage, the disclosure of the present value of the total determinable amounts of unrecorded unconditional purchase obligations for each of the five years after the latest balance sheet date [item (2) above]. In computing the present value of an obligation, the discount rate usually is the effective interest rate at the inception of the borrowings that (*a*) financed the project or (*b*) are associated with the unrecorded unconditional purchase obligations. If it is not practical to determine the discount rate, or if there are no borrowings associated with the obligations, the discount rate is the purchaser's incremental borrowing rate. The purchaser's incremental borrowing rate is the rate the purchaser would have incurred at the inception of the obligation to borrow funds, on similar terms, to discharge the unconditional purchase obligation (FAS-47, par. 8).

DISCLOSURE OF RECORDED OBLIGATIONS

In addition to requiring disclosure of information about unrecorded purchase obligations as described above, FAS-47 also requires disclosure of similar information for a variety of recorded obligations. The following specific disclosures must be made as of the date of the latest balance sheet presented (FAS-47, par. 10):

1. *Unconditional Purchase Obligations* For each of the five years immediately following the latest balance sheet date, the amount of payments for recorded unconditional purchase obligations that meet FAS-47 disclosure provisions must be disclosed. In addition, all amounts due after the fifth year shall be disclosed in a caption labeled "subsequent years." The disclosure provisions of FAS-47 require that an unconditional purchase obligation (*a*) be substantially noncancelable, (*b*) have a remaining term in excess of one year, and (*c*) be associated with the financing arrangements for facilities that will provide the contracted goods or services or relating to the costs of the contracted goods or services. (See Illustration of Take-or-Pay, Throughput, and Similar Contracts below.)

2. *Debt Payments* For each of the five years immediately following the latest balance sheet date, the combined total of maturities and sinking fund requirements for all long-term borrowings must be disclosed (see Illustration of Maturities and Sinking Fund Requirements below).

3. *Capital Stock Redemptions* For each of the five years immediately following the latest balance sheet date, the total of required redemptions (separately or combined) for all classes of capital stock that are redeemable at determinable prices on determinable dates must be disclosed (see Illustration of Redemption of Capital Stock below). (This requirement was carried forward into FAS-129 [Disclosure of Information about Capital Structure] unchanged.)

☛ **PRACTICE POINTER:** The requirement to disclose the payments due in each of the next five years on recorded obligations is sometimes overlooked, according to several studies of disclosure deficiencies in financial statements. This may be because FAS-47 is erroneously thought of as requiring disclosure only for unrecorded obligations. While it does cover unrecorded obligations, it also applies to recorded obligations.

Illustration of Take-or-Pay, Throughput, and Similar Contracts

X Company has entered into a long-term contract to purchase all of the widgets produced by a supplier. The contract expires in 19X9, and X Company must make minimum annual payments to the supplier, whether or not it is able to take delivery of the widgets. The minimum total payments for each of the five and later years succeeding December 31, 19X1, are as follows:

Year	Total Payments (in thousands)
19X2	$ 4,000
19X3	12,000
19X4	14,000
19X5	10,000
19X6	12,000
Subsequent years	28,000
Total	80,000
Less: Imputed interest	(30,000)
Present value of payments	$50,000

Illustration of Maturities and Sinking Fund Requirements

Maturities of long-term debt and sinking fund requirements on long-term debt for each of the five years* succeeding December 31, 19X1, are as follows:

Year	Long-Term Debt and Sinking Fund Requirements
19X2	$ 50,000
19X3	50,000
19X4	100,000
19X5	100,000
19X6	50,000

*FAS-47 does *not* require the disclosure of the above information for periods subsequent to the fifth year.

Illustration of Redemption of Capital Stock

Mandatory redemption requirements for all classes of capital stock for each of the five years* succeeding December 31, 19X1, are as follows:

Year	4% Preferred	7% Preferred
19X2	$ 200,000	$ 400,000
19X3	200,000	400,000
19X4	200,000	400,000
19X5	none	400,000
19X6	none	400,000

* FAS-47 does *not* require the disclosure of the above information for periods subsequent to the fifth year.

☛ **PRACTICE POINTER:** When disclosing unconditional obligations, much like operating leases, take care that the financial statements present both sides of the transaction. Thus, when recording an obligation, including a capital lease, both the asset (i.e., benefit) and the liability (i.e., obligation) are disclosed. Disclosure under FAS-47 applies only to the obligation side of the contract.

Paragraph 7a of FAS-47, which requires a statement about the nature and term of the obligation, may be the appropriate place for an enterprise to describe the associated benefits, if any. The last sentence of paragraph 19, Appendix A, of FAS-47 states, "The lack of explicit requirements to disclose associated benefits does not preclude an enterprise from describing those benefits."

OBSERVATION: FAS-47 contains specific disclosure requirements for recorded and unrecorded take-or-pay and throughput contracts. Both of these types of contracts are considered unconditional obligations under the provisions of FAS-47. However, a take-or-pay or throughput contract may, in substance, be a product financing arrangement. A product financing arrangement may also require unconditional periodic payments that are not dependent on the occurrence of a specified event or the fulfillment of a specified condition. Product financing arrangements are covered in the 1999 *Miller GAAP Guide* chapter titled "Product Financing Arrangements."

CHAPTER 33
NONMONETARY TRANSACTIONS

CONTENTS

CHAPTER 33
NONMONETARY TRANSACTIONS

OVERVIEW

As a general rule, GAAP require that exchanges be recorded based on the fair value inherent in the transaction. This applies to both monetary and nonmonetary transactions. Certain exceptions exist, however, for nonmonetary transactions. Different accounting bases may be required for these transactions, depending on the unique characteristics of the exchange transaction.

GAAP for nonmonetary transactions are found in the following pronouncements:

APB-29   Accounting for Nonmonetary Transactions

FIN-30   Accounting for Involuntary Conversions of Nonmonetary Assets to Monetary Assets

CROSS-REFERENCES

1999 MILLER GAAP GUIDE: Chapter 20, "Impairment of Loans and Long-Lived Assets"; Chapter 26, "Interim Financial Reporting"; Chapter 29, "Investments in Debt and Equity Securities"; Chapter 42, "Results of Operations"

1999 MILLER GAAP IMPLEMENTATION MANUAL: Chapter 21, "Nonmonetary Transactions"

1999 MILLER GAAP IMPLEMENTATION MANUAL: EITF: Chapter 21, "Nonmonetary Transactions"

1999 MILLER NOT-FOR-PROFIT REPORTING: Chapter 2, "Overview of Current Pronouncements"; Chapter 10, "Cash Flows"; Chapter 14, "Payroll and Miscellaneous Requirements"

BACKGROUND

Business transactions usually involve cash or monetary assets or liabilities that are exchanged for goods or services. These are identified as monetary transactions. Monetary assets or liabilities are fixed in terms of currency and usually are contractual claims to fixed amounts of money. Examples of monetary assets and liabilities are cash, accounts and notes receivable, and accounts and notes payable.

Some business transactions involve the exchange or transfer of nonmonetary assets or liabilities that are not fixed in terms of currency. These are identified as *nonmonetary transactions*. Nonmonetary assets and liabilities are those other than monetary assets and liabilities. Examples are inventory, investments in common stock, property, plant, and equipment, liability for advance rent collected, and common stock.

> ☛ **PRACTICE POINTER:** Under certain circumstances, management's intent may affect the monetary/nonmonetary classification of an asset or liability. For example, a marketable bond being held to maturity qualifies as a monetary asset because its face amount is fixed in terms of currency. If the same bond were being held for speculation, however, it would be classified as a nonmonetary asset, because the amount that would be received when sold would not be determinable and therefore not fixed in terms of currency.

ACCOUNTING FOR NONMONETARY EXCHANGES AND TRANSACTIONS

Exchanges (Reciprocal Transfers) and Nonreciprocal Transfers

An *exchange* is a reciprocal transfer in which each party to the transaction receives and/or gives up assets, liabilities, or services (APB-29, par. 3). Exchanges can be either monetary or nonmonetary, or a combination of both. Nonmonetary exchanges usually are for the mutual convenience of two businesses. Examples include an exchange of inventory for trucking services or a trade of a starting quarterback for three linemen and a future draft choice.

A *nonreciprocal transfer* is a transfer of assets or services in one direction, either from an enterprise to its owners or another entity, or from owners or another entity to the enterprise (APB-29, par. 3). Examples of nonreciprocal transfers are:

1. Declaration and distribution of a dividend

2. Acquisition of treasury stock
3. Sale of capital stock
4. Conversion of convertible debt
5. Charitable contributions

Fair Value

The transfer or distribution of a nonmonetary asset or liability generally is based on the fair value of the asset or liability that is received or surrendered, whichever is more clearly evident. Exceptions to this rule are (*a*) when fair value is not determinable, (*b*) with certain nonreciprocal transfers to owners, and (*c*) when the earning process is not completed. Fair value of the assets in a nonmonetary transfer is determined by reference to the estimated realizable value of similar assets that are sold for cash, quoted market prices, independent appraisals, and other available evidence. If cash could have been received in lieu of the nonmonetary asset, then the amount of cash may be the basis for the valuation of the nonmonetary asset (APB-29, par. 25).

> **OBSERVATION:** In a nonmonetary exchange, fair value inherent in the transaction is based on the value of either the consideration given or the consideration received, whichever is more readily determinable. Theoretically, in an arm's-length transaction in which each party represents its own interests, the value of consideration given and the value of consideration received are the same. While the value of consideration given generally is more consistent with the principle of historical cost, the fact that the values exchanged are expected to be substantially the same results in the value of consideration received being an acceptable measurement alternative, if that amount is more readily determinable than the fair value of consideration given.

Because of uncertainties, there may be situations in which the fair value of the nonmonetary assets received and surrendered cannot be determined with reasonable accuracy. In these situations, the only valuation available may be the recorded book values of the nonmonetary assets (APB-29, par. 26).

Nonreciprocal Transfers to Owners

If the fair value of the nonmonetary assets in a nonreciprocal transfer to owners can be determined objectively (e.g., realized in an outright sale at or near the date of transfer), the transfer is accounted for at fair value. In a reorganization or liquidation (including spin-offs), or in a rescission of a business combination, however, the nonreciprocal transfer of nonmonetary assets is accounted for at their recorded amount, less any necessary reduction for impairment in values (APB-29, par. 23). These types of nonmonetary transfers to owners are accounted for either at the assets' recorded amount or at the assets' net realizable value, as follows:

1. If the recorded amount of the nonmonetary assets is less than fair value, the transfer is accounted for at the recorded amount because there is no reduction necessary for impairment.

2. If the recorded amount of the nonmonetary assets is more than fair value, the transfer is accounted for at net realizable value, which is equal to the recorded amount less a reduction for impairment.

A pro rata distribution to owners of the shares of a subsidiary or investee that is or will be consolidated or accounted for by the equity method is considered a spin-off (APB-29, par. 23).

Earning Process Not Complete

Only when the earning process is complete and an exchange has taken place is the realization of revenue recognized. Two types of nonmonetary exchanges do *not* result in completion of the earning process (APB-29, par. 21):

- An exchange of property held for sale in the ordinary course of business for similar property to be held for the same purpose

- An exchange of productive assets used in business but not held for sale for similar property to be held for the same purpose

In these cases, accounting for the nonmonetary exchange is based on recorded amounts (i.e., book values) unless the following exceptions apply (APB-29, par. 22):

- A loss is indicated, in which case fair value is used to record the transaction and the loss is recognized.

- One party receives a small amount of monetary consideration, referred to as *boot*, in which case the recipient of boot recognizes a gain to the extent that the boot received exceeds a proportionate share of the recorded amount of the asset relinquished.

☛ **PRACTICE POINTER:** In implementing the boot provision of APB-29, the EITF established a guideline of 25% of the fair value inherent in the transaction to distinguish between nonmonetary and monetary transactions. If the recipient of boot receives cash that represents less than 25% of the fair value in the transaction, consider the transaction to be nonmonetary. On the other hand, if the cash received exceeds 25% of the value inherent in the transaction, consider the entire transaction to be monetary and account for it at fair value.

Gain or Loss

Gain or loss, when applicable, is recognized in nonmonetary transactions. A difference in the gain or loss for tax purposes and that recognized for accounting purposes may constitute a temporary difference in income tax provision (APB-29, par. 27). The following rules summarize the recognition of nonmonetary gains or losses.

1. The gain or loss on the transaction is the difference between the fair market value and the net book value of the asset surrendered.

2. Losses on nonmonetary transactions are always recognized in full.

3. Gains are recognized in full if the earning process has been completed.

4. If the earning process has not been completed, gains are recognized by the recipient of cash to the extent that the cash received exceeds a proportionate share of the recorded amount of the asset surrendered.

The process of determining the appropriate amount of gain or loss, if any, to be recognized in nonmonetary exchanges in accordance with APB-29 is summarized in Figure 33-1.

Illustration of the Major Provisions of APB-29

In all of the following cases, an enterprise is giving up nonmonetary Asset A, which has a recorded amount of $10,000.

Case 1: Asset A is exchanged for dissimilar nonmonetary Asset B, which is valued at $12,000. Entry to record:

Asset B	$12,000	
Asset A		$10,000
Gain on exchange		2,000

Explanation: Nonmonetary transaction is recorded at fair value because Assets A and B are dissimilar; any gain or loss is recognized.

Case 2: Asset A is exchanged for similar nonmonetary Asset C, which is valued at $9,500. Entry to record:

Asset C	$9,500	
Loss on exchange	500	
Asset A		$10,000

Explanation: Exchange of similar assets is recorded at fair value because loss is indicated; loss is recognized.

Case 3: Asset A is exchanged for similar nonmonetary Asset D, which is valued at $15,000. Entry to record:

Asset D	$10,000	
Asset A		$10,000

Explanation: Exchange of similar assets is recorded at book value because gain is indicated; gain is not recognized.

Case 4: Asset A is exchanged for similar nonmonetary Asset E, which is valued at $13,000; $2,000 cash is received. Entry to record:

Asset E	$8,667	
Cash	2,000	
Asset A		$10,000
Gain on exchange		667

Explanation: Exchange of similar assets is recorded at book value except to the extent that boot exceeds proportionate share of book value.

Asset E: [$13,000/($13,000 + $2,000)] x $10,000 = $8,667

Gain: [$2,000 – ($2,000/$15,000 x $10,000)] = $667

Case 5: Asset A is exchanged for similar nonmonetary Asset F, which is valued at $8,000; $4,000 cash is received. Entry to record:

Asset F	$8,000	
Cash	4,000	
Asset A		$10,000
Gain on exchange		2,000

Explanation: Transaction is treated as monetary because cash received is 25% or more of the fair value in the exchange: $4,000/[$4,000 + $8,000] = 33.3%.

Involuntary Conversion of Nonmonetary Assets to Monetary Assets

When a nonmonetary asset is involuntarily converted to a monetary asset, a monetary transaction results, and FIN-30 requires that a gain or loss be recognized in the period of conversion (FIN-30, par. 2). The gain or loss is the difference between the carrying amount of the nonmonetary asset and the proceeds from the conversion.

Examples of involuntary conversion are the total or partial destruction of property through fire or other catastrophe, theft of property, or condemnation of property by a governmental authority (eminent domain proceedings).

Gain or loss from an involuntary conversion of a nonmonetary asset to a monetary asset is classified as part of continuing operations, extraordinary items, disposal of a segment, etc., according to the particular circumstances (FIN-30, par. 4). In addition, a gain or loss recognized for tax purposes in a period different from that for financial accounting purposes creates a temporary difference, for which recognition of deferred taxes may be necessary (FIN-30, par. 5).

The involuntary conversion of a LIFO inventory layer at an interim reporting date does not have to be recognized if the proceeds are reinvested in replacement inventory by the end of the fiscal year (FIN-30, par. 11).

> **OBSERVATION:** This is the same treatment afforded a temporary liquidation at interim dates of a LIFO inventory layer that is expected to be replaced by the end of the annual period.

In the event the proceeds from an involuntary conversion of a LIFO inventory layer are not reinvested in replacement inventory by the end of the fiscal year, gain for financial accounting purposes need not be recognized, providing the taxpayer does not recognize such gains for income tax reporting purposes.

Disclosure

Disclosure of the nature of the nonmonetary transaction, the basis of accounting for assets transferred, and gains or losses recognized are required in the financial statements for the period in which the transaction occurs (APB-29, par. 28).

Figure 33-1: Accounting for Nonmonetary Exchanges

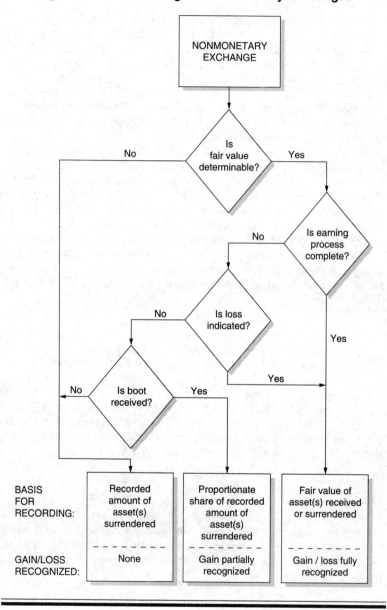

CHAPTER 34
PENSION PLANS—EMPLOYERS

CONTENTS

CHAPTER 34
PENSION PLANS—EMPLOYERS

OVERVIEW

GAAP for employers' accounting for pension plans center on the determination of annual pension expense (identified as net periodic pension cost) and the presentation of an appropriate amount of pension liability in the statement of financial position. Net periodic pension cost has often been viewed as a single homogeneous amount, but it is actually made up of several components that reflect different aspects of the employer's financial arrangements, as well as the cost of benefits earned by employees.

In applying principles of accrual accounting for pension plans, the FASB emphasizes three fundamental features:

1. *Delayed recognition*—Changes in the pension obligation and changes in the value of pension assets are recognized not as they occur, but systematically and gradually over subsequent periods.

2. *Net cost*—The recognized consequences of events and transactions affecting a pension plan are reported as a single net amount in the employer's financial statements. This approach results in the aggregation of items that would be presented separately for any other part of the employer's operations: the compensation cost of benefits, the interest cost resulting from deferred payment of those benefits, and the results of investing pension assets.

3. *Offsetting*—Pension assets and liabilities are shown net in the employer's statement of financial position, even though the liability has not been settled. The assets may still be controlled and substantial risks and rewards associated with both are clearly borne by the employer.

GAAP for accounting for pensions by employers are located in the following pronouncement:

FAS-87   Employers' Accounting for Pensions

FAS-132   Employers' Disclosures about Pensions and Other Post-retirement Benefits

CROSS-REFERENCES

BACKGROUND

Employment is based on an explicit or implicit exchange agreement. The employee agrees to provide services for the employer in exchange for a current wage, a pension benefit, and frequently other benefits such as death, dental, disability, etc. Although pension benefits and some other benefits are not paid currently, they represent deferred compensation that must be accounted for as part of the employee's total compensation package.

Pension benefits usually are paid to retired employees or their survivors on a periodic basis, but may be paid in a single lump sum. Other benefits, such as death and disability, may also be provided through a pension plan. Most pension plans also provide benefits upon early retirement or termination of service.

A pension plan may be contributory or noncontributory; that is, the employees may be required to contribute to the plan (contributory), or the entire cost of the plan may be borne by the employer (noncontributory). A pension plan may be funded or unfunded; that is, the employees and / or the employer may make cash contributions to a pension plan trustee (funded), or the employer may make only credit entries on its books reflecting the pension liability under the plan (unfunded). Pension plans are accounted for on the accrual basis, and any difference between net periodic pension cost charged against income and the amount actually funded is recorded as an accrued or prepaid pension cost.

> **OBSERVATION:** A qualified pension plan under the Employee Retirement Income Security Act (ERISA) has to be funded. Every year the plan actuary must determine the minimum funding for the defined benefit pension plan. If the plan fails to meet the minimum funding requirement, a penalty tax is imposed on the employer on the funding deficiency.

Although interest cost on the pension liability and the return (or loss) on a pension plan's assets will increase or decrease net periodic pension cost, they are considered financial costs rather than employee compensation costs. Financial costs can be controlled by the manner in which the employer provides financing for the pension plan. An employer can eliminate interest cost by funding the plan completely or by purchasing annuity contracts to settle all pension obligations. The return on plan assets can be increased by the contribution of more assets to the pension fund.

Pension Plan Accounting

The assets of a pension plan usually are kept in a trust account, segregated from the assets of the employer. Contributions to the pension trust account are made periodically by the employer and, if the plan is contributory, by the employees. The plan assets are invested in stocks, bonds, real estate, and other types of investments. Plan assets are increased by earnings and gains on investments and are decreased by losses on investments, payment of pension benefits, and administrative expenses. The employer usually cannot withdraw plan assets placed in a trust account. An exception arises, however, when the plan assets exceed the pension obligation and the plan is terminated. In this event, the pension plan agreement may permit the employer to withdraw the excess amount of plan assets, providing that all other existing pension plan obligations have been satisfied by the employer. Under GAAP, pension plan assets that are not effectively restricted for the payment of pension benefits or segregated in a trust are not considered pension plan assets.

Accounting and reporting for a pension plan (defined benefit plan) as a separate reporting entity are covered by FAS-35 (Accounting and Reporting by Defined Benefit Pension Plans).

Deferred Compensation Plan

A deferred compensation plan is a contractual agreement that specifies that a portion of the employee's compensation will be set aside and paid in future periods as retirement benefits. FAS-87 covers deferred compensation plans that are in substance pension plans.

Postemployment and postretirement benefits generally are considered a form of deferred compensation to an employee because an employer provides these types of benefits in exchange for an employee's services. Thus, these benefits must be measured properly and recognized in the financial statements and, if the amount is material, financial statement disclosure may be required.

> **OBSERVATION:** For a discussion of postemployment and postretirement benefits and their disclosure requirements, see the 1999 *Miller GAAP Guide* chapters titled "Deferred Compensation Contracts" and "Postemployment and Postretirement Benefits Other Than Pensions."

OVERVIEW OF FAS-87

Scope and Applicability

Most of the provisions of FAS-87 address *defined benefit pension plans* of single employers. A defined benefit pension plan is one that contains a pension benefit formula, which generally describes the amount of pension benefit that each employee will receive for services performed during a specified period of employment (FAS-87, par. 11). The amount of the employer's periodic contribution to a defined benefit pension plan is based on the total pension benefits (projected to employees' normal retirement dates) that could be earned by all eligible participants.

In contrast, a *defined contribution pension plan* does not contain a pension benefit formula, but generally specifies the periodic amount that the employer must contribute to the pension plan and how that amount will be allocated to the eligible employees who perform services during that same period. Each periodic employer contribution is allocated among separate accounts maintained for each employee, and pension benefits are based solely on the amount available in each employee's account at the time of his or her retirement.

For the purposes of FAS-87, any plan that is not a defined contribution pension plan is considered a defined benefit pension plan (see definition of *defined benefit pension plan* in Appendix D of FAS-87).

FAS-87 requires that its provisions be applied to any arrangement, expressed or implied, that is similar in substance to a pension plan, regardless of its form or method of financing. Thus, a pension plan arrangement does not have to be in writing if the existence of a pension plan is implied by company policy. A qualified plan, however, has to be in writing under ERISA, as well as for federal and state tax purposes. Frequently, defined contribution pension plans provide for some method of determining defined benefits for employees, as may be the case with some *target benefit* plans. A target benefit plan is a defined contribution plan. The benefit defined in the document is only for the purpose of determining the contribution to be allocated to each participant's account. It is not intended to promise any benefit in the future. If, in substance, a plan does provide defined benefits for employees, it is accounted for as a defined benefit pension plan.

Actuarial Assumptions

Actuarial assumptions are factors used to calculate the estimated cost of pension plan benefits. Employee mortality, employee turnover, retirement age, administrative expenses of the pension plan, interest earned on plan assets, and the date on which a benefit becomes fully vested are some of the more important actuarial assumptions (FAS-87, par. 39).

Under FAS-87, each significant actuarial assumption must reflect the best estimate for that particular assumption. In the absence of evidence to the contrary, all actuarial assumptions are made on the basis that the pension plan will continue in existence (going-concern concept) (FAS-87, par. 43).

Discount rates used in actuarial valuations reflect the rates at which the pension benefits could be settled effectively. In selecting appropriate interest rates, employers should refer to current information on rates used in annuity contracts that could be purchased to settle pension obligations, including annuity rates published by the Pension Benefit Guaranty Corporation (PBGC), or the rates of return on high-quality fixed-income investments that are expected to be available through the maturity dates of the pension benefits (FAS-87, par. 44).

An actuarial gain or loss is the difference between an actuarial assumption and actual experience. Under FAS-87, actuarial gains and losses are not included in net periodic pension cost in the year in which they arise, but may be recognized in subsequent periods if certain criteria are met (FAS-87, par. 29).

☛ **PRACTICE POINTER:** In accounting for pension plans—particularly defined benefit plans—the CPA relies heavily on the expertise of actuaries. Actuaries are educated in mathematics, modeling, and other areas that permit them to deal with the many uncertainties required to make estimates related to an enterprise's pension plan that are necessary for both funding and financial reporting. Actuarial assumptions are one area where the CPA is particularly vulnerable, because of the significant impact that different actuarial assumptions may have on the elements of the financial statements. Essentially, the CPA's responsibility is to be generally familiar with the actuary's work and to approach the results of the actuary's work with the professional skepticism that is typical of the CPA's work in many areas.

Pension Plan Assets

The resources of a pension plan may be converted into (*a*) plan assets that are invested to provide pension benefits for the participants of the plan, such as stocks, bonds, and other investments (FAS-87, par. 19) or (*b*) plan assets that are used in the operation of the plan, such as real estate, furniture, and fixtures. (FAS-87, par. 51). Plan assets must be segregated in a trust or otherwise effectively restricted so that the employer cannot use them for other purposes. Under FAS-87, plan assets do not include amounts accrued by an employer as net periodic pension cost, but not yet paid to the pension plan. Plan assets may include securities of the employer if they are freely transferable (FAS-87, par. 19).

Pension plan assets that are held as investments to provide pension benefits are measured at fair value (FAS-87, par. 23). Pension plan assets that are used in the operation of the plan are measured at cost, less accumulated depreciation or amortization (FAS-87, par. 51). All plan assets are measured as of the date of the financial statements or, if used consistently from year to year, as of a date not more than three months prior to that date (FAS-87, par. 52).

For the purposes of FAS-87, plan liabilities that are incurred, other than for pension benefits, may be considered reductions of plan assets (Appendix D of FAS-87, under definition of "Plan Assets").

Recording Pension Events

Under FAS-87, an enterprise makes two primary types of entries in its records each accounting period:

1. To record pension expense (called "net periodic pension cost" in FAS-87 and discussed later in this chapter)

2. To record funding of the pension plan

Depending on the circumstances, a third entry to record an additional pension liability may be required.

Illustration of Basic Entries to Record Pension Events

Maddux Co. determines its net periodic pension cost to be $10,000 for 19X5, its first year of operation. An equal amount is funded by transferring cash to the insurance company that administers the plan. No additional entry for an additional pension liability is required. The entries to record these events areas follow:

Pension expense	$10,000	
Accrued/prepaid pension cost		$10,000
Accrued/prepaid pension cost	10,000	
Cash		10.000

In this case, the pension expense is fully funded and no accrued/prepaid pension cost balance remains. If less than $10,000 had been funded, the balance in accrued/prepaid pension cost would have been a liability. If more than $10,000 had been funded, the balance in accrued/prepaid pension cost would have been an asset.

As this illustration shows, the accrued/prepaid pension cost carries the accumulated balance resulting from under- or over-funding of pension expense. The transfer of cash to the plan administrator is treated as a retirement of the pension liability. The pension asset and pension liability are effectively offset, and neither is presented in the employer's statement of financial position.

If the additional pension liability entry had been required, an intangible pension asset generally would have been debited and accrued/prepaid pension cost credited. The amount of the intangible pension asset is limited, however, to the amount of unrecognized prior service cost that may cause a negative element of stockholders' equity to emerge (i.e., excess of additional pension liability over unrecognized prior service cost). That procedure is explained later in this chapter.

Most of the provisions of FAS-87 pertain to the computation of the amount to be recorded in the first journal entry type in the above illustration as net periodic pension cost. This computation requires numerous worksheet calculations, which are illustrated throughout FAS-87.

Pension Plan Terminology

Each item appearing in the above reconciliation schedule is discussed briefly below. Further details are provided in subsequent text and illustrations.

Projected Benefit Obligation

Projected benefit obligation is the actuarial present value, as of a specified date, of the total cost of all employees' vested and nonvested pension benefits that have been attributed by the pension benefit formula to services performed by employees to that date.

The projected benefit obligation includes the actuarial present value of all pension benefits (vested and nonvested) attributed by the pension benefit formula, *including consideration of future employee compensation levels.* Vested benefits are pension benefits that an employee has an irrevocable right to receive at a date specified in the pension agreement, even if the employee does not continue to work for the employer. In the event a pension plan is discontinued, a vested benefit obligation remains a liability of the employer.

Payments of pension benefits decrease both the projected benefit obligation and the fair value of plan assets, while contributions to a plan decrease accrued pension cost (or increase the prepaid pension cost), and increase the fair value of plan assets.

The projected benefit obligation does not appear on the books of the employer. However, the employer maintains a worksheet record of the projected benefit obligation.

Accumulated Benefit Obligation

Accumulated benefit obligation is an alternative measure of the pension obligation; it is calculated like the projected benefit obligation, except that current or past compensation levels instead of future compensation levels are used to determine pension benefits. Under FAS-87, an employer must recognize an additional minimum liability in its statement of financial position, if its accumulated benefit obligation exceeds the fair value of pension plan assets as of a specified date. The amount of the additional minimum liability must at least equal the employer's *unfunded accumulated benefit obligation*, which is the amount by which the accumulated benefit obligation exceeds the fair value of plan assets. In the event a pension plan is discontinued, the balance of any unfunded accumulated benefit obligation remains a liability of the employer.

OBSERVATION: Basically, there are two types of pension benefit formulas: pay-related benefit and nonpay-related benefit. For a nonpay-related benefit formula, the accumulated benefit obligation and the projected benefit obligation are the same.

Fair Value of Plan Assets

Fair value of plan assets is the amount that a pension plan could reasonably be expected to receive from a current sale of plan assets, which are held to provide pension benefits, between a willing buyer under no compulsion to buy and a willing seller under no compulsion to sell. Plan assets that are used in the operation of the pension plan (building, equipment, furniture, fixtures, etc.) are valued at cost less accumulated depreciation or amortization.

Pension plan assets are recorded on the books of the pension plan. However, an employer maintains worksheet records of the cost and fair value of all pension plan assets.

Funded Status of Plan

For the employer's accounting purposes, *funded status of plan* is the difference between the projected benefit obligation and the fair value of plan assets as of a given date. If the projected benefit obligation exceeds the fair value of the plan assets, a pension plan liability exists. If the fair value of plan assets exceeds the projected benefit obligation, a pension plan asset exists.

Unrecognized Prior Service Cost

Unrecognized prior service cost is the portion of prior service cost that has not been recognized by the employer in net periodic pension cost of any period. Upon the initial adoption of a pension plan or through a plan amendment, certain employees may be granted pension benefits for services performed in prior periods. These retroactive pension benefits are referred to as *prior service costs,* and usually are granted by the employer with the expectation that they will produce future economic benefits, such as reducing employee turnover, improving employee productivity, and minimizing the need to increase future employee compensation. Under FAS-87, an employer is required to amortize any prior service cost in equal amounts over the future periods of active employees who are expected to receive the benefits.

An employer does not record unrecognized prior service cost on its books but maintains worksheet records of such amounts.

Unrecognized Net Gain or Loss

Unrecognized net gain or loss is the amount of actuarial gain or loss for a period that has not been recognized by the employer in net periodic pension cost of any period.

Actuarial gains or losses arise from the difference between (*a*) the actual and expected amount of projected benefit obligation at the end of a period and / or (*b*) the actual and expected amount of the fair value of pension plan assets at the end of the period. Under FAS-87, actuarial gains or losses are not recognized by the employer in the period in which they arise, but may become subject to recognition in subsequent periods if certain criteria are met.

An unrecognized net gain or loss that, as of the beginning of the year, exceeds 10% of the greater of (*a*) the projected benefit obligation or (*b*) the market-related value of plan assets is subject to recognition. Recognition for the year is equal to the amount of unrecognized net gain or loss in excess of 10% of the greater of the projected benefit obligation or the value of plan assets, divided by the average remaining service period of active employees expected to receive benefits under the plan. This frequently is referred to as the *corridor test* in applying FAS-87.

Actuarial gains and losses are recognized on the books of a pension plan as they occur. However, an employer does not record actuarial gains or losses on its books but maintains worksheet records of such amounts.

Unrecognized Net Obligation (or Net Asset) at Date of Initial Application of FAS-87

Unrecognized net obligation or net asset at date of initial application of FAS-87 is the difference between the projected benefit obligation and the fair value of plan assets, plus previously recognized unfunded accrued pension cost or minus previously recognized prepaid pension cost at the time FAS-87 was adopted. This unrecognized net obligation or net asset represents the difference between the funded status of a plan (projected benefit obligation less the fair value of plan assets) and the total amount of accrued or prepaid pension cost existing on the books of the employer as of the date of the initial application of FAS-87.

The unrecognized net obligation or net asset as of the date of initial application of FAS-87 is amortized on a straight-line basis over the average remaining service period of employees expected to receive benefits under the plan, except that (*a*) if the amortization period is less than 15 years, the employer may elect to use 15 years, and (*b*) if the plan is composed of all or substantially all inactive participants, the employer shall use those participants' average remaining life expectancy as the amortization period.

The amount of the employer's unrecognized obligation or net asset is included in the projected benefit obligation as of the date of the employer's initial application of FAS-87. However, an employer does not record its unrecognized net obligation or net asset on its books as of the date of the initial application of FAS-87, but maintains a worksheet record of such amount.

Accrued or Prepaid Pension Cost

Accrued pension cost is the total amount of net periodic pension cost that has been recognized but not funded. Prepaid pension cost is the total amount that has been funded in excess of the total amount of the net periodic pension cost that has been recognized.

Accrued or prepaid pension cost is recorded on the books of the employer.

NET PERIODIC PENSION COST

The employer's *net periodic pension cost* represents the net amount of pension cost for a specified period that is charged against income. Under FAS-87, the components of net periodic pension cost are (*a*) service cost, (*b*) interest cost on the projected benefit obligation, (*c*) actual return on plan assets, (*d*) amortization of unrecognized prior service cost (if any), (*e*) recognition of net gain or loss (if required by FAS-87), and (*f*) amortization of the unrecognized net obligation or net asset existing at the date of initial application of FAS-87 (FAS-87, par. 20).

All of the components of net periodic pension cost are not necessarily recognized on the books of the employer when they arise. For example, the total prior service cost that results from a plan amendment is determined in the period in which it arises. Under the provisions of FAS-87, however, the employer recognizes cost in equal amounts over the future service periods of each active employee who is expected to receive the benefits of the plan amendment that gave rise to the prior service cost (FAS-87, par. 24).

Net periodic pension cost is estimated in advance at the beginning of a period based on actuarial assumptions relating to (*a*) the discount rate on the projected benefit obligation, (*b*) the expected long-term rate of return on pension plan assets, and (*c*) the average remaining service periods of active employees covered by the pension plan. At the end of the period, adjustments are made to account for the differences (actuarial gains or losses), if any, between the estimated and actual amounts (FAS-87, par. 21).

The actuarial assumptions used to calculate the previous year's net periodic pension cost are used to calculate that cost in subsequent interim and annual financial statements, unless more current valuations of plan assets and obligations are available or a significant event has occurred, such as a plan amendment, which usually would require new valuations (FAS-87, par. 52).

The components of net periodic pension cost that are either partially recognized or not recognized at all on the employer's books in the period in which they arise are (a) unrecognized prior service cost, (b) unrecognized net asset gain or loss, and (c) unrecognized net obligation or net asset existing at the date FAS-87 is initially applied.

The following illustration shows how the different components of net periodic pension cost are estimated.

Illustration of Computing Net Periodic Pension Cost

Service cost component	$2,000
Interest cost component	3,000
Estimated return on plan assets	(2,500)
Amortization of unrecognized prior service cost	1,000
Amortization of unrecognized net (gain) or loss	1,000
Amortization of initial unrecognized net obligation (asset)	1,500
Total net periodic pension cost	$6,000

For simplicity, an assumption is made that there are no differences (actuarial gains or losses) between the estimated and actual amounts at the end of the period, and that the employer made no contributions to the pension fund during the period.

	Beginning of period	End of period
(a) Projected benefit obligation	$(115,000)	$(120,000)
(b) Fair value of plan assets	65,000	67,500
(c) Funded status of plan	$ (50,000)	$ (52,500)
(d) Unrecognized prior service cost	10,000	9,000
(e) Unrecognized net (gain) or loss	5,000	4,000

(f) Unrecognized net obligation or (net asset) at date of initial application of FAS-87	35,000	33,500
(g) (Accrued) or prepaid pension cost	$ 0	$ (6,000)

The following journal entry is recorded by the employer for net periodic pension cost:

Net periodic pension cost	$6,000	
Accrued pension cost		$6,000

The following explains the changes in the accounts that were affected by the net periodic pension cost accrual.

(a) *Projected benefit obligation*   An increase in the projected benefit obligation of $5,000, representing the service cost component of $2,000 and interest cost component of $3,000 for the period.

(b) *Fair value of plan assets*   The $2,500 increase in the fair value of plan assets, between the beginning and end of the period, represents the increase in the fair value of plan assets for the period.

(c) *Funded status of plan*   The $2,500 increase in the funded status of the plan, between the beginning and end of the period, is the difference between the $5,000 increase in the projected benefit obligation for the period and the $2,500 increase in the fair value of plan assets for the period.

(d) *Unrecognized prior service cost*   The $1,000 decrease in the unrecognized prior service cost, between the beginning and end of the period, is the amount of amortization of prior service cost that has been recognized by the employer as a component of net periodic pension cost.

Unrecognized prior service cost is not recorded on the books of the employer, but worksheet records are maintained for such amounts. Thus, the employer reduces the worksheet balance of the unrecognized prior service cost by $1,000.

(e) *Unrecognized net gain or loss*   The $1,000 decrease in the unrecognized net gain or loss (actuarial gain or loss), between the beginning and end of the period, is the amount of amortization that has been recognized by the employer as a component of net periodic pension cost.

Unrecognized net gain or loss (actuarial gain or loss) is not recorded on the books of the employer, but worksheet records are maintained for such amounts. Thus, the employer reduces the worksheet balance of the unrecognized net gain or loss by $1,000.

(f) U*nrecognized net obligation or net asset at date of initial application of FAS-87*   The $1,500 decrease in the unrecognized net obligation, between the beginning and the end of the period, is the amount of amortization that has been recognized by the employer as a component of net periodic pension cost for the period.

Unrecognized net obligation or net asset is not recorded on the books of the employer, but worksheet records are maintained for such amounts. Thus, the employer reduces the worksheet balance of the unrecognized net obligation or net asset by $1,500.

(g) *Accrued or prepaid pension cost* The $6,000 increase in the accrued or prepaid pension cost, between the beginning and the end of the period, is the amount of the net periodic pension cost for the period that has not been funded by employer contributions.

Accrued pension cost is the total amount of net periodic pension cost that has been recognized to date but not funded by contributions to the pension plan. Prepaid pension cost is the total amount that has been funded by contributions to date, in excess of the total amount of net periodic pension cost that has been recognized.

Service Cost Component

In a defined benefit pension plan, FAS-87 requires that a pension benefit formula be used to determine the amount of pension benefit earned by each employee for services performed during a specified period. Under FAS-87, attribution is the process of assigning pension benefits or cost to periods of employee service, in accordance with the pension benefit formula.

The service cost component of net periodic pension cost is defined as the actuarial present value of pension benefits attributed by the pension benefit formula to employee service during a specified period (FAS-87, par. 21). For example, a pension benefit formula may state that an employee shall receive, at the retirement age stated in the plan, a pension benefit of $20 per month for life, for each year of service. To compute the total future value of the pension benefit for the year, the monthly benefit is multiplied by the number of months in the employee's life expectancy at retirement age. This number of months is determined by reference to mortality tables. The actuarial present value of all employees' future pension benefits that are earned during a period is computed and included as the service cost component of the net periodic pension cost for the same period (FAS-87, par. 40).

If the terms of the pension benefit formula provide for benefits based on estimated future compensation levels of employees, estimates of those future compensation levels are used to determine the service cost component of net periodic pension cost. For example, if the pension benefit formula states that an employee's benefit for a period is equal to 1% of his or her final pay, an estimate of the employee's final pay is used to calculate the benefit for the period. Assumed compensation levels should reflect the best estimate of the future compensation levels of the employee involved and be consistent with assumed discount rates to the extent that they both incorporate expectation of the same future economic conditions (FAS-87, par. 202). Thus, future compensation levels in final-pay plans or career-average-pay plans are reflected in the service cost component of net periodic pension cost. Assumed compensation levels also shall reflect changes because of general price levels, productivity, seniority, promotion, and other factors (FAS-87, par. 46).

Changes resulting from a plan amendment that has become effective and automatic benefit changes specified by the terms of the pension plan, such as cost-of-living increases, are included in the determination of service cost for a period (FAS-87, par. 48).

An employer's substantive commitment to make future plan amendments in recognition of employees' prior services may indicate pension benefits in excess of those reflected in the existing pension benefit formula. Such a commitment may be evidenced by a history of regular increases in nonpay-related benefits, benefits under a career-average-pay plan, or other evidence. In this event, FAS-87 requires that the pension plan be accounted for based on the employer's substantive commitment, and that appropriate disclosure be made in the employer's financial statements (FAS-87, par. 41).

A plan's pension benefit formula might provide a nonvested benefit of $10 per month for life in the first 19 years of an employee's service and a vested benefit of $1,000 per month for life in the 20th year of an employee's service. If a pension plan benefit formula attributes all or a disproportionate portion of total pension benefits to later years, the employee's *total projected benefit* is calculated and used as the basis of assigning the total pension benefits under the plan. In this event, the employee's total projected benefit is assumed to accumulate in proportion to the ratio of the total completed years of service to date to the total completed years of service as of the date the benefit becomes fully vested (FAS-87, par. 42). An employee's total projected benefit from a pension plan is the actuarial present value of the total cost of pension benefits that the employee is likely to receive under the plan. If the pension benefit formula is based on future compensation, future compensation is used in calculating the employee's total projected benefit.

OBSERVATION: Under current pension law, the longest a single employer can make an employee wait before receiving vested benefits is five years. For a multiemployer plan, the longest period is 10 years.

In the event a pension benefit formula does not indicate the manner in which a specific benefit relates to specific services performed by an employee, the benefit shall be assumed to accumulate as follows (FAS-87, par. 42):

If the benefit is includable in vested benefits   The benefit is accumulated in proportion to the ratio of total completed years of service to date to the total completed years of service as of the date the benefit becomes fully vested.

A vested benefit is a benefit that an employee has an irrevocable right to receive. For example, an employee is entitled to receive a vested benefit whether or not he or she continues to work for the employer.

If the benefit is not includable in vested benefits   The benefit is accumulated in proportion to the ratio of completed years of service to date to the total projected years of service. (An example of a benefit that is not includable in vested benefits is a death or disability benefit that is payable only if death or disability occurs during the employee's active service.)

Interest Cost Component

The two factors used to determine the actuarial present value of a future pension benefit are (1) the probability that the benefit will be paid to the employee (through the use of actuarial assumptions), and (2) the time value of money (through the use of discounts for interest cost). The probability that a pension benefit will be paid is based on actuarial assumptions such as employee mortality, employee turnover, and the date the benefits become vested. An employer's liability for a retirement fund of $56,520 that is due in 10 years is not equal to a present liability of $56,520. At an 8% discount rate the $56,520 has a present value of only $26,169. The $26,169 increases each year by the employer's interest cost of 8%, and in 10 years grows to $56,520, if the 8% interest rate does not change.

FAS-87 requires an employer to recognize, as a component of net periodic pension cost, the interest cost on the projected benefit obligation. The interest cost is equal to the increase in the amount of the projected benefit obligation because of the passage of time (FAS-87, par. 16).

> **OBSERVATION:** FAS-87 specifies that the interest cost component of net periodic pension cost shall **not** be considered to be interest for the purposes of applying the provisions of FAS-34 (Capitalization of Interest Cost).

Actual Return on Plan Assets Component

The actual return on plan assets is equal to the difference between the fair value of plan assets at the beginning and end of a period, adjusted for employer and employee contributions (if a contributory plan) and pension benefit payments made during the period (FAS-87, par. 23). *Fair value* is the amount that a pension plan could reasonably be expected to receive from a current sale of an investment between a willing buyer under no compulsion to buy and a willing seller under no compulsion to sell. Plan assets that are used in the operation of the pension plan (building, equipment, furniture, fixtures, etc.) are valued at cost, less accumulated depreciation or amortization (FAS-87, par. 51).

A return on plan assets decreases the employer's cost of providing pension benefits to its employees, while a loss increases pension cost. Net periodic pension income can result from a significantly high return on pension plan assets during a period.

FAS-87 requires an employer to recognize, as a component of net periodic pension cost, the actual return (or loss) on pension plan assets (FAS-87, par. 34).

Amortization of Unrecognized Prior Service Cost Component

Upon the initial adoption of a pension plan or as the result of a plan amendment, employees may be granted pension benefits for services performed in prior periods. These retroactive pension benefits are assumed to have been granted by the employer in the expectation that they will produce future economic benefits, such as reducing employee turnover, improving employee productivity, and minimizing the need for increasing future employee compensation. The cost of pension benefits that are granted retroactively to employees for services performed in prior periods is referred to as *prior service cost* (FAS-87, par. 24).

Under FAS-87, only a portion of the total amount of prior service cost arising in a period, including retroactive benefits that are granted to retirees, is included in net periodic pension cost. FAS-87 requires that the total prior service cost arising in a period from an adoption or amendment of a plan be amortized in equal amounts over the future service periods of *active* employees who are expected to receive the retroactive benefits (FAS-87, par. 25).

> ☛ **PRACTICE POINTER:** Since retirees are not expected to render future services, the cost of their retroactive benefits cannot be recognized over their remaining service periods. FAS-87 requires that the total prior service cost arising from a plan

adoption or amendment, including the cost attributed to the benefits of retirees, shall be amortized in equal amounts over the future service periods of only the active employees who are expected to receive benefits.

If substantially all of the participants of a pension plan are inactive, the prior service cost attributed to the benefits of the inactive participants shall be amortized over the remaining life expectancy of those participants (FAS-87, par. 25).

> **OBSERVATION:** The last sentence of paragraph 25 of FAS-87 addresses the method of amortizing that portion of the cost of retroactive plan amendments that affect benefits of inactive participants of a plan composed of substantially all inactive participants, but does not address the method of amortizing the portion of the cost of the same retroactive plan amendments that affect benefits of the active participants of the same plan. Two alternatives appear to be available. The first is that the cost of the active participants' benefits is charged to income of the period of the plan amendment. The second is that the cost of the **active** participants' benefits is amortized in the same manner as if the plan were not composed of substantially all inactive participants. In this event, the cost attributed to the retroactive benefits of the **active** participants of a plan composed of substantially all **inactive** participants is amortized in equal amounts over the future service periods of each active employee who is expected to receive the retroactive benefits.

FAS-87 permits the consistent use of an alternative amortization approach that more rapidly reduces the amount of unrecognized prior service cost. For example, straight-line amortization of unrecognized prior service cost over the average future service period of active employees who are expected to receive benefits under the plan is acceptable. If an alternative method is used to amortize unrecognized prior service cost, it must be disclosed in the financial statements (FAS-87, par. 26).

The period in which an employer expects to realize the economic benefits from retroactive pension benefits that were previously granted may be shorter than the entire remaining future service period of all active employees. Under this circumstance, FAS-87 requires that a more rapid rate of amortization be applied to the remaining balance of the unrecognized prior service cost, to reflect the earlier realization of the employer's economic benefits and to allocate properly the cost to the periods benefited (FAS-87, par. 27).

An amendment to a pension plan usually increases the cost of employees' pension benefits and increases the amount of the projected benefit obligation. However, a pension plan amendment may decrease the cost of employees' pension benefits, which results in a decrease in the amount of the projected benefit obligation. Any decrease resulting from a pension plan amendment shall be applied to reduce the balance of any existing unrecognized prior service cost and any excess shall be amortized on the same basis as increases in unrecognized prior service cost (FAS-87, par. 28).

Gains and Losses Component

Gains and losses are changes in the amount of either the projected benefit obligation or pension plan assets, resulting from the differences between estimates or assumptions used and actual experience. Thus, a gain or loss can result from the difference between (*a*) the expected and actual amounts of the projected benefit obligation at the end of a period, and/or (*b*) the expected and actual amounts of the fair value of pension plan assets at the end of a period. Technically, both of these types of gains and losses are considered *actuarial gains and losses*. Under FAS-87, however, a gain or loss resulting from a change in the projected benefit obligation is referred to as an *actuarial gain or loss*, while a gain or loss resulting from a change in the fair value of pension plan assets is referred to as a *net asset gain or loss*. For the purposes of FAS-87, the sources of these gains and losses are not distinguished separately, and they include amounts that have been realized as well as amounts that are unrealized (FAS-87, par. 29).

Under FAS-87, the gains and losses component of net periodic pension cost consists of (*a*) the difference between the expected and actual returns on pension plan assets (net asset gain or loss) and (*b*) if required, amortization of any unrecognized gain or loss from previous periods (FAS-87, par. 34).

> **OBSERVATION:** The difference between the expected and actual returns on pension plan assets (net asset gain or loss) is not recognized in the period in which it arises. It is included in the gains and losses component of net periodic pension cost only as an offset or supplement to the actual return on pension plan assets, which is also a separate component of net periodic pension cost (FAS-87, par. 54).

As discussed in a previous section, the actual return on pension plan assets is equal to the difference between the fair value of pension plan assets at the beginning and end of a period, adjusted for any contributions and pension benefit payments made during that period. Fair value is the amount that a pension plan could reasonably be expected to receive from a current sale of an investment between a willing buyer under no compulsion to buy and a willing seller under no compulsion to sell.

The expected return on pension plan assets during the period is computed by multiplying the *market-related value* of plan assets by the *expected long-term rate of return*. The expected long-term rate of return is an actuarial assumption of the expected long-term interest rate that will be earned on plan assets during the period. Under FAS-87, the current rate of return earned on plan assets and the rates of return expected to be available for plan investments should be considered in estimating the long-term rate of return on plan assets. The expected long-term rate of return on plan assets should reflect the average rate of earnings expected on plan investments (FAS-87, par. 45).

To reduce the volatility of changes in the fair value of pension plan assets and the resulting effect on net periodic pension cost, FAS-87 requires the use of a market-related value for plan assets to compute the expected return on such assets during a period. Market-related value is used only to compute the expected return on pension plan assets for the period (expected return = market-related value x expected long-term rate of return) (FAS-87, par. 30).

Under FAS-87, the market-related value of a plan asset can be either (*a*) the actual fair value of the pension plan asset or (*b*) a calculated value that recognizes, in a systematic and rational manner, the changes in the actual fair value of the pension plan asset over a period of not more than five years (FAS-87, par. 30). Thus, in computing the market-related value of a pension plan asset, an enterprise may use actual fair value or a calculated value based on a five-year moving average of the changes in the actual fair value of the pension plan asset. In this event, the calculated market-related value would include only 20% of the total changes in the actual fair value of the pension plan asset that have occurred during the past five years. For example, if the actual fair value of a plan asset at the end of each of the last six years was $8,000, $10,000, $12,000, $14,000, $16,000, and $13,000, the net gain for the five years is $5,000 ($2,000 + $2,000 + $2,000 + $2,000 − $3,000 = $5,000). In this event, only 20% of the $5,000 gain ($1,000) is included in computing the calculated market-related value of the pension plan asset for the current year.

The difference between the actual fair value of a pension plan asset and its calculated market-related value is the amount of net gain or loss from previous years that has not yet been recognized in the calculated market-related value.

Market-related value may be computed differently for each class of plan assets, but the method of computing it must be applied consistently from year to year for each class of plan assets. For example, fair value may be used for bonds and other fixed income investments, and a calculated market-related value for stocks and other equities (FAS-87, par. 30).

Illustration of Computing Market-Related Value

For computing the market-related value of a particular class of plan assets as of the end of each period, an employer uses a calculated value that includes 20% of the gains and losses on the plan assets that have occurred over the last five years. The total market-related value of this particular class of plan assets at the beginning of calendar year 19X6 was $100,000. The total fair value of the plan assets was $120,000 at the beginning of 19X6 and $130,000 at the end of 19X6. Actual gains and losses for the past five years as of the beginning of 19X6 were: 19X1 $10,000; 19X2 $(8,000); 19X3 $12,000; 19X4 $10,000; 19X5 $(4,000); the result is a net gain of $20,000 for these five years. Employer's contributions to the plan for 19X6 are estimated at $2,000 and benefit payments expected to be paid from the plan in 19X6 are also $2,000. The expected long-term rate of return on plan assets for 19X6 is 10%. The computation of the estimated market-related value as of December 31, 19X6, for this particular class of plan assets is determined as follows:

Market-related value at the beginning of period	$100,000
Add:	
Expected return on assets for 19X6 (market-related value, multiplied by expected long-term rate of return ($100,000 x 10%)	10,000
20% of the net gain or loss for the last five years (20% x $20,000)	4,000
Employer's contribution	2,000
Benefit payments made from plan	(2,000)
Estimated market-related value, Dec. 31, 19X6 (Note:_____)	$114,000

Note: The difference between the fair value ($130,000) and market-related value ($114,000) of plan assets at the end of 19X6 is $16,000. This difference represents the amount of net gain from previous years that has not yet been recognized in the market-related value of plan assets.

The expected return on plan assets is based on market-related values, which do not include all of the net asset gains and losses from previous years (unless market-related values are equal to fair values). Thus, net asset gains and losses may include both (*a*) gains and losses of previous years that have been included in market-related value and (*b*) gains and losses of previous years that have not yet been included in market-related value (FAS-87, par. 31).

As mentioned above, FAS-87 does not require the recognition of any gains and losses as components of net periodic pension cost of the period in which they arise, except to the extent that the net asset gain or loss for the period offsets or supplements the actual return of pension plan assets for the period. In subsequent years, however, all gains and losses, except those which have not yet been recognized in the market-related values of pension plan assets, are subject to certain minimum amortization provisions of FAS-87.

FAS-87 requires recognition of unrecognized net gains or losses based on beginning-of-the-year balances. An unrecognized net gain or loss that, as of the beginning of the year, exceeds 10% of (*a*) the projected benefit obligation or (*b*) the market-related value of plan assets, whichever is greater, is subject to recognition. The minimum recognition for the year is calculated by dividing the average remaining service period of active employees who are expected to receive benefits under the plan into the amount of unrecognized net gain or loss that, as of the beginning of the year, exceeds 10 % of (*a*) the projected benefit obligation or (*b*) the market-related value of plan assets, whichever is greater. If substantially all of a plan's participants are inactive, however, the average remaining life expectancy of the inactive participants is divided into the excess unrecognized net gain or loss subject to amortization. The computation of the minimum amortization required by FAS-87 is made each year based on beginning-of-the-year balances of unrecognized net gains or losses (FAS-87, par. 32).

In lieu of the minimum amortization of unrecognized gains and losses specified by FAS-87, an employer may use an alternative amortization method provided that the method (*a*) is systematic and applied consistently, (*b*) is applied to both gains and losses similarly, (*c*) reduces the unamortized balance by an amount greater than the amount that would result from the minimum amortization method provided by FAS-87, and (*d*) is disclosed in the financial statements (FAS-87, par. 33).

Illustration of Gains and Losses Component of Net Periodic Pension Cost

ABC Corporation elected to apply the provisions of FAS-87 as of January 1, 19X7, and also elected to compute all pension-related amounts as of the end of the period. The unrecognized net obligation existing at the date of the initial application of FAS-87 was $400, of which $40 was amortized in 19X7. The net asset (gain) or loss for 19X7, resulting from changes in actuarial assumptions, was a loss of $400, which was deferred as an unrecognized net loss for the year. The market-related value of pension plan assets at 1/1/X8 is $1,600 and the average remaining service life of active employees is 10 years.

The expected net periodic pension cost for 19X8 is $340, determined as follows: the sum of service cost $200, interest cost $240 (10%), amortization of unrecognized net asset loss $20, and amortization of unrecognized net obligation $40, less a 10% expected return on plan assets of $160 (expected return = market-related value of plan assets of $1,600 x expected long-term rate of return of 10%). No contributions were made to the pension plan in 19X8.

		Actual 12/31/X7	Expected 12/31/X8	Actual 12/31/X8
(a)	Projected benefit obligation	$(2,400)	$(2,840)	$(2,900)
(b)	Fair value of plan assets	1,640	1,800	1,750
	Funded status of plan	$ (760)	$(1,040)	$(1,150)
	Unrecognized prior service cost	0	0	0
	Unrecognized net (gain) or loss	400	380	490
	Unrecognized net obligation existing at 1/1/X7	360	320	320
	(Accrued)/prepaid pension cost	$ 0	$ (340)	$ (340)

(a) The difference between the actual projected benefit obligation for 19X7 and the expected projected benefit obligation for 19X8 is $440, which consists of the expected service cost of $200, and the expected interest cost of $240. However, the actual projected benefit for 19X8 increased $500 over the actual projected benefit for 19X7. The difference between the expected increase in the projected benefit obligation of $440 and the actual increase of $500 represents a $60 actuarial loss. The $60 loss occurred because the actuarial assumptions used were different from actual experience.

The $40 amortization of the unrecognized net obligation does not affect the projected benefit obligation because the full amount of the net obligation was recognized in the projected benefit obligation as of the date of the initial application of FAS-87.

(b) The difference between the actual fair value of plan assets for 19X7 and the expected fair value of plan assets for 19X8 is $160, which represents the 10% expected return on plan assets (market-related value of plan assets of $1,600 x 10%). However, the actual fair value of plan assets for 19X8 of $1,750 increased only $110 over the actual fair value of plan assets of $1,640 for 19X7. The difference between the expected increase in the fair value of plan assets of $160 and the actual increase of $110 represents a $50 net asset loss for the period. The loss occurred because the actual rate of return on pension plan assets was less than the expected rate of return.

Cost Components of Net Periodic Pension Cost for 19X8

FAS-87 requires financial statement disclosure of the amount of net periodic pension cost for the period. The disclosure shall indicate separately the service cost component, the interest cost component, the actual return on plan assets for the period, and the net total of other components. The following illustrates this disclosure:

Service cost	$200
Interest cost	240
Actual return on plan assets	(110)
Net amortization and deferral (see below)	10
Net periodic pension cost for 19X8	$340

Net amortization and deferral computation:

Amortization of unrecognized net obligation	$ 40
Amortization of unrecognized prior service cost	0
Amortization of unrecognized net (gain) or loss	20
Net asset gain or (loss) for 19X8—deferred (Note 1)	(50)
Net amortization and deferral	$ 10

Note 1:   A net asset gain or loss is not recognized in the period in which it arises (FAS-87, par. 29); it is included in the gains and losses component of net periodic pension cost (FAS-87, par. 34), it only as an offset or supplement to the actual return on pension plan assets, which is a separate component of net periodic pension cost (FAS-87, par. 54).

Computation of the Amortization of the Unrecognized Gain or Loss for 19X8

Unrecognized net (gain) or loss 1/1	$400
Add asset gain or subtract asset loss not yet recognized in market-related values at 1/1 [difference between fair value of plan assets ($1,640) and market-related value ($1,600)]	40
Unrecognized net (gain) or loss subject to the minimum amortization provisions of FAS-87	440
10% of the greater of the projected benefit obligation or market-related value at 1/1	(240)
Unrecognized net (gain) or loss subject to amortization	$200
Amortization for 19X8 (over the 10-year average remaining service life of active employees)	$ 20

Note: The unrecognized net (gain) or loss at 1/1 must be adjusted to exclude asset gains and losses not yet reflected in market-related values, because gains and losses are not required to be amortized (FAS-87, par. 31).

Note: The $60 loss that occurred in 19X8 as a result of the difference between the expected and actual projected benefit obligation for 19X8, and the $50 loss that occurred in 19X8 as a result of the difference between the expected and actual fair value of plan assets for 19X8, will become subject to the minimum amortization provisions of FAS-87 as of 1/1/X9. The computation of the amount of unrecognized net (gain) or loss as of 1/1/X9, is as follows:

Unrecognized net asset (gain) or loss 1/1/X8		$400
Less: Amortization for 19X8		20
Unrecognized net asset (gain) or loss 12/31/X8		380
Add: Actuarial net (gain) or loss for 19X8	$60	
Net asset (gain) or loss for 19X8	50	110
Unrecognized net (gain) or loss as of 1/1/X9		$490

Amortization of the Unrecognized Net Obligation or Net Asset (as of the date of initial application of FAS-87)

The *funded status* of a pension plan for employer accounting purposes is equal to the difference between the projected benefit obligation and the fair value of pension plan assets. The funded status indicates whether the employer has underfunded or overfunded the pension plan.

The unrecognized net obligation or net asset of a pension plan is determined by the employer as of the date of its financial statements of the beginning of the year in which FAS-87 is first applied, or, if used consistently from year to year, as of a date not more than three months prior to that date. The unrecognized net obligation or net asset is equal to the difference between the projected benefit obligation and fair value of pension plan assets, plus previously recognized unfunded accrued pension cost or less previously recognized prepaid pension cost. In the event there is no accrued or prepaid pension cost on the employer's statement of financial position as of the date of transition to FAS-87, the funded status of the pension plan and the unrecognized net obligation or net asset are exactly equal (FAS-87, par. 77).

An unrecognized net obligation or net asset is amortized by the employer on a straight-line basis over the average remaining service period of employees expected to receive benefits under the plan, as of the date of initial application of FAS-87, except under the following circumstances (FAS-87, par. 77):

1. If the amortization period is less than 15 years, an employer may elect to use 15 years.
2. If the plan is composed of all or substantially all inactive participants, the employer shall use those participants' average remaining life expectancy as the amortization period.

The above amortization method is also used to recognize, as of the date of the initial application of FAS-87, any unrecognized net obligation or net asset of a defined contribution pension plan.

RECOGNITION OF LIABILITIES AND ASSETS

If an employer's total contribution to its pension plan for the period is not equal to the amount of net periodic pension cost as determined by the provisions of FAS-87, the difference is recognized by the employer either as a liability or as an asset (i.e., accrued/prepaid pension cost). A liability (unfunded accrued pension cost) is recognized if the amount of contribution is *less* than the amount of net periodic pension cost. If the amount of contribution is *more* than the amount of net periodic pension cost, an asset (prepaid pension cost) is recognized (FAS-87, par. 35).

An employer's *unfunded accumulated benefit obligation* is the amount by which the accumulated benefit obligation exceeds the amount of the fair value of plan assets as of a specific date. Under FAS-87, an *additional minimum liability* must be recognized in the employer's statement of financial position if an unfunded accumulated benefit obligation exists and (*a*) an asset has been recognized as prepaid pension cost, (*b*) a liability has been recognized as unfunded accrued pension cost in an amount that is less than the amount of the existing unfunded accumulated benefit obligation, or (*c*) no accrued or prepaid pension cost has been recognized. If an asset has been recognized as prepaid pension cost, the additional minimum liability is the amount of the existing unfunded accumulated benefit obligation plus the amount of the prepaid pension cost. If a liability has been recognized as unfunded accrued pension cost in an amount that is less than the amount of the existing unfunded accumulated benefit obligation, the additional minimum liability is the amount of the existing unfunded accumulated benefit obligation reduced by the amount of the unfunded accrued pension cost. If no accrued or prepaid pension cost has been recognized, the additional minimum liability is the amount of the existing unfunded accumulated benefit obligation (FAS-87, par. 36).

If an additional minimum liability is required to be recognized, generally an intangible asset in the same amount as the additional minimum liability is recognized. However, the amount of the intangible asset cannot exceed the total amount of any existing unrecognized prior service cost and any unrecognized net obligation. In the event that the intangible asset exceeds the total existing unrecognized prior service cost and unrecognized net obligation, the excess is reported as a separate negative component of stockholders' equity, net of related tax benefits (FAS-87, par. 37).

OBSERVATION: Limiting the intangible asset to the amount of unrecognized prior service cost is based on the circumstances that give rise to the need to record an additional pension liability. When a pension plan is amended and benefits to employees are increased, the company's pension obligation immediately increases. The amount of pension assets probably will increase slowly over time, however, because pension plan funding usually is tied to the amount of pension expense recognized, and the recognition of prior service cost will be made gradually as that cost is amortized as a component of net periodic pension cost. In this circumstance, it is logical to limit the amount of the intangible pension asset to the amount of unrecognized prior service cost, which is a surrogate measure of the unamortized cost of the "employee goodwill" acquired upon amendment of the pension plan.

When a new determination of the amount of additional liability is made to prepare a statement of financial position, the related intangible asset and separate component of equity are adjusted or eliminated, as necessary (FAS-87, par. 38).

Illustration of Calculation of the Additional Pension Liability

	As of End of Period		
	Year 1	Year 2	Year 3
Accumulated benefit obligation	$(3,762)	$(4,884)	$(4,848)
Fair value of plan assets	3,495	4,515	4,866
(Unfunded) or over-funded accumulated benefit obligation	$ (267)	$ (369)	$ 18
Projected benefit obligation	$(5,637)	$(7,326)	$(7,272)
Fair value of plan assets	3,495	4,515	4,866
Funded status of plan	(2,142)	(2,811)	(2,406)
Unrecognized prior service cost	2,145	3,942	3,516
Unrecognized net (gain) or loss	(753)	(1,671)	(1,380)
Unrecognized net obligation at date of initial application of FAS-87	840	780	720
(Accrued) or prepaid pension cost	$ 90	$ 240	$ 450

(Accrued) or prepaid pension cost at beginning of period	$ 0	$ 90	$ 240
Less: Net periodic pension cost	912	1,005	1,191
Add: Contributions paid	1,002	1,155	1,401
(Accrued) or prepaid pension cost at end of period	$ 90	$ 240	$ 450
(Unfunded) or overfunded accumulated benefit obligation (computed above)	$ (267)	$ (369)	$ 18
Required adjustment for additional minimum liability	(357)	(252)	609
Intangible asset	357	252	(609)
Cumulative balance of the additional minimum liability	(357)	(609)	0

Note: The adjustment necessary to record the additional minimum liability is equal to the unfunded accumulated benefit obligation, plus the amount of any prepaid pension cost or less the amount of any accrued pension cost (at the end of the period), less the previous balance of the additional minimum liability from the preceding year. Thus the adjustment in year 1 is $357, which is equal to the unfunded accumulated benefit obligation of $267, plus the prepaid pension cost of $90 at the end of the period (there was no previous balance of the additional minimum liability from the preceding year). The adjustment for year 2 is $252, which is equal to the unfunded accumulated benefit obligation of $369, plus the amount of prepaid pension cost of $240 at the end of the period, less the preceding year's balance of the additional minimum liability of $357.

In year 3, the balance of the unfunded accumulated benefit obligation was an $18 debit, which results in no unfunded accumulated benefit obligation. Thus, the adjustment consisted of eliminating the preceding year's balance of $609.

Note: The additional minimum liability that was required in all three years did not exceed the unrecognized prior service cost plus the unrecognized net obligation. Thus, no portion of the required additional minimum liability had to be reported as a separate component of stockholders' equity.

MISCELLANEOUS CONSIDERATIONS

Measurement of Plan Assets

All pension plan assets that are held as investments to provide pension benefits are measured at their fair values as of the date of the financial statements or, if used consistently from year to year, as of a date not more than three months prior to that date. Fair value is the amount that a pension plan could reasonably be expected to receive for a current sale of an investment between a willing buyer under no compulsion to buy and a willing seller under no compulsion to sell. If an active market exists for a plan investment, fair value is determined by the market price. If an active market does not exist for a particular plan investment, selling prices for similar investments, if available, should be considered appropriately. If no active market exists, an estimate of the fair value of the plan investment may be based on its projected cash flow, provided that appropriate consideration is given to current discount rates and the investment risk involved (FAS-87, par. 49).

Pension plan assets that are used in the actual operation of a plan are valued at amortized cost. Thus, buildings, leasehold improvements, furniture, equipment, and fixtures that are used in the everyday operation of a pension plan are valued at historical cost, less accumulated depreciation or amortization (FAS-87, par. 51).

Measurement Dates

For the purposes of FAS-87, plan assets and obligations are determined either (*a*) as of the date of the financial statements or (*b*) if used consistently from year to year, as of a date not more than three months prior to the date of the financial statements (FAS-87, par. 52).

Unless more current amounts are available for both the obligation and plan assets, the amount of additional minimum liability reported in interim financial statements shall be the same amount as reported by the employer in its previous year-end statement of financial position, adjusted for subsequent accruals and contributions (FAS-87, par. 52).

The same assumptions used to calculate the previous year-end net periodic pension cost are used to calculate the net periodic pension cost in subsequent interim and annual financial statements, unless more current valuations of plan assets and obligations are available or a significant event has occurred, such as a plan amendment that usually would require new valuations (FAS-87, par. 53).

Financial Statement Disclosure

The disclosure requirements that were originally included in FAS-87 (as well as in other pronouncements concerning pension and other postretirement benefits that are covered in other chapters) were replaced by the disclosure requirements of FAS-132 (Employers' Disclosures about Pensions and Other Postretirement Benefits). In addition to simplifying and streamlining disclosures about pensions, FAS-132 consolidates the disclosures about pensions, settlement and curtailment of pension plans, and retirement benefits other than pensions into a single set of requirements.

Guiding principles for applying these disclosure requirements are as follows (FAS-132, par. 6–7):

- Disclosures about defined benefit pension plans may be aggregated for all of an employer's plans, as is the case for all other postretirement plans.

- Disaggregated information may be presented if it is considered able to provide more useful information.

- Disclosures about plans with accumulated benefits in excess of assets may be combined with other plans (both pensions and other postretirement benefits), but disclosure is required of the aggregate benefit obligation and aggregate fair value of plans with benefit obligations in excess of assets.

- In the statement of financial position, prepaid benefit costs and accrued benefit liabilities shall be presented separately.

- Information about plans outside the U.S. may be combined with U.S. plans, unless the benefit obligation of the plans outside the U.S. are significant relative to the total benefit obligation and those plans use significantly different assumptions.

Following are the disclosure requirements about both pensions and other postretirement benefits for both public companies and nonpublic companies.

Disclosures about Pension and Other Postretirement Benefit Plans (FAS-132, par. 5)

1. Reconciliation of the beginning and ending balances of the benefit obligation, with separate disclosure of the following:
   a. Service cost
   b. Interest cost
   c. Contributions by plan participants
   d. Actuarial gains and losses
   e. Foreign currency exchange rate changes
   f. Benefits paid
   g. Plan amendments
   h. Business combinations
   i. Divestitures

    j. Curtailments

    k. Settlements

    l. Special termination benefits

2. Reconciliation of beginning and ending balances of the fair value of plan assets, including the effects of the following:

    a. Actual return on plan assess

    b. Foreign currency exchange rate changes

    c. Contributions by employer

    d. Contributions by plan participants

    e. Benefits paid

    f. Business combinations

    g. Divestitures

    h. Settlements

3. The funded status of the plan, including the following:

    a. Amount of any unamortized prior service cost

    b. Amount of any unrecognized net gain or loss

    c. Amount of any remaining unamortized, unrecognized net obligation or net asset at the initial application of FASB Statements 87 or 106

    d. Net pension or other postretirement benefit prepaid assets or accrued liabilities

    e. Any intangible asset and the amount of accumulated other comprehensive income

4. Amount of net periodic benefit cost recognized, showing separately:

    a. Service cost component

    b. Interest cost component

    c. Expected return on plan assets for the period

    d. Amortization of the unrecognized transition obligation or asset

    e. Amount of recognized gains and losses

    f. Amount of prior service cost recognized

    g. Amount of gain or loss recognized due to a settlement or curtailment

5. Amount included in other comprehensive income for the period arising from a change in the additional minimum liability recognized

6. On a weighted-average basis, the following assumptions used in accounting for the plan:

   a. Assumed discount rate

   b. Rate of compensation increased

   c. Expected long-term rate of return on plan assets

7. Assumed health care cost trend rate(s) for the next year used to measure the expected cost of benefits covered by the plan

8. A general description of the direction and pattern of change in the assumed trend rates, the ultimate trend rate(s), and when that rate is expected to be achieved

9. Effect of a 1% increase / 1% decrease in the assumed health care cost trend rates on the aggregate of the service and interest cost components of net periodic health care benefit cost and the accumulated postretirement benefit obligation

10. The amounts and types of securities included in plan assets

11. The amount of future annual benefits of plan participants covered by plan contracts issued by the employer or related parties

12. Any significant transactions between the employer or related parties and the plan during the year

13. Any alternative amortization method used to amortize prior service costs or unrecognized net gains and losses pursuant to FASB Statement 87

14. Any substantive commitment (e.g., past practice or a history of regular benefit increases) used as the basis for accounting for the benefit obligation recognized during the period and a description of the nature of the event

15. The cost of providing special or contractual termination benefits recognized during the period and a description of the nature of the event

16. An explanation of any significant change in the benefit obligation or plan assets not otherwise apparent in the above disclosures

Modified Disclosures about Pension and Other Postretirement Plans for Nonpublic Companies (FAS-132, par.8)

1. The benefit obligation

2. The fair value of plan assets

3. The funded status of the plan

4. Employer contributions

5. Participant contributions

6. Benefits paid

7. The amounts recognized in the statement of financial position:

   a. The net pension and net postretirement benefit prepaid assets or accrued liabilities

   b. Any intangible asset

   c. Amount of accumulated other comprehensive income

8. The amount of net periodic benefit cost recognized and the amount included in other comprehensive income arising from a change in the minimum pension liability

9. On a weighted-average basis, the following assumptions used:

   a. Assumed discount rate

   b. Rate of compensation increases

   c. Expected long-term rate of return on plan assets

10. The assumed health care cost trend rate(s) for the next year used to measure the expected cost of benefits covered by the plan

11. A general description of the direction and pattern of change in the assumed trend rates, the ultimate trend rate(s), and when rate is expected to be achieved

12. The amounts and types of securities of the employer and related parties included in plan assets

13. The approximate future annual benefits of plan assets

14. Participants covered by insurance contracts issued by the employer or related parties

15. Any significant transactions between the employer or related parties and the plan during the period

16. The nature and effect of significant events, such as amendments, combinations, divestitures, curtailments, and settlements

Employers with Two or More Pension Plans

If an employer sponsors more than one defined benefit pension plan, the provisions of FAS-87 are applied separately to each plan. An employer shall not apply the assets of one plan to reduce or eliminate the unfunded accrued pension cost and/or minimum additional liability of another plan, unless the employer clearly has the right to do so. An excess of plan assets over the accumulated benefit obligation or prepaid pension cost of one plan cannot be applied to reduce or eliminate a liability of another plan that is required to be recognized by FAS-87 (FAS-87, par. 55).

Annuity Contracts

All or part of an employer's obligation to provide pension plan benefits to individuals may be transferred effectively to an insurance company by the purchase of annuity contracts. An annuity contract is an irrevocable agreement in which an insurance company unconditionally agrees to provide specific periodic payments, or a lump-sum payment to another party, in return for a specified premium. Thus, by use of an annuity contract, an employer can effectively transfer to an insurance company its legal obligation to provide specific employee pension plan benefits. For the purposes of FAS-87, an annuity contract is not considered an annuity contract if the insurance company is a captive insurer or there is reasonable doubt that the insurance company will meet its obligation. A captive insurer is one that does business primarily with the employer and its related parties (FAS-87, par. 57).

An annuity contract may be participating or nonparticipating. In a participating annuity contract, the insurance company's investing activities with the funds received for the annuity contract generally are shared, in the form of dividends, with the purchaser (the employer or the pension fund). An annuity contract is not considered an annuity contract, for the purposes of FAS-87, unless all the risks and rewards associated with the assets and obligations assumed by the insurance company are actually transferred to the insurance company by the employer (FAS-87, par. 57).

The cost incurred for currently earned benefits under an annuity contract is the cost of those benefits, except for the cost of participating rights of participating annuity contracts, which must be accounted for separately (see below). Thus, the service cost component of net periodic pension cost for the current period is the cost incurred for nonparticipating annuity contracts that cover all currently earned benefits (FAS-87, par. 58). Pension benefits not covered by annuity contracts are accounted for in accordance with the provisions of FAS-87 that address accounting for the cost of pension benefits not covered by annuity contracts (FAS-87, par. 59).

The projected benefit obligation and the accumulated benefit obligation do not include the cost of benefits covered by annuity contracts. Except for the cost of participation rights (see below), pension plan assets do not include the cost of any annuity contracts (FAS-87, par. 60).

The difference in cost between a nonparticipating annuity contract and a participating annuity contract usually is attributable to the cost of the participation right. The cost of a participation right, at the date of its purchase, is recognized as a pension plan asset. In subsequent periods, a participation right is included in plan assets at its fair value, if fair value is reasonably determinable. If fair value is not reasonably determinable, a participation right is included in plan assets at its amortized cost and systematically amortized over the expected dividend period stated in the contract. In this event, amortized cost may not exceed the net realizable value of the participation right (FAS-87, par. 61).

Other Contracts with Insurance Companies

The purchase of insurance contracts that are, in substance, annuity contracts, is accounted for in accordance with the provisions of FAS-87 (see previous section). The purchase of other types of insurance contracts shall be accounted for as pension plan assets and reported at fair value. The best evidence of fair value for some insurance contracts may be their contract values. Under FAS-87, the cash surrender value or conversion value of an insurance contract is presumed to be its fair value (FAS-87, par. 62).

Multiemployer Plans

A multiemployer plan is a pension plan to which two or more unrelated employers make contributions, usually pursuant to one or more collective-bargaining agreements. In a multiemployer pension plan, assets contributed by one employer are not segregated in separate accounts or restricted to provide benefits only to employees of that employer. Thus, assets contributed by one employer in a multiemployer plan may be used to provide benefits to employees of other participating employers (FAS-87, par. 67).

The net periodic pension cost of an employer participating in a multiemployer plan is the amount of the required contribution for the period. An employer participating in a multiemployer plan shall also recognize as a liability any of its contributions that are due and unpaid (FAS-87, par. 68).

> **OBSERVATION:** A withdrawal from a multiemployer pension plan may result in a loss contingency if the withdrawing employer has a potential liability to the plan for a portion of its unfunded benefit obligation. Under FAS-87, if it is probable or reasonably possible that the loss contingency will develop into an actual loss, the withdrawing employer shall account for the loss contingency in accordance with the provisions of FAS-5 (Accounting for Contingencies) (FAS-87, par. 70).

An employer participating in a multiemployer plan shall disclose the following information separately from disclosures for a single-employer plan (FAS-87, par. 69):

1. A description of the multiemployer plan(s) including employee groups covered, the types of benefits provided (defined benefit

or defined contribution), and the nature and effect of significant matters affecting comparability of information for all periods presented

2. The amount of pension cost recognized during the period

Multiple-Employer Plans

Some pension plans to which two or more unrelated employers contribute are not multiemployer plans, but are groups of single-employer plans combined to allow participating employers to pool assets for investment purposes and to reduce the cost of plan administration. Under FAS-87, multiple-employer plans are considered single-employer plans and each employer's accounting shall be based on its respective interest in the plan (FAS-87, par. 71).

Non-U.S. Pension Plans

FAS-87 does not make any special provision for non-U.S. pension plans. In some foreign countries, it is customary or required for an employer to provide benefits for employees in the event of a voluntary or involuntary severance of employment. In this event, if the substance of the arrangement is a pension plan, it is subject to the provisions of FAS-87 (for example, benefits are paid for substantially all terminations) (FAS-87, par. 73).

Business Combinations

The total cost of a business combination accounted for by the purchase method must be allocated to the individual assets acquired and liabilities assumed (APB-16 [Business Combinations]). Each identifiable asset is assigned a cost equal to its fair value. Liabilities are accounted for at the present value of the amount that will eventually be paid and, if certain criteria are met, appropriate consideration should be given to contingent assets and liabilities (FAS-38 [Accounting for Preacquisition Contingencies of Purchased Enterprises]).

When a single-employer defined benefit pension plan is acquired as part of a business combination accounted for by the purchase method, an excess of the projected benefit obligation over the plan assets is recognized as a liability and an excess of plan assets over the projected benefit obligation is recognized as an asset. The recognition of a new liability or new asset by the purchaser, at the date of a business combination accounted for by the purchase method, results in the elimination of any (*a*) previously existing unrecognized net gain or loss, (*b*) unrecognized prior service cost, and (*c*) unrecognized net obligation or net asset that existed at the date of initial application of FAS-87 (FAS-87, par. 74).

In subsequent periods, the differences between the purchaser's net pension cost and contributions will reduce the new liability or new asset recognized at the date of combination to the extent that the previously unrecognized net gain or loss, unrecognized prior service cost, or unrecognized net obligation are considered in determining the amounts of contributions to the plan. In addition, the effects of an expected plan termination or curtailment shall be considered by the purchaser in calculating the amount of the projected benefit obligation at the date of a business combination accounted for by the purchase method (FAS-87, par. 74).

> **OBSERVATION**: FAS-87 amends APB-16 to provide that the assets and liabilities of a pension plan acquired by the purchase method of accounting shall no longer be accounted for in accordance with paragraph 88h of APB-16, but shall be accounted for in accordance with paragraph 74 of FAS-87, which is discussed above (FAS-87, par. 75).

DEFINED CONTRIBUTION PENSION PLANS

A defined contribution pension plan provides for employers' contributions that are defined in the plan, but does not contain any provision for defined pension benefits for employees. Thus, a defined contribution pension plan does not contain a defined benefit pension formula. Based on the amount of the employer's defined contributions, however, pension benefits are provided in return for services performed by employees (FAS-87, par. 63).

Under FAS-87, a defined contribution pension plan provides for individual accounts for each plan participant and contains the terms that specify how contributions are determined for each participant's individual account. Each periodic employer contribution is allocated to each participant's individual account in accordance with the terms of the plan, and pension benefits are based solely on the amount available in each participant's account at the time of his or her retirement. The amount available in each participant's account at the time of his or her retirement is the total of the amounts contributed by the employer, plus the returns earned on investments of those contributions, and forfeitures of other participants' benefits that have been allocated to the participant's account, less any allocated administrative expenses (FAS-87, par. 63).

Under FAS-87, the net periodic pension cost of a defined contribution pension plan is the amount of contributions in a period that are made to the individual accounts of participants who performed services during that same period. Contributions for periods after an individual retires or terminates shall be estimated and accrued during periods in which the individual performs services (FAS-87, par. 64).

The amount of the unrecognized net obligation of a defined contribution pension plan, at the date of initial application of FAS-87, is amortized on a straight-line basis over the average remaining service period of employees expected to receive benefits under the plan, except (a) if the amortization period is less than 15 years, the employer may elect to use 15 years, and (b) if the plan is composed of all or substantially all inactive participants, the employer shall use those participants' average remaining life expectancy as the amortization period (FAS-87, par. 77).

> **OBSERVATION:** The above amortization method is the same as that used to amortize the unrecognized net obligation or net asset of a defined benefit pension plan at the date of the initial application of FAS-87. Although not specified by FAS-87, this seems to imply that an employer who sponsors a defined contribution pension plan is also required to record an unrecognized net obligation or net asset at the date of the initial application of FAS-87.

An employer who sponsors one or more defined contribution pension plans shall disclose the amount of cost recognized for defined contribution pension and other postretirement benefit plans during the period. This disclosure shall include the nature and effect of any significant changes during the period affecting comparability (FAS-32, par. 9).

CHAPTER 35
PENSION PLANS—SETTLEMENTS AND CURTAILMENTS

CONTENTS

CHAPTER 35
PENSION PLANS—SETTLEMENTS
AND CURTAILMENTS

OVERVIEW

A *settlement of a pension plan* is an irrevocable action that relieves the employer (or the plan) of primary responsibility for an obligation and eliminates significant risks related to the obligation and the assets used to effect the settlement. Examples of transactions that constitute a settlement include (*a*) making lump-sum cash payments to plan participants in exchange for their rights to receive specified pension benefits and (*b*) purchasing nonparticipating annuity contracts to cover vested benefits.

A *curtailment* is a significant reduction in, or an elimination of, defined benefit accruals for present employees' future services. Examples of curtailments are (*a*) termination of employees' services earlier than expected, which may or may not involve closing a facility or discontinuing a segment of a business, and (*b*) termination or suspension of a plan so that employees do not earn additional defined benefits for future services.

GAAP for settlements and curtailments of pension plans are found in the following pronouncement:

FAS-88   Employers' Accounting for Settlements and Curtailments of Defined Benefit Pension Plans and for Termination Benefits

FAS-132   Employers' Disclosures about Pensions and Other Postretirement Benefits

CROSS-REFERENCES

1999 MILLER GAAP GUIDE: Chapter 34, "Pension Plans—Employers"; Chapter 36, "Postemployment and Postretirement Benefits Other Than Pensions"; Chapter 42, "Results of Operations"

1999 MILLER GAAP IMPLEMENTATION MANUAL: Chapter 23, "Pension Plans—Settlements and Curtailments"

1999 MILLER GOVERNMENTAL GAAP GUIDE: Chapter 17, "Claims, Judgements, and Special Termination Benefits"

BACKGROUND

In connection with the operation of a defined benefit pension plan, FAS-87 (Employers' Accounting for Pensions) provides for the delayed recognition of actuarial gains and losses, prior service costs, and the net obligation or asset that arises at the date of the initial application of FAS-87. As a result, at any given date, an employer's pension plan records may reflect a balance of an (*a*) unrecognized net gain or loss, (*b*) unrecognized prior service cost, and / or (*c*) unrecognized net obligation or net asset. Part or all of these unrecognized balances may be recognized in a settlement or curtailment of a pension plan.

In a settlement of a defined benefit pension plan, the employer or the pension plan is released irrevocably from its primary responsibility for all or part of its pension plan obligation, and all significant risks relating to the settlement are eliminated. For example, through the purchase of nonparticipating annuity contracts or cash payments to some or all of the plan participants in exchange for their pension benefits, an employer may be released irrevocably from the pension plan obligation related to the benefits involved in the exchange. After the settlement of a pension plan, an employer may continue to provide pension benefits in the same pension plan or a new plan.

In a curtailment of a defined benefit pension plan, some of the future pension benefits for present employees are reduced, generally resulting in a net decrease (gain) or increase (loss) in the projected benefit obligation. For example, if employees are terminated as a result of a plan curtailment, some or all of their pension benefits based on future compensation levels may cease to be an obligation of the employer or pension plan. In this event, the projected benefit obligation is decreased (a gain) by the amount of the pension benefits that are no longer an obligation of the plan. On the other hand, if terminated employees who are eligible for subsidized early retirement benefits accept the benefits at a date earlier than expected, there is an increase (loss) in the projected benefit obligation. Gain or loss on a plan curtailment is based on the net decrease (gain) or increase (loss) in the projected benefit obligation.

An employer may have to recognize an additional loss that is not included in the gain or loss on a plan curtailment, but is recognized as part of the total effects of a plan curtailment. This loss is equal to the amount of decrease in the unrecognized prior service cost of the pension benefits that are reduced by the plan curtailment. A separate loss computation is necessary for the unrecognized prior service cost of each plan amendment.

The pension benefits that are reduced or eliminated in a plan curtailment may have been granted to some or all of the employees who were working for the employer as of the date of the initial application of FAS-87. For this reason, any unrecognized *net obligation* that arose at the date of the initial application of FAS-87 and that remains unamortized at the date of the plan curtailment is also treated as a separate unrecognized prior service cost.

A pension plan settlement and a pension plan curtailment may occur simultaneously or separately. If the expected years of future service for some employees are reduced but the pension plan continues in existence, a curtailment has occurred, but not a settlement. If an employer settles all or a portion of its pension obligation and continues to provide defined benefits to employees for future services, either in the same plan or in a successor plan, a settlement has occurred, but not a curtailment. If an employer terminates its defined benefit pension plan without replacing it with another defined benefit pension plan, and settles its present pension plan obligation in full, a curtailment and settlement has occurred. Under these circumstances, it makes no difference whether or not some or all of the employees continue to work for the employer.

Employers frequently offer termination benefits as part of an overall plan to reduce employment levels, to increase productivity, or generally to decrease payroll costs. To induce certain groups of employees to terminate employment, many employers offer attractive termination benefits. This is particularly true for those employees who are close to, or have reached, the early retirement age specified in the employer's existing pension plan. Termination benefits may consist of periodic future payments, lump-sum payments, or a combination of both. The payment of termination benefits may be made from a new or existing employee benefit plan, from the employer's existing assets, or from a combination of these sources.

Under FAS-88, termination benefits are classified either as *special* or *contractual*. Special termination benefits are those that are offered to employees for a short period of time in connection with their termination of employment. Contractual termination benefits are those that are required by the terms of an existing plan or agreement and are provided only on the occurrence of a specified event, such as early retirement or the closing of a facility.

FAS-88 requires that the cost of termination benefits be recognized by an employer as a loss and a corresponding liability. The recognition date depends on whether the benefits are special or contractual.

Before applying the provisions of FAS-88, an employer should bring its defined benefit pension plan records up to date, preferably as of the day before the curtailment and/or settlement of the plan.

The effects of the pending curtailment and/or settlement are ignored in the updating process and all computations including the net periodic pension cost accrual are consistent with prior periods. The updating process includes the measurement of the fair value of pension plan assets and the computation of the net periodic pension cost accrual.

SETTLEMENTS OF DEFINED BENEFIT PENSION PLANS

Under FAS-88, a settlement of a defined benefit pension plan is an irrevocable transaction that (*a*) releases the employer or the pension plan from its primary responsibility for the payment of all or a portion of the pension plan obligation and (*b*) eliminates all of the significant risks associated with the assets and obligations used to effectuate the settlement (FAS-88, par. 3). A settlement of a defined benefit pension plan does not require that the plan be completely terminated (FAS-88, par. 26).

All or a part of an employer's obligation to provide pension plan benefits to individuals may be transferred effectively to an insurance company by the purchase of annuity contracts. An annuity contract is an irrevocable agreement in which an insurance company unconditionally agrees to provide specific periodic payments or a lump-sum payment to another party in return for a specified premium. For the purposes of FAS-87 and FAS-88, this definition of an annuity contract is not met if the insurance company is a *captive insurer* or there is reasonable doubt that the insurance company will meet its obligation. A captive insurer is one that does business primarily with the employer and its related parties (FAS-88, par. 5).

An annuity contract may be participating or nonparticipating. In a participating annuity contract the insurance company's investing activities with the funds received for the premium of the annuity contract generally are shared, in the form of dividends, with the purchaser of the contract (the employer or the pension fund). An annuity contract is not considered an annuity contract unless all the risks and rewards associated with the assets and obligations assumed by the insurance company are actually transferred to the insurance company by the employer (FAS-88, par. 5).

Gain or loss on a plan settlement is based on pension plan records that have been updated as of the day before the settlement. Under FAS-88, the maximum gain or loss on a settlement of a defined benefit pension plan is equal to the total balance of any (*a*) unrecognized net gain or loss arising after the date of the initial application of FAS-87 that remains unamortized at the date of the plan settlement, and (*b*) any unrecognized *net asset* that arose at the date of the initial application of FAS-87 that remains unamortized at the date of the plan settlement (FAS-88, par. 9).

If the total pension plan obligation is settled by the employer, the maximum gain or loss is recognized. If part of the pension benefit obligation is settled, the employer must recognize a pro rata portion of the maximum gain or loss, equal to the percentage reduction in the projected benefit obligation, unless the transaction qualifies as a "small settlement" (discussed below). Thus, if 40% of the pension plan obligation is settled, 40% of the maximum gain or loss on the settlement is recognized, and if 100% of the pension benefit obligation is settled, 100% of the maximum gain or loss is recognized (FAS-88, par. 9).

If the employer purchases a participating annuity contract to settle a pension obligation, the cost of the contract must be allocated between the cost of the pure annuity feature and the cost of the participation right. The amount of cost allocated to the participation rights reduces gain (but not loss) that would otherwise be recognized on a plan settlement. However, the participation rights do not affect the determination of the amount of loss that is recognized on a plan settlement (FAS-88, par. 10).

Reporting Gain or Loss on a Plan Settlement

Gain or loss on a plan settlement is reported as an ordinary gain or loss, unless it meets the criteria of an extraordinary item as specified in APB-30 (Reporting the Results of Operations) (FAS-88, par. 48).

Small Settlements for the Year

Part or all of a pension plan's obligation to an employee may be settled by the payment of cash or the purchase of an annuity contract.

The cost of a cash settlement of a pension plan obligation is the amount of cash paid to the employee. The cost of a settlement of a pension plan obligation involving a nonparticipating annuity contract is the cost of the contract. The cost of a settlement involving a participating annuity contract is the cost of the contract less the amount attributed to the participation rights (FAS-88, par. 11).

If the total cost of all plan settlements for the year is small or insignificant, gain or loss recognition may not be required. FAS-88 provides that an employer is not required, but is permitted, to recognize the gain or loss on all plan settlements for the year if the cost of all such settlements does not exceed the sum of the service cost and interest cost components of the net periodic pension cost for the current year. Once an accounting policy is adopted for small or insignificant settlements, it must be applied consistently from year to year. Thus, an employer that initially elects nonrecognition of gain or loss on all small settlements during a year must continue that same accounting policy from year to year (FAS-88, par. 11).

☛ **PRACTICE POINTER:** If the total cost of all plan settlements for the year is small or insignificant, the employer has discretion to decide whether or not to recognize gain or loss, provided only that the accounting policy is followed consistently from year to year. Question 45 of "A Guide to Implementation of Statement 88" indicates, however, that gains or losses should be recognized if the total cost of plan settlements is greater than the sum of the service and interest cost.

CURTAILMENT OF DEFINED BENEFIT PENSION PLANS

Under FAS-88, a curtailment of a defined benefit pension plan results from an event in which (*a*) the expected years of future service arising from a prior plan amendment are *significantly* reduced for present employees who are entitled to receive pension benefits from that prior plan amendment or (*b*) the accrual of defined pension benefits is eliminated for some or all of the future services of a *significant* number of employees (FAS-88, par. 6).

The total effects of a plan curtailment consist of (1) the decrease (loss) in the unamortized balance of unrecognized prior service cost (or unrecognized *net obligation*) that results from the significant reduction of the expected years of future service for present employees [see (*a*) above], and (2) the net decrease (gain) or increase (loss) in the projected benefit obligation that results from the elimination of the accrual of defined pension benefits for some or all of the future services of a significant number of employees [see (*b*) above]. Each of these two components that comprise the total effects of a plan curtailment are discussed separately below (FAS-88, par. 13).

Decrease (Loss) in Unrecognized Prior Service Cost

Retroactive pension benefits are sometimes granted by an employer, upon adoption of a plan or through a plan amendment, based on employees' services in prior periods. The costs of these retroactive pension benefits are referred to as prior service costs. Retroactive pension benefits are granted by an employer in expectation of future economic benefits, such as reduced employee turnover and higher productivity. FAS-87 requires that the prior service cost relating to a specific plan amendment be amortized in equal amounts over the expected years of future service of each active employee who is expected to receive benefits from the plan amendment. Periodic amortization for each expected year of future service is calculated by dividing the total expected years of future service into the total amount of unrecognized prior service cost. The total amount of unrecognized prior service cost represents the total cost of pension benefits that have been granted under the provisions of the plan amendment. If the expected years of future service are reduced as a result of a plan curtailment, the related unrecognized prior service cost also must be reduced and recognized as a loss by the employer.

The expected years of future service for present employees may be reduced significantly by the termination or suspension of pension benefits for future services so that employees are no longer allowed to earn additional benefits. In addition, the termination of some of the present employees earlier than expected may also result in a significant reduction in their total expected years of future service. As a result of the significant reduction in the expected years of future service, a loss is incurred by the employer in the amount of the decrease in the balance of the related unamortized unrecognized prior service cost at the date of the plan curtailment. To compute the loss, the percentage reduction in the total remaining expected years of future service at the date of the plan curtailment first must be calculated (number of expected years of future service that are reduced, divided by the total number of remaining expected years of future service before reduction). To determine the amount of the loss, the balance of the related unamortized unrecognized prior service cost at the date of the plan curtailment is multiplied by the percentage reduction in the total number of expected years of future service. For example, if the total remaining expected years of future service at the date of the plan curtailment is 1,000, and the number of years of future service that is reduced is 400, the percentage reduction is 40%. The balance of the related unamortized unrecognized prior service cost at the date of the plan curtailment is reduced by 40%, which represents the loss that the employer must recognize as part of the total effects of the plan curtailment.

For the purposes of FAS-88, the balance of any unrecognized *net obligation* that arose at the date of the initial application of FAS-87, which remains unamortized at the date of a subsequent plan curtailment, also is treated as a separate unrecognized prior service cost (FAS-88, par. 12). Thus, if the expected years of future service are reduced significantly for those employees employed at the date of the initial application of FAS-87, a separate loss must be calculated and recognized by the employer. This loss equals the amount by which the unamortized unrecognized *net obligation* is reduced when multiplied by the percentage reduction resulting from the expected years of future service that are significantly reduced for those employees who were employed at the date of the initial application of FAS-87.

The total of all decreases (losses) in unamortized balances of unrecognized prior service costs and/or unrecognized *net obligation* is included in the total effects of a plan curtailment (illustration 3A of Appendix B of FAS-88), but is not included in the gain or loss on the plan curtailment (FAS-88, par. 40).

The following steps are necessary to compute each decrease (loss) in the balance of the unamortized unrecognized prior service cost at the date of a plan curtailment arising from a significant reduction in the expected years of employees' future service:

Step 1.   Compute the percentage reduction in the total remaining expected years of future service, at the date of the plan curtailment, resulting from the expected years of future service that are significantly reduced. For example, if the expected years of future service that are reduced are 600 and the total remaining expected years of future service at the date of the plan curtailment is 1,000, the percentage reduction is 60%.

Step 2.   Multiply the balance of the unamortized unrecognized prior service cost (or unamortized unrecognized *net obligation*) of each plan amendment affected by the plan curtailment by the percentage calculated in Step 1. The result is the amount of loss that the employer must recognize as part of the total effects of the plan curtailment. The balance of the unamortized unrecognized prior service cost (or unamortized unrecognized *net obligation*) is also reduced by the same amount.

(From a practical standpoint, the dollar amount of amortization for each expected year of future service can be multiplied by the total number of expected years of future service that is reduced.)

Step 3.   The amount of loss recognized on the decrease in the balance of the unamortized unrecognized prior service cost (or unamortized unrecognized *net obligation*) is not part of the gain or loss on the plan curtailment (FAS-88, par. 40), but is included in the total effects of the plan curtailment (illustration 3A of Appendix B of FAS-88).

Decrease (Gain) or Increase (Loss) in the Projected Benefit Obligation

A plan curtailment may result in a net decrease (gain) or net increase (loss) in the projected benefit obligation. For example, if employees are terminated as a result of a plan curtailment, some or all of their pension benefits based on future compensation levels may cease to be an obligation of the employer or pension plan. In this event, the projected benefit obligation is decreased (a gain) by the amount of the benefits that are no longer an obligation of the plan. On the other hand, if terminated employees who are eligible for subsidized early retirement benefits accept those benefits at an earlier date than expected, there usually is an increase (loss) in the projected benefit obligation. Gain or loss on a plan curtailment is based on the net decrease (gain) or increase (loss) in the projected benefit obligation (FAS-88, par. 13).

A plan curtailment may result from the closing of a facility or the disposal of a discontinued business segment. If the event that results in the plan curtailment is related to the disposal of a discontinued business segment, gain or loss on the plan curtailment must be included in the total gain or loss on the disposal of the discontinued business segment.

The following steps are necessary to compute the gain or loss on a plan curtailment:

Step 1. Determine the total net gain (decrease) or net loss (increase) in the projected benefit obligation resulting from the plan curtailment. Do not include any increase (loss) in the projected benefit obligation that arises in connection with termination benefits (FAS-88, par. 13).

Step 2. Combine the remaining balance of any unrecognized *net obligation* that arose at the date of the initial application of FAS-87 and remains unamortized at the date of the plan curtailment, with the balance of any unrecognized net gain or loss that arose after the initial application of FAS-87 and also remains unamortized at the date of the plan curtailment. (**Note:** The remaining balance of any unrecognized *net obligation* that arose at the date of the initial application of FAS-87 and remains unamortized at the date of the plan curtailment is treated as an unrecognized prior service cost.)

The amount of gain or loss on the plan curtailment is recognized as follows:

If the change in the projected benefit obligation is a net gain (Step 1) and there is an unrecognized net gain (Step 2)   Curtailment gain is recognized in the amount of the net gain in the projected benefit obligation. (The unrecognized net gain computed in Step 2 is not used.)

If the change in the projected benefit obligation is a net gain (Step 1) and there is an unrecognized net loss (Step 2)   If the net gain in the projected benefit obligation does not exceed the unrecognized net loss, no curtailment gain or loss is recognized. If the net gain exceeds the unrecognized net loss, curtailment gain is recognized in the amount of the excess of the net gain in the projected benefit obligation over the unrecognized net loss.

If the change in the projected benefit obligation is a net loss (Step 1) and there is an unrecognized net gain (Step 2)   If the net loss in the projected benefit obligation does not exceed the unrecognized net gain, no curtailment gain or loss is recognized. If the net loss exceeds the unrecognized net gain, curtailment loss is recognized in the amount of the excess of the net loss in the projected benefit obligation over the unrecognized net gain.

If the change in the projected benefit obligation is a net loss (Step 1) and there is an unrecognized net loss (Step 2) Curtailment loss is recognized in the amount of the net loss in the projected benefit obligation. (The unrecognized net loss computed in Step 2 is not used.)

Recognition of the Total Effects of a Plan Curtailment

The total effects of a plan curtailment consist of (*a*) the decrease (loss) in the unamortized balance of unrecognized prior service cost and/or unrecognized net obligation that arose at the date of initial application of FAS-87, resulting from the significant reduction of the expected years of future service for present employees, and (*b*) the net decrease (gain) or increase (loss) in the projected benefit obligation that results from the elimination of the accrual of defined pension benefits for some or all of the future services of a significant number of employees.

If the total effects of a plan curtailment result in a loss, the loss is recognized when it is *probable* that the curtailment will occur and the effects of the curtailment can be *reasonably estimated*. If the total effects of a plan curtailment result in a gain, the gain is recognized only when the related employees terminate or the plan suspension or amendment is adopted (FAS-88, par. 14).

Reporting Total Effects of a Plan Curtailment

Gain or loss on the total effects of a pension plan curtailment is reported as an ordinary gain or loss, unless it meets the criteria of an extraordinary item as specified by APB-30 (FAS-88, par. 48).

Illustration of Computation of Expected Years of Future Service and Loss from the Decrease in Unrecognized Prior Service Cost Resulting from the Expected Years of Future Service That Are Significantly Reduced by a Plan Curtailment

Company X had 50 employees who were expected to receive pension benefits under a new pension plan amendment, which became effective January 1, 19X1. In the computation of the expected years of future service for each employee who was entitled to receive benefits under the new plan amendment, the company assumed that 10% of the employees would either quit or retire during the next 10 years. The total amount of unrecognized prior service cost arising from the new pension plan amendment was $27,500.

Employee Number	Expected Years of Future Service	Year									
		X1	X2	X3	X4	X5	X6	X7	X8	X9	YO
1–5	5	5									
6–10	10	5	5								
11–15	15	5	5	5							
16–20	20	5	5	5	5						
21–25	25	5	5	5	5	5					
26–30	30	5	5	5	5	5	5				
31–35	35	5	5	5	5	5	5	5			
36–40	40	5	5	5	5	5	5	5	5		
41–45	45	5	5	5	5	5	5	5	5	5	
46–50	50	5	5	5	5	5	5	5	5	5	5
	275										
Service years rendered		50	45	40	35	30	25	20	15	10	5
Amortization fraction		$\frac{50}{275}$	$\frac{45}{275}$	$\frac{40}{275}$	$\frac{35}{275}$	$\frac{30}{275}$	$\frac{25}{275}$	$\frac{20}{275}$	$\frac{15}{275}$	$\frac{10}{275}$	$\frac{5}{275}$

Amortization for each expected year of future service equals $100 ($27,500 unrecognized prior service cost divided by 275 years of expected future service).

Assume, at the beginning of X3, that 15 employees are terminated, resulting in a reduction of 90 years (given) of expected future service. The percentage reduction of expected future service years is 50%, determined as follows:

Expected years of future service, beginning of X3, before terminations (275, less amortization of 50 for X1 and 45 for X2)	180
Reduction due to terminations (given)	90
Percentage reduction: 90/180	50%

The remaining balance of unrecognized prior service cost relating to the new plan amendment at the beginning of year 3 was $18,000 (180 remaining years of expected future service multiplied by the $100 amortization rate per year). Thus, the pension plan curtailment, relating to the expected years of future service that were significantly reduced by the termination of 15 employees, results in a loss of $9,000 (50% of $18,000).

TERMINATION BENEFITS

Under FAS-88, termination benefits are classified as either *special* or *contractual*. Special termination benefits are those that are offered to employees for a short period in connection with the termination of their employment. Contractual termination benefits are those that are required by the terms of an existing plan or agreement and that are provided only on the occurrence of a specified event, such as early retirement or the closing of a facility (FAS-88, par. 15).

FAS-88 requires the recognition of the cost of termination benefits as a loss and corresponding liability. The recognition date depends on whether the benefits are special or contractual.

Special Termination Benefits

The recognition date on which the employer records the loss and corresponding liability for special termination benefits occurs when (*a*) the employees accept the offer of the special termination benefits and (*b*) the amount of the cost of the benefits can be reasonably estimated.

Contractual Termination Benefits

The recognition date on which the employer records the loss and corresponding liability for contractual termination benefits occurs when (*a*) it is probable that employees will be entitled to the benefits and (*b*) the amount of the cost of the benefits can be estimated reasonably (FAS-88, par. 15).

Reporting a Loss on Termination Benefits

A loss on termination benefits is reported as an ordinary loss, unless it meets the criteria of an extraordinary item as specified in APB-30 (FAS-88, par. 48).

DISPOSAL OF AN IDENTIFIABLE BUSINESS SEGMENT

Under APB-30, severance pay, additional pension costs, and employee relocation expenses are all costs directly associated with the decision to dispose of an identifiable business segment and are properly includable in the total gain or loss on disposal. Gains and losses resulting from the application of FAS-88 that are directly related to the disposal of an identifiable business segment are accounted for in accordance with APB-30 (FAS-88, par. 16).

The measurement date for determining a gain or loss on the disposal of an identifiable business segment is the date that management commits itself to a formal plan of action to sell or otherwise dispose of the segment. The disposal date is the closing date in the case of a sale, or the date operations cease in the case of an abandonment.

Determination of gain or loss on disposal of a business segment should be made as of the measurement date, based on estimates of net realizable values. The estimated loss on the disposal of a business segment is recognized as of the measurement date. A gain on the disposal of a business segment should not be recognized until it is realized, which usually is the disposal date.

> ☞ **PRACTICE POINTER:** Although a gain or loss on the disposal of an identifiable business segment is not an extraordinary item, it is treated in a similar manner on the income statement, preceded by the caption "Income from Continuing Operations."

FINANCIAL STATEMENT DISCLOSURE

The disclosure requirements for settlements and curtailments of plans are incorporated into a general set of disclosure requirements for all pension and other postretirement plans. They are covered in Chapter 35 of the 1999 *Miller GAAP Guide*.

Illustration of Curtailment and Settlement of a Pension Plan

The updated records of a defined benefit pension plan reflect the following:

Vested benefits	$ (30,000)
Nonvested benefits	(50,000)
Accumulated benefit obligation	$ (80,000)
Effects on benefits as a result of considering future compensation levels	(20,000)
Projected benefit obligation	$(100,000)
Fair value of plan assets	95,000
Funded status of plan	$ (5,000)
Unrecognized prior service cost	1,000
Unrecognized net (gain) or loss	(1,000)
Unrecognized net obligation or (net asset) at date of initial application of FAS-87	2,000
Accrued pension cost	$ (3,000)

Assume that the above plan is completely terminated without a successor plan. Under this circumstance, the effects on benefits as a result of considering future compensation levels are no longer an obligation of the employer or the plan, since all of the plan participants have been terminated. Assume also that the total projected benefit obligation was settled by the purchase of nonparticipating annuity contracts for $80,000, and the excess plan assets in the amount of $15,000 were withdrawn by the employer.

Computation of the total effects of a plan curtailment   The total effects of a plan curtailment consist of (*a*) the total loss resulting from the decreases in the balances of any unamortized unrecognized prior service costs and/or the unamortized unrecognized net obligation that arose at the date of the initial application of FAS-87, relating to the expected years of future service that were significantly reduced for present employees and (*b*) the net decrease (gain) or increase (loss) in the projected benefit obligation resulting from the elimination of the accrual of defined pension benefits for some or all of the future services of a significant number of employees.

The loss resulting from the decrease in the balance of any unamortized unrecognized prior service costs (or unamortized unrecognized net obligation) is computed as follows:

Step 1.   The percentage reduction, if any, in the balances of any unamortized unrecognized prior service cost and/or the unamortized unrecognized net obligation must be calculated (each loss must be computed separately, unless the pension plan is completely terminated). In the above illustration, the percentage reduction resulting from the significant reduction in the expected years of future service is 100%, because the plan is completely terminated. As a result, no separate computation is necessary.

Step 2.   Multiply the unamortized balance of each unrecognized prior service cost and unrecognized net obligation by its percentage reduction, if any. In the above illustration, the unamortized balance of the unrecognized prior service cost of $1,000 is multiplied by 100%, and the unamortized balance of the unrecognized net obligation of $2,000 is multiplied by 100%; the sum of the resulting amounts is a total loss of $3,000.

Step 3.   The $3,000 computed in Step 2 is treated as an effect of the plan curtailment, not as part of the gain or loss on the plan curtailment.

The net decrease (gain) or increase (loss) in the projected benefit obligation is computed as follows:

Step 4.   Calculate the net decrease (gain) or net increase (loss) in the projected benefit obligation resulting from the plan curtailment. Do not include any increase (loss) in the projected benefit obligation that arose in connection with termination benefits (FAS-88, par. 13, footnote 4). In the above illustration, the effects on benefits as a result of considering future compensation levels of $20,000 are no longer an obligation of the employer or the plan.

This results in a $20,000 net decrease (gain) in the projected benefit obligation, because there are no other decreases or increases.

Step 5. Compute the total of (*a*) the balance of any unrecognized net gain or loss arising after the initial application of FAS-87 that remains unamortized at the date of the plan curtailment and (*b*) the balance of any unrecognized net asset that arose at the date of the initial application of FAS-87 that remains unamortized at the date of the plan curtailment. In the above illustration, the total is a gain of $1,000 (unrecognized net gain of $1,000 and no unrecognized net asset).

Step 6. Compute the gain or loss on the plan curtailment, as follows:

- If Step 4 (projected benefit obligation) is a gain and Step 5 is also a gain, curtailment gain is recognized in the amount of Step 4 (the amount of gain in Step 5 is ignored).

- If Step 4 (projected benefit obligation) is a loss and Step 5 is also a loss, curtailment loss is recognized in the amount of Step 4 (the amount of loss in Step 5 is ignored).

- If Step 4 (projected benefit obligation) is a gain and Step 5 is a loss, curtailment gain is recognized in the amount by which the gain in Step 4 exceeds the loss in Step 5. If Step 5 exceeds Step 4, no gain or loss is recognized.

- If Step 4 (projected benefit obligation) is a loss and Step 5 is a gain, curtailment loss is recognized in the amount by which the loss in Step 4 exceeds the gain in Step 5. If Step 5 exceeds Step 4, no gain or loss is recognized.

In the above illustration, the net decrease (gain) in the projected benefit obligation was $20,000 (Step 4) and the total unrecognized net gain or loss is a gain of $1,000 (Step 5). Since both steps result in a gain, a gain on the plan curtailment in the amount of Step 4 is recognized, which is $20,000.

Settlement gain or loss As in Step 5 above, compute the total of (*a*) the balance of any unrecognized net gain or loss arising after the initial application of FAS-87 that remains unamortized at the date of the plan settlement and (*b*) the balance of any unrecognized net asset that arose at the date of the initial application of FAS-87 that remains unamortized at the date of the plan settlement.

If part of the pension obligation is settled, the employer must recognize a pro rata portion of the maximum gain or loss, equal to the total of the unrecognized net gain or loss and/or the unrecognized net asset multiplied by the percentage reduction in the projected benefit obligation. In the above illustration, there was an unamortized balance of an unrecognized net gain of $1,000 and no unamortized balance of any unrecognized net asset. Since the pension plan was terminated, the pension obligation completely settled, and the decrease in the projected benefit obligation was 100%, the pro rata portion that must be recognized is 100%, or $1,000. Thus, the gain on the settlement of the pension plan is $1,000.

Summary   The loss on the decrease in the unamortized balance of unrecognized prior service cost and unrecognized net obligation is $3,000, which was computed in Step 3. This loss is reported as a "Loss on Effects of Curtailment of Pension Plan." The net gain on the decrease in the projected benefit obligation is $20,000, which was computed in Step 6. This gain is reported as a "Gain on the Curtailment of Pension Plan." The "Gain on the Settlement of Pension Plan" is $1,000, which was computed separately above. Thus, the net gain on the pension plan curtailment and settlement was $18,000 ($3,000 loss, $20,000 gain, and $1,000 gain).

Journal entry   The journal entry and suggested financial statement presentation of the net gain on pension plan curtailment and settlement of $18,000 is as follows:

Cash (excess plan assets)	$15,000	
Accrued pension cost	3,000	
Gain from termination of pension plan		$18,000

Suggested financial statement presentation:

Gain on curtailment of pension plan	$20,000
Loss on effects of curtailment of pension plan	(3,000)
Total effects of plan curtailment	$17,000
Gain on settlement of pension plan	1,000
Net gain on pension plan curtailment and settlement	$18,000

CHAPTER 36
POSTEMPLOYMENT AND
POSTRETIREMENT BENEFITS
OTHER THAN PENSIONS

CONTENTS

CHAPTER 36
POSTEMPLOYMENT AND POSTRETIRE-
MENT BENEFITS OTHER THAN PEN-
SIONS

OVERVIEW

FAS-106 requires the accrual of postretirement benefits in a manner similar to the recognition of net periodic pension cost under FAS-87 (Employers' Accounting for Pensions). The provisions of FAS-106 are similar in most respects to those of FAS-87 and differ only where there are compelling reasons for different treatments.

Similar to FAS-87, FAS-106 incorporates the following features in the required accounting for postretirement benefits:

1. *Delayed recognition*—Certain changes in the obligation for postretirement benefits and in the value of plan assets are not required to be recognized as they occur. Rather, they can be recognized systematically over future periods.

2. *Net cost*—The recognized consequences of events and transactions affecting a postretirement benefit plan are reported as a single amount in the employers' financial statements. That amount includes at least three types of events or transactions that might otherwise be reported separately—exchanging a promise of deferred compensation for current employee services, the interest cost arising from the passage of time until those benefits are paid, and the returns from the investment in plan assets if the plan is funded.

3. *Offsetting*—Plan assets (assets that have been segregated and restricted for the payment of postretirement benefits) offset the accumulated postretirement benefit obligation in determining amounts in the employer's statement of financial position. Also, the return on plan assets reduces postretirement benefit cost in the employer's statement of income. That reduction is reflected, even though the obligation has not been settled and the investment in the assets may be largely controlled by the employer, and substantial risks and rewards associated with both the obligation and the assets are borne by the employer.

The FASB has also established accounting standards for employers that provide benefits for former or inactive employees after employment, but before retirement (*postemployment benefits*). FAS-112 requires employers to recognize the obligation to provide postemployment benefits in accordance with FAS-43 (Accounting for Compensated Absences) if the criteria for accrual established in that pronouncement are met. If the FAS-43 criteria are not met, the employer should account for postemployment benefits when it is probable that a liability has been incurred and the amount of that liability can be reasonably estimated, in accordance with FAS-5 (Accounting for Contingencies).

GAAP for postemployment and postretirement benefits are found in the following pronouncements:

APB-12   Omnibus Opinion—1967

FAS-106   Employers' Accounting for Postretirement Benefits Other Than Pensions

FAS-112   Employers' Accounting for Postemployment Benefits

FAS-132   Employers' Disclosures about Pensions and Other Postretirement Benefits

CROSS-REFERENCES

1999 MILLER GAAP GUIDE: Chapter 3, "Business Combinations"; Chapter 10, "Deferred Compensation Contracts"; Chapter 24, "Interest Costs Capitalized"; Chapter 34, "Pension Plans—Employers"; Chapter 35, "Pension Plans—Settlements and Curtailments"; Chapter 42, "Results of Operations"

1999 MILLER GAAP IMPLEMENTATION MANUAL: Chapter 25, "Postemployment and Postretirement Benefits Other Than Pensions"

1999 MILLER GAAP IMPLEMENTATION MANUAL: EITF: Chapter 24, "Postemployment and Postretirement Benefits Other Than Pensions"

1999 MILLER GAAS GUIDE: Chapter 8, "Evidence"; Chapter 20, "Audits of Employee Benefit Plans"

1999 MILLER GOVERNMENTAL GAAP GUIDE: Chapter 22, "Certain Postemployment Benefits"

BACKGROUND

FAS-106, issued in December 1990, establishes employers' accounting and disclosure for postretirement benefits other than pensions.

In general, FAS-106 was effective for fiscal years beginning on or after December 16, 1992. However, the effective date was extended for an additional two years, to fiscal years beginning on or after December 16, 1994, for (*a*) plans outside the United States and (*b*) defined benefit plans of nonpublic enterprises with no more than 500 participants in all of their plans in the aggregate.

For convenient discussion, this chapter uses the term *postretirement benefits* to mean postretirement benefits other than pensions. Practice sometimes uses the abbreviation "OPEB" (other postretirement employee benefits) with the same meaning.

GAAP ACCORDING TO FAS-106

FAS-106 establishes *accounting* as well as *disclosure* standards for employers with postretirement benefit plans. *Postretirement benefits* consist of all forms of benefits other than retirement income provided by an employer to retired workers, their beneficiaries, and their dependents (FAS-106, par. 6). The term does not include benefits paid after employment but before retirement, such as layoff benefits. Postemployment benefits are covered by FAS-112, which is the subject of a later section in this chapter. The disclosure requirements of FAS-106 have subsequently been replaced by FAS-132.

Postretirement benefit payments may begin immediately on employees' termination of service or may be deferred until retired employees reach a specified age. Benefits such as health-care, tuition assistance, or legal services are provided to retirees as the need arises. Other benefits, such as life insurance, are provided on the occurrence of specified events (FAS-106, par. 7).

A *postretirement benefit plan* is one in which an employer agrees to provide certain postretirement benefits to current and former employees after they retire. A postretirement benefit plan may be *contributory* (employees may be required to contribute to the plan) or *noncontributory* (the entire cost of the plan is borne by the employer).

A postretirement benefit plan may be *funded* or *unfunded*—that is, the employees and/or the employer may make cash contributions to a postretirement benefit plan trustee (i.e., funded), or the employer may make only credit entries on its books reflecting the postretirement benefit liability under the plan and pay all benefits from its general assets (i.e., unfunded).

General Approach of FAS-106—Deferred Compensation

According to FAS-106, postretirement benefits are a type of *deferred compensation* that is accounted for as part of an employee's total compensation package. A *deferred compensation plan* is an agreement specifying that a portion of an employee's compensation will be set aside and paid in future periods.

FAS-106 requires employers to account for postretirement benefit plans on the accrual basis. Any difference between net periodic postretirement benefit cost charged against income and the amount actually funded is recorded as an accrued or prepaid cost.

Comparison of FAS-106 to FAS-87 and FAS-88

Although there are some important differences, many provisions of FAS-106 are similar to the accounting and reporting requirements for pension accounting established by FAS-87 and FAS-88.

In accounting for postretirement benefits under FAS-106, an employer makes at least two types of journal entries to record its cost of these benefits—one to record the annual expense and related liability and a second to record the payment or funding of the liability, if any.

Illustration of Basic Entries for Recording Postretirement Benefits

Assuming a company determines its annual expense for postretirement benefits is $10,000 and funds that amount, the following entries are made:

1. Net periodic postretirement
   benefit cost $ 10,000
   Accrued postretirement
       benefit cost payable $ 10,000
   (To accrue postretirement benefit
   cost of $10,000 for a specific period.)

2. Accrued postretirement benefit
   cost payable $ 10,000
   Cash $ 10,000
   (To record cash contribution to
   postretirement plan trust or to
   pay benefits of $10,000.)

These entries are similar to those required for pension accounting under FAS-87, except for differences in the titles of the accounts.

Most of the provisions of FAS-87 and FAS-106 pertain to the computation of the amount to be recorded in journal entry type (1) above. This computation requires numerous worksheet calculations, which are illustrated throughout FAS-87 and FAS-106.

> **OBSERVATION**: A major difference between FAS-87 and FAS-106 is that under certain circumstances, FAS-87 requires the recognition of a minimum pension plan liability while FAS-106 does not require the recognition of a minimum liability for a postretirement benefit plan.

Financial statement disclosure under FAS-106 requires a reconciliation of the funded status of the postretirement benefit plan with certain amounts reported in the employer's statement of financial position. This reconciliation is similar to that required by FAS-87 for disclosure of pension plans.

Use of Reasonable Approximations

FAS-106 allows an employer to use estimates, averages, or computational shortcuts, provided that the employer reasonably expects that the results will not be materially different from those which would have been reached by a fully detailed application of the provisions of FAS-106 (FAS-106, par. 15).

Scope and Applicability of FAS-106

The applicability of FAS-106 is discussed in terms of five areas:

- Types of benefits
- Types of beneficiaries
- General rather than selective coverage of employees
- Source and form of payment
- Nature of the employer's undertaking

Types of Benefits

FAS-106 applies to an employer's undertaking to provide various types of nonpension benefits to employees after they retire. The benefits may commence immediately upon termination of the employee's active service, or may be deferred until the retired employee reaches a specified age.

The benefits include health care, life insurance outside of a pension plan, tuition assistance, day care, legal services, housing subsidies, and other types of postretirement benefits (FAS-106, par. 6). However, FAS-106 does not apply to pension or life insurance benefits provided by a pension plan. The GAAP for pensions and life insurance benefits provided by pension plans are established by FAS-87 and FAS-88 (FAS-106, par. 11).

> **OBSERVATION:** FAS-106 covers a broader range of benefits than FAS-81. Both FAS-106 and FAS-81 cover health care and life insurance benefits, but FAS-106 covers ad-ditional types of benefits, such as tuition, day care, legal services, and housing subsidies.

If an employer has established a plan to provide benefits to active employees as well as to retired employees, FAS-106 requires the employer to divide the plan into two parts for accounting purposes; one part covering benefits to active employees and the other part covering benefits to retired employees. The employer should use the accounting standards of FAS-106 only for the part covering benefits to retired employees (FAS-106, par. 10).

Types of Beneficiaries

The beneficiaries may be retired employees, disabled employees, any other former employees who are expected to receive benefits, or retirees' beneficiaries and covered dependents, pursuant to the terms of an employer's undertaking to provide such benefits. The beneficiaries may also be individuals who (*a*) have ceased permanent active employment because of disability, (*b*) have not yet completed formal procedures for retirement, or (*c*) are carried on nonretired status under the disability provisions of the plan so that they can continue accumulating credit for pensions or other postretirement benefits (FAS-106, par. 6).

General Rather Than Selective Coverage of Employees

The plan should cover employees in general, rather than selected individual employees. An employer's practice of providing postretirement benefits to selected employees under individual contracts with specific terms determined on an individual basis does not constitute a postretirement benefit plan under FAS-106. FAS-106 does apply to contracts with individual employees if these contracts, taken together, are equivalent to a plan covering employees in general (FAS-106, par. 9).

> **OBSERVATION**: An employer's commitment to selected individual employees is accrued in accordance with the terms of the individual contracts (see the 1999 *Miller GAAP Guide* chapter titled "Deferred Compensation Contracts"). Professional judgment is required whenever contracts with individual employees may be equivalent to a general plan. FAS-106 provides no guidance on how to make the determination.

Source and Form of Payment

A plan is covered by FAS-106 if it provides reimbursement or direct payment to providers for the cost of specified services as the need for those services arises, or if it provides lump sum benefits, such as death benefits. The plan may be either funded or unfunded (FAS-106, par. 6).

> **OBSERVATION**: If the plan is funded, the assets of a postretirement benefit plan usually are kept in a trust account, segregated from the assets of the employer. Contributions to the postretirement benefit plan trust account are made periodically by the employer and, if the plan is contributory, by the employees. The plan assets may be invested in stocks, bonds, real estate, and other types of investments. Plan assets are increased by earnings, gains on investments, and contributions by the employer (and employees if the plan is contributory), and are decreased by losses on investments and the payment of benefits and any related administrative expenses.

Nature of the Employer's Undertaking

FAS-106 applies to any arrangement that is in substance a plan for providing postretirement benefits, regardless of its form (FAS-106, par. 8).

> **OBSERVATION**: When it is not clear that a plan exists, professional judgment is required in determining whether a plan exists "in substance." FAS-106 provides little guidance on this issue.

FAS-106 applies not only to written plans, but also to unwritten plans if the existence of these plans can be perceived based on (*a*) the employer's practice of paying benefits or (*b*) the employer's oral representations to current or former employees. Once an employer pays benefits or promises to pay benefits, FAS-106 presumes that the employer has undertaken to provide future benefits as indicated by the past payments or promises, unless there is evidence to the contrary (FAS-106, par. 8).

> **OBSERVATION**: To indicate the existence of a plan, it appears that the employer's oral representations (a) should refer to a plan that is general in its scope and (b) should be communicated to current or former employees in general, or to individual employees as representatives of the employees in general.

One issue is whether FAS-106 applies only to legally enforceable obligations, or to a broader range of commitments including those that cannot be legally enforced.

> **OBSERVATION**: The Employee Retirement Income Security Act (ERISA) gives substantial legal protection to the expectations of employees under pension plans, but does not give the same level of protection to employee expectations of nonpension benefits. Courts have upheld the right of employers to terminate or curtail benefits under non-pension plans, unless the employers have entered into legally binding commitments to maintain benefits, such as collective bargaining agreements.

The "Basis for Conclusions" in FAS-106 explains in more detail the type of employer's obligation that is covered by FAS-106. Although the "Basis for Conclusions" is not part of the formal pronouncement, it provides significant guidance and states that an employer's undertaking comes within the scope of FAS-106 if the undertaking is a *liability* under CON-6 (Elements of Financial Statements).

The "Basis for Conclusions" in FAS-106 relies on CON-6 for the proposition that an obligation can qualify as a liability whether or not the obligation is legally enforceable. The test is whether the obligation "is effectively binding on the employer because of past practices, social or moral sanctions, or customs." FAS-106 concludes that an employer, by paying benefits or promising to do so, incurs a liability to be accounted for under FAS-106, in the absence of evidence to the contrary.

> **OBSERVATION:**
> 1. Accountants should obtain expert advice before (a) advising employers on the applicability of FAS-106 to existing

plans, (b) advising employers on the structuring of new plans or the restructuring of existing plans if the structure of the plan may determine whether the plan is within the scope of FAS-106, or (c) auditing the financial statements of an employer if there is a serious question as to whether the employer's plan is within the scope of FAS-106.

2. If a plan is covered by FAS-106, the next question is whether the plan is a defined benefit plan or a defined contribution plan. FAS-106 prescribes significantly different accounting and reporting requirements for these two categories. FAS-106 deals primarily with defined benefit plans. For the distinctive accounting and reporting requirements applicable to defined contribution plans, see the section titled "Defined Contribution Plans" in this chapter. When considering the structuring or restructuring of a plan, the employer and its advisors should consider whether the plan is covered by FAS-106 and, if so, whether the plan is governed by the accounting and reporting requirements for defined benefit plans or for defined contribution plans.

SINGLE-EMPLOYER DEFINED BENEFIT POSTRETIREMENT PLANS

FAS-106 deals primarily with an employer's accounting for a single-employer plan that provides defined benefits. FAS-106 also briefly covers multiemployer plans, multiple-employer plans, and defined contribution plans. Each is discussed later in this chapter.

> **OBSERVATION:** The accounting and reporting requirements for defined contribution plans differ significantly from those for defined benefit plans. If a plan has some characteristics of each type, FAS-106 calls for careful analysis of the substance of the plan. The difference in the accounting and reporting requirements, depending on whether the plan is a defined benefit plan or a defined contribution plan, may be a significant factor to be considered by employers attempting to structure or restructure their plans.

In a defined benefit plan, the benefit may be defined in terms of a specified monetary amount (such as a life insurance benefit), or a specified type of benefit (such as all or a percentage of the cost of specified surgical procedures). The benefits may be subject to a maximum (or *cap*), either per individual employee or for the plan as a whole, or the employer may agree to pay the full amount of benefits without regard to any maximum amount (FAS-106, par. 17).

The employee's entitlement to benefits is expressed in the benefit formula, which specifies the years of service to be rendered, age to be attained while in service, or a combination of both, which must be met for an employee to be eligible to receive benefits under the plan. The benefit formula may also define the beginning of the period of service during which the employee earns credit toward eligibility, as well as the levels of benefits earned for specific periods of service (FAS-106, par. 18).

The total amount of benefits depends not only on the benefit formula but also on actuarial factors, such as the longevity of the retired employee (and the longevity of the retiree's beneficiaries and covered dependents), and the occurrence of specific events entitling the individuals to benefits (such as illnesses) (FAS-106, par. 20).

Because of these factors, the employer cannot precisely calculate the amount of benefits to be paid in the future to any retired employee (or to the retiree's beneficiaries and covered dependents). The FASB is satisfied, however, that employers can make reasonable estimates useful for accounting purposes.

Accumulated Postretirement Benefit Obligation

FAS-106 requires the employer to accrue the accumulated postretirement benefit obligation. Once an employee has attained full eligibility, the amount of this obligation is the same as the employee's *expected* postretirement benefit obligation. Until then, the *accumulated* amount is the portion of the expected amount attributed to employee service rendered to a particular date (FAS-106, par. 21).

The accumulated and the expected amounts represent the actuarial present value of the anticipated benefits. Measurement of these amounts is based on assumptions regarding such items as the expected cost of providing future benefits and any cost-sharing provisions under which the employee, the government, or others will absorb part of these costs. If the benefits or cost-sharing provisions are related to the employee's salary progression, the calculation of benefits and cost-sharing reflects the anticipated impact of this progression (FAS-106, par. 22).

> **OBSERVATION:** FAS-106 differs from the accounting for pensions in FAS-87 in this respect, because FAS-87 does not anticipate salary progression in determining the accumulated pension benefit obligation.

Illustration of Relationship between Expected and Accumulated Postretirement Benefit Obligations

A plan provides postretirement health-care benefits to all employees who render at least 10 years of service and attain age 65 while in service. A

60-year-old employee, hired at age 45, is expected to terminate employment at the end of the year in which the employee attains age 67 and is expected to live to age 77. A discount rate of 8% is assumed.

At December 31, 19X2, the employer estimates the expected amount and timing of benefit payments for that employee as follows:

Age	Expected Future Claims	Present Value at Age 60	Present Value at Age 65
68	$ 2,322	$ 1,255	$ 1,843
69	2,564	1,283	1,885
70	2,850	1,320	1,940
71	3,154	1,353	1,988
72	3,488	1,385	2,035
73	3,868	1,422	2,090
74	4,274	1,455	2,138
75	4,734	1,492	2,193
76	5,240	1,530	2,247
77	7,798	2,108	3,097
	$40,292	$14,603	$21,456

At December 31, 19X2, when the employee's age is 60, the *expected* postretirement benefit obligation is $14,603, and the *accumulated* postretirement benefit obligation is $10,952 (15/20 of $14,603 because the employee has worked 15 of the 20 years needed to attain age 65 while in service and thus become fully eligible for benefits).

Assuming no changes in health-care costs or other circumstances, the obligations at later dates are as follows:

- December 31, 19X7 (age 65), the expected and the accumulated postretirement benefit obligations are both $21,456. These amounts are the same, because the employee is fully eligible.
- December 31, 19X8 (age 66), the expected and the accumulated postretirement benefit obligations are both $23,172 ($21,456 the previous year, plus interest @ 8% for 1 year).

Measurement of Cost and Obligations

In discussing the measurement of cost and obligations of single-employer defined benefit plans, FAS-106 addresses the following issues:

- Accounting for the substantive plan
- Assumptions
- Attribution

Accounting for the Substantive Plan

According to FAS-106, the accounting and reporting should reflect the substantive plan; that is, the plan as understood by the employer and the employees. Generally, the substantive plan is accurately reflected in writing. The employer's past practice or communications of intended future changes, however, may indicate that the substantive plan differs from the written plan (FAS-106, par. 23).

> ☛ **PRACTICE POINTER:** If an independent auditor is faced with a situation in which the substantive plan appears to be different from the written plan, the auditor should (a) seek expert advice, (b) consult with the highest levels of the employer's management, and (c) fully document the matter in the audit files.

FAS-106 discusses some areas in which the substantive plan may differ from the written plan, as follows:

- Cost sharing
- Benefit changes
- Plan amendments

Cost Sharing

In general, the employer's cost-sharing policy is regarded as part of the substantive plan if (*a*) the employer has maintained a consistent level of cost-sharing with retirees, (*b*) the employer consistently has increased or decreased the share of the cost contributed by employees or retirees, or (*c*) the employer has the ability to change the cost-sharing provisions at a specified time or when certain conditions exist, and has communicated to plan participants its intent to make such changes (FAS-106, par. 24).

An employer's past practice regarding cost sharing, however, is not regarded as the substantive plan if (FAS-106, par. 25):

- The cost sharing was accompanied by offsetting changes in other benefits or compensation.
- The employer was subjected to significant costs, such as work stoppages, to carry out that policy.

Along similar lines, an employer's communication of its intent to change the cost-sharing provisions is not regarded as the substantive plan if (FAS-106, par. 25):

- The plan participants would be unwilling to accept the change without adverse results to the employer's operations.
- The plan participants would insist on other modifications of the plan, that would offset the change in cost sharing, to accept the proposed change.

In estimating the amount of contributions to be received by the plan from active or retired employees, the employer should consider any relevant substantive plan provisions, such as the employer's past practice of consistently changing the contribution rates. If the employer is obliged to return contributions to employees who do not become eligible for benefits (together with interest, if applicable), the estimated amount of this obligation is (*a*) included in the employer's total benefit obligation and (*b*) factored into calculations of the contributions needed by the plan (FAS-106, par. 27).

Benefit Changes

The measurement of the obligation under the plan includes automatic benefit changes specified by the plan. An example is a plan that promises to pay a benefit in kind, such as health-care benefits, instead of a defined dollar amount. The obligation to pay the benefit automatically changes in amount when the cost of the benefit changes (FAS-106, par. 28).

Plan Amendments

Measurement also includes plan amendments as soon as they have been contractually agreed upon, even if some or all of the provisions become effective in later periods (FAS-106, par. 28).

> **OBSERVATION:** Even if a plan amendment has not been contractually agreed upon, it appears that an employer should reflect the amendment if it can be regarded as a change in the substantive plan. In general, a substantive plan may differ from the written plan in either of two cases: (1) when the employer has communicated its intention to adopt the amendment and certain conditions are met or (2) when the employer has engaged in consistent past practice.

Assumptions

An employer has to make numerous assumptions to apply FAS-106. Each assumption should reflect the best estimate of the future event to which it relates, without regard to the estimates involved in making other assumptions. FAS-106 describes this as an explicit approach to assumptions (FAS-106, par. 29).

> **OBSERVATION:** The FASB finds the use of **explicit** assumptions preferable to **implicit** assumptions, under which the reliability of assumptions would be judged in the aggregate, not individually (FAS-106, par. 181).

All assumptions should be based on the expectation that the plan will continue in the absence of evidence that it will not continue (FAS-106, par. 30). Some of the assumptions discussed in FAS-106 apply generally to all types of benefits, while other assumptions are unique to health-care benefits.

FAS-106 discusses the following general assumptions:

- Time value of money (discount rates)
- Expected long-term rate of return on plan assets
- Future compensation levels
- Other general assumptions

Time Value of Money (Discount Rates)

One of the essential assumptions relates to discount rates. Assumed discount rates are used in measuring the expected and accumulated postretirement benefit obligations and the service cost and interest cost components of net periodic postretirement benefit cost. Assumed discount rates should reflect the time value of money at the measurement date, as indicated by rates of return on high-quality fixed-income investments currently available with cash flows corresponding to the anticipated needs of the plan. If the employer could possibly settle its obligation under the plan by purchasing insurance (for example, nonparticipating life insurance contracts to provide death benefits), the interest rates inherent in the potential settlement amount are relevant to the employer's determination of assumed discount rates (FAS-106, par. 31).

Expected Long-Term Rate of Return on Plan Assets

Assumptions are also required in determining the expected long-term rate of return on plan assets. In general, plan assets are investments that have been segregated and restricted, usually in a trust, for the exclusive purpose of paying postretirement benefits.

The expected long-term rate of return on plan assets should reflect the anticipated average rate of earnings on existing plan assets and those expected to be contributed during the period (FAS-106, par. 32).

> **OBSERVATION:** This factor is used, together with the *market-related value* of plan assets, in computing the *expected return* on plan assets. The difference between the actual return and the expected return on plan assets is defined in FAS-106 as "plan asset gain or loss," discussed later.

If the return on plan assets is taxable to the trust or other fund under the plan, the expected long-term rate of return shall be reduced to reflect the related income taxes expected to be paid (FAS-106, par. 32).

When estimating the rate of return on plan assets, the employer should consider the rate of return on (*a*) assets currently invested and (*b*) assets that will be reinvested. If the income from plan assets is taxable, the anticipated amount of taxes should be deducted to produce a net-of-tax rate of return. If a plan is unfunded or has no assets that qualify as plan assets under FAS-106, the employer has no basis or need to calculate an expected long-term rate of return on plan assets (FAS-106, par. 32).

Future Compensation Levels

If the benefit formula provides for varying amounts of postretirement benefits based on the compensation levels of employees, the employer has to make further assumptions about the impact of anticipated future compensation levels on the cost of benefits and the obligation to pay them (FAS-106, par. 33).

Estimates of future compensation are based on anticipated compensation of individual employees, including future changes arising from general price levels, productivity, seniority, promotion, and other factors. All assumptions should be consistent with regard to general factors such as future rates of inflation. The assumptions should also include any indirect effects related to salary progression, such as the impact of inflation-based adjustments to the maximum benefit provided under the plan (FAS-106, par. 33).

Other General Assumptions

Other general assumptions involved in applying FAS-106 include the following:

- Participation rates for contributory plans
- The probability of payment (such as turnover of employees, dependency status, and mortality)

> ☞ **PRACTICE POINTER:** As is the case in pension accounting, the CPA is not expected to be an expert in actuarial science. In

fact, accounting for pensions and other retirement benefits is an area where the CPA relies heavily on the expertise of actuaries. However, the CPA still must have a general understanding of the work of the actuary, in-cluding the reasonableness of the underlying assumptions the actuary is using to prepare information that may have a significant impact on an enterprise's funding of benefit plans, as well as its financial statements.

Assumptions Unique to Postretirement Health-Care Benefits

Most postretirement benefit plans include health-care benefits. Measurement of an employer's postretirement health care obligation requires the use of special types of assumptions that will affect the amount and timing of future benefit payments for postretirement health care, in addition to the general assumptions required by all postretirement benefit plans.

FAS-106 discusses the following assumptions unique to postretirement health-care benefits:

- Per capita claims cost
- Assumptions about trends in health-care costs

Per Capita Claims Cost

An employer should estimate the net incurred claims cost at each age at which a participant is expected to receive benefits. To estimate this net cost, the employer first estimates the assumed per capita gross claims cost at each age, and then subtracts the effects of (*a*) Medicare and other reimbursements from third parties and (*b*) cost-sharing provisions that cause the participant to collect less than 100% of the claim. If plan participants are required to make contributions to the plan during their active service, the actuarial present value of the participants' future contributions should be subtracted from the actuarial present value of the assumed net incurred claims costs (FAS-106, par. 35).

The *assumed per capita claims cost* is the annual cost of benefits from the time at which an individual's coverage begins, for the remainder of that person's life (or until coverage ends, when sooner). The annual benefit cost is based on the best possible estimate of the expected future cost of benefits covered by the plan that reflects age and other appropriate factors such as gender and geographical location. If the employer incurs significant costs in administering the plan, these costs should also be considered part of the assumed per capita claims cost (FAS-106, par. 36).

If an employer does not have a reliable basis for estimating the assumed per capital claims cost by age, the employer may base its estimate on other reliable information. For example, the estimate may be based on the claims costs that have actually been incurred for employees of all ages, adjusted by factors to reflect health-care cost trends, age of the covered population, and cost sharing (FAS-106, par. 38).

A number of assumptions are based on the estimated effects of inflation. The employer should use consistent methods of estimating inflation, whether the assumption relates to discount rates, compensation levels, or health-care cost trend rates.

If the history of the plan is reliable enough to provide a basis for future estimates, the past and present claims data of the plan are considered in calculating the assumed per capita claims cost. If the plan does not provide any reliable data, the employer may base its estimates on other employers' claims information, as assembled by insurance companies, actuarial firms, or employee benefits consulting firms (FAS-106, par. 38).

> **OBSERVATION:** The independent auditor should verify that any outside information comes from reliable and independent sources, and that the audit files fully identify these sources.

The estimates derived from the experience of other employers should, however, be adjusted to reflect the demographics of the specific employer and the benefits available under its plan, to the extent they differ from those of the other employers. Relevant factors include, for example, health-care utilization patterns, expected geographical locations of retirees and their dependents, and significant differences among the nature and types of benefits covered (FAS-106, par. 38).

Assumptions about Trends in Health-Care Cost Rates

Assumptions about the trend in health-care cost rates represent the expected annual rate of change in the cost of health-care benefits currently provided under the plan (because of factors other than changes in the demographics of participants) for each year from the measurement date until the payment of benefits. The trend rates are based on past and current cost trends, reflecting such factors as health-care cost inflation, changes in utilization or delivery patterns, technological advances, and changes in the health status of plan participants. Examples include the possible future use of technology that is now being developed, or the reduction of the need for benefits resulting from participation in wellness programs (FAS-106, par. 39).

Different cost trend rates may be required for different types of services. For example, the cost trend rate for hospital care may differ from that for dental care. Further, the cost trend rates may fluctuate at different rates during different projected periods in the future. For example, there may be a rapid short-term increase, with a subsequent leveling off in the longer term.

Absent information to the contrary, the employer should assume that governmental benefits will continue as provided by existing law, and that benefits from other providers will continue in accordance with their existing plans. Future changes in the law are not anticipated (FAS-106, par. 40).

Attribution

Once the expected postretirement benefit obligation for an employee has been determined, an equal amount of that obligation is attributed to each year of service in the attribution period, unless the benefit formula of the plan is frontloaded and thus necessitates attribution on a different basis (FAS-106, par. 43).

The attribution period starts when the employee begins earning credit towards postretirement benefits. This generally occurs on the date of hire, but may be at a later date if the benefit formula requires a significant waiting period before the employee can earn credit. In any event, the attribution period ends when the employee reaches full eligibility for benefits. Thus, the cost of providing the benefits is attributed to the period during which the employee builds up full eligibility. The employer does not attribute any of the service cost to any period after the employee has achieved full eligibility (FAS-106, par. 44).

Illustration of Attribution Period

Under the postretirement benefit plan of Company Q, employees qualify by rendering at least five years of service and reaching age 65 while in service. The company hires an employee at age 61. Assume the expected postretirement benefit obligation for this employee is $10,000.

The attribution period is five years. (Note that the employee will not become eligible at age 65, because the employee will not yet have completed five years of service.) For each of the first five years of service, the annual service cost will be $2,000 (1/5 of $10,000). No service cost will be attributed after the first five years, even if the employee remains in service.

Illustration of Attribution under a Frontloaded Plan

A "frontloaded" plan is one in which a disproportionate share of the benefit obligation is attributed to the early years of an employee's service.

A life insurance plan provides postretirement death benefits of $200,000 for 10 years of service after age 45 and additional death benefits of $10,000 for each year of service thereafter until age 65. (The maximum benefit is therefore $300,000, consisting of the basic $200,000 plus 10 additional years @ $10,000.)

In this situation, the benefit obligation is attributed to periods corresponding to the benefit formula, as follows:

- The actuarial present value of a death benefit of $20,000 (1/10 of $200,000) is attributed to each of the first 10 years of service after age 45.

- The actuarial present value of an additional $10,000 death benefit is attributed to each year of service thereafter until age 65.

RECOGNITION OF NET PERIODIC POSTRETIREMENT BENEFIT COST

The amount of net periodic postretirement benefit cost is derived from the net change in the amount of the accumulated postretirement benefit obligation, after ignoring those components of the net change that do not pertain to the cost of benefits (FAS-106, par. 45).

The net periodic postretirement benefit cost recognized for a period consists of the following components (FAS-106, par. 46):

- Service cost

- Interest cost

- Actual return on plan assets, if any

- Amortization of unrecognized prior service cost, if any

- Gain or loss (to the extent recognized)

- Amortization of the unrecognized obligation or asset at the date of initial application of FAS-106 (if the full amount was not immediately recognized upon adoption of FAS-106)

> **OBSERVATION:** The employer makes one entry to accrue the net periodic postretirement benefit cost, the amount of which is the total of the components listed above, determined by worksheet calculations.

Basic Transactions and Adjustments

Illustration of Basic Transactions and Adjustments

Company A's date of transition to FAS-106 was the beginning of Year 1. At that time, the accumulated postretirement benefit obligation was $300,000. The plan was unfunded.

At the end of Year 1, Company A paid $65,000 of postretirement benefits. Service cost attributed to Year 1 was $60,000. The assumed discount rate was 10%.

Worksheets as of the end of Year 1 are as follows:

	Accrued Postretirement Benefit Cost	Accumulated Postretirement Benefit Obligation	Unrecognized Transition Obligation
Beginning of year	$ -0-	$(300,000)	$300,000
Recognition of components of net periodic post-retirement benefit cost:			
Service cost	(60,000)	(60,000)	
Interest cost (a)	(30,000)	(30,000)	
Amortization of transition obli-gation (b)	(15,000)		(15,000)
	$(105,000)	(90,000)	(15,000)
Benefit payments	65,000	65,000	
Net change	(40,000)	(25,000)	(15,000)
End of year	$ (40,000)	$(325,000)	$285,000

(a) 10% (assumed discount rate) of $300,000 (accumulated postretirement obligation at beginning of year)

(b) 20-year straight-line amortization of transition obligation (discussed later in this chapter)

The amounts on this worksheet are reflected in the reconciliation of the funded status of the plan with the amounts shown on the statement of financial position, as follows:

	Beginning of Year 1	End of Net Change	Year 1
Accumulated postretirement benefit obligation	$(300,000)	$(25,000)	$(325,000)
Plan assets at fair value	-0-		-0-
Funded status	(300,000)	(25,000)	(325,000)
Unrecognized transition obligation	300,000	(15,000)	285,000
Accrued postretirement benefit cost	$ -0-	$(40,000)	$ (40,000)

Service Cost Component

The *service cost component* of net periodic postretirement benefit cost is defined by FAS-106 as the portion of the expected postretirement benefit obligation attributed to employee service during a specified period, based on the actuarial present value of the expected obligation (FAS-106, par. 47).

A *defined benefit* postretirement benefit plan contains a benefit formula that defines the benefit an employee will receive for services performed during a specified period (service cost). FAS-106 requires that the terms of the benefit formula be used to determine the amount of postretirement benefit earned by each employee for services performed during a specified period. Under FAS-106, attribution is the process of assigning postretirement benefits or cost to periods of employee service, in accordance with the postretirement benefit formula.

Interest Cost Component

FAS-106 requires an employer to recognize as a component of net periodic postretirement benefit cost the interest cost on the accumulated postretirement benefit obligation. The interest cost is equal to the increase in the amount of the obligation because of the passage of time, measured at a rate equal to the assumed discount rate. FAS-106 specifies that the interest cost component of net periodic postretirement benefit cost is not considered interest expense for purposes of applying FAS-34 (Capitalization of Interest Cost) (FAS-106, par. 48).

Actual Return on Plan Assets Component

If a plan is funded, one component of periodic postretirement benefit cost is the actual return on plan assets. The amount of the actual return on plan assets is equal to the difference between the fair value of plan assets at the beginning and end of a period, adjusted for employer contributions, employee contributions (if the plan is contributory) and postretirement benefits paid during the period.

Fair value is the amount that reasonably could be expected to result from a current sale of an investment between a willing buyer and a willing seller, that is, a sale other than a forced liquidation. Plan assets that are used in the operation of the postretirement benefit plan (building, equipment, furniture, fixtures, etc.) are valued at cost less accumulated depreciation or amortization. The actual return on plan assets is shown net of tax expense if the fund holding the plan assets is a taxable entity (FAS-106, par. 49).

A return on plan assets decreases the employer's cost of providing postretirement benefits to its employees, while a loss on plan assets increases postretirement benefit cost. Net periodic postretirement benefit income can result from a significantly high return on plan assets during a period.

Illustration of Actual Return on Plan Assets

An employer may determine its actual gain or loss on plan assets as follows:

Plan assets, beginning of year, at fair value	$ 200,000
Add: Amounts contributed to plan	750,000
Less: Benefit payments from plan	(650,000)
	300,000
Less: Plan assets, end of year, at fair value	340,000
Actual (return) loss on plan assets	$ (40,000)

> **OBSERVATION:** Actual return on plan assets is one of the components of net periodic postretirement benefit cost. As discussed later in this chapter, FAS-106 requires this component to be disclosed on the financial statements. Another component of net postretirement benefit cost is gains and losses (discussed later in this chapter). The "gains and losses" component includes, among other items, "plan asset gains and losses," defined as the difference between the actual return and the expected return on plan assets.
>
> The following example illustrates the combined effect on net periodic postretirement benefit cost of (a) actual return on plan assets and (b) plan asset gains and losses: If the actual return on plan assets is $1,000,000 and the expected return is $700,000, the plan asset gain is the $300,000 difference be-

tween the actual return and the expected return. This $300,000 plan asset gain is part of the "gains and losses" component of net periodic postretirement benefit cost, while the $1,000,000 actual return on plan assets is another component. The combined effect is a net decrease of $700,000 in net periodic postretirement benefit cost, the result of offsetting the $300,000 plan asset gain against the $1,000,000 actual return. This $700,000 is equal to the expected return on plan assets. The total amount of net periodic postretirement benefit cost will include the $700,000 as well as other components, including service cost, interest cost, etc. The $300,000 plan asset gain will be taken into account in computing in future years (a) the expected return on plan assets and (b) amortization of deferred gains and losses. (See discussion and illustration later in this chapter.)

Amortization of Unrecognized Prior Service Cost Component

When a postretirement benefit plan is initially adopted or amended, employees may be granted benefits for services performed in prior periods. The cost of postretirement benefits that are granted retroactively to employees is referred to as *prior service cost* (FAS-106, par. 50).

Under FAS-106, only a portion of the total amount of prior service cost arising in a period is included in net periodic postretirement benefit cost. FAS-106 requires that the total prior service cost arising in a period from the adoption or amendment of a plan be amortized in a systematic manner. *Amortization* of prior service cost is a component of net periodic postretirement benefit cost (FAS-106, par. 50).

Initiation of a plan, or amendment that improves benefits in an existing plan When an employer initiates a plan or adopts an amendment that improves the benefits in an existing plan, the amount of prior service cost is the amount of increase in the accumulated postretirement benefit obligation that can be attributed to service of employees in prior periods (FAS-106, par. 50).

Illustration of Plan Amendment Increasing Benefits

At the beginning of Year 2, Company A amended its plan, causing the accumulated postretirement benefit obligation to increase by $84,000. Active plan participants had an average of 12 remaining years of service before reaching full eligibility for benefits.

At the end of Year 2, the employer paid $60,000 in benefits. Service cost was $50,000.

The worksheets as of the end of Year 2 are as follows:

	Accrued Postretirement Benefit Cost	Accumulated Postretirement Benefit Obligation	Unrecognized Transition Obligation	Unrecognized Prior Service Cost
Beginning of year	$ (40,000)	$(325,000)	$285,000	$ -0-
Plan amendment		(84,000)		84,000
Recognition of components of net periodic postretirement benefit cost:				
Service cost	(50,000)	(50,000)		
Interest cost (a)	(40,900)	(40,900)		
Amortization of transition obligation (b)	(15,000)		(15,000)	
Amortization of prior service cost (c)	(7,000)			(7,000)
	(112,900)	(174,900)	(15,000)	77,000
Benefit payments	60,000	60,000		
Net change	(52,900)	(114,900)	(15,000)	77,000
End of year	$ (92,900)	$(439,900)	$270,000	$77,000

(a) 10% (assumed discount rate) of $325,000 (accumulated postretirement benefit obligation at beginning of year), plus 10% of $84,000 (increase in obligation by plan amendment)

(b) 20-year amortization of original $300,000 transition obligation

(c) Straight-line amortization of prior service cost, based on average remaining years of service (12 years) of active plan participants before reaching full eligibility

Reconciliation of funded status:

	End of Year 1	Net Change	End of Year 2
Accumulated postretirement benefit obligation	$(325,000)	$(114,900)	$(439,900)
Plan assets at fair value	-0-		-0-
Funded status	(325,000)	(114,900)	(439,900)
Unrecognized prior service cost	-0-	77,000	77,000
Unrecognized transition obligation	285,000	(15,000)	270,000
Accrued postretirement benefit cost	$ (40,000)	$ (52,900)	$ (92,900)

Methods of amortizing prior service cost   FAS-106 provides a number of rules regarding the amortization of prior service cost, as follows:

- General rule
- Special rule if all or most employees are fully eligible
- Simplified computation
- Accelerated amortization

General rule: The general rule requires amortization of prior service cost in equal installments during each employee's remaining years of service until that employee reaches full eligibility under the new or amended plan (FAS-106, par. 51).

Special rule if all or most employees are fully eligible: If all or almost all employees are already fully eligible for benefits when the plan is initiated or amended, the employer amortizes prior service cost over the remaining life expectancy of those employees (FAS-106, par. 52).

Simplified computation: FAS-106 allows a simplified form of computation, provided it amortizes prior service cost more quickly than the methods described above. For example, instead of basing its amortization on the period during which each individual employee reaches full eligibility, an employer may amortize prior service cost over the *average* remaining years of service of all active plan participants until they reach full eligibility (FAS-106, par. 53).

Accelerated amortization: An enterprise uses an accelerated method of amortization if a history of plan amendments and other evidence indicates that the employer's economic benefits from the initiation or amendment of the plan will be exhausted before the employees reach full eligibility for postretirement benefits. In this situation, amortization should reflect the period during which the employer expects to receive economic benefits from the existence of the plan (FAS-106, par. 54).

Plan amendments that reduce obligation   If a plan amendment reduces the accumulated postretirement obligation, the reduction (a negative prior service cost) is amortized in accordance with the above rules after it is applied (*a*) to reduce any existing unrecognized (positive) prior service cost and (*b*) to reduce any unrecognized transition obligation (FAS-106, par. 55).

Gain or Loss Component

The approach to gains and losses in FAS-106 is similar to that in FAS-87. Gains or losses consist of certain types of changes in (*a*) the accumulated postretirement benefit obligation and (*b*) the plan assets. The changes may result from either (*a*) experience different from that assumed or (*b*) changes in assumptions (FAS-106, par. 56).

Gains and losses include amounts that have been realized (for example, the sale of a security) and amounts that have not been realized (for example, changes in the market value of plan assets) (FAS-106, par. 56).

Elements of the gain or loss component   The gain or loss component of net periodic postretirement benefit cost is the combination of three elements (FAS-106, par. 62):

- Plan asset gains and losses during the period
- Other gains and losses immediately realized
- Amortization of deferred gains and losses from previous periods

> ☞ **PRACTICE POINTER:** The gain or loss component of net postretirement benefit cost does not include the actual return on plan assets during the period, which is another component of net periodic postretirement benefit cost, discussed earlier in this chapter.
>
> The gain or loss component does include, among other items, the difference between the actual return and the expected return on plan assets, since this difference falls within the general concept of gains and losses according to FAS-106—changes resulting from experience different from that assumed or from changes in assumptions.

Plan asset gains and losses   Plan asset gains and losses are the difference between the actual return (including earnings and holding gains/losses) and the expected return for the same period (FAS-106, par. 57).

The computation of plan asset gains and losses starts with determining the expected return on plan assets, which is computed by multiplying the following two items: (1) the expected long-term rate of return on plan assets and (2) the market-related value of plan assets. Plan asset gains and losses include both changes reflected in the market-related value of plan assets and changes not yet reflected in the market-related value of plan assets (FAS-106, par. 58).

The market-related value may be either fair market value or a calculation that recognizes changes in fair market value systematically over a period of five years or less. The employer may use different methods of calculating market-related value for different categories of assets, but each category must be treated consistently during successive periods (FAS-106, par. 57).

FAS-106 requires plan asset gains and losses during the period to be included as a component of net periodic postretirement benefit cost. For purposes of financial statement disclosure, plan asset gains and losses are included in the "net total of other components" of net periodic postretirement benefit cost (FAS-106, par. 74b).

> **OBSERVATION:** As noted earlier, net periodic postretirement benefit cost includes (among other items): (a) plan asset gains and losses and (b) actual return on plan assets. The combined effect of these two items is equal to the expected return on plan assets.
>
> Plan asset gains and losses (excluding amounts not yet reflected in the market-related value of plan assets) are taken into account in computing the future expected return on plan assets. This year's plan asset gains and losses will therefore be reflected, in the computation of the expected return on plan assets, in future years' net periodic postretirement benefit cost. Plan asset gains and losses (excluding amounts not yet reflected in the market-related value of plan assets) are also taken into account in computing amortization of deferred gains and losses.

Other gains and losses immediately realized Immediate recognition of other types of gains and losses is required in some situations and permitted in others.

An employer recognizes an immediate gain or loss if it decides to deviate temporarily from its substantive plan, either by (*a*) forgiving a retrospective adjustment of the current or prior years' cost-sharing provisions as they relate to benefit costs already incurred by retirees or (*b*) otherwise changing the employer's share of benefit costs incurred in the current or prior periods (FAS-106, par. 61).

If immediate recognition of gains and losses is not required, an employer may elect to use a method that consistently recognizes gains and losses immediately, provided: (*a*) any gain that does not offset a loss previously recognized in income must first offset any unrecognized transition obligation and (*b*) any loss that does not offset a gain previously recognized in income must first offset any unrecognized transition asset (FAS-106, par. 60).

Amortization of deferred gains and losses from previous periods Any gains and losses not recognized immediately are deferred gains and losses. FAS-106 establishes a special formula to determine (*a*) whether an employer is required to amortize deferred gains and losses and (*b*) if amortization is required, the minimum amount of periodic amortization. FAS-106 allows other methods instead of those provided by the formula, if certain qualifications are met.

FAS-106 requires amortization of unrecognized gains and losses if the beginning-of-year balance of net unrecognized gain or loss (with a modification noted below) is more than a base figure used for comparison purposes (FAS-106, par. 59).

The base figure is 10% of the greater of the accumulated postretirement benefit obligation or the market-related value of plan assets.

For purposes of this comparison, the unrecognized gain or loss is modified, so as to exclude any plan asset gains or losses that have not yet been reflected in market-related value.

> ☞ **PRACTICE POINTER:** If unrecognized gains or losses are not greater than the base figure, they come within the 10% "corridor" and the employer need not recognize them. This procedure is similar to the corridor test for recognizing gains and losses on pensions in accordance with FAS-87.

If amortization is required under the formula, the amount to be amortized is the difference between the beginning-of-year balance of net unrecognized gain or loss (adjusted to exclude any plan asset gains or losses that have not yet been reflected in the market-related value) and the base figure.

The minimum amortization is the amount to be amortized, determined as above, divided by the average remaining service period of active plan participants. If all or almost all of the plan's participants are inactive, divide instead by the average remaining life expectancy of the inactive participants (FAS-106, par. 59).

Instead of using the minimum amortization method, an employer may use any other systematic method of amortization, provided that (a) the amortization for each period is at least as much as the amount determined by the minimum amortization method, (b) the method is used consistently, (c) the method applies consistently to gains and losses, and (d) the method is disclosed (FAS-106, par. 60).

Illustration of Gains and Losses

At the beginning of 19X5, Company L prepared the following projection of changes during that year:

	Prepaid Postretirement Benefit Cost	Accumulated Postretirement Benefit Obligation	Unrecognized Transition Obligation	Unrecognized Net Loss	Plan Assets
Beginning of year	$ 406,000	$(3,625,000)	$2,700,000	$ 302,500	$1,028,500
Recognition of components of net periodic postretirement benefit cost:					

Service cost	(180,000)	(180,000)			
Interest cost	(326,250)	(326,250)			
Amortization of transition obligation	(150,000)		(150,000)		
Amortization of unrecognized net loss	96,850				96,850
Expected return on plan assets [a]	(559,400)	(506,250)	(150,000)		96,850
Assets contributed to plan	956,250				956,250
Benefit payments from plan		450,000			(450,000)
Net change	396,850	(56,250)	(150,000)		603,100
End of year— projected	$ 802,850	$(3,681,250)	$2,550,000	$ 302,500	$1,631,600

(a) See Schedule 1.

As of the end of 19X5, Company L prepared the following worksheet and supporting schedules to reflect actual changes during the year:

	Projected 12/31/X5	Net Gain (Loss)	Actual 12/31/X5
Accumulated postretirement benefit obligation	$(3,681,250)	$ 118,630[b]	$(3,562,620)
Plan assets at fair value	1,631,600	(110,180)[c]	1,521,420
Funded status	(2,049,650)	8,450	(2,041,200)
Unrecognized net (gain) loss	302,500	(8,450)	294,050
Unrecognized transition obligation	2,550,000	—	2,550,000
Prepaid postretirement benefit cost	$ 802,850	$ -0-	$ 802,850

(b) Liability at year-end was $118,630 less than projected, because of changes in assumptions not detailed here.

(c) See Schedule 1.

Net Periodic Postretirement Benefit Cost

Service cost	$180,000
Interest cost	326,250
Actual loss on plan assets [(d)]	13,330
Amortization of transition obligation	150,000
Net amortization and deferral [(e)]	(110,180)
Net periodic postretirement benefit cost	$559,400

(d) See Schedule 3.
(e) See Schedule 4.

Schedule 1—Plan Assets

Expected long-term rate of return on plan assets	10%
Beginning balance, market-related value [(f)]	$ 968,500
Contributions to plan (end of year)	956,250
Benefits paid by plan	(450,000)
Expected return on plan assets	96,850
	1,571,600
20% of each of last five years' asset gains (losses)	(7,036)
Ending balance, market-related value	$ 1,564,564
Beginning balance, fair value of plan assets	$ 1,028,500
Contributions to plan	956,250
Benefits paid	(450,000)
Actual return (loss) on plan assets [(g)]	(13,330)
Ending balance, fair value of plan assets	$ 1,521,420
Deferred asset gain (loss) for year [(h)]	$ (110,180)
Gain (loss) not included in ending balance market-related value [(i)]	$ (43,144)

(f) This example adds 20% of each of the last five years' gains or losses.
(g) See Schedule 3.
(h) (Actual return on plan assets) – (expected return on plan assets). **Note:** The term *deferred asset gain (loss) for year* follows the terminology in the illustrations attached to FAS-106, although the text of FAS-106 refers to the same item as *plan asset gains and losses.*
(i) (Ending balance, fair value of plan assets) – (ending balance, market-related value of plan assets).

Schedule 2—Amortization of Unrecognized Net Gain or Loss

10% of beginning balance of accumulated postretirement benefit obligation	$ 362,500
10% of beginning balance of market-related value of plan assets (j)	96,850
Greater of the above	$ 362,500
Unrecognized net (gain) loss at beginning of year	$ 302,500
Asset gain (loss) not included in beginning balance of market-related value (k)	60,000
Amount subject to amortization	$ 362,500
Amount in excess of the corridor subject to amortization	None
Required amortization	None

(j) See Schedule 1.
(k) See Schedule 1.

Schedule 3—Actual Return or Loss on Plan Assets

Plan assets at fair value, beginning of year	$1,028,500
Plus: Assets contributed to plan	956,250
Less: Benefit payments from plan	(450,000)
	1,534,750
Less: Plan assets at fair value, end of year	(1,521,420)
Actual (return) loss on plan assets	$ 13,330

Schedule 4—Net Amortization and Deferral

Amortization of unrecognized net (gain) or loss (l)	$ -0-
Deferred asset gain (loss) for year (m)	(110,180)
Net amortization and deferral	$ (110,180)

(l) See Schedule 2.
(m) See Schedule 1.

Amortization of Transition Obligation/Asset Component

The final component of net periodic postretirement benefit cost is amortization of the unrecognized obligation or asset at the date of initial application of FAS-106.

MEASUREMENT OF PLAN ASSETS

Plan assets generally are stocks, bonds, and other investments. Such assets may include the participation rights in participating insurance contracts, but not other rights in insurance contracts. The employer's own securities may be included as plan assets, but only if they are transferable and otherwise meet the conditions under FAS-106 (FAS-106, par. 63).

Plan assets are increased by various means, including the employer's contributions, employees' contributions if the plan is contributory, and earnings from investing the contributed amounts. Plan assets are decreased by benefit payments, income taxes, and other expenses (FAS-106, par. 63).

All plan assets should be segregated and restricted for paying postretirement benefits. Usually, the assets are in a trust. Plan assets may be withdrawn only for the stated purposes of the plan. In limited circumstances, the plan may permit withdrawal when the plan's assets exceed its obligations and the employer has taken appropriate steps to satisfy existing obligations (FAS-106, par. 64).

If assets are not segregated or restricted effectively in some other way, they are not plan assets even though the employer intends to use them for paying postretirement benefits. Contributions that are accrued but not yet paid into the plan are not regarded as plan assets (FAS-106, par. 64).

For purposes of disclosure, FAS-106 requires the employer to use fair value as the measurement for all plan investments, including equity or debt securities, real estate, and other items. Fair value is the amount that reasonably could be expected to result from a current sale between a willing buyer and a willing seller. Value is not based on the estimated proceeds of a forced or liquidation sale (FAS-106, par. 65).

If an active market exists for the investment, fair value is measured by the market value. If no active market exists for the specific investment, but an active market exists for similar investments, the market value of those similar investments may provide helpful guidance on the market value of the plan's investment. If no active market exists for the investment or a similar one, the employer should consider basing fair value on a forecast of expected cash flows, discounted at a current rate commensurate with the risk involved (FAS-106, par. 65).

Plan assets used in plan operations, such as buildings, equipment, furniture and fixtures, and leasehold improvements, are measured at cost less accumulated depreciation or amortization (FAS-106, par. 66).

Insurance Contracts

Benefits covered by insurance contracts (defined below) are excluded from the accumulated postretirement benefit obligation. Insurance contracts are also excluded from plan assets, except for the amounts attributable to participation rights in participating insurance contracts.

Definition of Insurance Contracts

FAS-106 defines an *insurance contract* as a contract in which the insurance company unconditionally undertakes a legal obligation to provide specified benefits to specific individuals in return for a fixed premium. The contract must be irrevocable and must involve the transfer of significant risk from the employer (or the plan) to the insurance company. A contract does not qualify as an insurance contract if (*a*) the insurance company is a *captive insurer* doing business primarily with the employer and related parties or (*b*) there is any reasonable doubt that the insurance company will meet its obligations under the contract (FAS-106, par. 67).

Participating Insurance Contracts

Some contracts are *participating insurance contracts*, in which the purchaser (either the plan or the employer) participates in the experience of the insurance company. The purchaser's participation generally takes the form of a dividend that effectively reduces the cost of the plan. If, however, the employer's participation is so great that the employer retains all or most of the risks and rewards of the plan, the contract is not regarded as an insurance contract for purposes of FAS-106 (FAS-106, par. 68).

The purchase price of a participating contract ordinarily is higher than the price of a similar contract without the participation right. The difference between the price with and without the participation right is considered to be the cost of the participation right. The employer should regard this cost as an asset when purchased. At subsequent dates, the employer measures the participation right at its fair value if fair value can be estimated reasonably. Otherwise, the participation right is measured at its amortized cost, but this amount should not exceed the participation right's net realizable value. The cost is amortized systematically over the expected dividend period (FAS-106, par. 69).

Cost of Insurance

Insurance contracts, such as life insurance contracts, may be purchased during a period to cover postretirement benefits attributed to service by employees in the same period. In this situation, the cost of the benefits equals the cost of purchasing the insurance (after adjusting for the cost of any participation rights included in the contract) (FAS-106, par. 70).

Accordingly, if all postretirement benefits attributed to service by employees in the current period are covered by nonparticipating insurance contracts purchased during the same period, the cost of the benefits equals the cost of purchasing the insurance. If the benefits are only partially covered by nonparticipating insurance contracts, the uninsured portion of the benefits is accounted for in the same way as benefits under uninsured plans (FAS-106, par. 70).

Insurance Company Not Fully Bound

If the insurance company does not unconditionally undertake a legal obligation to pay specified benefits to specific individuals, the arrangement does not qualify as an insurance contract for purposes of FAS-106. The arrangement is accounted for as an investment at fair value (FAS-106, par. 71).

Fair value is presumed to equal the cash surrender value or conversion value, if any. In some cases, the best estimate of fair value is the contract value.

Measurement Date

The measurement date for plan assets and obligations is the financial statement date or an earlier date within three months, if such a date is used consistently from year to year. Information can be prepared ahead of the measurement date and projected forward to that date to adjust for events occurring between the preparation of the information and the measurement date (FAS-106, par. 72).

Net periodic postretirement benefit cost, as shown on interim and annual financial statements, generally is measured based on the assumptions carried over to the beginning of the current year from the previous year-end measurements. If, however, more recent measurements of plan assets and obligations are available, the employer should use them. Recent measurements may become available, for example, when a significant event occurs that requires a remeasurement, such as a plan amendment, settlement, or curtailment. Once a remeasurement has been made, the assumptions underlying that remeasurement should be used to remeasure net periodic postretirement benefit cost from the date of the significant event to the year-end measurement date (FAS-106, par. 73).

DISCLOSURES

The disclosure requirements of FAS-106 were replaced by FAS-132 and consolidated with the disclosure of information about pensions. They are covered in Chapter 34 of the 1999 *Miller GAAP Guide*.

EMPLOYERS WITH TWO OR MORE PLANS

FAS-106 deals with the questions of measurement and disclosure separately for an employer with two or more plans and for employers with one plan.

Aggregate Measurement

FAS-106 generally requires an employer with two or more plans to measure each plan separately. An employer may measure its plans as an aggregate rather than as separate plans, however, if the plans meet the following criteria (FAS-106, pars. 75 and 76):

1. The plans provide postretirement health-care benefits
2. The plans provide either of the following:
   a. Different benefits to the same group of employees
   b. The same benefits to different groups of employees
3. The plans are unfunded (without any plan assets)
4. The employer aggregates all of its plans that meet the preceding three tests.

An employer may make a separate aggregation of plans providing welfare benefits (that is, postretirement benefits other than health care), if requirements (2) through (4) above are met. However, a plan that has plan assets should not be aggregated with other plans, but should be measured separately (FAS-106, par. 76).

MULTIEMPLOYER PLANS

A *multiemployer plan* is one to which two or more unrelated employers contribute. Multiemployer plans generally result from *collective bargaining agreements*, and are administered by a joint board of trustees representing management and labor of all contributing employers. Sometimes these plans are called *joint trusts, Taft–Hartley*, or *union plans*. An employer may participate in a number of plans; for example, the employees may belong to a number of unions. Numerous employers may participate in a multiemployer plan. Often the employers are in the same industry, but sometimes the employers are in different industries, and the only common element among the employers is that their employees belong to the same labor union (FAS-106, par. 80).

The assets contributed by one employer may be used to provide benefits to employees of other employers, since the assets contributed by one employer are not segregated from those contributed by other employers. Even though the plan provides defined benefits to employees of all the employers, the plan typically requires a defined contribution from each participating employer, but the amount of an employer's obligation may be changed by events affecting other participating employers and their employees (FAS-106, par. 79).

A multiemployer plan can exist even without the involvement of a labor union. For example, a national not-for-profit organization may organize a multiemployer plan for itself and its local chapters.

Accounting for Multiemployer Plans

Distinctive accounting requirements apply to an employer that participates in a multiemployer plan. The employer recognizes as net postretirement benefit cost the contribution required for the period, including cash and the fair value of noncash contributions. The employer recognizes as a liability any unpaid contributions required for the period (FAS-106, par. 81).

> **OBSERVATION:**
> 1. This accounting resembles that required for the single employer that has a *defined contribution plan* (see section titled "Defined Contribution Plans").
> 2. By participating in a multiemployer plan, an employer that has a *defined benefit plan* accounts for it essentially as if it were a *defined contribution plan.* The financing of the plan is, in effect, off-balance-sheet.

The following disclosures are required for multiemployer plans, separate from disclosures for any single-employer plan (FAS-106, par. 82):

- Description of each multiemployer plan, including categories of employees covered, type of benefits provided (for example, whether the plan is a defined benefit or defined contribution plan), and the nature and effect of significant matters affecting comparability of the information for all periods shown on the financial statements.

- Amount of postretirement cost recognized during the period, if this information is available.

> **OBSERVATION:** The information may be unavailable if, for example, (a) a multiemployer plan provides health and welfare benefits to active employees as well as to retirees and (b) the employer is unable to determine how much of its contributions to the plan are attributable to postretirement benefits.

If information about the amount of postretirement cost recognized during the period is not available, the employer should disclose the total required contribution for the period to the plan for general health and welfare benefits for active employees as well as retired employees (FAS-106, par. 82).

Withdrawal from Multiemployer Plans

When an employer withdraws from a multiemployer plan, the employer may be contractually liable to pay into the plan a portion of its unfunded accumulated postretirement benefit obligation.

> **OBSERVATION:** Contractual obligations are the only ones facing the employer that withdraws from a multiemployer **postretirement** benefit plan. In contrast, an employer that withdraws from a multiemployer **pension** plan is subject not only to contractual obligations, but also to statutory ob-ligations under the Multiemployer Pension Plan Amendments Act of 1980.

An employer should apply FAS-5 if withdrawal from the plan is probable or reasonably possible, and the employer will incur an obligation as a result (FAS-106, par. 83).

Obligation under "Maintenance of Benefits" Clause

An employer should also apply FAS-5 if it is probable or reasonably possible that the employer's contribution to the multiemployer plan will increase during the remainder of the contract period under a "maintenance of benefits" clause, to make up for a shortfall in the funding of the plan to assure the full level of benefits described in the plan (FAS-106, par. 83).

MULTIPLE-EMPLOYER PLANS

A multiple-employer plan is distinct from a multiemployer plan. In a *multiple-employer* plan, individual employers combine their single-employer plans for pooling assets for investment purposes, or for reducing the costs of administration. The participating employers may have different benefit formulas; each employer's contributions to the plan are based on that employer's benefit formula. These plans generally are not the result of collective bargaining agreements.

Each employer should account for its interest in a multiple-employer plan as if that interest were a single-employer plan (FAS-106, par. 84).

> **OBSERVATION:** If an employer is a participant in a multiple-employer plan, the employer should consider disclosing this fact, as well as the other information included in the required disclosures about single-employer plans.

PLANS OUTSIDE THE UNITED STATES

FAS-106 applies to plans outside as well as inside the United States. The effective date is extended to fiscal years beginning after December 15, 1994, for plans outside the United States. If the accumulated postretirement obligation of the plans outside the United States is significant in proportion to the total of all the employer's postretirement benefit plans, the employer should make separate disclosure of the plans outside the United States. Otherwise, the employer may make combined disclosure of plans outside and inside the United States (FAS-106, par. 85).

> **OBSERVATION:**
> 1. FAS-106 does not define *outside the United States*. The following factors, among others, may be relevant: (a) where all or most of the employees and beneficiaries are located and (b) which country's law governs the relationships among employees, beneficiaries, and the employer.
> 2. If a plan is governed by the law of a foreign country that confers vested rights on employees, the employer may have to include this information in the description of the substantive plan, included in the disclosures required by FAS-106.

BUSINESS COMBINATIONS

If an employer sponsors a single-employer defined benefit postretirement plan, and the employer is acquired in a business combination treated as a purchase, the allocation of the purchase price must reflect the existence of the plan, once FAS-106 is adopted. To do this, the allocation should reflect either (a) a liability (for the excess of the accumulated postretirement benefit obligation over the plan assets) or (b) an asset (for the excess of the plan assets over the accumulated postretirement benefit obligation) (FAS-106, par. 86).

For purposes of this allocation, plan assets are measured at fair value. The accumulated postretirement benefit obligation is measured based on the benefits attributable to employee service rendered to the acquired employer before consummation of the business combination. This amount should be adjusted to reflect (a) any changes in assumptions based on the purchaser's assessment of future events and (*b*) any changes the purchaser makes in the substantive plan (FAS-106, par. 86).

Benefit Improvements Attributed to Prior Service

If benefits of an existing plan are improved in connection with a business combination treated as a purchase, and all or part of the improvement is attributable to employee service prior to the consummation date of the purchase, the accounting depends on whether the improvement was a condition of the purchase agreement.

If the improvement was a condition of the agreement, the improvement should be accounted for as part of the purchase agreement, and not as prior service cost, even though all or part of the improvement is attributable to prior service. On the other hand, if the improvement was not a condition of the agreement, the improvement should be accounted for as prior service cost to the extent the improvement is attributable to prior service (FAS-106, par. 87).

Termination or Curtailment

If a postretirement benefit plan is likely to be terminated or curtailed when an employer is acquired in a business combination accounted for as a purchase, the effect of the anticipated termination or curtailment should be taken into account in measuring the accumulated postretirement benefit obligation at the time of acquisition (FAS-106, par. 87).

Anticipate Additional Liabilities Only if Certain or Probable

In connection with a purchase-type acquisition, the purchaser should anticipate additional liabilities only if their occurrence is either (*a*) certain (for example, when the additional liability is a condition of the acquisition agreement) or (*b*) probable (as indicated by the circumstances).

> **OBSERVATION:** The "Basis for Conclusions" indicates that, in the context of purchase-type acquisitions, an enterprise participating in a **multiemployer** plan should not recognize additional liabilities to the plan, unless specific conditions exist that make additional liabilities probable. The FASB was not convinced that an obligation for future contributions to a multiemployer plan ordinarily exists, or that an employer should recognize any contractual withdrawal liability unless withdrawal is probable.

Elimination of Unrecognized Items

When an employer applies the preceding provisions for business combinations, the result will be the elimination of the following preexisting items of the acquired employer:

- Unrecognized net gain or loss
- Unrecognized prior service cost
- Unrecognized transition obligation or transition asset

After the acquisition, the difference between the amount contributed and the net periodic postretirement benefit cost will reduce the liability or asset recognized at the time of the acquisition, to the extent the net obligation assumed or the net asset acquired is taken into account in determining the amount of contributions to the plan (FAS-106, par. 88).

SETTLEMENT AND CURTAILMENT OF A POSTRETIREMENT BENEFIT OBLIGATION

According to FAS-106, a *settlement* is a transaction that has the following characteristics (FAS-106, par. 90):

- Is an irrevocable action
- Relieves the employer (or the plan) of primary responsibility for the postretirement benefit obligation
- Eliminates significant risks related to the obligation and the assets used to put the settlement into effect

Settlements take place, for example, in the following situations:

- The employer makes lump-sum cash payments to plan participants, buying their rights to receive future specified postretirement benefits.
- The employer purchases long-term nonparticipating insurance contracts to cover the accumulated postretirement benefit obligation for some or all of the participants in the plan (but the insurance company cannot be under the employer's control).

Settlements do *not* take place, however, in the following situations (FAS-106, par. 91):

- The employer purchases an insurance contract from an insurance company controlled by the employer. This does not qualify as a settlement because the employer is still exposed to risk through its relationship with the insurance company.

- The employer invests in high-quality fixed-income securities with principal and income payment dates similar to the estimated due dates of benefits. This does not qualify as a settlement because (*a*) the investment decision can be revoked, (*b*) the purchase of the securities does not relieve the employer or the plan of primary responsibility for the postretirement benefit obligation, and (*c*) the purchase of the securities does not eliminate significant risks related to the postretirement benefit obligation.

Accounting for a Plan Settlement

Maximum Gain or Loss

When a postretirement benefit obligation is settled, the maximum gain or loss to be recognized in income is the unrecognized gain or loss plus any unrecognized transition asset. This maximum gain or loss includes any gain or loss resulting from the remeasurement of plan assets and of the accumulated postretirement benefit obligation at the time of settlement (FAS-106, par. 92).

Settlement Gain or Loss When Entire Obligation Is Settled

If an employer settles the entire accumulated postretirement benefit obligation, a further distinction is made depending on whether the maximum amount subject to recognition is a gain or a loss.

If the maximum amount is a gain, the amount of this gain first reduces any unrecognized transition obligation, then any excess gain is recognized in income. If the maximum amount is a loss, the full amount of this loss is recognized in income (FAS-106, par. 93).

Settlement Gain or Loss When Only Part of Obligation Is Settled

If an employer settles only part of the accumulated postretirement benefit obligation, the employer recognizes in income a pro rata portion of the amount of gain or loss that would have been recognized if the entire obligation had been settled. The pro rata portion equals the percentage by which the partial settlement reduces the accumulated postretirement benefit obligation (FAS-106, par. 93).

Participating Insurance

If an employer settles the obligation by purchasing a participating insurance contract, the cost of the participation right is deducted from the maximum gain but not from the maximum loss, before the employer determines the amount to be recognized in income (FAS-106, par. 94).

Settlements at Lower Cost Than Current Cost of Service and Interest

FAS-106 defines the *cost of a settlement* as follows (FAS-106, par. 95):

- If the settlement is for cash, its cost is the amount of cash paid to plan participants.
- If the settlement uses nonparticipating insurance contracts, its cost is the cost of the contracts.
- If the settlement uses participating insurance contracts, its cost is the cost of the contracts, less the amount attributed to participation rights.

If the cost of all settlements during a year is no more than the combined amount of service cost and interest cost components of net postretirement benefit cost for the same year, FAS-106 permits but does not require the employer to recognize gain or loss for those settlements. The employer should apply a consistent policy each year (FAS-106, par. 95).

Accounting for a Plan Curtailment

A *curtailment* is an event that either (*a*) significantly reduces the expected years of future service of active plan participants or (*b*) eliminates the accrual of defined benefits for some or all of the future services of a significant number of active plan participants. The following events are examples of curtailments (FAS-106, par. 96):

- Termination of employees' services earlier than anticipated. (This may or may not relate to the closing of a facility or the discontinuation of a segment of the employer's business.)
- Termination or suspension of a plan, so that employees no longer earn additional benefits for future service. (If the plan is suspended, future service may be counted toward eligibility for benefits accumulated based on past service.)

Gain and Loss Recognition

Under the general provisions of FAS-106 for plans that continue without curtailment, the employer should recognize prior service cost on an amortized basis, on the theory that the employer receives economic benefits from the future services of employees covered by the plan.

When a plan is curtailed, the employer's expectation of receiving benefits from future services of its employees is reduced. Accordingly, curtailment requires the employer to recognize as a loss all or part of the remaining balance of unrecognized prior service cost. In this context, unrecognized prior service cost includes the cost of plan amendments and any unrecognized transition obligation (FAS-106, par. 97).

Curtailment Resulting from Termination of Employees

If a curtailment occurs as the result of the termination of a significant number of employees who were plan participants, the curtailment loss consists of the following components (FAS-106, par. 97):

1. The portion of the remaining unrecognized prior service cost (relating to this and any prior plan amendment) attributable to the previously estimated number of remaining future years of service of all terminated employees, **plus**

2. The portion of the remaining unrecognized transition obligation attributable to the previously estimated number of remaining future years of service, but only of the terminated employees who were participants in the plan at the date of transition to FAS-106

Curtailment Resulting from Terminating Accrual of Additional Benefits for Future Services

If a curtailment results from terminating the accrual of additional benefits for the future services of a significant number of employees, the curtailment loss consists of the following components (FAS-106, par. 97):

1. *The **pro rata** amount of the remaining unrecognized prior service cost*—This amount is based on the portion of the remaining expected years of service in the amortization period that originally was attributable to the employees (a) who were plan participants at the date of the plan amendment and (b) whose future accrual of benefits has been terminated, **plus**

2. *The **pro rata** amount of the remaining unrecognized transition obligation*—This amount is based on the portion of the remaining years of service of all participants who were active at the

date of transition to FAS-106, that originally was attributable to the remaining expected future years of service of the employees whose future accrual of benefits has been terminated.

Changes in Accumulated Postretirement Benefit Obligation

A curtailment may cause a gain by decreasing the accumulated postretirement benefit obligation, or a loss by increasing that obligation.

If a curtailment decreases the accumulated obligation, the gain from this decrease is first used to offset any unrecognized net loss, and the excess is a curtailment gain. If a curtailment increases the accumulated obligation, the loss from this increase is first used to offset any unrecognized net gain, and the excess is a curtailment loss. In this context, any remaining unrecognized transition asset is regarded as an unrecognized net gain, and is combined with the unrecognized net gain or loss arising after transition to FAS-106 (FAS-106, par. 98).

If a curtailment produces a net loss as the combined effect of the above calculations regarding unrecognized prior service cost and the accumulated postretirement benefit obligation, this combined net loss is recognized in income when it is *probable* that a curtailment will occur and the net effect of the curtailment is reasonably estimable. If the sum of these effects results in a net gain, however, the net gain is recognized in income when the affected employees terminate or the plan suspension or amendment is adopted.

Illustration of Curtailment

Company B reduced its workforce, including a significant number of employees who had been accumulating benefits under the postretirement benefit plan. An analysis of the terminated employees revealed:

1. At the time of curtailment, the terminated employees represented 22% of the *remaining years of expected service* of all employees who had been plan participants at the employer's date of transition.

2. At the time of curtailment, the terminated employees represented 18% of the *remaining years of service prior to full eligibility* of all employees who had been plan participants at the date of a prior plan amendment.

Company B's worksheet computation of the curtailment gain or loss is as follows:

	Before Curtailment	Curtailment	After Curtailment
Accumulated postretirement benefit obligation	$(514,000)	$108,000	$(406,000)
Plan assets at fair value	146,000		146,000
Funded status	(368,000)	108,000	(260,000)
Unrecognized net gain	(89,150)		(89,150)
Unrecognized prior service cost (a)	66,000	(11,880)	54,120
Unrecognized transition obligation (b)	390,000	(85,800)	304,200
(Accrued)/prepaid postretirement benefit cost	$ (1,150)	$ 10,320	$ 9,170

(a) Effect of curtailment is 18% of $66,000 (unrecognized prior service cost).
(b) Effect of curtailment is 22% of $390,000 (unrecognized transition obligation).

Relationship of Settlements and Curtailments to Other Events

An event may be either a settlement, or a curtailment, or both at the same time (FAS-106, par. 100).

- A curtailment occurs, but not a settlement, if the expected future benefits are eliminated for some plan participants (for example, because their employment is terminated), but the plan continues to exist, to pay benefits, to invest assets, and to receive contributions.

- A settlement occurs, but not a curtailment, if an employer purchases nonparticipating insurance contracts to cover the accumulated postretirement benefit obligation, while continuing to provide defined benefits for future service (either in the same plan or in a successor plan).

- A termination, or in effect both a settlement and curtailment, occurs if an employer settles its obligation and terminates the plan without establishing a successor defined benefit plan to take its place. This occurs whether the employees continue to work for the employer or not.

Illustration of Partial Settlement and Full Curtailment Resulting from Sale of Line of Business

Company C sold a line of business to Company D. Company C has a separate postretirement benefit plan that provides benefits to retirees of the division that is sold. In connection with the sale:

1. Company C terminated all employees of the sold division (a full curtailment).
2. Company D hired most of the employees.
3. Company D assumed the accumulated postretirement benefit obligation of $160,000 for postretirement benefits related to the former employees of Company C hired by Company D, and Company C retained the obligation for its current retirees (a partial settlement).
4. The plan trustee transferred $200,000 of plan assets to Company D, consisting of $160,000 for the settlement of the accumulated postretirement benefit obligation and $40,000 as an excess contribution.
5. Company C determined that its gain on the sale of the division was $600,000, before considering any of the effects of the sale on the postretirement benefit plan.

Company C's accounting policy is to determine the effects of a curtailment before determining the effects of a settlement when both events occur simultaneously.

For Company C, the net loss from the curtailment is $456,000, which is recognized with the $600,000 gain resulting from the disposal of the division. The effect of the curtailment is determined as follows:

	Before Curtailment	Curtailment-Related Effects Resulting from Sale	After Curtailment
Accumulated postretirement benefit obligation	$(514,000)	$ (20,000) [a]	$(534,000)
Plan assets at fair value	220,000		220,000
Funded status	(294,000)	(20,000)	(314,000)
Unrecognized net gain	(99,150)	20,000 [a]	(79,150)
Unrecognized prior service cost	66,000	(66,000) [b]	—
Unrecognized transition obligation	390,000	(390,000) [c]	—
(Accrued)/prepaid postretirement benefit cost	$ 62,850	$(456,000)	$(393,150)

(a) Loss from earlier-than-expected retirement of fully eligible employees (not detailed here)

(b) 100% (reduction in remaining years for service to full eligibility) of the unrecognized prior service cost

(c) 100% (reduction in remaining years for service to full eligibility) of the unrecognized transition obligation

The $16,255 loss related to the settlement and transfer of plan assets that is recognized with the gain from the sale is determined as follows:

	After Curtailment	Settlement and Transfer of Plan Assets	After Settlement
Accumulated postretirement benefit obligation	$(534,000)	$160,000	$(374,000)
Plan assets at fair value	220,000	(200,000)	20,000
Funded status	(314,000)	(40,000)	(354,000)
Unrecognized net gain	(79,150)	23,745 (d)	(55,405)
Unrecognized prior service cost	—	—	—
Unrecognized transition obligation	—	—	—
Accrued postretirement benefit cost	$(393,150)	$ (16,255)	$(409,405)

(d) The unrecognized net gain is computed as follows:

Step 1. Compute the percentage of the accumulated postretirement benefit obligation settled to the total accumulated postretirement benefit obligation ($160,000/$534,000 = 30%).

Step 2. Maximum gain is measured as the unrecognized net gain subsequent to transition plus any unrecognized transition asset ($79,150 + $0 = $79,150).

Step 3. The settlement gain is 30% of $79,150 = $23,745.

MEASUREMENT OF THE EFFECTS OF TERMINATION BENEFITS

If an employer offers postretirement benefits as special termination benefits that are not required by any preexisting contract, the employer recognizes a liability and a loss when the employees accept the offer and the amount is reasonably estimable. If the employer is contractually obliged to provide postretirement benefits as termination benefits, the employer recognizes a liability and a loss when it is probable that benefits will be paid and the amount is reasonably estimable (FAS-106, par. 101).

If an employer offers special or contractual termination benefits and curtails the postretirement benefit plan at the same time, FAS-106 requires the employer to account separately for the termination benefits and the curtailment (FAS-106, par. 101).

The amount of the liability and loss to be recognized when employees accept an offer of termination benefits in the form of postretirement benefits is determined as follows (FAS-106, par. 102):

Step 1.   Determine the accumulated postretirement benefit obligation for those employees (without including any special termination benefits), on the assumption that (*a*) any of those employees who are not yet fully eligible for benefits will terminate as soon as they become fully eligible, and (*b*) any of those employees who are fully eligible will retire immediately.

Step 2.   Adjust the accumulated postretirement benefit obligation as computed in Step 1 to reflect the special termination benefits.

Step 3.   Subtract the amount in Step 1 from the amount in Step 2.

DISPOSAL OF A SEGMENT

If an employer recognizes a gain or loss from settlement or curtailment of a postretirement benefit plan, or from offering postretirement benefits as special termination benefits, and the gain or loss is directly related to the disposal of a segment of a business or a portion of a line of business, the gain or loss should be included in determining the gain or loss from the disposal. The net gain or loss attributable to the disposal is recognized in accordance with APB-30 (Reporting the Results of Operations) (FAS-106, par. 103).

DEFINED CONTRIBUTION PLANS

A *defined contribution plan* provides an individual account for each participant, and specifies how to determine the amount to be contributed to each individual's account. The plan does not specify the amount of postretirement benefits to be received by any individual. This amount is determined by the amount of contributions, the return on the investment of the amount contributed, and any forfeitures of the benefits of other plan participants that are allocated to the individual's account (FAS-106, par. 104).

Accounting for Contributions

A defined contribution plan may require the employer to contribute to the plan only for periods in which an employee renders services, or the employer may be required to continue making payments for periods after the employee retires or terminates employment. To the extent an employer's contribution is made in the same period as the employee renders services, the employer's net periodic postretirement benefit cost equals the amount of contributions required for that period. If the plan requires the employer to continue contributions after the employee retires or terminates, the employer should make accruals during the employee's service period of the estimated amount of contributions to be made after the employee's retirement or termination (FAS-106, par. 105).

Disclosure

The disclosure requirements for defined contribution plans are consolidated with disclosure requirements for both pension and other postretirement plans. They are covered in Chapter 34 of the 1999 *Miller GAAP Guide*.

INTERIM FINANCIAL STATEMENTS

An employer may have to determine how to amortize its unrecognized transition obligation in interim financial statements if the employer anticipates recognition of an additional amount of this transition obligation later in the year because cumulative payments are likely to exceed cumulative accruals after the transition date. The interim statements should be based on the estimated amount to be amortized during the year, including any additional amounts the employer expects to recognize during the year because of cumulative payments exceeding cumulative accruals after the transition, with the following exception: The effects of a settlement should be recognized when the settlement itself is recognized, and should not be anticipated in interim statements (FAS-106, par. 113).

If the estimates reflected in an interim statement are revised by the time the next interim statement is prepared, the effects of the revision are recognized during the remainder of the fiscal year. The annual statement should reflect the employer's final determination of the amount of the unrecognized transition obligation to be amortized. Any difference between the year-end amount and the amounts shown in interim statements is recognized immediately (FAS-106, par. 113).

POSTEMPLOYMENT BENEFITS

FAS-112 specifies GAAP for postemployment benefits and generally applies to benefits provided to former or inactive employees, their beneficiaries, and covered dependents after employment, but before retirement. Benefits may be provided in cash or in kind and may be paid as a result of a disability, layoff, death, or other event. Benefits may be paid immediately upon cessation of active employment, or over a specified period of time.

Postemployment benefits that meet the following conditions of FAS-43 shall be accounted for in accordance with that Statement (FAS-112, par. 6).

1. The employer's obligation relating to employees' rights to receive compensation for future compensated absences is attributable to employees' services already rendered.

2. The obligation relates to rights that vest or accumulate.

3. Payment of the compensation is probable.

4. The amount can be estimated reasonably.

Postemployment benefits that are covered by FAS-112 but do not meet the above criteria of FAS-43 are accounted for in accordance with FAS-5. FAS-5 requires recognition of a loss contingency, including a liability for postemployment benefits, when the following conditions are met (FAS-112, par. 6):

1. Information available prior to issuance of the financial statements indicates that it is probable that an asset had been impaired or a liability incurred at the date of the financial statements.

2. The amount of loss can be reasonably estimated.

If an obligation for postemployment benefits is not accrued in accordance with either FAS-43 or FAS-5 only because the amount cannot be estimated, the financial statements shall disclose that fact (FAS-112, par. 7).

CHAPTER 37
PRODUCT FINANCING ARRANGEMENTS

CONTENTS

CHAPTER 37
PRODUCT FINANCING
ARRANGEMENTS

OVERVIEW

A *product financing arrangement* is a transaction in which an enterprise sells and agrees to repurchase inventory at a purchase price equal to the original sale price plus carrying and financing costs, or other similar transaction. In certain circumstances, a transaction labeled a *sale* is, in substance, a product financing arrangement and should be treated as such.

GAAP for product financing arrangements are included in the following pronouncement:

FAS-49   Accounting for Product Financing Arrangements

CROSS-REFERENCES

1999 MILLER GAAP GUIDE: Chapter 24, "Interest Costs Capitalized"; Chapter 32, "Long-Term Obligations"

BACKGROUND

Product financing arrangements usually provide for one entity to obtain inventory or product for another entity (the sponsor), which agrees to purchase the inventory or product at specific prices over a specific period. The agreed-upon prices usually include financing and holding costs. The following are examples of common types of product financing arrangements (FAS-49, par. 3):

1. A sponsor sells inventory or product to another entity and in a related arrangement agrees to buy the inventory or product back.

2. An entity agrees to purchase a product or inventory for a sponsor, who, in a related arrangement, agrees to buy the product or inventory from the first entity.

3. A sponsor, by arrangement, controls the product or inventory purchased or held by another entity.

In all of the above examples of product financing arrangements, the sponsor agrees to purchase, over a specified period, the product or inventory from the other entity at prearranged prices. The substance of a product financing arrangement, regardless of its legal form, is that of a financing arrangement rather than a sale or purchase by the sponsor.

> ☛ **PRACTICE POINTER:** Distinguishing a product financing arrangement from the outright sale of products may require careful professional judgment. Usually it will require an analysis and consideration of two related transactions rather than a single transaction. For example, if a sponsor sells inventory or product to another entity and in a separate agreement contracts to buy the inventory or product back, the initial transaction may appear to be a sale. Only when the two transactions (i.e., the "sale" and the later repurchase) are combined is the true substance of the transaction apparent. In applying GAAP for product financing arrangements, an important dimension is the follow-through analysis and understanding of the subsequent transaction.

Other factors that may be present in a product financing arrangement are (FAS-49, par. 4):

1. The entity that provides the financing arrangement to the sponsor is an existing trust, nonbusiness entity, credit grantor, or was formed for the sole purpose of providing the financing arrangement to the sponsor.

2. Small quantities of the product involved in the financing arrangement may be sold by the financing entity, but most of the product is ultimately used or sold by the sponsor.

3. The product is stored on the sponsor's premises.

4. The sponsor guarantees the debt of the other entity.

For purposes of FAS-49, unmined or unharvested natural resources and financial instruments are not considered products. Thus, they are not covered by the provisions of FAS-49 (FAS-49, par. 5).

> **OBSERVATION:** No mention is made in FAS-49 as to how a product financing arrangement involving unmined or unhar-

vested natural resources should be accounted for. For example, X Company enters into a financing arrangement with Y Company wherein Y Company acquires 10,000 acres of unharvested timberlands for the sole benefit of X Company. X Company guarantees the bank loan that was necessary to acquire the timberlands and agrees to purchase the processed timber from Y Company at specified prices over a specified period. The specified prices include (a) the cost of the timber, (b) processing costs, (c) interest costs on the bank loan, and (d) a handling fee. Only the standing timber was purchased and not the land.

It appears that the provisions of FAS-49 are appropriate for this type of transaction, but FAS-49 does not expressly cover this situation.

In a product financing arrangement, the specified prices that the sponsor must pay cannot be subject to change except for fluctuations because of finance and holding costs. The specified prices may be stated or determinable by reference to the substance of the arrangement, such as (*a*) resale price guarantees or (*b*) options that, in substance, compel or require the sponsor to purchase the product. In addition, the cost of the product and related costs to the other entity must be covered substantially by the specified prices that the seller must pay for the product. Related costs include interest, holding costs, and other fees charged by the other entity (FAS-49, par. 5).

ACCOUNTING FOR PRODUCT FINANCING ARRANGEMENTS

An arrangement that contains the characteristics of a product financing arrangement is accounted for by the sponsor of the arrangement as follows (FAS-49, par. 8):

1. If an entity buys a product from a sponsor and in a related arrangement agrees to sell the product, or a processed product containing the original product, back to the sponsor, no sale is recorded and the product remains an asset on the sponsor's books. Also, the sponsor records a liability in the amount of the proceeds received from the other entity under the provisions of the product financing arrangement.

2. If an entity buys a product for a sponsor's benefit and the sponsor agrees, in a related arrangement, to buy the product, or a processed product containing the original product, back from the other entity, an asset and the related liability are recorded by the sponsor at the time the other entity acquires the product.

Excluding processing costs, the difference between (*a*) the regular product cost the sponsor would have paid if there were no product financing arrangement and (*b*) the cost the sponsor actually pays under the terms of the product financing arrangement is accounted for by the sponsor as financing and holding costs. These financing and holding costs are recorded on the books of the sponsor in accordance with its regular accounting policies for such costs, even though the costs are incurred and paid directly by the other entity (FAS-49, par. 9).

Separately identified interest costs that the sponsor pays as part of the specified prices may qualify for interest capitalization under FAS-34 (Capitalization of Interest Cost). If not, the separately identified interest costs actually paid by the sponsor are included in the total interest costs incurred during the period (FAS-49, par. 9).

Illustration of Accounting for Product Financing Arrangements

Assume that each of the following situations meets the definition of a product financing arrangement (PFA) in accordance with FAS-49. In each situation, Walsh is the sponsor and Foster is the purchaser. Following are the appropriate journal entries for Walsh.

Case 1: Walsh sells inventory costing $800 to Foster for $1,000 and agrees to repurchase the same inventory for $1,050 in 30 days.

Cash (or receivable)	$1,000	
Due to Foster under PFA		$1,000
Inventory under PFA	800	
Inventory		800

Case 2: Walsh arranges for Foster to purchase inventory costing $1,000 from a third party and agrees to purchase that inventory from Foster for $1,050 in 30 days.

Inventory under PFA	$1,000	
Due to Foster under PFA		$1,000

Case 3: Walsh sells inventory costing $700 to Foster for $800 and agrees to a resale price of $1,000 to outside parties.

Cash (or receivable)	$800	
Due to Foster under PFA		$800
Inventory under PFA	700	
Inventory		700

Case 4: Walsh arranges for Foster to acquire inventory from an outside party for $750 and guarantees the resale price to outside parties for $850.

Inventory under PFA	$750	
Due to Foster under PFA		$750

CHAPTER 38
PROPERTY TAXES

CONTENTS

CHAPTER 38
PROPERTY TAXES

OVERVIEW

GAAP for real and personal property taxes are found in the following pronouncement:

ARB-43   Chapter 10A, Real and Personal Property Taxes

Generally, the basis for recognizing expense for property taxes is monthly accrual on the taxpayers' books over the fiscal period of the taxing authority for which the taxes are levied. At the end of the accounting period, the financial statements will show the appropriate accrual or prepayment.

> **OBSERVATION:** Accounting Research Bulletins were not intended to be officially promulgated GAAP at the time they were adopted by the Committee on Accounting Procedure. Instead, they reflected the views of the members and were intended as general guidance. ARBs were elevated to the status of GAAP by the Accounting Principles Board. As a result, obsolete and sometimes inappropriate material from ARBs now constitute GAAP. Moreover, ARBs were developed in an era in which the emphasis was primarily on revenue and expense reporting. That viewpoint contrasts with the asset–liability viewpoint of today. The asset–liability perspective of the FASB Concepts Statements suggests that a liability be measured for real and personal property taxes at the end of each reporting year. The amount of expense is the difference between two liability amounts.

CROSS-REFERENCES

1999 MILLER GAAP GUIDE: Chapter 9, "Current Assets and Current Liabilities"; Chapter 21, "Income Taxes"; Chapter 26, "Interim Financial Reporting"

1999 MILLER GOVERNMENTAL GAAP GUIDE: Chapter 9, "Revenues"

BACKGROUND

FASB Concepts Statements constitute the FASB's conceptual framework. In CON-6 (Elements of Financial Statements), *liabilities* are defined as probable future sacrifices of economic benefits arising from present obligations of a particular entity to transfer assets or provide services to other entities in the future as a result of past transactions or events. A liability has three essential characteristics:

1. It embodies a present duty or responsibility to one or more other entities that entails settlement by probable future transfer of assets at a specified or determinable date, on occurrence of a specific event, or on demand.

2. The duty or responsibility obligates a particular entity, leaving it little or no discretion to avoid the future sacrifice.

3. The transaction or other event obligating the entity has already happened.

Unlike excise tax, income tax, and Social Security tax, which are directly related to particular business events, real and personal property taxes are based on an assessed valuation of property as of a given date, as determined by law. For this reason, the legal liability for such taxes generally is considered to accrue when a specific event occurs, rather than over a period of time. Following are several dates that have been suggested as the point in time in which property taxes legally accrue (ARB-43, Ch. 10A, par. 2):

1. Assessment date
2. Beginning of the taxing authority's fiscal year
3. End of the taxing authority's fiscal year
4. Date on which the tax becomes a lien on the property
5. Date the tax is levied
6. Date(s) the tax is payable
7. Date the tax becomes delinquent
8. Tax period appearing on a tax bill

The date most widely accepted as obligating the entity is the date of assessment of the taxes by the appropriate taxing authority.

ACCOUNTING AND REPORTING STANDARDS

Although many states have different laws or precedents as to when the legal liability accrues for real and personal property taxes, the general rule is that it accrues on the date the taxes are assessed (ARB-43, Ch. 10A, par. 4). The exact amount of tax may not be known on the assessment date, however, and a reasonable estimate must be made. The inability to determine the exact amount of real and personal property taxes is not an acceptable reason for not recognizing an existing tax liability (ARB-43, Ch. 10A, par. 9).

In those cases in which the accrued amount is subject to a great deal of uncertainty, the liability should be described as estimated. Whether the amount of the accrued tax liability for real and personal property taxes is known or estimated, it should be reported as a current liability in the balance sheet (ARB-43, Ch. 10A, par. 16).

A monthly accrual over the fiscal period of the taxing authority is considered the most acceptable basis for recording real and personal property taxes. This results in the appropriate accrual or prepayment at any closing date (ARB-43, Ch. 10A, par. 14). An adjustment to the estimated tax liability of a prior year is made when the exact amount is determined. This adjustment is made in the income statement of the period in which the exact amount is determined, either as an adjustment to the current year's provision or as a separate item on the income statement (ARB-43, Ch. 10A, par. 11).

In most circumstances, however, real and personal property taxes are considered an expense of doing business and are reported in the appropriate income statement (*a*) as an operating expense, (*b*) as a deduction from income, or (*c*) allocated to several expense accounts, such as manufacturing overhead and general and administrative expenses. As a general rule, real and personal property taxes should not be combined with income taxes (ARB-43, Ch. 10A, pars. 17 and 18).

☞ **PRACTICE POINTER:** In interim financial reports, estimate the end-of-period liability in order to estimate the expense for the year. Reflect adjustments to the amount of the estimate in the interim period during which the adjustment becomes known.

Property taxes on property held for resale to customers or under construction are typically capitalized.

OBSERVATION: The promulgated GAAP do not describe the criteria for capitalizing or not capitalizing real estate taxes.

Illustration of Accounting and Reporting Standards for Property Taxes

On October 1, 19X1, the City assesses $12,000 of property taxes on Wilson, Inc., for the fiscal year, October 1, 19X1–September 30, 19X2. Wilson records the assessment as follows:

Oct. 1, 19X1

Deferred property taxes	$12,000	
Property taxes payable		$12,000

At December 31, 19X1, the end of Wilson's financial reporting year, Wilson adjusts the deferred property taxes account by recognizing three months of expense, as follows:

Dec. 31, 19X1

Property tax expense	$2,000	
Deferred property taxes		$2,000

At February 1, 19X2, Wilson pays the property taxes and makes the following entry:

Feb. 1, 19X2

Property taxes payable	$12,000	
Cash		$12,000

Throughout, or at the end of 19X2, the remaining 10 months of property taxes are recognized as expense:

Various dates, 19X2

Property tax expense	$19,000	
Deferred property taxes		$19,000

CHAPTER 39
QUASI-REORGANIZATIONS

CONTENTS

CHAPTER 39
QUASI-REORGANIZATIONS

OVERVIEW

Under carefully defined circumstances, contributed or paid-in capital generally may be used to restructure a corporation, including the elimination of a deficit in retained earnings. This procedure is called a *quasi-reorganization* or *corporate readjustment*. The circumstances in which this adjustment process is appropriate, as well as the specific procedures to be followed, are outlined in the following authoritative accounting pronouncements:

ARB-43	Chapter 7, Capital Accounts
	A. Quasi-Reorganizations
ARB-46	Discontinuance of Dating Earned Surplus

CROSS-REFERENCES

1999 MILLER GAAP GUIDE: Chapter 21, "Income Taxes"; Chapter 46, "Stockholders' Equity "

BACKGROUND

When a struggling business reaches a turnaround point and profitable operations seem likely, a quasi-reorganization may be appropriate to eliminate the accumulated deficit from past unprofitable operations. The resulting financial statements have more credibility and may make it possible for the company to borrow money for its profitable operations. In addition, by eliminating the deficit in retained earnings, the possibility of paying dividends in the foreseeable future becomes more likely.

The specific criteria that must be met for a quasi-reorganization to be appropriate are:

1. Assets are overvalued in the balance sheet.

2. The company can reasonably expect to be profitable in the future if a restructuring occurs so that future operations are not burdened with the problems of the past.

3. Formal shareholder consent is obtained.

Stockholders' equity usually is made up of the following:

1. Capital contributed for stock, to the extent of the par or stated value of each class of stock presently outstanding

2. Additional paid-in or contributed capital:

   a. Capital contributed in excess of par or stated value of each class of stock, whether as a result of original issues, any subsequent reductions of par or stated value, or transactions by the corporation in its own shares

   b. Capital received other than for stock, whether from shareholders or others (such as donated capital)

3. Retained earnings (or deficit), which represents the accumulated income or loss of the corporation.

Generally, items properly chargeable to current or future years' income accounts may *not* be charged to contributed capital accounts. An exception to this rule occurs in accounting for quasi-reorganizations, in which case a one-time adjustment to contributed capital is appropriate.

Although the corporate entity remains unchanged in a quasi-reorganization, a new basis of accountability is established. Net assets are restated downward to their fair values, and stockholders' equity is reduced. Retained earnings (deficit) is raised to a zero balance by charging any deficit accumulated from operations and the asset adjustments to either (*a*) capital contributed in excess of par or (*b*) capital contributed other than for capital stock. Contributed capital accounts must be large enough to absorb the deficit in retained earnings, including adjustments made as part of the quasi-reorganization.

☛ **PRACTICE POINTER:** Although the capital stock account may not be used to directly absorb a deficit in retained earnings, a corporation may reduce the par value of its existing capital stock and transfer the resulting excess to a capital contributed in excess of par account. This procedure frequently is used in a quasi-reorganization.

ACCOUNTING AND REPORTING

General Provisions

If a corporation restates its assets and stockholders' equity through a quasi-reorganization, it must make a clear report of the proposed restatements to its shareholders and obtain their formal consent (ARB-43, Ch. 7A, par. 3).

Assets are written down to their fair values; if fair values are not readily determinable, conservative estimates are used (ARB-43, Ch. 7A, par. 4). Estimates may also be used to provide for known probable losses prior to the date of the quasi-reorganization, when amounts are indeterminable (ARB-43, Ch. 7A, par. 5).

> ☞ **PRACTICE POINTER:** Determination of the fair value of assets may be a subjective process, requiring the use of different valuation and appraisal techniques for different asset categories.

If estimates are used and the amounts subsequently are found to be excessive or insufficient, the difference should be charged or credited to the capital account previously charged or credited and not to retained earnings (ARB-43, Ch. 7A, par. 5).

The steps in the accounting procedure are as follows:

1. All asset amounts to be written off are charged to retained earnings (ARB-43, Ch. 7A, par. 6).

2. After all amounts to be written off are recognized and charged to retained earnings, the negative (debit) balance is transferred to either (*a*) capital contributed in excess of par or (*b*) capital contributed other than for capital stock (ARB-43, Ch. 7A, par. 6).

   Capital contributed in excess of par value may have existed prior to the quasi-reorganization, or it may have been created as a result of a reduction of par value in conjunction with the quasi-reorganization.

3. If a deficit in retained earnings is transferred to an allowable capital account, any subsequent balance sheet must disclose, by dating the retained earnings, that the balance in the retained earnings account has accumulated since the date of reorganization (ARB-43, Ch. 7A, par. 10). For example:

   Retained earnings, since July 1, 19XX $1,234,567

The dating of retained earnings following a quasi-reorganization would rarely, if ever, be of significance after a period of 10 years. There may be exceptional circumstances that could justify a period of less than 10 years (ARB-46, par. 2).

4. New or additional shares of stock may be issued or exchanged for other shares or existing indebtedness. For example, stockholders may agree to subscribe to additional shares, or bondholders may agree to accept capital stock in lieu of principal or interest in arrears, to provide new cash for future operations. Accounting entries for these types of transactions are handled in accordance with GAAP. Consideration should include whether the issuance of new stock results in a change in control, in which case purchase accounting may be appropriate (ARB-43, Ch. 7A, par. 11).

5. Corporations with subsidiaries should follow the same procedures so that no credit balance remains in consolidated retained earnings after a quasi-reorganization in which losses have been charged to allowable capital accounts (ARB-43, Ch. 7A, par. 6).

   In those cases in which losses have been charged to the allowable capital accounts, instead of a credit balance in a subsidiary's retained earnings, the parent company's interest in such retained earnings should be regarded as capitalized by the quasi-reorganization in the same way retained earnings of a subsidiary are capitalized by the parent on the date of its acquisition (ARB-43, Ch. 7A, par. 7).

6. The effective date of the quasi-reorganization from which income of the corporation is thereafter determined should be as close as possible to the date of formal stockholders' consent and preferably at the start of a new fiscal year (ARB-43, Ch. 7A, par. 8).

Adjustments made pursuant to a quasi-reorganization should not be included in the determination of net income for any period.

Accounting for a Tax Benefit

Careful consideration must be given to the proper accounting for any tax attributes in a quasi-reorganization. Under FAS-109 (Accounting for Income Taxes), tax benefits of deductible temporary differences and carryforwards as of the date of the quasi-reorganization ordinarily are reported as a direct addition to capital contributed in excess of par if the tax benefits are recognized in subsequent years. An exception may exist for entities that have previously adopted

FAS-96 (Accounting for Income Taxes) and effected a quasi-reorganization; in that instance, subsequent recognition of tax benefits may be included in income and then reclassified from retained earnings to capital contributed in excess of par.

Disclosure

Adequate disclosure of all pertinent information should be made in the financial statements. A new retained earnings account dated as of the date of the quasi-reorganization should be established and reflected in subsequent financial statements.

Illustration of Accounting for a Quasi-Reorganization

The Centrex Company, founded in 19X0, experienced losses in each of its first six years of operation. In May 19X6, the company acquired two patents on an advanced solar-heating unit, which soon became the standard for the industry. The quarter ended September 30, 19X6, was extremely profitable, and the patent and accompanying licensing agreements indicate that continuing profitability is quite likely.

Centrex is closely held, and the stockholders have agreed in principle to a quasi-reorganization. Negotiations have been held with various creditors regarding capitalizing debts.

The balance sheet of Centrex at December 31, 19X6, appears as follows:

Assets:	
Cash	$ 25,000
Accounts receivable (net)	410,000
Plant and equipment (net)	1,670,000
Other assets	80,000
Total assets	$2,185,000

Liabilities and Equity:	
Accounts payable	$ 840,000
Notes payable—other	300,000
Equipment notes payable	240,000
Common stock	500,000
Paid-in capital in excess of par value—common stock	1,017,000
Retained earnings	(712,000)
Total liabilities and equity	$2,185,000

The stockholders and creditors have approved the following plan of informal reorganization effective January 1, 19X7:

1. The current shareholders will exchange their 100,000 shares of $5 par stock for 100,000 shares of $1 par stock.

2. The creditors have agreed to accept a new issue of 5% preferred stock valued at $300,000 for an equal amount of accounts payable.

3. The plant and equipment will be written down to its fair value of $1,100,000.

4. Accounts receivable of $70,000 will be written off as uncollectible.

5. Other assets will be written down to their fair value of $50,000.

The first step in a quasi-reorganization is to write down all assets to their fair values. In the example, the journal entry would be:

Retained earnings	$ 670,000	
Plant and equipment		
($1,670,000 – $1,100,000)		$ 570,000
Accounts receivable		70,000
Other assets ($80,000 – $50,000)		30,000

Next, the change in the par value of the common stock is recorded:

Common stock	$ 400,000	
Paid-in capital in excess of		
par value—common stock		$ 400,000

The following journal entry records the new preferred stock issued for $300,000 of accounts payable:

Accounts payable	$ 300,000	
5% Preferred stock		$ 300,000

After all the quasi-reorganization adjustments are made, the deficit in retained earnings ($1,382,000) is eliminated against the paid-in capital—common stock—leaving a zero balance in retained earnings:

Paid-in capital—common stock	$1,382,000	
Retained earnings		
($712,000 + $670,000)		$1,382,000

The Centrex Company balance sheet, after giving effect to the reorganization, appears as follows:

Assets:

Cash	$ 25,000
Accounts receivable (net)	340,000
Plant and equipment (net)	1,100,000
Other assets	50,000
Total assets	$1,515,000

Liabilities and Equity:

Accounts payable	$ 540,000
Notes payable—other	300,000
Equipment notes payable	240,000
5% Preferred stock	300,000
Common stock ($1 par)	100,000
Paid-in capital in excess of par value—common stock	35,000
Retained earnings since January 1, 19X7	-0-
Total liabilities and equity	$1,515,000

CHAPTER 40
RELATED PARTY DISCLOSURES

CONTENTS

CHAPTER 40
RELATED PARTY DISCLOSURES

OVERVIEW

Financial statement disclosure of related party transactions is required by GAAP in order for those statements to fairly present financial position, cash flows, and results of operations.

GAAP for related party transactions are presented in the following authoritative pronouncement:

FAS-57   Related Party Disclosures

CROSS-REFERENCES

1999 MILLER GAAS GUIDE: Chapter 8, "Evidence"

1999 MILLER NOT-FOR-PROFIT REPORTING: Chapter 2, "Overview of Current Pronouncements"

BACKGROUND

A *related party* is one that can exercise control or significant influence over the management and/or operating policies of another party, to the extent that one of the parties may be prevented from fully pursuing its own separate interests.

Related parties consist of all affiliates of an enterprise, including (*a*) their management and their immediate families, (*b*) their principal owners and their immediate families, (*c*) their investments accounted for by the equity method, (*d*) beneficial employee trusts that are managed by the management of the enterprise, and (*e*) any party that may, or does, deal with the enterprise and has ownership of, control over, or can significantly influence the management or operating policies of another party to the extent that an arm's-length transaction may not be achieved.

Transactions among related parties generally are accounted for on the same basis as if the parties were not related, unless the *substance* of the transaction is not arm's length. Substance over form is an important consideration when accounting for transactions involving related parties.

Common related party transactions include the following:

1. Sales, purchases, and transfers of realty and personal property

2. Services received or furnished (e.g., accounting, management, engineering, and legal services)

3. Use of property and equipment by lease

4. Borrowings and lendings

5. Maintenance of bank balances as compensating balances for the benefit of another

6. Intercompany billings based on allocation of common costs

7. Filing of consolidated tax returns

REPORTING AND DISCLOSURE STANDARDS

FAS-57 requires that material related party transactions that are not eliminated in consolidated or combined financial statements be disclosed in the financial statements of the reporting entity. Related party transactions involving compensation arrangements, expense allowances, and similar items incurred in the ordinary course of business, however, do not have to be disclosed (FAS-57, par. 2).

If separate financial statements of an entity that has been consolidated are presented in a financial report that includes the consolidated financial statements, duplicate disclosure of the related party transactions is not necessary. Disclosure of related party transactions is required, however, in separate financial statements of (a) a parent company, (b) a subsidiary, (c) a corporate joint venture, or (d) an investee that is 50% owned or less (FAS-57, par. 2).

Information required to be disclosed for material related party transactions is as follows (FAS-57, par. 2):

1. The nature of the relationship of the related parties

2. A description of the transactions, including amounts and other pertinent information necessary for an understanding of the effects of the related party transactions, for each period in which an income statement is presented (related party transactions of no or nominal amounts must also be disclosed)

3. The dollar amount of transactions for each period in which an income statement is presented; also, the effects of any change in terms between the related parties from terms used in prior periods

4. If not apparent in the financial statements, (*a*) the terms of related party transactions, (*b*) the manner of settlement of related party transactions, and (*c*) the amount due to or from related parties

If the operating results or financial position of a reporting entity can be altered significantly by the effects of common ownership or management control of the reporting entity and one or more other entities, even if there are no transactions among any of the entities, the nature of the ownership or management control must be disclosed in the financial statements (FAS-57, par. 4).

> **☞ PRACTICE POINTER:** The amount of detail disclosed for related party transactions must be sufficient for the user of the financial statements to be able to understand the related party transaction and its impact on the financial statements. Thus, all that is necessary may be disclosure of the total amount of a specific type of material related party transaction or of the effects of the relationship between the related parties. In other circumstances, however, more details may be required for the reader of the financial statements to have a clear understanding of the transaction.

One cannot assume that a related party transaction is consummated in the same manner as an arm's-length transaction. Disclosures or other representations of a material related party transaction in financial statements should not imply that the transaction was made on the same basis as an arm's-length transaction, unless the disclosures or representations can be substantiated (FAS-57, par. 3).

Illustrations of Related Party Disclosures

Transaction between company and officers/directors During 19X5, the company purchased land and buildings adjoining one of its plants from two company directors for $750,000. The board of directors unanimously approved the purchase, with the two directors involved in the transaction abstaining.

Transaction between company and profit-sharing plan During 19X5, the company purchased land from one of its profit-sharing plans for $750,000. Department of Labor exemption was received prior to the transaction.

Lease between company and officer/owner   Several years ago, the company leased land in upstate New York from John Doe, an officer and principal owner. The company constructed and furnished a residence on the property for use by the company's customers and distributors. The annual lease payment to Doe is $12,500, and the lease continues through December 31, 19X9. At that time, Doe has an option to purchase the residence and furnishings for $50,000 or to renew the lease at $10,000 per year for an additional five years.

Salary advance to officer   During 19X5, the company made a $100,000 salary advance to John Doe, an officer, as part of a new employment contract that required Doe to relocate to Atlanta, Georgia. According to the terms of the contract, Doe is required to repay the loan at $20,000 per year for the next five years, beginning in 19X6.

CHAPTER 41
RESEARCH AND DEVELOPMENT COSTS

CONTENTS

CHAPTER 41
RESEARCH AND DEVELOPMENT COSTS

OVERVIEW

Research and development (R&D) cost is carefully defined in the authoritative accounting literature. Once R&D costs are appropriately identified, GAAP require that they be expensed in the period incurred. Some costs related to R&D activities, however, are appropriately capitalized and carried forward as assets if they have alternative future uses. R&D-related assets typically include items of property, plant, and equipment and intangible assets used in the ongoing R&D effort of the enterprise.

The following pronouncements establish the promulgated GAAP for R&D costs:

FAS-2   Accounting for Research and Development Costs

FAS-68   Research and Development Arrangements

FAS-86   Accounting for the Costs of Computer Software to Be Sold, Leased, or Otherwise Marketed

FIN-4   Applicability of FASB Statement No. 2 to Business Combinations Accounted for by the Purchase Method

FIN-6   Applicability of FASB Statement No. 2 to Computer Software

CROSS-REFERENCES

BACKGROUND

Research is the planned efforts of a company to discover new information that will help create a new product, service, process, or technique or vastly improve one in current use. *Development* takes the findings generated by research and formulates a plan to create the desired item or to improve an existing one. Development in the context of this area of GAAP does not include normal improvements in existing operations. The following specific activities are *not* covered by the provisions of FAS-2:

- Activities that are unique to the extractive industries, such as prospecting, exploration, drilling, mining, and similar functions. Research and development activities that are comparable in nature to other companies not in the extractive industry, however, such as the development or improvement of techniques and processes, *are* covered.

- Research and development performed under contract for others, including indirect costs that are specifically reimbursable under a contract.

> ☛ **PRACTICE POINTER:** R&D does not include market research and testing, because these items specifically relate to the selling and marketing operations of a company. In addition, general and administrative expenses not *directly* related to the R&D activities are not included in R&D.

Because of the high degree of uncertainty of any resulting future benefit, the underlying basic principle in accounting for R&D is conservatism. Since at the time of performing R&D there is uncertainty concerning future success, the most conservative approach is to expense the item in the period incurred.

FIN-4 provides guidance in applying the provisions of FAS-2 to R&D costs acquired in a business combination accounted for by the purchase method. FIN-6 and FAS-86 provide guidance in applying the provisions of FAS-2 to computer software.

ACCOUNTING AND REPORTING RESEARCH AND DEVELOPMENT— GENERAL STANDARDS

All R&D costs covered by GAAP are expensed in the period when they are incurred. Assets used in R&D activity, such as machinery, equipment, facilities, and patents that have alternative future uses either in R&D activities or otherwise are capitalized. Depreciation and amortization on such capitalized R&D-related assets is charged to R&D expense. All expenditures in conjunction with an R&D project, including personnel costs, materials, equipment, facilities, and intangibles, for which the company has no alternative future use beyond the specific project for which the items were purchased, are expensed. Indirect costs, including general and administrative expenses, which are *directly* related to the R&D project also are expensed when incurred (FAS-2, par. 11).

Illustration of Determining R&D Expense

Lambert, Inc., develops new products and, therefore, engages in extensive research and development activities. Following is a description of current-period expenditures related to a current Lambert project:

1.	Material and labor directly related to the project	$150,000
2.	Purchase of machinery and equipment required to carry out the project:	
	a. Useful only for this project	75,000
	b. Useful for this and other R&D projects over an estimated five-year period	90,000
3.	Contract services acquired	15,000
4.	Overhead and administration allocation	50,000

Assuming the overhead and administration allocation is for activities closely related to the project, and assuming depreciation of machinery and equipment by the straight-line method with no expected salvage value, the R&D expense for the year is:

Material and labor	$150,000
Machinery and equipment	75,000
Depreciation of machinery and equipment	
($90,000/5 years)	18,000
Contract services	15,000
Overhead and administration	50,000
R&D expense	$308,000

The machinery and equipment with alternative future uses ($90,000 − $18,000 = $72,000 book value) is considered an asset available for use in future periods.

> ☞ **PRACTICE POINTER:** FAS-2 does not require assets related to R&D that have alternative future uses in R&D, production, or other activities to be expensed in the period incurred. Typical assets with alternative future uses include machinery, equipment, facilities, patents, and copyrights. Include amortization and depreciation of these assets in R&D expense as long as the assets are used in R&D activities. No asset described as "research and development" should appear in the balance sheet. Present R&D-related assets that are included in the balance sheet in the normal asset categories they represent—plant assets, intangible assets, etc.

Research and development costs acquired by the purchase method in a business combination are assigned their fair values, if any, in accordance with existing GAAP according to APB-16 (Business Combinations). The subsequent accounting by the acquirer of these R&D assets is that costs assigned to assets with alternative future uses are capitalized and all others are expensed at the date of consummation of the combination (FIN-4, pars. 4 and 5).

Disclosure

The amount of R&D charged to expense for the period must be disclosed in the financial statements for each period presented (FAS-2, par. 13).

COMPUTER SOFTWARE TO BE SOLD, LEASED, OR OTHERWISE MARKETED

FAS-86 applies to those costs incurred in purchasing or internally developing and producing computer software products that are sold, leased, or otherwise marketed by an enterprise. The costs covered by FAS-86 may be incurred (*a*) for separate computer software products or (*b*) for integral parts of computer software products or processes. FAS-86 does *not* cover those costs incurred for computer software that is (*a*) produced by an enterprise for others under a contractual arrangement or (*b*) created for the internal use of an enterprise (FAS-86, par. 2).

Under FAS-86, the terms *computer software product, software product*, and *product* are used interchangeably to mean either (*a*) a computer software program, (*b*) a group of programs, or (*c*) a product enhancement. A product enhancement represents improvement to an existing product that significantly improves the marketability or extends the estimated useful life of the original product. A product enhancement almost always involves a new design or redesign of the original computer software product.

The primary activities that are involved in the creation of a computer software product are the (a) planning function, (b) design function, and (c) production function. The planning function of a computer software product generally includes preliminary product specifications and design and the development of production and financial plans for the product. In addition, the planning function should include a marketing analysis and a marketing plan for the product. The planning function should generate sufficient documentation and detail information for an enterprise to make a determination of the overall feasibility of the proposed computer software product.

The design function of a computer software product includes the product design and the detail program design. The production of a product master generally involves coding, testing, and the development of training materials. Coding is the process in which the requirements of the detail program design are converted into a computer language. Testing includes the steps necessary to determine whether the computer software product works in accordance with its design specifications and documentation.

Computer Software Costs

FAS-86 specifies that all costs incurred in establishing the technological feasibility of a computer software product that is to be sold, leased, or otherwise marketed by an enterprise are research and development costs, which must be accounted for as required by FAS-2. Thus, until technological feasibility is established in accordance with FAS-86, all costs incurred through the purchase or internal development and production of a computer software product that is to be sold, leased, or otherwise marketed are accounted for as R&D costs and expensed in the period incurred (FAS-86, par. 3).

The development costs of a computer system that improves an enterprise's administrative or selling procedures are not considered R&D costs. All costs incurred for internally developed computer software products used in an enterprise's own R&D activities, however, should be charged to expense when incurred, because the alternative future use test does not apply to such costs (FIN-6, par. 8).

Production costs incurred for integral parts of a computer software product or process are expensed, unless (a) technological feasibility has been established for the computer software product or process and (b) all research and development activities have been completed for the other components of the computer software product or process (FAS-86, par. 5).

Technological Feasibility

Technological feasibility is established upon completion of all of the activities that are necessary to substantiate that the computer software product can be produced in accordance with its design specifications, including functions, features, and technical performance requirements. Thus, all planning, designing, coding, and testing activities that are required to substantiate that the computer software product can be produced to meet its design specifications must has been completed before technological feasibility is established (FAS-86, par. 4).

Under FAS-86, the method of establishing the technological feasibility of a computer software product depends on whether the process of creating the computer software product includes a detail program design or not. The following are the minimum requirements for establishing the technological feasibility of a computer software product (FAS-86, par. 4):

Including Detail Program Design

If the process of creating the computer software product includes a detail program design, the following criteria establish the technological feasibility of a computer software product:

1. An enterprise must complete the product design and detail program design for the computer software product and establish that it has available the necessary skills, hardware, and software technology to produce the product.

2. An enterprise must substantiate the completeness of the program design and its consistency with the product design by documenting and tracing the detail program design to the product specifications.

3. An enterprise must identify the high-risk development issues in the computer software product through review of the detail program design; if any uncertainties relating to the high-risk development issues are discovered, they must be resolved through coding and testing. High-risk development issues that may be encountered in the production of a computer software product may include novel, unique, or unproven functions and features, and/or technological innovations.

Not Including Detail Program Design

If the process of creating the computer software product *does not* include a detail program design, the following criteria establish the technological feasibility of a computer software product:

1. An enterprise must complete a product design and a working model of the computer software product.

2. An enterprise must substantiate the completeness of the working model and its consistency with the product design by testing the model.

Computer Software Costs That Must Be Capitalized

After technological feasibility has been established, FAS-86 specifies that all costs incurred for a computer software product that is sold, leased, or otherwise marketed by an enterprise shall be capitalized. Thus, the costs of producing product masters for a computer software product, including costs for coding and testing, are capitalized, but only after technological feasibility has been established (FAS-86, par. 5).

Production costs for computer software that is to be used as an integral part of a product or process are capitalized, but only after (*a*) technological feasibility has been established for the software and (*b*) all R&D activities for the other components of the product or process have been completed.

Capitalization of computer software costs is discontinued when the computer software product is available to be sold, leased, or otherwise marketed. Costs for maintenance and customer support are charged to expense when incurred or when the related revenue is recognized, whichever occurs first (FAS-86, par. 6).

> **OBSERVATION:** Under FAS-86, the amount of costs that an enterprise is required to capitalize depends primarily on its choice of production methods. Thus, an enterprise may control the amount of computer software costs that it capitalizes by establishing technological feasibility at a designated time during the production process.

Amortization of Capitalized Computer Software Costs

Amortization of capitalized computer software costs, on a product-by-product basis, begins when the product is available to be sold, leased, or otherwise marketed. Periodic amortization, on a product-by-product basis, is equal to the greater of (*a*) the amount computed by the straight-line method over the estimated useful life of the product or (*b*) the amount computed by using the ratio that current gross revenues bear to total estimated gross revenues (including current gross revenues) (FAS-86, par. 8).

Inventory Costs

Inventory costs are capitalized on a unit-specific basis and charged to cost of sales when the related revenue from the sale of those units is recognized. Inventory costs include duplicate copies of the computer software product made from the product master, documentation, training materials, and the costs incurred for packaging the product for distribution (FAS-86, par. 9).

Periodic Evaluation of Capitalized Computer Software Costs

Unamortized computer software costs that have been capitalized previously in accordance with FAS-86 are reported at net realizable value on an enterprise's balance sheet. Net realizable value is determined on a product-by-product basis and is equal to the estimated future gross revenues of a specific product, less estimated future costs of completing and disposing of that specific product, including the costs of performing maintenance and customer support on a product-by-product basis as required by the terms of the sale.

The excess of any unamortized computer software costs over its related net realizable value at a balance sheet date shall be written down. The amount of write-down is charged to periodic income. Capitalized costs that have been written down as a charge to income shall not be capitalized again or restored in any future period (FAS-86, par. 10).

Financial Statement Disclosure

The total amount of unamortized computer software costs that is included in each balance sheet presented shall be disclosed in the financial statements. The total amount of computer software costs charged to expense shall be disclosed for each income statement presented. The total amount of computer software costs charged to expense shall include amortization expense and amounts written down to net realizable value (FAS-86, par. 11).

All computer software costs that are classified as R&D costs shall be accounted for in accordance with FAS-2. These costs may include the costs of planning, product design, detail program design, and the costs incurred in establishing technological feasibility of a computer software product (FAS-86, par. 12).

RESEARCH AND DEVELOPMENT ARRANGEMENTS

FAS-68 covers an enterprise's research and development arrangements that are partially or completely funded by other parties. In this respect, the typical arrangement is for the parties to set up a limited partnership through which the R&D activities related to a specific project are funded. Although the limited partnership arrangement is used in FAS-68 for illustrative purposes, the legal structure of an R&D arrangement may take a variety of forms and is sometimes influenced by income tax implications and securities regulations.

In a typical R&D arrangement, an enterprise that has the basic technology for a particular project is the general partner and manages the R&D activities. The limited partners, who may or may not be related parties, provide all or part of the funds to complete the project. If the funds are not sufficient, the arrangement may allow or require the general partner to either (*a*) sell additional limited partnership interest or (*b*) use its own funds to complete the project. In addition, some funds may be provided in the form of loans or advances to the limited partnership. The repayment of the loans or advances may be guaranteed by the partnership.

Contract

The actual R&D activities usually are performed by the enterprise or a related party, under a contract with the limited partnership. The contract price is either fixed or cost plus a fixed or percentage fee and is performed on a *best efforts* basis, with no guarantee of ultimate success. The legal ownership of the results of the project vests with partnership. Frequently, the enterprise has an option to acquire the partnership's interest in the project or to obtain exclusive use of the results of the project. If the project is a success, the enterprise will no doubt exercise its option to acquire the project. Under some circumstances, however, even if the project is unsuccessful, the enterprise may still have reason to acquire the project, in spite of the fact that it is not legally required to do so. For example, the enterprise may want to prevent the final results of the project from falling into the hands of a competitor.

Many of the liabilities and obligations that an enterprise undertakes in an R&D project that is funded by others are specified in the agreements. Some liabilities and obligations, however, may exist in substance but may not be reduced to writing. For example, future payments by the enterprise to other parties for royalties or the acquisition of the partnership's interest in the project may, in substance, represent (*a*) the repayment of a loan or (*b*) the purchase price of a specific asset.

Nature of Obligation

In R&D arrangements that are partially or completely funded by other parties, accounting and reporting for R&D costs depend upon the nature of the obligation that an enterprise incurs in the arrangement. The nature of the obligation in such R&D arrangements can be classified in one of the following categories:

1. The obligation is solely to perform contractual services.
2. The obligation represents a liability to repay all of the funds provided by the other parties.
3. The obligation is partly to perform contractual services and partly a liability to repay some, but not all, of the funds provided by the other parties.

If the nature of the obligation incurred by an enterprise is solely to perform contractual services, all R&D costs are charged to *cost of sales*. If the nature of the obligation represents a liability to repay all of the funds provided by the other parties, all R&D costs are charged to *expense* when incurred.

If the nature of the obligation incurred by an enterprise is partly a liability and partly the performance of contractual services, R&D costs are charged partly to expense and partly to cost of sales. The portion charged to cost of sales is related to the funds provided by the other parties that do not have to be repaid by the enterprise. The portion charged to expense is related to the funds provided by the other parties that *are* likely to be repaid by the enterprise. Under FAS-68, the portion charged to expense is referred to as the enterprise's portion of the R&D costs. Under the provisions of FAS-68, an enterprise shall charge its portion of the R&D costs to expense in the same manner as the liability is incurred. Thus, if the liability arises on a pro rata basis, the enterprise's portion of the R&D costs shall be charged to expense in the same manner. If the liability arises as the initial funds are expended, the enterprise's portion of the R&D costs shall be charged to expense in the same manner (FAS-68, par. 9).

FAS-68 provides guidance in determining the nature of the obligation that an enterprise incurs in R&D arrangements that are partially or completely funded by other parties. FAS-68 requires that an enterprise report in its financial statements the estimated liability, if any, incurred in an R&D arrangement that is partially or completely funded by other parties. The estimated liability shall include any contractually defined obligations and any obligations not contractually defined but otherwise reasonably evident.

An important criterion in determining an enterprise's obligation is whether the financial risk involved in an R&D arrangement has been substantively transferred to other parties. To the extent that the enterprise is committed to repay any of the funds provided by the other parties regardless of the outcome of the research and development, all or part of the risk has not been transferred.

Under the provisions of FAS-68, if significant indications exist that the enterprise is *likely* to repay any funds, it is presumed that a liability has been incurred. This presumption can be overcome only by substantial evidence to the contrary. Circumstances in which significant indications exist that the enterprise is likely to repay funds and a liability is presumed are as follows (FAS-68, par. 8):

1. Regardless of the success of the R&D project, the enterprise has indicated the intent to repay all or part of the funds provided by other parties.

2. If it failed to repay any of the funds, the enterprise would suffer a *severe economic penalty.* Under FAS-68, an economic penalty is *severe* if an enterprise would probably elect, under normal business circumstances, to repay the funds rather than to incur the penalty.

3. At the inception of the R&D arrangement, a material related party relationship, as defined in FAS-57 (Related Party Disclosures), exists between the enterprise and any of the parties funding the R&D project.

4. At the inception of the R&D arrangement, the project is substantially complete. Under this circumstance, the financial risks involved in the R&D project are already known to all parties.

An obligation may represent a liability whether it is payable in cash, securities, or by some other means (FAS-68, par. 5).

Obligation for Contractual Services

If substantially all of the financial risks of the R&D project are transferred to the other parties and the enterprise is not committed to repay any of the funds provided by the other parties, the enterprise shall account for its obligation as contractual R&D services. If repayment by the enterprise of any of the funds provided by the other parties depends on the availability of a future economic benefit to the enterprise, the enterprise shall also account for its obligation as contractual R&D services. In these circumstances, the financial risks of the R&D arrangement have clearly been transferred to others and the enterprise is only obligated to perform contractual R&D services (FAS-68, par. 10).

Frequently, an enterprise makes a loan or advance to the other parties that is designated to be repaid as a reduction of the purchase price for the results of the project, or as a reduction of future royalty payments from the enterprise. In this event, the portion of the loan or advance that is designated to be repaid as a reduction of the purchase price for the results of the project, or as a reduction of future royalties, shall be accounted for by the enterprise as R&D expense, unless it can be attributed to activities other than R&D, such as marketing or advertising (FAS-68, par. 12).

At or before the completion of the R&D project, the enterprise may elect to exercise its option to purchase the partnership's interest, or to obtain exclusive rights to the results of the project. The enterprise shall account for the purchase of the partnership's interest, or the exclusive rights, in accordance with existing GAAP. Thus, any asset that results from the R&D project shall be assigned its fair value, and intangible assets shall be accounted for in accordance with APB-17 (Intangible Assets) (FAS-68, par. 11).

If an enterprise is required to issue warrants or similar instruments in connection with the R&D arrangement, a portion of the funds provided by the other parties shall be recorded as paid-in capital. The amount capitalized as paid-in capital shall be equal to the fair market value of the warrants or other instruments at the date the R&D arrangement is consummated (FAS-68, par. 13).

Financial Statement Disclosure

Notes to the financial statements shall include the following disclosures for R&D arrangements that are accounted for as contracts to perform R&D services for others (FAS-68, par. 14):

- The terms of the significant agreements relating to the R&D arrangement, including purchase provisions, license agreements, royalty arrangements, and commitments to provide additional funds as of the date of each balance sheet presented

- The amount of R&D costs incurred and compensation earned during the period for such R&D arrangements for each income statement presented

CHAPTER 42
RESULTS OF OPERATIONS

CONTENTS

CHAPTER 42
RESULTS OF OPERATIONS

OVERVIEW

Reporting the results of operations, primarily determining and presenting net income and comprehensive income, is one of the most important aspects of financial reporting. GAAP provide specific guidance concerning how certain items should be presented in the income statement.

There are several authoritative pronouncements in the area of reporting the results of operations, as follows:

APB-9   Reporting the Results of Operations

APB-20   Accounting Changes

APB-30   Reporting the Results of Operations—Reporting the Effects of Disposal of a Segment of a Business, and Extraordinary, Unusual, and Infrequently Occurring Events and Transactions

FAS-16   Prior Period Adjustments

FAS-130   Reporting Comprehensive Income (effective for fiscal years beginning after December 15, 1997)

FIN-27   Accounting for a Loss on a Sublease

> **OBSERVATION:** FAS-130 is amended by FAS-133 (Accounting for Derivative Instruments and Hedging Activities). This is effective for fiscal years beginning after June 15, 1999. FAS-133 applies in interim financial statements for periods that begin after the same date (e.g., the quarter beginning July 1, 1999). FAS-133 is covered in Chapter 16 of the 1999 *Miller GAAP Guide*.
>
> Because the effective date of FAS-133 is delayed as indicated above, and the first calendar year for which FAS-133 will be in effect is the year 2000, the impact of FAS-133 on FAS-130 is not reflected in the 1999 *Miller GAAP Guide*.

(IMPRESS™

CROSS-REFERENCES

1999 MILLER GAAP GUIDE: Chapter 1, "Accounting Changes"; Chapter 3, "Business Combinations"; Chapter 13, "Earnings per Share"; Chapter 15, "Extinguishment of Debt"; Chapter 17, "Foreign Operations and Exchange"; Chapter 20, "Impairment of Loans and Long-Lived Assets"; Chapter 26, "Interim Financial Reporting"; Chapter 29, "Investments in Debt and Equity Securities"; Chapter 48, "Troubled Debt Restructuring"

1999 MILLER GAAP IMPLEMENTATION MANUAL: Chapter 27, "Results of Operations"

1999 MILLER GAAP IMPLEMENTATION MANUAL: EITF: Chapter 25, "Results of Operations"

1999 MILLER NOT-FOR-PROFIT REPORTING: Chapter 2, "Overview of Current Pronouncements"; Chapter 11, "Display of Certain GAAP Transactions"

1999 MILLER GOVERNMENTAL GAAP GUIDE: Chapter 5, "Governmental Financial Reporting"

BACKGROUND

For many years, there were differences of opinion in the accounting profession as to what should be included in net income. Proponents of the *all-inclusive concept* (sometimes called "clean surplus") believed that all items affecting net increases in owners' equity, except dividends and capital transactions, should be included in computing net income. Alternatively, proponents of the *current operating performance concept* (sometimes called "dirty surplus") advocated limiting the determination of net income to normal, recurring items of profit and loss that relate only to the current period and recognizing other items directly in retained earnings. Differences between the two concepts are seen most clearly in the treatment of the following items:

- Unusual or infrequent items
- Extraordinary items
- Changes in accounting principles

- Discontinued operations
- Prior-period adjustments
- Certain items that are required by GAAP to be recognized directly in stockholders' equity rather than in net income

Current GAAP (primarily APB-9, APB-30, FAS-16) require the presentation of income in a manner that generally is consistent with the all-inclusive concept. Net income includes all items of revenue, expense, gain, and loss during a reporting period, except prior-period adjustments, dividends, and capital transactions, and a limited number of items that are required to be recognized directly in equity. Examples of items treated in this manner are certain foreign currency adjustments and certain changes in the value of debt and equity investments.

The FASB first introduced the term "comprehensive income" in its conceptual framework, CON-3 (Elements of Financial Statements), which was replaced subsequently by CON-6 of the same title. According to CON-6, *comprehensive income* is the change in equity of a business enterprise from transactions, other events, and circumstances from nonowner sources during a period. It includes all changes in equity during a period except those resulting from investments by owners and distributions to owners. CON-5 (Recognition and Measurement in Financial Statements of Business Enterprises) concluded that comprehensive income and its components should be reported as part of a full set of financial statements for a period and that earnings (i.e., net income) was a more narrow measurement of performance and, therefore, was a part of comprehensive income. FAS-130 (Reporting Comprehensive Income) requires the presentation of comprehensive income and its components in financial statements for years beginning after December 15, 1997.

IRREGULAR ITEMS REPORTED IN NET INCOME

Extraordinary Items

Extraordinary items are transactions and other events that are (*a*) material in nature, (*b*) of a character significantly different from the typical or customary business activities, (*c*) not expected to recur frequently, and (*d*) not normally considered in evaluating the ordinary operating results of an enterprise (APB-30, par. 20). Extraordinary items are disclosed separately in the income statement, net of any related income tax effect (APB-30, par. 11).

Identifying extraordinary items requires informed professional judgment, taking into consideration all the facts involved in a particular situation. Some areas of promulgated GAAP, however, require that an item be treated as extraordinary. The following are the more common items that, if material, should be reported as extraordinary items:

1. The profit or loss on disposal of a significant part of the assets, or a separate segment, of the previously separate companies of a business combination, when disposed of within two years after the date of the combination (APB-16 [Business Combinations])

2. Gains on restructuring payables (FAS-15 [Accounting by Debtors and Creditors for Troubled Debt Restructurings])

3. Most gains or losses on the extinguishment of debt (FAS-4 [Reporting Gains and Losses from Extinguishment of Debt])

4. Most expropriations of property (APB-30, par. 23)

5. Gains or losses that are the direct result of a major casualty (APB-30, par. 23)

6. Losses resulting from prohibition under a newly enacted law or regulation (APB-30, par. 23)

Disposal of a Segment

Discontinued operations result from the disposal of identifiable segments of a business. *Identifiable segments* of a business are components that represent a major class of a firm's business, usually taking the form of a subsidiary, division, department, or other identifiable entity.

Segments of a business have separate assets and results of operations and activities that can be distinguished clearly for financial reporting purposes. Facts that indicate there is no separate identity suggest that the disposal of that part of the business should not be classified as a segment of a business for purposes of discontinued operations accounting (APB-30, par. 13).

Measurement Date

The measurement date of the disposal of a segment of a business is the date management commits to a formal plan for action to sell or otherwise dispose of the segment (APB-30, par. 14).

> ☞ **PRACTICE POINTER:** The plan of disposal should be carried out within one year from the measurement date. If a plan of disposal is estimated to be completed within one year and subsequently is not, treat any revision of the net realizable

value of the segment as a change in an accounting estimate and account for it prospectively (APB-30, par. 15).

Disposal Date

The disposal date is the date of closing, in the case of a sale, or the date operations cease, in the case of abandonment (APB-30, par. 14).

Determination of Gain or Loss

An estimate of the gain or loss that ultimately will result from the disposal of a segment of a business is made at the measurement date, based on estimates of the net realizable value. Net losses from operations between the measurement date and the expected disposal date are provided for in the determination of gain or loss from the disposal. Estimates are based on the amounts that can be projected with reasonable accuracy (APB-30, par. 15).

An estimated loss on disposal of a segment of business is recognized at the *measurement date*. In the case of a gain, it should not be recognized until it is realized, which usually is the *disposal date* (APB-30, par. 15).

> ☛ **PRACTICE POINTER:** Cost, expenses, and other adjustments associated with normal business activities that should have been recognized prior to the measurement date are not included in the gain or loss on disposal of a segment, but are included in income (loss) from discontinued operations. Severance pay, additional pension costs, and employee relocation expenses are costs directly associated with the decision to dispose of the segment and properly are includable in the gain or loss on disposal (APB-30, pars. 16 and 17).

Long-Term Leases

FIN-27 reaffirms that estimated costs and expenses directly associated with a decision to dispose of a business segment should include future rental payments on long-term leases less any future rentals to be received from subleases of the same properties (APB-30, par. 17). The gain or loss is measured as the difference between the unamortized cost of the leased property (net carrying amount) and the present value of the minimum lease payments, which will be received under the terms of the sublease. The gain or loss is included in the overall gain or loss on the disposal of the business segment (FIN-27, par. 3).

> **OBSERVATION:** FIN-27 is not clear on its coverage of sub-leases that are classified as operating leases. There is a strong argument that gain or loss on an operating sublease be included as part of the overall gain or loss on disposal of a business segment. APB-30 specifically states that all costs and expenses that are directly associated with the decision to dispose of a business segment be included in the overall gain or loss on the disposal. If a business segment has a long-term operating lease that is subleased and classified as an operating lease as part of the overall disposal of the segment, then any gain or loss would be directly associated with management's decision to dispose of the segment. The gain or loss would be measured as the difference between the present value of the future rental payments that must be paid on the original lease and the present value of the future rental receipts that will be collected on the operating sublease. The journal entry to record a loss would be a debit to the gain or loss account for disposal of the business segment and a credit to a deferred account. The deferred credit account should be amortized each year in an amount that would make up the difference between the payment made on the original lease and the rental collected on the operating sublease.

Disclosure

Notes to the financial statements for the period encompassing the measurement date should include (APB-30, par. 18):

1. Identity of the segment of business
2. Expected date of disposal
3. Manner of disposal
4. Description of the remaining assets and liabilities of the segment of business
5. Income or loss from operations and other proceeds from disposal of the segment of business, from the measurement date to the balance sheet date

Income Statement Presentation

Discontinued operations from disposal of a segment are included in the determination of net income and presented after the caption "Income from Continuing Operations" and preceding extraordinary items, if any (APB-30, par. 8).

Discontinued operations are presented in two parts: (1) income (loss) from operations of the discontinued segment and (2) gain or loss on disposal. Each component is presented net of tax.

Unusual or Infrequent Items

If professional judgment dictates individual treatment of a material event or transaction that does not qualify as an extraordinary item (e.g., unusual or infrequent, but not both), it may be reported separately as a component of income from continuing operations with appropriate footnote disclosure. In this event, however, the separately identified item should not be reported net of its related tax effects or in a manner that implies that the item is an extraordinary item (APB-30, par. 26).

> ☞ **PRACTICE POINTER:** The FASB does not state precisely what should *not* be done in the presentation of an unusual or infrequent item in order for it to *not* be confused with an extraordinary item. In the presentation of unusual or infrequent items, avoid the following, which are characteristics of the presentation of extraordinary items:
>
> - Net-of-tax presentation
> - Presentation of earnings per share on the item
> - Presentation of income before and after the item

Prior-Period Adjustments

A *prior-period adjustment* is defined by FAS-16, amended by FAS-109 (Accounting for Income Taxes), as a correction of an error in a prior-period statement. Prior-period adjustments are excluded from the determination of net income (FAS-16, par. 16).

All other items of profit and loss (including accruals for loss contingencies) shall be included in the determination of net income for the period.

Interim-Period Adjustments

An adjustment of prior interim periods of a current fiscal year can include any of the following settlements (FAS-16, par. 13):

1. Litigation or similar claims
2. Income taxes
3. Renegotiation
4. Utility revenues governed by rate-making processes

In adjusting interim periods of the current year, any adjustment of prior periods is made to the first interim period of the current year. Adjustments to the other interim periods of the current year are related to the interim period affected (FAS-16, par. 14).

The effects (*a*) on income from continuous operations, (*b*) on net income, and (*c*) on earnings per share of an adjustment to a current interim period must be disclosed fully (FAS-16, par. 15).

Accounting Changes

The following accounting changes necessitate adjustments of prior periods for reporting purposes:

1. Reporting a change in an entity (APB-20, par. 34)
2. An accounting change from the LIFO method to any other method (APB-20, par. 27)
3. An accounting change in reporting long-term construction contracts (APB-20, par. 27)
4. A change to or from the full-cost method used in the extractive industries (APB-20, par. 27)
5. One-time change for closely held corporations in connection with a public offering of its equity securities, or when such a company first issues financial statements for obtaining additional equity capital from outside investors (APB-20, par. 29)
6. Change from the retirement-replacement-betterment method of accounting for railroad track structures to the depreciation method of accounting (FAS-73 [Reporting a Change in Accounting for Railroad Track Structures], par. 2)

In addition, a change in accounting methods made by constituents of a pooling-of-interest to conform with the parent company is applied retroactively, and financial statements presented for prior periods are restated.

In those rare material cases in which prior-period adjustments are recorded, the resulting effects should be disclosed in the period in which the adjustments are made by *restating the balance of retained earnings at the beginning of such period* (FAS-16, par. 16).

Both the gross and net effect (of related income taxes) of prior-period adjustments on net income should be disclosed in the year of adjustment and all years presented (APB-9, par. 26).

Illustration of Presentation of Net Income

The following illustrates the presentation of income in accordance with APB-30 and related pronouncements:

Income (loss) from continuing operations before provision for income taxes	$400,000
Provision for income taxes	(136,000)

Income (loss) from continuing operations		$264,000
Discontinued operations (Note:___)		
Income (loss) from operations of discontinued division A (less applicable income taxes $34,000)	$(66,000)	
Loss (gain) on disposal of division A, including provision of $10,000 for operating losses during phase-out period (less applicable income taxes of $17,000)	(33,000)	
Net income (loss) from discontinued operations		(99,000)
Net income (loss) before extraordinary items		$165,000
Extraordinary items (Note: ___) (less applicable income taxes of $41,000)		79,000
Cumulative effect on prior years (to December 31, 19X1) of a change in an accounting principle (less applicable income taxes of $26,000)		(54,000)
Net income		$190,000

Earnings per share (EPS) for extraordinary items is not required but is strongly recommended by APB-30 (APB-30, par. 12). EPS for discontinued operations and the resulting gain or loss on the disposal of the segment may or may not be presented (APB-30, par. 9).

REPORTING COMPREHENSIVE INCOME

Several accounting standards currently require that certain items that qualify as part of comprehensive income be reported directly in the equity section of the statement of financial position without having been recognized in the determination of net income. Examples of these items include:

- Foreign currency translation adjustments in accordance with FAS-52 (Foreign Currency Translation)
- Changes in the market value of a futures contract that qualifies as a hedge of an asset reported at fair value pursuant to FAS-115 (Accounting for Certain Investments in Debt and Equity Securities)

- Unrealized holding gains and losses on available-for-sale securities in accordance with FAS-115
- Negative equity adjustments recognized in accordance with FAS-87 (Employers' Accounting for Pensions) as an additional pension liability not yet recognized as net periodic pension cost

Despite the FASB's endorsement of the general concept of comprehensive income and its conclusion that comprehensive income should be included in a full set of financial statements, prior to FAS-130 no authoritative standard required the presentation of comprehensive income or provided guidance on how to present it.

FAS-130 applies to all enterprises that provide a full set of financial statements reporting financial position, results of operations, and cash flows. It does *not* apply to:

- Enterprises that have no items of other comprehensive income in any period presented
- Not-for-profit organizations that must follow FAS-117 (Financial Statements of Not-for-Profit Organizations).

FAS-130 deals with the presentation and display of comprehensive income, but it does not specify when to recognize or how to measure the components of comprehensive income. Those subjects are covered in other current standards or will be covered in future standards.

Comprehensive Income Defined

Comprehensive income is a broad concept of an enterprise's financial performance, in that it includes all changes in equity during a period from transactions and events from nonowner sources (e.g., revenue and expense transactions with external parties). The only changes in equity that are excluded from comprehensive income are those resulting from investments by owners and distributions to owners.

The term *comprehensive income,* as used in FAS-130, includes net income plus all other components of comprehensive income. The term *other comprehensive income* denotes revenues, expenses, gains, and losses that are included in comprehensive income but not in net income in accordance with GAAP. While the terms *comprehensive income* and *other comprehensive income* are used throughout FAS-130, those precise terms are not required to be used in an enterprise's financial statements.

Before FAS-130, some elements of comprehensive income were presented in the income statement and others were reported directly in the equity section of the statement of financial position. All elements were *not* required to be brought together in a single amount of comprehensive income, however.

The FASB believes that information an enterprise provides by reporting comprehensive income—along with related disclosures and other information in the financial statements—will help investors, creditors, and others to assess the enterprise's activities and the timing and magnitude of its future cash flows. Given the diverse nature of the components of other comprehensive income, the FASB indicates that detailed information about each component is important. In fact, the FASB states that information about the components of comprehensive income may be more important than the total of comprehensive income, and the required disclosures are intended to support this stance.

Reporting and Display

FAS-130's reporting and display requirements for comprehensive income and other comprehensive income are summarized as follows:

1. An amount of net income

2. A total amount of comprehensive income in the statement where the components of other comprehensive income are reported

3. All components of other comprehensive income, with items classified based on their nature (e.g., foreign currency items, minimum pension liability items, and unrealized gains and losses on investment securities)

☞ **PRACTICE POINTER:** Classifications within net income, such as the following, are *not* affected by FAS-130:

- Continuing operations
- Discontinued operations
- Extraordinary items
- Cumulative effect of changes in accounting principles

If a company has no components of comprehensive income other than net income, it is not required to report comprehensive income.

OBSERVATION: Apparently, the FASB believes that in a situation in which there are no elements of other comprehensive income, to designate a single amount as both net income and comprehensive income is potentially confusing to financial statement users. In this situation, the amount is comparable with net income of an enterprise that presents both net income and comprehensive income, so the FASB determined that no reporting of comprehensive income is appropriate. This should limit the applicability of FAS-130 considerably, because it is reasonable to assume that many enterprises do not have transactions that would create a difference between net income and comprehensive income. *Accounting Trends & Techniques* (AICPA, 1996) indicates that 400 of the 600 companies included in their survey had a cumulative foreign currency translation balance in stockholders' equity. Considerably fewer companies had other components of other comprehensive income (e.g., 105 of 600 had unrealized gains or losses on investments).

Items recognized in other comprehensive income that are later recognized in net income require a reclassification adjustment in order to prevent double counting of transactions in the determination of comprehensive income. Perhaps the easiest example of these transactions is accumulated gains or losses on available-for-sale investment securities that are accumulated in stockholders' equity under FAS-115 until the securities are sold. At the time of the sale, any previously recognized gains or losses that were accumulated in stockholders' equity (i.e., an element of other comprehensive income) are reversed in comprehensive income and then recognized as an element of net income. The reversal of the previous recognition in other comprehensive income offsets the recognition from the previous period and effectively moves the recognition from other comprehensive income to net income when the gain or loss is actually realized in a sale. Illustration I demonstrates how this reclassification would be done in a situation similar to the one just described.

> ☞ **PRACTICE POINTER:** Reclassification adjustments may be displayed on the face of the financial statement in which comprehensive income is reported, or they may be disclosed in notes to the financial statements. For all reclassification adjustments other than the minimum pension liability, an enterprise may use either a gross display on the face of the financial statement or a net display on the face of the financial statement or in notes to the financial statements. A reclassification adjustment is not made for the minimum pension liability adjustment, so an enterprise must use a net display for that item.

Illustration of Reclassification Adjustment

A company accounts for its available-for-sale investments in debt and equity securities at fair value in accordance with FAS-115. Information on these investments prior to 19X5—the year in which the investment were sold—is as follows (all numbers in thousands):

	19X3	19X4
Purchase	$100	$125
Market value	$120	$260

In 19X3, $20 ($120 − $100) would be recognized by increasing the investment and recording an accumulated unrecognized gain in stockholders' equity. In 19X4, a gain of $15 [$260 − ($125 + $120)] would be recognized in a similar fashion.

Assuming the investments are sold in 19X5 for $260, the accumulated unrecognized gain of $35 ($20 + $15) is offset by the recognition of a $35 reclassification loss in other comprehensive income, and a $35 realized gain is recognized in net income. This transaction results in the following presentation over the three-year period:

	19X3	19X4	19X5
Net income	None	None	$35
Other comprehensive income	$20	$15	($35)
Comprehensive income	$20	$15	None

If the reclassification of ($35) had not been recognized in other comprehensive income in 19X5, a $35 gain would have been recognized in comprehensive income *twice*—once as an element of other comprehensive income and once as an element of net income.

Alternative Display Formats for Comprehensive Income

FAS-130 does not require a single display presentation for elements of comprehensive income and the total of comprehensive income, but it does require that these items be presented in a financial statement that is displayed with the same prominence as other financial statements, which together constitute a full set of financial statements.

Three alternative presentation formats are acceptable, either of the first two being preferable to the third.

1. In a single statement of income and comprehensive income that extends a traditional income statement to include (following net income) the elements of other comprehensive income and the total of comprehensive income.

2. In two statements of income. The first is a traditional income statement that ends with an amount of net income. The second begins with net income and includes the elements of other comprehensive income and then a total of comprehensive income.

3. In another financial statement, such as a statement of (changes in) stockholders' equity.

These alternatives are described by example in the following Illustration.

Illustration of Alternative Presentations of Comprehensive Income

Warner, Inc., has revenues of $1,559,231, expenses of $790,000, and two components of other comprehensive income, as follows:

- Accumulated gains of $100,000 on available-for-sale investments
- Foreign currency translation adjustments (losses) of $25,000

Net income is $500,000 for 19X1, the current year. Warner's income tax rate is 35%.

Format 1—One Income-Statement Format

Warner, Inc.
Statement of Income and Comprehensive Income
For year 19X1

Revenues		$1,559,231
Expenses		790,000
Income before income tax		$769,231
Income tax		269,231
Net income		$500,000
Other comprehensive income, net of income tax:		
Unrealized holding gains	$65,000	
Foreign currency translation	(16,250)	48,750
Comprehensive income		$548,750

Format 2—Two Income-Statement Format*

Warner, Inc.
Statement of Comprehensive Income
For year 19X1

Net income	$500,000	
Other comprehensive income, net of income tax:		
Unrealized holding gains	$65,000	
Foreign currency translation	(16,250)	48,750
Comprehensive income		$548,750

---

*Income statement unchanged by FAS-130.

Format 3 shows how comprehensive income might be presented in another statement with prominence equal to that of Formats 1 and 2. Appendix B of FAS-130 also illustrates other ways of presenting comprehensive income, as well as the note disclosures that might accompany the presentations.

With any of these alternatives, the components of other comprehensive income may be displayed net of related income taxes, as done in this Illustration, or before related income taxes with one amount shown for the aggregate income-tax effects of all the components of other comprehensive income. Whether the components are displayed net of tax or not, the amounts of income tax expense or benefit allocated to each component of other comprehensive income, including reclassification adjustments, are required to be disclosed.

Equity Section of the Statement of Financial Position

At the end of the reporting period, the total of other comprehensive income is transferred to a separate stockholders' equity account, much like net income is transferred to retained earnings. This separate stockholders' equity account should have an appropriate descriptive title, such as *Accumulated Other Comprehensive Income.* Disclosure of the accumulated balances for each classification of that separate component of equity shall be made on the face of the statement of financial position, in a statement of changes in stockholders' equity, or in notes to the financial statements.

The classifications used in the disclosure of the balances of individual components of other comprehensive income must correspond to the classifications used elsewhere in the same financial statements.

Effective Date and Transition

FAS-130 is effective for fiscal years *beginning* after December 15, 1997, which essentially means that it is effective for 1998. Enterprises may apply it early, and the mid-year timing of the pronouncement should permit early adoption in 1997 financial statements for periods that end late in the calendar year (e.g., December 31, 1997).

When first applying FAS-130, financial statements for earlier periods that are provided for comparative purposes are required to be reclassified to reflect application of the provisions of FAS-130 with the following exception: The provisions of FAS-130 that require display of reclassification adjustments (paragraphs 18–21) are not required, but are encouraged, in comparative statements for earlier periods.

FAS-130 must be adopted at the beginning of an enterprise's fiscal year, or if the statement is adopted later in the year, information presented for all prior interim periods of that year is required to be restated in accordance with FAS-130.

Format 3—Statement of Changes in Stockholders' Equity*

Warner, Inc.
Statement of Changes in Stockholders' Equity
For year 19X1

	Total	Comprehensive income	Retained earnings	Accumulated other comprehensive income	Common stock	Additional paid-in capital
Beginning balances	$XXX		$XXX	$XXX	$XXX	$XXX
Comprehensive income:						
Net income	$500,000	$500,000	$500,000			
Unrealized holding gains	65,000	65,000				
Foreign currency translation	(16,250)	(16,250)				
Other comprehensive income		48,750		$48,750		
Comprehensive income		$548,750				
Common stock issued					$XXX	$XXX
Dividends declared on common stock			($XXX)			
Ending balances	$XXX		$XXX	$XXX	$XXX	$XXX

*Income statement unchanged by FAS-130.

CHAPTER 43
REVENUE RECOGNITION

CONTENTS

CHAPTER 43
REVENUE RECOGNITION

OVERVIEW

GAAP, as well as recognized industry practices, generally call for revenue recognition at the point of sale. One aspect of a sale that complicates this generally simple rule is a right of return on the part of the buyer. Revenue from sales in which a right of return exists is recognized at the time of sale only if certain specified conditions are met. If those conditions are met, sales revenue and cost of sales are reduced to reflect estimated returns and costs of those returns. If they are not met, revenue recognition is postponed.

The authoritative literature dealing with revenue recognition when the right of return exists is as follows:

FAS-48   Revenue Recognition When Right of Return Exists

CROSS-REFERENCES

1999 MILLER GAAP GUIDE: Chapter 2, "Accounting Policies "; Chapter 7, "Contingencies, Risks, and Uncertainties"; Chapter 22, "Installment Sales Method of Accounting"; Chapter 31, "Long-Term Construction Contracts"; Chapter 54, "Franchise Fee Revenue"; Chapter 62, "Real Estate—Recognition of Sales"

1999 MILLER GAAP IMPLEMENTATION MANUAL: Chapter 28, "Revenue Recognition"

1999 MILLER GAAP IMPLEMENTATION MANUAL: EITF: Chapter 26, "Revenue Recognition"

1999 MILLER NOT-FOR-PROFIT REPORTING: Chapter 2, "Overview of Current Pronouncements"; Chapter 3, "Revenues"; Chapter 9, "Note Disclosures"; Chapter 11, "Display of Certain GAAP Transactions"

1999 MILLER GOVERNMENTAL GAAP GUIDE: Chapter 9, "Revenues"

1999 MILLER AUDIT PROCEDURES: Chapter 19, "Revenue and Expenses"

1999 MILLER HUD AUDIT PROCEDURES: Appendix L, "Revenue and Expenses"

BACKGROUND

The realization principle requires that revenue be earned before it is recognized. Revenue usually is recognized when the earning process is complete and an exchange has taken place. The earning process is not complete until collection of the sales price is assured reasonably.

In some industries, dealers and distributors of personal property have the right to return unsold merchandise. The right to return merchandise usually is an industry practice but may also occur as a result of a contractual agreement. The return period can last for a few days, as in the perishable food industry, or it can extend for several years, which is not infrequent for some types of publishers. The rate of return of some companies may be high, while in other industries, such as perishable foods, the rate of return may be insignificant.

As long as a right of return exists and the returns could be significant, the seller is exposed to reacquiring the ownership of the property. The risks and rewards of ownership have not, in substance, been passed on to the buyer. Because the earning process is not complete until collection of the sales price is assured reasonably, certain accounting problems arise in recognizing revenue when the right to return exists.

FAS-48 contains the specialized accounting and reporting principles and practices that were originally published in the AICPA SOP 75-1, titled "Revenue Recognition When Right of Return Exists." FAS-48 does not cover real estate or lease transactions and does not apply to accounting for revenue of service industries.

REVENUE RECOGNITION FOR
RETURNABLE MERCHANDISE

When a buyer has the right to return merchandise purchased, the seller may not recognize income from the sale, unless *all* of the following conditions are met (FAS-48, par. 6):

1. The price between the seller and the buyer is substantially fixed, or determinable.

2. The seller has received full payment, or the buyer is indebted to the seller and the indebtedness is not contingent on the resale of the merchandise.

3. Physical destruction, damage, or theft of the merchandise would not change the buyer's obligation to the seller.

4. The buyer has economic substance and is not a front, straw party, or conduit, existing for the benefit of the seller.

5. No significant obligations exist for the seller to help the buyer resell the merchandise.

6. A reasonable estimate can be made of the amount of future returns.

If all of the above conditions are met, revenue is recognized on sales for which a right of return exists, provided that an appropriate provision is made for costs or losses that may occur in connection with the return of merchandise from the buyer.

> **OBSERVATION:** An exchange of one item for a similar item of the same quality and value is not considered a return for the purposes of FAS-48.

If all of the conditions of FAS-48 are met, an appropriate provision for costs or losses that may occur in connection with the return of merchandise from the buyer must be made by the seller. The provision for costs or losses must be in accordance with FAS-5 (Accounting for Contingencies) (FAS-48, par. 7). Under FAS-5, a provision for a loss contingency is accrued, by a charge to income, provided that both of the following conditions exist:

1. It is *probable* that at the date of the financial statements, an asset has been impaired or a liability incurred, based on information available prior to the issuance of the financial statements.

2. The amount of loss can be estimated reasonably.

The second requirement for the accrual of a loss contingency under FAS-5 is satisfied when all of the conditions of FAS-48 are met. This is because FAS-48 requires that a reasonable estimate can be made of the amount of future returns, which also means that the amount of loss on the returns, if any, should be reasonably estimable. Thus, if returns are *probable* and all of the conditions of FAS-48 are met, an accrual is required by FAS-5. This accrual results in a reduction of sales revenue and a related cost of sales in the income statement, which is consistent with the requirements of FAS-48.

> ☛ **PRACTICE POINTER:** If all of the conditions of FAS-48 are not met, the seller cannot recognize the sales revenue until the right of return privilege has substantially expired or the provisions of FAS-48 are subsequently met (FAS-48, par. 6). The seller has several alternatives in accounting for these transactions: First, do not record the transaction on the books at all and maintain a **memorandum account** for these types of transactions. Second, record the transaction as a debit to a deferred receivable account and a credit to a deferred sales account. Last, handle the transaction as a consignment. In any

event, maintain control for these types of transactions, particularly if they are a part of recurring business activities.

REASONABLE ESTIMATES OF RETURNS

Reasonable estimates of returns depend on individual circumstances. An enterprise must take into consideration its individual customers and the types of merchandise involved in determining the estimated amount of returns that may occur. The following factors may impair the ability to make a reasonable estimate of returns (FAS-48, par. 8):

1. Possible technological obsolescence or changes in demand for the merchandise
2. The length of the period that the customer has to exercise the right of return
3. Little or no past experience in determining returns for specific types of merchandise
4. Little or no past experience in determining returns for similar types of merchandise
5. A good chance that future marketing policies of the seller and/or the relationship with its customers will change

☛ **PRACTICE POINTER:** The above factors are to be considered in conjunction with the past experience with a specific customer and the individual product involved in the sale. One or more of these factors may or may not impair the ability of an enterprise to make a reasonable estimate of the amount of future returns.

Illustration of Reasonable Estimates of Returns

The right to return merchandise to a seller may apply to only a portion of a total sale. For example, X Company sells 100,000 widgets to Y Company on January 1 for $1 per widget (cost $0.65). In the sales agreement, X Company grants to Y Company the right to return up to a maximum of 30% of the widgets within six months from the date of sale. Under these circumstances, FAS-48 would only apply to the 30% of the widgets that can be returned by Y Company. Assuming that all of the conditions imposed by FAS-48 are met and it is *probable* that one-half (50%) of the widgets subject to return will actually be returned and the estimated cost that X Company expects to incur in connection with the returns is $1,000, the computations would be as follows:

Total sale	$100,000
Less: Portion of the sale not subject to FAS-48	70,000
Balance of the sale subject to FAS-48	$ 30,000
Less: Provision for estimated returns (50% of $30,000), plus estimated cost to be incurred on reacquiring the returns ($1,000)	16,000
Balance of sale which is recognized	$ 14,000
Balance of sale not subject to FAS-48	70,000
Total revenue recognized at date of sale	$ 84,000
Provision for returnable merchandise (allowance)	$ 15,000
Provision for related estimated costs	1,000
Total provision for expected merchandise returns and related costs	$ 16,000

Under FAS-48, X Company reports $84,000 of revenue on the date the title to the widgets passes to Y Company. X Company also sets up a provision for returnable merchandise and related costs of $16,000. Sales and related cost of sales are reported at their gross amounts in the income statement and the sales and related cost of sales for the *probable* returns are deducted from the gross amounts. The journal entries to record the transactions on the books of X Company are as follows:

Accounts receivable	$100,000	
Sales		$100,000
(To record the gross sales to Y Company.)		
Cost of sales	65,000	
Inventory		65,000
(To record cost of sales for Y Company order.)		
Estimated sales returns	15,000	
Deferred cost of sales ($0.65 per widget)	9,750	
Deferred cost of reacquiring returns	1,000	
Cost of sales		9,750
Provision for estimated returns		15,000
Provision for cost of reacquiring returns		1,000
(To defer sales of $15,000, related cost of sales of $9,750, and estimated cost of $1,000 to reacquire estimated returns.)		

The provisions for estimated returns and cost of reacquiring returns are contra accounts to accounts receivable. The deferred cost of sales represents the cost of inventory that is expected to be returned; it is most logically classified as inventory. The deferred cost of reacquiring returns is difficult to classify and may be added to the inventory amount above or classified as a deferred charge.

CHAPTER 44
SEGMENT REPORTING

CONTENTS

CHAPTER 44
SEGMENT REPORTING

OVERVIEW

The term *segment reporting* refers to the presentation of information about certain parts of an enterprise, in contrast to information about the entire enterprise. The need for segment information became increasingly apparent in the 1960s and 1970s as enterprises diversified their activities into different industries and product lines, as well as into different geographic areas. Financial analysts and other groups of financial statement users insisted on the importance of disaggregated information—in order for them to assess risk and perform other types of analyses. These needs resulted in the issuance of FAS-14 (Financial Reporting for Segments of a Business Enterprise) and several other pronouncements that amended FAS-14, which together provide the authoritative literature in effect through 1997. That literature is replaced by the following standard, which provides authoritative guidance for segment reporting beginning in 1998:

FAS-131   Disclosures about Segments of an Enterprise and Related Information (effective for financial statements for periods beginning after December 15, 1997)

CROSS-REFERENCES

1999 MILLER GAAP GUIDE: Chapter 6, "Consolidated Financial Statements"; Chapter 14, "Equity Method"; Chapter 17, "Foreign Operations and Exchange"; Chapter 26, "Interim Financial Reporting"; Chapter 42, "Results of Operations"

1999 MILLER GAAP IMPLEMENTATION MANUAL: Chapter 29, "Segment Reporting"

1999 MILLER GOVERNMENTAL GAAP GUIDE: Chapter 26, "Proprietary Funds"

1999 MILLER NOT-FOR-PROFIT REPORTING: Chapter 7, "Organizational Issues"; Chapter 11, "Display of Certain GAAP Transactions"

BACKGROUND

The objective of presenting disaggregated information about segments of a business enterprise is to produce information about the types of activities in which an enterprise is engaged in and the economic environment in which those activities are carried out. Specifically, the FASB believes that segment information assists financial statement users to:

- Understand enterprise performance
- Assess its prospects for future net cash flows
- Make informed decisions about the enterprise.

> **OBSERVATION:** The FASB does not specifically discuss the objective of providing information to assist in risk assessment. Risk assessment, however, is an important dimension of financial analysis and underlies, to some extent, the need for segment information. The requirements of FAS-131, like its predecessor FAS-14 (Financial Reporting for Segments of a Business Enterprise), include information about products and services, information about activities in different geographic areas, and information about reliance on major customers. All relate to areas of significant risk to an enterprise and to areas where risk may vary considerably from situation to situation, including different levels associated with different products, operating in different geographic areas, and differing levels of reliance on major customers.

Since FAS-14 was issued in 1976, various studies and professional groups have emphasized the importance of segment information and described it as essential, fundamental, indispensable, and integral to the investment analysis process (Association of Management and Research). Financial analysts consistently have pointed out two weaknesses of FAS-14: (1) its failure to require an adequate degree of disaggregation, and (2) its failure to require segment information in interim financial statements. Both the Canadian Institute of Chartered Accountants and the FASB issued research reports in the early 1990s on the subject. They subsequently decided to jointly pursue a project to improve segment reporting, which resulted in FAS-131 and a comparable standard in Canada.

In 1994, the AICPA's Special Committee on Financial Reporting (the "Jenkins Committee") issued its report, which suggests that for users analyzing a company involved in diverse business segments, information about those segments may be as important as information about the company as a whole. That study suggests that standard setters should give a high priority to improving segment reporting, and that segment information should be reoriented toward the way management operates the business enterprise. In identifying operating segments, FAS-131 requires a management approach that is generally consistent with the AICPA special committee's recommendations.

IDENTIFYING SEGMENTS

Scope

FAS-131 applies to public business enterprises. Any single aspect or combination of the following identifies an enterprise as a public enterprise:

- Has issued debt or equity securities that are traded in a public market (a domestic or foreign stock exchange or an over-the-counter market)
- Is required to file financial statements with the Securities and Exchange Commission
- Provides financial statements for the purpose of issuing securities in a public market

FAS-131 does *not* apply in the following situations:

- Nonpublic business enterprises
- Not-for-profit enterprises
- The separate financial statements of parents, subsidiaries, joint ventures, or equity-method investees if those enterprises' separate statements are consolidated or combined and both the separate company statements and the consolidated or combined statements are included in the same financial report

While FAS-131 is not required for *nonpublic* business enterprises, FAS-131 encourages them to provide the same information as public business enterprises.

Operating Segments

The concept of operating segments is instrumental to understanding FAS-131. Operating segments are components of an enterprise (FAS-131, par. 10):

1. That engage in business activities from which revenues may be earned and in which expenses are incurred

2. Whose operating results are reviewed by the enterprise's chief operating decision maker for purposes of making decisions with regard to resource allocation and performance evaluation

3. For which discrete financial information is available.

FAS-131 includes several guidelines that help implement these general criteria for identifying an enterprise's operating segments, as follows:

1. Having earned revenues is not a requirement for a component of a business to be an operating segment (FAS-131, par. 10). For example, a start-up component of the business, which has yet to earn revenue, may be an operating segment.

2. Not every component of an enterprise is an operating segment or part of an operating segment (FAS-131, par. 11). For example, corporate headquarters may not be an operating segment.

3. Concerning personnel involved in segments (FAS-131, par. 12–14:

   a. The term *chief operating decision maker* is intended to refer to a function, not a specific position title. The intent is to identify that person who performs two functions: (*i*) makes decisions relative to the allocation of resources and (*ii*) evaluates the performance of the segments of the enterprise. The chief operating decision maker could be an individual (e.g., chief executive officer, chief operating officer) or it may be a group of individuals.

☛ **PRACTICE POINTER:** FAS-131 is careful not to use a specific position title that might mean different things in different enterprises. The term *chief operating decision maker* was developed to apply to whatever position within an enterprise that meets certain criteria. A chief operating decision maker makes decisions relative to the allocation of resources and evaluates the performance of segments of the enterprise.

   b. The term *segment manager* is intended to refer to the functions having direct accountability to and regular contact with the chief operating decision maker to discuss operating activities, financial results, forecasts, and similar matters. A segment manager may be responsible for more than one segment. The chief operating decision maker also may be a segment manager for one or more operating segments.

4. Other factors that may be important in identifying an enterprise's operating segments are (*a*) the nature of the business activities of each component of the enterprise, (*b*) the way the business is organized in terms of managerial responsibility for components of the enterprise, and (*c*) the manner in which information is presented to the board of directors of the enterprise (FAS-131, par. 13).

5. The three primary characteristics of an operating segment may apply to two or more overlapping components of an enterprise (i.e., a matrix organization). For example, one individual may be responsible for each product and service line and another individual may be responsible for each geographic area in which those product and service lines are distributed. The chief operating decision maker may use information both based on products and services and on geographic areas to make decisions about resource allocation and segment performance. In this situation, the components based on products and services are considered operating segments (FAS-131, par. 15).

Reportable Segments

Reportable segments are operating segments that meet the criteria for separate reporting under FAS-131. Essentially, a reportable segment is one that accounts for a sufficient amount of an enterprise's activities to warrant disclosure of separate information.

Quantitative Thresholds

A logical starting point is the quantitative thresholds for identifying reportable segments. These criteria state that an operating segment is a reportable segment if any of the following quantitative criteria is met (FAS-131, par. 28):

1. The operating segment's total revenues (both external, such as sales to other enterprises, and intersegment, such as sales between operating segments) make up 10% or more of the combined revenue of all reported operating segments.

2. The absolute amount of the reported profit or loss of the operating segments 10% or more of the greater (absolute amount) of the total profit of all operating segments reporting a profit or the total loss of all operating segments reporting a loss.

3. The operating segment's assets make up 10% or more of the combined assets of all operating segments.

In determining its reportable segments that meet these quantitative criteria, management may combine the activities of two or more operating segments, but only if certain similar economic characteristics are present in both (or all) operating segments. These operating segments' segment characteristics include (FAS-131, par. 17):

- The nature of their products and services
- The nature of their production processes
- The types of their customers
- Their distribution methods
- The nature of their regulatory environment (if applicable).

Another quantitative criterion is that the identified reportable segments must constitute at least 75% of the total consolidated revenue (FAS-131, par. 20). If the operating segments that are initially identified as reportable segments do not meet this threshold, additional operating segments must be identified, even if they do *not* meet the quantitative criteria presented earlier. Information about those operating segments for which separate information is not presented can be combined and presented in the aggregate with an appropriate description (e.g., "all other segments").

Comparability

Comparability among years is an important factor in identifying reportable segments, as evidenced by the following requirements that relate to changes in segments meeting the quantitative criteria from one year to the next (FAS-131, pars. 22–23):

1. If a prior-year reportable segment fails to meet one of the quantitative criteria but management believes it to be of continuing significance, information about that segment shall continue to be presented.

2. If an operating segment meets the criteria as a reportable segment for the first time in the current period, prior-year segment information that is presented for comparative purposes shall be restated to reflect the new reportable segment as a separate segment.

As a practical matter, FAS-131 indicates that ten reportable segments is probably a reasonable maximum number for purposes of disclosing separate segment information (FAS-131, par. 24). While the maximum of ten is not stated as an absolute requirement, management is advised that when the number of reportable segments exceeds ten, consideration should be given to whether a practical limit has been reached.

DISCLOSURE OF INFORMATION ABOUT MULTIPLE REPORTABLE SEGMENTS

Segment information is required in four areas:

1. General information
2. Information about segment profit or loss and assets
3. Reconciliation of segment information to aggregate enterprise amounts
4. Interim period information

If complete financial statements are provided, the information required by FAS-131 must be reported for each period, including prior periods presented for comparative purposes.

The following sections cover the specific disclosure requirements in the four general areas identified above.

General Information

General information is necessary for financial statement users to understand the specific information about segments that is required to be disclosed. The general information logically would precede the information about segment profit or loss and assets and reconciliations, which are identified in the following two sections (FAS-131, par. 26):

1. Factors used to identify the enterprise's reportable segments
2. Types of products and services that are the basis for revenues from each reportable segment

In identifying the enterprise's reportable segments, an explanation of the basis for organization is required. Management may have used the following organizational alternatives, for example:

- Products and services
- Geographic areas
- Regulatory environment
- Combination of factors

Information about Segment Profit or Loss and Assets

The heart of the segment reporting requirements of FAS-131 is information about segments' profit or loss and assets. A measure of profit or loss and total assets is required for each reportable segment. This amount should be based on the information reported to the chief operating decision maker for making decisions about allocating resources to segments and assessing segment performance. Similarly, in presenting asset information, used by the chief operating decision maker is the basis for identifying information to be disclosed in the financial statements (FAS-131, par. 27).

If the chief operating decision maker uses only one measure of segment profit or loss and only one measure of assets, those are the measures that should be reported. On the other hand, if the chief operating decision maker uses multiple measures of segment profit or loss or segment assets in resource allocation decisions and performance evaluation, the information reported to satisfy FAS-131 should be that which management believes is determined most consistently with that used in the determination of the corresponding amounts in the enterprise's consolidated financial statements (FAS-131, par. 30).

In presenting segment profit or loss, the following information is required for each segment if the specific amounts are included in the measure of segment profit or loss reviewed by the chief operating decision maker (FAS-131, par. 27):

- Revenues from external customers
- Revenues from other operating segments
- Interest revenue
- Interest expense
- Depreciation, depletion, and amortization
- Unusual items
- Income recognized on equity-method investments
- Income tax expense or benefit
- Extraordinary items
- Significant noncash items other than depreciation, depletion and amortization

Following are guidelines included in FAS-131 for the determination of the information items listed above:

1. In identifying unusual items, APB-30 (Reporting Results of Operations—Reporting the Effects of Disposal of a Segment of a Business, and Extraordinary, Unusual, and Infrequently Occurring Events and Transactions) is the primary source of authority.

2. Interest revenue and expense should be presented separately (i.e., not net) unless the net amount is the figure used by the chief operating decision maker to assess performance and make resource allocation decisions.

Additional information about assets of each reportable segment is required, as follows, if the specified amounts are included in the determination of segment profit or loss (FAS-131, par. 28):

1. The amount of investment in equity-method investees
2. Total expenditures for additions to long-lived assets (except financial instruments, long-term customer relationships of a financial institution, mortgage and other servicing rights, deferred policy acquisition costs, and deferred income taxes)

In addition to the specific information items about segment profit or loss and segment assets, enterprises are required to present explanatory information that should assist users of the financial statements in better understanding the meaning of that information, as follows (FAS-131, par. 31):

1   The basis of accounting for transactions between reportable segments
2. Differences in the measurement of the reportable segments' profit or loss and the enterprise's consolidated income before income taxes, extraordinary items, discontinued operations, and cumulative effect of changes in accounting principle
3. Differences in the measurement of the reportable segments' assets and the enterprise's consolidated assets
4. Any changes from prior years in the measurement of reported segment profit or loss, and the effect, if any, of those changes on the amount of segment profit or loss
5. The nature of any asymmetrical allocations to segments

In further explaining the second and third requirements above, FAS-131 points out that the required reconciliation information (explained below) may satisfy this requirement. It also indicates that enterprises should consider whether differences in accounting policies with regard to the allocation of centrally incurred costs are necessary for understanding the segment information and, if so, to explain those allocation policies. In further explaining the fifth requirement above, FAS-131 illustrates an "asymmetrical allocation" as an enterprise allocating depreciation to a segment without allocating the related depreciable asset to that segment.

Reconciliations

Reconciliations of certain segment information to the enterprise's consolidated totals are an important part of the disclosure requirements of FAS-131, as indicated in the following table (FAS-131, par. 32):

Segment information	Reconciled to	Consolidated information
1. Reportable segments' revenues		1. Consolidated revenues
2. Reportable segments' profit or loss		2. Consolidated income before income taxes, extraordinary items, discontinued operations, and cumulative effect of change in accounting principle
3. Reportable segments'		3. Consolidated assets
4. Reportable segments' amounts for other significant items		4. Corresponding consolidated amounts

In presenting these reconciliations, all significant reconciling items must be separately identified and described.

> **OBSERVATION:** FAS-131, like many authoritative accounting standards, establishes minimum required disclosures. Generally, enterprises are encouraged to disclose additional information beyond the minimum requirements. In the case of segment information, the illustration in paragraph 32d implies that a decision to disclose information beyond the minimum requirements carries with it a responsibility to provide reconciling information about that item for the segments and for the consolidated enterprise. The wording of paragraph 32d is important: "... an enterprise *may choose* to disclose liabilities for its reportable segments, *in which case the enterprise would reconcile* the total of reportable segments' liabilities for each segment to the enterprise's consolidated liabilities if segment liabilities are significant." (Emphasis added.)

Interim Period Information

FAS-131 requires abbreviated segment information in interim financial statements. The following is an abbreviated categorized listing of the information required to be disclosed in condensed interim financial statements issued to shareholders (FAS-131, par. 33):

> Revenue
>> From external customers
>> Intersegment
> Segment profit or loss
> Material changes from last annual report
>> Total assets
>> Basis of segmentation
>> Basis of measuring segment profit or loss
> Reconciliation of segment profit or loss to enterprise consolidated income

In meeting the reconciliation of segment profit or loss requirement, enterprises have two alternatives, depending on whether they allocate items such as income taxes and extraordinary items to segments. If they do *not* allocate these items, the reconciliation should be from reportable segments' profit or loss to enterprise consolidated income before income taxes, extraordinary items, discontinued operations, and the cumulative effect of a change in accounting principle. On the other hand, if the items indicated above are allocated to segments, the reconciliation may be from segments' profit or loss to consolidated income after those items. In either case, significant reconciling items are to be separately identified and described in that reconciliation.

> ☛ **PRACTICE POINTER:** If an enterprise allocates items such as income taxes and extraordinary items to segments, it would be reasonable to expect fewer reconciling items between the total of the reportable segments' profit or loss and the related consolidated totals than would be the case if these same items were *not* allocated to segments and, therefore, were required to be part of the reconciliation. In other words, the more items that are allocated down to the segments in determining their profit or loss, the closer the total of the reportable segments' profit and loss will be to the consolidated enterprise's net income and the fewer the items required to meet the reconciliation requirement.

Restatement of Previously Reported Information

An enterprise may change the structure of its internal organization in a manner that causes information about its reportable segments to lack comparability with previous-period information. In this situation, and where practicable, previous-period information presented for comparative purposes should be restated in accordance with the revised organization. This requirement applies to both previous interim and annual periods. In addition to restating the financial information presented, an explanation of the change is required, including that previous-period information has been restated.

Should restatement of previous period information not be practicable in the year of the internal organization change, disclosure is required of current-period information under both the previous and the new organizational structure if it is practicable to do so.

DISCLOSURE OF ENTERPRISE-WIDE INFORMATION

The previous discussion has focused on disclosure of information about multiple reporting segments. An enterprise is required to report certain disaggregated information, even if it functions as a single operating unit.

Enterprise-wide information is required in the following three areas:

1.   Information about products and services
2.   Information about geographic areas
3.   Information about major customers

Enterprises that are organized around reporting segments may have satisfied these requirements already as a result of satisfying the disclosure requirements for multiple reporting segments. If not, they are required to present the enterprise-wide information, as are enterprises that are not subject to the requirements of those enterprises with multiple reportable segments. Information required in the three areas identified above is as follows:

Products and Services (FAS-131, par. 37)

- Revenues from external customers for each product and service or group of related products and services

Geographic Areas (FAS-131, par. 38)

- Revenues from external customers:
  — Attributable to the enterprise's country of domicile
  — Attributed to all foreign countries in total from which revenue is derived

- Revenues from individual foreign countries if the amounts are material
- The basis for attributing revenues from external customers to individual countries

Major Customers (FAS-131, par. 39)

- Revenues from a single customer that accounts for 10% or more of revenue
- The segment(s) from which sales to each major customer were made

In preparing the information about products and services and geographic areas, amounts should be based on the same information used to prepare the enterprise's general purpose-financial statements. If this is impracticable, the information is not required, but an explanation should be provided.

In preparing the information about major customers, the following additional guidance is provided:

- Neither the identity of the major customer nor the amount of revenue that each segment reports from that customer is required
- A group of entities under common control is considered a single customer.
- For purposes of identifying major *governmental* customers, the federal government, a state government, a local government, or a foreign government is considered a single customer.

EFFECTIVE DATE AND TRANSITION

FAS-131 is effective for fiscal years beginning after December 15, 1997. For calendar-year companies, this means that it is effective in 1998, although earlier application is encouraged. Once FAS-131 is adopted, comparative information for previous years is required to be restated to comply with FAS-131's reporting requirements (FAS-131, par. 40).

While FAS-131 requires certain information be presented in interim financial statements, that information is not required in the first year of implementation. In subsequent years in which the first year of implementation is a comparative year, however, interim information for the initial year of implementation is required to be presented, in conformity with FAS-131, even though it was not presented earlier.

> ☛ **PRACTICE POINTER:** Not requiring interim information in the first year of implementation gives companies considerably longer to get prepared for the new requirements of FAS-131. If this relief had not been granted, calendar-year companies would have been required to implement the interim reporting requirements of FAS-131 as early as March 31, 1998, whereas they are required to first implement the standard in annual financial statements at December 31, 1998.

Examples of several of the major disclosure requirements are presented in the following illustration.

Illustration—Sample Disclosures of Segment Information

FAS-131 requires the disclosure of extensive information about an enterprise's operating segments. Following are brief examples of how some of these requirements might appear in notes to the financial statements. In all cases, dollar figures (in thousands) are assumed for illustrative purposes. For more complete examples, see Appendix B of FAS-131.

Management Policy in Identifying Reportable Segments

Company A's reportable business segments are strategic business units that offer distinctive products and services that are marketed through different channels. They are managed separately because of their unique technology, marketing, and distribution requirements.

Types of Products and Services

Company B has four reportable segments: food processing, apparel manufacturing, insurance, and entertainment. Food processing is a canning operating for sales to regional grocery chains. The apparel segment produces mid-price clothing for distribution through discount department stores. The insurance segment provides primarily property insurance for heavy manufacturing enterprises. The entertainment segment includes several theme parks and multiple-screen theaters.

Segment Profit or Loss

Company C's accounting policies for segments are the same as those described in the summary of significant accounting policies. Management evaluates segment performance based on segment profit or loss before income taxes and nonrecurring gains and losses. Transfers between segments are accounted for at market value.

| | Segments | | | | | Consolidated |
	A	B	C	D	Other	Totals
Revenues from external customers	$200	$200	$300	$400	$100	$1,200
Intersegment revenues		50		60		110
Interest revenue	10	15		40		65
Interest expense	20	10	40	30		100
Depreciation and amortization	50	60	100	120		330
Segment profit	40	75	80	180		375
Segment assets	$180	$220	$280	$450	$250	$1,380
Expenditures for segment assets	20	70	30	80	20	220

Reconciliation of Segment Information to Consolidated Amounts

Information for Company D's reportable segments relates to the enterprise's consolidated totals as follows:

Revenues

Total revenues for reportable segments	$1,800
Other revenues	250
Intersegment revenues	(200)
Total consolidated revenues	$1,850

Profit or Loss

Total profit or loss for reportable segments	$250
Other profit or loss	40
Intersegment profits	(35)
General corporate expenses	(50)
Income before income taxes	$205

Assets

Total assets for reportable segments	$3,000
Assets not attributed to segments	200
Elimination of intersegment receivables	(300)
General corporate assets not attributed to segments	500
Total consolidated assets	$3,400

Geographic Information

Company E attributes revenues and long-lived assets to different geographic areas on the basis of the location of the customer. Revenues and investment of long-lived assets by geographic area are as follows:

	Revenues	Long-lived Assets
United States	$1,200	$800
Mexico	500	400
Brazil	450	375
Taiwan	300	200
Other	800	720
Total	$3,250	$2,495

Major Customer Information

Company F has revenue from a single customer that represents $800 of the enterprise's consolidated revenue. This customer is served by the automotive parts operating segment.

CHAPTER 45
STOCKHOLDERS' EQUITY

CONTENTS

CHAPTER 45
STOCKHOLDERS' EQUITY

OVERVIEW

The various elements constituting stockholders' equity in the statement of financial position are classified according to source. Stockholders' equity may be classified broadly into four categories: (1) legal capital, (2) additional paid-in capital, (3) minority interests, and (4) retained earnings. Detailed information is presented in the body of the statement, in related notes, or in some combination thereof.

GAAP for stockholders' equity are found in the following pronouncements:

ARB-43	Chapter 1, Prior Opinions
	A. Rules Adopted by Membership
	B. Opinions Issued by Predecessor Committee
APB-6	Status of Accounting Research Bulletins
	Paragraph 12, Treasury Stock
APB-12	Omnibus Opinion—1967
	Paragraphs 9 and 10, Capital Changes
APB-14	Paragraph 16, Debt with Stock Purchase Warrants
FAS-129	Disclosure of Information about Capital Structure (Effective for financial statements for periods ending after December 15, 1997)

CROSS-REFERENCES

BACKGROUND

Stockholders' equity represents the interest of the owners of a corporation in the corporation's assets. It represents the residual interest in the enterprise's assets, after liabilities have been subtracted, arising from the investment of owners and the retention of earnings over time.

In the balance sheet, stockholders' equity usually is displayed in two broad categories—*paid-in* or *contributed capital* and *retained earnings*. Paid-in or contributed capital represents the amount provided by stockholders in the original purchase of shares of stock or resulting from subsequent transactions with owners, such as treasury stock transactions. Retained earnings represent the amount of previous income of the corporation that has not been distributed to owners as dividends or transferred to paid-in or contributed capital.

Illustration of Balance Sheet Presentation
of Stockholders' Equity
December 31, 19X5

Preferred stock, $50 par value, 10,000 shares authorized, 7,000 shares authorized and outstanding	$ 350,000
Common stock, $25 par value, 100,000 shares authorized, 75,000 shares issued	1,875,000
Paid-in capital in excess of par value on common stock	500,000
Common stock dividend to be distributed	262,500
Total paid-in capital	$2,987,500
Retained earnings	1,000,000
Total paid-in capital and retained earnings	$3,987,500
Treasury stock, 10,000 shares of common stock at cost	(300,000)
Total stockholders' equity	$3,687,500

STOCKHOLDERS' EQUITY TERMINOLOGY
AND RELATIONSHIPS

Legal (or *stated*) *capital* usually is defined by state law. It refers to the amount of capital that must be retained by a corporation for the protection of its creditors. Legal capital may consist of common or preferred shares. Preferred shares may be participating or nonparticipating as to the earnings of the corporation, may be cumulative or noncumulative as to the payment of dividends, may have a preference claim on assets upon liquidation of the business, and may be callable for redemption at a specified price. Usually, preferred stock does not have voting rights.

Common stock usually has the right to vote, the right to share in earnings, a preemptive right to a proportionate share of any additional common stock issued, and the right to share in assets on liquidation.

Generally, stock is issued with a par value. No-par value stock may or may not have a stated value. *Par or stated value* is the amount that is established in the stock account at the time the stock is issued. When stock is issued above or below par value, a premium or discount on the stock is recorded, respectively. A discount reduces paid-in or contributed capital; a premium increases paid-in or contributed capital. A premium on stock is often referred to as "paid-in capital in excess of par value." Because the issuance of stock at a discount is not legal in many jurisdictions, discounts on stock are not frequently encountered.

A corporation's charter contains the types and amounts of stock that it can legally issue, which is called the *authorized capital stock*. When part or all of the authorized capital stock is issued, it is called *issued capital stock*. Since a corporation may own issued capital stock in the form of treasury stock, the amount of issued capital stock in the hands of stockholders is called *outstanding capital stock*.

A corporation may sell its capital stock by subscriptions. An individual subscriber becomes a stockholder upon subscribing to the capital stock; and upon full payment of the subscription, a stock certificate evidencing ownership in the corporation is issued. When the subscription method is used to sell capital stock, a subscription receivable account is debited and a capital stock subscribed account is credited. On payment of the subscription, the subscription receivable account is credited and cash or other assets are debited. On the actual issuance of the stock certificates, the capital stock subscribed account is debited and the regular capital stock account is credited.

Illustration of Capital Stock Relationships

A company has the following capital stock structure: The numbers below represent shares of a particular class of stock (e.g., common stock) and indicate the relationships among the various components of authorized stock. The number of shares authorized is 10,000, of which 8,000 have been issued and 2,000 are unissued. Of the 8,000 issued shares, 7,000 are outstanding (i.e., in the hands of investors) and 1,000 represent treasury shares (i.e., shares that were issued and outstanding at one time, but have been reacquired by the company). Of the 2,000 unissued shares, 500 have been subscribed and 1,500 are unsubscribed. The 500 subscribed shares have been partially paid and are considered unissued until they are fully paid, at which time they will be considered issued and outstanding shares.

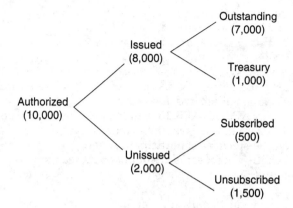

Following are examples of how the numbers of shares change for several independent common capital stock transactions:

1. *Sale of 700 shares of previously unissued stock*—Unsubscribed stock declines by 700 shares, as does the number of unissued shares. Outstanding shares and issued shares increase by 700. As a result, unissued shares number 1,300 and issued shares number 8,700, of which 7,700 are outstanding.

2. *Sale of 100 shares of treasury stock*—Treasury stock declines to 900 shares and outstanding increases to 7,100 shares. The total number of unissued and issued shares remains unchanged.

3. *Subscribed shares (500) are paid in full*—Subscribed shares become zero, reducing unissued shares to 1,500. Outstanding and issued shares increase to 7,500 and 8,500, respectively.

DISCLOSURE OF INFORMATION ABOUT STOCKHOLDERS' EQUITY

When financial statements are prepared in conformity with GAAP, capital changes must be disclosed in a separate statement(s) or note(s) to the financial statement. This requirement is in addition to disclosure of the changes in retained earnings, although all capital changes may be included in one statement. Capital accounts may have to be disclosed because of changes during the year in capital stock, additional paid-in capital accounts, retained earnings, treasury stock, and other capital accounts. (APB-12, pars. 9 and 10).

FAS-129 establishes standards for disclosing information about an entity's capital structure. It consolidates the disclosure requirements that were previously covered in APB-10 (Omnibus Opinion—1966), APB-15 (Earnings per Share), and FAS-47 (Disclosure of Long-Term Obligations). FAS-129 eliminates the exemption for nonpublic entities from certain disclosure requirements about capital structure included in APB-15 as amended by FAS-21 (Suspension of the Reporting of Earnings per Share and Segment Information by Nonpublic Enterprises).

FAS-129 applies to all entities and is effective for financial statements for periods ending after December 15, 1997. It does not change the dis-closure requirements for entities for which the reporting requirements of APB-10, APB-15, and FAS-47 were applicable.

Three terms are particularly important in understanding and applying FAS-129—securities, participating rights, and preferred stock (FAS-129, par. 2). These terms are defined as follows:

Securities   Evidence of debt or ownership or a related right, including options and warrants as well as debt and stock

Participating rights   Contractual rights of security holders to receive dividends or returns from the issuer's profits, cash flows, or returns on investments

Preferred stock   A security that has preferential rights over common stock

FAS-129 requires information about capital structure to be disclosed in three separate categories—information about securities, liquidation preference of preferred stock, and redeemable stock.

Information about Securities

The entity shall provide within its financial statements a summary explanation of the pertinent rights and privileges of the various securities that are outstanding (FAS-129, par. 4–5). Examples of information that is to be disclosed are:

- Dividend and liquidation preferences
- Participating rights
- Call prices and dates
- Conversion or exercise prices or rates and dates
- Sinking-fund requirements
- Unusual voting rights
- Significant terms of contracts to issue additional shares

In addition to the information about rights and privileges associated with securities, the number of shares issued upon conversion, exercise, or satisfaction of required conditions during the most recent annual fiscal period and any subsequent interim period shall be disclosed.

Liquidation Preference of Preferred Stock

Preferred stock or other senior securities may have a preference in involuntary liquidation that is in excess of the security's par or stated value. In this situation, the issuing entity shall disclose the liquidation preference of the stock (i.e., the relationship of the liquidation preference and the par or stated value of the shares). Under the following guidelines, this disclosure should be (FAS-129, par. 6–7):

- Presented within the equity section, either parenthetically or "in short" (i.e., included in the body of the financial statement, but not added in the total of stockholders' equity).

- Presented as an aggregate amount.

  ☞ **PRACTICE POINTER:** Take care not to overlook the requirement that the liquidation preference of preferred stock must be presented in the aggregate and in the body of the equity section of the balance sheet rather than in notes to the financial statements. This is an unusual requirement and could be easily overlooked.

Other disclosures, which may be made either in the financial statements or in related notes, are:

- The aggregate *or* per-share amounts at which preferred stock may be called or are subject to redemption through sinking-fund operations or otherwise

- The aggregate *and* per-share amounts of cumulative preferred dividends in arrears

Redeemable Stock

Redeemable stock must be repurchased by the issuing entity. In this situation, the issuing entity is required to disclose the amount of redemption requirements, separately by issue or combined, for all issues of stock for which the redemption prices and dates are fixed or determinable. This information is required for each of the next five years following the date of the latest statement of financial position that is presented (FAS-129, par. 8).

Illustration of Capital Structure Disclosures

Following are examples of the disclosures required by FAS-129. Disclosures of information about securities, the liquidation preference of preferred stock, and redeemable stock are the direct result of specific circumstances that exist within the reporting entity. No example can include all possible information that may require disclosure. Care should be taken in relying on these or other examples because of differences that may exist among reporting entities.

Information about Securities

ABC Company's capital structure includes common and preferred stock that is described as follows in its statement of financial position and in the note to the financial statements:

Statement of financial position:

Convertible preferred stock—$40 par value, 5 million shares authorized, 4 million shares and 3.8 million shares issued and outstanding in 1996 and 1995, respectively

Common stock—$10 par value, 10 million shares authorized, 6 million shares issued and outstanding in 1996 and 1995

Note to the financial statements:

Each share of ABC preferred stock is convertible into four shares of ABC common stock at any time through December 31, 1999. The preferred stock is entitled to a cumulative annual dividend of $2.50.

Liquidation Preference of Preferred Stock

DEF Company has preferred stock outstanding, as described below in the body of the statement of financial position:

Preferred stock—$10 per share par value, 1 million shares authorized. Issued and outstanding: 1996 and 1995—.8 million and .75 million shares, respectively. Aggregate liquidation preference: 1996 and 1995—$12 million and $11.25 million, respectively.

Redeemable Stock

GHI Company has redeemable preferred stock outstanding, as described below in notes to the financial statements:

Preferred stock—Each share of GHI preferred stock is convertible into four shares of GHI common stock. On December 31, 1998, the preferred shares are redeemable at the company's option at $50 per share. Based on the current market price of the stock, the company expects the majority of the preferred shares to be converted into common stock prior to December 31, 1998.

ADDITIONAL PAID-IN CAPITAL

All stockholders' equity that is not classified as legal capital, minority interests, or retained earnings usually is designated as additional paid-in capital. The common sources of additional paid-in capital are:

1. Excess of par or stated value paid for capital stock
2. Sale of treasury stock
3. The issuance of detachable stock purchase warrants (APB-14, par. 16)
4. Donated assets
5. Capital created by a corporate readjustment or quasi-reorganization

If capital stock is issued for the acquisition of property and it appears that, at about the same time and pursuant to a previous agreement or understanding, some portion of the stock so issued is donated to the corporation, the par value of the stock is not an appropriate basis for valuing the property. Generally, donated stock should be recorded at fair value at the time it is received. Fair value may be determined by the value of the stock or the value of the asset, services, or other consideration received (ARB-43, Ch. 1A, par. 6).

Charges should not be made to paid-in capital, however created, that are properly chargeable to income accounts of the current or future years (ARB-43, Chapter 1A, par. 2).

☞ **PRACTICE POINTER:** Under the cost and par value methods, adjustments to paid-in capital from treasury stock transactions are recognized at different times and determined in different ways. Under the cost method, base adjustments to paid-in capital on the relationship between the purchase price and the subsequent selling price; they are recognized at the time of the sale of the treasury stock. Under the par value method, base adjustments to paid-in capital on the relationship between the original selling price of the stock and the purchase price; they are recognized at the time of the purchase of the treasury stock. These relationships are summarized as follows:

	Cost Method	Par Value Method
Timing of adjustment to paid-in capital	Point of sale	Point of purchase
Paid-in capital increased	Selling price greater than purchase price	Purchase price less than original selling price
Paid-in capital decreased	Selling price less than purchase price	Purchase price greater than original selling price
Retained earnings decreased	Loss on sale greater than paid-in capital from previous treasury stock transactions	Purchase price is so high that all paid-in capital from previous treasury stock transactions is eliminated

Keep in mind that the cost method is much more widely used in practice than the par value method.

MINORITY INTERESTS

The *parent company theory* is used widely in practice for presenting minority interests in a consolidated balance sheet. Under this theory, minority interests are *not* considered part of stockholders' equity and are disclosed in the consolidated balance sheet between the liability section and the stockholders' equity section. When minority interests are insignificant and do not warrant a separate classification in the consolidated balance sheet, some enterprises disclose them among other liabilities. Minority interests in consolidated net income are shown as a deduction of consolidated net income.

Under the *entity theory*, minority interests are disclosed within and as part of the consolidated stockholders' equity section of the consolidated balance sheet. Although the entity theory has much theoretical support, it is seldom used in practice, because under GAAP, consolidated financial statements represent the results of operations, cash flows, and financial position of a single entity.

TREASURY STOCK

Treasury stock is a company's own capital stock that has been issued and subsequently reacquired. It is ordinarily presented as a reduction in the amount of stockholders' equity. Treasury stock is not considered an asset, because it is widely held that a corporation cannot own part of itself. The status of treasury stock is similar to that of authorized but unissued capital stock. Dividends on a company's own stock are not considered a part of income (ARB-43, Ch. 1A, par. 4).

Accounting and Reporting

Under GAAP, both the cost method and the par value method of accounting for treasury stock are acceptable. Under the cost method, each acquisition of treasury stock is accounted for at cost. In addition, separate records are maintained to reflect the date of purchase of the treasury stock, the number of shares acquired, and the reacquisition cost per share. Treasury stock may be kept based on an acceptable inventory method, such as FIFO or average cost basis. Upon the sale or other disposition, the treasury stock account is credited for an amount equal to the number of shares sold, multiplied by the cost per share and the difference treated as paid-in capital in excess of par (stated) value. The cost method of accounting for treasury stock is more commonly used in practice than the par value method.

Under the par value method of accounting for treasury stock, the treasury stock account is increased by the par or stated value of each share reacquired. Any excess paid per share over the par or stated value is debited to paid-in capital in excess of par (stated) value, but only for the amount per share that was originally credited when the stock was issued. Any excess cost per share remaining over the par or stated value per share and the amount per share originally credited to paid-in capital in excess of par (stated) value is charged to retained earnings. If the cost per share of treasury stock is less than the par or stated value per share and the amount per share originally credited to paid-in capital in excess of par (stated) value the difference is credited to paid-in capital from treasury stock transactions. Under the par value method, all of the original capital balances related to the shares reacquired are removed from the books.

When treasury stock is acquired with the intent of retiring the stock (whether or not retirement is actually accomplished), the excess of the price paid for the treasury stock over its par or stated value may be allocated between (*a*) paid-in capital arising from the same class of stock and (*b*) retained earnings. The amount of excess that can be allocated to paid-in capital arising from the same class of stock, however, is limited to the sum of (*a*) any paid-in capital arising from previous retirements and net gains on sales of the same class of treasury stock and (*b*) the pro rata portion of paid-in capital, voluntary transfers of retained earnings, capitalization of stock dividends, etc., on the same class of stock. For this purpose, any paid-in capital arising from issues of capital stock that are fully retired (formal or constructive) is deemed to be applicable on a pro rata basis to all shares of common stock. As an alternative, the excess of the price paid for the treasury stock over its par or stated value may be charged entirely to retained earnings, based on the fact that a corporation can always capitalize or allocate retained earnings for such a purpose (APB-6, par. 12).

When the price paid for the acquired treasury stock is less than its par or stated value, the difference is credited to paid-in capital.

When treasury stock is acquired for purposes other than retirement, it is disclosed separately in the balance sheet as a deduction from stockholders' equity.

A gain on the sale of treasury stock acquired for purposes other than retirement is credited to paid-in capital from the sale of treasury stock. Losses are charged to paid-in capital, but only to the extent of available net gains from previous sales or retirements of the same class of stock; otherwise, losses are charged to retained earnings (ARB-43, Ch. 1B, par. 7).

If a state law prescribes the manner in which a corporation accounts for the acquisition of treasury stock, the state law is followed, even if the state law is in variance with existing GAAP. Restrictions on the availability of retained earnings for the payment of dividends or any other restrictions required by state law are disclosed in the financial statements (APB-6, par. 13).

If treasury stock is donated to a corporation and then subsequently sold, the entire proceeds shall be credited to paid-in capital from the sale of donated treasury stock (ARB-43, Ch. 1A, par. 6).

Purchase Price of Treasury Stock

If treasury shares are reacquired for a purchase price significantly in excess of their current market price, it is *presumed* that the total purchase price includes amounts for stated or unstated rights or privileges. Under this circumstance, the total purchase price is allocated between the treasury shares and the rights or privileges that are identified with the purchase of the treasury shares based on the fair value of the rights or privileges, or the fair value of the treasury shares, whichever is more clearly evident.

Treasury Stock Not an Asset

Ordinarily, treasury stock is not presented as an asset in the statement of financial position. It may be reported as an asset under certain circumstances (not described), if disclosed adequately (ARB-43, Ch. 1A, par. 4 and APB-6, par. 12b). For example, some corporations have reported treasury stock as an asset if the treasury stock was held to liquidate a specific liability that appeared on the balance sheet.

DIVIDENDS

A *dividend* is a pro rata distribution by a corporation, based on shares of a particular class, and usually represents a distribution based on earnings.

Cash Dividends

Cash dividends are the most common type of dividend distribution. Preferred stock usually pays a fixed dividend, expressed in dollars or a percentage.

Three dates usually are involved in a dividend distribution:

1. *Date of declaration*: The date the board of directors formally declares the dividend to the stockholders
2. *Date of record*: The date the board of directors specifies that stockholders of record on that date are entitled to the dividend payment
3. *Date of payment*: The date the dividend is actually disbursed by the corporation or its paying agent

Cash dividends are recorded on the books of the corporation as a liability (dividends payable) on the date of declaration. Dividends are paid only on authorized, issued, and outstanding shares, thereby eliminating any dividend payment on treasury stock.

Stock Dividends

Stock dividends are distributions of a company's own capital stock to its existing stockholders in lieu of cash. Stock dividends are accounted for by transferring an amount equal to the fair market value of the stock from retained earnings to paid-in capital. The dividend is recorded at the date of declaration by reducing retained earnings and establishing a temporary account, such as "Stock Dividend to Be Distributed." Because no asset distribution is required for a stock dividend, that account is part of stockholders' equity, in contrast to a cash dividend payable account, which is a liability. When the stock is distributed, the stock dividend account is eliminated and permanent capital accounts (e.g., common stock and paid-in capital in excess of par (stated) value) are increased (ARB-43, Ch. 7B, par. 10).

Illustration of Stock Dividends

LPS Corporation declares a 5% stock dividend on its 1,000,000 shares of outstanding $10 par common stock (5,000,000 authorized). On the date of declaration, LPS stock is selling for $25 per share.

Total stock dividend (5% of 1,000,000)		50,000 shares
Value of 50,000 shares @ $25 per share (market)		$1,250,000
Date of declaration:		
Retained earnings	$1,250,000	
Stock dividend to be distributed		$1,250,000
Date of Distribution:		
Stock dividend to be distributed	$1,250,000	
Common stock (50,000 x $10)		$500,000
Paid-in capital in excess of par value		750,000

Stock Splits

When a stock distribution is more than 20% to 25% of the outstanding shares immediately before the distribution, it is considered a stock split, sometimes referred to as a "stock split-up" (ARB-43, Ch. 7B, par. 13). A stock split increases the number of shares of capital stock outstanding, and a reverse stock split decreases the number of shares of capital stock outstanding.

In both straight and reverse stock splits, the total dollar amount of stockholders' equity does not change. The par or stated value per share of capital stock, however, decreases or increases in proportion with the increase or decrease in the number of shares outstanding. For example, in a stock split of 4 for 1 of $40 par value capital stock, the new stock has a par value of $10 and the number of shares outstanding increases to four shares for each share of stock previously outstanding. In a reverse stock split of 1 for 4 of $40 par value capital stock, the new stock has a par value of $160 per share and the number of shares outstanding decreases to one share for each four shares of stock previously outstanding.

A stock split is used by a corporation to reduce the market price of its capital stock to make the market price of the stock more attractive to buyers (ARB-43, Ch. 7B, par. 2). Thus, in a 4 for 1 straight stock split, the new shares would probably sell for about one-fourth of the previous market price of the old shares prior to the split. Reverse stock splits are unusual and are used to increase the market price of a corporation's stock. For example, a reverse stock split of 1 for 4 of stock selling for $3 would probably increase the market price of the new shares to about $12 per share.

No journal entry is required to record a stock split except a memorandum entry in the capital stock account to indicate the new par or stated value of the stock and the number of new shares outstanding after the split. Stock splits should not be referred to as dividends (ARB-43, Ch. 7B, par. 11).

A stock split may, however, be accomplished in the form of a stock dividend. In this case, the distribution of stock is called *a stock split issued in the form of a stock dividend*, and the percentage distribution is large enough (i.e., in excess of 20% to 25% of the outstanding stock) that the market value of the stock reacts accordingly. Accounting in this situation is similar to a stock dividend, except that only the par or stated value of the stock, rather than the market value, is transferred from retained earnings to paid-in capital.

Stock dividends and stock splits are similar in that they result in increased numbers of outstanding shares of stock for which stockholders make no payment. They differ, however, in size, in their impact on the stock's market price, and, most important, in managerial intent. In the case of a stock dividend, management intent usually is to make a distribution to owners while preserving present cash; in the case of a stock split, management intent is to affect (reduce) market price. Accounting for stock dividends and stock splits is summarized in Figure 45-1.

STOCK RIGHTS

No accounting entry is necessary for the entity issuing the stock right or warrant, except for detachable stock purchase warrants or similar rights, which are accounted for separately and assigned a value (see the 1999 *Miller GAAP Guide* chapter titled "Convertible Debt and Debt with Warrants").

Figure 45-1:   Accounting for Stock Dividends and Stock Splits

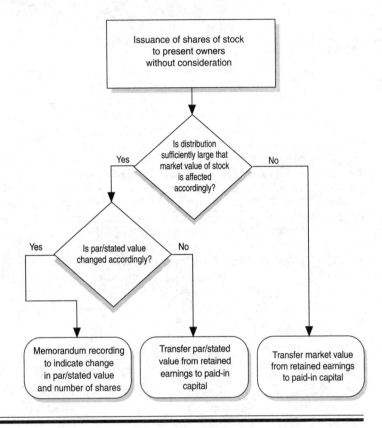

CHAPTER 46
STOCK ISSUED TO EMPLOYEES

CONTENTS

CHAPTER 46
STOCK ISSUED TO EMPLOYEES

OVERVIEW

Stock issued to employees may include compensation (compensatory plan) or may not include compensation (noncompensatory plan). A *compensatory plan* is one in which services rendered by employees are partially compensated for by the issuance of stock. The measurement of compensation expense included in compensatory plans is the primary problem encountered in accounting for stock issued to employees.

GAAP for stock issued to employees are found in the following pronouncements:

APB-25	Accounting for Stock Issued to Employees
ARB-43	Chapter 13B, Compensation Involved in Stock Option and Stock Purchase Plans
FAS-123	Accounting for Stock-Based Compensation
FIN-28	Accounting for Stock Appreciation Rights and Other Variable Stock Option or Award Plans
FIN-38	Determining the Measurement Date for Stock Option, Purchase, and Award Plans Involving Junior Stock

CROSS-REFERENCES

1999 MILLER GAAP GUIDE: Chapter 1, "Accounting Changes"; Chapter 7, "Contingencies, Risks, and Uncertainties"; Chapter 13, "Earnings per Share"; Chapter 21, "Income Taxes"; Chapter 45, "Stockholders' Equity"

1999 MILLER GAAP IMPLEMENTATION MANUAL: Chapter 31, "Stock Issued to Employees"

1999 MILLER GAAP IMPLEMENTATION MANUAL: EITF: Chapter 28, "Stock Compensation to Employees and Others"

BACKGROUND

GAAP for stock-based compensation plans are established primarily in APB-25 and FAS-123. APB-25 is based on the intrinsic value method of accounting. FIN-28 and FIN-31 are interpretations of APB-25. FAS-123 established a method of accounting for stock-based compensation that is based on the fair value of stock options and similar instruments; adoption of that method is encouraged but not required.

Descriptions of the more common types of plans follow:

Fixed Plan

In a typical fixed plan, terms are fixed at the date of grant to determine the number of shares of stock involved and the option price to the employee. Transferability of the stock acquired by the employee usually is restricted, and the plan generally provides that the employee must perform current and/or future services.

Stock Option and Purchase Plan

In a stock option and purchase plan, an employee is granted the right to purchase a fixed number of shares at a certain price during a specified period.

Stock Bonus and Award Plan

In a stock bonus and award plan, an employee is granted a bonus or award of a fixed number of shares or a specified dollar amount, which is payable in shares. The employee usually makes no payment to receive the bonus or award of stock.

Shadow or Phantom Stock Plan

In a shadow or phantom stock plan, the employee receives cash, stock, or a combination of both, in an amount equal to a specified increase in the market price of the employer corporation's stock or an amount equal to a specified increase in the dividend distributions of the employer corporation.

Combination and Elective Plan

In a combination and elective plan, the employee is granted rights to more than one plan, or the right to select alternatives under one plan. The separate rights may be granted at different intervals or simultaneously and may run concurrently or for different periods. These plans are sometimes referred to as tandem or alternate stock plans.

NONCOMPENSATORY PLANS

Certain stock options and stock purchase plans are not intended to compensate employees. For example, a corporation's intent may be to raise additional capital or to diversify its ownership to include employees and officers. A plan is *noncompensatory* if the cash received per share is very close to the amount of cash that would be received if the same deal were offered to all shareholders. In these types of transactions, a company generally does not recognize any compensation costs.

The essential characteristics of noncompensatory stock options or stock purchase plans are (APB-25, par. 7):

1. Substantially all full-time employees meeting limited employment qualifications may participate. Officers and employees who own more than a specific amount of the outstanding stock in the corporation may be excluded.

2. Stock is offered equally to eligible employees, but the plan may limit the total amount of shares that can be purchased.

3. The time permitted to exercise the rights is limited to a reasonable period.

4. Any discount from the market price is no greater than would be a reasonable offer of stock to shareholders or others.

Plans that do not have these characteristics are classified as compensatory plans (APB-25, par. 8).

COMPENSATORY PLANS

Compensatory plans give rise to compensation, usually out of an offer or agreement by a corporation to issue shares to one or more officers or employees (grantees) at a stated price less than the prevailing market. In some instances the grantees' options are exercisable under certain conditions, such as the length of employment of an employee. In other cases, the grantees may agree to take the shares only for investment purposes and not for resale.

Fixed Plans

Under traditional stock option and stock purchase plans, an employer corporation grants options to purchase shares of its stock, sometimes at a price lower than the prevailing market, making it possible for the individual exercising the option to have at least a potential profit at the time of acquisition. Many option agreements provide that the purchaser must retain the stock for a minimum period, thus eliminating the possibility of speculation.

Compensatory plans result in compensation expense on the books of the corporation and in compensation income to the recipient. Under APB-25, the cost of compensation is measured by the excess of the quoted market price of the stock over the option price on the measurement date (APB-25, par. 10). This is referred to as the intrinsic value method.

Measurement Date

The quoted market price of the shares granted under an option may vary considerably over the period of the option. This creates a problem in determining a date that may be used to measure the cost of compensation if the shares are offered at less than market. At least six dates are possible:

1. Date of adoption of the option plan
2. Date on which the option is granted to an employee
3. Date on which the grantee has performed any conditions precedent to the exercise of the option
4. Date on which the grantee may first exercise the option
5. Date on which the option is exercised by the grantee
6. Date on which the grantee disposes of the stock acquired

APB-25 states that the measurement date for determining compensation costs in stock options is the first date on which *both* of the following are known (APB-25, par. 10b):

1. Number of shares an employee is entitled to receive
2. Option or purchase price

For fixed plans, this information is known at the grant date, making the grant date and the measurement date the same. Compensation is measured as the excess of the market price over the option price times the number of shares on the measurement date.

Illustration of Accounting for Stock Options—Basic

An officer of a corporation is granted an option to purchase 100 shares of $20 par value stock for $30 when the market price is $40.

Compensation—officers	$1,000	
Outstanding stock options (100 x [$40 – $30])		$1,000

Subsequently, when the stock options are exercised, the journal entry is:

Cash (100 x $30)	$3,000	
Outstanding stock options	1,000	
Common stock (100 x $20)		$2,000
Paid-in capital in excess of par value		2,000

Outstanding stock options are part of the stockholders' equity and usually are classified as paid-in capital until they are exercised.

In a stock option for current services, the measurement date may be the end of the fiscal period if the following conditions are met (APB-25, par. 11c):

1. An established formal plan provides the terms of the award.

2. The plan details how to determine the total dollar amount due to an employee. It is possible that the *actual* amount will be indeterminable at the end of the period because it is dependent on an item, such as net income, which will not be known at that time.

3. The employee is being compensated for services rendered in the current period.

If a company transfers stock to a trustee, agent, or other third party, the measurement date becomes the date of transfer to the trustee if the following items are irrevocable (APB-25, par. 11e):

1. Transfer of the stock to the trust

2. Terms of the trust agreement

3. Specified employee(s) who will receive the stock

In essence, if all three of the above are met, the company has given up any alternative use of the shares except for the ones specifically stipulated in the stock option agreement.

If treasury stock is distributed in a stock option plan, it is unacceptable to measure compensation costs by the amount paid to reacquire such treasury stock. The only exception to this rule is when a company meets all the conditions in a stock option for current services (above). In this event, the company may elect to measure its compensation costs by the amount paid to reacquire treasury stock, provided the treasury stock is reacquired during the same period in which the award is made and distribution to the employee occurs shortly after the close of the period (APB-25, par. 11a).

The measurement date for stock options consisting of convertible securities can be determined only after the conversion ratio is known. Compensation is measured on the measurement date by the market price of the convertible security or the security into which it is convertible, *whichever is higher* (APB-25, par. 11f).

If a company renews a stock option or extends the period during which the recipient can exercise the option, then a new measurement date is established as if a new option had just been granted (APB-25, par. 11d). The measurement date does not change merely because the agreement stipulates that termination of employment alters the number of shares an employee will receive (APB-25, par. 11b).

Variable Plans

Variable plans include stock appreciation rights and other plans in which the number of shares, exercise price, or both are contingent on a future event. The measurement date follows the grant date because the number of shares of stock that an employee can acquire or the exercise price, or both are not determinable at the date of grant (FIN-28, par. 2).

The vesting period in variable plan awards usually runs from the date of grant to the exercise date. For the purposes of GAAP, the variable plan awards become vested on the date that the employee's right to receive the benefits under the plan are not contingent on any additional services to be performed by the employee (FIN-28, par. 3).

Compensation expense is charged to the *service period*, which is the period(s) in which the related services are performed by the employee. If the service period cannot be determined by the terms of the plan or otherwise, then the service period is presumed to be the same as the vesting period. If the variable plan award is for past services, compensation costs are charged as an expense of the period in which the plan was granted (FIN-28, par. 3).

When the service period of a variable plan award covers more than one fiscal period, compensation costs between the date of grant and the measurement date are estimated as follows (FIN-28, par. 4):

1. In the year of grant or first fiscal period, compensation cost is measured with whatever information is available. If the num-

ber of shares are known but not the exercise price, then an exercise price is estimated. If the exercise price is known but not the number of shares, then the number of shares is estimated. If both the number of shares and the exercise price are unknown, then reasonable estimates are made based on all information available.

2. Compensation cost initially is measured as the difference between the quoted market price and the option price multiplied by the number of shares involved.

3. In subsequent periods, compensation costs are adjusted, but not below zero, for any increase or decrease in the quoted market price. The adjustment is made to compensation expense of the period in which the change in the quoted market price occurs.

4. The accrued compensation cost for a right that is canceled or forfeited is adjusted by decreasing compensation expense in the period of cancellation or forfeiture. Such adjustments are considered changes in accounting estimates and are made in the period of change and/or future periods.

5. Accrued compensation cost is charged to expense over the period (service period) in which the employee performs the related services.

Illustration of Stock Appreciation Rights

Fox, Inc., grants stock appreciation rights to its chief executive officer on January 1, 19X1. After the three-year holding period, the rights entitle the CEO to the appreciation in share price over the market value of the $20 par value common stock. The rights have the following terms:

Service period:	January 1, 19X1–December 31, 19X3
Number of shares:	1,000
Exercise date:	January 1, 19X4
Form of compensation:	Cash or purchase common stock ($25 per share)

The quoted market price of Fox's capital stock is as follows:

January 1, 19X1	$25
December 31, 19X1	30
December 31, 19X2	29
December 31, 19X3	34

Compensation expense is determined for each year as follows:

Year	Market Price	Predetermined Price	Compensation to Date	Service Period Allocation	Annual Expense
19X1	$30	$25	$5,000*	1/3	$1,667
19X2	$29	$25	4,000**	2/3	$2,666
					(1,667)
					$1,000
19X3	$34	$25	9,000***	3/3	$9,000
					(2,667)
					$6,333

* ($30 − $25) x 1,000
** ($29 − $25) x 1,000
*** ($34 − $25) x 1,000

Compensation expense is recognized each year on a cumulative basis, using the current market price and giving consideration to compensation recognized in previous years. Entries to record compensation expense each year are:

	19X1	*19X2*	*19X3*
Compensation expense	$1,667	$1,000	$6,333
Compensation payable	$1,667	$1,000	$6,333

On January 1, 19X4, if the CEO takes the cash option, the entry is as follows:

Compensation payable	$9,000	
Cash		$9,000

On January 1, 19X4, if the CEO takes the option to purchase stock at $25 per share, the entry is as follows:

Cash (1,000 x $25)	$25,000	
Compensation payable	9,000	
Common stock		$20,000
Paid-in capital in excess of par value		14,000

Junior Stock Plans

Junior stock is a separate class of stock sold to employees for a fraction of the price of the company's regular common stock. The junior stock pays a lower dividend and has fewer voting rights than the company's common stock and usually is not transferable, except back to the issuing company. The junior stock is convertible into the company's regular common stock if certain performance goals, such as specified levels of sales or profits, are met.

FIN-38 requires that all junior stock options be accounted for as variable stock options because at the date of grant of a junior stock option there is no way to determine the number of shares of regular common stock that will ultimately be issued on the date the junior shares are converted by an employee. Thus, under the rules for variable stock options, the date for measuring compensation cost for junior stock plans is the first date on which the following are known: (*a*) the number of shares of regular common stock an employee is entitled to receive in exchange for the junior stock and (*b*) the option or purchase price, if any, that the employee pays for the junior stock (FIN-38, par. 2).

> **OBSERVATION:** Restricted junior stock that is issued to employees and becomes unrestricted when certain performance goals are achieved is also subject to the provisions of FIN-38 (FIN-38, par. 1).

Compensation cost is calculated on the measurement date as the difference between (*a*) the quoted market value of the shares of regular common stock that an employee is entitled to receive upon conversion of the junior stock and (*b*) the amount paid or to be paid by the employee for the junior stock. Compensation cost is charged to expense over the service period specified in the option agreement, which is the period(s) in which the related services are performed by the employee (FIN-28, par. 3). In junior stock options, however, accrual of compensation cost cannot begin until the date it becomes *probable* that the employee will qualify for conversion of the junior stock to regular common stock, through the achievement of performance goals or the occurrence of transactions specified in the plan (FIN-38, par. 3). Once it has become *probable* that an employee will qualify for conversion of junior shares to regular common shares, compensation cost is accrued. If the plan specifies a period during which performance must occur, the accrual of compensation cost is allocated to that same period. If no period is specified in the plan, compensation cost is accrued over the period that starts on the date that performance becomes *probable* and ends on the date that performance is *most likely* or when a required service period ends (FIN-38, par. 5).

> **OBSERVATION:** As used in FIN-38, *probable* has the same meaning as it has in FAS-5 (Accounting for Contingencies) (see the 1999 *Miller GAAP Guide* chapter titled "Contingencies, Risks, and Uncertainties"), namely, that it is *likely* that the

events will take place. However, the meaning of *most likely* is not clear. Evidently, *most likely* is a higher degree of probability, although not explained in either FIN-38 or FAS-5.

If, as a result of vesting provisions, junior stock becomes convertible to regular common stock after the measurement date, compensation cost is recognized during the period from (*a*) the first date that performance becomes *probable* or the date that performance occurs to (*b*) the date that the junior stock becomes convertible or the end of the service period, whichever occurs first. If cash is paid to the employee to reacquire previously issued junior stock, compensation cost is equal to the excess of the amount of cash paid to the employee, over the amount of cash or other assets received from the employee for the junior stock (FIN-38, par. 6).

For the purpose of determining diluted earnings per share, junior stock options are considered potential common stock, to the extent they are convertible into the employer's regular common stock (FIN-38, par. 7).

Measuring Compensation Costs

Under APB-25, the amount of compensation, or the value of the stock option, is the excess of the unadjusted quoted market price of the stock at the measurement date over the amount the employee must pay in cash or other assets. Often, the market quotations for a closely held or nonpublic corporation are not available, and other methods of valuation must be used. No compensation is recorded if the employee purchases the stock for an amount equal to or greater than the market price (APB-25, par. 10).

> ☛ **PRACTICE POINTER:** The value of a stock option may be affected by many factors, such as transferability and other restrictions. In spite of the recognition of these factors, promulgated GAAP require (as a practical solution) the use of a quoted market price to measure compensation costs relating to both restricted or unrestricted stock. Only if a quoted market price is not available can an estimate be used.

Compensation cost related to options for convertible stock is based on the higher market price of either the convertible stock awarded or the underlying security for which the convertible stock can be exchanged (APB-25, par. 11f).

Cash paid to settle an earlier option right with an employee is the measure of compensation, and the earlier measure of compensation (date the option was granted) should be adjusted. If a company uses cash to reacquire stock shortly after the stock was issued to an employee through a stock option plan, then the cash paid is used to measure the compensation cost (APB-25, par. 11g).

If compensation cost is to be measured at a date in the future, a company must make a reasonable estimate of what the compensation cost will be. Since the measurement date is unknown, the price of the stock at the end of each period is used (APB-25, par. 13). If the number of shares is also unknown, a reasonable estimate, given the known facts, must be made.

> ☛ **PRACTICE POINTER:** Make adjustments to estimates in future periods as a change in an accounting estimate. Make a change in an accounting estimate in the period of change and/or in future periods. Do not restate prior financial statements.

When a stock option plan combines two or more plans, compensation cost for each subplan may be measured separately. If the plan gives the employee a choice as to which section of the plan is to be exercised, the measurement at the end of each period should be based on an estimate of which part of the plan the employee is most likely to elect at that time (APB-25, par. 11h). For purposes of applying this provision to stock appreciation rights (and other variable plan awards), FIN-28 indicates that compensation expense shall be measured according to the terms the employee is most likely to elect based on the facts available each period. The enterprise usually shall presume that the employee will elect to exercise the stock appreciation rights (or other variable plan awards), but that presumption may be overcome if past experience or the terms of a combination plan that limit the market appreciation available to the employee provide evidence that the employee will elect the related stock option. If the employee elects to exercise the stock option, any compensation that has been accrued is recognized as consideration for the stock issued (FIN-28, par. 5).

Related Tax Effects

A company usually realizes a tax deduction for any amount the employee declares as ordinary income. The tax deduction is taken in the year in which the employee includes the benefits from the stock option in gross income. This corporate tax reduction results in a temporary difference, because on the company's books the compensation cost is reflected as an expense during the period of related employee service, but is recognized on the tax return in the year the employee includes the benefit in gross income. In such cases deferred taxes are recorded (APB-25, par. 16).

If a tax reduction exists above and beyond that which is recognized as a deferred tax, it is added to paid-in capital in excess of par in the period of the tax deduction (APB-25, par. 17).

It is also possible that recorded compensation cost will be greater than the allowable tax deduction. In such cases, a company may deduct the difference from paid-in capital in the period of the tax reduction. This reduction is limited to the amount that the tax reduction for the same plan previously increased paid-in capital (APB-25, par. 17).

A company can incur additional compensation costs by reimbursing an employee for the tax benefit derived from the stock option plan. This reimbursement is recognized as an additional expense against income (APB-25, par. 18).

Illustration of Accounting for Stock Options—Complex

An officer of a corporation is granted an option to purchase up to 1,000 shares of stock ($50 par value) at the end of two years at 80% of the then market price. The amount of the option will be determined by the total net income of the corporation for the two years in accordance with the following schedule:

Number of Shares	Net Income
200	0 to $500,000
500	$500,001 to $1,000,000
700	$1,000,001 to $1,500,000
1,000	above $1,500,000

At the end of the first year, assume the following facts:

Market price of stock	$ 100
Corporate net income	$700,000
Corporate tax rate	40%

Compensation costs at the end of the first year are determined as follows:

500 shares x 20% x market price = $10,000

or

500   x $20   = $10,000

The journal entry at the end of the first year is:

Compensation costs	$10,000	
Deferred taxes	4,000	
Outstanding stock options		$10,000
Income tax expense		4,000

At the end of the second year, corporate net income is $1,200,000 and the market price of the stock is $110.

The journal entry at the end of the second year to record the stock option is:

Compensation costs	$5,400	
Deferred taxes	2,160	
Outstanding stock options		$5,400
Income tax expense		2,160

The compensation costs and deferred taxes were found by valuing the entire option at the end of two years and subtracting the previous year's compensation costs and related deferred taxes.

700 shares x 20% x $110 =	$ 15,400
Recognized in first year	(10,000)
Recognized in second year	$ 5,400

The journal entry when the officer exercises the stock option is:

Cash ($110 x 0.80 x 700 shares)	$61,600	
Outstanding stock options	15,400	
Common stock ($50 par x 700 shares)		$35,000
Paid-in capital in excess of par value		42,000

Recognition of Compensation Cost

Compensation cost is recognized as an expense over the period of employment attributable to the option. If this period is not stated, a reasonable estimate must be made, taking into account the circumstances implied by the terms of the agreement (APB-25, par. 12).

Stock issued in accordance with a plan for past and future services of an employee is allocated between expired costs and future costs. Future costs are charged to the periods in which the employee performs services. In the event stock options are exercised before the related compensation cost is actually incurred, a deferred or prepaid compensation account is set up. Unearned compensation cost should be written off to the period(s) in which they were actually earned, and any balances at a reporting date should be deducted from stockholders' equity (APB-25, par. 14).

☛ **PRACTICE POINTER:** Recognition of a stock option is made in accordance with the substance of the transaction. Therefore, if an employee gives an employer a nonrecourse note as consideration for stock issued with the stock as collateral, the transaction may be in substance the grant of a stock option. In this event, compensation cost is measured and the nonrecourse note is reported as a reduction of stockholders' equity and not as an asset.

FAS-123 REPORTING REQUIREMENTS

FAS-123 establishes a method of accounting for stock compensation plans based on fair value and encourages employers to adopt that method instead of continuing to apply the provisions of APB-25, which have been described earlier in this chapter.

> **OBSERVATION:** The FASB was asked by the AICPA's Accounting Standards Executive Committee, the Securities and Exchange Commission, large accounting firms, industry representatives, and others to reconsider the accounting method for stock-based compensation in accordance with APB-25, FIN-28, and other pronouncements. In a 1993 Exposure Draft of a proposed Statement of Financial Accounting Standards, the FASB indicated its plan to require the fair value method in lieu of that specified in the current authoritative literature. Amid much controversy, however, the FASB relaxed that position in FAS-123 by encouraging, but not requiring, its new method.

FAS-123 establishes a method of accounting for stock compensation plans that is based on the fair value of employee stock options and similar equity instruments. The method is in contrast to that described in APB-25, which is based on the intrinsic value of equity instruments. The fair value method of FAS-123 is preferable for justifying a change in accounting principle in accordance with APB-20 (Accounting Changes) (FAS-123, par. 11). Companies are permitted to continue using the method of accounting described in APB-25 but are required to disclose pro forma net income and earnings per share (for public companies), determined as if the fair value method of FAS-123 had been used to measure compensation cost. Once an entity adopts the fair value method, that election cannot be reversed. The method used must be disclosed, and the same method must be used for all stock compensation arrangements (FAS-123, par. 14).

Applying Fair Value to Stock Compensation

The general principle underlying FAS-123 is that equity instruments are recognized at the fair value of the consideration received for them. In a transaction with third parties for goods and services, fair value may be the value of the consideration received or the value of the equity instruments issued, whichever is more reliably measurable (FAS-123, par. 8).

Applying this general principle to stock compensation results in the equity instruments being measured and recognized at their fair value and the compensation cost being the excess of that amount over any amount paid by the employee. For example, if an employee pays $10 for a stock option valued at $30, $20 is the amount of compensation attributed to employee services (FAS-123, par. 16).

The objective of the measurement process described in FAS-123 is to estimate the fair value, based on the stock price at the grant date, of equity instruments to be issued to employees when they have satisfied all conditions required to earn the right to benefit from the instruments (FAS-123, par. 17). The definition of *fair value* in FAS-123 is the same as given in FAS-121 (Accounting for the Impairment of Long-Lived Assets and for Long-Lived Assets to Be Disposed Of) and described in the chapter titled "Impairment of Loans and Long-Lived Assets" in the 1999 *Miller GAAP Guide*. The fair value of a stock option granted by a public entity shall be estimated in accordance with FAS-123 by an option-pricing model (e.g., the Black–Scholes or binomial model) that takes into consideration, as of the grant date, the following factors (FAS-123, par. 19):

- Exercise price of the option
- Expected life of the option
- Current price of the underlying stock (not applicable for nonpublic entities)
- Expected volatility of the underlying stock
- Expected dividends on the stock
- The risk-free interest rate for the expected term of the option

The fair value of an option estimated at the grant date is not subsequently adjusted for changes in the price of the underlying stock or other variables (e.g., changes in volatility, the life of the option, dividends on the stock, or the risk-free interest rate) (FAS-123, par. 19).

In unusual circumstances where it is not possible to estimate the fair value of stock options and other equity instruments when they are granted, the final measure of compensation cost shall be the fair value based on the stock price and other pertinent factors at the first date it is possible to estimate that value (FAS-123, par. 22).

If an employee stock purchase plan satisfies all of the following criteria, the discount from market price is not stock-based compensation and simply reduces the proceeds from issuing the shares of stock (FAS-123, par. 23):

1. The plan incorporates no option features.

2. The discount from the market price does not exceed the greater of (*a*) a per-share discount that would be reasonable in an offer of stock to stockholders or others or (*b*) the per-share amount of stock issuance costs avoided by not having to raise a significant amount of capital by a public offering of the stock.

3. Substantially all full-time employees meeting limited employment qualifications may participate on an equitable basis.

Awards Requiring Settlement in Cash

Some stock-based compensation arrangements require the employer to settle the award by paying cash to employees rather than issuing equity securities. For these plans, the effects of changes in the stock price during the service period are recognized as compensation cost over the service period in accordance with FIN-18, as described earlier in this chapter (FAS-123, par. 25).

Recognition of Compensation Cost

Following are summaries of some of the most significant principles included in FAS-123 concerning the recognition of compensation cost:

*   The amount of compensation cost recognized is based on the number of instruments that eventually vest (FAS-123, par. 26).

*   A stock-based compensation award becomes vested when an employee's right to shares of stock or to cash does not depend on the employee performing additional services (FAS-123, par. 27).

*   Compensation cost may be estimated based on the number of options or other equity instruments that are expected to vest; that estimate may be revised if subsequent information indicates that actual forfeitures will differ from the original estimates. Alternatively, compensation cost may be accrued as if all instruments granted will vest and the effects of actual forfeitures are recognized as they occur (FAS-123, par. 28).

*   The effect of changes in the number of shares or options expected to vest is a change in estimate, and the cumulative effect of the change on current and prior periods is recognized in the period of change (FAS-123, par. 29).

*   Compensation cost is recognized ratably over the period(s) during which the related employee services are rendered; if the

award is for future services, this recognition is shown by charging compensation cost and crediting equity if the award is for future services (FAS-123, par. 30).

- Compensation cost for an award with a graded vesting schedule is recognized in accordance with FIN-28 if the fair value of the award is determined based on different expected lives for the options that vest each year. If the expected life (or lives) of the award is determined in another manner, compensation cost is recognized on a straight-line basis (FAS-123, par. 31).

- Dividends paid to employees on the portion of an award that is expected to vest are charged to retained earnings. Nonforfeited dividends paid on shares of stock that do not vest are recognized as additional compensation cost (FAS-123, par. 32).

- If employees do not receive the dividends paid on the class of stock granted them until the stock becomes vested, the value of the award at the grant date is reduced by the present value of dividends expected to be paid on the stock during the vesting period, discounted at the appropriate risk-free interest rate. The fair value of an award of stock options on which dividend equivalents are paid to employees or are applied to reduce the exercise price pursuant to antidilution provisions are estimated based on a dividend payment of zero (FAS-123, par. 33).

Income Tax Implications

Compensation expense based on the fair value of an award issued to an employee will ordinarily result in a future deductible difference in applying FAS-109 (Accounting for Income Taxes). Any resulting deferred tax asset must be evaluated for future realization under the provisions of FAS-109 and reduced by a valuation allowance if evidence indicates it is more likely than not that some or all of the amount will not be realized solely because of insufficient future income (FAS-123, pars. 41–43).

If a deduction reported on a tax return for a stock-based award exceeds the cumulative compensation expense recognized in the financial statements, the related tax benefit is recognized in the financial statements as additional paid-in capital. If the tax deduction is less than the cumulative compensation cost recognized in the financial statements, the write-off of any related deferred tax asset in excess of the benefits of the tax deduction, net of any related valuation allowance, is recognized in the income statement, unless there is additional paid-in capital from previous awards under employee stock-based compensation arrangements accounted for by the fair value method against which the balance can be charged (FAS-123, par. 44).

DISCLOSURE REQUIREMENTS

FAS-123 requires that the following information be disclosed, regardless of the method used to account for employee stock-based compensation arrangements (FAS-123, pars. 45–48):

1. If the APB-25 method is used, for each year for which an income statement is provided: (*a*) the pro forma net income and earnings per share (public entities) must be disclosed as if the fair value–based accounting method were used to account for stock-based compensation and (*b*) the difference between compensation cost recognized by APB-25 and the fair value method of FAS-123 must be disclosed.

> ☛ **PRACTICE POINTER:** Take particular care to not overlook the disclosure requirement of pro forma information if the fair-value method is applied when the intrinsic-value method is retained. This requirement forces companies to become familiar with the fair-value method, even though they may choose to continue to report information in the primary financial statements using the intrinsic value method.

2. A description of the stock-based compensation plan, including the general terms of awards under the plan, the maximum term of options granted, and the number of shares authorized for grants of options or other equity instruments, must be given.

3. For each year for which an income statement is provided, entities must disclose:

   a. The number and weighted-average exercise prices of options for each of the following groups of options: (1) outstanding at the beginning of the year, (2) outstanding at the end of the year, (3) exercisable at the end of the year, and those (4) granted, (5) exercised, (6) forfeited, or (7) expired during the year.

   b. The weighted average grant-date fair value of options granted during the year. If the exercise prices of some options differ from the market price of the stock on the grant date, weighted-average exercise prices and weighted-average fair values of options must be disclosed separately for options whose exercise price (1) equals, (2) exceeds, or (3) is less than the market price of the stock on the date of grant.

   c. The number and weighted-average grant-date fair value of equity instruments, other than options granted during the year.

    d. Method and significant assumptions used to estimate the fair values of options must be disclosed.

    e. Total compensation cost recognized in income for stock-based compensation awards must be disclosed.

    f. Terms of significant modifications to outstanding option grants must be disclosed.

4. For options outstanding at the date of the latest balance sheet presented, the range of exercise prices, the weighted-average exercise price and the weighted-average remaining contractual life must be disclosed.

5. The number and weighted-average exercise price of options exercisable.

Illustration of Fair Value Method

On January 1, 19X1, Hammer Co. grants to its employees 5,000 stock options, in which the $50 exercise price is equal to the market price of the stock at that time. Applying an appropriate option pricing model, a fair value of $18 per option is determined. Hammer Co. expects 3% of the options to be forfeited each year during the three-year vesting period. The corporate income tax rate is 35%.

The number of stock options expected to be exercised is determined as follows, applying the assumption of 3% forfeitures per year:

$$5{,}000 \times .97 \times .97 \times .97 = 4{,}563$$

Estimated total compensation cost is $82,134 (4,563 x $18), or $27,378 per year during the three-year vesting period.

Journal entries for the fair value method (FAS-123) compared with the intrinsic value method (APB-25) follow.

Dec. 31, 19X1, 19X2, 19X3

	Fair Value Method (FAS-123)		Intrinsic Value Method (APB-25)
Compensation expense	$27,378		NONE
Additional paid-in capital		$27,378	
Deferred tax asset	9,582		NONE
Deferred tax expense ($27,378 x .35)		9,582	

Dec. 31, 19X4 (assume all options are exercised when the market price is $65)

	Fair Value Method (FAS-123)			Intrinsic Value Method (APB-25)
Cash (4,563 x $50)	$228,150		Cash	$228,150
Additional paid-in capital (4,563 x $18)	82,134		Common stock	$ 45,630
			Capital in excess of par	182,520
Common stock (4,563 x $10)		$ 45,630		
Capital in excess of par—common		264,654		
Deferred tax expense	28,746			NONE
Deferred tax asset		28,746		

CHAPTER 47
TRANSFER AND SERVICING OF FINANCIAL ASSETS

CONTENTS

CHAPTER 47
TRANSFER AND SERVICING OF
FINANCIAL ASSETS

OVERVIEW

Transfers of financial assets take many forms and, depending on the nature of the transaction, the transferor may have a continuing interest in the transferred asset. Accounting for transferred assets in which the transferor has no continuing involvement with the transferred asset or with the transferee has been relatively straightforward and not controversial. Transfers of financial assets in which the transferor has some continuing interest, however, have raised issues about the circumstances in which the transfer should be considered a sale of all or part of the assets or a secured borrowing, and how transferors and transferees should account for sales of financial assets and secured borrowings.

GAAP for transactions involving the transfer of financial assets are established in the following authoritative pronouncements:

FAS-125   Accounting for Transfers and Servicing of Financial Assets and Extinguishments of Liabilities

FAS-127   Deferral of the Effective Date of Certain Provisions of FASB Statement No. 125

FAS-125 establishes accounting and reporting standards for transfers and servicing of financial assets and extinguishments of liabilities based on the consistent application of the financial-components approach. This approach requires the recognition of financial assets and servicing assets that are controlled by the reporting entity, the derecognition of financial assets when control is surrendered, and the derecognition of liabilities when they are extinguished. Specific criteria are established for determining when control has been surrendered in the transfer of financial assets.

FAS-125 originally was effective for transfers and servicing of financial assets and extinguishments of liabilities occurring after December 31, 1996. In response to concern about the ability of certain entities to comply with the requirements of FAS-125 on a timely basis, FAS-127 defers for one year the effective date of FAS-125 for secured borrowings and collateral (paragraph 15 of FAS-125) and for repurchase agreements, dollar-rolls, securities lending, and similar transactions (paragraphs 9–12 and 237(b) of FAS-125).

> **OBSERVATION:** FAS-125 is amended by FAS-133 (Accounting for Derivative Instruments and Hedging Activities). This is effective for fiscal years beginning after June 15, 1999. FAS-133 applies in interim financial statements for periods that begin after the same date (e.g., the quarter beginning July 1, 1999). FAS-133 is covered in Chapter 16 of the 1999 *Miller GAAP Guide*.
>
> Because the effective date of FAS-133 is delayed as indicated above, and the first calendar year for which FAS-133 will be in effect is the year 2000, the impact of FAS-133 on FAS-125 is not reflected in the 1999 *Miller GAAP Guide*.

CROSS-REFERENCES

1999 MILLER GAAP GUIDE: Chapter 15, "Extinguishment of Debt"; Chapter 16, "Financial Instruments Disclosures"; Chapter 29, "Investments in Debt and Equity Securities"

1999 MILLER GAAP IMPLEMENTATION MANUAL: EITF: Chapter 29, "Transfers of Financial Assets"

BACKGROUND

Definitions

The term *financial asset* is defined in FAS-125 as: cash, evidence of an ownership interest in an entity, or a contract that conveys to a second entity a contractual right (*a*) to receive cash or another financial instrument from a first entity or (*b*) to exchange other financial instruments on potentially favorable terms with the first entity.

The term *financial liability* refers to a contract that imposes a contractual obligation on one entity (*a*) to deliver cash or another financial instrument to a second entity or (*b*) to exchange other financial instruments on potentially unfavorable terms with the second entity.

The term *transfer* refers to the conveyance of a noncash financial asset to someone other than the issuer of that financial asset. Examples are selling a receivable, putting it into a securitization trust, or posting it as collateral. It excludes the origination of the receivable, the settlement of the receivable, or the restructuring of the receivable into a security in a troubled debt restructuring. The *transferor* is the party that transfers a financial asset (or part of a financial asset or a group of financial assets) that it controls to another entity. The *transferee* is the entity that receives a financial asset from the transferor.

Transfers of financial assets may take many forms, and accounting for those transfers in which the transferor has no continuing involvement with the transferred asset or with the transferee is uncontroversial. Accounting for transfers of financial assets in which the transferor has a continuing involvement with the assets or with the transferee, however, is less straightforward and requires clarification. Examples of this type of transaction include:

- Recourse.
- Servicing.
- Agreements to reacquire.
- Options written or held.
- Pledges of collateral.

Issues raised by these types of transactions include the circumstances in which the transfers should be considered as sales of part or all of the assets or as secured borrowings. Also, accounting by transferors and transferees for sales and secured borrowings requires clarification.

The FASB has stated two broad objectives in establishing standards for the transfer and servicing of financial assets and the extinguishment of liabilities. The first objective is for each party to the transaction to recognize only assets it controls and liabilities it has incurred, to derecognize assets only when control has been surrendered, and to derecognize liabilities only when they have been extinguished. (The term *derecognize* means the opposite of recognize, namely, to remove previously recognized assets or liabilities from the statement of financial position.) For instance, if an entity sells a portion of a financial asset it owns, only the portion sold is derecognized, and the portion retained continues to be carried as an asset.

The second broad objective is that recognition of financial assets and liabilities not be affected by the sequence of transactions that result in their acquisition or incurrence unless the effect of those transactions is to maintain effective control over a transferred financial asset. For example, if a transferor sells financial assets and at the same time writes a put option on those assets, it should recognize the put obligation in the same manner as would an unrelated entity that writes an identical put option on assets it never owned. Certain agreements to repurchase or redeem transferred assets, however, are intended to maintain effective control over the assets and should be accounted for differently than agreements to acquire assets never owned.

FAS-125 addresses accounting and reporting for (*a*) servicing assets and servicing liabilities and (*b*) interest-only strips, securities, loans, other receivables, or retained interests in securitizations that contractually can be prepaid or otherwise settled in such a way that the holder would not recover substantially all of its recorded investment. A *servicing asset* is a contract to service financial assets under which the estimated future revenues are expected to more than adequately compensate the servicer for performing the service. A *servicing liability* is a similar contract in which the estimated future revenues are *not* expected to adequately compensate the servicer for providing the servicing. An *interest-only strip* is a contractual right to receive some or all of the interest due on a bond, mortgage loan, collateralized mortgage obligation, or other interest-bearing financial asset.

CONTROL CRITERIA AND TRANSFEROR ACCOUNTING

Determining when control has been surrendered is particularly important in applying FAS-125. Three conditions, all of which must be met, for the transferor to have surrendered control over transferred assets are specified (FAS-125, par. 9):

1. The transferred assets have been isolated from the transferor (i.e., they are beyond the reach of the transferor and its creditors)

2. One of the following is met:
   a. The transferee obtains the unconditional right to pledge or exchange the transferred assets
   b. The transferee is a qualifying special-purpose entity and the holders of beneficial interests in that entity have the unconditional right to pledge or exchange those interests

3. The transferor does not maintain effective control over the transferred assets either through an agreement that obligates the transferor to repurchase or redeem the assets before their maturity or through an agreement that entitles the transferor to repurchase or redeem transferred assets that are not readily obtainable.

If these conditions are met, the transfer is accounted for as a sale to the extent that consideration other than *beneficial interests* in the transferred assets is received in exchange. *Beneficial interests* are defined as rights to receive all or a portion of specified cash inflows to a trust or other entity (including senior and subordinated shares of interest, principal, or other cash inflows to be "passed-through" or "paid-through," premiums due to guarantors, and residual interests.)

Transfers of financial assets that meet the above criteria are accounted for as follows (FAS-125, pars. 10–11):

1. All assets sold are derecognized.

2. All assets obtained and liabilities incurred in consideration as proceeds are recognized. (*Proceeds* refers to cash, derivatives, or other assets that are obtained in a transfer of financial assets, less any liabilities incurred.)

3. Assets obtained and liabilities incurred are measured at fair value, if practicable, and otherwise by alternative measures.

4. Any gain or loss on the sale is recognized in income.

After a transfer of financial assets has been recorded in accordance with FAS-125, the transferor shall continue to carry in its statement of financial position any retained interest in the transferred assets, the amount of which is determined by an allocation of the previous carrying amount based on fair value. Examples of retained interests in the transferred assets are:

- Servicing assets.

- Beneficial interests in assets transferred to a qualified special-purpose entity in a *securitization* (i.e., a process by which financial assets are transformed into securities).

- Retained *undivided interests* (i.e., partial legal or beneficial ownership of an asset as tenant in common with others).

ACCOUNTING FOR SERVICING ASSETS AND LIABILITIES

Four specific principles specify accounting for servicing assets and liabilities (FAS-125, pars. 13–14):

1. For each obligation to service financial assets, the entity shall recognize either a servicing asset or a liability, unless it securitizes the assets, retains all of the resulting securities, and accounts for them as held-to-maturity securities in accordance with FAS-115 (Accounting for Certain Investments in Debt and Equity Securities).

2. A servicing asset or liability that was purchased or assumed rather than undertaken in a sale or securitization of the financial assets being serviced shall be initially recorded at its fair value.

3. Servicing assets and liabilities are amortized in proportion to and over the period of estimated net servicing income or loss, and are subject to assessment for impairment or increased obligation based on fair value.

4. Interest-only strips, loans, other receivables, or retained interests in securitizations that can contractually be prepaid or otherwise settled in a manner that the holder would not recover substantially all of its recorded investment are measured like investments in debt securities and classified as either available-for-sale or trading in accordance with FAS-115.

☛ **PRACTICE POINTER:** In applying the standards for servicing assets and liabilities in FAS-125, accounting for debt investments in accordance with FAS-115 is particularly important. That standard requires investments in debt securities to be classified into three categories: trading, available-for-sale, or held-to-maturity. Trading investments are expected to be held for only a short time and are carried at fair value with periodic adjustments in fair value recognized in income. Held-to-maturity investments are ones for which management has the intent and ability to hold to maturity; they are carried at amortized cost. Available-for-sale investments are those that are neither trading nor held-to-maturity investments, and they are carried at fair value with changes in value accumulated in stockholders' equity until their sale.

SECURED BORROWINGS AND COLLATERAL

A debtor may grant a security interest in assets to a lender (identified below as the secured party) as collateral for its obligation under a borrowing. If collateral is transferred to the secured party, the arrangement is often referred to as a *pledge*. In some circumstances, a secured party is permitted to sell or repledge collateral it holds under a pledge.

Accounting for collateral by the debtor and the secured party depends on the specific rights and obligations present in the collateral agreement. If the conditions specified below are *not* present, the debtor continues to carry the collateral as its asset and the secured party does not recognize the pledged asset. This treatment is modified as indicated for the following specified conditions (FAS-125, par. 15).

Condition	Accounting Requirements
The secured party is permitted to sell or repledge the collateral and the debtor does not have the right and ability to redeem the collateral on short notice	*Debtor*—Reclassifies the asset and reports it separately from other assets not so encumbered *Secured party*—Recognizes the collateral as an asset (at fair value) and a related liability to return it
The secured party sells or repledges the collateral on terms that do not give it the right and ability to repurchase or redeem the collateral on short notice (i.e., the debtor's right to redeem it is impaired)	*Secured party*—Recognizes the proceeds and an obligation to return the asset (to extent not already recognized) in accordance with FAS-125
The debtor defaults and is no longer entitled to redeem the collateral	*Debtor*—Derecognizes the collateral *Secured party*—Recognizes the collateral as its asset at fair value (to extent not already recognized)

DISCLOSURES

FAS-125 includes eight disclosure requirements related to transfers and servicing of financial assets and extinguishment of liabilities. The first four state a condition that, if met, leads to a specific disclosure requirement. If the condition is *not* met, that disclosure is not applicable. The last four disclosures are required for *all* servicing asset and servicing liabilities. These disclosures are summarized as follows (FAS-125, par. 17):

Disclosures Required in Specified Situations

Condition Requiring Disclosure	Information Required to Be Disclosed
1. Entity has entered into repurchase agreements or securities lending transactions.	Policy for requiring collateral or other security
2. Debt was considered extinguished under FAS-76 (Extin-	General description of the transaction and the amount of debt

guishment of Debt) prior to the effective date of FAS-125.	that is considered extinguished at the end of the period so long as that debt is outstanding
3. Assets are set aside after the effective date of FAS-125 solely for satisfying scheduled payments of a specific obligation.	Description of the nature of restrictions placed on such assets
4. It is not practicable to estimate the fair value of certain assets obtained or liabilities incurred in transfers of financial assets during the period.	Description of those items and the reasons why it is not practicable to estimate fair value

Disclosures Required for All Servicing Assets and Liabilities

1. Amounts of servicing assets or liabilities recognized and amortized during the period

2. Fair value of recognized servicing assets and liabilities for which it is practicable to estimate that value, the method used, and significant assumptions used

3. The risk characteristics of underlying financial assets used to stratify recognized servicing assets for purposes of measuring impairment

4. Activity in the valuation allowance for impairment of recognized servicing assets for each period for which results of operations are presented

IMPLEMENTATION GUIDANCE

Appendix A of FAS-125 describes certain provisions of the standard in more detail and describes how they apply to certain types of transactions.

The specific areas for which implementation guidance is provided are as follows:

- Assessing isolation of transferred assets
- Accounting for transfers of partial interests
- Servicing of financial assets
- Securitizations
- Transfers of sales-type and direct financing lease receivables
- Securities lending transactions

- Repurchase agreements (including "dollar rolls" and "wash sales")
- Loan syndications and participations
- Risk participations in banker's acceptances
- Factoring arrangements
- Transfers of receivables with recourse
- Extinguishment of liabilities

The following illustrations highlight two of the most important aspects of FAS-125 for which implementation guidance is provided. These illustrations also provide a flavor of the type of implementation guidance included in Appendix A for all of the areas listed above.

Financial-Components Approach

The financial-components approach recognizes that financial assets and liabilities are divisible into a variety of components. The approach requires accounting recognition of these different components, rather than treating a financial asset as an inseparable unit that has been entirely sold or entirely retained. This approach is applied in the following illustration, in which the primary transaction is the sale of loans for cash, but in which separate financial assets are recognized for a call option and an interest rate swap, and a separate financial liability is recognized for the recourse obligation.

Illustration of Financial-Components Approach

Fowler Company receives $2,625 in cash by selling loans with a fair value of $2,750 and a carrying amount of $2,500, retaining no servicing responsibility. Fowler Company obtains from the transferee an option (valued at $160) to purchase loans similar to those sold and assumes a recourse obligation (valued at $120) to purchase delinquent loans. Fowler Company simultaneously enters into an interest rate swap agreement (valued at $100) with the transferee in which it receives fixed interest at an above-market rate and pays a floating rate.

The net proceeds and gain on the sale are determined as follows:

Net proceeds:

Cash received	$2,625
Plus: Call option	160
Interest rate swap	100
Less: Recourse obligation	(120)

	$2,765
Carrying amount of loans	(2,500)
Gain on sale	$ 265

The general journal entry to record the transfer and recognize related assets and liabilities is:

Cash	$2,625	
Call option	160	
Interest rate swap	100	
Loans		$2,500
Recourse obligation		120
Gain on sale		265

Allocation of Fair Value

For purposes of recording financial instruments with multiple components, the carrying amount is allocated to the components based on their relative fair values. If no fair value can reasonably be estimated for a component, it is assigned a zero value. The following illustration demonstrates these procedures in three situations in which a company sells loans with a recourse obligation, acquires a call option to repurchase the loans, and agrees to service the loans: where fair values can be estimated for each component, where the fair value of the servicing asset cannot be estimated, and where the fair value of the recourse obligation cannot be estimated.

Illustrations of Allocation Process and Fair Value Determination

Anderson Company sells loans with a carrying amount of $2,600 to another entity for cash and a call option to repurchase the loans. Anderson Company agrees to service the transferred loans for the other entity and also incurs a recourse obligation to repurchase any delinquent loans.

Fair values are as follows: servicing asset, $90; call option, $175; recourse obligation, $150. Anderson received $2,730 in cash.

The net proceeds are determined as follows:

Cash received	$2,730
Plus: Call option	175
Less: Recourse obligation	(150)
Net proceeds	$2,755

This carrying amount is allocated to the loans sold and the servicing asset based on relative fair values as follows:

	Fair value	Percentage of total fair value	Allocated carrying amount
Loans sold	$2,755	97	$2,522
Servicing assets	90	3	78
Total	$2,845	100	$2,600

The general journal entry to record the transfer is as follows:

Cash	$2,730	
Servicing asset	78	
Call option	175	
Loans		$2,600
Recourse obligation		150
Gain		233

This illustration assumes that fair value can be determined for both the servicing asset and the recourse obligation. If fair value cannot be determined for the servicing asset, it is assigned a zero amount and the gain is reduced from $233 to $155, resulting in the following entry:

Cash	$2,730	
Servicing asset	-0-	
Call option	175	
Loans		$2,600
Recourse obligation		150
Gain		155

On the other hand, if no fair value is available for the recourse obligation, the gain is eliminated and the recourse obligation is increased from $150 to $383, which is the amount that results in zero gain. The recording entry would be as follows:

Cash	$2,730	
Servicing asset	78	
Call option	175	
Loans		$2,600
Recourse obligation		383
Gain		-0-

CHAPTER 48
TROUBLED DEBT RESTRUCTURING

CONTENTS

CHAPTER 48
TROUBLED DEBT RESTRUCTURING

OVERVIEW

Debt may be restructured for a variety of reasons. A restructuring of debt is considered a troubled debt restructuring (TDR) if the creditor, for economic or legal reasons related to the debtor's financial difficulties, grants a concession to the debtor that it would not otherwise consider. The concession may stem from an agreement between the creditor and the debtor, or it may be imposed by law or court.

A loan is impaired if, based on current information and events, it is probable that the creditor will be unable to collect all amounts due according to the contractual terms of the loan agreement.

GAAP for TDR by both debtors and creditors and for impairments of loans by creditors are included in the following pronouncements:

FAS-15   Accounting by Debtors and Creditors for Troubled Debt Restructurings

FAS-114   Accounting by Creditors for Impairment of a Loan

CROSS-REFERENCES

1999 MILLER GAAP GUIDE: Chapter 7, "Contingencies, Risks, and Uncertainties"; Chapter 15, "Extinguishment of Debt"; Chapter 20, "Impairment of Loans and Long-Lived Assets"; Chapter 25, "Interest on Receivables and Payables"; Chapter 42, "Results of Operations"

1999 MILLER GAAP IMPLEMENTATION MANUAL: Chapter 32, "Troubled Debt Restructuring"

1999 MILLER GAAP IMPLEMENTATION MANUAL: EITF: Chapter 30, "Troubled Debt Restructuring"

1999 MILLER NOT-FOR-PROFIT REPORTING: Chapter 2, "Overview of Current Pronouncements"; Chapter 6, "Liabilities"

BACKGROUND

A troubled debt restructuring is one in which the creditor grants the debtor certain concessions that would not normally be considered. The concessions are made because of the debtor's financial difficulty, and the creditor's objective is to maximize recovery of its investment. Troubled debt restructurings are often the result of legal proceedings or of negotiation between the parties.

Troubled debt restructurings include situations in which:

1. The creditor accepts a third-party receivable or other asset(s) of the debtor, in lieu of the receivable from the debtor.
2. The creditor accepts an equity interest in the debtor in lieu of the receivable. (This is not to be confused with convertible securities, which are *not* troubled debt restructurings.)
3. The creditor accepts modification of the terms of the debt, including but not limited to:
   a. Reduction in stated interest to below the current market rate
   b. Extension of maturity at a favorable interest rate
   c. Reduction in face amount of the debt
   d. Reduction in accrued interest

The reductions mentioned in (*a*), (*c*), and (*d*) can be either absolute or contingent.

For the purposes of FAS-15, troubled debt restructurings do *not* include the following:

1. Changes in lease agreements
2. Employment-related agreements, such as deferred compensation contracts or pension plans
3. A debtor's failure to pay trade accounts that do not involve a restructure agreement
4. A creditor's legal action to collect accounts that do not involve a restructure agreement

A troubled debt restructuring by a debtor in bankruptcy proceedings would be permitted under FAS-15 provided that the restructuring did *not* constitute a *general restatement* of the debtor's liabilities.

FAS-114 was issued by the FASB to address inconsistencies in the measurement and recognition of loan impairment. FAS-114 amends FAS-15 to require a creditor to account for all loans that are restructured as part of a TDR involving a modification of terms as an impaired loan.

Not all debt restructuring is considered troubled, even though the debtor is in financial difficulty. Circumstances in which the restructuring is not troubled include (FAS-15, par. 7):

1. The debtor satisfies the debt by giving fair value of assets or equity that at least equals either:

   a. The creditor's recorded receivable, or

   b. The debtor's carrying amount of the payable.

2. The creditor reduces the interest rate primarily in response to changes in market rates.

3. In exchange for the debtor's debt, the debtor issues new debt securities that have an effective interest rate that is at or near the current market interest rate of debt with similar maturity dates and interest rates issued by nontroubled debtors.

> **OBSERVATION:** If the debtor can obtain funds at current market rates and conditions, this provides evidence that the restructuring is not a troubled debt restructuring.

ACCOUNTING AND REPORTING STANDARDS

Debtors and creditors account for troubled debt restructurings by the type of restructuring. Types of restructuring include:

1. Transfer of asset(s) in full settlement.
2. Transfer of an equity interest in full settlement.
3. Modification of terms of the debt.
4. Combinations of the above three types.

Transfer of Asset(s)

The debtor recognizes a gain equal to the excess of the carrying amount of the payable (including accrued interest, premiums, etc.) over the fair value of the asset(s) given up. The gain is reported in net income of the period and presented as an extraordinary item because it results from the extinguishment of debt. The difference between the fair value and the carrying amount of the asset(s) given up is the gain or loss on the transfer of asset(s), which is also included in net income in the period the transfer occurs (not presented as an extraordinary item) (FAS-15, pars. 13 and 14).

☛ **PRACTICE POINTER:** Determine fair value either by the assets given up or by the amount payable, whichever is more clearly evident. In the case of a partial settlement, however, use the value of the asset(s) given up. This eliminates the need to allocate the fair value of the payable between the settled portion and the remaining outstanding balance.

When the creditor receives assets as full settlement of a receivable, they are accounted for at their fair value at the time of the restructuring. The fair value of the receivable satisfied can be used if it is more clearly determinable than the fair value of the asset or equity acquired. In partial payments the creditor *must* use the fair value of the asset or equity received (FAS-15, par. 28).

The excess of the recorded receivable over the fair value of the assets received is recognized as a loss. The creditor accounts for these assets as if they were acquired for cash (FAS-15, pars. 28 and 29).

Illustration of Transfer of Assets

A debtor owes $20,000, including accrued interest. The creditor accepts land valued at $17,000 and carried on the debtor's books at its $12,000 cost, in full payment.

Under FAS-15, the debtor recognizes two gains: $5,000 ($17,000 − $12,000) on the transfer of the assets, and $3,000 ($20,000 − $17,000) on the extinguishment of debt. Only the latter is an extraordinary item.

The creditor recognizes a loss of $3,000 ($20,000 − $17,000). That loss is not classified as extraordinary because it is not the creditor's debt that is extinguished.

Transfer of Equity Interest

The difference between the fair value of the equity interest and the carrying amount of the payable is recognized as an extraordinary gain by the debtor (FAS-15, par. 15).

The creditor records the receipt of an equity interest as any other asset by recording the investment at its fair value and recognizing a loss equal to the difference between the fair value of the equity interest and the amount of the receivable (FAS-15, par. 28).

Illustration of Transfer of Equity Interest

A debtor grants an equity interest valued at $10,000, consisting of 500 shares of $15 par value stock, to retire a payable of $12,000. Under FAS-15, the debtor records the issuance of the stock at $10,000 ($7,500 par value and

$2,500 additional paid-in capital) and an extraordinary gain on the extinguish-ment of debt of $2,000 ($12,000 – $10,000). The creditor records an invest-ment asset of $10,000 and an ordinary loss of $2,000 ($12,000 – $10,000) on the TDR.

> ☞ **PRACTICE POINTER:** Determining the fair value of an equity interest of a debtor company involved in a troubled debt restructuring may be particularly difficult in implementing FAS-15. In many cases, the company's stock will not be pub-licly traded, and there may be no recent stock transactions that would be helpful. Even if a recent market price were available, consider whether that price reflects the financially troubled status of the company that exists at the time the troubled debt restructuring takes place.

Modification of Terms

A restructuring that does not involve the transfer of assets or equity often involves the modification of the terms of the debt. The debtor accounts for the effects of the restructuring prospectively and does not change the carrying amount unless the carrying amount exceeds the total future cash payments specified by the new terms. The *total future cash payments* are the principal and interest, including any accrued interest at the time of the restructuring that will be payable by the new terms. *Interest expense* is computed by a method that results in a constant effective rate (such as the interest method). The new effective rate of interest is the discount rate at which the carry-ing amount of the debt is equal to the present value of the future cash payments (FAS-15, par. 16).

When the total future cash payments are less than the carrying amount, the debtor reduces the carrying amount accordingly and recognizes the difference as an extraordinary gain. When there are several related accounts (discount, premium, etc.), the reduction may need to be allocated among them. All cash payments after the restruc-turing go toward reducing the carrying amount, and *no* interest expense is recognized after the date of restructure (FAS-15, par. 17).

When there are indeterminate future payments, or anytime the future payments might exceed the carrying amount, the debtor recog-nizes no gain. The debtor assumes that the future contingent pay-ments will have to be made at least to the extent necessary to obviate any gain. In estimating future cash payments, it is assumed that the maximum amount of periods (and interest) is going to occur (FAS-15, par. 18).

A creditor in a TDR involving a modification of terms accounts for the restructured loan in accordance with FAS-114 (FAS-114, par. 22). FAS-114, as amended by FAS-118 (Accounting by Creditors for

Impairment of a Loan—Income Recognition and Disclosures), requires that impaired loans be measured at their present value of expected future cash flows discounted at the loan's contractual interest rate, the loan's observable market price, or the fair value of collateral if the loan is collateral-dependent.

> **OBSERVATION:** According to FAS-114, a loan is impaired if it is probable that a creditor will be unable to collect all amounts due according to the contractual terms of the loan agreement. A loan whose terms are modified in a TDR will have already been identified as impaired. For purposes of applying FAS-114, a loan is considered collateral-dependent if repayment is expected to be provided solely by the underlying collateral.

Illustration of Modification of Terms

A debtor has a loan to a creditor, details of which are as follows:

Principal	$10,000
Accrued interest	500
Total	$10,500

They agree on a restructuring in which the total future cash payments, both principal and interest, are $8,000. The present value of these payments is $7,500.

Under FAS-15, the debtor recognizes an extraordinary gain of $2,500 ($10,500 – $8,000) at the time of the restructuring, and all future payments are specified as principal payments. Under FAS-114, the creditor recognizes a loss of $3,000 ($10,500 – $7,500).

> **OBSERVATION:** The FASB recognized that FAS-114 introduces asymmetry between creditors' and debtors' accounting for TDR involving a modification of terms. They determined, however, that FAS-114 should deal only with creditor accounting, because to include debtor accounting would delay issuance of a final Statement. Presumably, at some future date, the asymmetry suggested in the above example will be addressed and resolved.

Combination of Types

When a restructuring involves combinations of asset or equity transfers and modification of terms, the debtor first uses the fair value of any asset or equity to reduce the carrying amount of the payable. The difference between the fair value and the carrying amount of any asset(s) transferred is recognized as gain or loss. The remainder of the restructuring is accounted for as a modification of terms in accordance with FAS-15 (FAS-15, par. 19).

The creditor reduces the recorded investment by the fair value of assets received, including an equity interest in the debtor. Thereafter, the creditor accounts for the TDR in accordance with FAS-114 (FAS-15, par. 33).

Related Issues

Amounts contingently payable in future periods are recognized as payable and as interest expense in accordance with the treatment of other contingencies. The criteria for recognizing a loss contingency are the following:

1. It is probable that the liability has been incurred.
2. The amount can be reasonably estimable.

If any contingently payable amounts were included in the total future cash payments, they must now be deducted from the carrying amount of the restructured payable to the extent they originally prevented recognition of a gain at the time of the restructuring (FAS-15, par. 22).

In estimating future payments subject to fluctuation, estimates are based on the interest rate in effect at the time of restructure. A change in future rates is treated as a change in accounting estimate. The accounting for these fluctuations cannot result in an immediate gain. Rather, the future payments will reduce the carrying amount, and any residual value is considered gain (FAS-15, par. 23).

If a loss from a troubled debt restructuring has been previously provided in a valuation allowance account, the loss is charged first to the valuation allowance and not directly to net income (FAS-15, par. 35).

Interest rates that fluctuate after a restructuring are accounted for as changes in an accounting estimate in the period they occur. The creditor recognizes a loss and reduces its restructured receivable when fluctuations in interest rates cause the minimum future cash receipts to fall below the recorded investment in the restructured receivable (FAS-15, par. 37).

Legal fees and other direct costs resulting from a TDR are expensed by the creditor when incurred (FAS-15, par. 38).

Legal fees and other direct costs that a debtor incurs in granting an equity interest to a creditor reduce the amount otherwise recorded for that equity interest. All other direct costs that a debtor incurs to effect a TDR are deducted in measuring the gain on restructuring of payables or are included in expense for the period, if no gain on restructuring is recognized (FAS-15, par. 24).

A receivable obtained by a creditor from the sale of assets previously obtained in a TDR is accounted for in accordance with APB-21 (Interest on Receivables and Payables), regardless of whether the assets were obtained in satisfaction of a receivable to which APB-21 was not intended to apply (FAS-15, par. 39).

For creditors, a troubled debt restructuring may involve substituting debt of another business enterprise, individual, or governmental unit for that of a troubled debtor. That kind of restructuring should be accounted for according to its substance (FAS-15, par. 42).

DISCLOSURE REQUIREMENTS

Debtors

The debtor must disclose the following regarding any debt restructuring during a period (FAS-15, par. 25):

1. Description of the terms of each restructuring
2. Aggregate gain on the restructuring and the related tax effect
3. Aggregate net gain or loss on asset transfer
4. Per share amount of aggregate gain on the restructuring and the related tax effect

The debtor also should disclose contingently payable amounts included in the carrying amount of restructured payables and the total of contingently payable amounts and the conditions under which the amounts become payable or are forgiven (FAS-15, par. 26).

Creditors

The creditor shall disclose the following regarding troubled debt restructurings (FAS-15, par. 40; FAS-114, par 6i):

1. As of the date of each statement of financial position presented, the total recorded investment in the impaired loans at the end of each period, as well as (a) the amount of the recorded investment for which there is a related allowance for credit losses, and the amount of that allowance; and (b) the amount of the recorded investment for which there is no related allowance for credit losses

2. The creditor's policy for recognizing interest income on impaired loans, including how cash receipts are recorded

3. For each period for which results of operations are presented, the average recorded investment in the impaired loans during each period; the related amount of interest income recognized during the time within that period that the loans were impaired; and, if practicable, the amount of interest income recognized (cash-basis method of accounting) during the time within that period that the loans were impaired

4. Amount(s) of any commitment(s) to lend additional funds to any debtor who is a party to a restructuring

All four disclosures may be made in the aggregate or by major category (FAS-15, par. 41).

Banking and Thrift Institutions

CHAPTER 49
BANKING AND THRIFT INSTITUTIONS

CONTENTS

CHAPTER 49
BANKING AND THRIFT INSTITUTIONS

OVERVIEW

Specialized industry GAAP for banking and thrift institutions focus on business combinations, with particular emphasis on the determination of goodwill and other assets acquired.

GAAP for banking and thrift institutions are located in the following pronouncements:

FAS-72   Accounting for Certain Acquisitions of Banking or Thrift Institutions

FIN-9   Applying APB Opinions No. 16 and 17 When a Savings and Loan Association or a Similar Institution Is Acquired in a Business Combination Accounted for by the Purchase Method

FAS-72 amends APB-17 (Intangible Assets) with regard to the amortization of unidentifiable intangible assets (i.e., goodwill) recognized in certain business combinations accounted for by the purchase method.

FIN-9 concludes that the net-spread method should not be used in determining the amount of goodwill or other intangible assets that are acquired in a business combination accounted for by the purchase method. FIN-9 also discusses the circumstances in which goodwill recorded in an acquisition of a banking or thrift institution can be amortized by accelerated methods.

CROSS-REFERENCES

BACKGROUND

FAS-72 is applicable to the acquisition of a troubled banking or thrift institution, and specifically to that portion of goodwill that arises from the excess of the fair value of assumed liabilities over the fair value of acquired identifiable assets. In respect to this portion of goodwill, FAS-72 provides for a different method of amortization from that required by APB-17. Although a shorter period of amortization generally is provided for the portion of goodwill covered by FAS-72, the amortization period can still be as much as 40 years. Any other goodwill that arises in the acquisition of a troubled banking or thrift institution is accounted for in accordance with existing GAAP.

FAS-72 covers accounting and reporting for financial assistance that may be granted by a regulatory authority in connection with an enterprise's acquisition of a troubled banking or thrift institution and applies to acquisitions of commercial banks, savings and loan associations, mutual savings banks, credit unions, and other similar depository institutions.

FAS-72 amends and interprets APB-17, interprets APB-16 (Business Combinations), and amends FIN-9.

> **OBSERVATION:** A provision in a final rule regarding Delegated Merger Approvals, issued in 1985 by the Federal Home Loan Bank Board, states, "Where goodwill has been included in the resulting association's assets (as a consequence of a merger), the applicant must submit an opinion of a certified public accountant...." Apparently, an opinion must be submitted, satisfactory to the principal supervisory agent, that the goodwill's use and value are accounted for in accordance with GAAP. The effective date of the rule is December 23, 1985.

Certain economic and competitive conditions may adversely affect the financial position of savings and loan associations and mutual savings banks. Fluctuating interest rates may erode profit margins, and may result in banking and thrift institutions carrying long-term, low-interest-earning assets that suffer losses when the marketplace interest rate increases.

GOODWILL

When a troubled banking or thrift institution is acquired and accounted for by the purchase method, the excess of the fair value of the liabilities assumed over the fair value of the individual identifiable assets acquired is accounted for as goodwill.

Under existing GAAP (APB-17), goodwill must be amortized over its estimated life, which may not exceed 40 years. In addition,

APB-17 requires that the straight-line method be used for amortizing goodwill, unless another systematic and rational method can be justified.

The FASB concluded that goodwill arising in the acquisition of a troubled banking institution should be amortized over a relatively short period because of the uncertainty about the nature and extent of the estimated future benefits related to the goodwill, because (FAS-72, par. 32):

1. Goodwill has always been related to the excess future profits a business is likely to earn. It is extremely difficult to justify goodwill in the acquisition of a troubled banking institution that has been incurring large losses.

2. CON-3 (Elements of the Financial Statements of Business Enterprises) defines an asset as a probable future economic benefit obtained or controlled by an entity as a result of a past transaction or event. It is doubtful whether goodwill resulting from the acquisition of a troubled banking institution can be classified properly as a *probable future economic benefit.*

> **OBSERVATION:** The above factors could lead to the conclusion that any goodwill arising in the acquisition of a troubled banking institution should be written off to expense at the time of acquisition. The FASB prefers a special amortization period and method as a middle ground between the two extremes of (a) complete write-off immediately upon acquisition and (b) 40-year amortization as provided by APB-17.

Because goodwill usually is related to future excess profits and profitable operations, a more acceptable method of accounting for the goodwill that arises in the acquisition of a troubled banking or thrift institution may be to treat it as a *preacquisition contingency* as described by FAS-38 (Accounting for Preacquisition Contingencies of Purchased Enterprises).

FAS-38 requires that a portion of the total acquisition cost under the purchase method be allocated to contingent assets, liabilities, and impairments. If it is *probable* that the contingent item existed at the consummation date of the combination, and the amount of the contingent item can be *reasonably estimated*, FAS-38 requires that it be recognized.

Paragraphs 5 and 6 of FAS-72 are applicable only to acquisitions of banking and thrift institutions in which the fair value of the liabilities assumed exceeds the fair value of all identifiable assets acquired. Paragraphs 5 and 6 provide for a different amortization method for goodwill from the method that is permitted under APB-17.

NET-SPREAD METHOD AND
SEPARATE-VALUATION METHOD

The two methods available to record the acquisition of a savings and loan association are the *net-spread method* and the *separate-valuation method*.

Under the net-spread method, the spread between interest paid on deposits and interest received on mortgages is used to evaluate whether the difference is normal, subnormal, or above normal for a particular market area. If the spread is normal, the principal assets and liabilities that are being acquired are recorded at the carrying amounts shown on the financial statements of the association being acquired. If the spread is subnormal or above normal, an adjustment is made to compensate for the difference. The acquisition is viewed as the purchase of an entire business and not of separate individual assets. The net-spread method is not acceptable for the purposes of GAAP (FIN-9, par. 4).

The separate-valuation method is based on recording the acquired identifiable assets at fair value at the date of purchase. Any difference between the fair value of assets acquired less liabilities assumed is recorded as purchased goodwill.

Fair value of assets is influenced by the ability of the assets to generate future income and/or new business within the territory served. Therefore, if the amount paid for the assets to generate future income or new business can be determined reliably, it is not recorded as goodwill, but as a separate identifiable intangible asset and amortized over its estimated life. Any portion of the purchase price that cannot specifically be allocated to identifiable tangible or intangible assets is recorded as goodwill (FIN-9, par. 8).

Goodwill recorded in an acquisition of a savings and loan association may be amortized by accelerated methods (contrary to the general rule) if (FIN-9, par. 9):

1. An indeterminable amount for the acquired assets to generate future income or new business is included in goodwill, but cannot be valued separately.

2. The expected benefits are projected to decline over their useful lives.

ACQUISITIONS OF TROUBLED
BANKING INSTITUTIONS

Upon acquisition of a banking or thrift institution, the excess of the fair value of liabilities assumed over the fair value of the acquired identifiable assets is classified as goodwill (FAS-72, par. 5).

OBSERVATION: Under the purchase method of accounting for a business combination, goodwill is the difference between the cost of the acquisition and the fair value of the net assets acquired. However, FAS-72 does not necessarily apply to the amount of goodwill computed in this manner. FAS-72 applies only to the excess of the fair value of the liabilities assumed over the fair value of the identifiable tangible and intangible assets acquired.

Allocating the Cost of an Acquisition

Independent appraisals and/or subsequent sales of acquired assets may provide evidence of fair value. Each identifiable tangible and intangible asset acquired is assigned a portion of the acquisition cost, equal to its fair value at the date of acquisition (APB-16, par. 87).

The fair value of a long-term interest-bearing asset is the present value of the amount that will be received, less an allowance for uncollectible accounts. The fair value of an assumed liability is its present value at the prevailing interest rates at the date of acquisition (APB-16, par. 88). A portion of the total acquisition cost is allocated to contingent assets, contingent liabilities, and contingent impairments of assets, if any, provided that (FAS-38, par. 5):

1. It is *probable* that the contingent item existed at the consummation date of the business combination accounted for by the purchase method
2. After the consummation date, but prior to the end of the *allocation period*, the facts in (1) above are confirmed
3. The amount of the asset, liability, or impairment can be *estimated reasonably*.

If the above conditions are met, the purchase method requires that a portion of the total cost of acquiring a banking institution be allocated to any contingent items. The allocation period is that which is required by the purchaser to identify and quantify the acquired assets and assumed liabilities for the purposes of allocating the total cost of the acquisition in accordance with APB-16. The allocation period usually will not exceed one year from the closing date of the purchase transaction (FAS-38, par. 4).

Identifiable Intangible Assets

Identifiable assets include intangible assets at appraised values that can be identified and named, including (FIN-9, par. 6):

- Contracts.
- Patents.

- Franchises.
- Customer lists.
- Supplier lists.
- Leases.

Identifiable intangible assets of a banking or thrift institution may include existing depositor or borrower relationships, such as the capacity of existing savings and loan accounts to generate future income and/or additional business or new business (FIN-9, par. 8). The fair value of these types of identifiable intangible assets must be determined reliably based on existing facts at the date of acquisition without regard to future events (FAS-72, par. 4). If an acquisition of a banking or thrift institution includes any of these types of identifiable intangible assets, a portion of the cost of the acquisition should be assigned to such assets and amortized over their estimated useful lives, in accordance with APB-17.

Maximum Amortization Period

The amount of goodwill and the related periodic amortization, computed in accordance with FAS-72, are calculated at the date of acquisition. The periodic amortization expense is not adjusted in subsequent periods, except as provided by FAS-72 (see below). The maximum period of amortization should not exceed the lesser of 40 years or the estimated remaining life of the long-term interest-bearing assets with maturities in excess of one year, if any, which were acquired in the transaction. If a significant amount of long-term interest-bearing assets with maturities of over one year is not part of the acquisition, goodwill is amortized over the estimated average remaining life of the acquired existing customer deposit base (FAS-72, par. 5).

Method of Amortization

Amortization must be calculated by the use of a constant percentage rate applied to the carrying amount of the long-term interest-bearing assets, which is expected to be outstanding at the beginning of each period. The carrying amount that is expected to be outstanding at the beginning of each period is determined by reference to the terms of the instruments themselves. If any prepayment assumptions are used to calculate the fair value of the acquired long-term interest-bearing assets at the date of acquisition, the same prepayment assumptions must be used to determine the expected carrying amount of long-term interest-bearing assets that will be outstanding in each subsequent period (FAS-72, par. 5).

> **OBSERVATION:** The carrying amount of long-term interest-bearing assets is equal to their face amount, increased or decreased by any related unamortized premium or discount (FAS-72, par. 5).

Subsequent Revision of Amortization

In periods subsequent to the date of acquisition, an enterprise must continually reevaluate the remaining periods of amortization of its unamortized intangible assets to determine whether revision of such amortization periods is necessary (FAS-72, par. 6). If the remaining amortization period is revised, the unamortized cost of the intangible asset must be allocated to the revised period (the total amortization period for an intangible asset can never exceed 40 years from the date of its acquisition). New estimates may indicate the necessity of significantly reducing the carrying amount of an unamortized intangible asset (APB-17, par. 31). Under these circumstances, a charge to net income is made in the applicable year.

If a significant portion of a segment or severable group of the operating assets of an acquired banking or thrift institution is subsequently sold or otherwise disposed of, a proportionate amount of the unamortized goodwill is allocated and charged to the cost of the sale. The sale of acquired long-term interest-bearing assets may result in the loss of the customer base. If the estimated value or benefits of the related unamortized goodwill are significantly reduced as a result of such a sale or liquidation, the reduction must be recognized as a charge to income in the year of sale or liquidation (FAS-72, par. 7).

> ☞ **PRACTICE POINTER:** The amount of goodwill that results from the application of FAS-72 may not be revised upward (FAS-72, par. 6). If there is a permanent impairment in the value of an unamortized intangible asset, its carrying amount should be reduced to net realizable value by a charge to income in the year in which the impairment is discovered.

Additional Goodwill

In the acquisition of a banking or thrift institution, the amount of goodwill may exceed the difference between the fair value of the liabilities assumed and the fair value of the assets acquired. If so, additional goodwill is recognized and accounted for in accordance with the provisions of APB-17.

ACCOUNTING FOR REGULATORY ASSISTANCE

An enterprise may receive financial assistance from a regulatory agency such as the Federal Deposit Insurance Corporation (FDIC) or the Federal Savings and Loan Insurance Corporation (FSLIC) for the acquisition of a banking or thrift institution. The assistance may be immediate or granted in periods subsequent to the date of acquisition. Assets and/or liabilities may be transferred to the regulatory agency.

Additional Interest

A regulatory agency often provides periodic financial assistance that is approximately equal to the difference between the average yield on the long-term interest-bearing assets acquired in the acquisition and the current interest cost of carrying such assets.

Under FAS-72, the computation of this type of financial assistance is made at the date of acquisition and is based on the difference between the average yield on the long-term interest-bearing assets and the current interest cost of carrying such assets. The amount thus computed is treated as additional interest on the long-term interest-bearing assets. The additional interest is included in determining the present value (fair value) of the long-term interest-bearing assets at the date of acquisition, and is reported in income of the period in which it accrued (FAS-72, par. 8). No other adjustment is made in the carrying amount of the long-term interest-bearing assets for subsequent changes in the estimated amount of financial assistance.

Long-term interest-bearing assets that the acquiring enterprise intends to sell must be reported at an amount not exceeding current market value (FAS-72, par. 8).

Other Types of Financial Assistance

Other types of financial assistance granted by a regulatory agency are accounted for as part of the combination if (*a*) the assistance is *probable* and (*b*) the amount of assistance can be *reasonably estimated.* Under the purchase method, assets that are, or will be, received as a result of regulatory financial assistance must be assigned a portion of the total acquisition cost of the banking or thrift institution (FAS-72, par. 9).

> **OBSERVATION:** FAS-72 does not cover a situation in which the amount of financial assistance by a regulatory agency exceeds the amount of goodwill that would otherwise be

recorded in the transaction. In this event, the fair value of the assets acquired will exceed the fair value of the liabilities assumed. Under the purchase method, the excess of acquired assets over assumed liabilities is accounted for as *negative goodwill.* Under APB-16, negative goodwill is not recorded unless the fair values of the noncurrent assets acquired, if any, except long-term investments in marketable securities, are proportionately reduced to zero. If a credit still remains after the noncurrent assets have been reduced to zero, the credit is classified as a deferred credit and amortized to income over the period that is expected to benefit, but not to exceed 40 years (APB-16, par. 91).

Transfer of Assets or Liabilities

Assets and/or liabilities may be transferred to a regulatory agency as part of the plan of financial assistance. The fair value of the assets and/or liabilities that are transferred to the regulatory agency is excluded from the fair market value of the assets and liabilities acquired in the transaction (FAS-72, par. 9).

Financial Assistance After Date of Acquisition

Financial assistance may not be recognized at any time, unless (*a*) it is *probable* and (*b*) the amount of assistance can be *reasonably estimated.* Financial assistance may become *probable* and the amount *reasonably estimable* after the date of acquisition of the banking or thrift institution. Here, the financial assistance is recognized in the financial statements of the period(s) in which it becomes *probable* and the amount *reasonably estimable.* When this occurs, the financial assistance is reported as a reduction of the balance of the unamortized goodwill. Amortization for subsequent periods is adjusted proportionately (FAS-72, par. 9).

☛ **PRACTICE POINTER:** All types of regulatory financial assistance, except assistance in the form of additional interest, must be **probable** and the amount **reasonably estimable** before such assistance is recognized and reported in the financial statements of an enterprise. Financial assistance in the form of additional interest is recognized in accordance with existing GAAP; all other types of financial assistance are recognized only if they are probable and the amounts reasonably estimable.

Under existing GAAP, the accounting recognition of financial assistance depends on the substance of the transaction or the contractual agreement between the parties. Financial assistance may represent (*a*) a bona fide receivable, *(b)* a gain contingency, or *(c)* a contingent asset. A receivable generally is recognized when an exchange takes place, collection of the amount is assured reasonably, and the earning process is complete. A gain contingency should not be recognized prior to its realization, and financial disclosure is necessary (FAS-5). Under the purchase method of accounting, a contingent asset is allocated a portion of the total acquisition cost if certain conditions are met (FAS-38).

Repayment of Financial Assistance

An enterprise may agree to repay (based on the attainment of future profitability levels) all or part of the financial assistance granted by a regulatory agency. Repayment of financial assistance is recognized as a liability and a charge to income of the period in which the repayment is probable and the amounts can be reasonably estimated, in accordance with FAS-5 (FAS-72, par. 10).

Disclosure of Financial Assistance

The nature and amount of financial assistance received by an enterprise from a regulatory agency in connection with the acquisition of a banking or thrift institution must be disclosed in the financial statements (FAS-72, par. 11).

Loan and Commitment Fees

Loan origination and commitment fees and direct loan origination costs are accounted for as prescribed in FAS-91 (Accounting for Nonrefundable Fees and Costs Associated with Originating or Acquiring Loans and Initial Direct Costs of Leases). (**Note:** A discussion of FAS-91 can be found in the 1999 *Miller GAAP Guide* chapter titled "Mortgage Banking Industry.")

Entertainment Industry

CHAPTER 50
BROADCASTERS

CONTENTS

CHAPTER 50
BROADCASTERS

OVERVIEW

A *broadcaster* is an entity that transmits radio or television program material. Exhibition rights acquired under a licensing agreement for program material shall be accounted for as a purchase of rights by the licensee (broadcaster); the licensee should record an asset and a liability for the right acquired and the obligation incurred, respectively. The licensee reports the asset and liability for a license agreement when the license period begins and certain other specified conditions are met.

GAAP for accounting by broadcasters are found in the following pronouncement:

FAS-63   Financial Reporting by Broadcasters

CROSS-REFERENCES

1999 MILLER GAAP GUIDE: Chapter 23, "Intangible Assets"; Chapter 25, "Interest on Receivables and Payables"; Chapter 32, "Long-Term Obligations"; Chapter 33, "Nonmonetary Transactions"

BACKGROUND

FAS-63 contains the specialized accounting and reporting principles and practices that were originally published in the AICPA Statement of Position 75-5 (Accounting Practices in the Broadcasting Industry).

A significant change from the specialized accounting principles in SOP 75-5 has been made in FAS-63 concerning the application of APB-21 (Interest on Receivables and Payables) to license agreements for program material rights of broadcasters. Under SOP 75-5, the licensor and licensee were required to apply the provisions of

APB-21 to license agreements for program material rights. Under FAS-63, the application of APB-21 is optional.

A broadcasting station may be completely independent or may be affiliated with a network. Independent broadcasters purchase or otherwise provide for all of their programming. A network-affiliated broadcaster obtains much of its programming from its affiliated network and usually receives an affiliation fee and has lower programming costs than an independent.

Revenues of broadcasters arise from the sale of advertising time. Independent broadcasters sell all of their advertising time, whereas much of an affiliated broadcaster's advertising time is sold by the network. When the broadcaster airs the sponsor's advertising, revenue is recognized. Network-affiliated broadcasters receive revenue from their affiliated networks on a monthly basis. The revenue is based on a formula, and the affiliates submit weekly reports of revenue to their networks .

Advertising rates usually are based on the size of the estimated audience reached by the broadcaster and the quality of the station's programming. Rates vary significantly from market to market. Local and regional rates generally are less than national advertising rates. Rate cards that contain the advertising rates of a broadcaster are determined during rating periods (so called "sweep months") in which the size and demographics of the broadcaster's audience are measured along with the quality of the broadcaster's programming. Rate cards usually are broken down into broadcasting periods called *dayparts* and are revised on a regular basis.

A broadcaster may exchange advertising time for services or products. Such "barter" transactions could result in a broadcaster becoming part of an "ad hoc" network by allowing the programmer to retain a certain number of spots in the telecast. The programmer then sells such spots to a national advertiser. There is no accounting impact to the broadcaster.

Programming costs usually are the largest expense of television broadcasters. Programming costs generally are higher for independent broadcasters, who must obtain all of their programming themselves, than they are for network-affiliated broadcasters. Program material for television broadcasters is purchased under television licenses from producers and distributors. These producers and distributors generally package several films and license the material for one or more exhibitions or for a specified period, at which time the license expires. The license agreement usually provides for installment payments over a period, which is almost always less than the license period. Thus, the producer or distributor receives all of its money for the license prior to the expiration of the license.

Many television broadcasters produce some of their programming material either live or on videotape. Local news broadcasts and local interview shows are popular programs produced by television broadcasters.

Television and radio broadcasters are regulated by the Federal Communications Commission (FCC). Broadcasters are licensed periodically to use frequencies in specific areas, which are assigned by the FCC. In licensing a broadcaster, the FCC may consider the (*a*) financial position of the broadcaster, (*b*) advertising policies, (*c*) quality of the programming, and (*d*) contribution made to the community in which the broadcaster operates. Advertising rates are not regulated by the FCC, but guidelines have been established for advertising rates by the National Association of Broadcasters.

The major assets of a broadcaster are its FCC license and its network affiliation agreement. Thus, network-affiliated broadcasters usually are more valuable than independent broadcasters.

FAS-63 covers three specific aspects of the broadcasting industry: (1) program material license agreements, (2) barter transactions, and (3) intangible assets.

PROGRAM MATERIAL LICENSE AGREEMENTS

FAS-63 requires that broadcasters record the assets and liabilities that are involved in a program material license agreement as a purchase of a right or group of rights (FAS-63, par. 2). The license agreement is reported in the financial statements of the licensee when the license period begins and all of the following conditions are met (FAS-63, par. 3):

1. The cost of each license fee for each program is known or is reasonably determinable.

2. The broadcaster has accepted the program material in accordance with the terms of the license agreement.

3. The program is available for its first showing or telecast under the license agreement.

FAS-63 requires that the balance sheet of broadcasters be classified. Thus, assets and liabilities are classified as current or noncurrent based on the normal operating cycle of the enterprise (FAS-63, par. 3).

The asset and liability that arise from the purchase of program material rights are reported by the licensee or licensor at either (*a*) the gross amount of the liability (the predominant practice) or (*b*) the present value of the liability computed in accordance with APB-21. Under the provisions of APB-21, the present value of the liability (over one year) is reported as an asset, and the difference between the present value and the face amount of the liability is reported as deferred interest expense. The deferred interest expense is amortized to income in proportion to the payments made on the liability (FAS-63, par. 4).

☛ **PRACTICE POINTER:** One purpose of APB-21 is to require that interest be imputed on liabilities that bear an unreasonable rate of interest or no interest at all. Thus, if a reasonable rate of interest is charged on a liability, the provisions of APB-21 would not apply and the liability would be recorded at its gross amount.

APB-21 is based on the pervasive principle of **substance over form**. Allowing the licensee or licensor to report the liability or receivable either **gross** or at **present value** is equivalent to permitting the licensee or licensor to report either the **substance** or the **form** of the transaction.

The cost of rights to a package of programs is allocated to each program right in the package, based on the relative value of each program right to the broadcaster. Amortization of program material rights is computed on the estimated number of times that the program will be aired by the broadcaster. Program rights purchased for unlimited broadcasts may be amortized over the term of the license agreement if the estimated number of future showings is not determinable (FAS-63, par. 5).

Feature programs are amortized on an individual basis. Series programs, however, are amortized on a series basis. An accelerated method of amortization must be used when the first broadcast of a program is more valuable than its reruns, which usually is the case. Thus, the straight-line method of amortization is appropriate only when each broadcast is expected to produce approximately the same amount of revenue (FAS-63, par. 6).

Unamortized program rights shall not exceed their net realizable value or a writedown is required. Program rights are reported in the balance sheet at the lower of their unamortized cost or their estimated net realizable value (FAS-63, par. 7).

☛ **PRACTICE POINTER:** FAS-121 (Accounting for the Impairment of Long-Lived Assets and for Long-Lived Assets to Be Disposed Of) exempts assets covered by certain other FASB pronouncements related to specialized industries, including FAS-63. Therefore, the general standards concerning impairment losses included in FAS-121 do not apply to program rights, and accounting for impairment is based on FAS-63 standards.

BARTER TRANSACTIONS

FAS-63 requires that all barter transactions be recorded in accordance with APB-29 (Accounting for Nonmonetary Transactions). Revenue from such transactions is recorded at the time the commercials are broadcast, and barter expense is recorded at the time the services are used. If the services or products have not been received at the date the commercial is aired, a receivable is reported. On the other hand, if services or products are received before the date the commercial is aired, a liability is reported (FAS-63, par. 8).

> ☞ **PRACTICE POINTER:** APB-29 requires that nonmonetary exchanges be accounted for at the fair value of the assets or services received or surrendered, whichever is more clearly evident. If fair value is indeterminable, the only valuation available may be the recorded book value of the nonmonetary assets exchanged.

INTANGIBLE ASSETS

FAS-63 requires that intangible assets in the broadcasting industry be accounted for in accordance with APB-17 (Intangible Assets). Thus, intangible assets in the broadcasting industry generally are amortized by the straight-line method, over a period not to exceed 40 years.

If a network affiliation is terminated, any unamortized network affiliation costs are charged to expense unless a replacement agreement exists. In this event, if the fair value of the replacement agreement exceeds the unamortized network affiliation cost of the terminated agreement, no gain is recognized. If the fair value of the replacement agreement is less than the unamortized network affiliation cost of the terminated agreement, however, a loss is recognized to the extent of the difference (FAS-63, par. 9).

Under the provisions of APB-17, a company records as assets the cost of intangible assets acquired from other enterprises or individuals. Costs of developing, maintaining, or restoring intangible assets that are not specifically identifiable, have indeterminate lives, or are inherent in a continuing business and related to an enterprise as a whole, are deducted from income when incurred.

DISCLOSURE

Unrecorded program material license agreements that have been executed and do not meet the criteria of FAS-63 must be disclosed in the notes to the financial statements (FAS-63, par. 10).

> **OBSERVATION:** FAS-63 is silent on the extent of note disclosure that is necessary for unrecorded license agreements that have been executed but do not meet the criteria of FAS-63. It appears that the provisions of FAS-47 (Disclosure of Long-Term Obligations), however, may apply to some unrecorded

license agreements that have been executed. FAS-47 requires that unrecorded unconditional purchase obligations that (a) are substantially noncancelable, (b) are related to the costs of the specific goods or services in the contract, or are part of the financing arrangement for the facilities that will provide the specified goods or services in the contract, and (c) are for a remaining term in excess of one year must be disclosed by note in the purchaser's financial statements. The disclosures include:

1. A description of the nature and term of the obligation.
2. The total determinable amount of unrecorded unconditional purchase obligations as of the latest balance sheet date, and for each of the five years after the latest balance sheet date.
3. A description of the nature of any variable component of the unrecorded unconditional purchase obligations.
4. For each income statement presented, the amounts actually purchased under the unconditional purchase obligations.

CHAPTER 51
CABLE TELEVISION COMPANIES

CONTENTS

CHAPTER 51
CABLE TELEVISION COMPANIES

OVERVIEW

GAAP for all companies generally apply to cable television companies. Certain accounting problems have arisen, however, with regard to the initial recording of assets and the treatment of hookup costs and franchise costs.

The pronouncement that applies GAAP to cable television companies is as follows:

FAS-51   Financial Reporting by Cable Television Companies

CROSS-REFERENCES

1999 MILLER GAAP GUIDE: Chapter 11, "Depreciable Assets and Depreciation"; Chapter 20, "Impairment of Loans and Long-Lived Assets"; Chapter 23, "Intangible Assets"; Chapter 24, "Interest Costs Capitalized"

BACKGROUND

FAS-51 contains the specialized accounting and reporting principles and practices that were originally published in the AICPA Statement of Position 79-2 (Accounting by Cable Television Companies).

Cable television (CATV) systems are organized and built to provide uninterrupted program entertainment. The distribution of the television programs by a CATV system usually is made over coaxial or fiber optic cables or satellites to a defined area. CATV systems cover approximately 60% of U.S. households.

Ordinarily, a cable TV company, which is regulated by the Federal Communications Commission, obtains a franchise from a local governmental authority, which permits the distribution of CATV programs in a specified area. The franchise agreement usually provides for payment of fees to the granting authority and contains, among other provisions, the maximum fees that the company can charge a subscriber. In addition, franchise agreements may include many provisions pertaining to the type and quality of service that must be provided, number of TV channels, type of construction, and duration of the franchise. If all of the terms of the franchise agreement are not met, the governmental authority may retain the right to terminate the contract with the cable TV company.

The operation of a CATV system begins with the purchase of program entertainment. Program entertainment from major suppliers and motion picture studios usually is acquired on a long-term contract. The transmission signals of a cable programming company are picked up by the CATV system by microwave relay, antennas, or satellite, then amplified and distributed to subscribers via coaxial cables. The subscriber usually pays an initial hookup charge and thereafter, a monthly subscription fee.

Key provisions of 1992 federal cable law include use of reasonable subscriber rates, better customer service standards, and sale of program entertainment on a nondiscriminatory basis. A cable operator with more than 12 usable channels must set aside four to carry local commercial TV stations upon demand.

The size of the franchise area and the density of the population usually determine the construction period required to install a CATV system. The type of system being built, however, may also affect the period of construction. For example, if the coaxial cables must be installed underground rather than on utility poles, the period of construction will likely take longer. The construction period is completed when all of the equipment used to receive transmissions (head-end equipment) is installed, all main (head-end) and distribution cables are in place, and most subscriber drops (installation hardware) are installed. The CATV system is *energized* when the first transmission is made to subscribers. It is not unusual to energize part of a CATV system before the entire system is built, because large CATV systems generally are built in sections over several years. When this occurs, a *prematurity period* is established. A prematurity period begins when the first subscriber's revenue is earned and ends when construction of the system is completed or when the first major stage of construction is completed. The prematurity period will vary in direct relation to the size of the franchise area and the density of the population.

The capital investment necessary for even a small CATV system is quite substantial. The acquisition of a franchise and the cost of the physical facilities are expensive, and the operating overhead during the construction period requires a great deal of working capital. Space on utility poles or in underground ducts usually is leased from utility companies.

INITIAL RECORDING OF ASSETS

In the construction of a cable TV company, the *prematurity period* begins on the date that subscribers' revenue is earned and ends on the date that the construction of the CATV system is completed or when the first major stage of construction is completed. Some cable TV companies, however, have determined that the prematurity period begins on the date that subscribers' revenue is earned and ends on the date that a predetermined number of subscribers is reached.

The prematurity period must be determined by management prior to the recognition of any earned revenue from the first subscriber. FAS-51 contains a presumption that the prematurity period usually should not exceed two years. Unless very unusual circumstances arise, a prematurity period is not changed after it is established by management (FAS-51, par. 4).

A portion of a CATV system that meets most of the following conditions is in a prematurity period and is accounted for separately from the rest of the system (FAS-51, par. 5):

1. It is a separate franchise area or a different geographic area.

2. It has separate equipment or facilities.

3. It has a separate construction period, break-even point, and/or separate accountability.

4. It has a separate budget and/or separate accountability.

FAS-51 distinguishes between capitalized costs attributable to the main cable television plant and other related capitalized costs of a fully operational system, such as the cost of leases on utility poles or underground ducts, leases on satellite or microwave installations, property taxes, and capitalized interest costs. FAS-51 requires that these other related capitalized costs of a fully operational system be amortized over the same period used to depreciate the main cable television plant (FAS-51, par. 10).

All costs of constructing the physical facilities of a CATV system, including materials, direct labor, and construction overhead are capitalized. During the prematurity period, however, some subscribers are receiving service while construction continues on the system. Thus, during the prematurity period a distinction must be made between costs related to (*a*) the current period, (*b*) future periods, and (*c*) both current and future periods (FAS-51, par. 6).

Costs Related to Current Period

Selling, marketing, administrative expenses, and all costs related to current subscribers are accounted for as period costs.

Costs Related to Future Periods

During the prematurity period, all costs of constructing the physical facilities of the CATV system, including materials, direct labor, and construction overhead, continue to be capitalized.

Costs Related to Both Current and Future Periods

Programming costs and other system costs (such as the costs of leases on utility poles or underground ducts, leases on satellite or microwave installations, and property taxes) that are incurred in anticipation of servicing a fully operating system and that will not vary significantly regardless of the number of subscribers should be allocated to both current and future periods.

FAS-51 requires that during the prematurity period, charges for capitalized costs other than those of the main cable television plant are allocated to both current and future periods based on a fraction. The denominator of the fraction is the total expected subscribers at the end of the prematurity period; the numerator of the fraction is the estimated number of subscribers at the end of each month of the prematurity period. The fraction results in the amount of amortization, which is charged to expense in the current period (FAS-51, par. 7).

During the prematurity period, depreciation of the cost of the main cable television plant of the CATV system is allocated by the same fraction. Instead of computing depreciation on the costs incurred to date, however, the total depreciable base of the main cable television plant is estimated, and the total amount of depreciation is determined by applying the depreciation method normally used by the company. After the total amount of depreciation is computed, the fraction described in the previous paragraph is applied to arrive at the amount of depreciation expense that should be charged to the current period (FAS-51, par. 8).

Under the provisions of FAS-34 (Capitalization of Interest Cost) certain interest costs, if material, are capitalized and added to the acquisition cost of assets that require a period of time to get ready for their intended use. The cost of assets to which capitalized interest is allocated includes the cost of both those assets acquired for a company's own use and those acquired for sale in the ordinary course of business (FAS-51, par. 9).

Interest cost is capitalized during the prematurity period on that portion of the CATV system which is undergoing development activities to get it ready for its intended use and is not being used in the earning activities of the system.

☛ **PRACTICE POINTER:** Several requirements of FAS-34 may pose particularly difficult problems for CATV systems. For example, capitalization of interest ceases when the asset being constructed is ready for its intended purpose. This requirement is particularly important in the construction of large CATV systems that are completed and placed into service in phases. Take care to ensure that interest is not capitalized on phases of the project that are complete and ready for service.

FAS-34 also specifies that if the enterprise suspends substantially all activities related to acquisition of the asset, interest capitalization shall cease until activities are resumed. Brief interruptions in activities, interruptions that are externally imposed, and delays that are inherent in the asset acquisition process do not require cessation of interest capitalization. Judge carefully to determine whether delays in CATV system construction require an interruption in the capitalization of interest.

HOOKUP REVENUE AND FRANCHISE COSTS

Hookup revenue is recognized currently to the extent of direct selling costs. Direct selling costs include those costs that are incurred in obtaining and processing new subscribers. Hookup revenue in excess of direct selling costs is deferred and amortized to revenue over the estimated average subscription period (FAS-51, par. 11).

Initial hookup costs for subscribers are capitalized, and subsequent disconnects and connects are charged to expense as incurred. The depreciation period for initial hookup costs for subscribers should not exceed the depreciation period of the main cable television plant (FAS-51, par. 12).

Usually, a CATV company makes a formal franchise application to a local governmental unit to provide cable television service in its geographical area. The costs associated with any successful application may be significant and are accounted for in accordance with APB-17 (Intangible Assets). These successful franchise costs are capitalized and amortized to income over the lesser of their estimated useful life or the life of the franchise, but not longer than 40 years. The straight-line method is used for amortization purposes unless a different method can be justified (FAS-51, par. 13).

The costs associated with unsuccessful franchise applications and abandoned franchises are charged to expense in the period in which it is determined that they cannot benefit any future period (FAS-51, par. 13).

PERIODIC REVIEW OF RECOVERABILITY

Capitalized assets not only benefit a future period, but their costs should be recoverable from the expected future revenue. Thus, a periodic review of the capitalized costs of a cable TV company must be made to determine whether the costs are recoverable through future successful operations or future sale of the assets or a write-down to recoverable values is necessary (FAS-51, par. 14).

> **OBSERVATION:** FAS-121 (Accounting for the Impairment of Long-Lived Assets and for Long-Lived Assets to Be Disposed Of) includes a list of pronouncements related to specialized industries that are exempt from the standards of FAS-121. FAS-51 is **not** on that list, and FAS-121 specifically modifies FAS-51 to indicate that capitalized plant and certain identifiable intangible assets of CATV companies are subject to the provisions of FAS-121.

CHAPTER 52
MOTION PICTURE FILMS

CONTENTS

CHAPTER 52
MOTION PICTURE FILMS

OVERVIEW

GAAP for motion picture films include specialized accounting and reporting principles primarily for producers and distributors of motion picture films. Motion picture companies and independent producers and distributors (licensors) shall consider a license agreement as a sale of a right or a group of rights. The sale is recognized by the licensor when the license period begins and certain specified conditions are met.

As used in FAS-53, the term *motion picture films* includes all types of films and video cassettes and disks, including feature films, television specials, television series, and cartoons that are (*a*) exhibited in theaters; (*b*) licensed for exhibition by individual television stations, groups of stations, networks, cable television systems, or other means; or (*c*) licensed for the home video market.

The following pronouncement contains GAAP for accounting for motion picture films:

FAS-53   Financial Reporting by Producers and Distributors of Motion Picture Films

CROSS-REFERENCES

BACKGROUND

FAS-53 contains the specialized accounting and reporting principles and practices that were originally published in the AICPA industry accounting guide titled "Accounting for Motion Picture Films" and the AICPA Statement of Position 79-4 (Accounting for Motion Picture Films). These principles and practices were extracted from these publications without significant change.

The exhibition rights to a film usually are licensed by the licensor, who may be the original producer of the film or a distributor of the film. The rights licensed may be for one showing of the film or for multiple showings of the film over a specified period. Generally, only one first-run showing of a film is licensed in a given market at a given time.

A film starts with the acquisition of a story property (book, stage play, original screenplay, etc.), goes through the various stages of film production, and is then distributed for exhibition. The production-to-distribution cycle includes exploitation in theatrical, television (both "free" and "pay"), home video, and other ancillary markets.

REVENUE RECOGNITION

Revenue for motion picture film rights is recognized in accordance with the basic realization principles embodied in GAAP. FAS-53 requires that certain events occur, however, before revenue is recognized.

Theatrical Exhibitions

In larger markets, exhibition rights are sold on a percentage of box office receipts, sometimes with a nonrefundable guarantee. In smaller markets, the film rights usually are sold on a flat-fee basis. In foreign markets, nonrefundable guarantees generally are considered outright sales because additional revenues based on percentage of box office receipts infrequently are remitted to the licensor, and the licensor has no control over distribution (FAS-53, par. 3). Thus, nonrefundable guarantees for completed films in a foreign market are recognized as revenue on the execution of a noncancelable agreement.

Under normal domestic conditions, revenue is recognized for percentage and flat-fee contracts on the date the film is exhibited by the licensee. Normal nonrefundable guarantees against a percentage of box office receipts are deferred and recognized as revenue on the date of the exhibition of the film (FAS-53, par. 4).

Television Exhibitions

Exhibition contracts of film rights for television usually provide for more than one exhibition over a specific period. In addition, most television contracts include a package of several films. These types of contracts expire on the date of the last authorized telecast, or on a specific date, if it occurs sooner. Payment for the contract usually is made in installments over a period that is shorter than that of the licensing agreement. Under FAS-53, revenue is recognized on a television exhibition contract when the license period begins and all of the following conditions are met (FAS-53, par. 6):

1. The license fee for each film is known.

2. The cost of each film can be reasonably determined.

3. Collection of the full contract is reasonably assured.

4. The licensee has accepted the film in accordance with the conditions of the license agreement.

5. The film is available for its first showing or telecast. The licensor can deliver the contractual right and the licensee can exercise the right.

Revenue recognition is postponed if an option or any other condition creates a doubt as to the ability or obligation of both parties to perform (FAS-53, par. 7).

Revenue from the licensing of a film is recognized in the same sequence as the market-by-market exploitation of the film and at the time the licensee is able to exercise rights under the agreement. That time is the later of the commencement of the license period or the expiration of a conflicting license (FAS-53, par. 8).

If a receivable from the sale of film rights extends over a long period and is either noninterest-bearing or has an unreasonable rate of interest, the provisions of APB-21 (Interest on Receivables and Payables) are applied. The present value of the long-term receivable is recorded as a sale, and the difference between the present value and face amount of the receivable is recorded as deferred interest income (FAS-53, par. 9).

COSTS AND EXPENSES

Production costs of motion picture films usually consist of (*a*) costs for acquisition of story rights, (*b*) pre-production costs, (*c*) principal photography costs, and (*d*) post-production costs. Production costs, which are capitalized as film cost inventory, generally are accounted for on a film-by-film basis and include overhead allocated on a systematic and rational basis in accordance with GAAP.

Amortization of production costs and other amortizable amounts (including talent participation compensation) begins with the release of the film for exhibition purposes. FAS-53 generally requires the *Individual Film Forecast Computation Method* for amortizing film production costs (FAS-53, par. 10). This method amortizes the film costs in the same ratio that current revenues bear to total estimated gross revenues. Estimated gross revenues are management's best estimates of a film's financial performance. The computation is similar to the percentage-of-completion method used in long-term construction-type contracts.

> ☛ **PRACTICE POINTER:** The individual-film-forecast computation requires the determination of a fraction, the numerator being gross revenues from the film for the period and the denominator being the anticipated total gross revenues from the film during its useful life, including future estimated total gross revenues from exploitation in all markets. The resulting fraction is applied to capitalized film costs (inventory) to determine the amortization for each period.

Care must be exercised in determining the *total estimated gross revenues* because long-term noninterest-bearing revenues can be included only to the extent of their present values (APB-21). Thus, the difference between the present value of the estimated long-term gross revenue and its face amount is recorded as deferred interest income at the inception of the contract. The *total revenues to date* in the fraction (numerator) must also exclude any interest income collected to date. In other words, neither the numerator nor the denominator of the fraction include any imputed interest (FAS-53, par. 11).

Reviews should be made of the total estimated gross revenue as of each reporting date, and appropriate revisions made when current information dictates. When anticipated total gross revenues are revised, a new denominator is determined to include only the anticipated total gross revenues from the beginning of the year; the numerator (actual gross revenues for the current period) is not affected. The revised fraction is applied to the net capitalized film costs as of the beginning of the current years (FAS-53, par. 12). Revisions are made prospectively as a change in accounting estimate, in accordance with APB-20 (Accounting Changes).

If compensation under a participation agreement is anticipated, the total expected participation is charged to expense in the same manner as amortization of production costs described above (FAS-53, par. 14). Exploitation costs (i.e., costs to exploit a film) that clearly benefit future periods should be capitalized as film cost inventory and amortized as described above (FAS-53, par. 15).

Illustration of Individual-Film-Forecast Method of Amortization
(FAS-53, pars. 40–42)

Assume the following:

Film cost	$10,000,000
Actual gross revenues:	
First year	12,000,000
Second year	3,000,000
Third year	1,000,000
Anticipated total gross revenues:	
At end of first year	24,000,000
At end of second and third years	20,000,000

Amortization in each of the first three years is calculated as follows:

First-year amortization:

$$\frac{\$12,000,000}{\$24,000,000} \times \$10,000,000 = \$5,000,000$$

Second-year amortization (anticipated total gross revenues reduced from $24,000,000 to $20,000,000):

$$\frac{\$3,000,000}{\$8,000,000\text{(a)}} \times \$5,000,000\text{(b)} = \$1,875,000$$

Third year amortization:

$$\frac{\$1,000,000}{\$8,000,000\text{(c)}} \times \$5,000,000\text{(c)} = \$625,000$$

(a) $20,000,000 minus $12,000,000 or anticipated gross revenues from beginning of period.

(b) $10,000,000 minus $5,000,000 or cost less accumulated amortization at beginning of period.

(c) The $8,000,000 and $5,000,000 need not be reduced by the second-year gross revenue ($3,000,000) and second-year amortization ($1,875,000), respectively, because anticipated gross revenues did not change from the second to third year. If such reduction were made, the amount of amortization would be as follows:

$$\frac{\$1,000,000}{\$5,000,000} \times \$3,125,000 = \$625,000$$

OTHER ACCOUNTING ISSUES

Inventory Adjustments

The inventory of motion picture films consists of the unamortized production and other properly capitalized costs. A periodic review must be made of each individual film to determine whether the total estimated gross revenues for the film are enough to recover the unamortized costs, talent participation percentages, and all direct distribution expenses. When total estimated gross revenues are insufficient, an inventory write-down to net realizable value is necessary (FAS-53, par. 16).

> ☛ **PRACTICE POINTER:** FAS-121 (Accounting for the Impairment of Long-Lived Assets and for Long-Lived Assets to Be Disposed Of) exempts assets covered by certain other FASB pronouncements related to specialized industries, including FAS-53. Therefore, the general standards concerning impairment losses included in FAS-121 do not apply to motion picture films, and accounting for impairment is based on FAS-53 standards.

If the estimate of future gross revenues for a particular film is subsequently increased during the same fiscal period in which the film was written down to net realizable value, the film may be written back up in an amount that does not exceed the current year write-down. Any film costs that have been reduced to net realizable value at the end of a fiscal period may not be written back up in subsequent fiscal periods (FAS-53, par. 16).

It may become necessary to reduce unfinished and/or unreleased films to their net realizable value. This can occur in situations in which the film costs have significantly exceeded budgeted costs, or in which major downward revisions by management of estimated gross revenue are required because of existing circumstances (FAS-53, par. 16).

The inventory of story costs (rights to books, stage plays, original screenplays, etc.) is reviewed as of each reporting date to determine whether it will be used in the production of a motion picture film. A presumption exists that story costs held for more than three years that have not been set for production of a film should be charged to current production overhead. Once charged off, story costs are not reinstated if subsequently set for production (FAS-53, par. 17).

Loans and Interest Costs

Loans, guarantees, and advances by motion picture companies to independent producers are recorded to reflect the substance of the transaction. Loans and/or advances to independent producers for the production of motion picture films are recorded as film cost inventory by the motion picture film company. All other items of revenue and expense are accounted for in accordance with the provisions of FAS-53 (FAS-53, par. 18).

> **OBSERVATION:** Although the original AICPA industry accounting guide specifically covered the interest costs incurred in the production of a motion picture film, FAS-53 does not. FAS-34 (Capitalization of Interest Cost), however, does allow the capitalization of interest costs for qualifying assets that require a period of time to be completed for their intended use. The cost of assets to which capitalized interest may be allocated includes the cost of both those assets acquired for a company's own use and those acquired for sale in the ordinary course of business. Thus, interest costs may be capitalized in the production of motion picture films that qualify under the provision of FAS-34.

Home Market

Motion picture films licensed for use at home on video cassettes, pay-per-view, laser disks, or through cable television are accounted for in accordance with the provisions of FAS-53 (FAS-53, par. 22).

Barter Syndications

When the distributor furnishes programming to an ad hoc network in exchange for the retention of advertising time, revenue recognition is upon broadcast and barter transaction accounting is governed by EITF 87-10 (Revenue Recognition by Television [Barter] Syndicators).

FINANCIAL STATEMENTS AND DISCLOSURE

Financial Statements

FAS-53 allows a motion picture company to use a classified or unclassified balance sheet for reporting purposes. While the unclassified balance sheet is more common, motion picture companies that segregate assets and liabilities between current and noncurrent classifications should use the following guidelines:

1. Unamortized film inventory in release to a primary market; completed films not released, reduced by secondary market allocations, if any; and television films in production that are under contract for sale are classified as current assets (FAS-53, par. 20).

2. Secondary market allocations of films that will not be realized within 12 months and all related film production costs are classified as noncurrent (FAS-53, par. 21).

3. Production costs that are allocated to secondary television markets are classified as noncurrent. These costs are amortized as revenues and recorded from secondary television markets. (**Note:** This treatment of production costs allocated to secondary television markets is expected to avoid reclassification of items, back and forth, between current and noncurrent classifications [FAS-53, par. 21].)

4. Liabilities are recorded in accordance with existing GAAP. Thus, current liabilities are obligations whose liquidation is reasonably expected to require the use of current assets or the creation of other current liabilities.

5. From the time of execution to the time of revenue recognition, license agreements for the sale of motion picture rights are to be considered as executory and are not reported on the balance sheet until revenues are recognized. Amounts may be received in advance and classified as current or noncurrent according to the circumstances (FAS-53, par. 19).

Disclosure

FAS-53 requires disclosure of film inventories, including films that are (*a*) released, (*b*) completed but not released, and (*c*) in process. In addition, the amount of story rights should be disclosed (FAS-53, par. 23). In addition, the Securities and Exchange Commission requires public companies to disclose the percentage of released costs expected to be amortized within three years from the balance sheet date and, if less than 60%, the period required to reach 60%. Many non-public companies voluntarily make this disclosure.

> **OBSERVATION:** The AICPA industry accounting guide titled "Accounting for Motion Picture Films" required that accounting policies peculiar to the industry be disclosed in accordance with APB-22 (Disclosure of Accounting Policies) (see the 1999 *Miller GAAP Guide* chapter titled "Accounting Policies"). The accounting guide also required that a description of the amortization methods of film costs used by a company be disclosed in accordance with APB-17 (Intangible Assets). Although FAS-53 does not mention these disclosures, it is apparent that they are still required by existing GAAP.

CHAPTER 53
RECORDS AND MUSIC

CONTENTS

CHAPTER 53
RECORDS AND MUSIC

OVERVIEW

Primary sources of revenue include sales of recorded music product (compact discs, cassettes, etc.), the licensing of others to use music, royalties from public performances, revenue from music used in motion pictures, and revenue from the sale of sheet music. If a license agreement is, in substance, a sale and if collectibility of the fee is reasonably assured, GAAP require the licensor to recognize the licensing fee as revenue.

Promulgated GAAP that specify accounting for these various types of revenue are found in the following pronouncement:

FAS-50   Financial Reporting in the Record and Music Industry

CROSS-REFERENCES

1999 Miller GAAP Guide: Chapter 43, "Revenue Recognition"

BACKGROUND

FAS-50 contains the specialized accounting and reporting principles and practices that were originally published in the AICPA Statement of Position 76-1 (Accounting Practices in the Record and Music Industry).

Music publishers control the copyrights on their music, which may be owned by an artist-composer. On the other hand, record companies usually depend on an artist who is employed under a personal service contract to produce the record master that is used in manufacturing the ultimate product. The caliber and reputation of the recording artist has a direct effect on the success of any album or individual record.

A record master is produced by an expert sound engineer. Each instrument and voice is first recorded separately on magnetic tape. The sound engineer then combines each instrument and voice, emphasizing and de-emphasizing as he or she deems appropriate. This process is called mixing and is an important phase of manufacturing a record. The mixing process produces a record master, which is used to make acetate discs that are coated with metal. The metal coated disc is used to produce the mold that is eventually used to make the final product. Record masters also are utilized to produce tapes for the manufacturer of tape cartridges, cassettes, and compact discs. The following costs usually are incurred in the production of a record master:

1. Costs for the recording studio
2. Costs for engineers, mixing experts, directors, and other technical talent
3. Costs for musicians, arrangers, vocal background, and other similar talent
4. Costs for manufacturing the record master itself

The more successful recording artists are paid a nonrefundable advance against future royalties and bear no cost of producing the record master.

Music publishers license others, on a royalty basis, to use their music. Additional sources of income for music publishers include royalties from public performance, revenue from the music used in motion picture films, and revenue from the sale of sheet music.

Music publishers usually are members of ASCAP (American Society of Composers, Authors, and Publishers), BMI (Broadcast Music Incorporated), or some other society or association. Copyright laws provide that each time music is played publicly, the publisher and/or composer are entitled to a minimum royalty for public performance and mechanical rights, i.e., rights to reproduce musical composition by any mechanical means—records, tapes, and diskettes. By monitoring radio and TV stations and live performances, ASCAP or BMI collects the royalties due to various publishers and/or composers. After collecting the royalties, ASCAP or BMI make periodic remittances to the publisher and/or composer.

One of the major accounting problems in the record and music industry is the timing of the recognition of a sale. This is because of the return privileges that manufacturers and distributors must make available to their customers. In addition, some manufacturers create discounts by including a certain number of free records in proportion to the size of the order.

> **OBSERVATION:** Accounting and reporting for revenue when a right of return exists is covered by FAS-48 (Revenue Recognition When Right of Return Exists).

LICENSOR ACCOUNTING

Owners of music copyrights or record masters usually enter into license agreements based on a minimum guarantee, which generally is paid in advance by the licensee. The licensor records the receipt of a minimum license guarantee as deferred income (liability), which is recognized as it is earned in accordance with the license agreement. If the license agreement is unclear as to when the guarantee is earned, the only alternative may be to recognize the guarantee over the term of the license agreement (FAS-50, par. 8).

Fees that are not fixed in amount by the terms of the license agreement are not recognized as revenue by the licensor until a reasonable estimate is made of such fees or the license agreement expires (FAS-50, par. 9).

When a licensee receives from the licensor a noncancelable contract for a specified fee granting specific rights to the licensee, who may use these rights at any time without restriction, an outright sale has been consummated. In this event, the earning process is complete and revenue is recognized if collectibility of the balance of the fee, if any, is assured reasonably (FAS-50, par. 7).

☞ **PRACTICE POINTER:** GAAP generally prohibit accounting for revenue by installment accounting except where significant doubt exists concerning collectibility. In such cases, a company can use either the cost recovery method or the installment sales method of accounting [APB-10 (Omnibus Opinion—1966)], depending on the extent of the uncertainty.

ARTIST COMPENSATION COST

Royalties earned by artists, adjusted for anticipated returns, are charged to expense in the period in which the related record sale takes place. Royalty advances are recorded as prepaid royalties (an asset) if the past performance and current popularity of the artist to whom the advance is made indicate that the advance will be recoverable from future royalties to be earned by the artist. Advances made to new or previously unsuccessful artists, as well as those not having current popularity, are expensed in the current period. Capitalized advances are charged to expense as subsequent royalties are earned by the artist. If any capitalized advances subsequently appear not to be fully recoverable from future royalties to be earned by the artist, such advances should be charged to expense during the period in which the loss becomes evident. Advance royalties should be classified as current and noncurrent assets, as appropriate (FAS-50, par. 10).

> **OBSERVATION:** FAS-121 (Accounting for the Impairment of Long-Lived Assets and Long-Lived Assets to Be Disposed Of) exempts assets covered by certain other FASB pronouncements related to specialized industries, including FAS-50. Therefore, the general standards concerning impairment losses included in FAS-121 are not applicable for record and music assets, and accounting for asset impairment is based on FAS-50 standards.

Future royalty guarantees, artist advances payable in the future, and other commitments, if material, should be disclosed in the financial statements (FAS-50, par. 13).

The cost of a record master is recorded as an asset if it is assured reasonably that such cost will be recovered from expected future revenue. This cost should be disclosed separately in the balance sheet. The cost of a record master is amortized to income in proportion to the net revenue that is expected to be realized (FAS-50, par. 11).

Any portion of the cost of a record master that is recoverable from the artist's royalties is accounted for as a royalty advance and disclosed separately in the financial statements (FAS-50, par. 12).

LICENSEE ACCOUNTING

As mentioned previously, license agreements usually are based on a minimum guarantee that generally is paid in advance to the licensor by the licensee. The licensee records this minimum payment as a deferred charge (an asset). The deferred charge is then amortized to expense in accordance with the terms of the license agreement. Any other fees required by the licensing agreement that are not fixed in amount by the terms of the license agreement before the agreement expires must be estimated and accrued on a license-by-license basis by the licensee (FAS-50, par. 15).

CHAPTER 54
FRANCHISE FEE REVENUE

CONTENTS

CHAPTER 54
FRANCHISE FEE REVENUE

OVERVIEW

A franchise agreement transfers rights owned by the franchisor to a franchisee. The rights transferred for a specified period of time may include the use of patents, secret processes, trademarks, trade names, or other similar assets.

The primary accounting problem associated with accounting for franchise fee revenue is the timing of the revenue recognition (i.e., determining when the franchise fee revenue is earned). Accounting standards prescribe specific criteria that must be met for revenue to be recognized.

GAAP for franchise fee revenue are found in the following pronouncement:

FAS-45   Accounting for Franchise Fee Revenue

CROSS-REFERENCES

1999 MILLER GAAP GUIDE: Chapter 3, "Business Combinations"; Chapter 22, "Installment Sales Method of Accounting"; Chapter 31, "Long-Term Construction Contracts"; Chapter 43, "Revenue Recognition"

BACKGROUND

Payment for franchise rights may include an initial franchise fee and/or continuing fees or royalties. The agreement usually also provides for any continuing services that are to be rendered by the franchisor, and any inventory or purchases that may be required of the franchisee. In addition, the franchise agreement typically sets forth the procedure for cancellation, resale, or reacquisition of the franchise by the franchisor.

FAS-45 contains the specialized accounting and reporting principles and practices that were originally published in an AICPA industry accounting guide titled "Accounting for Franchise Fee Revenue." This guide was published in 1973 and covered the accounting problems of the party granting the franchise (franchisor).

REVENUE RECOGNITION

Individual Franchise Fees

The two major accounting issues in revenue recognition of initial franchise fees are (1) the time the fee is properly regarded as earned and (2) the assurance of collectibility of any receivable resulting from unpaid portions of the initial fee.

> **OBSERVATION**: These accounting issues are not unique to franchise accounting and merely represent an application of the principle of revenue realization. The realization principle requires that be considered earned before it is recognized. GAAP require that the realization of revenue be recognized in the accounting period in which the earning process is substantially completed and an exchange has taken place. Revenue usually is recognized at the amount established by the parties to the exchange except for transactions in which collection of the receivable is not assured reasonably.

FAS-45 requires that revenue on individual franchise fees be recognized on the consummation of the transaction, which occurs when all material services or conditions of the sale have been substantially performed. Substantial performance by the franchisor occurs when the following conditions are met (FAS-45, par. 5):

1. The franchisor is not obligated in any way (trade practice, law, intent, or agreement) to excuse payment of any unpaid notes or to refund any cash already received.

2. The initial services required of the franchisor by contract or otherwise (e.g., training, site selection, etc.) have been substantially performed.

3. All other material conditions have been met that affect the consummation of the sale.

The earliest that substantial performance is presumed to occur is when the franchisee actually commences operations of the franchise. This presumption may be overcome, however, if the franchisor can demonstrate that substantial performance occurs at an earlier date (FAS-45, par. 5).

Another accounting issue involved in the recognition of individual franchise fees is the collectibility of any receivable resulting from unpaid portions of the initial franchise fee. An adequate provision for estimated uncollectible amounts from individual franchise fees must be established, if necessary. If the collection of long-term receivables from individual franchise fees is not assured reasonably, the cost recovery or installment sale accounting methods should be used to recognize revenue (FAS-45, par. 6).

Installment Method

Under the installment method of accounting, each payment collected consists of part recovery of cost and part gross profit, in the same ratio that these two elements existed in the original sale. (For a more detailed discussion of the cost recovery and installment methods, see the 1999 *Miller GAAP Guide* chapter titled "Installment Sales Method of Accounting.")

Cost Recovery Method

The cost recovery method is used in situations in which recovery of cost is extremely uncertain. Initially, all amounts received are considered recoveries of cost. Once all cost has been recovered, any other collections are recognized as revenue.

Continuing Franchise Fees

Continuing franchise fees are consideration for the continuing rights granted by the franchise agreement and for general and specific services during the life of the franchise agreement. Continuing franchise fees are recognized as revenue when actually earned and receivable from the franchisee. This is true, even if the continuing franchise fee is designated for a specific purpose. If an agency relationship is established by the franchise agreement and a designated portion of the continuing franchise fee is required to be segregated for a specific purpose, however, the designated amounts are recorded as a liability. Any costs incurred for the specific purpose would be charged against the liability. All other costs relating to continuing franchise fees are expensed as incurred (FAS-45, par. 14).

In the event that the continuing franchise fees appear to be insufficient to cover the costs and reasonable profit of the franchisor for the continuing services required by the franchise agreement, a portion of the initial franchise fee, if any, is deferred and amortized over the term of the franchise. The amount deferred should be sufficient to cover all the costs of the continuing services plus a reasonable profit (FAS-45, par. 7).

> **OBSERVATION:** Apparently, FAS-45 assumes that continuing services required by the franchisor coincide with the term of the franchise and amortization should be based on the term of the franchise. An alternate approach would be to relate the amortization period to the period in which the continuing services will be provided by the franchisor, which may not necessarily be the entire term of the franchise.

Area Franchise Fees

Area franchises transfer franchise rights within a geographic area, permitting the opening of a number of franchise outlets. Accounting for revenue recognition from an area franchise is essentially the same as that for individual franchise fees. The only difference is that substantial performance of the franchisor may be more difficult to determine. The terms of the franchise agreement must be used to determine when substantial performance has occurred. In addition, it may be necessary to use the percentage-of-completion method of recognizing revenue in some franchise agreements. For example, an area franchise agreement may require the franchisor to provide specific initial services to any franchise opened in the area. In this event, the franchisor should estimate reasonably the number of franchises that are expected to be opened in the area and should recognize a portion of the total area franchise fee as substantial performance occurs for each franchise in the area. Thus, it is necessary to determine the cost of servicing each individual franchise within the area and the total cost of all individual franchises that are expected to be opened in the area. The next step is to determine the percentage of costs that have been substantially performed to the total costs of all individual franchises that are expected to be opened in the area. The resulting percentage is applied to the total initial area franchise revenue to determine the amount of area franchise revenue that can be recognized (FAS-45, pars. 8 and 9).

> ☛ **PRACTICE POINTER:** The percentage-of-completion method of recognizing revenue should be used only in those situations in which costs can be estimated with reasonable reliability.

Estimates of the number of franchises that are expected to be opened in an area franchise are determined by reference to the significant terms and conditions of the franchise agreement (FAS-45, par. 9).

If the franchisor's substantial performance under the terms of the franchise agreement is related to the area franchise, and not to the individual franchises within the area, revenue recognition occurs when all material services and conditions relating to the area franchise have been substantially performed. Thus, this type of area franchise is treated similarly to an individual franchise (FAS-45, par. 8).

Any portion of the franchise revenue that is related to unperformed future services that may have to be refunded is not recognized by the franchisor until the right to refund has expired (FAS-45, par. 8).

OTHER FRANCHISE ACCOUNTING ISSUES

Franchisee and Franchisor—Unusual Relationships

Unusual relationships may exist between the franchisee and the franchisor, besides those created by the franchise agreement. For example, the franchisor may guarantee debt of the franchisee, or contractually control the franchisee's operations to the extent that an affiliation exists. In all these circumstances, all material services, conditions, or obligations relating to the franchise must be performed substantially by the franchisor before revenue is recognized (FAS-45, par. 10).

> **OBSERVATION:** The above requirements for unusual relationships between the franchisee and franchisor relate to both individual and area franchises. That is, substantial performance must occur before the franchisor may recognize any revenue.

The initial franchise fee is deferred if it is probable that the franchisor will acquire the franchise back from the franchisee because of an option or other understanding. In this event, the deferred amount is accounted for as a reduction of the cost of reacquiring the franchise when the option or understanding is exercised (FAS-45, par. 11).

Tangible Assets Included in the Franchise Fee

In addition to the initial services of the franchisor, the initial franchise fee may include the sale of specific tangible property, such as inventory, signs, equipment, or real property. Thus, a portion of the initial franchise fee must be allocated to such tangible property. FAS-45 requires that the amount allocated be the fair value of the property. The fair value of the tangible property is recognized as revenue when title to such property passes to the franchisee, even though substantial performance has not occurred for other services included in the franchise agreement (FAS-45, par. 12).

> **OBSERVATION:** FAS-45 does not specify the date on which fair value of the tangible property must be determined. Ordinarily, fair value would be determined at the date of the franchise agreement, which usually establishes the date of the sale.

The franchise agreement may also allocate a portion of the initial franchise fee to specific services that the franchisor will provide. If the various services that the franchisor will provide are interrelated to the extent that objective segregation is impossible, FAS-45 prohibits the recognition of revenue for any specific service until all the services required under the franchise agreement have been substantially performed. If actual prices are available for a specific service through recent sales of the specific service, however, FAS-45 permits recognition of revenue based on substantial performance of that service. In other words, if the franchisor has established objective prices for specific service, a portion of the total franchise fee may be recognized upon completion of substantial performance of the specific services (FAS-45, par. 13).

Continuing Product Sales

If the terms of the franchise agreement allow the franchisee to obtain equipment and supplies from the franchisor at bargain prices, a portion of the initial franchise fee must be deferred. That portion of the fee is either (*a*) the difference between the normal selling price of the equipment and supplies and the bargain purchase price or (*b*) an amount that will enable the franchisor to recover all costs and provide a normal profit. The deferred amount is accounted for as an adjustment of the initial franchise fee and an adjustment of the selling price of the bargain purchase items (FAS-45, par. 15).

> ☞ **PRACTICE POINTER:** The sale of equipment and supplies by the franchisor at normal selling prices, which should include a reasonable profit for the franchisor, is accounted for at the time the sale is complete. Find the amount of sale by reference to the franchise agreement; the cost of the sale is the cost of the equipment or supplies to the franchisor. If it is apparent that the franchisor is not making a reasonable profit on the equipment or supplies, then the rules for "bargain purchases" must be followed.

Agency Sales

Some franchise arrangements in substance establish an agency relationship between the franchisor and the franchisee. The franchisor acts as agent for the franchisee by reselling inventory, equipment, and supplies at no profit. FAS-45 requires that these transactions be accounted for on the franchisor's books as receivables and payables, and not as profit or loss items (FAS-45, par. 16).

Expense Recognition

Direct franchising costs should be matched to their related franchise revenue in accordance with the accrual basis of accounting. This may necessitate the deferral of direct costs incurred prior to revenue recognition and the accrual of direct costs, if any, not yet incurred through the date on which revenue is recognized. Total direct costs that are deferred or accrued must not exceed their estimated related revenue (FAS-45, par. 17).

Selling, general, administrative, and other indirect costs that occur on a regular basis regardless of the sales volume are required to be expensed when incurred (FAS-45, par. 17).

Repossessed Franchises

In repossessing a franchise, the franchisor may or may not refund the consideration previously paid by the franchisee. If a refund is paid by the franchisor, the accounting treatment is equivalent to a cancellation of the original sale. Any revenue previously recognized is treated as a reduction of the revenue of the current period in which the franchise is reacquired (FAS-45, par. 18).

> ☞ **PRACTICE POINTER:** Since substantial performance is required before any revenue is recognized, it is unlikely that a franchisor would grant a refund in the event that the revenue had already been recognized. Instead, it is more likely that the franchisor would enforce collection of any balance due rather than cancel the sale.

If a refund is not paid by the franchisor, the transaction is not considered a cancellation of the sale and no adjustment is made to the previously recorded revenue. If a balance is still owed by the franchisee, however, it may be necessary to review the allowance for uncollectible amounts for the transaction. Also, any deferred revenue on the original sale should be recognized in full (FAS-45, par. 18).

Business Combinations

When a franchisor acquires the operations of one of its own franchises in an arm's-length transaction, FAS-45 requires that the acquisition be accounted for in accordance with APB-16 (Business Combinations) (see the 1999 *Miller GAAP Guide* chapter titled "Business Combinations").

Pooling-of-Interests Method

If the acquisition of one of an entity's own franchises is accounted for as a pooling of interests, the financial statements of the two entities are combined as of the beginning of the year and all intercompany transactions are eliminated in the combined financial statements. Thus, the original sale of the franchise and any other sales of products or services do not appear on the combined financial statements. In addition, any prior years' financial statements that are presented would have to be retroactively restated to reflect the business combination (FAS-45, par. 19).

Purchase Method

If the acquisition of an entity's own franchises is accounted for as a purchase, the financial statements of the two entities are combined as of the date of the acquisition and no prior intercompany accounts are eliminated in the combined financial statements. In addition, details of the results of operations for each separate company prior to the date of combination that are included in current combined net income must be disclosed by footnote (FAS-45, par. 19).

DISCLOSURES

FAS-45 requires that the following disclosures be made in the financial statements or footnotes thereto:

1. The nature of all significant commitments and obligations of the franchisor, including a description of the services that have not been substantially performed (FAS-45, par. 20)
2. If the installment or cost recovery method is being used to account for franchise fee revenue, the following must be disclosed (FAS-45, par. 21):
   a. The sales price of franchises being reported on the installment or cost recovery method

    b. The revenue and related deferred costs (currently and cumulative)

    c. The periods in which the franchise fees become payable

    d. The total revenue that was originally deferred because of uncertainties and then subsequently collected because the uncertainties were resolved

3. If significant, separate disclosure for (*a*) initial franchise fees and (*b*) other franchise fee revenue (FAS-45, par. 22)

4. Revenue and costs related to non-owned franchises, as opposed to franchises owned and operated by the franchisor (FAS-45, par. 23)

5. If significant changes in the ownership of franchises occurs during the period, the following must be disclosed (FAS-45, par. 23):

    a. The number of franchises sold during the period

    b. The number of franchises purchased during the period

    c. The number of franchised outlets in operation during the period

    d. The number of franchisor-owned outlets in operation during the period

The following disclosures, while not required, are considered desirable:

1. A statement of whether initial franchise fee revenue will probably decline in the future because sales will reach a saturation point

2. If not apparent in the financial statements, the relative contribution to net income of initial franchise fee revenue

---

Illustration of Accounting for Franchise Fee Revenue

Abbott (franchisor) enters into a franchise agreement with Martin (franchisee) that permits Martin to operate a fast-food restaurant under the name of Hot Dog Haven. Abbott operates a large number of restaurants under this name, and via franchises permits others to use the name in geographic areas where Abbott does not have its own operating units.

    The initial franchise fee commitment is $10,000. Abbott receives $1,000 from Martin in 19X1 when the agreement is signed. Martin begins operations in 19X2 and is contractually obligated to pay Abbott 25% of the balance of the commitment each year from 19X2 through 19X5. Abbott considers the criteria for substantial performance to have been met in 19X2. Also, Abbott judges collection of the fee to be reasonably assured and makes an adequate allowance for uncollectible commitments based on the aggregate amount of all receivables from commitments to a large number of franchisees.

The agreement between Abbott and Martin also calls for Martin to pay Abbott 2% of total revenues each year as a continuing franchise fee. Abbott expects these amounts to adequately cover its costs of providing continuing service to Martin and to provide a reasonable profit on those costs. Martin reports revenue of $135,000 for 19X2.

General journal entries to record the above for Abbott for 19X1 and 19X2 are as follows:

19X1	Franchise fee receivable	$9,000	
	Cash	1,000	
	Unearned franchise fee revenue		$10,000
19X2	Unearned franchise fee revenue	$10,000	
	Franchise fee revenue		$10,000
	Cash ($9,000/4)	2,250	
	Franchise fee receivable		2,250
	Cash ($135,000 x 2%)	2,700	
	Franchise fee revenue		2,700

An entry identical to the second 19X2 entry will be made each year through 19X5. An entry similar to the third 19X2 entry will be made each year for 2% of Martin's revenue.

Insurance Industry

CHAPTER 55
INSURANCE ENTERPRISES

CONTENTS

CHAPTER 55
INSURANCE ENTERPRISES

OVERVIEW

GAAP for insurance industries contain specialized principles and practices from AICPA Insurance Industry Guides and Statements of Position. They establish financial accounting and reporting standards for insurance enterprises (hereinafter referred to as *insurers*) other than mutual life insurance enterprises, assessable mutuals, and fraternal benefit societies.

An important issue for insurance enterprises is the recognition of revenue on insurance contracts. GAAP require classification of insurance contracts (*policies*) as short-duration and long-duration as follows:

- Short-duration contracts—revenue over the policy period in proportion to coverage
- Long-duration contracts—revenue when premium is due from the policyholder

GAAP for insurers are found in the following pronouncements:

FAS-60	Accounting and Reporting by Insurance Enterprises
FAS-61	Accounting for Title Plant
FAS-91	Accounting for Nonrefundable Fees and Costs Associated with Originating or Acquiring Loans and Initial Direct Costs of Leases
FAS-97	Accounting and Reporting by Insurance Enterprises for Certain Long-Duration Contracts and for Realized Gains and Losses from the Sale of Investments
FAS-113	Accounting and Reporting for Reinsurance of Short-Duration and Long-Duration Contracts
FAS-120	Accounting and Reporting by Mutual Life Insurance Enterprises and by Insurance Enterprises for Certain Long-Duration Participating Contracts (effective for financial statements for fiscal years beginning after December 15, 1995)
FIN-40	Applicability of Generally Accepted Accounting Principles to Mutual Life Insurance and Other Enterprises

> **OBSERVATION:** FAS-60 and FAS-113 are amended by FAS-133 (Accounting for Derivative Instruments and Hedging Activities). This change is effective for fiscal years beginning after June 15, 1999. FAS-133 applies in interim financial statements for periods that begin after the same date (e.g., the quarter beginning July 1, 1999). FAS-133 is covered in Chapter 16 of the 1999 *Miller GAAP Guide.*
>
> Because the effective date of FAS-133 is delayed as indicated above, and the first calendar year for which FAS-133 will be in effect is the year 2000, the impact of FAS-133 on FAS-60 and FAS-113 is not reflected in the 1999 *Miller GAAP Guide.*

CROSS-REFERENCES

1999 MILLER GAAP GUIDE: Chapter 21, "Income Taxes"; Chapter 56, "Title Plant"; Chapter 57, "Mortgage Banking Industry"; Chapter 63, "Regulated Industries"

1999 MILLER GAAP IMPLEMENTATION MANUAL: EITF: Chapter 33, "Insurance Enterprises"

BACKGROUND

FAS-60 contains the specialized accounting and reporting principles and practices that were originally published in the following AICPA publications:

- Audits of Stock Life Insurance Companies
- Audits of Fire and Casualty Insurance Companies
- SOP 79-3, Accounting for Investments of Stock Life Insurance Companies
- SOP 80-1, Accounting for Title Insurance Companies

FAS-60 covers general purpose financial statements for stock life insurance companies and stock and mutual property and liability insurance companies, as well as for reciprocal or interinsurance exchanges. Title insurance companies are covered by FAS-60, except for accounting for a title plant, which is covered by FAS-61. Mortgage guaranty insurance companies are covered by FAS-60, except for premium revenue recognition, claim costs, and acquisition costs. Mutual life insurance companies, assessment enterprises, and fraternal benefit societies are excluded from the provisions of FAS-60.

FAS-91 amended FAS-60 to establish accounting and reporting standards for nonrefundable fees and costs associated with lending, committing, or purchasing a loan or group of loans. FAS-91 specifies accounting for fees and initial direct costs of leasing transactions.

FAS-91 applies to all types of loans and to all types of lenders. (See the *GAAP Guide* chapter titled "Mortgage Banking Industry.")

FAS-97 amends FAS-60 to establish accounting and reporting standards for interest-sensitive and flexible premium long-duration insurance contracts, including universal life and certain single premium annuity insurance contracts. The original GAAP for insurance enterprises did not include these recently developed products.

FAS-97 also amends FAS-60 to specify that realized gains and losses of insurance enterprises are to be included as a component of *other income* on a pretax basis. Under FAS-60, realized gains and losses were reported net of taxes in a separate income statement caption after operating income. Under FAS-97, realized gains and losses may not be deferred to future periods.

FAS-97 does not establish accounting and reporting standards for limited-payment and universal-life contracts that address (*a*) loss recognition (premium deficiency), (*b*) accounting for reinsurance, and (*c*) financial statement disclosure. The provisions of FAS-60 that apply to these items also apply to limited-payment and universal-life contracts.

FAS-113 specifies the accounting by insurance enterprises for reinsuring, or ceding, insurance contracts. It amends FAS-60 by eliminating the practice of reporting assets and liabilities related to reinsurance contracts net of the effects of reinsurance. FAS-113 requires reinsurance receivables and prepaid reinsurance premiums to be reported as assets. It establishes the conditions required for a contract with a reinsurer to be accounted for as reinsurance and prescribes accounting and reporting standards for such a contract. It requires ceding companies to disclose the nature, purpose, and effect of reinsurance transactions. It also requires disclosure of concentrations of credit risk associated with reinsurance receivables and prepaid reinsurance premiums in accordance with FAS-105 (Disclosure of Information about Financial Instruments with Off-Balance-Sheet Risk and Financial Instruments with Concentrations of Credit Risk).

FAS-120 extends the requirements of FAS-60, FAS-97, and FAS-113 to mutual life insurance companies. FIN-40 clarifies that enterprises, including mutual life insurance enterprises, that issue financial statements described as being in conformity with GAAP are required to apply all applicable authoritative accounting pronouncements in preparing those statements. While mutual life insurance companies, like many other regulated enterprises, prepare financial statements based on regulatory accounting practices that differ from GAAP, those financial statements should not be described as being prepared in conformity with GAAP.

A primer of insurance terminology is found in the Appendix to this chapter.

CLASSIFICATION OF INSURANCE CONTRACTS

FAS-60 requires that insurance policies be classified as either short-duration contracts or long-duration contracts. In a short-duration contract, the insurance carrier primarily provides insurance protection; in a long-duration contract the insurance company provides services and functions in addition to insurance protection, including loans secured by the insurance policy and various options for the payment of policy benefits.

In determining whether an insurance contract is of short duration or long duration, FAS-60 requires that the following factors be considered (FAS-60, par. 7):

Short-duration contracts The amount of premiums charged, the amount of coverage provided, or other provisions of the contracts can be adjusted or canceled by the insurance companies at the end of any contract period. Short-duration insurance contracts provide insurance protection and are issued for short, fixed periods.

Long-duration contracts The contracts usually are noncancelable, guaranteed renewable, or otherwise not subject to unilateral changes in their provisions. Long-duration insurance contracts provide insurance protection for extended periods and include other services and functions that must be performed.

Most property and liability insurance contracts and some specialized short-term life insurance contracts are classified as short-duration contracts. Most life insurance contracts, noncancelable disability income policies, and title insurance contracts are classified as long-duration contracts. Accident and health insurance contracts may be of short duration or long duration, according to their expected term of coverage (FAS-60, par. 8).

PREMIUM REVENUE RECOGNITION

Premium revenue recognition is based on short-duration or long-duration contract classification.

Short-Duration Contracts

FAS-60 specifies that premium revenue from short-duration contracts is to be recognized periodically in proportion to the insurance company's performance under the contract. The insurance company's performance under the contract is coverage on the insured risks. In insurance policies in which coverage is provided evenly over the term of the policy, premiums are recognized evenly over the term of the policy. If the period of coverage (risk) is different from the term of the insurance contract, however, the premium is recognized over the period of coverage (the premium income is *matched* to the coverage during which the insurance company is exposed to potential loss). In the event the amount of insurance declines over the term of the insurance, the premium is recognized in proportion to the amount of insurance over the term of the insurance (FAS-60, par. 13).

In some forms of insurance, such as workers' compensation, the final premium is determined on audit after the termination of coverage. Premiums are based on a rate per $100 of payroll. The insurance company receives a premium deposit at the inception of the policy, and a premium adjustment is made on audit. In this event, an estimate of the final premium adjustment is necessary to recognize the total premium revenue over the term of insurance coverage. If the final total premium cannot be estimated reasonably, the cost recovery method or the deposit method of accounting may be used until the final total premium is known (FAS-60, par. 14).

Over the term of a class of insurance policies, the premiums are expected to pay for losses, if any, and operational expenses and still provide the insurance company with a profit. The amount of losses that a single insurance policy may incur is based on the law of averages. In other words, the loss that a single policy may incur is based on the loss experience of the many policies. As long as an insurance policy is in force, there may be a claim for a loss. The unearned portion of the premiums, at any time, should be sufficient to pay losses, operational expenses, and a margin for profit to the insurer.

In most states, statutory laws provide that insurance companies maintain reserves for possible losses equal to the unearned premiums of all insurance policies outstanding. The most common method used to determine unearned premiums is the *monthly pro rata fractional basis*. This method assumes that the same dollar amount of insurance business is written each day of every month. Thus, the mean of all insurance business written in any month is the middle of the month. One year is divided into 24 periods, and a fraction is assigned to each month as follows: January 1/24, February 3/24, March 5/24, April 7/24, May 9/24, June 11/24, and so forth. The appropriate fraction is then applied to the total original premium to determine the amount of earned and unearned premium.

Most state statutes require that insurance companies maintain their records in a manner in which a determination can be made annually on December 31 of the (a) premiums in force on direct insurance business and any reinsurance business and (b) premiums in force on insurance policies that have been ceded for reinsurance to other insurance companies.

Long-Duration Contracts

FAS-60 requires that premium revenue from long-duration contracts be recognized when due from the policyholder. Thus, premiums for whole-life, endowment, renewable term, and other long-duration contracts are recognized as revenue when the premiums are due from the policyholders (FAS-60, par. 15).

Title insurance premiums are considered due from policyholders and recognized as revenue when the title insurance company is legally or contractually entitled to the premium. Either the effective date of the title insurance policy or the date of the binder is the likely date on which the title insurance company is legally or contractually entitled to collect the premium (FAS-60, par. 16).

> **OBSERVATION:** The reasoning behind recognizing the entire title insurance premium on the effective date of the policy is that the insurance company has performed all of the acts necessary to earn the revenue.

ACCOUNTING FOR INVESTMENT, LIMITED-PAYMENT, AND UNIVERSAL-LIFE CONTRACTS

The accounting specified by FAS-60 is designed for long-duration insurance contracts that generally provide for (a) insurance protection, (b) level premium payments, and (c) contract terms that are fixed and guaranteed. The long-duration insurance contracts addressed by FAS-97 are referred to as (a) investment contracts, (b) limited-payment contracts, and (c) universal-life contracts.

Interest-sensitive and flexible-premium long-duration insurance contracts do not have the fixed and guaranteed terms that are typical of most traditional insurance contracts. Instead, the terms of this type of contract usually allow the insurer to vary the amount of charges and credits made to the policyholder's account, and more often than not, the terms allow the policyholder to vary the amount of premium paid. FAS-97 concludes that the accounting methods established by FAS-60 for the recognition of revenue, based on a percentage of premiums, are not appropriate for insurance contracts in which the insurer has the discretion of varying amounts charged or credited to the policyholder's account or the policyholder has the discretion of varying the amount of premium paid.

An *investment contract* is one that does not subject the insurer to any significant risk of death or disability of the insured. Under FAS-97, investment contracts are accounted for in the same manner as other interest-bearing contracts. Payments received by the insurer are not reported as revenue (FAS-97, par. 15).

A *limited-payment contract* is one that subjects the insurer to risk over a period longer than the premium payment period. Under FAS-97, income from limited-payment insurance contracts is recognized over the period covered by the contract rather than the period that payments are received, (e.g., to age 65 or 70) (FAS-97, par. 16).

A *universal-life contract* is one that contains terms that give the policyholder significant discretion over the amount and timing of premium payments and allows the insurer to vary the amounts charged or credited to the policyholder's account. FAS-97 requires the use of the retrospective deposit method of accounting for universal-life contracts. Under this method, an insurer is required to record a liability for policyholder benefits equal to the amount of the policyholder's account balance. Premiums are not accounted for as revenue under this method (FAS-97, pars. 19 and 20).

FAS-97 specifies that when a traditional insurance policy (e.g., whole-life) is surrendered and replaced by an interest-sensitive or flexible-premium insurance contract (e.g., universal-life), the balance of any unamortized deferred policy acquisition costs related to the surrendered policy and any difference between the liability for policyholder benefits and the cash surrender value should be charged to operations (FAS-97, par. 26).

FAS-97 does not establish accounting and reporting standards for limited-payment and universal-life contracts that address loss recognition (premium deficiency), accounting for reinsurance, and financial statement disclosure. The provisions of FAS-60 that apply to these items also apply to limited-payment and universal-life contracts (FAS-97, par. 27).

Investment Contracts

FAS-97 defines an *investment contract* as one that does not expose the insurance enterprise to significant risks arising from policyholders' mortality (death) or morbidity (illness) (FAS-97, par. 7). Since the risk of loss from death or disability is almost nonexistent, an investment contract is viewed more as an investment instrument than as an insurance contract. Under FAS-97, an insurance enterprise shall account for an investment contract in the same way other financial institutions account for most other types of interest-bearing financial instruments. Amounts received by an insurance enterprise as payments for investment contracts shall be reported as liabilities and not reported as revenue (FAS-97, par. 15).

Some long-duration insurance contracts contain terms that permit the policyholder to purchase an annuity at a guaranteed price on settlement of the contract. Under FAS-97, there is no mortality risk involved in this type of contract until the right to purchase the annuity contract has been executed (FAS-97, par. 7).

An insurance enterprise may be required to make annuity payments regardless of whether the beneficiary lives or dies (annuities with a refund feature) and to make additional payments beginning on a specified date if the beneficiary is alive on that date. These types of policies are accounted for as insurance contracts, under both FAS-60 and FAS-97, unless (*a*) there is a remote chance that the beneficiary will be alive on the date that the additional payments begin or (*b*) the present value of the estimated additional payments is immaterial when compared with the present value of all payments that are estimated to be made under the contract (FAS-97, par. 8).

Limited-Payment Contracts

FAS-97 defines a *limited-payment insurance contract* as one in which the terms are fixed and guaranteed, and for which premiums are paid over a period shorter than the period over which benefits are provided. Under FAS-97, the benefit period includes the period during which (*a*) the insurance enterprise is subject to risk from policyholder mortality and morbidity and (*b*) the insurance enterprise is responsible for administration of the contract. The period in which the policyholder or beneficiary elects to have settlement proceeds disbursed is *not* included in the benefit period (FAS-97, par. 9).

The period in which an insurance enterprise is exposed to mortality and morbidity risks in connection with a limited-payment contract extends beyond the period in which premiums are collected. This occurs because premiums are paid over a period shorter than the period over which the insurance enterprise provides benefits. The liability for policyholders' benefits for this type of limited-payment insurance contract is set up and accounted for in accordance with FAS-60 (FAS-97, par. 16).

Here, the earnings process is not completed by the mere collection of premiums. The excess of gross over net premiums received must be deferred and amortized by a constant method over the period that the insurance enterprise provides services. Thus, for life insurance contracts, the deferred premiums are amortized in relationship to the amount of insurance in force. For annuity contracts, the deferred premiums are amortized in relationship to the estimated amount of benefits that are expected to be paid (FAS-97, par. 16).

FAS-97 does not establish accounting and reporting standards for limited-payment insurance contracts that address (*a*) loss recognition (premium deficiency), (*b*) accounting for reinsurance, and (*c*) financial statement disclosure. The provisions of FAS-60 that apply to these specific items also apply to limited-payment insurance contracts (FAS-97, par. 27).

Universal-Life Contracts

Universal-life insurance contracts do not have fixed and guaranteed terms that are typical of the types of insurance contracts for which the accounting specified in FAS-60 was designed. However, certain types of conventional forms of participating and nonguaranteed-premium contracts may be, in substance, universal-life contracts. Policyholders of universal-life insurance contracts frequently are granted significant discretion over the amount and timing of premium payments. In addition, insurers frequently are granted significant discretion over amounts that accrue to and that are assessed against policyholders. FAS-97 describes as *universal-life insurance contracts* policies that provide death or annuity benefits and have one or more of the following features (FAS-97, par. 10):

1. The terms of the contract do not fix and guarantee the amounts assessed by the insurer against the policyholder for mortality coverage, contract administration, initiation, or surrender.

2. Interest and other amounts that accrue to the benefit of the policyholder are not fixed and guaranteed by the terms of the contract.

3. Without consent of the insurer, the policyholder may change the amount of premium within certain limits set forth in the contract.

FAS-60 prescribed the appropriate accounting for conventional forms of participating and nonguaranteed-premium contracts. However, some conventional forms of participating and nonguaranteed-premium contracts may be, in substance, universal-life contracts, which are accounted for in accordance with the provisions of FAS-97. For the purposes of FAS-97, a *participating contract* is considered a universal-life contract if, without the consent of the insurer, the policyholder can change the amount of the premium, within limits set forth in the contract. In addition, both *participating* and *nonguaranteed-premium* insurance contracts are considered universal-life contracts if they contain either of the following features (FAS-97, pars. 12 and 13):

1. Under the terms of the contract, the insurer maintains a stated account balance for the policyholder, which is credited with premiums and interest and assessed for contract administration, mortality coverage, and initiation or surrender fees. The amounts credited to or assessed against the policyholder's account balance are not fixed and guaranteed.

2. Changes in interest rates or other market conditions are expected to be the primary cause of changes in any contract element. It is not expected that the primary cause of changes in any contract element will be related to the experience of a group of similar contracts or the enterprise as a whole.

Under FAS-60, a liability for future policy benefits relating to long-duration contracts (except title insurance contracts) is accrued when the insurance enterprise recognizes premium revenue. The liability is based on actuarial assumptions at the time the insurance contracts are executed, and it is presented in the balance sheet at present value. In subsequent periods, changes in the original actuarial assumptions that result in changes in future policy benefits or related costs and expenses are recognized in net income of the period of change (FAS-60, par. 18).

The *liability* for future policy benefits consists of the present value of future policy benefits and related expenses, less the present value of related future net premiums. *Gross premium* is the amount the policyholder pays, and it is equal to the net premium plus the profit made by the insurance enterprise. *Net premium* is that portion of the gross premium needed to cover future payments of all policy benefits and related costs and expenses.

Under FAS-97, an insurance enterprise computes its liability for policy benefits for universal-life contracts as the sum of the following (FAS-97, par. 17):

1. Any amounts that have been accrued to the benefit of policyholders at the date of the financial statements

2. Any amounts assessed against policyholders to compensate the insurance enterprise for services to be performed over future periods

3. Any amounts previously assessed against policyholders that the insurance enterprise must refund if the contract is terminated

4. Any loss that will probably (likely) occur as a result of premium deficiency (computed in accordance with FAS-60)

In determining its liability for policy benefits, an insurance enterprise shall not anticipate amounts that may be assessed against policyholders in future periods. In the event that no other amount can be established, the policyholder's cash surrender value in the insurance contract, at the date of the financial statements, represents the insurance enterprise's liability for policy benefits. The liability for policy benefits shall not include a provision for the risk of adverse deviation (FAS-97, par. 18).

An insurance enterprise shall not report premiums collected on universal-life contracts as revenue in its statement of earnings. Revenue on universal-life contracts is assessed against policyholders and reported in the period of assessment, unless it is evident that the assessed amount represents compensation to the insurance enterprise for future services to be provided over more than one period (FAS-97, par. 19).

Amounts assessed against policyholders' balances for future services to be provided by the insurance enterprise over more than one period are reported as unearned income in the period in which they are assessed. Amounts assessed against policyholders' balances as initiation or front-end fees are also unearned revenue. Unearned revenue shall be amortized to income over the periods benefited based on the same assumptions and factors that are used to amortize capitalized acquisition costs (FAS-97, par. 20).

An insurance enterprise shall not report as an expense in its statement of earnings any payments to policyholders that represent a return of policyholders' balances. The cost of contract administration, amortization of capitalized acquisition costs, and benefit claims that exceed related policyholders' balances shall be reported as expenses (FAS-97, par. 21).

Under FAS-97, the amortization of capitalized policy acquisition costs is recognized at a constant rate based on the present value of the gross profit that is expected to be generated by a book (group) of universal-life insurance contracts. The same interest rate used to accrue interest on a policyholder's account shall be used to compute the present value of the gross profit that is expected to be realized on a book of universal-life contracts. In those periods in which material amounts of negative gross profits arise, the present value of estimated gross profits, gross costs, or the balance of insurance in force shall be used as a substitute allocation base for calculating amortization (FAS-97, par. 22).

Estimated gross profit includes the best estimate of each of the following individual items, over the life of the book of universal-life contracts, without provision for adverse deviation (FAS-97, par. 23):

1. Assessments for mortality, less benefit claims in excess of related policyholder balances

2. Assessments for contract administration, less costs incurred

3. Investment income from, less interest credited to, policyholders' balances

4.   Assessments against policyholder accounts upon termination

5.   All other assessed amounts and credits

Under FAS-97, amortization of capitalized acquisition costs is based on the present value of estimated gross profits. Under FAS-60, amortization of capitalized acquisition costs is based on expected premium revenues. Under FAS-60, acquisition costs that are directly related to the production of insurance business include all direct costs and indirect costs, such as underwriting and policy issuance expenses. Collection expenses, professional fees, depreciation, and general and administrative expenses are not directly related to, nor do they vary directly with, the production of new or renewal insurance business; they should be expensed as incurred. Under FAS-97, acquisition costs that vary in a constant relationship to *premiums or insurance in force*, that are recurring in nature, or that tend to be incurred in a level amount from period to period shall be charged to expense in the period incurred (FAS-97, par. 24).

The computation of amortization under FAS-97 includes the accrual of interest on the unamortized balance of capitalized acquisition costs and the balance of any unearned income, at the same interest rate used to discount expected gross profits. Under FAS-97, estimates of expected gross profit must be evaluated periodically; if earlier estimates indicate that revision is necessary, total amortization to date shall be adjusted by a charge or credit to the statement of earnings (FAS-97, par. 25).

To compute the present value of revised estimates of expected gross profits, an insurance enterprise shall use either (*a*) the rate in effect at the inception of the book of universal-life contracts or (*b*) the latest revised interest rate applied to the remaining benefit period. The method used to determine the present value of revised estimates of expected gross profit shall be applied consistently in subsequent revisions (FAS-97, par. 25).

For universal-life insurance contracts, FAS-97 does not establish accounting and reporting standards that address (*a*) loss recognition (premium deficiency), (*b*) accounting for reinsurance, and (*c*) financial statement disclosure. The provisions of FAS-60 that apply to these specific items shall also apply to universal-life insurance contracts (FAS-97, par. 27).

Internal Replacement Transactions

A policyholder may use the cash surrender value of an old insurance contract to pay the initial lump-sum premium for a new universal-life contract. This is sometimes referred to as an *internal replacement transaction*. FAS-97 specifies that when a traditional insurance policy is surrendered and replaced by an interest-sensitive or flexible-premium insurance contract, the balance of any unamortized deferred policy acquisition costs related to the surrendered policy and any difference between the liability for policyholder benefits and the cash surrender value should be charged to operations (FAS-97, par. 26).

CLAIM COSTS AND FUTURE POLICY BENEFITS

Property and liability insurance companies must pay claims to policyholders who incur insured losses. At any time, claims may (*a*) be reported to the insurance company and be in the process of settlement or (*b*) be incurred but not reported to the insurance company.

A title insurance company insures title to real property. The company scrutinizes the chain of title to prevent losses. In practice, however, claims do occur and the title company incurs losses. Life insurance companies also pay losses.

FAS-60 contains specific GAAP for claim costs and future policy benefits.

Claim Costs

Title insurance companies should accrue estimated claim costs at the time the related insurance premiums are recognized as revenue. Claim costs for other types of insurance contracts are accrued as they occur. A provision for claim costs (liability) should include (*a*) reported losses in the process of settlement and (*b*) estimated losses incurred but not reported (FAS-60, par. 17).

The provision for reported claims in the process of settlement may be made by estimating each reported claim individually. Because there may be a large number of them, however, smaller reported claims may be estimated by an average dollar loss per claim. Thus, the provision for smaller claims frequently is made by multiplying the number of smaller claims by the estimated average loss per claim (FAS-60, par. 18).

Claims incurred but not reported are more difficult to determine and usually are estimated on a formula basis. Formulas use statistics on actual claim experience for prior years, which are then adjusted for current trends and other factors. This is accomplished by examining specific types of insurance policies for a selected period and then relating the loss experience to the premiums in force for the specific type of insurance policies. Formulas are used only for normal losses that are expected to recur. Large losses resulting from catastrophes are not included in the statistics used in determining formulas but are estimated separately, usually on the basis of judgment. Thus, a formula usually will consist of the loss experience determined for a prior period, adjusted for current trends, and a factor for large catastrophic losses.

Statutory Formula Reserves are required by most states for liability and workers' compensation insurance. Several states require minimum reserves for incurred but not reported (IBNR) losses on surety bonds and fidelity policies.

FAS-60 requires that a liability be accrued in the financial statements for reported losses in the process of settlement and unreported losses incurred but not reported. The liability for unpaid losses should not include the effects of inflation and other economic factors, and it should be based on the best good faith estimate of the cost of settlement, arrived at by using past loss experience adjusted for current trends. The cost of settlement may be reduced by estimated salvage expected to be recovered from the claim and the exercise of subrogation rights. Amounts of salvage and subrogation should be deducted from the liability for unpaid losses in the balance sheet, and the amount deducted should be disclosed in a footnote to the financial statements (FAS-60, par. 18).

Differences in and adjustments to estimates and actual claim payments, which result from periodic reviews, shall be recognized in net income of the period in which the differences or adjustments occur (FAS-60, par. 18).

> **OBSERVATION:** An insurance company may elect to report its liability for unpaid claims and the related claim adjustment expense for short-duration contracts at their present value. Under this method, the amount of the effects of such a presentation must be disclosed in the financial statements.

Title insurance companies and mortgage guaranty companies sometimes acquire real property as a result of settling a claim. Such property should be reported at estimated fair market value. Subsequent adjustments to the reported fair market value and realized gain or loss on the final disposition of the real property shall be reported in the financial statements as an increase or decrease of claim costs. Real property acquired in settling a claim should not be classified as an investment but should be reported separately in the balance sheet (FAS-60, par. 19).

Claim Adjustment Expense

Figuring the liability for reported claims in the process of settlement and for claims incurred but not reported requires an estimation of the amount of the claim. The claims adjustment expenses are the estimated expenses that will be incurred in settling the claims. Claims adjustment expense may be classified as allocated or unallocated (FAS-60, par. 20).

Allocated claims adjustment expenses are those that can be assigned to a specific claim. *Unallocated claims adjustment expenses* are those that cannot be assigned to a specific claim; they include indirect salaries, stationery, postage, rent, travel, and other similar expenses of the claims department.

The liability for the claims adjustment expense is determined by statistical formulas.

FAS-60 requires that a liability for claims adjustment expense for short-duration contracts be accrued for all reported claims in the process of settlement and for all claims incurred but not reported.

Future Policy Benefits

The normal costs of an insurance company include the payment of policy benefits and the expenses of doing business. These costs must be matched to their related premium revenue.

FAS-60 requires that a liability for future policy benefits on long-duration insurance contracts be accrued at the time that premium revenue is recognized. The liability includes the present value of future policy benefits and related expenses, less the present value of related future net premiums. Stated another way, the liability for future policy benefits for a particular group of insurance contracts is the excess of the total amount of net premiums collected over the total amount of related policy benefits paid to date. *Gross premium* is the total cost of the insurance contract to the policyholder. When accumulated with investment income, the gross premium creates a fund that will be sufficient to pay all policy benefits and related costs and expenses and provide a profit for the insurance company. *Net premium* is that portion of the gross premium that is needed to cover all policy benefits and related costs and expenses. Net premium should represent the gross premium, less a profit for the insurance company (FAS-60, par. 21).

Future policy benefits and related expenses are calculated by the use of actuarial assumptions, such as investment yields, mortality and morbidity rates, and estimated terminations or withdrawals. The liability for future policy benefits and related expenses is based on actuarial assumptions existing at the time the insurance contract is executed, and such liability is presented in the balance sheet at its present value (FAS-60, par. 22).

An insurance company pools the risks of many individuals and businesses. Thus, undertaking risks is the primary business of an insurance company. The real risk that an insurance company takes, however, is that actual experience will be worse than the actuarial assumptions used in calculating the premium. This is referred to as the *risk of adverse deviation*.

Changes in the original actuarial assumptions in subsequent periods are recognized in net income of the period of change (FAS-60, par. 21).

OTHER COSTS

Since the matching concept is applied to the recognition of premium revenue, it is logical that the same principal be used in accounting for the costs incurred in obtaining the premium revenue. Thus, variable acquisition costs that are directly or indirectly related to the production of new or renewal premium revenue are deferred and amortized as a charge against income as the related premium revenue is earned. Acquisition costs that are directly related to the production of insurance business include all direct costs and indirect costs, such as underwriting and policy issuance expenses (FAS-60, par. 29).

Deferred acquisition costs are amortized as a charge to income in the same manner the related premium revenue is earned. The method of amortization should be applied consistently from year to year. Unamortized acquisition costs are classified in the balance sheet as assets (FAS-60, pars. 29 and 30).

Actual acquisition expenses for long-duration contracts should be compared to those used in the actuarial assumptions and, when possible, the actual acquisition expenses should be used in the actuarial assumptions instead of estimates. When estimates are used to determine the acquisition expenses that should be deferred, it is necessary to adjust such estimates to actual amounts if the differences are significant (FAS-60, par. 31).

☛ **PRACTICE POINTER:** Under regulatory accounting practices, charge all acquisition expenses against income in the period incurred. Thus, a significant difference between regulatory accounting practices and GAAP is the deferral and amortization of acquisition expenses. This difference is reflected in stockholders' equity and net income determined under regulatory accounting practices and in stockholders' equity and net income determined under GAAP.

Other expenses of insurance companies are treated in accordance with existing GAAP. Thus, if an expenditure benefits future periods, it may be deferred and charged to the periods benefited. All other expenses, such as investment expenses, general administration, and policy maintenance, that are not directly related to the production of new or renewal insurance business should be charged to operations in the period incurred (FAS-60, par. 27).

DEFICIENCY IN PREMIUMS OR LIABILITY
FOR FUTURE POLICY BENEFITS

Insurance companies incur losses on short-duration and long-duration contracts. For the purposes of FAS-60, premium deficiencies are determined by reasonable grouping of similar insurance policies that are consistent with the company's usual system of acquiring, servicing, and measuring profitability for its insurance business (FAS-60, par. 32). Each of these types of deficiencies is discussed separately below.

Short-Duration Contracts

Premium revenue is intended to be sufficient to cover expected claims, claim adjustment expenses, acquisition costs, policy maintenance costs, estimated dividends to policyholders, and profit. Whenever unearned premiums are less than the total of (*a*) the related liability for unpaid claim costs and claim adjustment expenses, (*b*) related unamortized acquisition costs, (*c*) related estimated policy maintenance costs, and (*d*) related dividends to policyholders, a premium deficiency exists (FAS-60, par. 33).

Premium deficiencies should be recognized in the financial statements. Recognition should be made by reducing unamortized deferred acquisition costs by a charge to income in the amount of the deficiency. If the unamortized deferred acquisition costs are smaller than the amount of premium deficiency, all of the unamortized deferred acquisition costs should be charged to income, and an additional separate liability for the balance of the premium deficiency should be recorded by a charge to income (FAS-60, par. 34).

> ☛ **PRACTICE POINTER:** Make a provision for anticipated premium deficiencies when unearned premiums are insufficient to cover all related costs and expenses. Related costs and expenses should include expected claims and claims adjustment expenses, expected policyholder dividends, unamortized deferred acquisition costs, and any anticipated expenses expected to be incurred after the inception date of the policy. If a cost, after the inception date of the policy, is direct or can be attributed to maintaining the policy in force, include it in the determination of the premium deficiency.

If an insurance company includes anticipated investment income in the determination of a premium deficiency, FAS-60 requires that the effects, and the amount of the effects on the financial statements, be disclosed (FAS-60, par. 33).

Long-Duration Contracts

FAS-60 requires that the liability for future policy benefits for long-duration contracts be accrued at the time the premium revenue is recognized. The liability is based on actuarial assumptions at the time the insurance contracts are executed, and it is presented in the balance sheet at present value. In subsequent periods, changes in the original actuarial assumptions that result in changes in future policy benefits or related costs and expenses are recognized in net income of the period of change (FAS-60, par. 21).

The liability for future policy benefits consists of the present value of future policy benefits and related expenses, less the present value of related future net premiums. Net premium is that portion of the gross premium that is needed to cover future payment of all policy benefits and related costs and expenses. Gross premium is the amount the policyholder pays, and it is equal to the net premium plus the profit made by the insurance company.

At any given time, the present value of future gross premiums for a particular group of insurance contracts may be insufficient to cover the present value of future policy benefits and related expenses and the remaining unamortized acquisition costs. In this event, a gross premium deficiency occurs. The gross premium deficiency usually is the result of significant changes in the original actuarial assumptions. The procedures to determine a gross premium deficiency are as follows (FAS-60, par. 35):

1. Compute the present value of future policy benefits and related settlement and maintenance expenses using revised assumptions and updated experience.

2. Compute the present value of future gross premiums using revised assumptions and updated experience.

3. Subtract (1) from (2) to arrive at the new liability for future policy benefits based on revised assumptions and updated experience.

4. Compare the new liability for future policy benefits determined in (3) with the actual recorded liability for future policy benefits, reduced by the actual remaining unamortized acquisition costs. A deficiency exists if the newly computed liability exceeds the actual liability, reduced by the actual remaining unamortized acquisition costs.

A deficiency in the liability for future policy benefits must be recognized in net income by either increasing the liability for future policy benefits, or by decreasing unamortized acquisition costs. The revised assumptions and updated experience shall be used to determine changes in the liability for future policy benefits. A deficiency is not reported if its effect is to create income in future periods (FAS-60, par. 36).

A deficiency in the liability for future policy benefits usually is determined by groups or blocks of similar insurance policies. However, if a group or block of insurance contracts does not indicate a deficiency, but the aggregate liability for an entire line of insurance business does indicate a deficiency, the deficiency should be recognized (FAS-60, par. 37).

REINSURANCE

An insurance company may obtain indemnification against claims associated with contracts (policies) it has issued by entering into a reinsurance contract with another insurance company, referred to as the *reinsurer* or *assuming carrier*. The insurer, referred to as the *ceding company*, pays an amount to the reinsurer, and the reinsurer agrees to reimburse the insurer for a specified portion of claims paid under the reinsured contracts (policies), as shown in Figure 55-1. Usually, the policyholder is unaware of the reinsurance arrangement. The reinsurer may, in turn, enter into reinsurance contracts with other reinsurers. This process is known as *retrocession* (FAS-113, par. 1).

> **OBSERVATION:** Two particularly important terms are used in the previous paragraph: *insurer* (or ceding company) and *reinsurer* (or assuming company). These are formally defined in the appendix of FAS-113 as follows:
> **Insurer** (ceding company)—The party that pays a reinsurance premium in a reinsurance transaction. The ceding enterprise, or insurer, receives the right to reimbursement from the assuming carrier under the terms of the reinsurance contract.
> **Reinsurer** (assuming carrier)—The party that receives a reinsurance premium in a reinsurance transaction. The assuming company, or reinsurer, accepts an obligation to reimburse a ceding company under the terms of the reinsurance contract.

FAS-60 specified the accounting by insurance companies for reinsurance contracts. That Statement is an extraction of requirements of the AICPA Industry Audit Guides titled "Audits of Fire and Casualty Insurance Companies and Audits of Stock Life Insurance Companies." FAS-60 continued the practice that originated in statutory accounting whereby ceding companies reported insurance activities net of the effects of reinsurance. If the reinsurance contract indemnified the ceding company against loss or liability, FAS-60 required the ceding company to reduce unpaid claim liabilities by the estimated amounts recoverable from reinsurers and to reduce unearned premiums by related amounts paid to reinsurers (FAS-60, par. 38).

With FAS-113, the FASB reconsidered the accounting and reporting for reinsurance required by FAS-60 for the following reasons:

1. Increasing concerns about the effect of reinsurance accounting for contracts that do not indemnify the ceding company against loss or liability
2. The limited accounting guidance on reinsurance provided in FAS-60
3. The lack of disclosure requirements for reinsurance transactions
4. The established criteria for offsetting

FAS-113 applies to those insurance companies to which FAS-60 applied. FAS-60 sets accounting and reporting standards for general-purpose financial statements of:

*   Stock life insurance companies
*   Property and liability insurance companies
*   Title insurance companies
*   Mortgage guaranty insurance companies (except the sections of FAS-60 on premium revenue and claim cost recognition and acquisition costs)

FAS-60 does not apply to mutual life insurance companies, assessment companies, or fraternal benefit societies.

Some insurance contracts are *fronting arrangements,* wherein the ceding company issues a policy and reinsures all (or substantially all) of the risk with the assuming enterprise. FAS-113 provides guidance for determining whether those contracts meet the conditions for reinsurance accounting. If the conditions for reinsurance accounting are met, FAS-113 is applicable.

The specific accounting provisions in FAS-113 to be followed for reinsurance depend on whether the contract is long-duration or short-duration; if the contract is short-duration, it must be further classified as prospective reinsurance or retroactive reinsurance. In *prospective reinsurance,* an assuming company agrees to reimburse a ceding company for losses that may be incurred as a result of future insurable events covered under contracts subject to the reinsurance. In *retroactive reinsurance,* an assuming company agrees to reimburse a ceding company for liabilities incurred as a result of past insurable events covered under contract subject to the reinsurance.

Indemnification

The term *indemnify* means to make whole one who has suffered a loss, or to repair loss or damage already suffered.

Figure 55-1: Interrelationship among Policyholder, Ceding Company, and Reinsurers

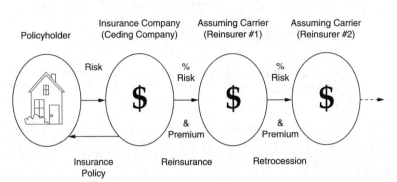

Figure 55-2 shows how, when a policyholder suffers a loss, the ceding carrier pays the loss to the policyholder and is indemnified under the reinsurance contract.

Determining whether a contract with a reinsurer provides loss or liability of insurance risk requires a careful understanding of the contract and other contracts or agreements between the ceding company and reinsurers. Of particular importance are contractual features that (FAS-113, par. 8):

- Limit the amount of insurance risk that is ceded to the reinsurer
- Delay the timely reimbursement of claims by the reinsurer

The following conditions generally must be met for the reinsurance of short-duration contracts to be considered indemnification contracts (FAS-113, par. 9):

- The reinsurer assumes significant insurance risk.
- It is reasonably possible that the reinsurer may realize a significant loss from the transaction.

A reinsurer is considered not to have assumed significant insurance risk if the probability of significant variation in either the amount or the timing of payments by the reinsurer is remote (e.g., there are no contractual provisions in the reinsurance contract that delay timely reimbursement to the ceding company) (FAS-113, par. 9). The ceding company's evaluation of whether it is reasonably possible for a reinsurer to realize a significant loss shall be based on the present value of all cash flows between the ceding and assuming companies under reasonably possible outcomes (FAS-113, par. 10).

> **OBSERVATION:** The terms *remote* and *reasonably possible* used in FAS-113 are borrowed from FAS-5 (Accounting for Contingencies). FAS-5 defines these terms as follows:
> **Remote**—The chance of the future event or events occurring is slight.
> **Reasonably possible**—The chance of the future event or events occurring is more than remote but less than likely.

In evaluating the significance of loss, the present value of all cash flows is compared with the present value of amounts paid or deemed to have been paid to the reinsurer. If the reinsurer is not exposed to the reasonable possibility of significant loss, the ceding company is considered indemnified against loss or liability relating to insurance risk only if the reinsurer has assumed essentially all the risk from the ceding company (FAS-113, par. 11).

For long-duration contracts, indemnification of the ceding company against loss or liability requires the reasonable possibility that the reinsurer may realize significant loss from assuming insurance risk as that concept is contemplated in FAS-60 and FAS-97. FAS-97 defines long-duration contracts that do not subject the insurer to mortality risks (life insurance) or morbidity risks (health insurance) as *investment contracts* (FAS-113, pars. 12 and 13).

Reporting Assets and Liabilities

Some reinsurance contracts represent legal replacements of one insurer by another. These are often referred to as *assumption* and *novation*. They extinguish the ceding company's liability to the policyholder and logically result in removal of related assets and liabilities from the financial statements of the ceding company, as shown in Figure 55-3 (FAS-113, par. 14).

Other reinsurance contracts do not result in the ceding company being relieved of its legal liability to policyholders and, accordingly, do not result in the removal of the related assets and liabilities from the ceding company's financial statements. Separate assets shall be shown by ceding companies for reinsurance receivables and for amounts paid to the reinsurer relating to the unexpired portion of reinsured contracts (e.g., prepaid reinsurance premiums) (FAS-113, par. 14). Amounts receivable and payable between the ceding company and an individual reinsurer are offset only when a right of setoff exists, as defined in FIN-39 (Offsetting of Amounts Related to Certain Contracts) (FAS-113, par. 15).

Figure 55-2: Ceding Company Indemnified by Reinsurer

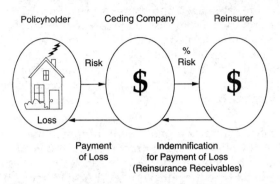

The amounts of earned premiums ceded and recoveries recognized under reinsurance contract shall be either (FAS-113, par. 16):

- Reported in the statement of earnings, as separate line items or parenthetically, or
- Disclosed in notes to the financial statements

Recognition of Revenues and Costs

To apply FAS-113, an entity must first determine whether the contract in question is considered reinsurance. For reinsurance contracts, a further classification must be made into long-duration or short-duration. Short-duration contracts are further classified as prospective or retroactive. This series of decisions is summarized in Figure 55-4 (FAS-113, par. 17).

FAS-113 first prescribes general accounting standards applicable to all reinsurance contracts (pars. 8–20), then discusses standards specifically applicable to short-duration contracts (pars. 21–25), and finally discusses standards specifically applicable to long-duration contracts (par. 26).

For contracts that do not meet the criteria for reinsurance accounting, FAS-113 has little to say, other than to incorporate certain provisions of FAS-60, summarized as follows (FAS-113, par. 18):

- Premiums paid, less the premium to be retained by the reinsurer, are accounted for as a deposit by the ceding company. A net credit resulting from the contract is reported as a liability by the ceding company. A net charge is reported as an asset by the reinsurer.

- Proceeds from reinsurance transactions that represent recovery of acquisition costs shall reduce applicable unamortized acquisition costs in such a manner that net acquisition costs are capitalized and charged to expense in proportion to net revenue recognized. If the ceding company has agreed to service the related insurance contracts without reasonable compensation, a liability shall be accrued for estimated excess future servicing costs under the contract. The net cost to the assuming company shall be accounted for as an acquisition cost.

Reinsurance contracts do not result in immediate recognition of gains unless the reinsurance contract represents a legal replacement of one insurer by another and, as a result, extinguishes the ceding company's liability to the policyholder (FAS-113, par. 19).

Reinsurance receivables are recognized in a manner consistent with the liability related to the underlying reinsured contracts. The assumptions used to estimate reinsurance receivables are to be consistent with the assumptions used to estimate the related liabilities (FAS-113, par. 20).

Standards for Short-Duration Contracts

Amounts paid for prospective reinsurance contracts are reported as prepaid reinsurance premiums and are amortized over the remaining contract period in proportion to the amount of insurance protection provided. If the amounts paid are subject to adjustment and can be estimated reasonably, the basis for amortization shall be the estimated ultimate amount to be paid (FAS-113, par. 21).

> **OBSERVATION:** FAS-113 defines the *contract period* as the period over which insured events that occur are covered by the reinsured contracts. This is commonly referred to as the *coverage period* or the period during which the contracts are in force (the *policy period*).

For retroactive reinsurance contracts, amounts paid are reported as reinsurance receivables to the extent those amounts do not exceed the recorded liabilities relating to the underlying reinsurance contracts. If the recorded liabilities exceed the amounts paid, reinsurance receivables are increased to reflect the difference, and the resulting gain is deferred. That deferred gain is amortized over the estimated remaining settlement period, applied as follows (FAS-113, par. 22):

Figure 55-3: Assumption and Novation

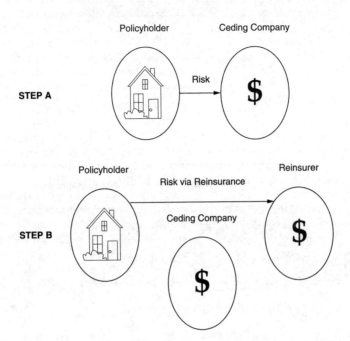

- If the amounts and timing of the reinsurance recoveries can be reasonably estimated, the deferred gain is amortized using the effective interest rate inherent in the amount paid to the reinsurer and the estimated timing and amounts of recoveries from the reinsurer (the interest method).

- Otherwise, the proportion of actual recoveries to total estimated recoveries determines the amount of amortization (the recovery method).

If the amounts paid for retroactive reinsurance exceed the recorded liabilities relating to the underlying reinsured contracts, the ceding company shall increase the related liability or reduce the reinsurance receivable, or both. This is done at the time the reinsurance contract is entered into, and the excess is charged to earnings (FAS-113, par. 23).

Fluctuations in liabilities tied to the underlying reinsurance contracts show as earnings for the relevant period and are reflected in reinsurance receivables. A gain will therefore be adjusted or established and must be deferred and amortized (FAS-113, par. 24).

Figure 55-4: Classification of Reinsurance

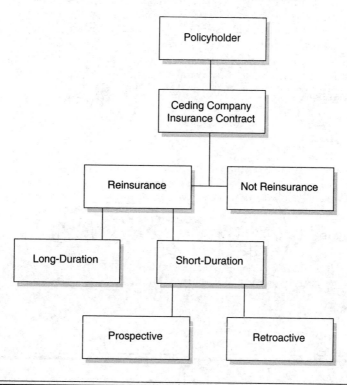

Changes in the estimated amount of the liabilities affect amounts recoverable from the reinsurer and therefore deferred gains, as shown in Figure 55-5 (FAS-113, par. 24).

When a single reinsurance contract contains both prospective and retroactive provisions, a separate accounting for each should be done when practicable, as shown in Figure 55-6 (FAS-113, par. 25).

Standards for Long-Duration Contracts

Amortization of the estimated cost of reinsurance of long-duration contracts depends on whether the reinsurance contract is long-dura-tion or short-duration. If the reinsurance contract is long-duration, the cost is amortized over the remaining life of the underlying rein-sured contracts (policies). (This is in contrast to amortization of the contract period of the reinsurance if the reinsurance contract is short-duration.) Determining whether a contract that reinsures a long-duration insurance contract is long-duration or short-duration in nature is a matter of judgment, requiring consideration of all of the facts and circumstances. The assumptions used in accounting for reinsurance costs should be consistent with those used for the reinsured contracts (policies). Any difference between amounts paid for a reinsurance contract and the amount of the liabilities for policy benefits relating to the underlying reinsurance contracts is part of the estimated cost to be amortized (FAS-113, par. 26).

Disclosure

Disclosure requirements for insurance companies are established in FAS-113.

These disclosure requirements can be summarized as follows:

1.   All insurance companies must disclose (FAS-113, par. 27):

     a.   The nature, purpose, and effect of ceded reinsurance transactions on the insurance company's operations (In addition, ceding companies shall disclose the fact that the insurer is not relieved of the primary obligation to the policyholder in a reinsurance transaction.)

     b.   For short-duration contracts, premiums from direct business, reinsurance assumed, and reinsurance ceded, on both a written and an earned basis

     c.   For long-duration contracts, premiums and amounts assessed against policyholders from direct business, reinsurance assumed and ceded, and premiums and amounts earned

     d.   Methods used for income recognition on insurance contracts

2.   Ceding companies must disclose (FAS-113, par. 28):

     a.   Concentrations of credit risk associated with reinsurance receivables and prepaid reinsurance premiums under FAS-105

POLICYHOLDER DIVIDENDS

Policyholder dividends are accrued and reported in the financial statements. If the amount is not known, the use of reasonable estimates is required (FAS-60, par. 41).

The amount of current income allocated to participating insurance contracts is excluded from stockholders' equity by a charge to current operations and a credit to a liability account. The liability account is reduced when dividends subsequently are declared or paid. Dividends declared or paid to participating insurance contracts in excess of the liability also are charged to current operations.

Life insurance companies usually do not pay or declare dividends on participating insurance policies during the first two years, because of the high initial policy acquisition costs. In determining the amount of dividends on participating insurance policies, consideration must be given to any restrictions on such amounts that may be imposed by the terms of the insurance contract, governing law, or company policy. When participating policy dividends are specified in the policy or projected at the time the policy is issued, they should be accrued ratably over the periods in which premiums are collected. Dividends to policyholders are not guaranteed payments, but are subject to a declaration by the insurer's directors. A "guaranteed dividend policy" may actually be a whole-life contract coupled with annually maturing endowments that pay out and appear to be dividends.

CONTINGENT COMMISSIONS

Insurance companies usually agree to pay additional commissions to agents if the business they generate results in a favorable loss experience.

FAS-60 requires that contingent commissions (receivable or payable) be accrued appropriately and appear in the income statement of the periods in which the related profits are recognized (FAS-60, par. 44).

INVESTMENTS

FAS-60 contains specific guidance in the valuation of investments of insurance companies.

Bonds

If the insurance company has the ability and intent to keep bonds to maturity, the bonds are carried at amortized cost, provided there has been no permanent decline in the market value of the bonds below amortized cost. Bonds held for speculation should be carried at

Figure 55-5: Relationship between Estimated Amount of Liabilities and Amount Recoverable from Reinsurer

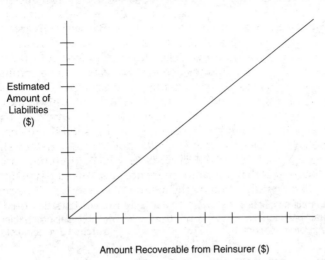

Amount Recoverable from Reinsurer ($)

market value, and unrealized gains or losses should be recognized periodically (FAS-60, par. 45).

Common and Nonredeemable Preferred Stock

Common and nonredeemable preferred stocks are carried at market value. If the insurance company has the ability and intent to keep redeemable preferred stock until redemption, the preferred stocks is carried at amortized cost, provided there has been no permanent decline in the market value of the preferred stock below amortized cost (FAS-60, par. 46).

Mortgages

Mortgages are carried at the balance of the unpaid principal. Mortgages purchased at a discount or premium are carried at amortized cost. An allowance should be used to reduce total mortgages to an expected collectible amount, if necessary, and changes in the allowance account should be included in realized gains and losses (FAS-60, par. 47).

Figure 55-6: Accounting for Reinsurance Contracts That Combine Prospective and Retroactive Provisions

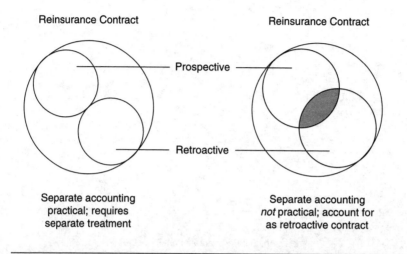

Reinsurance Contract

Reinsurance Contract

Prospective

Retroactive

Separate accounting
practical; requires
separate treatment

Separate accounting
not practical; account for
as retroactive contract

Real Estate Investments

Real estate investments are carried at depreciated cost. Amortization, depreciation, and other related costs or credits should be included in the determination of investment income (FAS-60, par. 48).

Loan and Commitment Fees

Loan origination and commitment fees and direct loan origination costs are accounted for as prescribed in FAS-91 (FAS-91, par. 26), as follows:

- Loan origination fees are recognized over the life of the related loan as an adjustment to yield.
- Certain direct loan origination costs are recognized over the life of the related loan as a reduction of the loan's yield.
- With limited exceptions, loan commitment fees are deferred and recognized over the loan commitment period.
- Loan fees, certain direct origination costs, and purchase premiums and discounts on loans are recognized as an adjustment of yield generally by the interest method based on the contractual terms of the loan.

Reporting Realized Gains and Losses

FAS-97 amends FAS-60 to eliminate the practice of reporting realized investment gains and losses in the statement of earnings, below operating earnings. FAS-97 requires insurance enterprises to report realized gains and losses as a component of other income, on a pretax basis, above earnings from operations in the statement of earnings. In addition, FAS-97 does not permit the direct or indirect deferment of realized investment gains and losses (FAS-97, par. 28).

Unrealized investment gains and losses are not included in the determination of net income, but are recognized, net of related taxes, as an addition to or reduction of stockholders' equity (FAS-60, par. 50).

Permanent declines in security investments, below cost or amortized cost, are recognized as realized losses. These security investments should be written down to their net realizable values, which subsequently become their new cost basis. Recovery in market value above the new cost basis is not recognized until sale, maturity, or other disposition of the security (FAS-60, par. 51).

REAL ESTATE USED IN BUSINESS AND SEPARATE ACCOUNTS

Real estate is classified in accordance with its predominant use either as property used in business or as an investment. Real estate operating expenses, including depreciation, are classified in a manner consistent with the related asset, as either investment expenses or operating expenses (FAS-60, par. 52).

Real estate that the insurance company uses in business should not be accounted for as investment income with a corresponding charge to operations for rental expense. An insurance company cannot include rental income in its financial statements for property it uses in the regular course of business (FAS-60, par. 52).

> **OBSERVATION:** Real estate is always classified as an investment for regulatory accounting purposes, regardless of its use. Rental expense is charged to operations, and rental income is included in investment income for real estate used by the insurance company in its own business.

As a fiduciary, an insurance company may maintain assets and liabilities in separate accounts to fund fixed-benefit plans. In this capacity, the insurance company usually receives a fee and does not assume any investment risk (FAS-60, par. 53).

Except for long-term separate accounts in which the insurance company has guaranteed a specific investment return, investments in separate accounts shall be valued at market. Long-term separate accounts with guaranteed returns shall be valued in the same manner as any other investment of the insurance company. Assets and liabilities of separate accounts shall be reported in the financial statements in summary totals (FAS-60, par. 54).

DEFERRED INCOME TAXES

The Life Insurance Company Act of 1959 covers the taxation of life insurance companies for federal tax purposes. For the purposes of GAAP, life insurance companies must comply with existing promulgated pronouncements, and thus must determine deferred income taxes when appropriate.

If circumstances indicate that the current tax effects of a temporary difference will not reverse in subsequent periods, an insurance company does not have to accrue deferred income taxes. Deferred taxes shall be accrued, however, if the reversal of the temporary difference cannot be determined reasonably. Deferred income taxes shall be accrued in accordance with existing GAAP.

Once it is determined whether deferred income taxes should or should not be provided on the tax effects of temporary differences, circumstances may change. If deferred taxes have not previously been provided, they should be accrued and reported as an income tax expense in the period of correction. Deferred taxes accrued under these circumstances should not be reported as an extraordinary item. Regardless of whether the gross change or net change method is used, previously accrued deferred income taxes should be included in income as the related temporary differences reverse, if the previously determined tax effects are expected to be different from those originally anticipated.

Policyholders' surplus of stock life insurance companies that create a difference between taxable income and pretax financial accounting income usually are considered permanent differences (because the company controls the events that create the tax consequence). If circumstances dictate that income taxes will be paid because of a reduction in policyholders' surplus, an income tax expense should be accrued on such reductions in the period in which they occur. In effect, these reductions create a temporary difference when they occur, and they should not be accounted for as an extraordinary item (FAS-60, par. 59).

DISCLOSURE

FAS-60 requires specific disclosures in the financial statements of insurance companies. These disclosures are listed below (FAS-60, par. 60):

1. The basis for estimating the following:
   a. The liability for unpaid claims
   b. The liability for claim adjustment expenses
2. The methods and assumptions used in calculating the liability for future policy benefits (In addition, FAS-60 encourages, but does not require, the disclosure of the average rate of assumed investment yields that are in effect for the current period.)
3. Capitalized acquisition costs
   a. The nature of such costs
   b. The method of amortizing such costs
   c. The amount of amortization of such costs for the current period
4. If the liabilities for unpaid claims and claim adjustment expenses for short-duration contracts are reported at their present values in the financial statements
   a. The carrying amount of those liabilities
   b. The range of interest rates used to discount those liabilities
5. Whether estimated investment income is used in calculating a premium deficiency for short-duration contracts
6. Reinsurance transactions of an insurance company
   a. The nature and significance of such transactions
   b. Estimated amounts recoverable from reinsurers that are related to unpaid claims and claim adjustment expenses
7. Participating insurance of an insurance company
   a. The relative percentage of participating insurance
   b. The method of accounting for participating insurance policyholders' dividends
   c. The amount of such dividends
   d. The amount of any additional income allocated to participating insurance policyholders
8. Stockholders' equity, statutory capital, and capital surplus
   a. The amount of statutory capital and capital surplus
   b. The amount of statutory capital and capital surplus required for regulatory purposes, if significant to the enterprise's total statutory capital and capital surplus
   c. The nature of statutory restrictions on dividends and the amount of retained earnings not available for dividends to stockholders
9. Policyholders' surplus of life insurance companies (When an insurance company is consolidated or accounted for by the

equity method, these disclosures also apply to the parent company.)

   a. The treatment of the policyholders' surplus under the provisions of the Internal Revenue Code

   b. The fact that income taxes may become payable if the company takes specific action, which should be disclosed appropriately

   c. The total amount of policyholders' surplus for which income taxes have not been provided

10. If no current or deferred federal income taxes have been provided by a life insurance company for any retained earnings in excess of policyholders' surplus

   a. The amount of such retained earnings

   b. The reasons for not accruing deferred federal income taxes

OBSERVATION: SEC-reporting companies should refer to Accounting Series Release 301 (October 21, 1981) for a complete list of disclosures required by the SEC for insurance companies.

MUTUAL LIFE INSURANCE ENTERPRISES

A mutual life insurance enterprise's main product is participating life insurance. These contracts provide certain guaranteed benefits and allow policyholders to share in the profits through dividends. Dividends are paid periodically at the direction of the board of directors, and they reflect the performance of the enterprise for investment activity, mortality experience, and overhead for each particular class of contracts. "Non-participating" contracts pay no dividends.

In 1972, the AICPA published an Industry Audit Guide, *Audits of Stock Life Insurance Companies.* That Guide did not apply to mutual life insurance enterprises. Since that time, the FASB has issued three Statements that exempt mutual life insurance enterprises from their requirements:

- FAS-60 (Accounting and Reporting by Insurance Enterprises)
- FAS-97 (Accounting and Reporting by insurance Enterprises for Certain Long-Duration Contracts and for Realized Gains and Losses from the Sale of Investments)
- FAS-113 (Accounting and Reporting for Reinsurance of Short-Duration and Long-Duration Contracts)

FAS-120 extends the requirements of these Statements to mutual life insurance enterprises, assessment enterprises, and fraternal benefit societies (FAS-120, par. 8). FAS-120 also permits stock life insurance enterprises to apply the provisions of the AICPA's Statement of Position 95-1 (Accounting for Certain Insurance Activities of Mutual Life Insurance Enterprises) to participating life insurance contracts that meet certain specified conditions. FAS-120 also amends FIN-40 (Applicability of Generally Accepted Accounting Principles to Mutual Life Insurance and Other Enterprises) to defer the effective date of the general provisions of that pronouncement to fiscal years beginning after December 15, 1995.

FAS-120 is effective for financial statements issued for fiscal years beginning after December 15, 1995.

OTHER ISSUES

There are significant differences between the accounting principles and practices used in reporting to insurance regulatory agencies and generally accepted accounting principles. The following are some of the more important exceptions to GAAP that are used in regulatory accounting practices:

1. Increasing the *policy reserves* account by a direct debit to unassigned surplus (retained earnings) instead of a charge to income
2. Charging unassigned surplus with prior service costs of pension plans instead of a charge to income
3. Netting liabilities against related assets
4. Debiting unassigned surplus for only the par value of certain stock dividends

Mandatory Securities Valuation Reserve

In most states, a mandatory securities valuation reserve (MSVR) must be established in accordance with a formula. Unassigned surplus is debited and a reserve account is credited. This procedure is unacceptable under GAAP.

Under GAAP, the MSVR represents an appropriation of retained earnings (surplus), which should be included in the equity section of the balance sheet.

Nonadmitted Assets

Under regulatory accounting practices, it is not permitted to show certain assets on the balance sheet of an insurance company. Nonadmitted assets are charged to surplus and thus eliminated from the regulatory balance sheet. The more common nonadmitted assets are the following:

1. Furniture and equipment
2. Automobiles
3. Prepaid and deferred expenses
4. Goodwill and other intangible assets
5. Unauthorized investments
6. Investments in excess of authorized amounts
7. Receivables from agents (debit balances)
8. Receivables from employees and officers
9. Accrued income on investments in default
10. Receivables from unauthorized reinsurers

In presenting financial statements in conformity with GAAP, nonadmitted assets must be restored. This is accomplished by debiting the various assets and crediting retained earnings (surplus). However, care must be exercised in determining the collectibility of receivables that are restored.

Stockholders' Equity

For financial statements to be presented in conformity with GAAP, it may be necessary to reclassify an insurance company's equity account. As mentioned previously, nonadmitted assets must be restored by a credit to retained earnings. If an insurance company has increased its policy reserves by a direct charge to surplus, the transaction will have to be redone to be in conformity with GAAP. Care must also be exercised in segregating appropriated surplus from unassigned surplus for financial statement purposes.

APPENDIX: INSURANCE PRIMER

PROPERTY AND LIABILITY INSURANCE COMPANIES

Other than the different products sold, property and liability companies (property and casualty companies) and life insurance companies are similar in that they are structured as:

- A mutual company (assessable or nonassessable, participating or nonparticipating)
- A capital stock company
- A reciprocal or interinsurance exchange

Regardless of the structure of the company, reinsurance typically is sought from other insurance companies or specialty reinsurers to spread the burden of losses.

The principal differences among mutual and stock insurance companies relate to ownership and the distribution of profits and losses.

Mutual vs. Stock Companies

	Ownership	Profits	Losses
Nonparticipating assessable mutual	Policyholders	Rates adjusted	Policyholders assessed and reinsurance
Nonparticipating nonassessable mutual	Policyholders	Rates adjusted downward	Rates adjusted upward and reinsurance
Participating assessable mutual	Policyholders	Dividends to policyholders	Policyholders assessed and reinsurance
Participating nonassessable mutual	Policyholders	Dividends to policyholders	Rates adjusted upward and reinsurance
Stock company (corporate form)	Shareholders	Shareholders	Reinsurance

RECIPROCALS AND INTERINSURANCE EXCHANGES

Reciprocals and interinsurance exchanges are unincorporated forms of cooperative insurance facilities. Such organizations hold approximately 2.4% of the insurance market. They are not insurance companies, but are organizations created by entities (factories, municipalities, etc.) that share similar risks of loss.

Each member agrees to pay its share of the losses of the entire group from its own assets (limited to an amount specified in the agreement among the members).

Most property and liability insurance companies sell multiple lines of insurance. The lines of property and liability insurance usually are grouped as the following:

1. Property coverage
2. Business liability
3. Business auto policies
4. Package policies
5. Crime insurance
6. Bonding
7. Workers' compensation and disability benefits coverage
8. Personal lines policies
   - Auto
   - Homeowners'
9. Boiler and equipment policies
10. Inland marine (floaters) coverage
11. Ocean marine (ships, cargo, yacht) coverage

From an economic standpoint, insurance is a method used to spread a specific risk among policyholders. The insurance company assumes the specific risk and charges a premium based on past loss experiences for the specific risk. The premiums collected by the insurance company are used to pay current losses and operational costs, and the balance is invested. Thus, the two main sources of income for a property and liability insurance company are (1) premiums and (2) investment income.

INSURABLE INTEREST

An owner of an insurance contract must have an insurable interest in the subject matter of the policy for the contract to be valid. An insurable interest in life insurance need only exist at the time the policy is issued, while an insurable interest in property insurance must exist at the time of the loss.

An insurable interest is a test of financial relationship. A husband may insure the life of his wife, an employer the life of an employee, a creditor the life of his or her debtor, and a partner the life of his or her co-partners. In life insurance the insurable interest must exist only at the time the policy is issued, and if the relationship is subsequently broken (e.g., divorce, dissolution of a partnership) the owner may still collect the benefits of the insurance contract.

In property insurance, the insurable interest must exist at the time a loss is incurred. If a landlord sells a piece of property, he or she has no further insurable interest on the property and is not entitled to collect for any losses on it.

DEPARTMENTAL FUNCTIONS

The departmental functions of a typical property and liability insurance company would consist of (*a*) an agency department, (*b*) an underwriting department, (*c*) a policy service department, (*d*) an investment department, and (*e*) a claims department.

The agency department is responsible for the marketing functions of the insurance company. Supervision and training of sales personnel, sales promotion, and other selling activities are handled by the agency department. Most property and liability companies market their policies through independent agents under a franchise arrangement.

The underwriting department is responsible for evaluating the risks that are submitted to the insurance company, and it controls the issuance of policies.

The policy service department is responsible for bookkeeping activities, such as premium notices and collection, changes in address, beneficiary and similar changes, and the payment of loss claims.

The investment department manages the insurance company's investments.

The claims department is responsible for assessing and approving claims.

CASH BASIS

Usually, insurance companies keep their general ledgers on a cash basis. Some reports required by regulatory agencies must be prepared on a cash basis, particularly details of income and expense. Assets that have been recorded on the books of an insurance company are called *ledger assets*. Others are called *nonledger assets*.

Nonledger assets arise from the adjusting journal entries necessary to convert the cash basis trial balance to the accrual basis. Liabilities are referred to in the same manner, so those recorded on the books are called *ledger liabilities* and others are called *nonledger liabilities*.

Because insurance companies use the cash basis, most liabilities are nonledger. An insurance company will have few nonledger assets, because most of its assets arise from cash transactions.

When adjusting journal entries are made for workpapers to convert the cash basis trial balance to the accrual basis, they are not posted to the books. Therefore, the books of insurance companies are on the cash basis. The insurance company will keep other records, such as a *claims register*, so that information is available to adjust easily to the accrual basis.

The claims register keeps track of claims pending, paid, negotiated, and rejected, while the cash basis trial balance reflects only the claims actually paid. The claims register is used to prepare some of the adjusting journal entries necessary for conversion to the accrual basis.

REINSURANCE

When an insurance company issues a policy (contract), it assumes the risk of loss from the policyholder in exchange for a premium. The policyholder, unable to bear the risk alone, passes it to the insurance company.

The insurer may hold the risk for the duration of the contract, or may itself seek to pass along all or a portion of the risk to another professional risk bearer, in exchange for a portion of the premium collected from the policyholder.

In the practice of reinsurance, the insurers are labeled:

- *Ceding carrier*   The company that issues the policy to the policy-holder
- *Assuming carrier*   The reinsurance company

Reinsurance is arranged between the ceding and assuming carriers under the following types of contracts:

- *Quota share reinsurance*   Each company pays a predetermined percentage of every loss.
- *Excess cover reinsurance*   The ceding carrier agrees to pay all losses up to a specified dollar amount over which the reinsurer pays all amounts.
- *Facultative reinsurance*   A single reinsurance contract for a specific policy or policyholder.

- *Blanket reinsurance*   The assuming carrier agrees to automatically reinsure the policies issued by the ceding carrier subject to prearranged conditions, costs, and limitations. The ceding carrier submits a monthly report of all policies issued under the agreement with payment of the premiums due.

REGULATION OF THE INDUSTRY

The insurance industry is state-regulated. The insurance department of each state monitors the solvency, dealings, and investments of insurance companies. The companies make mandatory periodic reports to the insurance departments.

The National Association of Insurance Commissioners (NAIC) is an organization composed of the insurance commissioners from each state. It meets semiannually and makes recommendations for new rules and procedures, which are almost always adopted by the states. NAIC is concerned with financial reporting and auditing of insurance companies, and has assisted in the development of uniform annual reports and an examiner's manual written in the form of an audit program for insurance companies.

MARKETING

Insurance companies market their policies through:

1. Company agents
2. Captive agents
3. Brokers
4. Independent agents
5. General agents

Company Agents

Company agents are employees of the insurer. They are paid a salary or a combination of salary and commissions on the policies they sell. A company agent may bind the insurer to a contract for insurance.

Captive Agents

Captive agents are independent contractors who have agreed to represent one insurer exclusively and sell only its products (some exceptions are made for risks the insurer will not accept). A captive agency carries all its own expenses, but it does not own the list of policyholders it produces. A captive agent may bind the insurer to a contract for insurance.

Brokers

Brokers are independent enterprises. A broker's function is to represent a client, not the insurer. The broker presents the client's proposal for insurance to any insurer willing to consider business from the broker. A broker has no powers of agency with the insurers, and coverage is effective only when deemed so by the insurer. A broker also may solicit coverage for a client from an agent of the insurer.

Independent Agents

Independent agents are independent contractors who are free to represent several insurers. The independent agent has the power to bind the insurers to insurance contracts within the prearranged limits and guidelines. The agency carries all its own expenses and typically also acts as a broker if so licensed and when required.

General Agents

General agents are independent contractors who have been given virtually all the powers and functions of the insurer itself, including:

- Binding the insurer on contracts of insurance
- Appointing agents
- Managing the insurer's business in a given exclusive territory
- Paying claims
- Issuing policies

CLAIM SERVICE

Insurance companies may handle their policy claims through salaried employees who investigate a claim and propose a settlement with the claimant. They also may use adjustment bureaus to investigate, adjust, and settle claims. Adjustment bureaus are sponsored by member insurance companies. The expenses of a bureau are paid by the members, usually based on the number of claims handled or the dollar value of the claims. Usually the right of final approval of all settlements made by an adjustment bureau is exercised by the insurance company. Members are not obligated to use the bureau.

Independent insurance adjustors, who work on a fee basis, are another alternative an insurance company may use.

Most of the accounting and statistical data used by a property and liability insurance company appears in the daily reports. A *daily report* is a copy of the front of the insurance policy that contains practically all the accounting and statistical data necessary to record the transaction. Copies of the daily reports are distributed to several departments at the home office of the insurance company.

STOCK LIFE INSURANCE COMPANIES

The proceeds of a life insurance policy are intended to provide financial security to one or more beneficiaries named in the policy. Upon death of the insured, the insurance company pays the beneficiary the face amount of the policy, less any outstanding indebtedness. The proceeds of the insurance policy are not always paid in a lump sum. One alternative, for example, is an election made by a policyholder for the insurance company to pay the beneficiary certain periodic amounts, or to pay the proceeds when the beneficiary reaches a specified age. In this event, the proceeds are held by the insurance company and usually will earn interest. Almost any type of arrangement can be made with a life insurance company for the payment of a policy's proceeds.

From an economic standpoint, insurance is a method of spreading a specific risk among many individuals. The insurance company assumes the specific risk, such as death, and charges a premium based on actuarial calculations.

In the case of death, mortality tables reflecting the frequency of deaths of individuals in various age groups are used to predict the life expectancy of the insured.

Illustration of Use of Mortality Tables

- For a group of 100,000 males, age 20, the death rate in a year is 179.
- Therefore, the rate per $1,000 of life insurance for one year for a 20-year-old male is $1.79.
- The insurance company then loads the rate to cover:
  — Costs of processing
  — Commissions
  — Profit

- A final rate per $1,000 of life insurance for a 20-year-old male would be approximately $2.14.

- The annual premium for pure life insurance of $100,000 for the 20-year-old male would be $214.

The premiums collected by the insurance company are used to pay current benefits and costs, and the balance is invested to yield investment income. Theoretically, if an individual dies in the year that the mortality tables predict, the accumulated net premiums collected by the insurance company, plus the investment earned on the accumulated premiums, should be sufficient to pay the face amount of the policy and still leave a profit. These accumulated premiums and investment income are reflected on the balance sheet of an insurance company as *policy reserves*.

Annuities

When life insurance policies project estates, annuities liquidate them. The function of an annuity contract is to pay out accumulated cash systematically to the beneficiary (*annuitant*). An annuity can be:

- A temporary annuity—payable for a fixed number of years.
- A whole-life annuity—payable for the life of the annuitant.

In its elemental form, the contract pays the annuitant only while he or she is alive. If the annuitant dies while collecting annuity benefits, the insurance company keeps the funds and uses them to pay other annuitants who are living beyond their predicted life expectancies.

Modern annuities have a refund option whereby a cash refund of unused money is paid to a contingent beneficiary upon the death of the annuitant. There are two types of annuities:

1. A *joint and survivorship contract* involves two or more annuitants and provides for guaranteed periodic payments to any surviving annuitant.

2. The periodic annuity payment from a *variable annuity* fluctuates in accordance with investment experience. Investments for variable annuities are kept in a separate fund, and the amount of the periodic annuity is based on the performance of the investments. Variable annuities may or may not include a minimum death benefit during the accumulation period.

Accident and health insurance policies are issued on an individual or group basis. The policies pay for hospital and medical care, and sometimes for the loss of income during periods that the insured is incapacitated.

Generally, life insurance companies are exempt from registration under the Securities Exchange Act of 1934. Many insurance companies have established holding companies, however, that are not considered life insurance companies and, thus, must be registered under the 1934 Act. In addition, some insurance companies have registered their shares under the 1934 Act so that the shares can be listed and traded on a national stock exchange. Public offerings of life insurance companies' stock must be registered under the Securities Act of 1933.

If an insurance company has registered under either of the securities acts, it must comply with annual and periodic reporting requirements and proxy solicitation rules.

An insurance company receives its revenues from premiums and investment income. Premium income may be derived directly from the owner of the policy or from reinsurance agreements with other insurance companies. Investment income is regulated by insurance statutes that set forth the types of investments that may be made.

Life insurance companies generally sell (*a*) life insurance, (*b*) annuity contracts, and (*c*) accident and health contracts. The more common policies are discussed below.

Whole-Life Policies

Benefits, which are paid upon death of the insured, are equal to the face amount of the policy, less cash value borrowed from the policy by the policyholder. Whole-life policies usually accumulate a cash surrender value, which increases over time. The owner of the policy can borrow from the insurance policy. The accumulated cash value can be used as collateral to secure a bank loan.

Premiums for whole-life insurance generally are level; that is, they are the same amount each year. They are payable annually, but more frequent payments can be made by payment of a small service fee. A whole-life policy can be paid in one lump-sum payment at the beginning of the policy term. Most policies are paid quarterly, semi-annually, or annually. A *straight-life* policy (also called *ordinary life*) requires that premiums be paid during the entire life of the insured (to age 100). A limited-payment policy requires that premiums be paid over a specified period, usually 10, 20, or 30 years. As a result, the premiums on a limited-payment policy are always higher than those of a straight-life policy, but the total cost of the policy usually is less. Coverage remains in force for the entire life of the insured.

Limited-Payment Life Contracts

A limited-payment plan is a modified form of whole-life insurance, made up of elements of whole-life and term insurance. Premiums are used to provide term insurance coverage and simultaneously accrue a cash reserve. At a specified date, the policyholder stops paying premiums and the accrued cash is used to purchase term coverage on the policyholder's life to an age of 61 or 70.

Universal-Life Contracts

In the late 1970s, interest rates soared (as high as 21% prime rate). Whole-life policyholders who were realizing 3% to 4% on the cash reserve in their policies found it beneficial to cancel the whole-life contract and invest the cash surrender value in a money market.

In response to mass cancellations, insurers developed the universal-life contract, which mated life insurance coverage with money market returns.

Projections of earnings are based on interest rates at the time of the inception of the policy; however, three factors inherent in the contract will affect the real net result:

1. The mortality rate upon which the contract price was quoted can be adjusted by the insurance company. If it is adjusted upward, more of the premium is used to provide life coverage, and less is used to accumulate a cash reserve.

2. The insurer can charge fees against the policy that may be subject to change at the insurer's option.

3. Interest rates are adjusted throughout the policy term.

Term Insurance Policies

Term insurance policies are issued for a specific period, and death benefits are paid only if the insured dies during the specified period. Benefits are equal to the face amount of the policy. Term insurance policies do not accumulate any cash surrender value.

Term insurance policies are written for short periods, usually one to five years. In most cases, however, the policyholder is granted the right to renew a term insurance policy up to a maximum age (60 or 65) without having to submit additional evidence of insurability. The term policy also may grant the policyholder the right to convert the term insurance to whole-life or some other type of coverage.

Premiums for term insurance policies usually increase with the age of the insured. Payments must be made annually, but they may be made at interim periods during the year for an additional service charge.

Since term insurance does not accumulate any cash value, the premiums constitute payment for insurance protection only. Thus, most people feel that term insurance is best when pure protection is sought.

An insurance company may issue group term life insurance policies. A group term policy insures a specific group of individuals under a single master contract, usually for one year. Premiums are calculated on the basis of the ages of the individuals in the group.

Endowment Insurance Policies

Endowment policies are issued for a specific time, called the *endowment period*, and they have a maturity date on which the insured receives the face amount of the policy, less any indebtedness to the insurance company. If the insured dies during the endowment period, however, the insurance company pays the face amount, less any indebtedness, to the beneficiary of the policy. Thus, the insured has insurance protection during the endowment period and, if living at the maturity date, receives the face amount of the policy, less any indebtedness to the insurance company. Endowment policies accumulate a cash value, which increases with time and may be used as collateral for a loan.

Premiums for endowment policies can be a single lump-sum payment or a limited-payment basis, but generally they are payable over the endowment period specified in the policy.

Basic insurance policies can be expanded by the use of riders that are attached to, and made part of, the insurance contract.

Nonforfeiture Benefits in Whole-Life Insurance

The standard nonforfeiture law of 1948 protects policyholders who allow their whole-life policy to lapse. The insurance company must offer the policyholder:

1. The cash surrender value of the policy in cash payment to the insured.
2. A reduced paid-up life policy to death (accumulated cash in the policy is used to purchase a lesser amount of permanent coverage).
3. Extended term coverage (the accumulated cash in the policy is used to purchase term insurance expiring at age 65 or 70).

Waiver of Premium Rider

This rider provides for the waiver of all premiums during periods of disability of the insured. An accidental death benefit rider (double indemnity) provides that, if the insured dies by accidental means, the insurance company will pay multiples (usually two or three times) of the face amount of the policy. An additional premium is charged for each rider.

Health Insurance

Health insurance typically is offered in these forms:

1. Basic hospital benefits
   - Providing scheduled coverage [a specified amount per day for room and board for a certain maximum number of days (no deductible)]
2. Basic doctor/surgical benefits
   - Providing scheduled coverage (a specified amount for certain listed procedures)
3. Major medical coverage
   - Providing coverage that applies in addition to the basic coverages when those coverages have been exhausted by a claim
   - Coverage for all other medical expenses not included in the basic coverages
   - The major medical coverage is payable after a deductible, either after the basic coverage is exhausted or before any payment for uncovered medical expenses.
   - After the deductible, the major medical coverage pays only 80% of the covered claim up to a specified dollar limit. Thereafter, the claim is covered 100% to the limit (if one exists) of the major medical policy (coinsurance).

TITLE INSURANCE COMPANIES

Title insurance provides financial security to buyers of real estate and their lenders. Thus, if a buyer obtains title insurance on real estate that is being purchased and subsequently suffers a loss because of a lien or defect in the title to the property, the title insurance company will pay the loss. Generally, mortgage lenders require a title insurance policy on the property being purchased before they will lend funds on a mortgage.

A title insurance policy is unique because the premiums are not refundable and the term of the policy is indefinite. However, the amount of title insurance and the date of title search are stated in the policy. Thus, any loss in excess of the amount of title insurance and any loss that occurs because of a lien or defect that did not exist up to the date of the title search will not be covered by the policy.

When the insurance company receives an application for title insurance, a title search is made. A *title search* consists of reviewing and scrutinizing public records of the chain of ownership of the property being insured up to the date of the title search. Some title searches may go back several hundred years. Each change of ownership is examined to make sure it was properly made and that there are no unpaid liens or defects against the title to the property. If a lien or defect is discovered, the title insurance policy usually is still issued but the discovered lien or defect is cited in the policy and not covered. In this event, the buyer may be able to cancel the purchase of the property or compel the seller to take care of the existing lien or defect. The seller must be given a reasonable amount of time to cure the defect up to the date of closing. Most contracts for the sale of real property contain a provision to the effect that the property is being sold free of any liens and/or defects and that the buyer has a specified period to determine whether any liens or defects against the property do exist.

The records that a title insurance company uses to search the chain of ownership of a parcel of real estate are called the *title plant*. The title plant consists of the public records of a specific geographic area (town, city, county, etc.) that have been indexed appropriately and integrated so that an individual parcel of real property may be located easily. From the title plant, the insurance company can prepare an abstract on any piece of real estate in the particular geographic area. An *abstract* is a short summary of the ownership history of a specified parcel of real property.

A title plant usually is kept up to date on a daily basis. A well-maintained title plant usually increases in value over time and seldom, if ever, decreases in value. In addition, the estimated useful life of a title plant generally is indefinite. These unusual characteristics make a title plant quite unique.

CHAPTER 56
TITLE PLANT

CONTENTS

CHAPTER 56
TITLE PLANT

OVERVIEW

GAAP for title plant include specialized principles and practices extracted from AICPA standards and apply to title insurance enterprises, title abstract enterprises, title agents, and other enterprises that use a title plant in their operations. GAAP require that the costs directly incurred to construct a title plant be capitalized until the enterprise can use the title plant to perform title searches. These capitalized costs are not depreciated, and the costs of maintaining a title plant and performing title searches are expensed as incurred.

GAAP for title plant activities are found in the following pronouncement:

FAS-61   Accounting for Title Plant

CROSS-REFERENCES

1999 MILLER GAAP GUIDE: Chapter 20, "Impairment of Loans and Long-Lived Assets"; Chapter 55, "Insurance Enterprises"

1999 MILLER GOVERNMENTAL GAAP GUIDE: Chapter 11, "Expenditures"

BACKGROUND

A title insurance company issues title insurance policies. Title insurance provides protection against losses incurred by a buyer or lender resulting from liens or other title defects on property purchased or secured. If a buyer obtains title insurance on real estate that is being purchased and subsequently a loss is incurred because of a lien or defect in the title to the property, the title insurance company will pay the loss up to the policy limit, or if so endorsed, up to the market value of the property. There are two types of policies: the owner's form and the lender's form. The owner's form protects the owner's equity interest in the property. The lender's form protects the lender for the amount loaned against the property. Lenders require an amount of insurance at least equal to the amount loaned in order to cover their interest.

A title insurance policy is unique because the premiums are not refundable and the term of the policy is indefinite. The amount of insurance and the date of title search are stated in the policy. Any loss in excess of the amount of title insurance and any loss that occurs because of a lien or defect which did not exist up to the date of the title search are not covered.

When a title insurer receives an application for title insurance, a title search is made. The search consists of reviewing and scrutinizing the chain of ownership of the property up to the date of the search. Each change of ownership is examined to make sure it was properly made and that no defects or unpaid liens exist against the title to the property. If a lien or defect is discovered, the title insurance policy is issued with the discovered lien or defect cited in the policy and not covered. The buyer may be able to cancel the purchase of the property or compel the seller to cure the existing lien or defect. Most contracts for the sale of real property contain a provision to the effect that the property is being sold free of any liens and/or defects, and that the buyer has a specified period to determine whether any liens or defects do exist against the property being purchased. The seller is given time up to the day of closing to cure the defect.

The records that a title insurance company uses to search the chain of ownership of a parcel of real estate are called the *title plant*. The title plant consists of the public records of a specific geographic area (town, city, county, etc.) that have been indexed and integrated so that an individual parcel of real property may be located easily. The title insurer or an abstractor prepares an abstract from the title plant records. An abstract is a short summary of the ownership history of a specific parcel of real property.

A title plant usually is revised on a daily basis. A well-maintained title plant usually will increase in value over time. The estimated useful life of a title plant generally is indefinite.

ACCOUNTING FOR TITLE PLANT

Capitalization of Title Plant

Until a title plant is ready for use, all direct costs incurred to acquire, organize, or construct the title plant are capitalized (FAS-61, par. 3).

☞ **PRACTICE POINTER:** A title plant may be constructed or purchased by an enterprise. In either case, capitalize costs directly identified with the title plant. A purchase may consist of (a) a copy of the title plant, (b) an un-divided interest in the title plant, or (c) the exclusive ownership (outright purchase) of the title plant (FAS-61, par. 4).

A title plant that is constructed or otherwise acquired will cover a definite period of time. For example, an enterprise may purchase a title plant of a particular geographic area that covers the period January 1, 1940 through December 31, 1981. Subsequently, the enterprise may construct or otherwise acquire a title plant for the same geographic area that covers the period from January 1, 1900 through December 31, 1939. This type of title plant is sometimes referred to as an *antecedent title plant* or *backplant*. The same rules for capitalization of direct costs apply. Thus, costs incurred to construct or otherwise acquire a backplant are capitalized if they can be identified directly with the acquisition of the backplant (FAS-61, par. 5).

FAS-61 states that capitalized costs of a title plant should not ordinarily be depreciated or otherwise charged to income. Unless there is an impairment in the carrying amount of the title plant, the undepreciated capitalized costs are reported as an asset indefinitely on the balance sheet. The impairment of a title plant below its carrying amount is recognized in the income of the period in which the impairment is discovered (FAS-61, par. 6).

☛ **PRACTICE POINTER:** The carrying amount of a title plant may become impaired if:

1. The title plant is not properly maintained on a current basis.

2. The title plant becomes partially or completely obsolete.

3. The title plant is abandoned or severely neglected.

4. Economics, competition, or legal factors result in a decline in the value of the title plant.

Maintenance and Operating Expenses

Costs incurred to revise a title plant may be expensed or deferred separately, but may not be added to the carrying amount of the title plant. If such costs are deferred separately, they are amortized over their estimated useful lives in a systematic manner (FAS-61, par. 8).

FAS-61 requires that all title plant maintenance and operational costs be expensed in the period incurred. The cost to update or maintain the title plant on a current basis and the cost of performing title searches to issue title policies are expensed as they are incurred (FAS-61, par. 7).

Sale of Title Plant

A sale of a title plant may consist of (*a*) an outright sale, (*b*) a sale of an undivided interest, or (*c*) a sale of a copy, or the right to use, the title plant. FAS-61 requires that gain or loss on any sale of a title plant be reported separately in the financial statements (FAS-61, par. 9).

Gain or loss on the sale of a title plant depends on the type of sale executed by the seller. In the event of an outright sale of the title plant, gain or loss is the difference between the selling price and the net carrying amount of the title plant on the date of sale (FAS-61, par. 9a).

In the event of the sale of an undivided interest in a title plant, gain or loss is the difference between the selling price and the pro rata portion of the title plant that is attributable to the sale of the undivided interest (FAS-61, par. 9b).

In a sale of a copy, or the right to use the title plant, no cost is allocated to the sale unless the value of the title plant decreases as a result of the sale. In the sale of a copy or the right to use the title plant, the sales price usually represents the gain on the sale (FAS-61, par. 9c).

Illustration of Accounting for Expenditures Related to Title Plant

Beta Co. engaged in the following activities related to the establishment of a title plant. It paid $50,000 of direct costs to construct and organize the title plant, $12,500 to perform title searches to support the issuance of title policies, and $10,000 to update the title plant. Beta Co. determined that the title plant had experienced a $7,000 impairment in value. Beta Co. sold the title plant for $52,000.

The $10,000 paid to update the title plant is to be capitalized separately and amortized over its estimated useful life of five years. The sale of the title plant occurred two years after the updating had been done.

Entries to record the above transaction are as follows:

To record the construction and organization of the title plant:

Title plant	$50,000	
Cash		$50,000

To record the cost of performing title searches:

Title search expense	$12,5000	
Cash		$12,500

To record the cost of updating the title plant:

Deferred title plant updating cost	$10,000	
Cash		$10,000

To record amortization of the cost of updating the title plant:

Amortization expense ($10,000 / 5)	$2,000	
Cash		$2,000

(A similar entry is made each year until the updating cost is fully amortized.)

To record the impairment in value of the title plant:

Impairment loss on title plant	$7,000	
Title plant		$7,000

To record sale of title plant:

Cash	$52,000	
Title plant ($50,000 – $7,000)		$43,000
Deferred title plant updating cost		
($10,000 – $4,000)		6,000
Gain on sale of title plant		3,000

Mortgage Banking Industry

CHAPTER 57
MORTGAGE BANKING INDUSTRY

CONTENTS

CHAPTER 57
MORTGAGE BANKING INDUSTRY

OVERVIEW

Mortgage banking activities primarily consist of three separate but interrelated activities: (1) the origination or acquisition of mortgage loans, (2) the sale of the loans to permanent investors, and (3) the subsequent long-term servicing of the loans. GAAP for mortgage banking activities, which prescribe principles in these and other related areas of accounting, are found in the following pronouncements:

FAS-65   Accounting for Certain Mortgage Banking Activities

FAS-91   Accounting for Nonrefundable Fees and Costs Associated with Originating or Acquiring Loans and Initial Direct Costs of Leases

FAS-122   Accounting for Mortgage Servicing Rights

> **OBSERVATION:** FAS-125 (Accounting for Transfers and Servicing of Financial Assets and Extinguishments of Liabilities) supersedes FAS-122 and is effective for transactions occurring after December 31, 1996. FAS-125 is covered in the 1999 *Miller GAAP Guide* chapter titled "Financial Instruments." Because this 1999 edition of the *Miller GAAP Guide* is available while FAS-122 is still in effect, coverage of the subject of mortgage servicing rights in accordance with that pronouncement is retained in this chapter.

> **OBSERVATION:** FAS-65 is amended by FAS-133 (Accounting for Derivative Instruments and Hedging Activities). This is effective for fiscal years beginning after June 15, 1999. FAS-133 applies in interim financial statements for periods that begin after the same date (e.g., the quarter beginning July 1, 1999). FAS-133 is covered in Chapter 16 of the 1999 *Miller GAAP Guide.*
> Because the effective date of FAS-133 is delayed as indicated above, and the first calendar year for which FAS-133 will be in effect is the year 2000, the impact of FAS-133 on FAS-65 is not reflected in the 1999 *Miller GAAP Guide.*

CROSS-REFERENCES

1999 MILLER GAAP GUIDE: Chapter 16, "Financial Instruments"; Chapter 23, "Intangible Assets"; Chapter 48, "Troubled Debt Restructuring"; Chapter 49, "Banking and Thrift Institutions"

1999 MILLER GAAP IMPLEMENTATION MANUAL: EITF: Chapter 34, "Mortgage Banking Industry"

1999 MILLER HUD AUDIT PROCEDURES: Chapter 15, "Compliance Audits of Issuers of Mortgage-Backed, Nonsupervised Mortgages, Loan Correspondents, and Lenders Payrolls and Other Liabilities"; Chapter 16, "Mortgagor's and Contractor's Cost Certifications"

BACKGROUND

FAS-65 contains the specialized accounting and reporting principles and practices that were originally published in SOP 74-12 (Accounting Practices in the Mortgage Banking Industry) and SOP 76-2 (Accounting for Origination Costs and Loan and Commitment Fees in the Mortgage Banking Industry).

FAS-65 establishes GAAP for an enterprise or that portion of an enterprise's operations engaged primarily in originating, marketing, and servicing mortgage loans for other than its own account. A financial institution or other enterprise that has operations that consist of originating, marketing, and servicing mortgage loans for others must apply the provisions of FAS-65 to those operations. FAS-65 has been amended by FAS-91 and FAS-122.

MORTGAGE LOANS

One of the more difficult problems in accounting for mortgage loans receivable and mortgage-backed securities of an enterprise engaged in mortgage banking activity is the valuation for reporting purposes. The valuation of mortgage loans receivable and mortgage-backed securities depends upon whether they are held for sale or for long-term investment. Most mortgage loans and mortgage-backed securities are held for sale in the ordinary course of business of a mortgage banker. Valuation of mortgage loans receivable and mortgage-backed securities for reporting purposes is determined as of the balance sheet date.

Held for Long-Term Investment

For a mortgage loan or mortgage-backed security to be classified as a long-term investment, the banking enterprise must have the requisite intent and ability to hold the loan to maturity or for an extended period. When a mortgage loan receivable or a security held for sale is reclassified as a long-term investment, the transfer must be made at the lower of cost or market on the date of transfer (FAS-65, par. 6). In the event of a permanent impairment in the value of a mortgage loan or security classified as a long-term investment, its carrying value is further reduced to net realizable value. The amount of reduction is reported in net income of the period in which the impairment is discovered. In subsequent periods, any market recovery from the net realizable value is realized only at the time of sale, maturity, or other disposition of the mortgage loan or security (FAS-65, par. 7).

Any difference between the carrying amount of the loan or security and its outstanding principal balance is recognized as an adjustment to yield and amortized to income by the interest method over the estimated life of the loan. The interest method is applied in accordance with paragraphs 18 and 19 of FAS-91 (FAS-91, par. 27).

Held for Sale

All mortgage loans receivable and mortgage-backed securities held for sale are valued at the lower of cost or market (as defined by FAS-65), according to the type of mortgage loan or mortgage-backed security. Write-downs of a mortgage loan or mortgage-backed security to the lower of cost or market are included in net income of the period in which the adjustment occurs (FAS-65, par. 4).

After write-down, write-ups to market values in subsequent periods are recorded, but total recorded market value is not permitted to exceed cost. The journal entry to record the recovery of market value is a debit to mortgage loans or mortgage-backed securities and a credit to an income account.

For the purposes of disclosure, mortgage loans and mortgage-backed securities are classified in at least the following two categories: (1) residential (one to four units) and (2) commercial. Lower of cost or market can be determined on the total of all mortgage loans in a particular category or for each individual mortgage loan or mortgage-backed security (FAS-65, par. 9).

Discounts resulting from the purchase of mortgage loans that are held for sale are not realized as income until the loans are actually sold.

Lower of cost or market is determined in accordance with the type of mortgage loan receivable or mortgage-based security, as follows (FAS-65, par. 9):

- *Loans and Securities Covered by Commitments* Mortgage loans and mortgage-backed securities that are covered by commitments are valued as specified in the commitment (the actual prices specified in the commitments). The mortgage banker is, at least, guaranteed those prices agreed upon in the commitment.

  Mortgage loans and mortgage-backed securities that do not conform to the required specifications in the commitments are classified as loans and securities *not* covered by commitments.

- *Loans Not Covered by Commitments* Market value for loans not covered by commitments is the market value of the loans as determined by reference to the normal market in which the mortgage banker operates.

  Quotations supplied by GNMA or by the FNMA Free Market System or other public markets should be used when appropriate. If no established market quotations are available, market prices should be determined by the enterprise's normal market outlets.

- *Mortgage-Backed Securities Not Covered by Commitments* GNMA mortgage-backed securities may be held by a mortgage banker for the purpose of trading on the open market. The current market value of the underlying mortgage loans that are pledged by the mortgage banker as collateral for the GNMA securities usually is the same as the current market value of the securities themselves. In other words, the market value of the mortgage loans held in trust as collateral for the GNMA securities should be approximately the same as the value at which the GNMA securities are being traded.

  Market value for GNMA mortgage-backed securities for the purposes of lower of cost or market depends upon whether the trust agreement that covers the mortgage banker's underlying mortgage loans can be terminated on short notice and the mortgage loans sold on the open market. In this event, market value for the GNMA securities is either the current market value of the GNMA securities or the current market value of the underlying mortgage loans.

  The choice of which current market to use is based on whether the mortgage banker intends to terminate the trust. If the mortgage banker does not intend to terminate the trust, market value for the purposes of lower of cost or market is the current market value of the GNMA securities. If the mortgage banker intends to terminate the trust, market value for the purposes of lower of cost or market is the current market value of the underlying mortgage loans.

If the trust cannot be terminated on short notice by the mortgage banker, market value of the GNMA securities for the purposes of lower of cost or market should be based on the published GNMA securities yield.

Block Purchases of Mortgage Loans

Block purchases of mortgage loans have been made by mortgage bankers from GNMA or other investors. Certain costs incurred in block purchases of mortgage loans that can be associated with future servicing income are capitalized and amortized over the estimated average term of the mortgage loans. When these costs are capitalized in accordance with FAS-65, they are added to the valuation of the loans, after cost or the lower of cost or market is determined (FAS-65, par. 10). If the costs have been inappropriately capitalized, they are included as part of cost, or the lower of cost or market, of the mortgage loans.

Repurchase Agreements

Frequently, a mortgage banking enterprise will enter into formal or informal repurchase agreements (repos) with a lending institution. In a repurchase agreement, the mortgage banking enterprise will give the lending institution a block of mortgage loans and/or mortgage-backed securities as collateral for a loan. On the surface, the transaction may appear as a sale of the mortgage loans and/or mortgage-backed securities to the lending institution, with an agreement, formal or otherwise, that the mortgage banking enterprise will repurchase the loans and/or securities at an agreed-upon price, usually equal to the amount of the loan. If the mortgage banking enterprise fails to repurchase the mortgage loans and/or mortgage-backed securities in accordance with the agreement, the lending institution exercises ownership of the loans and/or securities. The mortgage banking enterprise pays an agreed-upon rate of interest for the use of the funds (FAS-65, par. 8).

Formal and informal repurchase agreements are accounted for by the mortgage banking enterprise as a financing, and no sale is recorded (FAS-65, par. 8).

Historically, short-term interest rates have always been less than long-term interest rates. Thus, when a mortgage banker paid interest on short-term warehouse loans, the interest received on the pledged mortgage loans always exceeded the amount paid to carry them on a short-term basis. The difference between the short-term and long-term interest rates creates a *positive spread* for the mortgage banker. Sometimes interest rates reverse, however, and short-term rates exceed long-term rates. This results in a *negative spread*. Since the cost of warehousing mortgage loans by a mortgage banker is primarily a financing activity, negative spreads in interest rates should be charged to current operations as they are incurred.

Mortgage Servicing Fees

Mortgage loans require servicing, including collecting, sending notices, maintaining mortgage records, and other related chores. The owner of a loan or portfolio of loans may perform the servicing function, or it may contract with someone else to perform such services. Servicing fees are based on a percentage of the unpaid principal balance of the loans. Servicing revenue can be substantial.

Most mortgage bankers service their own outstanding loans, and they may also service a large number of mortgage loans for others.

A problem may arise when a mortgage banker sells a loan or a portfolio of loans and agrees to continue servicing the loans at a fee that is significantly different from prevailing servicing rates.

Ordinarily, a loan or portfolio of loans is sold and the buyer assumes the servicing function. Gain or loss on the sale of loans is the difference between the sales price and the net carrying amount of the loans. However, when loans are sold and the seller continues the servicing function for the buyer, a problem arises if the servicing fee charged is significantly different from prevailing service rates and the result is expected to affect current or future operating results materially. In this event, gain or loss on the sale of the mortgage loans must be increased or decreased to provide a normal profit on future servicing income, based on estimated prevailing servicing fee rates (FAS-65, par. 11).

The amount of adjustment, which is calculated on the date of sale, equals the difference between total servicing fee income based on the current prevailing servicing fee rate and total servicing fee income based on the contractually agreed-upon servicing fee rate. In the event that the contractually agreed-upon servicing fee rate is significantly lower than the current prevailing rate, the journal entry to record the adjustment is a debit to the gain or loss on the sale of mortgage loans and a credit to deferred servicing fee revenue. The deferred servicing fee revenue is amortized to income over the life of the related loans, so that each future period will include servicing fee revenue equal to the prevailing servicing fee rate at the date of sale of the mortgage loans.

Occasionally, estimated servicing costs may be expected to exceed normal servicing income over the estimated life of the related mortgage loans. The resulting loss is accrued on the date of sale or the date on which the loss is discovered (FAS-65, par. 11).

The adjustment of future servicing fees is made only when (*a*) the agreed-upon servicing fee rate at the date of sale is materially different from the current prevailing servicing fee rate and (*b*) the agreed-upon servicing fee rate is expected to affect current or future operating results significantly.

Normal Servicing Fees

Under FAS-65, a current (normal) servicing fee rate is representative of servicing fee rates most commonly used in comparable servicing agreements covering similar types of mortgage loans (FAS-65, par. 34). Federally sponsored secondary market makers for mortgage loans, such as Government National Mortgage Association (GNMA), Federal Home Loan Mortgage Corporation (FHLMC), and Federal National Mortgage Association (FNMA), set minimum servicing fee rates. For purposes of determining gain or loss on mortgage loans sold to those agencies with servicing retained, servicing fee rates that are specified in servicing agreements with GNMA, FHLMC, and FNMA generally are considered *normal servicing fee rates*, as that term is used in FAS-65.

If a seller-servicer sells mortgage loans directly to private-sector investors and retains the servicing of those loans, the seller-servicer should charge the private-sector investors a *current (normal) servicing fee rate* as defined in FAS-65. The seller-servicer should consider the normal servicing fee rates currently being charged by federally sponsored secondary market makers in comparable servicing agreements for similar types of mortgage loans.

If the servicing fee rate charged by the seller-servicer is not a normal servicing fee rate, an adjustment must be made to the sales price of the mortgage loans to the private-sector investors. In this event, gain or loss on the sale of the mortgage loans is adjusted to provide a normal profit on future servicing income, based on estimated prevailing normal servicing fee rates. The amount of adjustment is calculated on the date of sale and is equal to the difference between total servicing fee income based on current prevailing normal servicing fee rates and total servicing fee income based on the contractually agreed-upon servicing fee rate.

Prepayments of mortgage loans generally are taken into consideration at the time servicing rights are recorded on the books of a servicer of mortgage loans. The servicer sets up an allowance for future prepayments that may occur from refinancings or other sources. In this event, when there is a prepayment, no adjustment to the recorded amount of the servicing right is necessary. If the mortgage loan servicer did not set up an allowance for prepayments at the time the servicing right was originally recorded, however, an adjustment to the servicing right asset would be required when a prepayment is made.

Transactions with Affiliates

In separate financial statements of mortgage banking enterprises, special treatment is afforded sales of mortgage loans and/or mortgage-backed securities that are made to affiliated enterprises. The selling affiliate must first adjust the carrying amount of the mortgage loans and/or mortgage-backed securities to the lower of cost or market before computing gain or loss on the sale. Any adjustment is charged or credited to income by the selling affiliate. The gain or loss on the sale of mortgage loans and/or mortgage-backed securities to an affiliated enterprise is the difference between the sales price and the lower of cost or market of the loans and/or securities (FAS-65, par. 12).

Gain or loss on the sale or mortgage loans and/or mortgage-backed securities is determined as of the measurement date, which is the first date that management decides that the sale shall take place. The measurement date must be supported by formal approval of the sale by the purchasing affiliate and the issuance of a binding commitment. The binding commitment must be approved and accepted by the selling mortgage banker (FAS-65, par. 12).

A mortgage banker may act as an agent for an affiliated company. The affiliated company is principal and retains all risks of ownership. In its capacity as an agent, the mortgage banker will originate certain specified types of loans for, and authorized by, the affiliated company. Under these circumstances, the mortgage banker may charge an origination fee for services rendered in acquiring the loans. The affiliated company should record the loans acquired at the mortgage banker's acquisition cost (FAS-65, par. 13).

Agreements or arrangements that do not bind the affiliated company to purchase the loans originated by the affiliated mortgage banker, such as *right of first refusal* contracts, do not establish a principal–agency relationship (FAS-65, par. 13).

> **OBSERVATION:** This section on transactions with affiliates is applicable only to the separate financial statements of mortgage banking enterprises. Also, in separate financial statements of mortgage banking enterprises, material transactions with affiliates are subject to the disclosure provisions of FAS-57 (Related Party Disclosures).

Issuance Costs for GNMA Securities

A mortgage banking enterprise may use either the concurrent dates method (15 days) or the internal reserve method (45 days) to pay the holder(s) of GNMA mortgage-backed securities. Only under the internal reserve method is the mortgage banking enterprise required to deposit one month's interest on the mortgage loans with a trustee (FAS-65, par. 15).

Under the provisions of FAS-65, the one month's interest required by the internal reserve method is capitalized and amortized by a mortgage banking enterprise. Amortization of any amount deferred is over the period of, and in proportion to, the estimated net servicing income expected to be earned from the related underlying mortgage loans.

The total amount deferred by a mortgage banking enterprise for issuance costs or under any other provision of FAS-65 may not exceed the present value of the future net servicing income (FAS-65, par. 11). Future net servicing income is the difference between estimated future servicing revenue and the estimated future related servicing costs.

MORTGAGE SERVICING RIGHTS

FAS-65 treated capitalization of the cost of servicing rights through loan origination differently than capitalization of the cost of servicing rights acquired in a purchase transaction, as indicated in the following comparison:

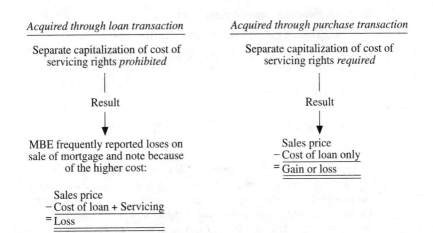

Acquired through loan transaction	*Acquired through purchase transaction*
Separate capitalization of cost of servicing rights *prohibited*	Separate capitalization of cost of servicing rights *required*
Result	Result
MBE frequently reported loses on sale of mortgage and note because of the higher cost:	Sales price − Cost of loan only = Gain or loss
Sales price − Cost of loan + Servicing = Loss	

FAS-122 (effective for fiscal years beginning after December 15, 1995) deletes this difference in the treatment of the cost of servicing rights acquired through loan origination and purchase transactions. Accounting for the cost of mortgage servicing rights in accordance with FAS-122, regardless of the origin of those costs, is as follows (FAS-122, par. 3):

1. Cost of acquisition includes the cost of related mortgage servicing rights.

2. If the mortgage banking enterprise sells a mortgage and a note (or securitizes same) and retains servicing rights, total cost of the mortgage loan should be allocated to:

   a. Mortgage servicing rights.

   b. Loan (without consideration of servicing rights).

3. Basis of allocation is the fair value of each (if practicably determinable).

4. If values are not practicably determinable, the entire cost of acquisition should be allocated to the loan only. (Any cost allocated to servicing rights constitutes a separate asset.)

See Figure 57-1.

FAS-122 further provides the following guidance for determining the fair value of servicing rights (FAS-122, par. 3):

1. Use most objective and relevant quoted market prices

2. (If 1. is not available) Estimate the fair value based on consideration of all available information.

   a. Compare prices for similar assets

   b. Use valuation techniques, such as:

      i. Present value of estimated future cash flows

      ii. Application of a discount rate reflective of risks involved

      iii. Option pricing models

      iv. Matrix pricing

      v. Option-adjusted spread models

      vi. Fundamental analysis

3. Consider possible impairment. Mortgage servicing rights are subject to devaluation resulting from prepayments of loans. As interest rates drop, borrowers will refinance (prepay loans) to take advantage of those rates. Other factors affecting impairment include loan type, loan size, note rate, date of origination, term, and geographic location.

Figure 57-1: Capitalization of Servicing Right

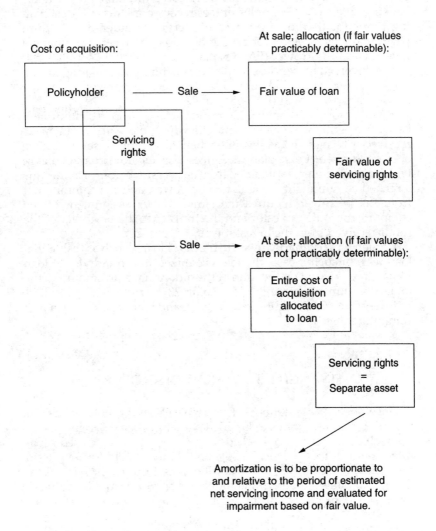

Cost of acquisition:

At sale; allocation (if fair values practicably determinable):

Policyholder —— Sale ——▶ Fair value of loan

Servicing rights

Fair value of servicing rights

—— Sale ——▶ At sale; allocation (if fair values are not practicably determinable):

Entire cost of acquisition allocated to loan

Servicing rights
=
Separate asset

Amortization is to be proportionate to and relative to the period of estimated net servicing income and evaluated for impairment based on fair value.

LOAN AND COMMITMENT FEES

Nonrefundable loan and commitment fees representing compensation for a variety of services may be received or paid by a mortgage banking enterprise. Examples of fees received are fees for designating funds for the borrower, fees for services rendered by a third party, and fees received for arranging a loan between a permanent investor and a borrower (FAS-65, par. 21).

Fees received for services rendered by a third party relating to loan origination costs, such as appraisal fees, are recognized when the services are performed (FAS-65, par. 22).

When a mortgage banking institution arranges a loan commitment between a permanent investor and a borrower, the loan placement fee received is recognized as revenue when all significant services have been performed. Loan placement fees also include transactions in which a commitment is obtained from an investor before or at the time a related commitment is made to a borrower, and the commitment from the borrower requires the simultaneous assignment of the commitment to the investor and the transfer to the borrower of the funds received from the investor (FAS-65, par. 24).

Certain fees ordinarily relate to blocks of loans, such as residential loan fees. In such a case, the fee recognized for an individual loan transaction is based on the ratio of the individual loan amount to the total commitment amount (FAS-65, par. 23).

FAS-91 provides additional guidance in accounting for loan and commitment fees.

FINANCIAL STATEMENT DISCLOSURE

Balance sheet presentations of mortgage banking enterprises for reporting purposes may be classified or unclassified. Mortgage loans receivable and mortgage-backed securities must be disclosed separately as to: (*a*) those held for sale and (*b*) those held for long-term investment (FAS-65, par. 28). In addition, disclosure must be made of the method used to determine the lower of cost or market value of mortgage loans receivable and mortgage-backed securities (FAS-65, par. 29).

In connection with the capitalization of any *servicing rights* acquired by purchase during the period, the following disclosures must be made (FAS-65, par. 30):

1. The amount capitalized
2. The method of amortization used
3. The amount of amortization

☞ **PRACTICE POINTER:** Under FAS-65, the above disclosures pertain only to servicing rights acquired by bulk purchases made during the current period. Since servicing rights are intangible assets, they are subject to the provisions of APB-17 (Intangible Assets). Thus, disclose servicing rights acquired during the current period in a business combination and all servicing rights acquired in prior periods, if material, in accordance with APB-17. APB-17 generally requires that a description of intangible assets, method of amortization, and estimated useful lives be disclosed appropriately in the financial statements or in footnotes. In the event that a large part or all of the amortized cost of an intangible asset is included as an extraordinary charge in the determination of current net income, APB-17 requires that the reasons for the extraordinary deduction be disclosed fully.

NONREFUNDABLE FEES AND COSTS ASSOCIATED WITH ORIGINATING OR ACQUIRING LOANS (FAS-91)

Loan origination fees and commitment fees represent a primary source of revenue to a mortgage banking enterprise. In addition, a mortgage banker may pay a fee to a permanent investor for that permanent investor's commitment to purchase certain specified mortgage loans from the mortgage banker during a specified term.

FAS-91 establishes accounting and reporting standards for nonrefundable fees and costs associated with lending, committing to lend, or purchasing a loan or a group of loans. FAS-91 also specifies the appropriate accounting for fees and initial direct costs associated with leasing transactions.

FAS-91 applies to all types of loans, including debt securities, and to all types of lenders, including banks, thrift institutions, insurance companies, mortgage bankers, and other financial and nonfinancial institutions. FAS-91 does *not* apply to nonrefundable fees and costs associated with originating or acquiring loans carried at market value.

Appendix C of FAS-91 contains the following definitions of terms used in FAS-91:

Commitment fees Fees charged for entering into an agreement that obligates the enterprise to make or acquire a loan or to satisfy an obligation of the other party under a specified condition. For purposes of this Statement [FAS-91], the term *commitment fees* includes fees for letters of credit and obligations to purchase a loan or group of loans and pass-through certificates.

Credit card fees The periodic uniform fees that entitle cardholders to use credit cards. The amount of such fees generally is not dependent upon the level of credit available or frequency of usage. Typically the use of credit cards facilitates the cardholder's payment for the purchase of goods and services on a periodic, as-billed basis (usually monthly), involves the extension of credit, and, if payment is not made when billed, involves imposition of interest or finance charges. For the purposes of this Statement [FAS-91], the term *credit card fees* includes fees received in similar arrangements, such as charge card and cash card fees.

Incremental direct costs   Costs to originate a loan that (*a*) result directly from and are essential to the lending transaction and (*b*) would not have been incurred by the lender had that lending transaction not occurred.

Origination fees   Fees charged to the borrower in connection with the process of originating, refinancing, or restructuring a loan. This term includes, but is not limited to, points, management, arrangement, placement, application, underwriting, and other fees pursuant to a lending or leasing transaction and also includes syndication and participation fees to the extent they are associated with the portion of the loan retained by the lender.

Direct Loan Origination Costs

Under FAS-91, there are only two categories of direct loan origination costs on completed loans that may be offset against any related loan origination fees or any related commitment fees. The first category includes those incremental direct costs that are incurred in originating loan transactions with independent third parties. *Incremental direct costs* are costs that are incurred to originate loans that (*a*) result directly from and are essential to the lending transaction and (*b*) would not have been incurred by the lender if that lending transaction had not occurred (FAS-65, pars. 5 and 6).

The second category includes certain costs that are directly related to the following activities performed by the lender in connection with a loan or a loan commitment:

1. Evaluating the prospective borrower's financial condition
2. Evaluating and recording guarantees, collateral, and other security arrangements
3. Negotiating the terms of the loan
4. Preparing and processing loan documents
5. Closing the transaction

Direct loan origination costs include only that portion of the lender's total employee compensation (including payroll-related fringe benefits) that is directly related to time spent performing the above activities for a specific loan and other costs related to those activities that would not have been incurred if not for that specific loan (FAS-91, par. 6).

All other lending-related costs are expensed by the lender as incurred. Costs related to activities performed by the lender for advertising, soliciting potential borrowers, servicing existing loans, and performing other ancillary activities related to establishing and monitoring credit policies, supervision, and administration are charged to expense as incurred. Employees' compensation and fringe benefits related to those activities, unsuccessful loan origination efforts, and idle time are charged to expense as incurred. Administrative costs, rent, depreciation, and all other occupancy and equipment costs are considered indirect costs and are charged to expense as incurred (FAS-91, par. 7).

Loan Origination Fees

An enterprise may acquire an individual loan contract by originating a loan directly with the borrower or by purchasing a loan from a party other than the borrower. Although the provisions of FAS-91 generally must be applied to each individual loan contract, similar individual loan contracts may be grouped together for the purpose of recognizing net fees or costs and purchase premiums or discounts, provided the amounts do not differ materially from the amounts that would have been recognized on an individual loan-by-loan basis (FAS-91, par. 4).

> **OBSERVATION:** Individual loan contracts that are grouped together must have sufficiently similar characteristics and approximately the same level of net fees or costs to permit the recalculation of the carrying amount of individual loan contracts. Thus, if an individual loan contract in the group is sold, its carrying amount must be recalculable.

Loan origination fees and direct loan origination costs that are incurred on a specific loan are offset against each other and accounted for as follows (FAS-91, par. 27c):

- *If Loan Is Held for Resale* The loan origination fee and the related direct loan origination costs are deferred and recognized at the time the loan is sold.

- *If Loan Is Held for Investment* The net difference between the loan origination fee and the related direct loan origination cost is deferred and recognized over the life of the loan as an adjustment of the yield on the loan. The interest method is used to amortize the net fee or cost over the life of the loan.

Commitment Fees

A loan commitment is a written offer from a lender to a borrower to lend funds for a specific purpose and term. A commitment term may be as short as one week, as long as one year, or longer. A floating rate commitment is one in which the interest rate to be charged on the loan is determined by the prevailing rate of interest at the time the loan is drawn upon. A fixed rate commitment is one in which the interest rate is specified in the commitment.

The recognition of revenue from loan commitment fees varies with the type and substance of the commitment. Income is recognized on all commitments if the loan is not made and the term of the commitment expires. In this event, the lender has no further obligation to perform, and the loan commitment fee is earned (FAS-91, par. 8).

If a loan commitment is exercised before the expiration of the commitment period, the related commitment fee and direct loan origination cost are deferred and recognized over the life of the loan as an adjustment of the yield on the loan. The interest method is used to amortize the net fee or cost over the life of the loan (FAS-91, par. 8).

If only a *remote* (unlikely) possibility exists that a commitment will be exercised based on an enterprise's past experience with similar types of commitments, the commitment fee is recognized as service fee income on a straight-line basis over the commitment period. If the commitment is exercised before the end of the commitment period, the balance of the remaining unamortized commitment fee on the date the commitment is exercised is recognized over the life of the loan as an adjustment of the yield on the loan (FAS-91, par. 8a).

The commitment fee is recognized as service fee income as of the determination date if (*a*) the amount of a commitment fee is determined retrospectively as a percentage of an available line of credit unused in a previous period, (*b*) the percentage is nominal in relation to the stated interest rate on any related borrowing, and (*c*) borrowing will bear a market interest rate at the date the loan is made (FAS-91, par. 8b).

Credit Card Fees

Credit card fees that are charged periodically to cardholders' accounts are considered loan commitments. Under FAS-91, credit card fees are deferred and recognized on a straight-line basis over the period in which the cardholder is entitled to use the card. Other similar card arrangements that involve the extension of credit by a card issuer are accounted for in the same manner (FAS-91, par. 10).

Syndication Fees

Loan syndication fees are recognized upon completion of the syndication loan, unless a portion of the syndication loan is retained by the syndication manager. The yield on the portion of the syndication loan retained by the syndication manager shall not be less than the average yield of all syndication loans, including fees, that are held by the other syndication participants (FAS-91, par. 11).

If the yield on the portion of the loan retained by the syndication manager is less than the average yield to the other syndication participants, the syndication manager shall defer a portion of the syndication fee in an amount that will produce a yield on the portion of the loan retained that is not less than the average yield of the loans held by the other syndication participants (FAS-91, par. 11).

Fees and Costs in Refinancings or Restructurings

A refinanced loan, other than a troubled debt restructuring, as discussed in FAS-15 (Accounting by Debtors and Creditors for Troubled Debt Restructurings), is accounted for as a new loan if its terms are at least as favorable to the *lender* as the terms for comparable loans to other customers with similar collection risks who are not refinancing or restructuring a loan with the lender. This means that the effective yield of the new loan should be at least equal to the effective yield of comparable loans of other customers with similar collection risks who are not refinancing (FAS-91, par. 12).

> **OBSERVATION:** The comparison of effective yields takes into consideration the level of nominal interest rate, commitment and origination fees, and direct loan origination costs. In addition, the comparison of other factors, such as compensating balance arrangements, should be considered when appropriate.

Any unamortized net fees or costs and any prepayment penalties from the original loan are recognized in interest income when the new loan is granted (FAS-91, par. 12).

If the terms of a refinancing or restructuring are not at least as favorable to the lender as the terms for comparable loans to other customers with similar collection risks who are not refinancing or restructuring loans with the lender, or if only minor modifications are made to the original loan contract, the unamortized net fees or costs from the original loan and any prepayment penalties are carried forward as a part of the net investment in the new loan. The investment in the new loan consists of (*a*) the remaining net investment in the original loan, (*b*) any additional amounts loaned, (*c*) any fees received, and (*d*) any direct loan origination costs that are associated with the refinancing or restructuring. The remaining net investment in the original loan consists of the unpaid loan principal, any remaining unamortized net fees or costs, any remaining unamortized purchase premium or discount, and any accrued interest receivable (FAS-91, par. 13).

For the purposes of applying paragraph 30 of FAS-15, fees received in connection with a modification of terms of a troubled debt restructuring shall be applied as a reduction of the recorded investment in the loan. All related costs, including direct loan origination costs, are charged to expense as incurred (FAS-91, par. 14).

Purchase of a Loan or Group of Loans

The initial investment in a purchased loan or group of loans shall include the amount paid to the seller plus any fees paid or less any fees received. The difference between the initial investment in a purchased loan or group of loans and the principal amount at the date of purchase is recognized as an adjustment of the yield over the life of the loan or group of loans. All other costs incurred in connection with acquiring purchased loans or committing to purchase loans are charged to expense as incurred (FAS-91, par. 15).

For the purposes of FAS-91, the initial investment made for loans purchased as a group may be accounted for in the aggregate or may be allocated to the individual loans in the group. The cash flows generated by the payment terms of the underlying loan contracts are used to calculate the constant effective yield necessary to apply the interest method. Prepayments of principal are not anticipated in calculating the constant effective yield, unless the conditions specified by FAS-91 are met. If prepayments of principal are not anticipated and prepayments occur or a portion of the purchased loans is sold, a proportionate amount of the related deferred fees and purchase premium or discount is recognized in income so that the effective interest rate on the remaining portion of loans continues unchanged (FAS-91, par. 16).

Application of the Interest Method

Except for demand loans and revolving lines of credit (see following discussion), the interest method is used to amortize net fees or costs that are required under FAS-91 to be recognized as yield adjustments over the life of their related loans. The interest method produces a constant effective rate of interest income on the remaining net investment in the loan receivable. The net investment in the loan receivable consists of the principal amount of the loan receivable adjusted for any unamortized fees or costs and purchase premium or discount. The amount of periodic amortization is equal to the difference between the stated interest on the outstanding principal amount of the loan receivable and the amount of periodic interest income calculated by the interest method (FAS-91, par. 18).

During those periods in which interest income on a loan is not being recognized because of concerns about realization of the loan principal or interest, deferred net fees or costs are not amortized (FAS-91, par. 17).

Under FAS-91, when the stated interest rate is not constant throughout the term of a loan, the interest method is applied as follows (FAS-91, par. 18):

- *Interest Rate Increases* If the stated interest rate increases during the term of the loan, the amount of interest accrued in the early periods under the interest method will exceed the stated amount of interest for the same periods. In this event, the net investment in the loan could increase to an amount greater than the amount at which the borrower could settle the obligation. Under FAS-91, no interest income is recognized during any period in which the borrower can settle the obligation for less than the amount of the net investment in the loan. In determining the amount at which the borrower can settle the obligation, prepayment penalties are considered only to the extent that such penalties are imposed throughout the loan term.

- *Interest Rate Decreases* If the stated interest rate decreases during the term of the loan, the amount of periodic interest accrued in the early periods under the interest method will be less than the stated amount of interest received for the same periods. In that circumstance, the excess stated interest received during the early periods of the loan is deferred and recognized in those future periods when the constant effective yield under the interest method exceeds the stated interest rate.

- *Interest Rate Varies* The stated interest rate on a loan may be based on the future changes that occur in an independent factor, such as the prime interest rate, the London Interbank Offered Rate (LIBOR), or the U.S. Treasury bill weekly average rate. In this event, the calculation of the constant effective yield necessary to recognize fees and costs is based either on the independent factor in effect at the inception of the loan or on the independent factor as it changes over the life of the loan.

Prepayments of Principal Anticipated

The cash flows generated by the payment terms of the underlying loan contracts are used to calculate the constant effective yield necessary to apply the interest method, and prepayments of principal are not anticipated to shorten the loan term. If an enterprise holds a large number of similar loans for which prepayments are *probable* (likely) and the timing and amount of prepayments can be estimated reasonably, an enterprise may consider estimates of future principal prepayments in calculating the constant effective yield necessary to apply the interest method (FAS-91, par. 19).

> ☛ **PRACTICE POINTER:** To permit the recalculation of their carrying amounts, individual loan contracts that are grouped together must have sufficiently similar characteristics and have approximately the same levels of net fees or costs. Thus, if an individual loan contract in the group is sold, that loan's carrying amount must be recalculable.

If the enterprise anticipates prepayments in applying the interest method and a difference arises between the prepayments anticipated and actual prepayments received, the enterprise shall recalculate the effective yield to reflect the actual payments received to date and the remaining anticipated future payments. In this event, the net investment in the loans is adjusted to the amount that would have existed if the new effective yield had been applied since the acquisition of the loans. The investment in the loans is adjusted to the new balance with a corresponding charge or credit to interest income (FAS-91, par. 19).

Enterprises that anticipate prepayments shall disclose that policy and the significant assumptions underlying the prepayment estimates. The practice of recognizing net fees over the estimated average life of a group of loans shall no longer be acceptable (FAS-91, par. 19).

> **OBSERVATION:** Most of the above information is included in paragraph 19 of FAS-91, which sets forth the conditions that must exist for an enterprise to anticipate prepayments of principal in calculating the constant effective yield necessary to apply the interest method. Absent a reasonably large number of loans with similar characteristics, the FASB believes the reliability of reasonably projecting cash flows is diminished to an unacceptable level (FAS-91, par. 58). When the conditions of paragraph 19 are not met, the FASB concluded that anticipation of prepayments is not appropriate and that recognition of fees and costs and purchase premiums or discounts should be in accordance with the repayment terms provided in the loan contract, with any unamortized amount recognized in income

if and when prepayment occurs. In this respect, the practice of recognizing net fees over the estimated average life of a group of loans shall no longer be acceptable (FAS-91, par. 19).

Demand Loans and Revolving Lines of Credit

A demand loan does not have scheduled repayment terms, because it is payable on demand. A revolving line of credit usually grants the borrower the option of making multiple borrowings up to a specified maximum to repay portions of previous borrowings, and then to reborrow more funds under the same contract. As mentioned above, net fees or costs that are incurred in connection with demand loans and revolving lines of credit are not recognized by the interest method, but are recognized as follows (FAS-91, par. 20):

- *Demand Loans* Net fees or costs on demand loans may be recognized as an adjustment of yield on a straight-line basis over a period that is consistent with (*a*) the understanding between the borrower and lender and (*b*) if no understanding exists, the lender's estimate of the period in which the loan will remain outstanding. At the time the loan is paid in full, any unamortized balance of net fees or costs shall also be recognized in full.

- *Revolving Lines of Credit* Net fees or costs on revolving lines of credit or similar arrangements are recognized in income on a straight-line basis over the period in which the revolving line of credit is active, provided that borrowings are outstanding for the maximum term specified in the loan agreement.

  At the time all borrowings are repaid in full by the borrower, and no additional funds can be borrowed under the terms of the loan agreement, the balance of any unamortized net fees or costs are recognized in income.

  When the loan agreement specifies a repayment schedule for the funds borrowed and no additional funds can be borrowed under the terms of the loan agreement, the interest method is used to recognize any net unamortized fees or costs.

Balance Sheet and Income Statement Classifications

The unamortized balance of loan origination, commitment, and other fees and costs and purchase premiums and discounts that are being recognized as an adjustment of yield is reported on the balance sheet of an enterprise as part of the related loan receivable balance (FAS-91, par. 21).

Amortization of loan origination, commitment, and other fees and costs recognized as an adjustment of yield is reported as part of interest income. For commitment fees and other fees that are being amortized on a straight-line basis over the commitment period or included in income when the commitment expires, amortization is reported in the income statement as service fee income (FAS-91, par. 22).

MORTGAGE BANKING INDUSTRY
IMPORTANT NOTICE FOR 1999

As the 1999 *Miller GAAP Guide* goes to press, the FASB has outstanding an Exposure Draft* titled "Accounting for Mortgage-Backed Securities and Certain Other Interests Retained after the Securitization of Mortgage Loans Held for Sale by a Mortgage Banking Enterprise." This proposed standard would amend FAS-65 (Accounting for Certain Mortgage Banking Activities), as amended by FAS-115 (Accounting for Investments in Debt and Equity Securities).

The term *beneficial interests* is defined as rights to receive all or portions of specified cash inflows to a trust or other entity. This includes senior and subordinated shares of interest, principal, or other cash inflows to "passed through" or "paid through" premiums due to guarantors and residual interests.

Based on the same criteria used for identifying mortgage loans held for sale in accordance with FAS-65, a mortgage loan enterprise would be required to determine whether retained beneficial interests are held for sale at the time the mortgage loans are transferred. Retained beneficial interests that would be held for sale are classified as trading. All other retained beneficial interests would be classified as trading, available-for-sale, or held-to-maturity in accordance with FAS-115.

The FASB has indicated its intent to issue a final statement in the third quarter of 1998.

---

*Note: For in-depth discussion and analysis of this Exposure Draft, read *Miller GAAP Update Service* Commentary Vol. 98, No. 6.

CHAPTER 58
NOT-FOR-PROFIT ORGANIZATIONS

CONTENTS

CHAPTER 58
NOT-FOR-PROFIT ORGANIZATIONS

OVERVIEW

Historically, accounting principles for not-for-profit organizations have been fragmented into industry-specific pronouncements prepared by the AICPA and other groups. The result of this fragmentation is that the practices followed by the various types of organizations were inconsistent. The FASB has undertaken a broad project to address many of these inconsistencies and to attempt to improve the accounting and reporting of not-for-profit entities.

GAAP for not-for-profit organizations are found in the following pronouncements:

FAS-93	Recognition of Depreciation by Not-for-Profit Organizations
FAS-99	Deferral of the Effective Date of Recognition of Depreciation by Not-for-Profit Organizations
FAS-116	Accounting for Contributions Received and Contributions Made
FAS-117	Financial Statements of Not-for-Profit Organizations
FAS-124	Accounting for Certain Investments Held by Not-for-Profit Organizations
FIN-42	Accounting for Transfers of Assets in Which a Not-for-Profit Organization Is Granted Variance Power

> **OBSERVATION:** FAS-124 is amended by FAS-133 (Accounting for Derivative Instruments and Hedging Activities). This is effective for fiscal years beginning after June 15, 1999. FAS-133 applies in interim financial statements for periods that begin after the same date (e.g., the quarter beginning July 1, 1999). FAS-133 is covered in Chapter 16 of the 1999 *Miller GAAP Guide.*
>
> Because the effective date of FAS-133 is delayed as indicated above, and the first calendar year for which FAS-133 will be in effect is the year 2000, the impact of FAS-133 on FAS-124 is not reflected in the 1999 *Miller GAAP Guide.*

CROSS-REFERENCES

1999 MILLER GAAP GUIDE: Chapter 4, "Cash Flow Statement "; Chapter 7, "Contingencies, Risks, and Uncertainties"; Chapter 11, "Depreciable Assets and Depreciation"; Chapter 29, "Investments in Debt and Equity Securities"; Chapter 33, "Nonmonetary Transactions"

1999 MILLER GAAP FOR NOT-FOR-PROFIT ORGANIZATIONS: Chapter 2, "Overview of Current Pronouncements"; Chapter 8, "Overview of External Financial Reporting"

1999 MILLER GAAS GUIDE: Chapter 22, "Audits of Not-for-Profit Organizations"

1999 MILLER GOVERNMENTAL GAAP GUIDE: Chapter 31, "Voluntary Health and Welfare Organizations"; Chapter 32, "Colleges and Universities"; Chapter 33, "Certain Nonprofit Organizations"

1999 MILLER HUD AUDIT PROCEDURES: Chapter 13, "Special Considerations for Not-for-Profit Organizations"

BACKGROUND

Prior to the issuance of FAS-93, the FASB and its predecessors did not provide guidance on the subject of accounting for not-for-profit organizations. The primary sources of GAAP for these entities were contained in the following AICPA Audit Guides and Statements of Position, such as the following:

* Audits of Colleges and Universities
* Audits of Voluntary Health and Welfare Organizations (1974)
* SOP 78-10, Accounting Principles and Reporting Practices of Certain Non-Profit Organizations (1978)
* Audits of Providers of Health Care Services (1990)

FAS-93 extends the provisions of paragraph 5 of APB-12 (Omnibus Opinion—1967) to not-for-profit organizations, requiring disclosure of information about depreciable assets and depreciation. FAS-93 also supersedes (*a*) those sections of the College and University Audit Guide that made depreciation optional and (*b*) SOP 78-10, which exempted certain long-lived tangible assets from depreciation.

FAS-116 and FAS-117 provide for significant changes in the standards for accounting for contributions received and made by all entities, as well as for the format and content of financial statements of all not-for-profit organizations. Accordingly, these two Statements supersede all inconsistent portions of the above AICPA Audit Guides and SOP 78-10. FAS-124 establishes standards of financial accounting and reporting for equity investments with readily determinable fair values and for all investments in debt securities.

FINANCIAL STATEMENTS OF
NOT-FOR-PROFIT ORGANIZATIONS

FAS-117 establishes standards for external financial statements of not-for-profit organizations. It requires not-for-profits to present a statement of financial position, a statement of activities, and a statement of cash flows. Operating cash flows of (*a*) unrestricted net assets, (*b*) temporarily restricted net assets, and (*c*) permanently restricted net assets must be disclosed separately in the statement of activities, and the statement of financial position must distinguish among these three classes of net assets. FAS-117 amends FAS-95 (Statement of Cash Flows), extending its provisions to not-for-profit entities. Not-for-profit entities are also required to disclose expenses by functional classification. Voluntary Health and Welfare Organizations (VHWO) are required, and Other Not-for-Profit Organizations (ONPO) are encouraged, to disclose expenses by natural classification as well.

Financial Statements Required

FAS-117 (*a*) specifies three financial statements that must be present in external financial reports and (*b*) standardizes the approach to the disclosure of operating cash flows from unrestricted, temporarily restricted, and permanently restricted net assets. FAS-117 reviews and discusses the fundamental concepts governing financial reporting; it emphasizes that general-purpose financial statements can be prepared to serve a wide range of user needs, including an assessment of management's stewardship responsibilities to safeguard entity assets and use them for authorized activities. FAS-117 further specifies that the user's primary informational needs include:

- Information about assets and liabilities
- Inflows and outflows of resources

- Cash flows
- Service efforts of the organization

Three financial statements are necessary to provide this information:

- Statement of financial position
- Statement of activities
- Statement of cash flows

FAS-117 also requires specific notes to the financial statements which complete the disclosures relevant to the information needs listed above.

Previous authoritative literature separately addressed financial statements for each type of not-for-profit entity. Table 59-1 illustrates the inconsistencies existing prior to FAS-117.

> **OBSERVATION:** FAS-117 significantly reduces the inconsistencies that appear when comparing the financial statements specified by the AICPA Audit Guides and SOP 78-10. It does not (a) require reporting on a fund basis or (b) use the terms *fund balance* or *changes in fund balance*. Instead, FAS-117 requires presentation of net assets taken as a whole, and reporting of changes in the three net asset categories and the total changes in net assets. The disclosure requirements in FAS-117 do not, however, preclude reporting of individual fund balance changes, although the FASB has stated that the focus of financial reporting is on the entity as a whole.

FAS-117 also emphasizes that the disclosure requirements contained in all authoritative literature that do not specifically exempt not-for-profit entities remain in effect. Another noteworthy aspect of FAS-117 is that the degree of disaggregated fund information is not limited. Preparers have flexibility regarding the amount of detail provided, the order of line items, and the grouping of assets, liabilities, revenues, expenses, and gains. However, it is expected that the exercise of this flexibility will be similar to that used by business enterprises.

FAS-117 does not address issues related to measurement focus, basis of accounting, or measurement methods.

Statement of Financial Position

According to FAS-117, the objective of the statement of financial position is to present information about assets, liabilities, and net assets to facilitate analysis of credit, liquidity, ability to meet obligations, and the need to obtain external financing (FAS-117, par. 9). In particular, FAS-117 emphasizes the need to distinguish between unrestricted assets and permanently or temporarily restricted assets. However, the focus of FAS-117 is on the organization as a whole, and therefore, the total amounts for assets, liabilities, and net assets must be reported (FAS-117, par. 10).

The statement of financial position must provide information about the entity's liquidity. This disclosure can be accomplished (*a*) by sequencing assets in the order of diminishing liquidity or by current/noncurrent classification or (*b*) by sequencing liabilities according to their nearness to maturity (FAS-117, par. 12).

Particular attention should be paid to disclosing which elements of the statement of financial position have donor-imposed restrictions on their use. Restrictions exist because assets cannot be used until a future period, because they may be used only for certain types of expenditures, or because only the investment income from the assets may be used. Internally imposed restrictions made by the governing board of an entity must also be disclosed. Preparers are given flexibility about where to show disclosures about restrictions: on the face of the statements or in notes to the statements (FAS-117, pars. 14 and 15).

The principle difference between previous not-for-profit balance sheets and the format required by FAS-117 is in the net assets (equity) section. Instead of presenting a balance sheet with different columns for each fund, entities present a single, combined balance sheet with a net assets section distinguishing between classes of asset restrictions (FAS-117, par. 13):

Net assets:

Unrestricted	$ xxx
Temporarily restricted	xxx
Permanently restricted	xxx
Total liabilities and net assets	$ xxx

While accounts may be maintained on a fund basis, the above example emphasizes that the reporting focuses on the nature of the restrictions and not on the particular fund in which an asset is carried.

☛ **PRACTICE POINTER:** FAS-117 makes no recommendations about whether the statement of financial position should show assets and liabilities by fund. Indeed, the terms fund and fund balance are not used in FAS-117. In its discussion of the statement of activities, FAS-117 explicitly states that reporting by fund groups is not precluded, but is not a necessary part of external reporting. Accordingly, it seems clear that entities may prepare a statement of financial position that includes disaggregated fund groups, as long as those groups aggregate with net asset classes. It is also important to note that the statement of activities change in net asset class must articulate with the net assets shown on the statement of financial position. FAS-117 emphasizes that information should be simplified, condensed, and aggregated into meaningful totals, and that the statements should not be obscured by unnecessary fund or line item details.

FAS-117 requires that either the statements or the notes thereto give information describing the amount and nature of the various types of restrictions that exist within the major categories of *temporarily restricted* or *permanently restricted* assets. For example, disclosures must be made to show the amount of assets temporarily restricted as to time of availability or as to type of use allowed. Within the category of permanently restricted assets, differentiation should be made regarding assets of an endowment nature, which earn income, and assets that may be part of a collection (of art objects, historical treasures, etc.) (FAS-117, par. 14). Entities may disclose board designations on unrestricted assets either on the face of the statements or in notes (FAS-117, par. 16).

Illustration of Format of Statement of Financial Position

NFP Organization #1
Statement of Financial Position
December 31, 19X1
(in thousands)

Assets:

Cash and cash equivalents	$ 15
Accounts and interest receivable	425
Inventories and prepaid expenses	120
Contributions receivable	600
Short-term investments	300
Assets restricted to investment in land, buildings, and equipment	1,050
Land, buildings, and equipment	12,300
Long-term investments	43,600
Total assets	$58,410

Liabilities and net assets:

Accounts payable	$ 500
Refundable advance	75
Grants payable	100
Notes payable	200
Annuity obligations	330
Long-term debt	900
Total liabilities	$ 2,105

Net assets:

Unrestricted	$23,010
Temporarily restricted (Note B)	4,800
Permanently restricted (Note C)	28,495
Total net assets	56,305
Total liabilities and net assets	$58,410

Statement of Activities

The statement of activities is the operating statement for a not-for-profit entity, analogous to an income statement for a business. This statement combines the revenues, expenses, gains, and losses with the changes in equities. The statement should use the term *changes in net assets* or *changes in equities* to describe equity (FAS-117, par. 18). As noted above, FAS-117 does not use the terms *fund balance* or *changes in fund balance*. Rather, FAS-117 sees net assets or equities as encompassing the whole of the net assets of the entity, while *fund balance* has historically been used to refer only to certain groups of assets. The statement of activities must report the changes in total net assets and the change in each net asset class (FAS-117, par. 19). Thus, an important dimension of reporting operations for not-for-profit entities by FAS-117 is the use of net asset classes instead of fund groups. The requirement is to report changes in unrestricted, temporarily restricted, and permanently restricted net assets in the statement of activities. Therefore, the statement will contain sections for changes in unrestricted net assets (which includes revenues and gains), changes in temporarily restricted net assets (both inflows and outflows), and a line for total changes in net assets.

Illustration of Format of the Statement of Activities

NFP Organization #2
Statement of Activities for Year Ending June 30, 19X5
(in thousands)

Changes in unrestricted net assets:
  Revenues and gains:

Contributions	$ 900
Fees	450
Investment income	25
Other	10
Total unrestricted income	$ 1,385

Net assets released from restrictions:

Program restrictions satisfied	$ 250
Equipment acquisition restrictions satisfied	200
Time restrictions expired	100
Total assets released from restrictions	550
Total support	1,935

Less: Expenses and losses:

Program A	600
Program B	750
Management and administrative	400
Fund-raising expenses	100
Total expenses and losses	1,850
Increase in unrestricted net assets	85

Changes in temporarily restricted net assets:

Contributions	650
Investment income	250
Net assets released from restrictions	(110)
Increase in temporarily restricted net assets	790

Changes in permanently restricted net assets:

Contributions	310
Investment income	80
Net realized and unrealized losses on investments	(550)
Decrease in permanently restricted net assets	(160)

Increase in net assets	715
Net assets, beginning of the year	2,600
Net assets, end of the year	$ 3,315

FAS-117 states that the term *changes in net assets* or *change in equity* should be used in the statement (FAS-117, par. 18).

> ☛ **PRACTICE POINTER:** FAS-117 does not specifically state that the operating statement must be titled "Statement of Activities." The operating statement may be disaggregated into a "Statement of Unrestricted Revenues, Expenses, and Other Changes in Unrestricted Net Assets" (changes in unrestricted net assets in the previous illustration) together with a second statement, "Statement of Changes in Net Assets" (changes in temporarily and permanently restricted net assets in the previous illustration). FAS-117 states unequivocally, however, that the focus must be on net assets and the three major classes of restrictions: unrestricted, temporarily restricted, and permanently restricted.

Several provisions in FAS-117 simplify reporting requirements for restricted resources. When donor-restricted assets are received, they normally are reported as restricted revenues or gains. In cases in which the restrictions are met in the same period the resources are received, it is permissible to classify the receipts as unrestricted, provided the policy is disclosed and applied consistently (FAS-117, par. 21). In addition, gains and losses on investments are unrestricted, regardless of the nature of the restrictions on the investment assets, unless the governing board determines that the law requires that such gains and losses be restricted (FAS-117, par. 22). Finally, FAS-117 allows reporting of subtotals for operating and nonoperating items, expendable and nonexpendable items, or other terms as desired to provide additional detail within the three classes of net assets. This additional detail is not required, but preparers can make such distinctions as they deem necessary (FAS-117, par. 23).

FAS-117 allows the reporting of gains and losses as net amounts if they result from peripheral transactions, such as disposal of assets. In its basis for conclusion, the FASB clearly states that this approach should not be used for special events that are ongoing major activities (FAS-117, par. 25).

Service Efforts   One of the most important disclosures for not-for-profit organizations is information about service efforts. In health-care entities, colleges and universities, and ONPOs, this disclosure is accomplished by arranging the statement of activities along functional lines. For VHWOs, this information traditionally has been contained in the Statement of Functional Expenses. Functional expense disclosure involves informing the statement users of the different types of expenses (e.g., salaries, rent, professional fees) incurred for the major types of programs or functions the entity conducts.

FAS-117 requires all not-for-profits to report expenditures by functional classification and encourages ONPOs, health-care providers, and colleges and universities to also provide disclosure of expenses by natural classification (FAS-117, par. 26).

Health-care providers, colleges and universities, and ONPOs can comply with the functional expense disclosure standards by reporting expenses by function in the statement of activities. VHWOs are required to show expenses by both functional and natural classifications. This must be done by showing, in a matrix-formatted statement, the amounts and types of expenses allocated to programs compared with the amounts spent on administration and fundraising. The matrix format is accomplished by using multiple columns for each type of program or support expenditure while retaining line item expense categories in vertical format. This approach enables statement users to understand the basis of program expenditures and total expenditures and to compare the amounts of expenditures for programs with those for support.

> **OBSERVATION:** While an ONPO's disclosure of expenses in a functional-natural matrix is **not required** by FAS-117, any ONPO whose primary mission is to conduct public service, educational, research, or similar programs will have to disclose these data to fulfill the concept of full disclosure. FAS-117 has an expressed goal of describing the minimum disclosures necessary. Preparers are expected to exercise their professional judgment and go beyond the minimum disclosures as needed.

Proper classification of expenditures between program and support is a fundamental disclosure principle. FAS-117 provides detailed guidance about the appropriate classification of items of a support nature. Supporting activities are divided into three categories: (1) management and general, (2) fund-raising, and (3) membership development (FAS-117, par. 28).

> **OBSERVATION:** FAS-117 specifies that membership development is an element of support activity and should be so reported.
>
> Also, it is important to emphasize that much information about service efforts may not be presentable in the body of the financial statements. Accordingly, preparers should ensure that notes provide full disclosure of information describing service accomplishments, including program descriptions, statistical

data relevant to program inputs and outputs, and narratives about accomplishments.

Statement of Cash Flows

The requirement that the statement of cash flows be included in the reports of all not-for-profit entities removes a significant inconsistency in previous statements. FAS-117 amends several sections of FAS-95 to require that not-for-profit organizations now include a statement of cash flows in their financial statement package. All these changes involve minor wording changes or additions to FAS-95 to clarify that FAS-95 is applicable to not-for-profit entities. As is the case for business entities, either the direct or indirect method may be used to present the cash flow information. The cash flow statement is best presented on an aggregated basis for the three classes of net assets; to do otherwise would result in a very detailed statement.

> ☛ **PRACTICE POINTER:** The statement of cash flows as required by FAS-117 is essentially the same as that required by FAS-95 for business enterprises. The only substantive difference is the substitution of "change in net assets" of the not-for-profit organization for "net income" of the business organization. For that reason, an illustration of the statement of cash flows is not presented here; see the 1999 *Miller GAAP Guide* chapter titled "Cash Flow Statement."

DEPRECIATION

FAS-93 requires that not-for-profit entities recognize the cost of using up the future economic benefits or service potential of long-lived tangible assets by reporting depreciation on those assets. In addition, disclosure of the following items is required for those assets (FAS-93, par. 5):

- Depreciation expense for the period
- Balances of major classes of depreciable assets by nature or function
- Accumulated depreciation by major class or in total
- A description of the methods of depreciation used

Depreciation is not required to be taken on works of art or historical treasures considered to have an indefinite service potential or an extraordinarily long useful life. Verifiable evidence should exist which indicates that (*a*) the historical treasures or works of art are of such value that they are worth preserving perpetually and (*b*) the entity has the capacity to preserve the undiminished service potential of the asset for an indefinite period, and is doing so (FAS-93, par. 6).

CONTRIBUTIONS RECEIVED AND MADE

FAS-116 eliminates inconsistencies in the method of accounting for contributions of cash and other assets, provides guidance for contributions received and contributions given, and promises to give cash or other assets, contributed services, collections of works of art, and gifts with donor-stipulated conditions. FAS-116 also specifies when to recognize the expirations of donor-imposed restrictions. (Prior to the issuance of FAS-116, accounting practices for contributions varied depending on the type of entity involved, the form of the contribution (whether cash, other assets, or services), and the purpose of the gift. To determine the correct practice for a particular financial reporting question, accountants were required to refer to the AICPA Audit Guide or SOP that specifically addressed the type of entity in question). FAS-116 also eliminates inconsistencies in the terminology used to describe the contributions and in the timing of recognition of income for the contributions received and expense for contributions given.

> **OBSERVATION:** FAS-116 is consistent with the general trend in recent standards toward a full accrual approach to the recognition of revenue and expenses, as well as an emphasis on fair market value as a basis for measuring nonmonetary transactions.

FAS-116 applies to contributions of cash, nonmonetary assets, and services, and to promises to give the same. It applies to exchange transactions in which the value received is substantially different from the value given. It does *not* apply to (*a*) bargained arm's-length transactions without a gift element or (*b*) transactions in which the entity is an intermediary or is acting in some form of agency capacity (FAS-116, par. 4).

> **OBSERVATION:** Transfers of assets in which the reporting entity acts as an agent are not contributions. Accordingly, the guidance in AICPA Audit Guides for agency funds continues to be authoritative. However, FAS-116's basis for conclusion provides an analysis that differentiates between receipt of funds by an agent or intermediary and receipt of funds by an entity as a donee. This analysis indicates that the United Way organizations and other federated fund-raising entities are donees, not agents. In instances in which a donor uses an inter-

mediary that acts as an agent to transfer assets to a third-party donee, neither the receipt nor the disbursement by the agent is a contribution received or made. Furthermore, a recipient of funds that makes disbursements in accordance with strict donor instructions (i.e., the recipient has discretion regarding the use made of those funds) is also an agent.

Also expressly excluded from the scope of FAS-116 are transactions that convey only contingent or indirect benefits, such as tax abatements. Transfers of assets from governments to businesses also are not covered by the Statement. The FASB concluded that these transactions pose specific complexities that may require further study, and so excluded them from the scope of the Statement (FAS-116, par. 4).

Contributions in FAS-116 include cash, assets, or services—or unconditional promises to give these in the future (FAS-116, par. 5). The Statement emphasizes the word *promise* and requires verifiable documentary evidence that a promise has been made (FAS-116, par. 6). It also distinguishes between donor-imposed *conditions* and donor-imposed *restrictions* to provide a basis for differentiating the way these items are reported (FAS-116, par. 7). Imposing restrictions on how a gift is to be used does not delay recognition of income or expense. However, recognition of conditional gifts is delayed until the conditions are substantially met.

Contributions Received

FAS-116 generally requires that all unconditional contributions—whether assets, services, or reductions of liabilities—be measured at fair market value on the date received and be recognized currently as revenue or gains (FAS-116, par. 8). FAS-116 takes the current recognition, fair value approach, which embraces the characteristics of relevance and reliability and the qualities of comparability and consistency that are discussed in FASB Concepts Statement 2 (Qualitative Characteristics of Accounting Information).

> **OBSERVATION:** The FASB Statements of Financial Accounting Concepts are intended to provide conceptual guidance in selecting the economic events recognized and reported in financial statements. Concepts Statement 2 examines the characteristics of accounting information and is useful as a reference to understanding the importance attached to various concepts that are emphasized in the FASB Standards.

FAS-116 also provides new guidance in accounting for donated services. In particular, it holds that donated services must create or enhance nonfinancial assets, must be of a specialized nature, must be provided by individuals possessing those skills, and typically need to be purchased, before they can be included as revenue or gains in the operating statement (FAS-116, par. 9). Thus, routine volunteer services requiring no particular expertise may not be reported as contribution revenue. Finally, FAS-116 requires explanatory footnotes that describe the programs or activities for which contributed services are used and other information that aids in assessing the success or viability of the entity (FAS-116, par. 10).

Assets to be included in a collection are recognized as revenue or gains if they are capitalized, but may not be included in revenue or gains if they are not capitalized (FAS-116, par. 13). To be part of a collection, the assets must be (FAS-116, par. 11):

- Held for public exhibition, education, or research rather than held for financial gain

- Protected, preserved, and not used as collateral or otherwise encumbered

- Subject to a policy that requires the proceeds of collection items sold to be reinvested in collections

Entities are encouraged by FAS-116 to capitalize collections retroactively or on a prospective basis; however, capitalization is *optional*. Capitalization of selected items is not permitted (FAS-116, par. 12). An entity that does not capitalize collections is required to disclose additional information as described later in this chapter.

Contribution Standards Applicable Only to Not-for-Profit Entities

FAS-116 requires that not-for-profit organizations distinguish the use of assets and support as *unrestricted, temporarily restricted,* or *permanently restricted* (FAS-116, par. 14). This separation could be accomplished through fund accounting by having a different fund for each of the three classes of net assets. Support that is restricted by donors as being available only in future accounting periods is reported as restricted support (FAS-116, par. 15).

Expiration of donor-imposed restrictions requires reclassification of net assets from restricted to unrestricted, or from a restricted to an unrestricted fund. FAS-117 provides guidance on financial statement format. Since restricted contributions are reported as support in the temporarily restricted class of net assets when first received, they are reclassified in the operating statement when restrictions lapse. FAS-117 supersedes the requirement in SOP 78-10 that support or revenue restricted for certain operating purposes be deferred until the restrictions are met. The classification "capital additions" required by SOP 78-10 for contributions to be added to endowments or plant funds is also superseded. FAS-116 requires that contributions to acquire fixed assets or contributions of plant assets be reported as restricted support over the life of the asset if (*a*) the donor restricts the use and disposition of the asset or (*b*) the donee has a policy of imposing a time restriction that expires over the life of the donated assets or the life of assets acquired with donated money (FAS-116, par. 16).

When restrictions lapse, recognition is required in the statement of activities. In general, a restriction expires when the period of the restriction has lapsed or when an expenditure for an authorized purpose is made. If an expense is incurred for a purpose for which both unrestricted and temporarily restricted net assets are available, the donor-imposed restriction is met (FAS-116, par. 17).

Contributions Made

FAS-116 continues the emphasis on full accrual and fair market value in providing guidance for contributions made. The fair market value emphasis is particularly evident in the directions given for accounting for contributions of nonmonetary assets. Contributions of nonmonetary assets are recognized as expenses and decreases in assets (or increases in liabilities) in the period made. Donors should find the most objective way possible to determine the fair market value of nonmonetary assets (FAS-116, par. 18).

> **OBSERVATION:** Absence of a definite valuation does not justify use of historical cost as a basis for recording the transaction.

FAS-116 states that appraisals, present value of estimated cash flows, net realizable value, and quoted market prices are all acceptable ways of determining the fair market value of donated nonmonetary assets (FAS-116, par. 19). The difference between the book value and the fair market value of donated assets is a realized gain or loss on disposition in accordance with APB-29 (Accounting for Nonmonetary Transactions) (FAS-116, par. 18). When a promise is recorded as a liability, any interest accruals on the promise should be accounted for as contribution expense by the donor and as contribution revenue by the donee. No interest income or expense should be reported (FAS-116, par. 20).

Conditional Promises

Material gifts or promises subject to conditions present accounting problems regarding the appropriate time to recognize the gift revenue or expense. They may also create the need for additional note disclosures describing the nature of the conditions. FAS-116 requires that a promise to give be recognized when the conditions of the promise are substantially met (FAS-116, par. 22). Conditional promises are essentially contingent events. If the contingent event (condition) is remote, it may be ignored and the promise accounted for as an unconditional promise. Otherwise, the gift is not recognized until the conditions have been substantially met. Although FAS-116 requires note disclosure by recipients of conditional promises, there is no similar requirement for the promisor.

Recognition problems also occur for donees when ambiguous wording makes it difficult to determine if conditions for recognition exist. Conditional promises are essentially contingent revenue for the donee. FAS-5 (Accounting for Contingencies) prohibits recognition of contingent gains, and FAS-116 is consistent with FAS-5 in that regard (FAS-116, par. 23). The donee need only prepare a note to the financial statements describing the nature and conditions of the promise and the amounts promised (FAS-116, par. 25). Accrual of conditional promises is not permitted unless the probability that the condition will not lapse is remote. For unconditional promises, the notes to the financial statements should indicate the timing of the cash flows as well as amounts, and should disclose the balances in any allowances for uncollectibles (FAS-116, par. 24).

Additional Disclosures for Collections

As described previously, capitalization of collections by donees is optional. FAS-116 requires that the financial statements disclose the cash flows associated with collections *whether the collection is capitalized or not*. The choice of capitalization policy affects the way that these cash flows are disclosed. If collections are capitalized, the cash consequences of collection activities are a result of routine transactions recorded in the ledger, and would appear in the statement of activities (FAS-116, par. 26).

If collections are *not* capitalized, the cash consequences of collection activities appear in the statement of activities within a separate category called "changes in permanently restricted net assets." This category follows the revenue and expense categories. Substantial descriptive notes regarding the collections are required when collections are not capitalized. These disclosures must include the relative significance of the collection, along with the accounting and stewardship policies followed. In addition, the notes should indicate the values of items sold, lost, or destroyed. A line in the financial statements must refer to the collections note (FAS-116, par. 27).

> **OBSERVATION:** The note disclosures required for uncapitalized collections are extensive. They emphasize that readers of

the financial statements must be made aware of the details of all significant changes in the collection. In particular, statement users must be advised regarding casualty losses, insurance recoveries, accounting policies, and managerial controls in place. The concept of *full disclosure* is very much in evidence in this standard.

ACCOUNTING FOR INVESTMENTS

Definitions and Applicability

FAS-124 establishes standards for certain investments in debt and equity securities. The term *securities* is defined in FAS-124 as a share, participation, or other interest in property or in an enterprise of the issuer or an obligation of the issuer that has the following characteristics:

- It is represented by an instrument issued in bearer or registered form, or it is registered in books maintained to record transfers by or on behalf of the issuer.
- It is of a type that is commonly dealt in on securities exchanges or markets or, when it is represented by an instrument, commonly recognized as a medium for investment in any area in which it is issued or dealt in.
- It is one of a class or series, or by its terms is divisible into a class or series of shares, participations, interest, or obligations.

Equity securities represent an ownership interest in an enterprise (e.g., common and preferred stock) or the right to acquire (e.g., warrants, rights, call options) or dispose of (e.g., put options) an ownership interest at fixed or determinable prices. Convertible debt and preferred stock that by their terms either must be redeemed by the issuing enterprise or are redeemable at the option of the investor are not considered equity securities.

Debt securities represent a creditor relationship with an enterprise. Debt securities include U.S. Treasury securities, U.S. government agency securities, municipal securities, corporate bonds, convertible debt, commercial paper, securitized debt instruments and interest-only and principal-only strips. Preferred stock that must be redeemed by the issuing enterprise or that is redeemable at the option of the investor, as well as collateralized mortgage obligations that are issued in equity form but are required to be accounted for as nonequity instruments regardless of how the instruments are classified, are considered debt securities. The term excludes option contracts, financial futures contracts, forward contracts, lease contracts, and swap contracts.

A final term that is particularly important for understanding FAS-124 is *fair value*. *Fair value* is the amount at which an asset could be bought or sold in a current transaction between willing parties, other than in a forced or liquidation sale. If a quoted market price is available for a financial instrument, the fair value of an investment is the number of trading units multiplied by the market price per unit.

> ☛ **PRACTICE POINTER:** The measurement standards of FAS-124 are applicable for investments in equity securities that have readily determinable fair values (with limited exceptions) and for all investments in debt securities. The exceptions for equity securities that have readily determinable fair values are investments that are accounted for by the equity method and investments in consolidated financial statements.

An equity security is deemed to have a readily determinable fair value if one of the following criteria is met:

1. Sales prices or bid-and-asked quotations for the security are available on a securities exchange registered with the Securities and Exchange Commission (SEC) or in the over-the-counter market. For over-the-counter market prices to qualify, they must be publicly reported by the National Association of Securities Dealers Automated Quotations (NASDAQ) system or by the National Quotation Bureau.

   > **OBSERVATION:** Restricted stock does not meet this criterion. The term *restricted stock* refers to equity securities for which sale is restricted at acquisition by governmental or contractual requirement, other than in connection with being pledged as collateral, except if that requirement terminates within one year or if the holder has the power by contract or otherwise to cause the requirement to be met within one year. Any portion of the security that can be reasonably expected to qualify for sale within one year is not considered restricted.

2. For an equity security traded only in a foreign market, that market is of a breadth and scope comparable to a U.S. market referred to in (1) above.

3. For an investment in a mutual fund, the fair value per share or unit is determined and published and is the basis for current transactions.

Measurement and Recognition Standards

The most important measurement and recognition requirement is that qualifying investments in equity securities (i.e., investments that have readily determinable fair values and are not accounted for by the equity method or consolidation) and all investments in debt securities are to be accounted for at fair value in the statement of financial position (FAS-124, par. 7).

> **OBSERVATION:** FAS-115, which specifies requirements for debt and equity investments for business enterprises, includes a category of investments labeled "held to maturity," which includes only certain debt securities that are accounted for at amortized cost. While the requirements of FAS-115 for business organizations and FAS-124 for not-for-profit organizations are comparable in many respects, an important difference is that FAS-124 does not include a category of investment for debt securities that are **not** measured at fair value as FAS-115 does for business enterprises.

Building on the general reporting requirements of FAS-117 (Financial Statements of Not-for-Profit Organizations), FAS-124 provides the following guidance for the income effects of measuring investments at fair value (FAS-124, pars. 8–10):

- Gains and losses on investments resulting from their measurement at fair value are to be reported in the statement of activities as increases or decreases in unrestricted net assets, unless their use is temporarily or permanently restricted by donor stipulation or by law.

- Dividend, interest, and other investment income is to be reported in the period earned as increases in unrestricted net assets, unless the use of the assets received is limited by donor restrictions.

- Donor-restricted investment income is to be reported as an increase in temporarily restricted net assets or permanently restricted net assets, depending on the nature of the donor restriction.

- Gains and investment income that are limited to specific uses by donor restriction may be reported as increases in unrestricted net assets if the restrictions are met in the same reporting period as the gains and income are recognized (provided the organization has a similar policy for reporting contributions received, applies that policy consistently, and discloses that policy).

FAS-124 also deals with accounting for a *donor-restricted* endowment fund, which is an endowment fund created by a donor stipulating that the gift be invested in perpetuity or for a specified term. Gains and losses on investments in a donor-restricted endowment fund are classified as changes in unrestricted net assets, unless they are temporarily or permanently restricted by a donor's stipulation or by law that extends the donor's restriction to them (FAS-124, par. 11).

> **OBSERVATION:** FAS-117 states that gains and losses on restricted net assets are unrestricted unless the donor stipulates otherwise. Thus, in a permanent endowment three possibilities exist:
>
> 1. Neither the donor nor law stipulates that the endowment restriction extends to gains and losses, in which case the gains and losses are unrestricted income.
> 2. The donor stipulates that gains and losses are to be used for some restricted purpose, often the same purpose for which the endowment income is restricted. In this case, the gains and losses are temporarily restricted income.
> 3. Either the donor or law stipulates that gains and losses become part of the endowment principle. In this case, the gains and losses are permanently restricted income. FAS-124 mentions the situation in which an endowment cannot be sold (i.e., must be held in perpetuity), in which case gains and losses on that security would be permanently restricted income.

As a general rule (i.e., unless otherwise restricted by donor stipulation or law), losses on investments in a donor-restricted endowment reduce temporarily restricted net assets to the extent that donor-imposed temporary restrictions on net appreciation of the fund have not been met before the loss occurs. Further losses reduce unrestricted net assets. If losses reduce the assets of a donor-restricted endowment fund below the level required by donor stipulation or law, gains that restore the fair value of the assets to the required level are classified as increases in unrestricted net assets.

Disclosure Standards

The FAS-124 disclosure requirements can be separated into three classifications.

First, the following information related to the statement of activities is required (FAS-124, par. 14):

1. Composition of investment return, including at least the following components:

   a. Investment income (e.g., dividends, interest)

   b. Net realized gains or losses on investments reported at other than fair value

    c. Net gains or losses on investments reported at fair value

2. A reconciliation of investment return to amounts reported in the statement of activities, if the investment is separated into operating and nonoperating amounts and if an explanation is given of the policy, including any changes in policy, used to make that classification

Second, the following information related to the statement of financial position is required (FAS-124, par. 15):

1. Aggregate carrying amount of investments by major type

2. Basis for determining the carrying amount for investments other than equity securities with readily determinable fair values and all debt securities

3. The method(s) and significant assumptions used to determine fair values (related to the FAS-107 requirement)

4. The aggregate amount of the deficiencies for all donor-restricted endowment funds for which the fair value of the assets at the reporting date is less than the level required by donor stipulations or law

Third, for the most recent period for which a statement of financial position is presented, the nature of and carrying amount for each individual investment or group of investments that represents a significant concentration of market risk are required (related to the FAS-105 requirement) (FAS-124, par. 16).

ACCOUNTING FOR TRANSFERS OF ASSETS

FAS-116 (Accounting for Contributions Received and Contributions Made) includes the following statement (paragraph 4):

> This Statement does not apply to transfers of assets in which the reporting entity acts as an agent, trustee, or intermediary, rather than as a donor or donee.

> **OBSERVATION:** Community foundations and others interested parties asked the FASB whether a transfer by a resource provider to a community foundation or other recipient organization should be accounted for as a contribution received by the organization, in accordance with FAS-116, if the resource provider (1) specifies that the organization distribute the assets contributed, income from the assets, or both to specified third-party beneficiary and (2) grants the organization the unilateral power to redirect the use of the transferred assets away from the specified third-party beneficiary.

Other not-for-profit organizations asked the FASB to expand the project's scope to include a description of the circumstances in which transfers of assets would be contributions received by them even though the assets ultimately would be transferred to another organization. These organizations were concerned that if paragraph 4 of FAS-116 were broadly interpreted, many of their current activities no longer would be accounted for as contributions received and contributions made. In light of these and similar concerns, the FASB decided to address the applicability of paragraph 4 of FAS-116 for all not-for-profit organizations that receive and distribute assets for charitable purposes.

In December 1995, the FASB issued an Exposure Draft titled *Transfers of Assets in Which a Not-for-Profit Organization Acts as an Agent, Trustee, or Intermediary.* That Exposure Draft was intended to clarify the use of the terms *agent, trustee,* and *intermediary.* It would have established specific criteria for determining when an organization was acting as an agent or trustee.

The FASB decided to issue an Interpretation that has a more limited scope than the Exposure Draft. FIN-42 is limited to situations in which the resource provider specifies a third-party beneficiary but permits the recipient organization the unilateral power to redirect the use of the assets to another beneficiary. The FASB plans to consider the other issues raised in its December 1995 exposure draft, as well as those that came up in the comment letters and public hearing, in another phase of the project.

FIN-42 (Accounting for Transfers of Assets in Which a Not-for-Profit Organization Is Granted Variance Power) indicates that an organization that receives assets from a resource provider for purposes of distributing the transferred assets, income from the assets, or both to a specified third-party beneficiary acts as a donee and donor, rather than as an agent, trustee, or intermediary, if the resource provider explicitly grants the recipient organization the unilateral power to redirect the use of the transferred assets to another beneficiary (FIN-42, par. 2). Two terms are particularly important in understanding this statement—*explicitly grants* and *unilateral power.*

Explicitly grants means that the unilateral power granted to the recipient organization to redirect the use of the assets is referred to in the instrument transferring the assets. *Unilateral power* means that the organization receiving the assets can override the resource provider's instructions without the resource provider's approval or the approval by the third-party beneficiary or any other interested party. In other words, the power granted to the organization by the resource provider is specifically stated and unqualified, and requires no additional action to be available to the organization.

NOT-FOR-PROFIT ORGANIZATIONS
IMPORTANT NOTICE FOR 1999

As the 1999 *Miller GAAP Guide* goes to press, the FASB has outstanding an Exposure Draft* titled "Transfers of Assets Involving a Not-for-Profit Organization That Raises or Holds Contributions for Others."

FAS-116 (Accounting for Contributions Received and Contributions Made) indicates that it is not applicable for transfers of assets in which the reporting entity acts as an agent, trustee, or intermediary, rather than as donor or donation recipient. The proposed statement would clarify the terms *agent, trustee,* and *intermediary* and would establish standards for transfers to those organizations and other not-for-profit organizations that serve as recipient organizations. In addition, it would establish standards for organizations that benefit from these transfers.

Generally the standard would require a recipient that accepts cash or other financial assets from a donor and agrees to disburse them to a specified beneficiary to recognize the fair value of the assets as a liability as well as an asset received from the donor. If the donor grants the recipient variance power, or if the recipient and the specified beneficiary have a relationship that causes one organization to have an economic interest in the net assets of the other, the recipient organization would be required to recognize the fair value of any assets it receives as a contribution received in accordance with FAS-116.

The FASB has indicated its plan to issue a final standard in the first quarter of 1999.

---

*Note: For in-depth discussion and analysis of this Exposure Draft, read *Miller GAAP Update Service* Commentary Vol. 98, No. 10.

Oil and Gas Producing Companies

CHAPTER 59
OIL AND GAS PRODUCING COMPANIES

CONTENTS

CHAPTER 59
OIL AND GAS PRODUCING
COMPANIES

OVERVIEW

Oil and gas producing activities of a business enterprise include the acquisition of mineral interests in properties, exploration, development, and production of crude oil, including condensate and natural gas liquids, and natural gas. These are referred to collectively as oil and gas producing activities in the authoritative accounting literature.

GAAP for oil and gas producing activities are established in the following pronouncements:

FAS-19	Financial Accounting and Reporting by Oil and Gas Producing Companies
FAS-25	Suspension of Certain Accounting Requirements for Oil and Gas Producing Companies
FAS-69	Disclosures about Oil and Gas Producing Activities
FAS-89	Financial Reporting And Changing Prices
FIN-33	Applying FASB Statement No. 34 to Oil and Gas Producing Operations Accounted for by the Full Cost Method
FIN-36	Accounting for Exploratory Wells in Progress at the End of a Period

CROSS-REFERENCES

1999 MILLER GAAP GUIDE: Chapter 1, "Accounting Changes"; Chapter 2, "Accounting Policies"; Chapter 5, "Changing Prices"; Chapter 21, "Income Taxes"; Chapter 24, "Interest Costs Capitalized"; Chapter 26, "Interim Financial Reporting"; Chapter 33, "Nonmonetary Transactions"; Chapter 44, "Segment Reporting"

BACKGROUND

GAAP concerning accounting and reporting by oil and gas producing companies are specified in FAS-19, which was to be effective for fiscal years beginning after December 15, 1978. Because the SEC rejected the successful-efforts accounting method, FAS-19 was amended in February 1979 by FAS-25, which suspends FAS-19 by eliminating its effective date for requiring the effective method of accounting. Nonpromulgated GAAP, in the form of industry practices, exist for alternative methods (full-cost, current-value, and discovery-value accounting methods).

FAS-69 establishes comprehensive financial statement disclosures for oil and gas producing companies. FAS-89 (Financial Reporting and Changing Prices) amends FAS-69, eliminating the required disclosure of supplementary current cost information by oil and gas producing companies.

FAS-19 covers only producing activities and specifically excludes the transporting, refining, and marketing of oil and / or gas. In addition, the promulgated GAAP do *not* cover the following:

1. Production of other wasting (nonregenerative) natural resources

2. Production of geothermal steam

3. Extraction of hydrocarbons as a by-product of the production of geothermal steam (Geothermal Steam Act of 1970)

4. Extraction of hydrocarbons from shale, tar sands, or coal

5. Accounting for interest on funds borrowed to finance oil and / or gas producing activities.

FAS-25 specifically states that for the purposes of the promulgated GAAP on accounting changes the provisions of FAS-19 pertaining to the successful-efforts method remain in effect. Since FAS-19 expresses a preference for the successful-efforts method of accounting and rejects other methods, an enterprise that changes to any method other than the successful-efforts method will have the burden of justifying such change (APB-20 [Accounting Changes]).

OIL AND GAS ACCOUNTING TERMINOLOGY

A major challenge in understanding the activities pertaining to the oil and gas producing industry is understanding the specialized terminology that is used. Following is a discussion of several of the key terms that must be understood.

Properties

Properties include any ownership in, or an interest representing the right to, or the participation in, the extraction of oil and / or gas. The term *properties* also includes a nonoperating interest, such as royalty interests, or production interests payable in oil and / or gas. Properties exclude contracts representing the right to purchase oil and / or gas (supply contracts).

Reservoir

Reservoir refers to a separate confined underground formation containing a natural accumulation of producible oil and / or gas.

Field

Field refers to one or more reservoirs related to the same individual geological structural feature and / or stratigraphic condition.

Proved Area

A *proved area* is that part of the property in which proved reserves have been attributed specifically.

Proved Reserves

The following definitions of *proved reserves* are those that were adopted by the SEC on December 19, 1978 (ASR-257), and were current at the date of publication. These definitions were developed by the Department of Energy for its financial reporting purposes.

Proved Oil and Gas Reserves

Proved oil and gas reserves are the estimated quantities of crude oil, natural gas, and natural gas liquids, which geological and engineering data demonstrate with reasonable certainty to be recoverable in future years from known reservoirs under existing economic and operating conditions; that is, prices and costs as of the date the estimate is made. Prices include consideration of changes in existing prices provided only by contractual arrangements, but not on escalations based upon future conditions.

1. Reservoirs are considered proved if economic productibility is supported by either actual production or conclusive formation test. The area of a reservoir considered proved includes (*a*) that portion delineated by drilling and defined by gas–oil and/or oil–water contacts, if any, and (*b*) the immediately adjoining portions not yet drilled, but which can be reasonably judged as economically productive based on available geological and engineering data. In the absence of information on fluid contacts, the lowest known structural occurrence of hydrocarbons controls the lower proved limit of the reservoir.

2. Reserves which can be produced economically through application of improved recovery techniques (such as fluid injection) are included in the *proved* classification when successful testing by a pilot project, or the operation of an installed program in the reservoir, provides support for the engineering analysis on which the project or program is based.

3. Estimates of proved reserves do *not* include the following: (*a*) oil that may become available from known reservoirs but is classified separately as *indicated additional reserve*; (*b*) crude oil, natural gas, and natural gas liquids, the recovery of which is subject to reasonable doubt because of uncertainty as to geology, reservoir characteristics, or economic factors; (*c*) crude oil, natural gas, and natural gas liquids that may occur in undrilled prospects; and (*d*) crude oil, natural gas, and natural gas liquids that may be recovered from oil shales, coal, gilsonite and other such sources.

Proved Developed Oil and Gas Reserves

Proved developed oil and gas reserves are reserves that can be expected to be recovered through existing wells with existing equipment and operating methods. Additional oil and gas expected to be obtained through the application of fluid injection or other improved recovery techniques for supplementing the natural forces and mechanisms of primary recovery should be included as *proved developed reserves* only after testing by a pilot project or after the operation of an installed program has confirmed through production response that increased recovery will be achieved.

Proved Undeveloped Reserves

Proved undeveloped oil and gas reserves are reserves that are expected to be recovered from new wells on undrilled acreage, or from existing wells where a relatively major expenditure is required for recompletion. Reserves on undrilled acreage shall be limited to those drilling units offsetting productive units that are reasonably certain of production when drilled. Proved reserves for other undrilled units can be claimed only where it can be demonstrated with certainty that there is continuity of production from the existing productive formation. Under no circumstances should estimates for proved undeveloped reserves be attributable to any acreage for which an application of fluid injection or other improved recovery technique is contemplated, unless such techniques have been proved effective by actual tests in the area and in the same reservoir.

Wells, Related Equipment, and Facilities

These include the cost of drilling and equipping *completed* wells, access to proved reserves, and facilities for extracting, treating, gathering, and storing the oil and / or gas.

Uncompleted Wells, Equipment, and Facilities

These include the costs of all uncompleted wells, equipment, and facilities.

Support Equipment and Facilities

These include the cost of support equipment and facilities used in producing oil and / or gas. Examples are construction and grading equipment, seismic equipment, vehicles, repair shops, warehouses, camps, and division, district, or field offices.

Stratigraphic Test Wells (Expendable Wells)

These wells generally are drilled without the intention of being completed for production, and are a geological drilling effort to gather information about specific geologic conditions. Core tests and other expendable holes are classified as stratigraphic test wells.

A stratigraphic test well drilled in a proved area is called a *development-type stratigraphic test well*. When drilled on an unproved area, these wells are called exploratory-type stratigraphic test wells.

Service Wells

These are wells drilled to service or support production in an existing field. Examples are injection wells (gas, water, steam, air, etc.) and observation wells.

Development Wells

These are wells drilled for producing oil and/or gas in a proved area known to be productive.

Exploratory Wells

These are wells drilled for exploration or discovery, usually on unproved areas. If a well is classified as a development, service, or stratigraphic test well, it cannot be an exploratory well.

Supply Agreements

These are long-term contracts or similar agreements that represent the right to purchase oil and/or gas, including agreements with foreign governments.

Discovery-Value Accounting

This refers to estimated methods used to determine the value of oil and/or gas reserves, either when discovered or when developed at a later date. The most common estimated valuation methods are:

1. *Current cost*—The amount of cash that currently would have to be paid to acquire the same asset. Similar to current reproduction cost or current replacement cost.

2. *Current exit value in orderly liquidation*—The net amount of cash that would be received in the current orderly liquidation of the asset.

3. *Expected exit value in due course of business*—The nondiscounted amount of cash the asset is expected to bring in the due course of business, less any direct costs incurred in its disposal (net realizable value). Under this method, the oil and/or gas reserves would be valued at an amount equal to the estimated net cash flow from the reserves.

4. *Present value of expected cash flow*—The present value of the expected cash inflows from the reserves, less the present value of the expected related cash outflows to produce the cash inflows. Various different discount rates have been recommended, such as the prime rate, company's cost of capital, and the rate on long-term government bonds.

Under the discovery-value accounting method, property acquisition and other prediscovery expenditures would be deferred and written off when the areas to which the costs apply have been explored and the reserves, if any, determined and valued.

Under FAS-19, the discovery-value accounting method is unacceptable.

Current-Value Accounting

One of the four valuation methods mentioned above in discovery-value accounting is applied on a continuous basis, and oil and/or gas reserves are revalued at each financial statement date using the most current information available. Property acquisition and other prediscovery expenditures are deferred and written off when the areas to which the costs apply have been explored and the oil and/or gas reserves, if any, determined and valued.

The uncertainties and inherent unreliability in using estimates to value oil and/or gas reserves render the discovery-value and current-value methods undesirable.

Under FAS-19, the current-value method is unacceptable.

Full-Cost Accounting

Full-cost accounting considers all costs of unsuccessful and successful property acquisition and exploration activities as a cost of discovering reserves. Thus, all costs are considered an integral part of the acquisition, discovery, and development of oil and/or gas reserves; and costs that cannot be directly related to the discovery of specific reserves are capitalized nonetheless.

In full costing, a country usually is selected as a cost center, and all costs incurred within the cost center are capitalized and subsequently amortized against the proved oil and/or gas reserves produced within the cost center by either the units of production or gross revenue methods. There is a limitation that capitalized costs of a cost center should not exceed the present value of the oil and/or gas reserves of the same cost center.

Under FAS-19, the full-cost accounting method is unacceptable. Because FAS-25 suspends the effective date of FAS-19, however, many companies continue to apply the full-cost method.

The promulgated rules for the full cost accounting method are contained in Rule 4-10 of Regulation S-X of the Securities and Exchange Commission (SEC). The Rule is titled "Financial Accounting and Reporting for Oil and Gas Producing Activities Pursuant to the Federal Securities Laws and the Energy Policy and Conservation Act of 1975." Additional interpretations of the rules are contained in "Topic 12: Oil and Gas Producing Activities" of the SEC's Staff

Accounting Bulletins and Sections 405 and 406 of the SEC's Codification of Financial Reporting Releases.

Successful-Efforts Costing

A cause-and-effect relationship between costs incurred and the discovery of specific reserves is required. The incurrence of a cost with no identifiable future benefit usually is expensed under the successful-efforts method.

Under the successful-efforts method of accounting, certain costs are capitalized while others are expensed when incurred. The types of costs capitalized include:

1. Mineral interests in properties, which include fee ownership or a lease, concession, or other interest representing the right to extract oil or gas, including royalty interests, production payments payable in oil and gas, and other nonoperating interests in properties operated by others

2. Wells and related equipment and facilities, the costs of which include those incurred to:

   a. Obtain access to proved reserves and provide facilities for extracting, treating, gathering, and storing the oil and gas, including the drilling and equipping of development wells (whether those wells are successful or unsuccessful), and service wells

   b. Drill and equip exploratory wells that have found proved reserves

3. Support equipment and facilities used in oil and gas producing activities

4. Uncompleted wells, equipment, and facilities

Costs other than the above incurred in oil and gas producing activities are charged to expense. Examples include geological and geophysical costs, the costs of carrying and retaining undeveloped properties, and the costs of drilling exploratory wells that do not find proved reserves.

Under successful-efforts costing, all property acquisition costs are capitalized when incurred, though different methods subsequently may be used to dispose of these costs by independent oil and gas exploration companies but not by integrated companies.

Under present tax law, intangible drilling costs generally are deductible as an expense in the year incurred.

FAS-19 generally is based on the successful-efforts costing method.

LEGAL BACKGROUND

In 1975, Congress enacted the Energy Policy and Conservation Act. Title V, Section 503, of the act grants the following powers to the Securities and Exchange Commission:

> ...to prescribe rules applicable to persons engaged in the production of crude oil or natural gas, or make effective by recognition, or by other appropriate means indicating a determination to rely on, accounting practices developed by the Financial Accounting Standards Board, if the Securities and Exchange Commission is assured that such practice will be observed by persons engaged in the production of crude oil or natural gas to the same extent as would result if the Securities and Exchange Commission had prescribed such practices by rule.

In addition, the act requires that certain information about national energy be compiled for both domestic and foreign operations, and consist of the following data:

1. The separate calculation of capital, revenue, and operating cost information pertaining to:

    a. Prospecting

    b. Acquisition

    c. Exploration

    d. Development

    e. Production

    The calculation of capital, revenue, and operating cost information includes geological and geophysical costs, carrying costs, unsuccessful exploratory drilling costs, intangible drilling and development costs on productive wells, the cost of unsuccessful development wells, and the cost of acquiring oil and gas reserves by means other than development. Any such calculation shall take into account disposition of capitalized costs, contractual arrangements involving special conveyance of rights and joint operations, differences between book and tax income, and prices used in the transfer of products or other assets from one person to any other person, including a person controlled by, controlling, or under common control with such person.

2. The full presentation of the financial information of persons engaged in the production of crude oil or natural gas, including:

   a. Disclosure of reserves and operating activities, both domestic and foreign, to facilitate evaluation of financial effort and result

   b. Classification of financial information by function to facilitate correlation with reserve and operating statistics, both domestic and foreign

3. Such other information, projections, and relationships of collected data as shall be necessary to facilitate the compilation of such base data

Securities Act Release No. 5706, issued on May 12, 1976, requires that certain information relating to oil and/or gas properties, reserves, and production be disclosed in registration statements, proxy statements, and reports filed with the Commission.

Securities Act Release No. 5801, issued on January 31, 1977, states that the Commission, consistent with its policy established in Accounting Series Release No. 150, will look to the FASB to provide leadership in setting forth accounting standards and principles for the producers of oil and/or gas.

Securities Act Release No. 5837, issued on June 30, 1977, solicits comments from interested parties with respect to the Commission's responsibility under the Energy Policy and Conservation Act of 1975. The release also states that the Commission will attempt to coordinate the reporting requirements promulgated by the FASB in its own disclosure and reporting requirements.

Securities Release No. 5861 and Securities Release No. 5877, issued on August 31, 1977, and October 26, 1977, respectively, generally adopt as a Commission regulation the accounting standards and disclosures that are contained in FAS-19. These releases apply to filings with the SEC and to reports filed with the Department of Energy.

Securities Release No. 5878, also issued on October 26, 1977, deals with replacement cost information (ASR-190) for certain registrants. In lieu of replacement cost information, the release requires the disclosure of the present value of future net revenues estimated to be received in the future from the production of proved oil and/or gas reserves. This release becomes effective for filings covering fiscal years ending after December 24, 1978.

On August 31, 1978, the SEC issued ASR-253 which included the following:

1. Adopted the successful-efforts accounting method and disclosure requirements of FAS-19

2. Indicated that a form of full-cost accounting for oil and gas producing companies will be developed by the SEC as an acceptable reportable alternative for the SEC

3. Concluded that the full-cost and successful-efforts methods based upon historical costs fail to provide sufficient information for gas and oil producing companies, and that the SEC would take steps to develop an accounting method based on current valuation of proved oil and gas reserves

4. Adopted disclosure rules for certain information regardless of the accounting method used

5. Adopted the definition of *proved reserves*, which differed from that prescribed by FAS-19

On December 19, 1978, the SEC issued ASR-257 and ASR-258, which included the following:

1. Reaffirmed the conclusions the SEC prescribed in ASR-253 (enumerated above)

2. Adopted definitions of proved reserves developed by the Department of Energy for its reporting purposes

3. Described the form of full-cost accounting for gas and oil producing companies that would be acceptable as an alternative to the successful-efforts method for reporting to the SEC

In 1982, the SEC issued ASR-300, adopting the disclosure requirements of FAS-69, discussed later in this chapter. The SEC issued Financial Reporting Release (FRR) 14 in 1983 and FRR-17 in 1984, clarifying the full-cost method of accounting.

ACCOUNTING PRINCIPLES—BASIC CONCEPTS

FAS-19 does not address the transporting, refining, and marketing aspects of oil and/or gas production. The functions covered by the promulgated GAAP are (*a*) acquisition of properties, (*b*) exploration, (*c*) development, and (*d*) production.

Generally, the incurrence of a cost that results in the acquisition of an asset is capitalized and subsequently amortized, unless the asset becomes impaired or worthless, in which case it is reduced in value or written off (FAS-19, par. 12). Costs that do not result in the acquisition of an asset, such as carrying costs of undeveloped properties, geological and geophysical (G&G) costs, and the costs of drilling exploratory wells that do not find proved reserves, are charged to expense when incurred (FAS-19, par. 13).

Costs incurred to operate and maintain producing wells, related equipment, and facilities become part of the total production costs (also known as *lifting costs*). The other part of production costs comprise depreciation, depletion, and amortization of the costs capitalized as property acquisition, exploration, and development costs.

Before the accounting treatment of a cost can be determined, it must be first classified as a cost of acquiring properties, exploring, developing, or producing. For example, support equipment and labor can be classified as any of the functional activities in the oil and gas industry. Labor used in developing a producing well is capitalized and subsequently amortized, whereas labor costs incurred in operating producing wells become part of production costs.

The following is a brief discussion of the accounting principles and basic concepts involved in each function of the oil and gas industry:

Acquisition of Properties

Acquisition of properties includes all costs to purchase, lease, or otherwise acquire a proved or unproved property, including brokers' fees, legal fees, and recording fees, and other costs incurred in acquiring properties (FAS-19, par. 15). The acquisition of properties may include the transfer of all or part of the rights and responsibilities of operating the properties (operating interest) or none of the rights or responsibilities of operating (nonoperating interest).

If the interest in the property acquired is in substance a borrowing repayable in cash or its equivalent, it is treated as a borrowing and not as the acquisition of an interest in the property.

If part or all of an interest in a property is sold and substantial uncertainty exists in the recovery of the applicable costs involved or if the seller has a substantial future performance obligation to drill a well or to operate the property without reimbursement, no gain is recognized on these types of conveyances.

As in all nonmonetary exchanges of like property, gain or loss is recognized only to the extent of any *boot* received, as follows:

1. Exchange of assets used in oil and gas producing activities for other assets used in oil and gas producing activities

2. A joint pooling of assets to find, develop, or produce oil and / or gas from a particular property

Unproved properties are reclassified to proved properties when proved reserves are attributed to the property. Periodic assessment of unproved properties is made to determine whether they have been impaired. Impairment is likely if a dry hole has been drilled and there are no future plans to continue drilling, or if the end of a lease approaches and drilling has not commenced on the property. Losses for impairment of unproved properties are made by a charge to income and a credit to a valuation account in the year the impairment occurs (FAS-19, par. 28).

If an unproved property is abandoned or becomes worthless, all related capitalized costs are charged first against any related allowance for impairment account, and any excess charged to income of the period that the unproved property is abandoned or becomes worthless (FAS-19, par. 40). If only a small portion of an amortization base is abandoned or becomes worthless, then that portion is considered fully amortized and its cost charged to the accumulated depreciation, depletion, or amortization account, and no gain or loss is recognized (FAS-19, par. 41).

The unit-of-production method is used to amortize (deplete) all capitalized property acquisition costs of proved properties. As stated previously, this amortization (depletion) becomes part of the production costs (lifting costs). Amortization rates should be reviewed at least annually and revisions should be accounted for prospectively as changes in accounting estimates as described by APB-20 (FAS-19, par. 30).

In proved properties that contain both oil and gas reserves, a common unit of measure based on the approximate relative energy content of the oil and gas should be used as the unit of production in the current period. Amortization is then based on the converted common unit of measure. In the event that either oil or gas dominates the content of both reserves and current production, unit-of-production amortization may be computed on the dominant mineral only (FAS-19, par. 38).

Exploration

Exploration includes all costs relating to the search for oil and/or gas reserves, including depreciation and applicable costs of support equipment and facilities, drilling exploratory wells, and exploratory-type stratigraphic test wells. Exploration costs may be incurred before the actual acquisition of the property, and in this sense they are sometimes referred to as *prospecting costs* (FAS-19, par. 16).

Some exploration costs do not represent the acquisition of an identifiable asset, and are therefore charged directly to expense when incurred. The cost of carrying and maintaining undeveloped properties is an expense, because such costs do not increase the potential that the properties will contain proved reserves. Examples of these types of expenses are delay rentals, taxes on properties, legal costs, and loan maintenance (FAS-19, par. 17).

Geological, topographical, and geophysical studies (G&G costs) and related salaries and other expenses also are expensed, because they do not represent the acquisition of an identifiable asset. The studies frequently are made before the acquisition of the property and represent research or information costs. More often than not, G&G costs are incurred and the properties are never acquired (FAS-19, par. 18).

Pending the determination of whether a well has proved reserves, all costs of drilling exploratory wells are capitalized and are classified as uncompleted wells, equipment and facilities. The disposition of exploratory wells and their related costs usually is made shortly after completion, and if the well has proved reserves, the costs are capitalized and reclassified as wells, related equipment and facilities. If no proved reserves are found, however, the capitalized costs of drilling the well, less any salvage value, are charged to expense (FAS-19, par. 19). If an exploratory well is in progress at the end of an accounting period and the well is determined not to have found proved reserves before the financial statements for the period are issued, the costs incurred through the end of the period, net of any salvage value, should be charged to expense for that period (FAS-19, par. 33). However, previously issued financial statements are not restated retroactively to account for subsequently learned information (FIN-36, par. 2).

Sometimes an exploratory well cannot be classified as having found proved reserves on completion of drilling, because justification for major capital expenditures, such as a trunk pipeline, must be made, which may depend on the success of additional exploratory wells in the same area. In this event, the exploratory well and its related costs may be carried on the books as an asset for a period not exceeding one year, providing both of the following conditions are met (FAS-19, par. 31):

1. A sufficient quantity of reserves was found to justify the completion as a producing well if the required capital expenditures are made.

2. Drilling of other exploratory wells has commenced or is firmly planned for the near future.

If the above conditions are not met, the exploratory well and all its related costs are charged to expense.

Costs incurred for an exploratory well or stratigraphic test well, net of salvage value, are charged to expense for the period, if the following conditions exist (FAS-19, par. 34):

1. The well is in progress (uncompleted) at the end of the period.

2. A determination has been made prior to the issuance of the financial statements that the well has not located any proved reserves. In other words, the well has proved to be dry.

FIN-36 requires that only the costs incurred through the end of the reporting period, net of any salvage value, need be charged to expense. The amount charged to expense should include costs incurred during the current period, as well as costs that were incurred and capitalized in prior periods (FIN-36, par. 2). Thus, estimated costs to complete the uncompleted "dry well," if necessary, should not be accrued, since they will be charged to expense when incurred in subsequent periods.

The unit-of-production method is used to amortize all capitalized exploration costs, including support equipment and facilities. As stated previously, this amortization becomes part of the cost of production (lifting costs) (FAS-19, par. 35).

An enterprise may conduct G&G studies and other exploration activities on a property owned by another party. In exchange, the enterprise is contractually entitled to receive an interest in the property if proved reserves are found or to be reimbursed by the owner for the G&G and other costs incurred if provided reserves are not found. The enterprise conducting the G&G studies and other exploration activities shall account for those costs as a receivable when they are incurred. If proved reserves are found, the receivable then becomes the cost of the proved property acquired (FAS-19, par. 20).

Development

Development includes all costs incurred in creating a production system of wells, related equipment, and facilities on proved reserves so that the oil and/or gas can be produced (lifted). Development costs are associated with specific proved reserves; exploration costs are associated with unproved reserves. The cost of building a road to gain access to proved reserves is a development cost, as is the cost of providing facilities for extracting, treating, gathering, and storing the oil and/or gas. Development costs also include depreciation and operating costs of support equipment and facilities used in development activities (FAS-19, par. 21).

Development costs are associated with previously discovered proved reserves with known future benefits. Therefore, under promulgated GAAP, unsuccessful development wells (dry holes) are capitalized as a cost of creating the overall production system for proved reserves (FAS-19, par. 22).

The unit-of-production method is used to amortize (deplete) all capitalized development costs. As stated previously, this amortization (depletion) becomes part of the production costs (lifting costs). Amortization rates should be reviewed at least annually, and revisions should be accounted for prospectively as changes in accounting estimates (APB-20) (FAS-19, par. 35).

In proved properties that contain both oil and gas, a common unit of measure based on the approximate relative energy content of the oil and gas should be used as the unit of production for the purpose of determining the number of units produced in the current period. Amortization is then based on the converted common unit of measure. In the event that either oil or gas dominates the content of both reserves and current production, unit-of-production amortization may be computed on the dominant mineral only (FAS-19, par. 38).

Production

Production includes all costs incurred in lifting the oil and/or gas to the surface, and gathering, treating, field processing, and field storage. FAS-19 provides that the production function terminates at the outlet valve on the leased property or the field production storage tank, or under unusual circumstances, at the first point at which the oil and/or gas is delivered to a main pipeline, refinery, marine terminal, or a common carrier (FAS-19, par. 23).

Production costs include labor, fuel, and supplies needed to operate the developed wells and related equipment, repairs, property taxes, and insurance on proved properties, and wells, related equipment, and facilities (FAS-19, par. 24).

Costs incurred to operate and maintain the production system become part of the total production costs (lifting costs). The other part of the production costs consists of the depreciation, depletion, and amortization of the costs capitalized as property acquisition, exploration, and development costs (FAS-19, par. 25).

Support Equipment and Facilities

Costs for support equipment and facilities may be incurred for exploration, development, or production activities. Generally, these costs are capitalized and depreciated over their estimated useful lives or the life of the lease, whichever is appropriate. The depreciation expense and related costs of operating the support equipment and facilities are charged to the related activity (exploration, development, or production). When support equipment and facilities are utilized for more than one activity, the depreciation expense and operating costs should be allocated between the activities on a reasonable basis (FAS-19, par. 26).

Residual salvage values and estimated costs of dismantlement, restoration, and abandonment should be considered in determining depreciation and amortization rates (FAS-19, par. 37).

Balance Sheet—Subsequent Information

GAAP require that information that becomes available subsequent to the balance sheet date and prior to the issuance of the financial statements should be taken into consideration in determining conditions that existed at the balance sheet date. The determination at the balance sheet date of whether an exploratory well has found proved reserves, the impairment of unproved properties, and similar conditions may be based on information that becomes available subsequent to the balance sheet date and prior to the issuance of the financial statements (FAS-19, par. 39).

MINERAL CONVEYANCES AND RELATED TRANSACTIONS

Mineral interests in properties frequently are conveyed to others. Conveyances of those interests may involve the transfer of all or part of the rights and responsibilities of operating a property. The transferer may or may not retain an interest in the oil and gas produced that is free of the responsibilities and costs of operating the property (i.e., a nonoperating interest). A transaction may involve the transfer of a nonoperating interest to another party and the retention of the operating interest (FAS-19, par. 42).

Certain transactions, referred to as *conveyances*, are in substance borrowings repayable in cash or its equivalent, and are accounted for as borrowings. In the following types of conveyances, gain or loss should not be recognized at the time of the conveyance:

1. A transfer of assets used in oil and gas producing activities in exchange for other assets also used in oil and gas producing activities

2. A pooling of assets in a joint undertaking intended to find, develop, or produce oil or gas from a particular property or group of properties (FAS-43, pars. 43 and 44)

In the following types of conveyances, gain shall not be recognized at the time of the conveyance:

1. A part of an interest owned is sold and substantial uncertainty exists about recovery of the costs applicable to the retained interest.

2. A part of an interest is sold and the seller has a substantial obligation for future performance, such as an obligation to drill a well or to operate the property without proportional reimbursement for that portion of the drilling or operating costs applicable to the interest sold (FAS-19, par. 45).

For conveyances other than the types listed in the previous two paragraphs, gain or loss shall be recognized at the time of the conveyance unless there are other aspects of the transaction that would prohibit such recognition under generally accepted accounting principles for all enterprises (FAS-19, par. 46).

INCOME TAX CONSIDERATIONS

Deferred income taxes should be recognized for items that enter into the determination of pretax accounting income and taxable income in different periods (temporary differences). A future tax benefit arising from an excess of statutory depletion over cost depletion, however, is not treated as a temporary difference, but is accounted for as a permanent difference in the period in which it is allowed as a deduction for income tax purposes (FAS-19, par. 62).

As discussed in FAS-109 (Accounting for Income Taxes), deferred tax liabilities and assets are required to be recognized for the expected future tax consequences of events that have been included in the financial statements or tax returns. Deferred tax liabilities and assets are established to reflect the future tax consequences of carryforwards and credits as well as differences between the financial statements and tax bases of assets and liabilities using the provisions of enacted tax laws and rates in effect for the year in which the differences are expected to reverse.

DISCLOSURES

Most of the disclosure requirements of FAS-69 pertain to *publicly held enterprises,* as that term is defined in FAS-89 (Financial Reporting and Changing Prices). FAS-89 defines a *public enterprise* as "a business enterprise (*a*) whose debt or equity securities are traded in a public market on a domestic stock exchange or in a domestic over-the-counter market (including securities quoted only locally or regionally), or (*b*) that is required to file financial statements with the Securities and Exchange Commission. An enterprise is considered to be a public enterprise as soon as its financial statements are issued in preparation for the sale of any class of securities in a domestic market."

General Disclosures

Interim financial reports are not required to contain the disclosures mandated by FAS-69. However, interim financial reports are required to contain disclosure of favorable or adverse events concerning an enterprise's proved oil and gas reserves. A major oil or gas discovery is the type of favorable event that must be disclosed in interim financial reports. A major accident, such as a fire, that consumes significant quantities of proved oil and gas reserves is the type of adverse event that must be disclosed in interim financial reports (FAS-69, par. 9).

The method of accounting for costs incurred in oil and gas producing activities and the manner of disposing of capitalized costs must be disclosed fully by both public and nonpublic enterprises that are engaged in oil and gas producing activities (FAS-69, par. 6).

☛ **PRACTICE POINTER:** Disclosure of accounting policies is required by APB-22 (Disclosure of Accounting Policies). Both the accounting principle and the method of applying the principle should be disclosed, but accounting principles and their methods of application in the following areas are considered particularly important:

a. A selection from existing acceptable alternatives

b. The areas that are peculiar to a specific industry in which the entity operates

c. Unusual and innovative applications of GAAP

Any, or all, of these may come into play in applying APB-22 by oil and gas producing companies.

When a complete set of annual financial statements is presented, publicly held enterprises that have significant oil and gas producing activities shall also disclose, as supplementary information to the financial statements, the following information relating to gas and oil producing activities (FAS-69, par. 7):

a. Proved oil and gas reserve quantities

b. Capitalized costs

c. Costs incurred for property acquisition, exploration, and development activities

d. Results of operations

e. A standardized measure of discounted future net cash flows

The above supplementary information should be disclosed in complete sets of annual financial statements by publicly traded enterprises that have significant oil and gas producing activities. The test of whether an enterprise has significant oil and gas producing activities must be applied separately for each year that a complete set of annual financial statements is presented (FAS-69, par. 8).

Generally, an enterprise has significant oil and gas producing activities if its oil and gas producing activities qualify as an industry segment under the provisions of FAS-14. Thus, if an enterprise satisfies one or more of the following tests, it is considered as having significant oil and gas producing activities (FAS-69, par. 8):

1. Its *revenue* from oil and gas producing activities (defined below) is at least 10% of the total revenue from all of the enterprise's *industry segments* (defined below).

2. Its operating profit from oil and gas producing activities is at least 10% of the total operating profit of all of the enterprise's industry segments that reflect operating profits.

3. Its operating loss from oil and gas producing activities is at least 10% of the total operating losses of all of the enterprise's industry segments which reflect operating losses.

4. Its *identifiable assets* (defined below) relating to oil and gas producing activities are at least 10% of all of the identifiable assets of all of the enterprise's industry segments.

The following definitions are used in applying the above tests for significant oil and gas producing activities:

Revenue

Revenue includes sales to unaffiliated organizations in connection with (*a*) networking interests, (*b*) royalty interests, (*c*) oil payment interests, and (*d*) net profit interests of the reporting enterprise. Intercompany sales or transfers are also included as revenue, based on appropriate market prices, which are equivalent to an arm's length transaction at the point of delivery from the producing unit. Excluded from gross revenue are (*a*) royalty payments and (*b*) net profit disbursements. Production or severance taxes are included as part of production costs and are not deducted in determining gross revenue.

Industry Segment

An *industry segment* is a component of an enterprise that sells its products or services primarily to outsiders for a profit.

Identifiable Assets

Indentifiable assets are tangible and intangible assets used exclusively by a segment of an enterprise, or the allocated portion of assets used jointly by more than one segment. General corporate assets are not allocated to segments and loan and investment accounts are not considered assets unless income from them is included in segment profit or loss.

Goodwill, less any amortization, is included in an industry segment's identifiable assets. An industry segment's identifiable assets are computed net of any valuation account, such as allowance for doubtful accounts, accumulated depreciation, etc.

Loans and advances between industry segments whose principal operations are financial (banking, leasing, insurance, etc.) and whose income is derived from such loans and advances, should be included as an identifiable industry segment asset.

Disclosures—Proved Oil and Gas Reserve Quantities

Publicly held enterprises disclose, as supplementary information to each of their annual financial statements presented, the net quantities of proved reserves and proved developed reserves of crude oil and natural gas (FAS-69, par. 10).

The net quantities of crude oil, which includes condensate and natural gas liquids, are stated in barrels. The net quantities of natural gas are stated in cubic feet (FAS-69, par. 15). Net quantities of crude oil and gas, if significant, are reported for the company's home country and each foreign geographic area (country or group of countries) in which significant reserves are located (FAS-69, par. 12).

In determining net quantities, the following rules apply:

1. Net quantities exclude oil and gas subject to purchase under long-term supply, purchase, or similar agreements including those with governments. If the company participates in the operation of the oil and / or gas producing properties or otherwise acts as a producer, however, this information is reported separately (see below) (FAS-69, par. 13).

2. Companies issuing consolidated financial statements include all the net quantities attributable to the parent company and all the net quantities attributable to the consolidated subsidiaries, whether or not wholly owned (FAS-69, par. 14).

    A significant portion of the net quantities at the end of the year may be attributable to a consolidated subsidiary that has a significant minority interest. In this event, disclosure of these facts and the approximate portion attributable to the consolidated subsidiary is required by FAS-69.

3. Net quantities of investments that are proportionately consolidated include the proportionate share of the investee's net quantities of oil and gas reserves (FAS-69, par. 14).

4. Net quantities of investments that are accounted for by the equity method are excluded. (This information is reported separately; see below) (FAS-69, par. 14).

5. Net quantities include any from royalty interest owned if the information is available. If the information is not available, a statement of that fact must be made and net quantities *produced* attributable to the royalty interest must be disclosed for each period presented (FAS-69, par. 10).

6. Net quantities include operating and nonoperating interest in properties (FAS-69, par. 10).

7. Net quantities do not include interest of others in properties (FAS-69, par. 10).

Beginning and ending net quantities in proved reserves and proved developed reserves of crude oil (including condensate and natural gas liquids) and natural gas and net changes during the year must be reported at the end of each year in which a complete set of financial statements is presented.

Illustration of Disclosing Net Quantities

(Oil in thousands of barrels, natural gas in millions of cubic feet)	Total Worldwide		United States		Foreign Geographic Area A		Foreign Geographic Area B		Other Foreign Geographic Areas	
	Oil	Gas	Oil	Gas	Oil	Gas	Oil	Gas	Oil	Gas
Proved developed and undeveloped reserve:										
1. Beginning of year	765	4,096	500	2,300	120	1,416	125	360	20	20
2. Revisions of previous estimates	10	(33)	(32)	25	25	(16)	20	(45)	(3)	3
3. Improved recovery	5	10	3	10	2	0	0	0	0	0
4. Purchases of minerals-in-place	7	5	5	5	2	0	0	0	0	0
5. Extensions, discoveries, and other additions	77	305	65	185	10	80	1	35	1	5
6. Production	(109)	(433)	(76)	(250)	(12)	(135)	(18)	(40)	(3)	(8)
7. Sales of minerals-in-place	(4)	(3)	(4)	(3)	0	0	0	0	0	0
8. End of year	751	3,947	461	2,272	147	1,345	128	310	15	20
9. Proved developed reserves:										
Beginning of year	693	3,320	500	1,800	80	1,200	105	300	8	20
End of year	668	3,295	475	1,875	78	1,150	110	250	5	20

	Total Worldwide		United States		Foreign Geographic Area A		Foreign Geographic Area B		Other Foreign Geographic Areas	
	Oil	Gas	Oil	Gas	Oil	Gas	Oil	Gas	Oil	Gas
Oil and gas applicable to long-term supply agreements with foreign governments or authorities in which the company acts as producer:										
10. Proved reserves at end of year	—	—	—	—	—	—	—	—	125	—
11. Received during the year	—	—	—	—	—	—	—	—	25	—
12. Company's proportionate interest in reserves of investees accounted for by the equity method, end of year	—	—	—	—	6	90	—	—	—	—

An explanation of each item in the chart follows:

1. **Beginning of year**   The total net quantities at the beginning of the year

2. **Revisions of previous estimates**   Upward or downward revision of proved reserves resulting from new information or changes in economic factors

3. **Improved recovery**   Changes during the year resulting from new recovery techniques

4. **Purchases of minerals-in-place**   Purchases during the year of proved developed and undeveloped reserves

5. **Extensions, discoveries, and other additions**   Proved reserves resulting from the extension of previously discovered reservoirs, discovery of new fields or new reservoirs in old fields, and other additions

6. **Production**   The total amount of net quantities produced for the year

7. **Sales of minerals-in-place**   Sales during the year of proved developed and undeveloped reserves

8. **End of year**   The total net quantities at the end of the year (All items above this item should add up to this item.)

9. **Proved developed reserves**   Net quantities of proved developed reserves only for the beginning and ending of the year. Proved developed reserves include oil and/or gas expected to be recovered through existing wells using existing equipment and operation methods. Proved undeveloped reserves are those in which oil and/or gas is expected to be recovered from new wells on undrilled acreage or from existing wells that require major expenditures for completion.

Net quantities subject to purchase under long-term supply agreements with governments or authorities and net quantities received during the year under such agreements (as indicated in items 10 and 11) must be disclosed separately (FAS-69, par. 28).

An investor's share of net quantities of an investment accounted for by the equity method (as indicated in item 12) shall be disclosed separately at the end of the year (FAS-69, par. 20).

If important economic factors or significant uncertainties are involved in any of the net quantities reported by an enterprise, an explanatory note should accompany the supplementary oil and gas information. Important economic factors or significant uncertainties would include (*a*) exceptionally high future development or lifting expenditures and (*b*) contractual obligations requiring the enterprise to sell significant quantities of oil or gas at substantially lower prices than the expected market price at the time of production (FAS-69, par. 16).

If a government restricts or prohibits the disclosure of any of the net quantities of oil and gas reserves required by FAS-69, or requires disclosure of a different nature than required by FAS-69, an enterprise must disclose the fact that (*a*) the net quantity reserves from that particular country are excluded from the supplementary information, or (*b*) the net quantity reserves from that particular country are not reported (FAS-69, par. 17).

Disclosures—Capitalized Costs

Publicly held enterprises shall disclose in each of their annual financial statements presented the total amount of capitalized costs and related accumulated depreciation (depletion) (amortization) and valuation allowances relating to oil and gas producing activities. Under FAS-19, capitalized costs are classified as follows (FAS-19, par. 11):

1. Mineral interest in properties which must be classified as (*a*) proved properties or (*b*) unproved properties

2. Wells, related equipment and facilities

3. Support equipment and facilities used in oil and gas producing activities

4. Uncompleted wells, equipment and facilities

Existing GAAP (APB-12 [Omnibus Opinion—1967]) require that the balances of major classes of depreciable assets, by nature or function, be disclosed in the financial statements of an enterprise. Thus, to comply with existing GAAP, it would appear appropriate to use the above classifications for capitalized costs relating to oil and gas producing activities. However, FAS-69 states that it often may be appropriate to combine one or more, or two or more, of the classifications of capitalized costs and offers the following illustration:

(in thousands of dollars)	*Total*
Unproved oil and gas properties	$ 300,000
Proved oil and gas properties	2,972,000
	$3,272,000
Less: Accumulated depreciation, depletion amortization, and valuation allowances	515,000
Net capitalized costs	$2,757,000
Proportionate share of capitalized costs of investments accounted for by the equity method	$ 125,000

FAS-69 expressly requires that capitalized costs of unproved properties, if significant, be disclosed separately (FAS-69, par. 19).

Under the provisions of FAS-69, capitalized costs of support equipment and facilities may be disclosed separately or included as appropriate with capitalized costs of proved and unproved properties.

An enterprise's proportionate share of the total capitalized costs relating to oil and gas producing activities of an investment accounted for by the equity method must be disclosed separately in each annual financial statement presented (FAS-69, par. 20).

Disclosures—Incurred Functional Costs

Publicly held enterprises shall disclose in each of their annual financial statements presented the total capitalized or expensed costs for the following functional activities of oil and gas producing companies (FAS-69, par. 21):

1. Property acquisition costs
2. Exploration costs
3. Development costs

Exploration and development costs include the depreciation expense of support equipment and facilities, but exclude the expenditures to acquire such equipment and facilities. Any of these functional costs that are incurred in a foreign country are disclosed separately by geographic areas in the same manner that net quantities of oil and gas are disclosed (FAS-69, par. 22).

An enterprise's proportionate share of the total property acquisition, exploration, and development costs relating to oil and gas producing activities of an investment accounted for by the equity method must be disclosed separately, in total and by geographic area, in each annual financial statement presented (FAS-69, par. 23).

If costs to acquire mineral interest in proved reserves are significant, FAS-69 requires that they be disclosed separately from costs to acquire interests in unproved reserves.

Illustration of Disclosure of Property Acquisition, Exploration, and Development Costs Required by FAS-69

(in millions)	Total Worldwide	United States	Foreign Geographic Area A	Foreign Geographic Area B	Other Foreign Geographic Areas
Property acquisition costs:					
Proved	$ 15	$ 3	$ 2	$ 2	$ 8
Unproved	5	5	—	—	—
Exploration costs	250	150	50	40	10
Development costs	660	420	110	80	50
Proportionate share of the property, acquisition, exploration, and development costs from investments accounted for by the equity method	10	—	10	—	—

Disclosures—Results of Operations

Publicly held enterprises shall disclose in each of their annual financial statements presented the results of operations (as defined below) for oil and gas producing activities. If the enterprise is subject to the segmentation provisions of FAS-14, however, the results of operations shall be included with the other segment information required by FAS-14.

Results of operations include an enterprise's interest in proved oil and gas reserves and oil and gas subject to purchase under long-term supply contracts and similar agreements.

Under FAS-69, results of operations for oil and gas producing activities are disclosed in total and for each geographic area for which related reserve quantities are disclosed (FAS-69, par. 12).

The following information is disclosed for results of operations for oil and gas producing activities (FAS-69, par. 24):

Revenue

Revenue includes sales to unaffiliated organizations in connection with (*a*) networking interests, (*b*) royalty interests, (*c*) oil payment interests, and (*d*) net profit interests of the reporting enterprise (FAS-69, par. 25).

Regarding gas sales, production is not always sold in accordance with the respective joint revenue interest of the owners of the well for various reasons. In these situations, revenue is recorded on either the entitlements method or the sales method. Under the entitlements method, each unit of gas sold is assumed to be jointly owned by the owners of the well, and each joint revenue interest owner records a proportionate share of the gas sold from the well, regardless of whose customer the gas is sold to or who collects the revenue from the sale. Normally, a receivable or payable is recorded under these circumstances to reflect the imbalance. Receivables should be net of selling expenses. Under the sales method of accounting, an owner of a revenue interest in a well records only the gas it sells to its customers for which it collects the revenue. The method of accounting for gas imbalances should be disclosed in the footnotes to the financial statements.

Intercompany sales or transfers also are included as revenue, based on appropriate market prices, which are equivalent to arm's length transactions at the point of delivery from the producing unit (FAS-69, par. 25).

Excluded from gross revenue are royalty payments and net profit disbursements. Production or severance taxes are included as part of production costs and are not deducted in determining gross revenue (FAS-69, par. 25).

Production

Includes all costs incurred in lifting the oil and / or gas to the surface, and gathering, treating, field processing, and field storage. The production function terminates at the outlet valve on the leased property or the field production storage tank, or under unusual circumstances, at the first point at which the oil and / or gas is delivered to a main pipeline, refinery, marine terminal, or a common carrier (FAS-19, par. 23).

Production costs include labor, fuel, and supplies needed to operate the developed wells and related equipment, repairs, property taxes, and insurance on proved properties, and wells, related equipment, and facilities (FAS-19, par. 23).

Costs incurred to operate and maintain the production system become part of the total production costs (lifting costs).

Depreciation, depletion, amortization, and valuation allowances related to capitalized costs are excluded from production costs and disclosed under a separate caption (see below).

Exploration

Exploration includes all costs relating to the search for oil and / or gas reserves, including applicable costs of support equipment and facilities, drilling exploratory wells, and exploratory-type stratigraphic test wells. Exploration costs may be incurred before the actual acquisition of the property, and in this sense they are sometimes referred to as prospecting costs (FAS-19, par. 16).

Some exploration costs do not represent the acquisition of an identifiable asset, and are therefore charged directly to expense when incurred. The cost of carrying and maintaining undeveloped properties is an expense, because such costs do not increase the potential that the properties will contain proved reserves. Examples of these types of expenses are delay rentals, taxes on properties, legal costs, and land maintenance (FAS-19, par. 17).

Geological, topographical, and geophysical studies (G&G costs) and related salary and other expenses also are expensed, because they do not represent the acquisition of an identifiable asset. The studies frequently are made before the acquisition of the property and represent research or information costs. More often than not, G&G costs are incurred and the properties are never acquired (FAS-19, par. 18).

Depreciation, depletion, amortization, and valuation allowances related to capitalized costs are excluded from exploration expenses and disclosed under a separate caption (see below).

Depreciation, Depletion, Amortization, and Valuation Allowances

Depreciation, depletion, amortization, and valuation allowances related to oil and gas producing activities, except those which are part of general overhead and financing costs, are disclosed separately under this caption.

> ☞ **PRACTICE POINTER:** Interest capitalized under the provisions of FAS-34 on qualifying assets used in oil and gas producing activities is charged to net income as depreciation, depletion, or amortization of the cost of the related asset.

Income Tax Expense

The determination of *income tax expense* reflects any permanent differences relating to oil and gas activities, provided that such permanent differences are reflected appropriately in the enterprise's consolidated income tax expense for the period (FAS-69, par. 26).

Results of Operations

Results of operations are equal to revenues, less (*a*) production costs, (*b*) exploration expenses, (*c*) depreciation, depletion, amortization, and valuation allowances, and (*d*) income tax expense. Results of operations for oil and gas producing activities do not include general corporate overhead and financing costs. However, corporate overhead or expenses incurred at a central administrative office may include operating expenses of oil and gas producing activities and should be accounted for as such. In determining whether an expenditure is or is not an operating expense of oil and gas producing activities, the nature of the expense governs. The location in which the expense is recorded or paid is irrelevant (FAS-69, par. 27).

Illustration of Disclosure of Results of Operations (as Defined Herein)

(in millions)	Total Worldwide	United States	Foreign Geographic Area A	Foreign Geographic Area B	Other Foreign Geographic Areas
Revenues	$1,800	$1,200	$450	$100	$ 50
Production costs	(630)	(380)	(210)	(25)	(15)
Exploration expenses	(250)	(150)	(50)	(40)	(10)
Depreciation, depletion, amortization, and valuation provisions	(700)	(475)	(175)	(40)	(10)
	220	195	15	(5)	15
Income tax expense	(81)	(66)	(6)	(2)	(7)
Results of operations for producing activities (excluding corporate overhead and financing costs)	$ 139	$ 129	$ 9	$ (7)	$ 8
Enterprise's share of equity method investees' results of operations for producing activities (excluding corporate overhead and financing costs)	$ 10	$ —	$ 10	$ —	$ —

Results of operations do not include an enterprise's proportionate share of the results of operations (as defined herein) of oil and gas producing activities from investments accounted for by the equity method. An enterprise's proportionate share of the results of operations (as defined herein) from an investment accounted for by the equity method must be disclosed separately, in total and by geographic area, in each annual financial statement presented (FAS-69, par. 29).

Disclosures—Discounted Future Net Cash Flows

Publicly held enterprises disclose, in each of their annual financial statements presented, a statement of the present value of future net cash flows, in total and by geographic area, from (*a*) the net quantities of proved reserves and proved developed reserves of crude oil and natural gas and (*b*) the net quantities of oil and gas subject to purchase under long-term supply contracts and similar agreements, and contracts in which the enterprise participates in the operation of the oil or gas producing properties or otherwise acts as a producer. Items (*a*) and (*b*) may be combined into one statement of the present value of future net cash flows (FAS-69, par. 30).

Under the provisions of FAS-69, a standardized measure of discounted future net cash flows is achieved by utilizing a 10% discount rate. The statement of the present value of future net cash flows must include the following detail (FAS-69, par. 30):

Future Cash Inflows

Future cash inflows are calculated by multiplying the current year-end net quantities of oil and gas reserves [items (*a*) and (*b*) above] by their respective current year-end prices. Future price changes are considered, but only to the extent of existing contractual agreements. In other words, prices that appear in existing agreements may be used, but only to the extent of the quantities involved in the agreement.

Future Development and Production Costs

Future development and production costs are estimated expenditures which should be incurred in producing the future cash inflows. Future development and production costs are estimated based on current year-end costs and existing economic environment. If significant, future development costs are disclosed separately.

Future Income Tax Expenses

Future income tax expenses are calculated by applying the current year-end statutory income tax rates to the total pretax future cash flows from the net quantities of oil and gas reserves, less (a) the tax basis of the properties involved and (b) the tax effects of any permanent differences, such as investment tax credits and the excess of statutory depletion over the tax basis.

Future tax rates are used if legislated before issuance of the financial statements.

Future Net Cash Flows

Future net cash flows are calculated by deducting future development and production costs and future income tax expenses from the future cash inflows.

Discount

Discount is calculated by applying a standardized 10% rate per year, which shall reflect the timing of the receipts of the future net cash flows from the net quantities of oil and gas reserves.

Standardized Measure of Discounted Future Net Cash Flows

The *standardized measure of discounted future net cash flows* is calculated by deducting the discount from the future net cash flows.

A significant portion of the consolidated standardized measure of discounted future net cash flows may be attributable to a consolidated subsidiary that has a significant minority interest. In this event, disclosure of these facts and the approximate portion attributed to the consolidated subsidiary is required (FAS-69, par. 31).

The standardized measure of discounted future net cash flows does not include an enterprise's proportionate share of the standardized measure of discounted future net cash flows from investments accounted for by the equity method. An enterprise's proportionate share of the standardized measure of discounted future net cash flows from investments accounted for by the equity method must be disclosed separately, in total and by geographic area, in each annual financial statement presented (FAS-69, par. 32).

An enterprise shall disclose, in each annual financial statement it presents, a statement of the changes in the standardized measure of discounted future net cash flows, in total and by geographic area. The factors that cause these changes shall be disclosed separately, if significant, under the following categories (FAS-69, par. 33):

1. Sales and transfers of oil and gas produced during the period, net of production costs
2. Net changes in sales and transfer prices, and changes in future development and production (lifting) costs
3. Previously estimated future development costs incurred during the period
4. Net changes for extensions, discoveries, additions, and improved recovery, less related future development and production costs
5. Net changes for revisions in quantity estimates
6. Net changes because of purchases and sales of minerals in place
7. Accretion of discount
8. Net changes in income taxes
9. Other (including the effect of changes in estimated rates of production)

> **OBSERVATION:** *Accretion of discount* (item [7] above) is a term the SEC uses to refer to the annual amount of imputed interest that is calculated on the standardized measure of discounted future net cash flows (see Illustration below).

Illustration of Standardized Measure of Discounted Future Net Cash Flows

A newly formed oil company spends $200,000 to drill for oil and discovers a commercially exploitable well. At year-end it is estimated that this well will produce 10,000 barrels of oil for the next three years, for a total of 30,000 barrels. The year-end price of oil is $35 per barrel, and future development and production costs and future income tax expenses are estimated, at year-end prices, to be $5 per barrel. The standardized measure of discounted future net cash flows at 10% is $30 ($35 − $5) x 10,000 = $300,000 x 2.48685 (present value of an ordinary annuity at 10% for 3 periods) = $746,055. The amortization table for the three-year period is as follows:

Year	Present Value (A)	Interest (B)	Total	Net Cash Flow	Present Value Balance
1	$746,055	$74,606	$820,661	$300,000	$520,661
2	520,661	52,066	572,727	300,000	272,727
3	272,727	27,273	300,000	300,000	-0-

(A) = Standardized measure of discounted future net cash flows
(B) = Accretion of discount

In computing the changes in the standardized measure of discounted future net cash flows, the effects of price changes are calculated before the effects of quantity changes, so the latter will be priced at year-end prices. The effect of changes in income taxes includes the effect of the income taxes incurred during the period and the effect of changes in future income tax expenses. All other changes except the accretion of discount and income taxes shall be reported pretax (FAS-69, par. 33).

Footnotes are required for any additional information that is needed to prevent the disclosures from being misleading (FAS-69, par. 34).

> ☞ **PRACTICE POINTER:** FAS-19 requires information that becomes available after the balance sheet date and before the issuance of the financial statements to be taken into consideration in determining conditions that existed at the balance sheet date. The determination at the balance sheet date of whether an exploratory well contains proved reserves, the impairment of unproved properties, and similar factors may be based on information that becomes available after the balance sheet date and before the issuance of the financial statements.

Illustration of Disclosure of Standardized Measure of Discounted Future Net Cash Flows and Changes Therein

(in millions)	Total	United States	Foreign Geographic Area A	Foreign Geographic Area B	Other Foreign Geographic Areas
Future cash inflows*	$ 19,890	$ 11,340	$ 6,800	$ 1,500	$ 250
Future production and development costs*	(8,725)	(5,200)	(2,800)	(600)	(125)
Future income tax expenses*	(4,835)	(2,835)	(1,600)	(325)	(75)
Future net cash flows	6330	3,305	2,400	575	50
10% annual discount for estimated timing of cash flows	(3,000)	(1,635)	(1,100)	(250)	(25)
Standardized measure of discounted future net cash flows relating to proved oil and gas reserves	$ 3,330	$ 1,670	$ 1,300	$ 325	$ 25
Enterprise's share of equity method investees' standardized measure of discounted future net cash flows relating to proved oil and gas reserves	$ 100	$ —	$ 100	$ —	$ —

Beginning of year	$ 3,700
Changes resulting from:	
Sales and transfers of oil and gas produced, net of production costs	(1,170)
Net changes in prices, and production costs	(450)
Extensions, discoveries, additions, and improved recovery, less related costs	500
Development costs incurred during the period	535
Net changes in future development costs	25
Revisions of previous quantity estimates	55
Net change in purchases and sales of minerals-in-place	25
Accretion of discount	375
Net change in income taxes	(215)
Other	(50)
End of year	$ 3,330

*Future net cash flows were computed using year-end prices and costs and year-end statutory tax rates (adjusted for permanent differences) that relate to existing proved oil and gas reserves in which the enterprise has mineral interests, or for which the enterprise has long-term supply, purchase, or similar agreements where the enterprise serves as the producer of the reserves.

Pension Plan Financial Statements

CHAPTER 60
PENSION PLAN FINANCIAL STATEMENTS

CONTENTS

CHAPTER 60
PENSION PLAN FINANCIAL
STATEMENTS

OVERVIEW

GAAP for pensions encompass accounting and reporting for pension plans for employers and, in addition, financial reporting for pension plans as separate reporting units. The subject of this section is pension plan financial statements. Disclosure of the following information, either in statement form or otherwise, is required:

- Net assets available for benefits
- Changes in net assets available for benefits
- Actuarial present value of accumulated plan benefits
- Effects of certain factors affecting the year-to-year change in the actuarial present value of accumulated plan benefits

GAAP establishing accounting and reporting standards for defined benefit pension plans are included in the following pronouncements:

FAS-35	Accounting and Reporting by Defined Benefit Pension Plans
FAS-75	Deferral of the Effective Date of Certain Accounting Requirements for Pension Plans of State and Local Governmental Units
FAS-110	Reporting by Defined Benefit Pension Plans of Investment Contracts

CROSS-REFERENCES

1999 MILLER GAAP GUIDE: Chapter 2, "Accounting Policies"; Chapter 34, "Pension Plans—Employers"; Chapter 35, "Pension Plans—Settlements and Curtailments"; Chapter 36, "Postemployment and Postretirement Benefits Other Than Pensions."

1999 MILLER GOVERNMENTAL GAAP GUIDE: Chapter 27, "Fiduciary Funds"

BACKGROUND

A defined benefit plan is a plan that provides for a determinable pension benefit to be paid on retirement or the occurrence of certain other events. Based on the benefits expected to be paid, the employer's contributions can be computed actuarially. A plan that specifies a fixed rate of employers' contributions is considered to be a defined benefit pension plan for the purposes of FAS-35, if employers' contributions are periodically adjusted to allow for payment of defined benefits that are described in the plan.

The main objective of the financial statements of defined benefit pension plans is to provide financial information that may be utilized to assess the present and future ability of the pension plan to pay benefits as they become due. The financial statements contain information about (*a*) the resources of the pension plan, (*b*) the accumulated plan benefits of participants, (*c*) the transactions affecting the plan's resources and benefits, and (*d*) other additional information, as necessary to provide clarity to the financial statement presentation.

> ☞ **PRACTICE POINTER:** FAS-35 does not require that financial statements be prepared and distributed for defined benefit plans. When financial statements of defined benefit plans *are* prepared and presented, however, they must comply with the provisions of FAS-35 to be in conformity with GAAP.

> **OBSERVATION:** FAS-75 indefinitely defers the applicability of FAS-35 to pension plans of state and local governmental units.

All financial statements and information should be prepared and presented for the same fiscal or calendar period. Thus, net assets available for benefits and the actuarial present value of accumulated plan benefits are presented as of the same date and the changes in both are presented for the same period. Financial statements for the most recent year-end period are preferred by FAS-35. If the information on the actuarial present value of accumulated plan benefits is not available or cannot be determined reasonably for the most recent year-end period, however, then such information shall be presented as of the beginning of the year. In this event, all other financial statements and changes in financial statements must be presented for the same period (i.e., all financial statements must be in comparative form).

The information concerning the actuarial present value of accumulated plan benefits and its year-to-year changes may be presented on the face of the statement of net assets, as a separate statement, or in notes to the financial statements. However, each category of information must be presented in its entirety in the same location on the financial statements regardless of the format in which it is presented.

Benefit information may become available during a fiscal year and not at the beginning or end of the year. In this event, FAS-35 allows the use of averages or approximations in determining benefit information at the beginning or end of the fiscal year. However, the method used to estimate benefit information must produce results similar to those required by FAS-35 (FAS-35, par. 29).

PENSION PLAN INFORMATION

Net Assets Available for Benefits

The pension plan's resources should be identified in reasonable detail and presented on the accrual basis of accounting (FAS-35, par. 9).

> ☛ **PRACTICE POINTER:** Comparison of the current year and the immediate prior year is used in FAS-35 only when the benefit information date is at the beginning of the current year. If the benefit information date is at the end of the current year, only the current year is presented. In footnote 1 of FAS-35, however, it is suggested that comparative financial statements for several plan years are more useful in assessing a plan's ability to provide future benefits. In addition, financial reporting required by the Employee Retirement Income Security Act (ERISA) requires that the statement of net assets be in comparative form.

Investments

All pension plan investments that are held to provide benefits for the plan's participants, excluding insurance contracts, must be identified in reasonable detail and presented at fair value in the financial statements. FAS-35 defines *fair value* as the amount that could reasonably be expected to be received in a current sale between a willing buyer and a willing seller, neither of whom is compelled to buy or sell. Plan investments include debt or equity securities, real estate, and other types of investments held to provide benefits for the plan's participants. Quoted market values, in an active market, are used as fair value when available (FAS-35, par. 11). If fair value is determined by some other method, the method should be disclosed adequately in the financial statements or footnotes thereto (FAS-35, par. 13).

Illustration of Presentation Suggested by FAS-35

Statement of Net Assets Available for Benefits

	December 31	
	19X5	19X4
Assets:		
Investments at quoted market values (Note:_____)		
Federal and state debt securities	$ 500,000	$ 1,000,000
Corporate debt securities	3,500,000	3,000,000
Common stock	6,000,000	5,500,000
	$10,000,000	$ 9,500,000

	December 31	
	19X5	19X4
Investments at estimated fair value (Note:_____)		
Corporate debt securities	$ 500,000	$ 600,000
Preferred stock	400,000	400,000
Mortgages	1,100,000	1,000,000
Real estate	500,000	600,000
	$ 2,500,000	$ 2,600,000
Deposit administrative contract at contract value* (Note:_____)	1,100,000	1,050,000
Total investments	$13,600,000	$13,150,000
Cash	100,000	110,000
Contributions receivable— employers	600,000	500,000
Accrued interest and dividends	90,000	80,000
Total assets	$14,390,000	$13,840,000
Liabilities:		
Accounts payable and accrued	(80,000)	(75,000)
Net assets available for benefits	$14,310,000	$13,765,000

*If issued prior to 3/20/92.

Insurance Contracts

FAS-110 requires insurance contracts to be presented in the same manner as specified in the annual report filed with certain governmental agencies pursuant to ERISA. Such contracts are presented either at fair value or at amounts determined by the insurance enterprise (contract value). A plan not subject to ERISA presents its insurance contracts as if the plan were subject to the reporting requirements of ERISA (FAS-110, par. 4).

Insurance contracts generally are characterized by the following:

- The purchaser of the insurance contract makes an initial payment or deposit to the insurance enterprise in advance of the possible occurrence or discovery of an insured event.

- When the insurance contract is made, the insurance enterprise ordinarily does not know if, how much, or when amounts will be paid under the contract (FAS-110, par. 5).

Contracts that do not subject the insurance enterprise to risks arising from policyholders' mortality or morbidity are investment, rather than insurance, contracts. A *mortality or morbidity risk* is present if the insurance enterprise is required to make payments or forego required premiums contingent upon the death or disability (life insurance contracts) or the continued survival (annuity contracts) of a specific individual or group of individuals (FAS-110, par. 6).

Contributions Receivable

Contributions receivable from employees, employers, state or federal grants, and other sources should be identified separately in the financial statements. Contributions receivable should be reported on the accrual basis pursuant to actual legal or contractual obligations or formal commitments (FAS-35, par. 10). The fact that an employer accrues a liability to a pension plan does not, by itself, provide a basis for a pension plan to record a corresponding receivable.

In order for a pension plan to record an employer's contribution receivable, the receivable must be supported by a formal commitment or an actual legal or contractual obligation. However, FAS-35 states that evidence of a formal commitment may include (*a*) the formal approval of a specified contribution, (*b*) a consistent pattern of payments made after the pension plan's year-end pursuant to an established funding policy that attributes the payments to the preceding plan year, and (*c*) a federal tax deduction taken for the contribution by the employer for periods ending on or before the reporting date for the pension plan (FAS-35, par. 10).

☞ **PRACTICE POINTER:** Many pension plans allow a company, at its discretion, to discontinue contributions and/or the plan itself. The resulting legal position is that the company has no legal liability for future pension fund contributions, and employees have no rights to any benefits beyond those already provided for in the pension fund. However, the position of GAAP is one of substance over form and that a business is viewed as an entity that will continue to exist (going-concern concept). Therefore, GAAP require that the "no future legal liability clauses" of a pension plan be ignored for the purposes of determining the annual pension costs of employers.

Operating Assets

Assets that are used in the actual operation of a pension plan are reported at amortized cost on the financial statements. For example, buildings, leasehold improvements, furniture, equipment, and fixtures that are used in the everyday operation of a pension plan are presented at historical cost, less accumulated depreciation or amortization (FAS-35, par. 14).

Changes in Net Assets Available for Benefits

Significant changes in net assets available for benefits should be identified in reasonable detail in the Statement of Changes in Net Assets Available for Benefits.

Illustration of Presentation Suggested by FAS-35

Statement of Changes in Net Assets Available for Benefits
Year Ended December 31

	19X5
Investment Income:	
Interest	$ 315,000
Dividend	475,000
Rental	50,000
Increase (decrease) in investments at quoted market values (Note:____)	145,000
Increase (decrease) in investments at estimated fair values (Note:____)	(210,000)
	$ 775,000

Less: Investment expenses	120,000
	$ 655,000
Contributions from employers (Note:_____)	800,000
Total	$ 1,455,000
Less: Direct benefit payments to participants	$ 460,000
Less: Annuity contracts purchased (Note:_____)	400,000
Less: Expenses of administration	50,000
Total	910,000
Net increase in net assets	$ 545,000
Net assets available for benefits:	
Beginning of year	13,765,000
End of year	$14,310,000

The minimum disclosures required by FAS-35 that appear in the Statement of Changes in Net Assets Available for Benefits or its related footnotes are as follows (FAS-35, par. 15):

1. Investment income other than from realized or unrealized gains or losses on investments is disclosed separately in reasonable detail.

2. Total realized and unrealized gains or losses on investments presented at quoted market values are reported separately from those of investments presented at estimated fair value.

3. Contributions from employers, participants, and others are reported separately. Cash and noncash contributions from employers are disclosed. Noncash contributions are recorded at their fair value on the date of receipt and, if significant, are fully described in the financial statements or footnotes thereto.

4. Direct benefit payments to participants are reported separately.

5. Purchases of insurance contracts that are excluded from the plan's assets are reported separately. Dividend income on insurance contracts that are excluded from the plan's assets may be netted against the purchase of such contracts. The dividend income policy on insurance contracts should be disclosed in a footnote to the financial statements.

6. Expenses of administering the plan are reported separately.

Accumulated Plan Benefits of Participants

FAS-35 requires that certain specified information regarding the actuarial present value of accumulated plan benefits of participants be disclosed as part of the financial statements. The present value of the accumulated plan benefits must be determined as of the plan benefit information date. Thus, if the plan benefit information date is the beginning of the year, the present value of the accumulated plan benefits must be determined as of the beginning of the year (FAS-35, par. 6).

In addition, financial statements as of the beginning of the year must also be included in the presentation. On the other hand, if the plan benefit information is dated as of the end of the year, the present value of the accumulated plan benefits must be determined as of the same date, and financial statements as of the end of the year must also be included in the presentation. FAS-35 states a preference for the use of end-of-year benefit information (FAS-35, par. 7).

FAS-35 allows considerable flexibility in presenting the actuarial present value of accumulated plan benefits and the changes therein from year to year (FAS-35, par. 8).

FAS-35 requires that the total actuarial present value of accumulated plan benefits be separated into at least three categories: (1) vested benefits of participants currently receiving payments, (2) vested benefits of other participants, and (3) nonvested benefits. Vested benefits of participants currently receiving payments include benefits due and payable as of the benefit information date. Disclosure of the accumulated contributions of present employees, including interest, if any, as of the benefit information date should be made in a footnote to the financial statements. In addition, the rate of interest, if any, should also be disclosed (FAS-35, par. 22).

For the purposes of FAS-35, the assumption is made that a pension plan will continue to exist (going-concern concept). The best estimates should be used in each actuarial assumption to reflect the pension plan's most likely expectations. The following specific assumptions must be applied (FAS-35, par. 20):

1. Assumed rates of return shall reflect the expected rates of return during the periods for which payment of benefits is deferred and shall be consistent with returns realistically achievable on the types of assets held by the plan and the plan's investment policy. To the extent that assumed rates of return are based on values of existing plan assets, the values used in determining assumed rates of return shall be the values presented in the plan's financial statements pursuant to the requirements of this Statement.

2. Expected rates of inflation assumed in estimating automatic cost-of-living adjustments shall be consistent with the assumed rates of return.

Illustration of Presentation Suggested by FAS-35

Statement of Accumulated Plan Benefits
Year Ended December 31

	19X5
Actuarial present value of accumulated plan benefits (Note:_____)	
Vested benefits	
Participants currently receiving payments	$ 4,650,000
Other participants	7,100,000
	$11,750,000
Nonvested benefits	1,100,000
Total actuarial present value of accumulated plan benefits	$12,850,000

---

3. Administrative expenses expected to be paid by the plan (not those paid by the sponsor) that are associated with providing accumulated plan benefits shall be reflected either by adjusting appropriately the assumed rates of return or by assigning those expenses to future periods and discounting them to the benefit information date. If the former method is used, the adjustment of the assumed rates of return shall be disclosed separately.

An acceptable alternative in determining the actuarial present value of accumulated plan benefits as of the benefit information date is to use the same assumptions an insurance company would use if it were to issue an insurance contract providing the same accumulated plan benefits to the same participants (FAS-35, par. 21).

Accumulated plan benefits are determined at the benefit information date in accordance with the provisions of the pension plan. Accumulated plan benefits include those expected to be paid to (*a*) retired or terminated employees or their beneficiaries, (*b*) beneficiaries of deceased employees, and (*c*) present employees or their beneficiaries (FAS-35, par. 16).

Pension plan benefits usually can be determined by reference to the provisions in the plan. In most pension plans, benefits usually are based on each year of service (employment) rendered by the employee. If the benefits are not clearly determinable from the provisions of the plan, FAS-35 requires the following computation to determine the accumulated benefits (FAS-35, par. 17):

Benefits Includable in Vested Benefits

$$\frac{\text{Number of years of service completed to the benefit information date}}{\begin{array}{c}\text{Number of years of service that will}\\ \text{have been completed when the benefits}\\ \text{will first be fully vested}\end{array}} = \begin{array}{c}\text{Percentage}\\ \text{of plan benefits}\\ \text{accumulated}\end{array}$$

The above computation is used to determine the amount of plan benefits that have been accumulated to the benefit information date; it is used for plan benefits that are classified as vested benefits.

The following computation is used to determine the amount of plan benefits that are not includable in vested benefits that have been accumulated to the benefit information date. This type of plan benefit includes death or disability benefits that are payable only if death or disability occurs during active service.

Benefits Not Includable in Vested Benefits

$$\frac{\text{Number of years service completed to the benefit information date}}{\begin{array}{c}\text{Estimated number of years' service}\\ \text{upon anticipated separation from covered}\\ \text{employment}\end{array}} = \begin{array}{c}\text{Percentage}\\ \text{of plan benefits}\\ \text{accumulated}\end{array}$$

Number of years service completed
to the benefit information date

FAS-35 requires that the following procedures be applied in determining accumulated plan benefits (FAS-35, par. 18):

1. Accumulated plan benefits shall be determined as of the benefit information date based on employees' history of earnings and service, and other appropriate factors.

2. In the case of periodic benefit increases, death benefits, early retirement benefits, and disability benefits, accumulated plan benefits should be based on employees' projected years of service.

3. All automatic benefit increases that are specified in the plan, such as cost-of-living increases, which are expected to occur subsequent to the benefit information date, shall be recognized in determining accumulated plan benefits.

4. Benefits that are covered by allocated insurance contracts that are not included as plan assets (in accordance with FAS-35)

are not included in determining accumulated plan benefits, provided that payment for the allocated insurance contract has been made to the insurance company.

5. Benefits arising from plan amendments adopted subsequent to the benefit information date shall not be included in determining accumulated plan benefits.

6. In computing Social Security benefits, employees' earnings as of the benefit information date shall be used to determine future compensation. Increases in Social Security benefits or in compensation base arising from present or future Social Security laws shall be excluded in determining future compensation.

Changes in Accumulated Plan Benefits

Certain factors that cause changes in the actuarial present value of accumulated plan benefits between the current and prior benefit information dates, if significant either individually or in the aggregate, shall be identified in the financial statements or the footnotes thereto. Significant changes that are caused by individual factors shall be identified separately. The minimum disclosure required by FAS-35 includes the effects of the following factors, if significant (FAS-35, par. 25):

1. Plan amendments
2. Changes in the nature of the plan, such as a merger with another plan, or a spin-off of a plan
3. Changes in actuarial assumptions

> **OBSERVATION:** An acceptable alternative permitted by FAS-35 to determine the actuarial present value of accumulated plan benefits as of the benefit information date, is to use the same assumptions an insurance company would use if it were to issue an insurance contract to provide the same accumulated plan benefits to the same participants. If a pension plan uses this method, it should disclose, if practical, the effects of changes in the actuarial present value of accumulated plan benefits that are caused by changes in actuarial assumptions. If the effects cannot be disclosed separately, they should be included in determining accumulated benefits.

Other factors that may cause significant changes in the actuarial present value of accumulated plan benefits are events and transactions that affect (*a*) the amount of accumulated benefits, (*b*) the discount period, and (c) the amount of benefits paid. These factors may be identified in the financial statements. Actuarial gains and losses may be disclosed separately, or included with the effect of additional accumulated benefits (FAS-35, par. 25).

Amounts paid to an insurance company for the purchase of insurance contracts are included in determining the amount of benefits paid. However, amounts paid by an insurance company for benefits, in accordance with an insurance contract that has been excluded from the plan's assets (in accordance with FAS-35), are not included in determining the amount of benefits paid (FAS-35, par. 25).

Changes in actuarial assumptions that result from changes in a plan's expected experience are treated as changes in accounting estimates. Accounting estimates are accounted for in the year of change and, if necessary, future years. Prior years' financial statements are not restated in accounting for a change in an accounting estimate in accordance with APB-20 (Accounting Changes) (FAS-35, par. 23).

Changes in the actuarial present value of accumulated plan benefits may be presented in the form of a separate reconciliation statement, or elsewhere in the financial statements. If the reconciliation statement is used, it should reflect the actuarial present value of accumulated plan benefits at both the beginning and the end of the year. The amount of detail between the beginning and end of year depends on whether a full presentation is made, or only the required minimum disclosures. If a full presentation is made, then all changes are identified and disclosed. If only the required minimum disclosures are made, however, it is necessary to include all other changes on one line to reconcile the beginning and ending balances (FAS-35, par. 26).

Illustration of Presentation Suggested by FAS-35

*Statement of Changes in Accumulated
Plan Benefits*

| | Year ended
December 31, 19X5
Increase (Decrease) |
|---|---|
| Actuarial present value of accumulated
plan benefits, at beginning of year | $12,705,000 |
| Plan amendment | 370,000 |
| Changes in actuarial assumptions | (210,000) |
| Other factors | (15,000) |
| Actuarial present value of accumulated
plan benefits, at end of the year | $12,850,000 |

If the minimum required disclosures pertaining to the changes in the actuarial present value of accumulated plan benefits are made elsewhere in the financial statements and not in a reconciliation statement format, FAS-35 requires that the actuarial present value of accumulated plan benefits, as of the preceding benefit information date, also be disclosed (FAS-35, par. 25).

Other Financial Statement Disclosures

In addition to the financial statement and footnote disclosures mentioned previously, FAS-35 requires two specific, additional note disclosures and several other disclosures if they are applicable. The two required note disclosures appear in the plan's significant accounting policies in accordance with APB-22 (Disclosure of Accounting Policies). They are as follows (FAS-35, par. 27):

1. The significant assumptions and method used to determine fair value of investments and the value of reported insurance contracts must be described adequately.

2. The significant assumptions and method used to determine the actuarial present value of accumulated plan benefits must be described adequately. In addition, any significant changes in assumptions or methods that occur during the reporting period must be described.

Other required financial statement disclosures (if applicable) are as follows (FAS-35, par. 28):

1. A brief description of the important provisions of the pension plan agreement. If this information is made generally available from sources other than the financial statements, however, reference to such sources may be made in the financial statements, instead of providing the brief description.

2. Significant amendments to the pension plan that are adopted on or before the latest benefit information date should be described. In the event that significant plan amendments are adopted between the latest benefit information date and the end of the plan's year, disclosure should be made to the effect that the present value of accumulated plan benefits does not include the effects of those amendments.

3. The order of priority for plan participants' claims to the assets of the plan upon termination of the plan should be described generally. In addition, a description of any benefits guaranteed by the Pension Benefit Guaranty Corporation (PBGC)

and a description of the applicability of any PBGC guaranty to any recent plan amendment should be included.

If the information required above is made generally available from sources other than the financial statements, reference to such sources may be made in the financial statements, provided that the following (or similar) disclosure is made in the financial statements:

> "Should the pension plan terminate at some future time, its net assets generally will not be available on a pro rata basis to provide participants' benefits. Whether a particular participant's accumulated plan benefits will be paid depends on both the priority of those benefits and the level of benefits guaranteed by the Pension Benefit Guaranty Corporation at that time. Some benefits may be fully or partially provided for by the then existing assets and the Pension Benefit Guaranty Corporation, while other benefits may not be provided for at all."

4. Significant plan administration costs that are being absorbed by the employer should be disclosed.

5. The policy for funding the pension plan and any changes in policy during the plan's year should be described. The method for determining participants' contributions, if any, should be described and plans subject to ERISA must disclose whether ERISA minimum funding requirements have been met. The status of minimum funding waivers should be disclosed, if applicable.

6. The pension plan's policy concerning purchased insurance contracts that are excluded from the pension plan's assets should be disclosed.

7. Disclosure of whether or not a favorable "determination letter" has been obtained for federal income tax purposes should be made.

8. Disclosure of any plan investments that represent 5% or more of the net assets available for benefits should be made.

9. Disclosure of any significant real estate or other transactions between the plan and the (*a*) employer, (*b*) sponsor, or (*c*) employee organization should be made.

10. Unusual or infrequent events and the effects of such events that occur subsequent to the latest benefit information date but prior to the issuance of the financial statements and that may significantly affect the plan's present and future ability to pay benefits should be disclosed. In the event that the effects of such events are not reasonably determinable, all substantive reasons should be disclosed.

Illustration of Financial Statement Notes Required or Applicable under FAS-35

Summary of Significant Accounting Policies

Description of Pension Plan   This pension plan is called the ABC Company Defined Benefit Pension Plan and covers substantially all of the employees of the ABC Company. The Plan is subject to the provisions of the Employee Retirement Income Security Act of 1974 (ERISA).

Annual pension benefits begin at the normal retirement age (65) for employees with five or more years of service to the company. The amount received at age 65 is equal to 1 1/2% of the final five-year average annual compensation for each year of service. Employees may elect to retire early from ages 55 to 64. The portion of the accumulated plan benefits attributable to the Company's contributions to an employee is forfeited if an employee discontinues employment before rendering five years of service. Several elections are available to employees for the distribution of pension benefits. Employees may elect to receive their pension benefits in the form of a joint and survivor annuity, single life annuity, or as a lump-sum distribution upon termination or retirement. The minimum amount that an employee may receive upon electing a life annuity is the greater of the annuity for five years or the employee's accumulated contributions to the plan, plus interest.

Death benefits are paid to the beneficiary equal to the value of the employee's accumulated pension benefits if the active employee was 55 years or older. Annual disability benefits are paid to an active employee who has become disabled, equal to the normal retirement benefits that have been accumulated at the time of disability. At normal retirement age, the disabled employee would begin receiving normal retirement benefits computed as if he or she had retired at the date of disability.

Investment Valuation   Investments are valued at quoted market prices when available. Securities for which no quoted market price is available are valued at a fair value. Fair value is based upon a combination of different factors. In most cases, corporate bonds are valued through comparison of similar securities' yields. Restricted common stock usually is valued at the quoted price of the issuer's unrestricted stock, reduced by a discount to reflect the restriction. If neither a quoted market price is available nor an unrestricted stock of the issuer exists, then a value is determined on a multiple of current earnings reduced by comparison of similar companies' earnings with a quoted price.

Mortgages are valued at their present values based on prevailing interest rates applied to the future principal and interest payments. Real estate leased to third parties is valued at the present value of all future rental receipts and estimated residual values. The interest rate used to discount future values varies with the risks inherent in each real estate investment.

The value of the Plan's deposit administration contract with American Insurance Company, dated October 2, 19X1, is contract value. Contract value is determined by the contributions made plus interest at the rate specified in the contract less funds used to purchase annuities and pay expenses. The Plan's assets do not include those funds used to purchase annuities. When an annuity is purchased, American Insurance Company is required to pay all related pension benefits to a particular employee.

Actuarial Present Value of Accumulated Plan Benefits   All future periodic benefit payments, including any lump-sum distributions provided for under the provisions of the Plan, are included in Accumulated Plan Benefits. Accumulated plan benefits include all benefits that may be paid to present employees or beneficiaries, retired or terminated employees or beneficiaries, and beneficiaries of employees who have died. The plan provides for benefits that are based on the employee's compensation during the last five years of eligible service. The basis of the accumulated plan benefits for active employees is the average compensation during the last five years of service. All benefits are included, up to the valuation date, providing that they are related to services rendered by the employee. Any benefits that are provided from assets that are excluded from the Plan's assets, are excluded from accumulated plan benefits.

The actuarial present value for the accumulated plan benefits is computed by American Appraisal Inc. Certain assumptions are utilized to adjust the accumulated plan benefits to reflect the present value of money and the probability of payment. Significant actuarial assumptions utilized in the valuations presented as of December 31, 19X4, and December 19X3 are as follows: Participants' life expectancy based on mortality tables (_____), average retirement age of 62.

Termination of the Plan   In the event of termination, the net assets of the plan will be allocated, in accordance with ERISA and its related regulations. The order of priority is as follows:

1. Any benefits related to the contributions of the employees
2. Any annuity benefits that have been received for at least the past three years by former employees or their beneficiaries or that employees eligible to retire for that three-year period would have received if they had retired with benefits under the Plan. (The priority amount is the lowest benefit payable or paid during the five-year period before termination of the Plan.)
3. Insured vested benefits by the Pension Benefit Guaranty Corporation (PBGC) up to certain limitations
4. All uninsured vested benefits
5. All nonvested benefits

Annuity contracts for which the American Insurance Company is obligated to pay benefits are not included in the above priority schedule.

PBGC insurance benefits include most vested normal age retirement benefits, early retirement benefits, and certain disability and survivor's pensions. However, not all benefits under the Plan are guaranteed by PBGC and certain limitations are placed on some of the benefits guaranteed. Vested benefits are guaranteed at the level in effect at the Plan termination date, but are subject to a statutory ceiling that limits individual monthly benefits. The ceiling in 19X4 and 19X3 was XXX,XXX and XXX,XXX, respectively, for employees who are 65 years old and elect a single life annuity. All other annuitants are subject to a downward adjustment. Benefit improvements as a result of a Plan amendment are not automatically fully guaranteed by PBGC. PBGC guarantees the greater of 20% or $20 for each year following the effective date of an amendment. Thus, the full increase in benefits would be completely guaranteed within five years after an amendment assuming primary ceilings are in effect.

Investments Other Than Insurance Company Contract All of the Plan's investments are held by a bank-administered trust fund, except for the deposit administration contract. The fair values of those investments for 19X4 and 19X3 were XXX,XXX and XXX,XXX, respectively.

Insurance Contract The company entered into a deposit administration contract with the American Insurance Company in 19X1. The Plan deposits a minimum of $100,000 annually, which is placed in an unallocated fund. American adds interest to the fund at a stated rate of 7%. The interest rate can be changed after 19X9, but the different rate only affects deposits made after the date of change. Withdrawals are made from the fund under the direction of the Plan's administration to purchase an annuity. American Insurance Company premiums on purchased annuities are fixed for the term of the contract. Periodic dividends, if any, increase the unallocated fund. Dividends received in 19X4 and 19X3 were XXX and XXX, respectively. These dividends are deducted from the purchased annuity contract payments on the Statement of Changes in Net Assets.

Plan Amendment There is an amendment to the plan expected in 19X7, which will increase the annual pension benefits for each year of service.

Real Estate Transactions

CHAPTER 61
REAL ESTATE COSTS AND INITIAL
RENTAL OPERATIONS

CONTENTS

CHAPTER 61
REAL ESTATE COSTS AND INITIAL
RENTAL OPERATIONS

OVERVIEW

Promulgated GAAP establish standards for the acquisition, development, construction, and selling and rental costs related to real estate projects. In addition, they cover accounting for initial rental operations and include rules for ascertaining when a real estate project is substantially completed and available for occupancy.

The authoritative accounting pronouncement that establishes GAAP in the areas cited above is:

FAS-67   Accounting for Costs and Initial Rental Operations of Real Estate Projects

CROSS-REFERENCES

1999 MILLER GAAP GUIDE: Chapter 1, "Accounting Changes"; Chapter 20, "Impairment of Loans and Long-Lived Assets"; Chapter 62, "Real Estate—Recognition of Sales"

1999 MILLER GAAP IMPLEMENTATION MANUAL: EITF: Chapter 36, "Real Estate Transactions"

BACKGROUND

FAS-67 contains the specialized accounting and reporting principles and practices that were originally published in the following AICPA publications:

SOP 78-3   Accounting for Costs to Sell and Rent, and Initial Rental Operations of Real Estate Projects

SOP 80-3   Accounting for Real Estate Acquisition, Development, and Construction Costs

In addition, FAS-67 includes those portions of the Industry Accounting Guide titled "Accounting for Retail Land Sales" that relate to costs of real estate projects.

The following items are expressly *excluded* from the provisions of FAS-67:

1. Real estate projects that are not for sale or rent and are developed by an entity for its own use. This includes real estate reported in consolidated financial statements that was developed by one affiliated member of the group for use in the operations of another member of the group.

2. Initial direct costs of leases, including sales-type leases

3. Direct costs that are related to commercial activities such as manufacturing, merchandising, or service-oriented activities

4. Real estate rental periods of less than one month in duration

Real estate acquisition costs may be classified as (*a*) preacquisition costs and (*b*) postacquisition costs. Preacquisition costs are those that are incurred prior to the acquisition of the property, such as appraisals, surveys, legal fees, travel expenses, and costs to acquire options to purchase the property. Postacquisition costs are those that are incurred after the property has been acquired, such as development and construction costs. Postacquisition costs may be classified further as (*a*) direct costs, (*b*) indirect costs, (*c*) costs of amenities, and (*d*) incidental operational costs.

Direct costs are those that can be directly identified with the real estate project. Indirect costs may or may not be related to a specific real estate project. Indirect costs of several real estate projects may be allocated to each project on a reasonable allocation basis. Incidental operations of a real estate project occur during the development stage of the project and are intended to reduce the cost of the real estate project. Incidental operations do not include activities that result in a profit or return on the use of the real property.

Capitalized costs of a real estate project are allocated to the individual components within the project. The allocation usually is accomplished by the specific identification method, if the individual components within the project can be identified specifically. If specific identification is not possible, capitalized land cost and all other common costs, including common costs of amenities, are allocated based on the relative fair value of each land parcel benefited prior to any construction. Capitalized construction costs are allocated based on the relative sales value of each individual component within the real estate project. Individual components of a real estate project may consist of lots, acres, or some other identifiable unit.

Costs incurred to sell real estate projects may be accounted for as (*a*) project costs, (*b*) prepaid expenses, or (*c*) period costs, according to the accounting periods that are benefited.

Costs to rent real estate projects under operating leases are either chargeable to future periods or chargeable to the current period, according to whether their recovery is reasonably expected from future rental revenue.

PREACQUISITION COSTS

Costs frequently are incurred before the actual date on which a parcel of real property is acquired. These costs are referred to by FAS-67 as *preacquisition costs*. Practically any type of cost may be classified as a preacquisition cost if it is incurred prior to the date of acquisition of a parcel of real property. For example, the cost of an option to purchase real property at a future date is a preacquisition cost and usually is capitalized. If the option is not exercised on or before its expiration date, however, the option becomes worthless and should be expensed.

All other types of preacquisition costs are expensed when incurred, unless they can be identified specifically to the real property being acquired and (FAS-67, par. 4):

1. The preacquisition costs would be capitalized if the property were acquired.

2. The acquisition of the property is probable (e.g., the prospective purchaser is actively seeking to acquire the property and can obtain financing).

> **OBSERVATION:** *Probable* implies that the property is available for sale, the purchaser is currently trying to acquire the property, and the necessary financing is reasonably expected to be available.

Thus, preacquisition costs of a real estate project consist of (*a*) unexpired options to purchase real property and (*b*) other costs that meet all of the above conditions. Preacquisition costs that do not qualify for capitalization should be expensed when incurred (FAS-67, par. 5).

After a parcel of real property is acquired, preacquisition costs are reclassified as project costs. In the event that the property is not acquired, capitalized preacquisition costs shall not exceed the amount recoverable, if any, from the sale of options, developmental plans, and other proceeds. Capitalized preacquisition costs in excess of recoverable amounts are charged to expense (FAS-67, par. 5).

Illustration of Preacquisition Costs

Omega Company incurred the following preacquisition costs related to a piece of property:

1. Option to purchase land parcel, $10,000
2. Architectural consultation concerning feasibility of constructing warehouse facility on land parcel, $14,000

Situation 1: At the end of the year in which the above costs were incurred, Omega was actively seeking financing for the land and warehouse facility. Management believes it is probable that financing will be found and the land will be purchased, after which time the warehouse facility will be constructed.

In this situation, the $10,000 option and the $14,000 feasibility study should be capitalized as preacquisition costs, to be reclassified as project costs when the land purchase and warehouse construction commence.

Situation 2: At the end of the year in which the above costs were incurred, preliminary results of the feasibility study were not optimistic. Omega has suspended its search for financing, pending the final outcome of the feasibility study. The company considers the probability of purchasing the land and constructing the facility as no more than reasonably possible, but is optimistic that it can sell the option for at least its $10,000 cost.

In this situation, the $10,000 option cost should be carried as an asset, but the $14,000 for the feasibility study should be expensed in the current period.

PROJECT COSTS

Project costs of real estate projects may be direct or indirect. Direct costs that are related to the acquisition, development, and construction of a real estate project are capitalized as project costs (FAS-67, par. 7).

Indirect costs of real estate projects that can be identified clearly to specific projects under development or construction are capitalized as project costs. Indirect costs that are accumulated in one account, but clearly relate to several real estate projects under development or construction, are allocated on a reasonable basis to each of the projects (FAS-67, par. 7).

Indirect costs on real estate projects not under development or construction are expensed as incurred. In addition, indirect costs that cannot be identified clearly with specific projects such as general and administrative expenses are charged to expense when incurred (FAS-67, par. 7).

Illustration of Direct and Indirect Project Costs

Zeta Co. incurs the following direct and indirect project costs for two major real estate construction projects, identified as L and M:

Direct project costs:	
Project L	$ 150,000
Project M	740,000
Indirect project costs:	
Identified with Projects L and M	270,000
Identified with projects not currently under development	145,000
General and administrative	250,000
Total	$1,555,000

The indirect costs associated with Projects L and M are allocable one-third to Project L and two-thirds to Project M.

Treatment of the $1,555,000 of project costs for the year is as follows (in thousands of dollars):

	Project L	Project M	Current Expense
Direct costs	$150	$740	
Indirect costs:			
Project L ($270 x 1/3)	90		
Project M ($270 x 2/3)		180	
Not allocable ($145 + $250)			$395
	$240	$920	$395

Taxes and Insurance

Property taxes and insurance are capitalized as project costs only during periods in which activities necessary to get the property ready for its intended use are in progress (FAS-67, par. 6).

> **OBSERVATION:** Under the provisions of FAS-67, real estate taxes, insurance, and interest related to the tract of land are not capitalized unless activities necessary to get the property ready for its intended use are in progress. This position apparently differs from the AICPA Industry Accounting Guide titled "Accounting for Retail Land Sales." Paragraph 51 of this Guide states, "Costs directly related to inventories of unimproved land . . . are properly capitalizable until a salable condition is reached." Paragraph 51 further states, "Those costs would

include interest, real estate taxes, and other direct costs incurred during the inventory and improvement periods."

After real property is substantially completed and ready for its intended use, FAS-67 also requires that property taxes and insurance costs be expensed as incurred (FAS-67, par. 6).

Amenity Costs of Real Property

Golf courses, swimming pools, tennis courts, clubhouses, and other types of amenities frequently are included in the overall plans of a real estate project. The ultimate disposition of an amenity, however, may vary from one real estate project to another. Thus, accounting for the costs of amenities is based on the developer's (management) ultimate plans for the disposition of the amenity. In this respect, a developer may decide to retain ownership of the amenity and to either (*a*) operate the amenity or (*b*) eventually sell the amenity. On the other hand, the developer may be required under the terms of the individual sales agreements to sell or otherwise transfer ownership of the amenity to the purchasers of the individual components within the project. In this event, the purchasers of the individual components within the project usually form an association for the purposes of taking title to the amenity and operating the amenity for the common benefit of all owners of individual components within the project.

Accounting for the costs of amenities under the provisions of FAS-67 is as follows:

Ownership Not Retained by Developer

When the ownership of an amenity is to be transferred to the individual components within the real estate project, the net cost of the amenity is accounted for by the developer as a capitalized common cost of the project. The capitalized common cost of an amenity is allocated to the individual components within the project that are expected to benefit from the use of the amenity. Thus, the total cost of each individual component in the project that benefits from the amenity will include a proportionate share of the costs of the amenity (FAS-67, par. 8a).

The developer's net cost or gain that is accounted for as a common cost (reduction) of the real estate project may include the sales price, if any, and all other proceeds, if any, from the transfer of the amenity, less the following items:

1. Direct costs that clearly are identifiable to the amenity

2. Indirect costs that clearly are related to the amenity

3. The developer's cost of operating the amenity until the amenity is transferred to the individual components in the project in accordance with the sales contract or other contractual agreement

4. Common costs of the project that are allocated appropriately to the amenity

If an amenity clearly benefits specific individual components within a real estate project, the common cost (reduction) of the amenity is allocated only to those specific individual components.

Ownership Retained by Developer

When a developer retains ownership of an amenity, the total cost of the amenity is capitalized as a separate asset. The total cost of an amenity includes direct costs, indirect costs, and the allocation of common costs, including operating results of the amenity prior to its date of substantial completion and availability for its intended use. Under FAS-67, however, the amount capitalized cannot exceed the estimated fair value of the amenity at its expected date of substantial completion. Any costs in excess of the estimated fair value of the amenity at the expected date of its substantial completion are accounted for as common costs of the real estate project (FAS-67, par. 8b).

After it is substantially completed and ready for its intended use, further revision of the final capitalized cost of an amenity not in excess of its estimated fair value is not permitted. This cost becomes the basis of the amenity for any future sale. The subsequent basis for determining gain or loss on the sale of the amenity is the capitalized cost of the amenity not in excess of its estimated fair value at its date of substantial completion, less any allowable depreciation to the date of the sale.

After its date of substantial completion and availability for its intended use, the operational results of an amenity that is owned by the developer shall be included in the developer's current net income (FAS-67, par. 9).

Incidental Operations of Real Property

Incidental operations of a real estate project usually occur during the holding or development stage of the project and are intended to reduce the cost of the project. Incidental operations do not include activities that result in a profit or return from the proposed development of the real property. For example, revenue received from billboard advertisements placed on the property or miscellaneous concession income would be classified as incidental operations.

If the incremental revenue received from incidental operations exceeds the related incremental costs, the difference is accounted for as a reduction of the capitalized costs of the real estate project. Thus, when incidental operations of a real estate project result in a profit, the capitalized costs of the project are reduced by the amount of profit. Under FAS-67, however, the same does *not* hold true if the incidental operations result in a loss: if the incremental costs of incidental operations exceed the related incremental revenue, the difference is charged to expense when incurred (FAS-67, par. 10).

Allocation of Capitalized Costs

All capitalized costs of a real estate project are allocated to the individual components within the project. If practicable, FAS-67 requires that capitalized costs be allocated by the specific identification method. Under this method, capitalized costs are identified specifically with the individual components within the real estate project. However, if it is impractical to use the specific identification method to allocate capitalized costs, FAS-67 requires that allocation be made, as follows (FAS-67, par. 11):

Land Costs

Only capitalized costs associated with the land prior to any construction are allocated as land costs. Land costs prior to any construction include capitalized land costs and other preconstruction common costs related to the land, including preconstruction common costs of amenities.

Total capitalized land costs are allocated based on the relative fair value of each land parcel prior to any construction. A land parcel may be identified as a lot, an acre, acreage, a unit, or a tract.

Construction Costs

Capitalized construction costs are allocated based on the relative sales value of each individual structure or unit located on a parcel of land. In the event capitalized costs of a real estate project cannot be allocated by the specific identification method or the relative sales value method, the capitalized cost shall be allocated on area methods or other methods appropriate under the circumstances.

Revisions of Estimates

Estimates are used extensively in the acquisition, development, and construction of a real estate project. As a result, revisions of estimated costs occur frequently, and past, present, and future accounting periods may be affected by the revisions.

Revisions of estimates that occur in the acquisition, development, and construction stages of a real estate project are accounted for as changes in accounting estimates (APB-20). The effects of a change in accounting estimate are accounted for (*a*) in the period of change, if the change affects only that period or (*b*) in the period of change and future periods, if the change affects both. A change in an accounting estimate caused in part or entirely by a change in accounting principle should be reported as a change in accounting estimate. APB-20 requires that disclosure be made in current period financial statements of the effects of a change in an accounting estimate on (*a*) income before extraordinary items, (*b*) net income, and (*c*) related per share data. However, ordinary accounting estimates for uncollectible accounts or inventory adjustments, made each period, do not have to be disclosed, unless they are material (FAS-67, par. 12).

Abandonments and Changes in Use

Occasionally a real estate project is partially or completely abandoned, or there is a significant change in the use of the property in the project. Under the provisions of FAS-67, if part or all of a real estate project is abandoned, the related capitalized costs must be expensed immediately. The capitalized costs of an abandoned real estate project should not be allocated to other real estate projects (FAS-67, par. 13).

The cost of land donated to a governmental authority is not accounted for as abandoned. Under this circumstance, the cost of the donated land is accounted for as a common cost of acquiring the project. Thus, the cost of the donated land is allocated to the other land in the project, based on the relative fair value of each parcel of land prior to construction of any buildings or structures (FAS-67, par. 14).

After significant development and construction costs have been capitalized in a real estate project, there may be a change in the use of part or all of the land within the project. Under the provisions of FAS-67, capitalized costs incurred prior to a change in use of all or part of the land within a real estate project are charged to expense, except in the following circumstances:

1. The enterprise has developed a formal plan that indicates that the change in use of the land will result in a higher economic

yield than was originally anticipated. In this event, the maximum costs that can be capitalized must not exceed the estimated value of the revised project at the date of substantial completion and availability for its intended use. Capitalized costs in excess of the estimated value of the revised project when substantially completed, if any, are charged to expense (FAS-67, par. 15).

2. The enterprise has not developed a formal plan, but the change in use of the land is expected to yield a higher economic return than was originally anticipated. In this event, the maximum cost that can be capitalized at the date of change in use cannot exceed the net realizable value of the project based on the assumption that, on the date of the sale, the property will be sold *as is*. Capitalized costs incurred prior to the change in use which exceed the net realizable value must be expensed (FAS-67, par. 16).

SELLING COSTS

Costs incurred to sell real estate projects are accounted for as (*a*) project costs, (*b*) prepaid expenses, or (*c*) period costs.

Project Costs

Project costs are capitalized as part of the construction costs of the real estate project provided that both of the following conditions are met (FAS-67, par. 17):

1. They are incurred for tangible assets that are used as marketing aids during the marketing period of the real estate project, or for services performed in obtaining regulatory approval for real estate sales in the project.

2. The costs incurred are reasonably expected to be recovered from sales.

☛ **PRACTICE POINTER:** Costs to sell real estate that qualify as project costs, less recoverable amounts from incidental operations or salvage value, include legal fees for prospectuses, sales offices, and model units, with or without furnishings.

Costs to sell real estate projects that qualify as project costs become part of the capitalized cost of the project and are allocated to the individual components of the project as common costs.

Prepaid Expenses

Prepaid expenses, which are sometimes called *deferred charges,* are capitalized and amortized over the period that is expected to benefit from the expenditure. If the prepaid item can be identified with certain future revenue, however, it is amortized to the periods in which the future revenue is earned. Costs incurred as prepaid expenses to sell real estate projects must meet the following conditions (FAS-67, par. 18):

1. They do not qualify as project costs.
2. They are incurred for goods or services that will be used in future periods.

Advances on commissions, future advertising costs, and unused sales brochures are examples of costs to sell real estate projects that qualify as prepaid expenses.

Period Costs

Period costs are charged to expense in the period incurred because they do not meet the criteria for project costs or prepaid expenses. Costs to sell real estate projects that do not benefit future periods should be expensed in the period incurred as period costs. Grand opening expenses, sales salaries, sales overhead, and used advertising costs are examples of period costs (FAS-67, par. 19).

RENTAL COSTS OF REAL ESTATE PROJECTS

Initial Rental Operations

Initial rental operations commence when a real estate project is substantially completed and available for occupancy. A real estate project is considered *substantially completed and available for occupancy* when tenant improvements have been completed by the developer, but in no event later than one year after major construction activity has been completed, excluding routine maintenance and cleanup (FAS-67, par. 22).

The actual rental operation of a real estate project shall commence when the project is substantially completed and available for occupancy. At this time, rental revenues and related operating costs are recognized on an accrual basis. Operating costs include amortization of deferred rental costs, if any, and depreciation expense.

Some portions of a real estate rental project may still require major construction for completion, and other portions of the same project may be substantially completed and available for occupancy. In this event, each portion should be accounted for as a separate project (FAS-67, par. 23).

Operating Leases

Costs incurred to rent real estate projects under operating leases are either chargeable to future periods or chargeable to the current period.

Chargeable to Future Periods

If the costs can be identified to, and reasonably expected to be recovered from, specific revenue, such costs are capitalized and amortized to the periods in which the specific revenue is earned. If the costs are for goods not used or services not received, such costs are charged to the future periods in which the goods are used or services are received.

If deferred rental costs can be associated with the revenue from a specific operating lease, such costs are amortized over the lease term. The amortization period commences when the rental project is substantially completed and available for occupancy. If deferred rental costs cannot be identified with the revenue from a specific operating lease, such costs are amortized over the periods benefited. The amortization period commences when the rental project is substantially completed and available for occupancy (FAS-67, par. 21).

> ☞ **PRACTICE POINTER:** Expense unamortized rental costs that subsequently become unrecoverable from future operations when they are determined to be unrecoverable. For example, unamortized rental costs related to specific leases which have been, or will be, terminated should be charged to expense.

Chargeable to the Current Period

If the costs to rent real estate projects under operating leases do not qualify as chargeable to future periods, they are accounted for as period costs and expensed as incurred (FAS-67, par. 20).

RECOVERABILITY

Under the provisions of FAS-67, the net carrying amount of a real estate project under development or held for sale shall not exceed its estimated net realizable value. In the event that the net carrying amount of a real estate project exceeds its estimated net realizable value, a provision to reduce the net carrying amount of its estimated net realizable value shall be established in the books of account. The difference between the net carrying amount of the project and the provision, or allowance account, equals the estimated net realizable value of the real estate project. Each individual project is analyzed separately to determine whether its net carrying amount exceeds its estimated net realizable value. An individual project is considered to consist of similar components within the real estate project, such as (a) individual residences, (b) individual apartments or condominiums, or (c) individual lots, acres, or tracts. Thus, a real estate project that includes 50 individual residences, 10 condominium buildings, 20 multifamily buildings, and 100 residential lots would be accounted for as four separate projects for the purposes of determining net realizable values. The net carrying amount of the 100 residential lots may exceed their net realizable value, while the individual net carrying values of the 50 individual residences, 10 condominium buildings, and 20 multifamily buildings may not exceed their individual estimated net realizable values (FAS-67, par. 24).

Suspension of major construction activity may occur because of a decline in rental demand. In this event, the carrying costs of the real estate rental project may be permanently impaired and a provision for losses may be required. Impairment of the net carrying amount of a real estate project may occur from insufficient rental demand even if construction is not suspended (FAS-67, par. 25).

CHAPTER 62
REAL ESTATE—RECOGNITION OF SALES

CONTENTS

CHAPTER 62
REAL ESTATE—RECOGNITION OF SALES

OVERVIEW

The primary financial reporting issue encountered in accounting for real estate transactions is the timing of revenue recognition. Promulgated GAAP address this important issue by classifying real estate transactions into the following three categories:

1. Real estate sales, except retail land sales
2. Sale-leasebacks involving real estate
3. Retail land sales

The following pronouncements include standards of financial reporting for these three types of real estate transactions:

FAS-66   Accounting for Sales of Real Estate

FAS-98   Accounting for Leases:
- Sale-Leaseback Transactions Involving Real Estate
- Sales-Type Leases of Real Estate
- Definition of the Lease Term
- Initial Direct Costs of Direct Financing

CROSS-REFERENCES

BACKGROUND

The matching principle requires that revenue and related costs be recognized simultaneously in determining net income for a specific period. If revenue is deferred to a future period, the associated costs of that revenue are also deferred. Frequently, it may be necessary to estimate revenue and / or costs to achieve a proper matching.

GAAP require that the realization of revenue be recognized in the accounting period in which the earning process is substantially completed and an exchange has taken place. In addition, revenue usually is recognized at the amount established by the parties to the exchange, except for transactions in which collection of the receivable is not reasonably assured. In the event that collection of the receivable is not reasonably assured, the installment method or cost-recovery method may be used [APB-10 (Omnibus Opinion—1966)]. Alternatively, collections may be recorded properly as deposits in the event that considerable uncertainty exists as to their eventual collectibility.

FAS-66 and FAS-98 address the recognition of revenue from real estate sales. FAS-98 specifically addresses sale-leaseback transactions involving real estate, and FAS-66 contains many of the specialized accounting and reporting principles and practices that were originally published in the following AICPA publications:

- Industry Accounting Guide (Accounting for Profit Recognition on Sales of Real Estate)
- Industry Accounting Guide (Accounting for Retail Land Sales)
- SOP 75-6 (Questions Concerning Profit Recognition of Sales of Real Estate)
- SOP 78-4 (Application of the Deposit, Installment, and Cost Recovery Methods in Accounting for Sales of Real Estate)

FAS-66 does not include those portions of the Industry Accounting Guide titled "Accounting for Retail Land Sales," which cover costs of real estate projects. These costs are covered in FAS-67 (Accounting for Costs and Initial Rental Operations of Real Estate Projects).

FAS-66 establishes GAAP for the recognition of revenue on all real estate transactions for any type of accounting entity. It provides separate criteria for the recognition of revenue on (*a*) all real estate transactions except retail land sales and (*b*) retail land sales. The following items are expressly excluded from the provisions of FAS-66:

1. Exchanges of real estate for other real estate
2. Sales and leasebacks

In extracting the specialized accounting principles and practices from the various AICPA publications, the FASB has made the following changes:

1. Sales of "Time-Sharing Interests in Real Estate" that represent fee simple ownership, or that are sales-type leases under FAS-13 (Accounting for Leases), are accounted for as sales of real estate and are included in the provisions of FAS-66.

2. The discount rate that is applied to the total contract price of a retail land sale has been changed to a rate that produces an amount at which the receivable could be sold on a volume basis without recourse to the seller.

3. The disclosure requirements of the Retail Land Sales Guide have been condensed and certain disclosures omitted because of duplication with other existing GAAP.

FAS-98 contains financial accounting and reporting standards that establish:

- A new definition of *lease term* for all leasing transactions

- The appropriate accounting for a seller-lessee in a sale-leaseback transaction involving real estate, including real estate with equipment, such as manufacturing facilities, power plants, and furnished office buildings.

- The appropriate accounting for a sale-leaseback transaction in which property improvements or integral equipment is sold to a purchaser-lessor and leased back by the seller-lessee who retains the ownership of the underlying land (The term *property improvements or integral equipment* refers to any physical structure or equipment attached to the real estate, or other parts thereof, that cannot be removed and used separately without incurring significant cost.)

- The appropriate accounting for sale-leaseback transactions involving real estate with equipment that include separate sale and leaseback agreements for the real estate and the equipment (*a*) with the same entity or related parties and (*b*) consummated at or near the same time, suggesting that they were negotiated as a package

Sale-leaseback transactions are addressed by FAS-28 (Accounting for Sales with Leasebacks) and FAS-13, except for sale-leaseback transactions involving real estate, which are addressed by FAS-98. A *sale-leaseback* transaction is one in which an owner sells property and then leases that same property back again from the purchaser. The parties to a sale-leaseback transaction are the *seller-lessee* and the *purchaser-lessor*.

If the lease portion of a sale-leaseback transaction meets the criteria for capitalization under FAS-13, the purchaser-lessor records the acquisition of the property as a purchase and the lease as a direct financing lease. If the lease portion of a sale-leaseback transaction does not meet the criteria for capitalization under FAS-13, the purchaser-lessor records the acquisition of the property as a purchase and the lease as an operating lease.

The seller-lessee accounts for the lease in a sale-leaseback transaction based on the portion of the property that is leased back. Under FAS-28, a seller-lessee can lease back (*a*) a minor portion of the property, (*b*) substantially all of the property, or (*c*) somewhere between more than a minor portion of the property and less than substantially all of the property.

Before the issuance of FAS-98, some enterprises recorded a sale of real estate in a sale-leaseback transaction ignoring the provisions of the sale-leaseback agreement, while other enterprises considered the provisions of the sale-leaseback agreement in evaluating whether the sale recognition criteria of FAS-66 were met. This difference in recording resulted from different interpretations of paragraph 40 of FAS-66. Paragraph 40 of FAS-66 required that the *amount* of profit recognized on a sale-leaseback transaction be determined at the date of the sale in accordance with the provisions of FAS-66, but the amount of profit determined in this manner was to be accounted for in accordance with the provisions of FAS-13 and FAS-28. FAS-98 solves this problem by requiring that a sale-leaseback involving real estate, including real estate with equipment, be accounted for as a sale only if it qualifies as a sale under the provisions of FAS-66 and the seller makes active use of the leased property during the lease term.

Under FAS-66, a real estate sale must be consummated before it qualifies as a sale. Consummation of a real estate sale usually requires the seller to transfer title to the buyer. Before the issuance of FAS-98, FAS-13, as amended by FAS-26 (Profit Recognition on Sales-Type Leases of Real Estate), provided that a sale of real estate could be recognized in a sales-type lease even if the title were never transferred. This resulted in a conflict between FAS-66 and FAS-13, which FAS-98 eliminates by prohibiting leases involving real estate from being classified as sales-type leases, under the provisions of FAS-13, unless the lease agreement provides for the title to the property to be transferred to the lessee at or shortly after the end of the lease term.

Under FAS-13, as amended by FAS-98, the lease term may be affected if the lessee provides financing to the lessor and the loan is considered a *guarantee of the lessor's debt*. The lease term may also be affected by the interpretation of the term *economic penalty*. The lease term includes all periods covered by ordinary renewal options during which a guarantee by the lessee of the lessor's debt directly or indirectly related to the leased property is expected to be in effect or a loan from the lessee to the lessor related to the leased property is expected to be outstanding. The lease term also includes all periods for which failure to renew the lease imposes a penalty on the lessee in an amount that makes renewal appear to be reasonably assured. The term *penalty* is defined by FAS-98 as "any requirement that is imposed or can be imposed on the lessee by the lease agreement or by factors outside the lease agreement to disburse cash, incur or assume a liability, perform services, surrender or transfer an asset or rights to an asset or otherwise forego an economic benefit, or suffer an economic detriment" (FAS-98, par. 22b).

REAL ESTATE SALES
(EXCEPT RETAIL LAND SALES)

In a real estate sale, a significant portion of the sales price usually is represented by a long-term receivable, which is not backed by the full faith and credit of the buyer. Usually, the seller can recover the property only in the event of default by the buyer. Another unusual facet of real estate sales is the seller's possible continuing involvement in the property. For instance, the seller may be legally bound to make certain improvements to the property or to adjacent property.

To ensure the collection of the long-term receivable, which usually is part of a real estate transaction, FAS-66 requires minimum down payments for all real estate sales before a seller is permitted to recognize a profit. FAS-66 emphasizes the timing of the recognition of profits but does not cover other aspects of real estate accounting.

Real estate transactions that are *not* considered "retail land sales" include the following:

1. Sales of homes, buildings, and parcels of land

2. Sales of lots to builders

3. Sales of corporate stock or a partnership interest in which the economic substance of the transaction is actually a sale of real estate

4. Sales of options to acquire real estate

5. Sales of time-sharing interests in real estate

For a seller to report the total profit on a sale of real estate (other than a retail land sale) by the full accrual method, FAS-66 requires that the transaction meet specific criteria, as follows (FAS-66, par. 5):

1. A sale must be completed (consummated).
2. The buyer's initial and continuing payments (investment) must be adequate.
3. The seller's receivable is not subject to future subordination, except to (a) a primary lien on the property existing at the date of sale or (b) a future loan or an existing permanent loan commitment the proceeds of which must first be applied to the payment of the seller's receivable.
4. All of the benefits and risks of ownership in the property are substantially transferred to the buyer by the seller.
5. The seller does not have a substantial continued involvement with the property after the sale.

If a sale of real estate, other than a retail land sale, meets all of the above criteria, the seller must recognize the entire profit on the sale in accordance with the full accrual method of accounting. If a real estate sale fails to meet all of the above criteria, profit on the sale is recognized by (a) the deposit method, (b) the installment sales method, (c) the cost-recovery method, (d) the reduced profit method, or (e) the percentage-of-completion method. The method that is used is determined by the specific circumstances of each real estate sale.

When a Real Estate Sale Is Consummated

FAS-66 contains four criteria that must be met for a sale of real estate to be considered "consummated" (FAS-66, par. 6):

1. The contracting parties are legally bound by the contract.
2. All consideration required by the terms of the contract has been paid.
3. If the seller is responsible by the terms of the contract to obtain permanent financing for the buyer, the seller must have arranged for such financing.
4. The seller has performed all of the acts required by the contract to earn the revenue.

As a general rule, the above criteria are met at the time of, or after, the closing of the real estate sale. These criteria rarely are met before closing or at the time a sales agreement is executed.

An exception to the "consummation rule" may occur if, after the date of sale, the seller has continued involvement with the property to construct office buildings, condominiums, shopping centers, or other similar improvements on the land that take a long time to complete. As will be discussed later, FAS-66 permits some profit recognition under certain circumstances even if the seller has this type of substantial continued involvement with the property.

Buyer's Initial and Continuing Investment

In determining whether the buyer's minimum initial investment is adequate under the provisions of FAS-66, the *sales value* of the property—not the stated sales price in the contract—is used. The *sales value* is defined as the stated sales price of the property, increased or decreased for other considerations included in the sale that clearly represent greater or smaller proceeds to the seller on the sale. Thus, any payments made by the buyer that are not included in the stated sales price in the contract and that represent additional proceeds to the seller are included as part of the buyer's minimum investment. These additional proceeds enter into the determination of both the buyer's minimum investment and the *sales value* of the property. Examples of additional proceeds to the seller are (*a*) the exercise price of a real estate option to purchase the property, (*b*) management fees, (*c*) points to obtain financing, (*d*) prepaid interest and principal payments, (*e*) payments by the buyer to third parties that reduce previously existing indebtedness on the property, and (*f*) any payments made by the buyer to the seller that will be applied at a future date against amounts due the seller (FAS-66, par. 7a). However, payments by the buyer to third parties for improvements to the property or payments that are not verifiable are not considered as additional proceeds to the seller (FAS-66, par. 10).

Decreases in the stated sales price that are necessary to arrive at the *sales value* of the property may include, but are not limited to, the following (FAS-66, par. 7b):

1. The amount of discount, if any, necessary to reduce the buyer's receivable to its present value. Thus, if the buyer's receivable does not bear interest or if the rate of interest is less than the prevailing rate, a discount would be required to reduce it to its present value according to APB-21 (Interest on Receivables and Payables).

2. The present value of services that the seller agrees to perform without compensation or, if the seller agrees to perform services at less than prevailing rates, the difference between (*a*) the present value of the services at prevailing rates and (*b*) the present value of the agreed-upon compensation.

The effects of an underlying land lease must also be included in computing the *sales value* of the property. If a seller sells a buyer improvements that are to be built on property subject to an underlying land lease, the present value of the lease payments must be included in the *sales value* of the property. The present value of the lease payments is computed over the actual term of the primary indebtedness of the improvements, if any, or over the usual term of primary indebtedness for the type of improvements involved. The present value of the land lease payments is tantamount to additional indebtedness on the property. If the land lease is not subordinated, the discount rate to determine the present value of the land lease payments should be comparable to interest rates on primary debt of the same nature. If the land lease is subordinated, however, a higher discount rate comparable to secondary debt of the same nature should be used.

Illustration of Computation of Sales Value

XYZ, Inc., agrees to build improvements for ABC Company for a total price of $1,750,000. The improvements are to be built on land leased by ABC from a third party. The payments on the land lease are $18,000 per year, payable monthly in advance, and the lease term is for 45 years. ABC Company will pay for the improvements as follows:

Cash down payment	$ 250,000
10% unsecured note payable in five annual payments of $20,000 plus interest	100,000
Primary loan from insurance company secured by improvements to the property, payable in equal monthly payments over 28 years at 8 1/2% interest	1,400,000
Total stated sales price of improvements	$1,750,000

The computation of the *sales value*, as required by FAS-66, is as follows:

Present value of land lease payments for 28 years, payable $1,500 monthly, discounted at 8 1/2% interest	$ 193,361
Primary loan from insurance company	1,400,000
Total equivalent primary debt	$1,593,361
Unsecured note from buyer to seller	100,000
Cash down payment	250,000
Sales value*	$1,943,361

* The adequacy of the buyer's minimum initial investment in the property is based on the *sales value* of the property and not on the stated sales price.

If a land lease exists between the buyer and a third party, its effects on the sales value of the property are used only to determine the adequacy of the buyer's initial investment. When the seller of the improvements is also the lessor of the land lease, however, the computation of the profit on the sale of the improvements is also affected. Since it is impossible to separate the profits on the improvements from the profits on the underlying lease, FAS-66 requires a special computation limiting the amount of profit that can be recognized. The amount of profit that can be recognized on the improvements is equal to the *sales value* of the property, less the cost of improvements and the cost of the land. However, the present value of the lease payments in the sales value may not exceed the actual cost of the land (FAS-66, par. 39).

The result of limiting the amount of profit that can be recognized on the sale of improvements is to defer any residual profit on the land from being recognized until the land is sold or the future rental payments actually are received.

If a land lease between a buyer and a seller of improvements on the land is for a term of less than 20 years or does not substantially cover the economic life of the improvements being made to the property, the transaction should be accounted for as a single lease of land and improvements (FAS-66, par. 38).

The buyer's minimum initial investment must be made in cash or cash equivalency at or before the time of sale. A buyer's note does not qualify for the minimum initial investment unless payment of the note is unconditionally guaranteed by an irrevocable letter of credit from an established unrelated lending institution. A permanent loan commitment by an independent third party to replace a loan made by the seller is not included in the buyer's initial investment. Any funds that have been loaned or will be loaned, directly or indirectly, to the buyer by the seller are deducted from the buyer's initial investment (down payment) to determine whether the required minimum has been met. For the purposes of this provision, the seller must be exposed to a potential loss as a result of the funds loaned to the buyer. For example, if a buyer made an initial cash investment of $200,000 in a real estate transaction, $25,000 of which was a loan from the seller, the buyer's minimum initial investment under the provisions of FAS-66 would be $175,000. However, if an unrelated banking institution unconditionally guaranteed the timely repayment of the $25,000 to the seller, the entire $200,000 would be eligible as the buyer's initial investment (FAS-66, par. 9).

A direct relationship exists between the amount of a buyer's first investment (down payment) and the probability that the seller eventually will collect the balance due. The larger the down payment, the more likely it is that the buyer will pay the balance due. A reasonable basis for establishing the amount of a buyer's initial investment is the prevailing practices of independent lending institutions. Thus, the difference between the amount of primary mortgage an independent lending institution would lend on a particular parcel of real estate and the *sales value* of the property is a realistic guide to figure the amount of the buyer's initial investment (FAS-66, par. 11).

To apply the full accrual method of accounting to a real estate transaction (other than a retail land sale), FAS-66 provides that the minimum initial investment (down payment) of the buyer should be the *greater* of (1) or (2) below:

1. The percentage of the sales value of the property as indicated in the following (FAS-66, par. 53a):

	Minimum Down Payment (% of Sales Value)
Land:	
Held for commercial, industrial, or residential development to commence within two years after sale	20%
Held for commercial, industrial, or residential development after two years	25%
Commercial and Industrial Property:	
Office and industrial buildings, shopping centers, etc.:	
Properties subject to lease on a long-term lease basis to parties having satisfactory credit rating; cash flow currently sufficient to service all indebtedness	10%
Single tenancy properties sold to a user having a satisfactory credit rating	15%
All other	20%
Other Income-Producing Properties (hotels, motels, marinas, mobile home parks, etc.):	
Cash flow currently sufficient to service all indebtedness	15%
Start-up situations or current deficiencies in cash flow	25%
Multi-Family Residential Property:	
Primary residence:	
Cash flow currently sufficient to service all indebtedness	10%
Start-up situations or current deficiencies in cash flow	15%
Secondary or recreational residence:	
Cash flow currently sufficient to service all indebtedness	15%
Start-up situations or current deficiencies in cash flow	25%
Single Family Residential Property (including condominium or cooperative housing):	
Primary residence of the buyer	5%*
Secondary or recreational residence	10%*

*If collectibility of the remaining portion of the sales price cannot be supported by reliable evidence of collection experience, a higher down payment is called for and should not be less than 60% of the difference between the sales value and the financing available from loans guaranteed by regulatory bodies, such as FHA or VA, or from independent financial institutions. This 60% test applies when independent first-mortgage financing is not utilized and the seller takes a receivable from the buyer for the difference between the sales value and the initial investment. When independent first-mortgage financing is utilized, the adequacy of the initial investment on sales of single family residential property should be determined in accordance with FAS-66.

2. The *lesser* of the following (FAS-66, par. 53b):

   a. The difference between the *sales value* of the property and 115% of the maximum permanent mortgage loan or commitment on the property recently obtained from a primary independent lending institution, or

   b. Twenty-five percent (25%) of the *sales value* of the property

---

Illustration of Determination of Buyer's Minimum Initial Investment in Accordance with FAS-66

The *sales value* of property being sold is $200,000, and the maximum permanent mortgage loan recently placed on the property from an independent lending institution is $150,000. The property being sold is commercial land, which will be developed by the buyer within two years after the date of sale. For the full accrual method of accounting to be applied to this real estate transaction, FAS-66 provides that the minimum initial investment (down payment) of the buyer should be the greater of (1) or (2) below:

1. The percentage of the *sales value* of the property as indicated on the table is $40,000 (20% of $200,000).

2. a. The difference between the *sales value* of the property and 115% of the recently placed permanent mortgage loan is $27,500 (115% of $150,000 = $172,500 and the difference between $200,000 [sales value] and $172,500 is $27,500).

   b. 25% of the sales value ($200,000) is $50,000.

The lesser of 2a ($27,500) and 2b ($50,000) = $27,500.
The greater of 2a ($27,500) and 1 ($40,000) = $40,000.

Thus, the minimum down payment of the buyer is $40,000.

OBSERVATION: The above method of determining the buyer's initial minimum investment (down payment) is described differently in the AICPA Industry Accounting Guide titled

"Accounting for Profit Recognition of Sales of Real Estate."
The AICPA Guide permits the use of two independent methods
to determine the buyer's minimum initial investment (down
payment). The first and simpler is that the minimum initial
investment of the buyer be not less than 25% of the sales value
of the property. The other method is that the minimum initial
investment of the buyer be the greater of:

1. The difference between the sales value of the property and
   115% of the primary permanent commitment or loan on the
   property, or

2. The percentage of the sales value of the property as indicated on the table.

Apparently, in extracting the specialized accounting principles from the AICPA Guide, the FASB concluded that the
method promulgated in FAS-66 either (a) is a better method
than that in the Guide or (b) produces the same results as the
method described in the AICPA Guide.

☛ **PRACTICE POINTER:** Even if the buyer makes the required
minimum initial investment, make a separate assessment to
determine the collectibility of the receivable. In other words,
there must be reasonable assurance that the receivable will be
collected after the seller receives the minimum initial investment; if there is not, do not record the sale by the full accrual
method. The buyer must make the minimum initial investment,
and the seller must be reasonably assured that the balance of
the sales price will be collected, before the real estate sale is
recorded and any profits are recognized. The assessment of the
receivable by the seller should include credit reports on the
buyer and an evaluation of the adequacy of the cash flow from
the property.

In addition to an adequate initial investment, FAS-66 requires that
the buyer maintain a continuing investment in the property by
increasing his or her investment each year. The buyer's total indebtedness for the purchase price of the property must be reduced each
year in equal amounts, which will extinguish the entire indebtedness
(interest and principal) over a specified maximum period. The specified maximum period for land transactions is 20 years. The specified
maximum period for all other real estate transactions is no more than
that offered by independent financial institutions at the time of sale
for first mortgages (FAS-66, par. 12).

The buyer's commitment to pay the full amount of his or her
indebtedness to the seller becomes doubtful if the total indebtedness
is not to be paid within the specified maximum period.

A buyer's payments on his or her indebtedness must be in cash or
cash equivalency. Funds provided directly or indirectly by the seller

cannot be considered in determining the buyer's continuing investment in the property.

Release Provisions

Real estate agreements involving land frequently provide for the periodic release of part of the land to the buyer. The buyer obtains the released land free of any liens. The conditions for the release usually require the buyer to have previously paid sufficient funds to cover the sales price of the released land, and often an additional sum is required to effectuate the release. In these types of transactions involving released land, the requirements for a buyer's initial and continuing investment must be determined based on the *sales value* of property not released or not subject to release (FAS-66, par. 13). In other words, for a seller to recognize profit at the time of sale, a buyer's investment must be enough to pay any amounts for the release of land and still meet the specified initial and continued investment required by the provisions of FAS-66 (FAS-66, par. 14). If the buyer's initial and continuing investment is not sufficient, then each release of land should be treated as a separate sale and profit recognized at that time (FAS-66, par. 15).

Future Subordination

If, at the time of sale, a seller's receivable is subject to future subordination, other than (*a*) to a primary (first mortgage) lien on the property existing at the date of sale or (*b*) to a future loan or existing permanent loan commitment the proceeds of which must first be applied to the payment of the seller's receivable, no profit should be recognized, because the effect of future subordination on the collectibility of a receivable cannot be evaluated reasonably. The cost-recovery method should be used to recognize profit at the time of sale if the seller's receivable is subject to future subordination, other than the exceptions (*a*) and (*b*) noted above (FAS-66, par. 17).

Nontransfer of Ownership and Seller's Continued Involvement

Real estate transactions must be analyzed carefully to determine their economic substance. Frequently, the economic substance of a real estate sale is no more than a management fee arrangement or an indication that the risks and benefits of ownership have not really been transferred in the agreement. Accounting for a real estate transaction can become quite complicated because of the many types of continuing relations that can exist between a buyer and a seller. The substance of the real estate transaction should dictate the accounting method that should be used.

> ☛ **PRACTICE POINTER:** As a general rule, before a profit is recognized, a sale must occur, collectibility of the receivable must be reasonably assured, and the seller must perform all of the acts required by the contract to earn the revenue. Profit also may be recognized—at the time of the sale—on contracts that provide for the continued involvement of the seller if the maximum potential loss of the seller is expressly limited and defined by the terms of the contract. In this event, recognize the total profit on the sale, less the maximum potential loss that could occur because of the seller's involvement, at the time of the sale.

Two important factors in evaluating the economic substance of a real estate sale are (1) the transfer of the usual risks and rewards of ownership in the property and (2) the full performance by the seller of all acts required by the contract to earn the revenue. Generally, both of these factors must be accomplished before full profit can be recognized on the sale of real estate. The more common types of real estate transactions and how they should be accounted for are discussed in the following paragraphs.

Profit Recognition Other Than Full Accrual Basis

If a sale of real estate, other than a retail land sale, meets all of the FAS-66 criteria discussed earlier, the seller must recognize the entire profit on the sale in accordance with the full accrual basis of accounting.

When one (or more) of the FAS-66 criteria is not met in a real estate sale, an alternative method of recognizing revenue from the sale must be used. The alternative method selected may be required by FAS-66 or may be a matter of professional judgment. The four accounting methods recommended by FAS-66 are (1) the deposit method, (2) the cost-recovery method, (3) the installment sales method, and (4) the reduced profit method.

Deposit Accounting

The uncertainty about the collectibility of the sales price in a real estate transaction may be so great that the effective date of the sale is deferred and any cash received by the seller is accounted for as a deposit. However, cash received that is designated by contract as nonrefundable interest may be applied as an offset to existing carrying charges on the property, such as property taxes and interest, instead of being accounted for as a deposit (FAS-66, par. 65).

All cash received, except that appropriately used as an offset to the carrying charges of the property, must be reflected in the seller's balance sheet as a liability (deposit on a contract for the sale of real estate). No change is made in accounting for the property subject to the contract and its related mortgage debt, if any. However, the seller's financial statements should disclose that these items are subject to a sales contract. Depreciation expense should continue as a period cost, in spite of the fact that the property has been sold legally. Until the requirements of FAS-66 are met for profit recognition, the seller does not report a sale and continues to report all cash received (including interest income) either as a deposit or, in the case of nonrefundable interest, as an offset to the carrying charges of the property involved (FAS-66, par. 65). If the buyer forfeits a nonrefundable deposit, or defaults on the contract, the seller should reduce the deposit account appropriately and include such amounts in income of the period (FAS-66, par. 66).

Cost Recovery Method

If a seller's receivable is subject to subordination that cannot be reasonably evaluated, or if uncertainty exists as to the recovery of the seller's cost on default by the buyer, the cost recovery method should be used. Even if cost has been recovered by the seller but additional collections are highly doubtful, the cost-recovery method is appropriate. Frequently, the cost recovery method is used initially for transactions that would also qualify for the installment sales method.

> **OBSERVATION:** Both the cost recovery method and the installment sales method defer the recognitions on the sale until collections actually are received.

Under the cost recovery method, all collections (including interest income) are applied first to the recovery of the cost of the property; only after full cost has been received is any profit recognized (FAS-66, par. 62). The only expenses remaining to be charged against the profit are those relating to the collection process. When the cost recovery method is used, the total sales value is included in the income statement for the period in which the sale is made (FAS-66, par. 63). From the total sales value in the income statement, the total cost of the sale and the deferred gross profit on the sale are deducted. On the balance sheet, the deferred gross profit is reflected as a reduction of the related receivable. Until full cost is recovered, principal payments received are applied to reduce the related receivable, and interest payments received are added to the deferred gross profit. At any given time, the related receivable, less the deferred gross profit, equals the remaining cost that must be recovered. After all cost is recovered, subsequent collections reduce the deferred gross profit and appear as a separate item of revenue on the income statement.

Installment Sales Method

Promulgated GAAP prohibit accounting for sales by installment accounting except under exceptional circumstances in which collectibility cannot be assured or estimated reasonably. Collectibility can be in doubt because of the length of an extended collection period or because no basis of estimation can be established.

> ☞ **PRACTICE POINTER:** The installment sales method frequently is more appropriate for real estate transactions in which collectibility of the receivable from the buyer cannot be reasonably assured because defaults on loans secured by real estate usually result in the recovery of the property sold.

Under the installment sales method of accounting, each payment collected consists of part recovery of cost and part recovery of gross profit, in the same ratio that these two elements existed in the original sale. In a real estate transaction, the original sale is equal to the *sales value* of the property. Thus, under the installment sales method, profit is recognized on cash payments made by the buyer to the holder of the primary debt assumed and on cash payments to the seller. The profit recognized on the cash payments is based on the percentage of total profit to total *sales value* (FAS-66, par. 56).

Illustration of Installment Sales Method

Jones Company sells real property to Smith for $2,000,000. Smith will assume an existing $1,200,000 first mortgage and pay $300,000 in cash as a down payment. The $500,000 balance will be in the form of a 12% second mortgage to Jones Company payable in equal payments of principal and interest over a 10-year period. The cost of the property to Jones is $1,200,000.

Computation of Sales Value and Gross Profit

Cash	$ 300,000
Second mortgage	500,000
First mortgage	1,200,000
Total sales value (which is the same as the stated sales price)	$2,000,000

Less: Cost of property sold	1,200,000
Total gross profit on sale	$800,000
Gross profit percentage ($800,000/$2,000,000)	40.0%
Profit to be recognized on down payment (40% of $300,000)	$ 120,000

Assuming that the $300,000 down payment is insufficient to meet the requirements of full profit recognition on the sale (accrual basis of accounting), Jones recognizes $120,000 gross profit at the time of sale. Several months later Smith makes a cash payment of $100,000 on the first mortgage and $50,000 on the second mortgage. The amount of gross profit that Jones recognizes on these payments would be as follows:

Payment on first mortgage	$100,000
Payment on second mortgage	50,000
Total cash payments	$150,000
Gross profit realized (40% of $150,000)	$ 60,000

Even though Jones does not receive any cash on Smith's payment on the first mortgage, gross profit is still realized because the gross profit percentage was based on the total *sales value*, which included the first mortgage liability.

When the installment sales method is used, the total sales value is included in the income statement of the period in which the sale is made. From the total sales value in the income statement, the total cost of the sale and the deferred gross profit are deducted (FAS-66, par. 59). On the balance sheet, the deferred gross profit on the sale is deducted from the related receivable. As cash payments are received, the portion allocated to realized gross profit is presented as a separate item of revenue on the income statement and deferred gross profit is reduced by the same amount. At any given time, the related receivable, less the deferred gross profit, represents the remaining cost of the property sold (FAS-66, par. 58). Since realized gross profit is recognized as a portion of each cash collection, a percentage relationship will always exist between the long-term receivable and its related deferred gross profit. This percentage relationship will be the same as the gross profit ratio on the initial sales value.

Reduced Profit Method

The buyer's receivable is discounted to the present value of the lowest level of annual payments required by the sales contract. The discount period is the maximum allowed under the provisions of

FAS-66, and all lump-sum payments are excluded in the calculation. The discount rate cannot be less than that stated in the sales contract, if any, or than the prevailing interest rate in accordance with existing GAAP (APB-21). The buyer's receivable discounted as described above is used in determining the profit on the sale of real estate and usually results in a "reduced profit" from that which would be obtained under normal accounting procedures. Lump-sum and other payments are recognized as profit when the seller receives them (FAS-66, par. 68).

Change to Full Accrual Method

After the cost-recovery method or the installment sales method is adopted for a real estate transaction, the receivable should be evaluated periodically for collectibility. When it becomes apparent that the seller's receivable is reasonably assured of being collected, the seller should change to the full accrual accounting method. The change is a change in accounting estimate. When the change to the full accrual accounting method is made, any remaining deferred gross profit is recognized in full in the period in which the change is made (FAS-66, pars. 61 and 64). If the change creates a material effect on the seller's financial statements, full disclosure of the effects and the reason for the change should be appropriately made in the financial statements or footnotes thereto (SOP 78-4).

Profit Recognition When Sale Is Not Consummated

If a real estate sale has not been consummated in accordance with the provisions of FAS-66, the deposit method of accounting is used until the sale is consummated (FAS-66, par. 20).

As mentioned previously, an exception to the "consummation rule" occurs if the terms of the contract require the seller to sell a parcel of land and also construct on the same parcel a building that takes an extended period to complete. In other words, the seller is still involved with the property after the sale because he or she must construct the building. In most jurisdictions a "certificate of occupancy" must be obtained, indicating that the building or other structure has been constructed in accordance with the local building regulations and is ready for occupancy. Thus, a certificate of occupancy usually is necessary to consummate the real estate transaction. However, FAS-66 contains a special provision for profit recognition when a sale of real estate requires the seller to develop the property in the future. If the seller has contracted (*a*) for future development of the land; (*b*) to construct buildings, amenities, or other facilities on the land; or (*c*) to provide offsite improvements, partial recognition of profit may be made if future costs of development can be estimated reasonably at the time of sale. In this event, profit can be recognized for any work performed and finished by the seller when (*a*) the sale of the land is consummated and (*b*) the initial and continuing investments of the buyer are adequate. In other words, if the sale of the land meets the first two criteria for the use of the full accrual method of accounting, any profit allocable to (*a*) the work performed before the sale of the land and (*b*) the sale of the land can be recognized by the percentage-of-completion method. Thus, the total profit on the sale may be allocated to work performed before the sale of the land and before future construction and development work. The allocation of the total profit is based on the estimated costs for each activity using a uniform rate of gross profit for all activities. If significant uncertainties exist or if costs and profits cannot be reasonably estimated, however, the completed contract method should be used.

If a buyer has the right to defer until completion payments due for developmental and construction work, or if the buyer is financially unable to pay these amounts as they come due, care should be exercised in recognizing any profits until completion or satisfactory payment.

The terms of a real estate transaction accounted for by the deposit method may indicate that the carrying amount of the property involved is more than the sales value in the contract and that a loss has been incurred. Since the seller is using the deposit method, no sale is recorded and thus no loss. However, the information indicates an impairment of an asset that should be appropriately recorded by the seller in the period of discovery by a charge to income and the creation of a valuation allowance account for the property involved (FAS-66, par. 21).

Profit Recognition When Buyer's Investment Is Inadequate

If all of the criteria for the full accrual method of accounting are met except that the buyer's initial investment is inadequate, the seller accounts for the sale by the installment sales method, provided the seller is reasonably assured of recovering the cost of the property if the buyer defaults. If the seller is not reasonably assured of recovering the cost of the property, or if cost recovery has been made but future collections are uncertain, the seller uses the cost-recovery method or the deposit method to account for the sale (FAS-66, par. 22).

If all of the criteria for the full accrual method of accounting are met except that the buyer's continuing investment is inadequate, the seller shall account for the sale by the reduced profit method, provided the buyer's periodic payments cover both of the following items (FAS-66, par. 23):

1. Amortization of principal and interest based on the maximum primary mortgage that could be obtained on the property

2. Interest, at an appropriate rate, on the excess amount, if any, of the total actual debt on the property over the maximum primary mortgage that could be obtained on the property

If both of the above conditions are not met, the seller shall not use the reduced profit method. Instead, the seller should account for the sale by either the installment sales method or the cost-recovery method, whichever is more appropriate under the specific circumstances (FAS-66, par. 23).

Profit Recognition—Subordinated Receivable

As mentioned previously, the cost-recovery method is used to recognize profit at the time of sale if the seller's receivable is subject to future subordination (FAS-66, par. 24).

This restriction does not apply in the following circumstances (FAS-66, par. 17):

1. A receivable is subordinate to a first mortgage on the property existing at the time of sale.

2. A future loan, including an existing permanent loan commitment, is provided for by the terms of the sale, and the proceeds of the loan will be applied first to the payment of the seller's receivable (FAS-66, par. 17).

Profit Recognition—Seller's Continued Involvement

In some real estate transactions the seller does not transfer the benefits and risks of ownership to the buyer, or the seller maintains a substantial continued involvement with the property after the date of sale. These types of real estate transactions require careful examination to determine the appropriate method of accounting to be applied.

In legal form a real estate transaction may be a sale, but if in substance the contract is a profit-sharing, financing, or leasing arrangement, no sale or profit is recognized. If a real estate contract contains any of the following provisions, it should be accounted for as a profit-sharing, financing, or leasing arrangement:

1. The return of the buyer's investment in the property is guaranteed by the seller (FAS-66, par. 28).

2. The buyer can compel the seller to repurchase the property (FAS-66, par. 26).

3. An option or obligation exists for the seller to repurchase the property (FAS-66, par. 26).

4. The seller is required to operate the property at its own risk for an extended period (FAS-66, par. 29).

5. The seller, as general partner, holds a receivable from the limited partnership as a result of a real estate sale. The collection of the receivable depends on the successful operation of the limited partnership by the general partner, who is also the seller and holder of the receivable (FAS-66, par. 27).

6. The seller guarantees a specific return on the buyer's investment for an extended period of time (FAS-66, par. 28).

7. The sale includes a leaseback to the seller of all or part of the property (FAS-66, par. 23).

In real estate transactions in which the seller guarantees for a limited period (*a*) to return the buyer's investment or (*b*) to give the buyer a specific rate of return, the seller shall account for the sale by the deposit method of accounting. After the operations of the property become profitable, the seller may recognize profit based on performance. After the limited period has expired and all of the criteria for the full accrual method of accounting are met in accordance with FAS-66, the seller may recognize in full any remaining profit on the sale of real estate.

Initiating and Supporting Operations

As part of a real estate transaction, the seller may be required to initiate or support the operations of the property for a stated period of time or until a certain level of operations has been achieved. In other words, the seller may agree to operate the property for a certain period or until a certain level of rental income has been reached.

Even if there is no agreement, there is a presumption that a seller has an obligation to initiate and support operations of the property he or she has sold in any of the following circumstances (FAS-66, par. 27):

1. The seller sells to a limited partnership an interest in property in which he or she is a general partner.

2. The seller retains an equity interest in the property sold by the seller.

3. A management contract between the buyer and seller provides for compensation that is significantly higher or lower than comparable prevailing rates and that cannot be terminated by either the buyer or the seller.

4. The collection of the receivable from the sale held by the seller is dependent on the operations of the property and represents a significant portion of the sales price. A *significant receivable* is defined as one in excess of 15% of the maximum primary financing that could have been obtained from an established lending institution.

If the seller has agreed to the initiating and supporting operations for a limited period, the seller may recognize profit on the sale based on the performance of the required services. The measurement of performance shall be related to the cost incurred to date and the total estimated costs to be incurred for the services. However, profit recognition may not start until there is reasonable assurance that estimated future rent receipts will cover (*a*) all operating costs, (*b*) debt service, and (*c*) any payments due the seller under the terms of the contract. For this purpose, the estimated future rent receipts shall not exceed the greater of (*a*) leases actually executed or (*b*) two-thirds of the estimated future rent receipts. The difference between the estimated future rent receipts and the greater of (*a*) or (*b*) shall be reserved as a safety factor (FAS-66, par. 29).

If the sales contract does not specify the period for which the seller must initiate and support operations of the property, a two-year period shall be presumed. The two-year period shall commence at the time of initial rental, unless rent receipts cover all operating cost, debt service, and other commitments before the time of initial rental (FAS-66, par. 30).

Services Without Compensation

As part of the contract for the sale of real estate, the seller may be required to perform services related to the property sold without compensation or at a reduced rate. In determining profit to be recognized at the time of sale, a value should be placed on such services at the prevailing rates and deducted from the sales price of the property sold. The value of the compensation should then be recognized over the period in which the services are to be performed by the seller (FAS-66, par. 31).

Sale of Real Estate Options

Proceeds from the sale of real estate options shall be accounted for by the deposit method. If the option is not exercised by its expiration date, the seller of the option shall recognize profit at that time. If an option is sold by the owner of the land and subsequently exercised, the proceeds from the sale of the option are included in determining the *sales value* of the property sold (FAS-66, par. 32).

Sales of Partial Interests in Property

A seller may continue to be involved in property sold by retaining an interest in the property and by giving the buyer preference as to profits, cash flow, return on investment, or some other similar arrangement. In this event, if the transaction is in substance a sale, the seller shall recognize profit to the extent that the sale proceeds, including receivables, exceed the seller's total cost in the property (FAS-66, par. 36).

A seller may retain a partial interest in the property sold, such as an undivided interest or some other form of equity. If a seller sells a partial interest in real estate property and the sale meets all of the criteria for the full accrual method, except for the seller's continued involvement related to the partial interest in the property, the seller shall recognize the proportionate share of the profit that is attributable to the outside interests in the property. If the seller controls the buyer, however, profit on the sale shall not be recognized until realized from transactions with outside individuals, or through the sale of the property to outside parties (FAS-66, par. 34).

A seller may sell single-family units or time-sharing interests in a condominium project. If the units or interests are sold individually, the seller shall recognize profit on the sales by the percentage-of-completion method, provided all of the following conditions are met (FAS-66, par. 37):

1. Construction has progressed beyond the preliminary stage, which means that the engineering and design work, execution of construction contracts, site clearance and preparation, and excavation or completion of the building foundation have all been completed.

2. The buyer cannot obtain a refund, except for nondelivery.

3. The property will not revert to rental property, as evidenced by the number of units or interests that have been sold. In determining the sufficiency of the number of units or interests sold, reference shall be made to local and state laws, the provisions of the condominium or time-sharing contract, and the terms of the financing agreements.

4. Total sales and costs can be estimated reasonably in accordance with the percentage-of-completion method of accounting.

Until all of the above conditions are met, the seller shall account for the sales proceeds from the single-family units or time-sharing interests by the deposit method of accounting (FAS-66, par. 37).

Disclosures

FAS-66 does not contain any specific disclosure requirements for the sale of real estate, other than retail land sales. However, professional judgment may require that a significant sale of real estate be disclosed appropriately in the financial statements.

If interest is imputed on a receivable arising out of a real estate sale, certain disclosures are required by APB-21. In addition, if commitments or contingencies arise in a real estate sale, disclosure may be required by FAS-5 (Accounting for Contingencies).

SALE-LEASEBACKS INVOLVING REAL ESTATE (FAS-98)

Under FAS-98, the sale portion of a sale-leaseback transaction involving real estate is accounted for as a sale only if it qualifies as a sale under the provisions of FAS-66. In addition, FAS-98 prohibits a lease involving real estate from being classified as a sales-type lease unless the lease agreement provides for the title of the leased property to be transferred to the lessee at or shortly after the end of the lease term (FAS-98, par. 5).

Under *sale-leaseback accounting*, the sale portion of the sale-leaseback transaction is recorded as a sale by the seller-lessee, the property sold and all of its related liabilities are eliminated from the seller-lessee's balance sheet, gain or loss on the sale portion of the sale-leaseback transaction is recognized by the seller-lessee in accordance with the provisions of FAS-13 (as amended by FAS-28, FAS-66, and FAS-98), and the lease portion of the sale-leaseback transaction is accounted for in accordance with the provisions of FAS-13 (as amended by FAS-28). Sale-leaseback accounting under FAS-98 is analogous to the full accrual method under FAS-66.

Under FAS-98, a seller-lessee applies sale-leaseback accounting only to those sale-leaseback transactions containing payment terms and provisions that provide for (*a*) a normal leaseback (as defined by FAS-98), (*b*) an adequate initial and continuing investment by the purchaser-lessor (as defined by FAS-66), (*c*) the transfer of all of the other risks and rewards of ownership to the purchaser-lessor, and (*d*) no other continued involvement by the seller-lessee, other than the continued involvement represented by the lease portion of the sale-leaseback transaction (FAS-98, par. 7).

Normal Leaseback

Under FAS-98, a normal leaseback is one in which the seller-lessee actively uses substantially all of the leased property in its trade or business during the lease term. The seller-lessee may sublease a minor portion of the leased property, equal to 10% or less of the reasonable rental value for the entire leased property, and the lease will still qualify as a normal lease. Thus, for the leaseback to qualify as normal under FAS-98, the seller-lessee must actively use substantially all of the leased property in its trade or business in consideration for rent payments, which may include contingent rentals based on the seller-lessee's future operations (FAS-98, par. 8).

If occupancy by the seller-lessee's customers is transient or short-term, the seller-lessee may provide ancillary services, such as housekeeping, inventory control, entertainment, bookkeeping, and food service. Thus, active use by a seller-lessee in its trade or business includes the use of the leased property as a hotel, bonded warehouse, parking lot, or some other similar business (FAS-98, par. 8).

Adequate Initial and Continuing Investment by the Purchaser-Lessor

To qualify for sale-leaseback accounting under FAS-98, the purchaser-lessor's initial and continuing investment in the property must be adequate as prescribed by FAS-66. In determining whether the purchaser's minimum initial investment is adequate under the provisions of FAS-66, the *sales value* of the property is used and not the stated sales price that appears in the sales contract.

In addition to an adequate initial investment, FAS-66 requires that the purchaser maintain a continuing investment in the property by increasing the investment each year. The purchaser's total indebtedness for the purchase price of the property must be reduced each year in equal amounts that will extinguish the entire indebtedness (interest and principal) over a specified maximum period. The specified maximum period for land transactions is 20 years. The specified maximum period for all other real estate transactions is no more than that offered at the time of sale for first mortgages by independent financial institutions. (The purchaser's initial investment, continuing investment, and the stated sales price in the property are discussed fully earlier in this chapter.)

Transfer of All Other Risks and Rewards of Ownership

To qualify for sale-leaseback accounting under FAS-98, the seller-lessee must transfer all of the risks and rewards of ownership in the property to the purchaser-lessor.

No Other Continuing Involvement

FAS-98 considers the leaseback portion of a sale-leaseback transaction to be a form of continued involvement with the leased property by the seller-lessee (FAS-98, par. 48). Other than the continued involvement represented by the leaseback portion of the sale-leaseback transaction, a normal leaseback excludes any *other* continuing involvement in the leased property by the seller-lessee. Thus, sale-leaseback accounting cannot be used to account for a sale-leaseback transaction in which the seller-lessee has any other continuing involvement in the property besides that represented by the leaseback portion of the transaction. (The continuing involvement of the seller in the property is discussed fully earlier in this chapter.)

An exchange of some stated or unstated rights or privileges is indicated in a sale-leaseback transaction if the terms of the transaction are substantially different from terms that an independent third-party lessor would accept. In this event, the stated or unstated rights or privileges shall be considered in evaluating the continued involvement of the seller-lessee. Terms or conditions indicating stated or unstated rights or privileges may involve the sales price, the interest rate, and terms of any loan from the seller-lessee to the purchaser-lessor (FAS-98, par. 9).

Recognition of Profit by Full Accrual Method

A sale-leaseback transaction must meet the criteria of FAS-98 before the seller-lessee can account for the transaction by the sale-leaseback accounting method (full accrual method). Under the sale-leaseback accounting method, the seller-lessee (*a*) records a sale, (*b*) removes the sold property and its related liabilities from the balance sheet, (*c*) recognizes gain or loss on the sale portion of the transaction in accordance with FAS-66, and (*d*) classifies the lease portion of the transaction as either a capitalized lease or an operating lease, in accordance with the provisions of FAS-13, as amended by FAS-28.

Once a sale-leaseback transaction qualifies for sale-leaseback accounting in accordance with the provisions of FAS-98, the steps below are followed to determine the amount of gain (loss) and the time of recognition of the gain (loss):

Step 1. Compute the *amount* of gain (loss) on the sale portion of the sale-leaseback transaction in accordance with the provisions of FAS-66. (Disregard the fact that the sale is part of a sale-leaseback transaction.)

> **Note:** A loss must be recognized immediately on the sale portion of a sale-leaseback transaction if the undepreciated

cost of the property sold is more than its fair value. The maximum amount of loss that is recognized immediately cannot exceed the difference between the fair value of the property and its undepreciated cost. If the indicated loss exceeds the difference between the fair value of the property sold and its undepreciated cost, the loss is possibly, in substance, a prepayment of rent. Under this circumstance, it is appropriate to defer the indicated loss and amortize it as prepaid rent (FAS-13, par. 33c, as amended by FAS-28, par. 3).

Step 2. Classify the lease portion of the sale-leaseback transaction in accordance with the provisions of FAS-13, as amended by FAS-28. [Depending on the percentage amount of the property that the seller-lessee leases back, a lease may be classified under FAS-28 as involving (*a*) substantially all of the property, (*b*) a minor portion of the property, or (*c*) more than a minor portion of the property but less than substantially all.]

Note: A *minor* portion of the property has been leased back if the present value of the total rents to be paid by the seller-lessee under the terms of the lease agreement is reasonable and is equal to 10% or less of the fair value of the property at the inception of the lease. *Substantially all* of the property has been leased back if the present value of the total rents to be paid by the seller-lessee under the terms of the lease agreement is reasonable and is equal to 90% or more of the fair value of the property at the inception of the lease.

Step 3. Determine whether the lease portion of the sale-leaseback transaction qualifies as a capital lease or an operating lease under the provisions of FAS-13.

Note: Under FAS-13, a lease is classified as a capital lease if it meets one or more of the following criteria:

a. Ownership of the property is transferred to the lessee by the end of the lease term.

b. The lease contains a bargain purchase option.

c. At its inception, the lease term is substantially (75% or more) equal to the estimated economic life of the leased property, including earlier years of use. [This particular criterion cannot be used for a lease that begins within the last 25% of the original estimated economic life of the leased property.]

d. The present value of the minimum lease payments at the beginning of the lease term, excluding executory costs and profits thereon to be paid by the lessor, is 90% or more of the fair value of the property at the inception of the lease, less any investment tax credits retained and expected to be realized by the lessor. [This particular criterion cannot be used for a lease that begins within the last 25% of the original estimated economic life of the leased property.]

Step 4. Recognize the amount of gain (loss) computed in Step 1, based on the percentage amount of the property that the seller-lessee leases back in Step 2 (substantially all of the property, a minor portion of the property, or more than a minor portion of the property but less than substantially all), *and* determine whether, in Step 3, the lease is classified as a capital lease or an operating lease.

If, under Step 2, the lease portion of the sale-leaseback transaction is classified as *substantially all*, any gain (loss) on the sale is deferred and amortized by the seller-lessee, according to whether the lease is classified, under Step 3, as a capital lease or an operating lease, as follows:

Capital lease—If the lease is classified as a capital lease, the gain (loss) on the sale is amortized in proportion to the amortization of the leased property.

Operating lease—If the lease is classified as an operating lease, the gain (loss) on the sale is amortized in proportion to the gross rental charged to expense over the lease term.

If, under Step 2, the lease portion of the sale-leaseback transaction is classified as *minor*, the sale and leaseback are accounted for as two independent transactions based on their separate terms. The lease must provide for a reasonable amount of rent, however, considering prevailing market conditions at the inception of the lease. The seller-lessee must increase or decrease the gain (loss) on the sale of the property by an amount that brings the total rental for the leased property to a reasonable amount. Any amount resulting from a rental adjustment shall be amortized as follows:

Capital lease—The deferred or accrued amount of rental adjustment is amortized in proportion to the amortization of the leased property.

Operating lease—The deferred or accrued amount of rental adjustment is amortized in proportion to the gross rental charged to expense over the lease term.

If, under Step 2, the lease portion of the sale-leaseback transaction is classified as *more than minor but less than substantially all*, the seller-lessee shall recognize any excess gain determined at the date of the sale, according to whether the lease is classified under Step 3 as a capital lease or an operating lease, as follows:

Capital lease—The excess gain (if any) is equal to the amount of gain that exceeds the seller-lessee's recorded amount of the property as determined under the provisions of FAS-13 (the lesser of the fair value of the leased property or the present value of the minimum lease payments). For example, if the seller-lessee's recorded amount of the sale-leaseback property is $100,000 as determined under the provisions of FAS-13, and the amount of gain on the sale portion of the sale-leaseback transaction is $120,000, the excess gain that is recognized by the seller-lessee is $20,000. The balance of the gain ($100,000) is deferred and amortized in proportion to the amortization of the leased property.

Operating lease—The excess gain (if any) on a sale-leaseback transaction is equal to the amount of gain that exceeds the present value of the minimum lease payments over the term of the lease. The amount of gain on the sale portion of the sale-leaseback transaction that is not recognized at the date of the sale is deferred and amortized over the lease term in proportion to the gross rentals charged to expense.

For a complete discussion of sale-leaseback transactions, see the 1999 *Miller GAAP Guide* chapter titled "Leases."

Profit Recognition Other Than by the Full Accrual Method

A sale-leaseback transaction must qualify under the provisions of FAS-98 and under most of the provisions of FAS-66 before the full amount of the profit on the sale portion of the transaction can be recognized by the sale-leaseback accounting method (full accrual method).

When one (or more) of the criteria for recognizing the full amount of profit on the sale portion of a sale-leaseback transaction is not met, an alternative method of recognizing revenue from the sale must be used. The alternative method selected may be required by FAS-66 or may be a matter of professional judgment. The four accounting methods recommended by FAS-66 are (1) the deposit method, (2) the cost-recovery method, (3) the installment sales method, and (4) the reduced profit method. (The four alternative methods are discussed earlier in this chapter.)

The collectibility of the receivable should be evaluated periodically. When it becomes apparent that the seller's receivable is reasonably assured of being collected, the seller should change to the full accrual accounting method. (Change to the full accrual method is discussed thoroughly earlier in this chapter.)

Regulated Enterprises—Sale-Leaseback Transactions

FAS-98 applies to regulated enterprises that are subject to FAS-71 (Accounting for the Effects of Certain Types of Regulation). The application of FAS-98 for financial accounting purposes (GAAP) may result in the recognition of income and expense in a different accounting period than that in which the same income and expense are recognized for regulatory purposes (rate-making). Under income tax accounting, this results in a temporary difference. If a temporary difference represents part or all of a phase-in plan as defined by FAS-92 (Regulated Enterprises—Accounting for Phase-In Plans), a specific method of accounting is prescribed by FAS-98. For all other types of temporary differences, a different method of accounting is specified (FAS-98, par. 14).

If a temporary difference represents part or all of a phase-in plan, as defined by FAS-92, it is accounted for in accordance with the provisions of FAS-92. In all other circumstances, a temporary difference is modified to conform with FAS-71. For example, the sale portion of a sale-leaseback transaction may be recognized for regulatory purposes and not recognized for financial accounting purposes because the transaction is accounted for by the deposit method. In this event, amortization of the asset should be modified to equal the total amount of the rental expense and gain or loss allowable for regulatory purposes. Also, the sale portion of a sale-leaseback transaction may be recognized for regulatory purposes and not recognized for financial accounting purposes because the transaction is accounted for as a financing. In this event, amortization of the asset and the total amount of interest imputed under the interest method for the financing should be modified to equal the total rental expense and gain or loss allowable for regulatory purposes (FAS-98, par. 15).

If it is not part of a phase-in plan as defined by FAS-92 and it meets the criteria of FAS-71, a temporary difference between the amount of income or expense allowable for regulatory purposes and the amount of income or expense recognized by the deposit method or as a financing shall be capitalized or accrued as a separate regulatory asset or liability (FAS-98, par. 16).

Financial Statement Disclosure and Presentation

The financial statements of the seller-lessee shall include a description of the terms of the sale-leaseback transaction, including future commitments, obligations, or other provisions that require or result in the seller-lessee's continuing involvement (FAS-98, par. 17).

A seller-lessee that has accounted for a sale-leaseback by the deposit method or as financing shall disclose in the aggregate and for each of the five succeeding fiscal years (FAS-98, par. 18):

- The obligation for future minimum lease payments as of the date of the latest balance sheet presented
- The total of minimum sublease rentals, if any, to be received in the future under noncancelable subleases

RETAIL LAND SALES

The development of a large tract of land, usually over several years, is typical for a company in the retail land sales industry. Master plans are drawn for the improvement of the property, which may include amenities, and all necessary regulatory approvals are obtained. Large advertising campaigns are held at an early stage, frequently resulting in substantial sales before significant development of the property. In most retail land sales, a substantial portion of the sales price is financed by the seller in the form of a long-term receivable secured by the property. Interest and principal are paid by the buyer over an extended number of years. In the event of default, the buyer usually loses his or her entire equity and the property reverts back to the seller. Frequently, the retail land sales contract or existing state law provides for a period in which the purchaser may receive a refund of all or part of any payments made. In addition, the seller may be unable to obtain a deficiency judgment against the buyer because of operation of the law. Finally, many project-wide improvements and amenities are deferred until the later stages of development, when the seller may be faced with financial difficulties.

Because of small down payments, frequent cancellations and refunds, and the possibility that the retail land sales company may not be financially able to complete the project, certain specific conditions must be met before a sale can be recognized.

Profit Recognition

FAS-66 requires that profit on all retail land sales within a project be recognized by a single accounting method. As conditions change for the entire project, the method of profit recognition changes in accordance with the provisions of FAS-66. The provisions of FAS-66 require that the profits on a retail land sales project be recognized by (*a*) the full accrual method, (*b*) the percentage-of-completion method, (*c*) the installment sales method, or (*d*) the deposit method. FAS-66 contains specific criteria that must be met before a particular profit recognition method can be used.

A *retail land sales project* is defined as a "homogeneous, reasonably contiguous area of land that may, for development or marketing, be subdivided in accordance with a master plan" (FAS-66, par. 44).

Profit Recognition—Full Accrual Method

A retail land sales project must meet all of the following conditions for the full accrual method of accounting to be used for the recognition of profit (FAS-66, par. 45):

1. The down payment and all subsequent payments have been made by the buyer, through and including any period of cancellation, and all periods for any refund have expired.

2. The buyer has paid a total of 10% or more, in principal or interest, of the total contract sales price.

3. The seller's collection experience for the project or for prior projects indicates that at least 90% of the receivables in force for six months after the sale is recorded will be collected in full. A down payment of 20% or more is an acceptable substitute for this experience test.

   OBSERVATION: Profit may be recognized before the end of six months if collection experience is based on a prior project. The six-month period is an eligibility test for the full accrual method of accounting.

   The collection experience of a prior project may be used if (*a*) the prior project was similar in characteristics to the new project and (*b*) the collection period was long enough to determine collectibility of receivables to maturity dates.

4. The seller's receivable for the property sold is not subject to subordination of new loans. However, subordination is allowed for construction of a residence, provided the project's collection experience for such subordinated receivables is approximately the same as that for those receivables that are not subordinated.

5. The seller is not obligated to construct amenities or other facilities or to complete any improvements for lots that have been sold.

If all of the above conditions are met for the entire retail land sales project, the seller shall recognize profits by the full accrual method of accounting.

Illustration of Procedures for Accrual Method

The actual procedures that must be used to record retail land sales under the full accrual method of accounting are as follows:

1. The total contract price of the retail land sale, before any deductions, is recorded as a gross sale. The total contract price includes the total amount of principal and interest that is expected to be received from the sale.

2. The down payment on the sale is recorded. The difference between the total contract price of the retail land sale and the down payment is the gross receivable.

3. The gross receivable is discounted at the date of sale to yield an amount at which it could be sold on a volume basis without recourse to the seller. The discount on the gross receivable is referred to as a "valuation discount."

4. The valuation discount is amortized to income over the life of the retail land sales contract. The interest method should be used to produce a constant rate of amortization.

5. An allowance for contract cancellations is established based on estimates of contracts that are not expected to be collected in subsequent periods. Canceled contracts are charged directly to the allowance account.

   For the purpose of determining the adequacy of the allowance for contract cancellations in subsequent periods, all receivables that do not conform to the criteria in the following table shall be considered uncollectible and the allowance account adjusted appropriately:

Percentage contract price paid	Delinquency period
Less than 25%	90 days
25% but less than 50%	120 days
50% and over	150 days

   If a buyer is willing to assume personal liability for his or her debt and apparently has the means and ability to complete all payments, the delinquency periods in the above table may be extended.

6. The following items represent deductions from the gross sale to arrive at net sales for the period:
   a. Valuation discount
   b. Allowance for contract cancellations
   c. Deferred portion of gross sale (to be matched with future work or performance of the seller)

7. Cost of sales should be computed on net sales for the period.

8. A sale that is made and canceled in the same reporting period should be included in, and also deducted from, gross sales or disclosed appropriately in some other manner.

9. The unamortized valuation discount (discount on receivables) and the allowance for contract cancellations are shown on the balance sheet as deductions from the related receivables.

10. Deferred revenue, less any related costs, is shown on the balance sheet as a liability. Deferred revenue should be recognized in future periods as the work is performed by the seller.

Profit Recognition—Other Than Full Accrual Method

Percentage-of-Completion Method

If the first four criteria for applying the full accrual method of accounting are met for the entire retail land sales project and the fifth criterion is not met (see "Profit Recognition—Full Accrual Method" above), the seller shall recognize profits by the percentage-of-completion method of accounting, provided the following additional criteria are met for the entire project (FAS-66, par. 46):

1. Progress on the entire project has passed the preliminary stages and tangible evidence exists to indicate that the project will be completed according to plans. Tangible evidence of such progress includes the following:

   a. Funds have actually been expended.

   b. Work on project improvements has been initiated.

   c. Engineering plans and construction commitments pertaining to lots that have been sold are in existence.

   d. Access roads and amenities are substantially completed.

   e. There is no evidence of any significant delay to the project, and dependable estimates of costs to complete the project and extent of progress are reasonable.

2. At the end of the normal payment period, it is reasonably expected that the property clearly will be useful for its intended purposes as represented by the seller at the time of sale.

If the above criteria are met for the entire project and the first four criteria for applying the full accrual method of accounting are met for the entire project, the seller recognizes profits on retail land sales by the percentage-of-completion method.

Installment Sales Method

If the first two criteria for applying the full accrual method of accounting are met for the entire project and the other three criteria are not met, the seller shall recognize profits by the installment sales method, provided the following additional criteria are met for the entire project (FAS-66, par. 47):

1. The current and prospective financial capabilities of the retail land sales company (seller) must reflect with reasonable assurance that the company is capable of completing all of its obligations under the sales contract and master plan.

2. Indications of the seller's financial capabilities include (*a*) the sufficiency of equity capital, (*b*) borrowing capacity, and (*c*) positive cash flow from present operations.

If the above criteria are met for the entire project and the first two criteria for applying the full accrual method of accounting are met for the entire project, the seller shall recognize profits on retail land sales by the installment sales method.

Deposit Accounting Method

If a retail land sale does not meet the criteria for accounting by the full accrual method, the percentage-of-completion method, or the installment sale method, the seller shall account for all proceeds from retail land sales by the deposit method of accounting (FAS-66, par. 48). Under the deposit method of accounting, the effective date of the sale is deferred and all funds received, including principal and interest, are recorded as deposits on retail land sales.

Change in Accounting Method

If a retail land sales entity has been reporting sales for the entire project by the deposit method and subsequently the criteria for the installment sales method, the percentage-of-completion method, or the full accrual method are met for the entire project, the change to the new method shall be accounted for as a change in accounting estimate (FAS-66, par. 49). Thus, the effects of the change shall be accounted for prospectively in accordance with APB-20 (Accounting Changes). If the effects of the change in an accounting estimate are significant, disclosure of the effects on (*a*) income before extraordinary items, (*b*) net income, and (*c*) the related per share data should be made in the financial statements of the period of change.

Initially, retail land sales may be accounted for by the installment sales method, and subsequently the criteria for the percentage-of-completion method may be met for the entire project. In this event, the percentage-of-completion method may be adopted for the entire project. The effects of the change to the percentage-of-completion method are accounted for as a change in accounting estimate and, if material, disclosure of the effects on (*a*) income before extraordinary items, (*b*) net income, and (*c*) related per share data should be made in the financial statements of the period of change.

In reporting the change from the installment sales method to the percentage-of-completion method, the following procedures should be observed:

1. If required, the receivables should be discounted to their present values at the date of change in accordance with APB-21.

2. The liability for the remaining future performance of the seller should be discounted to its present value at the date of the change.

3. The amount of discount, if any, on the receivables and the amount of discount, if any, on the liability for remaining future performance by the seller are deducted from the unrealized gross profit on installment sales at the date of the change to arrive at the net credit to income resulting from the change.

Disclosure—Retail Land Sales

Retail land sales companies, diversified entities with significant retail land sales operations, and investors who derive a significant portion of their income from investments involved in retail land sales must disclose specific information in the financial statements, as follows (FAS-66, par. 50):

1. The maturities of the receivables from retail land sales for each of the five years following the date of the financial statements

2. The amount of delinquent receivables and the method used to determine delinquency

3. The weighted average and range of stated interest rates on receivables from retail land sales

4. Estimated total costs and anticipated expenditures to improve major areas of the project from which sales are being made, for each of the five years following the date of the financial statements

5. The amount of recorded obligations for improvements

6. The method of recognizing profit

7. The effect of a change in accounting estimate, if the percentage-of-completion method is adopted for a retail land sales project originally reported using the installment method (APB-21)

Regulated Industries

CHAPTER 63
REGULATED INDUSTRIES

CONTENTS

CHAPTER 63
REGULATED INDUSTRIES

OVERVIEW

GAAP include specific coverage of regulated enterprises, indicating the applicability of GAAP to those enterprises and, in some instances, providing alternative procedures for them. In general, the type of regulation discussed is that which permits rates or prices to be set at levels intended to recover the estimated costs of providing regulated services and products.

An important accounting issue for regulated enterprises is the capitalization of costs and their associated recovery. Generally, if regulation provides assurance that incurred costs will be recovered, those costs should be capitalized. If current recovery is provided for costs that will be incurred in the future, regulated enterprises should recognize those costs as liabilities.

GAAP for regulated enterprises are found in the following pronouncements:

FAS-71	Accounting for the Effects of Certain Types of Regulation
FAS-90	Regulated Enterprises—Accounting for Abandonments and Disallowances of Plant Costs
FAS-92	Regulated Enterprises—Accounting for Phase-in Plans
FAS-101	Regulated Enterprises—Accounting for the Discontinuation of Application of FASB Statement No. 71
FAS-106	Employers' Accounting for Postretirement Benefits Other Than Pensions
FAS-109	Accounting for Income Taxes
FAS-121	Accounting for the Impairment of Long-Lived Assets and for Long-Lived Assets to Be Disposed Of

CROSS-REFERENCES

1999 MILLER GAAP GUIDE: Chapter 1, "Accounting Changes"; Chapter 6, "Consolidated Financial Statements"; Chapter 7, "Contingencies, Risks, and Uncertainties"; Chapter 20, "Impairment of Loans and Long-Lived Assets"; Chapter 21, "Income Taxes"; Chapter 24, "Interest Costs Capitalized"; Chapter 36, "Postemployment and Postretirement Benefits Other Than Pensions"

1999 MILLER GAAP IMPLEMENTATION MANUAL: Chapter 47, "Regulated Industries"

1999 MILLER GAAP IMPLEMENTATION MANUAL: EITF: Chapter 35, "Rate-Regulated Industries"

BACKGROUND

Over the years, state and federal regulatory agencies have been established by governmental authorities to regulate certain industries that provide essential services to the general public (i.e., public utilities, railroads, insurance companies, and cable television). One of the primary functions of regulatory agencies is to establish rates that the regulated enterprise can charge for its services or products. In connection with their regulatory authority, most agencies prescribe the types of accounting records and reports that the regulated enterprise must maintain. Frequently, these prescribed accounting rules conflict with GAAP.

The Addendum to APB-2 (Accounting Principles for Regulated Industries) required that financial statements of a regulated business intended for public use be based on existing GAAP, with appropriate recognition given to the rate-making process established by the regulatory agency. Under GAAS, an independent auditor must comply with the reporting standard that financial statements be presented in accordance with GAAP.

Different methods are used by regulatory agencies to set rates for regulated enterprises. The many different methods can be classified into (a) individual cost-of-service, (b) group rate-setting, and (c) a combination of both individual cost-of-service and group rate-setting.

Under the individual cost-of-service method of rate setting, the *allowable costs* that an enterprise usually is permitted to recover are all actual and/or estimated costs that are required to provide the service to the public, including a return on investment to compensate sources of long-term debt and equity capital. The rate or rates charged to different classes of customers are designed, but not guaranteed, to produce total revenue for the enterprise equal to the allowable costs. The individual cost-of-service method usually is used in setting rates for public utilities. An enterprise is more ensured of cost recovery under the individual cost-of-service method than any other method.

Under the group rate-setting method, the allowable costs that an enterprise may recover are based on rates established on an industry-wide, area-wide, or some other aggregate basis. Group rate-setting usually is utilized in more competitive industries, such as airlines, motor carriers, railroads, and insurance companies, than those in which the individual cost-of-service method is used.

Under the combination of individual cost-of-service and group rate-setting methods, the allowable costs that an enterprise can recover are based on some combination of both methods. Under the combination method, however, allowable costs usually do not include a provision for a return on investment, but may include an allowance for inflation or working capital.

Through the regulatory process, an enterprise is substantially assured of recovering its allowable costs by the collection of revenue from its customers. It must be noted that under some methods of rate-setting, allowable costs include a return on investment for the regulated enterprise. The economic effect of regulation is the substantiation that an asset exists or does not exist. As allowable costs are incurred by a regulated enterprise, they should be capitalized as assets. Costs that are not allowable under the regulatory process, however, are not substantially assured of being recovered and should be expensed as incurred.

FAS-71 establishes GAAP for enterprises whose regulators have the power to approve and/or regulate the rates that enterprises may charge customers for services or products. It contains the criteria that an enterprise must meet to be classified as a *regulated enterprise* and also establishes GAAP for the capitalization of allowable costs. FAS-90 amends FAS-71 to specify the appropriate accounting for abandonments of plants and the disallowances of costs of recently completed plants.

FAS-90 also amends FAS-71 to provide that an allowance for interest on funds used during the construction stage of an asset should be capitalized only if it is *probable* (likely) that such an allowance will be included subsequently by the governing regulatory authorities as an allowable cost of the constructed asset.

FAS-92 amends FAS-71 to specify the accounting for phase-in plans. FAS-92 specifically addresses those phase-in plans ordered by a regulator in connection with a plant on which construction was started before January 1, 1988.

FAS-101 establishes the appropriate accounting for situations in which an enterprise discontinues the application of the provisions of FAS-71.

FAS-121 amends FAS-71 and FAS-101 to establish accounting standards for the impairment of long-lived and certain other assets, except that impairment of (1) regulatory assets will continue to be governed by paragraph 9 of FAS-71 and (2) costs of recently complete plants will continue to be addressed by paragraph 7 of FAS-90.

For the purposes of FAS-71, a regulator may be an independent third party, or a governing board of the regulated enterprise empowered by statute or contract. FAS-71 supersedes the Addendum to APB-2. Paragraph 108 of FAS-71 amends APB-30 (Reporting the Results of Operations) to specify that utility refunds to customers be disclosed net of their tax effects, as a separate line item in the income statement. APB-30 generally prohibits net-of-tax disclosure of unusual or infrequently occurring items that do not qualify as extraordinary items.

FAS-71 does not identify any specific industry as *regulated*. Instead, the focus of FAS-71 is on the nature of regulation and its resulting financial effects on a specific enterprise. Thus, any enterprise in any industry that meets all of the criteria of FAS-71 must comply with its provisions.

FAS-71 does not change the fact that companies in regulated industries must comply with all existing and future authoritative accounting pronouncements. If a conflict arises between an authoritative accounting pronouncement and FAS-71, however, a regulated enterprise shall apply the provisions of FAS-71 instead of the conflicting pronouncement. The following conditions govern the application of FAS-71:

1. FAS-71 applies only to financial statements issued for external general purposes, not to financial statements submitted to a regulatory agency.

2. FAS-71 shall be applied only to regulated enterprises or those portions of the operations of a regulated enterprise that meet the specific criteria established by FAS-71.

3. FAS-71 does not apply to emergency governmental actions that are imposed under unusual circumstances, such as price controls during periods of high inflation.

CRITERIA FOR REGULATED OPERATIONS

FAS-71 applies to financial statements issued for general purposes by an enterprise that has regulated operations and meets all of the following criteria (FAS-71, par. 5):

1. An independent third-party regulator or a governing board of the regulated enterprise that has been empowered by statute or contract establishes or approves the rates the enterprise can charge its customers for its services or products.

2. The established or approved rates of the independent third-party regulator or governing board of the regulated enter-

prise are intended to recover the specific costs of the regulated services or products.

3. The rates set by the independent third-party regulator or governing board of the regulated enterprise to recover the costs of the regulated enterprise are reasonable and likely to be collected. (In applying this criterion, consideration must be given to the demand for the services or products and the level of direct and indirect competition.)

The thrust of FAS-71 is that the regulatory process can provide a basis for the regulated enterprise to recognize a specific asset. In this respect, FAS-71 requires that the following conditions be met for a regulated enterprise to recognize an incurred cost as a regulatory asset (FAS-71, par. 9):

1. The regulator's intent to provide recovery of a specific incurred cost must be clear.

2. Based on available evidence, it is expected that the regulated rates will produce revenue about equal to the specific incurred cost.

If at any time the above conditions are not met, the incurred cost should be charged to earnings (FAS-121, par. 32a).

An enterprise must first qualify as a regulated enterprise by meeting the specified criteria of FAS-71, and then both of the above conditions must be met before an incurred cost can be capitalized as an asset.

The essence of the first criterion in FAS-71 is the existence of a regulator that can approve and/or regulate the rates that the enterprise can charge its customers for its services or products. The regulator may be an independent third party or a governing board of the enterprise empowered by statute or contract. A contractual arrangement between an enterprise and its sole or principal customer may create the appearance of *regulation*. However, the sole or principal customer of the enterprise is also responsible for payment of the services or products and thus is not, in a strict sense, an independent third-party regulator or governing board empowered by statute or contract. Therefore, Medicare, Medicaid, and similar contractual arrangements are excluded from the scope of FAS-71.

The principal economic effect of the regulatory process covered by FAS-71 is that it can provide substantiation that an asset does or does not exist at the time a regulated enterprise incurs costs to provide services or products.

Under the provisions of FAS-71 the regulated rates must be designed to recover the specific costs of the regulated services or products. This usually is best accomplished by the individual cost-of-service method of rate-setting. Thus, the second criterion of FAS-71 requires that there be a cause-and-effect relationship between costs and revenues.

A cause-and-effect relationship usually does not exist if regulated rates are based on industry-wide costs. The cause-and-effect relationship is intended to be applied to the substance and not the form of the regulation. If regulated rates are based on the costs of a particular group of companies and there is a dominant company within the group, the costs of the dominant company may represent the costs of the entire group. Here, the second criterion of FAS-71 would be met.

The third criterion requires that the rates sufficient to recover incurred costs be reasonable to the ultimate consumer and likely to be collected.

If the regulatory process is based on the recovery of future costs and not specific incurred costs, the provisions of FAS-71 are not met. If a *rate order* authorizing regulated rates for an enterprise does not specify clearly the recovery of specific incurred costs, the provisions of FAS-71 are not met. The rate order must indicate clearly the specific incurred costs that are designated for recovery. These specific incurred costs are referred to as *allowable costs*, in accordance with FAS-121 and consistent with GAAP applicable to other enterprises in general.

In addition, if a regulator subsequently allows recovery through rates of costs previously excluded from allowable costs and written off, that action shall result in recognition of a new asset. The classification of that asset shall be consistent with the classification that would have resulted if those costs had been included initially in allowable costs (FAS-121, par 32c). This provision to reinstate costs previously written off under FAS-121 is unique to rate-regulated industries.

Sometimes the nature of an incurred cost, such as the abandonment of part or all of a particular facility, cannot be anticipated by the regulated enterprise or the regulator. Under these circumstances, the intent of the regulator may be inferred based on available evidence or regulatory precedent, and, as a result, it may be probable that the future rate increases will be provided by the regulator for the specific recovery of the unanticipated future cost.

On the other hand, the regulatory process may indicate the reduction or elimination of an existing asset or substantiate the existence of a new liability. If a cost or related asset is not classified as an allowable cost by the regulator, it will not produce future revenue through the regulatory process (FAS-71, par. 10). Here, the cost or related asset must be accounted for under existing GAAP, which are applied to other enterprises in general.

> **OBSERVATION:** If the regulatory process can create an asset, it appears that deregulation may result in the permanent impairment of an asset that owes its existence to regulation.

Additionally, as competition becomes more pervasive in the rate-regulated industries, costs (particularly plant costs) may become "stranded" in that the utility is unable to recover its cost or plant investment because the customer has changed the nature of the services it has historically received from the utility.

A regulated enterprise may be required by the regulator to refund revenue that was collected in prior periods; or the regulator may include in its regulated rates amounts that are intended to recover specific costs that may be incurred in the future, with the understanding that if the costs are not incurred, an adjustment will be made to future regulated rates. In either instance, the regulator has substantiated the existence of a liability (FAS-71, par. 11). In the event of customer refunds, FAS-71 requires that they be recorded as liabilities if they can be estimated reasonably and either (a) were ordered by the regulator and are unpaid or (b) are likely to occur and are not yet recorded.

If the regulator includes amounts in its rates that are intended to recover expected future costs that must be accounted for, a liability is created equal to the amount of revenue collected for the expected future costs.

The amount of revenue collected for the expected future costs is recorded as unearned revenue until those costs are actually incurred or an adjustment is made by the regulator. For example, a regulator may include in its regulated rates an amount for expected future uninsured storm damages. In this respect, the regulator may require that any amounts not actually incurred in the future for storm damages must be refunded to customers in the form of a future adjustment in the regulated rates. As the revenue attributable to the future storm damage is collected, FAS-71 requires that it be recorded as a liability and included in income only when the actual storm damage costs are incurred.

A regulator can substantiate the existence of another type of liability by requiring the regulated enterprise to credit customers over a future period for gains or other reductions of net allowable costs. The gains or other reductions in net allowable costs usually are amortized over the related future periods by a corresponding reduction in the approved regulated rates. In this event, FAS-71 requires that a liability be recorded in the amount of the future amortization (FAS-71, par. 11c). If a liability is recorded because of the regulatory process, it can only be reduced or eliminated by the regulatory process (FAS-71, par. 12).

An enterprise subject to FAS-71 must comply with all of its provisions. If there is a conflict between FAS-71 and existing GAAP, the provisions of FAS-71 must be applied (FAS-71, par. 4). In all other circumstances, however, existing GAAP must be followed and applied by a regulated enterprise. If a regulated enterprise is required by court order (affirmative injunction) to capitalize and amortize a particular cost and the cost does not qualify for capitalization under existing GAAP or FAS-71, the regulated enterprise cannot capitalize the cost in financial statements purported to be presented in accordance with GAAP.

ACCOUNTING FOR ABANDONMENTS (FAS-90)

Historically, utilities have abandoned plants in early stages of construction, rather than after incurring major construction costs. Prior to the issuance of FAS-71, most regulated enterprises accounted for the costs of abandoned plants on a cost-recovery basis (no loss was recorded if revenues promised by a regulator were expected to recover the recorded costs).

The cost-recovery approach of accounting for abandonments is based on the view that the regulator is disallowing future earnings, rather than disallowing a portion of the cost of the abandoned plant. Thus, the effect of the cost-recovery approach is to delay the recognition of losses that are known to have been incurred.

Originally, FAS-71 required that an abandoned plant be reported at the lesser of its cost or the probable *gross revenue* expected to be allowed on the portion of the cost of the abandoned plant that the regulator included in allowable costs for rate-making purposes. Thus, FAS-71 did not change the practice of accounting for the cost of an abandoned plant on a cost-recovery basis.

FAS-90 amended FAS-71 to require that the future revenue that is expected to result from the regulator's inclusion of the cost of an abandoned plant in allowable costs for rate-making purposes be reported at its *present value* when the abandonment becomes *probable*. If the carrying amount of the abandoned plant exceeds that present value, a loss is recognized.

FAS-90 further amended FAS-71 by requiring the definition of *probable* to be consistent with the use of the term in FAS-5 (Accounting for Contingencies), namely, that a transaction or event is likely to occur (FAS-90, footnote 1). Under FAS-90, the probability that an enterprise will abandon an asset may be classified as (*a*) probable, (*b*) reasonably possible, or (*c*) remote. For purposes of FAS-90, *probable* means that the abandonment is likely to occur, *remote* means that the abandonment is not likely to occur, and *reasonably possible* means that the probability of the abandonment occurring is somewhere between probable and remote.

On the date it becomes probable that an enterprise will abandon an operating asset or an asset under construction, the total cost of that asset is removed from the books of account (plant-in-service or construction work-in-process) and reclassified as a new asset (e.g., a regulatory asset). The amount of cost assigned to the new asset depends on the amount of the total cost of the abandoned plant that the enterprise estimates will be allowed by the governing regulatory authorities. Another factor is whether recovery of the allowed cost is likely to be provided with a full return on investment, or with partial or no return on investment from the date the abandonment becomes probable through the date recovery is completed.

If it is probable (likely) that all or part of the cost of the abandoned plant will be disallowed by the governing regulatory authorities and the amount of the disallowed cost can be estimated reasonably, the disallowed cost is recognized as a current loss and deducted from the total cost of the abandoned plant.

If Full Return on Investment Is Expected

The total cost of the abandoned plant, less the amount of the probable disallowed cost that is recognized as a loss, is recorded and reported as a separate asset (FAS-90, par. 3a).

If Partial or No Return on Investment Is Expected

The present value of the expected future revenue to be generated from the allowable cost of the abandoned plant, plus any return on investment, is reported as a separate new asset. Any excess of the total cost of the abandoned plant reduced by the amount of disallowed cost reported as a loss, over the amount of the separate new asset, is reported as an additional loss (FAS-90, par. 3b).

An enterprise shall use its incremental borrowing rate to compute the present value of the expected future revenue to be generated from the allowable cost of the abandoned plant. An enterprise's incremental borrowing rate is the rate that an enterprise would have to pay to borrow an equivalent amount for a period equal to the expected recovery period.

To compute the present value of expected future revenue to be generated from the allowable cost of the abandoned plant, an enterprise may be required to estimate the probable period before recovery is expected to begin and the probable period over which recovery is expected to be provided. If the estimate of either of these periods is a range (similar to a minimum-maximum), the present value is based on the minimum amount in the range, unless some other amount within the range appears to be a better estimate (FIN-14, par. 3).

Subsequent Period Adjustments to the Separate New Asset

In accounting for the abandonment of a plant, estimates that may be used by an enterprise to calculate and record the amount of the separate new asset include (FAS-90, par. 4):

1. The amount of any probable disallowed cost of the abandoned plant that can be estimated reasonably

2. Whether recovery of the allowed cost of the abandoned plant is likely to be provided with a full return on investment, a partial return on investment, or no return on investment

3. The period from the date the abandonment becomes *probable* through the date recovery is completed

4. The probable period before recovery is expected to begin and the probable period over which recovery is expected to be provided

FAS-90 requires that an adjustment be made to the recorded amount of the new asset if new information indicates that the estimates used by an enterprise to record the amount of the separate new asset have changed. The amount of the adjustment is recognized as a gain or loss in the net income of the period in which the adjustment arises. However, no adjustment is made to the recorded amount of the separate new asset for changes in the enterprise's incremental borrowing rate (FAS-90, par. 4).

Accrued Carrying Charges on the Separate New Asset

A carrying charge is accrued and added to the carrying amount of the recorded separate new asset during the period between the date on which the new asset is recognized by an enterprise and the date on which recovery begins.

The rate of the carrying charge is based on whether a full return on investment is likely to be provided, or a partial or no return on investment is likely to be provided (FAS-90, par. 5).

If Full Return on Investment Is Expected

A rate equal to the allowed overall cost of capital in the jurisdiction in which recovery is expected to be provided is used to calculate the amount of the accrued carrying charge.

If Partial or No Return on Investment Is Expected

The same rate that was used to compute the present value of the expected future revenue to be generated from the allowable cost of the abandoned plant is used to calculate the amount of the accrued carrying charge.

Amortization of Separate New Asset During Recovery Period

The separate new asset is amortized during the recovery period, based on whether a full return on investment is likely to be provided, or a partial or no return on investment is likely to be provided (FAS-90, par. 6).

If Full Return on Investment is Expected

The separate new asset is amortized during the recovery period in the same manner as that used for rate-making purposes.

If Partial or No Return on Investment Is Expected

The separate new asset is amortized during the recovery period at the same rate that was used to compute the present value of the expected future revenue to be generated from the allowable cost of the abandoned plant. (**Note:** This method of amortization will produce a constant return on the unamortized investment in the new asset equal to the rate at which the expected revenues were discounted.)

Accounting for Disallowances of Plant Costs

FAS-71 addresses the disallowance of costs by a regulator, indicating that when a disallowance occurs, "the carrying amount of any related asset shall be reduced to the extent that the asset has been impaired. Whether the asset [of a regulated enterprise] has been impaired shall be judged the same as for enterprises in general" (FAS-71, par. 10).

An enterprise's estimate of the cost of the abandoned plant that will be allowed should be based on the facts and circumstances related to the specific abandonment and should consider the past practice and current policies of the governing regulatory authorities.

Under FAS-90, if it becomes probable that part of the cost of a recently completed plant will be disallowed by the governing regulatory authorities and the amount of the disallowed cost can be estimated reasonably, the disallowed cost is recognized as a current loss and deducted from the total cost of the recently completed plant (FAS-90, par. 7).

☞ **PRACTICE POINTER:** If only a range of the amount of the disallowed cost (similar to the minimum or maximum) can be established, then use the minimum amount in the range, unless some other amount within the range appears to be a better estimate (FIN-14, par. 3).

If part of the cost of the recently completed plant is explicitly, but indirectly, disallowed, such as an explicit disallowance of return on investment on a portion of the plant, an equivalent amount of cost is deducted from the reported cost of the recently completed plant and recognized as a loss (FAS-90, par. 7).

ACCOUNTING FOR PHASE-IN PLANS (FAS-92)

Under traditional rate-making procedures, a utility is granted an increase in rates to provide for the recovery of the allowable costs of a newly completed utility plant that is placed in service. However, the impact of significantly increased costs such as those associated with nuclear plants and the high cost of capital has resulted in rate spikes. A *rate spike* is an unusually high, one-time increase in the rates of a regulated enterprise. To reduce the effect of such spikes, regulatory authorities and utilities have developed phase-in plans that allow for a gradual increase in rates.

Several different types of phase-in plans have been developed, all of which are designed to reduce the impact of rate spikes by (*a*) deferring a portion of the initial rate increase to future years and (*b*) providing the regulated enterprise with a return on the amounts deferred. Instead of the traditional pattern of an increase in allowable costs followed by a decrease in allowable costs for utility plants after the plants are placed in service, phase-in plans create a pattern of gradually increasing allowable costs for the initial years of the plant's service life.

The *allowable costs* that a regulatory authority usually permits a regulated enterprise to recover from the rates it charges to its customers include actual and/or estimated costs that are incurred to provide a product or service to the public, including a return on investment to compensate sources of long-term debt and equity capital. The rates that are approved by a regulatory authority are designed, but not guaranteed, to produce total revenue for a regulated enterprise that is approximately equal to its allowable costs.

Under the provisions of FAS-92, a phase-in plan is any method used to recognize allowable costs in the rates charged by a regulated enterprise to its customers that also meets all of the following criteria (FAS-92, par. 3):

1. The phase-in plan was adopted by the regulator in connection with a major plant of the regulated enterprise (or of one of its suppliers) that is newly completed or scheduled for completion in the near future.

2. The method defers the rates approved to recover the allowable costs of the regulated enterprise beyond the period in which those allowable costs would have been charged to expense under GAAP applicable to enterprises in general.

3. The method defers the rates approved to recover the allowable costs of the regulated enterprise beyond the period in which those rates would have been ordered by the enterprise's regulator under the rate-making method routinely used prior to 1982 for similar allowable costs of the same regulated enterprise.

> **OBSERVATION:** The definition of a *phase-in plan* under FAS-92 focuses on methods of rate-making that defer recognition of allowable costs (a) that would not be deferred under GAAP applicable to enterprises in general and (b) that would not have been deferred in the past under the methods of rate-making used by a regulated enterprise's regulator (FAS-92, par. 47).

Under FAS-92, accounting for the deferment of the allowable costs of a plant in connection with a phase-in plan ordered by a regulator depends on whether the physical construction of the plant was substantially completed *before* January 1, 1988.

> **OBSERVATION:** Paragraph 4 of FAS-92 addresses those phase-in plans ordered by a regulator in connection with a plant on which no substantial physical construction had been performed before January 1, 1988, while paragraph 5 of FAS-92 addresses those phase-in plans ordered by a regulator in connection with a plant on which substantial physical construction had been performed before January 1, 1988. Other than by implication, neither paragraph appears to address phase-in plans ordered by a regulator in connection with a plant on which construction was started after January 1, 1988.

Plant Not Substantially Completed Before January 1, 1988

If no substantial physical construction had been performed on a plant before January 1, 1988, *none* of the allowable costs that are deferred for future recovery under any phase-in plan ordered by a regulator may be capitalized for *financial reporting purposes* (FAS-92, par. 4). (**Note:** In this context, allowable costs that are deferred for future recovery are those that are deferred beyond the period in which they would otherwise be charged to expense under GAAP applicable to enterprises in general.)

Plant Completed or Substantially Completed Before January 1, 1988

If a plant had been completed or substantially completed before January 1, 1988, *all* allowable costs that are deferred for future recovery under any phase-in plan ordered by a regulator are capitalized as a separate asset (a deferred charge) for *financial reporting purposes* (FAS-92, par. 5). All of the following criteria must be met (**Note:** Under FAS-92, these criteria are used to determine whether capitalization is appropriate.):

1. The regulator has agreed, in a formal plan, to the deferral of the allowable costs.
2. The timing of the recovery of all allowable costs that are deferred to future periods is specified in the formal plan agreed to by the regulator.
3. The recovery of all allowable costs deferred to future periods is scheduled to occur within 10 years of the date on which the deferrals began.
4. The percentage increase in rates scheduled under the phase-in plan for each year cannot exceed the percentage increase of the immediately preceding year. The percentage increase in rates for year two of the phase-in plan cannot exceed the percentage increase in rates for year one of the phase-in plan, and the percentage increase in rates for year three cannot exceed the percentage increase for year two, and so forth.

If *all* of the above criteria are not met, *none* of the allowable costs that are deferred for future recovery under the regulator's formal plan shall be capitalized for *financial reporting purposes* (FAS-92, par. 5). (**Note:** In this context, allowable costs that are deferred for future recovery are those that are deferred beyond the period in which they would otherwise be charged to expense under GAAP applicable to enterprises in general.)

Modification, Replacement, or Supplement of an Existing Phase-In Plan

When an existing phase-in plan is modified or a new plan is ordered to replace or supplement an existing plan, the specific criteria required by FAS-92 to determine whether capitalization of allowable costs is appropriate for *financial reporting purposes* (discussed above) are applied to the combination of both the original plan and the new plan. The date at which deferrals begin, for the purpose of recovering all deferred allowable costs within 10 years (criterion 3, above), is the date of the earliest deferral under either the new or the old plan. The final recovery date is the date of the last recovery of all amounts deferred under the plan (FAS-92, par. 6).

ALLOWANCE FOR FUNDS USED DURING CONSTRUCTION (AFUDC)

FAS-71 requires that an enterprise capitalize an allowance for the funds used during the construction stage of an asset in lieu of capitalizing interest in accordance with FAS-34 (Capitalization of Interest Cost). AFUDC usually included interest costs on borrowing, or interest costs on a designated portion of equity funds, or both. The cost of the constructed asset is increased by the amount of AFUDC (FAS-71, par. 15). This increased cost is recovered through higher depreciation charges included in allowable costs over the life of the asset. The offsetting entry when this increase is recorded in the asset account is generally to increase "other income" for interest cost on equity funds and to reduce interest expense for interest costs on borrowings.

FAS-90 amends FAS-71 to specify that an allowance for funds used during the construction stage of an asset should be capitalized only if it is *probable* (likely) that the allowance for funds will be included subsequently by the governing regulatory authorities as an allowable cost of the constructed asset (FAS-90, par. 8). If it is *not probable* (not likely) that the allowance for funds used during the construction stage of an asset will be included as an allowable cost for rate-making purposes, a regulated enterprise may not alternatively capitalize interest cost in accordance with FAS-34 (FAS-90, par. 66).

A disallowance of a cost is the result of a rate-making action that prevents a regulated enterprise from recovering either some amount of its investment or some amount of return on its investment. Some existing phase-in plans have deferred allowable costs for recovery in future periods for rate-making purposes and have not provided a return on the investment on those deferred costs during the deferral period. This type of phase-in plan is in substance partially a deferral and partially a disallowance, and any disallowance should be accounted for in accordance with FAS-90.

After the initial application of FAS-92, any allowance for earnings on shareholders' investment that is capitalized for rate-making purposes other than for an asset during its construction stage or as part of a phase-in plan may not be capitalized for *financial reporting purposes* (FAS-92, par. 9).

CAPITALIZED AMOUNTS—
CLASSIFICATION AND DISCLOSURE

Cumulative amounts that are capitalized under phase-in plans are reported as a separate asset in the balance sheet. The net amount that has been capitalized in each period or the net amount of previously capitalized allowable costs that are recovered during each period is reported as a separate item of other income or expense in the income statement. Allowable costs that have been capitalized are not reported as reductions of other expenses (FAS-92, par. 10).

The terms of any phase-in plans in effect during the year or ordered for future years are disclosed in the financial statements. If allowable costs have been deferred for future recovery by a regulator for rate-making purposes, but not for *financial reporting purposes*, FAS-92 requires the financial statement disclosure of the net amount of such allowable costs that have been deferred for future recovery, and in addition, the disclosure of the net change in the related deferrals for those plans during the year (FAS-92, par. 11). FAS-92 also requires the financial statement disclosure of the nature and amounts of any allowance for earnings on shareholders' investment that has been capitalized for rate-making purposes but not capitalized for *financial reporting purposes* (FAS-92, par. 12).

SPECIFIC STANDARDS FOR
REGULATED ENTERPRISES

In addition to the items discussed above, regulated enterprises subject to the provisions of FAS-71 must comply with the following specific standards.

Intercompany Profits

Under existing GAAP, 100% of any intercompany profits must be eliminated in consolidated financial statements [ARB-51 (Consolidated Financial Statements)] and investments accounted for by the equity method [APB-18 (The Equity Method of Accounting for Investments in Common Stock)]. Under the provisions of FAS-71, however, a regulated enterprise shall not eliminate intercompany profits on sales to regulated affiliates if (FAS-71, par. 16):

1. The sales price is reasonable (as evidenced by the acceptance of the sales price by the enterprise's regulator, or in light of the specific circumstance).

2. It is expected (based on available evidence) that the approximate sales price which resulted in the intercompany profit will be recovered as an allowable cost.

If the above conditions are met, the realization of the intercompany profits are reasonably substantiated by the regulatory process. The intercompany profits shall not be eliminated because they are assured reasonably of being realized.

Deferred Income Taxes

Regulated enterprises (as defined by FAS-71) must comply with the following provisions of FAS-109:

1. The use of the net-of-tax accounting and reporting method is prohibited.
2. A deferred tax liability is required to be recognized for (*a*) the tax benefits of originating temporary differences that are passed on to customers and (*b*) the equity component of the allowance for funds used during construction.
3. A deferred tax liability or asset is adjusted for any enacted change in the tax laws or rates.

An asset is recognized by a regulated enterprise in the amount of the probable future revenue that will be received from customers if it is *probable* that the regulator will allow a future increase in rates for items (2) and (3) above. On the other hand, if it is probable that a future decrease in taxes payable for items (2) and (3) above will be returned to customers through a future decrease in rates, a regulated enterprise shall recognize a liability in the amount of the probable reduction in future revenue in accordance with FAS-71. Here, the asset or liability recognized by the regulated enterprise also is a temporary difference, and a deferred tax liability or asset shall be recognized for the deferred tax effects of that temporary difference (FAS-109 [Accounting for Income Taxes], par. 58).

Disclosure of Customer Refunds

Disclosure shall be made of any refunds that have a material effect on net income and that are not recognized in the same period as the related revenue. Disclosure shall include the effect on net income and indicate the years that the related revenue was recognized. The material effect on net income, net of related income taxes, may be disclosed as a separate line item in the income statement, but may not be presented as an extraordinary item (FAS-71, par. 19).

Disclosure of Certain Unamortized Costs

A regulator may exclude a specific cost in calculating the return on equity for a regulated enterprise, but may allow recovery of the actual cost over the current and future periods. For example, severe storm damage may be incurred for which the regulator allows the recovery over the current and future periods. The storm damage is not allowed to be included in determining the rate of return on equity for the regulated enterprise. The regulator allows recovery of the actual cost, but no profit is made on the incurred storm damage cost. The following disclosures are required by FAS-71 for major costs that do not provide a return on investment and are required to be amortized over the current and future periods (FAS-71, par. 20):

1. The unamortized amount of such costs
2. The remaining period of amortization

☛ **PRACTICE POINTER:** The result of the above disclosure requirements of FAS-71 is that if a cost is recoverable over an extended period and the regulator does not allow a return on investment (profit) for that specific cost, the unamortized balance of such costs must be disclosed along with the remaining amortization period.

Accounting for Postretirement Benefit Costs

FAS-106 requires most enterprises, including rate-regulated entities, to recognize postretirement benefit costs (OPEB costs) over the service periods of their employees rather than on a pay-as-you-go or terminal accrual basis. The predominant practice by rate-regulated companies before the adoption of FAS-106 was to include OPEB costs as an allowable cost on the pay-as-you-go basis (e.g., as the benefits were paid to retired employees). Regulators generally did not object to this treatment in rates. However, with the adoption of accrual accounting for these benefits costs, utilities were faced with the issue of how to account for the difference between the pay-as-you-go amount historically being recovered in rates and the incremental increase resulting from accrual under FAS-106.

Accounting for Alternative Revenue Programs

Some regulators have authorized the use of alternative revenue programs that provide alternatives to the traditional approved base rates that are designed to recover the utility's allowable costs, including a return on shareholders' investment. The two categories of alternative revenue programs follow:

- Type A—Adjust billings for the effects of weather abnormalities or broad external factors or to compensate the utility for demand-side management initiatives. Demand-side management programs are measures or programs undertaken by a regulated utility to reduce or otherwise influence the level of its customers' usage.

- Type B—Increase billings if the utility achieves certain objectives, such as reducing costs or reaching specified milestones.

Regulated entities may recognize the additional revenues if all of the following conditions are met:

- The regulator has approved an alternative program through an order that allows for the automatic adjustment of future rates;

- The amount of additional revenue for the period is objectively determinable and is probable of recovery; and

- The additional revenues will be collected within 24 months following the end of the annual period in which they are recognized.

GOING OFF FAS-71

The rate-regulated industry continues to undergo significant changes. Competition, deregulation, regulatory disallowances, and market-sensitive rate structures are driving these changes. Most of the regional telephone holding companies created upon the breakup of AT&T in 1984 no longer follow FAS-71. Many other companies in rate-regulated industries are evaluating the applicability of FAS-71 as these changes evolve.

Discontinuing Application of FAS-71

FAS-101 establishes the appropriate accounting that should be applied when an enterprise discontinues the application of the provisions of FAS-71. Under FAS-101, an enterprise shall discontinue the application of the provisions of FAS-71 as of the date it determines that its "regulatory" operations in a particular regulatory jurisdiction cease to meet the criteria of FAS-71.

If the application of FAS-71 is discontinued for one separable portion of "regulatory" operations in a particular regulatory jurisdiction, there is a presumption that the application of FAS-71 should be discontinued for all other "regulatory" operations within that same particular regulatory jurisdiction. However, an enterprise shall continue to apply the provisions of FAS-71 to any separable portion of "regulatory" operations that continues to meet the criteria of FAS-71, regardless of whether or not the other separable portions within the same particular regulatory jurisdiction meet the criteria of FAS-71 (FAS-101, par. 5).

Reporting the Discontinuance of FAS-71

FAS-101 requires an enterprise to record the net effects of discontinuing the application of the provisions of FAS-71. At the time an enterprise ceases to meet the criteria for applying FAS-71, assets or liabilities that were recognized as a result of the actions of a regulator must be removed from the enterprise's statement of financial position. Carrying amounts of plant, equipment, and inventory as reported under the provisions of FAS-71 shall not be adjusted for (a) an allowance for funds used during construction of an asset, (b) intercompany profits on sales to regulated affiliates, and (c) disallowances of costs of recently completed plants. On the other hand, carrying amounts of plant, equipment, and inventory shall be adjusted if those assets are impaired, with impairment being accounted for in the same manner as for enterprises in general (FAS-101, par. 6).

FAS-121 requires enterprises in general to evaluate as asset for impairment when events occur or conditions exist that indicate that the carrying amount of the asset may not be recoverable. Many of those conditions exist today for regulated enterprises. One example of such a condition, described in FAS-121, is a change in business climate that affects the value of an asset. As indicated above, competition and the introduction of new forms of rate-making are definitely changing the business climate in which regulated enterprises operate and may affect the value of their assets.

Once management determines that an asset should be evaluated for impairment, an enterprise is required to estimate the future undiscounted cash flows expected to be generated from the use of the asset and its eventual disposition less the future cash outflows expected to be necessary to obtain those inflows. If the carrying amount of the asset is greater than the estimated undiscounted cash flows, an impairment loss should be recognized. Assets should be grouped at the lowest level for which there are identified cash flows from the asset or group of assets that are largely independent of the cash flows of other assets or groups of assets (FAS-121, par. 8).

After all adjustments required by FAS-101 are recorded, the net effect of these adjustments shall be included in the income of the period in which the application of FAS-71 is discontinued, and the net amount shall be reported in the financial statements as an extraordinary item in accordance with APB-30 (Reporting the Results of Operations).

Disclosures and Amendment to APB-30

The following financial statement disclosures shall be made in the period in which an enterprise discontinues the application of FAS-71 to all or any portion of its regulated operations (FAS-101, pars. 8 and 9):

1. The reason(s) for the discontinuation of applying FAS-71
2. The identification of the portion(s) of operations to which the application of FAS-71 is being discontinued
3. Separate disclosure of the net adjustment, less related taxes, resulting from the discontinuation of applying FAS-71, as an extraordinary item in the statement of operations

APB-30 contains the criteria for classifying an amount as an extraordinary item in the financial statements of an enterprise. FAS-101 amends APB-30 by requiring the net adjustment resulting from the discontinuation of FAS-71 to be classified as an extraordinary item regardless of the criteria in paragraph 20 of APB-30 for classifying an extraordinary item (FAS-101, par. 10).

Disclosure Index

DISCLOSURE INDEX

CONTENTS

DISCLOSURE INDEX

This Disclosure Index includes many of the important disclosures required or recommended by current GAAP. Although great care has been taken in compiling this index, no index of this type can include all possible disclosures that might be appropriate in a particular circumstance. It is not intended to serve as a substitute for professional judgment nor for a thorough search of the accounting literature. Rather, it is intended to alert the reader to areas for which required or recommended disclosures are specified in the authoritative accounting literature and to summarize many of the most important disclosures.

Proper use of this Disclosure Index can assist preparers, reviewers, and auditors of financial statements in efficiently evaluating or preparing financial statements. In this edition of the *Miller GAAP Guide*, references to specific paragraphs in authoritative pronouncements have been included to assist users in locating the original text for those disclosures that are particularly important for a reporting enterprise.

Accounting Changes

- The nature, justification, and preferability (if applicable) of a change in accounting principle and its effects on income must be disclosed clearly in a note to the financial statements in the period in which the change is made (APB-20, par. 17).

- If an accounting change is considered immaterial in the year of change but is reasonably expected to become material in subsequent periods, it should be disclosed fully in the year of change (APB-20, par. 38).

- In reporting a change in an accounting principle in the income statement, pro forma disclosure of certain information is required for the current period and all prior periods presented. This includes (APB-20, par. 21):
  1. Income before extraordinary items.
  2. Net income.
  3. Related per share data for both primary and fully diluted earnings.

- The following disclosures concerning a cumulative-effect-type accounting change should be made in interim financial reports (FAS-3, par. 11):

1. The nature and justification of the change made in the interim period in which the new accounting principle is adopted

2. The effects of the accounting change on income from continuing operations, net income, and related per share data for:
   a. The interim period in which the change is made.
   b. Each, if any, prior interim period of the same year.
   c. Each, if any, restated prior interim period of the same year.
   d. Year-to-date and last twelve-months-to-date financial reports that include the adoption of the new accounting principle.
   e. Interim financial reports of the fiscal year, subsequent to the interim period in which the accounting change was adopted.

3. The pro forma effects of the accounting change on income from continuing operations, net income, and related per share data for:
   a. The interim period in which the change is made.
   b. Any interim period of prior fiscal years for which financial information is presented.
   c. Year-to-date and last twelve-months-to-date financial reports that include the adoption of a new accounting principle.

If no interim periods of prior fiscal years are presented, notes disclosures for the corresponding interim period of the immediate fiscal year in which the accounting change occurred are made for actual and pro forma income from continuing operations, net income, and related per share data.

- If a change in an accounting estimate affects future periods, the effect on income before extraordinary items, net income, and the related per share information of the current period should be disclosed in the income statement (APB-20, par. 33).

- A change in reporting entity must be disclosed by describing the nature of the change and the reason for it. Changes in income before extraordinary items, net income, and related earnings per share data should be disclosed adequately (APB-20, par. 35).

- Corrections of errors must be disclosed fully by reporting the nature of the error and the effect of its correction on income before extraordinary items, net income, and related per share data in the period in which the error is discovered and corrected (APB-20, par. 37).

Accounting Policies

- Accounting principles and the method of applying the principles should be disclosed for the significant accounting principles and methods that involve the following (APB-22, par. 12):
  1. A selection from existing acceptable alternatives
  2. The areas peculiar to a specific industry in which the entity functions
  3. Unusual or innovative applications of GAAP

Business Combinations

Combinations Accounted for by the Purchase Method

- The following disclosures are required in the period in which a business combination occurs (APB-16, par. 95):
  1. Name, brief description, and total cost of the acquisition
  2. Method of accounting (the purchase method)
  3. Period for which results of operations of the acquisition are included in the income statement
  4. If applicable, the number of shares of stock issued or issuable, including the amount assigned to the issued and issuable shares
  5. Description of the plan for amortization of acquired goodwill, including the amortization method and period
  6. Other pertinent information such as contingent payments, options, or other commitments

- Combining several minor acquisitions for disclosure purposes is acceptable (APB-16, par. 95).

- In the year of acquisition, the following supplemental information should be disclosed by all public enterprises (APB-16, par. 96):

  1. Results of operations for the current period, combining the acquisition as though is were acquired at the beginning of the period
  2. If comparative statements are presented, results of operations should include the acquisition as though it were

acquired at the beginning of the comparative statement period

Combinations Accounted for by the Pooling Method

- The following disclosures are required in the period in which a business combination occurs (APB-16, par. 64):

    1. Brief description of the companies combined

    2. Method of accounting (the pooling method)

    3. Description and amount of shares of stock issued to effect the combination

    4. Details of the results of operations for each separate company, prior to the date of combination, that are included in the current combined net income

    5. Description of the nature of adjustments in net assets of the combining companies to adopt the same accounting policies

    6. If any of the combining companies changed their fiscal year as a result of the combination, full disclosure of any changes in stockholders' equity that were excluded from the reported results of operations

    7. Revenues and earning previously reported by the acquiring company, reconciled with the amounts shown in the combined financial statements

- Any plan of combination that has been initiated but not consummated at a balance sheet date must be disclosed fully, including the effects of the plan on combined operations and any changes in accounting methods (APB-16, par. 65).

- The nature and effects on earnings per share of nonrecurring intercompany transactions involving long-term assets and liabilities that have not been eliminated should be disclosed (APB-16, par. 56).

Cash Flow Statement

- Noncash investing and financing activities in a period that affect assets or liabilities must be disclosed (FAS-95, par. 32).

- Amount of interest and income taxes paid must be disclosed separately if the indirect method is used (FAS-95, par. 29).

- Reconciliation of net income to cash provided by (used in) operating activities must be disclosed (FAS-95, par. 29).

Changing Prices

- Disclosure of the effects of changing prices are encouraged but not required (FAS-89, par. 3).

Comprehensive Income

- Total amounts of comprehensive income and net income (including in interim financial statements) (FAS-130, par. 14).
- Components of other comprehensive income, classified by their nature (FAS-130, par. 14).
- Classification adjustments to eliminate double-counting realized items in comprehensive income (FAS-130, par. 20).
- Accumulated comprehensive income in stockholders' equity with separate disclosure of the accumulated balances of each separate component (FAS-130, par. 26).

Consolidated Financial Statements

- The consolidation policy must be disclosed fully (ARB-51, par. 5).

Contingencies, Risks, and Uncertainties

- A loss contingency that is *probable* and can be estimated reasonably must be accrued as a charge to income (FAS-5, par. 8).
- All disclosure footnotes must describe the nature of the accrual and, in some circumstances, the amount accrued (FAS-5, par. 9). The note must indicate either the estimate of loss, the estimated range of the loss, or state that such an estimate cannot be made.
- Any *probable* or *reasonably possible* exposure to a loss in excess of the accrued amount must be disclosed in a note (FAS-5, par. 10).
- A loss contingency that is *probable* or *reasonably possible* but cannot be estimated must be disclosed (FAS-5, par. 10).
- A loss contingency that is classified as *probable* or *reasonably possible*, that occurs after the balance sheet date but before the issuance of financial statements, may have to be disclosed to keep financial statements from being misleading. In some circumstances, the historical financial statements may be supplemented with pro forma statements reflecting the loss as if it occurred at the date of the financial statements (FAS-5, par. 11).

- Loss contingencies that may occur as the result of a guarantee must be disclosed, even if they have a *remote* possibility of materializing. Examples are guarantees to repurchase receivables or related property, obligations of banks under letters of credit or stand-by agreements, guarantees of the indebtedness of others (both direct and indirect, as clarified by FIN-34), and unconditional obligations to make payments. Consideration should also be given to disclosing the amount, if estimable, that can be recovered in the event the guarantor is called upon to satisfy the guarantee (FAS-5, par. 12).

- Gain contingencies should be disclosed in the financial statements by footnote, but care should be exercised to avoid misleading implications as to the likelihood of revenue realization (FAS-5, par. 17).

- Disclosure of significant risks and uncertainties—Volatility and uncertainty in the business and economic environment result in the need for disclosure of information about the risks and uncertainties confronted by reporting entities. SOP 94-6 requires disclosure of significant risks and uncertainties that confront entities in the following areas:

  1. *Nature of operations*—A description of the major products or services an entity sells or provides and its principal markets and locations of those markets. Entities that operate in more than one market must indicate the relative importance of their operations in each market (SOP 94-6, par. 10).

  2. *Use of estimates*—An explanation that financial statements prepared in conformity with GAAP require the application of managements estimates (SOP 94-6, par. 11).

  3. *Significant estimates*—Disclosure regarding an estimate is required when *both* of the following conditions are met (SOP 94-6, par. 13):

     a. It is at least reasonably possible that the estimate of the effect on the financial statements of a condition, situation, or set of circumstances that existed at the date of the financial statements will change in the near term due to one or more future confirming events.

     b. The effect of the change would have a material effect on the financial statements. The disclosure requirements of FAS-5 for contingencies are supplemented by SOP 94-6 as follows (SOP 94-6, par. 16):

(1) If an estimate requires disclosure under FAS-5 or another pronouncement, an indication also shall be made that it is at least reasonably possible that a change in the estimate will occur in the near term.

(2) An estimate that does not require disclosure under FAS-5 (such as estimates associated with long-term operating assets and amounts reported under profitable long-term contracts) may meet the standards described above and, if so, requires disclosure of the nature of the estimate and an indication that it is reasonably possible that a change in the estimate will occur in the near term.

4. *Vulnerability from concentrations*—Information sufficient to inform financial statement users of the general nature of the risk associated with the concentration is required for the following specific concentrations (SOP 94-6, par. 22):

   a. The volume of business transacted with a particular customer, supplier, lender, grantor, or contributor

   b. Revenue from particular products, services, or fund-raising events

   c. The available sources of supply of materials, labor, or services, or of licenses or other rights used in the entity's operations

   d. The market or geographic area in which an entity conducts its operations

   In addition, for concentrations of labor subject to collective bargaining agreements, disclosure shall include both the percentage of the labor force covered by a collective bargaining agreement and the percentage of the labor force covered by a collective bargaining agreement that will expire within one year. For concentrations of operations located outside the entity's home country, disclosure shall include the carrying amounts of net assets and the geographic areas in which they are located (SOP 94-6, par. 24).

Convertible Debt and Debt with Warrants

- Disclosure of the features of debt, including any conversion options, is required.

Current Assets and Current Liabilities

- The more common disclosures that are required for current assets and current liabilities include the following:
    1. Method of valuing current marketable securities (FAS-12, par. 12)
    2. Classification of inventories and the method used (LIFO, FIFO, average cost, etc.) (ARB-43, Ch. 4, Statement 8)
    3. Restrictions on current assets (ARB-43, Ch. 3A, par. 6)
    4. Current portions of long-term obligations (FAS-6, par. 15)
    5. Description of accounting policies relating to current assets and current liabilities (APB-22, par. 13)

Depreciable Assets and Depreciation

- Required in the financial statements or notes thereto (APB-12, par. 5):
    1. Depreciation expense for the current period
    2. Balances of major classes of depreciable assets by nature or function, at the balance sheet date
    3. Accumulated depreciation allowances by classes of assets or in total, at the balance sheet date
    4. A general description of the methods used, by major classes of assets, in computing depreciation
- The effect of a change from one depreciation method to another must be disclosed (APB-20, par. 24).

Development Stage Enterprises

- Required financial statements (FAS-7, par. 11):
    1. A balance sheet presenting accumulated losses as "deficit accumulated during the development stage"
    2. An income statement including revenues and expenses for each period being presented and also a cumulative total of both amounts from the company's inception (This provision also applies to dormant companies that have been reactivated at the development stage. In such cases, the totals begin from the time development stage activities are initiated.)
    3. A statement of cash flows showing cumulative totals of cash inflows and cash outflows from the company's inception and amounts for the current period

4. A statement of stockholders' equity containing the following information:
    a. The date and number of shares of stock (or other securities) issued for cash or other consideration and the dollar amount assigned
    b. For each issuance of capital stock involving noncash consideration, a description of the nature of the consideration and the basis for its valuation

- Separate transactions of equity securities can be combined, provided that the same type of securities, consideration per equity unit, and type of consideration are involved and the transactions are made in the same fiscal period (FAS-7, footnote 9).

- Modification of the statement of stockholders' equity may be required for a combined group of companies that form a development stage company or for an unincorporated development stage entity (FAS-7, footnote 9).

OBSERVATION: GAAP do not indicate the types of modifications that might be necessary. Therefore, judgment must be exercised in the preparation of financial statements of development stage enterprises.

- The financial statements are to be identified as those of a development stage company and contain a description of the proposed business activities (FAS-7, par 12).

- The financial statements for the first year that the company is no longer in the development stage shall indicate that in the prior year it was in the development stage. If the company includes prior years for comparative purposes, the cumulative amounts specified for the income statement and the cash flow statement are not required (FAS-7, par. 13).

- When a development stage company that is a subsidiary adopts a new accounting principle, the parent should also reflect this accounting change by making the necessary adjustments on its financial statements in compliance with APB-20 (FIN-7, par. 5).

Earnings per Share

- For each period for which an income statement is presented:
    1. A reconciliation of the numerators and denominators of the basic and diluted EPS computations for income from continuing operations, including the individual income and share amount effects of all securities that affect EPS.

2. The effect that has been given to preferred dividends in determining the income available to common stockholders in computing basic EPS.

3. Securities that could potentially dilute EPS in the future, but which are not included in the calculation of diluted EPS because they are antidilutive in the current period (FAS-128, par. 40).

- For the latest period in which an income statement is presented, a description of any transaction that occurs after the end of the most recent period but before the issuance of the financial statements that would have changed materially the number of common shares or potential common shares (FAS-128, par. 41).

Equity Method

- The extent of disclosure should be evaluated in terms of the significance of the investment in relation to the investor's financial position and results of operations (APB-18, par. 20).

- Full disclosure must be made for investments accounted for by the equity method and include (APB-18, par. 20):

  1. The name of the investment

  2. The percentage of ownership

  3. The accounting policies of the investor in accounting for the investment

  4. The difference between the carrying value of the investment and the underlying equity in the net assets, and the accounting treatment of such difference

  5. The quoted market price of the investment, except if it is a subsidiary

  6. If material, a summary of the assets, liabilities, and results of operations presented as a footnote or as separate statements

  7. The material effect on the investor of any convertible securities of the investee

- For investments of 20% or more in which the equity method is *not* used, disclosure must be made of the name of the investment and the reason(s) the equity method was not used (APB-18, footnote 13).

- For investments of less than 20% in which the equity method *is* used, disclosure must be made of the name of the investment and the reason(s) the equity method was used (APB-18, footnote 13).

Extinguishment of Debt

- Disclosures of gains or losses from early extinguishment of debt that are classified as extraordinary items should include (FAS-4, par. 9):
  1. A description of the transaction, including any identifiable sources, of funds used to extinguish the debt
  2. The income tax effect for the period of extinguishment
  3. The gain or loss per share, net of any related income taxes

- Assets placed into an irrevocable trust to extinguish a specific debt must be disclosed as follows (FAS-76, par. 6):
  1. A general description of the transaction
  2. The total amount outstanding at the end of the period
  3. The total amount that is considered extinguished at the end of the period

Note: FAS-76 is superseded by FAS-125, which is effective for extinguishments of debt occurring after December 31, 1996. See Financial Instruments—Disclosures section of Disclosure Index.

Financial Instruments

- By class of financial instruments with off-balance-sheet risk, as defined by FAS-105:
  1. Face or contract amount (FAS-105, par. 17)
  2. Nature and terms of the class of instruments, including the credit and market risk, cash requirements of the instrument, and the related accounting policies (FAS-105, par. 17)
  3. Maximum amount of accounting loss that would be incurred if any party failed to perform according to the terms of the instrument (FAS-105, par. 18)
  4. Information regarding the collateral or other security required to support the instruments subject to credit risk (FAS-105, par. 18)

- For all financial instruments, except those excluded in paragraph 8 of FAS-107, the fair value of the instruments and the method(s) and significant assumptions used to estimate that value must be disclosed (FAS-107, par. 10).

- For all financial instruments (FAS-105, par. 20):

  1. Information that identifies the activity, region, or economic characteristics of each significant concentration of credit risk
  2. Maximum amount of accounting loss that would be incurred if any party failed to perform according to the terms of the instrument
  3. Information regarding the collateral or other security required to support the instruments subject to credit risk

- For derivative financial instruments that are not included in the scope of FAS-105, separately for those held for trading purposes and those held for other purposes (FAS-119, pars. 8–9):

  1. The face or nominal amount
  2. The nature and terms, including at a minimum:
     a. The credit and market risk of those instruments
     b. The cash requirements of those instruments
     c. The related accounting policy as required by APB-22

- For derivative financial instruments held for trading purposes (FAS-119, par. 10):

  1. The average and end-of-period amounts of fair value, distinguishing between assets and liabilities
  2. The net gains or losses arising from derivative financial instruments trading activities during the period disaggregated by class, business activity, risk, or other category that is consistent with management of those activities and where those net trading gains and losses are reported in the income statement

- For derivative financial instruments held or issued for purposes other than trading (FAS-119, par. 11):

  1. A description of the entity's objectives for holding or issuing the instruments, the context needed to understand those objectives, and the entity's strategies for achieving those objectives
  2. A description of how the derivative financial instruments are reported in the financial statements, including:
     a. Policies for recognizing and measuring the derivative financial instruments held or issued
     b. When recognized, and where those instruments are reported in the statement of financial position and income statement

3. For derivative financial instruments that are held or issued for purposes of hedging anticipated transactions:

   a. A description of the anticipated transactions for which risks are hedged with derivative financial instruments, including the period until the anticipated transactions are expected to occur

   b. A description of the classes of derivative financial instruments used to hedge the anticipated transaction

   c. A description of the transactions or other events that result in the recognition of earnings or gains or losses deferred by hedge accounting

- Encouraged qualitative information about all derivative financial instruments held or issued (FAS-119, par. 13):

   1. More details about current positions and perhaps activities during the period

   2. The hypothetical effects on equity, or on annual income, of several possible changes in market price

   3. A gap analysis of interest rate repricing or maturity dates

   4. The duration of the financial instruments

   5. The entity's value at risk from derivative financial instruments and from other positions at the end of the reporting period and the largest value at risk level during the year

- Information about transfers and servicing of assets and extinguishments of liabilities (FAS-125, par. 17):

   1. Disclosures Required for All Servicing Assets and Liabilities

      a. Amounts of servicing assets or liabilities recognized and amortized during the period

      b. Fair value of recognized servicing assets and liabilities for which it is practicable to estimate that value, the method used, and significant assumptions used

      c. The risk characteristics of underlying financial assets used to stratify recognized servicing assets for purposes of measuring impairment

      d. Activity in the valuation allowance for impairment of recognized servicing assets for each period for which results of operations are presented

2. Disclosures Required in Specified Situations

Condition Requiring Disclosure	Information Required to Be Disclosed
a. Entity has entered into repurchase agreements or securities lending transactions.	Policy for requiring collateral or other security
b. Debt was considered extinguished under FAS-76 (Extinguishment of Debt) prior to the effective date of FAS-125.	General description of the transaction and the amount of debt that is considered extinguished at the end of the period so long as that debt is outstanding
c. Assets are set aside after the effective date of FAS-125 solely for satisfying scheduled payments of a specific obligation.	Description of the nature of restrictions placed on such assets
d. It is not practicable to estimate the fair value of certain assets obtained or liabilities incurred in transfers of financial assets during the period.	Description of those items and the reasons why it is not practicable to estimate fair value

OBSERVATION: For interim and annual periods beginning after June 15, 1999, the following disclosures from FAS-133 replace those presented above from FAS-105 and FAS-119 and amend those from FAS-107.

- General disclosures—for instruments that qualify as hedging instruments:
  1. Objectives for holding or issuing the instruments
  2. The context needed to understand these objectives
  3. The entity's strategies for achieving those objectives
  4. Distinction concerning the above between derivative instruments designated as fair value hedging instruments,

cash flow hedging instruments, hedges of the foreign currency exposure of a net investment in a foreign operation, and all other derivatives

5. The entity's risk management policy for each type of hedge, including a description of the items or transactions for which risks are hedged

6. For instruments not designated as hedging instruments, the purpose of the derivative activity

- Fair value hedges—for derivative instruments, as well as nonderivative instruments, that may give rise to foreign currency transaction gains or losses under FAS-52, that have been designated and qualify as fair value hedging instruments:

  1. The net gain or loss recognized in earnings during the period representing:

     a. The amount of the hedges' ineffectiveness.

     b. The component of the derivative instruments' gain or loss, if any, excluded from the assessment of hedge effectiveness.

     c. A description of where the net gain or loss is reported in the statement of income or other statement of financial performance.

  2. The amount of net gain or loss recognized in earnings when a hedged firm commitment no longer qualifies as a fair value hedge

- Cash flow hedges—for derivatives that have been designated and qualify as cash flow hedging instruments and the related hedged transactions:

  1. The net gain or loss recognized in earnings during the reporting period representing:

     a. The amount of the hedges' ineffectiveness.

     b. The component of the derivative instruments' gain or loss, if any, excluded from the assessment of hedge effectiveness.

     c. A description of where the net gain or loss is reported in the statement of income or other statement of financial performance.

  2. A description of the transactions or other events that will result in the reclassification into earnings of gains or losses that are reported in accumulated other comprehensive income and the estimated net amount of the existing gains or losses at the reporting date that is expected to bereclassified into earnings within the next 12 months

3. The maximum length of time over which the entity is hedging its exposure to the variability in future cash flows for forecasted transactions excluding those forecasted transactions related to the payment of variable interest on existing financial instruments

4. The amount of gains and losses reclassified into earnings as a result of the discontinuance of cash flow hedges because it is probable that the original forecasted transactions will not occur

- Hedges of net investment in a foreign operation—for derivative instruments, as well as nonderivative instruments, that may give rise to foreign currency transaction gains or losses under FAS-52, that have been designated and qualify as hedging instruments for hedges of the foreign currency exposure of a net investment in a foreign operation:

  1. The net amount of gains and losses included in the cumulative translation adjustment during the reporting period

- Changes in the components of comprehensive income:

  1. Within other comprehensive income, a separate classification of the net gain or loss on derivative instruments designated and qualifying as cash flow hedging instruments

  2. As part of the disclosure of accumulated other comprehensive income in accordance with FAS-130 (Reporting Comprehensive Income), the beginning and ending accumulated derivative gain or loss, the related net change associated with current period hedging transactions, and the net amount of any reclassification into earnings

Foreign Operations and Exchange

- Disclosure must include the aggregate transaction gain or loss that is included in determining net income for the period, including gains or losses on forward exchange contracts (FAS-52, par. 30).

- Dealer gains and losses may be disclosed as dealer gains and losses, rather than as transaction gains and losses (FAS-52, par. 30).

- An analysis of the changes in the separate component of stockholders' equity for cumulative adjustments must include (FAS-52, par. 31):

  1. Beginning and ending amount of cumulative translation adjustments.

2. The aggregate increase or decrease for the period from translation adjustments and gains and losses from (*a*) hedges of a net investment in a foreign entity and (*b*) long-term intercompany transactions.

3. The amount of income taxes for the period allocated to translation adjustments.

4. The amount of translation adjustment transferred to net income during the period as a result of a sale or complete or substantially complete liquidation of a foreign investment.

- Disclosure must be made of any significant exchange rate changes and their effects on unsettled foreign currency transactions that occur after the financial statement date (FAS-52, par. 32).

- Adequate disclosure of foreign operations should be made (FAS-94, footnote 1).

Futures Contracts

- The following disclosures are required (FAS-80, par. 12):
  1. The nature of the items that are hedged or related to futures contracts
  2. A description of the accounting method(s) used for the futures contracts
  3. A description of the events or transactions that will result in recognition of income of the changes in value of the futures contracts

Government Contracts

- Offsetting of government advances against amounts due from the government under cost-plus-fixed-fee contracts must be disclosed clearly (ARB-43, Ch. 11A, par. 5).

- Reasonable estimates of renegotiation provisions are required to be disclosed. The enterprise must disclose the uncertainties, their significance, and the basis used in determining the provision (ARB-43, Ch. 11B, par. 5).

- When a significant part of a company's revenue (greater than 10%) is derived from the federal government, a state government, a local government, or a foreign government, disclosure is required of that fact and the amount of revenue from each government entity, as well as the identity of the industry segment(s) making the sales. If a concentration of the revenues is derived from a particular department or agency of government, disclosure of that fact and the amount of revenue derived from each source is encouraged (FAS-30, par. 6).

- Material amounts of termination claims should be disclosed separately (ARB-43, Ch. 11C, par. 5). If a termination claim is indeterminable but is believed to be material, full disclosure of the essential facts should be made (ARB-43, Ch. 11C, par. 4).

Impairment of Loans

- Creditors must disclose the following (FAS-118, par. 6i):

    1. As of the date of each statement of financial position, the total recorded investment in the impaired loan at the end of each period and:

        a. The amount of that recorded investment for which there is a related allowance for credit losses determined in accordance with FAS-118.

        b. The amount of the recorded investment for which there is no allowance for credit losses in accordance with FAS-118.

    2. The creditor's policy for recognizing interest income on impaired loans, including how cash receipts are recorded

    3. For each period for which results of operations are presented, the average recorded investment in the impaired loans during each period, the related amount of interest income recognized during the time within the period that the loans were impaired, and, if practicable, the amount of interest income recognized using a cash basis method of accounting during the time within that period that the loans were impaired

    4. For each period for which results of operations are presented, the activity in the allowance for credit losses related to loans, including the balances at the beginning and end of the period, additions charged to operations, direct write-downs charged against the allowance, and recoveries of amounts previously charged off

Impairment of Long-Lived Assets

- For long-lived assets to be held and used for which an impairment loss has been recognized in the current period, the following must be disclosed (FAS-121, par. 13):

1. Description of the impaired assets and the facts and circumstances leading to impairment

2. Amount of the impairment loss and how fair value was determined

3. The caption in the income statement or statement of activities in which the impairment loss is aggregated (if loss is not presented as a separate item)

4. The business segment(s) affected (if applicable)

- For long-lived assets to be disposed of for which a impairment loss has been recognized in the current period, the following must be disclosed (FAS-121, par. 19):

  1. Description of assets to be disposed of, the facts and circumstances leading to the expected disposal, expected disposal date, and carrying amount of the assets

  2. The business segment(s) affected (if applicable)

  3. The loss, if any, resulting from the application of FAS-121

  4. The gain or loss, if any, resulting from changes in the carrying amount of assets to be disposed of subsequent to the initial application of FAS-121

  5. The caption in the income statement or statement of activities in which gains or losses are aggregated, if they are not presented separately on the face of the statement

  6. The results of operations for assets to be disposed of, to the extent that those results are included in the entity's results of operations and can be identified

Income Taxes

- The following components of the net deferred tax liability or asset recognized in an enterprise's balance sheet must be disclosed (FAS-109, par. 43):

  1. The total of all deferred tax liabilities for taxable temporary differences

  2. The total of all deferred tax assets for deductible temporary differences and loss and tax credit carryforwards

  3. The total valuation allowance recognized for deferred tax assets

  4. The net change during the year in the total valuation allowance

- If a deferred tax liability is not recognized because of the exceptions identified in APB-23, the following must be disclosed (FAS-109, par. 44):

1. A description of the types of temporary differences for which a deferred tax liability has not been recognized and the types of events that would cause those temporary differences to become taxable

2. The cumulative amount of each type of temporary difference

3. The amount of the unrecognized deferred tax liability for temporary differences related to investments in foreign subsidiaries and foreign corporate joint ventures that are essentially permanent in duration if determination of that liability is practicable, or a statement that determination is not practicable

4. The amount of the deferred tax liability for temporary differences other than those listed in item (3) above that is not recognized on the basis of exceptions granted by APB-23

- Significant components of income tax expense attributable to continuing operations must be disclosed. This includes (FAS-109, par. 45) the following:

  1. Current tax expense or benefit

  2. Deferred tax expense or benefit

  3. Investment tax credit

  4. Government grants used to reduce income tax expense

  5. Tax benefits of operating loss carryforwards

  6. Tax expense resulting from allocating tax benefits either directly to contributed capital or to reduce goodwill or other noncurrent intangible assets of an acquired entity

  7. Adjustments to a deferred tax liability or asset for enacted changes in tax laws or rates or for a change in tax status of an enterprise

  8. Adjustments of the beginning balance of the valuation allowance

- The amount of tax expense or benefit allocated to continuing operations and the amounts allocated to other items must be disclosed separately (FAS-109, par. 46).

- A public company that is not subject to income tax because its income is taxed directly to its owners must disclose that information (FAS-109, par. 43).

- Companies with operating loss and tax credit carryforwards must disclose the amounts and expiration dates (FAS-109, par. 48).

- Companies must disclose any portion of the valuation allowance for deferred tax assets for which subsequently recognized tax benefits will be allocated to contributed capital or to reduce goodwill or other noncurrent intangible assets of an acquired entity (FAS-109, par. 48).

Intangible Assets

- Disclosure of intangible assets must include (APB-17, par. 30):
    1. Description of intangible assets.
    2. Method of amortization of intangible assets.
    3. Estimated useful lives of intangible assets.

- The reason for any unamortized costs of intangible assets included as an extraordinary charge to net income must be disclosed (APB-17, par. 31).

Interest Costs Capitalized

- Disclosure must be made of the amount of interest costs expensed during the period. If any interest costs have been capitalized, these also must be disclosed (FAS-34, par. 21).

Interest on Receivables and Payables

- Disclosure must include (APB-21, par. 16):
    1. A full description of the receivable or payable.
    2. The effective interest rate.
    3. The face amount of the note.

Interim Financial Reporting

- In the absence of reporting separate fourth quarter results in the annual report, disclosure should be made in the annual report of any disposals of business segments and any extraordinary, unusual, or infrequently occurring items, as well as any material year-end adjustments that have been recorded in the fourth quarter (APB-28, par. 31).
- Cumulative effects of an accounting change made in an interim period that are material in relation to the interim period but not the full fiscal year must be disclosed separately (APB-28, par. 29).

- Outstanding contingencies must be disclosed in each interim period statement (APB-28, par. 22).

Inventory Pricing and Methods

- Disclosures must include the following:
    1. A description of the accounting principles used and the methods of applying those principles (APB-22, par. 12)
    2. Any accounting principles or methods that are peculiar to a particular industry (APB-22, par. 12)
    3. The classification and the basis of pricing for inventories (ARB-43, Ch. 4, Statement 8)
    4. Any significant change in the basis of stating inventories, as well as its effect on income (ARB-43, Ch. 4, Statement 8)
    5. Any inventory stated above cost (ARB-43, Ch. 4, Statement 9)
    6. Material losses on firm purchase commitments (ARB-43, Ch. 4, Statement 10)

- Companies that depend on a limited number of sources for raw materials or inventory, or upon precarious sources (labor problems, foreign governments, etc.) should disclose these facts.

Investment Tax Credit

- Disclosure must be made of the method used to record the ITC (deferral or flow-through), and the amounts involved (APB-4, par. 11).
- Separate disclosure of the ITC benefit is required (FAS-109, par. 45).

Investments in Debt and Equity Securities

- Separately, for securities classified as available-for-sale and held-to-maturity (FAS-115, pars. 19–20):
    1. Aggregate fair value
    2. Gross unrealized holding gains and losses
    3. Amortized cost basis
    4. Contractual maturities of all securities
- For each period for which the results of operations are presented (FAS-115, par. 21):

1. Proceeds from the sale of available-for-sale securities and the gross unrealized gains and losses on those sales

2. The basis on which cost was determined in computing realized gain or loss

3. Gross gains and losses from transfers of securities for the available-for-sale category to the trading category that are included in earnings

4. Change in net unrealized holding gains or losses on available-for-sale securities that are included in the separate component of shareholders' equity

5. Change in net unrealized holding gain or loss on trading securities that are included in earnings

- For held-to-maturity securities, for each period for which results of operations are presented (FAS-115, par. 22):

1. The amortized amount of any sold or transferred security

2. The related realized or unrealized gain or loss

3. The circumstances leading to the decision to sell or transfer the security

Leases

- Disclosures required by lessees for capital leases (FAS-13, par. 16):

1. A general description of the leasing arrangements

2. Amount of capital lease assets by major category

3. Present value of future minimum lease payments, for the current and succeeding five years, less executory costs

4. Future minimum sublease rentals to be received under noncancelable leases

5. Total contingent rentals

- Disclosures required by lessees for operating leases (FAS-13, par. 16):

1. A general description of the leasing arrangements

2. Future minimum payments required for the latest balance sheet and the succeeding five years

3. Future rental amounts to be received under noncancelable subleases

4. Rental expense segregated by minimum rentals, contingent rentals, and sublease rentals

- Disclosures required by lessors, whose significant business activity is leasing, for sales-type and direct financing leases (FAS-13, par. 23a, and FAS-91, par. 25d):

  1. A general description of the leasing arrangements

  2. A schedule of the components of the net investment in leases, as of each balance sheet date, which includes future minimum lease payments, executory costs, allowance for uncollectibles, unguaranteed residual values accruing to the benefit of the lessor, unearned income, and contingent rentals

  3. A schedule of the minimum lease payments, in total and for the next five years

- Disclosures required by lessors, whose significant business activity is leasing, for operating leases (FAS-13, par 23b):

  1. A general description of the leasing arrangements

  2. A schedule of assets leased and available for lease, by major categories, less accumulated depreciation

  3. A schedule of minimum future rental payments on noncancelable leases, in total for the next five years

  4. The amount of contingent rentals included in each income statement presented

- The nature and extent of leasing transactions with related parties must be disclosed (FAS-13, par. 29).

- Significant leveraged leasing activities must be disclosed (FAS-13, par. 47).

Long-Term Construction Contracts

- An enterprise with long-term construction contracts should disclose whether it has used the percentage-of-completion method or the completed-contract method to account for the contract(s) (ARB-45, par. 15).

Long-Term Obligations

- Disclosure required for unrecorded unconditional purchase obligations (FAS-47, par. 7):

  1. A description of the nature and term of the obligation

  2. The total determinable amount of unrecorded unconditional purchase obligations as of the latest balance sheet date, and for each of the five succeeding years

3. A description of the nature of any variable component of the unrecorded unconditional purchase obligations

4. The amounts purchased under the unconditional purchase obligations for each period of the income statement

- Disclosure of the present value of the determinable amount of unconditional purchase obligations is encouraged (FAS-47, par. 8).

- Disclosure required for recorded obligations, for the latest balance sheet and for each of the following five years (FAS-47, par. 10):
  1. Payments for unconditional purchase obligations
  2. Debt payments
  3. Capital stock redemptions

Nonmonetary Transactions

- For the period in which a nonmonetary transaction takes place, disclosure must be made of the nature of the transaction, the basis of accounting for the transaction, and any gains or losses recognized (APB-29, par. 28).

Pension and Other Postretirement Benefit Plans

- For Publicly Held Companies (FAS-132, par. 5):
  1. Reconciliation of the beginning and ending balances of the benefit obligation, with separate disclosure of:
     a. Service Cost
     b. Interest Cost
     c. Contributions by plan participants
     d. Actuarial gains and losses
     e. Foreign currency exchange rate changes
     f. Benefits paid
     g. Plan amendments
     h. Business combinations
     i. Divestitures
     j. Curtailments
     k. Settlements
     l. Special termination benefits
  2. Reconciliation of beginning and ending balances of the fair value of plan assets, including the effects of:

    a. Actual return on plan assess

    b. Foreign currency exchange rate changes

    c. Contributions by employer

    d. Contributions by plan participants

    e. Benefits paid

    f. Business combinations

    g. Divestitures

    h. Settlements

3. The funded status of the plan, including:

    a. Amount of any unamortized prior service cost

    b. Amount of any unrecognized net gain or loss

    c. Amount of any remaining unamortized, unrecognized net obligation or net asset at the initial application of FASB Statements 87 or 106

    d. Net pension or other postretirement benefit prepaid assets or accrued liabilities

    e. Any intangible asset and the amount of accumulated other comprehensive income

4. Amount of net periodic benefit cost recognized, showing separately:

    a. Service cost component

    b. Interest cost component

    c. Expected return on plan assets for the period

    d. Amortization of the unrecognized transition obligation or asset

    e. Amount of recognized gains or losses

    f. Amount of prior service cost recognized

    g. Amount of gain or loss recognized due to a settlement or curtailment

5. Amount included in other comprehensive income for the period arising from a change in the additional minimum liability recognized

6. On a weighted-average basis, the following assumptions used in accounting for the plan:

    a. Assumed discount rate

    b. Rate of compensation increased

    c. Expected long-term rate of return on plan assets

7. Assumed health care cost trend rate(s) for the next year used to measure the expected cost of benefits covered by the plan

8. A general description of the direction and pattern of change in the assumed trend rates, the ultimate trend rate(s), and when that rate is expected to be achieved

9. Effect of a 1% increase / 1% decrease in the assumed health care cost trend rates on the aggregate of the service and interest cost components of net periodic health care benefit cost and the accumulated post retirement benefit obligation

10. The amounts and types of securities included in plan assets

11. The amount of future annual benefits of plan participants covered by plan contracts issued by the employer or related parties

12. Any significant transactions between the employer or related parties and the plan during the year

13. Any alternative amortization method used to amortize prior service costs or unrecognized net gains and losses pursuant to FASB Statement 87

14. Any substantive commitment (e.g., past practice or a history of regular benefit increases) used as the basis for accounting for the benefit obligation recognized during the period and a description of the nature of the event

15. The cost of providing special or contractual termination benefits recognized during the period and a description of the nature of the event

16. An explanation of any significant change in the benefit obligation or plan assets not otherwise apparent in the above disclosures

- Modified Disclosures for Nonpublic Companies (FAS-132, par. 8):
  1. The benefit obligation
  2. The fair value of plan assets
  3. The funded status of the plan
  4. Employer contributions
  5. Participant contributions
  6. Benefits paid
  7. The amounts recognized in the statement of financial position
     a. The net pension and net postretirement benefit prepaid assets or accrued liabilities
     b. Any intangible asset
     c. Amount of accumulated other comprehensive income

8. The amount of net periodic benefit cost recognized and the amount included in other comprehensive income arising from a change in the minimum pension liability

9. On a weighted-average basis, the following assumptions used:
   a. Assumed discount rate
   b. Rate of compensation increases
   c. Expected long-term rate of return on plan assets

10. The assumed health care cost trend rate(s) for the next year used to measure the expected cost of benefits covered by the plan

11. A general description of the direction and pattern of change in the assumed trend rates, the ultimate trend rate(s), and when the rate is expected to be achieved

12. The amounts and types of securities of the employer and related parties included in the plan assets

13. The approximate future annual benefits of plan assets

14. Participants covered by insurance contracts issued by the employer or related parties

15. Any significant transactions between the employer or related parties and the plan during the period

16. The nature and effect of significant events, such as amendments, combinations, divestitures, curtailments, and settlements

Quasi-Reorganizations

- The new earned surplus account created as the result of a quasi-reorganization must be dated and disclosed for a period not to exceed 10 years (ARB-46, pars. 1–2).

Related Party Disclosures

- Material related party transactions, including (FAS-57, par. 2):
  1. Nature of relationship
  2. Description of the transaction(s)
  3. Dollar amounts of the transaction(s)
  4. Amounts due from related parties at the balance sheet date, and the terms of settlement
- Existence of relationships of common control, even if no transactions occurred must be disclosed (FAS-57, par. 4).

Research and Development Costs

- The amount of R&D charged to expense for the period must be disclosed (FAS-2, par. 13).
- For computer software costs (FAS-86, par. 11):
  1. The unamortized software costs included in each balance sheet
  2. The amount charged to expense on the income statement for amortization and for write-downs to net realizable value

Results of Operations

- Information regarding a disposal of a segment, including (APB-30, par. 18):
  1. Identity of the business segment
  2. Expected date of disposal
  3. Manner of disposal
  4. Description of the remaining assets and liabilities of the segment
  5. Income and loss from operations and other proceeds from disposal of the segment

Segment Reporting

- General information (FAS-131, par. 26):
  1. Factors used to identify the enterprise's reportable segments
  2. Types of products and services that are the basis for revenues from each reportable segment
  3. An explanation of the basis for organization
- Information about segment profit or loss and assets (FAS-131, par. 27):
  1. Revenues from external customers
  2. Revenues from other operating segments
  3. Interest revenue
  4. Interest expense
  5. Depreciation, depletion, and amortization
  6. Unusual items
  7. Income recognized on equity-method investments
  8. Income tax expense or benefit
  9. Extraordinary items
  10. Significant noncash items other than depreciation, depletion and amortization

- Information about assets of each reportable segment if the specified amounts are included in the determination of segment profit or loss (FAS-131, par. 28):
    1. The amount of investment in equity-method investees
    2. Total expenditures for additions to long-lived assets (except financial instruments, long-term customer relationships of a financial institution, mortgage and other servicing rights, deferred policy acquisition costs, and deferred income taxes)
- Explanatory information that should assist users of the financial statements in better understanding the meaning of that information, as follows (FAS-131, par. 31):
    1. The basis of accounting for transactions between reportable segments
    2. Differences in the measurement of the reportable segments' profit or loss and the enterprise's consolidated income before income taxes, extraordinary items, discontinued operations, and cumulative effect of changes in accounting principle
    3. Differences in the measurement of the reportable segments' assets and the enterprise's consolidated assets
    4. Any changes from prior years in the measurement of reported segment profit or loss, and the effect, if any, of those changes on the amount of segment profit or loss
    5. The nature of any asymmetrical allocations to segments
- Reconciliations (FAS-131, par. 32):

    Reconciliations of certain segment information to the enterprise's consolidated totals as indicated in the following table (FAS-131, par. 32):

Segment information	Reconciled to	Consolidated information
1. Reportable segments' revenues		1. Consolidated revenues
2. Reportable segments' profit or loss		2. Consolidated income before income taxes, extraordinary items, discontinued operations, and cumulative effect of change in accounting principle
3. Reportable segments'		3. Consolidated assets
4. Reportable segments' amounts for other significant items		4. Corresponding consolidated amounts

- Interim period information (FAS-131, par. 33)

  Revenue

    From external customers

    Intersegment

  Segment profit or loss

  Material changes from last annual report

    Total assets

    Basis of segmentation

    Basis of measuring segment profit or loss

  Reconciliation of segment profit or loss to enterprise consolidated income

- Enterprise-wide information
  1. Products and services (FAS-131, par. 37)
     - Revenues from external customers for each product and service or group of related products and services
  2. Geographic areas (FAS-131, par. 38)
     - Revenues from external customers:
       — Attributable to the enterprise's country of domicile
       — Attributed to all foreign countries in total from which revenue is derived
       — Revenues from individual foreign countries if the amounts are material
       — The basis for attributing revenues from external customers to individual countries
  3. Major customers (FAS-131, par. 39)
     - Revenues from a single customer that accounts for 10% or more of revenue
     - The segment(s) from which sales to each major customer were made

Stockholders' Equity

- Information about securities (FAS-129, pars. 4–5):
  1. Pertinent rights and privileges (e.g., dividend and liquidation preferences, participation rights, call prices and dates, conversion or exercise prices or rates and pertinent dates, sinking-fund requirements, unusual voting rights, significant terms of contracts to issue additional shares)
  2. Number of shares issued upon conversion, exercise, or satisfaction of required conditions during at least the most recent annual fiscal period and any subsequent interim period presented

- Liquidation preference of preferred stock (FAS-129, pars. 6–7):
  1. Liquidation preference of preferred stock if considerably in excess of the par or stated value shown "short" or parenthetically (not in notes)
  2. Aggregate or per-share amounts at which preferred stock may be called or is subject to redemption through sinking-fund operations or otherwise
  3. Aggregate or per-share amount of arrearages in cumulative preferred stock

- Redeemable stock (FAS-129, par. 8):
  1. Amount of redemption requirements for all issues of capital stock that are redeemable at fixed or determinable prices on fixed or determinable dates in each of the five years following the date of the latest statement of financial position

- Treasury stock:
  1. Number of shares and basis for valuation
  2. The impact state laws may have on the availability of retained earnings for payment of dividends (APB-6, par. 13)

Stock Issued to Employees

- Status of all option plans (ARB-43, Ch. 13B, par. 15):
  1. Number of shares under option
  2. Option price
  3. Number of shares that can be exercised
  4. Number of shares exercised
  5. Option price of exercised shares

- For financial statements for fiscal years beginning after December 15, 1995, in accordance with FAS-123 and regardless of the method used to account for employee stock-based compensation arrangements (FAS-123, pars. 45–48):
  1. If the APB-25 method is used, for each year for which an income statement is provided, entities must disclose: (*a*) the pro forma net income and earnings per share (public entities) as if the fair value–based accounting method were used to account for stock-based compensation and (*b*) the difference between compensation cost recognized by APB-25 and the fair value method of FAS-123.

2. A description of the stock-based compensation plan, including the general terms of awards under the plan, the maximum term of options granted, and the number of shares authorized for grants of options or other equity instruments, must be given.

3. For each year for which an income statement is provided, entities must disclose:

    a. The number and weighted-average exercise prices of options for each of the following groups of options: (1) outstanding at the beginning of the year, (2) outstanding at the end of the year, (3) exercisable at the end of the year, and those (4) granted, (5) exercised, (6) forfeited, or (7) expired during the year.

    b. The weighted average grant-date fair value of options granted during the year. If the exercise prices of some options differ from the market price of the stock on the grant date, weighted-average exercise prices and weighted-average fair values of options must be disclosed separately for options whose exercise price (1) equals, (2) exceeds, or (3) is less than the market price of the stock on the date of grant.

    c. The number and weighted-average grant-date fair value of equity instruments, other than options granted during the year.

    d. Method and significant assumptions used to estimate the fair values of options must be disclosed.

    e. Total compensation cost recognized in income for stock-based compensation awards must be disclosed.

    f. Terms of significant modifications to outstanding option grants must be disclosed.

4. For options outstanding at the date of the latest balance sheet presented, the range of exercise prices, the weighted-average exercise price and the weighted-average remaining contractual life must be disclosed.

5. The number and weighted-average exercise price of options exercisable.

Transfer and Servicing of Financial Assets

-   If the transfer is recorded as a sale, the proceeds to the transferor for each period of the income statement must be disclosed (FAS-77, par. 9).

-   For instruments with off-balance sheet risk, for each class of financial instrument (FAS-105, pars. 17–18):

    1. Face or contract amount

    2. Nature and terms of the instrument

    3. Potential accounting loss if any party to the transaction failed to perform

    4. Information regarding the collateral or security policies of the company, as well as the collateral or security supporting each financial instrument subject to credit risk

- Information regarding each group concentration of credit risk must be disclosed (FAS-105, par. 20).

Note: FAS-77 is superseded by FAS-125, which is effective for transfers of receivables occurring after December 31, 1996. See Financial Instruments—Disclosures section of Disclosure Index.

Troubled Debt Restructuring

- A debtor must disclose the following (FAS-15, pars. 25–26):

    1. For each restructuring, a description of the changes in terms and / or the major features of the settlement

    2. Gain on restructuring including the related income tax effect

    3. Aggregate net gain or loss on transfers of assets

    4. Per share data

    5. Contingently payable amounts

- A creditor must disclose (FAS-15, pars. 40–41):

    1. Restructured receivables, by major category.

    2. Commitments to lend additional funds to a debtor as part of a restructuring.

- Effective for fiscal years beginning after December 15, 1994, creditors must disclose (FAS-114, par. 20):

    1. Investment amounts in loans in which impairment has been recognized and the total allowance for credit losses recorded.

    2. Credit loss account activity.

    3. Their income recognition policy.

Banking and Thrift Institutions

- The nature and amount of any financial assistance received by an enterprise from a regulatory agency in connection with the acquisition of a banking or thrift institution must be disclosed (FAS-72, par. 11).

Broadcasters

- License agreements that have been executed but that are not reported on the balance sheet because they do not meet the criteria outlined in FAS-63 must be disclosed (FAS-63, par. 10).

Motion Picture Films

- Film inventories, including films released, completed and in process must be disclosed (FAS-53, par. 23).

- The amount of story rights and scenarios must be disclosed (FAS-53, par. 23).

Records and Music

- Commitments for artist advances payable and future royalty guarantees must be disclosed (FAS-50, par. 13).

- The portion of the cost of record masters borne by the record company and recorded as assets must be disclosed (FAS-50, par. 14).

Franchise Fee Revenue

- The nature of all significant commitments and obligations from franchise agreements must be disclosed (FAS-45, par. 20).

- If the installment or cost recovery method is used to account for franchise fee revenue, the following must be disclosed (FAS-45, par. 21):
  1. Sale price of the franchise
  2. The revenue and related costs deferred, both currently and cumulatively
  3. The periods in which the franchise fees become payable
  4. Revenues originally deferred but recognized late

- Probable changes in the initial franchise fee revenue because of sales saturation and the relative contribution of initial franchise fees to total franchise fee revenue are recommended disclosures (FAS-45, par. 22).

- If there are significant changes in the number of franchiser-owned or franchised outlets during the period, the number of franchises sold, purchased, and in operation (segregated by franchiser-owned and franchised) must be disclosed (FAS-45, par. 23).

Insurance Enterprises

- The basis for estimating (FAS-60, par. 60):
  1. The liability for unpaid claims
  2. The liability for claim adjustment expenses

- The methods and assumptions used in calculating the liability for future policy benefits must be disclosed. In addition, FAS-60 encourages, but does not require, the disclosure of the average rates of assumed investment yields that are in effect for the current period (FAS-60, par. 60).

- Capitalized acquisition costs (FAS-60, par. 60):
  1. The nature of such costs
  2. The method of amortizing such costs
  3. The amount of amortization of such costs for the current period

- If the liabilities for unpaid claims and claim adjustment expenses for short-duration contracts are reported at their present values in the financial statements (FAS-60, par. 60):
  1. The carrying amount of the liabilities
  2. The range of interest rates used to discount the liabilities

- If estimated investment income is used in calculating a premium deficiency for short-duration contracts, this information must be disclosed (FAS-60, par. 60).

- Reinsurance transactions of an insurance company (FAS-113, par. 27):
  1. The nature, purpose, and effect of ceded reinsurance transactions (Ceding enterprises shall also disclose the fact that the insurer is not relieved of its primary obligation to the policyholder in a reinsurance transaction.)
  2. For short-duration contracts, premiums from direct business and reinsurance assumed and ceded, on both a written and an earned basis
  3. For long-duration contracts, premiums and amounts assessed against policyholders from direct business, rein-

surance assumed and ceded, and premiums and amounts earned

4. Methods used for income recognition on reinsurance contracts

- Participating insurance of an insurance company (FAS-60, par. 60):
  1. The relative percentage of participating insurance
  2. The method of accounting for participating insurance
  3. The amount of such dividends
  4. The amount of any additional income allocated to participating insurance policyholders

- Stockholders' equity, statutory capital, and surplus (FAS-60, par. 60):
  1. The amount of statutory capital and surplus
  2. The amount of statutory capital and surplus required for regulatory purposes, if significant to the enterprise's total statutory capital and surplus
  3. The nature of statutory restrictions on dividends and the amount of retained earnings not available for dividends to stockholders

- Policyholders' surplus of life insurance companies (when an insurance company is consolidated or accounted for by the equity method, these disclosures also apply to the parent company) (FAS-60, par. 60):
  1. The treatment of the policyholders' surplus under the provisions of the Internal Revenue Code
  2. The fact that income taxes may become payable if the company takes specific action, which should be disclosed appropriately
  3. The total amount of policyholders' surplus for which income taxes have not been provided

- If no current or deferred federal income taxes have been provided by a life insurance company for any retained earnings in excess of policyholders' surplus (FAS-60, par. 60):
  1. The amount of such retained earnings
  2. The reasons for not accruing deferred federal income taxes

- Ceding companies must disclose concentrations of credit risk associated with reinsurance receivables and prepaid reinsurance premiums under FAS-105 (FAS-113, par. 28).

- Amounts of salvage and subrogation deducted from the liability for unpaid losses in the balance sheet must be disclosed (FAS-60, par. 18).

Mortgage Banking Industry

- Mortgage loans receivable and mortgage-backed securities must be disclosed separately as those held for sale and those held for investment (FAS-65, par. 28).

- The method used to determine the lower of cost or market value of mortgage loans receivable and mortgage-backed securities must be disclosed (FAS-65, par. 29).

- Information about the capitalization of servicing rights acquired by purchase during the period (FAS-65, par. 30):
  1. Amount capitalized
  2. Method of amortization used
  3. Amount of amortization

- Information about the allocation of the cost of service rights (FAS-122, par. 3):
  1. The fair value of capitalized servicing rights and the methods and significant assumptions used to estimate fair value (if no cost is allocated to certain mortgage servicing rights, a description of those rights and the reasons why it is not practicable to estimate the fair value)
  2. The risk characteristics of the underlying loans used to stratify capitalized servicing rights for purposes of measuring impairment
  3. For each period for which results of operations are presented, activity in the allowance for capitalized servicing rights, including the aggregate balance of the allowance at the beginning and end of the period, aggregate additions charged and reductions credited to operations, and direct write-downs charged against the allowance

Note: FAS-122 is superseded by FAS-125, which is effective for mortgage servicing rights transactions occurring after December 31, 1996. See Financial Instruments—Disclosures section of Disclosure Index.

Not-for-Profit Organizations

- Information about depreciation (FAS-93, par. 5):
  1. Depreciation expense for the period
  2. Balances of major classes of depreciable assets by nature or function
  3. Accumulated depreciation by major class or in total
  4. A description of the depreciation methods used

Note: FAS-116 is effective for financial statements issued for fiscal years beginning after December 15, 1994, except for not-for-profit organizations with less than $5 million in total assets and less than $1 million in total annual expenses, for which the effective date is December 15, 1995.

- Information about unconditional promises to give (FAS-116, par. 24):

  1. The amount of promises receivable in less than one year, in one to five years, and in more than five years

  2. The amount of the allowance for uncollectible promises receivable

- Information about conditional promises to give (FAS-116, par. 25):

  1. The total of the amounts promised

  2. A description and the amount of each group of promises having similar characteristics, such as promises toward completing a new building or establishing a new program

- An entity that does not recognize and capitalize its collections (FAS-116, par. 26):

  1. Costs of collections purchased as a decrease in the appropriate class of net assets

  2. Proceeds from the sale of collection items as an increase in the appropriate class of net assets

  3. Proceeds from insurance recoveries of lost or destroyed items as an increase in the appropriate class of net assets

- An entity that capitalizes its collections prospectively (FAS-116, par. 26):

  1. Proceeds from sales and insurance recoveries of items not previously capitalized separately from revenues, expenses, gains, and losses

- An entity that does not recognize and capitalize its collections or that capitalizes its collections prospectively (FAS-116, par. 27):

  1. A description of its collections, including their relative significance

  2. Its accounting and stewardship policies

  3. Either a description of items given away, lost, destroyed, or damaged during the period, or their fair value

  4. A line on the face of the statement of financial position must refer explicitly to the note containing these disclosures

- Information about investments (FAS-124, pars. 14–16):
  1. Composition of investment return, including at least the following components: investment income (e.g., dividends, interest), net realized gains or losses on investments reported at other than fair value, and net gains or losses on investments reported at fair value
  2. A reconciliation of investment return to amounts reported in the statement of activities, if the investment is separated into operating and nonoperating amounts and if an explanation is given of the policy, including any changes in policy, used to make that classification

Also, the following information related to the statement of financial position is required:

  3. Aggregate carrying amount of investments by major type
  4. Basis for determining the carrying amount for investments other than equity securities with readily determinable fair values and all debt securities
  5. The method(s) and significant assumptions used to determine fair values (related to the FAS-107 requirement)
  6. The aggregate amount of the deficiencies for all donor-restricted endowment funds for which the fair value of the assets at the reporting date is less than the level required by donor stipulations or law
  7. For the most recent period for which a statement of financial position is presented, the nature of and carrying amount for each individual investment or group of investments that represents a significant concentration of market risk (related to the FAS-105 requirement)

Note: FAS-124 is effective for fiscal years beginning after December 15, 1995, and interim periods within those fiscal years.

Oil and Gas Producing Companies

- Methods of accounting for costs incurred and disposing of capitalized costs must be disclosed (FAS-69, par. 6).
- Publicly held enterprises must disclose (FAS-69, par. 7):
  1. Proved oil and gas reserve quantities
  2. Capitalized costs
  3. Costs incurred for property acquisition, exploration, and development activities
  4. Results of operations
  5. A standardized measure of discounted future cash flows

- Capitalized and expended costs classified by activity (FAS-69, par. 21):

  1. Property acquisition costs
  2. Exploration costs
  3. Development costs

- Long-term supply agreements with governments and net quantities received during the year under such agreements must be disclosed (FAS-69, par. 28).

- Government or authority restrictions on the disclosures of oil and gas reserves must be disclosed (FAS-69, par. 17).

- Important economic factors or significant uncertainties affecting proved reserves must be disclosed (FAS-69, par. 15).

- Capitalized costs, related depreciation, depletion, amortization, and valuation allowances classified by (FAS-19, par. 11):

  1. Mineral interests in property
  2. Wells, related equipment, and property
  3. Support equipment and facilities
  4. Uncompleted wells, equipment, and facilities

- Disclosure should include costs incurred by each geographic area for which reserve quantities are disclosed (FAS-69, par. 22).

- Costs incurred to acquire mineral interests that have proved reserves must be disclosed separately from costs incurred to acquire unproved properties (FAS-69, par. 22).

- Interim statements must disclose significant events (FAS-69, par. 9).

Pension Plan Financial Statements

- Disclosure should include description of the methods and significant assumptions used to determine fair value of investments and the reported value of contracts with insurance companies (FAS-35, par. 27).

- Disclosure should include description of the method and significant assumptions used to determine the actuarial present value of accumulated plan benefits (FAS-35, par. 27).

- Any significant changes of method(s) between benefit information dates must be disclosed (FAS-35, par. 27).

- General description of the plan agreement, including vesting and benefit provisions must be disclosed (FAS-35, par. 28a).

- Description of significant plan amendments adopted during the year must be disclosed (FAS-35, par. 28b).

- Brief, general description of (FAS-35, par. 28c):
  1. The priority order of participants' claims to the assets of plan upon plan termination
  2. Benefits guaranteed by PBGC, including any PBGC guarantee to any recent plan amendment(s)

- Funding policy and any changes in the policy during the plan year must be disclosed. Funds subject to ERISA must disclose whether the minimum funding requirements for ERISA have been met. Minimum funding waivers granted by or pending before the IRS must also be disclosed (FAS-35, par. 28d).

- Disclosure must include policy regarding the purchase of contracts with insurance companies that are excluded from plan assets. Dividend income related to these contracts must also be disclosed (FAS-35, par. 28e).

- Federal income tax status of the plan must be disclosed (FAS-35, par. 28f).

- Investments that represent 5% or more of the net assets available for benefits must be disclosed (FAS-35, par. 28g).

- Real estate or other transactions between the plan and either the plan sponsor, the employer(s), or the employee organization must be disclosed (FAS-35, par. 28h).

- Unusual or infrequent events or transactions occurring after the latest benefit information date but before the financial statements are issued that significantly effect an assessment of the plan's present and future ability to pay benefits must be disclosed. The effect of these events should be quantified, or the reason(s) they cannot be quantified should be discussed (FAS-35, par. 28i).

Real Estate—Recognition of Sales

- Financial statements of the seller-lessee must disclose the terms of the sale-leaseback transaction (FAS-98, par. 17):
  1. Future commitments, obligations, provisions or circumstances that require the seller-lessee's continuing involvement

- If the seller-lessee has accounted for the sale-leaseback transaction by the deposit method or a financing (FAS-98, par. 18):

1. The obligation for future minimum lease payments as of the date of the latest balance sheet
2. The total of minimum sublease rentals to be received in the future under noncancelable leases

- For enterprises with retail land sales (FAS-66, par. 50):
    1. Maturities of accounts receivable for each of the next five years
    2. Amount of delinquent accounts receivable and the method for determining delinquency
    3. The weighted average and range of stated interest rates of receivables
    4. Estimated total costs and estimated dates of expenditures for improvements to major areas of the project from which sales are being made, for the next five years
    5. Recorded obligations for improvements

Regulated Industries

- Customer refunds that are recognized in a period other than the period in which the related revenue was recognized (FAS-71, par. 19):
    1. Effect on net income
    2. Year that the related revenue was recognized
- Recovery of major allowable costs that do not provide for a return on investment during the recovery period (FAS-71, par. 20):
    1. The unamortized amount of such costs
    2. The remaining periods of amortization
- Information about any phase-in plans in effect during the year or ordered for future years (FAS-92, par. 11):
    1. The terms of the plan(s)
    2. Net amounts of allowable costs deferred for future recovery and the net change in the deferral account for the year
- The nature and amount of any allowance for earnings on shareholders' investment capitalized for rate-making purposes but not capitalized for financial reporting must be disclosed (FAS-92, par. 12).
- Discontinuation of the application of FAS-71 (FAS-101, pars. 8–9):
    1. Reason(s) for the discontinuation
    2. The portion(s) of the operations to which the application of FAS-71 is being discontinued

1999

MILLER

GAAP GUIDE CPE PROGRAM

Module 1—
Chapters 1–13, 49, and 57

Module 2—
Chapters 14–26, 59, and 63

Module 3—
Chapters 27–36, and 50–54, 60

Module 4—
Chapters 37–48, 55, 56, 58, 61, and 62

www.hbpp.com
TAKE YOUR CPE TEST ONLINE!

HARCOURT BRACE PROFESSIONAL PUBLISHING

A Division of
Harcourt Brace & Company
SAN DIEGO   NEW YORK   CHICAGO   LONDON

INTRODUCTION

Thank you for choosing this self-study CPE course from Harcourt Brace Professional Publishing. Our goal is to provide you with the clearest, most concise, and most up-to-date accounting and auditing information to help further your professional development, as well as the most convenient method to help you satisfy your continuing professional education obligations.

This CPE program is intended to be used in conjunction with your 1999 *Miller GAAP Guide*. This course has the following characteristics:

Prerequisites: None

Recommended CPE credits: 10 hours per module

Level of Knowledge: Basic

Field of Study: Accounting

The complete, four-module 1999 *Miller GAAP Guide* Self-Study CPE Program is designed to provide 40 hours of CPE credit if all tests are submitted for grading and earn a passing score. You may complete any or all of the four modules that make up the CPE Program.

In accordance with the standards of the National Registry of CPE Sponsors, each credit hour awarded for this program is based on 100 minutes of average completion time. Credit hours are recommended in accordance with the Statement on Standards for Formal Continuing Professional Education (CPE) Programs, published by the AICPA. CPE requirements vary from state to state. Your state board is the final authority for the number of credit hours allowed for a particular program, as well as the classification of courses, under its specific licensing requirement. Contact your State Board of Accountancy for information concerning your state's requirements as to the number of CPE credit hours you must earn and the acceptable fields of study.

This course currently is not recognized in Mississippi and North Carolina. Florida CPAs, please consult your state board.

To receive credit, complete the course according to the instructions on page 65.04. Each module costs $64.00. Payment options are shown on the answer sheets.

Each CPE test is graded within two weeks of its receipt. A passing score is 70% or above. Participants who pass the test will receive a Certificate of Completion to acknowledge their achievement. The self-study CPE Program offered in conjunction with the 1999 *Miller GAAP Guide* will expire on December 31, 1999. Participants may submit completed tests for the program until that date.

Instructions for Taking This Course

Each module consists of chapter learning objectives, reading assignments, review questions and suggested solutions, and an examination. Complete each step listed below for each module you want to submit for grading:

1. Review the chapter learning objectives.

2. Read the assigned material in the 1999 *Miller GAAP Guide.*

3. Complete the review questions, and compare your answers to the suggested solutions.

4. After completing all assigned chapters in the module, take the examination, writing "true," "false," or the corresponding multiple choice letter (a–d) to indicate your answer on the appropriate line on the answer sheet.

5. When you have completed the examination, remove the answer sheet, place it in a stamped envelope, and send it to the following address:

> *Miller GAAP Guide* CPE Coordinator
> Harcourt Brace Professional Publishing
> 525 B Street, Suite 1900
> San Diego, CA 92101-4495

Be sure to indicate your method of payment on the answer sheet.

SELF-STUDY CONTINUING PROFESSIONAL EDUCATION
Module 1

Accounting Changes

After completing this section you should be able to:

- Discuss how to distinguish and account for changes in accounting principles, changes in accounting estimates, and corrections of errors.
- Describe the financial statement presentation for accounting changes and corrections of errors.
- Explain the hierarchy of accounting principles set forth in Statement on Auditing Standards No. 69.

Read Chapter 1, "Accounting Changes," of the 1999 *Miller GAAP Guide*.

Answer review questions 1–2 on page 65.09.

Accounting Policies

After completing this section, you should be able to:

- Explain which accounting policies should be disclosed in the "Summary of Significant Accounting Policies."

Read Chapter 2, "Accounting Policies," of the 1999 *Miller GAAP Guide*.

Answer review questions 3–4 on page 65.09.

Business Combinations

After completing this section you should be able to:

- Discuss how to account for business combinations by the purchase method and the pooling of interests method.
- Describe the conditions under which the pooling of interests method is proper.
- Describe the disclosures that are required in the period in which a business combination occurs.

Read Chapter 3, "Business Combinations," of the 1999 *Miller GAAP Guide*.

Answer review questions 5–6 on page 65.09.

Cash Flow Statement

After completing this section, you should be able to:
- Explain how to classify activities as operating, investing, or financing
- Define cash equivalents.
- Describe the direct and indirect methods of reporting cash flows.
- Describe how to report noncash investing and financing activities.

Read Chapter 4, "Cash Flow Statement," of the 1999 *Miller GAAP Guide*.

Answer review questions 7–8 on page 65.09.

Changing Prices

After completing this section you should be able to:

- Explain the difference between current value accounting and general price-level accounting.
- Explain how to obtain current cost information.
- Describe the minimum supplementary information that the FASB encourages an enterprise to disclose.

Read Chapter 5, "Changing Prices," of the 1999 *Miller GAAP Guide*.

Answer review questions 9–10 on page 65.10.

Consolidated Financial Statements

After completing this section you should be able to:

- Discuss the conditions under which consolidation is required.
- Discuss the conditions under which combined financial statements are appropriate.
- Explain how consolidation differs from the equity method.
- Identify items that should be eliminated in consolidated financial statements.
- Describe how minority interests are disclosed.

Read Chapter 6, "Consolidated Financial Statements," of the 1999 *Miller GAAP Guide*.

Answer review questions 11–12 on page 65.10.

Contingencies, Risks, and Uncertainties

After completing this section you should be able to:

- Explain the conditions that require accrual of a loss contingency.
- Determine the proper amount to accrue for a loss contingency.
- Discuss how to account for and report gain contingencies.
- Discuss how to account for and disclose unasserted claims.

- Understand the disclosure requirements for significant risks and uncertainties.

Read Chapter 7, "Contingencies, Risks, and Uncertainties," of the 1999 *Miller GAAP Guide*.

Answer review questions 13–14 on page 65.10.

Convertible Debt and Debt with Warrants

After completing this section you should be able to:

- Discuss the characteristics of convertible debt.
- Explain the difference between convertible debt and debt with detachable warrants.
- Discuss how to account for the issuance of convertible debt and for its conversion.
- Discuss how to account for the issuance of debt with detachable warrants and for the exercise of the warrants.
- Recognize an induced conversion and explain how to account for it.

Read Chapter 8, "Convertible Debt and Debt with Warrants," of the 1999 *Miller GAAP Guide*.

Answer review questions 15–16 on page 65.10.

Current Assets and Current Liabilities

After completing this section you should be able to:

- Define *current assets* and *current liabilities*.
- Compute current and acid test ratios.
- Discuss the rules for offsetting assets and liabilities.
- Explain how to classify the cash surrender value of a life insurance policy and how to report increases.
- Describe objective and subjective acceleration clauses and their potential effects on financial statements and disclosures.
- Discuss the conditions that require accruals for future employee vacations, holidays, and sick-days.

Read Chapter 9, "Current Assets and Current Liabilities," of the 1999 *Miller GAAP Guide*.

Answer review questions 17–18 on page 65.10.

Deferred Compensation Contracts

After completing this section you should be able to:

- Recognize deferred compensation agreements.

- Explain how to determine the liability for deferred compensation agreements.
- Explain how to make periodic accruals.

Read Chapter 10, "Deferred Compensation Contracts," of the 1999 *Miller GAAP Guide*.

Answer review questions 19–20 on page 65.10.

Depreciable Assets and Depreciation

After completing this section, you should be able to:

- Explain which costs should be capitalized as fixed assets, including self-constructed assets.
- Explain how improvements affect accounting for fixed assets.
- Discuss how to apply common depreciation methods.
- Describe the disclosure requirements for depreciable assets.

Read Chapter 11, "Depreciable Assets and Depreciation," of the 1999 *Miller GAAP Guide*.

Answer review questions 21–22 on page 65.10.

Development Stage Enterprises

After completing this section, you should be able to:

- Explain how to account for costs incurred during the development stage.
- Describe the financial statements of a development stage enterprise.

Read Chapter 12, "Development Stage Enterprises," of the 1999 *Miller GAAP Guide*.

Answer review questions 23–24 on page 65.10.

Earnings per Share

After completing this section, you should be able to:

- Explain the concepts of the new earnings per share calculation under FAS-128.
- Compute basic earnings per share.
- Compute diluted earnings per share.
- Describe disclosure requirements related to earnings per share.

Read Chapter 13, "Earnings per Share," of the 1999 *Miller GAAP Guide*.

Answer review questions 25–26 on page 65.10.

Banking and Thrift Institutions

After completing this section you should be able to:

- Discuss how to account for the purchase of a savings and loan association.
- Discuss how goodwill and regulatory assistance are treated in the acquisition of a banking or thrift institution.

Read Chapter 49, "Banking and Thrift Institutions," of the 1999 *Miller GAAP Guide.*

Answer review questions 27–28 on page 65.10.

Mortgage Banking Industry

After completing this section, you should be able to:

- Explain how to account for mortgage loans receivable and mortgage-backed securities.
- Explain how to account for mortgage servicing fees.
- Describe how to account for loan origination and commitment fees.
- Define *collateralized mortgage obligations* and explain how to determine whether they should be recorded as liabilities in the financial statements of the issuer.

Read Chapter 57, "Mortgage Banking Industry," of the 1999 *Miller GAAP Guide.*

Answer review questions 29–30 on page 65.10.

REVIEW QUESTIONS

1. How is the cumulative effect of a change in accounting principle reported for interim periods?
2. What types of pronouncements and documents are included in the highest-weighted category (category A) of the GAAP hierarchy?
3. Provide some examples of areas where accounting policies are required to be disclosed.
4. Which accounting principles and methods should be disclosed under the caption "Summary of Significant Accounting Policies"?
5. Using the purchase method, how is the purchase price that is allocated to acquired assets recorded in a business combination accounted for?
6. Describe the nature of a business combination that is a pooling of interests.
7. List some types of transactions that would be reported as investing activities in a statement of cash flows.
8. Define *cash equivalents* according to FAS-95 for purposes of preparing a cash flow statement.

9. When is an entity required by FAS-89 to disclose the impact of changing prices on financial statements?

10. What items are considered monetary by FAS-89? Provide some examples of monetary items.

11. When are consolidated financial statements required?

12. What are some examples of intercompany receivables and payables that would be eliminated in consolidated financial statements?

13. When should financial statements disclose concentrations under SOP 94-6?

14. When would a loss contingency be accrued as a charge to income as of the date of the financial statements?

15. How should an entity account for the issuance of convertible debt?

16. How does a debtor account for an induced conversion of convertible debt under FAS-84?

17. What is the general rule about offsetting assets and liabilities?

18. Explain the allowance method of providing for uncollectible accounts receivable and how it is used.

19. Describe the accounting treatment under FAS-106 for deferred compensation plans that are not tantamount to a plan for pension or other postretirement benefits.

20. Describe the calculation of the accrued liability for deferred compensation contracts.

21. Under what condition should the cost of an improvement of a depreciable asset be capitalized?

22. What disclosures about depreciable assets and depreciation are required in the financial statements?

23. What is a *development stage enterprise*?

24. How are losses accumulated by a development stage enterprise presented on the balance sheet?

25. How do preferred stock dividends affect the calculation of basic earnings per share under FAS-128?

26. Distinguish between the reporting objectives of basic earnings per share and diluted earnings per share.

27. What is the focus of specialized industry GAAP for banking and thrift institutions?

28. What are the conditions for recognizing regulatory assistance in connection with the acquisition of a banking or thrift institution?

29. How should a mortgage loan receivable held for sale be valued?

30. How should a mortgage banking institution recognize revenue on loan placement fees?

SUGGESTED SOLUTIONS

1. The cumulative effect of a change in accounting principle is included in net income of the first interim period of the year in which a change is made, regardless of what period during the year the change occurs. If the accounting change occurs in other than the first interim period, the current and prior interim statements are restated to include the newly adopted accounting principle.

2. The pronouncements and documents that make up Category A of the GAAP hierarchy are:
   * FASB Statements
   * FASB Interpretations
   * APB Opinions
   * AICPA Accounting Research Bulletins

3. Examples of areas of accounting for which accounting policies should be disclosed are:
   * Basis of consolidation
   * Depreciation methods
   * Inventory methods
   * Amortization of intangibles
   * Recognition of profit on long-term construction contracts
   * Recognition of revenue from franchising and leasing operations

4. The following should be disclosed under the caption "Summary of Significant Accounting Policies": (*a*) a selection from acceptable alternatives, (*b*) peculiarities to a specific industry, (*c*) unusual or innovative applications of GAAP, and (*d*) when required by a specific pronouncement.

5. Under the purchase method of accounting for a business combination, acquired assets are recorded at their fair value. Any excess of the purchase price over the fair market value of identifiable assets acquired less liabilities assumed is recorded as goodwill, which is amortized by the straight-line method in accordance with APB-16.

6. The nature of a business combination that is a pooling of interests is that the shareholders of the combining companies neither withdraw nor invest assets, but exchange shares in accordance with a ratio that preserves their interests in the combined corporation.

7. Investing activities in a statement of cash flows would include:
   * Making or collecting loans
   * Acquiring and disposing of debt or equity instruments
   * Acquiring and disposing of property, plant, and equipment
   * Acquiring and disposing of assets held for or used in the production of goods or services by the enterprise (other than materials that are part of the enterprise's inventory)

8. Under FAS-95, cash equivalents are short-term, highly liquid investments that are (a) readily convertible to known amounts of cash and (b) so near their maturities that they present insignificant risk of changes in value because of changes in interest rates.

9. Disclosure of the impact of changing prices is not required. The FAS-89 disclosure standards for the impact of changing prices are optional.

10. Assets and liabilities are considered monetary items under FAS-89 if their amounts are fixed or determinable without reference to future prices of specific goods and services. Cash, accounts and notes receivable in cash, and accounts and notes payable in cash are examples of monetary items.

11. Consolidated financial statements are required when a parent company has a controlling financial interest in an investee, except those in which control of the investee is temporary or if significant doubt exists regarding the parent's ability to control the investee.

12. Some examples of intercompany receivables and payables that would be eliminated in consolidated financial statements are:

    • Accounts receivable and accounts payable

    • Advances to and from affiliates

    • Notes receivable and notes payable

    • Interest receivable and interest payable

13. Financial statements should disclose concentrations under SOP 94-6 if *all* of the following conditions are met:

    • The concentration existed at the date of the financial statements.

    • The concentration makes the enterprise vulnerable to the risk of a near-term severe impact.

    • It is reasonably possible that the events that could cause the severe impact will occur in the near term.

14. The following two conditions must be met for a loss contingency to be accrued as a charge to income as of the date of the financial statements:

    • It is probable that as of the date of the financial statements an asset has been impaired or a liability incurred, based on information available before the actual issuance date of the financial statements, and

    • The amount of the loss can be reasonably estimated.

15. When convertible debt is issued, no portion of the proceeds is accounted for by the entity as attributable to the conversion feature. The debt issue is treated entirely as debt, and no formal accounting recognition is assigned to the value inherent in the conversion feature.

16. In an induced conversion of convertible debt under FAS-84, a debtor does not recognize any gain or loss on the amount of equity securities required to be issued under the original conversion terms for each convertible bond converted. However, the fair value of equity securities or other consideration paid or issued by the debtor that exceeds the amount of equity securities required to be issued for each convertible bond converted under the original conversion terms is recognized as current expense on the date the bondholder accepts the inducement offer.

17. Offsetting assets and liabilities in the balance sheet is improper except when a right of setoff exists.

18. The allowance method of providing for uncollectible accounts receivable recognizes an estimate of uncollectible accounts receivable each period, even though the specific individual accounts that will not be collected are not known at that time. Estimates of uncollectible accounts usually are made as a percentage of credit sales or ending receivables.

19. For deferred compensation plans that are not tantamount to a plan for pension or other postretirement benefits, FAS-106 requires the employer to make periodic accruals, so that the cost of the deferred compensation is attributed to the appropriate years of an employee's service, in accordance with the terms of the contract between the employer and the employee.

20. The total liability for deferred compensation contracts is determined by the terms of the individual contract. The amount of the periodic accrual, computed from the first day of the employment contract, must total no less than the then-present value of the benefits provided for in the contract. The periodic accruals are made systematically over the active term of employment.

21. An enterprise should capitalize the cost of an improvement of a depreciable asset if the improvement is substantial and increases the capacity or operating efficiency of the asset.

22. Required in the financial statements or the notes thereto are the following disclosures that relate to depreciable assets and depreciation:
    - Depreciation expense for the periods presented
    - Balances of major classes of depreciable assets by nature or function
    - Accumulated depreciation allowances by classes or in total
    - The methods used, by major classes, in computing depreciation
    - The effect of a change from one depreciation method to another, where applicable

23. A *development stage enterprise* is one in which principal operations have not commenced or principal operations have generated an insignificant amount of revenue.

24. Losses accumulated by a development stage enterprise should be presented on the balance sheet as *deficit accumulated during the development stage.*

25. The amount of income (or loss) attributable to common stock used in the calculation of basic earnings per share is reduced (or increased) by dividends declared on preferred stock (whether paid or not paid) and by dividends on cumulative preferred stock (whether paid or not paid).

26. The objective of reporting basic earnings per share is to measure the performance of an entity over the reporting period based on its outstanding common stock. The objective of diluted earnings per share is to measure the performance of an entity over the reporting period based on its outstanding common stock and to give effect to all dilutive potential common shares that were outstanding during the period.

27. Specialized industry GAAP for banking and thrift institutions focuses on business combinations, particularly the valuation of goodwill and other assets acquired.

28. The conditions for recognizing regulatory financial assistance are that it must be probable and estimable.

29. A mortgage loan receivable held for resale should be valued at the lower of cost or market on the balance sheet date.

30. When a mortgage banking institution arranges a loan commitment between a permanent investor and a borrower, the loan placement fee received is recognized as revenue when all significant services have been performed.

Examination for Self-Study Credit— Module 1

1. *Multiple choice:* A change from an unacceptable accounting principle or method to an acceptable accounting principle or method is considered a:

    a. Change in accounting principle.

    b. Correction of an error.

    c. Change in accounting estimate.

    d. Change in accounting entity.

2. *Multiple choice:* The approach for handling a change in accounting estimate is the:

    a. Current and prospective method.

    b. Cumulative effect method.

    c. Retroactive restatement method.

    d. Any of the above.

3. *True or false:* Corrections of errors in financial statements are incorporated into financial statements by retroactively restating prior periods' financial statements.

4. *Multiple choice:* Which of the following would *not* be considered a change in accounting principle?

    a. Change in the method of inventory pricing from LIFO to FIFO

    b. Change in the method of depreciating previously recorded assets from straight-line to an accelerated method

    c. Change in the method of accounting for long-term construction contracts

    d. Change in subsidiaries comprising the group of companies for which consolidated financial statements are presented

5. *Multiple choice:* Which of the following accounting policies are required to be disclosed in the financial statements?

    a. Basis of consolidation

    b. Depreciation methods

    c. Inventory methods

    d. Amortization of intangibles

    e. All of the above

6. *Multiple choice:* In a business combination accounted for using the purchase method, what would be the accounting treatment in cases

where the value assigned to net assets exceeds the cost of the acquisition (i.e., where there is negative goodwill)?

a. The difference is recorded as a deferred credit and amortized into income over a period of 40 years.

b. The difference is recorded as a liability to provide for any unknown liabilities that may arise from the acquisition.

c. The values of noncurrent assets (excluding investments) are reduced proportionately by the amount of the difference. Any remaining difference is recorded as a deferred credit and amortized into income over a period of the expected benefit, but not more than 40 years.

d. The difference should be credited to net income in the period of the acquisition.

7. *Multiple choice:* When a single-employer defined benefit pension plan is acquired in a business combination accounted for by the purchase method, how should an excess of the projected benefit obligation over the plan assets be recorded?

a. As a liability

b. As an asset

c. Not recorded in the financial statements

d. As a charge to earnings in the period of the acquisition

8. *Multiple choice:* The allocation period for a purchaser in a business combination to identify and quantify the acquired assets and assumed liabilities to allocate the total cost of the acquisition should generally not exceed:

a. One month.

b. One quarter.

c. One year.

d. Two years.

9. *Multiple choice:* In preparing a statement of cash flows, interest paid should be classified as a(n):

a. Operating activity.

b. Investing activity.

c. Financing activity.

d. Noncash transaction.

10. *Multiple choice:* In preparing a statement of cash flows, income taxes paid resulting from a gain on an asset sale should be presented as a(n):

a. Operating activity.

b. Reduction of the gain.

c. Investing activity.

d. Financing activity.

11. *True or false:* Defined benefit pension plans that prepare their financial statements in accordance with FAS-35 (Accounting and Reporting by Defined Benefit Pension Plans) are not required to present a statement of cash flows.

12. *Multiple choice:* For purposes of FAS-89 (Financial Reporting and Changing Prices), which of the following is considered a nonmonetary asset?

    a. Accounts receivable

    b. Notes receivable

    c. Inventory

    d. Notes payable

13. *True or false:* The disclosures of the effects of changing prices described by FAS-89 are encouraged, but not required, by that statement.

14. *True or false:* Intercompany bonds that are purchased by an affiliate are treated in the year of acquisition as though they have been retired.

15. *Multiple choice:* Under the parent company theory, where are minority interests presented on a consolidated balance sheet?

    a. Liability section

    b. Equity section

    c. Between the liability and equity sections

    d. Asset section, as a reduction of total assets

16. *True or false:* Regardless of any minority interests, all of any intercompany profits on the sale of long-lived assets between affiliates are eliminated when preparing consolidated financial statements.

17. *Multiple choice:* If a loss contingency is classified as probable, but only a range of possible loss can be established, what amount should be accrued in the financial statements?

    a. No accrual should be made, since an actual estimate cannot be made.

    b. The maximum amount of the range should be accrued, unless some amount in the range appears to be a better estimate.

    c. The minimum amount of the range should be accrued, unless some amount in the range appears to be a better estimate.

    d. The average of the minimum and maximum amounts of the range should be accrued, unless some amount in the range appears to be a better estimate.

18. *Multiple choice:* Which degree of probability of a loss contingency would require disclosure, but not accrual, in the financial statements?

    a. Probable

    b. Reasonably possible

    c. Unlikely

    d. Remote

19. *True or false:* If it is probable that an unasserted claim will be asserted, and it is probable or reasonably possible that an unfavorable outcome will result, the unasserted claim must be disclosed in the financial statements.

20. *True or false:* A product or service warranty obligation is not a contingency that would be covered by the provisions of FAS-5 (Accounting for Contingencies).

21. *Multiple choice:* When convertible debt is issued, what portion of the proceeds is treated as equity?

    a. None, the proceeds are treated entirely as debt.

    b. A nominal amount of the proceeds are treated as paid-in-capital.

    c. The difference in the fair value of the bonds with and without the conversion feature is treated as paid-in-capital.

    d. All proceeds are treated as equity if it is likely that the conversion features will be exercised.

22. *True or false:* When a detachable purchase warrant that was issued with debt is exercised by the holder in accordance with the original purchase terms, no gain or loss is recognized on the transaction by the issuing entity.

23. *Multiple choice:* Which of the following employee benefits are not covered by FAS-43 (Accounting for Compensated Absences)?

    a. Vacation pay

    b. Sick pay

    c. Holiday pay

    d. Severance pay

24. *Multiple choice:* Which of the following is not included as an asset in the numerator of the acid-test ratio?

    a. Cash

    b. Accounts receivable

    c. Marketable securities

    d. Inventory

25. *Multiple choice:* The process by which a company uses existing accounts receivable as collateral for a loan is known as:

    a. Factoring with recourse.

    b. Factoring without recourse.

    c. Pledging.

    d. Assigning.

26. *True or false:* Offsetting of assets and liabilities in the balance sheet is improper *except* where a right of setoff exists.

27. *True or false:* An employer should record the expense for a deferred compensation contract when the actual payments are made.

28. *True or false:* An expenditure for repairing a piece of equipment that was damaged during shipment should be charged to expense and *not* capitalized.

29. *Multiple choice:* What amortization period should be used for amortizing leasehold improvements?

    a. Useful life of the leasehold improvement

    b. Length of the lease

    c. Shorter of the useful life of the leasehold improvement or the length of the lease

    d. None, leasehold improvements should be expensed when purchased or constructed

30. *Multiple choice:* The depreciation method that would be the most appropriate when there is no discernible pattern of decline in service potential of the asset over its useful life is:

    a. Straight-line method.

    b. Double declining balance method.

    c. Sum-of-the-years digits method.

    d. Units of production method.

31. *True or false:* In all circumstances, the amount of depreciation expense calculated for tax purposes in accordance with the Internal Revenue Code can be used for financial reporting purposes in accordance with GAAP.

32. *True or false:* The statement of cash flows of a development stage enterprise should present the cumulative totals of cash inflows and cash outflows from the company's inception, as well as amounts for the current period.

33. *Multiple choice:* In computing basic earnings per share, how are purchases and sales of treasury stock during the reporting period treated?

    a. Calculation treats all of the purchases and sales during the period as if they occurred at the beginning of the reporting period.

    b. Calculation treats all of the purchases and sales during the period as if they occurred at the end of the reporting period.

    c. Treasury stock transactions are weighted for the portion of the period they were outstanding during the reporting period.

    d. Calculation should ignore all treasury stock transactions.

34. *Multiple choice:* In computing basic earnings per share, how are dividends on cumulative preferred stock treated?

    a. Dividends on preferred stock should reduce the amount of net income used in the calculation.

    b. Dividends declared and paid on preferred stock should reduce the amount of net income used in the calculation; dividends declared but not paid have no effect on the calculation.

    c. Preferred stock dividends have no effect on the calculation of basic earnings per share.

    d. Preferred stock dividends should be added back to net income in calculating basic earnings per share.

35. *True or false:* In presenting earnings per share, any stock splits are retroactively recognized in all periods presented in the financial statements.

36. *True or false:* In calculating earnings per share, potential issuances of additional common shares that would have the effect of increasing earnings per share are excluded from the earnings per share calculation.

37. *Multiple choice:* The accounting method to record the acquisition of a savings and loan association which is based on recording the acquired identifiable assets at fair value at the date of acquisition is known as the:

    a. Net-spread method.

    b. Separate-valuation method.

    c. Pooling method.

    d. Regulatory method.

38. *Multiple choice:* In applying FAS-72 to the amortization of goodwill resulting from the acquisition of a troubled banking institution, what would be the preferable amortization period for this goodwill?

    a. None, it should be immediately expensed.

    b. It should always be amortized over a period of 40 years.

    c. Some time period between 1 and 40 years.

    d. An amortization period in excess of 40 years is permitted for this goodwill.

39. *Multiple choice:* What is the appropriate accounting treatment by a bank for credit card fees that are periodically charged cardholders' accounts?

    a. Recognized as income when the fee is charged to the cardholder's account

    b. Recognized as income when paid by the cardholder

    c. Deferred and recognized on a straight-line basis over the period in which the cardholder is entitled to use the card

    d. Recorded as an offset to credit card balances receivable to provide for doubtful collections of these accounts

40. *True or false:* When a loan portfolio is sold by a financial institution and the selling continues to service the loans for the buyer, gain or loss on the sale should *always* be deferred by the seller until the expiration of its commitment to service the loans that were sold.

1999 Miller *GAAP Guide* CPE Program
Module 1—Chapters 1–13, 49, and 57

Please record your CPE answers in the space provided on the left and return this page for scoring. Simply place the completed answer sheet in a stamped envelope and mail it to:

GAAP Guide CPE Coordinator
Harcourt Brace Professional Publishing
525 B Street, Suite 1900
San Diego, California, 92101-4495

METHOD OF PAYMENT

☐ **Payment enclosed ($64.00 per Module).**
(Make checks payable to Harcourt Brace & Company.)

Please add appropriate sales tax.
Be sure to sign your order below.

Charge my:
☐ MasterCard ☐ Visa ☐ American Express

Account number _____

Expiration date _____
Please sign below for all credit card orders.

☐ **Bill me.** *Be sure to sign your order below.*

NAME _____

FIRM NAME _____

ADDRESS _____

PHONE ( ) _____

CPA LICENSE # _____

ISBN (MODULE 1): 0-15-606724-2

TO ORDER: Call Toll-Free 1-800-831-7799

Signature _____

See the reverse side of this page for the CPE evaluation.

MODULE 1 CPE ANSWERS

1. _____	21. _____
2. _____	22. _____
3. _____	23. _____
4. _____	24. _____
5. _____	25. _____
6. _____	26. _____
7. _____	27. _____
8. _____	28. _____
9. _____	29. _____
10. _____	30. _____
11. _____	31. _____
12. _____	32. _____
13. _____	33. _____
14. _____	34. _____
15. _____	35. _____
16. _____	36. _____
17. _____	37. _____
18. _____	38. _____
19. _____	39. _____
20. _____	40. _____

GAAP Guide CPE Evaluation

1. Were you informed in advance of the:
   a. Objectives of the course? Y N
   b. Experience level needed to complete the course? Y N
   c. Program content? Y N
   d. Nature and extent of preparation necessary? Y N
   e. Teaching method? Y N
   f. Number of CPE credit hours? Y N

   c. Program content? Y N
   d. Nature and extent of advance preparation necessary? Y N
   e. Teaching method? Y N
   f. Number of CPE credit hours? Y N

2. Do you agree with the publisher's assessment of:
   a. Objectives of the course? Y N
   b. Experience level needed to complete the course? Y N

   3. Was the material relevant? Y N

   4. Was the presentation of the material effective? Y N

   5. Did the program increase your professional competence? Y N

   6. Was the program content timely and effective? Y N

Please make any other comments that you feel would improve this course. We appreciate the time you take to complete this questionnaire. Be assured that all of your comments will be considered carefully.

_____

_____

_____

_____

_____

_____

SELF-STUDY CONTINUING PROFESSIONAL EDUCATION
Module 2

Equity Method

After completing this section you should be able to:

- Discuss the conditions under which the equity method should be used.
- Explain how to apply the equity method.
- Describe the disclosure requirements when the equity method is applied.
- Discuss the conditions under which the equity method should be applied to real estate partnerships.

Read Chapter 14, "Equity Method," of the 1999 *Miller GAAP Guide*.

Answer review questions 1–2 on page 65.27.

Extinguishment of Debt

After completing this section you should be able to:

- Compute the gain or loss on the extinguishment of debt.
- Determine the reacquisition price.
- Explain how to report gain or loss.
- Explain how to account for gains or losses incurred to meet sinking fund requirements.

Read Chapter 15, "Extinguishment of Debt," of the 1999 *Miller GAAP Guide*.

Answer review questions 3–4 on page 65.27.

Financial Instruments

After completing this section you should be able to:

- Recognize and define financial instruments.
- Define *off-balance-sheet risk of accounting loss* and give examples of financial instruments that carry that risk.
- Describe the disclosure requirements for financial instruments with off-balance-sheet risk.
- Describe the disclosure requirements related to credit risk for financial instruments with off-balance-sheet credit risk.

- Describe the disclosure requirements related to concentrations of credit risk.
- Describe the disclosure requirements related to fair value of financial instruments.
- Describe the accounting for derivative instruments and hedging activities.

Read Chapter 16, "Financial Instruments—Disclosures," of the 1999 *Miller GAAP Guide.*

Answer review questions 5–6 on page 65.27.

Foreign Operations and Exchange

After completing this section, you should be able to:

- Define functional currency and reporting currency.
- Explain how to translate from the functional currency to the reporting currency of a foreign entity.
- Describe how to report gains and losses from translation.
- Describe how to account for and disclose gains and losses from foreign currency transactions.
- Discuss the disclosure requirements related to foreign currency translation and transactions.

Read Chapter 17, "Foreign Operations and Exchange," of the 1999 *Miller GAAP Guide.*

Answer review questions 7–8 on page 65.28.

Futures Contracts

After completing this section you should be able to:

- Identify the futures contracts and enterprises to which FAS-80 applies.
- Explain the process of hedging.
- Describe how to account for speculative futures contracts.
- Summarize the conditions that qualify a futures contract as a hedge.
- Describe how to account for hedges of existing items and for anticipatory hedges.

Read Chapter 18, "Futures Contracts," of the 1999 *Miller GAAP Guide.*

Answer review questions 9–10 on page 65.28.

Government Contracts

After completing this section you should be able to:

- Recognize cost-plus-fixed-fee government contracts.
- State the general rule for revenue recognition under cost-plus-fixed-fee contracts.
- Explain when the percentage-of-completion method may be used.
- Describe how a provision for renegotiation is determined and reported.

Read Chapter 19, "Government Contracts," of the 1999 *Miller GAAP Guide*.

Answer review questions 11–12 on page 65.28.

Impairment of Loans and Long-Lived Assets

After completing this section your should be able to:

- Explain when a loan should be considered impaired under FAS-114.
- Discuss the criteria for identifying an impaired loan and recognizing a loss contingency.
- Discuss how a loan is valued to measure impairment.
- Explain how to recognize changes in the present value of an impaired loan's expected cash flows.
- Discuss the requirements of FAS-121.

Read Chapter 20, "Impairment of Loans and Long-Lived Assets," of the 1999 *Miller GAAP Guide*.

Answer review questions 13–14 on page 65.28.

Income Taxes

After completing this section, you should be able to:

- State the four basic principles underlying FAS-109.
- Identify temporary differences.
- State the five steps required to compute deferred tax liabilities and assets.
- Determine the tax rate to use for computing deferred taxes.
- Discuss how to determine a valuation allowance.
- Explain how to classify deferred taxes.
- Describe disclosure requirements related to income taxes.

Read Chapter 21, "Income Taxes," of the 1999 *Miller GAAP Guide*.

Answer review questions 15–16 on page 65.28.

Installment Sales Method of Accounting

After completing this section you should be able to:

- Explain how revenue is recorded under the cost recovery and install-ment sales methods.
- Discuss the conditions under which each method is appropriate.
- Describe how to report unrealized gross profit in receivables for installment sales.

Read Chapter 22, "Installment Sales Method of Accounting," of the 1999 *Miller GAAP Guide.*

Answer review questions 17–18 on page 65.28.

Intangible Assets

After completing this section you should be able to:

- Discuss how to record intangible assets.
- Describe the disclosure requirements for intangible assets.

Read Chapter 23, "Intangible Assets," of the 1999 *Miller GAAP Guide.*

Answer review questions 19–20 on page 65.28.

Interest Costs Capitalized

After completing this section you should be able to:

- Identify qualifying assets.
- Explain when to capitalize interest.
- Describe how to determine the amount of interest to capitalize.

Read Chapter 24, "Interest Costs Capitalized," of the 1999 *Miller GAAP Guide.*

Answer review questions 21–22 on page 65.28.

Interest on Receivables and Payables

After completing this section you should be able to:

- Explain how to impute interest to a receivable or payable.
- Recognize receivables and payables that require imputing of interest.
- Discuss how a premium or discount is recorded and disclosed.

Read Chapter 25, "Interest on Receivables and Payables," of the 1999 *Miller GAAP Guide.*

Answer review questions 23–24 on page 65.28.

Interim Financial Reporting

After completing this section, you should be able to:

- Explain how to determine the amounts of revenues and expenses for interim financial statements.
- Describe disclosure requirements for contingencies in interim financial statements.

Read Chapter 26, "Interim Financial Reporting," of the 1999 *Miller GAAP Guide*.

Answer review questions 25–26 on page 65.28.

Oil and Gas Producing Companies

After completing this section you should be able to:

- Explain the successful-efforts method.
- Discuss the types of costs incurred in oil and gas production.

Read Chapter 59, "Oil and Gas Producing Companies," of the 1999 *Miller GAAP Guide*.

Answer review questions 27–28 on page 65.28.

Regulated Industries

After completing this section you should be able to:

- Give examples of the types of businesses to which these specialized industry principles apply.
- Describe the conditions under which a regulated enterprise can recognize an asset.
- Explain how a regulated enterprise capitalizes interest and other costs of funds used during construction of an asset.

Read Chapter 63, "Regulated Industries," of the 1999 *Miller GAAP Guide*.

Answer review questions 29–30 on page 65.28.

REVIEW QUESTIONS

1. When is an investor presumed to have significant influence over an investee?
2. How is the difference between the underlying equity in net assets of an investee and the cost of the investment accounted for?
3. How is the gain or loss on the extinguishment of debt computed?
4. What is the most significant impact of FAS-125 on accounting for the extinguishment of debt?
5. What organizations did FAS-126 make optional the fair value disclosures of FAS-107?
6. What are the four categories of derivative instruments specified by FAS-133?

7. When an entity has multinational operations, what determines the functional currency of the entity?

8. What exchange rates should be used to translate revenues and expenses denominated in foreign currencies?

9. What are the current criteria in FAS-80 for determining whether a futures contract qualifies as a hedge?

10. If a futures contract qualifies under FAS-80 as an anticipatory hedge, how should you account for changes in the market value of the futures contract?

11. When should profits be recognized on a cost-plus-fixed-fee government contract?

12. Describe the accounting for renegotiation provisions of cost-plus-fixed-fee government contracts.

13. When is a loan considered to be impaired under FAS-114?

14. Describe the general requirements of FAS-121 for determining the fair value of an asset.

15. What types of differences give rise to deferred tax assets and liabilities under FAS-109?

16. When should deferred tax assets be reduced by a valuation allowance?

17. When is the cost recovery method acceptable for revenue recognition?

18. Describe the installment sales method of accounting.

19. What factors might imply that a period of amortization shorter than the maximum, legal, or contractual life is appropriate?

20. Describe the requirements for the amortization of intangible assets.

21. During what period should an entity capitalize interest on a qualifying asset?

22. What is the maximum amount of interest that may be capitalized for an accounting period?

23. When is it necessary to impute interest on receivables and payables?

24. What rate should be used to determine the present value of a receivable or payable in accordance with APB-21?

25. How should the tax provision in interim financial statements be determined?

26. How should a company that uses a standard cost system handle variances when preparing interim financial statements?

27. Describe the successful-efforts method of accounting for oil and gas exploration activities.

28. Under what conditions should oil and gas producing companies charge the cost of exploratory wells to expense?

29. What conditions must be met for a regulated enterprise to recognize an incurred cost as a regulatory asset?

30. When does a regulated enterprise not eliminate intercompany profits on sales to regulated affiliates?

SUGGESTED SOLUTIONS

1. An investment (directly or indirectly) of 20% or more of the voting stock of an investee is presumed to indicate the ability to exercise significant influence over the investee.

2. The difference between the underlying equity in net assets of an investee and the cost of the investment is treated as goodwill and amortized over a period of 40 years or less.

3. Gain or loss on the extinguishment of debt is the difference between the reacquisition price and the net carrying amount of the debt on the date of the extinguishment.

4. The most significant impact of FAS-125 on the accounting for extinguishment of debt is the elimination of the in-substance defeasance as an alternative method of extinguishing debt.

5. FAS-126 makes optional the fair value disclosures of FAS-107 for entities meeting the following criteria:

   • The entity is a nonpublic entity.

   • The entity is small enough that it comes under the size criterion of less than $100 million of total assets on the date of the financial statements.

   • The entity has not held or issued any derivative financial instruments other than loan commitments during the reporting period.

6. The four categories of derivative instruments specified by FAS-133 are as follows:

   • No hedge designation

   • Fair value hedge

   • Cash flow hedge

   • Foreign currency hedge

7. The functional currency of an entity with multinational operations is the currency of the primary economic environment in which the entity operates and expends cash, which is generally the currency of the country in which the entity is located.

8. Generally, a weighted-average exchange rate for the period should be used for translating revenue and expenses denominated in foreign currencies.

9. Under FAS-80, a futures contract that hedges an existing or anticipated exposure to price or interest rate changes qualifies as a hedge if *all* of the following conditions are met:

   • Item must be designated as a hedge.

   • Hedge item must be exposed to the risk of changes in market prices or interest rates.

   • Changes in the market value of a futures contract must be highly correlated to the changes in the fair value of the hedged items.

   • Enterprises that hedge assets reported at fair value are required to include the changes in value of both the hedged assets and the related futures contract in income of the same accounting period.

10.   Changes in the market value of the futures contract are included in the ultimate gain or loss on the hedged transaction when a futures contract qualifies as an anticipatory hedge under FAS-80.

11.   As a general rule, profits on a cost-plus-fixed-fee (CPFF) government contract are not recognized until the right to full payment becomes unconditional, which is usually when the product has been delivered and accepted or the services fully rendered (completed-contract method).

   When CPFF contracts extend over several years, the percentage-of-completion method is acceptable, provided that costs and profits can be estimated reasonably and realization of the contract is reasonably assured.

12.   Cost-plus-fixed-fee government contracts usually include a provision for renegotiation of the original selling or contract price. When such a provision for adjustment is included in the contract, a provision for such probable adjustments is necessary. The provision for renegotiation is based on the contractor's past experience or the general experience of the particular industry, and is shown in the income statement as a reduction of the related sales or income. If a reasonable estimate cannot be made, this inability to provide for renegotiation should be disclosed in the financial statements or footnotes.

13.   A loan is impaired when it is probable that a creditor will be unable to collect all amounts due, including principle and interest, according to the contractual terms and schedules of the loan agreement.

14.   In applying the provisions of FAS-121, the fair value of the asset is the amount at which the asset could be bought or sold in a current transaction between willing parties. Fair value, however, is not intended to be determined by the value in a forced liquidation or sale. Three methods of determining fair value specified by FAS-121 are:

   • Quoted market prices in active markets

   • Estimate based on prices of similar assets

   • Estimate based on valuation techniques

15.   Taxable temporary differences give rise to deferred tax liabilities; deductible temporary differences give rise to deferred tax assets.

16.   A valuation allowance is required if it is more likely than not that some or all of the deferred tax assets will not be realized. *More likely than not* is defined as a likelihood of more than 50%.

17.   The cost recovery method, also known as the *sunk-cost theory*, is used in situations in which recovery of cost is undeterminable or extremely questionable.

18.   Under the installment sales method of accounting, gross profit is recognized only to the extent that cash has been collected. Each payment collected consists of part recovery of cost and part gross profit, in the same ratio under which these two elements existed in the original sale.

19.   Factors that might imply that a period of amortization shorter than the maximum, legal, or contractual life is appropriate would include:

- Effects of obsolescence.
- The service lives of employees who are critical to the realization of the asset.
- Expected actions of competitors or others.

20. The cost of intangible assets is amortized by systematic charges to income over the period estimated to be benefited, but not to exceed 40 years. The straight-line method of amortization is required unless a company demonstrates that another systematic method is more appropriate.

21. Interest is capitalized during the acquisition period, which begins with the first expenditure and ends when the asset is substantially complete and ready for its intended use.

22. The amount of interest capitalized may not exceed the actual interest cost during the period.

23. Imputation of interest on receivables and payables is required when the interest rate is not stated or when the stated interest rate is unreasonable, except for receivables or payables that are not specifically excluded by APB-21.

24. An estimate of the rate that would have been negotiated by an independent lender using the same terms and conditions should be used to determine the present value of a receivable or payable in accordance with APB-21.

25. In interim financial statements, income tax expense should be computed by applying an effective tax rate to income on a cumulative year-to-date basis.

26. For interim financial statements, inventory and product costs computed by the use of a standard cost accounting system are determined by the same procedures used at the end of a fiscal year. Variances from standard costs that are expected to be made up by the end of the fiscal year need not be included in interim-period statements.

27. The successful-efforts method of accounting for oil and gas exploration activities establishes a cause and effect relationship between costs incurred and the discovery of specific reserves. When a cost is incurred with no identifiable future benefit, the costs are usually expensed when incurred. Accordingly, costs related to oil and gas exploration activities may be capitalized; however, costs such as geological and geophysical costs, the costs of carrying and retaining undeveloped properties, and the costs of drilling exploratory wells that do not find proved reserves are expensed.

28. Oil and gas producing companies should charge the cost of exploratory wells, net of salvage value, to expense for the period if the following conditions exist:
    - The well is in progress (uncompleted) at the end of the period.
    - It has been determined, before the issuance of the financial statements, that the well has not located any proved reserves.

29. In order for a regulated enterprise to recognize an incurred cost as an asset, the regulator must have a clear intent to provide recovery of the

cost and available evidence must indicate that the rates will produce revenue about equal to the cost.

30. Under the provisions of FAS-71, a regulated enterprise does not eliminate intercompany profits on sales to regulated affiliates if the following conditions are met:
    • The sales price is reasonable (as evidenced by the enterprise's regulator accepting the sales price, or in light of the specific circumstances).
    • It is expected (based on available evidence) that the approximate sales price that resulted in the intercompany profit will be recovered as an allowable cost.

Examination for Self-Study Credit— Module 2

1. *Multiple choice:* Generally, the equity method of accounting would be used by an investor that owns what percentage of the currently outstanding voting stock of an investee corporation?

    a. Less than 20%

    b. Between 20% and 50%

    c. More than 50%

    d. Between 5% and 20%

2. *Multiple choice:* What is the effect on the carrying amount of an investment accounted for by the equity method when the investee corporation reports net income?

    a. The carrying amount of the investment is increased.

    b. The carrying amount of the investment is decreased.

    c. There is no effect on the carrying amount of the investment.

    d. The carrying amount of the investment is increased only to the extent that it was previously decreased by reported losses of the investee.

3. *True or false:* The equity method of accounting should be applied to unincorporated joint ventures that are subject to joint control.

4. *Multiple choice:* When should the gain or loss on the extinguishment of debt be recognized?

    a. Immediately, in the year of the extinguishment

    b. Amortized over the life of any refunding debt issued to obtain proceeds to extinguish the debt

    c. Amortized over a period not to exceed 40 years

    d. Amortized over the period of expected benefit from the assets acquired when the extinguished debt was originally issued

5. *True or false:* Gains or losses from the maturity of serialized debt are classified as extraordinary items.

6. *Multiple choice:* For purposes of preparing fair value disclosures required by FAS-107 (Disclosures about Fair Value of Financial Instruments), which of the following would be a market source of information?

    a. Exchange market

    b. Dealer market

    c. Broker market

    d. All of the above

7. *Multiple choice:* Under FAS-133, how are changes in the fair value of derivative instruments classified as no hedge designation reported?

    a. Included in current income

    b. Not included in current income, but included in other comprehensive income

    c. Reported on the balance sheet as deferred income or deferred losses

    d. There is no effect on reporting, since these derivative instruments are carried at cost

8. *True or false:* Under FAS-133, changes in the fair value of derivative instruments that qualify as fair value hedges are *not* recognized currently in earnings.

9. *Multiple choice:* What exchange rate would be used to remeasure the accumulated depreciation account under FAS-52 (Foreign Currency Translation)?

    a. Current remeasurement rate

    b. Historical remeasurement rate

    c. Current purchase cost remeasurement rate

    d. Future exchange rate

10. *Multiple choice:* FAS-52 defines a highly inflationary economy as one in which the cumulative inflation over a three-year consecutive period approximates:

    a. 30–35%.

    b. 100%.

    c. 300%.

    d. 600%.

11. *True or false:* Revenue and expense transactions are remeasured at the average exchange rate for the period according to FAS-52, *except* those expenses related to assets and liabilities.

12. *True or false:* Accounting for futures contracts under FAS-80 will *not* be affected by the recent issuance of FAS-133.

13. *True or false:* The accounting requirements for income recognition for cost-plus-fixed fee contracts with the government apply only to contracts for the manufacture of products and not to contracts that are for the performance of services.

14. *Multiple choice:* The profit on a five-year cost-plus-fixed-fee contract with the government that *cannot* be reasonably estimated should be accounted for under which of the following methods?

    a. Percentage of completion method

    b. Completed contracts method

    c. Installment sales method

    d. None of the above

15. *Multiple choice:* Which of the following would be cause to consider a loan to be impaired?
    a. There is an insignificant delay in the receipt of payments.
    b. There is an insignificant shortfall in amounts received under the loan.
    c. It is probable that all amounts due, principle and interest, will not be collected.
    d. All of the above.

16. *Multiple choice:* Which of the following would be included in the scope of FAS-121 for determining and measuring the impairment of long-lived assets?
    a. Financial instruments
    b. Deferred tax assets
    c. Mortgage and other servicing rights
    d. Fixed assets

17. *Multiple choice:* Which of the following is an acceptable method of determining fair value of a long-lived asset for purposes of measuring impairment?
    a. Quoted market prices in active markets
    b. Estimate based on prices of similar assets
    c. Estimate based on valuation techniques
    d. All of the above
    e. Only a and b

18. *Multiple choice:* The increase in taxes payable in the future as a result of a temporary difference at the end of the current year is reported as:
    a. Deferred tax asset.
    b. Deferred tax liability.
    c. Current tax liability.
    d. Current tax asset.

19. *True or false:* The requirements of FAS-109 (Accounting for Income Taxes) that pertain to the accounting for income taxes do *not* cover the accounting for the investment tax credit.

20. *Multiple choice:* The applicable tax rate used in measuring deferred tax assets and liabilities is:
    a. The marginal tax rate as of the date of the end of the period being reported upon.
    b. The rate expected to apply to taxable income in the periods in which the deferred tax liabilities and assets are expected to be settled or realized based on enacted tax law.
    c. The rate expected to apply to taxable income in the periods in which the deferred tax liabilities and assets are expected to be settled or realized based on anticipated future tax law.

    d. The average effective tax rate of the reporting entity for the immediately preceding three tax years.

21. *True or false:* FAS-109 precludes the consideration of tax planning strategies in determining deferred tax assets and deferred tax liabilities.

22. *Multiple choice:* FAS-109 uses a specific term to describe the case where a valuation account is needed for a deferred tax asset. The valuation account is needed when it is _____ that some or all of the asset may not be realized:

    a. Probable

    b. Reasonably possible

    c. More likely than not

    d. Remote

23. *Multiple choice:* Assuming that collection is both reasonably estimated and assured, what is the most acceptable method for accounting for a sale in which the buyer will pay for the purchase by making periodic payments after the date of the sale?

    a. Installment sales method

    b. Cost recovery method

    c. Profit or loss recognized at the time of the sale, when title to the purchased goods transfers to the buyer

    d. Income tax method

24. *True or false:* Under the installment sales method, selling and administrative costs should be charged to expense when incurred.

25. *Multiple choice:* Which of the following intangibles would be considered to have a determinate life?

    a. Brand loyalty

    b. Patents

    c. Secret processes

    d. Goodwill

26. *Multiple choice:* Unless a company can demonstrate that another systematic method is more appropriate, what method should be used to amortize intangible assets?

    a. Straight-line

    b. Declining balance

    c. Sum-of-the-year's digits

    d. Double declining balance

27. *True or false:* The costs of maintaining an intangible asset that is not separately identifiable and that is inherent in a continuing business are charged to expense when incurred.

28. *Multiple choice:* If there is no specific borrowing related to a qualifying asset for which interest is being capitalized, what interest rate should be used in the calculation of capitalized interest?

    a. The organization's long-term borrowing rate in effect at the end of the period being reported upon

    b. The organization's long-term borrowing rate in effect at the beginning of the capitalization period

    c. The weighted-average interest rate actually incurred on other borrows during the capitalization period

    d. The organization's short-term incremental borrowing rate

29. *Multiple choice:* When does the interest capitalization period end?

    a. The qualifying asset is substantially completed and ready for intended use.

    b. After the asset has been placed into production for a limited period of time.

    c. The majority of dependent parts of the asset have been completed.

    d. A brief interruption occurs in the development of the qualifying asset.

30. *True or false:* If an entity does not incur interest costs during the period of construction of a qualifying asset, interest should still be capitalized on the asset to reflect the opportunity cost of the funds used to construct the asset.

31. *Multiple choice:* Which of the following would be subject to the requirements of APB-21 (Interest on Receivables and Payables) for imputing interest?

    a. Accounts receivable arising in the ordinary course of business and due within one year

    b. Security deposits

    c. Receivables/payables between subsidiaries of a common parent

    d. A five-year note receivable between unrelated parties resulting from the sale of land with no stated interest rate

32. *True or false:* Interest that is imputed on certain payables in accordance with APB-21 is eligible for capitalization under the provisions of FAS-34 (Capitalization of Interest Cost).

33. *Multiple choice:* How are discounts and premiums resulting from imputing interest reported on the balance sheet?

    a. Reported separately as deferred charges or credits

    b. Added to or deducted from the related asset or liability

    c. Reported on separate lines in the balance sheet as assets or liabilities

    d. None of the above

34. *True or false:* In accounting for interim periods, the integral, or dependent, approach views an interim period as a component of the annual period rather than a separate or discrete period.

35. *True or false:* In determining whether an inventory loss has occurred in an interim period, temporary market declines that are expected to be made up by the end of the annual period need *not* be included in interim period statements.

36. *Multiple choice:* Which method of accounting for oil and gas exploration activities would generally require that the cost of exploratory wells that do not find proved reserves is expensed?

    a. Full-cost accounting

    b. Successful efforts accounting

    c. Both a and b

    d. Neither a nor b

37. *Multiple choice:* In oil and gas accounting terminology, which of the following refers to one or more reservoirs related to the same individual geological structural feature and/or stratigraphic conditions?

    a. Property

    b. Field

    c. Proved area

    d. Proved reserve

38. *True or false:* FAS-19 covers the accounting for activities relating to the exploration and production of oil and gas and the refining and marketing of these products.

39. *Multiple choice:* Which of the following industries are designated as regulated industries by FAS-71 (Accounting for the Effects of Certain Types of Regulation)?

    a. Electric and gas utilities

    b. Telephone utilities

    c. Water utilities

    d. All of the above

    e. None of the above (no specific industry is identified as regulated)

40. *True or false:* In order for an entity in a regulated industry to recognize an asset representing an incurred cost, the regulator's intent to provide recovery of the specific cost must be clear.

1999 *Miller GAAP Guide* CPE Program
Module 2—Chapters 14–26, 59, and 63

Please record your CPE answers in the space provided on the left and return this page for scoring.
Simply place the completed answer sheet in a stamped envelope and mail it to:

GAAP Guide CPE Coordinator
Harcourt Brace Professional Publishing
525 B Street, Suite 1900
San Diego, California, 92101-4495

METHOD OF PAYMENT

☐ **Payment enclosed ($64.00 per Module).**
(Make checks payable to Harcourt Brace & Company.)

Please add appropriate sales tax.
Be sure to sign your order below.

Charge my:
☐ MasterCard ☐ Visa ☐ American Express

Account number _____

Expiration date _____
Please sign below for all credit card orders.

☐ **Bill me.** *Be sure to sign your order below.*

NAME _____

FIRM NAME _____

ADDRESS _____

PHONE ( ) _____

CPA LICENSE # _____

ISBN (MODULE 2): 0-15-606725-0

TO ORDER: Call Toll-Free 1-800-831-7799

Signature _____

See the reverse side of this page for the CPE evaluation.

MODULE 2 CPE ANSWERS

1. _____   21. _____
2. _____   22. _____
3. _____   23. _____
4. _____   24. _____
5. _____   25. _____
6. _____   26. _____
7. _____   27. _____
8. _____   28. _____
9. _____   29. _____
10. _____   30. _____
11. _____   31. _____
12. _____   32. _____
13. _____   33. _____
14. _____   34. _____
15. _____   35. _____
16. _____   36. _____
17. _____   37. _____
18. _____   38. _____
19. _____   39. _____
20. _____   40. _____

GAAP Guide CPE Evaluation

1. Were you informed in advance of the:
   a. Objectives of the course? y n
   b. Experience level needed to complete the course? y n
   c. Program content? y n
   d. Nature and extent of preparation necessary? y n
   e. Teaching method? y n
   f. Number of CPE credit hours? y n

2. Do you agree with the publisher's assessment of:
   a. Objectives of the course? y n
   b. Experience level needed to complete the course? y n

   c. Program content? y n
   d. Nature and extent of advance preparation necessary? y n
   e. Teaching method? y n
   f. Number of CPE credit hours? y n

   3. Was the material relevant? y n

   4. Was the presentation of the material effective? y n

   5. Did the program increase your professional competence? y n

   6. Was the program content timely and effective? y n

Please make any other comments that you feel would improve this course. We appreciate the time you take to complete this questionnaire. Be assured that all of your comments will be considered carefully.

SELF-STUDY CONTINUING PROFESSIONAL EDUCATION
Module 3

Inventory Pricing and Methods

After completing this section, you should be able to:

- Discuss passage of title and how it affects inventory.
- Explain how to determine the lower of cost or market value.
- Describe the common methods for determining the cost of inventory.
- Describe the disclosure requirements related to inventory.

Read Chapter 27, "Inventory Pricing and Methods," of the 1999 *Miller GAAP Guide*.

Answer review questions 1–2 on page 65.46.

Investment Tax Credit

After completing this section, you should be able to:

- Explain how to account for investment tax credits by the deferred method and the flow-through method.
- Explain the effect of FAS-109 in accounting for the investment tax credit.

Read Chapter 28, "Investment Tax Credit," of the 1999 *Miller GAAP Guide*.

Answer review questions 3–4 on page 65.46.

Investments in Debt and Equity Securities

After completing this section you should be able to:

- Define *debt and equity securities* as applied in FAS-115.
- Describe the guidelines for determination of fair values for equity securities.
- Identify investments and enterprises to which FAS-115 does not apply.
- Identify the three accounting issues that must be addressed after securities are classified.
- Define *unrealized holding gains and losses* and describe how to account for them.

- Explain how to account for transfers of securities between categories.
- Explain how to account for permanent declines in fair value.
- Summarize how to classify securities as current or noncurrent assets.
- Explain how to report cash flows from securities transactions.
- Summarize disclosure requirements under FAS-115.

Read Chapter 29, "Investments in Debt and Equity Securities," of the 1999 *Miller GAAP Guide.*

Answer review questions 5–6 on page 65.46.

Leases

After completing this section you should be able to:

- State the criteria used by a lessee to classify a lease as capital or operating.
- State the additional criteria used by a lessor.
- Explain how a lessee records a capital lease and determines the value to record.
- Explain how a lessee amortizes the recorded assets and liabilities.
- Discuss how a lessee's rental expense is determined for operating leases.
- Summarize how a lessee should report and disclose operating and capital leases.
- Explain how to record sales-type and direct financing leases.
- Summarize how a lessor should report and disclose capital and operating leases.
- Explain the special rules for classifying leases that involve real estate.
- Summarize how a sale-leaseback transaction should be recorded by a lessor and lessee.

Read Chapter 30, "Leases," of the 1999 *Miller GAAP Guide.*

Answer review questions 7–8 on page 65.46.

Long-Term Construction Contracts

After completing this section you should be able to:

- Explain when it is appropriate to use the completed-contract and percentage-of-completion methods.
- Describe how accumulated costs and billings are reported in the balance sheet under each method.
- Discuss the conditions that require a loss accrual under each method.
- Discuss how income is determined under each method.

Read Chapter 31, "Long-Term Construction Contracts," of the 1999 *Miller GAAP Guide.*

Answer review questions 9–10 on pages 65.46 and 65.47.

Long-Term Obligations

After completing this section you should be able to:

- Define an *unconditional purchase obligation.*
- State the criteria that require disclosure of unconditional purchase obligations.
- Summarize disclosures required for recorded unconditional purchase obligations, long-term borrowings, and capital stock redemptions.

Read Chapter 32, "Long-Term Obligations," of the 1999 *Miller GAAP Guide.*

Answer review questions 11–12 on page 65.47.

Nonmonetary Transactions

After completing this section you should be able to:

- Define and give examples of an *exchange.*
- Define and give examples of a *nonreciprocal transfer.*
- Explain how generally to value the transfer of a nonmonetary asset or liability.
- Explain the exceptions to the general rule.
- Explain how to value nonreciprocal transfers to owners.
- Summarize the rules for recognition of nonmonetary gains or losses.

Read Chapter 33, "Nonmonetary Transactions," of the 1999 *Miller GAAP Guide.*

Answer review questions 13–14 on page 65.47.

Pension Plans—Employers

After completing this section you should be able to:

- Explain the difference between a defined benefit plan and a defined contribution plan.
- Describe the journal entries used to record pension costs and contributions.
- Identify the components of net periodic pension cost.
- Compute the funded status of a pension plan.
- Explain how to determine the accrued pension cost liability.
- Summarize financial statement disclosures for employers that sponsor defined benefit and defined contribution plans.

Read Chapter 34, "Pension Plans—Employers," of the 1999 *Miller GAAP Guide.*

Answer review questions 15–16 on page 65.47.

Pension Plans—Settlements and Curtailments

After completing this section you should be able to:

* Define settlements and curtailments of pension plans.
* Discuss how gains or losses are computed for settlements and curtailments.
* Define *termination benefits.*
* Describe how to account for the cost of termination benefits.

Read Chapter 35, "Pension Plans—Settlements and Curtailments," of the 1999 *Miller GAAP Guide.*

Answer review questions 17–18 on page 65.47.

Postemployment and Postretirement Benefits Other Than Pensions

After completing this section you should be able to:

* Define *postemployment benefits.*
* Explain how FAS-112 relates to FAS-43 and FAS-5.
* State the conditions under which a liability for postemployment benefits should be recorded under FAS-43.
* State the conditions under which an estimated loss contingency should be accrued under FAS-5.
* Discuss disclosure requirements under FAS-112.

Read Chapter 36, "Postemployment and Postretirement Benefits Other Than Pensions," of the 1999 *Miller GAAP Guide.*

Answer review questions 19–20 on page 65.47.

Entertainment Industry—Broadcasters

After completing this section you should be able to:

* Discuss the conditions for recording assets and liabilities related to program material license agreements.
* Explain how program rights are amortized.

Read Chapter 50, "Broadcasters," of the 1999 *Miller GAAP Guide.*

Answer review questions 21–22 on page 65.47.

Entertainment Industry—Cable Television Companies

After completing this section you should be able to:

- Discuss the business of a cable television company.
- Describe the prematurity period and how costs are treated during that period.
- Explain how hook-up revenue and installation costs are treated.
- Describe how to account for franchise costs.

Read Chapter 51, "Cable Television," of the 1999 *Miller GAAP Guide*.

Answer review questions 23–24 on page 65.47.

Entertainment Industry—Motion Picture Films

After completing this section you should be able to:

- Explain how licensors recognize revenues for films shown in movie theatres.
- Summarize the conditions for recognizing revenue for films shown on television.
- Explain how to account for production costs.

Read Chapter 52, "Motion Picture Films," of the 1999 *Miller GAAP Guide*.

Answer review questions 25–26 on page 65.47.

Entertainment Industry—Records and Music

After completing this section you should be able to:

- Discuss the business of a music publisher.
- Explain how revenue is recorded for minimum guarantees received by a licensor.
- Explain when a license agreement is, in substance, an outright sale.
- Describe how to account for the cost of a record master.

Read Chapter 53, "Record and Music," of the 1999 *Miller GAAP Guide*.

Answer review questions 27–28 on page 65.47.

Franchise Fee Revenue

After completing this section, you should be able to:

- Explain when revenue may be recognized for individual and area franchises.

- Explain when and how to use the cost recovery and installment sales methods.
- Discuss how to account for tangible assets included in a franchise fee, continuing franchise fees, continuing product sales, and agency sales.
- Describe disclosure requirements related to franchise sales.

Read Chapter 54, "Franchise Fee Revenue," of the 1999 *Miller GAAP Guide*.

Answer review questions 29–30 on page 65.47.

Pension Plan Financial Statements

After completing this section you should be able to:

- Summarize the contents of pension plan financial statements and disclosure requirements.
- Name the typical financial statements presented by a pension plan and summarize the contents of each.
- Discuss requirements related to presentation of accumulated plan benefits.
- Summarize disclosure requirements.

Read Chapter 60, "Pension Plan Financial Statements," of the 1999 *Miller GAAP Guide*.

Answer review questions 31–32 on page 65.47.

REVIEW QUESTIONS

1. In the phrase "lower of cost or market," what does the term *market* mean?
2. If inventory is sold "F.O.B.—Destination Point," when does the seller recognize the sale?
3. Describe the flow-through method of accounting for the investment tax credit.
4. Describe the deferral method of accounting for the investment tax credit.
5. Under FAS-115, when is it proper to value securities at amortized cost?
6. In applying FAS-115, what is meant by *trading securities,* and how are they valued on the statement of financial position?
7. Describe some of the reasons why identifying a capital lease can require a significant amount of professional judgment.
8. What is the amortization period for a lessee's capital lease asset?
9. When are losses recognized for long-term construction contracts when the percentage-of-completion method is used?

10. When should the completed-contract method be used in accounting for long-term construction contracts?

11. What conditions would cause an unrecorded unconditional purchase obligation to be subject to the disclosure requirements of FAS-47?

12. What disclosure is required by FAS-47 for long-term borrowings?

13. Generally, at what value should a nonmonetary exchange be recorded?

14. Distinguish between an exchange and a nonreciprocal transfer.

15. What is the projected benefit obligation of a pension plan?

16. When is it necessary to record an additional minimum liability on the balance sheet of the sponsor of a pension plan?

17. When should the cost of special termination benefits be recorded?

18. What are *special termination benefits* under FAS-88?

19. What is the *accumulated postretirement benefit obligation*?

20. What is the *interest cost* component of the net periodic postretirement benefit cost?

21. How does a broadcaster value the asset and liability that arise from the purchase of program material rights?

22. How should a broadcaster amortize the cost of program material rights?

23. What is the *prematurity period* of a cable television system?

24. How does a cable television operator account for administrative costs during the prematurity period?

25. Under normal domestic conditions, when does the licensor of a motion picture film recognize revenue for nonrefundable guarantees received from movie theatres?

26. Describe the accounting for production costs of motion picture films.

27. How is the sale of specific rights of music copyrights or record masters accounted for by the owners of these copyrights or masters?

28. When are royalties earned by recording artists charged to expense by a music company?

29. If the collection of long-term receivables from individual franchisees is not reasonably assured, what is the most appropriate accounting treatment?

30. What are the two significant accounting issues in revenue recognition of franchise fees?

31. In determining whether a pension plan should record an amount due from an employer, what circumstances would provide evidence that an employer has a formal commitment to make the contribution?

32. What are the characteristics of an insurance contract prescribed in FAS-110?

SUGGESTED SOLUTIONS

1. In the phrase "lower of cost or market," the term *market* means current replacement cost, whether by purchase or by reproduction, *but is limited to the following maximum and minimum amounts:*

   • *Maximum:* Cannot exceed the estimated selling price less any costs of completion and disposal. The maximum cost is also the net realizable value.

   • *Minimum:* The maximum, less an allowance for normal profit.

2. F.O.B. means *free on board* and requires the seller, at its expense, to deliver the goods to the destination indicated as F.O.B. Title passes to the buyer upon delivery to the destination, which generally is when the seller should recognize the sale.

3. Under the flow-through method of accounting for the investment tax credit (ITC), the amount of the ITC used in a year reduces the amount of income tax currently payable for the year, and thereby reduces income tax expense. Thus, the ITC flows into income.

4. Under the deferral method of accounting for the ITC, the ITC is recognized as a reduction in tax expense on a pro rata basis over the life of the asset that gives rise to the ITC. Unamortized deferred ITC is a deferred tax credit that will be recognized in the determination of income over time.

5. Under FAS-115, investments in debt securities should be valued at amortized cost only if the reporting enterprise has the intent and ability to hold them to maturity.

6. The trading securities category of FAS-115 includes both debt securities and equity securities with readily determinable fair values. They are measured at fair value in the statement of financial position and are characterized by the following:

   • Are bought and held primarily for purposes of selling them in the near term

   • Reflect active and frequent buying and selling

   • Generally are used with the objective of generating profits on short-term differences in price

7. While the criteria for identifying a capital lease appear very specific, the following factors can result in the need to exercise significant professional judgment:

   • Determining the term of the lease may require judgment.

   • Several of the criteria include terms—such as bargain purchase option, estimated useful life of the property, and fair value of the property—that require judgment when applying them to a specific lease.

   • The lease term and present value information of minimum lease payments are not available for leases that begin within the last 25% of the asset's estimated useful life, which is subject to judgment.

   • Determining the minimum lease payments for the lessee may require use of that party's incremental borrowing rate, which may involve judgment.

8. The amortization period for a lessee's capital lease asset is either (*a*) the estimated economic life or (*b*) the lease term, depending on which criterion was used to classify the lease. If the criterion used to classify the lease as a capital lease was either of the first two criteria (ownership of the property is transferred to the lessee by the end of the lease term or the lease contains a bargain purchase option), the asset is amortized over its estimated economic life. In all other cases, the asset is amortized over the lease term.

9. When current estimates of the total contract costs for a long-term construction contract indicate a loss, a provision for the loss on the entire contract should be made.

10. The completed-contract method should be used for long-term construction contracts when reliable estimates of degree of completion are not available.

11. FAS-47 requires disclosure of information for unrecorded unconditional purchase obligations that are:

    • Substantially noncancelable.

    • Associated with the financing arrangements for facilities that will provide the contracted foods or services or related to the costs of the contracted goods or services (such as carrying costs).

    • For a remaining term in excess of one year.

12. FAS-47 requires that or each of the five years immediately following the latest balance sheet date, the combined total of maturities and sinking fund requirement for all long-term borrowings be disclosed.

13. A nonmonetary exchange should be recorded at the fair value of the asset or liability that is received or surrendered, whichever is more clearly evident.

14. An exchange is a reciprocal transfer in which each party to the transaction receives and/or gives up assets, liabilities or services. A nonreciprocal transfer is a transfer of assets or services in one direction, either from an enterprise to its owners or another entity, or from owners or another entity to the enterprise.

15. The projected benefit obligation of a pension plan is the actuarial present value, as of a specified date, of a total cost of all employees' vested and nonvested pension benefits that have been attributed by the pension benefit formula to services performed by employees to that date.

16. An additional minimum liability is generally required to be recorded by the sponsor of a pension plan when the accumulated benefit obligation exceeds the fair value of plan assets.

17. The cost of special termination benefits should be recorded when the employee accepts the offer of the special termination benefits and the cost of the benefits can be estimated reasonably.

18. Under FAS-88, *special termination benefits* are those that are offered to employees for a short period in connection with the termination of their employment.

19. *Accumulated postretirement benefit obligation* is the portion of the expected postretirement benefit obligation that is attributed to employee service rendered to a particular date.

20. The *interest cost* is the increase in the amount of the accumulated postretirement benefit obligation due to the passage of time, measured at the assumed discount rate.

21. The asset and liability that arise from the purchase of program material rights are reported at either the gross amount of the liability or the present value of the liability computed in accordance with APB-21.

22. A broadcaster should amortize program material rights based upon the estimated number of times the broadcaster will air the program. An accelerated method of amortization should be used when the first broadcast of a program is more valuable than its reruns.

23. A *prematurity period* of a cable television system is the period from the time when the first subscriber's revenue is earned to the time when construction of the system is completed or the first major stage of construction is completed.

24. Administrative costs are recorded as period costs by a cable television operator during the prematurity period.

25. Receipts for nonrefundable guarantees from movie theaters are deferred and recognized as revenue on the date of the exhibition of the film.

26. Production costs of motion picture films are capitalized as film cost inventory. Production costs are accounted for on a film-by-film basis and include overhead allocated on a systematic and rational basis in accordance with GAAP. Amortization of production costs begins when the film is released for exhibition purposes.

27. When a licensee receives from the licensor a noncancelable contract for a specified fee granting specific rights to the licensee who may use these rights at anytime without restriction, the earning process is complete and revenue is recognized if collectibility is reasonably assured.

28. Royalties earned by recording artists, adjusted for anticipated returns, are charged to expense in the period in which the related record sale takes place. Royalty advances are recorded as prepaid royalties if the past performance and current popularity of the artist to whom the advance is made indicate that the advance will be recoverable from future royalties earned by the artist.

29. The cost recovery method or installment sales method should be used to recognize revenue if the collection of long-term receivables from individual franchises is not reasonably assured.

30. The two significant accounting issues in revenue recognition of initial franchise fees are (1) the time at which the fee is properly regarded as earned and (2) the assurance of collectibility of any receivable resulting from unpaid portions of the initial fee.

31. FAS-35 states that evidence of a formal commitment of an employer to contributed to a pension plan may include:

- The formal approval of a specified contribution.

- A consistent pattern of payments made after the pension plan's year-end pursuant to an established funding policy that attributes payments to the preceding plan year.

- A federal tax deduction take for the contribution by the employer for periods ending on or before the reporting date for the pension plan.

32. According to FAS-110, insurance contracts are characterized by the following:

- The purchaser of the insurance contract makes an initial payment or deposit to the insurance enterprise in advance of the possible occurrence or discovery of an insured event.

- When the insurance contract is made, the insurance enterprise ordinarily does not know if, how much, or when amounts will be paid under the contract. Contracts that do not subject the insurance enterprise to risks arising from policy holders' mortality or morbidity are investment, rather than insurance, contracts.

Examination for Self-Study Credit— Module 3

1. *Multiple choice:* At what value is inventory reported on the balance sheet?

   a. Cost

   b. Lower of cost or market

   c. Fair value

   d. Replacement cost

2. *Multiple choice:* Which inventory flow assumption matches the most recent costs incurred with current revenue, leaving the earlier costs incurred as inventory?

   a. FIFO

   b. LIFO

   c. Weighted-average cost

   d. Moving-average method

3. *True or false:* The exclusion of all overhead from inventory costs is *not* an acceptable accounting procedure.

4. *True or false:* When standard costs are used in determining inventory value at an interim period, unanticipated purchase price, volume, or capacity variances should be included in the results of operations of the interim period.

5. *Multiple choice:* Under FAS-109 (Accounting for Income Taxes), any investment tax credit carryforward is reported as:

   a. A deferred tax asset equal to the amount of the credit, not subject to a valuation allowance.

   b. A deferred tax asset equal to the amount of the credit, but subject to a valuation allowance.

   c. A deferred tax liability.

   d. Should not be reported in the financial statements until a reduction of tax expense is realized.

6. *Multiple choice:* Which method of accounting for an investment tax credit is acceptable under current GAAP?

   a. Flow-through method

   b. Deferral method

   c. Neither a or b

   d. Both a and b

7. *Multiple choice:* Under FAS-115 (Accounting for Certain Investments in Debt and Equity Securities), equity securities with readily determinable fair values that are bought and held primarily for purposes of selling them in the near term with the objective of generating a short-term profit would be categorized as:

   a. Available-for-sale securities.

   b. Trading securities.

   c. Held-to-maturity category.

   d. These securities are not included in the scope of FAS-115 and would be reported at cost on the statement of financial position.

8. *Multiple choice:* Held-to-maturity securities are reported in the statement of financial position at:

   a. Cost.

   b. Amortized cost.

   c. Fair value.

   d. Replacement cost.

9. *Multiple choice:* Unrealized holding gains and losses on securities categorized as trading securities are:

   a. Included in earnings.

   b. Excluded from earnings, but reported as part of comprehensive income.

   c. Reported as deferred assets or deferred credits.

   d. Not recognized, since trading securities are reported at cost.

10. *Multiple choice:* How should a lessee normally account for a lease in which the present value of the minimum lease payments at the beginning of the lease (excluding executory costs and profits thereon to be paid by the lessor) is more than 90% of the fair value of the property at the inception of the lease?

    a. Operating lease

    b. Capital lease

    c. Sales-type lease

    d. Direct-financing lease

11. *True or false:* In determining the term of a lease, any period covered by a bargain renewal option should be included in the lease term.

12. *Multiple choice:* A type of capital lease that results in a manufacturer's or dealer's profit or loss to the lessor is known as a(n):

    a. Direct-financing lease.

    b. Sales-type lease.

    c. Sale-leaseback.

    d. Operating lease.

13. *Multiple choice:* Which method of accounting for long-term construction contracts should be used when a reliable estimate of the costs to complete the work under the contract *cannot* be made?

   a. Percentage-of-completion method

   b. Completed-contracts method

   c. Installment sales method

   d. Cash basis

14. *Multiple choice:* In a long-term construction contract accounted for by the percentage-of-completion method, what is the appropriate accounting treatment when current estimates indicate that a loss will be incurred on the total contract?

   a. A percentage of the loss should be recognized in each period as work progresses on the contract.

   b. The loss should be recognized at the completion of the contract.

   c. A provision should be made in the current period for the total loss on the contract.

   d. The percentage of the loss on the work performed to date should be recognized as a loss in the current period.

15. *Multiple choice:* Which of the following recorded obligations would be subject to the disclosure requirements of FAS-47 (Disclosure of Long-Term Obligations)?

   a. Unconditional purchase obligations

   b. Debt payments

   c. Capital stock redemptions

   d. All of the above

   e. Both a and b

16. *True or false:* Minimum lease payments that are *not* required to be disclosed in accordance with FAS-13 (Accounting for Leases) would *not* be subject to any disclosure requirements under FAS-47.

17. *Multiple choice:* Which of the following would *not* be considered a nonreciprocal transfer?

   a. Declaration and distribution of a dividend

   b. Sale of capital stock

   c. Charitable contributions

   d. Exchange of inventory for office space

18. *True or false:* Gain or loss would *never* be recognized in nonmonetary transactions.

19. *True or false:* An exchange of property held for sale in the ordinary course of business for similar property to be held for the same purpose

would be an example of a nonmonetary transaction where the earnings process would not be complete and revenue would not be realized.

20. *Multiple choice:* The funded status of a pension plan for employer accounting purposes is equal to the difference between the fair value of pension plan assets and:

    a. Accumulated benefit obligation.

    b. Projected benefit obligation.

    c. Nothing, since the funded status is equal to the fair value of the plan assets.

    d. Net periodic pension cost.

21. *Multiple choice:* The total amount of net periodic pension cost that has been recognized by an employer but *not* funded is known as:

    a. Accrued pension cost.

    b. Prepaid pension cost.

    c. Unrecognized net obligation.

    d. Accumulated benefit obligation.

22. *True or false:* Actuarial gains and losses are *not* included in net periodic pension cost in the year in which they arise, but may be recognized in subsequent periods if certain criteria are met.

23. *True or false:* The interest cost on the projected benefit obligation should be included as a component of net periodic pension cost.

24. *Multiple choice:* A significant reduction in, or an elimination of, defined benefit accruals for present employees' future service is a pension plan:

    a. Termination.

    b. Curtailment.

    c. Redefinition.

    d. Reorganization.

25. *True or false:* Special termination benefits are those that are required by the terms of an existing plan or agreement and that are provided only on an occurrence of a specified event.

26. *Multiple choice:* Which of the following postretirement benefits would *not* be included within the scope of FAS-106?

    a. Health care

    b. Life insurance

    c. Legal services

    d. Pensions provided by a pension plan

27. *Multiple choice:* Which of the following interest rates would be used as a discount rate in measuring benefit obligations and costs for a postretirement benefit plan?

    a. Prime rate

    b. Employer's average cost of borrowing for the last five years

    c. Rate of return on high-quality fixed-income investments currently available with cash flows corresponding to the anticipated needs of the plan

    d. Rate on the measurement date of 10-year Treasury notes

28. *True or false:* An insurance contract with a captive insurer doing business primarily with the employer and related parties would *not* qualify for treatment as an insurance contract under FAS-106.

29. *Multiple choice:* Which of the following is the most appropriate method of amortization for the costs of program material rights by a broadcaster?

    a. Straight-line over the life of the license

    b. Declining balance method over the term of the license

    c. Computed based on the number of times that the program will be aired by the broadcaster

    d. No amortization should be recorded for program material rights

30. *True or false:* Network affiliation costs incurred by a local broadcaster should be charged to expense when paid.

31. *Multiple choice:* FAS-51 contains a presumption that the prematurity period for a cable television company should not exceed a period of:

    a. One year.

    b. Two years.

    c. Five years.

    d. Ten years.

32. *True or false:* A cable television company would capitalize selling and marketing expenses during the prematurity period.

33. *Multiple choice:* Which of the following methods should be used for amortizing film production costs:

    a. Straight-line over the estimated useful life of the film

    b. Based upon the total number of times that the film is expected to be shown

    c. In the same ratio that current revenues bear to total estimated gross revenues

    d. Declining balance method over the estimated useful life of the film

34. *True or false:* FAS-53 requires the disclosure of film inventories, including films that are completed but not released.

35. *True or false:* The owner of a music copyright should record the receipt of a minimum license guarantee as revenue in the period in which the cash is received.

36. *Multiple choice:* How should advance royalties to new or previously unsuccessful artists be recorded?

    a. As a deferred charge

    b. Expensed in the current period

    c. As a prepaid royalty

    d. As a deferred credit

37. *True or false:* The earliest that substantial performance by a franchisor under a franchise agreement is presumed to occur is when the franchisee actually commences operations of the franchise.

38. *True or false:* A portion of a franchise fee that includes the sale of specific tangible property should be allocated to such tangible property based on the fair value of the tangible property.

39. *True or false:* FAS-35 requires that a pension plan's benefit information date be at the end of the most recent period presented in the financial statements.

40. *Multiple choice:* Which of the following by itself would *not* provide sufficient evidence for a pension plan to record a receivable for a contribution relating to the current period that an employer will actually make after the date of the plan's financial statements?

    a. The employer has formerly approved a specific contribution

    b. The employer has a contractual obligation to make the contribution.

    c. The employer has taken a tax deduction for the contribution for a period ending on or before the date of the plan's financial statements.

    d. The employer has accrued a liability for the contribution in its financial statements.

1999 Miller *GAAP Guide* CPE Program
Module 3—Chapters 27–36, 51–54, 60

Please record your CPE answers in the space provided on the left and return this page for scoring. Simply place the completed answer sheet in a stamped envelope and mail it to:

GAAP Guide CPE Coordinator
Harcourt Brace Professional Publishing
525 B Street, Suite 1900
San Diego, California, 92101-4495

METHOD OF PAYMENT

☐ **Payment enclosed ($64.00 per Module).**

(Make checks payable to Harcourt Brace & Company.)

Please add appropriate sales tax.
Be sure to sign your order below.

Charge my:
☐ MasterCard ☐ Visa ☐ American Express

Account number _____

Expiration date _____
Please sign below for all credit card orders.

☐ **Bill me.** *Be sure to sign your order below.*

NAME _____

FIRM NAME _____

ADDRESS _____

PHONE ( ) _____

CPA LICENSE # _____

Signature _____

ISBN (MODULE 3): 0-15-606726-9

TO ORDER: Call Toll-Free 1-800-831-7799

See the reverse side of this page for the CPE evaluation.

MODULE 3 CPE ANSWERS

1. _____	21. _____
2. _____	22. _____
3. _____	23. _____
4. _____	24. _____
5. _____	25. _____
6. _____	26. _____
7. _____	27. _____
8. _____	28. _____
9. _____	29. _____
10. _____	30. _____
11. _____	31. _____
12. _____	32. _____
13. _____	33. _____
14. _____	34. _____
15. _____	35. _____
16. _____	36. _____
17. _____	37. _____
18. _____	38. _____
19. _____	39. _____
20. _____	40. _____

GAAP Guide CPE Evaluation

1. Were you informed in advance of the:
   a. Objectives of the course? Y N
   b. Experience level needed to complete the course? Y N
   c. Program content? Y N
   d. Nature and extent of preparation necessary? Y N
   e. Teaching method? Y N
   f. Number of CPE credit hours? Y N

2. Do you agree with the publisher's assessment of:
   a. Objectives of the course? Y N
   b. Experience level needed to complete the course? Y N
   c. Program content? Y N
   d. Nature and extent of advance preparation necessary? Y N
   e. Teaching method? Y N
   f. Number of CPE credit hours? Y N

3. Was the material relevant? Y N

4. Was the presentation of the material effective? Y N

5. Did the program increase your professional competence? Y N

6. Was the program content timely and effective? Y N

Please make any other comments that you feel would improve this course. We appreciate the time you take to complete this questionnaire. Be assured that all of your comments will be considered carefully.

_____

_____

_____

_____

_____

_____

SELF-STUDY CONTINUING PROFESSIONAL EDUCATION
Module 4

Product Financing Arrangements

After completing this section you should be able to:

- Identify a product financing arrangement.
- Explain how to account for product financing arrangements on the sponsor's books.
- Describe how the sponsor should determine and account for financing and holding costs.

Read Chapter 37, "Product Financing Arrangements," of the 1999 *Miller GAAP Guide*.

Answer review questions 1–2 on page 65.66.

Property Taxes

After completing this section, you should be able to:

- Explain the most acceptable method for recording property taxes.

Read Chapter 38, "Property Taxes," of the 1999 *Miller GAAP Guide*.

Answer review questions 3–4 on page 65.67.

Quasi-Reorganizations

After completing this section you should be able to:

- Define a *quasi-reorganization*.
- Discuss the criteria under which a quasi-reorganization is appropriate.
- Describe the steps for accounting for a quasi-reorganization.
- Explain what it means to date retained earnings.

Read Chapter 39, "Quasi-Reorganizations," of the 1999 *Miller GAAP Guide*.

Answer review questions 5–6 on page 65.67.

Related Party Disclosures

After completing this section you should be able to:

- Define and recognize related parties.
- Give examples of related party transactions.
- Discuss the disclosure requirements for related party transactions.
- Explain when it is necessary to disclose common ownership or management control of the reporting entity and other entities.

Read Chapter 40, "Related Party Disclosures," of the 1999 *Miller GAAP Guide*.

Answer review questions 7–8 on page 65.67.

Research and Development Costs

After completing this section you should be able to:

- Define and identify research and development (R&D) costs.
- Discuss how to account for R&D costs.
- Discuss how to account for R&D machinery equipment and facilities.
- Describe the computer software costs that are considered R&D.
- Explain which computer software costs should be capitalized.
- Explain how to amortize capitalized computer software costs.
- Discuss how to account for R&D costs incurred under arrangements such as R&D limited partnerships.

Read Chapter 41, "Research and Development Costs," of the 1999 *Miller GAAP Guide*.

Answer review questions 9–10 on page 65.67.

Results of Operations

After completing this section, you should be able to:

- Identify extraordinary items.
- Describe how to disclose extraordinary items and unusual or infrequent items.
- Explain how to account for and disclose the disposal of a segment.
- Describe how to present a prior-period adjustment.
- Understand how to report comprehensive income.

Read Chapter 42, "Results of Operations," of the 1999 *Miller GAAP Guide*.

Answer review questions 11–12 on page 65.67.

Revenue Recognition

After completing this section, you should be able to:

- Explain the realization principle.

- Discuss the conditions for revenue recognition when a buyer has the right to return merchandise.
- Discuss the factors that tend to decrease the possibility of making a reasonable estimate of returns.

Read Chapter 43, "Revenue Recognition," of the 1999 *Miller GAAP Guide*.

Answer review questions 13–14 on page 65.67.

Segment Reporting

After completing this section, you should be able to:

- Understand the reporting requirements about operating segments.
- Explain how to determine operating segments.

Read Chapter 44, "Segment Reporting," of the 1999 *Miller GAAP Guide*.

Answer review questions 15–16 on page 65.67.

Stockholders' Equity

After completing this section you should be able to:

- Discuss the types of capital stock.
- Describe the components of stockholders' equity.
- Explain the cost and par value methods of accounting for treasury stock.
- Describe how to account for stock dividends and splits.
- Discuss the disclosure requirements for an entity's capital structure.

Read Chapter 45, "Stockholders' Equity," of the 1999 *Miller GAAP Guide*.

Answer review questions 17–18 on page 65.67.

Stock Issued to Employees

After completing this section you should be able to:

- Describe the common types of stock plans.
- Discuss the features of compensatory and noncompensatory plans.
- Explain how to determine the cost of a compensatory plan.
- Define the measurement date for a compensatory plan.
- Describe the disclosure requirements for stock option plans.
- Describe the new accounting and reporting requirements for stock options.

Read Chapter 46, "Stock Issued to Employees," of the 1999 *Miller GAAP Guide*.

Answer review questions 19–20 on page 65.67.

Transfer and Servicing of Financial Assets

After completing this section, you should be able to:

- Describe the basic principles of accounting for the transfer and servicing of financial assets.
- Distinguish between transfers of financial assets with and without continuing involvement.

Read Chapter 47, "Transfer and Servicing of Financial Assets," of the 1999 *Miller GAAP Guide*.

Answer review questions 21–22 on page 65.67.

Troubled Debt Restructuring

After completing this section you should be able to:

- Define *loan* and *troubled debt restructuring*.
- Describe the bankruptcy proceedings that are considered to be troubled debt restructurings.
- Discuss how debtors and creditors account for each type of restructuring.
- Explain which gains and losses are considered extraordinary.
- Summarize disclosure requirements for impaired loans and for troubled debt restructurings.

Read Chapter 48, "Troubled Debt Restructuring," of the 1999 *Miller GAAP Guide*.

Answer review questions 23–24 on page 65.67.

Insurance Enterprises

After completing this section you should be able to:

- Distinguish short-duration contracts from long-duration contracts and give examples of each.
- Distinguish between limited-payment contracts and universal-life-type contracts.
- Explain how premium revenues should be recognized for short- and long-duration contracts.
- Explain how to account for the following: unpaid claims, catastrophe losses, future policy benefits relating to long-duration contracts, acquisition costs, premium deficiencies, and policyholder dividends.
- Explain when reinsurance contracts result in the removal of certain assets and liabilities from the ceding company's balance sheet.
- Describe how to report earned premiums ceded and recoveries recognized under reinsurance contracts.

- Discuss how to account for contracts that do not meet the criteria for reinsurance accounting.
- Describe how to account for prospective and retroactive short-duration contracts.
- Explain the rules for amortizing the estimated cost of reinsurance of long-duration contracts.
- Summarize the disclosures required for insurance companies.

Read Chapter 55, "Insurance Enterprises," of the 1999 *Miller GAAP Guide.*

Answer review questions 25–26 on page 65.67.

Title Plant

After completing this section you should be able to:

- Describe a title plant.
- Explain which costs related to a title plant are capitalized and which are expensed.

Read Chapter 56, "Title Plant," of the 1999 *Miller GAAP Guide.*

Answer review questions 27–28 on page 65.67.

Not-for-Profit Organizations

After completing this section you should be able to:

- Summarize the rules related to depreciation.
- Define *contributions* and determine the appropriate accounting treatment for contributions.
- Identify assets that are part of a collection and discuss the rules for recognizing contributions received consisting of such assets.
- Discuss how donor-imposed restrictions affect recognition of contributions received and classification of assets.
- Explain how a donor should account for contributions of nonmonetary assets.
- Discuss the rules for recognition of revenue or expense for conditional promises.
- Discuss the financial statements required by FAS-117.
- Explain how information about liquidity is presented in the statement of financial position.
- Discuss how to report revenues and expenses for ongoing special events.
- Discuss the requirements to report expenses by functional and natural classifications for various types of not-for-profit organizations.
- Describe how to report expenses for supporting activities.

- Discuss the content of the statement of cash flows.
- Summarize disclosure requirements related to the following: conditional and unconditional promises, collections, restrictions imposed by donors or the governing board, and the statement of activities.

Read Chapter 58, "Not-for-Profit Organizations," of the 1999 *Miller GAAP Guide.*

Answer review questions 29–30 on page 65.68.

Real Estate Costs and Initial Rental Operations

After completing this section, you should be able to:

- Describe which costs of real estate projects are capitalized and which are expensed.
- Explain how to account for income from incidental operations during the holding or development stage of a project.
- Discuss the conditions that indicate when a real estate project is substantially complete and available for occupancy.

Read Chapter 61, "Real Estate Costs and Initial Rental Operations," of the 1999 *Miller GAAP Guide.*

Answer review questions 31–32 on page 65.68.

Real Estate—Recognition of Sales

After completing this section, you should be able to:

- Discuss the criteria that a transaction must meet before a seller can report the total profit on a sale of real estate.
- Explain when it is appropriate to account for a sale-leaseback transaction as a sale.
- Identify the four methods for profit recognition from retail land sales projects and explain when each is appropriate.

Read Chapter 62, "Real Estate—Recognition of Sales," of the 1999 *Miller GAAP Guide.*

Answer review questions 33–34 on page 65.68.

REVIEW QUESTIONS

1. What is a *product financing arrangement*?
2. How should a sponsor record proceeds received in a product financing arrangement?

3. What is the most acceptable method for recording property taxes?

4. When does the legal liability for property taxes accrue?

5. What is a *quasi-reorganization*?

6. What specific criteria must be met for a quasi-reorganization to be appropriate?

7. What is a *related party*?

8. The sole stockholder of Company A also owns Company B. Company B uses offices without paying rent in a building owned by Company A. What information should be disclosed in the financial statements of A and B?

9. Distinguish between *research* and *development*.

10. At what point in the development of computer software is technological feasibility established?

11. What is the definition of the term *extraordinary items*?

12. Describe the concept of "comprehensive income."

13. When may a seller recognize income from a sale when the buyer has the right to return the merchandise purchased?

14. What general requirements must be met for revenue to be recognized?

15. How does an enterprise determine if the segment reporting requirements of FAS-131 apply to it?

16. What are the three characteristics of an operating segment under FAS-131?

17. What are the three categories of information about capital structure for which FAS-129 provides disclosure requirements?

18. What are some examples of the information that is required to be disclosed under FAS-129?

19. Describe FAS-123's general principles for stock compensation issued to employees.

20. How is compensation expense for stock options calculated under APB-25?

21. How does FAS-125 define the term *financial asset*?

22. What three conditions must all be met for a transferor to have surrendered control over transferred assets in applying FAS-125?

23. What is meant by troubled debt restructuring?

24. Describe some circumstances when a debt restructuring is not considered to be a troubled debt restructuring.

25. How does an insurance company recognize revenue on short-duration contracts?

26. When are premiums recognized as revenue under short-duration contracts?

27. What is a *title plant*?

28. Describe the accounting for the costs of a title plant.

29. Under what conditions should revenue be recorded for donated services received by a not-for-profit organization?

30. What three basic financial statements does FAS-117 require to be prepared for all not-for-profit organizations?

31. When is it appropriate to capitalize indirect costs of real estate projects?

32. When is a real estate project considered substantially complete and available for occupancy?

33. If a sale of real estate (other than a retail land sale) does not meet the criteria for full accrual of profit, what accounting methods does FAS-66 recommend be used?

34. List the four criteria in FAS-66 that must be met for a sale of real estate to be considered consummated.

SUGGESTED SOLUTIONS

1. A *product financing arrangement* is a transaction in which an enterprise sells and agrees to repurchase inventory at a price equal to the original sale price, plus carrying and financing costs.

2. Proceeds received by a sponsor in a product financing arrangement should be recorded as a liability.

3. A monthly accrual over the fiscal period of the taxing authority is considered the most acceptable basis for recording real and personal property taxes. This results in the appropriate accrual or prepayment at any closing date.

4. As a general rule, the legal liability for real and personal property taxes accrues on the date the taxes are assessed.

5. A *quasi-reorganization* is a restatement of assets and stockholders' equity in which assets may be written down to their fair values and a deficit in retained earnings may be charged to contributed or paid-in capital accounts.

6. The specific criteria that must be met for a quasi-reorganization to be appropriate are:
   - Assets are overvalued in the balance sheet.
   - The company can reasonably expect to be profitable in the future if the restructuring occurs in such a way that future operations are not burdened with the problems of the past.
   - Formal stockholder consent can be obtained.

7. In general, a *related party* is one that can exercise control or significant influence over the management or operating policies of another party, to the extent that one of the parties is or may be prevented from fully pursuing its own separate interests.

8. Assuming this transaction is material, the following information should be disclosed:
   - The relationship between A and B.
   - A description of the transaction and the effects it has on the financial statements. For example, the effect may be presented as the

amount of fair value of the rent that A is not charging B for the offices.

9. *Research* is the planned efforts of a company to discover new information that will help create a new product, service, process or technique or vastly improve one in current use. *Development* takes the finding generated by research and formulates a plan to create the desired item or improve the existing one.

10. Technological feasibility of computer software is established when all of the activities that are necessary to substantiate that the product can be produced in accordance with its design specifications have been completed.

11. *Extraordinary items* are transactions and other events that are (*a*) material in nature, (*b*) of a character significantly different from the typical or customary business activities, (*c*) not expected to recur frequently, and (*d*) not normally considered in evaluating the ordinary operating results of an enterprise.

12. Comprehensive income is a broad concept of an enterprise's financial performance in that it includes all changes in equity during a period from transactions and events from nonowner sources. The only changes in equity that are excluded from comprehensive income are those resulting from investments by owners and distributions to owners. Accordingly, equity changes, such as foreign currency translation adjustments and unrealized holding gains and losses from available-for-sale securities, would be included in the determination of comprehensive income.

13. When a buyer has the right to return merchandised purchased, the seller may not recognize income from the sale unless all of the following conditions are met:
    • The price between the seller and buyer is substantially fixed or determinable.
    • The seller has received full payment, or the buyer is indebted to the seller and the indebtedness is not contingent on the resale of the merchandise.
    • Physical destruction, damage, or theft of the merchandise would not change the buyer's obligation to the seller.
    • The buyer has economic substance and is not a front, straw party, or conduit existing for the benefit of the seller.
    • No significant obligations exist for the seller to help the buyer resell the merchandise.
    • A reasonable estimate can be made of the amount of future returns.

14. The general principle for revenue recognition is that revenue is recognized when the earnings process is complete and an exchange has taken place. The earnings process is not complete until collection of the sales price is reasonably assured.

15. FAS-131 applies to public business enterprises. Any one or combination of the following identifies an enterprise as being a public business enterprise:
    • Has issued debt or equity securities that are traded in a public market (a domestic or foreign stock exchange or an over the counter market)

- Is required to file financial statements with the Securities and Exchange Commission
- Provides financial statements for the purpose of issuing securities in a public market

16. Under FAS-131, operating segments have three essential characteristics. They are components of an enterprise:
    - That is engaged in business activities from which revenues may be earned and in which expenses are incurred
    - Whose operating results are reviewed by the enterprise's chief operating decision maker for purposes of making decisions with regard to resource allocation and performance evaluation
    - For which discrete financial information is available.

17. FAS-129 requires information about capital structure to be disclosed in three separate categories:
    - Information about securities
    - Liquidation preference of preferred stock
    - Redeemable stock

18. Some examples of the information that is required to be disclosed under FAS-129 are as follows:
    - Dividend and liquidating preferences
    - Participating rights
    - Call prices and dates
    - Conversion or exercise prices or rates and dates
    - Sinking-fund requirements
    - Unusual voting rights
    - Significant terms of contracts to issue additional shares

19. The general principle underlying FAS-123 is that equity instruments are recognized at the fair value of the consideration received for them. Applying this principle to stock compensation results in equity instruments being measured and recognized at their fair value and the compensation cost being the excess of that amount over any amount paid by the employee.

20. Under APB-25, the amount of compensation expense in a stock option plan is the excess of the unadjusted quoted market price of the stock at the measurement date over the amount the employee must pay in cash or other assets.

21. FAS-125 defines *financial asset* as cash, evidence of an ownership interest in an entity, or a contract that conveys to a second entity a contractual right (*a*) to receive cash or another financial instrument from a first entity or (*b*) to exchange other financial instruments on potentially favorable terms with the first entity.

22. The three conditions that all must be met for a transferor to have surrendered control over transferred assets are:
    - The transferred assets have been isolated from the transferor (i.e., they are beyond the reach of the transferor and its creditors)
    - One of the following is met:
      — The transferee obtains the unconditional right to pledge or exchange the transferred assets

— The transferee is a qualifying special-purpose entity and the holders of beneficial interests in that entity have the unconditional right to pledge or exchange those interests

— The transferor does not maintain effective control the transferred assets either through an agreement that obligates the transferor to repurchase or redeem the assets before their maturity or through an agreement that entitles the transferor to repurchase or redeem transferred assets that are not readily obtainable.

23. A troubled debt restructuring is one in which the creditor allows the debtor certain concessions that normally would not be considered. The concessions are made because of the debtor's financial difficulty and the creditor's objective to maximize recovery of its investment.

24. A debt restructuring is *not* considered to be a troubled debt restructuring in the following circumstances:
    - The debtor satisfies the debt by giving fair value of assets or equity that at least equals either:
      — The creditor's recorded receivable, or
      — The debtor's carrying amount of the payable.
    - The creditor reduces the interest rate primarily in response to changes in market rates.
    - The debtor issues at or near the current market new marketable securities in exchange for old securities.

25. FAS-60 specifies that premium revenue from short-duration contracts is to be recognized periodically in proportion to the insurance company's performance on the contract. The insurance company's performance under the contract is coverage on the insured risks.

26. Premium revenue from short-duration contracts is recognized periodically in proportion to the amount of coverage provided.

27. The records that a title insurance company uses to search the chain of ownership of a real estate parcel are called the *title plant.*

28. Until a title plant is ready for use, all direct costs incurred to acquire, organize, or construct the title plant are capitalized. Ordinarily, capitalized costs of a title plant should not be depreciated or otherwise charged to income unless there is an impairment in the carrying amount of the title plant.

29. Donated services must create or enhance nonfinancial assets, must be of a specialized nature, must be provided by individuals possessing those skills, and typically need to be purchased, before they can be included as revenue or gains in the operating statement.

30. The three basic financial statements that FAS-117 requires to be prepared for all not-for-profit organizations are:
    - Statement of financial position
    - Statement of activities
    - Statement of cash flows

31. It is appropriate to capitalize indirect costs of real estate projects that can be identified with specific projects under development or construction.

32. A real estate project is considered substantially completed and available for occupancy when the developer has completed tenant improvements, but in no event later than one year after major construction activity has been completed, excluding routine maintenance and cleanup.

33. The four accounting methods recommended by FAS-66 when a sale of real estate (other than a retail land sale) does not meet the criteria for full accrual of profit are (1) deposit, (2) cost-recovery, (3) installment sales, and (4) reduced profit.

34. The four criteria contained in FAS-66 that must be met for a sale of real estate to be considered consummated are that:
    - The contracting parties are legally bound by the contract.
    - All consideration required by the terms of the contract has been paid.
    - If the seller is responsible by the terms of the contract to obtain permanent financing for the buyer, the seller must have arranged for such financing.
    - The seller has performed all of the acts required by the contract to earn the revenue.

Examination for Self-Study Credit— Module 4

1. *True or false:* The substance of product financing arrangement is that of a financing arrangement, rather than a sale or purchase by the sponsor.

2. *Multiple choice:* Which of the following is the date most widely accepted as obligating an entity for real estate taxes?
   a. Tax period appearing on the tax bill
   b. End of the taxing authority's fiscal year
   c. Assessment date
   d. Date the tax is levied

3. *Multiple choice:* The most acceptable basis for recording real and personal property is:
   a. Monthly accrual over the fiscal period of the taxing authority.
   b. Record as an expense when paid.
   c. Record as an expense when taxes are levied.
   d. Record as an expense when the taxes are assessed.

4. *True or false:* A corporation desiring to enact a quasi-reorganization must obtain the formal consent of its shareholders.

5. *Multiple choice:* In enacting a quasi-reorganization, to what value are the assets of the organization adjusted?
   a. Cost before accumulated depreciation
   b. Cost after accumulated depreciation
   c. Fair value
   d. Zero

6. *Multiple choice:* Which of the following would be considered related parties of an organization?
   a. Management
   b. Owners
   c. Immediate families of management
   d. Immediate families of owners
   e. All of the above

7. *True or false:* Disclosures of a material-related party transaction in financial statements should not imply that the transaction was made on the same basis as an arm's length transaction, unless the representation can be verified.

8. *Multiple choice:* Under FAS-86, how are the costs that are incurred in establishing the technological feasibility of computer software accounted for?

   a. Accounted for as research and development costs and expensed when incurred

   b. Capitalized and amortized in accordance with FAS-17 as an intangible asset

   c. Expensed as incurred, however, the expense is reversed and recorded as an asset once technological feasibility is achieved

   d. Recorded as a deferred charge until the entity determines whether technological feasibility will be achieved

9. *True or false:* For accounting purposes, market research and testing activities are not considered to be research and development activities.

10. *Multiple choice:* Which of the following transactions are not usually accounted for as an extraordinary item (assume all amounts are material)?

    a. Gains on the restructuring of payables

    b. Gains and losses on the extinguishment of debt

    c. Gains or losses that are the direct result of a major casualty

    d. Loss due to the uncollectibility of a significant accounts receivable

11. *Multiple choice:* Which of the following circumstances would result in an organization having to report comprehensive income?

    a. Foreign currency translation adjustments in accordance with FAS-112

    b. Unrealized holding gains and losses on available-for-sale securities in accordance with FAS-115

    c. Changes in the market value of a futures contract that qualifies as a hedge of an asset reported at fair value in accordance with FAS-115

    d. Changes in the fair value of permanently restricted net assets of a not-for-profit organization

12. *True or false:* If a company has no components of comprehensive income other than net income, it is *not* required to report comprehensive income.

13. *Multiple choice:* Which of the following changes necessitate adjustment of prior periods for financial reporting purposes?

    a. Reporting a change in an entity

    b. A change in the estimate of the total profit on a long-term construction contract accounted for by the percentage-of-completion method

    c. A change in the estimated useful life of a depreciable asset

    d. A change to an accelerated depreciation method from the straight-line method

14. *True or false:* When a buyer has the right to return merchandise purchased, the seller should not recognize income from the sale if a reasonable estimate cannot be made of the amount of future returns.

15. *Multiple choice:* Which of the following factors would generally *not* tend to impair the ability of a seller to make a reasonable estimate of returns?

    a. Possible technological obsolescence or changes in the demand for merchandise

    b. Large volume of small dollar purchases

    c. Length of period that the customer has to exercise the right of return

    d. Little or no past experience in determining returns for similar types of merchandise

16. *Multiple choice:* To which of the following do the disclosure requirements of FAS-131 regarding segment information apply?

    a. All for-profit organizations

    b. Only public business enterprises

    c. All entities, including not-for-profit organizations

    d. Only public business enterprises and nonpublic enterprises with revenues in excess of $10 million

17. *Multiple choice:* What percentage of total consolidated revenues should be constituted by identifiable reportable segments?

    a. 50%

    b. 75%

    c. 90%

    d. 100%

18. *True or false:* FAS-131 has no segment information requirements for interim financial statements.

19. *Multiple choice:* Treasury stock is ordinarily presented on the balance sheet as:

    a. An asset.

    b. A liability.

    c. An addition to stockholders' equity.

    d. A reduction of stockholders' equity.

20. *Multiple choice:* Contractual rights of securities holders to receive dividends or returns from the issuer's profits, cash flows, or returns on investments are known as:

    a. Participating rights.

    b. Liquidation preferences.

    c. Redeemable rights.

    d. Detachable rights.

21. *True or false:* The capital structure disclosure requirements of FAS-129 (Disclosure of Information about Capital Structure) are applicable to all entities.

22. *Multiple choice:* Which of the following are acceptable accounting treatments for stock compensation plans?

    a. Calculate compensation expense in accordance with FAS-123.

    b. Calculate compensation expense in accordance with APB-25; disclose the amount of expense that would have been recorded under FAS-123.

    c. Calculate compensation expense in accordance with APB-25, no other disclosures required.

    d. All of the above.

    e. Both a and b are acceptable.

    f. Both b and c are acceptable.

23. *Multiple choice:* Under APB-25, which of the following is the appropriate measurement date?

    a. Date on which the grantee may first exercise the option

    b. Date on which the grantee disposes of the stock acquired

    c. Date on which the number of shares the employee is to receive and the option or purchase price is known

    d. Date of the adoption of the option plan

24. *Multiple choice:* A stock-based compensation plan in which an employee receives cash, stock, or a combination of both in an amount equal to a specified increase in the market price of the employer corporation's stock is known as a:

    a. Fixed plan.

    b. Stock option plan.

    c. Stock bonus plan.

    d. Phantom stock plan.

25. *Multiple choice:* A contractual right to receive some or all of the interest due on a bond, mortgage loan, or other interest-bearing obligation is known as a(n):

    a. Interest-only strip.

    b. Servicing right.

    c. Beneficial interest.

    d. Collateralized mortgage obligation.

26. *True or false:* Transfers of financial assets in which the transferor has no continuing involvement with the financial assets or with the transferee are *not* permitted under FAS-125 to be recognized as sales.

27. *Multiple choice:* Which of the following would be considered a *troubled debt restructuring*?

    a. Change in a lease agreement

    b. Change in a deferred compensation contract

   c. Reduction of stated interest to below the current market rate

   d. A debtor's failure to pay trade accounts that do not involve a restructure agreement

28. *True or false:* When a creditor receives assets as full settlement of a receivable, the assets are accounted for at their fair market value.

29. *True or false:* In a debt restructuring that only involves modification of the terms of the debt, the debtor accounts for the effects of the restructuring prospectively and does not change the carrying amount unless the carrying amount exceeds the total future cash payments specified by the new terms.

30. *Multiple choice:* Which of the following would be an example of a contract that would be categorized as a short-duration contract?

   a. Whole-life policy

   b. Renewable term insurance

   c. Endowment contracts

   d. Workers compensation policy

31. *Multiple choice:* When is revenue recognized on short-duration insurance contracts?

   a. In proportion to the insurance company's performance under the contract

   b. When the premium is received from the policyholder

   c. At the time the insurance contract is signed

   d. At the end of the term of the insurance contract

32. *True or false:* An investment contract does *not* expose the insurance enterprise to significant risks arising from the policyholder's death or illness.

33. *Multiple choice:* How should the costs to acquire, organize, or construct a title plant be accounted for?

   a. Capitalized

   b. Capitalized and depreciated over a period not exceeding 20 years

   c. Charged to expense in the period incurred

   d. Recorded as deferred charges until the title plant records begin to be used, at which time all title plant costs are charged to expense

34. *True or false:* In a sale of a copy or right to use a title plant, in determining the amount of gain or loss, no cost is allocated to the sale unless the value of the title plant decreases as a result of the sale.

35. *True or false:* Not-for-profit organizations are exempt from the requirement to present a statement of cash flows as part of their financial statements.

36. *Multiple choice:* At what value should a not-for-profit organization record investments in debt securities on its statement of financial condition?

    a. Cost

    b. Amortized cost

    c. Fair value

    d. Net realizable value

37. *True or false:* Real estate projects that are not for sale or rent and that are developed by an entity for its own use are excluded from the provisions of FAS-67.

38. *Multiple choice:* When is it appropriate to capitalize property taxes as a project cost of a real estate development project?

    a. Never appropriate, property taxes should always be treated as a period cost

    b. May be capitalized only during periods in which activities necessary to get the property ready for its intended use are in progress

    c. May be capitalized until all units are sold or leased

    d. May be capitalized for the entire expected life of the real estate development

39. *Multiple choice:* When a real estate sale does not meet the criteria of FAS-66 for revenue recognition, an accounting method in which all cash received, except that cash appropriately used as an offset to the carrying charges of the property, must be reflected in the seller's balance sheet as a liability is known as the:

    a. Deposit method.

    b. Cost recovery method.

    c. Installment sales method.

    d. Reduced profit method.

40. *True or false:* FAS-66 requires minimum down payments on all real estate sales before a seller is permitted to recognize a profit.

1999 *Miller GAAP Guide* CPE Program
Module 4—Chapters 37–48, 55, 56, 58, 61, and 62

Please record your CPE answers in the space provided on the left and return this page for scoring. Simply place the completed answer sheet in a stamped envelope and mail it to:

GAAP Guide CPE Coordinator
Harcourt Brace Professional Publishing
525 B Street, Suite 1900
San Diego, California, 92101-4495

METHOD OF PAYMENT

☐ **Payment enclosed ($64.00 per Module).**

(Make checks payable to Harcourt Brace & Company.)

Please add appropriate sales tax.
Be sure to sign your order below.

Charge my:

☐ MasterCard ☐ Visa ☐ American Express

Account number _____

Expiration date _____
Please sign below for all credit card orders.

☐ **Bill me.** *Be sure to sign your order below.*

Signature _____

NAME _____

FIRM NAME _____

ADDRESS _____

PHONE ( ) _____

CPA LICENSE # _____

ISBN (MODULE 4): 0-15-606727-7

TO ORDER: Call Toll-Free 1-800-831-7799

See the reverse side of this page for the CPE evaluation.

MODULE 4 CPE ANSWERS

1. _____   21. _____
2. _____   22. _____
3. _____   23. _____
4. _____   24. _____
5. _____   25. _____
6. _____   26. _____
7. _____   27. _____
8. _____   28. _____
9. _____   29. _____
10. _____   30. _____
11. _____   31. _____
12. _____   32. _____
13. _____   33. _____
14. _____   34. _____
15. _____   35. _____
16. _____   36. _____
17. _____   37. _____
18. _____   38. _____
19. _____   39. _____
20. _____   40. _____

GAAP Guide CPE Evaluation

1. Were you informed in advance of the:
   a. Objectives of the course? Y N
   b. Experience level needed to complete the course? Y N
   c. Program content? Y N
   d. Nature and extent of preparation necessary? Y N
   e. Teaching method? Y N
   f. Number of CPE credit hours? Y N

   c. Program content? Y N
   d. Nature and extent of advance preparation necessary? Y N
   e. Teaching method? Y N
   f. Number of CPE credit hours? Y N

2. Do you agree with the publisher's assessment of:
   a. Objectives of the course? Y N
   b. Experience level needed to complete the course? Y N

3. Was the material relevant? Y N

4. Was the presentation of the material effective? Y N

5. Did the program increase your professional competence? Y N

6. Was the program content timely and effective? Y N

Please make any other comments that you feel would improve this course. We appreciate the time you take to complete this questionnaire. Be assured that all of your comments will be considered carefully.

_____

_____

_____

_____

_____

Topical Index

TOPICAL INDEX

Purchase method. *See* Business
   combinations
Put options. *See* Debt and equity
   securities

Q

Quasi-reorganizations
   generally **39.01 et seq., 64.30**
   accounting and reporting **39.05–39.09**
   disclosures **39.07, 64.30**
   taxation **21.18–21.19, 39.06–39.07**

R

Railroad track structures, changes in
   accounting principles **1.07**
Real estate
   insurance enterprises, investments
      55.34
   See also Leases; Mortgages; Real estate
      costs; Real estate—recognition of
      sales
Real estate costs
   generally **61.01 et seq.**
   abandonment and changes in use
      61.11–61.12
   allocation of capitalized costs
      generally **61.10**
      construction costs **61.10**
      land costs **61.10**
   amenity costs
      generally **61.08–61.09**
      ownership not retained by
         developer **61.08–61.09**
      ownership retained by developer
         61.09
   direct and indirect project costs
      61.06–61.07
   incidental operations **61.09–61.10**
   leases. *See* Real estate costs, rental
      costs
   preacquisition costs **61.05–61.06**
   prepaid expenses, selling costs **61.13**
   project costs, generally **61.06–61.12**
   recoverability **61.15**
   rental costs
      generally **61.13–61.14**
      initial rental operations **61.13–61.14**
      operating leases, chargeable to
         current or future periods **61.14**
   revisions of estimates **61.11**
   selling costs

generally **61.12–61.13**
      period costs **61.13**
      prepaid expenses **61.13**
      project costs **61.12**
      taxes and insurance **61.07–61.08**
Real estate—recognition of sales
   generally **62.01 et seq., 64.44–64.45**
   changes in accounting method, retail
      land sales **62.37–62.38**
   consummation of sale **62.08–62.09**
   cost recovery method, profit
      recognition **62.17–62.18**
   deposit accounting **62.16–62.17, 62.37**
   full accrual method
      profit recognition **62.20**
      retail land sales **62.34–62.36**
      sale-leasebacks **62.28–62.31**
   future subordination **62.15**
   initial and continuing investment by
      buyer **62.09–62.15**
   installment sales method **62.18–62.19,
      62.37**
   nontransfer of ownership and seller's
      continued involvement **62.15–
      62.16**
   options, sales of **62.24–62.25**
   partial interests, sales of **62.25–62.26**
   percentage-of-completion method,
      retail land sales **62.36**
   profit recognition
      compensation, continued involve-
         ment of seller without **62.24**
      consummation of sale, absence of
         62.20–62.21
      continued involvement of seller
         62.22–62.26
      cost recovery method **62.17–62.18**
      deposit accounting **62.16–62.17**
      disclosures, continued involvement
         of seller **62.26**
      full accrual basis, other than **62.16–
         62.20**
      full accrual method, change to
         62.20
      initiating and supporting opera-
         tions, continued involvement
         of seller **62.23–62.24**
      installment sales method **62.18–
         62.19**
      investment of buyer, inadequacy of
         62.21–62.22
      options, sales of **62.24–62.25**